BARBARISM

AND

CIVILIZATION

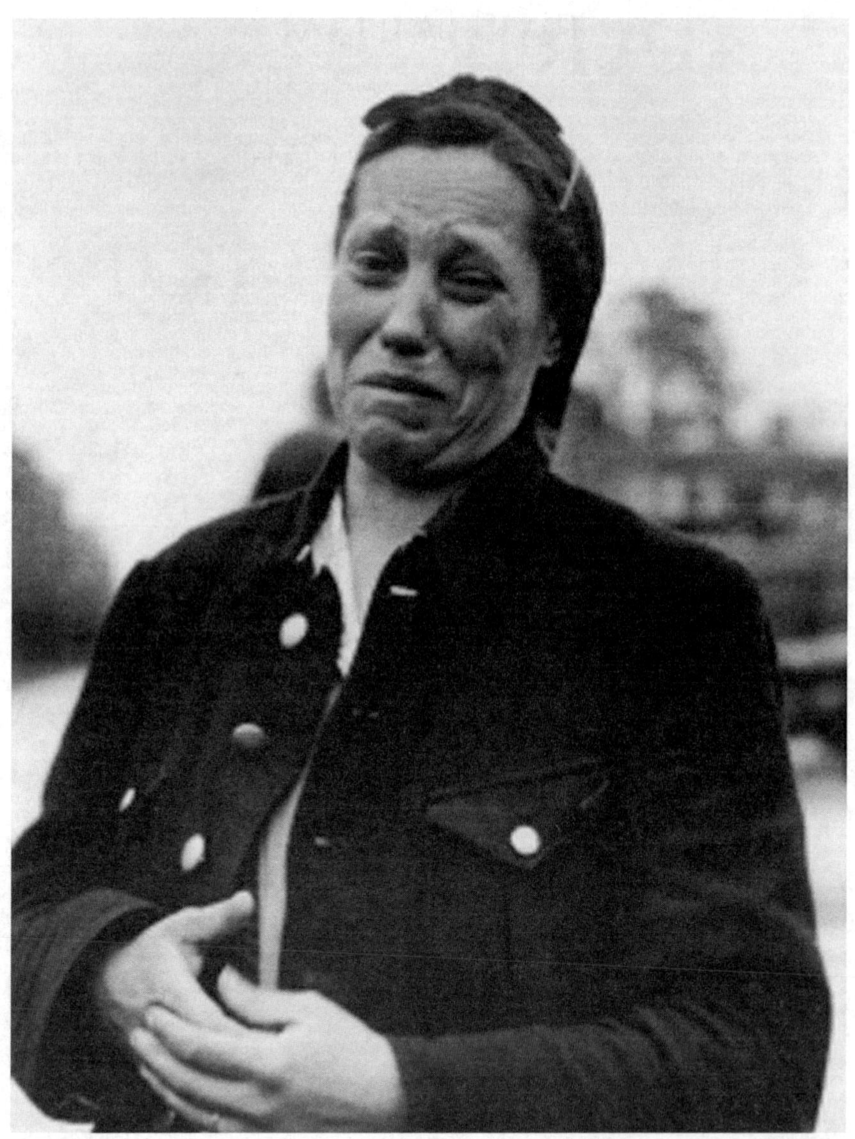

A slave labourer for the Nazis, liberated by US forces in Augsburg, 28 April 1945 (*Imperial War Museum*)

BARBARISM AND CIVILIZATION

A HISTORY OF EUROPE IN OUR TIME

BERNARD WASSERSTEIN

OXFORD
UNIVERSITY PRESS

Great Clarendon Street, Oxford OX2 6DP

Oxford University Press is a department of the University of Oxford.
It furthers the University's objective of excellence in research, scholarship,
and education by publishing worldwide in

Oxford New York

Auckland Cape Town Dar es Salaam Hong Kong Karachi
Kuala Lumpur Madrid Melbourne Mexico City Nairobi
New Delhi Shanghai Taipei Toronto

With offices in

Argentina Austria Brazil Chile Czech Republic France Greece
Guatemala Hungary Italy Japan Poland Portugal Singapore
South Korea Switzerland Thailand Turkey Ukraine Vietnam

Published in the United States
by Oxford University Press Inc., New York

First published 2007

British Library Cataloguing in Publication Data

Data available

Library of Congress Cataloging in Publication Data

Data available

Typeset by SPI Publisher Services, Pondicherry, India
Printed in Great Britain
on acid-free paper by
Clays Ltd, St Ives plc

ISBN 978-0-19-873074-3

1

To Celia

Preface

'There is no document of civilization', writes Walter Benjamin, 'that is not simultaneously a document of barbarism.'[1] During the past century Europe was the scene of some of the most savage episodes of collective violence in the recorded history of the human species. Yet the same period has also seen incontestable improvements in many aspects of the life of most inhabitants of the continent: human life has been extended, on average, by more than half; standards of living have increased dramatically; illiteracy has been all but eliminated; women, ethnic minorities, and homosexuals have advanced closer to equality of respect and opportunity. These and other changes have been so rapid and convulsive that any effort to distil their essence is a quixotic undertaking. Here is one historian's tilt at the windmill. This is a long book—necessarily so. Both the theme and the evidence are vast. Yet much has had to be omitted or boiled down: as the painter Max Liebermann put it: 'Drawing implies leaving out.'[2]

My primary objective has been to fashion a narrative of the main contours of the political, diplomatic, and military history of Europe in this period as well as to describe and account for the most striking features of demographic, economic, and social change. In the cultural sphere, I have had room to do no more than provide glimpses of areas that, it may be argued, affected society most broadly, such as film, broadcasting, and popular music. I also seek to furnish some basis for understanding the evolution of values in an era during which God has disappeared as a living presence for most Europeans.

Fifteen of the twenty chapters are structured along a linear, mainly political narrative. The other five (1, 6, 9, 15, and 20) seize specific moments (1914, the 1930s, the war years, the 1960s, and the dawn of the new millennium) and embark on a *tour d'horizon* of life in Europe at those junctures.

What are the limits of this enquiry in time and space? First, chronological: Europe in our time is understood as roughly one contemporary lifetime.

That takes us back to the early twentieth century. Of course, that is not the lifetime of most Europeans now living. But this is *our* time, the time of all of us, on the principle, enunciated by Cicero, that 'not to know what happened before one was born is to remain always a child'.[3] An investigation of the history of our time necessarily extends back to the origins of the institutions, the events, the ideas that shape our immediate environment. How far back we must go to attain a mature perspective is a matter of argument. The twentieth century has been called the shortest on record, beginning with the outbreak of the First World War in August 1914 and ending with the collapse of European communism in 1989–91.[4] The date 1914 has been selected as a starting-point neither conventionally nor arbitrarily. It chooses itself by dint of the profound shock to the European system that was administered by the First World War—an earthquake of which Europe even today still feels the after-tremors. As for the end, although the fall of communism in eastern Europe marks a decisive turn, I have chosen to bring the narrative as close to the present as possible. This enables me to outline the emerging shape of post-Cold War Europe, to examine the violent national conflicts that have appeared since 1989, most notably the Balkan wars of the 1990s, and to discuss problems connected with the enlargement of the European Union.

As for the geographical limits, 'Europe' includes, for the purposes of this book, European Russia and European Turkey, as well as the islands adjacent to the European land mass to the north-west and south. To state those inclusions is to expose a nakedness and untidiness: 'Europe' for much of the period covered by this book is a fiction. It did not exist as a focus of loyalty or even as a meaningful category for most inhabitants of the continent. To take the cases just mentioned, the British islanders have always thought of themselves as separated from Europe not only by twenty-one miles of water but also by a larger sense of a distinctive identity. British history was for long heavily conditioned by a lingering extra-European imperial role. The Russians and the Turks have lived in an uneasy, ambiguous, and often antagonistic relationship with what they perceived as Europe—very different in the two cases. Russian history does not halt at the Don or the Urals. Consideration of European Turkey makes little sense without reference to Anatolia. All this means that the geographical limitations mentioned above should be taken as no more than roughly indicative.

Two minor vexations of modern European history are the problems of alternative dates and place names. In Russia, the Ottoman Empire, and the

Balkan states in 1914, the Julian calendar had not yet been replaced by the Gregorian. The 'new style' was not adopted in Russia until after the Bolshevik revolution: by a decree of 26 January 1918 (Julian), 1 February 1918 (old style) was declared to be 14 February 1918 (new style). (Hence, the dates 1–13 February 1918 are said to have been the happiest in Russian history, since not a single calamity was recorded!) In other countries the new dating system was introduced at various points between 1915 and 1923. The difference between the two calendars in the twentieth century is thirteen days. To avoid confusion, all dates in this book are rendered in the new style.

The second problem is less easily solved. Many cities and regions, particularly in eastern Europe in the early part of the twentieth century, were known by two or even three names, reflecting mixed populations and changes in sovereignty. For instance, Bratislava, today the capital of Slovakia, contained only a small minority of Slovaks in 1914; at that time the city was under Hungarian rule; its two largest population groups were Germans, who called it Pressburg, and Hungarians, who called it Pozsony. Similarly, Klausenburg in Transylvania, established by Saxon colonists in the late twelfth century, was under Hungarian rule in 1914 and known as Kolozsvár; subsequently it changed hands three times between Hungary and Romania. Since the end of the Second World War it has found itself in Romania and its current name is Cluj.

Other names have changed altogether for political reasons as in the cyclical nomenclature St Petersburg (until 1914), Petrograd (1914), Leningrad (1924), and again St Petersburg (since 1991). In some instances it is impossible to reconcile the competing principles at stake, such as national pride, local usage, and universal recognition. Occasionally inhabitants themselves are at a loss. For example, in Kaliningrad, today a small Russian enclave on the Baltic coast, formerly Königsberg, founded in the thirteenth century as a fortress of the Teutonic knights, later the coronation city of kings of Prussia, the mainly Russian inhabitants were reported in the 1990s to be nonplussed by the problem of what to call their town: they had no desire to cling to a name imposed in 1946 to commemorate a now reviled Soviet politician; on the other hand, the previous historic name had become meaningless in the absence not only of a Prussian king but of the city's entire German population who fled at the end of the Second World War. For want of any obvious alternative, Kaliningrad was thus one of the few city names of the Communist era to remain unchanged—for the time being.

The spelling of names also presents problems. In the early part of this century R*ou*mania was the common form; later R*u*mania became the accepted spelling; since the 1960s R*o*mania has been generally adopted. Behind the apparently trivial changes in form lies a historico-nationalist ideology—the so-called Daco-Roman theory of the origins of the Romanian people—that remains central to the self-conception of Romanian nationalism to this day.

Total consistency is unattainable in such circumstances—and perhaps undesirable. As a rule of thumb I have used the name that seems most appropriate at the period with which I am dealing. Where there may be ambiguity I have included the alternative form in brackets. In some cases I have used throughout the form that is most familiar to the English reader: R*o*mania, East Germany (rather than German Democratic Republic), and Fiume, Strasbourg, Londonderry, and Dubrovnik, rather than Rijeka, Strassburg, Derry, and Ragusa. Historically, such choices have often carried a political freight: no such intention should be imputed here.

The epigraphs have been selected from European poets of the period covered by each chapter. Some of these fragments deal with public events and may be read as illustrative documents; others are more personal. They have been chosen with an eye to seizing, if only fleetingly and on the wing, the evolution of civilized sensibilities in this most brutish of ages.

Acknowledgements

Ivon Asquith and the late John Roberts invited me to write this book. Both were founts of advice and encouragement over a long period. I am sorry, in particular, that John did not live to see it completed.

I wish to thank the following who read parts of the book in manuscript and made helpful comments: David Barchard, Rudolph Binion, Eugene C. Black, Vernon Bogdanor, Sean Dunwoody, Julia Fein, Sheila Fitzpatrick, Gregory Freeze, Israel Getzler, John Grenville, Paul Jankowski, Paulina Kewes, Ulrika Mårtensson, Susan Pedersen, Antony Polonsky, Dagfinn Rian, David Satter, Philip Spain, Norman Stone, and Maria Todorova. I owe a special debt to my brother, David Wasserstein, of Vanderbilt University History Department, who read the entire book in draft and made many valuable suggestions.

For other information and help I am grateful to my late father, mother, and sister as well as to Chris Baggs, Gábor Betegh, Patricia Clavin, Samuel K. Cohn Jr., Richard Crampton, Shmuel Eisenstadt, Teddy Fassberg, Jürgen Förster, Thomas Fuller, Avis Furness, Dieter Grimm, Hajo Grundmann, Lars-Erik Gustafsson, Alois Hahn, Revd. Brian Hehir, Peter Hodgkinson, Jan van Impe, Dermot Keogh, James Knowlson, Madeline Levine, John Löwenhardt, Andrew Martin, Katherine McSharry, Evan Mawdsley, Helen Murphy, Rodney Needham, Phillips O'Brien, Katiana Orluc, Göran Rosenberg, Robert Schwandl, Wolfgang Seibel, Bozena Shallcross, Marek Swinarski, George Szirtes, Thomas Weber, Michael Wood, and David Young.

In the early stages of my work on this project I was fortunate in enjoying research assistance at Brandeis University from John Hill, Paul Salstrom, David Soule, Sandra Gereau, Maura Hametz, and Ruth Abrams. More recently at the University of Chicago I have benefited from the assistance of Robert Stern, Alexander Joskowicz, Zsolt Nagy, Julia Fein, Ronen Steinberg, Charles Miller, and Sean Dunwoody.

The maps are based on drafts by Mike Shand of the University of Glasgow Department of Geography and Geomatics.

I am grateful to the many libraries and archives that have made materials available to me, most particularly the university libraries of Brandeis, Oxford, Glasgow, Chicago, and Jerusalem. I also thank the Centre for European Studies at Harvard University and the Wissenschaftskolleg zu Berlin at each of which I spent a year as a visitor, working on the book. Finally, I wish to thank a long line of patient editors at Oxford University Press, culminating in Matthew Cotton, as well as my indefatigable copy-editor, Mary Worthington, and the tireless production editor, Catherine Berry.

Contents

List of Maps

List of Plates

List of Figures

Abbreviations

The following abbreviations are used in the notes and bibliography:

AHR	*American Historical Review*
AHYB	*Austrian History Yearbook*
BDEE	*British Documents on the End of Empire*
CoEH	*Contemporary European History*
CWIHPB	*Cold War International History Project Bulletin*
DBFP	*Documents on British Foreign Policy 1919–1939*
DBPO	*Documents on British Policy Overseas*
DDF	*Documents diplomatiques français*
DGFP	*Documents on German Foreign Policy 1918–1945*
EAS	*Europe–Asia Studies* (formerly *Soviet Studies*)
EHR	*English Historical Review*
EcHR	*Economic History Review*
FA	*Foreign Affairs*
FHS	*French Historical Studies*
FRUS	*Foreign Relations of the United States*
FT	*Financial Times*
HQ	*Hungarian Quarterly*
HJ	*Historical Journal*
IA	*International Affairs* (London)
JCH	*Journal of Contemporary History*
JCWS	*Journal of Cold War Studies*
JEEH	*Journal of European Economic History*
JMH	*Journal of Modern History*
JMilH	*Journal of Military History*
MGW	(*Manchester*) *Guardian Weekly*
NYT	*New York Times*
NZZ	*Neue Zürcher Zeitung*
PS	*Politics and Society*

RR	*Russian Review*
SR	*Slavic Review*
SS	*Soviet Studies*
TLS	*Times Literary Supplement*
VfZ	*Vierteljahrshefte für Zeitgeschichte*

In everything I want to reach
The very essence . . .

The essence of past days
And where they start,
Foundations, roots,

The very heart . . .
If only I could . . .

(Boris Pasternak, 1956)*

*From 'When the Weather Clears', translated from the Russian by Jon Stallworthy and Peter France. Boris Pasternak, *Selected Poems*, London, 1984, 141–4.

I

Europe at 1914

What are we waiting for, assembled in the forum?
The barbarians are due here today.

*C. P. Cavafy, Alexandria, 1904**

Anticipations

There are two possible ways of looking at Europe on the eve of war in 1914. We can look backwards and see the end of a period of relatively settled, peaceful, and stable existence in what was still the world's richest, most culturally productive, and politically and militarily dominant continent; or we can look forwards and see the early tremors of social and international upheaval—the beginning of the end of the Eurocentric world. Both views contain elements of truth, but the first has one special significance: contemporaries could look back much more easily than they could see ahead. While perceptive observers in 1914 saw much that was deeply unsettling in the world around them, the idea of progress remained deeply ingrained in the consciousness of educated Europeans and few foresaw that they stood on the edge of an abyss.

One of the most popular social forecasters of the day, H. G. Wells, in his *Anticipations* (1902), had analysed the effects of technological change on population distribution, social organization, and warfare. He predicted the growth of giant metropolitan areas that would swallow up vast tracts of countryside, the decay of existing political systems, and the mechanization of warfare.[1] In *The War in the Air* (1908) he drew a graphic and prescient representation of aerial

* From 'Waiting for the Barbarians', translated from the Greek by Edmund Keeley and Philip Sherrard. Peter Forbes, ed., *Scanning the Century: The Penguin Book of the Twentieth Century in Poetry*, London, 2000, 5–6.

combat, which, he suggested, would put an end to the distinction in warfare between combatant and civilian that had been recognized by civilized nations in the Hague Conventions of 1899 and 1907. In France Emile Durkheim warned in 1905 that while war between his nation and Germany 'would be the end of everything', an even greater danger was presented by revolutionary socialism which threatened to destroy all social organization, creating in its place not 'the sun of a new society' but rather 'a new Middle Ages, a new period of darkness.'[2] In Italy the poet F. T. Marinetti issued a 'Futurist Manifesto' in 1909 in which he embraced extreme bellicosity: 'We want to glorify war—the only hygiene of the world—militarism, patriotism, the anarchist's destructive gesture, the fine Ideas that kill, and the scorn of woman. We want to demolish museums, libraries, fight against moralism, feminism, and all opportunistic and utilitarian cowardices.'[3] In Germany Max Weber spoke in 1909 of his horror at the prospect that 'the world could one day be filled with nothing but those little cogs, little men clinging to little jobs and striving towards bigger ones'.[4] He discerned the threat that rootless, dislocated social groups could give rise under modern democratic conditions to a demagogic Caesar. Yet such dark ruminations notwithstanding, all these thinkers fundamentally remained social optimists, wedded to what Wells himself later called 'the peculiar fatuous hopefulness of the Nineteenth Century'.[5]

Unique in his genius of precognition was the writer who in Prague in July 1914 began to set down on paper a prophetic, nightmarish vision of the individual deprived by mysterious social forces of all control over his own destiny. *The Trial* was first published only in 1925, a year after Franz Kafka's death; even then it was ahead of its time in its eerie foresight into the world of the Gestapo and the NKVD. No conventional social analyst could have ventured such a wild imaginative leap merely by extrapolating from current conditions in the summer of 1914. What were those conditions and why was the European *Zeitgeist* on the eve of catastrophe basically optimistic? Was it really so, or should we be more cautious in ascribing to the population in general a mood perhaps prevalent only among social philosophers and intellectuals?

Empires and nation-states

Four great land empires dominated the greater part of the east and central European land mass in 1914. The largest in both area and population was

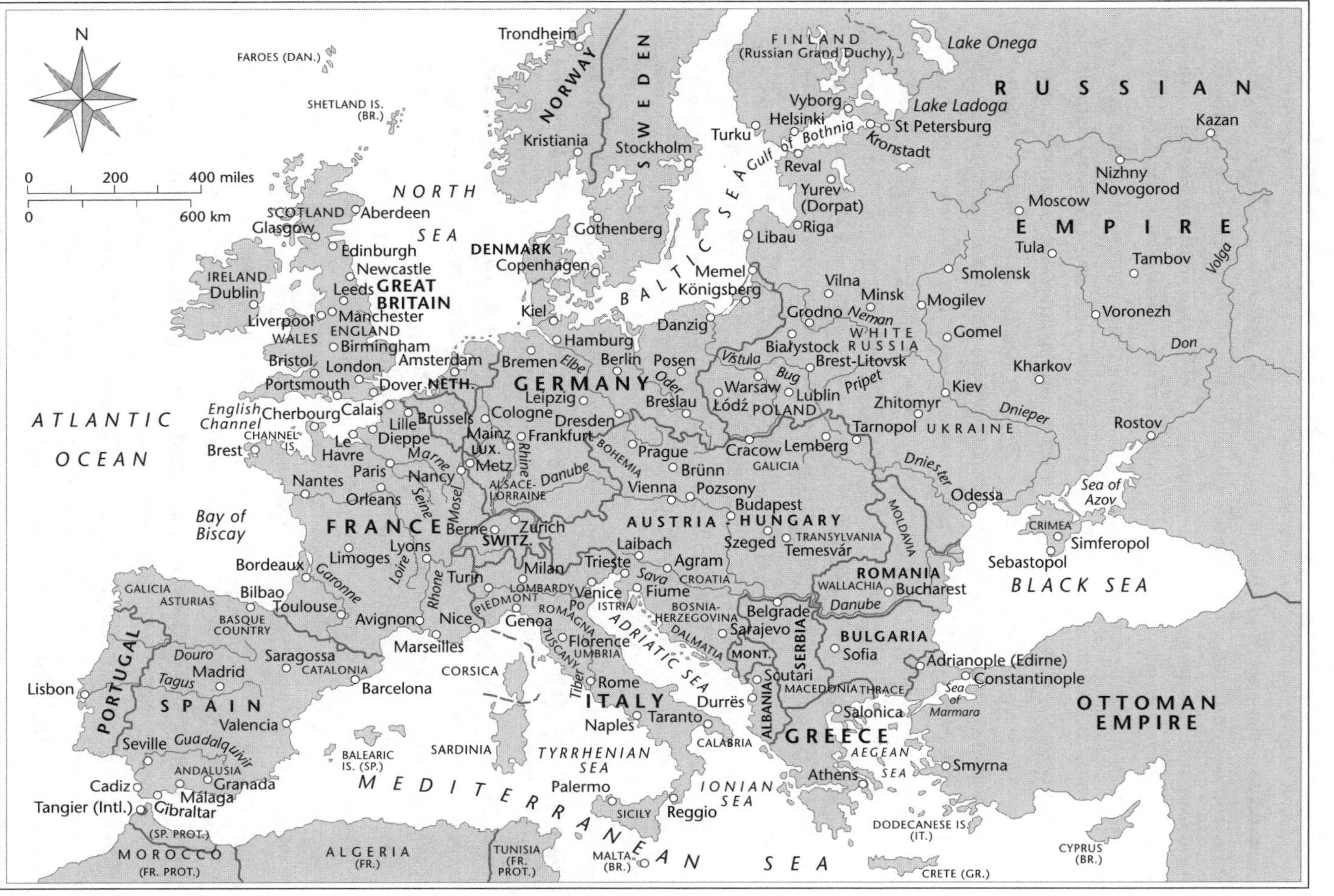

Map 1. Europe in 1914

the Russian Empire, which had expanded in the course of the nineteenth century to the shores of the Pacific and the borderlands of China and the Indian subcontinent. The empire's population of 166 million, of whom 140 million lived in European Russia, was larger than that of Germany, Britain, and France put together. More than 80 per cent of the population was rural and the peasant problem remained the 'question of questions' confronting the government and society. Although Russia's was by some measures the largest economy on the continent, her per capita income was the lowest of any major European power.[6] The economy was overwhelmingly agricultural. Even the industrial sector was dominated by primary products such as lumber, coal, and oil. Manufacturing industry, in enterprises such as the textile factories of Łődź (in Russian Poland) and the Putilov metals, machinery, and armaments works in St Petersburg, had grown rapidly since 1890, albeit from a very low base. Industrial development was characterized by heavy state involvement, large production units, and considerable dependence on foreign, especially French, capital. Overall, economically, socially, and, in the eyes of many, politically, Russia was one of the most backward countries in Europe. Defeat in the Russo-Japanese War of 1904–5 had revealed the vulnerability of her army and navy. Revolutionary convulsion in 1905 had shaken but not overthrown the Tsarist autocracy. The conservative, unimaginative Nicholas II, who had reigned since 1894, remained on the throne. Many of the political reforms that flowed from that revolution had gradually been withdrawn once the crisis passed. In particular the franchise for the Duma (lower house of parliament) was narrowed and parliamentary powers restricted. Government remained repressive, corrupt, and hostile to subject nationalities, particularly the large Jewish population concentrated in Poland, Lithuania, and Ukraine, who were victims of discriminatory laws and periodic pogroms. The Tsarist empire was an authoritarian structure but not, in the modern sense, a police state. The repressive machine at the disposal of the government was quite small: in the whole of the empire in 1914 there were under 15,000 gendarmes or uniformed police. The autocratic regime was confronted in the years before 1914 with challenges from non-Russian nationalists, particularly Poles, and from revolutionary Socialists whose more extreme elements carried out sporadic assassinations and attacks. The professional bourgeoisie, and its political expression the Constitutional Democrat (Kadet) Party, formed a narrow, unrepresentative sliver of society whose influence barely extended beyond St Petersburg and Moscow. Mass political parties such as the Socialist Revolutionaries, whose support was drawn largely from the peasantry, and the Social

Democrats, based mainly on the urban working class, were driven underground. Was Russia in 1914 poised for an economic leap forward that would catapult her into the ranks of the leading industrial powers? Or was she so riven by social and economic contradictions that she was bound to collapse into revolution? Both views seemed plausible in 1914.

The Habsburg Empire, known since the Ausgleich (compromise) with Hungary of 1867 as the Dual Monarchy, was headed by the longest-reigning European monarch, Franz Josef, who had ascended the imperial throne in 1848. Its population of fifty million in 1914 was the third largest in Europe, after Russia and Germany. The Habsburgs formed 'the only connecting tie of the state' (as the playwright Franz Grillparzer had put it in 1830). Slavs and other subject races together outnumbered Germans and Hungarians, the two 'hegemonic' nationalities of the Habsburg dominions. Vienna, with 2.1 million inhabitants, was the third city of Europe, after London and Paris, and could claim to be one of Europe's cultural capitals. As an internal free-trade unit sheltering behind high tariff walls, Austria-Hungary's economy grew at a fair pace in the half-century before 1914. In the period 1904–12 Austria experienced a spurt in industrial growth that some historians have interpreted as a 'take-off'. But there were wide regional variations and overall per capita national income and standard of living remained substantially lower than in Germany or France. Austrian administration was relatively efficient, the social and cultural atmosphere mildly tolerant, and political expression and organization more or less free. The main sources of internal political disturbance arose from the growth of the anti-Semitic Christian Social Party and from conflict between Pan-German nationalists and Habsburg loyalists. Although the monarch retained significant powers, Austria-Hungary was, in a measure, a constitutional monarchy. Since 1907 Austria had enjoyed universal male suffrage. In Hungary, on the other hand, only limited electoral reform had been enacted in 1913; universal suffrage was resisted by the ruling Magyars, for fear that non-Hungarians, forming over half the total population, would supersede Magyar political predominance. By 1914 the most ominous problem facing the two ruling nations was the growing autonomist and nationalist ferment among subject peoples, particularly Czechs, Poles, Serbs, and Croats. Still, the Habsburg monarchy presented an outward mien of solid durability. Recalling his childhood in pre-war Vienna, Stefan Zweig later wrote that his parents had regarded it 'as if it had been a house of stone'. 'Today, now that the great storm has long since smashed it, we finally know that that world of security was naught but a castle of dreams.'[7]

The feeblest and least modernized of the four empires was that of the Ottoman Turks, whose European dominions had reached their zenith in 1683 and thereafter had been steadily squeezed back by nationalist movements, often supported by other European powers—the British in the case of Greece, the Russians in the cases of Romania and Bulgaria. Nationalism was heightened by religious difference: the greater part of the Muslim sultan's European subjects were Christians; even in the capital, Constantinople, Muslims were a minority of the population. After the Russo-Turkish War of 1877–8, the Congress of Berlin had limited Russia's gains. Nevertheless, the area in Europe directly ruled by Constantinople was reduced by 1881 to Macedonia and Thrace. In 1908 a revolution against the autocracy of Sultan Abdülhamid II had installed a constitutional regime. The empire's Christian neighbours took advantage of the succeeding period of turmoil to wrench away yet more of what remained of Ottoman power in Europe. Bulgaria, an autonomous tributary of the sultan since 1878, declared her complete independence in October 1908. Italy defeated the Turks in a war in 1911–12 in the course of which she occupied the Dodecanese Islands and Libya. Greece, led from 1910 by the Cretan Eleftherios Venizelos (see plate 15), succeeded by 1912 in incorporating Crete, since 1898 autonomous under nominal Ottoman suzerainty, into the national state.

In 1912 Serbia, Bulgaria, Greece, and Montenegro, taking advantage of the Ottomans' preoccupation with the Italians, and enjoying the support of Russia, banded together as the Balkan League for a frontal assault on Turkey-in-Europe, pushing back the Turkish army almost to Constantinople itself. As a result of this First Balkan War Turkey-in-Europe was reduced to a small rump and, at the insistence of the powers, Albania achieved independence. Military defeat produced a *coup d'état* in Constantinople. Power was seized by three generals, Enver, Cemal, and Talât. This triumvirate ruled Turkey until 1918. They were threatened not only by assault from without but also by dissidence within, particularly from the large Christian Armenian population who had suffered massacres by the Turks, the latest in 1909, and who looked to Russia as their protector and potential liberator. Russia had traditionally exploited the cause of the Christians in the Ottoman Empire in order to advance her ambition to control Constantinople and the Straits, control that would give her naval access to the Mediterranean. During much of the nineteenth century the Ottomans had been able to rely on British support against Russian designs. But after the 1890s Britain, firmly ensconced as effective ruler of nominally Ottoman Egypt, abandoned the traditional commitment to maintenance of Ottoman territorial integrity. Thus the Turkish rulers, like those of the other three empires, could reasonably feel that they were beset on all sides by enemies.

The Russian, Habsburg, and Ottoman empires all belonged to the relatively less developed region of Europe. Germany, the fourth and youngest empire, presented, by contrast, the most impressive spectacle of economic and social dynamism on the continent in the period between 1871 and 1914. With sixty-five million citizens she was the most populous country in Europe after Russia. Berlin, with over two million inhabitants, was growing rapidly and seemed set to overtake Vienna to become the third city of the continent. In the course of the previous two generations Germany had catapulted herself into the vanguard of industrial nations. At the same time she presented strange contrasts of sophisticated modernization and reactionary conservatism. Her Reichstag (lower house of parliament) was elected by universal male suffrage; but parliamentary authority was limited; governments were not responsible to it; and the *Länder* (states) of the empire retained considerable powers. The erratic Kaiser Wilhelm II retained significant authority, exercised with arrogant irresponsibility. Interest groups representing the large landowners of the east, heavy industry of the Ruhr, and commercial and financial sectors, constantly manoeuvred for advantage. Germany enjoyed some of the most progressive welfare provisions in Europe; her engineering, science, and humane scholarship were considered the finest in the world. Yet as Ralf Dahrendorf has put it: 'Not even industrialization managed, in Germany, to upset a traditional outlook in which the whole is placed above the parts, the state above the citizen, or a rigidly controlled order above the lively diversity of the market, the state above society.' The political framework of imperial Germany was an uneasy mixture of authoritarianism, bureaucracy, and parliamentarism. Instead of reinforcing the liberal principle, Dahrendorf argues, industrialization in Germany swallowed it.[8]

Around the edges of the empires clustered a number of small, more homogeneous nation-states. Spain, Portugal, France, Britain, and the Netherlands were polities of long standing and had built up large overseas empires. Others were creations of the previous hundred years, either breakaways from empires, like Romania, Bulgaria, Greece, and Serbia, or from neighbouring states, as in the cases of Belgium, which had separated from the Netherlands in 1830, and Norway, which split off from Sweden in 1905. Several of these states had border disputes with the empires: Italy coveted 'Italia irredenta', the Trentino, Istria, and Dalmatia. Serbia dreamed of becoming the 'Piedmont of the Balkans' to form a unified south Slav state (as Piedmont-Sardinia had been the kernel of a unified Italy in the mid-nineteenth century). France still resented Germany's annexation of Alsace-Lorraine after the Franco-Prussian War in 1871. Of all these countries only two, Britain and France, counted as great powers.

Britain's status, which derived essentially from her economic primacy and her imperial role, was unique in resting mainly on naval rather than military power. Her small standing army, although highly efficient, could not compare with the vast conscript armies of the continental powers. Her overseas empire endowed her with immense prestige although military humiliation by the Boers in South Africa in the war of 1899–1902 had punctured the rising imperialist spirit and given rise to misgivings among some members of the elite that Britain's imperial responsibilities were dangerously over-extended. In 1907 the Permanent Under-Secretary (the most senior official) of the Foreign Office, Sir Thomas Sanderson, wrote that 'to a foreigner reading our press the British empire must appear in the light of some huge giant sprawling over the globe, with gouty fingers and toes stretched in every direction, which cannot be approached without eliciting a scream'.[9] Britain was socially, economically, and temperamentally disengaged from Europe in 1914. She was by far the largest foreign investor in the world but only 6 per cent of the capital flow went to Europe. Her investments were primarily directed towards the Americas, India, Australasia, South Africa, and China. Her main commercial links were also extra-European, although Germany was an increasingly important trading partner in the decade before 1914. Unlike all the other European powers, Britain could still afford to cling to free trade, in spite of the views of some businessmen and influential figures in the opposition Conservative Party who were increasingly inclined to favour tariffs.

For all the surface snobbism and flummery that continued to mark its social life, Britain in 1914 was the most bourgeois of the major powers. Unlike France, where the peasant smallholder remained the single most influential political force, and unlike Germany, where the values of the old aristocratic and military castes lived in improbable and uneasy symbiosis with those of the rising middle class, Britain in 1914 was suffused with a bourgeois spirit in politics and society. The Liberal government, which had held power since 1905, embodied the enlightened middle-class ethos in its devotion to free trade, its cautious social reformism, its reluctance to spend on armaments, and its efforts to balance the contending interests of labour and capital, of Irish Catholics and Protestants, of supporters and opponents of women's suffrage, of empire and free trade. Under the effortlessly benign leadership of H. H. Asquith, with the radical Welsh populist David Lloyd George snapping at his heels, the Liberal Party seemed the natural party of government in Britain. In fact both it and the delicately balanced social structure of which it formed a seemingly perfect expression were on the verge of extinction.

The heart of European civilization in 1914, however, was unquestionably France. Nouveau riche Germany could not claim such a role and semi-disengaged Britain did not aspire to it. Educated Europeans looked to Paris as the pre-eminent cultural capital of Europe, its chief source of artistic vitality, the fount of aesthetic modernism, and the city more than any other where an intellectual of whatever nationality might feel at home, more so, perhaps, than many a newly arrived French provincial. The previous year this 'central station of Europe', as it was called by the painter Jacques-Emile Blanche, had witnessed the scandalous first performance of Stravinsky's *Sacre du printemps*, a collaboration of the composer with the impresario/director Diaghilev and the dancer Nijinsky ('massacre du printemps' some called it).[10] The politics of 'la république des camarades', with its corruption, financial scandals, and factionalism, hardly provided an attractive advertisement for parliamentary republicanism. A bizarre and tragic climax was attained in July 1914: Mme Caillaux, wife of the former Prime Minister, was tried on a charge of murdering a newspaper editor who had attacked her husband (she was acquitted); and Jean Jaurès, Socialist leader, scholar, and orator, was assassinated. Yet France still represented some sort of ideal for those throughout Europe who cherished the principles of 1789. She had long ago been overtaken by Germany according to most demographic, economic, and educational indices. The republic remained deeply riven by social conflicts, strikes, and the eternal struggle between Church and State. On the other hand, France possessed an overseas empire and foreign investments second only to those of Britain; and she was the only one of the six major European powers with no 'national question' within her borders.

Europe was thus divided politically into two state systems: dying empires (though few realized how close at hand their demise was) and rising nation-states (some of which also possessed overseas empires). But the pattern of Europe's diplomatic alignments did not reflect these political divisions. The rough contours of the coalitions that were to engage in a life-and-death struggle in and after 1914 had become visible as much as two decades earlier. The two polar alliances in Europe were those of Austria-Hungary and Germany on the one hand, and of France and Russia on the other. Berlin's alliance with Vienna had been concluded by Bismarck in 1879 and was regarded as fundamental by all his successors as German Chancellor. It had broadened into a Triple Alliance in 1882 with the adhesion of Italy, though Italian participation in a war on the side of Austria could not be taken for granted. France's alliance with Russia, concluded between 1891 and 1894, marked a critical turning-point. Bismarck had sought to prevent such a dangerous alignment of Germany's eastern and western neighbours by means of a 'Reinsurance Treaty' signed with Russia in 1887. His successors, however, allowed the treaty to lapse. The Anglo-French Entente of 1904 and the Anglo-Russian Entente of 1907, originally intended primarily as settlements of colonial differences in North Africa and Persia, led many to see those three powers as a bloc, though Britain did not regard the ententes as in any sense an alliance.

Russia and Austria-Hungary had much more in common with each other than with their allies. Both were over-extended multi-national empires with pockets of modernity and vast stretches of backwardness. Similarly, Britain and Germany, the two most advanced economies and societies among the major European powers, were seen by some as natural allies. But efforts at the turn of the century by the British statesman Joseph Chamberlain and others to effect such an alignment came to nothing. Britain's only formal alliance with a major power in these years was that of 1902, concluded with Japan and designed to allow Britain to reduce her naval presence in Far Eastern waters. The leaders of Russia and France abhorred each other's political system and, apart from large French loans and investments in Russia, had few positive interests in common: the French had little enthusiasm for becoming embroiled in the long-standing Austro-Russian rivalry in the Balkans; the Russians had no interest in fighting a war to restore Alsace-Lorraine to France. Nor did they evince much inclination to support France against Germany in a crisis over Morocco in 1911. Nevertheless, in the long run France and Russia were drawn together by a common fear of Germany.

Economy and demography

Europe in 1914 was essentially divided economically and socially between the north-west and the rest. Much of England, south Wales, central Scotland, Belgium, and north-eastern France, as well as parts of the Netherlands, Germany (especially the Ruhr and Silesia), Bohemia, Switzerland, and northern Italy formed a region of advanced industrial development. Most of the rest of

Europe consisted of large expanses of primitive agrarianism, dotted with small pockets of industry, more often extractive than manufacturing. The striking variations in the distribution of the labour force in Europe clearly illustrate the division. In Britain in 1914, no more than 13 per cent of the workforce was engaged in agriculture, forestry, or fishing. This figure contrasts with that for every other country in Europe. The equivalent for Belgium was 23 per cent, for the Netherlands 29 per cent, and for Germany 35 per cent. In no other country was less than 40 per cent of the working population engaged in these pursuits. In all the countries of southern and eastern Europe over half the economically active population still worked on the land.

Britain was still the strongest economic power in 1914, although her relative position had slowly eroded since the 1870s. All her major competitors, particularly Germany and the United States, grew faster between 1900 and 1914. Industrial production in Germany in 1914 grew by nearly two-thirds in this period as against only a quarter in Britain. Germany had already overtaken Britain in the production of steel by 1900 and was producing more than three times as much electric energy by 1914. Nevertheless, though Britain's economic dominance was slipping, it had not disappeared. She was in 1914 still ahead of Germany in the volume of her exports of manufactured goods and in industrial productivity. She had more cotton spindles in operation in that year than the whole of the rest of Europe put together. Her share of world trade had declined from 20 per cent in 1876–80 to 14 per cent in 1911–13 but she remained the world's largest trader. Her merchant fleet was the largest in the world and represented half of world steam and motor tonnage. In terms of value British ships carried a little over half of all world shipping trade in the years immediately before 1914. In 1913 British shipyards launched twice as much tonnage as the rest of the world together. Britain had more motor vehicles on her roads than there were in Germany, France, and Italy. Her total foreign investments of between £2.5 billion and £4 billion were as great as those of Germany, France, and the United States combined. In Britain the joint-stock, limited-liability company was the characteristic vehicle by which enterprises raised capital. Britain had an estimated fifty thousand such companies in 1910 compared with only five thousand in Germany. British banks occupied a less central role in the national economy than German, French, Belgian, and Swiss banks, which dominated their countries' industrialization and the largest of which, in each case, was bigger than the country's largest industrial company. Yet the City of London was still the financial capital of Europe.

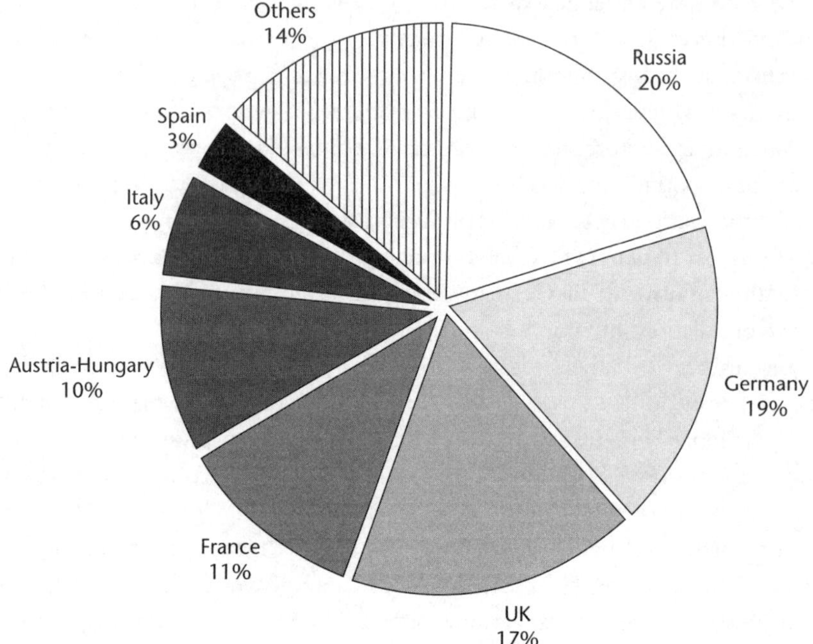

Figure 1. GNP of selected countries as share of total European product, 1913

Source: Paul Bairoch, 'Europe's Gross National Product, 1800–1975', *Journal of European Economic History*, 5: 2 (1976), 282.

British finance commanded the international economy and gold-backed sterling remained the world's reserve currency.

By comparison with the rest of the century, the most striking feature of the European industrial economy before 1914 was the stable and low price of money, labour, and goods. Currencies backed by gold maintained their internal and external values. Inflation was non-existent or low. The constant replenishment of the industrial labour pool by immigration from the countryside ensured cheap labour costs. Coal provided abundant low-cost energy. Capital too was cheap: the bank rate in London in the summer of 1914 stood at 3 per cent, in Vienna at 4 per cent.

Government spending in many countries had increased over the previous few years because of social legislation and the armaments race. In Russia defence costs in 1913–14 rose to 5 per cent of national income, one-third of all government expenditure, but in most other countries the percentage was much lower. As a proportion of national product, central government expenditures before 1914 were low by the standards of the rest of the century. The range was from as little as 3 per cent in Germany, though the constituent states of the empire bore a large share of its burden, to 13 per cent in France, with Denmark, Sweden, and the Netherlands near the lower end, and Spain and Italy near the upper. In Britain the central government spent about 7 per cent of GNP.

The tax burden was correspondingly light and mainly took indirect forms. In Austria in 1913 only 20 per cent of government revenue came from direct taxation. In Germany the central government was precluded from imposing an income tax since this was a prerogative of the states (a limited form of capital levy was introduced in 1913 to finance army reforms). In Russia there was no income tax at all. In France there was none until July 1914 when it was adopted at a rate of 2 per cent, though collection did not start until 1916. The standard rate of income tax in Britain in 1913–14 stood at 5.8 per cent; it was levied only on the one million people with annual earned incomes above £160, thus excluding the working class altogether.

An important accelerator of economic growth was ever-greater ease of communications. The prevalent long-distance modes were still by water and rail; motorized road traffic was relatively light and air transport in its infancy. Rail travel was often slow even on main lines. The night express from Vienna to Trieste (a distance by rail of 367 miles) in 1914 left at 9.30 p.m. and arrived at 9.15 a.m. The journey from Paris to Berlin (626 railway miles) in 1910 took about 18 hours, and from Berlin to St Petersburg (1,020 miles) 28 hours. All the major countries had substantial railway networks. Russia boasted 62,300 kilometres of track, Germany 61,749, France 37,400, the United Kingdom 32,623, and Italy 19,125. But these figures must be measured against the size of each country; on that basis Britain and Germany appear near the top and Russia and Italy near the bottom of a comparative table. Figures for freight traffic provide a more illuminating basis for comparison. A total of 132 million metric tons of freight were carried on Russian railways in 1913; British railways transported 571 million and German 676 million. Similarly in the case of passenger traffic: a total of 1,798 million passenger journeys were undertaken by rail in Germany in 1913; the figure for Britain was 1,199 million, for France 529 million, for Russia 185 million, and for Italy only 99 million. Patterns of railway ownership varied greatly. In most countries the state owned part of the system: in Germany more than 90 per cent and in Italy more than 80 per cent of railway track was state-owned; in Denmark, Belgium, the Netherlands, and Switzerland public and private shares were about equal; in France the state owned less than 20 per cent. In Russia, although foreign investors had played an important role in railway construction, the state had come to own a large part of the system by 1914. Only in Britain, Spain, Greece, and Turkey-in-Europe were the railways wholly in private hands.

Roads were only beginning to be adapted to the requirements of motor traffic. In big cities many streets were cobbled. Inter-urban roads had only one lane in each direction and motor traffic would frequently be held up by horse-drawn carts. In 1914 there were 132,000 private cars in use in Britain; France had 108,000, Germany only 61,000. In the absence of means of private locomotion, except for the popular bicycle, most cities had complex systems of public transportation, relying mainly on trains and trams. Underground railways existed in only six cities: London, Glasgow, Paris, Berlin, Hamburg, and Budapest (unless one counts the Istanbul Tünel, a short funicular railway between Galata and Beyoğlu, opened in 1875). By 1914 electricity had displaced steam, horse and other forms of traction on most tramways in Britain. But out of 762 large towns and cities in European Russia, only thirty had electric tramways in 1909 and only another twelve had trams of any kind. In Warsaw, one of the most modern cities in the Russian Empire, the trams were still horse-drawn in 1914.

Telephones were widely used by governments and business but even in the most advanced countries could be found only in a small minority of private homes. Germany led the field with 1,420,000 telephones in 1914. Among European capitals Berlin had the largest number of telephones in proportion to population—6.6 per hundred persons—but even there most homes had no telephone. Britain had barely half as many telephones, 780,512, and France came a poor third with 330,000. In this as in other spheres Russia was far behind, although making rapid progress. In the whole of Russia in 1907 there were only 36,000 telephones. Only 137 large towns in European Russia had a telephone service in 1910. But in the years immediately preceding the First World War the Russian telephone system expanded fast: by 1914 the number of telephones in European Russia was 320,000. Moscow by 1914 had more telephones in proportion to population (3.1 per hundred) than Manchester (2.5 per hundred). International telephone service was in its infancy and urgent messages, whether inland or abroad, were generally sent by telegram. Russians sent the largest number of telegrams in 1913 (97.6 million), followed by Britain (87.1 million), France (65.5 million), and Germany (60.9 million), the high Russian figure perhaps reflecting the relative inadequacy of the telephone network.

The basic economic structure of Europe was, with few exceptions, reflected in demographic patterns. During the period 1900 to 1914 population growth had been faster than in almost any other period in modern European history. The population of the continent in 1914 stood at an unprecedented 450 million. Growth was most rapid in eastern Europe, somewhat less so in north-west Europe, and particularly slow in France and Spain. Infant mortality in many countries was still high: in Russia and Romania 200 out of every thousand children died before the age of one year; in most other countries, even Britain and Germany, the rate was above 100 per thousand. Only in Scandinavia, the Netherlands, and Switzerland did it dip below 100. Life expectancy at birth was between forty and fifty in most European countries. But since nearly half of all deaths in much of Europe occurred before the age of five, the life chances of those who survived childhood were quite favourable: most might expect to live into their sixties.

Although historical demographers since the Second World War have tended to regard declining population growth rates as characteristic of more developed societies, contemporaries linked population to power and worried that low fertility would diminish national strength both economically and militarily. The French in particular speculated gloomily on this theme in the early years of the century as they contemplated the widening gap

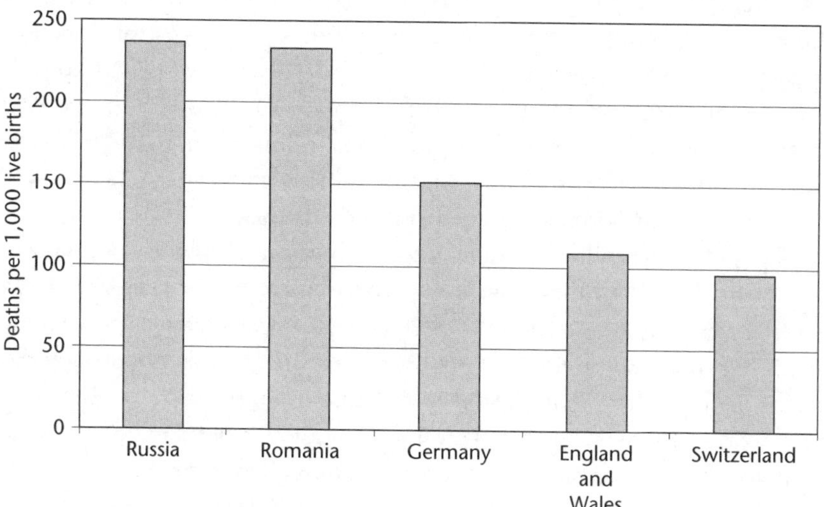

Figure 2. Infant mortality rates in 1913

Source: B. R. Mitchell, *European Historical Statistics 1750–1975* (New York, 1980).

between their available manpower and the Germans'. In the eighteenth century theirs had been the largest population in Europe; since then they had been overtaken by Russia, Germany, Austria-Hungary, and Britain. This rapid increase in population elsewhere on the continent occurred in spite of diminishing birth rates and very heavy emigration. The main reason was a swiftly falling death rate.

Notwithstanding this rapid population increase until 1914, the crucial signal of an impending demographic transition was already apparent, although it was only dimly perceived as such at the time. This was the fall in fertility rates that, particularly when combined with the effects of the high death rate during the First World War, reduced population growth in the inter-war period to little more than replacement level in many countries. The drop in fertility was already reflected before 1914 in shrinking absolute numbers of births, particularly in richer societies. In England and Wales, where fertility rates had diminished by more than a quarter since the 1870s, the number of live births declined from 945,000 in 1904 (an absolute level never surpassed before or since) to 882,000 in 1913. Austria, Belgium, Germany, and Sweden also recorded declines.

The causes of the decline in fertility are difficult to discover but one in particular stands out: urban populations were starting to have recourse to birth control. *Coitus interruptus*, abortion, and various crude forms of contraception were common but by the early years of the century the rubber contraceptive sheath was becoming available in western Europe. Artificial birth control was still, however, largely restricted to the bourgeoisie. Moralists expressed concern at the prospect of its spread to the lower classes: 'We are now beginning to suffer', wrote an English social reformer in 1907, 'from that wild orgy of individualism into which the nineteenth century plunged with all the reckless abandonment of desperate and insensate folly.'[11]

If population increase in general may be regarded as a crude index of optimism, the decline in fertility is open to varying interpretations and should perhaps alert us to the dangers of defining the *Zeitgeist* by reference only to the views expressed by writers and publicists. The same holds true for another major demographic phenomenon of the period: migration from Europe to other continents, which in this period was at its highest level in history. More than a million Europeans a year, on average, registered their dissatisfaction with conditions in their home countries by leaving Europe in the years 1900 to 1914. Poor agricultural regions, notably Ukraine, southern Italy, Ireland, and Austrian Galicia, tended to furnish the highest proportion of emigrants.

The largest numbers went from Italy (mainly to the Americas), Britain (mainly to the USA, Canada, Australia, and South Africa), Austria-Hungary (to the USA), Spain (to Latin America), and Russia (overwhelmingly to the USA). More than five million people left Italy alone between 1900 and 1914. Some smaller countries also had very high emigration rates, among them Portugal (mainly to Brazil) and Sweden (to the USA). French emigration was mainly to the French possessions in North Africa. Of the major countries Germany had the lowest emigration rate in this period: in 1913 only 26,000 people emigrated, fewer than left small countries such as Greece, Belgium, or Sweden. Far more males tended to emigrate than females: many of the emigrants were single young men; others were husbands who hoped to establish themselves in new lands and bring over their wives and families later. Yet except in Ireland, emigration did not lead to net loss in population.

Simultaneously with overseas migration, movement within Europe transferred large numbers from the country to the city. Germany's rapid economic expansion since the foundation of the empire in 1871 had led to a big shift in population. Then two-thirds of the population had been rural; by 1914 nearly two-thirds was urban. Germany pursued a vigorous policy of internal colonization, providing incentives for Germans to settle on the land, especially in East Prussia and Prussian Poland where Germans feared being outnumbered by Slavic elements; but the flow of population to the cities continued inexorably, a symptom of the crisis facing the largest social group on the continent: the peasantry.

Country life

In spite of the explosive growth of cities, most of European society was still rural—defined by size of settlement (generally 2,000 or fewer inhabitants), economic function (especially agriculture, forestry, and fishing), and traditional cultural patterms.[12] Although Britain and Belgium had large urban majorities and Germany a somewhat smaller one, the bulk of the population almost everywhere else lived in small rural settlements. This was particularly true of southern and eastern Europe and European Russia where the population was more than four-fifths rural.

The peasant was consequently the representative European social type in 1914 and the village the basic social milieu. Country life in most parts of Europe had changed vastly over the previous century. Improved communications had brought town and country closer together. But village existence remained brutish by comparison with the conditions of even the poorest city-dwellers. Hardly any villages had paved ways, electricity, or piped water.

Clothing was simple, often sordid and filthy. The colourful 'traditional' costumes that we associate with peasant life in east-central Europe were worn only on special occasions; in some cases they were nationalist revivals, in others inventions. In the more prosperous country areas of Britain, France, and Germany ready-made clothing was becoming available by 1914, undergarments were increasingly popular, and nightgowns were replacing unchanged dayclothes in bed. Elsewhere clothing was generally home-made, spun and sewn by women or woven by men. Most male peasants wore undyed, colourless smocks or floppy shirts over loose trousers. Worn clothes were patched rather than replaced. Children would wear hand-downs. Washing of clothes, as of persons, was rare. 'By 1914', it has been estimated, 'the family wash was undertaken perhaps two or four times a year in relatively advanced areas like Mayenne, still only once a year in Morbihan.'[13] Better-off men might have one Sunday suit that would have to last them the whole of their adult lives. Poorer peasants dressed in rags and sometimes lacked shoes. Good working boots were expensive and many had to make do with wooden clogs. Even those who could afford shoes would seldom wear them for daily pursuits, reserving them for church: they would carry them to the door lest they got muddy, dusty, or worn out. Peasant women and children in Poland, for example, wore shoes only in the winter or when going to market.

Rural housing remained rudimentary. Poor peasants, sharecroppers, and landless labourers might live in mud huts or log cabins with dirt floors. Outside western Europe glass windows were found only in more recently built homes. In Russian Poland the typical peasant hut was built of square-hewn timbers laid across one another as in American log cabins. The interstices between the logs would be stuffed with moss. In the poorer eastern regions such as Belorussia (White Russia) many cottages lacked chimneys. In Romania in 1912 there were still 32,367 traditional *bordeie*, half-buried, low-roofed, one-room, windowless, hovels. It was not uncommon for peasants to share their homes with farm animals. Few children had beds of their own. Such conditions were typical in eastern and south-eastern Europe but they existed in many other areas—in southern Italy, for instance, and in the outlying Celtic parts of Britain. In the Western Isles of Scotland the typical crofter's 'black house' was built of undressed stones, without cement. For lack of wood on the windswept islands, few of the dwellings had windows. There were generally three rooms. The living-room was divided from the *bathach* (byre) by a partition extending only part of the way up to the thatched roof—there were no ceilings. Only the bedroom had a wooden floor. The byre floor was thick with manure, stored there lest the rain dilute its nutrient properties. There was no chimney and the smoke from the perpetually lit peat fire mingled with other animal and vegetable odours and darkened the walls and rafters until it found its way out through the door or a hole in the roof.

The peasant diet was monotonous but rarely unhealthy, save that hygienic precautions were minimal. Most food was home-made. In France by 1914 home-baking had given way in most places to purchase from bakeries, but elsewhere on the continent bread was still commonly baked at home. In eastern Europe peasants rarely ate meat. Pork and lamb were reserved for holidays or special occasions. Otherwise smoked bacon, salami, or sausages would be the only meat consumed. In Orthodox Russia and Romania meat and milk products were in any case forbidden on Wednesdays and Fridays as well as during the four annual fast periods that lasted several weeks. Black bread, often coarse and unappetizing, was the staple in Russia, supplemented by potatoes, turnips, and cabbage. Milk from sheep or goats would be used to make cheese. The best fruit and eggs would generally be sent to the market; for themselves peasants made do with bruised apples and broken eggs. Among peasants in the Brescian hill country of northern Italy the average adult male was estimated to consume 2 kilograms of corn-meal porridge a day. Sicilian peasants ate mainly bread, macaroni, and vegetables. In Greece the rural diet consisted primarily of bread, olives, cheese and garlic; not much meat was eaten save among the Vlach shepherds of the Pindos mountains. In Transylvania the relatively prosperous German farmer ate a rich diet of roast pork, sausage, smoked meats, cheese, sauerkraut, and fruit; his poor Romanian neighbour ate little except corn mush and onions.

In some areas diseases arising from malnutrition and dirt were widespread: peasants in southern Europe, whose corn diet lacked niacin, suffered from chronic pellagra. In most countries, tuberculosis was gradually declining as a killer disease, but in south-east Europe it remained a deadly scourge of the peasant population and even in Britain more than fifty thousand people died of it in 1914. In country areas medical care was often rudimentary. The application of leeches was still the most commonly prescribed remedy for a wide range of illnesses. A typical procedure was that of the village of Vannes, near Orléans: a horse would be driven into shallow water at the edge of a pond and made to stand there for a quarter of an hour.

When it emerged, large numbers of leeches would be found attached to its legs. These would be detached and a dozen or so of the fattest ones selected for application to the patient. The leeches would be placed in position behind the ears and would remain there until gorged with blood whereupon they would be replaced as often as indicated by the doctor.[14]

Population growth, soil exhaustion, and inheritance laws pressed down on land usage, increasing the impetus to migrate to cities or overseas. Many peasants would emigrate temporarily, sometimes returning seasonally to work on the family farm. This was true even of transatlantic migrants, particularly from southern Italy. The Italian economist (later Prime Minister) F. S. Nitti, who conducted an inquiry into social conditions among peasants in Calabria and Basilicata in the period 1906–10, wrote: 'Emigration has lost its quasi-dramatic character. People come and go from America with the greatest of ease.'[15]

Peasants were heavily dependent on the vagaries of the agrarian cycle. When blessed with good harvests, as in Russia immediately before 1914, they might succeed in accumulating a small surplus. But if crops failed they would often be compelled by the threat of starvation to mortgage or even sell their land. In Russia and Prussian Poland, the expansion of land banks, credit unions and co-operatives in the years before 1914 helped peasants to acquire or retain title to their land, to buy farm implements, and to market products. In Bulgaria, Bohemia, Slovenia, and Croatia too co-operatives and agrarian savings banks played an important role. But they tempered rather than eradicated the prevailing peasant misery.

The money economy had not yet fully penetrated those parts of eastern and southern Europe where subsistence farming was the norm. In the Polesian marshes, for example, trade was commonly by barter. Peasants still preferred to keep their money in gold under the bed, not in banks. But in other areas financial institutions were beginning to venture into the countryside, as, for example, in France, where peasants increasingly placed their savings in the government-guaranteed postal savings banks. In Britain and France shops were quite common in small country towns but in eastern Europe most retail trade was conducted in markets or by itinerant pedlars, generally Jews.

Patterns of landholding varied greatly. The small peasant proprietor was the characteristic landholder in Scandinavia, France, Serbia, Greece, Bulgaria, and parts of the Galician region of Spain. In Britain most farms were medium-sized tenancies (the mean size of holdings was about 115 acres); very large holdings generally existed only in unproductive grazing lands on the Celtic fringe.

Large estates, generally belonging to the aristocracy and gentry, predominated in much of the Russian Empire (except Finland), most of Austria-Hungary, East Prussia, parts of Romania and southern Italy, as well as some regions of Spain (notably Andalusia). In some countries, such as Hungary, the great territorial magnates retained their traditional roles and power virtually intact. In others, such as France, the nobility had been legally abolished and survived as little more than a quaint relic. But even where they no longer held direct economic power over the peasantry, the aristocracy and gentry still often dominated rural society, inspiring deference where they could no longer wield authority. In Britain rural labourers had had the vote since 1884 and aristocratic political influence had declined, particularly since the Liberal government's emasculation of the power of the House of Lords in 1911; nevertheless working men in the English countryside still routinely touched their forelocks in the presence of their betters. Such attitudes were partly a matter of mystique but they also reflected the considerable indirect power that the aristocracy continued to enjoy. Great aristocratic fortunes, although declining by comparison with industrial wealth, remained important in Germany and even in Britain. In Bavaria in 1914 forty-nine out of the sixty-six richest inhabitants were classified as belonging to royalty or nobility. Forty out of the sixty-four richest individuals in Prussia belonged to the nobility, although, as Anatole Lieven points out, such figures can be misleading since wealth itself often provided a passport into the titled class: twenty-eight of the forty, among them thirteen Jews, had been ennobled within the previous half-century and all these were financiers or businessmen rather than landowners.[16] Increasingly, the old aristocracy, while often subscribing theoretically to rural ideals, moved their homes and capital to the cities, and were infiltrated by and intermarried with urban financial and business classes.

Living side by side with the owners of great estates in the less-developed parts of Europe were large numbers of smallholders, sometimes tenants of neighbouring magnates. Such peasants scraped a precarious living off tiny plots of land, often working for part of the year as day-labourers on nearby estates. In Romania, for example, 49 per cent of the cultivable area was held by 7,790 large proprietors (in lots larger than 50 hectares), while 51 per cent was owned by 957,000 peasant smallholders. Of these, 921,000 held lots smaller than 10 hectares and 423,000 farmed less than 3 hectares, which was well below the minimum regarded as necessary for subsistence. In general, agriculture in eastern and southern Europe was much less efficient than in Germany, the Low Countries, Scandinavia and England. In the poorer regions artificial fertilizers were little used and few even among the most prosperous farmers could dream of buying the recently invented petrol-driven tractor. On Russian peasant farms the primitive hand sickle was still in general use. Most miserable was the lot of the landless labourers, the *braccianti* on the *latifondi* (great estates) of Sicily and Calabria, and their counterparts elsewhere.

In most parts of Europe women worked in the fields alongside their menfolk at least at some times of year. In Romania the number of women engaged in agriculture, 1.6 million, almost exactly equalled the number of men in that sector. Similar conditions prevailed in several more advanced countries. In France 3.2 million women worked in agricultural pursuits in 1911, compared with 2.5 million in manufacturing industry. In Germany the 4.6 million women agriculturalists in 1907 exceeded the number of women workers in all other sectors combined. Nor were women limited to milking, fruit-picking, or other light tasks. Often they performed backbreaking labour: Millet's female hay-binders, faggot-gatherers, potato planters, sheep-shearers, and gleaners were still hard at work in the early twentieth century.

Denmark provides an example of one of the most efficient agricultural economies in Europe. Her farms were highly specialized and succeeded in expanding productivity fast in the years before 1914. Danish farmers were well educated and quick to adopt new techniques and machinery. Co-operatives also played an important role in production and marketing. By 1913 there were more than 1,100 dairy co-ops. Agricultural exports, particularly of butter and bacon to Britain, accounted for nearly 90 per cent of all exports in the decade before 1914, an increase from about 80 per cent thirty years earlier.

Spain furnishes a striking contrast of agricultural inefficiency and stagnation. Once she had been self-sufficient in grain production, but in the three decades before 1914 grain imports exceeded exports, this in spite of tariffs raised against imports. Nor could she comfort herself, as did Britain, that this food deficit was the price of population growth and industrial advance: by contemporary European standards her population grew slowly and industrialization was minimal.

Nowhere was the crisis of agrarian society more pressing than in Russia. Pyotr Stolypin, Interior Minister and Prime Minister from 1906 until his assassination in 1911, had vigorously promoted reform of the peasant economy. His particular object had been to free peasants from the bonds of the *mir* (village commune). The holding of peasant land in communal tenure had been regarded by conservatives as an important safeguard against political unrest ever since the emancipation of the serfs in 1861. But the *mir* was a barrier against agricultural modernization and productivity. When Stolypin took office in 1906 more than 80 per cent of all peasant land was held in communal tenure. By eliminating the rigidities of the commune, Stolypin aimed to create a solid class of small peasant proprietors (his 'wager on the strong'). In the years before 1914 the inefficient strip system of cultivation began to be replaced by more efficient, consolidated holdings. Better-off peasants started using more advanced implements and machinery. Consumption of artificial fertilizers multiplied sevenfold between 1900 and 1913. Population pressure was eased by the encouragement of migration to Siberia. In 1913 Russia was the world's largest grain exporter. Yet although Russian agricultural productivity improved as a result of Stolypin's measures, it continued to lag far behind west European standards. Average wheat yields in the three decades before 1913 were less than half those in France, a third of those in Germany and Britain, and lower even than those of India. Meanwhile the land reform had unsettling effects on agrarian social relationships; as the surplus population of poorest peasants was driven off the land, discontent and unrest in the countryside grew rather than diminished.

The crisis of rural Europe was not merely demographic and economic; one of its symptoms was also mass ignorance. Illiteracy was still a widespread condition in Europe in 1914. Universal or near-universal literacy (more than 90 per cent of the population) was found in Britain, France, Germany, and Switzerland. On the other hand, more than half the population was illiterate in Greece, Portugal, Romania, Spain, and the Russian Empire. Levels of literacy varied greatly between regions. Scotland was more literate than England, the Baltic provinces and Poland more so than Russia. Northern Italy's literacy rate was closer to that of France than to that of southern Italy: Piedmont, for instance was 89 per cent literate in 1911, whereas the rate in Calabria was only 30 per cent. The rate also varied between the sexes: almost everywhere men were more literate than women. And among national groups: in the Austrian Empire most Germans, Czechs, and Jews could read and write, but among other nationalities, particularly Serbs, Croats, and Ruthenians, illiteracy was widespread. The rate varied greatly between town and country: the urban upper and middle classes everywhere were wholly literate; the rural poor had the largest percentage of illiterates. But above all, it varied according to age, since in most countries the extension of compulsory elementary schooling was a relatively recent event.

By 1914 compulsory, free education at the primary level was the European norm. But the gap between legislation and realization was wide. In rural eastern and southern Europe many children did not attend school at all. A law calling for universal primary education had been enacted in the Russian Empire in 1908 but its implementation was to be stretched out over many years and was not expected to be complete until 1922. Russia had made impressive educational strides since the 1860s, thanks particularly to the efforts of the *zemstva* (local councils). As many as 68 per cent of Russian army recruits were literate in 1913. In Moscow and St Petersburg 90 per cent of young men could read in that year. But the contrast between urban and rural areas was sharp. In the province of Moscow 84 per cent of children between the ages of eight and eleven were enrolled in 1911 in schools under the jurisdiction of the Ministry of Education or of the Orthodox Church. But in Bessarabia enrolment was only 40 per cent and in the province of Kovno only 22 per cent. Even allowing for some children who attended other schools (for example, those of ethnic minorities, particularly Jews), this left a large part of the rural poor totally uneducated. The wage of a village schoolteacher in Russia barely sufficed even to cover the cost of food for a family, so that many teachers were compelled to moonlight as caretakers or porters or to cultivate small plots of land. As for secondary education, it was largely the reserve of the gentry and the urban middle class. Overall, Russia's educational system was by far the worst of the major European powers. Teacher training and instructional aids, including books, were minimal in much of Europe. Class sizes were large—over forty on average in primary schools in Russia, near fifty in Spain and Bulgaria. Educational methods usually included a large measure of rote memorization as well as corporal punishment. Throughout the continent provision for the education of girls was far lower than for boys: in Russia, for example, only 7 per cent of the Ministry of Education's budget for secondary education in 1914 was earmarked for girls' schools.

Throughout the continent religion was the most powerful institutional and ideological force in the countryside. Secularization had eroded the intellectual and social power of the Church in the course of the previous century. In this as in other respects the impact was greatest in north-west Europe but even there organized religion maintained powerful redoubts. In Britain, where urban working-class attendance at church declined steadily, the churches retained significant social influence in rural areas and the non-conformist conscience continued to hold part of the governing Liberal Party, in power since 1905, in thrall. In many countries the Church retained authority over much of the educational system; in others it contested the state for control over it. The majority of schools in Hungary were under church administration. German public elementary schools were largely organized on a confessional basis, with all-Catholic or all-Protestant pupils and teaching staffs. French anti-clerical governments under the Third Republic had struggled since the 1880s to reduce the influence of the Church in education and state schools had been almost completely laicized; but in the countryside the long-running conflict between the village schoolteacher and the *curé* still raged, churches were full on Sundays, and ecclesiastical influence in politics had by no means been vanquished.

Alongside institutionalized religion, and often mixed up with it, countryside superstitions, magical remedies, and folk customs died hard. In some places witches would still be called upon to remove evil spirits from troublesome cows or pigs. In the Polish countryside, fires were lit on the eve of St John (24 June) to help crops grow. Polish peasants would not dare to touch a swallow's nest or even to look too closely at a bird flying in or out of it. Belief was widespread in wood-sprites, banshees, cloud-dwelling spirits, old women who ate children, and local devils in the guise of owls, cats, bats, or reptiles. W. B. Yeats, in an essay written in 1914, recalled: 'When I was a boy in Sligo, a stable boy met his late master going round the yard, and having told him to go and haunt the lighthouse, was dismissed by his mistress for sending her husband to haunt so inclement a spot.'[17] All sorts of rituals were performed to ward off the evil eye. Hungarian peasants believed that the recital of incantations could have medicinal effects: a man with a pustule on his tongue would say, 'A lump's appeared on my tongue, pray take it to Mrs Deák's bum.'[18]

While city and village were, in many senses, worlds apart, they were not rigidly separated. Although most peasants rarely travelled further than the market town nearest their villages, several forces were drawing town and country closer together. Railways had ended the hermetic isolation of many rural areas. Universal conscription in all the major countries except Britain plucked young men out of villages in their formative years and deposited them in garrison towns often far from their homes. The extraordinary pace of industrialization and urbanization over the previous two generations left many families with half a foot in the countryside. In Russia, France, Germany, and elsewhere, urban dwellers often retained some rural land and worked it as a part-time venture, or on a sharecropping basis, or, in the case of smaller plots, as allotments. It was not uncommon for town-dwellers to work in the fields as seasonal migrant labour. Conversely, peasants with marginally productive units would take jobs in nearby factories leaving some or all of the farm work to be done by their wives.

Urban civilization

Urban living conditions for the poor, while dismal, were generally less miserable and uncertain than the rural poverty that the immigrants to the cities had fled. Overcrowding in tumbledown rural housing was frequently even worse than in the city slums. Concentrations of urban squalor affronted social consciences and led well-meaning theorists to advocate resettlement of workers on the land. But such bucolic utopianism rarely achieved meaningful results. The great density of urban populations, it is true, afforded dangerous breeding conditions for epidemic disease; on the other hand, preventive public health measures reached urban populations before being extended to more remote rural areas. Most big cities had piped water (not always purified) and drainage systems although working-class homes rarely had bathrooms or inside toilets and one tap often served several households. In eastern Europe hygienic conditions were a major threat to health. The great Polish textile manufacturing centre of Łődź, 'Manchester of the Russian Empire', with a population of nearly half a million people, was one of many cities that had no sewerage system at all in 1914.

Daily life was a hard grind for most of the urban population. Men rather than machines or horses performed a great deal of heavy labour at the coal-face, in dockyards, and on building sites. But unlike peasants, whose working hours were in principle unregulated (though in effect they varied according to the agricultural cycle), industrial working hours were increasingly limited by legislation. Most countries had set an outer limit of ten or eleven hours of work in any twenty-four-hour period. In some industries eight- or nine-hour days had been established by collective agreement and in some cases enshrined in law. Many industries, particularly mining, which employed over a million men in both Britain and Germany, were physically dangerous and gave rise to terrible industrial diseases. Of the 1.1 million miners in Britain in 1913, 177,000 suffered injury and 1,753 were killed as a result of industrial accident or disease in that year alone. Agricultural accidents could not compare with this grim annual toll of just one branch of the industrial economy. But industrial workers, unlike peasants, could sometimes claim some form of compensation for injury and their workplaces were generally subject to regulation and inspection for hygiene and safety.

Women frequently worked long hours in factories for much lower wages than men but in most countries legislation provided them with some minimal safeguards. Women peasants enjoyed no such protection, while many states, for example, prohibited night-work by women in factories or workshops. In western Europe labour laws also forbade or limited the employment of children in industry. Even Hungary, hardly in the vanguard of social experimentation, forbade the employment of children under ten, and limited it, albeit not very strenuously, up to the age of sixteen. The administration of such laws, however, was often imperfect, inspection was lax, and loopholes were eagerly exploited by employers. In eastern and southern Europe peasants often preferred that their children work on the land rather than attend school.

Domestic service, the largest category of women's employment in towns in Britain and some other countries, remained almost completely unregulated. Britain had 1.7 million domestic servants in 1914, the largest single occupational group; in Germany the figure (for 1907) was 1.3 million. In both countries women constituted an ever-larger proportion of the group as men increasingly turned to industrial occupations. Servants' hours were long and they worked without mechanical aids. Heating in middle-class homes was by logs or coal that had to be carried regularly to the grate by servants. The portable vacuum cleaner and the electric washing machine, recently invented luxuries, had barely yet been purchased by most households.

The urban diet was more varied and perhaps more nourishing than that of the subsistence farmer. In Germany a typical working-class household budget in 1907 was estimated to allocate a little under half of family income to food, a lower proportion than in 1927, 1937, or 1950 and only slightly higher than in 1962 when German workers were certainly not starving. This suggests a certain margin of discretionary income. Average weekly meat consumption of all classes in Britain and Germany in 1914 was over 2 lb per person. In poorer countries less meat was eaten, but so long as they had jobs few urban workers starved. In most of central and eastern Europe imported oranges, grapefruit, or bananas were exotic luxuries available only to the wealthy. Locally produced vegetables were cheap and some workers grew their own on plots in the country or suburban allotments. Sections of the urban population, however, ate miserable fare. Slum children in Britain often contracted rickets for lack of vitamin D. The standard English workhouse provision of the early years of the century was designed more as a deterrent than as a nutrient: for breakfast the inmate received 4 oz of bread and 1.5 oz of porridge; for lunch, vegetables (12 oz) were served four times a week and meat (4.5 oz of beef or pork) three times; supper consisted of more bread plus 1.5 oz of gruel; broth and cheese appeared occasionally; tea was available only on Sundays. The British had the sweetest national tooth in Europe: 87 lb of sugar was consumed per head in 1914. Perhaps for this reason Britain had more than three times as many dentists as France.

Urban working-class incomes tended to be higher and to grow faster than rural ones, although this might hardly be noticeable to city people weighed down by the pressure for money payments of all sorts. In Germany, for example, real wages in industry are estimated to have doubled between 1871 and 1913. They varied greatly, however, by area: wages in Hamburg and Berlin were more than double those in Silesia. Average earnings of rural day-labourers in the same period also increased—but only by about three-quarters. Continuity of employment for unskilled urban workers was far from assured but in 1913–14 unemployment was low. It was estimated at 4.7 per cent in France, 2.9 per cent in Germany, and 2.1 per cent in Britain (we have no exact figures because governments hardly yet recognized the concept of unemployment, often seeing it as a moral rather than an economic problem; consequently regular statistics on the unemployed were not collected). Unemployment insurance, generally organized by benefit societies, municipalities, or trade unions, covered mainly skilled workers. Britain introduced a broader compulsory state system in 1911, covering, however, only certain industries. Nevertheless, many urban workers could rely to some extent on state insurance schemes against accidents, disability, sickness, and old age: these had been initiated in Germany by Bismarck and were later emulated in other advanced economies.

Some degree of protection for urban workers was also provided by trade unions. Relative prosperity in the years before 1914 had led to fast growth in trade union membership: in Britain the numbers had grown from 2.2 million in 1906 to 4.1 million in 1913; and in Germany from 2.3 million in 1907 to three million in 1913. Although unions had not yet captured a majority even of the non-agricultural workforce in any country, they were making headway, particularly in extractive and manufacturing industries. In spite of economic growth and low unemployment, the years immediately before the outbreak of the First World War saw heightened industrial tensions in several countries. Syndicalist doctrines, popularized in France, spread through much of western Europe and between 1910 and 1914 both Britain and Germany suffered record numbers of workdays lost in strikes.

In the industrial societies of north-west Europe, most observers in 1914, if asked to identify the most dangerous sources of social conflict, would have pointed to the profound class divisions that rent Britain, Germany, Belgium, and France. These found ideological form in the various streams of socialism characteristic of each country: revisionist Marxist in Germany and Austria, Marxist, Blanquist, Proudhonist, and syndicalist in France, and various radical, generally non-Marxist traditions in Britain. They found institutional form in the working-class movements that had grown up over the previous two generations. Socialist political parties were advancing in partnership with labour unions. In the elections to the German Reichstag in 1912 the Social Democrats had won a third of the votes and 110 seats, thereby becoming the largest party in the chamber. In France too election results in May and June 1914 showed significant Socialist gains. Socialists also gained ground in elections in Norway in 1912, in Italy in 1913, and in Sweden in the spring of 1914. Within the Socialist parties conflict raged between revolutionaries and constitutionalists; trade unions were often divided between syndicalists, who dreamed of a revolutionary general strike, and reformists, who sought gradual economic gains for their members within the existing social order. Internal splits notwithstanding, the Second International, an alliance of national Socialist parties founded in 1889, seemed in 1914 to be a major political force. But the advanced economies, in which socialism was moving ahead, were not representative of Europe as a whole. The urban proletariat, to whom socialism made its chief appeal, might take courage from the forecast that they represented the wave of the future. In most countries, however, they were outnumbered by the peasantry and in the cities outgunned and outmanoeuvred by the class that stamped its interests, its values, and its tastes on urban civilization: the bourgeoisie.

Of all classes this was the most difficult to define. The term embraced a number of quite disparate social groups, sometimes with conflicting interests: high financiers and entrepreneurs, petty traders and shopkeepers, the independent professions and government officials. One simple way of recognizing a 'bourgeois' household that has been suggested by historians probably makes sense: it generally could not exist without servants. But even this litmus test was not universally valid, since it might exclude many teachers, librarians, clerks, shop assistants, and other white-collar workers spawned by commerce and bureaucracy, some of whom subsisted on wages only marginally above those of the skilled working-class.

At the outer fringes of the bourgeoisie was another floating element that defied rigid classification: the intelligentsia. The word first came into use in several European languages at this period, originally with special application to Russian radical intellectuals. This was the group of whom Marx had written in the *Communist Manifesto*: 'Just as . . . at an earlier period, a section of the nobility went over to the bourgeoisie, so now a portion of the bourgeoisie goes over to the proletariat, and in particular a portion of the bourgeois ideologists who have raised themselves to the level of comprehending theoretically the historical movement as a whole.' If the bourgeoisie is defined narrowly as the owners of movable capital, then the intelligentsia might be excluded; but their intangible capital of ideas gave them a special power that, in truth, enabled them to transcend class, although by no means all of them 'comprehended the historical movement' sufficiently to adopt the role allotted to them by Marx.

For the archetype of the bourgeois city in 1914, we may turn to the largest provincial city in Europe (leaving aside only Moscow): with a population of one million, Glasgow, now at the height of its importance as an industrial centre and port, exemplified the creative vitality of middle-class civilization in its industrial importance particularly in shipbuilding, its international trading connections, its architecture, and its cultural life. A greater tonnage of ships was produced on the Clyde in 1913 than in the whole of Germany. The stolid grandeur of Glasgow's mercantile thoroughfares, its municipal buildings, and its university, the confident sweep of the terraces in its western suburbs, and the ornamented fantasy of its French Renaissance-style art gallery, built for the Glasgow International Exhibition in 1901, all gave expression to the self-satisfaction of the city's regnant merchant class. 'No city has rivalled, far less surpassed, the commercial metropolis of Scotland,' boasted its Town Clerk in 1915, adding, 'This has chiefly arisen from the city being—if the expression may be used—*cosmopolitan* in its commerce and manufactures.'[19] The architect and designer Charles Rennie Mackintosh, a pioneer of modernist functional design, achieved his masterpiece in the interior decoration of the Willow Tea Rooms on Sauchiehall Street—setting for that most sacred ritual of Scottish life, high tea. Cheek by jowl with this splendour were the tenements of the Gorbals, among the vilest slums in Europe. Free Church Presbyterians from the Highlands, Catholics from Ireland, and Jews from Lithuania crowded into the poorer areas of the city, sucked into its booming, diversified economy.

Of all the institutions of bourgeois Europe in 1914, two were at their apogee: the department store and the café. Every European city worthy of the name possessed several large retailing emporiums. The Bon Marché in Paris claimed to be the largest in the world; the other large Paris stores in order of 1910 sales volume were the Louvre, La Samaritaine, and Printemps. In

London Whiteley's, 'the Universal Provider', founded in 1863, claimed to be the oldest; the newest and most glamorous was Selfridge's, founded in 1909. Berlin had more than thirty major stores, of which the best known were the Kaufhaus des Westens ('Kadewe'), the palatial Wertheim store on the Leipzigerstrasse, and the Hermann Tietz ('Hertie') store on the Alexanderplatz. The two latter were regarded as architectural marvels on account of the grandeur and sumptuousness of their design. Some stores expanded into nationwide and even cross-national chains. Lewis's spread from Liverpool all over Britain. Tietz bought stores in various parts of Germany as well as the De Bijenkorf store in Amsterdam. These were huge concerns. Harrod's building in Knightsbridge, London, covered 4.5 acres by 1911 and had a staff of six thousand. Even a provincial store, Cockayne's in Sheffield, employed over five hundred permanent staff. Such stores were veritable temples of consumerism. Their staff were commonly subjected, like regular clergy, to iron discipline: at La Samaritaine, we are told, 'regulations governed every detail of behaviour, from prohibiting the wearing of silk stockings and décolleté dresses by the assistants, to the requirement that each of the eight thousand employees should always sit in the same place at the free lunch'.[20] Although department stores controlled only a small share of trade, they set standards and modernized retailing practices. Trademarked brand-name goods, packaged in factories, attractively displayed, and advertised on a national scale (features satirized in Wells's *Tono-Bungay* (1909)), were gradually displacing the old-style system whereby goods were weighed, measured, and wrapped only at the point of sale. In eastern Europe, however, this process was still in its infancy. Marc Chagall's painting *Shop in Vitebsk* (1914), shows equal-armed balances for weighing goods that were stored in sacks, jars, and boxes.

This was the great era of the café as a social and intellectual centre throughout most of continental Europe. The coffee-house culture of Budapest, Prague, and Vienna provided a home, workplace, club, salon, reading-room, debating-hall, advertising agency, and stock exchange for gossip. The café was a forum that was classless in the sense that it was open to all who could pay its modest charges, yet a place where bourgeois manners and mannerisms were cultivated to the highest degree of refinement—and the lowest depths of vulgarity. In the early years of the century Paris had around thirty thousand cafés. Budapest had over six hundred, of which the most luxurious was the Café New York, whose architect, Alajos Hauszmann, was also responsible for the reconstruction of the Hungarian royal palace. The café was an alien concept in Britain where the club, the public house, and the tea-room each performed some, but not all, of its functions. No central European intellectual of the period would have disagreed with the conservative Hungarian publicist Jenő Rákosi who later recollected that 'every intelligent person had spent a part of his youth in the coffeehouse . . . without that, the education of a young man would be imperfect and incomplete'.21 The café was an ersatz university for the half-educated, finishing-school for the semi-civilized, and drawing-room for the *demi-mondaine*. Everybody went there, but it was the peculiar haunt of people at the margin of society: prostitutes, conmen, faddists, *flâneurs*, layabouts, 'resting' actors, freelance feuilleton writers hoping to be published, and discontented would-be artists waiting to be 'discovered'. Among the latter in the cafés of Vienna and Munich in 1913 and 1914, engaging in violent arguments, or muttering to himself as he ate cream cakes and read the newspapers, was the young Adolf Hitler.

To some extent the café was merely a respectable transmogrification of the tavern. Drunkenness was a major social problem in most European countries in the years before 1914. In France 34 gallons of wine were drunk per head of population in 1905. Consumption of beer in Britain in 1914 was 27 gallons per head and the figures were similar for Germany and Denmark. In Belgium, where children often drank beer, an astonishing 48.8 gallons per head were consumed in 1905; however, the alcoholic content there was relatively low. In Russia, where vodka was the main alcoholic drink, nearly a gallon a year per head was consumed. The effects on health and social behaviour were far-reaching: in Russia half of all prisoners were said to have committed their offences while drunk. Temperance groups in several countries conducted energetic propaganda campaigns but achieved little or no reduction in alcohol consumption.

For many working-class people drink was the chief escape from drudgery and squalor, a partial substitution for old-style recreations still popular among country folk. Among the Vlach mountain people of northern Greece, for example, young people played vigorous outdoor games, *Muma ku Preftlu* (The Mother with the Priest) and *ku Gámila* (With the Camel). Traditional rural or small-town entertainments, hurdy-gurdies, bear-baiting, cock fights, and circuses, were being replaced by urban mass amusements: music halls in Britain, Grand Guignol melodramas in France, and the silent cinema almost everywhere. Germany alone had two thousand picture houses by 1914. Variations on the café incorporated old styles of entertainment in a new setting, as in the café-concert in Paris and the art-nouveau-style Café Jama Michalika in Cracow, which presented cabaret, *szopki* (a form of political satire), and a puppet theatre. Games and sport too were adapting to the constraints of city life. Urban workers could not afford to play middle-class sports, such as tennis, golf, or badminton, let alone upper-class ones like polo, fencing, and yachting; they had few open spaces in which to play games of any sort. Cycling, however, was a relatively classless sport that attracted a large following in England, France, and the Low Countries. The working classes flocked to old spectator sports, horse-racing and boxing, as well as newer ones, particularly football. The average professional football match in Britain on Saturday afternoon attracted a crowd of thirty thousand. The modern Olympics, held quadrennially since 1896 (at Stockholm in 1912), attracted huge crowds. In north-western Europe day trips by railway to the seaside were common and the beginning of a mass tourism industry was discernible.

The rise of literacy extended the market for popular fiction, while the growth of public libraries, particularly in Britain, brought all literature within the reach of urban workers. Autodidacts used the libraries as night schools, betting men as a place to ascertain the odds, and tramps as shelter from the rain—leading some authorities to institute separate reading rooms to protect ladies from unpleasant odours. Over sixty million books a year circulated from public libraries in Britain in the years before 1914. Although Britain led the field, most of western Europe was well endowed with various types of public library: in 1906 Berlin had 268, Dresden 78, and Vienna 165. In this respect too eastern Europe lagged behind.

This was very much a man's world. Most governments, institutions, and businesses were run by men. In 1906 Finland (an autonomous Grand Duchy under the suzerainty of the Tsar) had become the first European country to enfranchise women and also allowed them to stand for election to parliament. But only Denmark and Norway followed suit before the First World War. Women were beginning to gain admission to some professions but were barely represented save in nursing and teaching, both low-paid and low-status by comparison with the 'free' professions such us law and medicine. Married women were generally regarded, in legal form and social practice, as subject to the authority of their husbands. The proper object of the single woman was held to be the finding of a husband. Women, even if they worked outside the home, were expected to bear primary responsibility for household tasks and to cultivate domestic arts such as sewing, knitting, and embroidery.

In general, European society in 1914 was settled and peaceful. Crime, both against persons and against property, was low. In Britain the average number of murders per annum in the years 1910–14 was 153; the rate had been going down steadily since 1890. Elsewhere the rate was higher (it was at least four times as high in Italy) but still low by the standards of the second half of the century. Capital punishment, while on the statute books of most countries, was generally regarded as exceptional and unusual; it had disappeared altogether in Belgium, Finland, the Netherlands, Italy, Portugal, and Romania. By and large the bourgeoisie remained confident that the future was on its side; alarmists might take fright from syndicalist threats of a general strike or from occasional eruptions by violent anarchists but in general social peace prevailed. Yet there was an insidious force at work that would shortly destroy this world.

The nationalist canker

The root of European disorder in 1914 was not, as some thought, class, but ethnicity. Solidarities and antagonisms based on ethnicity, for reasons that lie buried in human hearts, answer to some of the most deeply rooted and instinctive social feelings of our species. European history in our time shows how futile it is to ignore them.

Nationalism, not socialism, was the most explosive political force in much of central and eastern Europe, all the more so because it was frustrated and pent up by the authoritarian structures of the multi-national empires. Even in some of the advanced economies national questions had become acute in these years: in Britain the struggle over Irish home rule reached its parliamentary climax; in Belgium conflict between advocates of French and Flemish in education and the army divided the country bitterly. National feeling was dismissed as 'false consciousness' by Marxists and derided as irrational by many others. Its force derived from the fact that for large numbers of people it provided the most intelligible framework into which to fit their understanding of the world around them. For some it became, as James Joll has put it, 'an all-demanding, all-excusing nationalism'[22] that defied the conventional cost-accounting of rational men and pressed the quest for national fulfilment to the ultimate extremes of glory or death.

The national question took different forms in different places. Sometimes it was bound up with property relations, sometimes with language disputes, and sometimes with religion. In Ireland nationalism was mainly supported by Catholic peasants and opposed by Protestant landowners and urban workers. Although some romantics sought to revive the Gaelic tongue, most Irishmen already spoke English and the language question was not at the forefront of political controversy. In Croatia, by contrast, resentment of enforced linguistic Magyarization was a primary grievance of nationalists; Croatian peasants' demands for land reform at the expense of Magyar and German landowners also featured prominently in the nationalist programme. Most Croats shared the Roman Catholic religion of their Austrian and Hungarian rulers but religious affinity barely abated nationalist enthusiasm. In Finland, we find a third pattern: here the Finnish language and the Lutheran religion formed a basis for national identity and resistance to forcible Russification; but since most agricultural land was farmed by Finnish peasant proprietors, the land question did not figure in nationalist politics.

The national question was most acute in Austria-Hungary. To some extent, however, this is more apparent in retrospect than it was to contemporaries. The common picture of the empire as a 'prison of nations' is overdrawn, a product of the nationalist historiographies of the subject peoples and of some of their foreign champions. In reaction against this tradition, one historian has described pre-1914 Austria as 'a tolerant, open society, without forcible Germanization or blind centralism'.[23] Limited freedoms enabled Czechs, Poles, Ukrainians, and others to fashion national cultures and organize political parties under the Habsburg umbrella. Jews, unlike their co-religionists in Russia, enjoyed civil equality and in Vienna, Budapest, and elsewhere many moved into the professions and upper bourgeoisie and played important economic and civic roles. On the other hand, the demands of Czechs and others for political autonomy in the empire were not granted. The national question remained the Achilles heel of the Habsburgs. It arose most dangerously in its Balkan extremities.

The twin provinces of Bosnia and Herzegovina had been under Ottoman suzerainty from 1463 but since 1878 had been occupied by Austro-Hungarian forces. At the time of the 1910 census the population of 1.9 million consisted of 43 per cent Serbs, 32 per cent Muslims, and around 20 per cent Croats; there was also a small Jewish community. The Muslims, descendants of Christian converts to Islam, were ethnically and linguistically indistinguishable from their Serb and Croat neighbours. There was very little industry and 87 per cent of the population lived off the land. Most large estates belonged to Muslim *begs* and *agas* and were worked by Christian tenants, *kmets*, who were little more than serfs. This was one of the last areas in Europe where a system akin to serfdom still existed. There were, in addition, large numbers of smallholders, both Muslim and Christian. Following the Young Turk Revolution of 1908 the Habsburgs, fearing a resuscitation of Turkish power in the Balkans, formally annexed Bosnia-Herzegovina (in order not to upset the balance between Austria and Hungary it was annexed to neither but was ruled as a *corpus separatum* by the joint Austro-Hungarian Minister of Finance). The annexation exacerbated Serbian resentment and anti-Habsburg feeling. Habsburg rule was relatively efficient and began construction of a modern infrastructure in the region. The Austrians conceded a Diet (assembly) with limited powers and governed with the support of a coalition of Muslim landowners, Croats, and some Serbs. But the rulers were seen as alien by all major elements of the population. Croats sought links with neighbouring Hungarian-ruled Croatia. Muslims hankered after Ottoman rule. Serbian nationalists, both in Serbia herself and in Bosnia, had for several years harboured the ambition to acquire the province for Serbia. Terrorist groups, encouraged by elements in the Serbian government, became active in Bosnia. Such groups were hostile both to the feudal agrarian order and to Habsburg rule. On 28 June 1914 Gavrilo Princip, a young Bosnian Serb member of one such group, the 'Young Bosnians', assassinated the Archduke Franz Ferdinand, nephew and heir-apparent of the Austrian emperor, as he visited Sarajevo.

There was no inevitability about the spiral that descended from the assassination in Sarajevo to the outbreak of world war. Nevertheless, if the archduke had left Sarajevo unscathed, some similar incident elsewhere would probably have led to a similar war. The murder was a precipitant, not a cause. The conflict between national aspirations and imperial structures was not unique to Bosnia. It existed in different forms over much of Europe. In particular, a dangerous vacuum had opened up in the Balkans as a result of the virtual elimination of Ottoman power in Europe. Russia and Austria-Hungary found themselves drawn in by way of vindication of the principles on which they believed their empires were based. Russia had long championed the rights of the south Slavs to independence. To abandon that position now, Russia's leaders believed, would be to abdicate her role as a great power. Austria-Hungary's leaders felt that the very survival of the Habsburg monarchy was threatened by the resurgence of south Slav nationalisms. Meanwhile Germany's dynamic economy and military strength demanded, in the minds of many political, military, and business leaders, some outlet, whether in the form of territorial acquisitions in eastern Europe (a German-dominated *Mitteleuropa*) or colonies (*Mittelafrika*). War, while not inevitable, was a logical outcome.

2

Europe at War 1914–1917

I stood on my own, the last
of the species that fight,
seeing these brothers, with feet turned upwards, growing
until they reached the sky, in death,
to kick it. I saw
the moon like an animal
rub a silver face on the worn nails in the boots
of upturned soldiers.

*Uri Zvi Greenberg, Balkan front, 1915/16**

Outbreak

The First World War has been called 'the Third Balkan War'.[1] The most immediate explanation for the outbreak of this third war, at the local level, is the situation resulting from the previous two. The First Balkan War, which ended with the Treaty of London in May 1913, had demonstrated that Turkish power in the Balkans was at an end and that the final stage of the scramble for succession was at hand. In the Second Balkan War, in the summer of 1913, the Bulgarians, angered that Athens and Belgrade had come to an agreement to partition Macedonia, attacked their former allies, Greece and Serbia. They were joined by Romania, which had stood on the sidelines in the First Balkan War. Ottoman forces renewed the struggle against Bulgaria. The result was the defeat of Bulgaria's bid to become the dominant state in the region. The Turks regained Adrianople. In the Treaty of Bucharest, signed in August 1913, Greece gained Salonica, Crete, and part of Macedonia.

* From 'Naming Souls', translated from the Hebrew by Jon Silkin and Ezra Spicehandler. Jon Silkin, ed., *The Penguin Book of First World War Poetry*, London, 1996, 277–8.

Romania took the northern Dobrudja. The biggest victor was Serbia, which doubled in size as a result of her acquisition of Kosovo and much of Macedonia.

This result had serious consequences for Austria-Hungary since both the Romanians and the Serbs, whose territorial ambitions had vaulted higher with their military successes, had long-standing designs on Habsburg-held lands: Romania hoped one day to annex Transylvania and Serbia had her eye on Bosnia-Herzegovina, as well as Slovenia, Croatia, and other Slav-populated areas. Romania's membership of the Triple Alliance with Germany and Austria-Hungary and her comparative military weakness prevented her for the time being from taking any steps to realize her ambition. Not so Serbia. Emboldened by sympathetic voices in Russia, also to some extent in France and Britain, militarist elements in Belgrade gave overt and covert support to nationalist groups in Bosnia-Herzegovina that engaged in anti-Habsburg agitation, conspiracies, and terrorism. As early as January 1913, the British ambassador in Vienna wrote: 'Servia will some day set Europe by the ears and bring about a universal war on the Continent, and if the French press continues to encourage Servian aspirations as it has done during the last few months, the Serbs may lose their heads and do something aggressive against the Dual Monarchy which will compel the latter to put the screw on Servia.'[2]

The Archduke Franz Ferdinand was generally known to have toyed with a 'Trialist' solution of the nationalities problem in the Habsburg Empire; but the prospect of transforming the Dual into a Triple Monarchy in which Slavs would share power with Germans and Magyars found little favour among Slav nationalists who viewed the idea as a cunning device to stave off real independence. In any case, by 1914 the archduke had abandoned the proposal. The Sarajevo assassins, fervent nationalist visionaries who abjured sex and alcohol for fear of contaminating their revolutionary purity, sought the unity of all Yugoslav (south Slav) peoples and believed that tyrannicide and martyrdom would further their cause. Gavrilo Princip, the nineteen-year-old Bosnian Serb who fired the fatal shot, told the court at his trial: 'I do not feel like a criminal because I put away the one who was doing evil... Austria represents the evil for our people, as it is, and therefore it should not exist.'[3] Within the Serbian political establishment counsels were divided on the wisdom of promoting the efforts of such idealistic juvenile hotheads. Prior to the assassination, the Serbian government, headed by Nikola Pašić, had sought to curb arms smuggling across the Austro-Serb frontier and to limit the support given to the nationalist secret societies by the head of military intelligence, Colonel Dragutin Dimitrijević, known by his *nom de guerre* 'Apis'. Pašić was an arch-enemy of Apis; the story that he gave the Austrians warning of the impending attack on the archduke seems unfounded, but the Prime Minister certainly disapproved of such terrorism and took action to try to stop it.

Austria-Hungary's leaders had no intention of following the fate of the Ottomans in Europe and allowing small Balkan states, backed by Russia, to nibble away at their empire. Serbia seemed to pose a threat to the Habsburgs' rule over their south Slav subjects that, if not nipped in the bud, might well grow more formidable. Even before the assassination, influential figures in Vienna had reached the conclusion that if the Habsburgs were to avoid disaster they would sooner or later have to assert themselves militarily against the impudently assertive Balkan states. The Austro-Hungarian Chief of Staff, Franz Conrad von Hötzendorf, was one of those who had long advocated a preventive war against Serbia. In a letter to his German counterpart, Helmuth von Moltke, in February 1914, he had urged the necessity for forceful action to 'break the ring that once again threatens to enclose us'.[4] The assassination of Franz Ferdinand four months later has been called 'an unexpected gift from Mars to the Viennese war party'.[5] Worried about potential disloyalty among the subject nationalities, the Hungarian Prime Minister, Count István Tisza, exercised a certain restraining influence in the ensuing discussions. In the end, he agreed to firm action, provided that the delicate balance of the Dual Monarchy were not upset by any accretion of Serbian territory.

After nearly a month of deliberation, Austria-Hungary presented an ultimatum to Serbia on 23 July 1914. This accused the Serbian government of having tolerated the activity of the subversive groups directed against the Dual Monarchy; it alleged that officials of the Serbian government had been directly involved in the conspiracy to bring about the assassination; and it dictated the text of an announcement, to be issued by the Serbian government, acknowledging the role of its officials in the murder. It further demanded the immediate dissolution of the anti-Habsburg secret societies, the arrest of two named officials, the enforced retirement of others, and the acceptance by the Serbian government of collaboration by Habsburg officials in the suppression of subversive movements and in a judicial inquiry into the assassination. The Austrians set a time limit of forty-seven hours for receipt of a reply. The Serbian Foreign Minister was told by the Austrian Minister in Belgrade that he had been instructed, failing an unqualified acceptance by the deadline, to leave immediately for Vienna with all the legation staff.

The ultimatum was deliberately designed to elicit a Serbian rejection that might then be used as justification for a declaration of war by Austria-Hungary. This ulterior purpose of the document was immediately recognized by the Russian Foreign Minister, Sergei Sazonov, whose first reaction on being presented with a copy was recorded by the Austrian ambassador: 'In the course of reading he said he knew how it was, we wanted to make war with Serbia and here was the pretext.'[6] The Serbian government, aware that Austria meant business, came very close to accepting the ultimatum. Its reply was conciliatory and chastened in tone. The Serbs agreed to publish an announcement along the lines dictated by the Austrians, though not completely identical with it. They also acquiesced in virtually all the other demands. Only the participation of Austro-Hungarian representatives in the proposed judicial inquiry was rejected outright, on the ground that such a procedure would constitute a 'violation of the constitution and of the law on criminal procedure'.[7] The Austrian Minister in Belgrade, upon receiving this reply, immediately withdrew with his staff to Vienna. On 28 July Austria-Hungary, strongly encouraged by Germany, declared war on Serbia.

It is doubtful whether even this local war would have broken out had it not been for the support given to the two potential antagonists by their allies. During the month between the assassination and the Austrian ultimatum the Austrians looked to Berlin for support. The clear tendency of the advice received by Vienna, both through regular diplomatic channels and in communications between the two military staffs, was in favour of strong action against Serbia. This was the famous 'blank cheque'—'indeed blank', as Hew Strachan points out, since the Germans did not limit their support to any specific course of action.[8] The German Emperor told the Austro-Hungarian ambassador in Berlin that Vienna could 'reckon on full support from Germany' even in the event of a war between Austria-Hungary and Russia.[9]

As for Serbia, she depended even more critically on Russia than did Austria on Germany. Serbia too was not disappointed by her ally. During the crises of 1912 and 1913 Sazonov had exercised a restraining influence on the Serbs. Even then, however, he had given hostages to fortune in the shape of assurances of future support 'in order later, when the time comes, to lance the Austro-Hungarian abscess'.[10] In July 1914 the Russian government felt that to withhold support from Serbia, threatened as she was with total humiliation by Vienna, would imply that Russia could no longer perform the role of a great power in European affairs. This time the Russians were determined they would not blink, as they had in the Bosnian crisis of 1908. Sazonov did not give Serbia quite the blank cheque that Austria received from Germany. He told the Serbian Minister that Serbia could count on Russian aid without specifying its form. At the same time he suggested that, if it came to war, the Serbs should permit the Austrians to enter the country without offering resistance. Potential Serbian doubts about the implications of this advice, however, were thrust aside with the news that the Russians had decided on a partial mobilization against Austria. The Russians seem to have intended the move as a deterrent against Austria and an aid to diplomacy. Its effect was quite different. The Serbian government had been on the verge of accepting the Austrian ultimatum unreservedly, but the assurance of Russian support stiffened its back and led it to redraft its reply. Thus the local war itself came about in large measure as a consequence of the broader involvement of the powers.

The involvement of great powers did not necessitate their direct participation in the war. Why, then, was this third Balkan war not successfully localized? This question has received a variety of answers over the years. In the early months of the war each of the combatant powers published selective dossiers of diplomatic documents designed to show that the war was caused by the aggressive designs of the enemy. Many left-wing opponents of the war were persuaded by V. I. Lenin's *Imperialism, the Highest Stage of Capitalism*, published in 1916, which argued that the war arose from a crisis of capitalism in which imperialist powers, thwarted of outlets for 'excess capital', struggled for world domination. In the inter-war period, liberals, particularly in the United States, stressed the evil consequences of 'secret diplomacy' as a prime cause of the war. None of these explanations is taken very seriously today.

More recently historians have laid stress on such factors as railway timetables which dictated reciprocal mass mobilizations: Germany, France, Russia, and Austria had each prepared elaborate mobilization and deployment plans, based on the use of rail transport to move vast numbers of men, horses, heavy guns, and other equipment rapidly into position. The pre-war arms race, both in the form of naval rivalry between Britain and Germany and in the military build-up of the continental powers, has been seen as another major cause of the war. While investment in armaments need not have increased the propensity to use them, military staffs in 1914 were haunted by the fear of being overtaken by the modernization programmes of their rivals. In the 1960s the German historian Fritz Fischer steered historiographical debate in a different direction by emphasizing the determination of leading political, military, and business circles in Germany to enable her to attain the status of a 'world power', if necessary by war. Opponents of the Fischer thesis complained that this came close to a resuscitation of the charge against Germany of 'war guilt'. Nevertheless, other historians have followed Fischer in turning from a scrutiny of the diplomatic record alone to examine the internal politics of each of the powers for clues to their decisions for war. Beyond the search for, as it were, intelligible causes, some have focused on an indefinable but nevertheless palpable atmosphere in 1914 that impelled Europe to war: 'The mood of 1914 must be seen partly as the product of a widespread revolt against the liberal values of peace and rational solutions of all problems which had been taken for granted by so many people for much of the nineteenth century,' writes Joll.[11] Each of these explanations, which are not mutually exclusive, sheds light on the larger picture, although their significance varies in the case of each of the powers.

The view from Vienna was coloured not only by the nationalist pressures within the empire and at its borders but by its frustratingly unequal relationship with its major ally, Germany. Austria-Hungary's position as junior partner in the alliance was irksome to policy-makers in Vienna. To some extent Austrian policy in 1914 can be seen as an attempt to reassert Habsburg power not only vis-à-vis Serbia and Russia but also in relation to her domineering ally. Austria's last-ditch effort to prove that she was a great power, however, flew in the face of military reality. Paul von Hindenburg, German Chief of Staff from 1916 to 1918, remarked aptly: 'To me as a soldier, the contrast between Austria-Hungary's political claims and her domestic and military resources was particularly striking.'[12] (It should be noted, however, that Hindenburg wrote this after the war when he was, of course, anxious to shuffle off responsibility for Germany's defeat.) The Austro-Hungarian army's permanent strength of about 450,000 men was the weakest of the major continental powers' armed forces. The *kaiserliche und königliche* (*k.u.k.*) army was one of the few Habsburg institutions, other than the monarchy itself, that transcended the national divisions of Franz Josef's dominions. At the same time, however, there existed separate territorial forces, the Austrian *kaiserliche-königliche* (*k.k.*) *Landwehr* and the Hungarian *königlich ungarische* (*k.u.*) *Honvéd*, the latter an object of endless bickering between German and Hungarian politicians. National differences did not appear to impair the cohesion of the officer corps of the common army, though non-Germans were heavily under-represented and conflicts had erupted repeatedly over the language of command. Austria-Hungary spent far less on armaments than any other major European power. While she certainly had the capacity to crush Serbia on her own, albeit probably at some considerable military cost, she could not contemplate with equanimity the prospect of war with Russia. Hence the need to lean on German support. Even then, given the likely German preoccupation with the danger in the west from France, Austrian military planners could not be sanguine about the outcome of a general war. Indeed, Conrad von Hötzendorf, recognizing the comparative weakness of the forces at his disposal, seems, like Brutus on the eve of Philippi, to have harboured a strangely fatalistic expectation of defeat. In a letter to his mistress immediately after the assassination of the archduke, he wrote: 'It will be a hopeless struggle, but nevertheless it must be, because such an ancient monarchy and such an ancient army cannot perish ingloriously.'[13] Some more sober heads in Vienna hoped to localize the conflict but there, as in several other capitals, notably Berlin and St Petersburg, military staffs exercised a powerful, sometimes predominant, influence on decision-making in the later stages of the crisis. This influence led the Dual Monarchy to overreach itself in a desperately ill-calculated bid to ensure its survival.

Russia's leaders too were influenced by the notion that inaction might spell doom for their empire. Beyond that, not only conservatives but also many liberals in Russia felt a national obligation to support their Slav brethren in the Balkans. Less idealistic goals also entered the minds of Sazonov and others in the Russian government who saw war as offering the long-sought opportunity to gain Constantinople for the empire. The Russian standing army was the largest in the world, with over a million men under arms. Moreover, Russia's large population gave her an unparalleled manpower reserve on which she might draw to build new armies. On the other hand, the Tsar's 'steamroller' moved slowly and inefficiently: the Russian army was more primitively equipped and trained than the German and suffered from severe logistical problems arising from poor communications and a backward industrial base. In spite of heavy military spending in recent years, the army and navy had still not fully recovered from the crushing blows inflicted by the Japanese in 1904–5. After 1910 the Russians had begun a programme of military modernization and, with the help of French loans, had invested heavily in railway improvements on their western frontiers. These, however, would not be completed until 1916 at the earliest. In a war with Austria-Hungary alone in 1914, Russia might anticipate success. But if Germany were to take the field against Russia, the outcome was much less certain. Everything would depend on whether France would fulfil her alliance obligations and turn Germany's flank in the west.

On this point the Russians received throughout the crisis categorical assurances from the French ambassador in St Petersburg, Maurice Paléologue, and also, it appears, from the French President, Raymond Poincaré, who happened to be visiting St Petersburg in late July.

Germany's leaders were driven by a long-standing desire to win for the Reich the status and appurtenances of a 'world power'. Among the driving forces was the German officer corps. Still highly aristocratic in composition and suffused with antiquated political and social attitudes, it enjoyed a prestige and authority that enabled it to defy civilian control by parliament and, in matters that it regarded as of critical importance, to impose its will on the government. Together with other dominant elements in German society, including business leaders, Junkers (Prussian landowners), and nationalist politicians, German military leaders aimed to break out of what they saw as Germany's 'encirclement' by winning control, direct or indirect, over a broad expanse of territory in eastern Europe. In addition, they sought a powerful navy and colonies, of which they felt unjustly deprived by comparison with Britain and France. The idea that Germany would have to go to war to attain these aims had become deeply entrenched in the collective mentality of the German political elite by 1914. Among popular tracts that gave expression to this concept was General Friedrich von Bernhardi's *Deutschland und der Nächste Krieg* (Germany and the Next War). Building on a crude social Darwinism, Bernhardi wrote of the 'biological necessity of war'; he quoted the dictum of the influential historian Heinrich von Treitschke, that 'a country which owns no colonies will no longer count among the European Great Powers' and declared that the choice facing the country was 'world power or downfall'.[14] First published in 1912, Bernhardi's book went through six printings by 1914. During the war it was interpreted in Britain and elsewhere as evidence of Germany's aggressive intentions. The German Chancellor, Theobald von Bethmann Hollweg, in his memoirs, written in 1919, protested that the public never read Bernhardi.[15] But Bernhardi's work certainly impressed the Kaiser, whose influence in the July crisis was, with only occasional hesitations, in a violently bellicose direction. Bethmann, while sharing many of the objectives of the military leaders and the Kaiser, leant towards a somewhat more cautious policy designed, in particular, to secure British neutrality in the event of war. The Chancellor was weakened, however, by sniping from nationalists who impugned his patriotic zeal. Furthermore, Bethmann, like other European statesmen, found himself increasingly overshadowed by military leaders, especially the army chief, Moltke.

The German army was the most professional and, in most branches, the best equipped in the world. Since 1911 military spending had more than doubled. Peacetime army strength had increased from 628,000 in 1913 to 840,000 by August 1914, not including the large number of excellently trained reserves who would become available upon mobilization, and a potential manpower pool of nearly six million. German military planning was based on the famous Schlieffen Plan, named after its creator, Moltke's predecessor as Chief of the General Staff. Actually, there was a series of plans, reformulated each year in the light of changing conditions. But they all shared a similar basic approach. This envisaged a two-front war in which the Germans, threatened with encirclement by Russia and France, would take advantage of their excellent internal lines of communication to win a quick victory in the west while Russia's cumbersome mobilization, calculated to take at least six weeks, proceeded. During the initial phase, limited German forces in the east, supported by the Austrians, would contain the Russians. The bulk of the German army would meanwhile launch an all-out offensive through Belgium and Luxembourg with the objective of destroying the defensive capability of the French army. Ample forces could then safely be moved east to deal with the Russians. By 1914 they were on the threshold of being able to mobilize two-thirds of their army within eighteen days. The railway timetable thus confronted the Germans with both a short- and a medium-term incentive to move fast. If they waited for a few more years, the entire strategic approach on which they had based their plans for a two-front war was in danger of collapsing. All this accentuated, in the minds of the German General Staff, the need for a short, sharp victory in the west—dictating an attack through Belgium and Luxembourg.

French policy in the later stages of the July crisis was hamstrung by the absence from Paris of the President and Prime Minister, on their way home by sea from their visit to Russia. President Poincaré, a Lorrainer, was a bitterly anti-German nationalist. Unlike most presidents of the Third Republic, he sought to play an energetic role in formulating foreign policy. The vacillation of the Prime Minister, René Viviani, enabled Poincaré to exert himself effectively in this sphere. France did not actively pursue war in 1914 but Poincaré expected that it would come at some stage and was determined to take advantage of the opportunity, with Russia's help, to regain Alsace and Lorraine.

The French army was smaller than the German and not nearly so well equipped. In August 1914 France had 540,000 men under arms and could call on another 1.3 million reservists. A higher proportion of Frenchmen than Germans had received some military training since France habitually called up larger numbers of each age cohort in order to try to compensate for the lower total manpower pool on which she could potentially draw. In 1913 the length of compulsory military service had been extended from two to three years—another incentive to the Germans to seek a military decision sooner rather than later. French heavy artillery was woefully deficient compared with German, both in numbers and in quality. Only in the as yet little regarded field of military aviation could France boast technical and numerical superiority over any other power.

The Austrian declaration of war on Serbia did not make a general conflict inevitable. The Serbs might have followed Sazonov's advice and yielded without fighting. Even if they resisted, the war might have been contained at the regional level, as in the previous Balkan wars. Much depended on the action of Russia, Serbia's ally and great-power patron. Under pressure from the French, the Russians decided on 30 July to order a general mobilization. This was the fateful move that most immediately precipitated a general war. The German government decided that it was now or never. On 1 August Germany declared war on Russia. That night all telephone and telegraph communications between Germany and France were cut. German troops mobilized and prepared for an attack in the west. The French felt they had no choice but to respond with their own mobilization. Not only their treaty obligations to Russia but their own national security was at stake. On 3 August Germany declared war on France.

Britain was the last of the great powers to declare war. She was the only one among the belligerents that did not have a large standing army in August 1914. Her small professional force numbered no more than 125,000 men. Germany, gambling on a quick military victory in the west, did not rate the possibility of British intervention as a serious threat since British military power was so slight in the short term. In any case the German government hoped that Britain might be induced to remain neutral. Within the British Liberal Cabinet were several ministers who adhered to the tradition of hostility to militarism and to involvement in foreign wars. But Britain was more deeply bound to France than was publicly realized or than even some senior British politicians knew. British and French military staffs had been conducting secret conversations since 1906. Naval talks had led in 1912 to secret understandings whereby the French would concentrate their navy in the Mediterranean while the British would take responsibility for defence of the English Channel. These arrangements had not been approved by the

British Cabinet, many of whose members would not recognize any moral obligation to go to war at the side of France. The Cabinet hesitated until near the end, reluctant to commit the country to support France and Russia unless British interests seemed directly threatened.

The crucial determinant was the German decision to launch her offensive against France by means of an attack through Belgium and Luxembourg. Bethmann Hollweg was conscious that such an attack would threaten his objective of securing British neutrality since Britain was a guarantor of Belgian neutrality under a treaty of 1839. Moreover, the threat of German domination over the Channel ports was regarded as a direct peril to Britain's security. But as Bethmann later recalled: 'The offence against Belgium was obvious, and the general political consequences of such an offence were in no way obscure.... Moltke was not blind to this consideration, but declared that it was a case of absolute military necessity. I had to accommodate my view to his.'[16] The last comment indicates the extent to which, by this stage, civilian leaders were obliged to yield ground to military chiefs, particularly in Berlin. On 2 August the Germans demanded that Belgium permit the German army free passage across her territory. The Belgians refused and prepared to resist. The aggression against Belgium caused a great revulsion of feeling in Britain. The German ultimatum and its rejection by the Belgians led the British Cabinet, with some misgivings and four dissenters, to issue an ultimatum of their own to Germany that led to a state of war on 4 August.

The shape of the warring coalitions had now been clarified: Germany and Austria-Hungary (the 'Central Powers') were at war with Russia, France, and Great Britain (the 'Entente Powers') as well as Serbia and Belgium. Enver Pasha, the most pro-German member of the ruling Turkish triumvirate, induced his government to sign a secret alliance treaty with Germany on 2 August but Turkey bided her time before joining the belligerents. The United States observed the rush to war in Europe with concern but the question of American involvement was not seriously raised at this stage. Italy too, notwithstanding her membership of the Triple Alliance with Germany and Austria-Hungary, renewed as recently as December 1912, stayed neutral for the time being, as did Portugal, Romania, Greece, and Bulgaria. The Netherlands, close to the arena of combat in Belgium, also chose neutrality and, unlike all the rest, maintained it for the duration of the war. So too, at some cost in internal dissension, did Spain, which enjoyed an economic spurt by supplying both the Entente and Central Powers with raw materials and industrial goods.

Few images in collective memory are more familiar or more poignant than the cheering crowds in the capital cities of Europe in the early days of August 1914. The war everywhere seemed wildly popular. For masses of people across Europe, patriotism overcame all other emotions, both public and private. Young men looked forward to a great adventure. Socialists who had until recently spoken of international working-class solidarity as an invincible barrier to future wars voted for war credits in the French and German parliaments. In France two left-wing Socialists, Jules Guesde and Marcel Sembat, joined the government. In the spirit of the *union sacrée*, invoked by Poincaré, old enmities were forgotten; left and right laid aside their differences. Poincaré himself was reconciled with his bitter political enemy, Georges Clemenceau. They talked of Alsace and shed tears of emotion. 'When men have wept together,' said Clemenceau, 'they are united forever.'[17] The German equivalent of the *union sacrée* was the *Burgfrieden* (truce of the fortress): 'We can say that on the day of mobilization the *society* which existed until then was transformed into a community,' declared a German economist in 1914.[18] In Russia the outbreak of war evoked a similar access of emotional patriotism, particularly from the liberal professional classes represented by the Kadet Party. When the Tsar reconvened the Duma for a special session on 26 July, nearly all members, including most Socialists and members of non-Russian nationalities, followed the lead of the Kadet leader, Pavel Milyukov, who called for national unity. Not a single vote was cast against war credits, although a few Socialists walked out.

We should not deduce from all this that Europe as a whole succumbed to a wave of bellicosity. Political leaders, journalists, and intellectuals were not necessarily representative of the politically unconscious or half-conscious masses, in particular the rural majorities. Peasants responded readily enough to the call to arms, but neither they nor their families could be delighted that they were obliged to abandon their fields on the eve of the harvest. This was the first of five harvests gathered by women, children, and old folk through most of continental Europe.

Western front

The Germans took the initiative in the west in accordance with their pre-war plans—and came close to succeeding. They achieved their first victory on the morning of 7 August when the as yet little-known General Erich

Ludendorff captured the Liège citadel: 'No German soldier was there when I arrived. The citadel was still in enemy hands. I banged on the closed gate. It was opened from the inside. The few hundred Belgians gave themselves up at my order.'[19] This, at any rate, was Ludendorff's self-dramatizing account of the episode, for which he was awarded Prussia's highest military decoration, the *Pour le mérite* (the 'Blue Max'). The ring of fortresses surrounding the city put up more stubborn resistance; the last one did not fall to the Germans until 16 August. The consequent delay in the German advance played a critical part in the ultimate failure of their plan of campaign. The bulk of the German army in the north-west, however, swept on ahead and, on 20 August, entered Brussels.

The French meanwhile launched an offensive against Alsace and Lorraine. This was in accordance with their pre-war 'Plan XVII', based on the theory of 'mass plus velocity', that had been embraced by their Commander-in-Chief, General Joseph Joffre (see plate 4). In the eyes of some military historians the plan 'was one of pathetic simplicity'.[20] 'The essential principle that guided me was the following: to go into battle with all my forces', Joffre later wrote.[21] Actually, French planning was more sophisticated than that.[22] But it was based on a number of erroneous assumptions, derived in part from faulty intelligence: among these were the expectations that the Germans would concentrate their main strength on the common frontier rather than moving through central Belgium; and that, in the initial phase of the war, the Germans would use only regular forces rather than deploying reserves. The French played directly into German hands by charging headlong into the centre of the German defensive line in Lorraine. Attackers and defenders were roughly equal in strength. After initial advances against light opposition, the French were driven back in Lorraine, the Argonne, and the Ardennes.

While Moltke thus achieved his strategic aim of drawing the weight of the French army away from the northern sector, German forces advanced rapidly through central Belgium. Joffre had not expected this. In Plan XVII he had opposed any significant French deployments that might appear to infringe on Belgian neutrality. Confronting the most powerful elements of the German army near the Franco-Belgian frontier were only light French forces and four British divisions that had been hastily rushed across the Channel. At Mons on 26–27 August the British Expeditionary Force, commanded by Sir John French, put up a stiff holding action. They were now known as the 'Old Contemptibles', adopting the nickname with pride after the Kaiser was alleged to have spoken, a few days earlier, of 'General

French's çontemptible little army'. A British journalist sent a dispatch describing the appearance on the battlefield of St George and the angels, dressed in white, who beat back the advancing Germans. In the inflamed public mind this flight of fancy was transformed into authenticated fact and a legend was born. With or without supernatural assistance, the British and French were compelled to withdraw as the Allied generals engaged, through interpreters, in mutual recriminations. Altogether, by the end of August they had suffered 300,000 casualties in what became known as the 'Battle of the Frontiers'. The German right wing now wheeled round to threaten Paris.

One month after the outbreak of the war the French faced the imminent prospect of catastrophic and total defeat. On 2 September the government and parliament crept miserably out of Paris under cover of darkness and took temporary refuge in Bordeaux. They were followed by hordes of refugees who clogged the roads as they fled the regions overrun by the Germans. Parisians awoke to find the city under military government and to read *affiches* announcing unconvincingly that the government had left the city 'to give a new impetus to national defence'.[23]

Moltke, however, made several strategic and tactical errors. In his pre-war planning he had made a crucial change from the original conception of Schlieffen, reducing the balance of forces between the northern and southern sectors from 7:1 to 3:1. The result was to weaken the aggressive capability of the forces in Belgium that were to conduct the great wheeling motion towards Paris. Moltke compounded this error by diverting further precious troops from Belgium to help contain the Russians in the eastern theatre, by detailing other forces to besiege Belgian fortresses, and by sending yet others to reinforce the resistance to the French attacks in the centre. As a result of Moltke's dispositions, the overstretched German right, instead of circling to the west of Paris, as Schlieffen had envisaged, found itself compelled to move towards Paris from the north-east, a more direct but more hazardous direction from which to launch their assault on the capital.

Between 6 and 10 September, the fate of the German offensive was decided when the French initiated a counter-offensive that came to be known as the Battle of the Marne. The Germans found themselves logistically over-extended. Their communications were inadequate and, most importantly, Moltke's weakening of the German right wing prevented them from pressing home their initial advantage. Having found an opening in the German line, the French rushed in additional troops from Paris. At a crucial

GOUVERNEMENT MILITAIRE DE PARIS

Armée de Paris,
Habitants de Paris,

Les Membres du Gouvernement de la République ont quitté Paris pour donner une impulsion nouvelle à la défense nationale.

J'ai reçu le mandat de défendre Paris contre l'envahisseur.

Ce mandat, je le remplirai jusqu'au bout.

Paris, le 3 Septembre 1914.

Le Gouverneur Militaire de Paris,
Commandant l'Armée de Paris,

GALLIÉNI

Wall poster announcing the abandonment of Paris, September 1914 (*Imperial War Museum*) stage in the battle, six thousand soldiers were hastily delivered to the front by taxi-cab: the story of the taxis ballooned until it was believed that a whole army had been mobilized by this means. In fact, most of the reinforcements arrived by train. The Germans, whose advanced units had reached almost within sight of the capital, were driven back to a line along the Aisne. By 11 September Joffre was able to claim a '*victoire incontestable*'. Although he took the credit, the main author of the victory was General Joseph Gallieni, military commander of Paris, who persuaded Joffre to order an attack on the Germans' overstretched and enfeebled right wing.[24] The Battle of the Marne saved France and shattered the entire strategic concept with which the Germans had entered the war. Thirty-three German generals were dismissed. Among these was Moltke, who was replaced as Chief of Staff by the Prussian Minister of War, Erich von Falkenhayn, though, for fear of upsetting public morale, the change was not announced until 3 November.

There followed the 'race for the sea', in which both antagonists belatedly moved large forces north to try and outflank each other. On 10 October the Germans captured Antwerp in spite of a quixotic effort by Winston Churchill, First Lord of the Admiralty in Asquith's government, to take personal charge of the defence of the port city. The Germans occupied the whole of Belgium except a tiny segment in the north-west. After a series of battles, at the Yser in October–November, at Ypres in November, and in Champagne in late December, with very heavy casualties on both sides, the 'race' ended in a draw. Neither side was able to outflank the other and renewed attempts by both Germans and French to punch through enemy lines also failed.

War on the western front settled down to static trench warfare along a front that wound from the Swiss border to the Channel. Neither side wanted this; neither knew of any alternative. For the next four years millions of men endured a nightmarish world of mud, barbed wire, sandbags, and constant danger of death or mutilation. The overwhelming superiority of defence, coupled with the irrepressible determination of generals to attack at all costs, produced the highest death rates in battle in the history of man. Hordes of infantrymen were repeatedly ordered to charge with bayonets drawn into the fire of waiting machine-guns. By 20 November 1914 the French army alone estimated that its casualties already numbered 581,000.

Numbers consequently became critical and the massive French losses were only gradually alleviated by the arrival of British troops. Liberal tradition in Britain was hostile to conscription and to large standing armies, considered to be characteristic of militaristic continental empires. For nearly two years after the outbreak of the war Britain adhered to the voluntary principle. Over a million men volunteered before the end of 1914, and by June 1916, when universal compulsory service was introduced, 2,675,000 had been recruited into the army. Inevitably a gap yawned between donning uniforms and receiving the necessary armaments and training. By contrast with the highly efficient and disciplined 'Old Contemptibles', the raw recruits who were rushed to France in the first two years of the war were sometimes a poor match for their well-trained opponents.

Until the end of 1915 there was hardly such a thing as an Allied grand strategy. Neither of the two warring coalitions had prepared detailed plans for coordinating their strategies; nor did they do so until the disastrous offensive failures they both suffered in the early part of the war compelled them to subordinate national *amour-propre* to more pressing objectives. The preponderance of the French over the British in numbers of troops meant that they in effect dictated Allied strategy on the western front. As the British built up their forces they acquired a greater share in decision-making but strategic coordination remained imperfect and there was no joint Allied Commander-in-Chief until 1918.

On the western front in 1915 the French pursued a strategy of *grignotage* (nibbling). Again and again massive artillery assaults, designed to 'soften up' the enemy, would be followed by infantry attacks 'over the top' of the trenches. Generally attackers were mown down by enemy fire before they reached the enemy lines. In successive Allied attacks in the course of the year the would-be 'nibblers' were themselves devoured. The Allies suffered hundreds of thousands of casualties.

In the second Battle of Ypres, in April 1915, the Germans were the first to use poison gas as a weapon of war (though they had fired shells containing a kind of sneezing powder at Neuve-Chapelle in October 1914 and the French had occasionally used *cartouches suffocantes* of tear gas). But the Germans failed to follow through the initial advantage that they gained by this loathsome (and, under the Hague Convention of 1899, illegal) killing method. The development of efficient gas masks soon reduced its impact.

Successive failures on the western front led in November 1915 to the dismissal of General French, who was replaced as British Commander-in-Chief by Sir Douglas Haig. At the same time Sir William Robertson became Chief of the Imperial General Staff. Both Haig and Robertson believed that the war must be decided on the western front: the war of attrition thus continued in France with terrible losses.

In early 1916 the Germans resorted to a new strategy. On 21 February nine German divisions attacked the French fortress of Verdun. The purpose of the battle as conceived by Falkenhayn was less to break through the Allied lines than to draw the French into a trap in which, as Falkenhayn put it in a memorandum to the Kaiser, the French army would 'bleed to death'.[25] The Germans assembled an artillery concentration of 1,220 big guns including thirteen 'Big Berthas' (supposedly named after Bertha Krupp, wife of the armaments manufacturer, Gustav Krupp von Bohlen), huge 17-inch mobile howitzers each weighing 43 tons and firing a shell that weighed over a ton. The battle lasted ten months. On 25 February General Philippe Pétain was appointed to command French forces at Verdun (he had to be summoned from his mistress's bed at the Hotel Terminus of the Gare du Nord). Pétain was popular with his troops and had an unusual reputation among western-front commanders for being parsimonious with the lives of his men. The Germans had cut the main railway line into Verdun. Pétain solved the problem by ordering the construction of an eighty-four-mile-long dirt road that became known as the *Voie Sacrée*. The supply of Verdun was an impressive feat of organization. Thousands of lorries were assembled to bring in arms, food, and men. The opening of the road enabled Pétain to ease the strain on the defenders by frequent rotation of troops: eventually more than two-thirds of the entire French army on the western front came to serve at Verdun.

Unwilling to allow Falkenhayn to dictate the terms of the battle, Pétain considered a tactical withdrawal with the object of drawing the Germans into a trap. But Joffre would not hear of retreat and was impatient for Pétain to launch an attack. When he found Pétain unwilling to take the offensive he decided to promote him out of Verdun into command of the entire Army Group Centre. While Verdun remained within his general sphere of operations, command of the battle was transferred to General Robert Nivelle, whose strategic ideas were more in line with those of Joffre. It was Nivelle, not Pétain, who famously declared '*ils ne passeront pas*'.[26] Nivelle scrapped Pétain's rapid rotation system in order to free troops for a projected late-summer Anglo-French offensive further north on the Somme.

In late June 1916 the Germans came close to capturing the fortress. They used newly developed phosgene gas shells, against which French gas masks were at first ineffective. French losses were so heavy that Verdun became known as the 'mincing machine'. But on 1 July the long-planned offensive by British and French armies on the Somme drew off German forces and prevented Falkenhayn from pushing the attack on Verdun through to a conclusion. By December the French had succeeded in recapturing their lost ground around Verdun and the Germans were obliged to call off their effort to capture the fortress. In the sense that they had beaten off an intensive and concentrated German attack, the French could claim a victory. But the cost for both sides was almost beyond endurance. According to the best estimates, 162,000 Frenchmen and 140,000 Germans were killed at Verdun.[27] Even larger numbers were wounded. Identification and normal burial of the dead was often impossible; the French piled their bones into ossuaries.

On 29 August 1916 Falkenhayn was dismissed, to be replaced by Hindenburg. Bethmann Hollweg had argued for the change in the hope that Hindenburg's immense popularity might provide cover for a possible compromise peace: 'The name Hindenburg is a terror to our enemies; it electrifies our army and our people who have boundless faith in it. Even if we should lose a battle, which God forbid, our people would accept that if Hindenburg were the leader, just as they would accept any peace covered by his name.'[28] Bethmann Hollweg's manoeuvre rebounded against himself. Rather than providing a cloak for his diplomatic moves, the authority of the new Chief of Staff soon overshadowed his own. Hindenburg and Ludendorff, now Quartermaster-General, formed a duumvirate direction of the German army for the remainder of the war (see plate 8). Their power soon expanded far beyond the military sphere to encompass all aspects of government. In his post-war apologia, in which he tried to lay the blame for Germany's defeat on everybody but the German High Command, Ludendorff complained: 'The Government departments only with difficulty accustomed themselves to the idea that on the outbreak of the war an authority, the General Headquarters, had come into being, which not only shared responsibility with the Imperial Chancellor, but bore such an enormous share of it that it was obliged to take ever more energetic measures to compensate for the lack of them in Berlin.'[29] Ludendorff, who often took decisions in the name of his nominal superior, Hindenburg, came close to being dictator of the German Empire.

In response to desperate pleas from Joffre and from the French Prime Minister, Aristide Briand, Haig had agreed to move forward the date of the offensive on the Somme in order to alleviate pressure on the beleaguered French position at Verdun. The Anglo-French attack was launched on 1 July 1916 after a massive week-long artillery bombardment with 1,738,000 shells. As usual, the bombardment was intended to 'soften up' the enemy but instead merely indicated the location of the coming attack. Twenty-five British and fourteen French divisions went 'over the top'. The ground had been ill-chosen: in many places the attackers had to fight uphill, each man carrying 66 lb of equipment. On the first day the British lost 60,000 men, a third of them dead. The hoped-for 'breakthrough' again failed to materialize. The British were by this time making a major contribution to the alliance in both men and *matériel*: 128,000 tons a week of stores and ammunition were crossing to France in September 1916. The gargantuan supply effort failed, however, to change the military balance. By the time the battle ground to a halt in mid-November, the British had lost over 400,000 men and the French 200,000. The Germans lost over half a million but they had prevented Haig from making any significant territorial gain for this horrendous sacrifice.

On 15 September, in the course of the Battle of the Somme, a new weapon, developed by the British, made its first appearance in combat—the tank, which, in the words of one of its greatest champions, 'changed the face of war by substituting motor-power for a man's legs as a means of movement on the battlefield and by reviving the use of armour as a substitute for his skin or for earth-scrapings as a means of protection'.[30] Early models, however, were slow, cumbersome, prone to frequent breakdowns, and unbearably hot for crews. They tended to be used as a moving shield for infantry rather than as mobile armoured formations and were deployed in 'penny packets' rather than en masse. Over the next two years enthusiasts for mechanical warfare argued that imaginative use of the tank and the aeroplane could break the stalemate on the western front. Improvements in tank construction proceeded rapidly and several hundred were used in action in the final year of the war (see plate 5). The Germans failed to match Allied technological advances in this area. But British army chiefs, in particular Haig, remained sceptical of the claims made for the tank. The French were even more dubious. The tank's revolutionizing effect on strategy was not fully realized until a later conflict.

Eastern and southern Europe

From the outset, the war on the eastern front took a very different course from the conflict in the west. By contrast with the trench battles in the west, the war in the east was primarily one of movement. Even before the failure of the initial German offensive in the west, German forces in the east, originally earmarked merely for a holding operation pending the arrival of reinforcements, achieved brilliant success.

The Russians had mobilized more quickly than expected. But their armies were ill-equipped and inadequately supplied. Unlike the other major powers, the Russians' supreme command failed to execute a coherent war plan or to assert supreme coordinating authority over the war machine. In late August 1914 the German armies in East Prussia, commanded by Hindenburg and Ludendorff, won a great victory. Ninety thousand Russian soldiers and nearly four hundred big guns were captured and the Russian commander, Aleksandr Samsonov, shot himself in the head. Ludendorff's draft report of the battle was prepared at the village of Frögenau, but at the suggestion of Lieutenant-Colonel Max Hoffmann, he gave the site of the battle as the nearby village of Tannenberg, scene of the defeat of the Teutonic Knights by the Polish-Lithuanian army in 1410. Two weeks later a second Russian army under Paul Rennenkampf was routed in the Battle of the Masurian Lakes. Hindenburg and Ludendorff were acclaimed as saviours of the fatherland, though much of the credit for the triumph at Tannenberg may have been due to Hoffmann, who later claimed that he had been the author, and Hindenburg and Ludendorff merely the executors, of the envelopment manoeuvre that brought victory. But it was Hindenburg who was awarded a *Pour le mérite* and literally elevated to pedestal: a gigantic wooden statue of him was erected in the Königsplatz in Berlin and citizens who offered 1, 5, or 100 marks to the war loan were accorded the privilege of driving in iron, silver, or gold nails.

Further south, in Austrian Galicia, an initial Russian offensive had greater success. The Austrians, like the Germans, were constricted by the need to fight a two-front war—but without the resources of the Germans. At the outset Conrad von Hötzendorf committed the serious error of concentrating his main effort not on the Russian front but against the Serbs. The Russians quickly rolled back the feeble Habsburg forces and captured Lemberg, the main city of eastern Galicia. In March 1915 they captured the fortress of Przemyśl, with its garrison of 120,000 men, and advanced into western Galicia. The Austro-Hungarian army seemed on the verge of collapse. A German liaison officer reported to Falkenhayn that it was 'exhausted, rotten'.[31] To a large degree the Dual Monarchy's critical situation was of its own making, a product of poor leadership, disorganization, and faulty priorities. That summer, we are told, half a million soldiers were diverted from military duties to help gather the Hungarian harvest.[32]

Conrad appealed to the Germans for help and even threatened a separate peace if his allies were not forthcoming. Eight German divisions under General Mackensen were sent to bolster Conrad's armies. Mackensen quickly turned the tables on the Russians. In early May the Germans achieved a decisive breakthrough between Tarnow and Gorlice in Galicia. They captured 140,000 prisoners and 200 guns in six days. In June the Austrians recaptured Lemberg. Lublin, Brest-Litovsk, Grodno, and Vilna also fell to the Central Powers in the course of 1915. In August Warsaw fell: as the Russians retreated from the city they destroyed the bridges across the Vistula and other landmarks, incurring the indignation of the Polish civilian population. The Russians, grievously short of shells and even of rifles, suffered catastrophic casualties and lost over a million men captured by the enemy in 1915 alone. By March 1916 they had been driven back hundreds of miles to a line stretching from Riga in the north to Czernowitz in the south. A further defeat in that month at Lake Narotch, east of Vilna, seemed virtually to eliminate the offensive capability of the Russian army.

Remarkably, within three months they achieved a striking reversal of fortunes. On 4 June 1916 forty Russian infantry divisions and fifteen cavalry divisions under General Aleksei Brusilov attacked the Austrians on a broad front in Galicia. Brusilov achieved tactical surprise, in spite of Austrian intelligence warnings that an attack was imminent. As Ludendorff put it, 'the *k. und k.* [Austro-Hungarian] troops showed such small powers of resistance that with one blow the situation on the eastern front was in dire peril'.[33] The Austrians were routed. Their collapse was attributed at the time to the poor quality of their troops, particularly those of subject nationalities. A recent study, however, suggests that the primary explanation was the over-confidence and poor leadership of the Austrian command.[34] The Central Powers were also weakened on the Galician front by Falkenhayn's withdrawal of German forces to feed the attack on Verdun and to meet the Anglo-French attack on the Somme. The Brusilov offensive turned out to be the most successful Russian operation of the war. The Austrians lost over 750,000 men, at least 380,000 of whom were captured by the enemy. The army of the Habsburgs was shattered and henceforth virtually ceased to exist on the eastern front, save as an appendage of the Germans. Brusilov's forces occupied the Bukovina and eastern Galicia. On the other hand, Russian losses were hardly less than those of the enemy. Russia by this time had more than seven million men under arms but casualties on this scale were near the limit of what even the most populous of the warring European empires could bear.

Meanwhile, in early November 1914, the Ottoman Empire had been drawn into the war by a German-inspired *coup de main*. Two German ships, the battlecruiser *Goeben* and the light cruiser *Breslau*, both of which had evaded British naval patrols in the Mediterranean, entered the Dardanelles on 10 August and were transferred, complete with their crews, to the Turks. On 29 October the Ottoman navy, thus reinforced, opened fire from sea on the Russian naval base at Sebastopol. The Russians declared war on Turkey on 2 November and Britain and France did so three days later. The Germans did not set great store by their new ally's military capacity. A few months earlier Moltke had pronounced Turkey 'militarily a nonentity'.[35] But Turkish belligerency carried serious implications for Russia. It opened a new front that would drain troops from the struggle against Germany and Austria. It also deprived Russia of access through the Straits to the Mediterranean from her only year-round warm-water ports. The effect on supply to Russia of armaments from Britain and France was immediate and damaging.

The Ottoman entry, however, opened up in some British minds the possibility of a new grand strategy. The Dardanelles campaign was Churchill's project—and temporarily his nemesis. He envisaged the scheme as a way of knocking the Ottoman Empire out of the war, attacking the Central Powers at their weakest point, and reopening a warm-water supply route to Russia. As an alternative to the stalemate and carnage on the western front, the basic concept was sound: it has been called 'the one imaginative strategic idea of the war on the Allied side'.[36] But its execution was flawed by poor planning, faulty tactics, inadequate commitment of resources, lack of coordination, delays, logistical difficulties, and poor leadership. Churchill initially proposed a joint naval and military attack on the Dardanelles. But this was opposed by the War Secretary, Lord Kitchener, who was reluctant to deplete military strength on the western front. The scheme was revived as a purely naval assault. The Cabinet supporters of the plan had so low an opinion of the Turks that they persuaded themselves that a demonstration of naval might would of itself be enough to topple the government in Constantinople. The Foreign Secretary, Sir Edward Grey, told the War Council on 28 January 1915, the day they decided on the attack, that 'the Turks would be paralysed with fear'.[37] Ominously, Captain Wyndham Deedes, one of the few British officers who had served with the Turkish army, told Kitchener that he opposed the enterprise. So did the First Sea Lord, Admiral Fisher: 'Damn the Dardanelles!' he wrote to his political master, Churchill, on 5 April, 'They will be our grave!'[38]

A major element in British thinking was an appeal from Russia for some diversionary venture against the Turks to ease the pressure on her southern front against the Ottoman Empire. The Russians declined to participate themselves in the attack and also vetoed a Greek offer to send troops to support the British. At the same time they anxiously demanded assurances from Britain that Constantinople and the Straits would be theirs after the war. The British and French acquiesced, on condition that their own territorial demands were met elsewhere in the near east. The French contributed a division, but their high command was even more sceptical than the British, and they pursued a limited liability policy throughout this campaign. The British Cabinet took one of the most disastrous decisions of the war on the basis of unjustified hope and unqualified greed.

The attack began on 19 February 1915 with a naval bombardment of the Turkish fortifications on the shore of the Dardanelles. This failed to achieve its purpose, at the expense of severe Allied losses: six out of eighteen battleships were lost or disabled by mines. The conception then changed to an amphibious operation. On 25 April a seventy-thousand-strong force under General Sir Ian Hamilton began landing on the Gallipoli peninsula. Hamilton, who had enjoyed a glittering early military career, proved to be one of the least effective military leaders of the war. When the attackers encountered fierce resistance from the Turkish garrison, led by the German General Liman von Sanders, they became bogged down on the beaches in hopeless positions. The British, French, Australian, and New Zealand troops suffered fearful losses. So abominable was the stench of the thousands of dead of both sides that an eight-hour armistice was agreed on 24 May while bodies were collected for burial. Staff officers of the two armies talked as they watched the macabre operation. A Turkish captain said to a British officer: 'At this spectacle even the most gentle must feel savage, and the most savage must weep.'[39] The truce over, the two armies returned to the business of killing each other.

The failure of the early attacks had already precipitated the resignation of Fisher and the dismissal of Churchill from the Admiralty. The Conservative opposition was invited to join a coalition government, under Asquith's leadership, in which the former Conservative Prime Minister A. J. Balfour took Churchill's place at the Admiralty. The War Office delayed sending vitally needed reinforcements until July, by which time the Turks too had brought in large reinforcements. In the intense heat of the summer fearsome new enemies appeared: lice, maggots, and millions of green flies that feasted on carrion in no man's land, then moved to the army latrines. 'Boots the chemists' sent out a special powder from England but it did not get rid of vermin in the trenches. By August 80 per cent of the Allied army was suffering from dysenteric diarrhoea.

On 6 August a British force effected a successful new landing at Suvla Bay, at the north-western end of the peninsula, but poor leadership prevented them from following this through by ousting the small defending force on the neighbouring hills. Lack of fresh water in the blazing heat was one reason given for the inaction, although water was to be had if the troops had gone to look for wells. Instead they were allowed to go bathing in the sea. By the time they tried to advance, the local Turkish commander, Mustafa Kemal, was able to bring in reinforcements and throw the British back on to the beaches. Hamilton was relieved of his command and his successor advised immediate evacuation. By January 1916 the last Allied troops were withdrawn in a humiliating rout. The Allies suffered over 250,000 casualties in the campaign, the Turks even more—but they won a defensive victory.

The fiasco became one of the most fiercely refought campaigns in military history—a debate to which Churchill himself made a major contribution. Gallipoli was above all an indictment of poor leadership. But it was also a failure of military organization, which on all fronts in this war proved the critical determinant of success. In undertaking that most difficult of military operations, amphibious attack against defended positions, the British had failed to prepare serious plans and had gravely underestimated their opponents. Gallipoli discredited all 'sideshows' in the minds of British and French strategic policy-makers for the rest of the war. The decisive arena would be the western front, they now concluded, and Allied grand strategy henceforth adhered undeviatingly to this premiss.

Even the Serbian front, where the conflict had begun, was regarded as peripheral by the major contestants—'emphatically a subsidiary operation', declared Falkenhayn.[40] The Austrians, however, felt that their honour was at stake, and invaded Serbia at the outset of the war, expecting an easy victory. Against all expectations the Serbs, who had organized a modern conscript army, succeeded in rebuffing three successive assaults in the autumn of 1914 and drove the enemy off their territory altogether by the end of the year. The situation changed in October 1915, when Bulgaria, led by her king, 'Foxy' Ferdinand (or 'the Balkan Richelieu') (see plate 7) entered the war on the side of the Central Powers, hoping to regain Macedonian lands lost in the Second Balkan War. Bulgarian troops joined German and Habsburg forces in a renewed attack on Serbia which was overrun within six weeks.

Upon the British withdrawal from Gallipoli shortly afterwards, the Central Powers dominated the Balkans. A substantial Anglo-French force in Salonica, which had arrived in October 1915, was the only remaining Allied army in the region. Greece was divided over its presence and over the question of entry into the war: the Prime Minister, Venizelos, favoured entry on the side of the Allies, but King Constantine was opposed. Venizelos eventually formed a rival government in Salonica and in June 1917, with the aid of Allied naval power, returned to Athens, deposed Constantine, and took Greece into the war. In the meantime half a million Allied troops were tied down in Salonica to no very clear purpose. The Germans called Salonica their 'largest internment camp'.[41]

One Allied objective in remaining in Salonica was to support Romania if she entered the war on the Allied side. Romania was a signatory to the Triple Alliance, but like Italy had declined to go to war in 1914. In July 1916 she secured from the Allies a promise of territorial gains if she joined the coalition against the Central Powers. The next month, encouraged by Russian advances in the Brusilov offensive, Romania declared war against Austria. Her army made some initial headway against the Austrians in Transylvania. But most of her territory was quickly overrun by German-Austrian armies aided by Bulgarian and Turkish forces. By December 1916 Bucharest had fallen and the Romanian army, government, and king were forced to take refuge behind Russian lines at Jassy.

Unlike the Balkan states, Italy considered herself a great power. In August 1914 she declined to join the war, complaining of lack of consultation about the attack on Serbia. Conrad von Hötzendorf fumed at Italy's treachery and looked forward to settling accounts. Moltke agreed and wrote to him that Italy's failure to fulfil its obligations under the Triple Alliance constituted a 'felony' that would be 'revenged in history'.[42] During the first ten months of the war Italy held what amounted to an auction of her services, whether as neutral or belligerent. The Prime Minister, Antonio Salandra, in a speech in October 1914, defined his country's policy as 'sacro egoismo', a phrase that was variously interpreted. Eventually the Entente offered the highest bid. In the secret Treaty of London, in April 1915, Britain, France, and Russia promised Italy that, in return for waging war against 'all their enemies', Italy would receive substantial territorial acquisitions, including the South Tyrol, the Istrian peninsula, and Dalmatia. Her sovereignty would be recognized over the Dodecanese islands, occupied by Italy 'temporarily' since 1912. More vaguely, the Entente also promised Italy 'a just share' in any partition of Turkey and 'some equitable compensation' in the event of a further imperial share-out in Africa.

In May 1915 Italy declared war on Austria-Hungary. Contrary to her engagement in the Treaty of London, she did not declare war on the Ottoman Empire until the following August, nor on Germany until a year after that. In purely numerical terms Italy, with 875,000 men in her armed forces, seemed a formidable antagonist; eventually nearly five million were called up. Some units, such as the Alpini and Bersaglieri, were highly effective, but the artillery and infantry were poor, the desertion rate was high, and the leadership displayed by officers was variable. Between 1915 and 1917 the Italians fought eleven inconclusive battles on their north-eastern frontier with Austria along the River Isonzo. By the end of 1915 they had lost a quarter of a million men. Several hundred thousands more fell or were captured in the battles of 1916.

Disaster came at Caporetto in October 1917 when a combined Austro-German army of fifty-five divisions inflicted a crushing defeat on the Italians. Demoralized Italian units surrendered en masse. A young German officer, Erwin Rommel, who displayed great skill in the battle, recorded that in one engagement, several hundred Italians thrust aside their officers and ran up to him. 'In an instant I was surrounded and hoisted on Italian shoulders. "*Evviva Germania!*" sounded from a thousand throats.'[43] Italian officers wept with shame at such surrenders but seemed powerless to prevent them. The entire Second Italian Army fled in disarray and clogged the roads in the rear, joined by a rabble of civilian refugees. By the end of December 1917 the Italians had lost 450,000 men, killed, wounded, missing, or taken prisoner at Caporetto, quite apart from the disintegration of the Second Army. But the Austrians failed to follow through after their victory, partly because the German High Command rejected pleas from Conrad for reinforcements. Almost miraculously, the Italians, reinforced by British and French forces amounting eventually to eleven divisions, made a stand on the River Piave, and held their ground.

Sea and air warfare

The First World War was primarily a land war. Sea power, except in the case of Britain, was generally regarded as subsidiary and air power as merely ancillary. In both cases, however, rapid technological advances produced new machines and dictated new battle tactics that, especially in the later part of the war, helped shape the course of the conflict.

In 1914 the British Navy, with seventy capital ships, remained the most formidable on the waves. Since 1897 the Germans had embarked, amidst a great blast of patriotic fervour, on a programme of naval expansion under the direction of Admiral Tirpitz and with the enthusiastic support of the Kaiser. The British countered with a revamped naval building programme centred on the Dreadnought class of battleships, of which the first was launched in 1906. The Germans lost the race. In 1914 they could muster only forty battleships. The British had fifty-six submarines to the Germans' twenty-eight, but these were as yet primitive vessels. Few naval strategists appreciated the enormous potential of this weapon. The French, Russian, and Austro-Hungarian navies were much smaller and less modern than either the British or the German and played only a minor role in the naval war.

The war at sea began on 1 November 1914 with an engagement off the coast of Coronel, Chile, between the powerful German East Asiatic Squadron commanded by Vice-Admiral Maximilian Graf von Spee and the weaker British West Atlantic Squadron under Rear-Admiral Sir Christopher Cradock. The Germans sank two British armoured cruisers, including Cradock's flag-ship, HMS *Good Hope*. Following this defeat, the Royal Navy dispatched a force of nearly thirty ships, including two Dreadnoughts, under Rear-Admiral Sir Doveton Sturdee, with orders to seek out and destroy Spee's squadron. In the Battle of the Falklands, on 8 December, Sturdee won a decisive victory, sinking four of Spee's five ships (the fifth was later scuttled to avoid capture). In January 1915 the British scored another success in an encounter at the Dogger Bank (a shoal in the North Sea, about sixty miles off the coast of Northumberland), in which a German heavy cruiser was sunk. Thereafter the Germans limited themselves to occasional hit-and-run raids on merchant ships and on the British North Sea coast, while the British devoted their main naval energies to the enforcement of an economic blockade of the Central Powers. Until 1916 both navies desisted from large clashes with each other in northern waters, the Germans because they were outnumbered, the British because they preferred to avoid German mines and impose their blockade on Germany from a prudent distance.

In May 1916, however, the German Grand Fleet, under Admiral Reinhard Scheer, emerged en masse into the North Sea, hoping to ambush British ships. British intelligence, however, had obtained the German naval cipher and succeeded in decoding most German naval communications. In the ensuing

Battle of Jutland (or Skagerrak) on 31 May/1 June 1916, the British, under Admiral Sir John Jellicoe, outnumbered the Germans in capital ships by more than three to two and their advantage in firepower was even wider. Each side lost several ships in the battle, which ended as something of a draw, though in a strategic sense the British may be said to have won since the German imperial fleet never again ventured out in force from its territorial waters.

Although there were no more large-scale naval encounters, this was not the end of the war at sea. In early 1917 the German navy was finally permitted to unleash a new weapon that, it hoped, would break the stalemate in the west: the U-boat. In attacking unarmed or lightly armed merchantmen rather than battleships, the Germans thought they had found a vulnerable point. The German High Command had been pressing since the end of 1915 for a campaign of 'unrestricted submarine warfare' against Britain. Falkenhayn pointed out that it would 'strike at the enemy's most sensitive spot, because it aims at severing his overseas communications'.[44] Bethmann Hollweg rejected the proposal then, and again in April 1916, for fear of upsetting the United States. But the assumption of semi-dictatorial power by Hindenburg and Ludendorff in August that year led to a change in policy. The new rulers in Berlin believed, as Ludendorff put it, that unrestricted submarine warfare was 'the only means left to secure in any measurable time a victorious end to the war'.[45] Initiated on 1 February 1917, with a fleet of 111 submarines, the new strategy was intended to prevent supplies from reaching Britain, which was critically dependent on imported food. This was a daring initiative since it challenged British power in the arena where it was strongest—the sea.

In order to be effective, however, the German onslaught had to be directed not only against British shipping but also against neutral vessels carrying supplies to Britain. The Germans thereby ran the risk that other powers, notably the United States, might enter the war. The sinking of the British transatlantic liner *Lusitania* in May 1915, with the loss of more than 1,100 lives, among them 124 Americans, had already provoked outrage in America. The German decision for unrestricted submarine warfare led President Woodrow Wilson to decide that the United States must go beyond its earlier policy of 'armed neutrality'. The declaration of war on Germany by the United States on 6 April 1917 (as an 'Associated' rather than an 'Allied' Power) held out to the Allies the long-term prospect of access to almost unlimited new resources of raw materials, capital, armaments production, food, and manpower.

The U-boat campaign reached its peak in April 1917 when 869,000 tons of Allied and neutral merchant shipping were sunk by the Germans. Had losses on this scale continued Britain must have succumbed. As so often in warfare, however, new weapons evoked counter-measures. In May 1917 the British Cabinet, overruling Admiralty resistance, adopted the convoy system whereby large groups of commercial vessels were escorted by an outer ring of naval ships (sometimes also by aircraft). The success of convoys and the development of new anti-submarine devices reduced Britain's monthly tonnage losses by more than half by the late autumn. At this level new ships could be constructed quickly enough to replace the losses. Thereafter the U-boat remained an irritant but no longer a weapon that might decide the war.

If naval power seemed to decline in importance as an element in the overall strategic equation during the war, the opposite was true of air power. Aircraft, in the form of tethered balloons, had first been used in warfare by the French at the Battle of Fleurus in 1794. The Italians were the first to deploy heavier-than-air machines in the invasion of Libya in 1911–12. In Europe they were first used by the Bulgarians in their siege of Adrianople in 1913. By 1914 all the powers were beginning to invest in military air power though none yet recognized its potential for dominating the battlefield. France entered the war with about 600 military aircraft, Germany with 450; but only 136 French planes were ready for combat upon mobilization as against the Germans' 220. General staff officers tended to regard aviation as little more than a sporting enthusiasm. Strategists had not yet reformulated military or naval doctrine to take account of this new arm. Experience soon changed such attitudes. As early as November 1914 Joffre recognized that air power was 'not only, as could once be imagined, merely an instrument of surveillance', but 'by launching powerful explosive projectiles' might 'act as an offensive arm both on long-range missions and in liaison with other troops'.[46] The translation of this insight into battlefield doctrine took some time. In the early years, aerial warfare tactics were almost laughably primitive: pilots dropped hand grenades on trenches and shot with pistols at enemy planes. Apart from reconnaissance and leaflet drops, aircraft did not play a significant role until the final campaigns of the war.

For civilians the best-known sight of the air war was the Zeppelin dirigible airship used by the Germans in bombing raids over London and Paris from early 1915 onwards. Paris newspapers had assured their readers only a few weeks earlier that Zeppelins would not fly over Paris. When they appeared after all, one newspaper declared unabashedly that they were 'even less fearsome when viewed at close quarters'.[47] But a German observer was thrilled: 'Now war, with all its terrors, [has been] driven home to the country of lies and slander.'[48] Count Ferdinand Zeppelin dreamed that his invention might be the miracle weapon that would save Germany and end the war with one overwhelming and decisive blow. In the event, the airships caused some alarm and interfered with production but their huge size and ready combustibility rendered them tempting targets for attacks by aircraft and ground fire. Of Germany's 125 military and naval airships, 79 were lost in five thousand offensive sorties in the course of the war. Airship bombardments caused 556 British deaths, but almost as many German airship crewmen perished. The cost of such attacks to Germany probably outweighed their offensive value.

In the last two years of the war, machines and tactics developed fast. Allied bombers played a useful role at Verdun and in the Battle of the Somme. The price was high: the British alone lost over seven hundred planes over the Somme; the Germans lost more. For a while the Germans gained a crucial technological edge by developing Fokker fighters equipped with a forward-firing gun whose bullets would not hit the propeller (gun and propeller operated as one machine), but this was soon copied by the Allies. By 1918 Britain, France, and Germany were producing much more sophisticated planes, among them the fast-climbing Fokker DVII, the British Sopwith Camel, and the French Spad XIII. These had maximum speeds of between 113 and 134 miles per hour and were manufactured in large numbers. Spectacular but strategically irrelevant duels between solo 'aces' gave way to battles between squadrons of fighters operating in formation. The British and the French conducted some not very effective air raids on German industrial targets in the Saar, the Ruhr, and Lorraine. Neither side, however, yet realized the potential disruption to rail and sea communications that might be caused by concentrated air attack.

By late 1918 the Allies had won overwhelming superiority not just in the air over the battlefield but in aircraft production, where the Germans were limited by shortages of skilled labour and raw materials. Germany and Austria manufactured altogether about 47,200 planes of all types during the war, the British and French as many as one hundred thousand. The creation in Britain of the Royal Air Force in April 1918, the first independent air arm in the world, reduced inter-service rivalries over the uses to be made of air power and increased pressure for the development and supply of modern aircraft. With the great expansion of British production capacity in the final year of the war, and the gearing-up of American manufacturing potential, the Germans lost any hope of achieving superiority in the air.

State, economy, and society in wartime

The phrase 'total war' appears to have been coined by the German aphorist Georg Christoph Lichtenberg in or around 1776.[49] Now it acquired a grim reality. The new forms taken by both the sea and the air wars pointed to the transformation of the nature of warfare itself. This was a war in which, in the end, access to raw materials and production capacity were the keys to victory. Not only fortresses and cities but virtually the entire civilian populations of countries found themselves, in effect, under siege.

Recognition of the changed character of modern war was slow. On 4 August 1914 the British Chancellor of the Exchequer, David Lloyd George, had announced that the government's policy was 'to enable the traders of this country to carry on business as usual'.[50] At that time he and his fellow ministers, except Kitchener, anticipated a short war, as did most governments throughout Europe. The reality, of course, was very different, and its effects on European economies far-reaching. In all the belligerent states economic blockade, massive demand for armaments and other war goods, and the mobilization of huge armies led to pressures on the supply of labour and of raw materials, the flow of trade, and the stability of prices. All this overwhelmed the free-market system. None of the powers had prepared economic plans for a war that would last more than a few months. None had laid in large stockpiles of strategic materials or food. The immense expansion of industrial production was nowhere foreseen. The need for mobilization of labour did not immediately become apparent; at the start of the war, governments were more worried about war 'distress' and the threat of unemployment arising from a decline in normal economic activity.

As soon as the scale of the conflict became apparent, governments, whatever their economic philosophy, found themselves compelled to intervene in the market. Before the war liberals and socialists had debated the exact limits of proper governmental intervention in the economy; now conservatives swept aside theoretical constraints and helped impose sweeping moves towards economic socialization. By February 1915 Lloyd George was demanding 'legislation . . . to commandeer all the works in the United Kingdom'.[51] Large-scale planning became the order of the day. Imports, transportation, mining, manufacture, and distribution all came under government control. Government bureaucracies swelled to an unprecedented size. When the stalemate on the western front generated demand for munitions and supplies of every kind on a scale unimagined before the war, the trade union movements in Germany, Britain, and France behaved in strikingly similar manners: they cast aside the class struggle and harnessed their memberships to production for the war effort. The great pre-war strike movements in France and Britain virtually evaporated. In Britain strikes in war industries were banned by law, compulsory arbitration was introduced, and the government took powers to direct labour. In France the productive effort was severely affected by enemy occupation of the north-eastern region, which produced 16 per cent of French industrial output; mass conscription created an urgent need for industrial mobilization. The Socialist Albert Thomas, who headed the French munitions effort from October 1914 to September 1917, obtained the collaboration of labour leaders for his *dirigiste* measures. Workdays lost in strikes fell in France from 2.2 million in 1913 to just 55,000 in 1915. In Germany the fall was even steeper. In both countries, they remained at a low level until 1917.

Women's participation in the workforce increased and spread to industries that had hitherto been male preserves. The number of women gainfully employed in Britain rose during the war from a little under six million to 7.3 million. In 1914 they constituted 31 per cent of the total British labour force; by 1918 they were 37 per cent. By the end of the war almost a million British women were employed in metal and chemical industries or in government arsenals. In France the increase in women's share of employment during the war was from 38 per cent to 46 per cent. A quarter of the 1.7 million workers in war factories in France in 1918 were female. In Russia too women's employment increased, not only in those sectors where they were already strongly represented, such as textile manufacturing, but in industries in which they had previously played little part: by 1917 they were a third of the workforce in the chemical industry and one seventh in iron, steel, and engineering works.

As an economic struggle the First World War was first and foremost one between Britain and Germany. Upon their ascent to supreme power in 1916, Hindenburg and Ludendorff called for drastic measures whereby the entire workforce would be militarized, on the principle 'he who does not work shall not eat'. Women too were to be subjected to compulsory labour. 'The entire German people should live only in the service of the Fatherland,' the army chiefs declared.[52] On the face of it, this pronouncement might appear akin to Lloyd George's Cabinet memorandum a year earlier, which laid down that 'the population ought to be prepared to suffer all sorts of deprivations and even hardships' in the interest of maximizing war production.[53] The British, however, were more successful than the Germans in translating such ideas into a coherent strategic equation. The adoption in 1916 of the 'Hindenburg Programme' seemed to indicate that Germany was mobilizing her economy according to an integrated plan that would yield the highest productive potential of war materials. The outcome, according to one authority, was different: 'In his pursuit of an ill-conceived total mobilization for the attainment of irrational goals, Ludendorff undermined the strength of the army, promoted economic instability, created administrative chaos, and set loose an orgy of interest politics.'[54] The programme subordinated economic planning to supposed military necessity to such a degree as to ignore the balancing of industrial with military manpower needs. No consideration was given to such matters as financial or transportation constraints. The inevitable results were inflation, supply bottlenecks, and shortages, particularly of food.

By 1917 military spending accounted for more than half of Germany's national income and more than a third of Britain's. The huge growth in government expenditures generated by the war led to unprecedented increases in taxation in all countries. In France, a country with a historic aversion to any form of direct taxation, income tax rose to 20 per cent. In Britain the standard rate of income tax rose from one shilling and three pence in the pound (6.25 per cent) in 1914 to six shillings (30 per cent) by 1918. The tax net was extended downward into the working class, most of whom had hitherto paid no direct taxes at all. Even so, taxation could not meet Britain's increasing need for hard currency to pay for war supplies. By April 1917 barely three weeks' supply of dollars remained. Only the providential entry of the USA into the war that month saved Britain from a collapse of sterling. Until after the end of the war the British currency was propped up at a 2 per cent discount on its pre-war parity of $4.86 by American financial support to the tune of some $100 million a month. In Germany existing taxes were increased and indirect ones were imposed on such goods as tea, coffee, and chocolate; but in general the imperial government resorted less to taxation than to giant war loans, building a mountain of debt that was to bankrupt post-war Germany. Britain too raised a large war loan to which millions of patriotic small investors subscribed: its real value to the subscribers proved far from 'gilt-edged' and it was eventually repaid in heavily depreciated pounds. In all countries large sums were raised for war charities by voluntary subscription drives. But neither taxation, nor loans, nor gifts sufficed: all the major belligerents ran large deficits.

An inevitable consequence was inflation. In Britain and France prices more than doubled during the war, a phenomenon that was disconcerting and frightening to a generation that had not known inflation in its lifetime. In Vienna the price of fresh eggs multiplied four times in the first two years of the war. Inflation in Austria and Germany accelerated under the pressure of the Allied blockade.

Rationing consequently grew steadily more stringent. It extended to soap, clothing, and fuel but its effects were felt most immediately in food. The civilian population in Germany, where a bread ration was introduced in June 1915, suffered ever-increasing hardship from lack of food. Shortages of livestock, accentuated by inadequate fodder, became acute. Imports to Germany from the Netherlands, Sweden, and Switzerland could not make up the shortfall. Meat and milk became ever scarcer. Ersatz replacements were marketed for bread, butter, cooking oil, eggs, beer, coffee, and many other products. In October 1916 meat was rationed at 250 grams a week. By the winter the ration was lowered to 80 grams. Meat was in any case obtainable only two days a week. One egg and 20 grams of butter per week were available in Berlin for each person. Soup kitchens were set up in the streets to feed the starving. During the 'turnip winter' of 1916/17 that unloved vegetable replaced potatoes in German cooking pots. Conditions were not much better in other countries. In Italy in 1918 the bread ration was reduced to 250 grams per day, meat was available only twice a week, and confectionery was banned. In rural areas, of course, rationing could not be enforced; quite soon urban dwellers were going off to the countryside at weekends to forage for food and in many areas a black market quickly grew up in rationed products. In some parts of the continent, particularly in eastern Europe, food shortages by 1917 attained famine proportions. In Germany average civilian body weight declined, according to a contemporary reckoning, by 20 per cent—a total of 'more than half a million tons of "human mass"'.[55] But such estimates failed to take account of the growth of the black market. Avner Offer has argued that while the German people 'were often cold and hungry', by and large wartime Germany 'did not starve'.[56] Elsewhere, rationing had beneficial effects. In Britain life expectancy for civilians rose and the general health of the civilian population, particularly of children, improved during the war, mainly due to improved nutrition. Infant mortality fell in Britain, but in Belgium it rose as a result of the privations induced by the Allied blockade; it also rose in France and Italy. The disruptive impact of the war on conventional social norms was reflected in an increase in illegitimate births: nearly one-third of all births in Paris and one-fifth in Berlin during the war occurred outside wedlock.

The neutral states, Switzerland, Spain, the Netherlands, and the Scandinavian countries, found that their economies could not be cocooned from the effects of the war. Economic blockades and embargoes led to loss of markets and to changes in trade patterns. Reductions in imports produced shortages that necessitated rationing. Norway enjoyed an unprecedented trade boom in spite of Allied trade restrictions and German attacks on Norwegian shipping that destroyed the equivalent in tonnage of nearly half of the pre-war mercantile fleet. Sweden too enjoyed a wartime boom, with tremendous stock market activity. Sales volume on the Stockholm stock exchange in 1918, measured in constant prices, was not exceeded until 1980. The role of banks in the economy expanded greatly and bank mergers increased the size while decreasing the number of institutions. Both Sweden and Norway, however, suffered severe food shortages in the last year of the war: in Norway government price controls led to the disappearance of butter from the open market; in Sweden by 1918 the price of bread had nearly doubled since 1914, that of milk and eggs tripled, and meat prices quintupled. Animals as well as people went hungry. In Denmark the milk yield of cows fell by more than a third during the war.

The war brought some notable medical advances: X-rays were used on the battlefield and in hospitals in order to locate bullets and shrapnel. But it also brought previously unknown illnesses. The filth of the trenches led to outbreaks of 'trench fever', a mysterious illness spread by the excreta of lice, and other infectious diseases. Another hazard was 'trench foot', a fungal growth that occurred when wet boots were worn for long periods. A new psychological condition, 'shell shock', was diagnosed, although many officers refused to recognize it as anything other than cowardice and punished sufferers accordingly: some were shot.

Venereal disease was a widespread scourge. The Germans and French tried to cope by hygienic control of prostitutes. Unlike the Germans, the British had no civil or military brothels; and unlike the French, the British military authorities did not license prostitutes. Instead, they relied on a printed letter from Lord Kitchener that was handed to every soldier: 'In this new experience you may find temptations . . . and while treating all women with courtesy, you should avoid any intimacy. Do your duty. Fear God. Honour the King.'[57] This piece of paper was of limited prophylactic value. British soldiers frequented brothels in Belgium, France, and Egypt.

In 1917 one-fifth of the British forces were infected by venereal disease. Reluctantly the War Office decided to distribute condoms to the soldiers. As for the eastern front, the standard of sexual (mis)conduct—and its predictable consequences—may be gauged from the experience of the most famous recruit to the Austro-Hungarian army, the immortal 'Good Soldier Švejk', as recorded in the crude, bawdy, vivid masterpiece of the Czech writer Jaroslav Hašek.

Prolonged war inevitably increased the power of central governments, threatened civil liberties, and diminished the ability of parliaments, courts, or public opinion to check the authority of governments and armed forces. Censorship of mail, telegrams, and the press was introduced or extended in all belligerent countries. In France publication of casualty lists was forbidden for fear of affecting morale on the home front. French censors were also ordered to strike out all items 'liable to harm our relations with Allied countries or neutrals, or relating to political negotiations' as well as 'anything that might be taken for peace propaganda'.[58] Clemenceau protested against the imposition of political censorship, whereupon his paper was suspended from publication.

Most of the press needed no official encouragement to adopt a tub-thumping patriotic colouring that produced much exaggeration and frequent absurdities. Writers flocked to enlist their pens in the cause of their country. Maurice Barrès, who wrote of the 'blessed wounds' of French soldiers, was dubbed 'nightingale of carnage' by the anti-war Romain Rolland.[59] Thomas Mann in Germany and Gilbert Murray in Britain rallied divisions of intellectuals to their respective flags. The rectors and senates of Bavarian universities issued an appeal at the outbreak of war: 'Students! The muses are silent! The issue is battle, the battle forced on us for German *Kultur*, which is threatened by the barbarians from the east, and for German values, which the enemy in the west envies us. And so the *furor teutonicus* bursts into flame once again.'[60] The French philosopher Henri Bergson complained that such pronouncements were evidence of 'barbarism reinforced by civilization'.[61] From Oxford to Petrograd university professors issued calls to arms. Propaganda aimed at popular audiences was hardly subtle: the German satirical magazine *Simplicissimus*, for example, carried a sarcastic caricature of a bloated John Bull, 'protector of the oppressed', crushing Egypt, India, the Transvaal, Ireland, and Belgium; a famous French poster calling for subscriptions to the national defence loan showed a *poilu* advancing cheerfully with the words 'On les aura!'; an Italian cartoon showed the Kaiser as '*L'Ingordo*', the glutton who tries to bite off a chunk of the globe but finds it is 'too tough'. Film of war scenes began, for the first time, to be used as propaganda; often, however, the fighting was staged for the cameras. Governments also used the cinema to keep up morale at home and for more utilitarian purposes including proposed menus for coping with food rationing: the British government, for example, produced a short film showing the British housewife how to make suet pudding—without suet.

In spite of the horrors of the front and hardships at home, opposition to the war was rare. Three streams of anti-war feeling, sometimes intermingled, may be distinguished. The first was socialist internationalism. Objection on this ground was at first much more limited than had been anticipated by many, including Socialists themselves. Most German, French, and British Socialists initially supported the war; the Russian Socialists included significant anti-war elements but many adopted a 'defencist' rather than a 'defeatist' position. In Germany the first vote against war credits was cast in the Reichstag by Karl Liebknecht in December 1914. But his was a lonely voice and in 1916 he was arrested for anti-war agitation, his parliamentary immunity was lifted, and he was sentenced to imprisonment with hard labour for four years and one month. International conferences of anti-war Socialists at the small Swiss towns of Zimmerwald in September 1915 and Kienthal a year later produced no significant results. The second source of opposition to the war was humanitarian pacifism. In Britain this was represented in the Union of Democratic Control, headed by E. D. Morel, which campaigned against the war, against secret diplomacy, and against compulsory military service. Romain Rolland was one of the few French writers who opposed the war publicly almost from the outset. In his pamphlet *Au-dessus de la mêlée* (1915), he called on intellectuals to work for peace. He condemned the use of colonial troops by the would-be 'guardians of civilization'; it reminded him of 'the Roman Empire at the time of the tetrarchy calling upon the hordes throughout the world to tear each other to pieces'. But Rolland's critique aroused a violently hostile reaction and few sympathetic echoes.

The third type of opposition was conscientious objection, generally on religious grounds. This appeared chiefly in Britain. Some conscientious objectors were sent to prison, but approximately 16,500 'conchies' were officially recognized. Most undertook some form of alternative service. Conscription aroused strong opposition in Ireland and the government avoided introducing it there. About 210,000 Irishmen nevertheless volunteered to fight for Britain and nearly 50,000 were killed.

In their treatment of prisoners of war and of conquered civilian populations, the behaviour of armies was less barbaric than in other twentieth-century wars.

The major powers generally treated captured enemy soldiers and occupied civilian populations in accordance with humanity and with the provisions of the Hague Conventions of 1899 and 1907. But there were many glaring exceptions.

In Belgium, nearly the whole of which was occupied by Germany for most of the war, the population suffered from the combined effects of German requisitions and the Allied blockade. British propaganda alleging widespread atrocities was later deemed to have been exaggerated but about 6,500 civilians were killed, often victims of exaggerated German fear of *francs-tireurs*. The university town of Louvain was sacked and its priceless university library burned to the ground. Thousands of unemployed workers were forcibly deported to Germany to work in labour battalions. An electrified fence was installed along the entire Dutch–Belgian frontier to prevent illicit crossings by Belgians seeking to join the Belgian army in France. The occupation authorities attempted to weaken potential Belgian resistance by crude attempts to divide the Flemish-speaking population from the francophone Walloons. In 1916 the country was divided into three linguistic zones: Flemish, German, and Walloon. This was followed, in 1917, by the virtual partition of the country between Flanders and Wallonia. The University of Ghent was turned into a Flemish-speaking institution. Some Flemish nationalists welcomed these measures but the bulk of the population in Flanders, as elsewhere in the country, remained loyal to King Albert.

Occupied areas in eastern Europe suffered much more severely, especially those near front lines that moved to and fro repeatedly. In Galicia many villages were totally destroyed. The retreating Habsburg armies took reprisals against local inhabitants suspected of being Russian spies. Jews on the eastern front fled from the ravages of the Russian army to the civilized embrace of Austria or Germany. Many Ukrainian nationalists from Galicia took refuge in Vienna and remained there until the end of the war. The most savage attacks on civilian populations took place in the Balkans and in Anatolia where national and religious animosities fuelled massacres, particularly by Turks against Armenians suspected, often correctly, of supporting Russia.

No atrocity stories were needed to persuade most soldiers on the front line anywhere in this war of the foul obscenity of warfare even if played strictly by Hague Convention rules. They had only to lie awake at night listening to the moans from the wounded men bleeding helplessly to death in no man's land. For years on end millions of men were subjected compulsorily to nauseating and dehumanizing conditions of living and constant danger of death. Why did they put up with it? The fear that they would not was a source of constant anxiety for governments and army staffs. In fact, none of the combatant armies was immune from disciplinary problems, and of the major European powers only the British (perhaps because of their lower rates of mobilization and of deaths in action) managed to avert mutinies, large-scale desertions, or revolution. By 1917 the strain on all the warring societies had produced political changes, industrial unrest, and a rising tide of calls for peace.

To what end?

One by one the leaders who had taken their countries into the war disappeared from power, to be replaced by men of a different stamp. In Britain, the reverses of 1916 led to criticism of Asquith's leadership. His placid demeanour seemed ill-suited to the prosecution of a savage modern war. In April an Irish nationalist rebellion in Dublin was brutally put down. Asquith was displaced in December as the result of a palace revolution by members of his own government. The head of the conspiracy was Lloyd George. Its chief organizer was the Canadian newspaper-owner Sir Max Aitken (later Lord Beaverbrook). As Prime Minister, Lloyd George brought vigour and determination to his new post. He created a small War Cabinet, most of whose members were free of any departmental duties. Bypassing the civil service, he mobilized his 'garden suburb' of expert advisers, housed in temporary huts at the back of 10 Downing Street. He swept away some of the cobwebs of traditional practice in British government, creating for the first time a Cabinet Secretariat, one of whose functions was to record Cabinet meetings (hitherto no minutes had been kept).

In Germany, Bethmann Hollweg's support for the installation of Hindenburg and Ludendorff as army chiefs soon became his own undoing. In the autumn of 1916 informal peace feelers, encouraged by the Chancellor, led to unofficial talks in Sweden between Germans and Russians. In December Bethmann issued a 'peace note', declaring Germany's readiness to negotiate, but the army chiefs prevented his including any specific proposals that might have lent the offer an air of substance. Six weeks later, against his own better judgement, he gave way to the High Command's insistence on unrestricted submarine warfare. In April 1917 a major political crisis erupted. Bethmann found himself caught between a left demanding peace with no annexations or indemnities and a right calling for German economic domination of the continent and large territorial acquisitions in eastern and western Europe.

Under pressure from Hindenburg and Ludendorff, he resigned on 13 July. His successors were lesser figures who allowed themselves to be dominated by the high command. Six days after Bethmann's resignation, the Reichstag, whose left-centre majority was increasingly out of tune with the high command's annexationist war aims, passed a 'peace resolution' renouncing conquest and calling for 'a peace of understanding and permanent reconciliation of peoples'. The Chancellor, Georg Michaelis, accepted it, but added the caveat 'as I interpret it'.

In France too the top military and political leadership changed. In December 1916 Joffre was removed from his command. The disastrous offensive on the Somme spelt his demise. He was succeeded by Nivelle, whose charm and command of English (his mother was British) commended him to British generals and politicians. The change in command did not, however, portend any renovation in strategy. By early 1917 the combined strength of British, French, and Belgian forces on the western front was 3.9 million; they faced about 2.5 million Germans. The French, however, were nearing the end of their manpower resources. In April 1917 Nivelle launched another offensive on the western front. The *poilus* walked into yet another bloodbath: the French army suffered 120,000 casualties within the first two days. Nivelle refused to resign and had to be dismissed. His successor was Pétain.

The low point of French morale, both civilian and military, was probably the aftermath of this disastrous offensive. For the first time since 1914 major strikes broke out in Paris, Toulouse, and in the mining district of Saint Etienne. Although not anti-war in spirit, the stoppages showed the danger of large-scale social conflict. Reports by prefects and postal censors suggested a widespread war-weariness.[62] This mood began to be reflected even in public print. Some newspapers, including the recently founded *Canard enchaîné*, had begun to react against the propagandistic *bourrage de crâne* (eyewash) that had been the daily diet served up by most of the press since August 1914.

At the same time the morale of the French army threatened to crack. More than 21,000 men deserted in 1917 compared with just under 9,000 the previous year. In April mutinies broke out among the troops on the western front. Over the next nine months between thirty and forty thousand soldiers participated in at least 250 episodes of collective indiscipline. In a typical incident on 1 June at Ville-en-Tardenois, near Rheims, two thousand soldiers gathered outside the town hall. When their commanding general tried to intervene he was attacked amid shouts of '*Assassin!... Buveur de sang!... A mort!... Vive la Révolution!*'[63] Altogether two-thirds of all French divisions on the western front were affected by the mutinies, a fifth of them seriously. The movement seems to have been more an inchoate protest than a revolutionary challenge. The main cause was disgust at the apparently pointless waste of lives in endless unsuccessful offensives. Pétain handled the incidents with a deft mixture of firmness and sensitivity. Several hundred mutineers were condemned to death, but most had their sentences commuted. Food and conditions at the front were improved, leave periods were made more frequent. Publication of news of the mutinies in the French press was prohibited. Remarkably, the German High Command did not get wind of the movement in time to try to take military advantage of it. Although limited in extent, the mutinies caused serious concern in the French High Command and helped steer it towards a new strategy in the final year of the war.

At Passchendaele in Flanders in the second half of 1917 British and Canadian forces engaged in what Lloyd George later called 'the battle which, with the Somme and Verdun, will always rank as the most gigantic, tenacious, grim, futile and bloody fights ever waged in the history of war'.[64] Haig, who conceived this disastrous offensive, persuaded himself and a sceptical Prime Minister that the long-hoped-for 'breakthrough' was within his grasp and that, upon the capture of the Passchendaele ridge, the cavalry would be able to move forward and capture Ostend, Bruges, and the Belgian coastline. In the most ferocious chapters of his memoirs Lloyd George recalled how he was induced to agree to this 'muddy and muddle-headed adventure': 'When Sir Douglas Haig explained his projects to the civilians, he spread on a table or a desk a large map and made a dramatic use of both his hands to demonstrate how he proposed to sweep up the enemy—first the right hand brushing along the surface irresistibly, and then came the left, his outer finger touching the German frontier with the nail across.' The attack began on 31 July 1917 and ground on until early December. Although the British used large numbers of tanks, they failed to overwhelm the German defences. The Germans inflicted severe casualties on the attackers, particularly by the use of mustard gas. There was no breakthrough and, as Lloyd George put it, 'not a single cavalry horse had wetted his hooves in the slush'.[65] The Allies lost over 400,000 men and gained about five miles of mud; German casualties numbered about 300,000. The Allies thus ended the year as they had begun it—in a bloody stalemate.

Meanwhile, the military impasse unsettled the French political class. Briand, who had served as Prime Minister since 1915, fell from power on 17 March; he was succeeded over the next few months by uninspiring ministries headed by Alexandre Ribot and then Paul Painlevé. In France, as in Germany in 1917, the idea of a compromise peace found an advocate, here in the former Prime Minister Joseph Caillaux. Left-wing opinion turned increasingly against the war and in September the Socialist members of the government resigned. But in an atmosphere of heightened Germanophobia and spy fever (in which the German agent Mata Hari was executed), opponents of the war found few supporters. In November Painlevé resigned and Poincaré was compelled to call on his old enemy Clemenceau to form a government. Clemenceau was seventy-six years old but he was the toughest politician in France. He embodied the fighting Jacobin tradition. His was the militant patriotism of the left. 'We present ourselves before you,' he announced in Parliament on 19 November, 'possessed by the single thought of total war ['une guerre intégrale']—his original draft said 'défense' but he scored that out and wrote 'guerre'[66] . . . war. Nothing but the war!'[67] The new government's firm rejection of the concept of peace without victory was signalled by the prosecution of Caillaux on charges of defeatism and contact with the enemy. The former Interior Minister, Louis Malvy, was also indicted and the two men were found guilty. Malvy was exiled and Caillaux was sentenced to three years' imprisonment. Although both were later amnestied and returned to political life, the prosecutions were an indication of the mood of intransigent nationalism into which the French political class, with the exception of the far left, had now plunged.

By November 1917, therefore, Britain, Germany, and France were all led by men determined to fight to the end. Like George Canning in 1826, Lloyd George could draw encouragement from the expectation that the New World would redress the balance of the Old. American military unpreparedness, however, left the Central Powers a breathing-space: victory still seemed attainable if the long-awaited decisive battle could materialize during the year or so before American strength began to be effectively mobilized in Europe. Reversing their original strategic conception, German military leaders began to dream of triumphing over the enemy in the east and then turning their full strength against the western front for the final struggle. In November 1917, as a result of events in Russia, their dream seemed about to come true.

3

Revolutionary Europe 1917–1921

Come brothers, hail this great and twilight year,
Come, celebrate the dusk of liberty.

*Osip Mandelshtam, Russia, 1918**

Revolution in Russia

By early 1917 military reverses, economic collapse, and social distress had given birth to a revolutionary situation in Russia. Nearly fifteen million men were under arms; at least 1.6 million soldiers had been killed, two million were wounded, and another two million had been captured by the enemy. A serious munitions shortage in the army, caused not so much by lack of production as by inefficient distribution, led to dark rumours of sabotage, plots, and war profiteering. As the army retreated, morale plummeted, officers were murdered, and desertion became pandemic. Hundreds of thousands of refugees fled eastwards from the front, choking transport bottlenecks and adding to pressure on food supplies. Fuel shortages in the cities led to frequent interruptions in supply of electricity and gas. Strikes by industrial workers, irate at price rises and lack of food, led to almost as many lost workdays in the first two months of 1917 as in the whole of the previous year.

Central government in Russia had never been very adaptable and it did not rise effectively to the challenges posed by total war against a technologically superior enemy. Voluntary organizations such as the Central War Industries

* From 'The Twilight of Liberty', translated from the Russian by Babette Deutsch. Avrahm Yarmolinsky, ed., *Two Centuries of Russian Verse: An Anthology from Lomonosov to Voznesensky*, New York, 1966, 163–4.

Committee and the All-Russian Union of *Zemstva* rather than the imperial government took the initiative in organizing industrial production, social welfare, and transportation. In response to demands for more effective mobilization of industry, government controls were extended over production, distribution, and prices. Councils were set up to regulate key commodities but these bodies faced immense difficulties. The economy was severely affected by the closure of Russia's European land frontiers and of her sea outlets in the Black Sea and the Baltic. Only Vladivostok, Murmansk, and the Finnish ports remained open to international traffic. Manufacturing industry, still in its infancy, was starved of imported raw materials and unable to meet the vast demands imposed on it by the army. Coal shortages particularly affected the railway system, crucial to military transportation. With the loss of the Polish coalfields to the Central Powers, Russia became dependent on coal from the Donets basin and on imports; railway capacity, however, proved insufficient to move coal to where it was needed. The rate of railway construction during the war was substantial (it was never surpassed in the Soviet period) but in spite of this the system could not cope with the demands of war. As railways were increasingly monopolized by the army, civilian distribution channels were clogged. Food ran short in urban areas even though agricultural production had fallen only about 6 per cent below pre-war levels. Economic decline soon turned to economic meltdown, reflected in rapid inflation. During the first two years of the war prices more than doubled. By early 1917 they doubled again.

Opposition to the government coalesced in the Duma, where the mood of patriotic unity at the outset of the war gradually evaporated. In August 1915 a Progressive Bloc, dominated by the Kadets, gathered the support of a majority of the assembly and demanded a 'government of public confidence'. The government presented a spectacle of disarray as its members were repeatedly changed in what became known as 'ministerial leapfrog'. Court intrigue rather than administrative competence or public reputation became the basis for official appointments; far from inspiring confidence, each successive ministerial change heightened the loss of political legitimacy.

Criticism focused increasingly on the court. In August 1915 the Tsar, acting contrary to the advice of most of his ministers, had taken supreme command of the armed forces from his uncle the Grand Duke Nikolai. So long as the army enjoyed successes, as in the Brusilov offensive of 1916, the Tsar could bask in reflected glory; but when the war began, once again, to go badly, blame was heaped on the imperial Commander-in-Chief. On the opening day of the new session of the Duma on 14 November 1916, the Kadet leader, Milyukov, startled the assembly with a venomous attack on the miserable incompetence of the government, his speech culminating in the famous recurring query, or rather challenge: 'Is this stupidity or is it treason?'[1] Public antipathy focused on the Empress, accused of treasonous pro-Germanism. The reputation of the royal family was further damaged by gossip about the evil influence exerted by the miracle-working holy man (often inaccurately called a monk) Grigory Rasputin. His assassination in December 1916 by Prince Felix Yusupov and other members of the nobility was a sign that disaffection had penetrated even the ruling class.

The 'February Revolution' (March, according to the western calendar) was almost entirely bloodless. Although some anti-government politicians had been talking for months about a coup, it began as something closer to a spontaneous mass outburst than a putsch. The immediate precipitant was a strike, followed by a lockout, at the giant Putilov metalwork factory in Petrograd. Protests by strikers stirred the general anger about food shortages into an explosive brew. Demonstrators chanted 'We want bread!', 'Down with the war!', and 'Down with the Autocracy!' At first neither the government nor the Duma paid much attention, regarding the demonstrations as a matter for the police. The civil authorities, however, proved incapable of restoring order and troops were marshalled to confront the crowds. The ensuing street fighting left several dozen dead and wounded, enraging the populace and denting military morale. Several units of the Petrograd garrison, including regiments of the imperial guard, mutinied and many soldiers joined the rioters. Government ministers, isolated from the political class, from popular opinion, and to a large degree from reality, found that their orders were no longer obeyed.

By 12 March the Tsar's government had ceased to exist. Prince G. E. Lvov, a left-wing Kadet who was head of the All-Russian Union of *Zemstva*, formed a Provisional Government, composed mainly of liberals of various hues. The new Prime Minister, believer in 'a curious brand of Slavophil-anarchic populist liberalism,'[2] was an ineffective leader. Milyukov became Foreign Minister. Aleksandr Guchkov, a leader of the Octobrists (right-wing liberals who had accepted the Tsar's reformist promises in his October Manifesto of 1905), became War Minister, and Aleksandr Kerensky, a lawyer who was close to the Socialist Revolutionary Party, was appointed Minister of Justice. The Provisional Government, an emanation from the Duma, was neither elected by the people nor appointed by the Tsar. 'We were chosen by the Russian revolution' was Milyukov's response to those who questioned its legitimacy.[3] On 15 March the Tsar abdicated in favour of his brother, Grand Duke Mikhail. Milyukov favoured the continuation of the monarchy in the form of a regency, which, he believed, would bolster the authority of the new government, but he found himself overridden by a wave of antagonism against the Romanov dynasty and all it stood for. The Grand Duke in any case declined to accept the throne and Russia thus passed effectively from empire to republic, though the formal declaration came only in September.

The revolution was welcomed almost universally throughout the empire and beyond. Workers burnt effigies of the Tsar in the streets; servicemen hoisted red flags on naval vessels and in the trenches; towns and villages held parades and festivals to celebrate. 'A miracle has happened,' the poet Alexander Blok wrote to his mother.[4] The liberal bourgeoisie too hailed the revolution as a new dawn of liberty. In Britain, France, and the United States, enlightened opinion celebrated Russia's entry into the comity of democratic nations.

From the outset the Provisional Government faced a challenge to its authority from the Petrograd Soviet. This elected assembly, formed by Socialists on 12 March (on the model of a similar body in October 1905) represented the workers of the capital. The Soviet's 'Order No. 1', issued the next day, called on the city's garrison to elect committees and representatives to the Soviet and ordered troops to obey the Soviet rather than their officers or the Military Commission of the Duma. Soon Soviets of Soldiers' and Workers' Deputies sprang up across the country. The phrase 'dual power' was heard, signifying the Provisional Government's failure to stamp its authority on the Soviet. Following negotiations between the government and leaders of the Soviet, an agreed eight-point programme was issued. This called for (1) an immediate political amnesty, (2) freedoms of press, speech, and assembly, as well as the right to strike, (3) abolition of religious discrimination, (4) immediate preparations for a constituent assembly, (5) replacement of the police by a militia with elected officers, (6) election to local self-governing bodies by universal, direct, equal, and secret suffrage, (7) retention of arms by the revolutionary soldiery, and (8) observance of strict military discipline during actual service with full civil freedom to soldiers when not on duty. The government granted independence to Poland (a theoretical undertaking since the Central Powers controlled all ethnic Polish territory) and restored autonomy to Finland. This was an impressive programme but the new regime was weakened by internal strife. Several ministers resented the fact that, as Guchkov put it as early as 22 March, 'one could say bluntly that the Provisional Government exists only as long as the Soviet permits'.[5]

Within nine months the parliamentary system was toppled with only minimal resistance. Why were the fervid hopes of February so quickly dashed? The keyholders to power were not the urban middle class but the rebellious urban workers, mutinous soldiery, and discontented peasants. Many of the latter, like their French predecessors in 1789, saw revolution as a licence for land seizures. The government issued a warning against arbitrary action but its slowness in tackling the critical issue of agrarian reform discredited it in the eyes of the radicalized rural population. Even more destructive of support for the government was its determination to continue the war and the continued military reverses and rising social unrest that flowed from that decision.

In the rumbustious Petrograd Soviet, leadership initially devolved on the Mensheviks (the moderate wing of the Social Democrat Party) and their allies, the Socialist Revolutionaries. Most Mensheviks, though not Julius Martov and his faction of Menshevik Internationalists, advocated a 'revolutionary defencist' policy of continuing the war until a 'democratic peace' could be achieved; but they repudiated Milyukov's expansionist policy of 'war until victory'. In spite of much revolutionary rhetoric they were, in fact, ready to cooperate with the Provisional Government. Gradually, however, as the war became ever more unpopular, the Mensheviks found themselves outshone and outflanked by a little regarded but formidable opponent on the left.

Vladimir Ilyich Lenin, leader of the Bolshevik wing of the Social Democrats, was in Zurich when the revolution broke out in Russia. He had not foreseen the upsurge and his party had not played a major role in the events in Petrograd. From exile he could not exert much influence within Russia. At this critical juncture, however, an angel of deliverance appeared from an unexpected quarter: Berlin. The significance of German aid to the Bolsheviks has been much debated. That it was given, and on a substantial scale, is not in doubt, but 'German gold', while helpful to the Bolsheviks, was probably only marginal to their success. More important was the Germans' decision to facilitate the return home of the one Russian party leader they could rely on to promote a militantly anti-war policy. Lenin obtained German government approval for his journey to Russia by train across the German lines. Contrary to myth, this was *not* a 'sealed train'. Single-minded in his ambition for a revolutionary seizure of power, infinitely flexible in his tactics, and ruthless in his methods, Lenin returned to his homeland to seize the day.

On 16 April Lenin arrived at Finland Station in Petrograd and was welcomed by supporters in the former imperial waiting room. In his 'April Theses', enunciated in a speech to a Bolshevik Party meeting, he evinced an attitude of intransigent hostility to the Provisional Government. He reiterated his implacable opposition to the war, 'which also under the new government of Lvov and Co. unquestionably remains on Russia's part a predatory imperialist war owing to the capitalist nature of that government'. He denounced the doctrine of 'revolutionary defencism'. The slogan of the moment, he declared, was 'All power to the Soviets!' He called for an alliance of the proletariat with 'the poorest strata of the peasantry'. He urged a change in the party's name: 'we must call ourselves a *Communist* Party.'[6] The April Theses outraged many veteran Bolsheviks, who were much more cautious and regarded Lenin's ideas as wild, even insane, but he succeeded in enforcing his authority and his programme on the party.

Shortly afterwards the Provisional Government faced its first major crisis. On 1 May Milyukov sent a diplomatic note to Russia's allies in which he denied that Russia sought a separate peace, affirmed 'the aspiration of the entire nation to conduct the World War to a decisive victory', and promised that the Provisional Government would 'observe fully the obligations undertaken towards our Allies'.[7] In the ensuing uproar, Guchkov resigned and Prince Lvov formed a new government without Milyukov but with several Socialists. Kerensky became War Minister. The Mensheviks and Socialist Revolutionaries joined the coalition as junior partners but soon found themselves compromised by its failure. The government's leaders were soon expressing despair at their inability to control events. 'We are tossed about like débris on a stormy sea,' the Prime Minister confessed privately.[8] Renewed strains within the government led on 20 July to the replacement of Lvov by Kerensky, who personified the Provisional Government for the remainder of its short life. Enemies regarded him as a would-be Bonaparte, admirers (and perhaps he himself) as a potential saviour of the nation. 'Hot hurricane, young dictator', the poet Marina Tsvetaeva called him.

Kerensky staked everything on a final military effort against the Central Powers. It was a desperate gamble. The army was in a chaotic state. Bolshevik propaganda, capitalizing on low troop morale, called for an end to the war and for fraternization with the enemy. The 'Kerensky offensive' began on 1 July. The Prime Minister seemed to believe that his theatrical oratory alone could inspire the army to triumphant offensives. 'Kerensky displayed astonishing activity, supernatural energy, and the greatest enthusiasm,' the Social Democrat Nikolai Sukhanov noted in his diary. 'Crowds thronged into the streets he passed through. Flowers were showered on his car. Standing up in it Kerensky hailed "the people". He was at the peak of his popularity. He was a hero and object of adoration—[Sukhanov, a political opponent, added] for philistines and nondescripts.'[9] The 'Supreme-Persuader-in-Chief' discovered, however, that wars were not won by speeches alone. After initial successes in Galicia, the offensive was a disastrous failure that by September assumed the dimensions of a rout.

As enemy forces advanced inexorably, the Provisional Government faced two challenges at home, the first from the left, the second from the right. In mid-July growing popular unrest brought an uprising in Petrograd. The Bolsheviks found themselves drawn in despite Lenin's warning that they were still a minority: 'One wrong move on our part can wreck everything... if we were now able to seize power, it is naïve to think that we would be able to hold on to it. ... Events should not be anticipated. Time is on our side.'[10] Some soldiers nevertheless joined workers from the Putilov works in street fighting against security forces. Moscow, however, remained relatively unaffected and the unrest did not spread to the rest of the country. After two days troops loyal to the government repressed the movement. Lenin fled to Finland.

Reeling from defeat, Russia fell into virtual anarchy. The right called for a strong hand and some thought the new Commander-in-Chief, General Lavr Kornilov, could provide it. Kornilov was said to have 'the heart of a lion and the brain of a sheep'.[11] In September the Prime Minister and the general quarrelled violently. Kornilov accused the government of acting in collusion with the Germans, and, ignoring Kerensky's attempt to dismiss him, ordered troops to positions around the capital. Socialists of all parties rallied to the defence of the revolution and railwaymen halted Kornilov's troop trains outside Petrograd. The coup failed and Kornilov was arrested. Kerensky, falling into the same error as the Tsar, appointed himself Commander-in-Chief.

By late 1917 the Russians had suffered over seven million casualties since the start of the war. Military and economic disaster had totally discredited the Kerensky government. Since all significant anti-Tsarist parties except the Bolsheviks had participated in the Provisional Government, all shared to some extent in its fall from grace. A last failure, surprising given the regime's original commitment to constitutional liberalism, was the repeated postponement of the promised elections to a constituent assembly.

The delay was partly due to red tape, perhaps also to the mistaken hope of some members of the government that their electoral prospects might improve with time. The possibility was thus lost that elections might provide the necessary basis of legitimacy for a reconstituted government.

In these circumstances the Bolsheviks alone could claim to have clean hands. Riding the wave of working-class and military discontent, they recovered from the debacle of the 'July Days' and, in early September, secured majorities on the Petrograd and Moscow Soviets. Revising classic Marxist theory, which predicated the success of a proletarian revolution on a lengthy phase of bourgeois capitalist rule, the Bolsheviks argued that the bourgeois stage might be foreshortened and, with support from peasants and soldiers, catapulted directly into the proletarian revolution. Moving clandestinely to and fro between Finland and Petrograd, Lenin directed party strategy. His message to the Russian people was crude, direct, and in tune with the popular mood. He demanded peace, bread, land, and '*All power* to the Soviets of Workers' and Soldiers' Deputies![12]

The Bolshevik revolution involved elements of both a popular movement and a conspiratorial coup. In a meeting of the Bolshevik Central Committee, convened secretly on 23 October, Lenin moved a resolution declaring that the time was 'fully ripe' for 'an armed uprising'. Two members, Grigory Zinoviev and Lev Kamenev, opposed immediate action which, they argued, would be 'to gamble not only the fate of our party but the fate of the Russian and international revolution as well'. They pointed out that the Bolsheviks' prospects in the elections to the Constituent Assembly were excellent. With the strong support they now enjoyed among the urban proletariat and the army, they might win as many as a third of the seats. On the other hand, the majority of the peasants, they correctly forecast, would vote for the Socialist Revolutionaries, who retained overwhelming support in the countryside. The two dissenters warned that support for revolution in the rest of Europe was far from assured. A rising now, they concluded, would involve 'declaring war on the whole bourgeois world', a conflict in which they could by no means be certain of victory.[13] Lenin's resolution, however, was supported by all the other members and preparations immediately began for a rising.

The coup, when it came, seemed almost an anticlimax. The chief organizer of the seizure of power was not Lenin but Trotsky, at whose behest the Petrograd Soviet, on 2 November, appointed a Military-Revolutionary Committee (MRC) that supervised the details of the insurrection. The committee included some Left Socialist Revolutionaries as well as Bolsheviks. The MRC and the Bolshevik-dominated soviets served as fronts for Bolshevik control of the revolution, effectively muffling the opposition of the Mensheviks and most Socialist Revolutionaries. The committee's first objective was to secure the support of the Petrograd garrison, partly on the pretext that a renewed attack on the capital was threatened by Kornilovite forces. The Bolsheviks meanwhile recruited as reinforcements to their cause eight thousand sailors from the Kronstadt naval base near Petrograd. There was little fighting. On 6 and 7 November troops loyal to the Bolsheviks captured the Peter and Paul fortress and the General Staff headquarters and seized control of telephone and telegraph communications in the capital.

A single blank shell fired at 9.40 p.m. on 7 November from the battleship *Aurora*, which had entered the River Neva and trained its guns on the seat of the Provisional Government in the Winter Palace, was the signal for an assault. Inside the building ministers (minus Kerensky, who had rushed to the front in a hopeless effort to rouse loyal troops) found that even their food supply had been blocked by the rebels. They rejected an ultimatum demanding surrender. An armed mob overwhelmed the barely defended barricades and pillaged the palace, burning much of the imperial library, smashing precious plate, bayoneting pictures, and consuming large quantities of vintage wine. The ministers were arrested and narrowly escaped being lynched before being imprisoned in the fortress of Peter and Paul.

Meanwhile a Second All-Russian Congress of Soviets had opened in the capital. Unlike the first such congress, the previous June, in which the Bolsheviks had been a small minority, this body had a large Bolshevik representation—at least 300 out of 670—and together with allies among the left wing of the Socialist Revolutionaries they were able to dominate the proceedings. When news of the attack on the Winter Palace reached the congress, the Mensheviks and most Socialist Revolutionaries as well as the Jewish-Socialist Bund walked out in protest. Trotsky scornfully cried: 'You are pitiful isolated individuals; you are bankrupts; your role is played out. Go, where you belong from now on—into the rubbish-bin of history!'[14]

Secure in control of the congress, the Bolsheviks presented a manifesto drafted for the occasion by Lenin:

> Supported by an overwhelming majority of the workers, soldiers, and peasants, and basing itself on the victorious insurrection of the workers and the garrison of Petrograd, the congress hereby resolves to take governmental power into its own hands. The Provisional Government is deposed and

> most of its members are under arrest. The Soviet authority will at once propose a democratic peace to all nations and an immediate armistice on all fronts. It will safeguard the transfer without compensation of all land—landlord, imperial, and monastery—to the peasant committees; it will defend the soldiers' rights, introducing a complete democratization of the army; it will establish workers' control over industry; it will ensure the convocation of the Constituent Assembly on the date set; it will supply the cities with bread and the villages with articles of first necessity; and it will secure to all nationalities inhabiting Russia the right of self-determination.... Long live the Revolution![15]

The resolution passed with only two negative votes. 'All power to the Soviets' was quietly forgotten as the Bolsheviks formed a new government styled Council of People's Commissars (*Sovnarkom*). Its composition was exclusively Bolshevik: Lenin was declared Chairman, Trotsky became Commissar for Foreign Affairs, and a little-known Georgian, Josef Stalin, took the Nationality Affairs portfolio.

Having lambasted Kerensky's tardiness in organizing the elections to the Constituent Assembly, Lenin could not avoid them, although he briefly considered further postponement. Between 25 November and 9 December 1917 forty-four million votes were cast in the first relatively free nationwide election in Russian history. There was some intimidation, particularly of Kadets, but in general the vote provided a fair representation of opinion. The Bolsheviks performed well among urban workers and the armed forces, but the overwhelming victors were the Socialist Revolutionaries who won 17.5 million votes to the Bolsheviks' 9.8 million. The Mensheviks, whose support had waned over the previous few months, secured only 1.2 million and the Kadets just under two million. These results hardly represented an enthusiastic endorsement of the regime under whose auspices the ballots had been cast. But Socialist Revolutionaries' support was dispersed across the Russian countryside whereas the Bolsheviks had by now secured firm control of Petrograd and Moscow.

The Constituent Assembly convened on 18 January 1918 at the Tauride Palace in Petrograd. That night two former Kadet ministers who had been arrested and held in hospital were murdered in their beds. Russia's first freely elected parliament met for only a few hours. Shortly after it opened the Bolsheviks walked out. The assembly remained in session and attempted, in the face of barracking from the galleries, to transact business. Early the following morning, however, a sailor who commanded the sentries protecting the building ordered the deputies to disperse on the ground that 'the guard is tired'. In an awkward draft decree attempting to justify the dissolution, Lenin argued that the Assembly 'was an expression of the old relation of political forces which existed when power was held by the compromisers and the Kadets'. For the Soviets, which were the most authentic representatives of the working classes, to relinquish power 'for the sake of bourgeois parliamentarism . . . would now be a retrograde step and [he confessed] cause the collapse of the October workers' and peasants' revolution'.[16] The suppression of the Constituent Assembly, condemned at the time by Socialists such as Maxim Gorky and Rosa Luxemburg, gave a clear signal of the dictatorial intentions of the Bolsheviks—as Lenin declared in conversation with Trotsky: 'The dissolution of the Constituent Assembly by the Soviet Government means a complete and frank liquidation of the idea of democracy by the idea of dictatorship. It will serve as a good lesson.'[17]

War endings

The Bolsheviks rapidly made good on their pledge of peace. On their first day of power, they issued a decree calling for the immediate conclusion of 'a just and democratic peace . . . without annexations . . . and without indemnities'.[18] Soon afterwards, the new regime greatly embarrassed Britain and France by publishing the texts of secret treaties concluded in the early stages of the war, showing the extent of Allied territorial ambitions at the expense of the Central Powers. Talks between the Bolsheviks and the Germans began almost immediately and on 15 December an armistice was signed, to be followed in short order by similar agreements with Austria-Hungary and the Ottoman Empire. A week later Russia and Germany, with Germany's allies in attendance, opened negotiations for a peace treaty at the Germans' eastern front military headquarters at Brest-Litovsk.

The Allied reaction was one of alarm and confusion. The former French ambassador to Russia, Maurice Paléologue, suggested that the French might turn the Russian defection to their advantage by negotiating a peace of their own with Germany; he hoped that France would thereby regain Alsace and Lorraine in exchange for allowing the Germans to annex former Russian territories in the east. But this approach found few supporters among the Allies since it would leave Germany even more powerful than at the beginning of the war. Instead, the French moved towards a policy of creating an 'eastern barrier' of new states between a weakened Germany and a weakened Russia. Hence the decision to declare support for an independent Poland—a war aim that the British, Americans, and Italians eventually endorsed in a note issued on 3 June 1918. The British and French angrily rejected Soviet proposals that they join in a peace without annexations. They refused to recognize the legitimacy of the Bolshevik government and began to cast around for some means of preserving an eastern front and safeguarding the vast stockpiles of war *matériel* that they had shipped to Russia and that they feared might fall into German hands.

At Brest–Litovsk the Germans, taking full advantage of their strong military position, made far-reaching territorial demands. Ludendorff, in particular, pushed the government towards maximalist claims: 'If Germany makes peace without profit, Germany has lost the war,' he declared.[19] Trotsky, who took charge of the Russian delegation on 8 January 1918, hoped that revolution in central Europe might spring to the aid of revolution in Russia and he therefore resisted the German demands. But in spite of some signs of working-class unrest in Austria and Germany no such revolutionary *deus ex machina* materialized. Trotsky's policy of 'neither war nor peace' provided no defensive rampart against a renewed German advance which began in the east on 17 February 1918. Meeting no opposition at all, the Germans captured Estonia and Livonia and within a few days threatened an occupation of Petrograd. Hastily and, as it turned out, irrevocably, the Bolsheviks moved the Russian capital to Moscow. Some Bolsheviks, including Nikolai Bukharin and Karl Radek, favoured a revolutionary war of resistance. But they had no army capable of waging such a campaign. With some difficulty, Lenin imposed his authority and insisted that peace must be signed at almost any cost in order to preserve the Soviet state.

In the Treaty of Brest–Litovsk, concluded on 3 March 1918, Russia was compelled to make far-reaching territorial and other concessions (see plate 9). She gave up Finland, the Baltic provinces, Russian Poland, and the Ukraine. She also returned to Turkey three sanjaks (provinces) in the Caucasus that she had held since 1878. The treaty added insult to injury by stating that Russia was to have no say whatsoever in determining the future status of the areas she thus yielded; Germany and Austria-Hungary alone would decide about that 'in agreement with their populations'. Russia undertook to recognize the independence of Ukraine, with which the Central Powers had signed a separate treaty on 9 February, and to withdraw all her troops from Ukrainian territory. What remained of the Russian army was to be demobilized. The Russian navy was to be disarmed or detained in port. Under the terms of the treaty Russia lost 34 per cent of her population, 54 per cent of her industry, and 89 per cent of her coal mines. There was no choice, however, but to yield. The Russian delegate declared that his country, 'grinding its teeth', was ready under duress to accept these terms.[20] Two days later Romania too signed a peace treaty under which she accepted German–Austrian occupation and became an economic satellite of the Central Powers. As a consolation, and as a further way of weakening the new Soviet state, the Russian province of Bessarabia, where about half the population were ethnic Romanians, was recognized as belonging to Romania.

Peace in the east gave Germany renewed breathing-space and hope. The prospect of abundant grain supplies from Ukraine enabled the government to increase the bread ration for German civilians in 1918. The Brest–Litovsk treaty was generally applauded in the Reichstag. In spite of considerable unease on the left, only the Independent Socialists voted against ratification. By the end of 1917 Germany had nearly six million men under arms. For the 1918 campaign she could still muster over two hundred divisions and as a result of Brest–Litovsk the bulk of these could be concentrated for the great struggle in the west. The build-up of American forces there proceeded slowly. In January 1918 there were not more than 175,000 American soldiers in Europe. But US troop strength could be expected to expand steadily. As the Germans confronted the spring campaign of 1918, they therefore summoned up all their strength for what must be their make-or-break effort to win the war in the west as they had already done in the east.

On 21 March 1918 the Germans at last achieved a breakthrough on the western front. Thanks to the transfer of thirty-six divisions from the eastern front and another eight from Italy, they enjoyed clear numerical superiority in the west for the first time in the war: 192 divisions against 169 Allied divisions. In the initial attack the Germans achieved tactical surprise. Using mustard gas on a massive scale, they advanced rapidly against the British, threatening to drive a wedge between them and their allies. Fierce quarrels broke out between Haig and Lloyd George and between Haig and Pétain. In the hope of composing these disputes, Clemenceau and Lloyd George agreed to promote Ferdinand Foch, Pétain's Chief of Staff, over his head to the position of supreme Allied Commander-in-Chief on the western front. At last the Allies had a single generalissimo, although still not a fully integrated command structure. On 12 April, as the British front in Flanders seemed about to give way, Haig ordered his men 'to fight it out. . . . With our backs to the wall and believing in the justice of our cause, each one of us must fight on to the end.'[21] The British line buckled and nearly broke but Ludendorff failed to exploit his temporary superiority and the arrival of five French divisions two days later helped stabilize the Allied position in the north.

In the summer of 1918, as in the autumn of 1914, the Germans seemed on the verge of conquering Paris. The Kaiser Wilhelm Geschütz, one of the largest guns ever constructed, with a range of 76 miles, shelled Paris from the Forest of Crépy. The bombardment caused widespread panic although the number of casualties, at least compared with those at the front, was small: 250 people were killed and 678 injured in the capital. At the same time Paris came under renewed air attack although from this quarter too casualties were slight. On 27 May the Germans launched a great offensive in the west; again they achieved tactical surprise; they crossed the Aisne and broke through Allied lines. Within a week they were once more on the Marne. In a speech to a tumultuous session of Parliament on 4 June, Clemenceau made it clear that on this occasion there was no thought of abandoning the capital: 'I will fight in front of Paris, I will fight in Paris, I will fight behind Paris.'[22] French manpower resources were on the verge of exhaustion. More than 200,000 American troops a month were arriving in France, offering the Allies hope for the future, but they were judged unready for frontline service until they had received another three or four months of training. On 15 July the Germans made their final lunge towards Paris and crossed the Marne. This time the French line did not break.

Three days later the French launched a successful counter-attack south of Soissons, pushing the Germans back over the Aisne. By 24 July Foch glimpsed the prospect of victory: 'it passed before my eyes like a flash!'[23] A decisive turning-point came with a British attack at Amiens on 8 August, the 'black day' of the German army. The British achieved total surprise, partly because they eschewed the ritual preliminary artillery bombardment. They deployed 462 tanks for this battle as well as nearly 800 aircraft and they manoeuvred their mechanical forces in coordination with the infantry. German morale cracked. Hindenburg later wrote: 'I had no illusions about the political effects of our defeat on August 8th.' But he evidently still retained at least a glimmer of hope, for he added: 'In the middle of August I did not consider that the time had come for us to despair of a successful conclusion of the war.'[24]

Now began the 'hundred days' that vindicated Haig's command or at least extenuated his earlier failures. In six weeks the Allies captured 254,000 prisoners, 3,670 heavy guns, and 23,000 machine guns. The Allied armies, among them ever-increasing numbers of Americans, pierced the great German defensive fortifications known as the Hindenburg Line and threatened the borders of Germany herself.

Germany's allies too were on the brink of defeat. Austria-Hungary had been searching for an exit from the war for the previous two years. Following the death of the Emperor Franz Joseph on 21 November 1916 (see plate 7), his great-nephew, Karl, who succeeded him, announced that he would seek 'to put an end to the horrors and sacrifices of the war at the earliest possible moment and to restore the sadly missed blessings of peace to my peoples'.[25] Through his brother-in-law, Prince Sixtus of Bourbon-Parma, Karl opened contacts with the Entente Powers. Generous with what belonged to others, Karl declared himself ready to support the return of Alsace and Lorraine to France; he was less prepared to meet Italy's insistence on her claim to Trieste and the Trentino. In any case, his feelers were disowned by his own ministers and by his senior ally. The German Kaiser was furious when he found out about Karl's support for the French claim to Alsace and Lorraine, though the Germans themselves had had no compunction about offering Austrian territory to Italy.

Karl's diplomatic overtures led nowhere and in the end the Habsburgs, like their allies, pursued the struggle to its bitter end. The Dual Monarchy made a prodigious, last-gasp military effort: eight million men, one third of the adult male population, served in the armed forces during the war. But by 1918 the Austrians, running short of horses and able to produce aircraft only half as fast as the Italians, were thrown on the defensive. In October the Italians were even able to drive the Austrians back and inflict a severe defeat on them at Vittorio Veneto. On 27 October the Habsburg government sought an armistice and sued for a separate peace. In the meantime the Allied expeditionary force at Salonica had at last proved its value as General Louis Franchet d'Esperey's French, Italian, Serbian, Greek, and British troops advanced into Bulgaria, which signed an armistice on 29 September. The last European state to enter the war was thus the first to exit it. Allied forces occupied Belgrade and moved into Bosnia. The Turks capitulated on 30 October after a mainly British army under General Allenby had completed the conquest of Palestine and Syria.

Abandoned by her allies, her forces in headlong retreat in the field, her civil population restive, Germany could resist no longer. By the beginning of November the Americans, under General John Pershing, had two million men and 240,000 horses on the western front. The balance of forces turned more decisively against the Germans every day. In the hope of at least preserving the German army intact as the bulwark of a society by now on the edge of open revolt, Ludendorff and Hindenburg, on 28 September, urged a speedy armistice. A new government, headed by the liberal Prince Max of Baden, took office on 2 October. Hindenburg insisted on an immediate halt to the fighting 'in order to spare the German nation and its allies useless sacrifices. Each day that is lost costs the lives of thousands of brave soldiers.'[26] Accordingly the new government sent a note to US President Woodrow Wilson requesting an armistice and peace negotiations on the basis of the 'Fourteen Points' programme that he had proposed the previous January. Pershing and Pétain wanted to move ahead and occupy Germany but they were overruled in the interest of preventing further bloodshed.

The armistice was signed by German representatives in Foch's railway carriage at Compiègne a little after 5.00 a.m. on 11 November. The Germans had tried to negotiate terms but their efforts were brushed aside by Foch who insisted on imposing harsh conditions that had been previously decided among the Allies. The Germans were to hand over five thousand heavy guns, twenty-five thousand machine-guns, three thousand trench mortars, 1,700 aeroplanes, five thousand railway locomotives and 150,000 wagons, five thousand lorries, and 150 submarines. All Allied prisoners of war were to be repatriated immediately and 'without reciprocity'. Ten battleships and six battlecruisers of Tirpitz's Grand Fleet were to be interned.

Other terms of the armistice foreshadowed the Allies' demands and preoccupations at the forthcoming peace conference. Within fifteen days the German army was to evacuate all occupied territories in western Europe as well as Alsace-Lorraine. The Allies would occupy the left bank of the Rhine as well as bridgeheads on the right bank. In eastern Europe the Germans were to withdraw their forces from the territories of their former allies. As for German troops in Russia, these were to return to Germany 'as soon as the Allies shall think the moment suitable, having regard to the internal situation of these territories'. The treaty of Brest-Litovsk was declared annulled. At the insistence of Clemenceau a clause was inserted demanding German payment of 'reparation for damage done' on a scale to be determined later. The economic blockade of Germany was to continue although the Allies would 'contemplate the provisioning of Germany . . . as shall be found necessary'.[27] The head of the German delegation, Matthias Erzberger, declared: 'The German people, who stood steadfast against a world of enemies for fifty months, will preserve their freedom and unity no matter how great the external pressure. A nation of seventy millions can suffer, but it cannot die.'[28] Foch said, '*Eh bien, messieurs, c'est fini, allez*!'[29]

Foch drove back to Paris and presented the document to Clemenceau with the words, 'My work is finished; your work begins.'[30] Fighting stopped on the western front at 11.00 a.m. that day. Hindenburg recalled the end in Wagnerian terms: 'Like Siegfried stricken down by the treacherous spear of savage Hagen, our weary front collapsed.'[31] In Paris and London huge crowds rejoiced in the streets. Clemenceau was one of many who broke into tears. Later in the day he smiled as he was kissed by five hundred girls. On 8 and 9 December he accompanied Poincaré to Strasbourg and Metz as the French President made a triumphal return to his native province, now restored to French rule. 'A day of sovereign beauty. Now I can die,' Poincaré wrote.[32]

Revolution in central Europe

Germany had been defeated on the battlefield but her army had not been destroyed and at the signing of the armistice hardly any enemy soldiers stood on German soil. Her defeat was as much psychological as military, confirming what Liddell Hart called 'the immemorial lesson of history—that the true aim in war is the mind of the enemy command and Government, not the bodies of their troops, that the balance between victory and defeat turns on mental impressions and only indirectly on physical blows'.[33] A consequence, not a cause, of that psychological defeat was the revolution that broke out in Germany in the last days of the war.

The roots of the German revolution can be traced back to the grim winter of 1917/18. At that time Bolshevik hopes of avoiding an imposed peace were concentrated on the prospect of a revolution in Germany, home of the oldest and strongest Social Democratic Party in Europe and of a large and politically conscious proletariat. Average urban workers' earnings in real terms declined by more than a third between 1914 and 1917. With food, fuel, and clothing in short supply, the German working class became increasingly discontented. This mood was exploited by the Independent Socialist Party (USPD), founded in 1917 on an anti-war platform. Mass strikes in many German cities in January 1918, demanding the Bolshevik formula of a 'peace without annexations or indemnities', were soon snuffed out by a firm government response. Socialist and liberal newspapers were suppressed. Strikers were arrested and major industrial enterprises placed under military control.

The revolutionary contagion was contained for the time being but the deterioration of the military position in the summer and early autumn brought renewed unrest and the 'revolution from above' in which Ludendorff, in order to evade responsibility for the debacle, insisted on handing over power to the Reichstag and the civilian government.

In the course of October the new government revised the German constitution in order to transform the country into a constitutional monarchy. The Reichstag completed the revisions on 26 October. That day Ludendorff resigned his position as Quartermaster-General, expecting 'to see the country given over to Bolshevism'.[34] His successor was General Wilhelm Groener, a provocative appointment since he had been responsible for repressing the strike movement the previous January. Two days later a naval mutiny broke out at Wilhelmshaven, quickly spreading to Kiel and other naval bases. The sailors' basic demand was for peace. They were soon joined by shipyard workers. By 7 November virtually the entire fleet had mutinied. Meanwhile the spirit of revolt had infected the army. Soldiers' and workers' councils, on the model of the Russian soviets, were set up in a number of cities. In Cologne the mayor, Konrad Adenauer, reached a modus vivendi with such a council. Elsewhere established authority was entirely overthrown. A Bavarian government headed by Kurt Eisner, a USPD leader, deposed the thousand-year-old Wittelsbach dynasty and declared a republic.

The German Empire gave way without a struggle. On 9 November a general strike broke out in Berlin. Soldiers at many barracks in Berlin fraternized with revolutionary crowds. Shorn of the means of repression, the Kaiser agreed to abdicate. He and his family fled to neutral Holland. Subsequently the victorious powers applied strong pressure for his surrender to stand trial for war crimes. The Dutch government had nothing but its self-respect to lose by yielding to the clamour; but it refused. Wilhelm survived just long enough to applaud the destruction in 1940 of the state that had so punctiliously protected him and to congratulate Adolf Hitler on succeeding where he had failed—in presiding over a German-dominated Europe.

Philipp Scheidemann, a leading Social Democrat, proclaimed a republic. Another Social Democrat, Friedrich Ebert, a former saddler, took over the government, not as Chancellor but as chairman of the Council of People's Representatives, composed of Socialists of various stripes. Within the new government tensions soon appeared between moderate and extreme elements. The Social Democrats, conscious of their lack of administrative experience, had taken over and preserved intact the profoundly conservative imperial bureaucratic apparatus. Ebert also formed a tacit alliance with the army high command, who were anxious to avert social revolution. On the other hand, the USPD and other left-wing groups regarded the soldiers' and workers' councils as the legitimate source of authority and as foundation-stones of a German Soviet Republic.

In December fighting broke out in Berlin between government forces and left-Socialist adherents of the Spartacist League. On 29 December, at a conference attended by Karl Radek as a fraternal delegate from Soviet Russia, the Spartacists split away from the USPD and formed the German Communist Party (KPD). Led by Karl Liebknecht and Rosa Luxemburg (see plates 13 and 14), the Spartacists sought to establish a soviet republic and on 5 January 1919 launched a rebellion in Berlin. They occupied a number of buildings, including the offices of the Social Democrat newspaper *Vorwärts*. The revolt, which was joined by many left-wing Socialists, was crushed with great severity by military units under the direction of Gustav Noske, the Social Democrat minister for military affairs. At least twelve hundred people were killed in a week of fighting in the capital. Liebknecht and Luxemburg were captured and murdered by right-wing officers. Luxemburg's body was thrown into a canal.

Gangs of ex-servicemen loosely organized into *Freikorps* played a prominent part in suppressing the Spartacist revolt and in exacting savage revenge. Inspired by reactionary, militarist, nationalist, and anti-Semitic propaganda, these units were fertile ground for the *Dolchstosslegende* ('stab in the back legend') of the cause of German defeat—the notion that Germany had been beaten not on the battlefield but by subversive elements at home. The *Freikorps* took to the streets as vigilantes, attacking leftists and, in some cases, Jews. Over the next year or two they evolved into right-wing private armies to which the republic, paradoxically and dangerously, became indebted for help in repressing left-wing agitation. The army high command, seeing in the volunteers of the *Freikorps* a politically more reliable buttress for their political aims than the conscripted troops of the old imperial army, gave its blessing to the movement. For unemployed veterans of the trenches the *Freikorps* provided a focus of companionship and loyalty and a sense of meaning and purpose. For such men, any inhibitions about the use of political violence had been shattered by the experience of war. A return to arms, whether in punch-ups with leftists or in more disciplined combat and training, became an outlet for the frustrations and disappointments of civilian life in the harsh post-war economic climate.

Under these dubious auspices, the new regime, a strange alliance of moderate Social Democrats and the reactionary army command, survived its initial ordeal by fire. In January 1919 a Constituent Assembly was elected on the basis of universal suffrage for all men and women over the age of twenty. The elections confirmed the dominance of the Social Democrats who won 39 per cent of the vote; the Catholic Centre Party, together with its Bavarian pendant, drew 20 per cent, the liberal Democrats 15 per cent, the conservative nationalists 8.5 per cent, and the USPD only 7.6 per cent (although it won 27.6 per cent in Berlin). The Communists, still dreaming of revolution, decided not to participate. For fear of disturbances, the assembly met not in Berlin but at Weimar and elected Ebert President. Scheidemann formed a coalition government of Social Democrats, the Catholic Centre Party, and Democrats which turned to the difficult tasks of political, diplomatic, and economic reconstruction.

After the suppression of the Berlin Spartacists, revolutionary effervescence, mainly organized by soldiers' and workers' councils, continued for several months in various parts of the country. The most spectacular such movement emerged, a little embarrassingly for Marxist theory, not in the more industrialized regions but in agrarian, Catholic Bavaria. Eisner, the leader of the November revolution in Munich, had formed a government in alliance with the Bavarian Peasants' League. But in an election to the Bavarian Diet in early January 1919, his USPD won only 2.5 per cent of the vote and he was obliged to step down. On 21 February 1919, on his way to the opening session of the Diet, Eisner was assassinated. The murder radicalized the left-wing Socialists who declared a Bavarian Councils' Republic (*Räterepublik*) on 7 April. The new regime, composed of assorted leftist intellectuals, among them the writers Ernst Toller and Gustav Landauer, had a distinctly amateurish air. The elected government headed by the Social Democrat Johannes Hoffmann nevertheless took fright and fled to Bamberg. An attempted counter-revolution in Munich on 13 April was thwarted but led to the installation there of a second *Räterepublik* dominated by Communists. The new leaders looked to Bolshevik Russia for inspiration and guidance. But direct communication between Moscow and Munich was very limited. When Lenin and the Soviet Foreign Affairs Commissar, G. V. Chicherin, succeeded in making brief radio contact with the government of the first *Räterepublik*, asking for information, they were told by Dr Franz Lipp, its 'Foreign Minister', that 'the proletariat of Upper Bavaria is happily united' but that 'the fugitive Hoffmann . . . has taken with him the key to my ministry toilet'.[35] This seems to have been the only significant communication between Moscow and Munich during the short life of the Bavarian Soviet Republic. Comic opera ended in tragedy. On 1 May, after heavy fighting between the 'Red Army' of the infant soviet republic and *Freikorps* contingents aided by troops dispatched by Noske in Berlin, the Hoffmann government was reinstalled in power. At least six hundred people were killed, among them many prisoners murdered by the *Freikorps*.

The German revolution was part of a general revolutionary tremor throughout central Europe. Conservatives discerned the insidious hand of Moscow behind the outbreaks; the Bavarian episode demonstrated that, whatever the inspirational attraction of the Soviet idea, Lenin's ability to project power abroad was very limited. Bolshevism, in any case, was but one of a number of ideological strands in the revolutions of 1918–19. In Austria-Hungary, in particular, demands for political and social liberty were mixed up with pressure from subject nationalities for national freedom. This explosive mixture led, in the case of the Habsburg lands, not merely to the overthrow of a regime, but to the break-up of an entire system.

The end of the Habsburg monarchy in November 1918, like that of the Hohenzollerns, was precipitated by military defeat, but it can be attributed also to the growing instability of the social and political structure of which it formed the apex. An early portent was the assassination in October 1916 of the Austrian Prime Minister, Count Stürgkh, as he sat in a café in Vienna. The death of Franz Josef a few weeks later, after a reign of sixty-eight years, had long been expected and caused sadness but little surprise. He had commanded deep reserves of loyalty and respect; by contrast, the new Emperor and his wife, Zita, were unpopular and the subjects of malicious rumours. Karl sought to move with the tide of public opinion both in seeking peace and in constitutional reform. He advocated universal suffrage in Hungary. He granted an amnesty to political prisoners in mid-1917. Censorship was relaxed. All to no avail. Food riots, demonstrations, strikes, and marches erupted in Vienna. A study of Viennese children in the spring of 1918 found that out of 56,849, only 4,637 could be classified as healthy. The inflationary spiral continued to rise inexorably. By June fresh eggs in the city cost more than seven times the July 1914 price. In October food rations provided only 831 calories per person per day. Deaths from influenza, tuberculosis, and hunger multiplied. The imperial capital, according to one observer, was in a state of 'social decomposition'.[36]

On 30 October the German members of the Reichsrat, who had constituted themselves a 'Provisional National Assembly' nine days earlier, declared the creation of 'German-Austria'. A coalition government, composed of Socialists, nationalists, and members of the conservative Christian Social Party, took power. The army was by now crumbling. The imperial government, shorn of all support, gave up without a fight and simply faded out of existence. The emperor went into exile though he did not abdicate the imperial throne (later, under pressure, he did abdicate the Hungarian throne). On 12 November the National Assembly unanimously declared a republic and simultaneously announced that German-Austria was part of Germany. The latter declaration indicated the lack of any real sense of Austria as a country: it was simply the 'home-farm' of the dynasty, what was left over when the non-German parts of the empire severed their links with Vienna.

The passing of the Habsburg dynasty was merely the outward sign of profound shifts in political identification that had already dissolved the multi-national empire. As the historian Lewis Namier (born in Austrian Galicia and a British Foreign Office official at the time) put it, 'Austria-Hungary disappeared when it vanished from the consciousness of those concerned'.[37] In 1914 the aspirations of the Slavic subject peoples had, with few exceptions, been limited to the securing of equal status with Germans and Magyars within the imperial system. In the early years of the war the subject nationalities had remained surprisingly loyal to the empire. There had been few desertions from the Austrian army. But by the autumn of 1918 the prospect of imminent Habsburg defeat produced a jostling for the inheritance. 'Successor states' suddenly emerged, led by nationalist governments that threw off all allegiance not only to the Habsburgs but to any alien authority: a resurrected Poland, a newly minted Czechoslovakia, and a Serbia enlarged to incorporate most of the other south Slav lands.

During the war Polish nationalists had been united in their desire to restore the independence that had been lost since 1795. They were deeply divided, however, over the means of attaining it and their divisions reflected to some extent the lines of the partition of their country. Both warring coalitions assembled Polish military units and sought to woo recruits with promises of post-war freedom. Some Polish nationalists, adherents of Roman Dmowski, declared support for Russia, hoping to gain some measure of autonomy from the Tsar; others followed the lead of the former leader of the Polish Socialist Party, Józef Piłsudski, whose Polish Legions, formed in Galicia, fought for Austria against the Russians. In November 1916 Wilhelm II and Franz Josef met at Pless in Silesia and issued the 'Two Emperors' Declaration' promising the Poles independence. A Polish Regency Council was established in Warsaw in which Piłsudski served for a short time as Minister of War. In July 1917, however, he refused to serve as a puppet leader under the Germans. As a result he was placed in a German prison. The treaty signed between Germany and the Ukrainians at Brest-Litovsk involved recognition of their rule over the province of Cholm, regarded by the Poles as belonging to Poland. Polish public opinion reacted with outrage. The Regency Council as well as Polish representatives in the Austrian Reichsrat protested bitterly. Henceforth the Central Powers' protestations of sympathy for Polish nationalism were dismissed by most Poles as hypocritical opportunism. Increasingly, they turned instead towards the Entente Powers.

The eviction of Russian and then of German and Austrian authority in the Polish lands left a political vacuum that was immediately filled. When Piłsudski returned to Warsaw on 10 November 1918 he was the hero of the day and immediately made himself master of the situation. He took over from the Regency Council as 'Chief of State'. The new Poland had ill-defined borders that were quickly called into question when fighting broke out between Poles and Ukrainians in eastern Galicia. The Ukrainians sought the area's incorporation in an independent Ukraine; the Poles considered it part of their national state. The population of the region (east of the River San) was predominantly Ukrainian but Piłsudski nevertheless insisted that it must form part of Poland and sent troops to conquer it. Poland, Lloyd George said, was 'drunk with the new wine of liberty supplied to her by the Allies' and 'fancied herself as the resistless mistress of Central Europe'.[38] Piłsudski's attitude on the Galician issue reflected a broader objective of constructing a large Poland, extending beyond areas of mainly ethnic Polish concentration, a policy that soon led the new state into wars with almost all its neighbours.

The territories that came to form the Czechoslovak state had never in history formed a unified political entity. Czechs and Slovaks spoke closely related languages but their historic experiences had been different. Under the Habsburgs Slovak-speaking areas had been ruled by Hungary, while Bohemia, Moravia and Czech Silesia formed part of the Austrian Empire.

The national revival of the nineteenth century had imparted to the Czechs a collective identity and sense of shared nationhood with the Slovaks but until 1914 there had been no serious thought of an independent state. After the outbreak of the war, however, the philosopher Tomáš Masaryk (see Plate 16) contacted the Entente Powers and acted as chief spokesman for the cause of national independence. He formed and headed a Czechoslovak National Council in Paris. Between 1914 and 1918 Masaryk conducted an effective lobbying campaign in London, Paris, and Washington, to assemble political support for a Czechoslovak state. He was aided by sympathetic British and French intellectuals and propagandists, notably the historian R. W. Seton-Watson, who viewed the liberation of the subject Habsburg peoples as both a high ideal and a useful tactic in political warfare. Just as the Germans regarded support for revolutionary and nationalist movements as a device for destabilizing the Russian Empire, the Allies (no doubt with less cynicism) hoped that the Habsburg edifice might be weakened by their invigoration of Slav nationalisms.

Advocates of a Czechoslovak state were strengthened by the creation of distinct national fighting units, composed mainly of prisoners of war from the Austrian army. Over forty thousand Czechs, mainly former Austrian soldiers captured by the Russians, joined a Czech Legion that fought at the side of the Russians on the eastern front. After the Treaty of Brest-Litovsk, the soldiers of this force found themselves in a quandary as to how to get home. In mid-1918, in order to effect their exit, they captured the main stations along the 4,900 miles of the Trans-Siberian railway. They then headed east from European Russia all the way to Vladivostok, giving heart to the enemies of the Bolsheviks in Siberia—and further afield. By a strange quirk of history this military feat on the other side of the world helped secure diplomatic support for the fledgling Czechoslovak government-to-be. When Masaryk was received by President Wilson in Washington, he was able to present himself on the one hand as 'formally a private man', but on the other as effectively 'master of Siberia and half Russia'.[39] On this peculiar basis the Allied powers granted recognition to the Czechoslovak National Council in September 1918 'as a *de facto* belligerent government' representing the Czechoslovak people.

As the Habsburg edifice cracked, the National Council moved fast to forestall any second thoughts on the part of the Powers. On 21 October it declared Czechoslovakia's independence and established a provisional government. On 28 October it took over the administrative reins in Prague.

Here the revolution was predominantly nationalist, not Socialist. Czech units of the former Austrian army immediately transformed themselves into an army of the new state. Two weeks later a National Assembly unanimously elected Masaryk President of the republic. At first the Czechoslovak government's writ ran only in those parts of Bohemia and Moravia where Czechs predominated. In German-majority districts the inhabitants sought incorporation in the new German–Austrian state. Gradually, however, those areas were brought under Czech military occupation. Local Germans protested, but were unable to organize a military force of their own and so could do little. Here, as in the case of the ethnically mixed regions of Poland, the seed of a great tragedy was sown.

The expansion of Serbia into the Kingdom of Serbs, Croats, and Slovenes, or Yugoslavia as it came to be known, was the cruellest blow to the Habsburg system since it represented a triumphant assertion of the principle against which Austria–Hungary had launched the war—that of south Slav unity. Proportionately Serbia had suffered more than any other country in the war. She lost a fifth of her population from the direct and indirect effects of the fighting—among the latter a terrible typhus epidemic. Hundreds of thousands of people had been forced to leave their homes with their oxen and carts. They were turned into a horde of refugees (see plate 3). Joined by army deserters and harassed by bandits, they wandered across the wild countryside in an exodus that nationalist poets and historians later described as a Calvary: 'By the waters of Albania, by the waters of Death, we halted our soldiers. By the waters of the Chkoumba, Séména, Voyoucha, we halted to rest our bones. . . . We were laid low on earth, but we wept not at all, we died in silence, as a great mourning is silent—silent like the Great Passion on the Cross at Jerusalem.'[40]

In December 1914, flushed with success in driving back the Austrian invaders, the Serbian Prime Minister, Pašić, had issued a declaration calling for the creation of a unified state of Serbs, Croats, and Slovenes. The Austrian conquest of Serbia and the exile of her government did not put an end to such plans. Rivalry and suspicion between Serbs and Croats complicated the efforts of the south Slav nationalists but in July 1917 leaders of both major nationalities issued a declaration at Corfu calling for the creation of a common state. The question whether the country should be a federation of national units or a centralized state (which would inevitably be dominated by the largest national group, Serbs) was not resolved. It was never resolved—with poisonous consequences for the entire history of the south Slav state that was born out of the ashes in late 1918.

Meanwhile, revolution in Hungary at the end of October 1918 led to the appointment of the liberal Count Mihály Károlyi as Prime Minister. His first act was to secure the relatively peaceful establishment of a republic—although the revolution claimed one prominent victim: Count Tisza, the former Prime Minister, was shot dead. Károlyi was able to give Hungary only a brief taste of liberal government. In March 1919 extreme leftist revolutionaries assumed power and declared a Socialist Federated Soviet Republic. Its nominal head was a Social Democrat, but the real moving force in the new regime was a Communist, Béla Kun, who became Commissar for Foreign Affairs. The acting Education Commissar was György Lukács, later famous as a Marxist theoretician. Only a few weeks earlier the Károlyi government had imprisoned most of the Communist leaders, but Károlyi's position had become impossible on 26 February when the victorious Allies presented Hungary with proposals for a peace treaty that he declared totally unacceptable. Rather than make the large territorial and other concessions demanded by the Allies, he handed over the government to the left whose leaders thus found themselves catapulted from prison cells to supreme power.

Kun's government sought military aid from the Russian Bolsheviks and tried to rally the country. But it failed to win popularity. Kun had a far from prepossessing manner: he 'somehow left the impression of an inflated frog', according to the Finnish Communist Arvo Tuominen.[41] The Kun regime created a Red Army, a Red Guard, and revolutionary courts. It nationalized industries, banks, schools, and even private homes. It decreed land reform, breaking up the large estates and ordering the creation of large co-operatives.

The Entente Powers sent the South African General Jan Smuts to Hungary to treat with Kun, but the emissary abandoned his task after one day during which he did not leave his railway carriage. Kun's forces moved into Slovakia and set up a Slovak Soviet Republic. It lasted only a fortnight. Britain and France then encouraged Romania to intervene. French military advisers were attached to the Romanian army which quickly advanced into eastern Hungary, capturing Debrecen on 23 April 1919. Meanwhile right-wingers, headed by Count Gyula Károlyi and Count István Bethlen, set up a rival regime at Szeged under the protection of French forces. The Minister of War in this government was the last chief of the Austro-Hungarian navy, Admiral Miklós Horthy. The Kun government was now faced with enemies from within as well as without and resorted to a common device of revolutionary regimes *in extremis*. A Committee of Public Safety under Tibor Szamuely unleashed a 'red terror' against suspected counter-revolutionaries and killed three hundred people.

On 31 July the Romanians began entering Budapest and the next day Kun's regime, which had lasted only 133 days, collapsed. The Romanians remained in occupation of the Hungarian capital until November while all parties manoeuvred for position. In a bizarre turn of events on 6 August, the Habsburg Archduke Josef temporarily assumed the presidency of the republic, allegedly having been appointed Regent by the deposed King Karl. Josef appointed a right-wing government but its authority was not generally recognized. Meanwhile the occupying troops pillaged the countryside energetically. According to an American military observer, they 'cleaned the country out of private automobiles, farm implements, cattle, horses, clothing, sugar, coal, salt, and in fact everything of value'. Sixteen wagon-loads of supplies were taken from the Children's Hospital in Budapest with the result that eleven children died within the next twenty-four hours. Clemenceau and Balfour sent stiff rebukes to the Romanians and even discussed the possibility of military or naval action. Romania, for her part, pointed out that by destroying the Bolshevik regime in Hungary she had rendered a great service to the general weal; she insisted on her right to take all that her army required 'and 30% besides for her own population'.[42] Meanwhile, the Hungarian Whites, organized in groups such as the 'Awakening Magyars', launched a White terror by way of revenge against the Reds. An estimated five thousand people were killed. The traditional anti-Semitism of the Hungarian right was reinforced by a general tendency to identify Jews with Bolshevism, arising from the fact that many of the leaders of the Kun regime had been deracinated Jews. As a result, large numbers of Jews who had nothing at all to do with communism were among the victims.

On 16 November a 25,000-man Hungarian army headed by Horthy made a formal entry to Budapest as the Romanians completed their evacuation in compliance with arrangements brokered by an inter-allied commission. Horthy had close connections with militant groups of nationalist officers and others involved in the White terror. Under his authoritarian rule, 75,000 people were imprisoned for involvement in the Kun government. An estimated 100,000 others, including many intellectuals, fled abroad. But for all his reliance on the radical right, Horthy was an essentially conservative figure whose attitudes were a throwback to the Habsburg period. On 1 March 1920 he assumed the title of Regent. For the remainder of the inter-war period this Admiral without a navy presided paternalistically over a kingdom without a king.

The revolutions in central Europe were emulated elsewhere, but with even less success. In the industrial areas of northern Italy widespread strikes and unrest continued to agitate society well into 1920. In Spain syndicalist and anarchist strikes broke out, particularly in Barcelona, and civil–military conflict intensified in March 1921 with the assassination of the conservative Prime Minister, Eduardo Dato. Ripples of Bolshevism even washed onto British shores. In January 1919 at a demonstration in George Square, Glasgow, called in support of a general strike, Willie Gallacher and Emanuel Shinwell addressed a crowd of thirty thousand as the red flag was hoisted above the City Chambers. Fighting with police erupted and twelve thousand troops were called out to maintain order. Tanks rolled across the cobbled city streets and parked incongruously in the Cattle Market. In spite of the fiery temper of the labour movement in red Clydeside, the Scottish soviet republic was aborted before birth.

Civil war and intervention in Russia

While the revolutionary tide on the continent receded, the conflict between Bolshevism and its enemies in Russia continued and assumed an international dimension. Anti-Bolshevik 'White' armies, financed and supplied by the Allied powers, were joined by foreign expeditionary forces.

The Russian Civil War was waged against the background of an effort by the Bolsheviks to achieve socialism virtually overnight. Almost immediately upon assuming power, Lenin's government issued a number of far-reaching decrees. Landed estates were to be nationalized, with the proviso that 'the land of ordinary peasants and ordinary Cossacks shall not be confiscated'.[43] In effect, large estates were divided and distributed in small lots to peasants. A decree on the nationalities question emphasized the equality of all the peoples of Russia and abolished 'all national and national-religious disabilities', thus emancipating the Jews. The same ordinance asserted 'the right of the peoples of Russia to free self-determination, even to the point of separation and the formation of an independent state', a commitment that was soon to be put to the test.[44] In February 1918 the government repudiated Russia's $3.6 billion foreign debt, thus wiping out at a stroke both Russia's liabilities and her ability to borrow on the world's capital markets. This was one of several actions by which the new Soviet state excluded itself from the comity of respectable governments.

Russia's foreign trade dwindled to almost nothing. What came to be known as 'War Communism' was a disorganized, helter-skelter rush towards a socialized society. All enterprises were declared state property. 'Communist Saturdays' were introduced during which volunteers worked extra shifts, particularly on the railways. Banks were seized and loans annulled. Money became worthless. The Russian economy almost totally seized up. In part this was a natural result of war conditions but in large measure it was a self-inflicted disaster.

The ideological justification for this policy grew out of the Bolsheviks' fear that their revolution would succumb in the absence of support from revolutions in the more advanced industrial states of Europe. Given Russia's primitive economic and social development, and the strong support for other parties demonstrated in the election to the Constituent Assembly, the Bolsheviks were pessimistic about the long-term prospects for their regime unless, by a rapid series of institutional and economic changes, they could implant socialism irrevocably in Russian society. They recognized that the greatest single block of potential opposition to their rule was the Russian peasantry. Although the new regime had secured its authority in the major cities, its hold on the Russian countryside was much weaker. It therefore held out to the peasants what has been called 'a quid pro quo': 'The Bolsheviks sanctioned land seizures while the peasantry would hand over grain to the cities and the army.'[45] But after five years of war and tumult the food distribution system barely functioned. The collapse of money values and markets led naturally to hoarding which in turn stimulated forcible requisitioning by Bolshevik commissars determined to feed the cities and the Red Army. In May 1918 the government declared a Food Dictatorship, according carte blanche to urban 'food supply detachments' to roam the countryside and seize produce. Bolshevik use of force against peasants and against their political opponents fed growing hostility to the regime within Russia.

News in July 1918 of the murder at Yekaterinburg of the Tsar and his family sent a shudder through Europe. This was still a time when many people regarded the person of a monarch as sacrosanct. Moreover, unlike the English regicide of 1649 and the French of 1793, these killings, ordered by Lenin himself, bore no semblance of judicial sanction. Here was another action by which the new rulers of Russia placed themselves outside the conventional bounds of acceptable behaviour.

Already at the outset of their rule the Bolsheviks had demonstrated readiness to take ruthless measures against their enemies. The secret police force, the *Cheka* (or *VeCheKa*: All-Russian Extraordinary Commission for

Combating Counterrevolution and Sabotage, later to be known under various other grim acronyms) was founded in December 1917. As successor to the Tsarist *okhranka*, it took over its predecessor's headquarters, its files, some of its personnel, and many of its techniques, including the use of torture. The first head of the *Cheka* was Felix Dzerzhinsky, a Pole from Vilna (he attended the same school there as Piłsudski). The secret resolution creating the *Cheka* defined its function as the suppression of counter-revolution and sabotage; it rapidly acquired not merely investigative but also executive and secret judicial functions that facilitated its development into the most feared instrument of state authority.

Sanction for terrorist methods came from the top. Asserting that the 'last decisive battle' with the kulaks (literally 'tight-fists', the term applied to the upper stratum of private farmers) was under way, Lenin's orders to Bolsheviks in Penza province, south-east of Moscow, in August 1918 were explicit:

> An example must be demonstrated:
>
> 1. Hang (and make sure that the hanging takes place *in full view of the people) no fewer than one hundred* known kulaks, rich men, bloodsuckers.
> 2. Publish the names.
> 3. Seize *all* their grain from them.
> 4. Designate hostages in accordance with yesterday's telegram.
>
> Do it in such a fashion that for hundreds of kilometers around the people might see, tremble, know, shout: *they are strangling* and will strangle to death the bloodsucking kulaks.[46]

This message (which remained unpublished until the fall of the Soviet Union) was not in any way exceptional. In tone and substance, such instructions became a norm—and a precedent to be followed and multiplied by Lenin's successor.

Creation of a revolutionary dictatorship necessarily implied elimination of political competitors. At first only right-wing and 'bourgeois' political parties, such as the Kadets, were outlawed. But in July, following the assassination of the German ambassador, Count Wilhelm von Mirbach-Harff, by two Socialist Revolutionaries, the Bolsheviks turned on the Left Socialist Revolutionaries, hitherto their allies. Alleging that the SRs were engaged in an uprising, the Bolsheviks arrested their leaders. Some were shot, others later put on trial. An unsuccessful attempt on Lenin's life on 30 August was pinned on the SRs and was used to justify terror against all opponents of the government. Soon all opposition parties were banned.

Press freedom had already been curbed: one of the first decrees issued by the Bolshevik regime ordered the closure of all newspapers 'inciting to open resistance or disobedience' to the new government or 'sowing confusion by means of an obviously calumniatory perversion of fact'. Anticipating complaints that this decree represented an attack on press freedom, the government declared that the measure was 'of a temporary nature and [would] be revoked by a special *ukaz* when the normal conditions of life will be reestablished'.[47] Even left-Socialist papers such as *Novaya zhizn* were banned. By February 1919 all non-Bolshevik papers had been suppressed and a one-party press was firmly established.[48]

Within a few months of the Bolshevik revolution, rival governments and military forces had sprung up in several regions of the former empire. The challenge to the Bolsheviks came from all points of the compass. In the east an army under a self-proclaimed 'Supreme Ruler and Supreme Commander-in-Chief', Admiral A. V. Kolchak, claimed to control vast tracts of territory in Siberia. In the south the White armies were led by Kornilov and, after he was killed by a Red shell in May 1918, by General Anton Denikin. In the north, General Nikolai Yudenich threatened to occupy Petrograd. In the west, Ukrainian nationalists, anarchist peasants led by Nestor Makhno, and motley White armies waged a confusing multi-sided war against the Bolsheviks and against one another. As the central power weakened, some regions sought complete independence. By August 1918 as many as thirty governments were said to be operating on the territory of the former Tsarist empire. Finland, under the leadership of General Gustaf Mannerheim, and the Baltic states of Estonia, Latvia, and Lithuania succeeded in vindicating their claims to independence. Others, such as the Menshevik regime in Georgia, maintained a precarious hold on power only for a short time.

Foreign intervention in the Russian Civil War was not animated primarily by a desire to overthrow the Bolshevik regime. In the initial stages a predominant motive was strategic: the Allied powers' desperate wish to keep open some sort of eastern front in order to preoccupy German forces that might otherwise be transferred to the west.

At first, the French tried to persuade the Bolsheviks to renew the war against Germany. They seemed to have succeeded momentarily in February 1918, when the Russo-German talks at Brest-Litovsk broke down and the Russian Council of People's Commissars decided to accept the aid of 'the brigands of French imperialism against the German brigands'.[49] In early

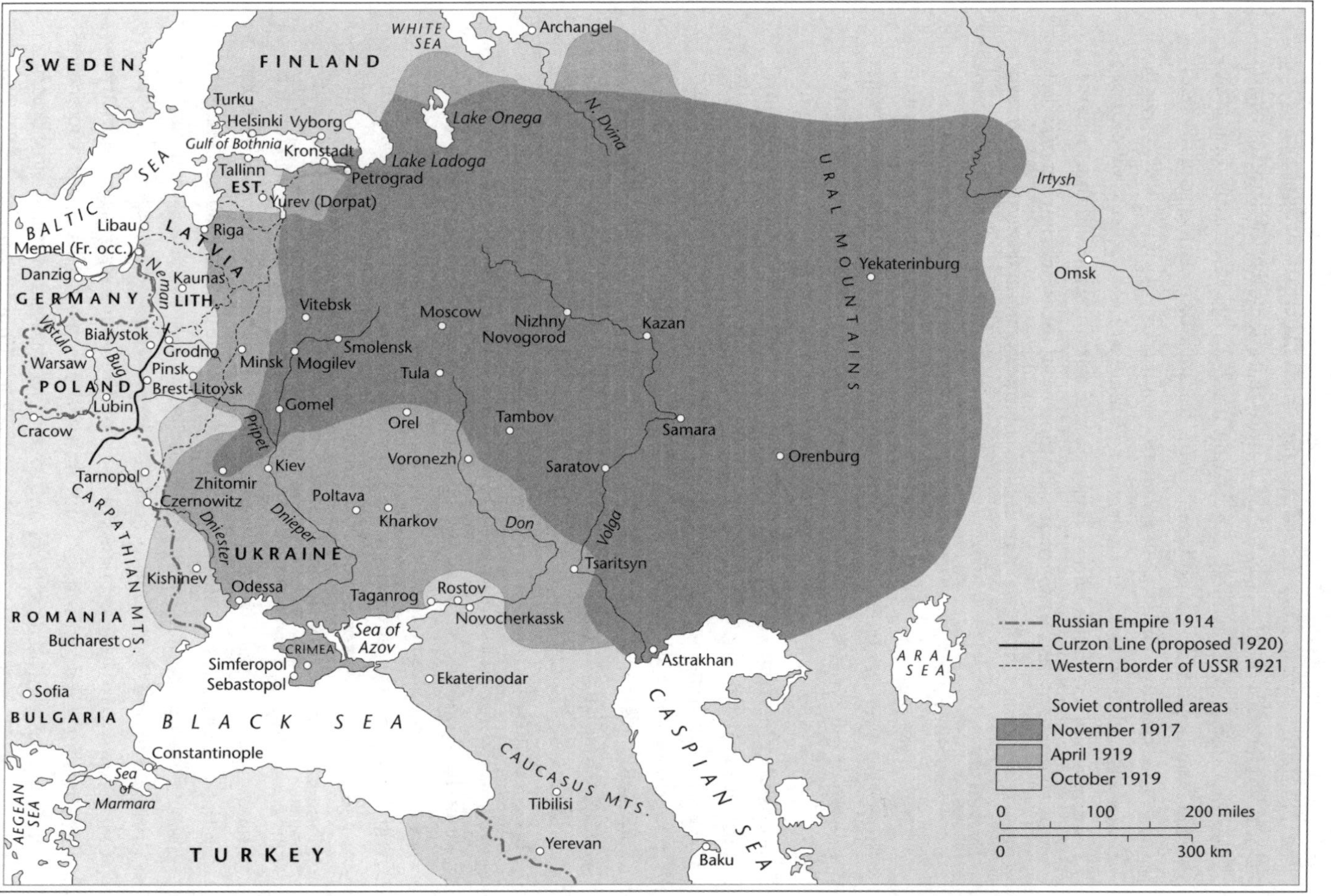

Map 2. Russian Civil War

March British troops landed at Murmansk with the apparent approval of the local Soviet. But in Moscow Lenin's more realistic policy of acquiescing to German demands prevailed. After submitting to the Germans' draconian terms, the Bolsheviks toyed briefly with the idea of securing support from the United States, Britain, and France, against Germany. Those powers, however, had no interest in buttressing Bolshevism; nor were they eager to become involved in the efforts of the White armies gathering to overthrow it. But a desire to distract German attention from the western front gradually drew them into half-hearted and ill-planned entanglements in Russia. Eventually soldiers of a dozen or more nationalities were to become embroiled in the war of intervention.

In August 1918 a mixed force of fifteen thousand British, Canadian, American, French, Italian, and Serb troops landed at Archangel. A huge pile-up of imported war *matériel* had developed there awaiting transportation down the single-track, low-capacity railway line that was the only feasible overland goods route to the south. Protection of these supplies was a primary goal of the force. Beyond that, the interventionist powers were of no very clear mind as to the purpose of their enterprise and the troops never advanced more than two hundred miles south of Archangel. Under their protection an anti-Bolshevik government was formed, at first Socialist Revolutionary in complexion, later acknowledging the authority of Kolchak. With the defeat of Germany, Lloyd George soon lost what little enthusiasm he had had for this adventure, though Churchill, Secretary of State for War from January 1919, urged robust support for the Whites against 'the Bolshevik tyranny', which he pronounced 'of all the tyrannies in history . . . the worst, the most destructive, the most degrading'.[50] In September 1919 the British nevertheless withdrew from the northern theatre altogether.

Meanwhile, however, in November 1918, a mixed force of twelve thousand French, Polish, and Greek troops had landed at Odessa under the command of Franchet d'Espérey, fresh from his victory in Bulgaria. Enemies of the revolution hoped that he might stiffen the forces of Denikin on the southern front. But d'Espérey was unimpressed by Denikin's rabble-like army and his orders were in any case limited. French statesmen, like the British, dithered, reluctant to become deeply engaged in eastern Europe. On 5 April 1919 the French sailed from Odessa, taking with them five thousand of Denikin's men and thirty thousand civilians. In October Denikin was defeated at Orel and over the next six months was beaten back to the Crimea. Wrangel, who succeeded him in command of White forces in the south, achieved some initial successes but by November 1920 he was obliged to evacuate the remnants of his army to Constantinople.

Meanwhile, in Siberia Kolchak was bolstered for a while by the Czech Legion, strung out along the Trans-Siberian railway, and by American and Japanese troops who landed at Vladivostok. But his regime never gained more than tenuous control over the vastness of Asiatic Russia. In November 1919 he retreated from his headquarters at Omsk. The withdrawal was chaotic and slowed down by thirty-six freight cars holding the imperial gold reserve. In January 1920 he was captured by the Czechs. They handed him over to the Bolsheviks who shot him and threw his body into a river. In the course of 1920 the Czechs and Americans left Vladivostok and the last Japanese withdrew in October 1922. Long before then all the intervening powers had decided to cut their losses and abandon any attempt to depose Lenin's regime.

As the White governments on Russian soil evaporated, waves of refugees boarded ships at Odessa and Vladivostok. Altogether more than a million (by some estimates double that number) fled, settling in western Europe, the Americas, and China. Substantial Russian communities concentrated in Paris, Berlin, and Brussels. They founded Russian-language schools, churches, and newspapers, and, in the common way of exiles, plotted their return and argued acrimoniously among themselves about the causes of their misfortunes.

In addition to the Whites and the Allied powers, two other forces of opposition to the Bolshevik regime posed determined and serious military challenges. The first was Ukraine, the second Poland.

Ukrainian nationalists, like the Poles, had been divided during the war. Some saw their destiny as lying in the creation of an autonomous region within the Habsburg Empire, others sought full separation. After the February Revolution in Russia an opportunity seemed to arise for autonomy under Russian auspices. The first, short-lived Ukrainian government sprang into being in April 1917 when a 'Central Rada' (council) was formed at Kiev, initially loyal to the Provisional Government in Petrograd. In elections in November 1917 the Bolsheviks won only 10 per cent of the seats in the Rada, whereupon they set up a rival Ukrainian Soviet regime at Kharkov. On 24 January 1918 the Rada declared Ukraine an independent state. Two weeks later the Germans and Austrians signed a peace treaty with representatives of the Rada whereby Ukrainian independence was recognized against Ukrainian promises of large supplies of food and raw materials. But peasants refused to hand over their grain and the Germans found themselves drawn into an expensive occupation of the whole territory up to the Don. Tiring of the Rada, they decided to eliminate it and replace it with a pro-German puppet government headed by General Pavel Skoropadsky, a former Tsarist officer who was proclaimed *Hetman* (chieftain) of Ukraine. Deprived in November 1918 of its German buttress, Skoropadsky's regime fell and was in its turn replaced by a 'Directory' headed, from February 1919, by Simon Petliura. Over the next few years he battled the Bolsheviks, the Poles, Denikin's Whites, and Makhno's anarchist bands in the hope of vindicating the Ukrainian claim to nationhood. Kiev changed hands sixteen times in the course of the war.

The Russo-Polish War of 1919–21 coincided in time and overlapped in space with the later stages of the Russian Civil War, the Ukrainian independence conflict, and the Allied intervention against Bolshevism. But it should really be considered separately, since Piłsudski's government had its own distinctive war aims. Responsibility for the outbreak of hostilities must be shared between the antagonists. The Poles aimed to take advantage of the elimination of Russia's power on its western marches in order to secure a large swath of territory in Belorussia and Ukraine. The Bolsheviks, hardly less than the Tsars, considered these areas to be part of the historic Russian patrimony. In the first phase of the war, between February 1919 and May 1920, the Poles advanced virtually unchallenged and captured Wilno (Vilna/Vilnius), Piłsudski's birthplace, and moved deep into Belorussia and Ukraine. In the second phase, between June and August 1920, tables were turned: soldiers of the Red Army, led by the youthful Mikhail Tukhachevsky, launched a successful counter-offensive that carried them to the gates of Warsaw.

In an effort to resolve the conflict, the British Foreign Office delineated the Curzon line (named after the British Foreign Secretary of the time), a proposed frontier between Russia and Poland that followed approximately the ethnographic border between Poles and their eastern neighbours, Ukrainians and Belorussians. The British threatened to intervene if the line was not accepted. But this was a bluff. The proposal was rejected by Poles and Russians alike, although the line retained a strange diplomatic half-life and was partly translated into reality a generation later.

In the third and final phase of the war, after August 1920, Polish forces under General Władisław Sikorski succeeded in enveloping and destroying the bulk of Tukhachevsky's army. This 'miracle of the Vistula' (allegedly achieved with assistance from the Black Madonna of Częstochowa) decided the outcome. Over the next few weeks Bolshevik forces were driven back hundreds of miles. Facing disaster, the Bolsheviks offered peace at almost any price. They signed an armistice in October and a peace treaty at Riga in March 1921. The treaty awarded the Poles a band of territory in western Belorussia and Ukraine, from Latvia in the north to Romania in the south. This frontier between Poland and Russia remained intact until 1939.

In the final stages of the Russo-Polish war, the Ukrainian leader Petliura allied himself with the Poles. The Poles' price for supporting him was Ukrainian recognition of their rule in Galicia, the eastern part of which had long been a stronghold of Ukrainian nationalism. The Treaty of Riga required Russia to recognize the independence of Ukraine. But that provision was ignored. The reassertion of Russian central authority spelt the doom of Ukraine's fragile independence. The country was partitioned: western areas, including Galicia, where a 'West Ukrainian People's Republic' had maintained a precarious existence in 1918–19, followed by a 'Galician Socialist Soviet Republic' from July to September 1920, were allocated to Poland; the rest went to the Bolsheviks. Squeezed between the Russians and the Poles, Petliura fled to Poland and later to France, where he was assassinated in 1925.

In the Civil War the Bolsheviks had virtually the whole world and a large part of the former Russian Empire ranged against them. Yet they won. The primary reason was the disunity of their enemies, who shared neither common aims nor a common strategy. Unlike their enemies, the Bolsheviks enjoyed the advantage of holding the centre and consequently of relatively secure internal lines of communication. They controlled the bulk of the population and of war industry. The Russian railway system, decrepit though it was, and capable of carrying only a fraction of its pre-war traffic, proved a godsend to the Red Army. Armoured trains were used by both sides in this '*eshelonaya* war' ('railway war'), though horses still drew much military traffic. Victory in the Civil War was Trotsky's greatest hour. His followers later inflated his role and his enemies devalued it. Yet his achievement was real. As Commissar for War, he created the Red Army out of the debris of the old imperial army. Bolsheviks permeated the army: a party cell was formed in each unit. At the same time, Trotsky had no compunction about drawing on the professional expertise of members of the old officer class. A total of 48,000 of these *voyenspets* ('military specialists') served the Bolsheviks in the Civil War, some voluntarily, others under compulsion. To ensure their good behaviour, they were flanked by an 'iron corset' of political commissars and their families were often held as hostages. 'Let the turncoats realize', wrote Trotsky, 'that they are at the same time betraying their fathers, mothers sisters, brothers, wives, and children.'[51]

The Russian Civil War was the bloodiest in any European country in the twentieth century. A total of 800,000 combatants are estimated to have died (more from disease than in combat). Tens of thousands more were killed in White terror and Red terror. Terrible atrocities were committed on all sides. In the Far East the demented White general Baron R. F. Ungern-Sternberg was guilty of horrific barbarities. The Red Army combined old-fashioned military professionalism with the ruthlessness of revolutionary warfare. It probably behaved no worse than most of its opponents. Where its leaders distinguished themselves was in making a virtue out of their inhumanity. Trotsky justified the use of terror tactics in rhetoric that married the fervour of Robespierre and Saint Just in 1793 to the class analysis of Marx in 1871:

> The State terror of a revolutionary class can be condemned 'morally' only by a man who, as a principle, condemns every form of violence whatsoever.
>
> 'But in that case, in what do your tactics differ from the tactics of Tsarism?' we are asked.
>
> You do not understand this, holy men? We shall explain to you. The terror of Tsarism was directed against the proletariat. The gendarmerie of Tsarism throttled the workers who were fighting for the Socialist order. Our Extraordinary Commissions shoot landlords, capitalists, and generals who are striving to restore the capitalist order. Do you grasp this distinction? Yes? For us Communists it is quite sufficient.[52]

This primitive philosophy helped the Bolsheviks cling to power against overwhelming odds. Ultimately it destroyed both its author and millions of his comrades, along with the utopian social vision that animated their revolutionary zeal.

The expansion of the Russian Civil War into something close to a European one led in almost every country to schism within Socialist movements between pro- and anti-Bolshevik elements. The separation had its roots in the divisions within the Second International over the issue of support for the war. In 1919 the foundation of the Third International (Comintern) confronted every Socialist party with the question whether to affiliate with the new organization. The second congress of Comintern in August 1920 issued twenty-one conditions for membership. These included adherence to the principle of 'democratic centralism', refusal to recognize 'bourgeois laws', 'a complete and absolute rupture with reformism', the institution of periodic purges of party membership 'in order systematically to free the party from the petty bourgeois elements which penetrate into it', the obligation 'to render every possible assistance to the Soviet Republics in their struggle against all counter-revolutionary forces', and the waging of 'a decisive war against the entire bourgeois world, and all yellow Social Democratic parties'.[53] Every member party of the Comintern thus surrendered policy-making authority to the Moscow centre. As an instrument of Soviet foreign policy, however, the Comintern turned out to be more concerned with battling its Socialist competitors than its capitalist enemies. Surveying the failures to realize revolutionary hopes in central Europe, Lenin postponed world revolution and focused on stabilization at home. By 1921 an implicit armistice in the European class war took effect: the Allies called off intervention in Russia; Communists elsewhere halted insurrectionary efforts and began to play the parliamentary and trade union game.

Peace treaties

The Peace Conference, the greatest assembly of nations since the Congress of Vienna in 1815, opened in Paris in January 1919 and lasted for a whole year. Three powerful currents dominated its proceedings: first, the determination of the European victors, above all France, to create a new continental structure that would permanently disable Germany militarily and, as a corollary, to exact territorial and financial compensation for the sacrifices of war; secondly, the anxiety, particularly of the British, to staunch the flow of revolutionary poison from Russia to the rest of the world; and thirdly, the desire of the United States, more specifically of Wilson, to erect a supra-national authority that would prevent future wars. Reflecting these underlying objectives, the conference was dominated by Clemenceau, Lloyd George, and Wilson. The heads of government and foreign ministries of the powers moved *en bloc* to Paris for several months so that the city took on the aspect of capital of a new world in the making. Altogether thirty-two countries were admitted to membership of the conference but major decisions were reached by the five 'Principal Allied and Associated Powers', the British Empire, France, Italy, Japan, and the United States, who arrogated to themselves the exclusive right to participate in all the sessions. Others attended only as and when summoned.

In concluding the armistice in November 1918 the German government had conceived of the forthcoming peace conference as a negotiation among equals. But, like the Russians at Brest-Litovsk a year earlier, they were speedily disabused of such notions. As a guarantee against any German attempt to renew hostilities, the blockade was maintained throughout the period of the conference. Deprived again of their eastern granaries, the Germans faced mass starvation and were in no condition to resist Allied demands. The defeated powers were further humiliated by being refused admission to formal sessions of the conference, with the bizarre result that countries such as Liberia, Panama, and Siam were seated, while Germany, Austria, Hungary, Bulgaria, and Turkey were excluded. Delegations of the smaller powers as well as suitors, supplicants, and petitioners of almost every political cause populated the corridors of the conference. Among them were ghost-like figures claiming to represent the deceased Russian imperial government and the dying Ottoman one.

The French entered the Peace Conference puffed up with the delirium of victory and keen to avenge the agony of war. Clemenceau, dubbed *père-la-victoire*, initially adopted a proposal by Foch that France should sponsor a Rhineland republic to act as a buffer between France and Germany. This, however, was opposed by the British and the Americans on the ground that it conflicted with the principle of self-determination. Reluctantly, Clemenceau settled for a compromise whereby the Rhineland would be temporarily occupied by the Allies and permanently demilitarized. Foch angrily opposed this arrangement and French military commanders in the Rhineland secretly colluded with local separatists who were plotting the creation of a Rhenish mini-state with its capital at Wiesbaden. Clemenceau, however, disavowed the conspiracy while resisting attempts to water down the more stringent anti-German provisions of the peace treaty.

This was an imposed peace. Of its 440 articles, the most humiliating for Germany was number 231, the so-called 'war guilt clause', which stated: 'The Allied and Associated Governments affirm and Germany accepts the responsibility of Germany and her allies for causing all the loss and damage to which the Allied and Associated Governments and their nationals have been subjected as a consequence of the war imposed upon them by the aggression of Germany and her allies.' On the basis of this judgement, the Allies imposed on Germany far-reaching territorial cessions, military limitations, and financial impositions.

The territorial losses significantly reduced Germany's land area and included some of her most valuable industrial regions. 'Recognizing the moral obligation to redress the wrong done by Germany in 1871 both to the rights of France and to the wishes of the population of Alsace and Lorraine',

Germany was obliged to return those two provinces to France. The Saar was placed under international trusteeship with provision for a plebiscite after fifteen years. The small districts of Moresnet, Eupen, and Malmédy were ceded to Belgium after a plebiscite in 1920. A plebiscite was to be held in Schleswig on the basis of which a new frontier would be drawn with Denmark (eventually northern Schleswig was awarded to Denmark). In Upper Silesia, after the Ruhr Germany's most important industrial zone, a plebiscite in 1921 produced a 60 per cent vote in favour of Germany. After local fighting and diplomatic argument, the region was partitioned: Germany retained 70 per cent of the territory and 57 per cent of the inhabitants but lost most of the industry, including the city of Kattowitz (Katowice). Another plebiscite, in Allenstein (Masuria), the south-eastern part of East Prussia, produced a 98 per cent vote in favour of Germany; accordingly the area remained in Germany (Allenstein's Masurian Slavs were Lutheran and pro-German). A belt of territory running north–south through the provinces of Posen and Pomerania to the sea was also ceded in order to give Poland access to the sea. This was the area that came to be known as the 'Polish corridor'. Danzig was made a free city under the League of Nations. German sovereignty over Memel was to end and its fate to be decided by the Allies. In the meantime Memel was occupied by French troops and governed by a French High Commissioner. Germany was forced to yield all her colonies in Africa and the Far East. She was also obliged to abrogate the Treaty of Brest-Litovsk (which had in any case been renounced by the Bolsheviks) as well as all other agreements 'with the Maximalist Government of Russia'.

Under the military provisions of the treaty, the German army was restricted to one hundred thousand men, all volunteer professionals, to be 'devoted exclusively to the maintenance of order within the territory and to the control of the frontiers'. The army was to have no tanks, armoured cars, or gas weapons, and hardly any heavy guns. Even the number of rifles was strictly limited. The armaments industry was placed under Allied supervision. Compulsory military service was to be abolished. The remains of Tirpitz's fleet had been scuttled by their crews in June 1919 in order to prevent the ships falling intact into Allied hands. The future German navy was to have no more than fifteen thousand men, six battleships, thirty smaller warships, and no submarines. Germany was allowed no air force at all.

The treaty formally recognized the claim of the German representatives 'that the resources of Germany are not adequate, after taking into account permanent diminutions of such resources which will result from other provisions of the present Treaty, to make complete reparation for all such loss and damage'. The Allies nevertheless required 'compensation for all damage done to the civilian population of the Allied and Associated Powers and to their property'. In order to determine the amount of reparations payable by Germany a Reparation Commission was to be established.

As a guarantee for Germany's observance of the treaty, the Rhineland was to be occupied by Allied troops; the northernmost section (2,500 square miles) would be evacuated after five years, the central zone (approximately the same size) after ten, and the remainder (6,690 square miles) after fifteen. Thereafter the entire area, to a line fifty miles east of the Rhine, was to be permanently demilitarized.

The German government at first refused to accept the treaty. Scheidemann declared that the hand that signed it should wither. His government resigned and was replaced by a new coalition of Social Democrats and the Centre Party. The new government attempted to secure the elimination of what were regarded as the most obnoxious clauses but all attempts at negotiation were rebuffed by the Allies. Erzberger of the Centre Party called the treaty 'the work of the devil'[54] but he nevertheless took the lead in persuading his reluctant party and the Parliament to accept the inevitable. Some German officers attempted to organize resistance. But in reply to an enquiry from Ebert, Groener admitted that any thought of fighting a threatened Allied advance on Berlin was hopeless. Two German representatives signed the treaty under protest at Versailles on 28 June.[55] With deliberate symbolism the French staged the ceremony in the Hall of Mirrors, where the German Empire had been declared forty-eight years earlier. It was the first major treaty-signing ceremony to be recorded by newsreel cameras, thus helping to imprint its significance on the consciousness of the generation. Max Weber, an adviser to the German delegation, had earlier warned his countrymen that 'a polar night of icy darkness and austerity' was about to descend on them, and he predicted that 'in ten years . . . the reaction [will] long since [have] set in'.[56] The French were more sanguine: '*C'est une belle journée*', said Clemenceau.[57]

No less than the Germans, their former allies were treated with disdain by the victors. Harold Nicolson, a member of the British delegation at the Peace Conference, recorded his scorn for these lesser peoples. The Hungarians: 'I confess that I regarded, and still regard, that Turanian tribe with acute distaste.' For the Bulgarians Nicolson 'cherished feelings of contempt'. And as for the Turks, 'I had, and have no sympathy whatsoever'.[58] Such prejudices were not uncommon in the corridors of the conference.

The Treaty of St Germain with Austria, signed on 10 September 1919, reduced the former empire to a small German-speaking rump. Most former Austrian territory went to the 'successor states'. Austria was required to recognize the incorporation of Bohemia and Moravia in Czechoslovakia, of south-east Carinthia and South Styria into Yugoslavia, and of Galicia into Poland. Bukovina was ceded to Romania and the Trentino to Italy. Several of these cessions aroused controversy and even resistance by German-speaking populations in the areas affected. In Carinthia, which had a mixed German-speaking and Slovene population, Italian, Austrian, Yugoslav, and Carinthian separatist tendencies had vied for power since the armistice. Fighting between Carinthian and Yugoslav forces led to a Yugoslav occupation of Klagenfurt in June 1919. A plebiscite ordered by the Entente Powers was held in part of the disputed region in October 1920: 59 per cent of those voting rejected incorporation in Yugoslavia—a remarkable rejection of Slav nationalism given that a majority of the population in the plebiscite area was Slovene-speaking. As a result most of Carinthia remained in Austria. On Austria's eastern frontier, the Burgenland region, formerly part of Hungary, was transferred to Austria, mainly because of the Allies' concern about Béla Kun. The regional capital, Sopron (Ödenburg), was restored to Hungary in 1921 after a plebiscite in which the Hungarians won nearly 73 per cent of the vote in Sopron itself while the Austrians gained a smaller majority in the surrounding countryside. The Social Democrat government of Austria protested bitterly against the imposition of Czechoslovak rule on the more than three million Germans of 'German Bohemia and the Sudetenland'. (The term 'Sudetenland' derived from the name of a mountain range in northern Bohemia; in the inter-war period it was used loosely to refer to all the German-inhabited border areas of western Bohemia.) Even Edvard Beneš, the first Foreign Minister, had some misgivings about whether the Germans there would be digestible in the new state; but the powers were in no mood to add any territory to Germany and Czechoslovakia's need for a secure, natural frontier was regarded as paramount.

Like Germany, Austria was presented with a demand for reparations: a 'reasonable sum' was to be paid immediately and more later, the precise figures to be fixed by a commission. She too was subjected to strict limitations on her armed forces: the Austrian army could have a maximum of thirty thousand men. The treaty also laid down that Austria would not be permitted to unite with Germany. All-German unity had been a dream as much of liberals and Socialists as of right-wing nationalists since 1848. In Austria its only significant opponents were a minority in the Christian Social Party, Catholics who feared Protestant predominance in a united Germany. Otto Bauer, the Social Democrat Austrian Foreign Minister, argued strenuously for *Anschluss*, which he regarded as the best safeguard against a Habsburg restoration. In February 1919 the German Constituent Assembly at Weimar had adopted a unanimous resolution in favour of union with Austria. But with the Allied veto embedded in the treaty, the aspiration went into cold storage.

The Treaty of Neuilly with Bulgaria, signed in November 1919, followed the common pattern of territorial cessions, reparations (£90 million to be paid over thirty-seven years), and military limitations. The treaty confirmed Romania in possession of the southern Dobrudja, an area of very mixed population which she had gained from Bulgaria in the Second Balkan War in 1913. Greece and Yugoslavia similarly retained territory in Macedonia that they had won in 1913. Bulgaria gave up western Thrace, which was transferred by the Allies to Greece. Article 48, never implemented, gave Bulgaria the right to economic access to the Aegean.

The Treaty of Trianon with Hungary, signed on 4 June 1920, took away more than two-thirds of pre-war Hungary's territory and left one-third of the Hungarian people under alien rule. Transylvania and most of the Banat were added to Romania. The 1.3 million Hungarians in Transylvania, 29 per cent of the population of the historic province, were thereby placed under Romanian rule, a source of lasting bitterness for Hungary and one that she was eventually to avenge. The Hungarians and Germans of the annexed areas abhorred rule by the Romanians, whom they regarded as racial inferiors. Croatia, Slavonia and the remainder of the Banat were handed over to Yugoslavia. Slovakia, including Pressburg (Bratislava), and Sub-Carpathian Ruthenia and Spiš were ceded to Czechoslovakia. The Hungarian army was henceforth to be limited to a professional force of thirty-five thousand. Hungary too was to pay reparations and also to give up all her merchant shipping. The treaty left Hungary embittered and fuming with irredentist ambitions.

One question left unresolved by the Austrian and Hungarian peace treaties was that of Italy's eastern border. Italy lodged far-reaching claims to Trieste, the Istrian peninsula, Fiume, the islands of the Adriatic and part of the Dalmatian coastline. During the conference, the venal French press was heavily bribed by the Italians to support these demands. But a decision on the Italian–Yugoslav frontier was left for subsequent negotiation between the two states. The ink was hardly dry on the Austrian peace treaty, however, when the Italian poet-adventurer Gabriele D'Annunzio led a band of desperadoes, Garibaldi-style, in a seizure of Fiume, formerly Hungary's only port. This act of political theatre and brigandage humiliated the Italian government and shocked opinion elsewhere. In November 1920, Italy and Yugoslavia agreed that Trieste and the Istrian peninsula would become Italian, while most of the Dalmatian coastline would become Yugoslav. Fiume would become a free state, separate from both countries. D'Annunzio was ejected from the city by Italian forces on 29 December but his exploit and the feeble response of the powers had set an ugly precedent.

The harshest of the peace treaties was the Treaty of Sèvres with Turkey. The country was to be virtually eliminated as an independent state, restricted to a tiny area around the shores of the Sea of Marmara. Greece was to receive most of what remained of Turkey-in-Europe. The bulk of Anatolia was to be partitioned among France, Italy, Greece, and a nascent Armenian state. Britain assumed mandates over Iraq, Palestine, and Trans-jordan, France over Syria and Lebanon. This treaty, in effect a sentence of death, was signed in August 1920 by the wraith that was all that survived of the imperial Ottoman government. The Sèvres Treaty, however, was never ratified. It was soon superseded by new political realities that extinguished not merely the Ottoman dynasty but a Greek presence in Asia Minor that had lasted nearly three millennia.

The unwitting agent of this historic retreat was the Greek Prime Minister, Venizelos, who laid claim to Smyrna, the largely Greek-populated city on Turkey's Aegean coast. In order to press the demand, which was contested by Italy, Greek forces landed at Smyrna on 15 May 1919 with British, French, and American naval support. They advanced into Anatolia, committing atrocities against civilians on the way, with the aim of conquering the hinterland and realizing the 'great idea' of the re-establishment of the Greek Empire with its capital at Constantinople.

In Mustafa Kemal (later known as Atatürk) the Turkish army and people found a leader able to lead them to victory over the invaders and to national regeneration. He formed a nationalist government at Ankara which displaced the totally discredited Ottoman regime, defied the invaders, and repudiated the Treaty of Sèvres. Nascent Armenian and Kurdish regimes, as well as rival Turkish forces, were crushed by the Kemalists. In early 1921 successive Greek offensives at İnönü were held back by Kemalists under İsmet Pasha (thereafter known as İsmet İnönü). In August Mustafa Kemal won a brilliant victory over a superior Greek force at the Sakarya River. Meanwhile Soviet Russia, France, and Italy signed agreements with the Turks and withdrew their forces from Anatolia. By September 1922 the Turks had driven the Greek army out of Anatolia and recaptured Smyrna, henceforth to be known by its Turkish name, İzmir. Much of the ancient city was sacked and burned to the ground (the source of the conflagration was variously ascribed); the Greek population was driven out amidst scenes of great brutality. In the autumn of 1922 Britain, France, and Italy momentarily considered using their occupation forces in Constantinople to resist the Turkish advance towards the Straits. But there was little public appetite at home for such an enterprise. The French and Italians withdrew precipitately and the British signed an armistice with the Turks on 11 October. A further peace conference at Lausanne resulted in a wholesale revision of the Sèvres diktat. The Treaty of Lausanne, signed in July 1923, restored the whole of Anatolia and eastern Thrace to Turkey. Allied occupation forces evacuated Constantinople, which reverted to Turkey. Italy retained the Dodecanese. King Constantine abdicated and Greek politics dissolved into a chaotic and bloody settling of internal accounts.

Greece and Turkey negotiated a large-scale forced migration, euphemistically termed an 'exchange of populations', whereby most Christians were removed from Turkey to Greece and most Muslims from Greece to Turkey. Fifty thousand Greeks had already fled Istanbul. The remainder were spared for the time being, as were those of the Turkish islands of Imbros and Tenedos and the Pomaks (Slavic Muslims) and Turkish Muslims in western Thrace. Altogether around 1.3 million Christians and 400,000 Muslims fled between 1912 and 1923 or were driven out of their homes by 1925 under the supervision of a commission appointed by the League of Nations and headed by the Norwegian explorer and humanitarian Fridtjof Nansen. Large numbers of Greek refugees were resettled in Macedonia and western Thrace; hundreds of thousands of others congregated like a 'swarm of wasps' in shanty-towns on the outskirts of Athens and became a troubling element in the Greek economy and in Greek politics for the next generation. Similar exchanges took place with Bulgaria, which additionally was compelled to absorb at least two hundred thousand refugees from Romania, Yugoslavia, and Turkey. About 125,000 Turks left Bulgaria between 1928 and 1939—in the period after 1934 mainly as a result of pressure or expulsion. The disruption of patterns of settlement stretching back to ancient times set an internationally endorsed precedent that was soon to be copied elsewhere in Europe.

The diplomacy of the peacemakers, clothed in the garb of national self-determination and peaceful resolution of disputes, was sullied at several points by the crude imposition of national interests and by acquiescence in the use of force. The illusion was nevertheless created of a new order in which righteousness would reign supreme. The cornerstone of the new international system was to be the League of Nations. Conceived by British liberal and Socialist thinkers, notably Viscount Bryce, H. N. Brailsford, J. A. Hobson, and G. Lowes Dickinson, the idea had been taken up by statesmen such as Lord Robert Cecil, Jan Smuts, and, most influentially, President Wilson. The basic concept was the creation of an organized legal framework for international relations that would include mechanisms for resolving problems and provision for enforcement action in the case of egregious breaches of the agreed rules. The Covenant of the League, its foundation document and a sort of world constitution, was incorporated in the Treaty of Versailles. Article X of the Covenant defined the League's primary task: 'to respect and preserve as against external aggression the territorial integrity and existing political independence of all Members of the League.' From the outset the League was hamstrung by institutional weaknesses and international realities. It had no standing armed force of its own and although the Covenant provided for the imposition of economic and, if necessary, military sanctions against an aggressor, these clauses proved weak reeds. While it seemed to claim universal authority, the League never attained anything approaching universal membership. The defeated powers were initially excluded and American membership was blocked by the United States Senate. The Soviet Union did not join until 1934. In spite of its lofty ambitions, the imposing headquarters that were eventually built at Geneva, and its dedicated corps of international civil servants, the League never quite shook off the appearance of an Anglo-French club.

The treaties were condemned by the defeated powers and by some others as a Carthaginian peace. Critics pointed out that the peacemakers paid lip-service to the principle of national self-determination while in reality stripping the Central Powers of much of their territory and their economic viability. The treaties owed more to Clemenceau's realism than Wilson's idealism. Nevertheless, compared with what she had imposed on Russia at Brest-Litovsk, Germany had little ground for complaint at Versailles. She remained potentially a great power.

The most trenchant and influential critic of the treaties was John Maynard Keynes, who served on the British delegation in Paris as an economic expert but resigned in 'misery and rage'[59]. In *The Economic Consequences of the Peace* (1919), he denounced the Versailles Treaty on both moral and practical grounds, arguing that the economic demands on Germany represented 'an act of spoliation and insincerity'. After a pessimistic analysis of Germany's capacity to pay, he concluded that the vast reparations bill presented by France and Belgium 'skins [Germany] alive year by year in perpetuity'. He also drew attention to the dangers inherent in the American reluctance to forgive or reduce the large debts of her allies, amounting in total to over $7 billion. Failing a renegotiation of these debts, he predicted that 'the war will have ended with the intolerable result of the Allies paying indemnities to one another instead of receiving them from the enemy'. He warned: 'If we aim deliberately at the impoverishment of Central Europe, vengeance, I dare predict, will not limp.'[60] His mother thought he was committing himself 'too much to a prophecy of a Jeremiah type'.[61] But as his biographer writes, Keynes felt 'a brooding sense of menace; a sense of a civilization *in extremis*; of the mindless mob waiting its turn to usurp the collapsing inheritance'.[62]

4

Recovery of the Bourgeoisie 1921–1929

We are the hollow men
We are the stuffed men
Leaning together
Headpiece filled with straw. Alas!
Our dried voices, when
We whisper together
Are quiet and meaningless
As wind in dry grass
Or rats' feet over broken glass
In our dry cellar.

*T. S. Eliot, England, 1925**

Transition pains

The European transition from war and revolution to more stable conditions was a painful and imperfect process everywhere. Victors and vanquished alike were left with enduring scars that proved difficult or impossible to repair. The notion that the defeated powers could pay for the damages resulting from the war was a delusive mirage. The costs were registered not only in human lives, but in devastated economic infrastructures, shattered social bonds, toppled political edifices, and traumatized collective psychologies.

The number of war dead in most of the belligerent countries was so great as to effect a significant shift in the balance of populations. A total of 9.5 million military lives were lost. Germany and Russia suffered the largest absolute

* From 'The Hollow Men'. T. S. Eliot, *Selected Poems*, London, 1954, 77.

numbers of losses. Between 1.6 and 1.8 million German soldiers were killed. Russia counted at least 1.7 million military dead by November 1917 plus hundreds of thousands more in the ensuing Civil War. France, with her smaller population, felt the loss of 1.4 million as an even more acute demographic shock. At least 1.2 million men died in Austro-Hungarian military uniform, many of them neither Austrians nor Hungarians. British military losses, not including those of the empire, were officially given as 548,749 but recent research suggests that 723,000 may be closer to an accurate figure. Italy's appallingly wasteful campaigns on the Isonzo raised her death toll to 560,000. The Turkish armed forces lost 437,000. The Balkan states also lost hundreds of thousands of military and civilian dead. In many cases exact numbers remain unknown: estimates varied widely and were inflated or minimized for nationalist purposes. Hundreds of thousands died, particularly in eastern Europe, due to war-related hunger and disease. A worldwide influenza pandemic in 1918–19 claimed millions more.

The dead—or at least those of them that could be found—were buried: in Flanders, Belgium, and north-east France the war cemeteries, with their geometric lines of identical white slabs, sometimes stretching to the far horizon, left a permanent mark of Cain on the landscape.

Even more visible, for the next generation, were the much larger numbers of war wounded. Altogether eight million men were permanently disabled. Italy was left with over nine hundred thousand injured. In Germany half a million men had endured amputations. Others bore psychological scars that were either not recognized or not fully understood. Much lip-service was paid to the predicament of the wounded but sympathy had its limits. The rasping voices and racking coughs of those permanently affected by gas burns were offensive to the ear. Many people found it unpleasant to contemplate men hobbling around without limbs or with terrible facial disfigurements. In France the *invalides de guerre* were allocated special seats on public transportation and 1.2 million were given small pensions and free medical care for life. In Germany and Austria from 1919 public and private employers were obliged to hire war disabled as 2 per cent of their work forces. One-fifth of the entire national budget of Germany in the 1920s was allocated to war pensions (compared with 7–8 per cent in Britain). But for the most part the disabled were thrown on the scrap heap by ungrateful societies. Most of the injured had difficulty reintegrating into the workforce and, even more than veterans in general, they became an alienated and embittered segment of inter-war society.

The economic effects of the war were far-reaching and in some respects irreparable. Trade patterns had been disrupted, currencies destabilized, capital stock destroyed. Railways, in particular, were in a state of decrepitude bordering on collapse. Reconstruction required huge amounts of investment that war-weary and tax-resistant populations were reluctant to pay. In terms of sheer physical destruction of buildings and fixed industrial capital, Belgium and north-east France had suffered the most devastating damage. Nevertheless, harbours, bridges, canals, and railways were quickly reconstructed, mines and factories reopened, and the region soon resumed its pre-war industrial primacy. Some parts of eastern Europe suffered no less heavily. In Latvia, when the successive invaders had departed, a quarter of all farms had been devastated (11 per cent of buildings entirely destroyed, and 14 per cent partly destroyed). In Poland it was estimated that 1,651,892 buildings had been destroyed. Less tangible economic wounds healed more slowly or not at all. The disintegration of Austria-Hungary and the alacrity with which the successor states erected tariff barriers against their former oppressors and against each other stunted the growth of the entire east-central European economy for the whole of the inter-war period.

The most significant long-term change in relative economic standing, however, was that of Britain. Her position in the world economy, although not destroyed, was severely dented. British overseas investments were probably reduced by about 15 per cent as a result of the demands of war financing and loss of assets in Russia and enemy countries. Japan overtook Lancashire as the world's largest producer and exporter of cotton piece-goods. Britain's war debts, mainly to the United States, were immense. As the trade deficit widened, the status of the pound as a reserve currency weakened. New York replaced London as the world's foremost financial centre. The British imperial economy was no longer the slowly cooling sun around which the rest of the world revolved. The American and Japanese economies grew rapidly in the 1920s but neither could replace Britain's pre-war role as a centre of economic gravity.

All European countries had experienced wartime inflation which, after a brief pause when the fighting stopped, resumed everywhere. In March 1919 Britain was forced by the withdrawal of American support to devalue the pound: by the end of the year the value of sterling fell from \$4.76 to \$3.81. This helped fuel an inflationary boom. In 1920 the cost-of-living index in Britain was 2.8, in France 4.2, and in Germany 11.6 times the pre-war level. By the end of 1920, inflation had been arrested in Britain, France, and

Scandinavia. But this was at a great cost. In Britain the 'Geddes Axe' (after Sir Eric Geddes who headed a government committee that called for drastic reductions in spending) lowered government expenditure by 20 per cent. The policy succeeded in reversing inflation: the cost of living index fell from 152 to 107 between 1920 and 1924. The boom turned quickly to deep recession. Hundreds of thousands of demobilized soldiers moved straight onto the unemployment rolls. Unemployment rose from 2 per cent in 1920 to 10 per cent of the workforce in 1924 and remained stubbornly above that level through most of the inter-war period.

In most of central and southern Europe the rise in prices continued, and in Austria, Germany, Hungary, Poland, and Russia, it accelerated into hyperinflation. This was a new and frightening phenomenon on a continent that had hardly experienced it for a century or more. In Germany the massive wartime debt, the prospect of onerous reparations transfers, and government efforts to resist payment destroyed all confidence in paper money. The mark, which had been linked to gold at 24 US cents up to 1914, was worth 12 cents in December 1919. It declined to 1 cent by February 1920. After a short respite, it resumed its fall in September 1921, reaching 349 to the dollar in June 1922 and 7,500 by November. The inflation nearly wiped out the life savings of much of the German middle class who had invested, as they thought conservatively, in financial instruments. Not only their expectations but their confidence as a class was shattered. Civil servants and pensioners were particularly hard hit. The experience deeply scarred German society, instilling a profound fear of inflation that haunted policy-makers over the next decade.

Underlying these worldwide economic dislocations were the massive burdens of war debt and reparations. Inter-Allied war debts, mainly to Britain and the United States, amounted to nearly $16 billion. The greatest creditor was the United States, which was owed over $9 billion. The largest debtor was France, which owed $3.7 billion, a little over half to the USA, the rest to Britain. Britain and France were owed $3.4 billion by Russia, which had defaulted altogether. Most of the Russian debt was to Britain; but the impact was felt most widely in France, where Russian bondholders, estimated to number 1.5 million, most of them small investors, reacted with impotent fury. (In 1986 the Soviet government finally agreed to pay $120 million in compensation to British holders of pre-1917 Russian bonds. In 1990 the USSR agreed in principle to compensate French bondholders too—but no money had changed hands by the time the Soviet

Union disintegrated in 1991.) All the debtor countries found immense difficulty in paying and sought to renegotiate their debts. American public hostility to any loan forgiveness or moratorium was encapsulated in President Coolidge's famous dictum: 'They hired the money, didn't they?' Between 1923 and 1926, the US War Debts Commission reached settlements with all the debtor countries (except Russia) that stretched out payment periods and reduced interest rates. But the burden of repayment remained heavy and Britain and France depended on reparations from Germany to meet the payments to the United States. When reparations stopped flowing, so did debt repayments. In the end only Finland, which had a relatively small debt, paid up in full—one source of the special affection for that country felt by Americans in mid-century.

Reparations after a war were nothing new in European history. Germany herself had exacted an 'indemnity' of $1 billion from France after the Franco-Prussian War in 1871 and had sought vast sums from Russia after the Treaty of Brest-Litovsk. The impositions on Germany after her defeat appeared astronomical, although, viewed in economic as distinct from political terms, they were within the capacity of the country to pay. The total bill was set by the Reparation Commission in 1921 at $33 billion, payable to France (52 per cent), Britain and the British Empire (22 per cent), Italy (9.3 per cent), Belgium (8 per cent), Yugoslavia (5.9 per cent), and others (3 per cent). Germany protested her inability to pay and tried unsuccessfully to bargain the Allies down. Poincaré, who became French Prime Minister in January 1922, was determined to force Germany to comply in full.

In January 1923, exasperated with German recalcitrance, France and Belgium sent troops to occupy Germany's prime industrial region, the Ruhr, as a '*gage par excellence*' to extract payment. The German government responded by calling for passive resistance by the population of the occupied region. Strikes by civil servants and workers on the railways and in mines and steelworks prevented the Allies from taking possession of 'productive guarantees'. Hoping to seize the opportunity to secure their eastern frontier once and for all, the French promoted a separatist movement in the Rhineland. Fighting broke out and several hundred people were killed. The German government made large credits available to the Ruhr industrialists. The resulting increases in expenditure brought about a sudden widening of the government deficit.

The consequence was an acceleration of hyperinflation and the total collapse of the mark. By June 1923 the mark had dropped to 100,000 to the dollar. In later years the myth spread that the over-zealous Allied exaction of reparations had been the cause of the hyperinflation; this was at most a half-truth. The immediate cause of the final paroxysm was the German government's financing of resistance to reparations. Shops refused to accept money, food shortages developed, many died of hunger, and riots broke out.

In August 1923 the centrist politician Gustav Stresemann (see plate 17) formed a new coalition government with Social Democrat support. Stresemann was a nationalist but he was also a realist. He called off passive resistance and began to look for a way out. By 21 November the mark stood at 4,210,500,000,000 to the dollar. Stresemann capitulated to Allied demands and succeeded in stabilizing the currency. At the end of the month it was replaced by a new currency, the Rentenmark, at a rate of one to 1,000 billion old marks. The new currency was not gold-backed; it was based on a fictional mortgage of Germany's entire productive land. Its immediate success was based less on that than on the government's restriction of the money supply and its efforts to eliminate the budget deficit. This, however, depended on a settlement of the reparation question.

A committee headed by an American general, Charles G. Dawes, recommended a new basis for reparation. Payment was rescheduled, starting at $250 million in the first year, rising after five years to $625 million per annum. The total amount to be paid was left open. The Dawes Plan was approved by an international conference in London in August 1924. The German government balanced its budget and replaced the Rentenmark with the Reichsmark, tied to gold at the pre-war value. A loan to support the reparation payments was raised, mainly in the United States, where it was oversubscribed eleven times. This recycling of capital flows solved the problem—for as long as Americans were willing to lend. The total amount paid by the Germans in reparations between 1918 and 1932 was a little under $6 billion. In terms of the disruption to the international economic system and to diplomatic relations, it was of very doubtful value to the recipients.

The settlement of the debt and reparations problems seemed, for a time, to restore international financial stability. The new confidence was marked, in April 1925, by Britain's return to the gold standard, a move that betokened an effort to reassert London's primacy as the world's financial centre. The Chancellor of the Exchequer, Winston Churchill, with some misgivings but relying on the advice of most experts, restored the pound to its pre-war parity of $4.86. The Governor of the Bank of England, Montagu Norman, strongly advocated the change; Keynes opposed it. The 'Norman conquest' appealed to patriotic instincts and was justified accordingly: *The Times* asserted sterling's 'need to face the dollar in the eye'.[1] Keynes attacked the decision in *The Economic Consequences of Mr Churchill*. The experience of the next six years vindicated Keynes's arguments. Sterling's over-valuation severely impaired Britain's capacity to sell abroad. In 1929 her export of manufactured goods was still 19 per cent below that of 1913 whereas most of her west European competitors except Germany and Switzerland had far surpassed their pre-war export performance. Within a few years, the 'return to par' proved to be unsustainable and a costly economic and political error.

The apparent restoration of international financial stability inaugurated a short period of expansion and relative prosperity. Industrial production in the advanced economies of Europe (Austria, Britain, Czechoslovakia, France, Germany, Scandinavia, and the Low Countries) rose by 23 per cent between 1925 and 1929. GNP grew in Sweden by 19 per cent, in France by 18 per cent, in Germany by 10 per cent, and in Britain by 7 per cent. Britain's relatively poor performance was symptomatic of her failure to diversify out of old, declining industries such as cotton manufacturing and shipbuilding, neither of which could now compete effectively on world markets. Nevertheless, changes in economic structure were taking place even in Britain. New science-based industries grew rapidly in western Europe: electrical engineering, chemicals, rayon, radio, automobile, and household appliance manufacture. In France, for example, annual production of private cars grew from 121,000 in 1925 to 212,000 in 1929, a level that was not attained again until 1950. Growth in productivity was achieved by the application of rationalized production-line methods and 'Taylorist' scientific management techniques adopted from America. A new managerial class began to displace old-fashioned, paternalist entrepreneurs.

The capitalist system, which had seemed on the edge of collapse in 1917–19, thus staged an impressive, if temporary, comeback. But the recovery was fragile, patchy, and flawed by the high level of structural unemployment that prevailed stubbornly in most European economies. The social and political costs would become apparent with the next downturn of the economic cycle.

Revolution contained

In Russia, as in capitalist Europe, stabilization was the order of the day after the spring of 1921. The basic institutional structure of the Soviet regime now crystallized. The Russian Socialist Federal Soviet Republic, founded in

1918, expanded its rule over most of the former Tsarist empire except for the belt of territory on its western marches. The new empire was given constitutional form on 30 December 1922 with the creation of the Union of Soviet Socialist Republics. Originally there were four republics: Russia, Ukraine, Belorussia, and the Transcaucasus. Later, Azerbaijan, Georgia, Armenia, and five central Asian regions were recognized as separate republics. All were supposedly equal and had a theoretical right to secede. In practice, Russia, larger both in area and population than all the others put together, dominated the rest. This was a single-party state in which the Communist Party (as the Bolsheviks called themselves after 1918) held a monopoly of power. Within the party a limited form of political debate was permitted in the early years, provided that, once decisions had been made, they were adhered to without further question. But the stern disciplinarian principles that had characterized the Bolsheviks since the schism in the Russian Social Democrat Party in 1903 soon moved to the fore. Internal critics were stifled and, in 1921, in the first of many 'purges' that characterized the new regime, a quarter of the party's 650,000 members were expelled. Party membership became the key to advancement in state positions. Over the next two decades a new elite, composed predominantly of non-proletarian, especially white-collar elements, gradually took the helm of the proletarian state. At the head of the party stood the Central Committee and its inner ruling group, the Political Bureau (Politburo), consisting, on its formation in 1919, of five members: Lenin, Trotsky, Stalin, Kamenev, and Nikolai Krestinsky.

At the end of the civil war, Russia's new rulers presided over a social and economic disaster area. 'War Communism' had reduced the country to chaos, anarchy, and misery. As money became worthless, people resorted to barter and black market exchanges and crime. Seven million orphans were estimated to be living rough. Gangs of famished children roamed the country, turning to theft, begging, or prostitution. Industrial production virtually ceased. Transportation ground to a halt. Fuel was unavailable. Disease was rampant: 834,000 died of typhus alone in 1920. The Tambov region in the western Volga uplands was convulsed by a widespread peasant uprising in the autumn of 1920. Thousands joined a 'Green Army' that was suppressed with ruthless zeal by a Special Commission for Struggle with Banditry. The Commission's head reported to Lenin: 'In general the Soviet régime was, in the eyes of the majority of peasants, identified with flying visits by commissars or plenipotentiaries who were valiant at giving orders to the [district] Executive Committees and village soviets and went around imprisoning the representatives of these local organs of authority for the non-fulfilment of frequently quite absurd requirements.'[2] The 1920 harvest was barely half the normal volume. The next year a severe drought in the Lower Volga region reduced it even further. Peasants desperately resisted attempts to requisition grain and impress them into forced labour battalions. Famine stalked the land. Hordes of starving people left the cities, scouring the countryside in search of food. Dark rumours of cannibalism circulated. A village woman in the Lower Volga Valley, found with her child eating her dead husband, protested: 'We will not give him up. We need him for food. He is our own family and no-one has the right to take him away from us.'[3] Perhaps as many as five million died of starvation in 1920–3. Humiliatingly, in August 1921 the Soviet regime was compelled to accept charity from the capitalists: an American relief mission organized by Herbert Hoover and Fridtjof Nansen imported more than sixty million dollars worth of food and medical supplies. At the peak of the operation in mid-1922 the mission was feeding more than ten million people a day.

Meanwhile, Lenin had been forced onto a new course. The main precipitant of this change of direction was the outbreak in early March 1921 of an anti-Bolshevik revolt in the naval base of Kronstadt a little to the west of Petrograd. Disillusioned sailors there were joined by soldiers and workers, many of whom had earned revolutionary laurels by participating in the events of 1917. The rebels issued a manifesto condemning the October Revolution: it had promised emancipation but produced 'even greater enslavement of the individual man'. They denounced the 'torture-chambers of the Cheka, which in their horrors surpass many times the gendarme administration of the czarist régime'. And they uttered a criticism which, in the mouths of working men, not intellectuals, took on a special force: 'But the most hateful and criminal thing which the Communists have created is moral servitude: they laid their hands even on the inner life of the toilers and compelled them to think only in the Communist way.'[4] The government condemned the revolt as a counter-revolutionary conspiracy. An initial assault on Kronstadt by the Red Army failed, whereupon fifty thousand men, including several thousand Bolshevik Party volunteers, were dispatched to subdue the insurgents. Thousands died in the fighting; surviving rebels fled across the ice to Finland or were captured and summarily executed.

Kronstadt was a terrible warning to the Bolshevik government. If these stalwart proletarians could turn against the Soviet regime, it was plain that it could not survive without a radical shift in policy. Even before Kronstadt signs of an impending change of line had been evident; but the rebellion 'was the flash', Lenin said, 'which lit up reality better than anything else'.[5] It led directly to the New Economic Policy (NEP). If the revolution in Russia could not be sustained by the support of proletarian governments in the west, it would, of necessity, have to make concessions to the peasants at home. That, at any rate, was the theoretical justification of the shift. Lenin admitted that 'the effect will be the revival of the petty bourgeoisie and of capitalism on the basis of a certain amount of free trade (if only local)'. But he admitted what was already plain to see—that further attempts to abolish markets altogether would be suicidal.[6] NEP involved a wholesale abandonment of 'War Communism'. Requisitioning of grain ended. Rationing was abolished. Nearly all sown areas of land were handed over to the peasants. A limited return to private enterprise was permitted. Although the state retained control of banks, railways, mines, heavy industry, and foreign trade, small private industrialists and shopkeepers were allowed to resume operation. Western capital was welcomed, although not much arrived. A foreign trade agreement with Britain was signed. In 1922 an attempt at currency reform, backed by gold, failed. It was followed by the 'scissors crisis' of 1923 in which industrial prices rose precipitately while agricultural ones declined. For 1923–4 the government adopted a balanced budget: there was even a surplus in the following year. A new rouble was introduced in 1924 and inflation was at last arrested. By 1925 a measure of economic order had been restored. About half of all internal trade was by this time back in private hands. In 1926 railway traffic returned to 1913 levels. By then the New Economic Policy had proved a clear success: the huge losses in livestock since 1913 had nearly been made up. In spite of a chronic shortage of grain for the market, overall economic activity had returned to 1913 levels in many sectors. As a by-product, a new personality-type appeared, the 'NEP-man', the small entrepreneur, a kind of new bourgeois—soon to be turned into a hate figure.

Lenin's final achievement thus lay in restoring some semblance of order, cohesion, and economic functionality to Soviet Russia. In May 1922 he suffered a stroke: he continued as head of government until the end of 1923 but his hitherto inexhaustible energy was reduced and power slipped imperceptibly out of his hands. He died in January 1924, aged fifty-three. His body, embalmed and placed in a tomb in front of the Kremlin, became an object of worship and pilgrimage in the secular religious ritual of the

Soviet state. His image became an icon, his *Collected Works* holy writ and compulsory texts in Soviet schools and universities. In Moscow alone 130 shrines dedicated to his memory were enumerated in 1980. His legacy to his successors was a centralized party machine solidly entrenched in power over the greater part of the former Russian Empire. Control of that machine was the key to victory in the ensuing party struggle: since April 1922 the dominant figure in the party apparatus had been its newly elected General Secretary, Josef Stalin.

In his famous 'testament', written in December 1922 but not published until 1926 (abroad; in 1956 in the Soviet Union), Lenin had warned against the danger of a split in the Communist Party, based on the differences between Trotsky and Stalin. As General Secretary, Stalin had concentrated 'boundless power in his hands', Lenin wrote, adding, 'I am not sure whether he will always know how to use this power with sufficient caution.' Trotsky was pronounced 'the most able man in the present Central Committee' though 'prone to excessive self-confidence'. Lenin urged that neither Trotsky's non-Bolshevik past nor Zinoviev's and Kamenev's wobbling on the eve of the October Revolution be held against them. And he expressed favourable opinions of Bukharin and G. L. Pyatakov. All five of these men were later to die by order of a sixth—Stalin. In a postscript on 4 January 1923, Lenin wrote more forcefully: 'Stalin is too rude, and this failing, entirely tolerable in relations between us Communists, becomes intolerable in the office of General Secretary. I therefore recommend that the comrades give thought to means of transferring Stalin from this job and nominate to it another person . . . more tolerant, more loyal, more polite and more attentive to comrades, with less capriciousness etc.'[7] But Lenin's mental and physical debilitation in the final months of his life prevented him from directly influencing the choice of his successor.

The obvious successor was Trotsky, the outstanding political brain and public figure among the revolutionary leaders. Anatoly Lunacharsky, himself a noted speaker, declared Trotsky the greatest orator of the age: 'His impressive appearance, his handsome, sweeping gestures, the powerful rhythm of his speech, his loud but never fatiguing voice, the remarkable coherence and literary skill of his phrasing, the richness of imagery, scalding irony, his soaring pathos, his rigid logic, clear as polished steel—those are Trotsky's virtues as a speaker.'[8] But Lunacharsky also noted: 'His colossal arrogance and an inability or unwillingness to show any human kindness or to be attentive to people, the absence of that charm which always surrounded

Lenin, condemned Trotsky to a certain loneliness.'[9] In the eyes of many Bolsheviks, Trotsky was too clever by half. They favoured the safe (as they thought) mediocrity over the dangerously inspired intellectual.

In the manoeuvring for position after Lenin's death, Stalin succeeded in picking off his opponents one by one. First he secured the support of Kamenev and Zinoviev against Trotsky, who was isolated at the head of a small 'left opposition'. Too late Stalin's allies realized that he aimed at sole power. At the fourteenth Communist Party congress in December 1925, Kamenev declared, 'I have come to the conclusion that Comrade Stalin cannot fulfil the role of unifier of the Bolshevik general staff. . . . We are against the doctrine of one-man rule, we are against the creation of a leader.'[10] When Lenin's testament was published abroad, Stalin was brazen in his response. Posing modestly as 'a minor figure', he admitted to the charge that he was 'rude': 'That is quite true. Yes, comrades, I am rude to those who perfidiously wreck and split the party.' He accused Trotsky and his allies of 'a scurrilous campaign of slander against Lenin'.[11] Attention was drawn to the fact that Trotsky, Zinoviev, and Kamenev were all Jews. Trotsky gave as good as he got: he called Stalin 'the grave-digger of the revolution'. Condemned as a 'petty-bourgeois deviationist', Trotsky was expelled from the party, deported to Kazakhstan, and in 1929 banished from the USSR. Meanwhile Zinoviev and Kamenev were sidelined. Over the next decade, in Turkey, France, Norway, and finally in Mexico, Trotsky pursued a ferocious propaganda campaign against Stalin, terminated only by his assassination by a Stalinist hit-man in 1940.

The struggle for the political succession was bound up with ideological debate over the direction of Soviet economic policy. Trotsky, disappointed in his hopes of revolution in industrialized Europe, believed that the only hope of survival for Bolshevism lay in a push for rapid industrialization in Russia. He called in 1923 for a 'dictatorship of industry': a centrally planned programme of state-owned industrial development. He was supported by the economist Yevgeny Preobrazhensky who argued for 'primitive Socialist accumulation', that is for the extraction from the peasants, by means of taxation and pricing policies, of capital for industrial investment. Such a policy would, of course, have revived the town–country antagonism that had been stilled by the adoption of NEP. The so-called 'rightists', led by Nikolai Bukharin, maintained that this would be political suicide for the Bolsheviks. They advocated continued concessions to rural interests even while recognizing that these would entail the construction of socialism 'at a snail's pace'. Echoing Guizot, Bukharin told the peasants in 1925 '*Enrichissez-vous*!' These phrases would later be used against him. Having defeated the 'left', Stalin turned his attention to the so-called 'rightists'. At the sixteenth party congress in 1929, he defeated Bukharin and his supporters who were accused of 'a masked form of struggle against the party'.[12] All were ousted from leadership positions. Stalin was now undisputed master of the USSR.

A former seminarian from Georgia, the son of a shoemaker and a washer-woman, Stalin was neither a brilliant intellectual like Trotsky, nor a magisterial political analyst like Lenin. But he was no plodder. In the Tiflis Spiritual Seminary, he scored top marks in nearly all subjects, including Holy Scripture, mathematics, and Greek-Slavonic singing. Recently claims have been made for the quality of his juvenile poetry, though the admiration is not widely shared.[13] He owed much of his early success to underestimation by his colleagues. His nickname in the 1920s, reflecting the view of him as a dutiful bureaucrat, was 'Comrade Card-Index'. In his biography of Stalin (a literary equivalent of the ice-pick that Stalin's hatchet-man later wielded against him as he was in the final stages of writing the book) Trotsky wrote: 'Stalin took possession of power, not with the aid of personal qualities, but with the aid of an impersonal machine. And it was not he who created the machine, but the machine that created him.'[14] Later a cult of fawning adulation would accrete around Stalin. But in his early years of power he almost emulated Lenin's personal modesty. Puffing away sagely at his Dunhill pipe, he exhibited a stolid, reliable persona—almost a Russian Baldwin. Under this reassuring captain, the Soviet Union in 1927–8 seemed, like the rest of Europe, to be sailing into calmer waters.

Locarno diplomacy

Germany remained the critical centre of European politics. Like a wounded beast, she was observed fearfully by her neighbours: they worried about her rage so long as she was in pain, about her power if she recovered. The basic fear of France and of all the successor states was that the defeated powers would seek to revise the peace treaties at their expense. The French attempted to create a *cordon sanitaire* between Russia and Germany by sponsoring an alliance of Czechoslovakia, Yugoslavia, and Romania known as the Little Entente. Poland hovered at the edge of this grouping but never joined it. In 1921, however, she signed an alliance treaty with France as well as a secret military agreement providing for common action in the event of attacks by

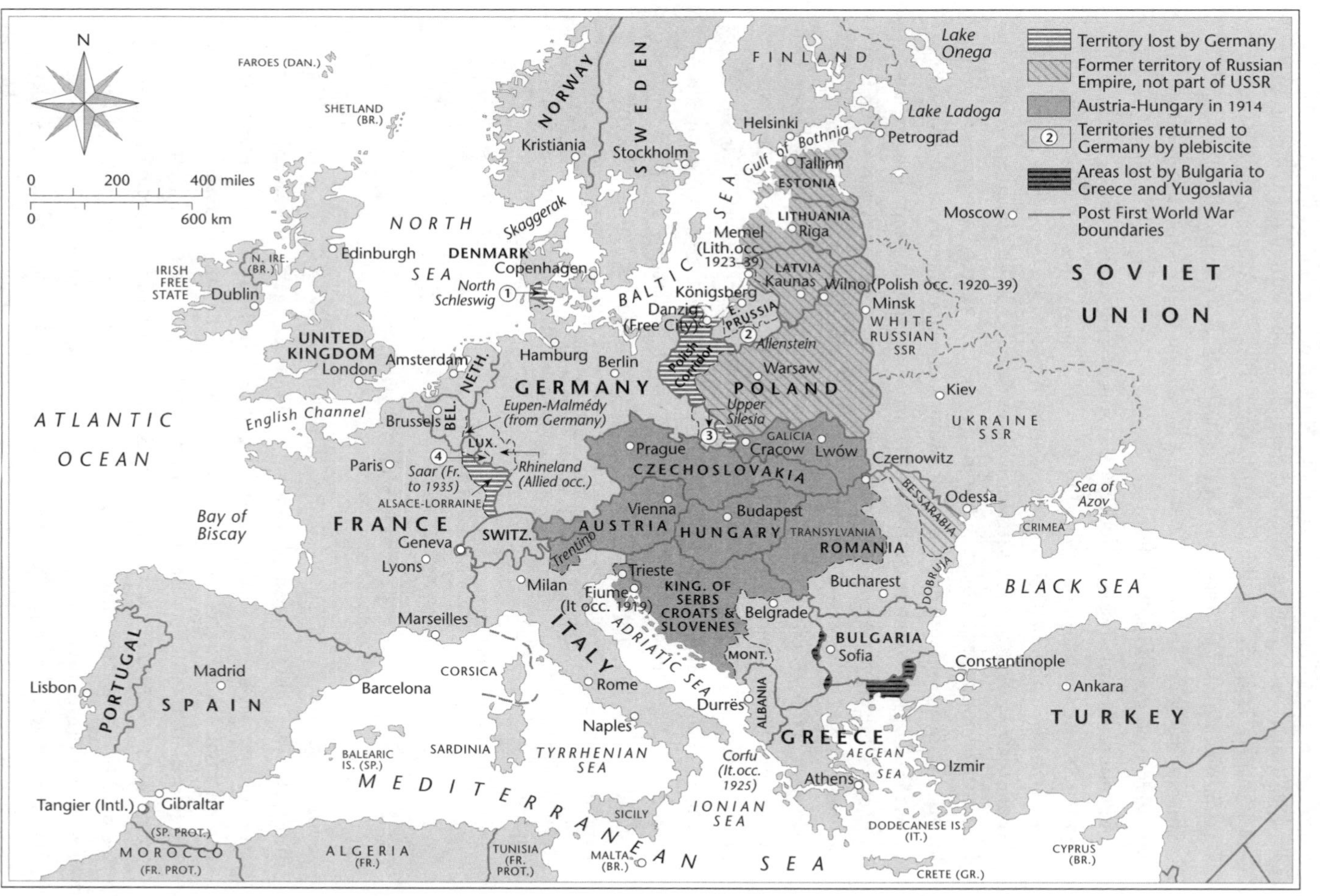

Map 3. Europe after the First World War

either Germany or Russia. After her defeat of the Russians, Poland flattered herself that she was a major European power. Yet she saw her very existence as predicated on the weakness of neighbours who had partitioned her three times. Accordingly, she maintained an extraordinarily high rate of military expenditure—one-third of total government outlays in 1923. All these eastern European states, however, remained second-rate military powers and the French remained nervous.

In 1922 Germany sprang a surprise on the Allies by concluding a pact with the other great outcast, Soviet Russia. The Treaty of Rapallo of 16 April 1922 represented, at one level, an effort by the two pariah states of Europe to break out of isolation. The agreement settled outstanding claims, restored diplomatic relations, and held out the promise of increased trade between the two countries. Its chief architect was the German Foreign Minister, Walther Rathenau, who signed it together with the Soviet representative, G. V. Chicherin, on a 'Sunday outing' at Rapallo. Rathenau was at first hesitant about the reaction of Britain and France and finally came to terms only out of fear that the Russians might conclude a separate agreement with the Allies.[15] News of the treaty outraged the Allied leaders who were gathered at a conference in Genoa, negotiating on reparations with the Germans. They were furious at having been two-timed by Rathenau. Lloyd George demanded the annulment of the treaty—but in vain. Rapallo was thus the first indication that a resolute Germany might successfully defy her conquerors.

The atmosphere created by the treaty facilitated secret military cooperation between Germany and Russia. Contacts between German military experts and Soviet agents had begun as early as 1919, when Karl Radek was in Berlin, and had continued sporadically since then. From 1921 the German General Staff pursued close relations with the Russians on a separate track from the German Foreign Office. The army chief, General Seeckt, strongly promoted Russo-German military cooperation. In February 1922, in a personal discussion with Seeckt, Radek is even alleged to have suggested that Russia, supplied by Germany, would be prepared to join in a joint attack on Poland the next spring, though this seems to have been a personal effort by Radek to 'play the Polish card', rather than settled Soviet policy.[16] The idea chimed with Seeckt's own thinking. In a memorandum in September 1920, he had written: 'Poland's existence is intolerable, incompatible with the survival of Germany. It must disappear, and it will disappear through its own internal weakness and through Russia—with our assistance.'[17] At a meeting with

Russian representatives in July 1923, Chancellor Wilhelm Cuno responded to criticism that Germany was not doing enough to prepare against possible attack by Poland. Cuno pointed out that Germany 'had to avoid giving the impression of preparing for a war of revenge. The more inconspicuous the preparations were made, the more advantageous they were.'[18] Soon thereafter, planning began for expansion of Russian armaments industries, with German help, in order to produce war *matériel* for Germany beyond the Versailles Treaty limitations. Cuno's successor, Stresemann, although privately anxious to restore Germany's eastern frontier, was initially opposed to military dealings with Russia, but the *Reichswehr* nevertheless continued direct contacts with the Russians. After 1924 experimental and training stations, operated by the *Reichswehr*, were set up in the USSR for tanks, aircraft, and gas, all prohibited to Germany under the Versailles Treaty. Although these arrangements were secret, word of them got out in the mid-1920s, and it was even rumoured incorrectly that the Rapallo Treaty contained secret military clauses.

Eventually the French came to the conclusion that their best hope of long-term security rested in agreement with the Germans. After the defeat of Poincaré in the general election of May 1924, the new Prime Minister, Edouard Herriot, reversed his predecessor's bellicose anti-German line and instead embarked on a policy of reconciliation. French troops withdrew from the Ruhr in August 1925. In October the Locarno Treaties were signed. In the first, the wartime Allies, Britain, France, Belgium, and Italy, mutually guaranteed the territorial status quo on Germany's western frontier and the demilitarization of the Rhineland. At the same time, Germany signed Arbitration Treaties with France, Belgium, Poland, and Czechoslovakia. The reason for this complex arrangement was British refusal to guarantee the borders of Germany's eastern neighbours. Bismarck in 1876 had famously pronounced that the Balkans were not worth 'the healthy bones of a single Pomeranian musketeer'; now the British Foreign Secretary, Sir Austen Chamberlain, said that Germany's eastern marches were a region 'for which no British government ever will or ever can risk the bones of a British grenadier'.[19] (As prophecies, both were disastrously wrong.) In any case, Germany, bolder since Rapallo, would not sign a multilateral treaty legitimizing and perpetuating her eastern frontier. The Czechoslovak and Polish Foreign Ministers were not even admitted to the early meetings of the Locarno conference and the agreements were seen by some as an indication of faltering French commitment to their defence. At home, right-wingers accused Stresemann of having signed a 'treaty of renunciation'. Stresemann, a nationalist, in fact saw Locarno rather as a first step towards undermining the Versailles system and revising Germany's eastern frontier. It was he, not Hitler, who declared, 'I consider myself the protector of all Germans abroad.'[20] But Stresemann's preferred method was diplomacy; Hitler's was force. Thomas Mann later wrote, Stresemann 'was able... to grow out from and above all the traditions he had inherited... into the world of a European society of nations in thought, conviction, and deed, which no one would have dreamt possible on the basis of his early adulthood'.[21] France was represented at the conference by the self-styled 'pilgrim of peace', Aristide Briand (see plate 18), who served as French Foreign Minister for most of the period 1925 to 1932. He rejoiced that Locarno eliminated the threat of any further Russo-German combination. Briand and Stresemann shared the 1926 Nobel Peace Prize but the failure to provide equally solid guarantees on Germany's eastern and western frontiers was a harbinger of future lack of resolve by Britain and France. Paul Reynaud, who as French Prime Minister in the spring of 1940 had to deal with the consequences, later reflected: 'Perhaps... there was already the spirit of Munich in Locarno.'[22]

The Locarno 'tea parties' nevertheless led to a general easing of international tension. In 1926 Germany was admitted to the League of Nations. In 1928 the Pact of Paris, popularly known as the Kellogg–Briand Pact (after the US and French Foreign Ministers who drafted it) brought agreement on the renunciation of war as an instrument of national policy. In mid-1929 a committee chaired by an American, Owen D. Young, recommended a reduction in reparation payments, now to be stretched out over fifty-nine years. In spite of Anglo-French differences over the proposals, the Young Plan was approved in April 1930. Three months later the Allies completed their evacuation of the Rhineland. Amid this general outbreak of reasonableness, preparations advanced for convening an international conference on disarmament.

Bourgeois ascendancy

After a decade of wars, revolutions, economic dislocations, border changes, and refugee movements, Europe thus finally settled down after about 1923 to a short period of relative peace and prosperity. Outside the USSR the danger from the extreme left that had seemed so imminent in 1919 had either been suppressed or could safely be dismissed as a fringe political phenomenon. As the threat to lives and to property receded, politics in most European countries assumed less the form of a Manichaean struggle between forces of light and darkness and became more concerned with narrower bread-and-butter issues.

In Britain the Conservatives ruled, in government or coalition, for all but three of the inter-war years. 'Hang the Kaiser' had been a popular enough cry to help secure the re-election of Lloyd George's governing coalition in Britain in December 1918. The Parliament was dominated by Conservatives who were content to shelter under the aura of the victorious war leader. Stanley Baldwin, himself a Conservative, described the new House of Commons privately to Keynes as dominated by 'hard-faced men who looked as if they had done well out of the war'.[23] They maintained the former radical Prime Minister in office for another four years while he postured on the world stage and presided over a government composed largely of his former political enemies.

Lloyd George's last significant achievement was the treaty of December 1921, which brought a half-century's respite in the tortured Anglo-Irish struggle. Ireland had been in a state of turmoil since the suppression of the 1916 Easter rising. In the 1918 general election, the nationalist Sinn Féin Party, led by Arthur Griffith, Michael Collins, and Éamon De Valera, had won 73 out of 105 seats in Ireland, including all but three of those outside Ulster. The constitutionalist Irish Party, which had sought home rule within the United Kingdom, was almost obliterated. The Sinn Féin victors refused to take up their seats at Westminster and in January 1919 met in Dublin as an Irish parliament, the Dáil, and declared independence. British efforts to reassert authority proved unavailing and the island was consumed for the next three years by ferocious terrorism and counter-terrorism. The Anglo-Irish treaty recognized the Irish Free State as having a status similar to that of a Dominion, that is, something close to but not absolute independence. But Britain retained sovereignty over Northern Ireland, in which the large Protestant majority was determinedly Unionist. Although the Irish nationalists never accepted partition in principle, they were obliged to put up with it. In the ensuing civil war in southern Ireland, the anti-treaty faction, led by De Valera, was defeated and in 1927 agreed to enter parliamentary politics. For all the Free State's anti-British fervour and in spite of the retrograde influence of the Catholic Church on intellectual and social life, the country's institutions remained deeply marked by British influences.

Independence did not end economic stagnation. Population decline was perpetuated by migration to Britain and the United States. In the more prosperous north, the Catholic minority never accepted the legitimacy of the self-governing institutions under which Protestant domination was ensured but until the late 1960s they were relatively quiescent.

In October 1922, as Kemalist forces neared British- and French-occupied Constantinople, the Conservatives seized the opportunity to withdraw their support from Lloyd George. He left 10 Downing Street never to return. His Liberal Party had virtually expired (some said he had murdered it) and although he made heroic efforts to breathe new life into the corpse, power slipped inexorably away from the centre to the two poles of the electoral spectrum. In the general election of December 1923 the Labour Party received 30 per cent of the vote and 191 out of 615 seats in the House of Commons. Although the Conservatives were still the largest party, Labour formed a government, relying on the parliamentary support of the Liberals. This first Socialist administration turned out to be a very tame affair. Anxious lest he lose Liberal support, the Prime Minister, Ramsay MacDonald, refrained from introducing any Socialist measures. He was out within a year, defeated by a red scare based on the publication by the *Daily Mail* of a forged letter from the Comintern leader, Grigory Zinoviev. The Conservatives regained power and, under the stolid leadership of Stanley Baldwin, governed Britain for the next five years.

The most serious immediate problem facing Baldwin was the crisis in the coal mines. Employing over a million men, this was the largest industry in Britain. Like many of Britain's older, heavy industries, it had entered a long decline since the end of the war. The government had pumped tens of millions of pounds into it since 1917 but to little effect. It suffered from under-capitalization, overseas competition, and bitter labour relations. The Franco-Belgian withdrawal from the Ruhr and the resumption of large-scale German production, together with the return of the pound to the gold standard, dealt savage blows to British coal mining. In mid-1925 60 per cent of all coal in Britain was being produced at a loss. Since labour costs were the largest single component in production, the mine-owners protested that they had no alternative but to cut wages. In April 1926 the government subsidy was withdrawn and the miners were locked out unless and until they accepted lower pay. On 4 May the Trades Union Congress called a general strike in sympathy. It was the largest labour stoppage in British history, though not in truth general since not all workers were unionized and, even of those who were, not all struck. It was a very British affair, less a strike than a striking of class attitudes: upper-class gentlemanliness confronted working-class deference. Neither side was really prepared to mount barricades. Enthusiasts on both sides got a bad name. The government's *British Gazette*, edited by Churchill (who had left the Liberals and rejoined the Conservative Party), spouted vehement anti-strike propaganda that was felt by many to be out of tune with British peacetime traditions. The TUC's heart was not really in it, and from the outset the union leaders squirmed uncomfortably and sought a decent exit route. This was a world away from the syndicalist apocalypse. After nine days, the TUC gave up and abandoned the miners to their fate. They were starved into submission by November. The following year the government introduced legislation prohibiting sympathy strikes or any 'designed or calculated to coerce the government'. Continuing high unemployment weakened the trade union movement and it was not until the 1950s that, in conditions of full employment, it re-emerged as a major force.

French inter-war politics were characterized by the failure of the institutions of the Third Republic to provide stable ministries or strong executives. Forty-four ministries held office between the armistice of 1918 and that of 1940. Most were weak coalitions formed around the shifting centre of French politics, the Radical Party, radish-like (red on the outside, white on the inside), corrupt, and enjoying strong support among peasants and the petty bourgeoisie. Through the perpetually revolving doors of ministries, the same figures kept appearing. Briand, for example, served three times as Prime Minister and four times as Foreign Minister in the decade after 1921.

Excluded from government and from the spoils of office was the far left. In December 1920 a conference of the French Socialists at Tours split irrevocably, with the majority forming the French Communist Party, loyal to the Comintern, and the minority maintaining their adhesion to the reformist, parliamentary socialism of the Second International, though they continued to employ the rhetoric of revolutionary Marxism. The official name of the Socialist party until as late as 1969 remained Section Française de l'Internationale Ouvrière. The Communists took with them more than 80 per cent of the membership as well as title to the party newspaper, *l'Humanité*. Tainted from the outset by their slavish subservience to Moscow, the French Communists remained a sect rather than the party of the organized working class. The Socialists were at first greatly weakened by the defection of the Communists, though they soon overtook them in support. Fearful of the dilution of principle unavoidable in coalition politics, they disdained to accept ministerial office until such time as they might control the main levers of power and effect a transformation of society rather than mere reformist policies. The rigid sectarianism of the Communists and the refusal of the Socialists, anxious to maintain doctrinal purity, to join 'bourgeois' parties in government condemned the French left to fifteen years of futile opposition.

The conservative Bloc National held power for five years from 1919. Its main preoccupation was with foreign affairs, particularly reparations. By 1924 the decline of the franc forced retrenchment in public finances. After a bitter fight, Poincaré, Prime Minister from 1922 to 1924, secured parliamentary approval for the *double décime*, an all-round 20 per cent increase in taxes. The measure temporarily restored the currency but heightened voter discontent. The revived Socialists joined in an electoral pact and 'minimum programme' with the Radicals.

This Cartel des Gauches triumphed in the general election of May 1924. The victors' first action was to oust the sitting President of the Republic, Alexandre Millerand, who was hated as a traitor to the left. After a futile effort at resistance he gave way, confirming the supremacy of the legislature over the presidency in the political system of the Third Republic. The new government aroused great hopes for reform but like the first Labour government in Britain, this was one of those turning-points that failed to turn. The Socialists shied away from the offer of ministerial offices by the Radical leader, Herriot. They would merely give the new government support from without. Herriot, '*la République en personne*', intelligent, witty, and warm-hearted, a *normalien* (graduate of the *Ecole normale supérieure*), biographer of Philo and of Madame Récamier, and mayor of Lyons since 1905, was an admired orator and a much-loved statesman. But as Prime Minister he proved to be an inept political tactician: he created needless enemies and alienated allies. His promise of 'total transformation' remained unfulfilled. The government's achievements were mainly limited to symbolic acts such as the transfer of the body of Jaurès to the Pantheon. The franc tumbled again and the left complained that it had been defeated by the '*mur d'argent*'.

After barely two years, the same Chamber of Deputies that had installed Herriot in office approved the return to power of Poincaré and granted him powers to rule by decree. He accepted Locarno, increased indirect taxes, and imposed reductions in government spending. The franc stabilized and in 1928 it returned to the gold standard, though at a fifth of its pre-war value. The economy revived but the opportunity was lost to reform public finances (most taxation remained indirect), to modernize the still primitive French countryside, still at that time the home of a little over half the population of the country, or to grapple with social problems, in particular the abominable housing conditions in urban slums.

The critical test case for liberal political institutions in Europe was Germany where the republic had survived the initial challenge from the left only by compromising with the right. The Weimar constitution provided for a federal system in which the states (now to be called *Länder*) retained considerable powers. The federal government was responsible to the lower house of parliament, the Reichstag, elected by a pure proportional system on the basis of universal franchise for men and women over the age of twenty (hitherto voting had been restricted to men over twenty-five). The President too was elected by universal suffrage: he was to have power to appoint the Chancellor, dissolve the Reichstag, and issue decrees in emergencies provided they were counter-signed by the Chancellor or the responsible minister. An upper chamber, the Reichsrat, composed of members of the state governments, retained limited powers. After a bitter left–right struggle, the old imperial black-white-red flag was replaced by the black-red-gold colours of 1848.

This was, on the face of things, a model parliamentary regime. The old social order, however, remained largely intact. The officers of the new *Reichswehr*, under Seeckt, inherited the attitudes of the imperial officer corps from which they were largely drawn. The rank-and-file were heavily recruited from the right-wing *Freikorps*. The army high command, particularly Seeckt, wielded substantial behind-the-scenes influence and enjoyed considerable autonomy. Similarly, the old imperial bureaucracy remained in office in seamless continuity from old to new order and, even when ostensibly serving Social Democrat masters, steered policy away from left-wing experimentation. In these senses, the German revolution was stillborn.

Established on this uncertain basis, the Weimar Republic nevertheless survived renewed challenges in the early 1920s, this time from the right rather than the left. In March 1920 a short-lived military revolt in Berlin, known as the Kapp putsch, lasted only six days and collapsed in general ridicule. The left persuaded themselves that the rebellion had been defeated by a general strike. No doubt that helped. But the chief causes of the failure of the coup were the limited support the revolt evoked in the armed forces and the astonishing incompetence of the putschists, headed by a colourless official, Wolfgang Kapp, and supported by militarists including Ludendorff and his former right-hand man, Colonel Max Bauer. The only lasting consequence of the putsch was the fall of the Social Democrat government in Bavaria and its replacement by conservatives. A swing to the right was manifested in Germany as a whole in the first elections held under the Weimar constitution in June. The governing coalition of Social Democrats, Centre, and Democrats lost power. The Social Democrats' vote was reduced from 38 per cent to 22 per cent. They never again attained more than 30 per cent of the vote under Weimar. A new government of the centre-right took office. But the far right remained unreconciled to the republic and a dangerous force for violence and instability. In August 1921 the Centre Party leader, Erzberger, who had made himself deeply unpopular with the extreme nationalists, was assassinated. The following summer, Rathenau was shot dead in the street in Berlin. Jew, industrialist, philosopher, and a member of the small, liberal Democratic Party, he too had been targeted for venomous attack by the right. His funeral in the Reichstag chamber was a great demonstration of republican faith. In November 1923 Ludendorff joined a young nationalist street orator, Adolf Hitler, in an attempted revolt in Munich. The 'beerhall putsch' was almost as much of a comic-opera fiasco as the 1920 coup. It never spread beyond Munich. The ringleaders were quickly rounded up and Hitler was sentenced to a short prison term, which he used to write a rambling, incoherent statement of racist faith, *Mein Kampf*.

With the defeat of revolutionaries of left and right, the restoration of the currency, and renewed, if sluggish, economic growth, the political class settled down to a more normal, certainly less exciting, life. The late 1920s were the halcyon years of the Weimar Republic. Since no political party ever won an overall majority, all governments were coalitions—from 1924 to 1928 of the centre-right, then until 1930 a grand coalition stretching from the moderate right to the Social Democrats. The foremost political figure was Stresemann who, after his short but critical term as Chancellor in 1923, served as Foreign Minister until his death in 1929. Stresemann's doctoral dissertation had been a study of the Berlin bottled beer trade and his first job had been as a clerk for the Association of Chocolate Manufacturers in Dresden. As leader of the small German People's Party, representing middle-class, business elements, Stresemann personified the stolid bourgeois virtues. The perceptive diarist Count Harry Kessler considered that he possessed 'a robust determination' but that he lacked 'fine moral sensibility'.[24] Yet he was the most creative German statesman of the age. Although his primary achievement was in diplomacy, Stresemann played a significant role in containing social tensions in Germany and resisting political polarization. Welfare state provisions, enshrined in the Weimar constitution, were given legislative effect, notably by the introduction in 1924 of basic state welfare provision for those in dire poverty, and legislation in 1927 for state unemployment insurance. Public spending on education, hospitals, and housing rose quickly with the result that state expenditure averaged 26 per cent of national income in the period 1925–9.

Although the Weimar system had certainly stabilized after its rocky beginnings in 1918–23, fundamental weaknesses remained. Though owners of bank accounts, mortgages, and bonds that had been made worthless during the great inflation received some compensation after 1925, its modesty increased middle-class resentment and demoralization, driving many into the arms of the extreme right. The paramilitary groups refused to fade away: a new right-wing veterans' group, the *Stahlhelm*, confronted its leftist mirror, the *Reichsbanner*, dedicated to defence of the republic. Their presence indicated the incipient tendency towards recurrence of civil war that simmered just below the surface of Weimar politics. The party system remained fragmented, with deep schisms within the left, the liberals, and the right. The only parties with a positive commitment to the Weimar constitution were the Social Democrats and the Democratic Party. Significant elements in society remained alienated. The Communists participated in the parliamentary system but awaited the first opportunity to destroy it. The army regarded itself as a kind of guarantor, not of the republic, but of the German state, tending to see the President, rather than government or parliament, as the legitimate fount of authority. The election of Hindenburg as President in 1925 gave the Weimar system a degree of respectability in the eyes of the traditional right; but the new head of state's adhesion to the republic was questionable and, in the end, he joined its destroyers rather than its defenders.

The peacemakers had sought to recreate the world in their own image of liberal parliamentarianism. In large measure they failed. Liberalism remained the characteristic political form only in the prosperous, industrialized societies of north-west Europe, barely touched by the tide of revolution or the fierce ethnic antagonisms that afflicted most of the rest of the continent.

Successor states

All the 'successor states' on the territory of the former multi-national empires in east-central Europe, stretching in a great arc from Finland in the north to Yugoslavia in the south, shared basic common features: they were weak, they were poor, and they were frightened. As for the defeated countries of eastern Europe, Hungary and Bulgaria, they were weaker and poorer than they had been—and they were both frightened and vengeful.

The weakness of these countries was an unavoidable consequence of the application of the principle of nationality in the post-war settlement. With the exception of Poland, which had a population of twenty-seven million in 1921, none of the states between Russia and Germany held more than twenty million inhabitants. In descending order of size, Romania, which had roughly doubled her population as a result of the peace treaties, had about seventeen million, Czechoslovakia thirteen million, and Yugoslavia twelve million. The remainder were all under ten million, ranging from Hungary's eight million to Latvia and Estonia, each with about 1.5 million. Most of the countries in the region nevertheless felt over-populated because of the pressure of a growing peasantry on limited cultivable land. The only significant exceptions were Hungary, which had the lowest population growth in eastern Europe, and Czechoslovakia, with her industrialized western provinces. One outlet for agrarian over-population closed in the early 1920s when the United States enacted restrictive immigration laws. Although France permitted some immigration from eastern Europe, mainly Poland, in the hope of making up the population deficit caused by the war, few other emigration opportunities existed from eastern Europe.

Most of the successor states adopted democratic parliamentary constitutions. Poland's, for example, was modelled in large measure on that of the French Third Republic. But formal democratic mechanisms did not prevent a slide towards authoritarian regimes. Apart from Czechoslovakia and Finland, none of the states in the region succeeded in implanting democratic institutions in political cultures that were highly inhospitable to liberal ideas.

Although each of the successor states had its own special characteristics, the political life of all of them in the inter-war period was dominated by four great and often interrelated issues: the land question; the failure to achieve a transition towards a modern industrial economy; problems of minorities; and the threat to regional stability—and to the very existence of the successor states—posed by demands for revision of the post-war settlement.

The eastern European economies remained predominantly agrarian throughout the inter-war period. The populations of all the states of the region, again with the exception of Czechoslovakia, were more than 50 per cent rural. In all the countries peasant parties were formed that claimed, with varying degrees of verisimilitude, to represent agrarian interests.

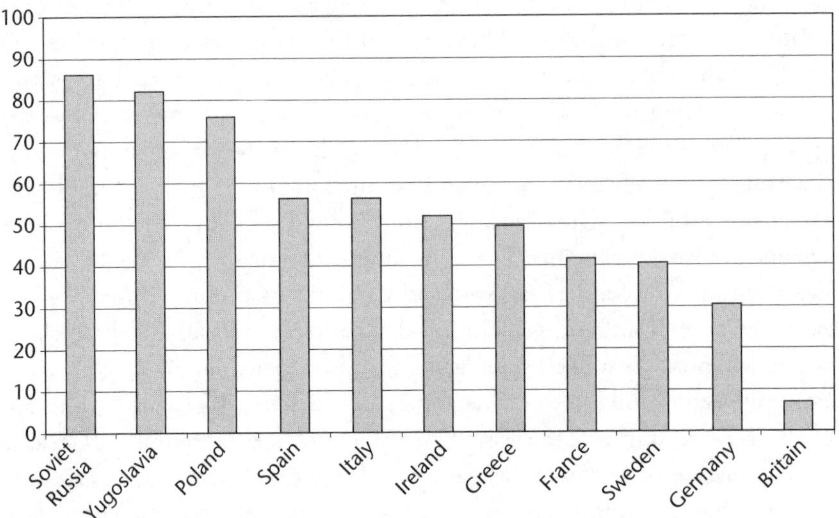

Figure 3. Proportion of workforce engaged in agriculture, *c.*1921

Source: Paul Bairoch et al., eds., *The Working Population and its Structure* (Brussels, 1968).

Peasant majorities in the electorate compelled all such parties and most governments to pay at least lip-service to the ideal of redistributive land reform that would break up large tracts and enable cultivators to become owners of the land they worked. In the case of Poland the concept was even enshrined in the constitution adopted in 1921 which called for the creation of 'private farming units capable of adequate productivity'.[25] But in this as in other matters the constitution-makers' ideals were not realized.

Land reforms were initiated in Romania, Czechoslovakia, Greece, and Yugoslavia. The Romanian legislation, enacted in December 1918, was perhaps the most far-reaching: it expropriated most large estates and distributed the land to 1.4 million peasants. The power of the old landowning class was decisively broken. In Poland and Hungary, on the other hand, especially the eastern provinces of both countries, the majority of large estates remained intact throughout the inter-war period and landowning magnates, especially in Hungary, remained a major political force. In 1921, 1 per cent of landowners in Poland held more than half of all the land. On the other hand, ten million people depended for survival on holdings of less than 5 hectares, the produce of which barely sufficed to keep them alive. Some redistribution of Church, state, and private landholdings took place, but this barely kept pace with pressure on land. By 1935 it was (conservatively) estimated that

2.4 million peasants in Poland were economically 'superfluous', that is, they could leave the land without injuring its output given existing methods of production. But such people had nowhere to go.

Not coincidentally, Poland and Hungary, the two countries in which significant land reform did not occur, were those in which the landowning class belonged mainly to the dominant nationality of the state, whereas in the other three countries a large number of dispossessed landowners were members of the former 'hegemonic' nationalities. A Romanian Academy study, published in the 1930s, congratulated the authors of the Romanian land reform on their 'breadth of view and genuinely social sentiment' in distributing land not only to ethnic Romanians but also to members of ethnic minorities, 206,000 of whom received land under the reform.[26] But the study neglected to mention that those expropriated, particularly in Transylvania, were disproportionately Hungarians or Germans. Although the former owners received compensation this was often in money that had depreciated in value. Some Romanian politicians made no bones about the nationalist tinge to the land reform: 'We regard the agrarian reform as the most potent instrument in the Romanization of Transylvania,' said the poet-politician Octavian Goga in 1920.[27] National resentments were consequently often aggravated rather than mitigated. The land question thus continued to be bound up with the national question in the successor states.

Neither in the countries that redistributed land nor in those that retained large estates did efficiency in agriculture approach the levels of north-west Europe. Where land was redistributed, lots were often too small, and on the death of the owner were often sub-parcelled out into ever tinier portions: in Romania, where such parcelling reached the furthest extreme, 83 per cent of agricultural land in 1936 was held in lots of less than 5 hectares. In Bulgaria, the average holding shrank from 6.3 hectares in 1908 to 5.75 in 1929. In much of eastern Europe there were few medium-sized farms of the sort common in Britain and Germany. In Poland holdings of between 20 and 100 hectares constituted under 3 per cent of the total (and amounted to no more than 10 per cent of the land). In contrast, such middle-size farmers in Holland numbered 7 per cent (39 per cent of the land). The millions of east European 'dwarf holders' had no access to capital, could barely afford to buy even the simplest tools, such as ploughs, and were ignorant of modern techniques. They could not dream of replacing horse-power with the tractors that were starting to operate on British farms. The average milk yield from their cows (more often a single cow) was a fraction of that of the continent's most efficient farmers, the Danes. As for large estates, they were in general more highly capitalized and produced for national and international markets; but their productivity was well below that of the most efficient farms in Britain, Germany, or Scandinavia. Many were not run as *latifundia* but were leased out in small units to tenant farmers whose production methods remained primitive.

With the exception of Czechoslovakia, none of the successor states boasted a modern manufacturing industrial base. Czechoslovakia attained the highest rate of growth in manufacturing output of the east European states between 1920 and 1929. But even in Czechoslovakia, industry was largely confined to Bohemia, Moravia, and Silesia, whereas the eastern regions, Slovakia and Sub-Carpathian Ruthenia, remained mainly agrarian. Poland and Romania had large extractive industries of coal and oil, but manufacturing, with the exceptions of textiles and metalworking in Poland, was less well developed. The transportation infrastructure was weak and had been severely disrupted by the war and the break-up of empires. The five-foot railway gauge in eastern Poland, built to the imperial Russian standard, was 3.5 inches wider than those in ex-Prussian and ex-Austrian Poland. By 1929 industrial production in Poland was still only 86 per cent of the level for the same regions in 1913—which indeed was never attained during the inter-war period. Access to capital markets was limited by a weak domestic banking sector and competitive devaluations that failed to jump-start foreign trade and deterred foreign investment. In Poland, as elsewhere, a 'new mercantilism', fuelled by a short-sighted desire for 'self-sufficiency', hindered trade and stifled economic development. Figures for output of electric energy in 1929 provide a telling index of the comparative economic backwardness of the region: Bulgaria, Greece, Hungary, Poland, Romania, and Yugoslavia together produced less electricity than Norway.

All of the states of eastern Europe were rent, to greater or lesser degrees, by national conflicts or minority problems that threatened their cohesion, and in some cases their very existence. In Poland in 1921, only 69 per cent of the population were ethnic Poles. As a result of the conquest of large swathes of territory from Soviet Russia, the country held nearly four million Ukrainians and over a million Belorussians, in addition to a million Germans, mainly in the 'Polish corridor', and nearly three million Jews. All these minorities suffered from nationalistic policies and petty persecution by the Polish majority. The disproportionate representation of Jews and Germans in trade, ownership of manufacturing industry, and the liberal professions, in Poland as elsewhere, fed nationalist jealousy. Everywhere there was reluctance to employ minorities in official positions and barriers were set against their admission to universities. The Allied powers had attempted to enforce good behaviour on Poland, Czechoslovakia, Romania, and Yugoslavia by imposing treaties for the protection of minorities as part of the peace settlement. By 1924 thirteen states in east-central Europe had signed minorities treaties. But rather than protecting minorities, the main effect was further to embitter ethnic antagonisms.

In Czechoslovakia, quite apart from the large German minority, relations were not always easy between the Czechs, more urbanized, more westward-looking, more sophisticated, and the Slovaks, a mainly peasant people who tended to resent the sometimes patronizing attitude of their western neighbours. Under the leadership of Masaryk, a Moravian, an imperfect effort was made to inculcate a sense of 'Czechoslovak' national identity. Perhaps, with time and in the absence of external pressures, this might have succeeded. But the country was not afforded that luxury for long and her enemies eventually used the wedge of Czech-Slovak differences to drive a dagger into her heart.

Of all the countries in eastern Europe, none exhibited deeper or more complex ethnic divisions than Yugoslavia, officially known until 1929 as the Kingdom of Serbs, Croats, and Slovenes. The name was intended to convey the equality of the constituent nationalities of the state. But rather than a federation of south Slav provinces, Yugoslavia developed into a centralized, Serb-dominated kingdom. Serbs constituted 43 per cent of the population, Croats 25 per cent, Slovenes 9 per cent. The rest were Montenegrins, Bosnian Muslims, Albanians, Germans, Hungarians, Romanians, Turks, Gypsies, Jews, Bulgars, Macedonians, Czechs, Slovaks, Ruthenians, Vlachs, and 'others'. The Catholic Croats, who generally considered themselves a cut above the Orthodox Serbs, resented their subjugation. Yugoslav politics bogged down in a morass of intrigue and ethnic conflict. In 1928 the Croat Peasant Party leader, Stjepan Radiç, was assassinated. The violence culminated in January 1929 in the declaration by King Alexander of a royal dictatorship.

All the new or enlarged states of eastern Europe lived in perpetual terror of territorial revisionism on the part of those countries that had lost land in the post-war settlement. Greece, for example, feared a renewed Bulgarian attempt to cut through Thrace to gain an outlet to the Mediterranean. Romania's relations with Hungary were poisoned by the Hungarian obsession with regaining Transylvania. The Baltic states eyed their neighbours with no less unease. The Polish occupation of Vilna, captured in a supposedly unauthorized attack by the Polish General Lucjan Żeligowski in October 1920, continued until 1939. This was a lasting source of embitterment in relations with the

Lithuanians who insisted that it was their capital, although Vilna's population in 1916 had been 50 per cent Polish-speaking and 42 per cent Yiddish-speaking; only 2.6 per cent spoke Lithuanian. By way of self-consolation, in January 1923, the Lithuanians seized the formerly German city of Memel, drove out the French garrison that was holding it on behalf of the Allies, and annexed the city. The national question and reaction against the peace treaties thus destabilized both internal and external relations throughout the region.

The retreat from democracy became visible first in the two defeated states, Hungary and Bulgaria. From 1920 until almost the end of the Second World War, Admiral Horthy presided over a backward-looking, conservative political system in Hungary that paid only the faintest of lip-service to liberal principles. Although the White terror was terminated and Hungary remained a *Rechtsstaat*, the rule of law was often limited by arbitrary bureaucratic and police practices. The franchise was restricted to 27 per cent of the adult population, a return to the electoral law of 1913. Except in towns possessing municipal charters, the vote was exercised in public rather than by secret ballot. The landowning aristocracy controlled most of the levers of power. The Communist Party was banned and the Social Democrats were subjected to various restrictions. Parliament exercised little influence. The dominant political figure of the 1920s, Count István Bethlen, a Transylvanian nobleman who had lost his ancestral estates in what was now Romania, succeeded in restoring a measure of social peace and in restabilizing the currency after a catastrophic hyperinflation; but his long-term goal of revising the Treaty of Trianon precluded any possibility of harmonious relations with Hungary's Little Entente neighbours.

If Hungary at least could boast a measure of internal peace after the upheavals of the immediate post-war period, Bulgaria descended into a maelstrom of political violence. In 1923 the Prime Minister, Alexandŭr Stamboliiski, a popular peasant leader, was assassinated in a militarist *coup d'état* that enjoyed at least the tacit approval of King Boris. The dead premier's ears and hands were cut off and his head removed to Sofia in a tin box. In 1925 extremist elements in the Communist Party bombed Sofia cathedral, killing 128 worshippers and precipitating a bloody right-wing backlash in which thousands of left-leaning elements, among them many intellectuals, perished. For much of the period the Internal Macedonian Revolutionary Organization (IMRO), a congerie of bandits, ultra-nationalists and anarchists, engaged in murderous attacks that embroiled Bulgaria in disputes with Greece and Yugoslavia.

In the successor states, Poland led the way in the descent to authoritarianism. Polish politics throughout the inter-war period was dominated by conflict between the supporters of Piłsudski and those of Roman Dmowski. Piłsudski, a fierce anti-Russian, was more a nationalist than a democrat; although he had initially been a Socialist, his socialism withered away in later years. He enjoyed support particularly in the army and his movement degenerated in later years into authoritarian militarism. Dmowski, a fierce anti-German, had started out as an advocate of Polish autonomy within the Russian Empire rather than of independence; but his National Democrat or 'Endek' movement was disfigured by a xenophobic and anti-Semitic streak and he developed into as much of a nationalist as his rival and hardly more of a democrat. The minorities question contributed to the extreme party fragmentation that characterized Polish politics, though this has also been explained as the result of oppositionist attitudes formed before 1914 by Polish politicians in all three partitions. To overcome the bias against small parties in the voting system, the Ukrainian, White Russian, German, and Jewish parties often formed electoral pacts, as did other groups. In 1925 no fewer than thirty-two parties were represented in the Sejm (lower house of parliament). All Polish governments between the wars depended on parliamentary coalitions. In May 1926 Piłsudski seized power in a *coup d'état*, with military support. He remained, in effect, the ruler of Poland until his death in 1935, although for much of the period his only official title was Minister of War. A façade of parliamentary government was maintained, but for the rest of the life of the second Polish republic the army was the ultimate repository of power. The Polish example was followed in December 1926 by Lithuania, where a military revolt dislodged the constitutional government and installed an extreme-right regime.

One country succeeded in the 1920s in reinventing herself and carrying through a transformative social and cultural revolution. This was Turkey, which under the leadership of Mustafa Kemal made a decisive transition away from her imperial past. After the Treaty of Lausanne and the completion of the population exchange with Greece, Turkey set about turning herself into a secular, national state. The institutions of the old empire were replaced and thoroughly overhauled. Turkey was declared a republic. The Sultanate and the Caliphate were abolished. The capital was relocated from Constantinople to Ankara in Asia Minor—in principle, even if not geographically, a move towards, not away from, Europe. Islam ceased to be the official religion; Islamic courts and other religious institutions lost most of their power. The western calendar and day of rest were introduced. The Swiss civil code was adopted, with some variations, as the law of the land. New, western-style commercial and criminal codes followed. The Latin script replaced the Arabic in the written language, thus within a generation cutting off nearly all Turks from access to books in Turkish printed before the war. The fez was banned and men were advised to wear wide-brimmed Homburgs or Panamas. Women showed greater reluctance to abandon the veil. On the other hand, women were granted full equality and many middle-class urban women embraced secondary and higher education as well as European fashions. All Turks were obliged by law to adopt a surname; Mustafa Kemal himself became Kemal Atatürk ('Father Turk'). The Turkish republic was a 'guided democracy' rather than a liberal polity. The army retained considerable power as the ultimate political arbiter. The Atatürk revolution encountered resistance from traditionalists and was accomplished only at the expense of some interference with civil liberties, including limitation of freedom of expression, bloody suppression of Kurdish uprisings, and, in a few cases, execution of opponents by public hanging. But compared with all the other European revolutions of the first half of the century, such excesses were few. Atatürk took care at an early stage to maintain neighbourly relations with Soviet Russia and he made it an axiom of Turkey's foreign policy that she would not seek to regain non-Turkish territories formerly ruled by the Ottomans. Internally and externally, therefore, this was a relatively peaceful revolution. The contrast with another would-be revolution-from-above was both instructive and painful.

Fascism

The capture of power by Fascism in Italy in 1922 prefigured the collapse of democracy in most of southern, central, and eastern Europe in the inter-war period and arose from similar causes: economic dislocation; an extreme law-and-order reaction to left-wing revolutionary activity; wartime wrenching apart of social bonds; and post-war disgruntlement with the sour fruits of peace. Italy, moreover, like many of the successor states, was an imperfectly nationalized polity whose political institutions had never struck firm roots. Apart from the small German and Slovene minorities acquired at the peace, Italy was one of the most nationally homogenous states in Europe. But she was also one of the most deeply riven by regionalism and localism. The *Risorgimento* ideals of Mazzini and Garibaldi were widely felt to have degenerated into corruption and ineffectiveness.

Like other countries Italy suffered from the difficulties of economic adjustment to peace. The middle classes were shaken by inflation: the lira lost two-thirds of its value between March 1919 and December 1920. Widespread industrial unrest, factory occupations and syndicalist riots and revolts in northern Italy in 1919–20 alarmed the forces of order. The Liberal political establishment, now represented by Giovanni Giolitti, a Piedmontese, had dominated Italian politics since unification. The old Liberal strategy of *trasformismo* (originally a term for coalition-building) came to be seen as cynical manoeuvring and wire-pulling. In the elections of 1919 and 1921 the Liberals lost votes to Socialists and the *Popolari*, a new Catholic party led by a priest, Luigi Sturzo. The Fascists too entered parliament for the first time, though with only thirty-five seats. One weak coalition government after another was formed and collapsed. A general despair with the parliamentary system set in, paving the way for a demagogue who promised easy solutions. All sections of the Italian political spectrum shared some responsibility for creating the conditions that permitted Mussolini's capture of power. All paid bitterly for its consequence—more than two decades of arbitrary, erratic, and often brutal despotism.

The son of a village blacksmith, Benito Mussolini was a former Socialist journalist who had become a violent proponent of war against Austria. A boor, a brute, an exhibitionist, and at times a buffoon, Mussolini was an impulsive adventurer whose journalistic energy and oratorical gifts propelled him into nationalist politics. His motto was '*Vivere pericolosamente*' ('Live dangerously!'). He despised his own people—'a race of sheep'.[28] As for his political colleagues, they were 'all rotten to the core'.[29] Indeed, he felt contempt for humanity in general. He extolled a cult of violence, vaunted a posturing machismo, and boasted openly of having committed rape. 'Action', he maintained, was desirable for its own sake—'even when it is wrong'.[30] In his maiden speech as a member of the Chamber of Deputies, on 21 June 1921, Mussolini referred to what he called 'the civil war'. 'For us', he declared, 'violence is not a system, it is not a form of aesthetics, and even less is it a sport. It is a hard necessity to which we have had to submit.'[31]

How could such a mountebank gain power in a civilized country? By force: the Fascist seizure of power was a pseudo-constitutional *coup d'état*, in which the threat or promise of violence was used to attract support and cow opposition. By chicanery: Mussolini simultaneously intrigued with the respectable political parties and plotted their downfall. By theatricality: Fascism introduced a note of melodrama into political rhetoric and a thrilling excitement, akin to the blood lust of the hunt, into the political activity of its early adherents. By the abject submission of the political class: the left spouted revolutionary rhetoric but crumpled in the face of a real insurrection; the respectable right initially went along with Mussolini's brutal methods, thinking that he would restore order and then enable them to assume power.

As an expression of hyper-nationalist solipsism, Fascism could be traced back to some elements in the *Risorgimento* and to the wartime mood of *sacro egoismo*. Nationalist distress at the slim pickings left to Italy by the peacemakers, seen as a paltry reward for the country's immense wartime sacrifices, was inflamed by D'Annunzio's exploit at Fiume which seemed to provide an example of what could be achieved by the application of violent methods to political problems.

As a set of ideas Fascism was a primitive rationalization of gangsterism rather than a political philosophy in the conventional sense. It offered neither a coherent theory of society nor a consistent political programme. It represented no particular social class nor set of interest groups, except in so far as it volunteered as the vigilante defender of order against Socialist and syndicalist revolutionaries. On the other hand, it rejected liberal principles, parliamentarism, intellectual freedom, and the rule of law.

Yet Fascism was vastly appealing to many. It promised to cut through the hypocrisy of the Giolittian spoils system, to restore order to society and the economy, to recreate the glory of the Roman Empire. Old soldiers were attracted by its talk of discipline, young men by the opportunities for licensed hooliganism, by the hyperbole of Fascist propaganda, and by the spirit of dynamism that seemed to infuse the movement.

The first *Fasci* (literally, 'bundles', recalling the ancient Roman *fasces*: a bundle of rods bound up with an axe in the middle, carried by lictors as an emblem of authority) had been organized during the war as groups of vehemently bellicose nationalists. After the war they and the *Arditi* (literally 'daring'—shock-troops) recruited ex-servicemen and students, similar in outlook to the German *Freikorps*. In March 1919 Mussolini called a national congress of *Fasci di Combattimento* at Milan. Only a few dozen people attended. Early Fascist policy proposals included several radical-sounding elements: capital taxes, a universal eight-hour day, expropriation of church properties, a minimum wage, and workers' participation in industrial management. But by November 1921 such Socialistic ideas had given way to an emphasis on nationalism. The call for expropriation of clerical properties disappeared. The principles of the 'so-called League of Nations' were rejected and Italy's role 'as a bulwark of Latin civilization in the Mediterranean' was affirmed.[32] A Fascist agrarian programme drawn up in 1921 rejected the distribution of land to peasants and called instead for the reorganization of large estates into efficient economic units.

More important than what Fascists said was what they did. As the country drifted into incipient civil war in 1920 and 1921, *squadristi* of young Fascist thugs, particularly in the Po Valley, Tuscany, Umbria, and Apulia, beat up Socialists and clericalists, closed down meetings of opponents, broke strikes, and intimidated officials. Their claim that they were merely restoring social order convinced many elements in the police and the army. As they attracted attention by such exploits, the Fascists quickly grew from a fringe movement into a national political force.

In October 1922, Fascists seized a number of provincial towns and Mussolini dared his opponents to suppress the movement by force or appoint him Prime Minister. Liberal politicians and King Vittorio Emmanuele III floundered, proclaimed and then withdrew a state of siege, and finally gave in. The so-called 'March on Rome' was a typical piece of Fascist myth-making: the *Duce* and most of his supporters arrived by train (see Plate 12). There was little fighting: the mere threat of force proved enough to frighten the state machine into submission. Mussolini formed a coalition government that included *Popolari*, some Liberals, and nationalists, as well as Fascists. He arrogated to himself the positions of Prime Minister, Foreign Minister, and Interior Minister. Wearing the blackshirt of his movement, he was invested with office by the king to whom he allegedly declared: 'Majesty, I come from the battlefield—fortunately bloodless.'[33]

In his first speech to the Chamber as Prime Minister, on 16 November, Mussolini demanded full powers. His party still held only a tiny minority of seats: yet he won a vote of confidence by 306 to 116, with only the Socialists and Communists voting solidly against him. He soon set about transforming the liberal state into a dictatorship. In 1923 a new electoral law stated that the party with the largest number of votes, provided it won more than 25 per cent, would hold two-thirds of the seats in the Chamber. In a general election in April 1924, intimidation and official pressure assured the Fascists' victory. Many Liberal leaders still backed Mussolini and even Benedetto Croce, Italy's most respected liberal thinker, urged support for the Fascists. 'Mussolini is now our prisoner,' he said by way of justification.[34] He soon rued this epic misjudgement. Henceforth Parliament became a rubber stamp.

A few weeks after the election, the Socialist leader, Giacomo Matteotti, was seized in Rome by a Fascist gang and killed. Mussolini was accused of complicity. Opposition deputies withdrew from the Chamber in protest and set themselves up on the Aventine Hill, the ancient *ager publicus* of the *plebs*. But the 'Aventine secession' merely sealed the fate of the parliamentary system. On 3 January 1925, in what was, even for him, an extraordinarily shameless speech, Mussolini told those deputies who remained: 'I now declare before this assembly and before the entire Italian people that I assume, I alone, full political, moral, and historical responsibility for all that has happened.'[35] The assassination was a turning-point in the history of Fascism. After this there could be no turning back. In October 1925 the Socialist Party was banned. Four attempts to assassinate Mussolini in 1925–6 provided a pretext for suppressing all remaining opposition parties. Such opposition as remained was seduced, repressed, neutered, or pushed into internal or foreign exile. The Liberal Francesco Nitti, the Communist Palmiro Togliatti, and the Socialist Pietro Nenni fled abroad. Don Sturzo was ordered to leave the country by the Vatican. The *fuoriusciti* (exiles) were joined by some anti-Fascist intellectuals, notably the conductor Arturo Toscanini (who had sympathized with Fascism in the early 1920s but became an implacable opponent), the physicist Enrico Fermi, the historian Gaetano Salvemini, and his pupils Carlo and Nello Rosselli. The Rosselli brothers founded the anti-Fascist group *Giustizia e Libertà*. Both were later murdered by French right-wing extremists. Most of the country's university professors, journalists, and writers, however, accommodated themselves one way or another to the new dispensation. In November 1926 leading Communists, headed by Antonio Gramsci, were arrested. He spent the remaining eleven years of his life in prison (later in a clinic under guard), writing his famous *Lettere del carcere*.

Italy was now a one-party dictatorship. Mussolini consolidated his internal hold over the Fascist Party, sidelining dangerous rivals such as Italo Balbo. The Mafia was squared, then broken. Police powers were expanded to provide for arbitrary powers of arrest, search, and deportation. Freemasonry, which Mussolini particularly detested, was outlawed. By 1925 Fascists effectively controlled the whole of the Italian press, though the Socialist and Communist papers maintained a shadow existence in censored form until 1926. The liberal editor of the *Corriere della Sera*, Luigi Albertini, who had come to regret his early support for Mussolini, was edged out.

School curricula were revised to include Fascist indoctrination. History school books gloried in the new order: 'The Fascist state is, therefore, *totalitarian*, because it seeks to permeate the entire nation. From which comes the Mussolinian dictum: "Everything for the state, nothing beyond the state, nothing against the state".'[36]

In place of the discredited institutions of the liberal state, Mussolini invented new bodies: a Fascist Grand Council, designed to act as a bridge between party and government; a Militia, formed out of the *squadristi*, and a 'Special Tribunal for the Defence of the State' to try political opponents. Local party chiefs or *ras* (a word borrowed from Ethiopia), such as Carlo Scorza in Lucca or Roberto Farinacci in Cremona, aggregated enough power to develop into petty local despots. The *Dopolavoro* ('after-work') organization sought to organize and regiment Italians' leisure activities. Much was made of the supposed efficiency of this new, allegedly totalitarian state. But by and large Mussolini governed through the existing civil service and state institutions, sometimes, as in the case of OVRA, the secret police, adapted to his special purposes. And apart from the minor inconvenience of the absence of political freedom, to which many Italians did not attach a primary value at any rate in the form it had taken in Liberal Italy, day-to-day life for most people did not change radically—at first.

Fascist economic policy was a rag-bag of protectionist, étatist, and neo-liberal ideas that lacked much coherence or substance. Mussolini insisted that agriculture took precedence over all other branches of the economy: in 1925 a tariff was introduced on imported grain and a 'battle of wheat' was declared. Prices went up and so did production. But agricultural rents also rose so that most peasants, who in any case consumed most of such wheat as they grew, were further impoverished. Moreover, in order to meet Mussolini's grandiose production targets, unsuitable land was often diverted to wheat from cultivation of other more productive crops. Ambitious land reclamation schemes were launched with fanfares of publicity. Some, such as the draining of the Pontine marshes, were successful; most belonged to the realm of propaganda rather than economics. In 1927 the lira was returned to the gold standard: mainly for reasons of prestige, its value was set at a grossly over-valued rate. The *quota novanta* (the rate of 90 lire to the pound) harmed Italian export trade, increased unemployment, and accelerated the tendency towards the policy of 'autarky' pursued in the 1930s. The left-wing labour unions were replaced with ones wholly controlled by the Fascists. Strikes were made illegal. A 'corporativist structure', uniting capital and labour, was supposed to manage the economy and was trumpeted as a great Fascist achievement, amounting to the abolition of class conflict. But behind the façade of the 'corporations' the capitalist structure of industry remained intact, reinforced by harsh labour discipline.

Mussolini's foreign policy was noisy, aggressive, bombastic, and showy but often sacrificed real interests to the pursuit of empty propaganda victories. In September 1923 he seized on the pretext of the murder of an Italian general to dispatch Italian troops to occupy Corfu; they withdrew only after Greece agreed to pay an indemnity. (Greece got the message: she in turn defied international pressure to hand back fourteen border villages that she had taken from Albania.) In 1924 the Italians, breaking their treaty obligations, annexed Fiume. As compensation, Yugoslavia received most of the city's hinterland. But in spite of heavy Italian subsidies and lucrative smuggling rackets, prosperity was slow to return to the former Hungarian port. In February 1929 Mussolini secured his greatest diplomatic achievement: the signature of the Lateran Pact between the Vatican and the Kingdom of Italy marked for the first time the mutual recognition of the two states; the 'Roman question', which had dogged relations between the two since 1871, was at last resolved. Catholics were reconciled to the regime. Pope Pius XI called Mussolini 'the man of Providence'.[37] In the late 1920s Mussolini pursued a policy of alignment with the would-be revisionist states, Hungary, Austria, and Bulgaria, as against the Little Entente. The returns were nugatory. It was not until the next decade that Mussolini discovered a powerful ally, cast in his own image, who first saved his regime, then brought it, and much of Europe, crashing to disaster.

5

Depression and Terror 1929–1936

This happened when only the dead wore smiles
They rejoiced at being safe from harm.
And Leningrad dangled from its jails
Like some unnecessary arm.

*Anna Akhmatova, Leningrad, 1935**

Slump

The stock-exchange crash on Wall Street in October 1929 inaugurated the worst international depression of all time, from which Europe suffered not only economic but also long-term political and social consequences. The American origins of the crisis reflected the changed economic geography of the world after the First World War. Not only had the United States replaced Britain as the world's financial centre but American production of manufactured goods in the late 1920s exceeded that of the whole of Europe put together. The USA also led the world in the application of new technologies and management methods to many areas of industry. Although European economies suffered to different degrees and at different stages, the Depression is best understood as a crisis of the world capitalist system as a whole.

While the Wall Street crash was the clearest starting-point of the slump, it was not the primary cause of the catastrophe. There was, in fact, no single cause. Several have been proposed. Among these, the return to the gold

* From 'Requiem', translated from the Russian by Lynn Coffin. Anna Akhmatova, *Poems*, New York, 1983, 83–4.

standard by Britain and most other major industrial powers has been indicted as perhaps the chief culprit. Other elements in an explanation include: the agricultural depression that began before the Wall Street crash; the effects of the reparations/war debts crisis; changes in the composition of production, in particular, the decline of old industries and growth of new ones producing consumer durables that were peculiarly susceptible to cyclical fluctuations; structural unemployment in Britain and Germany during the 1920s; and weaknesses in the international monetary system and in the banking systems of Germany, Austria, and Hungary.

The initial stages of recession might to some degree be explained as an adjustment to a speculative boom, the decline in economic activity as a natural downturn of the business cycle. But the pervasive effects of the slump in international trade, industrial production, commodity prices, and employment require some deeper structural explanation. The fragile recovery of the 1920s had not repaired the profound damage caused to the international financial system by the Great War. The withdrawal of American capital flows to Europe, first because of the investment bubble at home in 1928–9, then because of the crash, exposed the vulnerability of the circulatory pattern of capital movement that had evolved between Europe and the United States. Suddenly bereft of American funds, and finding no alternative source, Germany could no longer pay reparations nor finance her budget deficit, which was heavily dependent on short-term loans. As a result of the German default in reparations payments, Britain and France could no longer pay their debts. The Young Plan eased Germany's obligations somewhat but provided no fundamental solution.

Economic contraction in Germany was more severe than in any other major economy. At the lowest point of the Depression, in 1932, industrial production was only 61 per cent of its 1929 level. More than six million people were registered as unemployed, a third of the workforce. Since not all those out of work were registered, the real rate was even higher. Economists (and, retrospectively, some economic historians) criticized the large-scale borrowing by German governments in the 1920s, both national and local, as well as the allegedly over-generous welfare provisions of the Weimar Republic. These, it was suggested, were the primary cause of the collapse of Germany's credit. It is true that the German Parliament had, in 1927, enacted an unemployment insurance law that, as it turned out, was inadequately funded: but no reasonable person could have foreseen or should reasonably have been expected to plan for the bottomless pit of unemployment into which Germany collapsed three years later. The resultant government deficits were not, in fact, very large; but taken together with the reparations problem and the recent memory of hyperinflation, they severely damaged financial confidence and deterred foreign investors.

Heinrich Brüning, a member of the Catholic Centre Party who served as Chancellor from March 1930, pursued a savage deflationary policy. His minority government, 'a Cabinet not bound to parties', depended for its existence on the support of the President. Using emergency decree powers sanctioned by Hindenburg, Brüning raised taxes and introduced drastic cuts in government expenditure. Compulsory contributions to the unemployment insurance fund were increased and benefits were lowered. The result was to reduce economic activity and drive unemployment figures even higher without reassuring financial markets. During the first seven months of 1931 the Reichsbank lost nine tenths of its disposable gold reserves. The insolvency in May of the Creditanstalt, the largest commercial bank in Austria, brought the financial crisis to a head. Although the collapse of the bank was staved off, the news led to a general run on banks in central Europe, particularly in Germany. Meanwhile, in the teeth of French opposition, the German Cabinet daringly adopted the long-mooted idea of a customs union with Austria. Fearing such a union as a first step towards political unification of the two countries, prohibited under the peace treaties, the French refused new credits to Germany and Austria. Brüning visited Paris and London to plead for support: the British were sympathetic but said they had troubles of their own; the French granted a $100 million credit for the Reichsbank—too little, too late.

As the financial crisis deepened, President Hoover, on 20 June, announced a year's moratorium on reparations and war debts. Although it reduced Germany's immediate outgoings, the moratorium failed to restore market confidence. On 13 July a major German bank failed and all German banks closed for three days. When they reopened, the Reichsbank imposed strict foreign-exchange controls and put up interest rates. Foreign-owned assets were frozen and Germans were forbidden to withdraw more than a small amount from their bank accounts. Foreign travel was restricted and other measures were taken to staunch the flight of capital. Germany remained nominally committed to the gold standard but with a currency that was no longer freely convertible and tightening restrictions on the movement of capital and goods.

The financial contagion now moved to Britain where MacDonald's second Labour government, elected in 1929, was struggling unsuccessfully to stem a rising tide of unemployment. It hesitated to resort to full-fledged Socialistic measures both because of the moderation of most of its ministers and out of concern lest it lose the support of the Liberals on whom it again depended for a parliamentary majority. As economic activity continued to decline, pressure on the pound grew. In late July a committee of experts under Sir George May recommended cuts in public spending, including a reduction in the unemployment benefit, the 'dole'. This hit the Labour government at its most sensitive point and the Cabinet split on the issue. When the Bank of England sought new loans, international bankers set compliance with the May recommendations as a condition. Socialists complained of a 'bankers' ramp'. King George V, unusually for a constitutional monarch, took the initiative and discussed proposals for a 'National Emergency Government'. In late August MacDonald formed such an administration, with Conservative and Liberal support but without most of his own party, who crossed to the opposition benches in the House of Commons.

The ostensible purpose of the National Government was to defend the sterling parity with gold through a short crisis period. In the event, MacDonald failed to prevent devaluation, which was forced on the government in September by a renewed run on sterling. The decision was taken by a group of senior ministers and civil servants in a meeting with Bank of England officials; the Cabinet was not consulted. 'Nobody told us we could do this,' was the reported reaction of one astounded former Labour minister.[1] Keynes rejoiced 'at the breaking of our gold fetters'.[2] Sterling depreciated by 30 per cent against gold-backed currencies by December. Britain's retreat from gold, soon followed by other countries in the so-called sterling bloc (the Scandinavian countries, Portugal, Yugoslavia, Greece, most members of the British Commonwealth, and some other non-European states), heightened the division of the world into currency blocs and also the tendency towards trade protectionism everywhere.

Those countries, headed by France, that still adhered to the gold standard were next to experience pressure. France initially weathered the storm a little better than others. From the late 1920s she had built up a huge hoard of gold, thus protecting the value of the currency but inhibiting capital investment in industry. 'We shall cling to it [gold] as we did to Verdun,' said Pierre-Etienne Flandin, the French Finance Minister.[3] Given the human cost of the defence of the fortress, it was, to say the least, an unfortunate analogy. Following Britain's devaluation, France sought to protect herself by raising tariffs on British imports. The other members of what became the 'gold bloc', including Italy, the Low Countries, and Switzerland, followed suit. The creeping protectionism of the 1920s (even Britain, though nominally wedded to free trade, had imposed low duties on some imports between 1915 and 1930) now gave way to the erection of high tariff walls by all countries. In 1932, at a conference at Ottawa, the British government announced its conversion to a system of 'imperial preference'. Britain was the last major trading country to abandon free trade. The average incidence of import duties in Europe was now about 50 per cent *ad valorem*. The intention was to revive internal economies: the actual effect was further to depress international trade.

Meanwhile reparations and war debts had both expired. When the Hoover moratorium ended in June 1932, the French stopped paying. The British continued for a while—but in depreciated silver. An international conference convened at Lausanne in the summer of 1932 in the hope of agreeing on a settlement of reparations and war debts. The conference approved a final lump sum reparations payment by Germany of £150 million. 'No more reparations! They have gone! . . . They have been an affliction on all nations,' MacDonald declared at the final conference session.[4] The Lausanne agreement, however, was supposed to be dependent on American readiness to cancel war debts. Facing its highest peacetime federal government deficit thus far in history, the United States would not forgo payment. The British and French governments both defaulted on their American debts, whereupon the US Congress in January 1934 passed a law prohibiting new loans to any countries in default (twelve European ones were on the list).

As the financial crisis spread like a plague between 1929 and 1932, economic activity declined sharply. The overall GDP of European countries fell by at least 10 per cent. Industrial production in Europe declined in value to 72 per cent of its 1929 level. Industrial raw materials prices in 1932 were 44 per cent of their 1929 levels.

Throughout industrialized Europe, the effects of the Depression were disproportionately concentrated in certain countries, regions, and economic sectors. In the period 1929–32, Germany, Austria, Poland, and the Low Countries all suffered declines in industrial output of more than one-third, whereas in Sweden the reduction was only 11 per cent and in Britain 17 per cent. In Britain, however, the old, declining industries of the north, coal, iron and steel, shipbuilding, and cotton manufacturing, were disproportionately affected: unemployment in north-east England and Scotland reached 28 per cent in 1932—double the rate in London and the south-east. The shrinking world market for luxury goods hit some industries and regions particularly hard blows. One example was the silk industry in France and Italy, already hurt by changing public tastes, competition from China and Japan, and the development of new, artificial fibres. Italian silk production in 1934 was 45 per cent lower than before the First World War. All stages of the industry were affected, from sericulture to the manufacture of silk piece-goods. The price of raw 'classical' silk on the Milan exchange fell by 57 per cent between 1927 and 1930. In Lyons the export of silk goods fell by 80 per cent between 1929 and 1937 and sales to the French market also decreased substantially.

In Switzerland the silk ribbon industry in the canton of Basel was dealt a death-blow from which it never recovered. The embroidery industry in St Gallen, which had employed half of all the workers in the canton in 1905, went into precipitous decline:

> In the middle of the 1930s, St Gallen had become like a ghost town. The pompous office blocks in *Jugendstil* which had housed firms with English names like 'Atlantic,' 'Union' and 'Worldwide' were empty. The misery in the countryside was unimaginable. The tens of thousands of smallholders who had adapted their lives to the outwork system of the embroidery industry were destitute. The fragility of the Swiss economy had never been more evident: an entire region ruined by a change in fashion.[5]

On the other hand, the Swiss watchmaking industry, at first seriously affected by US tariffs, staged an impressive revival. Swiss exports declined from 20.8 million watches and watch movements in 1929 to 8.2 million in 1932. Then the Swiss government intervened and created a strong cartel of Swiss producers. By 1937 exports had recovered to 23.9 million units (and these were merely the official figures—according to David Landes, 'high duties made contraband flourish like the psalmist's green bay tree').[6]

In eastern Europe the Depression reversed the limited industrial growth that had taken place in the late 1920s. Industry was starved of new investment. Internal and export markets dried up. On the agrarian sector of these still mainly pre-industrial economies the Depression had a catastrophic effect. In the late 1920s productivity gains in North America, particularly through mechanization, had led to overproduction of wheat, sugar, and other crops. As a result, prices of all major agricultural products had already been falling before 1929; after the Wall Street crash they collapsed. In the period 1929–30, the average price of wool fell by 46 per cent, of wheat by 19 per cent. Prices of manufactured goods declined less sharply, with the result that peasants were again caught in 'price scissors' that greatly reduced their purchasing power. They could not afford to buy chemical fertilizers, let alone mechanize their farms. As a League of Nations report put it in 1931:

> The complaints of the farmers are heard in almost every country.... It is not merely a question of bad harvests caused by natural or atmospheric disorders, such as continuous rain or drought. The evil is deep-rooted and its progress may be traced throughout the world.... The general character of the price movement completely changed in 1930. A fall, sometimes catastrophic, spread with extreme violence to almost all agricultural produce.... Modern economic history gives few instances of such a decline.[7]

In Hungary, for example, total agricultural production was 3 per cent higher in terms of volume in 1932 than in 1923; but measured by value, there had been a decline of 50 per cent. The price of some crops fell to such an extent that production became uneconomic: in Yugoslavia the area devoted to hop production was reduced by one-third in 1929 but half of the crop from that limited area was not harvested and left to rot.

In many parts of eastern Europe peasant proprietors were forced to sell their land, with the consequence, in some cases, that the redistributive effects of land reform were annulled. Meat vanished altogether from poor peasants' diet. Eggs were sold, not eaten. Sugar was regarded as a luxury. In 1935 the Polish Institute of Social Economy published *Peasant Memoirs*, descriptions of daily life that illustrate the effects of the slump. A typical case came from a village near Tarnopol in Galicia:

> The floors in the stables and pigsties are ruined and the farmer cannot afford to repair them.... The hut is made of mud and has no floor; stench and moisture are constant. The stables are no better and the barns often have no walls. The dog has no shelter and we pity him. Before we had a latrine made of planks; now it is made of straw because the planks were used to make a table for the hut, and then the table was used to make doors for the pigsty, and the pig finally put its tusks [*sic*] through it.... One bucket for the whole household and landholding. This bucket serves to carry water to the kitchen, to feed the horse, the cow and the pig, to draw water from the well. The wagon and the plough are rotting in the rain for there is no shelter for them and one cannot build for lack of means. The food for the pigs is cooked in pots that we use for ourselves. And the housewife, poor thing, is dissatisfied and complains.[8]

Given such conditions it is hardly surprising that in Poland rural disturbances became endemic in the late 1930.

The response of all countries to the Depression illustrated the inefficacy of international economic cooperation and the almost universal tendency to resort to beggar-my-neighbour policies that inhibited a general recovery. One after another, currencies were devalued in the hope of undercutting competitors in export markets, whereupon tariffs were raised in order to protect home industries from 'dumping'. Exports to the United States of European luxury goods collapsed, especially after the enactment of the Smoot–Hawley tariff in June 1930. International trade was throttled. Altogether, between 1929 and 1932, it declined by no less than 60 per cent.

The international institutions created after the Great War were ill-equipped to come to grips with the crisis. An International Economic Organization had been formed under the auspices of the League of Nations following a conference in Brussels in 1920. Further international economic conferences gathered in Genoa in 1922 and Geneva in 1927: these criticized economic nationalism and called for reductions in tariffs. But as a later study of the League's economic activities put it, 'While the governments of the world recognized the dangers of the movement towards increased economic isolation, they felt unable to pay the price required to arrest it.'[9] A Bank for International Settlements, with headquarters at Basel, had been founded in 1929–30 as a successor to the Reparation Commission, but its functions were initially restricted to technical operations concerning reparations and it played no effective role in international support for beleaguered currencies.

In June 1933 a further International Monetary and Economic Conference opened at the Geological Museum in London. A preparatory commission of experts had called for a programme that included general reflation by means of low interest rates, currency stabilization, and eventual abolition of exchange controls, and a truce in the tariff wars. But two months earlier the newly elected President of the United States, F. D. Roosevelt, had taken the dollar off the gold standard. The US currency took some time to stabilize at a lower level. In the meantime the new administration tried to persuade the British to agree to tariff reductions in return for US concessions on war debts. No such bargain was reached and as a result the conference failed to agree on anything else of significance. Internationalist central bankers continued to try to cooperate but almost everywhere internal political considerations were now paramount.

In Britain a prophet came forth who was retrospectively judged to have discovered a means of moderating the savage gyrations of the economic cycle. Keynes provided the theoretical framework for a rejection of the neoclassical economics that guided the policies of most governments until after the Depression. In addition to the traditional method of monetary controls, he advocated the deployment of new weapons, most notably fiscal policy which, he maintained, should be driven not merely by the requirements of government revenue but by the objective of managing demand. In bad times, he argued, the state should promote public works and deliberately pursue deficit budgeting in order to stimulate aggregate demand. Keynes's *General Theory* was not published until 1936, although some of its ideas had circulated earlier and had sprung to the attention of a few politicians. In the 1929 general election, Lloyd George, claiming 'We Can Conquer Unemployment', embraced many of the pump-priming proposals advocated by Keynes. But this last great Liberal push failed. The only minister in the second Labour government who urged adoption of Keynesian measures was the Chancellor of the Duchy of Lancaster (i.e. minister without portfolio), Sir Oswald Mosley. When his ideas failed to win approval he left the government and the Labour movement, first forming a 'New Party', then heading down the cul-de-sac of British Fascism. Although Keynes's doctrines gradually made converts, a decade was to pass before they were to be reflected consciously in government policy-making. For the time being, *laissez-faire* prevailed. Nowhere were the political consequences more monstrous than in Germany.

Hitler

Son of a minor Austrian customs officer, former resident of a dosshouse in Vienna, a man of little education, poor work habits, lack of any sense of proportion or limits, total self-centredness, and apparent inability to forge normal human relationships, Adolf Hitler possessed neither the curriculum vitae nor the personal qualities that in normal times propel men to leadership. His dominant characteristic was the advocacy of force as an instrument of both internal politics and external expansion. This abnormal figure was a product of times profoundly out of joint. His emergence was possible only against the background of the brutalization of the First World War and its aftermath and the further dislocation of values during the Depression. His chief personal assets were supreme self-assurance, demagogic oratorical gifts of the first order, a crafty ability to balance potential rivals and to take advantage of other men's weaknesses, and a capacity to win the loyalty of subordinates and to enthuse millions with quasi-messianic faith and hope.

Hitler was not a politician in the conventional sense: he had little time for policies, position papers, or the routine business of party leadership or government responsibility. Like Mussolini, he was less interested in platforms than in propaganda. His movement was a revolt of the gutter, of losers who felt that, through no fault of their own, they had been thrown aside by respectable society and were determined to rise up and wreak their revenge. Apart from ill-defined dreams of racial domination, Hitler's politics were inspired by no social vision. On the contrary, underlying his thought and actions was a barely hidden sociopathy: 'What is stable', he said, 'is emotion, hatred.'[10] Hitler claimed to offer the German people a restoration of their national self-respect. As a public speaker his rasping screech was perfectly attuned to the psychology of masses of defeated individuals who felt betrayed by selfish elites and conventional values which they held responsible for inflicting successive disasters on them. War, revolution, inflation, and now depression had knocked the stuffing out of millions of individuals who sought salvation by submergence in the mass. Nazism gave a sense of community to lost souls who felt thwarted, frustrated, and abandoned. It provided a sense of common purpose to the many ordinary Germans who vaguely believed that decency and honour meant subsuming selfish individualism within a larger cause. It held aloft a visionary ideal to a people who had lost their moral bearings. It was an angry creed but it contained a promise of great joy—and for a while it brought many Germans happiness. Nazism could not have triumphed and survived in power for twelve years if it had not served these vital psychosocial needs.

For Hitler, as for so many of his generation, the formative episode in his life was service in the Great War. His views and attitudes were characteristic of those of embittered ex-servicemen of the *Freikorps*, who formed the nucleus of membership of his National Socialist Party, formed in 1920. The SA (*Sturmabteilung*) brownshirts, headed by Ernst Röhm, and the SS (*Schutzstaffel*), under the command of Heinrich Himmler, were the shock troops of the movement. They were by no means unique in Weimar Germany, where several political parties organized such militias. But the

Nazis went out of their way to provoke confrontation as a means of gaining publicity, as a stimulus to their own ranks, and out of a fundamental belief in violence as a political tactic.

Hitler's first attempt to seize power, in November 1923, ended in embarrassing failure. Nineteen people were killed in the abortive 'beerhall putsch' in Munich. Hitler was tried and imprisoned for a year in a castle at Landsberg am Lech in Bavaria. In *Mein Kampf*, the long-winded ranting, ideological tract that he began while in prison, he expounded his primitive doctrine. This did not differ significantly from the extreme nationalism that had been the common coin of *völkisch* propagandists for a generation. The myth of the *Dolchstoss*, rejection of 'war guilt', resentment of reparations, racial anti-Semitism, contempt for parliamentarism, hatred of communism, and demands for *Lebensraum* in Europe and colonies overseas—all this was unoriginal and far from unique to Hitler. In various degrees these ingredients formed part of the general world-view of large parts of the German right. What Hitler added was a readiness to jettison the *Rechtsstaat* and a willingness to use violence to push each of these objectives to its uttermost limit—and then not know where to stop.

The Nazis' support was not concentrated in any one social group. There were significant class, regional, and religious variations. The sections of society most resistant to the appeal of the Nazis were, on the one hand, the old landowning aristocracy and the Prussian officer class, and on the other the employed working class. Protestants were more supportive than Catholics, the countryside more than towns, and at first men more than women (though later that changed). Nazi supporters were disproportionately represented among white-collar workers, the lower-middle classes generally, shopkeepers, craftsmen whose skills were being rendered obsolete by industrialism, university students, and small farmers.

It used to be suggested, particularly by Marxist historians, that Hitler owed his ascent to power to the support given him by 'big business'. This, however, has been shown to be a myth.[11] True, the Nazis enjoyed some support from business leaders. So did most parties except the Communists. Businessmen saw such financial backing as a kind of insurance policy. But business leaders in general evinced no special attraction to Nazism and business support was not the main explanation for Hitler's rise to power, except perhaps in the negative sense that businessmen did little to give succour to the parliamentary regime, in which few of them placed much faith.

Can Hitler's ascent be attributed to the intervention of the military in politics? In the final years of the Weimar Republic the behind-the-scenes military influence of the *Reichswehr*, already strong, greatly increased. Hindenburg's invitation to Brüning to form a government in March 1930 owed much to military pressure. The general outlook and political sympathies of the officer class were certainly close to the nationalist right: organizations such as the *Stahlhelm* were seen as upholders of order and as worthy of cooperation, whereas the republican *Reichsbanner* was regarded with suspicion. As civilian politicians flailed and floundered under the impact of the Depression, the inclination towards the man on horseback grew. Yet in the end it was the army's reluctance to intervene in politics to *prevent* Hitler's assumption of power that administered the final blow to the Weimar regime.

Was the Weimar Republic betrayed by a failure on the part of its adherents to defend it with sufficient vigour? The ineradicable divisions among the liberals and the left undoubtedly weakened their capacity to resist. The Communists conducted a fierce campaign against the Social Democrats, whom, in accordance with instructions from the Comintern after 1928, they labelled 'social fascists'. Communists were happy to engage Nazis in street fighting, though whether the parliamentary system was most usefully defended in such brawls is questionable. Some intellectuals spoke out. The greatest German writer of the age called, in October 1930, for the bourgeoisie to join with the Social Democrats in defence of the values of Goethe and against the 'eccentric barbarity', 'epileptic ecstasy', and 'mass narcosis' of Nazism.[12] Thomas Mann was the most significant intellectual voice of the liberal elite. But that was in disarray and losing its grip on events.

None of these interpretations of Hitler's triumph bears close examination, though no doubt each was a contributory agent. In the final analysis, the central feature of any explanation must be the extreme and catastrophic effects of the Depression on the self-confidence and self-respect of the German middle class and on the day-to-day survival of the petty bourgeoisie and the urban and rural working classes. Hitler's *Machtergreifung* (seizure of power) was not a coup, like Lenin's in 1917, but rather, like Mussolini's advent in 1922, a knife-twist in the back of a liberal state that had already swallowed deadly poison.

Intelligent, upright, and determined as he was, Brüning was an uninspiring political leader, ill-equipped for the democratic age let alone for a democracy in terminal crisis. A monarchist at heart, he was a democrat more by circumstance than conviction. Yet he became the last defender of the republic. In July 1930, his invocation of emergency powers to pass his austerity programme was defeated in the Reichstag by the combined votes of the Social Democrats, Communists, Nazis, and right-wing nationalists. Brüning attempted to restore the authority of his minority government by an appeal to the people. It was one of the most disastrous miscalculations in the history of democracy. The Reichstag elections of September 1930 gave a sharp boost to extremism of both right and left. By this time the roll of registered unemployed had passed three million. Whatever economists might maintain, the unemployed found their situation intolerable and were increasingly driven to favour those who proposed easy solutions even at the expense of the parliamentary regime. The Communists were the chief direct beneficiaries of the votes of the unemployed: they advanced to 77 seats (13 per cent of the vote); but the Nazis benefited from the broader fears of other threatened social groups and made their crucial breakthrough, winning 107 seats (18 per cent). The Social Democrats remained the strongest party with 143 seats but the liberals and moderate right lost heavily. In Berlin electoral polarization was reflected in street fighting between rival Nazi and Communist militias.

Brüning remained Chancellor, supported in the Reichstag by the Social Democrats, but his authority had been weakened and foreign political and financial opinion was growing alarmed. In December 1931 further cuts were ordered in all wages, salaries, prices, rents, fares, and interest payments. But what was now required was stimulation not deflation. Brüning and his advisers, however, felt an overwhelming obligation to restore Germany's shattered credit. He also evidently hoped to use deflation as a means of securing an end to reparations. The 'hunger Chancellor' paid too little heed to the domestic social and political consequences of his *politique du pire*. The German economy was close to paralysis and millions were on the edge of starvation. In late 1931 the average unemployment benefit to a family man in Berlin was 51 marks a month. After rent and utilities, he would be left with 18.50 marks for food, which would force the family to survive on a diet of bread, potatoes, and cabbage with an occasional herring thrown in as a luxury. By the winter of 1932/3 the unemployment benefit had been reduced to 16 marks a month in large cities and less elsewhere. Nearly half of German working families were by this time dependent on some form of public assistance. Historians have argued about whether there was any serious alternative to Brüning's policies. He himself had no doubt that he had none. In January 1932 a group of Socialists, Wladimir Woytinsky, Fritz

Tarnow, and Fritz Baade, recommended an expansionary programme of public works. But their ideas were opposed by the Social Democrat former Finance Minister, Rudolf Hilferding, and the proposal was stillborn.

In the spring of 1932 the octogenarian Hindenburg's term of office as President came to an end. He was persuaded to stand for re-election against Hitler (who acquired German citizenship just in time to be eligible) and against a Communist, Ernst Thälmann. The result fell far short of a triumph for Hindenburg, who secured 53 per cent of the vote in the second round. The election marked a further advance for Hitler, who won 13.4 million votes (37 per cent). The Nazi leader won most of the votes of the right whereas Hindenburg was compelled to rely on the support of his former enemies, the Social Democrats, the Liberals, and the Centre Party, all of whom saw the aged symbol of German conservatism as the last remaining bulwark against Hitler. Hindenburg blamed Brüning for the fact that a corporal had secured more conservative votes than a field marshal. When the Chancellor, under pressure from the Social Democrats, on whose votes his government depended in the Reichstag, banned the Nazi SA militia, Hindenburg refused to authorize any more emergency decrees submitted by Brüning. Without the support of the President, the minority government could not survive.

On 29 May 1932 Hindenburg dismissed Brüning, telling him, 'At long last, I must go toward the right; the newspapers and the whole nation demand it.'[13] Brüning fell, as he put it, 'one hundred metres from the goal'.[14] At the Lausanne Conference in July, his policy at last bore a belated, stunted fruit, when reparations effectively came to an end. But his hope that this would transform the internal political scene was not fulfilled.

Brüning's successor was Franz von Papen, a right-wing fellow member of the Catholic Centre Party, society figure, and former cavalry officer who had married the heiress to Germany's largest manufacturer of lavatory pans. Papen was a less scrupulous character than Brüning and carried little political weight. He was in effect installed by General Kurt von Schleicher, a military intriguer, who became Defence Minister. One of the first acts of Papen's 'Cabinet of gentlemen', using presidential decree powers, was to rescind the ban on the SA. Street fighting between Nazis and Communists in Berlin resumed. On 'bloody Sunday', 17 July, eighteen people were killed in gun-battles in Hamburg. Three days later Papen again invoked emergency powers, this time to impose direct rule on Prussia. A coalition headed by a Social Democrat premier, the state government was virtually bankrupt and unable to pay its officials. Papen himself became 'National Commissioner' for Prussia. At the same time Social Democrats were purged from the Prussian civil service. The closing-down of parliamentary government in Germany's largest state presaged the end of democracy in the country as a whole. In new Reichstag elections on 31 July, the Nazis became the largest party in Germany, with 37 per cent of the vote, their best performance ever in a free election. The Communists moved slightly ahead to 14 per cent while the Social Democrats declined to 22 per cent. The Nazis now held 230 seats out of 608 in the Reichstag. Hitler demanded the Chancellorship. When Schleicher and Papen offered to make him Vice-Chancellor he demurred. According to a statement from the President's office, the Nazi leader 'demanded the same sort of position for himself as Mussolini had possessed after the March on Rome'. But the President replied that 'neither his private conscience nor his public obligations' would permit him to install the Nazis in power.[15]

Papen's Cabinet, however, could not muster a majority in the Reichstag and the Nazis succeeded in forcing new elections in November. The final stages of the campaign took place against the background of a transport strike in Berlin jointly directed by Nazis and Communists. The hostility of Hindenburg and public outrage at Nazi street violence led to an electoral setback for the Nazis. Their vote declined a little to 33 per cent (196 seats), while the Communists climbed to 17 per cent (100 seats), their best performance under Weimar. The Social Democrats secured only 20 per cent (121 seats), their worst showing in the life of the republic. For a moment the defenders of the republic breathed more freely, encouraged by the reverse suffered by the Nazis. But it was a false dawn. Papen now produced a scheme for the replacement of parliamentary government by an authoritarian regime; but his support, such as it was, had disintegrated and he was compelled to resign. On 2 December a weeping President appointed Schleicher Chancellor.

Schleicher tried unsuccessfully to mobilize support from Socialist, Catholic, and Nazi labour unions. After two months of ineffectual manoeuvring, he resigned in a huff on 28 January 1933. Hindenburg toyed with the idea of reappointing Papen but there was little support for such a government. Nor, in spite of their impatience with the palpable failure of parliamentarism, did the Reichswehr chiefs have the stomach to impose direct military rule.

On 30 January 1933 Hindenburg gave way and appointed Hitler Chancellor, with Papen as his deputy. 'We've hired him,' said Papen.[16] It was a colossal misjudgement, akin to Croce's early view of Mussolini. Apart from Hitler, the eleven-member cabinet contained only two Nazis: Wilhelm Frick as Minister of the Interior and the sly, corrupt vulgarian Hermann Göring as Minister without Portfolio. Hitler swore to uphold the constitution. Within a few months all constitutional constraints and all political competitors had been swept aside. The Nazis had made themselves sole masters of Germany.

Four weeks after Hitler's assumption of power, the Reichstag building was seriously damaged in a fire. The opportunity was taken the next day to issue a presidential decree suspending all civil liberties. The following month the decree was entrenched in law, turning Germany from a *Rechtsstaat* (a state applying the rule of law) into a police state. In a celebrated piece of political theatre that rebounded on the Nazis, the Bulgarian Communist Georgi Dimitrov, head of the Comintern's West European Bureau in Berlin, was put on trial with others, accused of plotting to set the fire. But he succeeded in turning tables on his accusers and won an acquittal. At the time suspicions were rife that the SA had torched the building in order to destroy the home of parliamentary democracy. In fact, the fire was set by a Dutch Communist, Marinus van der Lubbe, acting on his own. He was sentenced to death and guillotined.

New Reichstag elections on 5 March, held against a background of Nazi intimidation, produced a vote of 52 per cent for the government parties, though still no overall majority for the Nazis. On 23 March Hitler submitted an Enabling Bill to the Reichstag, which met in a Berlin opera house with a baying mob outside and a gauntlet of SA men at the entrance. Hitler promised that the dictatorial powers he was requesting would not be used to curtail the rights of the Reichstag, the Reichsrat, the presidency, the German states, or the churches. Reassured on the last point, the Centre Party voted for the bill, though some of its members expressed misgivings. Even the liberal parties persuaded themselves that it would make tactical sense to vote in favour. The Communist deputies had all been arrested or gone into hiding. Only the 94 remaining Social Democrats courageously voted against. This was the end of the Reichstag as an institution, save as an occasional audience for Hitler's tirades. The practice of legislating by decree, initiated by Brüning, became the norm. The way was open to the subordination of German society to the new order.

Gleichschaltung ('coordination', 'bringing into line') was the Nazi term used to describe the process whereby hitherto autonomous institutions were to be brought under the control of the Nazi Party and state. It had mixed results. On 7 April a Law for the Coordination of the States with the Reich effectively disposed of the autonomous powers of the *Länder*. On the same day a Law for the Restoration of the Professional Civil Service as well as a further law in July provided for the dismissal of Jews, Socialists, and Communists from official positions. While the purge affected nearly all Jewish civil servants, by no means all non-Nazis were fired. The personnel records of the SS, captured by the Allies at the end of the Second World War, show that it was possible even for known former Social Democrats to continue to hold jobs in the security apparatus without apparently suffering on that account. In this and other respects there was considerable continuity between the late Weimar and Nazi regimes.

By July 1933 all political parties other than the Nazis, as well as non-Nazi trade unions, had been dissolved. Non-Nazi mayors, for example, Konrad Adenauer in Cologne, were generally replaced by Nazis. The Communists' secretive cell structure, which supposedly equipped them for underground and insurrectionary activity, availed them nothing: their leaders were herded into prison camps or hounded out of Germany; the cadres quietly shed their political identity and tried to stay out of trouble. The Stahlhelm was incorporated into the SA and its youth organizations merged with the Hitler Youth. On 1 December a Law for the Unity of Party and State declared the Nazi Party 'the bearer of the concept of the German State', though exactly what this meant in practical or legal terms was not made clear. Tension between party and state organs remained a permanent characteristic of the Nazi regime.

In 1934 came two further stages in Hitler's progress to absolute power. The first involved the repression of rival centres of authority within the Nazi movement. On 29/30 June 1934, the 'Night of Long Knives' (*Nacht der langen Messer*), the SA chief, Ernst Röhm, who was suspected of plotting a putsch, as well as dozens of other SA leaders, were summarily shot on Hitler's orders. Among others murdered at the same time were Gregor Strasser, leader of the 'left wing' of the Nazi movement, and the retired General Schleicher, who thus paid for his contumely in blocking Hitler's demand for the Chancellorship in 1932. Papen was arrested and later packed off to serve as ambassador to Austria and thereafter to Turkey. The SA henceforth dwindled in importance, while the SS and SD (*Sicherheitsdienst*) became the mainstays of the regime. The open acknowledgement by the German government of such a gangster-style settling of scores shocked enlightened opinion. But most Germans seemed satisfied that the SA, feared for their bully-boy behaviour, had been curbed and 'order' restored. A month later Hindenburg died. While the old soldier was still on his deathbed, Hitler put in place a law abolishing the office of President and declaring himself 'Führer and Reich Chancellor', a post that would concentrate in his own hands all the powers hitherto reserved to the presidency, including that of Supreme Commander of the armed forces. A plebiscite endorsed the change with a vote of 90 per cent in favour.

Control of the police, hitherto a function of state governments, was centralized in Berlin. The Gestapo (secret police), under the authority of Heinrich Himmler, who also commanded the SS, operated independently of any political controls. Himmler's security apparatus developed into a vast empire, with special divisions for concentration camps, intelligence, censorship, and repression of Marxists, Jews, the churches, homosexuality, and abortions. Court decisions confirmed the right of the security apparatus to operate without restraint of the law. The first concentration camp, at Dachau near Munich, opened in March 1933. It became a model for the hundreds of others set up in the course of the next twelve years. Inmates were subjected to forced labour, torture, humiliation, starvation, arbitrary beatings, and death. By July 1933 about 27,000 political prisoners had been detained. The number diminished to ten thousand by the end of 1936 as the regime consolidated its power. Millions would later be drawn into its python-like embrace. Special courts were instituted to try political cases. The German League of Judges was absorbed into the League of National Socialist German Lawyers. The legal principle of *nulla poena sine lege* (no penalty without law) was eroded. In 1935 an edict was passed requiring judges to consider not only the letter of the law but also whether an act 'deserved punishment according to the principles of the penal code or according to popular feeling'.[17]

A vice gradually tightened round Germany's half million Jews. A commercial boycott, called by the Nazis in April 1933, met with a tepid public response and strong criticism overseas. The Nuremberg Laws, enacted in 1935, set out legalistic definitions of 'Aryans' and 'non-Aryans' and prohibited marriage between Jews and 'Aryan' Germans. Deprived of their livelihoods, subjected to a barrage of officially sponsored hate propaganda, Germany's half million Jews began to look abroad for possible refuge. But as the numbers seeking to emigrate grew, the barriers against refugee migration were raised in country after country.

With the extension of *Gleichschaltung* to education, law, the media, and other institutions, Nazi ideology began to pervade all sections of German society. Schoolteachers were forced to join the National Socialist Teachers' League. Universities had already been purged of Jews and anti-Nazis. The tone was set by the Bavarian Minister of Culture, Hans Schemm, who told an audience of professors in Munich in 1933, 'From now on, it will not be your job to determine whether something is true, but whether it is in the spirit of the National Socialist revolution.'[18] The University of Berlin lost a third of its academic staff. The academic community, by and large, submitted without protest to the new dispensation. Germany's leading philosopher, Martin Heidegger, who became Rector of the University of Freiburg in May 1933, declared: 'Not theses and ideas are the laws of your being! The Führer himself, and he alone, is Germany's reality and law today and in the future.'[19] A Reich Institute for the History of the New Germany, founded in 1935, was assigned the task of rewriting German history according to Nazi principles. The historian Ulrich Kahrstedt told his colleagues at the University of Göttingen: 'We renounce international science, we renounce the international republic of scholars, we renounce research for the sake of research. *Sieg Heil!*'[20]

Many scholars and scientists were forced into exile. Germany before 1933 had been the world's pre-eminent centre of scientific research. Abruptly and for ever, this ended. Between 1901 and 1932 Germany had won thirty-three out of a hundred Nobel prizes awarded in science. Several of these laureates now emigrated. Germany won only eight prizes between 1933 and 1960. But in the same period an additional fourteen were awarded to scientists who had been compelled to emigrate from Nazi Europe, mostly to Britain or the United States. At Göttingen only eleven out of the thirty-three academic staff of the physics and mathematics institutes remained. Albert Einstein, who held a chair in Berlin in 1933, was visiting America when Hitler came to power: he decided not to return and settled at Princeton for the rest of his life. Max Born, Hans Bethe, Otto Frisch, Rudolf Peierls, and other émigré physicists provided the essential basis for the development of nuclear weapons by the Allies in the Second World War. The transfer of intellectual capital was no less significant in other fields of science and scholarship (including history). 'Hitler's gift' to Britain and the United States grew out of an obtuse anti-intellectualism deeply rooted both in his personality and in Nazi doctrine. In response to protests, he was reputed to have replied: 'Our national policies will not be revoked or modified even for scientists. If the dismissal of Jewish scientists means the annihilation of contemporary German science, then we shall do without science for a few years.'[21]

School curricula were reformed to lay special emphasis on gymnastics, eugenics, biology, and 'race lore'. Special 'Adolf Hitler Schools' and *Ordensburgen* ('order castles'—echoing the medieval Germanic military orders), academies for special instruction in athletics, military drill, and political ideology, were founded for a selected elite of 'racially pure' students. Their object, as set down by the leading Nazi ideologist, Alfred Rosenberg, was to create 'a nucleus of men to whom the special task of state leadership will be entrusted, whose members grow from youth on into the idea of an organic politics'.[22] The Hitler Youth absorbed most other youth movements. By the end of 1934, it had over 3.5 million members. From December 1936 all other youth movements were abolished and nearly all children between the ages of ten and eighteen were compelled to join it or its affiliate the Bund Deutscher Mädel (League of German Girls). All members swore loyalty to the Führer and were subjected to nationalistic indoctrination and regimented training.

Two institutions, the churches and the army, retained vestiges of autonomy, but to little effect and at the price of their self-respect. The atavistic paganism that was half-buried in Nazism surfaced as soon as Hitler came to power. Nazi ideologists attacked the existing institutions of Christianity as outgrowths of Judaism and some wished to create a new 'German Christian' religion in which 'the Reich our life' would replace 'Christ our life' (Col. 3: 4) and 'the children of God' would give way to 'the children of our Führer'.[23] The German *Volk*, it was suggested, were the new Chosen People. Alfred Rosenberg propagated a '*Volk*-religion' that rejected the Old Testament, attacked St Paul, and dwelt on the Nordic myths of Odin and Valhalla. Writings of Nietzsche and Goethe were distorted and perverted in the effort to provide a lineage for this racist faith. Such ideas were given political support by the deputy Führer, Martin Bormann, who maintained that Nazism had superseded Christianity, which had therefore outlived its usefulness. Hitler despised the faithful. Yet he had a healthy respect for the institutional power of the churches and restrained the more enthusiastic de-Christianizers among his followers. He used, or rather paraphrased and manipulated, scriptural texts in his speeches and even Cardinal Michael von Faulhaber of Munich, a genuine opponent of Nazism, could come away from a long private meeting with the Führer persuaded that he 'undoubtedly lives in belief in God' and 'recognizes Christianity as the builder of western culture'.[24] These internal contradictions were never wholly resolved and the twelve years of Nazi rule witnessed, on the one hand, efforts to reconcile the churches to the Nazi system and on the other a 'Church struggle' in which organized Christianity was subjected to state direction and persecution.

Overall, Protestant Germany was more receptive to the Nazi message than Catholic, as reflected in voting patterns, institutional behaviour, and theological pronouncements. The Protestant Evangelical (Lutheran) Church submitted to the control of the state and to the infusion of Nazi doctrines. A German Christian Movement (Glaubensbewegung Deutsche Christen), headed by a 'Reich Bishop', Ludwig Müller, styled themselves 'stormtroopers for Christ' and sought to synthesize Nazi and Protestant doctrines. They won more than half a million adherents. A smaller Lutheran group, the Bekennende Kirche (Confessing Church), led by Martin Niemöller, Karl Barth, Otto Dibelius (who had, however, supported early Nazi attacks on the Jews) and Dietrich Bonhoeffer, refused to submit. By 1937 seven hundred pastors had been arrested. Many were driven into exile and some died in concentration camps.

In spite of distaste for Nazi doctrines and methods, the general view in the Vatican was that Nazism was a lesser evil than Communism. In March 1933 Faulhaber deplored the tendency of Pope Pius XI to 'judge National Socialism, like Fascism, as the only salvation from Communism and Bolshevism'. He feared that this attitude would have 'tragic' consequences for the Church in Germany.[25] But the dominant influence in Vatican policy-making was that of the Secretary of State, Cardinal Eugenio Pacelli, the former Papal Nuncio in Berlin (and later Pope Pius XII). In July 1933 he negotiated a Concordat between the Vatican and Germany that helped disarm such pockets of opposition to Nazism as remained in the Catholic Centre Party, which was dissolved in the same month. In 1937 Nazi racialism finally compelled Pius XI to issue the encyclical *Mit brennender Sorge* ('With burning concern'), complaining of Nazi encroachments on the rights of the Church and condemning 'the idolatrous cult of Race and Nation'. But neither Hitler nor any of those who followed his sacrilegious orders was ever threatened with excommunication. A few Catholic voices bravely spoke out against Nazism, notably Faulhaber, Cardinal Count Galen of Münster, and Bishop Preysing of Berlin. Yet the great majority of believing Christians in Germany, even as they attended church every Sunday, felt little compunction about fitting in with the new order.

The leaders of the German army, like those of the churches, were ambivalent in their attitude to the Nazi regime. They were disturbed by the power of the SA (until 1934) and of the SS. Some of the old Prussian officer class despised Hitler as a guttersnipe and upstart. At the same time, they appreciated the resources that were devoted to rebuilding Germany's armed strength. In March 1935, plans for a 36-division, 300,000-strong army, under way since 1933, were made public in the form of a decree that constituted open defiance of the Versailles Treaty. Great store was set by the oath of unconditional loyalty that all soldiers were compelled to swear to the Führer. Political indoctrination was applied with special intensity to recruits to the armed forces and the High Command was gradually cleared of those unsympathetic to Nazism.

Banks too were subjected to *Gleichschaltung*. They had traditionally played a central role, not only in finance, but in the industrial economy, because of their heavy participation in investment and the presence of bankers in prominent positions on many company boards. Nazis now exercised influence in most banks and Jews were removed. With the help of banks, the 'aryanization' of all large businesses was expedited. Meanwhile, the appointment in March 1933 of Dr Hjalmar Schacht as President of the Reichsbank and Minister for Economic Affairs helped reassure foreign financial opinion.

Schacht invented a cunning device, the so-called 'MeFo bill' to camouflage Germany's short-term debt. The bills were drawn by armament contractors and accepted by a dummy limited liability company, Metallurgische Forschungsgesellschaft (hence 'MeFo'). They were guaranteed by the Reich and could be presented at any German bank. Their secrecy was assured by the fact that they were published neither in the accounts of the Reichsbank nor in government budget figures. Budget deficits, for which the governments of the Weimar Republic had been strongly criticized, increased under the Nazis to 6.7 per cent of GNP in 1936–7 as against 1.1 per cent in 1931–2. These might have harmed Germany's credit but they were concealed from the rest of the world. In any case, Germany no longer sought large foreign loans. She paid no more reparations and defaulted on loans or offered repayment in non-convertible marks. Instead of paying for all her imports in foreign currency, she sought barter deals with politically dependent foreign countries, particularly in eastern Europe, though recent research suggests that Germany's economic imperialism in *Mitteleuropa* up to 1939 was more a matter of propaganda than reality.[26]

Behind a wall of exchange controls and tariff barriers, Germany recovered rapidly from the Depression. Large-scale public works, which contributed to the reflation of the economy, had been planned and initiated in the final stages of the Weimar Republic by the governments of Papen and Schleicher. They were taken up and developed by the Nazis under whom disciplinary and coercive features, already present under Weimar, were extended. What became, in effect, forced labour schemes for afforestation and the building of roads and the new autobahns (the first, between Bonn and Cologne, had been opened in 1932) helped reduce unemployment. But the public works programmes were not in themselves a primary cause of economic recovery. They have even been dubbed an 'optical illusion', since total public spending on housing, transport, and (at least until 1935) roads, remained below Weimar levels.[27] Rearmament and associated indirect expenditures were what made a decisive difference. In the period 1933–5 twice as much was spent on rearmament as on work creation schemes. These were merely part of a general tendency towards state intervention in the economy. The recovery in the labour market was rapid. By December 1934, registered unemployment had fallen to 2.6 million. Big business profited from Nazism even though its initial direct investment in it had been small. But contrary to left-wing myth-making of the period, the German business community exercised little influence on policy-making in the Third Reich.

The Nazis thus had much to celebrate in their first three years in power. Dr Joseph Goebbels, appointed Minister of Public Enlightenment (*Volksaufklärung*) and Propaganda in March 1933, supervised the reduction of the mass media to instruments of state policy. *Gleichschaltung* in this sphere was ensured by a Reich Chamber of Culture, with seven sub-'chambers' for literature, theatre, music, film, fine arts, the press, and broadcasting. A new press law in October 1933 denied newspapers the right to criticize the government and turned editors into censors of their own papers. The Jewish-owned Mosse and Ullstein press empires were taken over, their owners murdered or forced into exile. The left-wing press disappeared as did the venerable *Vossische Zeitung*. The Nazi Party organ, the *Völkischer Beobachter*, *Der Stürmer*, Julius Streicher's vicious weekly, and Goebbels's pet *Der Angriff* flourished as the non-Nazi press, including the respected, serious *Frankfurter Zeitung*, fell into line. News and commentaries were issued through the single, state-owned news agency, Deutsches Nachrichtenbüro (DNB), and the Reich Press Chief, Otto Dietrich, issued daily directives with detailed instructions on news treatment and policy guidelines. The state-owned radio system became the most effective propaganda medium, particularly in its broadcasts of Hitler's speeches.

Beyond all these conventional means of spreading the Nazi gospel, Goebbels stage-managed some incandescent *coups de théâtre*: torchlight processions, party rallies, and Hitler's oratorical set pieces. On 10 May 1933 Nazi students in Berlin organized a bonfire of books by authors disapproved of by the regime, among them Heine, Marx, Freud, Erich Kästner (author of the classic children's book *Emil and the Detectives*), the satirist Kurt Tucholsky, and the anti-war writers Erich Maria Remarque and Carl von Ossietzky. In Leni Riefenstahl's film, *The Triumph of the Will* (1935), the 1934 party rally at Nuremberg was transfigured into a joyous pictorial hymn to *völkisch* ideals, dominated by rippling swastika banners and punctuated by the rhythm of marching boots. The high point of the first period of Nazi rule was reached in the summer of 1936 when Hitler welcomed the nations of the world to Berlin for the Olympic Games. The German capital was sanitized of offensive racist slogans and brownshirts were on their best behaviour. The episode was a triumph of Nazi propaganda that dazzled and entranced Germans and impressed the world.

Nazism was neither an aberration from the course of German history nor its logical end, a product of Germany's 'unmastered past' (*unbewältigte Vergangenheit*), as it later came to be called. It was not the product of any uniquely German essence but rather, first and foremost, of the impact on German society of the First World War and the Great Depression. Nazi Germany was savagely authoritarian but the label 'totalitarian' that used to be applied to it is no longer generally accepted by historians. Some have seen Nazism as a form of 'political messianism'. But unlike other modern apocalyptic movements, its aspirations were diffuse and vague: save in its racialism, it offered no clearly formulated social agenda. It was 'Socialist' in name only; but the left, which portrayed it as an outgrowth of 'late capitalism' allied to militarism and extreme reaction, failed to grasp its animalistic attraction for the masses. It contained elements of revolt against modernism but it can also be seen as an expression of the amoralism of modern industrial society. It was inherently expansionist and aggressive but then so were most other ultra-nationalist movements of the period. Nazism was not unique but part of larger international tendencies in the inter-war period towards authoritarian government, though, given Germany's exceptional power, it carried those tendencies to their ultimate extremes.

One of the more sophisticated and influential, though not universally accepted, interpretations of Nazism has been advanced by those historians who stress the 'polycratic' character of the regime. The term was actually coined by Carl Schmitt, the leading Nazi legal theorist, but has been adopted in recent decades by the historians Martin Broszat and Hans Mommsen to analyse and explain the dynamics of the Nazi system. While by no means attenuating the centrality of Adolf Hitler as a primary generating force of the regime, they emphasize its lack of consistent planning and the way in which German elites were sucked into complicity with criminal acts. Citing a Nazi official's description of the system as 'temporarily well-organized chaos', Mommsen argues that Nazism 'was not a hierarchical system at all but a competitive leadership system. . . . The mechanism by which the old elites became implicated in the regime's criminal policies and were systematically corrupted by them arose primarily from the ever greater willingness of authorities in all areas to keep pace with the progressive radicalization of the regime so as not to be circumvented or altogether excluded from the system. They bought their right to continue to exist by perpetually conceding ground on legal points or on the substance of the rule of law itself. This process had to lead to a precipitous slope from which there could be no retreat.'[28] Such an approach has at least the merit, essential to all political understanding, of knitting together social analysis with an attempt to define and explain collective psychologies. Thus it was that decent men in the civil service, army, banks, judicial system, schools and universities, and even the churches were seduced into collaboration with barbarism.

Stalin

Soviet Russia, which had in large measure withdrawn from economic relations with the outside world, appeared little affected by the Depression, an illusion proudly upheld by the Communist movement, oblivious to the self-destructive effects of the economic policies being pursued in Russia in this period. At the world Economic Conference in London in 1933, the Soviet People's Commissar for Foreign Affairs, Maxim Litvinov, boasted that the world crisis had been unable to affect the steady economic development of the Soviet Union. Whereas the rest of the world had seen a fall in industrial output between 1928 and 1932 of 33 per cent, the USSR, he said, had enjoyed growth of 219 per cent in the same period.[29] The figures were exaggerated and glossed over the effects on rural living standards of the decline in prices obtainable for grain exports. Nevertheless, behind the propaganda lay a transformation of the economic structure of the Soviet Union.

Having defeated Trotsky by 1927, Stalin stole his clothes and embarked on a drastic switch away from the quasi-capitalist policies of NEP. In June 1927 a decree ordered preparations to begin for an 'all-union plan' that would bring about 'the maximum utilization of... resources for the purpose of industrialization of the country'.[30] This was the origin of the first five-year plan, which took effect from 1928. The plan was similar in inspiration to, although much more ambitious than the proposals of Trotsky and Preobrazhensky that had been ridiculed by Stalin.

> We have assumed power in a country whose technical equipment is terribly backward [Stalin told the Communist Party Central Committee in a speech in 1928].... We must overtake and outstrip the advanced technology of the developed capitalist countries.... We must systematically achieve a fast rate of development of our industry.... Either we accomplish this task—in which case the final victory of socialism in our country will be assured, or we turn away from it and do not accomplish it—in which case a return to capitalism may become inevitable.[31]

In its definitive version, prepared by Gosplan, the State Economic Planning Commission, the plan called for investment at the unusually high level of between a quarter and a third of all national income; one-third of this was to be directed to industry, and of that three-quarters to heavy industry. The targets set by the plan were almost incredibly high: production of electricity was to rise over the five-year period by 236 per cent, of iron ore by 163 per cent, of steel by 107 per cent. The object was to effect not only a rapid increase in production and productivity but a change in the structure of the Soviet economy away from agriculture, small industry, and consumer goods towards very large enterprises in iron and steel, machinery, and armaments.

Any hope of fulfilling the ambitious targets set by the plan depended above all on availability of investment capital. Initially this was financed by the issuing of bonds and an increase in taxes on 'NEP-men' and kulaks. But in the end the massive amounts required could come from only one source: the peasantry. Depression of farm incomes by downward adjustment of prices of agricultural goods led to peasant resistance. Had not the peasants been told to 'enrich themselves'? As in the period of 'War Communism', agricultural produce was withheld from the market. Grain was buried in pits, hidden in churches, bogs, and forests. Sometimes peasants set fire to crops or threw them into rivers rather than hand them over. A severe shortage of grain developed.

Bukharin argued for gradualism and for raising agricultural prices back to realistic levels. In a savage outburst in early 1929, Stalin denounced Bukharin's group as 'right deviators and capitulators who advocate not the elimination, but the free development of the capitalist elements in town and country'.[32] In the ensuing purge, the 'rightists' as well as 'bourgeois specialists', 'non-party engineers', 'NEP-men', 'wreckers', and 'counter-revolutionaries' were removed from positions of influence.

Stalin's alternative means of financing industrialization was a sudden and massive collectivization drive throughout the countryside. Peasant-owners, 97 per cent of all peasant households in 1928, were to be subjected to confiscation of their land and compulsory incorporation in giant *kolkhozy*, state-owned collective farms. Primitive agricultural techniques (74 per cent of grain was still sown by hand in 1928) were to be eradicated. Farming was to be mechanized by a massive increase in tractor production and the creation of 'machine-tractor stations' that would serve the new *kolkhozy*. Agricultural productivity would increase; labour requirements in the countryside would decline, releasing workers for expanding industrial enterprises.

Collectivization was carried out by force, helter-skelter, and at breakneck speed. By mid-1930 a quarter of all peasant households had been collectivized. The 'great turn' involved savagery and human suffering on an unprecedented scale. Resistance was widespread. The Soviet secret police recorded 22,754 'terrorist acts' by peasants in 1929 and 1930. Two million peasants participated in more than thirteen thousand riots and disturbances in 1930. Peasants slaughtered their livestock by the million rather than surrender them to collectives. The stock of cattle fell by 44 per cent, of horses by 50 per cent, and of pigs by 55 per cent between 1928 and 1933. Red Army units and urban 'collectivization brigades' were mobilized to enforce the policy by exhortation, bullying, or threats. The Soviet countryside was transformed. The village commune was dealt a death-blow. The Communist Party now assumed direct control over most aspects of life in rural areas.

The kulaks, Stalin declared, must be 'eliminated as a class'. Echoing this, with the edgy, heavy-handed humour typical of Bolsheviks, a speaker at the sixteenth party congress in 1930 attacked peasant saboteurs who were seeking to 'destroy the horse as a class'.[33] Soviet propaganda, as in Sergei Eisenstein's film *The General Line*, depicted the 'revolution' in the countryside as class warfare against a small exploiting class of wealthy peasants. The horrors attendant on 'dekulakization' were on a vast scale. Large numbers of petty agriculturists, tarred with the 'kulak' brush, were deported to Siberia or other remote regions, sent to labour camps, maltreated, or killed. Millions were driven off the land to feed the insatiable demands of the industrial labour force. The purpose was not, in fact, to destroy 'rural capitalists'; such a 'class' hardly existed: it was rather to terrorize the great mass of peasants into compliance with the directives of their urban masters.

In the years between 1928 and 1941 Soviet agriculture was transformed. Private farms ceased to exist. Peasants dragooned into *kolkhozy* were subjected to industrial-type work discipline. Total available tractor horse-power quadrupled between 1928 and 1931. But 92 per cent of all draught power was still animal at that stage rather than mechanical. Mechanization proceeded apace later in the 1930s but barely compensated for the huge losses of horse and other animal power in the early stages of collectivization. The total cattle stock fell from 60 million to 48 million. Grain production probably increased somewhat between 1928 and 1940, though the official figures, suggesting that the grain supply problem had been 'solved', were certainly exaggerated. The social convulsion in the countryside changed the structure of Soviet agriculture but it did not solve its longstanding problem of low productivity nor did it provide secure, continuous food supplies for the growing urban population.

Forced collectivization resulted in a terrible famine in 1929–30 across much of the Soviet Union. In 1931 and 1932 harvests were lower than in any year since the 1921 famine, though this was not revealed in government statistics. The food shortages brought renewed large-scale death to the countryside, particularly in Ukraine and in central Asia. Even more than the 1929–30 famine, which might be termed an unanticipated by-product of the collectivization campaign, the famine of 1931–2 may be called man-made, for it was a direct and foreseeable consequence of government policies. The Soviet media were forbidden to report on it. And unlike the famines of the early 1920s, this one was not alleviated by charitable aid from the west which was not to be admitted for fear of blotting the escutcheon of the Soviet Union's supposedly miraculous economic advance.

Meanwhile the attempt to build 'socialism in one country' brought a hectic dash for growth under the first five-year plan and its successor between 1933 and 1938. Soviet production statistics were tendentiously presented and sometimes falsified, especially after 1932 when the head of the government's statistical office was reprimanded by the Politburo for 'a bourgeois tendency concealed under the banner of "objective" statistics'.[34] National income, according to official figures, more than quintupled between 1928 and 1940. The most authoritative modern estimates give much lower estimates of economic expansion: GNP growth in that period was probably nearer 50 per cent, an average of around 6 per cent per annum. This was a respectable rate, particularly against the background of the international depression, but not the Socialist miracle proclaimed by Soviet propaganda.

The change in economic structure was, however, momentous. Between 1928 and 1940 the contribution of industry to Soviet national income rose from a fifth to a third. Coal production nearly tripled; iron and steel output quadrupled; electricity generation increased nearly tenfold. Overall industrial production grew by an average of at least 7 per cent per annum. New industries were created, for example aviation, machine tools, and heavy engineering. The urban population doubled. The industrial labour force tripled while the number of workers engaged in agriculture fell by a quarter. But Soviet productivity remained much lower than that of the advanced western countries and, save in a few restricted areas, mainly in the armaments industry, Soviet technology remained relatively backward.

This was to a remarkable degree an 'autarkic' economy. Foreign debt, except in 1931–2, was minimal. Foreign trade fell between 1928 and 1940; exports were generally limited to primary products such as grain, timber, and minerals. During the first five-year plan there were large-scale imports of machinery and technical expertise. But at no stage in the inter-war period did foreign trade even approach the level attained by the Russian Empire in 1913.

The rapid industrial growth rate was achieved only by a ruthless ploughing back of surplus capital at the expense of consumers. The standard of living of urban workers declined between 1928 and 1934 and never surpassed the level of the NEP period until after the Second World War. In 1937 real wages of Moscow workers were still only two-thirds of their 1928 level. The rapid growth of the urban proportion of the population, from 18 per cent in 1913 to 32 per cent by 1939, put enormous pressure on housing:

most families lived choc-a-bloc with others, crammed into decrepit apartments with shared kitchens and bathrooms. Between 1929 and 1935 rationing of foodstuffs was introduced, although some food was available on the black market. Privileged persons, with connections (*blat*), had access to goods beyond normal ration limits. During this period, the average urban worker's diet has been described as one of 'enforced vegetarianism, the bulk of it consisting of rye bread, potatoes, and cabbage'.[35] A growing proportion of the labour force worked in conditions akin to slavery. Soviet trade unions, toothless organs of party and state, formed part of the machinery of labour discipline rather than acting as effective representatives of workers' interests.

The Stalinist system fostered a new morality and conjured new social myths. Central to both were official cult heroes. Aleksei Stakhanov, a coal miner in the Donets basin, was hailed as a model worker in 1935 after he allegedly drilled 102 tons of coal in six hours, fourteen times his quota. The achievement was accomplished by attaching a large number of uncelebrated auxiliary workers to assist the hero. Stakhanov was rewarded with a new flat, a telephone, free cinema passes, and an inscription on the mine's honour board. *Pravda* hailed him as a 'Soviet Hercules'. His supposed feat was publicized throughout the country. Mines and a town were named after him. His name entered the language to denote a worker who exceeded work norms. Hosts of emulators were acclaimed in every branch of industry. Stakhanovites became a labour aristocracy who acquired prestige, privileges, medals, bicycles, superior rations, and new apartments, as well as, in some cases, the supreme accolade of party membership. They were acclaimed as 'Stalin's tribe'. Over-achieving norms by day, enjoying elevated culture by night, the Stakhanovite became the model 'New Soviet Man'—or woman: O. P. Chapygina, a Frunze factory worker, was noted for her love of opera and theatre and personal library of no fewer than 282 books.[36] In November 1935 Stalin addressed an All-Union Conference of Stakhanovites in Moscow and congratulated them on 'smashing antiquated standards of output and introducing amendments into the estimated capacity of industry and the economic plans prepared by the leaders of industry'.[37] But other workers often resented the increases in work norms and the attempts to speed them up that resulted from this system: Stakhanovites became unpopular and were attacked and sometimes killed. Credulous observers attributed considerable credit for increases in Soviet productivity in this period to the Stakhanovite phenomenon. But the recent analysis of Lewis Siegelbaum carries greater conviction: he argues that Stakhanovism, 'by making a fetish of individual performance . . . exacerbated the difficulties of achieving proportionality' and increased distortions and bottlenecks in the centrally planned system.[38] Stakhanovism was still being celebrated on its fiftieth anniversary in 1985. Meanwhile, its patron saint, poor Stakhanov himself, found that his personal privileges were short-lived; he was kicked upstairs to a desk job and died in obscurity in 1977.

A peasant lad, Pavel Morozov, became a hero of a different kind. In 1932 he denounced his father as a class enemy. After his father was sent to prison camp, young Pavel was murdered, allegedly by a group of peasants led by his uncles. The killers were executed. Such, at any rate, was the received version of the story. Recent research has cast doubt on several elements. It is not certain that the denunciation ever occurred. If so, it was probably inspired less by ideological zeal than by Pavel's resentment against his father for abandoning his family. Pavel's death (if, indeed, he was murdered) has plausibly been interpreted as the result of a brawl among youths rather than of a conspiracy by outraged villagers. Whatever the facts of the case, the Morozov story was transmuted into a powerful myth. Successive editions of the *Great Soviet Encyclopaedia*, until as late as 1974, carried articles commending the boy martyr's example. Edifying novels were published recounting little Pavlik's story. Schools, summer camps, and a street in Moscow were named in his memory. A statue was erected in his honour in the Moscow Children's Park. A museum dedicated to him was founded in his home village in the Urals.

Such phenomena were manifestations of the effort, not wholly successful, by the state to sunder traditional social bonds and replace them with its own values. The personnel, powers, and social reach of the secret police greatly expanded. The NKVD (People's Commissariat for Internal Affairs), which supervised the internal security system, became a law unto itself. The penetration of the state into social institutions was extended. The Church had long since been forced to bow down; its land and other property holdings were nationalized, place-servers and spies were appointed to leading positions, religious education was banned, no new churches were constructed, the average age of clergy increased as few young men entered holy orders, and the spiritual authority of the Church rapidly declined. Russia, nevertheless, remained, particularly in rural areas, a religious country at least in the sense that popular religion survived as a source of solace and inspiration to millions of persecuted, starved, or miserable people who mouthed the official slogans but lacked true faith in the new ideology.

Shorn of much of its institutional baggage, religion became a private, often secret loyalty. Although Christmas celebrations were banned, many people in the countryside continued to observe the holy days surreptitiously. When their priests disappeared, peasants would continue to gather in village churches and pray as best they knew. The grandparents of Mikhail Gorbachev, who were party members, kept icons at home, hidden behind portraits of Lenin and Stalin. Gorbachev's mother remained a believer and attended church services all her life. The potential price of such incorrect behaviour in the 1930s was high. The slightest expression of unorthodoxy or questioning of officially decreed values became a potential ground for arrest. Cultural and intellectual life surrendered to the dead hand of censorship and bureaucratic controls. Political debate, which until 1929 remained vigorous, was entirely snuffed out.

The murder in December 1934 of Sergei Kirov, the party chief in Leningrad, fired the starting-gun for Stalin's liquidation of a considerable part of the Russian political, intellectual, and military elite. Kirov had formerly been a boon companion of Stalin. Stalin's subordinate and eventual successor, Nikita Khrushchev, had no doubt that Stalin himself was behind Kirov's murder. He surmised that 'it was organized by [Genrikh] Yagoda [head of the NKVD], on Stalin's instructions'.[39] This is now generally accepted, though, even after the partial opening of Soviet archives, the evidence remains inconclusive. Whatever its origin, the assassination led to a cascade of arrests, trials, imprisonments, and executions and to a general atmosphere of terror. Zinoviev, Kamenev, and others were found guilty of 'moral complicity' in the murder and sent to prison.

In Germany, most people, provided they were not Jews or Marxists and conducted themselves circumspectly, could still, in the mid-1930s, live relatively normal lives; in the Soviet Union many came in this period to endure fear of arbitrary persecution as a regular component of daily life. The urban intelligentsia were the most closely watched and terrorized. 'We all felt as if we were constantly exposed to x-rays and the principal means of control over us was mutual surveillance,' recalled Nadezhda Mandelshtam.[40] Her husband, Osip Mandelshtam, was arrested after he wrote a poem in which he referred to Stalin's 'cockroach whiskers'.[41] He paid for this lèse-majesty with his life.

The labour camp system that grew up in the early 1930s held millions of people, most of whom had committed no crime. In the early years a majority of the detainees were kulaks. Later, political prisoners from all classes predominated, although there was also a sub-stratum of ordinary criminals. Most camps were in the frozen Arctic or Siberian regions of the USSR. Prisoners, who included women and children, worked in mines, lumber camps, or on construction projects. Those guilty of offences against discipline were confined to 'punishment compounds' where conditions were filthy, labour unremitting, and treatment savage. Sanitary, medical, and housing conditions in the camps were primitive. Rations were barely above starvation level. The death rate was high. Most of those who entered the camps were never seen again.

Prison camps, torture chambers, and much of the apparatus of the police state were hidden from direct public view. But in 1936 a series of great 'show trials' opened in which justice Soviet-style was displayed to the world. 'The case of the Trotskyite–Zinovievite Terrorist Centre' was heard before the Military Collegium of the Supreme Court of the USSR. The defendants, who again included Zinoviev and Kamenev, admitted all the charges of counter-revolutionary activity, responsibility for the murder of Kirov, plotting the murder of Stalin, collusion with the Gestapo and with Trotsky. Andrei Vyshinsky, Procurator-General of the USSR, delivered a violent speech for the prosecution, ending with the demand: 'Dogs gone mad should be shot—every one of them.'[42] The verdicts were a foregone conclusion and the exact wording of the final judgement was refined in advance by Stalin personally.[43] All the accused were executed.

In January 1937 it was the turn of Radek and sixteen others accused of 'treason against the country, espionage, acts of diversion, wrecking activities and the preparation of terrorist acts'.[44] Radek confessed to all the preposterous charges and received a long prison sentence: he was never heard of again. The arrest of Marshal Tukhachevsky, hero of the civil war and the Russo-Polish War, and suppressor of the Kronstadt rebellion, together with seven other generals in June 1937, was reported the following day by the Communist Party organ, *Pravda*, under the banner front-page headline: 'SPIES, DESPICABLE HIRELINGS OF FASCISM, TRAITORS TO THEIR COUNTRY—SHOOT THEM!' Similar headlines, all ending with the invocation 'SHOOT THEM!', emblazoned every page of the newspaper that day.[45] Tukhachevsky was tried in secret and met the usual fate.

The climax to the show trials came with the arraignment of Bukharin. In a letter to his fellow Soviet leaders on 20 February 1937, immediately before his arrest, he passionately protested his innocence, swearing 'on the last breath of Ilich [Lenin] who died in my arms' that the accusations were slander.[46] In March 1938 he was put on trial together with twenty co-defendants, including Yagoda, who, as former head of the NKVD, had been responsible for organizing the first show trial. Bukharin was accused of having been an enemy of the revolution from an early date. He was alleged to have plotted the murder of Lenin and Stalin in 1918, of being a member of a conspiratorial group called 'the Bloc of Rightists and Trotskyites', of collaborating with foreign intelligence services to carry out acts of terrorism and 'wrecking' that aimed at the dismemberment of the USSR, of having ordered the murder of Kirov, and of having colluded with doctors to poison other Soviet leaders—for example, by spraying poisonous substances in the study of Nikolai Yezhov, the new head of the Soviet security apparatus.

The trial was a bizarre travesty of legal procedure, enacted in the full glare of publicity. It took place in a courtroom draped with a banner that demanded 'To the mad dogs—a dog's death'. Vyshinsky resorted to viciously abusive epithets in his denunciation of the accused: 'putrefying heap of human scum', 'loathsome hybrid of fox and viper', and so forth. As in the previous trials, his interrogations resulted in astonishing expressions of self-abasement from most of the prisoners. Bukharin adopted the peculiar legal strategy of confessing his general guilt while denying the specific acts of sabotage of which he was accused. Perhaps he thought thereby to preserve his intellectual integrity or to send a signal to the world that his sole crime had been that of political opposition to Stalin. Some have read into his behaviour an attempt 'to use the trial in order to outwit his captors, and to convey, in Aesopian language, something of the ideals to which he had devoted his life'.[47] He was sentenced to death. In a final plea for mercy he repeated his grotesque admissions of guilt: 'There is not a single word of protest in my soul. I should be shot ten times for my crimes.'[48] He was probably executed the same day, shot in the head at the Lubyanka prison. E. H. Carr wrote that 'Bukharin's end can never lose its unique elements of pity and terror'. At the same time he justly pointed out that Bukharin himself had helped hound Trotsky, Zinoviev, and Kamenev out of the party, though he had not wanted to persecute them personally.[49] Bukharin was merely one among the countless horde of victims of judicial murder in Europe in this period but his fate was emblematic of the degeneration of a movement founded on the rights of man and the utopian vision of the enlightenment into systematized inhumanity and barbarism.

The show trials were held up as models of judicial practice at party cell meetings, schools, and institutions throughout the country. They fascinated foreign observers, few of whom could bring themselves to believe that the abject confessions to far-fetched crimes and conspiracies were the result of intimidation or torture. The leftist British barrister D. N. Pritt QC and other 'fellow travellers' with Communism hailed the trials as legally sound. The German-Jewish writer Lion Feuchtwanger wrote that there was no reason 'for imagining that there was anything manufactured, artificial or even awe-inspiring or emotional' about the show trials.[50] Dimitrov, hero of the Reichstag Fire trial, said that while the verdicts might be harsh, 'it was cutting into good flesh in order to get rid of bad'.[51] Even non-Communist experts on Russia, such as Sir Bernard Pares, took the trials at face value. A few foreign sympathizers had doubts. Romain Rolland criticized Stalinism as a '*régime de l'arbitraire incontrôlé le plus absolu*', but he uttered these heretical thoughts only in the privacy of his diary. In public he declared his confidence in the verdicts against Kamenev and Zinoviev, 'persons long despised, twice renegades and traitors'.[52]

In his influential novel *Darkness at Noon* (1940), which attempted to interpret these events, Arthur Koestler tried to explain the self-abasement of the Old Bolsheviks among the accused, men who had, after all, often endured, without breaking, the worst that Tsarist gaolers had to offer. Their conduct in court, according to Koestler, was not simply a surrender to physical pressure, but rather a manifestation of their ultimate loyalty to the party, reflecting their genuine conviction that, whatever their subjective feelings of guilt or innocence, what counted within the Marxist-Leninist thought system in the last resort was the 'objective reality' of what was needed by the party. If the party required that they confess to crimes and die, so be it; they would go to their deaths happy to render this final service to the cause. In an autobiography written fifteen years later Koestler returned to the theme and offered some evidence to support his view.[53] In retrospect, and in the light of new evidence available since the 1980s, Koestler's theory seems an over-intellectualized interpretation of what were almost certainly dictated statements made under extreme mental and physical pressure.

It is now known that before and after the trial Bukharin strenuously denied all the charges against him.[54] Dmitri Volkogonov, in his biography of Stalin, written in the late 1980s with access to Soviet archives, cites the case in 1938 of Nikolai Krestinsky, survivor of Lenin's first Politburo of 1919, who forgot, or ignored, his script and denied in court the accusation that he had been a paid agent of German intelligence since 1921. Stalin reportedly 'exploded angrily, "They prepared the good-for-nothing badly," and let it be known he would not stand for it again. Steps were taken and by the same evening Krestinsky had returned to "normal".'[55]

Whatever the explanation, the trials were judged a success by Soviet propagandists. Vyshinsky's treatise on 'The Problem of Evaluation of Proof in Criminal Trials' became a standard text and was awarded the Stalin Prize, First Class. His pseudo-legal concept that the accused's confession was the 'crown of evidence' became a basic element in Soviet jurisprudence, one that was put to renewed use in further political trials before and after the war. After a distinguished career in the service of Soviet law and diplomacy, Vyshinsky was buried in the Soviet pantheon at the Kremlin wall.

By 1939 nearly three million people were being held in the Gulag. Strictly speaking this was the Chief Administration of Camps but the term came to be used loosely to denote the entire penal system of Soviet labour camps, colonies, and prisons. Inmates were used as slave labour to build canals and railways, and to work in mines in Siberia, the far north, and other remote areas. Sanitation was rudimentary. Large numbers died of typhus, tuberculosis, malnutrition, and exhaustion. Camps were riddled with agents and informers. Denunciations were encouraged and harsh punishment beatings and torture were frequent. Suicides were common. Regional quotas were set for executions. Estimates of the total number of Stalin's victims vary widely.[56] Alexander Solzhenitsyn wrote of as many as 'sixty million victims of the Soviet regime'.[57] The unorthodox Soviet historian Roy Medvedev estimated in 1989 a total of forty million victims, including those arrested, driven from their land, or blacklisted; of these, he calculated, half died in labour camps, collectivization, famine, or by execution.[58] These figures include wartime and post-war victims in the whole period 1924 to 1953. Scholarly estimates of the number of 'excess deaths' between 1926 and 1939 have ranged from 5.5 to 14 million. A careful recent analysis suggests a total of ten million for the period 1927–38, most of these during the famine of the early 1930s.[59]

How can the terror be understood? Three basic lines of approach have emerged: the first based on Russian political culture, the second on the nature of the Communist Party system, and the third on the personality of Stalin. The first sees the Stalinist police state as heir to that of the Tsars. The second suggests that it was a logical progression from Lenin's rule which had already produced the one-party state, political murder, and show trials. In his revelatory speech in 1956, denouncing Stalin's crimes, Nikita Khrushchev placed the blame squarely on the character of the supreme leader: 'Stalin was a very distrustful man, sickly suspicious; we know this from our work with him. He could look at a man and say: "Why are your eyes so shifty today?" or "Why are you turning so much today and avoiding to look me directly in the eyes?" The sickly suspicion created in him a general distrust even towards eminent party workers whom he had known for years. Everywhere and in everything he saw "enemies", "two-facers" and spies.'[60] Stalin's paranoia, indeed, knew no bounds. But Khrushchev's indictment of the man he had happily served for many years was, of course, in part a self-exculpation, or rather an apologia for his entire generation of obsequious henchmen. None of these approaches by itself seems adequate to explain this colossal tragedy in which a society came close to committing genocide against itself. Only an interpretation that draws all three into meaningful relation can carry full conviction.

In an incisive article in 1962, Alec Nove asked: 'Was Stalin really necessary?' Could the USSR have been transformed by 1941 into a relatively advanced industrial state without massive coercion? The Soviet leaders, Nove notes, were generally agreed that the USSR's national strength and independence, as well as the survival of Communism, depended on swift progress in building a modern, economic infrastructure. Bukharin's policy of gradualism ran the risk, they feared, of permitting the growth of capitalist elements (kulaks and 'NEP-men') who might overcome the revolution from within; it might also leave the USSR open to renewed attack by 'imperialist interventionists' from without. Stalin first backed Bukharin's view, then swung against it. Perhaps this was merely a 'clever power-manoeuvre' but, argues Nove, the policies eventually adopted, though not the associated 'excesses', had widespread support in the party. 'If this be so,' he continues, 'the policy as such cannot be attributed to Stalin personally, and therefore the consequences adopted must be a matter of more than personal responsibility.' Collectivization, party leaders generally agreed, 'could not be voluntary'. And rapid industrialization could be achieved only if there were a reduction in living standards. Economic centralization and dictatorial party power were the only means by which the policy objectives could be attained. Nove nevertheless attributes to Stalin personal responsibility for the brutality of collectivization and the 'madly excessive pace of industrial development'. 'In each case,' he writes, 'we are dealing with "*excessive excesses*", since we have already noted that collectivization without coercion was impossible, and rapid industrialization was bound to cause stresses and strains.' Stalin's 'needless cruelty', police terror, and purges weakened rather than strengthened the Soviet Union. 'Purges not only led to the slaughter of the best military officers but also halted the growth of heavy industry.' Nove therefore concludes that the 'whole-hog of a Stalin' was not 'necessary' but at the same time that '*some* elements of Stalinism' were 'a necessary consequence of the effort of a minority group to keep power and to carry out a vast social-economic revolution in a very short time'.[61]

Subsequent debate has contested some elements in this analysis. Moshe Lewin, for example, denied that forcible collectivization was a necessary condition of rapid industrialization.[62] Roy Medvedev agreed with Lewin that Stalinism was not inevitable but the result of policy choices by Soviet leaders. He attributes these to social changes in the inter-war period, in particular the rapid increase in the size of the working class, which was 'bound to affect its psychology and behaviour' and the 'degeneration of some parts of the [party] *apparat*'. Stalinism, he argued, was not merely the doctrine of 'degenerates and careerists': 'There were also sincere believers, genuinely convinced that everything they did was necessary for the revolution. They believed in the political trials of 1936–8, they believed that the class struggle was intensifying, they believed in the necessity of repression. They became participants—and many of them subsequently became victims.'[63] The opening of Soviet archives since the late 1980s has provided more empirical evidence on which to base such arguments but the basic lines of approach remain little changed.

Boris Pasternak, the greatest Russian writer of the period, mocked Stalin as a 'pock-marked Caligula'. Of that Roman emperor it is reported that he not only laid claim to divinity but also gave orders that 'statues of the gods . . . should be brought from Greece in order to remove their heads and replace them with his own'.[64] Stalin had photographs of the epic events of 1917 doctored so as to remove the head of Trotsky while he himself took centre stage in photographic, film, and literary depictions.[65] One of the most degrading aspects of the terror was that it was accompanied by a chorus of hallelujahs from its millions of victims in praise of their voracious idol. Acclaim for Stalin was orchestrated on a vast scale and developed into a veritable civil religion. All public speeches rendered obligatory obeisance to Stalin at beginning and end. 'We talk a lot about a cult of personality [the Soviet writer Ilya Ehrenburg later recalled]. At the beginning of 1938 the term "cult" in its original religious sense would have described it more accurately. In the minds of millions of people Stalin had become a sort of mythological demi-god; everyone uttered his name with awe and believed that he alone could save the Soviet State from invasion and disruption.'[66] Even the Aztecs, in their ritual slaughter ceremonies, sacrificed only prisoners of war; the Soviets, under Stalin, sacrificed each other.

Stalin and Hitler continue to pose the most elusive challenges to historical understanding of the twentieth century, not only because they were the most destructive political leaders of their time, probably of all time, but also because, terrifyingly for those with any faith in the human spirit, they were wildly popular among their own peoples.

Nor was this merely a matter of their persons. Both Nazism and Communism became deeply attractive belief systems for millions. Both in their day offered emotional comfort to the disoriented, reassurance to the bewildered. Both demanded surrender of self to the mass, offering in return the comfort of suspension of individual moral responsibility. Both dispensed with the rule of law, elevated the secret police to the highest authority in the land, constructed vast systems of slave labour, and killed millions of their subjects. Yet in the supreme test of total war both sustained the morale and adhesion of their followers at least as well as the liberal democracies. Both succumbed on battlefields of their own choosing: Nazism by defeat in war, Communism by its failure to create a classless society free from material want. Yet so long as they could plausibly claim success, most of their subjects willingly did as they were told.

We should not, however, fall into the common error of imputing a false parallelism between the two great warrior ideologies. Nazism, for all its revolutionary jargon, represented in its essence a reaction against the nineteenth-century faith in human progress. It was an attempt to seize history by the collar and frog-march it in a direction determined primarily by the selfish interests and obsessive beliefs of those in power. From the outset it was an anti-intellectual movement, offering its adherents the spurious solidarity of the street gang and the prospective enjoyment of stolen booty.

Communism, by contrast, was a sophisticated and internally coherent framework of thought. It was not, as it is sometimes portrayed, a manic delusion of the intelligentsia but rather a modern transformation of the utopian chiliasm of the most enlightened elements in European thought since the seventeenth century. As distinct from the cave-man morality of Nazism and from the individualist ethic of liberalism, Communism sought to achieve a higher collective good that derived from Rousseau's concept of the general will and Gerard Winstanley's idea of the common weal. The source of its special appeal to several generations of European intellectuals, perhaps also one of the reasons why it survived in power so much longer than Nazism, was its (ultimately self-falsified) claim, derived from Marx, to be able to discern and to accelerate the underlying motive forces of history. That both Communism and Nazism developed into mechanisms of brute force and thuggery should not blind us to their distinctive origins and aspirations.

As the liberal structures created in 1919 broke down almost everywhere, and as first Hitler, then Stalin extended their empires over much of the continent, Europeans began to feel like the former citizens of the Roman Republic subjected to the rule of oppressive emperors: 'Under the reign of these monsters,' Gibbon wrote, 'the slavery of the Romans was accompanied by two peculiar circumstances, the one occasioned by their former liberty, the other by their extensive conquests, which rendered their condition more completely wretched than that of the victims of tyranny in any other age or country. From these causes were derived, 1, the exquisite sensibility of the sufferers; and, 2, the impossibility of escaping the hand of the oppressor.'[67] By the late 1930s this was the predicament of the greater part of the European continent.

6

Europe in the 1930s

Consider this and in our time
As the hawk sees it or the helmeted airman:
The clouds rift suddenly—look there
At cigarette-end smouldering on a border
At the first garden party of the year.

*W. H. Auden, London, 1930**

Populations

Radical social changes transformed the face of Europe in the inter-war period. For the first time in the history of the continent, more people lived in towns and cities than in rural areas. The values of urban civilization came increasingly to dominate society, undermining old-fashioned institutions and ways of living. The nature and shape of the family, relations between the sexes, patterns of work and of recreation, standards of housing and sanitation, modes of dress, of private and public conduct were all reconfigured. Fundamental to all these changes was a shift in the demographic prospect in Europe. The highly industrialized countries had already moved from high to low birth and death rates; less developed areas were at an earlier stage of the process but they too were entering the 'demographic transition'.

Between 1914 and 1939 the total population of Europe grew from 450 million to 540 million. The USSR, with 174 million, more than three-quarters of them in European regions, had by far the largest population of any European state. Germany (not including areas annexed after 1937) ranked second with 70 million, followed by Britain with 48 million, Italy with 44 million and France with 42 million. In general, population grew fastest in the poorest areas: the Soviet Union, the Balkans, and the Iberian peninsula. The highest proportional increase for any European country was

* From 'Consider', W. H. Auden, *Collected Poems*, ed. Edward Mendelson, New York, 1991.

in Greece (44 per cent), much of this due to the refugee influx from Turkey. Growth was much slower in north-western Europe, with the exception of the Netherlands. Ireland remained the only country in Europe to suffer population loss.

Population growth is determined by two variables: natural increase or decrease and inward or outward migration. In most of the continent in the inter-war period the rate of natural increase was falling. For Europe as a whole (excluding the USSR) in 1930 it stood at eight per thousand per annum, the lowest rate for any continent. Population growth was highest in eastern Europe and the Balkans but in Scandinavia, Britain, France, Germany, Austria, and Hungary it had fallen to around replacement level.

Natural increase is a combined outcome of birth and death rates. Both were declining in the inter-war period but there was a pronounced difference between developed and undeveloped regions: Albania, the most backward country in Europe by almost any measure, had the highest birth rate in Europe (35 per thousand) in 1940; the USSR came second (31). At the other end of the spectrum were England, France, Belgium, Sweden, and Norway, all of which recorded less than half the Soviet rate. The decline in numbers of births was partly a consequence of changes in social conditions and cultural attitudes. Another major reason was the carnage on the battlefield between 1914 and 1918 which had left a serious imbalance of sexes in many countries. This led, particularly in western Europe, to late marriage or, in many cases, non-marriage of women who might otherwise have borne children. The decline was most striking in southern France, Germany, Austria, and Estonia, where, in about 1930, the number of births was well below the level necessary to maintain population size. The rate was generally lower in urban than rural areas. This was true even in less-developed countries: Prague, Budapest, Belgrade, and Warsaw all had net reproduction rates well below replacement levels: they maintained or increased their populations only as a result of internal migration. The same was true of Moscow and Leningrad. In Italy, where fertility declined by one-third between 1901 and 1931, the rate for Turin, according to the 1931 census, was only one third that for Apulia (the 'heel' of the peninsula).

Lower birth and fertility rates were the prime cause of slowing population growth. This is easily demonstrated if we examine death rates, infant mortality, and migration patterns. Death rates were declining everywhere. They were lowest in 1936–9 in England, Germany, and Scandinavia, highest in the USSR, Spain, and Romania. Yet even in the latter group of countries they were declining fast. For example, in the Soviet Union between 1913 and 1940 the death rate fell from thirty per thousand to eighteen per thousand. As a result, average life expectancy at birth in Europe in the 1930s had risen to between fifty and sixty almost everywhere and as high as sixty-five in the Netherlands, though in the USSR it was still only forty-seven and in Romania only forty.

Fertility decline may be the result of worsening health conditions, a reduced frequency of sexual intercourse, or some form of deliberate birth control. Except in the famine-stricken regions of the Soviet Union in the early 1920s and early 1930s, health conditions were not so bad as to interfere with fertility. Infant mortality was generally declining, in part because more women during and after the war chose to breastfeed.[1] In Austria the rate fell from 169 per thousand in 1912 (for the territory that became the post-war republic) to 73 by 1939. Similar improvements were registered in other parts of Europe, though there were still great variations between industrialized and non-industrialized countries. In the early 1930s the rate ranged from 50 to 80 per thousand in north-west Europe to over 150 per thousand in the Balkans and as high as 181 in Romania. The sharpest decline over the inter-war period was probably in Russia—from 380 in 1918 to less than 140 in 1940–1.[2] Regional variations within countries remained great: around 1940 the rate for Berlin was 72 but 166 for Lower Bavaria; it was 46 in the

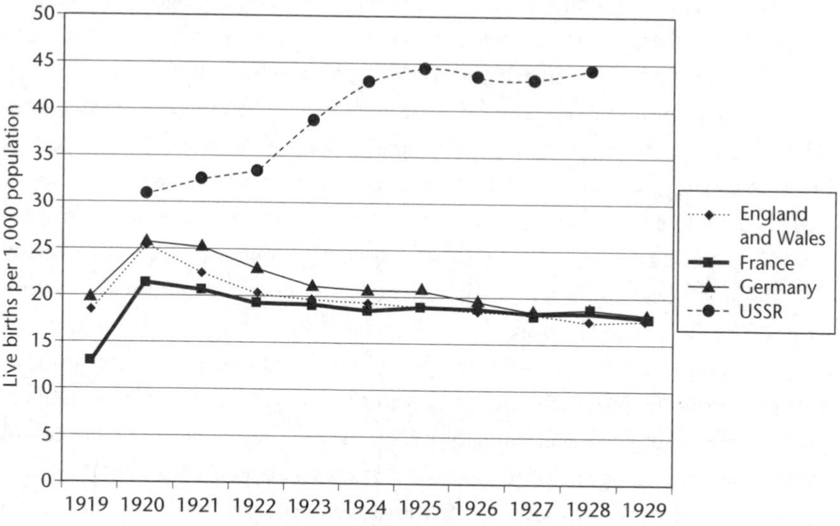

Figure 4. Birth rates in selected countries, 1919–1929

Source: B. R. Mitchell, *International Historical Statistica, Europe 1750–2000* (New York, 2003).

southern English county of Kent but 91 in west-central Scotland; 100 in Belorussia but 296 in the Ural oblast of Russia.

Some historians have proposed that lower fertility was, if only in part, caused by a lower level of sexual activity in this period; but such evidence as has been adduced is largely anecdotal and unconvincing. The main cause of the decline was almost certainly birth control. In less-developed areas, for instance southern Italy, the most widely used method was probably *coitus interruptus* (the local slang term was *marcia indietro*). Artificial birth control was practised on an increasing scale. Mass distribution of condoms to soldiers during the war probably increased their use thereafter. But the opposition of the Catholic Church (and of the Anglican Church until 1930) limited their spread. Catholic injunctions against birth control clearly affected fertility in some countries. It was significantly lower in Protestant than in Catholic cantons of Switzerland. Similar differences were recorded between Protestant and Catholic regions of the Netherlands and Germany. The rhythm method of birth control, the only one permitted by the Catholic Church, was hardly understood at this time. Indeed, in all classes there was a general ignorance of elementary facts about human reproduction. Many medical authorities, including the British Medical Association, opposed use of contraceptives as unnatural. In Ireland they were banned by law in 1935. In France, their sale, formally illegal, was pushed into a grey underworld. Elsewhere, even if legal, they were regarded with distaste. In Britain the eugenicist Marie Stopes, author of the best-seller *Married Love* (1918), promoted sex education and urged greater availability of artificial contraceptive devices: she opened the first birth-control clinic in London in 1921. A government-sponsored centre offering advice 'in all sexual matters, particularly reproduction' opened in Prenzlauer Berg, a working-class area of Berlin, in 1926. By the early 1930s there were more than two hundred such counselling centres across Germany. But these were concerned more with promoting eugenic reproduction by checking for venereal diseases or hereditary illnesses; under political pressure, particularly from the Catholic Centre Party, they did not actively promote birth control. It was left to other bodies, run by sexual reform associations, to distribute contraceptives. In Berlin and in some other cities they were easily available from public vending machines; elsewhere they were more difficult to obtain. In spite of opposition, however, their use began to percolate down to the working class, though with the advent of the Nazis, birth-control propaganda was made illegal in Germany and contraceptives were banned. Probably connected with the increased resort to birth control was the reduction in numbers of illegitimate births in the inter-war period, continuing a general decline since at least the early twentieth century.

Abortion, a crime in most countries, was nevertheless widely performed. In Germany in the 1920s, hospitals were reporting two to three times as many abortions as in the pre-war period. There, as in Britain, abortion was often sought not only by unmarried women but by married ones. In England an estimated five hundred women died each year between the wars from botched abortions. In France a 1920 law severely punished any person providing or obtaining an abortion; an estimated 400,000 terminations a year nevertheless took place in the 1930s. Everywhere, quack remedies and folk methods of abortion produced untold numbers of injuries and deaths. The first country to legalize abortion was Russia in 1921; the rest of the Soviet Union followed suit soon afterwards. But in the late 1920s the practice was increasingly controlled and repressed and in 1936 banned, apparently out of a political desire to promote population growth. In spite of the change in the law, the number of abortions recorded by the USSR Ministry of Health fell quite slowly: from about 800,000 in 1936 to half a million in 1940.[3] Abortion continued to be authorized on a broad range of medical grounds and, given the general unavailability in the USSR of other forms of contraception, illegal operations continued, often resulting in injury or death.

The massive loss of life in the First World War had aroused widespread fear in many countries of the effects of declining population and led to the adoption of governmental policies designed to encourage *familles nombreuses* and to discourage emigration. In France, whose population growth was slower than that of any other major power, concern over depopulation had been voiced as far back as the mid-nineteenth century. Social theorists argued that decline in population would weaken France militarily, sap her political, diplomatic, and cultural strength, slow her economic development, and result in foreign penetration and loss of national consciousness. Clemenceau warned after the First World War that if the French did not have more children 'France will be lost, because there will no longer be Frenchmen'.[4] He and other politicians called for a consciously expansive 'population policy' designed to make up the losses of the war years. Feminists did not rally to oppose the anti-abortion legislation in the 1920s although the anarchist 'neo-Malthusian' movement proposed a *grève de ventres* (strike of wombs) to counter the law. In 1932 France became the first country to introduce family allowances, though at first only in certain regions and industries; the allowances were paid out of funds compulsorily financed by employers. In 1939 a comprehensive Family Code was enacted. But all these efforts to raise the birth rate had limited effect. Not until 1950 did France once more attain her population (within the same territory) of 1914.

Demographic nationalism transcended ideological boundaries. In Sweden in 1934 the social scientists (and later Nobel laureates) Alva and Gunnar Myrdal published their *Kris i befolkningsfrågan* (*Crisis in the Population Question*), warning that Sweden was in danger of a dangerous decline in population. In response, the Social Democrat-dominated government set up a royal commission on the problem. Mussolini too was greatly concerned about the issue. In 1927 he launched a campaign for more births with the words: 'Every nation and empire has felt the deadly grasp of decadence when the number of its births diminishes.'[5] Denouncing the practice of *coitus interruptus*, the Fascist mayor of Bologna declared: 'Screw and leave it in! Orders of the Party!'[6] The Fascist regime's energetic population policy had other strands. It banned distribution of information on contraceptives, introduced extra taxes on bachelors and unmarried couples, and rewarded the (male) heads of large families with government jobs and tax incentives. Homosexuality was criminalized and restrictions were placed on emigration. Child allowances, payable to the family breadwinner (i.e. generally to the father), were introduced in 1936.

Similar measures were introduced in Nazi Germany where a law of August 1933 granted loans to newly married couples to enable the wife to withdraw from work: a quarter of the loan was forgiven on the birth of each child. The number of day nurseries greatly increased and the law against abortions was strictly enforced. Women who bore several children were awarded the Cross of Honour of the German Mother. The number of births in Germany increased each year between 1933 and 1939. Whether this was a result of such laws has been debated; some demographers have argued that the recovery in the birth rate was simply a natural response to mass re-employment. Even in the late 1930s, however, the number of births was still barely at replacement level. And after 1939 the figure fell back again. Nazi stress on natalism went hand in hand with a strong eugenicist thrust. Such doctrines had enjoyed a vogue under Weimar but after 1933 they combined with notions of the importance of pure Aryan breeding stock. As Goebbels's Ministry of Propaganda put it, 'The goal is not "children at any cost" but racially worthy, physically and mentally unaffected children of German families.'[7] Among the first laws promulgated by the Nazi regime was a 'Law for the Prevention of Hereditarily Diseased Offspring'. Voluntary sterilization had already been legalized in 1932, before the Nazis' ascent to power. The new law endowed 'Hereditary Health Courts' with authority to order compulsory sterilization of any person who suffered from one of a number of listed illnesses: 'congenital feeblemindedness', schizophrenia, manic depression, hereditary epilepsy, Huntington's chorea, hereditary blindness or deafness, 'serious physical deformities', or 'chronic alcoholism'. The law stipulated that 'if other measures prove insufficient, the use of force is permissible'.[8] By 1945 at least 360,000 Germans (not including 'non-Aryans'), half of them women, had been sterilized. (Compulsory sterilization was not unique to Nazi Germany; it was performed also in the United States, Norway, Sweden, and Denmark in this period, although on a much smaller scale.) A further law, enacted in 1936, prevented the marriage of persons suffering from such illnesses. Carried to their ultimate extreme, such ideas gave rise to the supposedly scientific breeding of human beings, like pigs, in the *Lebensborn* baby farms—maternity homes for women who bore children for SS-men and others judged racially pure.

Slower population growth cannot be explained by emigration. Movement out of Europe, such a marked demographic feature before 1914, dwindled in the inter-war period. Total overseas emigration from the continent fell from an average of well over a million a year in the period before 1914 to barely half that number in 1926–30. During the depression years of the 1930s almost all receiving countries stiffened conditions of entry with the result that emigration ceased to be a significant demographic factor: the average figure for European annual intercontinental emigration in 1931–5 was only 131,000, rising slightly to 147,000 in the period 1936–9 (a large part of these Jewish refugees from Nazism). The effect on countries that had been huge exporters of people before 1914 was pronounced: for example, net emigration from Italy fell from 477,000 in 1914 to only 47,000 in 1929. Poland as well as other countries that thought of themselves as grossly overpopulated and that had earlier been major exporters of population now had small net inflows as disappointed emigrants trickled home.

Within Europe too migration declined precipitously. The USSR under Stalin virtually sealed its borders to emigration—though not to immigration: a few enthusiasts moved there on ideological grounds. Germany in the 1930s enjoyed a net inflow of migration. The forced departure of nearly 400,000 Jewish and political refugees was more than balanced numerically by the arrival of a larger number of *Volksdeutsche* (the term used by German nationalists for ethnic Germans living outside the *Reich*), drawn in by the developing labour shortage in the late 1930s. France remained the largest recipient of immigrants. Fear of population decline led the French government in the 1920s to take active measures to promote immigration, particularly from Italy, Poland, Spain, and Belgium. The new arrivals settled mainly in the eastern and southern *départements* of the country. By 1929, nearly half of all employees in French mines were aliens as were more than 40 per cent of workers in the chemical, cement-manufacturing, public works contracting, and sugar-refining industries. Nearly three million aliens lived in France in 1931, constituting 7 per cent of the population. Not included in these figures were about a hundred thousand north Africans, precursors of what would, a generation later, become a great flood of immigration. Yet even France's traditional hospitality to immigrants began to show signs of serious strain in the 1930s under the impact of mass unemployment and rising xenophobia. Labour unions opposed immigration lest it dilute the labour market; and the nationalist right did so lest it dilute the 'racial stock'. Reduced but still significant numbers nevertheless continued to arrive, including many political refugees from Spain and central Europe. Altogether France had a positive net migration balance of 1.2 million between 1921 and 1940.

In most of Europe internal migration from rural to urban areas continued apace. In Paris, according to the 1931 census, only 37 per cent of the population were natives of Paris or its suburbs; 12 per cent were immigrants from other countries or from French overseas possessions; no fewer than 51 per cent had been born in other parts of France. In Scotland almost every county lost population in the 1920s, most of the migrants moving to Glasgow or Edinburgh. In Spain there was large-scale migration to Madrid and Barcelona; in Sweden to Stockholm, Göteborg, and Malmö; in Italy to Rome, Lombardy, Piedmont, and Liguria. Even in the poorer countries of southern Europe big cities were sucking in people from the countryside: in Bulgaria, for example, the fastest growing region was around the capital Sofia; similarly for Lisbon in Portugal. In the Soviet Union rural migration to the cities was a consequence of deliberate government policy. The exodus from the country continued even in Germany and Italy, in spite of strenuous government efforts to prevent it, although the *rate* of mobility to the cities declined in Germany by comparison with the pre-1914 period.

Half the population of the continent by the early 1930s lived in urban areas. The most urbanized countries were Scotland, Belgium, and the Netherlands, where four-fifths of the population lived in towns. In France, for the first time in history, there was an urban majority. By contrast, in Romania, Latvia, Portugal, and Yugoslavia, four-fifths of the population still lived in rural settlements. In the late 1930s London remained the largest city in Europe with 8.7 million people; Paris ranked second with five million, followed by Berlin with 4.4 million, Moscow with 4.1 million, and Leningrad with 3.2 million. No other European city had a population of more than two million. By about 1930 Europe had 182 cities with more than a hundred thousand inhabitants, representing nearly a fifth of the total population of the continent. The great majority were in north-western or central Europe: fifty-eight were in Germany, fifty-seven in Britain, and seventeen in France. Only sixteen cities boasted more than a million people. Nine were capitals, four provincial cities in Britain (Manchester, Glasgow, Liverpool, and Birmingham), and three major ports: Hamburg, Naples, and Leningrad.

Migration changed the ethnic balance of many cities, particularly in east-central Europe. Many towns there had been founded by German merchants and their inhabitants before the war had been largely German or Jewish. The immigration of large numbers of members of peasant nationalities from surrounding countrysides changed the composition of their populations. In Tallinn, the capital of Estonia, Germans, a quarter of the population in 1881, were only 5 per cent by 1939. In the Latvian capital, Riga, the proportion of ethnic Latvians rose from 45 per cent in 1897 to 63 per cent by 1939. In Salonica Sephardic Jews had been the largest element in the population in the late Ottoman period. After the Greek conquest in 1912 their position deteriorated. The great influx of Greek refugees from Turkey after the First World War turned them into a minority. Between the wars many emigrated to France or Palestine. By 1937, when the name of the city was changed by royal decree to Thessaloniki, its population was more than four-fifths Greek.

Social change

Movement of population to cities changed the age balance between town and country. The young left rural areas in pursuit of opportunities in urban society; the old stayed behind on the farms. The continued growth of cities reflected the general decline in agriculture as an occupation. This was the first period in history when a majority of Europeans did not earn their living from the land. In Europe as a whole (not including the USSR) an estimated 36 per cent of the population were dependent on agriculture in the 1930s. Regional variations remained great. In Britain in the early 1930s the agricultural labour force was no more than 5 per cent of the total; in Germany, France, and most of Scandinavia the proportion was between 20 and 30 per cent. But in most of eastern Europe, particularly in the Balkans, a half to three-quarters of the population were still peasants. These regional disparities were inversely related to agricultural productivity which was highest in England and Denmark and lowest in western Ireland, northern Portugal, the USSR, Poland, the eastern half of Czechoslovakia, and the Balkans. In general, it was estimated that agriculture in north-western Europe was three or four times as productive as in eastern and southern regions of the continent.

Driven out of the countryside by acute rural distress, the newcomers to the city encountered a barely less miserable quality of life in their new abode. In Berlin, according to the 1925 census, 117,430 people were homeless. Even where people had homes, working-class housing almost everywhere was congested, insanitary, and squalid. In the USSR the urban standard was one room per family in a communal apartment. Most Russian homes were still without bathrooms and people had to take weekly baths in public bathhouses—where these were available. Paris was the most densely populated capital in Europe, with over eighty thousand people per square mile (excluding the Bois de Boulogne and the Bois de Vincennes). In many parts of the city more than half the population lived at a density of more than one person per room. Living conditions were even worse in the decaying slum tenements of Glasgow or Lyons. They were almost unendurable in the cities of southern and eastern Europe that were swollen with the influx of peasants squeezed out of the countryside. In Athens the population had ballooned from 167,000 in 1907 to 642,000 (including 225,000 refugees from Turkey and Bulgaria) by 1926. In the initial stage of the refugee influx, overcrowding was so severe that the municipal theatre was turned into an emergency shelter, each box holding one family. Here, as in most other semi-developed countries of Europe, the magnitude of the housing problem overwhelmed any attempt to grapple with it effectively.

Under popular pressure to address this challenge, European states began to intervene in the housing market in these years, although, outside north-west and central Europe, rarely to great effect. In Sweden housing construction, encouraged by state loans and grants, reached record levels and new homes were built to higher standards: 90 per cent of all those completed between 1934 and 1939, for example, had central heating, regarded as a luxury in most other parts of Europe. In France rent controls discouraged both new construction and maintenance and led to the deterioration of much of the housing stock into slums. The *loi Loucheur* of 1930 envisaged the construction of half a million houses over ten years, a modest target that was only half achieved.

The British built six times as many homes as the French in the 1930s. The Housing Act of 1930 provided for clearance of nineteenth-century slums and the building of municipally owned 'council houses', modestly appointed but a great improvement on what they replaced. The 'garden city' concept, originating in private initiatives in England in the late nineteenth century, was developed on a large scale by public authorities in Britain in the inter-war period. Overall, British government expenditure on working-class housing nearly tripled between 1924 and 1936. In the year 1936/7 alone, 346,000 units were completed. In Vienna, where housing congestion was particularly acute, the city council, controlled by the Social Democrats, embarked on perhaps the most ambitious and certainly the most famous enterprise in public housing construction of the period. Between 1919 and 1934 64,000 units were built, housing 180,000 people. Most were large blocks of flats. The Karl-Marx-Hof, designed by Karl Ehn and completed in 1930, was a massive fortress-style apartment complex, containing 1,382 units; it became known as the 'Ring of the Proletariat'. Unusually for urban workers' housing of the time, flats contained running water and private lavatories as well as a community infrastructure of kindergartens and laundries.

Architectural style in the European city in this period was revolutionized. The dominant force was the Bauhaus, a college of architecture and design founded by Walter Gropius at Weimar in 1919 (it later moved to Dessau). In the Bauhaus-influenced International Modern style, the accent was on functionalism, light, simplicity, and geometrical harmony. Applied decoration was avoided as was detail not required by the underlying structure. In the interior of buildings completely enclosed rooms gave way to open-plan spaces divided by movable partitions. In some parts of Europe, notably the Netherlands, even sometimes in the 1920s in Russia, public housing projects were designed by imaginative, modernist architects. Nowhere was this more the case than in Weimar Germany, as for example in Frankfurt, where the city architect, Ernst May, used pre-cast slab construction to build thousands of attractive apartment blocks. Berlin boasted many of the finest examples of the International Style: the Shell building on Königin-Augusta-Strasse, designed by Emil Fahrenkamp, Hans Poelzig's vast Broadcasting Centre in Masurenallee, and Erich Mendelsohn's Columbushaus. The Bauhaus school's influence extended to commercial architecture and design, particularly through the department stores built by Mendelsohn in Berlin, Breslau, Stuttgart, Nuremberg, and Chemnitz, whose hallmark was the long horizontal bands of windows that gave natural light to interiors and a graceful lightness of touch to exteriors. In

Paris and London new emporiums eschewed the palatial grandeur and marble columns of the pre-war period: a prime example was the Peter Jones store on Sloane Square in London, which opened in 1936. Apart from Germany, the International Style particularly affected architecture in the Netherlands, Czechoslovakia, and Scandinavia, notably through the work of the Finnish architect and designer Alvar Aalto. In France the French-Swiss architect Le Corbusier (Charles-Edouard Jeanneret-Gris) became the outstanding proponent of the house as a '*machine à habiter*'. His workers' housing scheme at Pessac, near Bordeaux, built in 1925, expressed his purist, socially engaged, architectural modernism.

Le Corbusier's futuristic conception of a 'City of Towers' imagined sixty-storey blocks of flats soaring up 750 feet. In 1921 Ludwig Miës van der Rohe completed a pathbreaking design for a skyscraper in Friedrichstrasse in Berlin; but, like Le Corbusier's, this was a theoretical exercise, as the technology for such a construction did not yet exist. In 1926 Fritz Lang's dystopian science-fiction film *Metropolis* portrayed a mechanized slave-society set in the year 2026 in a vertical city, composed of towering skyscrapers. Europe's first skyscraper, the Boerentoren in Antwerp, also one of the first buildings in Europe with a load-carrying structured frame, was completed in 1930 in time for the city's World Exhibition. Originally 287 feet high, the structure was further extended later. But the European city did not move upwards quite yet. Most big cities set a height limit on buildings of between 60 and 75 feet. In Moscow, Stalin, an enthusiast for size though not for modernism, ordered the demolition of the Cathedral of Christ the Saviour in 1931 with a view to building a gigantic Congress of Soviets building; but construction had not begun by the time war broke out ten years later.

Under Hitler German architectural priorities changed. The Bauhaus was closed by the Nazis in 1933. Gropius, Mendelsohn, and many other architects and designers went into exile. Miës van der Rohe, who had once built for the German Communist Party, tried to ingratiate himself with the Nazis, but he too left Germany in 1937. Hitler took a personal interest in architecture. For him it was, like everything else, a form of propaganda. He favoured monumentalism, neoclassicism, stone rather than concrete, and large-scale city planning. Nazi architecture alternated between vainglorious bombast and backward-looking, supposedly *völkisch* traditionalism. Albert Speer, Hitler's chief state architect, redesigned the capital of the 'thousand-year Reich' with buildings that he thought would indeed last a millennium. Most of his plans never got beyond the blueprint stage. But his new Reich

Chancellery was built by eight thousand construction workers within twelve months in 1938–9. Its vast halls, grand vistas, and enfilades were designed to awe the visitor and elevate the ego of its chief occupant. 'When one enters the Reich Chancellery, one should have the feeling that one is visiting the Master of the World,' Hitler declared.[9] The Olympic sports complex, constructed in Berlin for the 1936 games, with a stadium for 100,000 spectators and an adjacent parade ground, catered to Nazi notions of a connection between 'Aryan blood' and ancient Greece. It furnished an alternative to Nuremberg for the 'human architecture' of mass patriotic rallies. The opening of the games provided a world stage for just such a demonstration, skilfully exploited by the Nazis. Such great prestige projects were what excited Hitler most. As for housing, Germany was an exception to the general pattern in affluent regions of Europe in that publicly financed construction sharply contracted after 1933.

The urban infrastructure in most of Europe failed to keep pace with growth in population. If, as Victor Hugo averred, sewage is the conscience of the city, then inter-war Europe was a place with few scruples. Waste water in the growing cities could be disposed of in three ways: by recycling for use in agriculture, by treatment in specialized plants, or, in the case of coastal or riverine cities, by pumping into lakes, estuaries, or the sea. In most German cities treatment plants were constructed before 1914. Improved means of dealing with the resultant sludge were developed in the 1920s. In 1925 a new method, the 'activated sludge' process, was employed for the first time at Essen-Recklinghausen. The largest and most advanced such plant in Europe, with a flow rate of 12,000 cubic metres a day, was built in the Free City of Danzig in 1930 (it also served the neighbouring Polish seaside resort of Sopot but not the nearby Polish port of Gdynia, regarded as a competitor against Danzig). Such technical advances, however, came to a stop with the Depression. The Nazis preferred to give priority to recycling waste water for agriculture as a form of subsidy to farmers. Elsewhere in Europe progress in waste-water purification was uneven. Leningrad had no effective sewerage system until 1930, when the Vasilievsky Island pumping station was completed. Athens relied until after the Second World War entirely on cesspools that contaminated the soil. A reservoir behind the Marathon dam, completed in 1929, improved the purity of the water supply but other Greek cities were not so fortunate: no doubt partly for this reason, the infant mortality rate in Greece, alone in Europe, soared by 50 per cent between 1922 and 1937. Even the capital of a rich, socially aware country like Sweden did not tackle its sewage problem much more effectively. Stockholm had no waste-water treatment plant in the 1920s and pollution levels rose alarmingly in the adjacent Mälaren Lake. In 1928 20 tons of dead fish were scooped out of the nearby Norrvik Lake and public anger was fanned by a newspaper campaign demanding action. The city opened its first, small treatment plant in 1933 but it did not use the 'activated sludge' method. Most of the city's waste water remained untreated until 1941. Outside big cities, piped running water was unusual in homes, not only in poor countries but even in parts of Switzerland and Norway: most householders had to rely on public wells, springs, or rivers. Where piped water was available, it was often contaminated by sewage leaking into the underground water table.

Nor was the urban or inter-urban road system adequate for the great increase in motor transport. Older towns and cities with centuries-old centres composed of winding, narrow streets found themselves choked with traffic. Even Paris and Berlin, with their broad, straight boulevards, found difficulty in adapting to the epidemic spread of the motor car. In early 1923 a survey in Berlin found traffic evenly balanced between horse-drawn carriages and motor vehicles. By 1932 only seventy-four horse-drawn carriages remained. In London in 1936 the Minister of Transport banned horse-drawn vehicles from several of the major streets in the centre of the city. But car ownership was still restricted to the upper-middle class and in eastern Europe the automobile was a rarity. Whereas Germany in 1935 had 11.9 cars per thousand people, and Sweden 22.6, Romania had only 1.8. Poland had four million horses but only 25,000 motor cars. A traveller on a main road near Nowogródek in eastern Poland in 1934 counted 500 horse-drawn wagons, twenty-five pedestrians, two bicycles and no motor cars at all passing in the course of an hour. She reported that crowds of curious onlookers would gather round her car when she stopped and horses would shy when she drove past.[10] In the second half of the decade European automobile production increased greatly. Britain manufactured 379,000 cars in 1937 compared with 269,000 in Germany. But Germany was catching up fast. At the Berlin Motor Show in February 1939 Hitler launched a world-beating line, the first Volkswagen ('people's car'), designed by Ferdinand ('Ferry') Porsche and produced by Mercedes-Benz. Hitler called it the KdF ('*Kraft durch Freude*', 'Strength through Joy'); the English moniker 'beetle' was pinned on it only after the war. Early models were primitive: there was no synchromesh in the gearbox; the driver had to double-declutch. Yet they became wildly popular.

Only a few thousand were built before the outbreak of the Second World War, whereupon the factory switched to military vehicles. But production resumed after the war and it eventually became the world's best-selling car, surpassing the Model T Ford. By 1939 Germany had 1.4 million private cars by comparison with Britain's two million and France's 1.75 million. But Germany had more motor-cycles than any other European country. To accommodate the vehicular hordes, Germany had begun construction of its Autobahn system in 1929. Under the Nazis road construction was the most important form of job creation and helped fuel the economic recovery. By 1939 more than 1,800 miles were complete. Britain at that time had only 27.5 miles of double-carriage highway.

In spite of the spread of the motor car, most travel was still by public transport—by rail across country, by bus, trolleybus, or tram in the city. Trams were generally single-level (except in Britain, where some cities retained double-deckers) and often double-car. Prague had no buses at all, only trams. Some tramways, for example Lisbon's, expanded in the 1930s. But many were bankrupted by the Depression and were replaced by buses. Only three underground railway systems were added to the existing six in the inter-war period: Madrid (1919), Barcelona (1924), and the Moscow subway, one of the great showpiece developments of Stalin's Russia, for which construction began in 1932. Seventy thousand workers, including many women, were enlisted for this 'shock' project: dozens died in underground accidents during construction. The first 12-kilometre section opened in 1935. This was a rare case of a national prestige enterprise that brought significant and lasting benefit to the masses.

By contrast with the underground, which was used by all classes, civil aviation was still an expensive means of travel, available only to a wealthy minority. Yet public enthusiasm for the feats of solo fliers and for spectacular aerial feats of technology and endurance reached a peak in this decade. Record-breaking pilots became overnight celebrities like the space travellers of the next generation. In Germany the giant airships *Graf Zeppelin* and *Hindenburg* became objects of mass enthusiasm. But the hopes invested in these ocean liners of the air disintegrated after the crash of the British-built R101 in October 1930 (which killed all fifty-four people on board) and the subsequent disasters of the American *Akron II* in 1933 and of the *Hindenburg*, the largest airship ever built, in 1937. Attention now switched to fixed-wing planes. The first transatlantic passenger aeroplane flights were inaugurated by Pan Am in June

1939 with the Yankee Clipper, a four-engine flying boat, that flew weekly from New York to Lisbon in twenty-six hours, with a stop in the Azores.

A technical change that came closer to most people was the spread of electrification. By the 1930s a majority of homes in all the advanced industrial economies were connected to the grid. Yet in spite of electrification and the rapid growth of electrical consumer-durables industries, few homes outside the affluent middle class had electric-powered goods other than lights and radio receivers. In Britain, which was ahead of most other European countries in this sphere in 1939, 33 per cent of electrically wired homes contained vacuum cleaners, but only 4 per cent had electric washing machines or boilers, and only 3 per cent had refrigerators. Large parts of Europe, meanwhile, were as yet in no position even to begin to participate in this consumer revolution. In 1939 two-thirds of Hungarian villages were without electricity. In the Balkans the connection rate was even lower.

Although the Depression brought acute misery to the peasantry and urban workers, it also greatly reduced the value of the assets of the possessing classes. Massive disparities in distribution of wealth and income remained in all European societies, as R. H. Tawney showed for Britain in his influential *Equality* (1931). Yet overall economic inequalities in western Europe did not increase in the 1930s and may even have diminished somewhat. Economic recovery in the second half of the decade restored Europe's pre-1914 position as producer of more than half of all the world's industrial production. Germany was the continent's largest producer in 1938 with 13 per cent of the world total. Britain came next with 9 per cent. Notwithstanding her great leap forward since 1928, the USSR still lagged behind. The most buoyant industrial sectors were chemicals, metallurgy, automobiles, electrical goods, and armaments. But in spite of Europe's increased share of world production, heightened tariff restrictions had reduced the continent's share of international trade. Economic recovery nevertheless brought a substantial reduction in unemployment. In Germany the official rate fell to 2 per cent by 1939 (although this was partly a result of the withdrawal of women from the labour force). Elsewhere the decline was less impressive: in Britain to 12 per cent; in the Netherlands to 20 per cent. The service sector was the fastest-growing area of employment in the advanced economies in the 1930s, employing half of all workers in Britain and more than a third in most other countries of western Europe. As a result, the distribution of classes began to change: growth was strongest in the white-collar lower-middle class.

The working class, although for the most part back at work, did not quickly regain the ground lost during the world economic crisis. Even after the abatement of the Depression, authoritarian governments hostile to labour organization prevented the recovery of labour unions. Divisions in many countries between Communist, Socialist, and Catholic unions weakened the movement as a whole. American methods of scientific management, associated with Frederick W. Taylor and the motor manufacturer Henry Ford, had begun to be adopted in the 1920s, especially in Germany where technical and organizational rationalization and mass production techniques were widely applied in the chemical, machine-tool, and automobile industries. The French labour leader Albert Thomas, who became head of the International Labour Organization, established by the Treaty of Versailles, was open to such ideas as offering potential benefits to employees as well as employers; but most organized labour resisted automation, assembly lines, shift work, and time-and-motion studies. The fears and resentments aroused by the Depression left a residue of class hatreds that added a keen edge of bitterness to political conflict between left and right.

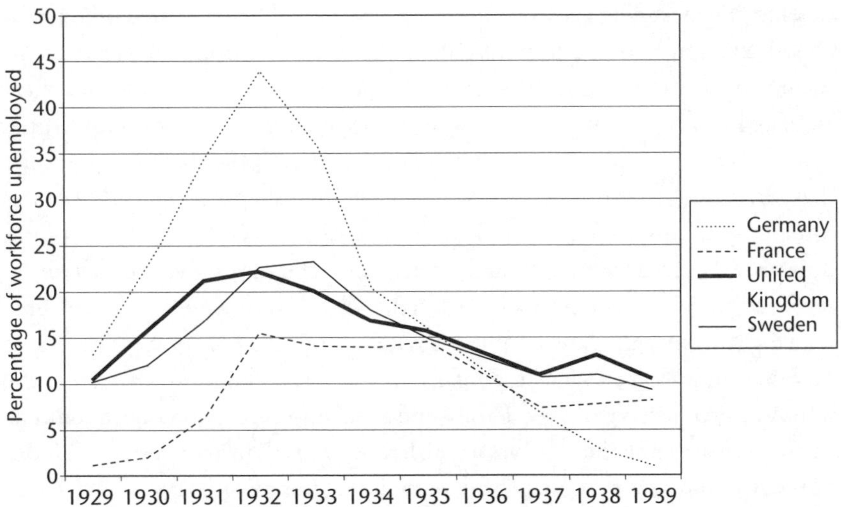

Figure 5. Unemployment in selected countries, 1929–1939

Source: B. Eichengreen and T. J. Hatton, eds., *Interwar Unemployment in International Perspective* (Dordrecht, 1988).

Domestic life

Demographic shifts had far-reaching effects on the family. In spite of the reduction in infant mortality, reduced fertility meant that average family size was becoming smaller. Demographers spoke grimly of the 'small family problem'. The structure of the family was changing in other ways too. Altogether the family seemed a less stable unit. The divorce rate, which had gone up almost everywhere during and after the First World War, remained at a high level in the 1930s. In Austria it was eight times, in Finland three times, and in Germany, Sweden and Denmark twice the pre-war rate. Yet all the churches continued to uphold traditional sexual roles and family values. In Italy, Ireland, and other Catholic countries, divorce remained illegal. In his encyclical *Casti Connubii* (31 December 1930), Pope Pius XI not only condemned divorce, adultery, contraception, abortion, and eugenics; he also denounced feminism as promoting 'false liberty and unnatural equality with man'. Within the family, he insisted on 'the superiority of the husband over the wife'.[11] But such pronouncements were gradually losing authority or effectiveness in shaping social practice.

The most radical attack on the sanctity of the family was launched in the Soviet Union during the first phase of Bolshevik rule. Reflecting the general onslaught against religion and bourgeois values, the USSR seemed on track to abolish the institution of the family altogether. In a notorious phrase attributed to the Russian feminist Alexandra Kollontai, who served as Commissar for Welfare in 1917–18, sex was to be as unremarkable an event as 'drinking a glass of water'. It is not clear, however, that Kollontai ever said that. She did write that 'the sexual act must be seen not as something shameful and sinful but as something which is as natural as the other needs of a healthy organism, such as hunger and thirst'—which, though no less unconventional, was perhaps more sensible.[12] In any case, Lenin repudiated the idea of free love: 'Would a normal man drink from a glass', he enquired, 'when its rim has been sullied by dozens of other lips?'[13] Kollontai and other avant-garde thinkers advocated the removal of children from the family and their upbringing in collective units. In these years cohabitation was regarded as equivalent to marriage. Under the 1926 family law, divorce became simply a matter of signing a piece of paper by either spouse at a registration office; the other would be notified within three days by mail—the so-called 'postcard divorce'. In the 1930s, however, a change set in. Stalin closed down Zhenotdel, the Women's Department of the Communist Party, and ordained a return to what might almost be called Victorian values. Expounding the new official view, *Pravda* declared that 'so-called "free love" and all disorderly sex life are bourgeois through and through'.[14] The virtues of marriage and motherhood were lauded. Bearers of many children were extolled as 'hero mothers'. A divorce tax was introduced: each successive divorce attracted a higher impost. Pornography was suppressed. Homosexuality, which had not hitherto been contrary to Soviet law, was criminalized in 1934. The divorce law was tightened: as a result, the divorce rate dropped by more than a third between 1936 and 1938.

As the European family grew smaller, the role of the woman within it was changing. Arranged marriages were becoming much less common, though they could still be found in traditionalist societies in much of the Balkans, Sicily, and rural Ireland, as well as among gypsies and orthodox Jews in eastern Europe. In central Italy the contractual veto power of landlords over marriage of sharecroppers had been removed by 1920 but in practice it survived much longer.

Women still found it difficult to become more autonomous actors politically, economically, or socially. The revolutions in Russia, Germany, Austria, and Atatürk's Turkey all granted women the vote as did the new states of Poland and Czechoslovakia. In Britain most women over thirty were enfranchised in 1918; in 1928 the bar against 'flappers' was removed and women over twenty-one could vote on the same basis as men. An amendment to the Swedish constitution in 1919 granted women suffrage and the right to stand for parliament. Elsewhere progress was slow. In Spain, where women remained disenfranchised until 1931, some Socialists opposed women's suffrage out of fear that it would strengthen the right, given alleged female susceptibility to clerical influence. In France, Italy, Belgium, Switzerland, and (with some exceptions) Bulgaria, women did not gain the vote in parliamentary elections until the end of the Second World War or even later. Women took some time to gain a foothold in parliaments, let alone governments. The first woman member, Lady Astor, took her seat in the British House of Commons in 1919. In 1924 Nina Bang was appointed Minister of Public Instruction in Denmark, thus becoming the first woman cabinet minister in Europe (apart from Kollontai). But these were isolated cases. Women would have to wait until long after the Second World War to make a significant dent in the masculine near-monopoly in European politics.

Nor were women free economic actors. In Britain, for example, a married woman could not sign hire purchase contracts (now becoming common, especially for buying vacuum cleaners, sewing machines, or other consumer durables) without her husband's permission. Women had entered the medical profession before 1914 but only in the inter-war period were they generally admitted to the bar (Hungary and Bulgaria resisted that until after 1945). Women could not become judges, save in Norway, Weimar Germany, and the USSR, until after the Second World War. They were granted improved access to the civil service in France and Italy in 1919. By 1926 women's share of employment in central government administration in France had risen to 45 per cent, compared with less than 3 per cent before 1914. But several ministries would not admit women to professional positions at all, and others limited their promotion. Almost everywhere, particularly if married, women found legal or practical impediments to attaining senior posts in the civil service, the universities, the armed forces, the diplomatic corps, and, of course, the church hierarchy.

The entry of working-class women into industrial employment during the First World War paved the way for an expansion of opportunities for women in factories in the inter-war period. But labour union leaders, concerned about competition for scarce jobs, often opposed women's encroachment into former male preserves. In France, for example, the National Bureau of the Confédération générale du travail declared in 1919: 'The woman's natural place is at home, and forcing her into workshop employment incurs the destruction of the family.'[15] In the final years of the Weimar Republic and also under the Nazis, policies were introduced against *Doppelverdiener* (two-earner) families. Nevertheless, in most countries more women entered the labour force in new light industries, for example food packaging, and in the service sector as secretaries, telephone operators, teachers, and nurses. Generally, domestic service now accounted for fewer women's jobs, though in Italy the number of female domestic servants rose from 381,000 in 1921 to 585,000 in 1936. In the Soviet Union women were mobilized into factories and mines in large numbers to help meet the targets of the five-year plans: their share of the industrial labour force rose from 29 per cent to 43 per cent between 1928 and 1939. Everywhere, including the USSR, women continued to be paid at lower rates than men. A male clerk in Berlin, for example, earned a starting salary 17.5 per cent higher than a female. In factories, in the USSR as well as elsewhere, women were often segregated from men on separate assembly lines.

Women's place under Fascism and Nazism was emphatically in the home. Italy set quotas limiting female employment in both official and private employment. *La donna a casa!* was the Fascist slogan. Hitler's attitude to women was primitive. 'The message of woman's emancipation', he declared in a speech in 1934, 'is a message discovered solely by the Jewish intellect. . . . We do not find it right when the woman presses into the world of the man. Rather we find it natural when these two worlds remain separate. . . . To the one belongs the power of feeling, the power of the soul . . . to the other belongs the strength of vision, the strength of hardness, the decisions and willingness to act.'[16] Woman's primary function, in the mind of the Fascist dictator, was to bear children for the perpetuation of the race.

The practice of sending children to paid wet-nurses, common in earlier periods, had almost died out. In 1910–14 30 per cent of infants in Paris were being sent *en nourrice*, often in the countryside. By 1920 only 7 per cent were being fed outside the home. Mercenary wet-nursing was already almost extinct elsewhere in Europe and soon disappeared in France too. Bottle-feeding had once been a major cause of infection and infant mortality but pasteurization of milk made bottle-feeding almost as healthy as breast-feeding. In Sweden in the late 1930s the first, rather primitive forms of disposable nappies (diapers) were introduced to the market. Meanwhile menstruation was somewhat mitigated by the introduction in the 1920s of industrially produced sanitary pads, though their use was not universal: they were hardly known, for example, in Italy, Spain, or most of eastern Europe and, as a result of pressure from the Church, were banned in Ireland.

In other ways too, women's social behaviour was changing. By the 1930s large numbers of women, at least in towns, were using make-up, particularly face powder, lipstick, and nail polish, to disguise or enhance their natural features. Once the prerogative of the harlot and the well-to-do, cosmetics developed into a major industry for all classes. In Sweden per capita consumption of face powder and rouge multiplied more than tenfold between 1914 and 1930; the sales graph dipped slightly during the Depression but then resumed its upward trajectory.

Cigarette smoking, before the First World War largely a male pursuit, became fashionable among women in the inter-war period, and spread rapidly, though more in the city than in the country. Swedish cigarette sales nearly tripled between 1916 and 1930; meanwhile, consumption of other forms of tobacco decreased somewhat, suggesting that men too, particularly in towns, were turning to cigarettes and away from cigars, pipes, chewing-tobacco, and snuff. The general European increase in smoking was to wreak its terrible revenge in the form of increased deaths from lung cancer and other diseases—but this would only become apparent a generation later.

In most other respects health conditions in Europe were improving. Purer water supplies and immunization helped lower the prevalence of infectious diseases that had been child-killers on a vast scale in earlier generations. In Sweden, for example, death from tuberculosis declined by more than half in the inter-war period. Even in Greece, one of the poorest countries in Europe, with a very primitive health system, the death rate from the disease declined significantly between the wars. Yet it remained a killer. In France an average of 49,000 people a year were still dying of TB in 1930–6. The BCG vaccine (Bacille Calmette et Guérin) had first been produced at the Pasteur Institute in 1923. But British doctors were dubious about it. The vaccine was not generally adopted in Britain until the 1950s. A catastrophe at Lübeck in 1930, when seventy-one children died after receiving contaminated vaccine, made many German parents suspicious too. The vaccine was nevertheless widely administered with beneficial results in France, Sweden, and elsewhere. The incidence of other diseases also declined, though with great regional variations. In 1937, 147,000 cases of diphtheria, a disease that particularly affected children, were reported in Germany, compared with only 19,000 in France. In Nazi Germany growth in public expenditure on rearmament and reduced spending on public health led to a fall in the general standard of health of the population between 1933 and 1939. Most other parts of Europe, however, registered improvements in health from the spread of vaccination as well as from the easier availability of medical facilities to urban populations, from the construction of more hospitals, and from the spread of medical insurance. The Soviet Union, which had decreed universal free health care in 1917, claimed significant advances in health provision in this period. The number of doctors was said to have doubled and of hospital beds tripled between 1928 and 1938. But in health, as in other spheres, the privileged party bureaucracy, the *nomenklatura*, enjoyed superior treatment. In France a landmark law, passed in 1928, extended medical insurance to hitherto uninsured sections of the population so that by 1940 more than half the population was covered. In the early stages of the industrial revolution European cities had been more unhealthy places than the countryside; now, thanks to cleaner water, better sewerage, and improved public health, most were healthier than rural areas.

Apart from the Soviet Union, no country in Europe experienced serious famine in the inter-war period. Urbanization, commercialization of food distribution, and technological advances led to changes in diet. Until the

1920s tinned (canned) food was rarely seen outside the armed services. But advances in canning technology led to the growth of a large civilian market for canned food and drink in the inter-war period. British breakfast tables began to carry American-style cereals rather than porridge. Potato crisps, originally a French speciality, were sealed in packets and became popular in Britain. Average British food consumption increased in the inter-war period: a study in 1934 concluded that the average person was eating 88 per cent more fruit, 64 per cent more vegetables (other than potatoes), 46 per cent more eggs, and 6 per cent more meat than before the war. Yet one-third of the population was found to be short of calories and protein and at least half was deficient in vitamins. If this was the case in Britain, the position in the poorer countries of Europe was much worse. In Romania, according to a contemporary report, 'the peasants cannot afford to have bread regularly; meat is a rare dish on their table and often enough the ordinary diet of *mamaliga*, a sort of maize-grits, is broken only at Easter time.'[17] The Depression accentuated the serious problems of malnutrition in several parts of the continent. So-called 'deficiency diseases', attributable to poor diet—rickets, beriberi, scurvy, and pellagra—remained widespread in rural areas of southern and eastern Europe.

Alcohol consumption was declining. Between 1929 and 1933 per capita consumption of beer in Germany fell by 43 per cent, partly because of successive large increases in the excise duty. In Britain beer consumption fell by nearly half between 1913 and 1938, although it was no longer regarded primarily as a working-class beverage: a Royal Commission report in 1931 'noted that beer was becoming a more respectable drink and is now taken by people whose fathers would never have tolerated it'.[18] In the Soviet Union, however, drink remained a serious problem. Prohibition, which had been enforced with limited success since the outbreak of the First World War, was abolished in 1925. Given the cost of manufactured alcohol, moonshine and *denaturat*, an alcohol-based cleaning fluid with a warning skull-and-crossbones on the label, were widely consumed, often with deleterious effects on health. A Soviet worker is said to have commented: 'The bourgeoisie's cognac carries stars, our cognac comes with bones.'[19]

Bad diet and poor health care had another consequence: few adults in Europe in the 1930s had all their own teeth intact. Preventive dentistry was almost unknown. Most people visited the dentist only if they had severe toothache. A mass dental examination of secondary-school children in Poland in 1928–9 found 79 per cent with diseased teeth. The growing consumption of confectionary and chocolate, especially by children, worsened the problem. In some segments of the British working class it was common for young people to have all their teeth extracted at once when they were fully grown: that way they could have a full set of false teeth installed immediately and so avoid future inconvenience.

Urban dress was gradually invading the countryside: the peasant smock was giving way to a blouse and breeches, though the old styles survived in more backward areas. Peasants still often made their own clothes. In Greece the *foustanella* (a white, pleated skirt) was still worn by mountain men. In the collectivized Soviet countryside domestic spinning and weaving declined and villagers started wearing factory-made clothes. In Soviet cities women's clothing, which in the early revolutionary days had approximated to men's, was newly feminized as elegant skirts and dresses became fashionable. The doctrine of *kulturnost* ('culturedness') permitted both men and women to smarten up. Of course, fashion Soviet-style did not extend beyond the *nomenklatura*; for the bulk of the population clothing remained primitive and choice almost non-existent. In western Europe women started wearing slacks and in 1935, for the first time, a woman was permitted to wear shorts in the Wimbledon tennis championship. Underwear too evolved. Philippe de Brassière's eponymous invention (both the etymology and the patent were contested) became fashionable as did the panty-top girdle which replaced the whalebone corset. Men's and women's briefs began to be marketed. Increasingly, these were made of artificial fabrics, especially rayon (marketed as 'synthetic silk'), rather than wool or cotton. By the late 1930s rayon's share of total production of textile fibres by weight had reached 28 per cent in Germany and 27 per cent in Italy. The 'fob pocket' lost its function as men in civilian life abandoned the pocket watch for the wrist watch, no longer regarded as effeminate since it had been widely used in armies in the Great War. The zip began to be sewn onto men's trousers in the 1930s. A 'hookless fastener' had been used in clothing manufacture in Germany as far back as 1912 but early versions were unreliable. The modern zip, invented by a Swedish immigrant to the USA, began as a fastener for tobacco pouches and boots but by the 1930s its use had spread to both men's and women's clothing. As its historian notes, the zip 'quickly became a symbol of the ingenuity of modern technology, and its use was itself a badge of modernity'.[20] By 1938 it was being manufactured in nineteen European countries and, we are told, annual European consumption was 'about three inches per capita'.[21]

Mass culture

Illiteracy was declining fast, especially in eastern Europe. In Poland, for example, the rate declined from 33 per cent in 1921 to 18 per cent by 1937. In Italy it ranged from 4 per cent in Piedmont to 15 per cent in Calabria. The highest illiteracy rates in the early 1930s were to be found in Portugal (60 per cent) and in rural areas of southern Europe, for example, 61 per cent in the western Thrace region of Greece. The great educational effort in the Soviet Union led to significant reductions in illiteracy by 1939 when, according to the Soviet census, four-fifths of the population was literate (though the census probably overrated the rapidity of progress, especially in the countryside). Most remaining analphabetics in Europe by 1939 were old people, so that there was a prospect, for the first time in history, of near-total literacy as the generation of almost-universal schooling came of age.

By the inter-war period universal compulsory elementary education up to the age of twelve or thirteen had become the norm throughout Europe. Class sizes, however, remained large: even in England a third in 1938 contained over forty pupils. In the same year only 12 per cent of English children between the ages of eleven and seventeen were in school. In other countries the percentage was even lower. In Hungary most peasant children received at most six years of schooling and 10 per cent received none at all. Venizelos, upon his return to power in Greece in 1928, set about making primary education compulsory and raising the school leaving age from ten to twelve. But the arrival of the Depression and Venizelos's fall in 1932 hampered realization of these modest goals. By the late 1930s most Greek children were receiving a primary education but the country's 15,573 teachers had to cope with 985,735 pupils, yielding an average class size of sixty-three. Fewer than 15 per cent of Greek children attended even the first two years of secondary school.

Education in most Catholic countries was heavily influenced by the Church. Even in France, where the separation of Church and State had taken education out of clerical hands at the turn of the century, about a fifth of elementary school pupils and a third of secondary pupils in the late 1930s attended schools controlled by the Church. In Germany 80 per cent of schoolchildren attended denominational schools in 1933.

In the Soviet Union the early 1930s were marked by disruptive social experiments in education: children were sent to work in factories and to participate in anti-illiteracy campaigns in the countryside. But by the end of the decade a reaction had set in: teaching methods and syllabuses returned to more traditional paths, although Marxism-Leninism was installed as a central feature of the curriculum at all levels of education. By 1940 two-thirds of children were attending school for at least seven years. Like everywhere else, urban children in the USSR enjoyed, on average, several more years of schooling than their rural counterparts.

Girls still received a poorer education than boys, though the gap was slowly narrowing. In most of western Europe around a third of secondary-school pupils and about a quarter of university students were female. But in Italy the proportion of girls among pupils attending a *liceo* (secondary school) rose from 18 per cent in 1920 to 26 per cent in 1937. Women constituted 15 per cent of the Italian university student body in 1935, as against 6 per cent in 1914. Most girls were steered into humanities subjects rather than science, law, or engineering. In Germany, on the other hand, the number of women university students declined from twenty thousand to 5,500 between 1933 and 1939. In 1937 women with advanced degrees lost the right to be addressed as 'Frau Doktor', a title now reserved to the wives of physicians.

The newly literate masses provided a fertile market for the picture papers and news magazines that became popular in this period. In pre-Hitler Germany the Communist John Heartfield developed the photo-montage as a forceful satirical weapon against militarism and Nazism. Photo-journalism was effectively a German invention. In this sphere too, the Nazi years took their toll, as some of the leading practitioners were driven abroad, for example, Stefan Lorant, editor of the innovative mass-circulation *Münchner Illustrierte Presse* (*MIP*) from 1929 to 1933. Arrested after Hitler's assumption of power, he was released after a worldwide campaign and eventually moved to Britain, where he created the vastly successful *Picture Post* news magazine which attained a circulation of 1.7 million. Such news magazines were printed only in black and white, although colour film was beginning to become readily available. The essential technological breakthrough for the success of the picture papers was the invention by Oskar Barnack of the Leica camera, which came onto the market in 1925. Light and handy, using 35-mm negative film, it set speed records and facilitated instant, candid photographs of the highest quality. The camera became a powerful instrument of propagandist suasion in the hands of the great, socially conscious documentary photographers of the day. Many were Hungarian-born: for example, Lászlό Moholy-Nagy, Robert Capa (Endre Ernö Friedmann), and Brassaï (Gyula Halász), all of whom worked in Paris in the 1930s.

The work of such photographers forms an important archive of social history, as in the case of Roman Vishniac, who, between 1934 and 1939, travelled through eastern Europe recording images of traditional Jewish life in what were almost its final moments.

In much of Europe the press in the 1930s was highly politicized: many newspapers were owned or controlled by political parties and adhered closely to the required line on all issues. With the exception of respectable, conservative newspapers of record, *The Times* of London, *le Temps* in Paris, the *Vossische Zeitung* in Berlin, and the German-language *Pester Lloyd* in Budapest, much of the press (notoriously in France) was venal and deeply embedded in a culture of political and commercial corruption. The British read newspapers more than any other nation in Europe. Increasingly their morning newspapers were national rather than local in circulation and in news coverage. Press ownership was more concentrated in Britain than in most other countries. Outside north-western Europe censorship of the press was widespread: in Stalin's Russia it was absolute; in Romania, Hungary, and elsewhere it stiffened or relaxed depending on the temper of the current regime. As a growing part of the European press was turned, in Goebbels's words, into 'a piano on which the government might play',[22] the *Neue Zürcher Zeitung* acquired a unique reputation for independence and enjoyed a serious readership far beyond the borders of Switzerland, not least because it was in German. Much of the press served up little more than commercialized pap, designed with special attention to the demands of the growing advertising industry, particularly in the case of women's magazines, popular in all sectors of society and in most countries, especially in cities. Rather than pressing for the extension of women's rights, they tended almost everywhere to reinforce rather than challenge conventional sexual attitudes, stressing the role of the woman as mother and housekeeper.

At the same time, serious literature found a growing audience thanks to the spread of paperback books. The first ten paperback Penguins were published in Britain in 1935. Priced at sixpence each, they were an immediate success and opened the possibility of book purchase to many for whom the public library had hitherto been the sole source of non-ephemeral reading matter. The Left Book Club, founded in 1936 by Victor Gollancz, became a powerful force for the dissemination of social criticism. Its two most celebrated titles were George Orwell's *The Road to Wigan Pier*, which appeared in March 1937, and Ellen Wilkinson's *The Town that was Murdered*, published in September 1939, an account of the 1936 Jarrow hunger march (of unemployed shipyard workers from the depressed Tyneside town that Wilkinson represented in Parliament). By 1938 16,000 book titles were being published annually in Britain. By contrast, book publishing in Russia, which had flourished in the 1920s, suffered a severe setback during the Stalinist terror. The number of titles published dropped drastically and the 1930 level was not attained again until 1953.

Censorship of literature extended to almost all countries in the 1930s. In Germany the Reich Office for Literature, under the control of Goebbels, issued regular black lists of 'un-German' books. Among those deemed to fall into that category were works of Thomas Mann, Stefan Zweig, and Franz Kafka. Under the military dictatorship of General Ioannis Metaxas in Greece between 1936 and 1941, censors interfered with the speeches of Pericles and with a performance of *Antigone*. The publishing history of James Joyce's *Ulysses* illustrates the difficulties that could be encountered by serious literature even in democracies. It was first published in a limited edition by Shakespeare and Co. in Paris in February 1922. When two further limited editions were issued in London, copies were seized by the authorities. Unlimited editions were published between 1924 and 1932 in Paris, Hamburg, and Bologna. The first unlimited edition in Britain did not appear until 1937 and the first edition in Ireland only in 1997.

In Germany and the Soviet Union censorship led to a cramping and philistine uniformity in all the arts. A conference 'for the mass organization of arts and literature' in Kharkov in 1930 ordained that artists must abandon petty-bourgeois individualism. Artistic creation was to be systematized, collectivized, and 'carried out according to the plans of a central staff like any other soldierly work'.[23] Henceforth modernist art, including even the Impressionists, could not be publicly displayed in the USSR. The low point of the Nazi campaign against the avant-garde was the grotesque exhibition of *Entartete Kunst* ('Degenerate Art') in Munich in 1937. Expressionist, Cubist, Futurist, Dadaist, Constructivist, and almost every other kind of modernist art was displayed in a framework of sneering ridicule. Among the 112 artists whose works were shown were Max Beckmann, Marc Chagall, Otto Dix, George Grosz, Paul Klee, Oskar Kokoschka, and Emil Nolde (an early member of the Nazi Party, though that did not help him). 'It is a pity one cannot lock up people like that,' Hitler said as he stood in front of a painting by Dix.[24] More than two million people attended in four months, after which the exhibition embarked on a tour of thirteen cities and was seen by a further two million. It ranks among the best-attended art shows in history. The following year the Nazis organized a 'Degenerate Music' exhibition, featuring, among others, the composers Webern, Schoenberg, and Kurt Weill. Goebbels seized the opportunity to decree the 'ten commandments for German music' ('Music is rooted in the *Volk*' etc.) and to press forward the 'dejudaization' of musical life in Germany. The nadir of this phase of the barbarization of German culture was a huge bonfire of five thousand so-called works of 'degenerate art' in the courtyard of the central fire station in Berlin.

Cinema and theatre were censored everywhere. Soviet film and drama, which had been inventively avant-garde in the 1920s, declined into slavish Stalin-worship, as modernist directors like Aleksandr Medvedkin and Vsevolod Meyerhold were tamed or eliminated. Russia's greatest director, Sergei Eisenstein, out of favour in the early 1930s, regained official approval with his relatively conventional *Aleksandr Nevsky* (1938). Elsewhere the emphasis was generally on excluding sexual scenes or seditious (left-wing) propaganda. Arthur Schnitzler's *Reigen* ('La Ronde'), with its theme of sexually transmitted disease, was removed from the stage in Vienna. Samuel Beckett's *More Pricks than Kicks* was banned in his native Ireland in 1934. In the 1930s the British Board of Film Censors sought to keep from the screen all 'references to controversial politics', refusing, under this rubric, to pass films depicting anti-Semitism in Germany or anti-Nazi films in general, or even, in some instances, newsreel footage showing events in Germany. In Weimar Germany film censors were relatively liberal, at any rate until December 1930 when Nazi and nationalist agitation forced the Censorship Board to reverse its original decision and ban Lewis Milestone's film version of Erich Maria Remarque's anti-war novel *All Quiet on the Western Front*. After 1933 Goebbels, who watched at least one movie every day, became the ultimate arbiter of the fate of German cinema. Lest his decisions be questioned, Goebbels issued an order in 1936 prohibiting any negative reviews of films he had approved.

With the development of the talkies after 1929 and the invention of genuine colour cinematography after 1932, film became the most popular medium of mass entertainment. In Warsaw, which had fifty-seven cinemas in 1929, twelve admission tickets were sold per head of population in that year. In Stockholm attendances were even higher. Germany had six thousand cinemas by the early 1930s, more than any other country. Berlin alone had nearly four hundred. Hollywood films penetrated every part of Europe except the Soviet Union, but all the major European countries produced large numbers of films for audiences that often transcended national boundaries. Feature films of the 1930s, particularly those regarded by contemporaries as of the highest artistic value, tended to convey ideological messages. This was true not only of the controlled cinema industries of totalitarian countries but also of films produced in the liberal democracies. Sometimes the message was quasi-pacifist, as in Jean Renoir's *La Grande Illusion* (1937). Another common theme was the enslavement of men to machines in modern industrial society, conveyed with a light touch (and a half-admiring eye for the clean lines of contemporary industrial design) by René Clair in *A nous la liberté* (1931). Soviet film, even in the hands of Eisenstein, adhered strictly to the ideological message of the moment. The German film industry was Europe's largest, but imaginative German cinema was devastated by the Nazi plague. The directors Fritz Lang, Anatol Litvak, and Billy Wilder, as well as the film stars Marlene Dietrich and Peter Lorre were only the most prominent among the cinematic talent lost to Hollywood. But the UFA studios continued, under Nazi control, to produce standard entertainment films as well as propaganda.

After films, dancing in large public dance-halls was the most popular leisure activity of the young. A succession of mainly American-inspired dance crazes swept the continent: the Charleston, the lindy-hop (named after the aviator Charles Lindbergh), the rumba (a Cuban import), the Lambeth Walk (a cockney dance first made popular by Lupino Lane) and, towards the end of the 1930s, the jitterbug. An elderly German liberal intellectual in 1937, contemplating the history of the previous generation, wrote: 'The craze for public dancing which marked the first few years after the War in many countries where a cold climate and an uncouthness of bodily construction make hopping a welcome exercise, and no one is offended by the absurdity of the spectacle, formed a horrible anticlimax to the events of 1918.'[25] He was not alone in this opinion. Goebbels (who had a club foot) shared it and at one point tried to ban public dancing in Germany altogether.

The most pervasive medium of mass culture of the period was radio, which had begun on an experimental basis in the Netherlands in 1919, followed by the first regularly scheduled programmes, put out by the British Broadcasting Company (later Corporation) in 1922. In the early days enthusiasts built their own 'crystal' receivers. But very soon the manufacture of more sophisticated valve sets developed into a major industry. The medium entered its golden age in 1930s Europe. Goebbels called it 'the Eighth Great Power'.[26] He quickly brought all radio stations in Germany under state control. The

Nazis encouraged the production of cheap *Volksempfänger* ('people's receiver', also known as *Goebbelsschnauze*, 'Goebbels's snout') radio sets with a limited range so as to diminish the audience for foreign stations. By 1939, radios were to be found in more than 70 per cent of German homes, one of the highest proportions in the world. They broadcast a diet of dance music, audio-gymnastics, Hitler's speeches, and Nazi propaganda, including exhortations to German women to bear more children. In 1928 the Deutsche Welle initiated a special '*Frauenfunk*' that broadcast programmes on motherhood, housewifery, women in the arts, and, during the Depression, exhorted listeners to hold '*Kopf hoch, nicht klagen*' (Chin up, don't complain).

Radio broadcasts in Russia in the 1930s were characteristically received on 'wired' sets either in the home or via loudspeakers in public places. In the countryside only a minority of village clubs had a radio and these were often out of order. In the 1930s reception was generally limited to one programme. In 1940 5.9 million radio sets in the USSR were 'wired' as against only 1.1 million 'over-the-air' receivers. This meant that listeners could tune in only to officially approved wavebands. While thus preventing reception of foreign broadcasts by the Soviet people, the Soviet Union was nonetheless the first country to develop external broadcasting in foreign languages in a systematic way. A special department for the purpose was formed in 1929 and by 1933 broadcasts were going out regularly in eight foreign languages. The BBC, by contrast, did not start broadcasting in foreign languages until 1938.

Radio bound nations together in a common culture. It flattened regional dialects and accents. It overwhelmed minority languages, which were rarely admitted to the airwaves. It connected far-flung provinces with each other and with capital cities. Its influence was greatest in heavily electrified areas. Britain led the way both in the quality of broadcasting output and in the number of listeners. By 1936 there were 7.7 million receiving sets in Britain. The most popular programmes there in 1939 were 'variety', theatre and cinema organ recitals, and military band music, though listeners under thirty preferred dance music. In eastern Europe radio was slower to penetrate beyond the cities. Poland in 1929 had a total of 202,586 receiving sets: nearly a quarter of these were in Warsaw; only 9,654 were registered as held by 'farmers'. In Italy, where few private homes boasted a radio, it could nevertheless be heard in cafés, factories, or other public places.

Although the Scotsman John Logie Baird had transmitted the first television image of a human face (of his office boy, William Taynton [see plate 21], aged fifteen, who received half a crown for his trouble) in 1925, it was another decade before public broadcasts started. Regular public transmissions began in Berlin in March 1935, at first for only an hour a day, three times a week, using a medium-definition 180-line system. The following year recorded television pictures of the Olympic Games were broadcast. They could be watched only in a few public viewing rooms in Berlin and Potsdam. High-definition 405-line broadcasts to domestic viewers began in Britain on 2 November 1936. By the outbreak of the war, when the BBC halted broadcasts (mid-programme) for the duration, about 25,000 homes had sets. German broadcasts continued until 1943. The only other country to initiate public broadcasts before the Second World War was the USSR, where transmissions began in Moscow on 10 March 1939. But only one hundred sets were able to receive the signal. And in Russia too television broadcasts were suspended during the war.

In most countries broadcasting was, or soon became, a state-controlled monopoly. The BBC, from 1927 a public corporation, unusually combined public ownership with some degree of independence: listeners paid a licence fee and an independent Board of Governors kept the government at arm's length. In France a few private commercial stations operated alongside the state network. Some were owned by politicians or politically minded entrepreneurs: for example, Pierre Laval, who served as Prime Minister twice during the decade, was proprietor of Radio Lyon. Britain prohibited commercial broadcasting but some enterprising broadcasters set up stations abroad directed at Britain: Radio Athlone in Ireland and Radio Normandie at Fécamp. The most important was the French-owned Radio Luxembourg, which defied international conventions on frequency allocation by broadcasting on long wave on the most powerful transmitter in Europe.

Popular music in Europe in the inter-war period was hugely influenced by America, both stylistically and in its commercial presentation. The birth of the talking picture at the end of the 1920s and the popularity of lavish Hollywood musical and dance extravaganzas further accentuated Americanization of this branch of popular culture. The invention of the electric gramophone and improvements in recording techniques helped sustain the musical recording industry against the competition of radio, although sales dropped during the Depression. The great singing stars of the era, such as Charles Trénet and Mistinguett in France, exemplified older traditions of *café-concert* and *guinguette* but commanded national and international audiences. Similarly in Britain, the Glaswegian Sir Harry Lauder, the first British artist to sell a million records, and the Mancunian George Formby, who accompanied himself on the ukelele, bridged the worlds of music-hall and mass-market popular music.

The husky-voiced Swedish chansonneuse Zarah Leander ('*Der Wind hat mir ein Lied erzählt*') moved to Berlin in 1936 and became the most popular film star in central Europe, entrancing even an initially hostile Goebbels. Similarly successful across frontiers was the Cairo-born Hungarian Marika Rökk, a child stage prodigy at the Moulin Rouge in Paris in 1923 and a star in musical films produced in Britain, Hungary, Germany, and Austria from 1930 onwards, including, in 1941, the first colour feature film made in Germany, *Frauen sind doch bessere Diplomaten*.

The most significant musical import from America appealed to smaller audiences but aroused violent hostility on all sides. In 1918 the Original Dixieland Jazz Band visited London and caused a sensation. Sidney Bechet, Coleman Hawkins and other leading American jazz stars soon followed. In Paris the 'revue nègre' was a *succès fou*: '*On s'extase sur ce néo-barbarisme*.'[27] Paris became the jazz capital of Europe in the 1930s with the creation of the Quintet of the Hot Club of France and its stars Django Reinhardt and Stéphane Grappelli. Prague and Warsaw were outlying stations of jazz mania. The new music form aroused the respectful interest of the conductor Ernest Ansermet and of Milhaud, Stravinsky, Hindemith, and other serious composers. But jazz was outlawed on German radio stations after 1935, though the ban was never consistently enforced: Nazi cultural controllers encountered some difficulty of definition, even with the help of a committee of experts. The saxophone fell into disrepute. Inspectors from the *Reichsmusikkammer* visited night clubs and bars to enforce the ban. In the end, popular dance music, even if jazz-influenced, was permitted while 'hot jazz' and 'swing' emanating from abroad were barred. The most popular big band conductor in Germany, James Kok, who was of partly Jewish origin, was forced to leave for Britain. Visiting foreign bands were tolerated for a while, though one Swiss bandleader who jazzed up the *Horst-Wessel-Lied* song was summarily expelled. The Nazis were not alone in denouncing jazz as 'nigger music'. The Frankfurt School theorist Theodor Adorno, who fled Nazi Germany, was unrestrained in his condemnation of the genre. And the Rector of Exeter College, Oxford, Dr Lewis Farnell, warned that 'Nigger music comes from the Devil'. It might not be as criminal as murder but, he maintained, it was far more degrading.[28] Jazz arrived in Soviet Russia in the early 1920s but there too found a mixed reception. 'Listening for a few minutes to these wails,' Maxim Gorky told the readers of *Pravda* in 1928, 'one involuntarily imagines an orchestra of sexually driven madmen conducted by a man-stallion brandishing a huge genital member'.[29] He was echoed at the First All-Russian Musical Congress in Leningrad in 1929 by the Soviet Cultural Commissar, Lunacharsky. But Soviet jazz enjoyed the powerful patronage of Marshal Voroshilov and of the First Secretary of the Moscow Communist Party, Lazar Kaganovich, who saw it as the 'friend of the jolly'.[30] An uneasy compromise was reached in 1938 with the inauguration of the State Jazz Orchestra of the USSR, a strictly party-line ensemble that condemned *dzhaz* to virtual suffocation.

The press, radio, and newsreels all stimulated public interest in spectator sports. The most popular was football (soccer), which had spread to most parts of the continent, including the USSR, by the 1920s. In many countries it was also a mass participatory sport: in Germany there were over a million registered players in 1932. The first football world cup competition, organized by the French president of FIFA, Jules Rimet, was held in 1930 but it was not until after the Second World War that a European championship competition began. Boxing also had a large following. Its greatest hero was Max Schmeling, world heavyweight boxing champion from 1930 to 1932. He regained the title in one of the great matches of the century, his 1936 bout with the American 'brown bomber', Joe Louis. This triumph was hailed by the Nazis as a victory of the Aryan over the Negro. When Schmeling was defeated after 124 seconds in the rematch in 1938, the German radio transmission mysteriously went silent as the referee declared the fight over. Other sports appealed to more select audiences. Motor racing was heavily promoted in these years, primarily as a marketing device by auto manufacturers. In inter-war Europe it became a popular spectator sport, dominated until 1934 by Italian teams (Bugatti, Alfa Romeo, and Maserati) and from then until 1939 by the Germans (Mercedes-Benz, Auto Union). For the affluent classes, skiing became popular in the 1930s, as a competitive sport and also as a recreational activity in Scandinavia, the Alps, and at Zakopane in the Tatra mountains of southern Poland. The spread of cable-car ski lifts after 1928 facilitated the growth of ski-tourism. The first winter Olympic games took place in 1924 though it was not until the 1936 games, held at Garmisch-Partenkirchen in Bavaria, that downhill skiing was recognized as an Olympic sport.

The Nazis, who shrewdly exploited the Berlin Olympics that year as a gigantic propaganda spectacle, were by no means alone in politicizing sport in this period. The Soviet Union was not even invited to participate in the Olympics. 'I am absolutely opposed,' wrote the president of the International Olympics Committee, Henri de Baillet-Latour, 'not wanting at any price to facilitate the corruption of the youth of the entire world by putting them in contact with these reds, who would take advantage [of participation] to make wild propaganda.'[31] Nor were such fears without some tincture of substantiation. The French Communist daily, *l'Humanité*, denounced the gruelling Tour de France, the premier international cycling event, for its 'ferocious and at times criminal exploitation' of the competitors, dubbed 'pedal workers'. Their ordeal, according to the newspaper, was 'the exact copy of the rationalized work, supervised by the warder, of galley slaves in the great factories'.[32]

The vast popularity of spectator sports, stimulated by press and radio coverage, encouraged the growth of associated gambling, often illegal or semi-legal. In Britain racecourse totalizators, betting on 'the dogs' (greyhound racing, initiated in 1925 and by the late 1930s drawing some 25 million attendances a year), gaming machines, and illegal street betting all prospered; but football pools were by far the most common form of regular 'flutter', indeed the most widespread working-class leisure activity: more than ten million people, mainly men, filled in their coupons each week. Other countries followed the British model. In Sweden, the government created a state-controlled monopoly in 1934 to run football pool betting, based on results of the English Football League.

The growth of such activities was partly an outcome of the increased leisure time available to the working class as a result of the widespread adoption in the 1920s of an eight-hour limit on the working day. The inter-war period also saw the extension to workers in many countries of the right, hitherto restricted mainly to the professional classes and civil servants, to paid annual vacations. Youth hostels opened in Britain and France after 1929. In Britain seaside 'holiday camps', such as those of Billy Butlin, catered to the new mass market in the late 1930s. Elsewhere the shadow of the state loomed large: in Russia, Italy, and Germany quasi-official organizations dragooned vacationers into approved locations and activities.

Whether from the state or the market, pressures for cultural uniformity grew throughout European society. Contemplating this development with some distaste, the Spanish thinker José Ortega y Gasset defended an elitist, or, as he called it, 'radically aristocratic' version of liberalism against the celebration of vulgarity and elevation of mediocrity that he saw in the collectivisms of the age, Fascist and Marxist alike. In *The Revolt of the Masses* (1930), he lamented that 'the mass crushes beneath it everything that is different, everything that is excellent, individual, qualified and select. Anybody who is not like everybody, who does not think like everybody, runs the risk of being eliminated.'[33]

In this age of dominant collective ideologies, the characteristic figure was the lost and abandoned individual—the refugee. S/he was the most visible outward manifestation of a deeper rootlessness in modern European society, in which war and social deformations had torn men and women away from established institutional structures and attachments (including from each other) without furnishing replacements that offered comparable emotional or physical security, other than the fool's gold of Communism and Fascism.

The age of anxiety

The apparent breakdown of capitalism, the discrediting of bourgeois social norms, the challenges to Christian moral verities, large-scale refugee movements, the palpable failure of the system of international law based on the League of Nations, as well as the looming shadow of a new world war—all this fed a pervasive public mood of insecurity and lost bearings in the 1930s, what Auden called 'the Age of Anxiety'.

One symptom of the emotional climate was a rise in the suicide rate, registered in much of the continent. It was highest in Hungary, which even had a special 'suicide anthem', the song 'Gloomy Sunday' (*Szomoru Vasárnap*), composed by Rezső Seress, who used to play it in the Kis Pipa restaurant in Budapest in the early 1930s. The song, which allegedly inspired several suicides, was banned on that account on many radio stations. (Seress killed himself in 1968.) Sigmund Freud is said to have regarded the song as a representation of his theory of the '*Sonntagsneurose*'.

Foremost interpreter of the sources of human neuroses, discoverer of the primacy of the unconscious in the determination of human behaviour, Freud enjoyed a fashionable reputation that was now at its peak. He had coined the term 'psychoanalysis' in 1895 and, in the decade before 1905, had published his pathbreaking works on hysteria, on the interpretation of dreams, on jokes and the unconscious, on the psychopathology of everyday life, and on infantile sexuality. But he initially encountered hostility from the medical establishment and it was not until 1920 that he was appointed a professor at the University of Vienna. In 1930 he was awarded the Goethe Prize for literature but his ideas remained controversial and were often fiercely contested. Yet his concepts of traumatic repression, of displacement, sublimation, and regression, and of the œdipus complex laid the basis not merely for a new therapy but for a revolution in human self-understanding.

By the 1930s psychology, although divided into warring schools, had become the modish social science of the period. Although fashionable as a treatment for many forms of mental illness, some hitherto unrecognized, as well as for generalized anxiety, psychoanalysis reached almost exclusively a narrow segment of upper bourgeois society in central and western Europe. The Bolsheviks opposed it and it made few inroads in the USSR. Under Nazism it fared little better, although many 'Aryan' psychoanalysts, headed by Carl Jung, tried to ingratiate themselves with the New Order. By the end of the 1930s the centre of gravity of the movement had shifted to the United States. The social and cultural impact of Freud's ideas in Europe, however, was far-reaching, extending into social work, the social sciences, religious thought, the arts, and literature. Like Darwinism half a century earlier, Freudianism permeated the public mind and, in the process, was vulgarized, distorted, and misrepresented. Although primarily concerned with the individual, Freudian concepts were loosely applied to collective behaviour and to 'mass-man'.

In *Civilization and its Discontents* (1930), Freud himself ventured into the territory of social psychology. 'Civilization', he maintained, was 'built up on renunciation of instinctual gratifications'. The repression of sexuality had reached a high water mark in contemporary western civilization. 'The standard which declares itself in these prohibitions,' he wrote, 'is that of a sexual life identical for all.' As a result, the sexual life of civilized man was 'seriously disabled'. The consequences of the inherent human tendency to aggression had led society to restrict sexuality and, further, by means of what he termed a 'narcissism in respect of minor differences', to channel hostility against other collectivities, such as Jews or neighbouring states. Given the sacrifices of both sexuality and aggressiveness that civilization demanded, it was hardly to be wondered that civilized man should be unhappy. The aggravated anxiety that seemed to afflict contemporary men, 'their dejection, their mood of apprehension', he attributed to the fact that 'men have brought their powers of subduing the forces of nature to such pitch that by using them they could now very easily exterminate one another to the last man'.[34] Freud was a pessimist who had no faith in the inherent goodness of man but even he could not know how soon, and with what wild abandon, Europeans would cast aside all civilizing inhibitions.

7

Spiral into War 1936–1939

I want to sleep the sleep of apples,
Far away from the uproar of cemeteries.
I want to sleep the sleep of that child
Who wanted to cut his heart out on the sea

*Federico García Lorca, Granada, c.1934**

Little dictators

By the late 1930s democracy was on the retreat throughout Europe. Of the main European states only the Scandinavian nations, the Low Countries, the British Isles, France, and Switzerland succeeded in maintaining plausibly democratic systems of government throughout the inter-war period. Authoritarian or military regimes, many of them aping the styles of Fascism and Nazism, gained power almost everywhere in eastern and southern Europe with the exception of Czechoslovakia—not coincidentally the most economically advanced and relatively prosperous of the east European states. The two chief motors of the trend were the effects of the Depression, particularly on agrarian populations, and the sharpening of ethnic conflicts and antagonisms against minorities in the highly nationalistic states of the region.

The drift to the right was visible from the Atlantic to the Baltic. A military coup in Portugal in 1926 displaced the parliamentary regime and launched a *ditadura* that by 1932 gave way to the so-called Estado Novo headed by the former Finance Minister, António de Oliveira Salazar.

* From 'Ghazal of Dark Death', translated from the Spanish by Catherine Brown. Federico García Lorca, *Selected Poems*, ed., Christopher Maurer, London, 1997, 245.

Denouncing 'the deficiencies, abuses, and vices of parliamentary systems',[1] he consolidated a corporatist, clericalist, and militarist regime, in which all political parties, save the governing União Nacional, were prohibited. In Greece General Metaxas established a military dictatorship in August 1936. This banned all political parties and labour unions, focusing its efforts on enhancing the battle-worthiness of the armed forces. Elsewhere in the Balkans the fashion was for royal dictatorships. A militarist putsch in Bulgaria in 1934 ended parliamentary government there. Eighteen months later Tsar Boris III orchestrated a prime-ministerial coup and became effective ruler of the country, remaining in power until his death in 1943. In Romania King Carol II, supported by the army and the Orthodox Church, took advantage of a financial crisis and political stalemate in early 1938 to suspend the constitution and assume quasi-dictatorial authority. In the Baltic states in 1934, Latvia and Estonia followed Lithuania's earlier example and abandoned democracy. In both countries political fragmentation and lack of consensus doomed the parliamentary system; the Depression administered the final blow. Although they became dictatorships, neither Latvia nor Estonia embraced Fascism: indeed, in each case the rulers used the threat from the extreme right as a pretext for seizing power.

Piłsudski's regime in Poland after 1926, which went by the name of Sanacja ('purification' or 'cleansing'), maintained the outward forms of democracy and limited parliamentary and press freedoms survived so long as he was alive. From 1930, and particularly after Piłsudski's death in 1935, a clique of his followers, known as the 'government of the colonels', concentrated power in their own hands. Constitutional safeguards were further eroded. The chief element in the opposition was the National Democrat (Endek) Party. Its leader, Roman Dmowski, an admirer of Hitler and Mussolini, posed as the defender of parliamentary prerogatives while cultivating support by a mixture of populist nationalism and anti-Semitism. Some opposition leaders were imprisoned or exiled. Hostility to national minorities intensified. Nationalist feeling grew among Ukrainians, a majority of the population in the eastern borderlands captured from Russia in 1921. Germans in the 'Polish corridor' were increasingly attracted to Nazism. Boycotts, discrimination, and violence were directed against Jews: 'Jew-benches' were set up in universities and a pogrom at Przytyk in central Poland in 1936 aroused Jewish fears of worse to come. Poland never recovered from the Depression before the outbreak of war; industrial and agricultural output figures in 1938 were both still below those for the same area in 1913. Twenty years of independence had left the Poles poorer and angrier than when they had been divided under the rule of three empires. The country did not degenerate into a dictatorship of the Nazi or Fascist variety; it was authoritarian but not totalitarian. But little remained of the bright hopes of 1918.

Hungary too, under the paternalistic conservatism of Admiral Horthy's regency, drifted further to the right. In 1932 a government took office headed by Gyula Gömbös, a fanatical Magyar nationalist (though he was of German origin). He aligned Hungarian foreign and trade policies with those of Nazi Germany. After 1934 the economy made an uncertain recovery from the Depression but Gömbös's efforts to bring about significant land redistribution were successfully resisted by large landholders, including the Church. His attempt to create a one-party corporatist regime in the Italian mould was cut short by his sudden death in 1936. Gömbös's successors were nationalist conservatives rather than Fascists. As in Poland the veneer of parliamentary institutions was maintained and limited freedom of speech and press endured. But a discriminatory anti-Semitic law was passed in 1938 and the government came under growing pressure from extreme-right movements financed and encouraged by Berlin.

Although many of these authoritarian regimes shared some characteristics with Fascism, most were traditionalist, militarist, conservative dictatorships rather than movements of the radical right. Some such regimes, indeed, came into conflict with more properly Fascist movements, as in Romania, where King Carol engaged in a bloody off-on courtship and feud with the green-shirted Iron Guard. This movement, an outgrowth of the Legion of the Archangel Michael, founded in 1927, attracted cross-class backing not only from gutter bully-boys but also among the educated middle class, the clergy, and some young intellectuals, like Mircea Eliade, later a professor of religion at the University of Chicago. Disgusted with the notorious corruption of the Romanian political class and with the camarilla around the king, including his supposedly Jewish mistress, Magda Lupescu, the Guardists embraced mystical nationalism, self-sacrificing idealism, and political redemption through violence: 'A state of combat is what we call politics... A nation is defined by the friend-foe equation.'[2] Their leader, Corneliu Zelea Codreanu, rode around villages on a white horse and won a fanatical personal following. A fervent Christian and ardent Romanian nationalist (although of Polish-German stock), he was believed to enjoy support and subventions from Nazi Germany, though the accusation was probably false.

The movement's songbook, the *Carticica de cantece*, echoed the Nazi *Horst-Wessel-Lied*. Guardists engaged in street rowdyism and assassinated several leading Romanian statesmen. Their star nevertheless rose: in the relatively free elections of 1937, they won 16 per cent of the votes. The movement was disbanded by the royal dictatorship in February 1938. In April Codreanu was arrested; in November he and thirteen of his henchmen were garroted to death (the government announced that they had been shot while trying to escape). His movement nevertheless survived underground and re-emerged to win governmental power for a few months in 1940.

Unlike Communism, Fascism was in no sense an international movement, although in the 1930s it seemed to be the wave of the future. Every country generated its own variant but all Fascist groups were at the same time authoritarian and populist as well as anti-parliamentary, anti-intellectual, hyper-nationalist, militarist, anti-Semitic, and violent. Some, such as the Arrow Cross in Hungary, succeeded in mobilizing significant support. Others, for example Sir Oswald Mosley's British Union of Fascists, remained on the political fringe. Even the Jews generated a quasi-Fascist movement, the Revisionist Zionist Party, later known as the New Zionist Organization, led by Vladimir Jabotinsky and popular in Poland in the 1930s. Each Fascist movement had its own symbols and rituals but all generated a cult of the leader, copied the uniforms and marching styles of the Italian and German prototypes, and, however nationalistic they might be, looked to Rome and Berlin for encouragement and inspiration.

Germany resurgent

The attraction of authoritarian and Fascist movements owed much to the dazzling foreign policy successes of Nazi Germany after 1933. The expansion of the Third Reich, between 1933 and 1938, beyond even the borders of the Wilhelmine empire, represented a signal diplomatic achievement, the more so as it was achieved without a shot fired in anger, albeit with repeated threats of force. Nazi foreign policy aimed from the outset at delegitimizing the Versailles Treaty and destabilizing the Locarno settlement. It was a policy of territorial expansion, of search for *Lebensraum* ('living space') for the German race in eastern Europe, and of hostility to the League of Nations and the collective security system. Foreign policy was the Führer's peculiar domain: his foreign ministers were mere executors of his instructions.

Hitler did not proceed according to any timetable or clearly formulated plan. But the fundamental thrust of his diplomacy was one of unlimited aggression. This derived partly from an inner psychological urge of the megalomaniac dictator and partly from the ideological imperatives of the Nazi movement: resurrection of German glory; subjugation of inferior races, first and foremost Jews and Slavs; and unrelenting hostility to parliamentary liberalism, social democracy, and Communism.

The essential prerequisite for a diplomacy of intimidation was rearmament. Long before Hitler's accession to power, the German armed forces had devised a variety of stratagems for evasion of the Versailles restrictions. Covert military cooperation with the USSR continued until 1933. Another avenue was government support for gliding clubs, 'flying Freikorps' that attracted thousands of aviators and tens of thousands of spectators at nationalistic gliding competitions. After 1926, when the Allies ended restrictions on civil aircraft production, German companies began secret manufacture of military planes under the guise of 'transport', 'mail carrier', and 'sporting planes'. By 1933 the German army already boasted 228 aircraft and 350 trained pilots. U-boats, similarly prohibited under the treaty, were manufactured in Holland, Spain, and Finland. The treaty limitation on military manpower was evaded by recruitment into armed police units. Sharpshooting clubs, long a feature of German towns, were encouraged to train marksmen. In 1932 the German army had already begun implementing secret plans for expansion far beyond the treaty limit of one hundred thousand men. Yet in spite of all this, Weimar Germany remained formally committed to its treaty obligations and the covert infractions were relatively small-scale compared with the period after 1933.

While Hitler was not, therefore, the initiator of rearmament beyond the treaty limits, he enormously extended it, at first secretly, after a time publicly. Arms expenditure grew from 3 per cent of GNP in 1933 to 17 per cent by 1938—more than double the level in either France or Britain. In 1934 a compulsory six-month 'labour service' was introduced, a first step towards universal military conscription. A Panzerwaffe (tank arm) and Luftwaffe (air force) were created. The Krupp works began building tanks in 1934—they were called 'tractors' in all the documentation. The number of workers in the aircraft industry grew from 5,000 in 1933 to 135,000 by 1936. In the same period the number of combat aircraft available to the Luftwaffe grew from (supposedly) zero to more than 1,800. By this time it had already overtaken the French air force in both quantity and quality of machines.

Hitler gave his first signal of defiance of the post-war international order in October 1933, when German delegates withdrew from the World Disarmament Conference which had been meeting in Geneva since February 1932 without achieving agreement. A few days later Germany resigned from the League of Nations. In January 1935, as stipulated in the Versailles Treaty, a plebiscite was held in the Saarland, hitherto under League of Nations administration. Voting was conducted under the protection of an international police force, the first—and last—international force ever organized by the League. Although the Nazi-sponsored 'Deutsche Front' threatened retribution to their enemies, there was no question about the genuineness of the result. Anti-Hitler Germans campaigned freely; on the other hand, the Catholic Church, very influential in the area, strenuously advocated reunion with Germany. More than 90 per cent of voters in the territory opted for reintegration. A few hundred spoilt ballots were marked as for Germany but 'against Hitler'. Church bells rang when the result was announced. 'Thus a great international problem has been amicably and satisfactorily settled,' concluded an American member of the electoral supervisory commission.[3] On 1 March German troops entered the region, thereby granting Hitler his first territorial victory.

Emboldened by this eminently legal triumph, Hitler permitted his supposedly Civil Aviation Minister, Göring, to acknowledge publicly the existence of the Luftwaffe. A few days after that Hitler announced the restoration of compulsory military service, with a view to enlarging the German army to thirty-six divisions with 550,000 men. Both steps were brazen violations of the peace treaty. The response of Germany's treaty partners was subdued. In April a conference of Britain, France, and Italy at Stresa condemned the German unilateral repudiation of the peace treaty. But the 'Stresa Front' was just that: a cover for disunity and indecision. 'Words, words! We got an agreement with dentures, not teeth, and tried to show them,' was the retrospective verdict of a senior British diplomat.[4] The French, in the following month, sought reinsurance by concluding a treaty with the USSR whereby each undertook to aid the other in the event of 'an unprovoked aggression on the part of a European State'.[5] Still hoping to entice the Germans back to the Disarmament Conference, the British concluded an agreement with Hitler in June setting limits on naval rearmament. German naval strength, according to the treaty, was not to exceed 35 per cent of the navies of the British Commonwealth.

The agreement was the first major step in what came to be known as the appeasement policy, which guided British diplomacy towards Germany until the spring of 1939. The common view, propagated by Winston Churchill and others, that this was based on pusillanimity or blindness is woefully over-simplified. It is true that *The Times* (often, to the government's frequent embarrassment, regarded abroad as an official organ) as well as a considerable body of opinion across the political spectrum regarded the Versailles Treaty as vindictive and outdated. It is also true that Hitler received warm approbation from some British visitors such as David Lloyd George and George Bernard Shaw. But the general attitude towards Nazism was hostile: one of disdain for its militarism and disgust at its racism and brutality.

British policy was formed out of a number of cross-cutting influences and considerations. Although the Soviet threat to capitalist societies appeared to have subsided, there remained a deep undercurrent of suspicion and hostility to the Soviet Union. But more immediate dangers were seen elsewhere. As early as March 1932, in response to Japanese aggression in Manchuria, Britain had 'suspended' the 'ten-year rule' under which the armed services' planners were permitted to count on a decade ahead without a major war. Politicians, diplomats, and armed service chiefs were divided between those who saw Japan as the main potential threat to British interests and those who regarded defence against Germany as the number one priority. The continental commitment was one that British defence planners dreaded, responsible, as they were, with resources stretched to breaking point, for protection of a worldwide empire. Nevertheless, in February 1934 it was agreed by defence planners that Germany was Britain's 'ultimate potential enemy'.[6] Public opinion at this stage was generally pacific in outlook but the British were acutely sensitive to the potential danger of air attack. In November 1932 the Conservative leader, Stanley Baldwin, had told the House of Commons, in a famous phrase, 'the bomber will always get through'.[7] And in July 1934 he acknowledged: 'The old frontiers are gone. When you think of the defence of England, you no longer think of the chalk cliffs of Dover, you think of the Rhine. That is where our frontiers are.'[8]

The logical response was rearmament and consolidation of alliances. But the Prime Minister, MacDonald, now in his dotage, dwelt in a rhetorical stratosphere of angelic international harmonies. In June 1935 he was replaced as head of the National Government by Baldwin who led the government to a smashing electoral victory the following November. Neither he nor the directors of British defence shared MacDonald's airy faith in an era of universal peace. The dominant influence on policy-making, however, throughout this period, was the Chancellor of the Exchequer, Neville Chamberlain. The Treasury was concerned above all with economy. Chamberlain agreed that the main threat emanated from Germany. But he used this as a basis for holding down naval spending while channelling limited expenditure increments to air force expansion. In 1932 British defence expenditure amounted to £103 million, its lowest point in the inter-war period (one-sixth of the 1919 level). Thereafter, it grew steadily, reaching £186 million by 1936. Only a small group of Conservatives, led by Churchill, argued for more. The small opposition Labour Party, while anti-Fascist, was strongly influenced by pacifism and wedded to the nostrums of collective security and disarmament; its leader, George Lansbury, opposed military sanctions even if authorized by the League of Nations.

Two precedents had already been set for the failure of collective security under the League. The first was the Japanese occupation of Manchuria in 1931, which had earned the invader a rap over the knuckles but little more from the League-appointed Lytton Commission in 1932. The second was the Italian invasion of Ethiopia in October 1935. Italian service chiefs warned the Duce that the attack might provoke Britain to a war that 'would reduce us to a Balkan level'.[9] But Mussolini reckoned he knew better. After a six-month war in which the primitive army of Emperor Haile Selassie was overwhelmed by Italian tanks, aircraft, and mustard gas, the capital, Addis Ababa, fell in May 1936. The Italian colonial regime in Ethiopia presented a challenge to British and French power in the Middle East, but London and Paris reacted in a tolerant spirit. Pierre Laval, who served at the time in a dual capacity as French Prime Minister and Foreign Minister, favoured close relations with Italy which he thought would open the door to rapprochement with Germany. In Britain the Permanent Under-Secretary (civil service head) of the Foreign Office, Sir Robert Vansittart, and others who favoured a resolute policy towards Germany, were ready to overlook Mussolini's peccadillo in Ethiopia in the hope of holding together the Stresa Front against Hitler. Even before the invasion the British Foreign Secretary, Sir Samuel Hoare, together with Laval, devised a plan that involved substantial concessions to Italy at Ethiopia's expense. Only a public outcry compelled withdrawal of the proposal. After the invasion, the League gingerly rebuked Italy and eventually imposed limited and ineffective economic sanctions against her. The deposed emperor made a dignified appearance in Geneva where he was reviled by Italian journalists. Liberal opinion in Britain condemned the Italians but Mussolini successfully defied his critics and exposed the League as impotent.

The Ethiopian crisis drove Mussolini closer to Hitler, rendering it unlikely that he would stand up to him. Conditions were thus favourable by early 1936 for Hitler to embark on his first open move in defiance of the post-war territorial settlement. On 7 March German forces entered the demilitarized zone of the Rhineland, a breach of the Versailles and Locarno treaties. The German General Staff supported the move but the Defence Minister, General Werner von Blomberg, was doubtful and Göring initially warned that it was a risky step. The Foreign Minister, Konstantin von Neurath, urged Hitler forward, reinforced in his view by intelligence information indicating that France would not respond.[10] The decision, however, was Hitler's alone. He knew that the British were not in a position to stop him and that Italian forces had been preoccupied with Ethiopia since late 1935. British politicians were outraged but public opinion was impassive. Hitler's move did not, after all, offend against the principle of national self-determination; quite the contrary. The German ambassador in London reported that the British War Secretary, Duff Cooper, had admitted to him over dinner that most people in Britain probably 'did not care "two hoots" about the Germans occupying their own territory'.[11]

The French, who at the end of the First World War had regarded demilitarization of the region as a fundamental national interest, did nothing. They consoled themselves with the reflection that developments in military air power and mechanized ground forces had diminished the strategic value of the Rhineland to their defence. But French military effort since the withdrawal from the region in 1930 had concentrated on the construction of the defensive 'Maginot Line' of fortresses. The cost of this had soared while budgets were cut back: as a result, spending on new weapons had been severely reduced. France's strategic obsolescence contrasted painfully with Germany's military modernization. On paper, the military balance in 1936 was still in France's favour but military chiefs warned that in a long war Germany's superiority in manpower and industrial potential would render the outcome uncertain. The French army did not even have operational contingency plans to meet the eventuality of a move by the Germans. Hitler's action came as no surprise to the French government, since the Deuxième Bureau, the French intelligence service, had learned in the autumn of 1935 of German plans to remilitarize the area. Only two ministers firmly advocated an immediate military response against Germany. The government decided on a diplomatic rather than a military reaction. With an election imminent, the country's generally pacific mood was the decisive factor. In the event, the French grossly overestimated German mobilized strength: they thought Hitler had sent 295,000 troops to the demilitarized zone; in fact, he dispatched 30,000.

Hitler's gamble had paid off. Not for the first or last time, he assured the world: 'In Europe we have no territorial claims to put forward.'[12] The Rhineland crisis was viewed by many afterwards as the last chance to stop Nazi expansionism without a major war—'*le relais où les destins changèrent de chevaux*', as the French Foreign Minister, Pierre-Etienne Flandin, called it.[13] German public opinion was enthusiastic. Goebbels's mother telephoned her son. 'She is beside herself,' he recorded in his diary.[14] The British Foreign Secretary, Anthony Eden, sought a negotiated solution: discussions dragged on for months and eventually the issue was overtaken by other more immediate concerns. The Rhineland triumph left Hitler ecstatic. In a speech in Munich he said, 'I go with the certainty of a sleepwalker along the path laid out for me by Providence.'[15] In October he announced the adoption of a Four-Year Plan with the aim of making the German economy self-sufficient and ready for war. Large-scale programmes were initiated for the replacement of imported raw materials, such as rubber and oil, by synthetic substitutes. German industrial output more than doubled between 1933 and 1939. As German power and ambition grew, the other European powers remained disoriented, divided, and distracted.

Popular Front

In France in the early 1930s the stability of democratic institutions seemed to be threatened by heightened political conflict in an atmosphere of ideological fervour, class hatreds, verbal violence, and polarization between left and right. The Depression accentuated an old French political phenomenon: scandal-mongering. Conspiracy theories were rife, with both left and right flinging around accusations against the 'two hundred families' who supposedly dominated the economy and corrupted the political life of the republic. The Stavisky affair, the greatest of the politico-financial scandals of the late Third Republic, destroyed the government of Camille Chautemps in January 1934. The shady confidence trickster Serge Alexandre Stavisky drew politicians, journalists, and officials into a complex web of corruption and intrigue. When he was found dead, newspaper reports claimed that the police had deliberately allowed him to die lest he reveal unfortunate secrets about persons in high places. The extreme right, in particular, enjoyed a field day in criticizing the republican parliamentary system that allegedly produced such outrages.

Action Française, the most important French ultra-nationalist movement, had been founded in 1898 as a product of the fierce battles over the Dreyfus affair. The movement was a hotchpotch of paradoxes. Staunchly monarchist, it was disavowed by the Bourbon pretender; archaically Catholic, it was condemned by the Pope; violently nationalist, it became the doctrinal source for a collaborationist regime. The movement's foremost intellectual spokesman was Charles Maurras. A nostalgic reactionary and an elitist, stone-deaf from his teens, Maurras drew some of the leading writers and thinkers of the day to his side. The historians Jacques Bainville, Frantz Funck-Brentano, Pierre Gaxotte, and Daniel Halévy, literary figures such as Robert Brasillach, Léon Daudet, and Georges Bernanos, and the future Socialist President, François Mitterrand, all hovered at one time or another around the Maurrassien flame. A newer phenomenon on the far right was the rise of quasi-Fascist 'leagues': the para-military Camelots du Roi (founded in 1908, an offshoot of the Action Française), the Jeunesses Patriotes (a student group founded in 1924 by Pierre Taittinger), and the militantly Catholic and anti-parliamentary Croix de feu. Originally a non-political ex-servicemen's association, founded in 1928, the Croix de feu was transformed by Colonel François de La Rocque, into a mass organization. The far right vehemently attacked Jews, Protestants, freemasons, and *métèques* (resident aliens). On 6 February 1934 a right-wing riot in Paris, in which fifteen people were killed and more than a thousand people and 120 horses injured, momentarily destabilized the republic. The episode was more *opéra bouffe* than genuine revolt but it jolted the political class and led to the resignation of another Radical Prime Minister, Edouard Daladier.

Meanwhile, the French economy had fallen into recession as even France's accumulated mountain of gold failed to protect her against the general decline in world trade brought about by the international depression. A succession of centre-right governments pursued orthodox deflationary policies that accentuated the slowdown in business activity. At the same time, the government deficit widened. A few French politicians, notably the independent-minded moderate rightist Paul Reynaud, recognized the need for devaluation but this was regarded as taboo. In mid-1935 Laval headed a new government with a mandate to 'save the franc'. It issued draconian decree-laws lowering prices of public utilities, civil service salaries, rents, and interest rates. The policy succeeded statistically (indices of economic activity rose sharply over the year to May 1936) but confidence was not restored and the outflow of gold continued. Laval's measures provoked a sharp political reaction and helped stimulate a *rassemblement populaire* of the left.

Foreign affairs, especially the growing threat of Fascism, further strengthened a coalescence of Radicals, Socialists, and Communists. In 1935 the Comintern ordered Communists worldwide to cease impugning Socialists as 'social Fascists' and instead to embrace them in a 'popular front'. And the Socialists, worried about the rise of Nazism and the heightened activity of the far right in France, began to reassess their policy of 'ministerial virginity' and to prepare to exercise power, if necessary with the Radicals, the hardy perennials of Third Republic coalitions. All the main elements of the French left, from the Radicals to the Communists, agreed in January 1936 on a common programme. It promised measures against the leagues, extension of the school leaving age, collective security abroad, reduction of the working week, revaluation of agricultural produce (i.e. higher prices to be paid to peasants), and nationalization of the Bank of France.

The parliamentary elections, held in two stages on 26 April and 3 May 1936, produced a decisive victory for the left. The Popular Front parties together won 409 out of the 614 seats in the Chamber of Deputies. The Socialists were the largest single party with 147 seats. The new government formed by Léon Blum (see plate 19) was the most left-wing of the inter-war period and the first ministry of the Third Republic to be headed by a Socialist. Bourgeois and Marxist, Jew and humanist, *normalien* and aesthete, moralist and advocate of sexual equality, Blum led a party of workers, peasants, teachers, and *fonctionnaires* that asserted its devotion to revolutionary goals but remained attached to legal parliamentarism. For the right Blum was the most hated man in France: 'Better Hitler than Blum!' was the slogan of the moment. '*Voilà un homme à fusiller, mais dans le dos!*' wrote Maurras.[16] Blum formed a government of Socialists and Radicals (among the ministers were, for the first time in French history, three women) but without Communists. Maurice Thorez, leader of the Communist Party, was (or claimed later that he had been) in favour of joining the government, but Dimitrov, now head of the Comintern, conveyed Stalin's instruction 'not to participate in the government but to support it against the right for the sake of implementing the program of the popular front'.[17] The Popular Front aroused huge hopes on the left for radical reform. New adherents flocked to the Communist and Socialist parties. Labour union membership rose from 786,000 in 1935 to four million by 1937.

So great was the surge of fervour among the working class that, even before the new government took office in June, large numbers of factories were occupied by striking workers in a spontaneous outburst of quasi-revolutionary enthusiasm. Blum's first act on taking office was to call together workers' and employers' representatives at his official residence, the Hôtel de Matignon. The participants agreed in short order to a far-reaching package of reforms. The Matignon Agreements provided for a five-day, forty-hour work week, collective bargaining (hitherto rare in French industry), across-the-board increases in wages of up to 15 per cent for all industrial workers, and the right to two weeks of paid holiday per annum. In return the workers eventually agreed to end the factory occupations and return to work. After this success, which went far beyond what had been foreshadowed in the *programme commun*, the government moved fast to enact further reforms. Public works were instituted, though fear of a budgetary deficit that would threaten market stability reduced their scale. Education was made compulsory to the age of fourteen. The Fascist leagues were dissolved, though they reappeared in other guises. The Croix de feu, in its new form as the Parti Social Français, grew into the largest political party in the country, gaining members especially in the petty bourgeoisie frightened by the Popular Front's economic policies.

These did not have the effect that had been forecast. Production fell back and the depletion of the gold reserve accelerated. In 1934 Blum had argued, against the conventional wisdom, that France need not fear devaluation. But the Popular Front had campaigned on the slogan: '*ni déflation, ni dévaluation*'. The Finance Ministry had by now come to accept the necessity for devaluation but popular opinion was strongly against it. The wisest course would have been to devalue immediately upon taking office but to Blum this seemed politically impossible. The newly installed Minister of Finance, Vincent Auriol, who recognized the economic logic of devaluation, was found by a colleague sitting in his office with his head in his hands: 'No, no, no. The whole world wants me to devalue. But I shall not devalue.'[18] Instead of taking an immediate decision, Blum and Auriol embarked on a lengthy process of consultation with the British and Americans. An expensive rearmament programme, announced in September, renewed the flight of capital. On 25 September the government was forced, after all, to devalue—a severe political blow, all the greater for being partly self-inflicted. Two further devaluations followed, so that within two years the franc had lost more than half its value against the dollar. Devaluation did indeed stimulate the economy briefly. But the government's insistence, from December 1936, on enforcing the forty-hour week undermined confidence and in the first half of 1937 economic activity again slackened.

Two dramatic incidents raised the political temperature to fever pitch. Both arose from the activity of the far right whose press launched vitriolic attacks on the government. The Minister of the Interior, Roger Salengro, was falsely accused of having deserted to the enemy when he was a military cyclist-courier during the First World War. Although exonerated by a specially constituted commission of inquiry headed by the army Chief of Staff, Salengro committed suicide in November 1936. Blum saw in the case an echo of the Dreyfus affair in which he had battled for justice forty years earlier. A million attended the martyr's burial of Salengro, reminiscent of that of Rathenau in Berlin in 1923. Blum eulogized his dead comrade and uttered an eloquent affirmation of faith in the national community and its republican institutions.

The second incident, in March 1937, arose from a public meeting at the Olympia cinema in Clichy, a working-class district of Paris, of the Parti Social Français. Police fired on Communist and Trotskyist protesters who had marched on the cinema. Six demonstrators and one *garde républicain* were killed and two hundred people injured. The episode was exploited gleefully by the right and mercilessly by the far left, including Blum's opponents in his own party. 'Who said this man has no French blood?' asked a right-wing caricaturist.[19] The Communists held their fire but after the fall of the Popular Front Thorez would denounce Blum as '*l'assassin des ouvriers de Clichy*'.[20] Shaken by the killings, Blum talked privately of resigning. He remained in office but it was the beginning of the end of his government.

Blum was later charged with weakening France's defences during his term of office. His government's rearmament expenditure represented an advance on his predecessors' effort; in retrospect it may be judged as too little too late, though it was perhaps the maximum possible politically at the time. In the early 1930s failure to focus on a small number of model lines for aircraft and other heavy equipment led to short production runs, greatly increasing costs. Now the Minister of National Defence, Daladier, aimed to restructure armaments manufacturing and shift gears towards mass production. The government obtained powers to nationalize war industries, although only the aircraft industry, under the vigorous leadership of Pierre Cot, the Air Minister, was fundamentally restructured. But the nationalization programme provoked resistance from industrialists that, in the short term, damaged rather than enhanced the rearmament effort. At the same time, inter-service rivalries limited the effectiveness of rearmament: in particular, the army and navy resisted priority being given to the enlargement of an offensive air force.

The cost of rearmament not only hastened devaluation: it also necessitated a 'pause' in social reforms in February 1937, which disappointed government supporters, particularly on the left. The Communists gave Blum nominal support while seizing every opportunity to criticize and undermine his authority. Blum declared that the 'pause' was not a 'retreat' but 'a phase of prudent consolidation'.[21] But the conservative *le Temps* commented 'It is not only a pause; it is a conversion'.[22] For the remainder of its life the Popular Front ministry eschewed new social reforms but the continued government deficit generated renewed pressure on the franc. In June 1937 the Senate rejected a government request for decree powers to cope with a continued exodus of capital. A constitutional crisis loomed over the power of the second chamber, an issue that had never in the history of the republic been settled with finality. The left urged demonstrations and defiance. But deserted by his Radical ministers, Blum decided to resign after a little over a year in power. A nominally Popular Front ministry under Radical Prime Ministers limped along in his wake. Blum himself returned to office briefly in the spring of 1938, but the life had gone out of the enterprise. The brave new world of June 1936 had given away to shattered illusions and cynicism.

The Popular Front left an ambiguous legacy. The far left condemned Blum for failing to seize the opportunity offered at the outset to enact thorough-going Socialistic measures. The right attributed to him the inadequate rearmament programme and the catastrophe that followed from that. Few of the Popular Front's social reforms endured: the forty-hour week was modified in September 1938 and abandoned a few months later. The wage increases of June 1936 were soon rubbed out in real terms. The left blamed a 'strike of capital' for the stalled economic recovery. But such excuses, while perhaps adequate for party faithful, failed to confront the underlying internal and external challenges to the Popular Front programme. Blum and Auriol zigged and zagged between soaring working-class expectations, mobilized in a suddenly revivified trade union movement, and deeply suspicious financial markets, but their craft ultimately foundered. In foreign policy the record was one of almost-frozen impotence in the face of Fascist advance. The rearmament programme remained incomplete at the outbreak of war in 1939 and was unaccompanied by the changes in military doctrine that might have rendered it effective in the crisis of 1940. Nevertheless, in a period when Fascism was in the ascendant, the Popular Front inspired almost millenarian enthusiasm on the left, not merely in France but throughout Europe. Nowhere were such hopes raised higher and nowhere were they dashed more cruelly than in Spain.

Civil War in Spain

Spain in the inter-war period was divided by conflicts even deeper than those in France. To class hatreds were added regional antagonisms and ideological absolutisms that ranged from the anarchism of Catalan workers, Andalusian peasants, and Asturian miners to the rigid conservatism of the Spanish Church, landowners, and military officers. The 'aimless drift towards nowhere' of the dictatorship of General Miguel Primo de Rivera between 1923 and 1930 failed to reconcile the country's divisions.[23] In April 1931 adverse results for monarchists in municipal elections persuaded King Alfonso XIII to leave Spain, although he did not abdicate. A republican regime was established under a Provisional Government. Elections to the Cortes (parliament) in June gave the left a large majority. The second Spanish Republic, like the first (1873–4), was short-lived. Politics continued to be characterized by class conflict, corruption, party fragmentation, and severe instability: eighteen governments held office over the next five years.

The Republic enacted sweeping reforms that aroused the ire of conservatives. Women aged twenty-three and over were granted the vote. Divorce and homosexuality were legalized. The stigma of illegitimacy was lifted from children born out of wedlock. Religious symbols, observances, and instruction were prohibited in public schools. An eight-hour day was introduced. Secularizing clauses in the new constitution of 1932, debate over which was accompanied by outbreaks of church-burning, evoked fury from the Church and cemented its alliance with the enemies of the

Republic. A botched agrarian reform and a Statute of Autonomy for Catalonia added to the anti-republican ferment. Attempts to reform the army were fiercely opposed by the officer corps whose cause was taken up by the right-wing press and political parties. An attempted military rising in 1932 was foiled but elections the following year returned a right-wing government to power. The ferocity with which it suppressed Asturian miners and Catalan nationalists in 1934 galvanized rather than intimidated opposition and helped unify the disparate elements of the left. In new elections in February 1936 the Popular Front won a clear victory, securing 34 per cent of the votes but two-thirds of the seats in the Cortes.

The Spanish Popular Front differed in its composition from its namesake in France: the main elements were Socialists and Left Republicans; at the outset Communists played an insignificant role. The new government, headed by the Left Republican intellectual Manuel Azaña, was initially composed only of Republicans, since the Socialists stood aside, offering only ambiguous encouragement from outside. The Socialists were deeply divided: their two most prominent leaders were Indalecio Prieto, the foremost advocate of unity with the Republicans, and Francisco Largo Caballero, the 'Spanish Lenin', a labour union organizer and speechifier in the language of class war, who lacked much political sense or tactical flexibility.

The Popular Front victory was the signal for an eruption of political violence. In May the Socialists engineered Azaña's elevation to the figurehead position of President. Infighting among the constituent elements of the Popular Front weakened his successors as Prime Minister. The spark for civil war was the assassination, on 13 July, of the conservative opposition leader, José Calvo Sotelo, a revenge killing by left-wingers for the murder of a Socialist the previous day. A military revolt four days later marked the start of large-scale hostilities.

The main initiator of the conspiracy was General Emilio Mola Vidal, military governor of Pamplona, but the officer who soon captured its leadership was Francisco Franco (see plate 22), Comandante General of the Canary Islands, who had won his spurs in the campaign against rebels in the Rif region of Spanish Morocco. The man who would dominate twentieth-century Spanish history came of an old but impoverished naval family. Thanks to his exploits in Morocco, he had earned rapid promotion and, by 1926, at the age of thirty-three, was the youngest general in Spain, indeed, so it was said, the youngest in Europe since Napoleon. Less impulsive than Mussolini, more socially respectable than Hitler, he long outlasted both as ruler of his people. Cunning, cynical, immensely ambitious and self-aggrandizing, a man of obsessively reactionary outlook and inflexible temperament, blessed with a strong bladder that enabled him to outsit opponents in long meetings, cursed with a squeaky voice that rendered him an indifferent public speaker, he was unemotional to the point of callousness, signing death warrants while drinking coffee after dinner. 'He is cold with that coldness which at times freezes the soul,' observed one of his closest associates.[24] The birth of the Republic filled Franco with disgust. In 1934 he was ordered to Asturias to suppress a rising by miners and peasants. He did so with ferocious zeal: two thousand miners were killed. Franco was at first reluctant to join Mola's conspiracy but after Calvo Sotelo's murder he banished all doubts and threw in his lot with the rebel junta. He declared martial law in the Canaries and then flew to Tetuán in Spanish Morocco where he issued a manifesto proclaiming 'Spain is saved'.[25]

The rebels' prospects at the outset seemed doubtful. The government was greatly superior in armed strength, retaining the loyalty of most of the air force, more than half the army and paramilitary forces, and much of the navy. The Republic controlled Spain's main industrial regions and three-quarters of the merchant fleet. The Popular Front enjoyed the support of the urban working class, nationalists in Catalonia and the Basque provinces, and much of the peasantry hungry for land reform. In addition the Republic could count on the leftist political militias who seized control of Madrid, Barcelona, and Bilbao. Yet the government threw away many of its initial advantages, almost collapsing in disarray and internal bickering.

The insurgent nationalists drew together monarchists, militarists, clericals, the landowning class, ultra-traditionalist Carlists in Navarre, and the small Fascist Falange Party founded in 1933 by José Antonio Primo de Rivera, son of the former dictator. For the nationalists the rising was a holy war against a hydra-headed monster of godlessness, disintegration, and freemasonry, a 'crusade against Communism to save religion, the nation, and the family', as the bishop of Salamanca put it in a pastoral letter.[26]

In the first phase of the war, between June and October, the nationalists succeeded in moving substantial forces from Morocco to the mainland and in bolstering strongholds at Seville in the south and at Burgos and Salamanca in the north. Nationalist victory in the Battle of Irún, near the French border in September was a dispiriting setback for the Republic. This was the

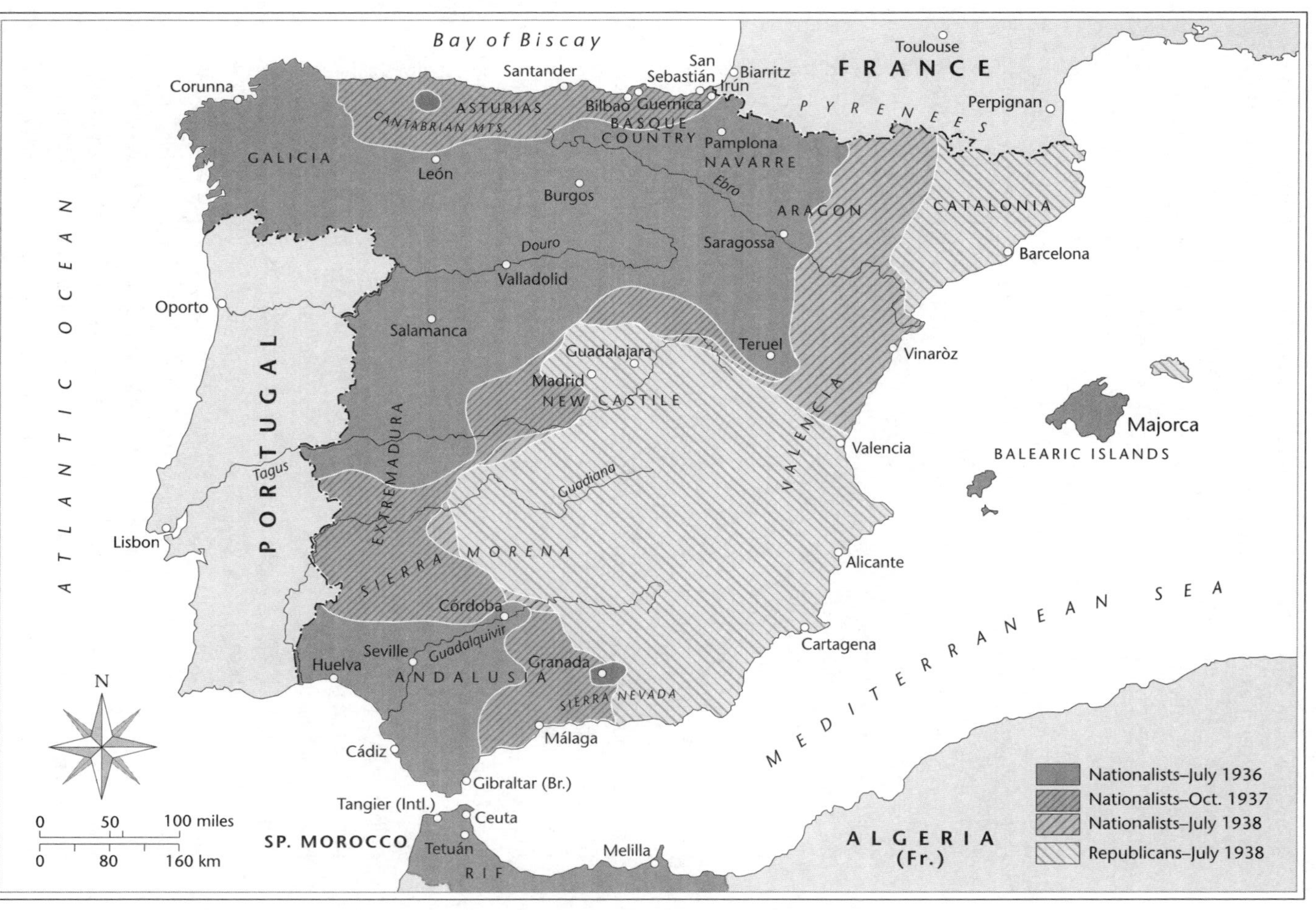

Map 4. Spanish Civil War

first battle in history to be broadcast live—in a CBS News radio transmission to the USA. The Basque and Asturias regions were now isolated from the rest of the Republic and from France.

Largo Caballero headed a new ministry that included Socialists, Republicans, Communists, a Basque nationalist, and later also anarchists. Working-class excitement knew no bounds. As nationalist forces headed towards Madrid, the government decided to 'arm the people', that is the left-wing militias. Across Spain 'spontaneous' collectivization of industry and agriculture alarmed the possessing classes. In many areas proletarian committees replaced the regular administration and, as the conflict intensified, lynch law became the order of the day. According to the new revolutionary code of manners one might not even say '*¡adios!*', since no presumption of the existence of a deity was permissible.

On the other side of the lines, Franco became undisputed master of nationalist Spain. On 1 October he was invested as Chief of State in a grandiose ceremony at Burgos. After its founder was shot in prison by republican forces, Franco took over the Falange and turned it into a mass movement on the model of the Italian Fascist Party. Nationalist Spain became a one-party state with a repressive apparatus of arbitrary police violence, political prisoners, censorship, and elimination of civil liberties. A cult of the Caudillo (warrior-leader: the title was taken from the medieval Caudillo Kings of Asturias) portrayed him as a worthy successor to El Cid, Charles V, and Philip II. Preening himself as the restorer of Spanish greatness, Franco looked forward to taking his place beside the Führer and the Duce as a world-class statesman.

Terror of right and left produced a bloodbath of civilians as well as fighters. During the early months of the war nearly seven thousand members of the Catholic clergy, including thirteen bishops and 283 nuns, were murdered, mostly by anarchists. Often victims were humiliated or tortured before death and their bodies mutilated afterwards. Massacres of nationalist prisoners imprisoned in Madrid in August 1936 reduced Azaña to despair and almost impelled his resignation from the presidency. The nationalists too committed barbaric crimes: among their victims was the poet Federico García Lorca, aged thirty-eight. A friend who saw Lorca being taken away yelled, 'Murderers! You're going to kill a genius! A genius! Murderers!' He was shot on a hillside at dawn together with a schoolmaster and two anarchist bullfighters. Lorca's executioner later boasted that, after Lorca had been killed, he fired 'two bullets into his arse for being a queer'.[27]

Outside intervention in the war was initiated on all sides by Spaniards themselves. The Germans and Italians sent help to the nationalists, the Russians and French to the Republic. At first, the Germans, especially the Foreign Office, were leery of becoming involved. But in response to an appeal from Franco, Hitler decided to dispatch transport aircraft and other supplies. The planes played a critical part in the airlift of rebel troops from Morocco to the mainland at the start of the war. In October Hitler decided to send the 'Condor Legion', an air group of five thousand men, including bombers and fighter planes, to take the field on behalf of the rebels. Its battle experience in tactical deployment of air power to support ground operations proved of great importance in the development of the combat doctrine with which the Luftwaffe later entered the Second World War. Later the Germans sent thousands more men, tanks, artillery, light arms, and communications equipment. Total German deliveries of war *matériel* to Spain (including the supply of the Condor Legion) were estimated by German experts to amount to 500 million Reichsmarks (a little over $200 million).[28] Hitler later complained that, when Germany demanded repayment of this debt, 'as a German one found oneself appearing to the Spaniards almost like a Jew who wished to do business in the most sacred human value'.[29] But Spanish iron ore and wolfram, the basis of tungsten, were vital to Germany's armaments industries and the Germans used the leverage of arms supplies to extract what they required.

Mussolini too decided to participate, rejecting the more cautious advice of his army Chief of Staff. He eventually dispatched fifty thousand men to Spain, mostly untrained volunteers attracted less by ideology or the prospect of glory than by exceptionally high pay rates. An Italian general described his own men as 'mostly scum'.[30] In addition, more than half the fighter strength of the Italian air force plus two thousand pilots, among them Mussolini's son, and formidable naval units were mobilized to support Franco. Their performance in battle was unimpressive and the main long-term effect of this large commitment was to help ensure that Italy entered the Second World War woefully under-equipped.

Meanwhile the Republic appealed to France and the Soviet Union for arms and equipment. The USSR, happy to see the Germans and Italians embroiled in a far corner of Europe, supplied the Republic with at least 331 tanks, 600 planes, and a large number of pilots. The Russians too exacted a price: three-quarters of Spain's gold reserve, the fourth largest in the world, worth over $500 million, was shipped to the Soviet Union. The entire

1. Slum children, London, *c.*1914 (Imperial War Museum)

2. Albanian mountain farmers, Scutari, *c.*1914 (Imperial War Museum)

3. Serbian refugees on the march under the protection of an armed monk, Macedonia, 1915 (Imperial War Museum)

4. Albert Thomas (French Under-Secretary for War), General Sir Douglas Haig (Commander in Chief, British Expeditionary Force), General Joseph Joffre (French Chief of Staff), and David Lloyd George (Secretary of State for War), at 14th Army Corps HQ, Méaulte, Western Front, 12 September 1916 (Imperial War Museum)

5. Tanks captured by the Germans, recaptured by the British, near Méaulte, Western Front, 20 September 1918 (Imperial War Museum)

6. An old woman refugee with her cow, Amiens, 28 March 1918 (Imperial War Museum)

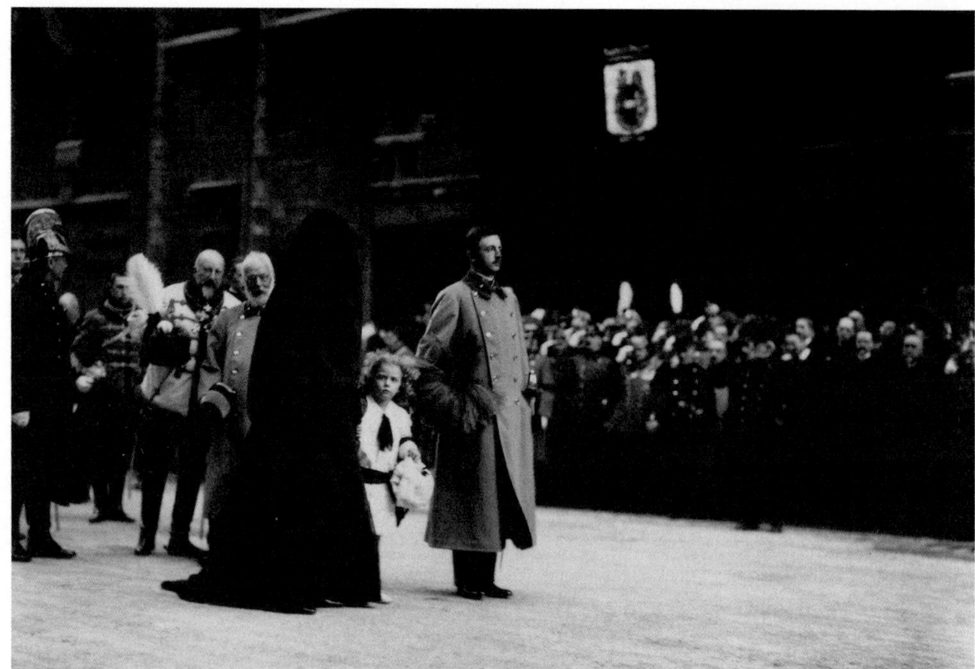

7. Funeral procession of Emperor Franz Josef, outside St Stephen's Cathedral, Vienna, 30 November 1916: (*left to right*) King 'Foxy' Ferdinand of Bulgaria (holding fur cap with plume), King Friedrich August III of Saxony, Empress Zita, Crown Prince Otto, Emperor Karl of Austria (Imperial War Museum)

8. Hindenburg and Ludendorff, July 1917 (Imperial War Museum)

9. Richard von Kühlmann, German Foreign Minister, signing Treaty of Brest-Litovsk, 3 March 1918. Looking on at right, Count Ottokar Czernin, Austro-Hungarian Foreign Minister (Imperial War Museum)

10. Demonstration against the peace terms, outside Hotel Adlon, Berlin, 14 May 1919 (Imperial War Museum)

11. Armoured train of a White unit in the Caucasus during the Russian Civil War (Imperial War Museum)

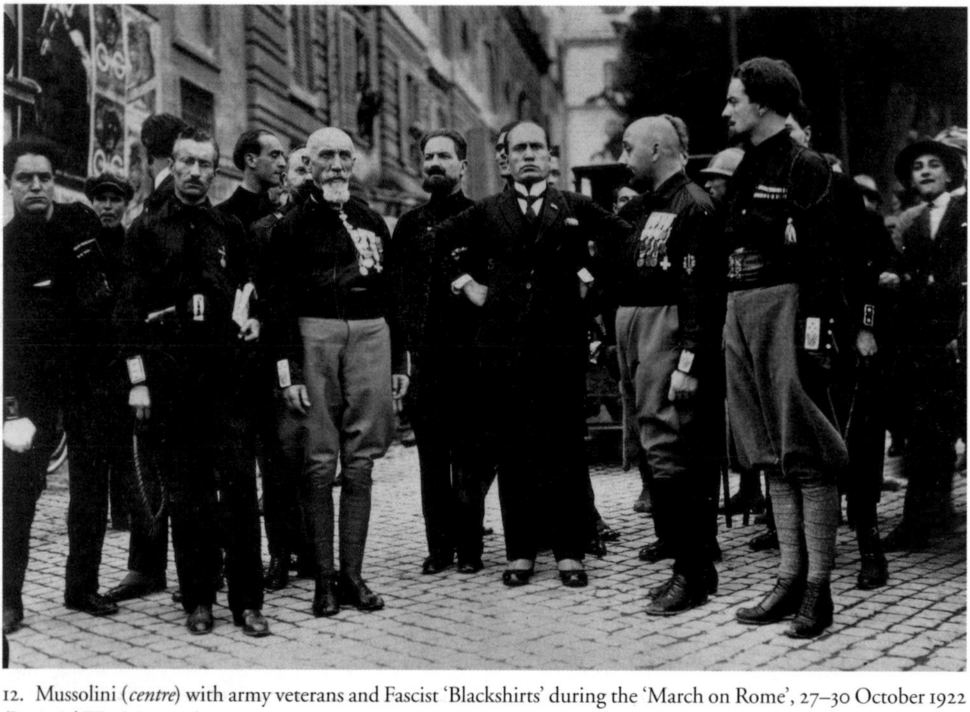

12. Mussolini (*centre*) with army veterans and Fascist 'Blackshirts' during the 'March on Rome', 27–30 October 1922 (Imperial War Museum)

13. Karl Liebknecht (1871–1919), leader of Spartacist revolt in Berlin, 1919, murdered in Berlin, January 1919 (Imperial War Museum)

14. Rosa Luxemburg (1871–1919), leader of Spartacist revolt in Berlin, 1919, murdered in Berlin, January 1919 (Imperial War Museum)

15. Eleftherios Venizelos (1864–1936), Prime Minister of Greece, protagonist of the 'great idea' of the re-establishment of a Greek empire with its capital at Constantinople, architect of the disastrous war against Turkey, 1919–23 (League of Nations Archives, UN Library, Geneva)

16. Tomás Garrigue Masaryk (1850–1937), philosopher-statesman, President of Czechoslovakia, 1918–1935 (League of Nations Archives, UN Library, Geneva)

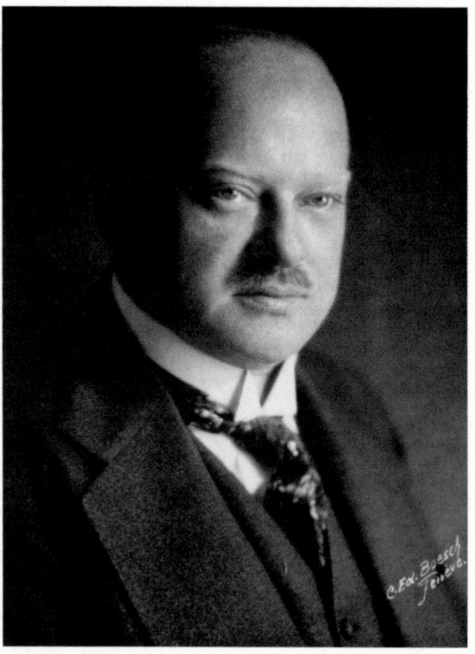

17. Gustav Stresemann (1878–1929), German Foreign Minister (League of Nations Archives, UN Library, Geneva)

18. Aristide Briand (1862–1932), French Foreign Minister, advocate of Franco-German amity (League of Nations Archives, UN Library, Geneva)

19. Léon Blum (1872–1950), Socialist leader of the Popular Front government in France, 1936–7 (League of Nations Archives, UN Library, Geneva)

20. Jean Monnet (1888–1979), 'father of the European Community' (League of Nations Archives, UN Library, Geneva)

amount was appropriated as payment for supplies sent to the Republic. The remnants of the loot of the conquistadores thus helped swell the coffers of the Kremlin.

As for the French, the Republic's plea for aid presented Blum with a terrible dilemma. On the one hand, the Spanish republicans were a Popular Front government ideologically akin to his own. The installation of a Fascist regime in Spain would potentially endanger French national security. The Communists as well as many of Blum's fellow Socialists clamoured for aid to Spain. But weighing against all this was the danger of a general European war for which France was ill-prepared. As he discovered on a visit to London, the British, who held 40 per cent of all foreign investments in Spain, were disinclined to become involved. France might thus face alone potential enemies on three fronts. There loomed the additional threat, which Blum took seriously, of civil war spilling over into France itself. Moreover, the army, itself seriously under-equipped, was loth to see much-needed supplies sent abroad. Blum's initial response to the Spanish government was nevertheless to agree to send aid secretly. Munitions, planes, and a few pilots were supplied to the Republic. But rebel sympathizers in the Spanish embassy in Paris informed the French right-wing press, which denounced the assistance as 'treason'. Within the government, many of the Radical ministers opposed sending aid to Spain. Reluctantly Blum decided it would be impossible for France to give open military support to the Republic.

On the advice of Alexis Léger, Secretary-General of the Foreign Ministry from 1933 to 1940 (also, under the nom de plume Saint-John Perse, later a Nobel-prizewinning poet), whose influence exceeded that of successive political masters at the Quai d'Orsay, Blum conjured up what seemed a reasonable compromise: non-intervention. Britain strongly supported the concept and in August Germany, Italy, and the USSR joined in signing a non-intervention agreement. But the committee set up to enforce the arms embargo at Spain's borders and sea coasts was hopelessly ineffective. Confidentially, a British Foreign Office official described the agreement as 'an extremely useful piece of humbug'.[31]

Spain became the cause of the generation, what America had been for Lafayette and Greece for Byron. Blum later wrote that as Mary Tudor had said 'Calais' was engraved on her heart, so on his was the word 'Spain'.[32] So it was, for a while, on the heart of Europe. The great ideological cause of both left and right, the conflict became a surrogate for the larger European civil war. The '*¡No pasarán!*' radio speech on 19 July by the Communist firebrand Dolores Ibárruri, known as La Pasionaria, was celebrated the world over.[33] The cause of republican Spain provided a perfect opportunity for the organization of Communist front organizations or 'innocents' clubs', a technique that had earlier been perfected by the 'red millionaire' and Comintern agent, Willi Münzenberg, 'patron saint of the "fellow traveller" '.[34] In a tactic that would be widely adopted over the next half-century, non-Communists were attracted to various committees and organizations for ostensibly non-partisan objectives; the bodies were secretly controlled by the Communists. As an extension of the same principle, the Comintern decided in August to recruit International Brigades to fight on behalf of the Republic. Although mobilized under a Popular Front banner, the brigades were heavily Communist in composition and direction. Their numbers and military effectiveness, although not their sacrifices, were exaggerated by propaganda: probably no more than 32,000 volunteers reached the Republic (no more than eighteen thousand at any one time) of whom a very high percentage died. Among those attracted to the cause were the French novelist André Malraux, who flew without a pilot's licence for the republicans, and the English novelist George Orwell (Eric Blair), who fought with the POUM (Partido Obrero di Unificación Marxista) militia (denounced as 'Trotskyist' by the Communists, though Trotsky himself disowned it).

In October the nationalists mounted a determined assault on Madrid. Some advanced units reached its outskirts and engaged in fierce hand-to-hand fighting. Air raids left hundreds of civilian casualties. The rebels came so close to taking the city that the government decamped to Valencia. In December four mobile columns tried to encircle the capital. A nationalist 'fifth column' (this was the origin of the phrase) was rumoured to be ready to rise within the city. The rebels were bolstered by large-scale Italian intervention, desperately needed but only grudgingly acknowledged by Franco. Soviet arms supplies, including tanks and fighter aircraft, as well as three thousand Russian pilots and technicians, helped the defenders to throw back Franco's forces.

Both sides now settled in for a long haul. Franco disregarded advice from all sides and determined on a war of attrition. Over the next two years the republicans launched several offensives but were never able to capitalize on initial successes. Mass conscription enabled the nationalists to recruit an army that eventually mobilized a million men.

In February 1937 Italian troops conquered an ill-defended Málaga; the nationalists celebrated the victory with a massacre of thousands of republicans. Next, three Italian divisions attacked Guadalajara. Inadequately equipped and poorly trained, they performed miserably and were driven back. The 'Spanish Caporetto', as it was exaggeratedly called by republican sympathizers, prompted Lloyd George to mock the 'Italian skedaddle' and greatly embarrassed the Duce.[35] Franco was not altogether displeased: he did not relish the prospect of advancing into Madrid in the baggage-train of a foreign army.

Abandoning hope of an imminent fall of the capital, Franco launched an offensive in the Basque country. On 26 April the small Basque town of Guernica, near Bilbao, was bombed by German and Italian aircraft operating under the command and at the request of the nationalists. Hundreds were killed and the centre of the town was almost entirely destroyed. Guernica, with its 'holy oak' monument, occupied a central place in the national mythology of the Basque people. This was not, in fact, the first large-scale aerial bombardment of civilians (the Germans had bombed English towns in the First World War) but it greatly shocked contemporary opinion. The nationalists asserted that the Basques themselves had set fire to the town; later they alleged that the Germans had operated wholly on their own initiative and therefore bore sole responsibility: the inconsistent claims were both brazen falsehoods.

The atrocity inspired the most compelling aesthetic response to the war, Pablo Picasso's *Guernica*, commissioned by the Republic and first exhibited in the Spanish pavilion at the Paris World's Fair a few weeks later. Picasso, a fervent supporter of the Popular Front, declared that his purpose was to give vent to his 'abhorrence of the military caste which has sunk Spain in an ocean of pain and death'.[36] The huge canvas (11′ 6″ × 25′ 8″) makes no attempt at a realistic portrayal of the bombing, apart, perhaps, from the figure of a weeping mother, her head upturned in anguish, her arms holding a dead child. Rather it conveys, through symbol and movement, Picasso's confused but intense emotions of tenderness and outrage at the violation of the innocent. Like Goya's *Los Desastres de la Guerra*, *Guernica* became an immensely influential expression of horror at man's capacity for cruelty to his own kind. But whereas Goya's etchings of the Peninsular War were not published until 1863, long after the death of their creator, Picasso allowed his painting to be exploited immediately for propaganda purposes. At the fair, *Guernica* stole the show from the rebarbative gigantism of the German and Russian pavilions. The painting then toured Europe and America, before settling in semi-permanent exile at the Museum of Modern Art in

New York. Picasso insisted it must not be sent to his homeland until the reinstallation of the Republic (later revised to restoration of 'public liberties') in Spain.[37]

As the republicans won a propaganda victory, the nationalist advance continued on the ground. Bilbao fell in June and within a few weeks Franco's forces controlled the whole of the Basque region and Asturias. Meanwhile, in early May food shortages, exacerbated by a large-scale influx of refugees from areas occupied by the nationalists, led to a revolt of anarchists, supported by POUM, in Barcelona. The *Generalitat* (Catalonian provincial government) was compelled to call on central government troops to restore order. Hundreds were killed during the 'May Days'. In the ensuing cabinet crisis, Largo Caballero's government fell. The new Prime Minister, Juan Negrín, also a Socialist, sought to consolidate the power of the central government at the expense of regional particularists and anarchists. He curbed revolutionary excesses in the hope of gaining the confidence of the liberal bourgeoisie and of London and Paris. But, dependent as he was on arms supplies from Moscow, he was himself obliged to fall back ever more heavily on the Communists who became the dominant force in the Republic. POUM was suppressed, its cadres killed or arrested, a process in which the Communists participated with a blood lust ideologically sanctioned by Moscow. Stalin personally signed the order for the POUM leader's liquidation.

The Soviets sent more tanks and planes and for a while the French adopted a policy, later termed *non-intervention relâchée* (relaxed non-intervention), under which transit of Soviet supplies was permitted and French arms were purchased, supposedly for delivery to Mexico and Lithuania, and then diverted to Spain. By this surreptitious and, as Blum later acknowledged, hypocritical behaviour, the French Popular Front, itself in its death throes, sought to salve its conscience. The Soviet Union was no less forthright in rhetorical support; its practical help, however, could not be sufficient to save the Republic.

In late 1937 the Italians, responding to an appeal by Franco to cut off Soviet seaborne supplies to the Republic, expanded their unacknowledged (and not very effective) submarine attacks on merchant shipping in the Mediterranean. By mistake a British destroyer was attacked. This was too much for the British to stomach. With French support they convened a conference at Nyon, near Geneva, to which all Mediterranean states, except Spain, plus Germany and the USSR were invited. Germany and Italy declined to participate. The conference agreed that an Anglo-French naval patrol would combat submarines, ships, or aircraft that threatened shipping in the Mediterranean. Nyon had little more effect than previous non-intervention efforts. As the British representative on the League of Nations Council confessed, 'The main, melancholy, unanswerable fact is that, to all appearance, the agreement is being violated in favour of both parties to the struggle.'[38] He might more accurately have said that non-intervention was being violated *against* both parties, since both Germany and the USSR cynically rationed their aid to Spain with a view to prolonging the war and serving their own interests rather than those of their protégés.

In October the republican government retreated to Barcelona. Italian aerial bombardment of the city inflicted massive death, property damage, and panic. The food crisis in the city deepened. The surrender of the nationalist stronghold of Teruel in January 1938 briefly heartened the republicans but they were evicted again by the end of February. In April the nationalists broke through to the coast at Vinaroz, cutting off Catalonia from the rest of the republic. From July to November a ferocious land and air battle was waged at the River Ebro. Both sides suffered immensely in this, the longest battle of the war. The nationalists could replace their losses; the republicans could not. The government in desperation resorted to a 'baby call-up' of teenagers.

The end of the Republic was now merely a matter of time. In January 1939 Barcelona fell. Madrid and Valencia held out only a few weeks longer. In early March an anti-Communist military *coup d'état*, headed by Colonel Segismundo Casado, ousted Negrín's government and sought a negotiated peace. But Franco demanded unconditional surrender. His forces entered Madrid unopposed and by the end of the month controlled the whole of Spain.

An estimated 365,000 people were killed in the war, of whom around 130,000 died not in action but from murders or executions behind the lines. Hundreds of thousands were wounded. At least thirty thousand opponents of the regime were executed in the five years after the end of the Civil War and many more were imprisoned. Some 300,000 refugees fled to France. The defeat of the Republic condemned Spain to thirty-five years of dictatorship, reinforced the social and cultural dominance of traditional forces, and retarded her modernization and economic development for a generation. Franco's Spain remained a highly militarized state: in 1946 the army, Civil Guard, and police still consumed 45 per cent of the total state budget.

The economy took years to recover from the ravages of the war: the 1940s were *años de hambre* (starvation years); only in 1951 did GDP attain the pre-civil-war level. Franco abolished the autonomy of the Basques and Catalans and banned public use of their languages. The dominance of the Church over education and cultural values was restored. Accordingly, the newly elected Pope Pius XII expressed his 'immense joy' at Franco's 'Catholic victory'.[39] But while the struggle in Spain ground to a blood-soaked conclusion, the diplomatic spotlight shifted elsewhere.

From Axis to *Anschluss*

In Austria, as in Spain, the onset of the Depression deepened the cleavage between left and right. The conservative Christian Social Party had dominated all governments after 1920. Their main rivals, the Social Democrats, controlled the capital but could make little headway in the rural hinterland. As in Weimar Germany, armed militias organized: the Social Democrat Republikanischer Schutzbund confronted the nationalist Heimwehr, led by Prince Ernst Rüdiger von Starhemberg, subsidized by Mussolini, and strongly supported by the Catholic Church. Tension between left and right was endemic and occasionally erupted into violence, as in July 1927 when government forces shot dead eighty-five people in Vienna after a mob set fire to the Palace of Justice.

The beginning of the end of the Republic came in May 1932 with the appointment as Chancellor, through constitutional processes, of Engelbert Dollfuss of the Christian Social Party. A trained economist (and the shortest European leader of the time: he stood four foot, eleven inches), Dollfuss faced an alarming economic crisis that seemed insurmountable by consensual decision-making. To this was added the political threat resulting from the accession to power in Germany of the Austrian-born Hitler, an event that gave Austrian Nazis a considerable boost. The new German government offered them strong support, hoping to effect a speedy *Anschluss* (union) of Austria with Germany. Like Brüning, Dollfuss sought salvation in rule by decree. Political meetings and parades, save those judged 'patriotic', were prohibited and press censorship was introduced. The Schutzbund was disbanded, while the Heimwehr was given quasi-official status. Capital punishment, which had been abolished at the institution of the republic, was reintroduced. In April 1933 Dollfuss announced, 'Austria's

Parliament has destroyed itself and nobody can say when it will be allowed to take up its dubious activities again.'[40] Echoing Madame de Staël's reference in 1810 to the Germans as a people of *Dichter und Denker* (poets and thinkers), the Viennese satirist Karl Kraus had quipped in 1919 that they had become a nation of *Richter und Henker* (judges and hangmen). Now the same might be said of his own countrymen.

Fearful of a putsch, Dollfuss banned all Nazi organizations in the summer of 1933. Relying on Italian support as a counterweight to Nazi pressure, he was urged by his allies in Rome to suppress the Social Democrats as he had the Nazis. In February 1934 a quasi-civil war broke out in Vienna between leftist militias and the army. The Social Democrats' leaders had opposed violence but they were arrested or fled and the party was banned. The government used artillery to subdue resistance in the Karl-Marx-Hof housing estate. Lesser disturbances also erupted in other cities. At least 314 people were killed (anti-government sources suggested much higher figures). Meanwhile, Nazi street violence, bombings, and killings increased and in July a German-inspired coup led to the assassination of Dollfuss. But the conspiracy was disorganized, the government regrouped, and Mussolini's mobilization of troops on the frontier deterred Hitler from pushing the enterprise further. For the next four years Austria, under clerico-Fascist rule, preserved a shaky independence between the upper and nether grindstones of Germany and Italy—or, as the new Chancellor, Kurt von Schuschnigg later put it, 'between hammer and anvil'.[41]

The changed nature of German–Italian relations in 1937 spelled the doom of Austrian independence. The wars in Ethiopia and Spain helped bring Germany and Italy together. In a speech in the Piazza del Duomo in Milan in November 1936 Mussolini declared: 'This vertical line between Berlin and Rome . . . is an axis round which all European States animated by the will to peace and collaboration can cooperate.'[42] A year later Mussolini signed the German–Japanese 'Anti-Comintern Pact'. But as Germany's international prestige ballooned, the Duce found that he was 'reduced from second violinist to broken-down viola player'.[43] He no longer dared to oppose Hitler's designs on Austria.

By early 1938 the last major German institution still semi-independent of Hitler, the army, had been neutered. In January the War Minister, Field-Marshal Werner von Blomberg, was dismissed when the Gestapo disclosed that his new wife was an ex-prostitute. A few days later the Army Chief of Staff, Colonel-General Werner Freiherr von Fritsch, was charged with homosexuality. Although later cleared by a military court, he was forced to retire 'on health grounds'. Hitler took the opportunity to purge the high command: twelve generals were removed. At the same time, a shake-up in the diplomatic service led to the fall of Neurath. His successor, Joachim von Ribbentrop, a former champagne salesman, was generally despised as an intriguer and social climber. 'He bought his name, he married his money, and he swindled his way into office,' was Goebbels's dismissive verdict on him.[44] For the previous three years he had been a disastrous ambassador in London (dubbed 'Brickendrop' by the London press): for the next seven he served as a notoriously inefficient and ineffective Foreign Minister. But in diplomacy, as in military matters, all important decisions were taken by Hitler.

On 12 February Schuschnigg was summoned to a meeting with Hitler at the Führer's Bavarian retreat at Berchtesgaden. Hitler presented his guest with a list of demands that amounted to the virtual abrogation of Austrian independence: among these was the insistence that a Nazi, Arthur Seyss-Inquart, be appointed Minister of the Interior, in charge of the security services. When Schuschnigg baulked, Hitler flew into a rage and threatened military action. Under intense pressure, the Austrian Chancellor eventually agreed to most of Hitler's requirements. Back home, Schuschnigg tried to organize a plebiscite on the issue of union with Germany. Hitler professed to regard this as a provocation. On 11 March, Schuschnigg, yielding to German demands, cancelled the plebiscite, and resigned in favour of Seyss-Inquart. In a farewell broadcast, Schuschnigg lamented, 'we have yielded to force'.[45] Fearful of renewed civil war, he announced that Austrian forces had been ordered to 'withdraw without resistance and to await the decisions of the coming hours'.[46] Hitler obtained an assurance of non-interference from Mussolini and, the next day, German troops entered Austria. They met no opposition. Austria was formally 'reunited' with Germany. Hitler immediately revisited his homeland, receiving a rapturous welcome in Vienna. In a speech to a vast crowd in the Heldenplatz he yet again declared that he had no further territorial demands—while, almost in the same breath, uttering new threats directed against the expanded Reich's eastern neighbours.

Union between Austria and Germany had been explicitly prohibited in the peace treaties. But international reaction was limited to ineffectual protests. France was in the throes of a ministerial crisis. Blum tried and failed to form a national unity government; the right refused to participate and he was able to scramble together only a short-lived Socialist-Radical ministry. In Britain, Eden, the foremost government advocate of resistance to the dictators, had resigned the Foreign Secretaryship three weeks earlier. His successor, Viscount Halifax, was a true believer in appeasement (the term had not yet acquired its malodorous reputation). And Mussolini, who had postured as protector of Austria since 1934, found himself powerless to intervene and humiliated by Hitler's success.

The idea of union with Germany had been widely popular in Austria, on left as well as right. This was 'a country that nobody wanted'.[47] But the *Anschluss* to which many Austrians had looked forward was a union of equals; what they got was conquest and absorption in the Third Reich as 'Ostmark'. A Nazi-conducted plebiscite on 10 April produced (it was announced) a 99.73 per cent vote in favour of union with Germany. Even the Socialist leader Karl Renner advocated a 'yes' vote. The police state was soon extended into Austria. One of the most brutal concentration camps opened at the citadel of Mauthausen, near Linz. The Nuremberg laws were automatically applied to the newly integrated territories. In Vienna, where anti-Semitism had a long political pedigree, the large Jewish community was subjected to maltreatment and violence. Tens of thousands tried to emigrate, but few countries were willing to admit significant numbers of refugees. *Gleichschaltung*, in the form of incorporation into the existing Nazi German framework, was applied to Austrian institutions from the postal service to the boy scouts. The proud ex-imperial capital was reduced to a provincial outpost. The Austrian National Bank was taken over and its stock of gold and foreign currency impounded. All Austrian sport was subjected to Nazi policy: professional football was abolished; 'race consciousness' was promoted. The Nazis' task was eased by a declaration of the Austrian Catholic bishops, headed by the Archbishop of Vienna, Cardinal Innitzer, acclaiming the fulfilment of 'the thousand-year-old longing of our people for union in a Great Reich of Germans', hailing the *Anschluss* 'with joy', and urging their flock, 'out of a sense of debt to their race' to vote affirmatively in the plebiscite.[48] Austrians bore a measure of responsibility for what had befallen them: yet the legend was born of their country as Hitler's 'first victim'.

Munich

Uniquely in inter-war eastern Europe, political conflict in Czechoslovakia was contained within parliamentary bounds. The chief problem facing the

Republic, that of relations between the Czech lands and the more backward Slovak region, had been exacerbated by the failure to enact promises of Slovak autonomy made by Masaryk in 1918. Slovak resentment of centralized government from Prague was at the root of the appeal of the Slovak People's Party headed by Father Andrej Hlinka, a militantly nationalist Catholic priest. But the most pressing issue facing the Czechoslovak government in the late 1930s was that of the three-million-strong German minority intermingled with Czechs all along the border regions of Bohemia and Moravia. The Germans, complaining, with some justice, that they were denied their fair share of civil service positions and that they had been discriminated against in land reforms, demanded autonomy.

Hitler seized on their grievances to destroy the last democracy in eastern Europe. The Sudeten Germans, as they had come to be called (after the Sudeten mountain region where some of them lived) were strongly nationalistic; an important minority nevertheless supported the German Social Democrat Party, which had participated in Czechoslovak governments. Since the rise of Hitler, however, Nazi influence had increased and in 1935 the Sudeten German Party, headed by Konrad Henlein, a gymnastics teacher, won the support of two thirds of German voters, thereby suddenly becoming the largest political party in Czechoslovakia. Like many of the European ultra-nationalists of the period, Henlein came of mixed ancestry: his father was German, his mother Czech. He acted as a stalking-horse for Hitler, receiving regular, secret subsidies from the German Foreign Ministry. Under pressure from Germany, the Czechoslovak government made a number of concessions to the German minority but drew the line at granting autonomy. In August 1938, alarmed by the ever more aggressive tone of Hitler's speeches on the issue, the British sent a former minister, Lord Runciman, to Czechoslovakia on a mission of mediation. On British and French advice, the Prague government reluctantly decided to satisfy most of Henlein's demands, including the claim to autonomy. This achieved nothing since Henlein obeyed orders from Hitler not to come to terms with the Prague government. On 12 September Hitler raised the stakes and demanded self-determination for the Sudeten Germans. Henlein fled to Germany and called for the incorporation of the Sudetenland into Germany. Czechoslovak troops were dispatched to quell disturbances in the area and the threat of German military intervention loomed.

As on previous occasions, Hitler proceeded in defiance of much expert opinion. He vowed to 'settle the Czech affair by force of arms'.

The State Secretary (civil service head) of the German Foreign Office, Ernst von Weizsäcker, expressed reservations, warning that such a policy involved 'an unjustifiable risk'. But Ribbentrop, ever a fervent Führer-worshiper, 'declared that the Führer had never yet made a mistake.... It was necessary to believe in his genius.'[49] In consultation with the General Staff, Hitler ordered plans to be prepared for the manufacture of 'an incident in Czechoslovakia which will provide Germany with a pretext for military intervention'.[50]

Confronted with Hitler's demands, the Czechoslovak government turned to their allies, France and the USSR, and to Britain, with which Czechoslovakia's political leaders had enjoyed a close relationship since Masaryk's days in London during the war. Jan Masaryk, son of the founder of the Republic, was now ambassador in London. His father's successor as President since 1935 and his political heir, Edvard Beneš, had spent the whole of his previous career under the great man's shadow and was, in truth, very much a lesser figure. His nickname at the Paris Peace Conference had been 'the little fox'. Decent, well-meaning, unhumorous, uninspiring, Beneš had become, suggests Hugh Seton-Watson, 'a man of words, believing that by a carefully phrased speech or by well-timed suggestions or pressure in private, he could fix any problem'.[51]

For France the basic consideration was the British attitude. The Prime Minister, Daladier, had a reputation as an energetic decision-maker but in this crisis he vacillated. The 'Bull of Vaucluse' did not dare commit France to war without Britain. The Quai d'Orsay favoured a negotiated settlement; indeed, the Foreign Minister, Georges Bonnet, was willing to go to almost any lengths to avoid war. French intelligence, as conveyed to the government, greatly overestimated the strength of the Wehrmacht and the Luftwaffe at this time; indeed, according to one historian, 'the French High command of the late 1930s seemed bent on frightening its own government rather than Hitler'.[52] Yet France was hardly in condition to fight. Only a few months earlier Daladier had learned, to his consternation, that the entire Maginot Line was dependent for its power supply on just two sources of electricity, one in Germany, the other in a vulnerable position on the border; it took several months to rectify this potentially disastrous error.

The Soviet Union was bound by treaty, signed in May 1935, shortly after the Franco-Soviet alliance, to come to Czechoslovakia's aid in the event of 'unprovoked aggression' against her. The Soviets now reminded the French that their military support for Czechoslovakia was conditional on France fulfilling her obligations too (a stipulation that had been inserted in the treaty at the request of Prague). This remained the Soviet position throughout the crisis. But Soviet military capability had been dealt a serious blow by a purge of the officer corps of the Red Army in 1937 in which the former chief of the general staff, Marshal Tukhachevsky, as well as twenty thousand other officers (including 90 per cent of generals' rank and 85 per cent of colonels) were arrested on trumped-up charges. Tukhachevsky initially denied some of the accusations. His subsequent confessional deposition was splattered with blood. He was among the thousands who were shot. Contemplating this bloodbath, British and French analysts did not set much store by Soviet military capability. Moreover, Chamberlain, British Prime Minister since 1937, 'warned of the great danger that would arise from the presence of Russian troops in central Europe since it would strengthen Bolshevism throughout the world'.[53]

The British, unlike the French and Russians, had no treaty commitment to defend Czechoslovakia other than their general obligations arising from membership of the League of Nations. In any case, much more hardheaded calculations now perforce came to the fore. While Britain maintained her historic concern to prevent domination of the continent by any one power, Czechoslovakia was not a prime area of British strategic or economic interest. British rearmament had accelerated since 1936 but the Chiefs of Staff warned the government in March 1938 that, even with French and other European allies, they could not prevent a German occupation of Czechoslovakia nor engage successfully in a world war that would be the likely consequence of such an enterprise. It would be important for Britain, if she went to war, to carry with her the independent Dominions of the British Commonwealth, Canada, South Africa, Australia, and New Zealand; but none of these was enthusiastic about such a prospect. On 22 March the British Cabinet formally decided that Britain would not undertake any commitment to go to war in defence of Czechoslovakia. In a conversation with Daladier in April, Chamberlain said that 'it made his blood boil to see Germany getting away with it time after time and increasing her domination over free peoples'. But he added that 'such sentimental considerations were dangerous and [he and Daladier] must remember the forces with which we were playing'.[54]

In the second half of September Chamberlain made three visits to Germany in an effort to preserve the peace. His first, on 15 September, was to Berchtesgaden, where the Führer persuaded him that German-majority areas of Czechoslovakia must be ceded to the Reich. Chamberlain found a justification for this position in Runciman's report, delivered after his return to London on 16 September following the collapse of his mission. Explaining that he considered Sudeten German grievances 'in the main justified', Runciman recommended that 'those frontier districts where the Sudeten [German] population is in an important majority should . . . *at once* be transferred from Czechoslovakia to Germany'.[55]

The Czechs refused to comply but sought to appear reasonable by proposing arbitration. On 21 September, however, the British and French presented the Czechoslovak government with an ultimatum demanding acceptance of the proposed terms. Beneš tried to play for time. The next day Chamberlain flew back to Germany and met Hitler at Bad Godesberg on the Rhine. While they met, the Czechoslovak army was ordered to mobilize. Hitler now raised his demands: he insisted on German annexation of the entire border area by 28 September plus satisfaction of Polish and Hungarian territorial claims against Czechoslovakia. Chamberlain was shocked by what he regarded as Hitler's bad faith. He expressed his outrage and received a paltry reward for his efforts: Hitler agreed to postpone the date for Czechoslovak evacuation to 1 October. 'You are the only man to whom I have ever made a concession,' he informed the Prime Minister.[56]

Anxious discussions in London and Paris over the next few days disclosed divisions within the British and French Cabinets. The French army began mobilizing. Chamberlain desperately sought a way out. On 27 September he broadcast to the nation: 'How horrible, fantastic, incredible it is that we should be digging trenches and trying on gas-masks here because of a quarrel in a far-away country between people of whom we know nothing.' Chamberlain said that he 'would not hesitate to pay even a third visit to Germany if [he] thought it would do any good'. Declaring himself 'a man of peace to the depths of my soul', he averred that he did not consider sympathy with 'a small nation confronted by a big and powerful neighbour' a sufficient reason for Britain to go to war: 'If we have to fight it must be on larger issues than that.'[57] In line with these sentiments, both the British and the French intensified their pressure on Beneš to cede territory.

Hitler now discerned the prospect of another great victory to be gained without firing a shot. In response to an 'appeal' from Mussolini, he convened a conference at Munich, to be attended by the leaders of Germany, Italy, Britain, and France. Stalin was not invited. Nor were representatives of the state most intimately concerned, Czechoslovakia. Chamberlain raised the question of their attending but was overruled. Nevertheless, he found

Hitler's opening attitude 'so moderate and reasonable that I felt instant relief'.[58] Daladier, who had never met Hitler before, felt immediately that he had 'fallen into a trap'.[59] The only significant difference between what Hitler demanded at Bad Godesberg and what he was granted at Munich was that, on the insistence of the British, an orderly procedure, with a veneer of international legitimacy, was now provided for the transfer of territory. German occupation of the Sudetenland was to begin on 1 October and to be completed by 10 October. A plebiscite would be held to determine the final frontier. In an annex to the Munich agreement, the signatories offered an international guarantee of Czechoslovakia's new frontiers against unprovoked aggression (the German and Italian governments made their participation in the guarantee conditional on the satisfaction of Polish and Hungarian claims against Czechoslovakia). The treaty was signed on the night of 29/30 September. The next day Chamberlain and Hitler met again and signed a joint declaration asserting that the pact symbolized 'the desire of our two peoples never to go to war with one another again'.[60] This was the document that Chamberlain waved in the air triumphantly on his return to a hero's welcome at Heston aerodrome (see plate 25).

The Czechs protested with dignified but bitter indignation. In a public statement Jan Masaryk said: 'If it *is* for peace that my country has been butchered up in this unprecedented manner, then I am glad of it. If it isn't, may God have mercy on our souls.'[61] There was to be no resistance. Could Czechoslovakia have taken a stronger line in 1938? She had a strong air force (1,200 planes of which more than half were first-line craft), well-fortified defences, a front-rank armaments industry, good internal lines of communication, and an army of thirty-five divisions with seven hundred tanks. She might have held the Germans at bay for a while (the French military intelligence service reckoned a month)[62]—perhaps long enough to induce the French or the Russians to intervene. But by the end of September Beneš realized that this was a vain hope. One of his successors, Václav Havel, summed up his dilemma:

> Beneš knew that a decision to reject the Munich Agreement would be met by resistance and by a lack of comprehension in the democratic world, which would see him as a Czech nationalist, a disturber of the peace, a provocateur and a gambler who hoped insanely to draw other peoples into a war which did not need to happen. He opted for capitulation without battle, because it seemed to him that this was more responsible than risking endless sacrifices which would ultimately end in surrender anyway.[63]

As a result of the Munich agreement, Czechoslovakia lost a third of her territory and 40 per cent of her industrial capacity. In the short interlude granted them prior to completion of the German occupation of the Sudetenland, Czechs, Jews, and German Socialists fled. Livestock, wagons, and machinery were driven helter-skelter across the demarcation line by farmers bearing cocked pistols lest their German neighbours prevent their departure. Beneš resigned the presidency on 5 October and departed into exile, first in London, then at the University of Chicago.

Under his successors, what was left of Czecho-Slovakia soon crumbled away—the hyphenation of the rump 'second Republic' was symptomatic of its disintegration. Slovakia and Sub-Carpathian Ruthenia acquired autonomy. Maggots soon began to gnaw at the carcass. On 2 October the Poles successfully demanded the Silesian border district of Teschen, important for its coal mines. A month later, by the so-called 'Vienna Award', in theory an arbitral judgement by Germany and Italy, Hungary was allowed to annex parts of Sub-Carpathian Ruthenia and southern Slovakia.

For the British and French, Munich was a diplomatic catastrophe that was acclaimed in both countries as if it were a triumph. Daladier, for one, had few illusions. He felt surprised and a little ashamed when he was welcomed by cheering crowds on his arrival home. He turned to a neighbour and muttered, '*Les cons!*'—or, according to another account, he said, '*Les gens sont fous.*'[64] Chamberlain, by contrast, felt elated by his wildly enthusiastic reception in London. Appearing at the window of 10 Downing Street, he exulted, 'My good friends, for the second time in our history, a British Prime Minister has returned from Germany bringing peace with honour. I believe it is peace for our time.'[65] Disraeli, on his return from the Congress of Berlin in 1878, had been a little more modest: 'Lord Salisbury and myself have brought you back peace—but a peace, I hope, with honour.' As soon as Chamberlain turned from the window he regretted the remark. In the short term, he need not have worried: his popularity soared and he received tens of thousands of letters from grateful citizens. James Maxton, the far left MP from 'red Clydeside', incongruously joined Lady Astor, châtelaine of the notoriously pro-appeasement 'Cliveden Set', in hymning the preservation of peace. Yet in both Britain and France the mood of relief was tinged with a sense of shame. *Punch* recalled the words of Sir Philip Francis in 1801: 'It is a peace which everybody is glad of, though nobody is proud of.'[66] The Peace of Amiens (finalized in March 1802) had earned

Britain fourteen months of respite; but Hitler was in a greater hurry than Napoleon.

Churchill expressed the minority view: he pronounced Munich an 'unmitigated defeat'. Over the previous three years he had battered Baldwin and Chamberlain with criticism for their failure to rearm, particularly to meet the threat of German air attack. Using information derived privately from a number of official sources, he assaulted the government with questions, speeches, and political ambushes, designed to show the inadequacy of their rearmament efforts. A few fellow Conservatives rallied to support him but he was generally regarded as an irresponsible warmonger. Out of office since 1929, he had damaged his reputation by a vehement campaign against concessions to Indian nationalism and by an ill-considered, albeit short-lived, effort in 1936, at the time of King Edward VIII's abdication (over his wish to marry an American divorcée), to form a 'king's party'. Most respectable opinion still regarded him as erratic, bellicose, and unfit for public office—'a Malay run amok', as the Liberal leader, Sir Herbert Samuel, had called him in 1935. He nevertheless now emerged as the main political alternative to Chamberlain.

The two men offered striking similarities and contrasts. Both were the sons of senior politicians who had just failed to reach the supreme position in British politics. They belonged to the same party and shared many fundamental political attitudes: on the importance to Britain of the imperial connection; on economic policy; on moderate social reform. Chamberlain was a product of middle-class, Unitarian, business-oriented, municipal politics; Churchill a scion of one of the great aristocratic families of England. The Prime Minister was narrow-minded, prudent, and cautious, his challenger large-spirited, impulsive, and theatrical. Chamberlain's manner on radio and cinema newsreels could be effective with contemporary audiences, but as a public speaker he lacked fire in the belly. The MP and diarist Harold Nicolson compared one of his speeches to that of 'the secretary of a firm of undertakers reading the minutes of the last meeting'.[67] Churchill's oratorical style already seemed old-fashioned but his orotund periods nevertheless commanded attention. As the disturbing implications of the Anglo-French surrender at Munich became evident over the next few months, the British public pricked up its ears and began to heed what Churchill had to say on the vital issue that now confronted the country.

After Munich spending on rearmament was increased significantly by both the French and British governments. French arms expenditure more than doubled in the 1939 budget: spending on re-equipment of the air force nearly quadrupled. British rearmament geared up to a level approximately equivalent to the German (expressed as a proportion of GNP). But total German military spending in 1938/9 remained higher than that of Britain and France together, as it had been since 1935. Moreover, financial constraints and mistaken priorities impeded the British build-up. Until early 1939 production of locomotives and railway wagons delayed that of tanks. Bombers were much cheaper to manufacture than fighter aircraft and were regarded as more valuable by the Air Ministry: it was not until after Munich that a decision was taken to give top priority to fighters. In late January and early February 1939 the British Cabinet, alarmed at the prospect of German aggression in the west, intensified staff talks with France and resolved to go to war if Germany attacked the Low Countries, Switzerland, or France. In the event, however, the challenge came from a different direction.

War over Danzig

Immediately after Munich Hitler began to apply pressure on Poland with the object of reducing her to the status of a satellite. On 24 October 1938 Ribbentrop outlined to the Polish ambassador in Berlin his conception of 'a general settlement of all possible points of friction'; the main item was a proposal that Danzig revert to Germany with an extraterritorial link to Germany across the Polish corridor. In return Germany offered a guarantee of Poland's frontier.

Like all the states of east-central Europe, Poland lived in permanent fear of her larger neighbours to the east and west. In 1934 the Poles had hoped to appease Hitler by signing a non-aggression pact with him. Since the death of Piłsudski in the following year, the chief architect of Polish diplomacy had been the foreign minister, Colonel Józef Beck. Inspired by hatred of Bolshevism and lack of confidence in British and French resolve, Beck steered Poland towards compliance with Hitler's designs on Czechoslovakia. He hoped thereby to deflect German ambitions to the south and, at the same time, to obtain a territorial *pourboire* for his own country. Ribbentrop's démarche showed the futility of this policy. The Polish government held an inflated opinion of their country's importance and military prowess: they imagined that they could deal with Germany as a fellow great power. Their response to Ribbentrop was conciliatory in tone but German sovereignty over Danzig was ruled out. Nazi propaganda over the next few months laid increasing stress on the supposed tribulations of Germans in Poland and on the German claim to Danzig.

The Free City of Danzig (actually an area of 754 square miles, including not only the municipality of Danzig but four other towns and 250 villages, with a total population of 400,000, the overwhelming majority Germans) had been self-governing under the authority of a League of Nations High Commissioner since 1920. Throughout the 1920s Poland, which was recognized as having certain special rights in Danzig, notably responsibility for foreign relations, had jostled to gain further advantages. Between 1920 and 1932 Poland and Danzig submitted sixty-six disputes to the League for resolution. In 1926 Poland began construction of a rival port, Gdynia, a few miles away on its own territory. By 1931 Gdynia was handling more goods than Danzig. In May 1933 the local Nazi Party had won a majority of the votes in elections. The process of *Gleichschaltung* was implemented more slowly than in Germany, but by 1939 all opposition parties had been banned, the Nuremberg laws introduced, and the High Commissioner, C. J. Burckhardt, a Swiss, reduced to a cipher.

In the hope of counter-balancing the pressure from Germany, the Poles tried to square Stalin. On 26 November Poland and the Soviet Union issued a joint declaration stressing 'the inviolability of peaceful relations between the two states'; but the Poles, profoundly suspicious of Russian intentions, were not prepared to take the plunge into an alliance with the USSR.[68]

On 15 March 1939 German troops marched into Prague and extinguished what little remained of Czecho-Slovak independence. The Czecho-Slovak army disintegrated. The rump of Czecho-Slovakia was carved up. Bohemia and Moravia were declared a 'Reich Protectorate', in effect a German colony, while Slovakia was accorded nominal independence under a clerical-nationalist puppet regime headed by Monsignor Jozef Tiso. In Czecho-Sub-Carpathian Ruthenia Ukrainian nationalists optimistically declared independence; but after twenty-four hours the region was occupied by Hungary.

One day after the occupation of Prague, Hitler sent an ultimatum to Lithuania, demanding the return of the formerly German Baltic port of Memel, which had been seized by Lithuania in 1923. There too Hitler could point in justification to a large German population allegedly suffering under alien rule and could argue that he was merely turning tables on an earlier action of *force majeure*. Lithuania gave way three days later.

The British and French governments had both received prior intelligence of the occupation of Prague. Nevertheless, it came as a shock, particularly for Chamberlain who felt he had been swindled and exposed as a dupe. For British public opinion, Prague marked a decisive turning-point. This was the first time that Hitler had occupied non-German-speaking territory. Germany's grievances against the Versailles Treaty were by now widely conceded to have merit, but Hitler's actions could no longer be justified by the principle of national self-determination. It was not so much, however, the substance of Hitler's diplomacy as its manner that upset the British. What stuck in the British craw was Hitler's defiance of all conventional norms of diplomatic behaviour: the bully-boy intimidation of smaller opponents; the brazen lying; the unabashed identification of might with right; and the cynicism manifest in Hitler's tearing up of agreements on which the ink was barely dry. Even *The Times*, hitherto an advocate of appeasement, now argued for strong action. In France a public opinion poll after Prague showed 77 per cent support for firm resistance to future German or Italian demands.[69]

The pace of British preparations for war was further stepped up. The Territorial Army (the reserve) was doubled. For the first time in British history, conscription was introduced in peacetime. No serious thought was devoted to giving effect to the guarantee that had been offered to Czecho-Slovakia at Munich. But on 31 March Britain and France issued a guarantee to Poland, promising that 'in the event of any action which clearly threatened Polish independence and which the Polish government accordingly considered it vital to resist with their national forces', Britain and France 'would feel themselves bound at once to lend the Polish Government all support in their power'.[70] Two weeks later further guarantees were distributed to Greece and Romania. The three undertakings were intended, optimistically, more as deterrent than *casus foederis*. At the end of April Chamberlain could still write, 'in cold blood I cannot see Hitler starting a world war for Danzig'.[71] Unknown to Chamberlain, Hitler had already issued a secret directive on 3 April ordering his High Command to be ready for an attack on Poland by 1 September.

Mussolini, like Chamberlain, viewed the developments in central Europe with chagrin. He too, after all, had been a party to the Munich agreement. His signature too had been shown to be worthless. As the senior Fascist statesman he resented being outwitted and outshone by his upstart ally. Casting around for some outlet for his seething frustration and jealousy, his eye lit on Albania. This little country of one million people, among the poorest and most primitive in Europe, struck him as easy prey.

Ruled by the Turks since the death of the Albanian national hero, Skanderbeg, in 1467, Albania had prised a precarious independence on the eve of the First World War. At the end of the war, and throughout the inter-war period, the Serbs of Yugoslavia saw in an independent Albania a threat to their rule over Albanian-populated areas in Kosovo and Macedonia. In 1918 Serbian troops penetrated deep into Albania and perpetrated large-scale destruction and massacres. Italian forces arrived, ostensibly as protectors, inaugurating a virtual Italian protectorate over the country. In the 1920s and 1930s Albania remained a shuttlecock between the two larger Adriatic powers. A republic was declared in 1925, headed by a tribal chief, Ahmet Bey Zogu, who had come to power by cooperating with Belgrade in repressing Albanian bandit movements in Kosovo and Macedonia. Once securely installed, he switched patrons from Belgrade to Rome. Three years later, supported by the Italians, he persuaded a constituent assembly to declare him 'King of the Albanians', thus alarming the Yugoslavs who suspected him of irredentist ambitions towards Kosovo. The reign of King Zog was a pitiful imposture from start to finish. Absurdly, he sought legitimacy by claiming descent from Skanderbeg. Italy supervised the country's finances, exploited its mineral deposits, and monopolized most of the country's trade. The headquarters of the national bank were at Rome and most of its capital was Italian-owned. The country's Muslim and Orthodox peasantry, divided between the Geg pastoralists of the north and the Tosks of the south, paid little attention to all this, their political sensibility rarely stretching beyond localized blood feuds between rival clans.

This was the pathetic object towards which the conqueror of Ethiopia now cast his rapacious gaze. Zog had already annoyed Mussolini by renewed attempts to play the Yugoslav card against Italy. The conquest of Albania would yield Italy less than nothing, since she had already extracted what little of value was to be found there. Formal rule would merely saddle her with the burden of Albania's chronic government deficit. Mussolini was fired, however, by a desire for prestige, not gross material gain. On 7 April 1939 he sent Italian forces into the country. Zog was deposed and Vittorio Emmanuele III assumed the dubious additional title of King of Albania. The Albanian adventure won the Duce some short-lived and hollow glory. But it proved a fatal blunder. From this first step into the Balkan quagmire Mussolini was drawn into an embarrassing and costly military involvement that, far from demonstrating his prowess as an equal of Hitler, exhibited his growing dependence on the man he had once thought to patronize.

On 22 May, fresh from his hollow Albanian triumph, Mussolini sent his son-in-law and Foreign Minister, Count Galeazzo Ciano, to Berlin to sign a 'Pact of Steel' with Germany. The alliance between the two dictators sent a further tremor of fear through the continent. Professional strategists were less impressed. British and French estimates of Italian strength were low: French military intelligence considered that Italy would be 'a deadweight for Germany' in the event of war.[72] The assessment proved to be only too accurate. Mussolini himself was obliged to confess privately to his ally that his armed forces, their weaponry depleted after their sacrifices in Ethiopia, Spain, and Albania, would be in no condition for the next three years to fight in any European conflict. Hitler was not in the least downcast. He was not relying on the Italians.

After the signature of the pact, Hitler told a group of senior military commanders that war was unavoidable: 'At present we are in a state of national ebullience as are two other states, Italy and Japan.... It is not Danzig that is at stake. For us it is a matter of expanding our living space in the East.... There is therefore no question of sparing Poland and we are left with the *decision: to attack Poland at the first opportunity*. We cannot expect a repetition of Czechia. There will be war.'[73]

In the late spring and summer the British and French cast around for some means of deterring Hitler from attacking Poland. The chief of the British Secret Intelligence Service believed that the Soviet armed forces 'could do nothing of real value', an assessment in which the French General Staff still concurred.[74] Chamberlain, so credulous in the case of Hitler, harboured deep suspicion of the Bolsheviks; he nevertheless sanctioned low-level talks with Moscow. But these bogged down on the issue of passage of Soviet troops through Poland in the event of the outbreak of war. British military opinion of Polish, as of Russian, military capacity was low, although the Chiefs of Staff considered that, on balance, if war had to be waged against Germany it would be better to do so with Poland as an ally than without. The Poles reckoned they could give a good account of themselves if it came to a war. A high-level Polish government conference in late March concluded that Hitler would come to his senses 'once he encounters determined opposition, which hitherto he has not met with.... The Germans are marching all across Europe with nine divisions; with such strength Poland would not be overcome.'[75] Fatally calculating that Hitler was bluffing, the Poles adamantly refused to sanction the entry of any Russian forces to their soil. Polish obstinacy on this point prevented any Anglo-Russian agreement and led to what has justly been called 'the most stunning volte-face in diplomatic history'.[76]

There had been some earlier straws in the wind. In March 1939 Stalin had warned that the USSR would 'not let our country be drawn into conflicts by warmongers who are accustomed to have others pull the chestnuts out of the fire for them'.[77] The 'chestnuts' speech was a sign that the policy of collective security, associated with Litvinov, was no longer the dominant trend in Moscow. On 3 May 1939 he was replaced as head of Narkomindel, the People's Commissariat for Foreign Affairs, by Vyacheslav Molotov. The removal of Litvinov, a Jew, indicated a possible impending change of course in Soviet policy towards Nazi Germany. The Germans had begun to woo the Soviets seriously in the spring. But Stalin's decision to throw in his lot with the Nazis, at least temporarily, was taken only in August as a result of the failure of Soviet discussions with the western powers.

The rapprochement between the two erstwhile enemies was formalized in talks between the German and Soviet foreign ministers in Moscow on 23–24 August. Two non-Nazi diplomats from the German embassy in Moscow, attending the airport reception for Ribbentrop, noticed with what alacrity NKVD men greeted Gestapo agents among the German delegation: 'Look how they're laughing with each other. They're delighted to be able to work together at last! That could be frightful! Imagine if they exchanged their files.'[78] Details of the agreement were quickly ironed out and at around 2.00 a.m. on 24 August Molotov and Ribbentrop signed a non-aggression treaty in which their two countries undertook 'to desist from any act of violence, any aggressive action, and any attack on each other'. Clearly foreseeing imminent war, the second clause stated that if either of the parties became 'the object of belligerent action by a third Power', the other party would 'in no manner lend its support to this third Power'.

Attached to the published text of the treaty was a secret protocol containing the conclusions of 'strictly confidential conversations' between the Germans and Russians on 'the question of the boundary of their respective spheres of influence in Eastern Europe'. The agreement allocated Finland, Estonia, and Latvia to the Soviet sphere, and Lithuania, including Vilna, to the Germans. Ribbentrop had originally proposed that a line along the

Daugava River should separate the projected Soviet and German zones: this would have placed Finland, Estonia, and northern Latvia under Soviet rule, and southern Latvia and Lithuania under German. Stalin, however, demanded the whole of Latvia. Hitler's wired agreement came within three hours—so quickly that, according to one historian, 'it made Stalin's head spin'.[79] The key element in the protocol was its provision for a renewed partition of Poland, with the western part allocated to Germany, and the rest to the USSR. 'In the event of a territorial and political rearrangement of the areas belonging to the Polish State', the protocol stated that the German and Soviet spheres would be demarcated by a line following the courses of the rivers Narev, Vistula, and San. The Russian zone, under this arrangement, would extend to the suburbs of Warsaw on the eastern bank of the Vistula. Finally, Germany declared 'its complete political disinterestedness' regarding Bessarabia, which the USSR claimed from Romania.[80]

Signature of the treaty was accompanied by champagne toasts, Stalin to Hitler, Molotov to Ribbentrop, Ribbentrop to Stalin. Ribbentrop repaired to the German embassy to report to Hitler. When the Führer heard the news he too called for champagne and declaimed, 'Now Europe is mine. The others can have Asia.'[81] Meanwhile Ribbentrop retired to bed. But Stalin's appetite for nocturnal revelry was not yet sated. Exulting in his diplomatic success, he went off to his dacha near Moscow to continue the celebrations at a late-night supper with cronies, Molotov, Anastas Mikoyan, and Lavrenty Beria, as well as Nikita Khrushchev, who had recently been elected a member of the Politburo. They dined on a duck that Khrushchev had shot the previous day. Stalin was in high spirits. He said 'Hitler wants to trick us, but I think we've got the better of him.'[82]

News of the Nazi–Soviet pact electrified Europe. Consternation in London and Paris recalled the reaction to the Treaty of Rapallo in 1922. Communist parties throughout the world suddenly halted all anti-Fascist propaganda. In Moscow anti-Nazi films, including Eisenstein's *Aleksandr Nevsky*, with its portrayal of thirteenth-century Russian resistance to invasion by Teutonic knights, were removed from cinemas. Some Communists, who had taken the previous five years of anti-Fascist rhetoric all too seriously, found the agreement hard to swallow. A few even left the party. Although the text of the additional protocol did not become available until after the war (and was not published in the Soviet Union until 1989), rumours of such a secret arrangement were rife almost from the moment of the pact's signature.

War now seemed inevitable. On 22 August Hitler addressed his army chiefs, portraying Germany's enemies as 'small worms' and insisting, 'We must act'. The current favourable military and diplomatic conditions, he warned, might not endure for long. 'Therefore better a conflict now.' He added: 'Close your hearts to pity. Act brutally. Eighty million people must obtain what is their right. Their existence must be made secure. The stronger man is right. The greatest harshness.'[83] Three days later he told the British ambassador in Berlin, Sir Nevile Henderson: 'People in England have tried to make out that I was bluffing last September. They were absolutely wrong. I can assure [you] that I was not bluffing then, any more than I am bluffing now.'[84] Hitler was indeed now ready to contemplate war with the western powers, though he forecast, correctly as it turned out, that they would be able to do nothing to help the Poles and that he would be able to wipe Poland off the map before turning the full strength of his forces to face the west.

In the face of a booming cacophony of anti-Polish complaints and demands emanating from Berlin, Bonnet again inclined towards negotiation. Daladier, however, put his foot down and said he would rather resign than attend a second Munich.[85] British ministers too were determined that they would not humiliate themselves by complicity in another *Diktat* in the German interest. Yet while they would not contemplate such an imposed capitulation, the British did not stint in advising the Poles that it would be in their own interest to come to some negotiated settlement with the Nazis. A year earlier Beneš had accepted such well-meant advice with disastrous results; now the Poles stubbornly refused to do so—with even more terrible consequences.

On the night of 31 August/1 September the Germans staged a deliberate provocation at Gleiwitz on the border with Poland in Upper Silesia. They then announced that Germany had been the victim of an unprovoked attack by the Poles. Exploiting this manufactured pretext, German armed forces immediately attacked Poland in strength. Britain issued an ultimatum demanding withdrawal of German troops from Polish territory. In a memorandum handed to the British ambassador in Berlin by Ribbentrop, the Germans refused 'to receive, accept, let alone to fulfil demands in the nature of ultimata'.[86] Diplomacy had now exhausted its resources. Shortly after 11.00 a.m. on 3 September Chamberlain lamented, in a broadcast address to the nation, that his 'long struggle to win peace ha[d] failed' and declared that Britain was at war with Germany.[87] France followed suit a few hours later.

8

Hitler Triumphant 1939–1942

Out of the libraries
Emerge the butchers.

*Bertolt Brecht, Lidingö, Sweden, Feb.–April 1940**

Polish collapse

'Poland', wrote Rousseau in 1771, on the eve of the first partition of Poland, 'is a great state surrounded by even greater ones that, with their despotism and military discipline, possess formidable offensive strength.... Notwithstanding Polish valour, she lies exposed to all their outrages.'[1] The sage of the enlightenment could not have begun to envisage the twentieth-century horrors that his words uncannily foretold.

On 1 September 1939 five German armies, comprising sixty divisions, invaded Poland. Their objective was to knock out the Poles swiftly before the Allies could mount an offensive in the west. Recalling their victory over the Red Army in 1921, the Poles flattered themselves that they were a significant military power but they found themselves hopelessly outnumbered and out-manoeuvred by the Germans. The Polish Commander-in-Chief, Marshal Edward Rydz-Śmigły, decided to mount his chief defensive effort near the frontier. The reasons were partly political (reluctance to yield the formerly German western border regions without a fight), partly economic (the presence, especially in Silesia, of important industrial resources), and partly strategic (the hope of buying time to complete mobilization of his vaunted fifty-four divisions). But the odds were against the defenders. They could deploy only 313 tanks, most of them distributed piecemeal to

* From '1940', translated from the German by Sammy McLean. Michael Hoffmann, ed., *The Faber Book of 20th-Century German Poems*, London, 2005, 74–6.

infantry units, against the Germans' 2,600, and only 388 warplanes, most of them obsolete, against the Germans' 1,900. Polish mechanized forces comprised only two brigades whereas the Germans fielded fourteen mechanized or partly mechanized divisions. The popular conception of the Polish army flinging horse cavalry, with drawn swords and lances, against tanks is overdrawn. Nevertheless, as the British strategic thinker Basil Liddell Hart later put it, 'the campaign in Poland was the first demonstration, and proof, in war of the theory of mobile warfare by armoured and air forces in combination'.[2] Heinz Guderian, architect of the German armoured corps, had gained Hitler's approval for a war of movement in which large concentrations of tanks, backed up by motorized support units, and enjoying close air support, would replace infantry as the decisive force on the battlefield. 'Blitzkrieg', as the strategy came to be known, lent the Germans an aura of invincibility that struck terror into Europe. By mid-September they had complete command of the air and Polish forces had been driven back to defence lines around Warsaw and behind the River San in the south.

The Poles' only hope was a diversionary attack by the French and British on Germany's western frontier. But this was not forthcoming. Britain and France had gone to war over Poland, not for Poland. Their guarantee notwithstanding, they sent no forces to aid the Poles. They did not even have contingency plans for doing so. Allied strategy was based on the expectation of '*la guerre de longue durée*'. A defensive posture would be maintained in the west while Allied resources were gradually built up. French military thinking remained mired in static defensive concepts drawn from the experience of the previous war. Apart from minor pinpricks, therefore, the Allies did not take the obvious military opportunity to attack Germany in the west while the bulk of German forces were engaged in the east. As for Britain, her army and air force were woefully inadequate to defend herself and her empire, let alone fulfil the European guarantees that Chamberlain had (in the end) distributed so freely. It would be a matter of years, not months, before Britain could contemplate a land campaign against a major military power. In default of any tangible aid, the head of the British military mission in Poland, General Adrian Carton de Wiart, was instructed that his primary task was 'inspiring confidence'.[3]

On 17 September the Soviet army moved into eastern Poland, advancing towards the line previously agreed between Ribbentrop and Molotov. The Chief of the British Imperial General Staff, General Ironside, put the most optimistic interpretation possible on the news when he told the Cabinet that 'the presence of large Russian forces on the German borders might compel the Germans to maintain a very considerable garrison on the Eastern frontier'.[4] Caught between two giant pincers, the Poles put up a spirited but hopeless resistance. The government and general staff, headed by Rydz-Śmigły, fled the country the next day, proceeding first to Romania, later to France, and finally to Britain. They were followed by some eighty thousand Polish troops, most of whom eventually joined the Allied war effort in the west or North Africa. But a million Polish soldiers fell into either German or Soviet captivity. Warsaw surrendered on 27 September.

Hitler's victory over Poland did not come cheap. His armed forces lost eleven thousand dead and thirty thousand wounded. Three hundred German armoured vehicles and 560 aircraft were put out of action. Altogether, the Poles knocked out the equivalent of nine months of German war production—though some of the losses were made up by captured Polish *matériel*. Calculating that time would work against Germany, as British and French production would grow fast, Hitler told his generals to prepare for an early attack in the west. He nevertheless issued a 'peace offer' to his enemies, more as propaganda than in earnest. If they would only recognize his latest acquisition, he would seek no further quarrel with them. But neither Chamberlain nor Daladier would yield; nor, in spite of some defeatist chatter, would the majority of public opinion in either country have countenanced a further such humiliation. Hitler was correct in thinking that Poland, 'this ridiculous state',[5] was not the main obstacle. That was now Hitler himself. The Polish guarantee thus turned out to be merely the precipitant of the larger war, not its fundamental issue. This was why the various attempts between the autumn of 1939 and the spring of 1940 to arrange a compromise peace collapsed.

Molotov justified the Soviet move into Poland by declaring that the Polish state had ceased to exist and that 'the Soviet Government deems it its sacred duty to extend a helping hand to our Brother Ukrainians and Brother White Russians who live in Poland'.[6] In a meeting with Dimitrov, Molotov, and Andrei Zhdanov on 7 September, Stalin articulated the Soviet position: 'We see nothing wrong in them [Hitler and the Allies] having a good hard fight and weakening each other.'[7] The Nazi–Soviet pact had called for the Soviets to occupy the whole of eastern Poland up to the Vistula. In the event, Stalin baulked at taking the entire area.

On a second visit to Moscow, during which he was greeted by a Soviet band playing the Nazi '*Horst-Wessel-Lied*', Ribbentrop revised the original agreement by a new treaty, dated 28 September. The demarcation line between the Soviet and German spheres in Poland was adjusted eastwards from the Vistula to the Bug. This left all those regions in which Poles were a majority in German hands. Russia reclaimed the Ukrainian and Belorussian territories she had lost in 1921. Most of Lithuania was assigned to the Russians to do with as they pleased. All three Baltic states were compelled to sign mutual assistance agreements with the USSR, whereby the Soviet army gained the right to station naval, military, and air bases on their territories. Vilna, which had been occupied by Poland since 1920, was presented by Stalin to Lithuania—'a condemned man's breakfast'.[8] But the transfer was effected only after the Red Army had occupied the city for forty days and stripped it of food, manufactured goods, and machinery. A report in the Red Army newspaper *Krasnaya zvezda* (*Red Star*) on 18 September summarized the reaction of the population to the Soviet takeover: 'The workers of the Western Ukraine and Western Byelorussia, thanks to the fraternal assistance of the Soviet people and its Red Army, were forever liberated from the class and national oppression of the Polish bourgeois. They acquired a new homeland for themselves—the land of happiness—the Soviet Union. . . . Warmed by the sunrays of Stalin's constitution, people are joyfully building a new life.'[9]

After elections in which more than 91 per cent of the votes were recorded as having been cast for official candidates, a 'People's Assembly' of the western Ukraine convened at Lwów on 26 October and requested incorporation of the area in the Ukrainian Soviet Socialist Republic, which petition was granted a few days later. A similar assembly in Białystok led to the annexation of western Belorussia into the Belorussian Soviet Socialist Republic. The apparatus of the Soviet state was extended to the annexed regions. A social revolution was launched with the object of eliminating all feudal, i.e. mainly Polish, and bourgeois, i.e. mainly Jewish, socio-economic elements. Banks, mines, factories, and railways were nationalized. Land belonging to large proprietors and churches was expropriated and a start was made to the collectivization of agriculture. In December the rouble suddenly replaced the złoty, which became virtually worthless: many lost their life savings.

These events confronted the Communist Parties of the belligerent countries with awkward dilemmas, particularly in France. Communist representatives had voted for war credits in parliament on 2 September 1939. But soon ideological guidance began to arrive from Moscow that the war was 'imperialist and predatory'. Following the Soviet entry into eastern Poland, the Comintern informed its members that it would not be regarded as 'a terrific misfortune if Poland were to disappear from the scene', that the war was 'seen as a war of two groups of imperialist countries for world domination', and that the differentiation between the Fascist and democratic countries had lost its former significance.[10] The party leadership immediately fell into step and the slogan of the hour became '*A bas la guerre impérialiste!*' The sudden switch led 21 out of 72 Communist deputies and several senators to leave the party. Some intellectuals, such as Paul Nizan, also resigned but most remained faithful to the dictates of Moscow.[11] The government, which had banned Communist newspapers as early as 25 August, declared the party illegal a month later. The party newspaper, *l'Humanité*, continued to appear illegally, denouncing the war of 'brigand capitalists'.[12] Communist anti-war propaganda and suspected sabotage activity in armaments factories led the government to arrest and intern large numbers of party members. Thorez deserted from the army in October and fled to Moscow. In January 1940 Communist deputies were expelled from parliament. In April forty-four of them were put on trial. On May Day 1940 Communists circulated among soldiers at the front an illegally produced edition of *L'Humanité du Soldat* containing defeatist propaganda.

Winter War

Meanwhile, Stalin, even as he digested his gains in Poland, had decided to reinforce Russia's northern defences by applying pressure on Finland. In October 1939 he presented a sheaf of territorial demands to Finnish representatives whom he had summoned to Moscow. These included a proposal for the cession to the USSR of 2,761 square kilometres of territory in the Karelian isthmus and elsewhere in return for double that area of land in eastern Karelia. By way of explanation, Stalin told his guests that he had to prepare for possible attack by England or Germany: 'We are on good terms with Germany now, but everything in this world may change.'[13] When the Finns rejected all but very limited concessions, Stalin retorted that what he was asking was 'nothing really'. Menacingly, he reminded them that Hitler, after all, had decided the Polish frontier was too close to Berlin for his liking and had grabbed a much larger swathe of territory.[14]

Intimidatory diplomacy having failed, Stalin resorted to other means. After a manufactured frontier incident, Nazi-style, the Russians attacked Finland on 30 November. At the border town of Terijoki they installed a puppet Finnish government, headed by Otto Kuusinen, a Comintern operative who had been a founder of the Finnish Communist Party in 1918. Misled by Soviet intelligence reports, Stalin expected the Finnish working class to rally to the Kuusinen regime and the Finnish army to crumple like the Poles a couple of months earlier. Instead, the Finns, once more led by the veteran Marshal Mannerheim, hero of their War of Independence, put up unexpectedly stiff resistance. Although much weaker in manpower and armaments, they were better trained and equipped for winter warfare than the invaders. By contrast, some Russian infantrymen arrived at the front line barefoot. Each was loaded down with 33.5 kg of equipment. Soviet armoured sledges were at first useless because they had no runners. Russian radio communications were inefficient and were tapped by the Finns. Lacking snow camouflage or skis, the Russians were harried by the 'white death' of enemy commandos. The Finns' staunch defence of their homeland evoked admiration in the democracies and elsewhere. The League of Nations, by this time a diplomatic dinosaur, expelled the Soviet Union—the organization's last political act. The Soviet news agency, Tass, commented that the League, dominated by the 'Anglo-French military bloc', had been converted 'from some kind of an "instrument of peace"... into a real instrument of war'.[15]

Sweden's neutrality came under severe strain. Her Prime Minister, Per Albin Hansson, insisted that the country must not be dragged into the war.[16] The Foreign Minister, Rickard Sandler, who advocated military intervention on behalf of the Finns, was compelled to resign. Swedish aid was, therefore, limited to the dispatch of military supplies, mainly small arms, and 8,500 volunteers. Britain and France sent military aircraft and ammunition; Italy and Spain too supplied some equipment. The British, however, had an ulterior motive: the government considered using aid for the Finns as a pretext for seizing the Swedish iron-ore fields, thereby denying them to Germany. The Swedes became alarmed by British naval movements in Norwegian territorial waters and by French demands for passage for their troops through Sweden to aid the Finns. The Swedish government feared that that would lead to German intervention. They had no desire to turn their country into a battlefield. The head of the Foreign Ministry told the British chargé d'affaires acidly: 'I should have thought that the British Government had the fate of a sufficient number of smaller states on their conscience as it is.'[17]

Before British or French forces could be assembled, however, the Winter War came to an end. In February Soviet forces under Marshal Timoshenko smashed through Finnish lines. Mindful of the bloody nose he had received in the initial phase of the war, Stalin decided not to press military action further than necessary and thereby incur the risk of Anglo-French intervention. On 12 March 1940 the Finns signed a treaty with the USSR yielding even more territory than Stalin had initially demanded. They gave up the Karelian isthmus and land around Lake Ladoga. Leningrad, previously just 25 kilometres from the border, thus acquired a territorial buffer. The Finns yielded with heavy hearts. Their losses were 23,000 dead and 44,000 wounded. Funereal music was played on Helsinki radio. But they maintained their independence, albeit on a reduced territorial base. The Russians' puppet regime was quietly disbanded. More than 400,000 refugees fled the Soviet-annexed territories. For the Soviet Union it was a Pyrrhic victory. The Russians suffered over 200,000 casualties, including at least 49,000 dead, as well as losing 1,600 tanks (a quarter of their modern armour), and 684 aircraft. A German military evaluation concluded: 'The Soviet "mass" is no match for an army and superior leadership.'[18] Hitler could not but be impressed by the proven incapacity of the Red Goliath against the Finnish David.

Phoney War

The Finnish collapse fatally weakened the position of Daladier, who stood accused of failing to offer proper support to the Finns. On 21 March he was replaced as French Prime Minister by Paul Reynaud. A conservative patriot, the new premier was a determined *belliciste*, committed to vigorous prosecution of the war. But his government, which included Socialist ministers, enjoyed only a narrow majority in a dispirited Chamber. France remained in a static, defensive posture behind the Maginot Line, the fortification system, named after a former war minister, that stretched along France's eastern frontier with Germany, from Switzerland to Luxembourg (see plate 24). The line was, however, broken by a gap at the Ardennes, since this mountainous region was regarded as providing a natural barrier.

Further north, the border with Belgium lay open. To have continued the fortifications along the Belgian border, it was argued, would be to condemn Belgium to occupation if attacked: the battle would best be conducted on French terms in the Belgian plain. But the Belgians, wary of antagonizing the Germans, had decided in 1936 to emulate their Dutch neighbours and adopt a policy of neutrality. Henceforth and until early 1940 they refused all military cooperation with the French and British.

The Germans had built the 480-mile-long 'West Wall' or Siegfried Line along the frontier. But it was weaker than the Maginot Line, designed more as a trip-wire than an impassable barrier, and a determined French attack on it could probably have succeeded. Why, then, did the French remain passive? The explanation was only partly the relative balance of forces. On paper, at any rate, French military strength in early 1940 was comparable with German. Each had about the same number of tanks and fighter planes. More important was the strategic outlook of the French High Command, which failed to appreciate the possibilities of mobile armour and of coordinated ground and air tactics. The revolution in warfare rendered possible by the development of tanks and military aircraft was not without its French exponents, notably Colonel Charles de Gaulle and, at the political level, Reynaud and, later and less decisively, Daladier. The Commander-in-Chief, Maurice Gamelin, an intelligent and sophisticated officer with a penchant for Bergsonian philosophy, was more open to new ideas of mechanized warfare than many of his colleagues. But the Army Council remained resistant to the idea of emulating the Germans' *Panzer* tactics. Memories of the carnage of the previous war led to a general caution and reliance on bloodless strategies such as economic blockade of Germany. Symptomatic of the mood was resistance by the French to a scheme for mining the Rhine; they feared German reprisals. Some British leaders were infected with similar scruples: Kingsley Wood, the air minister, opposed bombing German munitions works on the ground that the Germans might retaliate; moreover, he pointed out, these factories were private property. Until the spring of 1940, therefore, the war in the west froze in a state of suspended animation, dubbed 'phoney war', *drôle de guerre*, or *Sitzkrieg*.

Churchill, who had accepted Chamberlain's invitation to return to his old post of First Lord of the Admiralty upon the outbreak of war, pressed the Cabinet to undertake some form of offensive action. In early April the Royal Navy was ordered to mine Norwegian waters around Narvik. Churchill and others hoped that this might lead to Allied landings in

Norway and occupation of the Swedish iron-ore mines. But the Allies were forestalled by Hitler. On 9 April the Germans attacked Denmark and Norway. They achieved complete surprise. Denmark could not resist and surrendered within hours. In Norway, the Social Democrat government in power since 1935, bound by a tradition of hostility to the military as strike-breakers, had authorized only very limited expenditure on armaments. They declared Oslo an open city and fled to the interior with the royal family. Vidkun Quisling, leader of the far-right Nasjonal Samling, broadcast to the Norwegian people announcing that he had taken power (the first-ever radio *coup d'état*). His regime, which, in its initial phase lasted only a few days, failed to persuade most Norwegians to collaborate with the invaders. He was removed from office for the time being by the occupiers who explained to the Norwegians that they had arrived to protect the country from the Allies and set up a military administration.

The Germans soon overwhelmed the flimsy defences in southern Norway. Hastily dispatched Allied troops were pushed back onto the sea within a month, though British and Norwegian naval and ground forces continued to battle around Narvik for another few weeks. On 7 June King Haakon VII went into exile on a British cruiser, his government vowing to continue the war from exile in England. This decision was more than a moral gesture since it enabled the Allies to utilize the Norwegian mercantile marine; it was to play a useful role in the supply of Britain during the forthcoming Battle of the Atlantic.

On 7–8 May a tense debate in the House of Commons on the fiasco of British intervention in Norway spelt the doom of Chamberlain's administration. The climactic moment came when a Conservative rebel, Leopold Amery, pointing at the Prime Minister, echoed Cromwell's dismissal of Parliament in 1653: 'You have sat too long here for any good you have been doing. Depart, I say, and let us have done with you. In the name of God, *go!*'[19] As a Cabinet minister who shared responsibility for the debacle, Churchill was placed in the awkward position of having to defend a leader he privately hoped to displace. The aged but still rapier-sharp Lloyd George warned that Churchill 'must not allow himself to be converted into an air-raid shelter to keep the splinters from hitting his colleagues'.[20] Although the government won the vote with a reduced majority, the 'Norway debate' was a devastating political blow for Chamberlain.

Though a Conservative, Churchill was, in effect, imposed as leader on his reluctant and suspicious party by the Labour Party's refusal to serve under

Chamberlain, coupled with his own refusal to serve under Halifax. A wall-to-wall coalition government was now recognized as essential and Churchill alone commanded the support necessary to head it. The powerful trade union boss Ernest Bevin became Minister of Labour and took charge of the home front. Eden was sent to the War Office (he replaced Halifax as Foreign Secretary in December). Churchill assigned his old friend Lord Beaverbrook, a maverick Conservative newspaper proprietor, to the Ministry of Aircraft Production: he presided over an all-out effort to ginger up production of fighters that were to prove critical to Britain's survival in the air over the next few months.

Churchill appointed himself Minister of Defence (a new title) as well as Prime Minister. From the outset he made it clear that he intended to take a hand at the helm of the military direction of the war. Military experts, recalling Gallipoli and what were held to be his impulsive adventurism and love for theatrical 'sideshows', felt dark foreboding. Over the next five years his repeated interventions often drove his commanders to despair. At times, the Chief of the Imperial General Staff, Alan Brooke, felt 'like a man chained to the chariot of a lunatic'.[21] Venting his frustration in his diary, Brooke declared: 'Without him [Churchill] England was lost for a certainty, with him England has been on the verge of disaster time and again.'[22] But Brooke recognized Churchill's genius and slowly learned to rein in his temperamental master's galloping enthusiasms and direct his superabundant energy to constructive ends. Although Churchill argued vociferously in favour of his own ideas and constantly demanded offensive action, he never once during the war overruled his military advisers on a major strategic policy decision—in this unlike Hitler, whose sense of his own infallibility as a military leader led him into appalling blunders that his cowed and submissive generals dared not contradict. The new Prime Minister's puckish good humour and patriotic rhetoric, contrasting forcefully with his predecessor's awkward didacticism, cheered up the British people and steeled them for the trials ahead. But hardly was Churchill's government installed than successive disasters hailed down on Europe.

The fall of France

Hitler had decided the previous autumn to launch an offensive in the west at the earliest opportunity. The army general staff, which retained a certain respect for French military strength, urged caution. Hitler would have none of it. He forecast a swift and decisive victory that would wipe out the disgrace of 1918. The Commander-in-Chief of the army, Walther von Brauchitsch, was so dubious that he offered his resignation, which was not accepted. The Chief of the Army General Staff, Franz Halder, conducted cautious soundings about a military putsch but these were soon abandoned. Hitler faced down his top two hundred generals with a tirade in which he compared himself to Frederick the Great, berated them for their lack of fighting spirit, and insisted that his decision was unalterable. The elimination of France, he told Goebbels, would constitute 'an act of historical justice'.[23] After a number of postponements the date for attack was set for 10 May.

On the face of it, the order of battle on the western front slightly favoured the Allies. The Germans fielded 136 divisions, the Allies 144 (101 French, twenty-two Belgian, only eleven British, and ten Dutch). The German attack deployed about 2,500 tanks. Against these the French had at least as many and with the British and Dutch the Allied total reached 3,400. Only in the air were the Germans superior: they could operate about four thousand first-line warplanes as against the Allies' three thousand. The Allies' difficulties arose less from lack of military fire-power than from their failure to concentrate resources in the right place at the right time. One reason was poor inter-Allied coordination. Another was the rigidity of the French operational doctrine which led to a cascade of tactical blunders.

German strategy was based on the idea of a 'sickle cut' sweep through Holland, Luxembourg, and Belgium. In defiance of conventional military opinion, Hitler backed the unorthodox view of Generals Manstein and Guderian that it would be possible to pierce the Allied defences at their weakest point, the Ardennes, by moving heavy armour through this mountainous terrain. Guderian stressed the importance of concentrating maximal strength at a single point: '*Klotzen, nicht kleckern*' (Boot 'em, don't splatter 'em!).[24] The aim was to cross the Meuse near Sedan, the site of Prussia's decisive victory over France in 1870.

'The Battle of France', Liddell Hart later wrote, 'is one of history's most striking examples of the decisive effect of a new idea, carried out by a dynamic executant.'[25] Yet although implemented with new technology, the German battle-plan was, in fact, a practical illustration of the stress laid by the classical theorists of war, Jomini and Clausewitz, on the importance of concentrating strength 'at the decisive point'.[26] The French had not expected a major German attack in the Ardennes nor guarded against this contingency. Allied intelligence had noticed some evidence of German deployments in the region but failed to draw the necessary conclusions.[27] Guderian's Panzer divisions in the Ardennes, operating with close Luftwaffe support, achieved total surprise and swept all before them. Within three days, German tanks moved through Luxembourg and southern Belgium, captured the fortress of Sedan, and reached the Meuse. Defying orders to pause, Guderian struck north towards the Channel.

The Allies had responded to the German attack by plunging three French armies plus Lord Gort's British Expeditionary Force into neutral Belgium. But this belated resort to the offensive proved fatal. When Guderian's tanks crossed the Meuse and began to move towards the Channel, the Allied formations to the north found themselves in danger of being cut off. These were the Allies' most formidable and best-equipped forces: once they were trapped, the fate of France would be sealed. On 15 May Reynaud telephoned Churchill and told him that the road to Paris was open and that 'the battle was lost'.[28] The British now faced an awkward dilemma: should they respond to desperate French pleas for more fighter aircraft or should they hold them in reserve for the defence of the British Isles? Air Chief Marshal Dowding, head of RAF Fighter Command, said that if more fighters were sent to France they would not make a decisive difference there but they would greatly weaken Britain's home defences. Churchill agreed that it was a 'very grave risk' but he nevertheless decided to send over four squadrons.[29] The next day German troops were eighty miles from Paris. Churchill flew to France and agreed to the dispatch of a further six squadrons of Hurricanes, virtually the last the RAF had left. But Churchill was horrified by the air of defeatism and despair he encountered in Paris. At one point he asked Gamelin: 'Where is the strategic reserve?' To which the Commander-in-Chief responded, as Churchill recalled, 'with a shake of the head and a shrug, [and] said "*Aucune*"'.[30] 'In all the history of war', Churchill said disgustedly a few days later, 'I have never known such mismanagement.'[31]

The British resolve to continue the struggle was marked on 15 May by the first major British bombing assault on Germany. That night in Cologne, a dairyman on his way to the outside toilet became the first of the city's twenty thousand civilian dead from enemy action in the war. The next evening at Hamburg thirty-six fires were ignited, a fertilizer factory was destroyed, and thirty-four people killed. At Bremen a dock warehouse 'full of furniture confiscated from emigrating Jews' was destroyed. But these were only pinpricks and later air attacks on German railways, oil refineries, and other industrial and communications targets in May and June did not achieve much more. An absurd attempt to set fire to the Black Forest failed miserably.[32]

Holland had already capitulated after five days of resistance. Queen Wilhelmina was taken to England on a British destroyer. Brussels fell on 17 May, whereupon King Leopold III and the Belgian Cabinet moved to the south of the country where fighting continued for a further two weeks. British gunboats stood by to evacuate the king but he astonished his ministers by arguing that it would be dishonourable to abandon his subjects.[33] In the course of the fighting, the University Library of Louvain, which had been reconstituted following its destruction in the First World War, was shelled by the Germans and again destroyed by fire. After the departure of the Belgian government Leopold remained behind, effectively a prisoner of war in his own palace, until 1944 when he was removed to Germany. The government condemned the king, declared him incompetent, invalidated his surrender, and announced from London in December 1940 that, like the Norwegians and Dutch, it remained at war with Germany.

Panic overwhelmed the French capital as the Germans approached. Gamelin was replaced by Weygand, former Chief of Staff to Foch, but the new commander had to travel back from Syria and after his arrival on 19 May took a while to find his bearings. Although aged seventy-three, Weygand, 'a fighting cock' as Reynaud called him, seemed a more energetic figure than Gamelin. In reality, he was already convinced from the moment he took command that France had been defeated. The entry into the Cabinet of Marshal Pétain as Vice-Premier was designed to mollify the right; but the hero of Verdun became very soon a voice of defeatism within the council.

By 21 May the Germans reached the Channel coast and split the Allied forces in two. The British now fought a desperate battle to hold the Channel ports long enough to facilitate an orderly withdrawal. The evacuation from Dunkirk from 26 May to 4 June was a rout that British propaganda brilliantly turned into one of the epic myths of the war. The famous armada of fishing smacks and other little boats was improvised as a troop-carrying fleet. But most of the soldiers were carried on Royal Navy vessels. A total of 225,000 British troops of the British Expeditionary Force embarked from Dunkirk as well as a further 122,000 members of Allied forces (mostly French). The core of Britain's army was thus preserved, though much of their equipment was lost. A strange rumour later circulated that Hitler had deliberately restrained German forces in order to permit the British evacuation, this with a view to subsequent peace negotiations. In reality, he had ordered the army to hold back for several days while the Luftwaffe attempted to destroy enemy positions in and around Dunkirk.

The second phase of the war in the west, the battle for France, more specifically for Paris, was a confused rout that, from the German viewpoint, assumed the character almost of a mopping-up operation. On 5 June Reynaud reshuffled his ministry with the object of ridding it of defeatist elements. De Gaulle, recently promoted to general, was brought in, over protests from Pétain and Weygand, as Under-Secretary for War. Under the portrait, in his ministerial office, of Lazare Carnot, 'organizer of victory' in 1793–4, de Gaulle sought to give effect to his advanced ideas on armoured warfare. Since the Prime Minister, with whom he had long cooperated, was himself Minister for National Defence and War, de Gaulle's authority was, for the moment, substantial. But the high command was in a state of turmoil. Some hoped for a repetition of the 'miracle of the Marne'. The military chiefs, however, realized that such hopes were empty figments. A schism now emerged between those who wanted to continue the struggle by whatever means and those who were prepared to face the harsh necessity for an armistice and a negotiated peace. Weygand placed himself emphatically in the latter camp. He opposed withdrawal of the government from Paris (as had occurred in September 1914), suggesting that if the army abandoned the capital a revolutionary movement might develop.[34]

On 10 June, a 'day of agony' as de Gaulle called it, the French government nevertheless abandoned Paris.[35] Ministers moved first to Tours, then to Bordeaux. As the capital's defenders and a large part of the population fled south in a confused tidal wave of humanity, Paris was declared an open city. In a discussion with Weygand on 12 June, Reynaud opposed an armistice: '*Hitler, c'est Genghis Khan!*'[36] Two days later the Germans encountered no resistance as they entered Paris and paraded in triumph up the Champs-Elysées. A despairing Weygand meanwhile confessed to a British general that 'the French army had ceased to be able to offer organized resistance and was disintegrating into disconnected groups'.[37]

Grasping at a straw, Reynaud appealed in vain to Roosevelt for American help. Churchill too looked forward to intervention by this *deus ex machina*. He had already initiated a direct, secret correspondence with the US

President that he saw as a lifeline for the British Empire. While shaving on 18 May, he told his son: 'I shall drag the United States in.'[38] Two days later he warned Roosevelt of the 'nightmare' possibility that, while his government fully intended 'to fight on to the end in this Island', if things turned out badly, his government might be replaced by another that would be prepared 'to parley amid the ruins'.[39] Churchill returned to the theme later that summer, instructing the British ambassador in Washington: 'Never cease to impress on President and others that if this country were successfully invaded and largely occupied after heavy fighting some Quisling Government would be formed to make peace on the basis of our becoming a German Protectorate.'[40] In the meantime, such a government had been formed in France.

On 16 June Reynaud, a large part of whose Cabinet had no stomach for continuing a fruitless struggle, resigned and was replaced by Pétain, with Weygand as Minister of Defence and Admiral François Darlan as Minister of Marine. All three regarded the war as lost. The fortresses of the Maginot Line were encircled. French defensive lines had collapsed. German troops cut broad swathes south and east. Pétain broadcast to the nation, announcing that the fighting was at an end, and told his people that he was making them the 'gift of [his] person to attenuate their misfortune'.[41] On 19 June the last British forces, together with remnants of Polish and Czech units, were evacuated from Cherbourg. The new government immediately sued for an armistice. Formal negotiations with the Germans opened on 21 June in the forest of Compiègne, north-east of Paris. The Germans insisted for symbolic reasons that the meeting take place in the same railway dining carriage, number 2419D, in which the armistice had been signed in November 1918. Hitler sat on the chair once occupied by Foch. After some argument over minor details, the armistice was signed the next day. A week later Hitler paid a brief visit to Paris. He was thrilled by his latest acquisition, though film footage of him dancing a celebratory jig was a cunning concoction of Allied propaganda.

The armistice limited the size of the French army in metropolitan France to a hundred thousand men. This number was dictated not by military considerations but by a desire to wipe out the humiliation of the Versailles Treaty in which that same limit had been applied to the German army. The French were likewise forbidden to hold most categories of mechanized armour. France was carved into chunks and reduced to vassalage: the Nord and Pas-de-Calais departments were attached to Belgium and governed directly by German military command from Brussels; the rest of the area north of the Loire, and west down to the Spanish border, about two-thirds of the country, was occupied by Germany; most of the remainder survived as a rump French state, nominally sovereign and neutral, with its capital at the small spa town of Vichy. In a separate armistice treaty, Italy, which had declared war on France and Britain on 10 June, obtained a small area of occupation near the border. This morsel barely sated Mussolini's appetite but his negligible military contribution hardly entitled him to more.

A few weeks later Alsace and Lorraine were detached from France and returned to German sovereignty. The swastika was hoisted on Strasbourg (Strassburg) cathedral. Public use of French was banned: even the words *chaud* and *froid* were obliterated on water taps. The French public memory would long remember these slights, though local Germans could recall the discrimination that they had suffered at the hands of the French republic after the provinces' return to France in 1918. About 200,000 young men from the two recaptured provinces were called up to the Wehrmacht: forty thousand of these deserted; three-quarters of the remainder were later killed or reported missing in action.

Only a handful of politicians opposed the armistice. Daladier, Georges Mandel, Pierre Mendès France, and two dozen other parliamentarians sailed from Bordeaux on 21 June aboard the *Massilia*, bound for Morocco, where they hoped to maintain some form of French government. The departure of the president, government, and parliament had earlier been approved by the Cabinet, though, amid much confusion, it was later countermanded. After their arrival in Casablanca, the travellers were interned by French military authorities there who were loyal to Pétain's government. Right-wingers denounced the politicians' departure as treasonable and the Vichy regime put them on trial. Daladier spent most of the war in prison, first in France, later in Germany. Mandel, who had been the most outspoken opponent of the armistice in Reynaud's Cabinet, was, on Pétain's orders, sentenced to life imprisonment; later he was sent to Buchenwald concentration camp; in 1944 he was returned to French soil where he was shot by his French guards.

The greater part of the French political elite in the summer of 1940 rallied round Pétain. When the two chambers of parliament met together as the National Assembly at Vichy on 10 July, the members granted him virtually dictatorial powers. The vote was a lopsided 569 for and 80 against. Blum, who did not speak in the debate, voted against but he was supported by only thirty-four Socialists. The chamber that had been elected with such exultant hopes four years earlier thus, in its overwhelming majority, collaborated in the suicide of republican institutions. Pétain's regime was at first regarded almost universally as no less legitimate than any government of the Third Republic, though it rejected that label and instead forged a new 'Etat Français'. On 18 June de Gaulle, who had gone to London, broadcast (live) over the BBC his stentorian appeal to his homeland for resistance to continue: 'Must hope disappear? Is the defeat final? No! . . . Nothing is lost for France. . . . This war has not been decided by the Battle of France. This is a world war. . . . Whatever happens, the flame of French resistance must not and will not be extinguished.'[42] But de Gaulle's clarion call for Free France became famous only later. At the time few heard it and even fewer heeded it.

The fall of France produced agonized national self-criticism and even self-laceration. At one level the event was explicable as a straightforward military defeat by a better-equipped, better-led, more mobile enemy with a clearer strategy, better integration of air and land power, and more flexible tactics. But large events, people felt, must have large causes. The explanation was therefore sought in the politics of the Third Republic, both in the errors and crimes of politicians and, at a deeper level, in what was seen as the failure of the political system—a product, some argued, of profound social, organizational, intellectual, and even moral weaknesses in pre-war France. Paul Valéry argued that 'the war was lost during the peace'.[43] François Mauriac wrote in *le Figaro* that France must accept 'repose at the bottom of the abyss'. The historian Marc Bloch reflected something of this mood in his book *L'étrange défaite* (*Strange Defeat*), written during the war but published only in 1946, by which time he had been murdered by the Germans.

Anti-British feeling ran high. On 28 March 1940 Britain and France had solemnly declared that neither would enter into a separate peace or armistice. In the tumultuous last days before the collapse, the utopian idea had even been floated of a 'union' of the two countries. Mutual recrimination replaced amity and concord. The British now faced the question of what attitude they should adopt towards their erstwhile ally in the revolutionized circumstances. An immediate British concern was the French fleet, which Churchill was determined should not fall into German hands. Darlan was far from friendly to the British, often recalling that his great-grandfather had died at Trafalgar. He nevertheless promised that he would scuttle his ships rather than allow the Germans to make use of them. The British concluded, however, that they could not rely on his good faith. On 3 July all French ships in British ports were seized. The same day Operation *CATAPULT* was launched by the Royal Navy against the French fleet at the naval port of Mers-el-Kébir, near Oran. After the French naval commander rejected an ultimatum, the British opened fire, eventually destroying a battleship, incapacitating several smaller vessels, and killing 1,297 French sailors. The Vichy propaganda service and later the Germans too made hay with newsreel film footage of the British attack. This action spelled out, even more clearly than Churchill's speeches, that Britain would stop at nothing to defeat Hitler.

The German victory in the west had ripple effects throughout Europe. Mussolini, although mollified by a share of the spoils in France, barely concealed his chagrin at being outshone on the battlefield by Hitler. Speaking from his favourite oratorical position on his office balcony above the Piazza Venezia, he defined his war aims to a wildly enthusiastic crowd: 'After having solved the problem of our land frontiers, we are taking up arms in order to establish our maritime frontiers. We want to break the territorial and military chains that are strangling us in our own sea. A nation of forty-five million souls is not truly free unless it has free access to the ocean.'[44] At the same time he 'solemnly declared' that he did not 'intend to drag into the conflict' any of Italy's neighbours, naming specifically Switzerland, Yugoslavia, Greece, Turkey, and Egypt.

Just as the Italians had moved fast to seize a morsel, so Russia too sought hers. First she swallowed the three Baltic states. The Molotov–Ribbentrop pact had created the diplomatic foundation for the annexations. The arrangements the previous autumn, whereby the Baltic states granted the USSR bases on their soil, had provided the military framework. In mid-June the Russians demanded that all three states accept full Soviet occupation. Soon afterwards rigged elections installed Communist regimes that duly petitioned for admission to the Soviet Union. About half a million German residents were evacuated to the Reich. As these moved west, the Russians forcibly transported to the east tens of thousands of politically suspect citizens from the former newly incorporated regions.

Stalin's next objective was another former province of the Russian Empire, Bessarabia, which he considered his due under the Molotov–Ribbentrop pact, though the Germans had merely declared themselves 'disinterested' in respect of the territory. King Carol of Romania tried to forestall him by switching abruptly from the country's traditional pro-French alignment to a pro-German one. On 21 June all political parties were banned and power was transferred to the Iron Guard. The Soviet Union, fearing German intervention, demanded that Romania hand over not only Bessarabia but also the northern Bukovina, a territory that had never been ruled by Russia. The Germans manifested annoyance but in the end permitted the Russians to proceed. On 28 June Soviet forces occupied the two provinces without meeting resistance. Most of Bessarabia was incorporated in the Moldavian republic, which was separated from Ukraine and declared a full-fledged union republic of the USSR. The British and French had given Romania a guarantee in April 1939 but took no action now against the Soviet Union.

Romania, set upon by her enemies and abandoned by her friends, now stood, like Poland the previous autumn, on the verge of disintegration. Hungary, which for twenty years had smarted under the forced cession of Transylvania to Romania and which recalled grimly the horrors of Romanian occupation in 1919, was poised to seize the opportunity for revenge. Anxious to avoid a war between its satellite states, the Germans decided to force the issue. At a meeting in Vienna in August 1940, Ribbentrop and Ciano issued the 'second Vienna award' in which they decided that northern Transylvania must be returned to Hungary. What remained of Romania was taken under German protection. A few days later, under both German and Russian pressure, Romania retroceded the southern Dobrudja to Bulgaria. Carol abdicated in favour of his young son, Michael, and General Ion Antonescu took power as dictator. He requested German help in reorganizing the Romanian army and over the next few months Romania increasingly took on the aspect of a German-occupied country.

The Battle of Britain

After the fall of France, Hitler toyed briefly once more with the idea of making peace with Britain. On 19 July, in an address to the Reichstag, he made a public 'appeal to reason and common sense in Britain'.[45] This did not fall on completely stony ground. The consensus of expert military opinion in Britain after the fall of France was that the war was unwinnable by Britain alone. Various well-intentioned folk, from Pope Pius XII to a group of Labour MPs, urged the British government not to reject Hitler's offer out of hand. Leading strategic thinkers such as Liddell Hart and the Fascist General J. F. C. Fuller took a dim view of Britain's prospects of victory. But Churchill obdurately refused to contemplate any compromise peace. The majority of the British people supported him, though few had any conception of the magnitude of the task that confronted them. They prepared to defend their island by all and any means. Armed, more often than not, with wooden staves and pikes in lieu of rifles which were in short supply, old soldiers rallied to the Local Defence Volunteers (later known as 'Home Guard') and took literally Churchill's dictum, 'You can take one with you'. The south coast was declared a restricted military zone. Enemy aliens, including large numbers of refugees from Nazism, were rounded up and interned. Pots and pans and iron railings were contributed or confiscated as scrap metal, supposedly to be turned into planes.

When the British evinced no sign of interest in a negotiated peace on his—or any—terms, Hitler resolved to proceed with the invasion of Britain. He had already on 16 July ordered preparations to begin for a landing operation against England, code-named Operation *SEA-LION*, the aim being 'to eliminate the English homeland as a base for the prosecution of the war against Germany and, if necessary, to occupy it completely'.[46] Hitler did not underestimate the difficulties of this 'exceptionally daring undertaking'. He told the German naval commander, Admiral Raeder: 'operational surprise cannot be expected; a defensively prepared and utterly determined enemy faces us and dominates the sea area we must use.'[47] Raeder, for his part, pointed out that a landing in force in England would be impossible without air supremacy over the English Channel. In spite of intensive preparatory efforts by the German navy, including the assembly of barges in French Channel ports, the technical difficulties of such an amphibious operation forced a series of delays. As it became clear that a cross-Channel invasion would be a risky venture so long as the RAF was flying, Hitler instructed Göring's Luftwaffe 'to overpower the English Air Force with all the forces at its command in the shortest possible time'.[48]

The Battle of Britain pitted the world's two most advanced air forces against each other in a new kind of warfare. The German objective was to destroy RAF planes and ground installations as well as aircraft factories and Channel shipping. The battle took the form of engagements between British fighters and squadrons of German bombers and their fighter escorts. The British began with about 900 fighters against the Luftwaffe's 1,000 bombers and 750 fighters. Over the previous few years both countries had rushed to develop and produce high-performance fighters. The Messerschmidt 109 fighter presented a formidable challenge to the British Spitfire. The twin-engined Me 110 had a longer range but was less easily manoeuvrable and performed disappointingly against Spitfires and Hurricanes. The Germans, flying far from their home bases, could spend little time over the battlefield before having to turn towards home. The greatest threat to the British came from an acute shortage of pilots: Fighter Command had lost a third of its pilots in the Battle of France and neither new trainees nor replacements from the empire could quickly make up the deficit.

The British, however, possessed secret weapons that they put to good use. The most important at this stage was radar (acronym for 'radio detection and ranging'). Several countries, including Germany, had conducted research on radar before the war but Britain's was the most advanced and operationally effective, reflecting the acute official anxiety in the 1930s about the country's vulnerability to aerial attack from the continent. 'Chain Home', the line of radar stations strung out across southern England by Robert Watson-Watt, enabled the RAF to gain crucial early warning of approaching enemy air formations. Later, in the 'Battle of the Beams', British scientists succeeded in detecting and jamming German radio beams that directed bombers to their targets. As the Germans deployed jamming systems against radar, British 'boffins' (scientific experts) and their German counterparts devised ever more sophisticated counter-measures that were applied in what developed into high-intensity electronic warfare.

No less important was the British capacity to decipher German official communications that had been encoded using the Enigma cipher machines. Mathematicians, chess players, and linguists were recruited to the top-secret 'ULTRA' cryptanalytic headquarters at Bletchley Park. Among them was the Cambridge mathematician Alan Turing, whose work there paved the way for the invention of the electronic computer. The intercepts gave British commanders of all three services an extraordinary window into the thinking of their enemies, the German order of battle, movements, supplies, and plans. Large-scale access to Luftwaffe radio communications, which began in late May 1940, revealed vital information on German air strength, which turned out to be weaker than had hitherto been believed. ULTRA was so secret that, at first, even British commanders were deceived as to the source of the information, being told that it came from a highly placed British agent.

The battle was, in the main, waged in clear summer skies but an almost impenetrable fog of war enveloped the results since each side lied about its losses and neither could be sure of those it had inflicted. In the week 31 August to 6 September Fighter Command lost 151 planes and 10 per cent of its pilots. For a moment the Germans scented victory. But the Germans made mistakes in their choice of targets, for example not launching all-out attacks on radar stations. Believing that they had gained the upper hand in the air, they suddenly switched the main weight of their attacks from RAF stations to docks and power stations in London. The British changed their tactics to meet this new threat and achieved much better results. Over the next week they downed 175 German planes.

The turning-point came on 15 September. On that day the Germans lost 56 aircraft (the British claim for that day was 185 planes downed). Two days later Hitler postponed Operation *SEA-LION* indefinitely. By the end of October the British had shot down 1,294 German planes at a cost of 788 of their own (at the time the British, like the Germans, again made exaggerated claims). The British victory was won as much on the ground as in the air. Britain succeeded in building planes faster than the Germans could destroy them: during 1940 British factories produced more than fifteen thousand military planes of all types, including over four thousand fighters—far more than the Germans.

As the main thrust of the German attack switched to the bombing of cities, British civilians bore the brunt. The 'Blitz', seen by the Luftwaffe as a 'war of attrition',[49] remained intense until May 1941 and continued more sporadically until the end of the war. Ports and industrial centres were the main targets and London, Birmingham, Sheffield, Bristol, Southampton, and Coventry (where the medieval cathedral was destroyed) were hit repeatedly with bombardment by as many as six hundred bombers at a time. Later, so-called 'Baedeker' raids were launched against historic cities such as Bath, Canterbury, and York (but not Oxford, which, so it was said, Hitler intended to make the capital of a subjugated Britain). These attacks caused much suffering, destruction, and disruption. The House of Commons chamber was destroyed and the Commons had to meet for the remainder of the war in the House of Lords. But the Blitz failed to depress civilian morale or industrial production and did nothing to pave the way for a German landing in Britain.

Britain's long-term position was reinforced by help from the United States. In September 1940 the USA agreed to transfer fifty destroyers to

Britain in return for ninety-nine-year leases on bases in the British West Indies, Newfoundland, and Bermuda (the base on Jamaica closed in 1945, the one on Trinidad in 1967, those on Bermuda and Newfoundland in 1995). Most of the ships were unserviceable and were not even delivered for many months but the deal was the harbinger of a burgeoning alliance and gave a strong boost to morale in Britain. Britain, however, needed more than a few superannuated warships. By late 1940 her economic position was dire. As she depleted her foreign reserves and disposed of her overseas assets, the value of the pound sank. At its lowest point in 1940 sterling was quoted at $3.275, down from $4.687 before the outbreak of war. In November the British ambassador in Washington confessed publicly: 'Well, boys, Britain's broke; it's your money we want.'[50] 'For the first time in its history,' Robert Skidelsky writes, 'Britain found itself a suppliant for means-tested benefits, with Morgenthau [the US Treasury Secretary] running the benefits office.'[51] British propaganda in the USA gradually made some inroads into strongly isolationist public and Congressional opinion, thus providing a political basis for Roosevelt to enlarge aid to Britain. From the spring of 1941 onwards, 'Lend-Lease' expanded into a vast programme of economic aid, eventually dispensed to thirty-eight countries. By 1945 Britain and her Dominions had received more than half of the $42 billion (at a conservative estimate) of military and civilian supplies, including food and oil, supplied by the US to thirty-eight belligerent nations.

Britain's increasing dependence on the United States led logically to a German effort to cut the trans-oceanic supply lines. The Battle of the Atlantic came, in some ways, as a welcome diversion for what was still the strongest naval power in Europe. Yet in spite of British naval might, the Germans hoped that attacks on shipping by U-boats, surface raiders, mines, and bombers, could force Britain to her knees. In the winter of 1940/1 several convoys of merchant ships were severely damaged by U-boats that managed to slip through protective naval escort screens. But the German navy lacked sufficient strength to press the battle through to a successful conclusion: the total number of U-boats available for action in February 1941 was only twenty-seven. In May 1941 Allied and neutral shipping losses in the north Atlantic peaked at 325,000 tons. Thereafter, although German submarine strength increased, the British were able to use ULTRA decipherment of German naval codes to excellent effect. British merchant shipping losses meanwhile were rapidly replaced by new production at home and in the USA.

In spite of the failure of his onslaught on Britain, Hitler's strategic position in late 1940 was solid. At relatively small cost in men (96,500 German servicemen killed or missing) or armaments, he had conquered the most productive parts of the European land mass. He succeeded also in parlaying military gains into further diplomatic triumphs. On 27 September 1940 Germany, Italy, and Japan signed a Tripartitite Pact, promising mutual assistance in the event of an attack on any one of their number. By November Hungary, Romania, and Slovakia had added their signatures to the agreement which seemed to betoken a Fascist world hegemony. The only recalcitrants in the Balkans were Prince Paul of Yugoslavia (another royal dictator, nominally Regent for the son of King Alexander who had been assassinated in 1934) and Bulgaria's cunning Tsar Boris, both of whom refused to sign—for the time being.

The Balkan campaign

In reality, Germany's alliance with Italy, and her involvement in the Balkans, proved to be a source of weakness, not strength. On 13 September 1940 Mussolini ordered Italian forces in Libya, under Marshal Graziani, to advance against British-held Egypt. At a meeting of the two dictators at the Brenner Pass on 4 October, Mussolini boasted of impending victories in the Western Desert. Shortly after his return to Rome, he heard, with outrage, of the arrival of a German military mission in Romania (though Ciano had, in fact, been forewarned): 'Hitler always confronts me with *faits accomplis*. This time I shall pay him back in his own coin; he shall learn from the newspapers that I have occupied Greece. Thus will equilibrium be restored.'[52] Madly jealous of Hitler and desperate to show his own mettle, Mussolini embarked on another campaign that he thought would lead to easy victory. On 28 October, anniversary of the 'March on Rome', the Italian army in Albania attacked Greece.

The Italian armed forces, however, still recovering from their exertions in Ethiopia and Spain, were ill-equipped and poorly led. They suffered disastrous military setbacks in both theatres. In North Africa General Sir Archibald Wavell drove them back into Tripolitania by early 1941, capturing 130,000 prisoners and 380 tanks. The Italians were able to avoid total humiliation only thanks to the arrival of German forces. In February General Erwin Rommel arrived in Libya to take command of the *Deutsches*

Afrika-Korps. Although nominally under Italian command, he insisted on complete freedom of action and in effect consigned the Italians to a subordinate role. He quickly succeeded in stabilizing the Axis position and in early April reconquered most of Cyrenaica (but not the fortress port of Tobruk) for the Axis.

The Italian campaign in Greece, commanded by Marshal Badoglio, was 'as fatuous in execution as it was unnecessary in design' (the judgement of Guderian).[53] The Greek army rebuffed the Italians and pushed them back into Albania. French anti-Fascist wags allegedly posted signposts at Menton on the French/Italian border: 'Greeks stop here! This is France!' The Greek dictator, Metaxas, had disdained British aid against the Italians but after his death in January 1941 the new Greek government permitted the British army to reinforce the country against potential German attack. The Germans immediately put pressure on Bulgaria to sign the Tripartite Pact and on 1 March Tsar Boris yielded, thus paving the way for the Wehrmacht to enter Bulgaria and threaten Greece from the north. Mussolini tried to recapture the initiative by launching a fresh offensive against Greece from Albania, only to find his forces once again driven back and obliged to call on the Germans for help.

All eyes next turned to Yugoslavia, whose attitude would be crucial in the event of any broadening of the war in the Balkans. Yugoslav policy towards Germany had been notably complaisant since 1934. Prince Paul, although sentimentally Anglophile, now succumbed to intense pressure from Germany, whose troops in Bulgaria menaced not only Greece but also Yugoslavia. On 25 March Prince Paul's government signed the Tripartite Pact. But two days later a group of young officers in Belgrade, encouraged by British agents, initiated a successful coup that ousted Paul and installed a new regime that sought to disentangle itself from the German embrace, even to the extent of seeming to flirt with the Soviet Union. Hitler was enraged and immediately ordered the Wehrmacht 'to smash Yugoslavia militarily and as a state-form'.[54] The attack was to be launched by German troops operating out of Austria, Hungary, Romania, and Bulgaria.

The Hungarian Prime Minister, Count Pál Teleki, had signed a Treaty of Eternal Friendship with Yugoslavia just five months earlier. An old-fashioned Transylvanian aristocrat, with strong religious convictions and a reputation for incorruptibility, Teleki had staked his personal honour on refusing to allow Hungary to become a launching-pad for German attacks on neighbouring countries (see plate 26). When the Germans demanded passage for their troops across Hungary in order to attack Yugoslavia, Teleki realized that his policy was bankrupt. On 3 April he committed suicide, leaving a note in which he declared: 'We have become breakers of our word—out of cowardice. The nation feels this, and we have thrown away its honour. We have placed ourselves at the side of scoundrels. . . . We shall be robbers of corpses!'[55] His successors had fewer scruples and not only permitted the German army to pass through the country but offered their own forces as allies in the impending attack.

The German offensive in the Balkans was launched three days later. Twenty-nine German divisions subdued Yugoslavia in eleven days for a loss of only 151 dead. The Greeks had no illusions that the Germans could be dispatched towards the French Riviera with as much ease as the Italians; hence their invitation to the British. But British aid proved inadequate and confusion between British and Greek military planners led to another Allied debacle. The German advance was so fast that a British message to the Greek garrison in the northern town of Jannina evoked the reply, '*Hier ist das deutsche Heer!*' (This is the German army!).[56] On 18 April the Greek Prime Minister, Alexandros Koryzis, committed suicide. Nine days later German troops entered Athens. A calamitous effort to save Crete, to which the king and government had retreated with residual scraps of Greek, British, and Commonwealth forces, was overwhelmed by German airborne troops by the beginning of June. The Allies managed to evacuate around fifty thousand men from Greece but again lost most of their equipment and many ships.

The British position in the eastern Mediterranean and Middle East now looked very wobbly. Pro-German elements, under Rashid 'Ali Gailani, took power briefly in Iraq in April 1941. Anti-British rumblings by nationalists also began to be felt in Egypt. In Libya successive British counter-offensives failed to dislodge Rommel, who moved the battle onto Egyptian territory. On 21 June Wavell was abruptly dismissed and reinforcements were rushed to Egypt. The Allies won an inexpensive victory when British and Free French forces toppled the pro-Vichy regime in Syria. Meanwhile the British colony of Malta held out against Axis air and naval raids. But Britain's overlordship in the region owed as much to political artifice as to military might and probably survived the test only due to the preoccupation of her enemies with another theatre.

Barbarossa

War against Bolshevik Russia lay at the heart of Hitler's thinking. On 31 July 1940, long before the abandonment of Operation *SEA-LION*, he told a meeting of army and navy chiefs that Russia must be 'shattered to its roots with one blow'.[57] The 'turn to the east' took definitive shape on 18 December when he issued his directive for Operation *BARBAROSSA*, the invasion of the Soviet Union. 'The German Armed Forces', he declared, 'must be prepared, even before the conclusion of the war against England, to crush Soviet Russia in a rapid campaign.'[58] Preparations for the assault, in which he counted on the active support of Romania and Finland, were to be completed by 15 May 1941. During the intervening period, great stress was to be laid on concealing any offensive intentions. From a strategic point of view the decision to open up a second front in the east was foolhardy, even lunatic, and qualifies as one of the greatest errors ever committed by a political leader: it swung the odds heavily towards an ultimate German defeat. But Hitler's deep-seated anti-Bolshevism, his racist notions of Slav inferiority, his programmatic aim of conquering *Lebensraum* for German settlement, as well as the aggressive urge at the core of Nazism, all impelled him towards this fateful step. This would be a 'war of annihilation', he told his generals on 30 March 1941.[59] Brauchitsch and Halder, as well as other generals, had misgivings, though hardly any dared express them openly. When one did so hesitantly, Hitler brushed him aside: 'I am convinced that our attack will sweep over them like a hailstorm.'[60] Cowed and dazzled by Hitler's string of victories, the German High Command set aside their professional judgement and accepted Hitler's predictions.

The Balkan campaign forced Hitler to delay the planned attack on the Soviet Union by seven weeks. Historians have long debated whether the diversions in North Africa and the Balkans fatally wounded his chances of victory in the east. The conclusion of Guderian was that these commitments led, at any rate, 'to a weakening of our strength in the decisive theatres of the war'.[61] Hitler later used this delay as an excuse for his failure to knock out the Soviet Union in the autumn of 1941. But it was at most a contributory cause rather than a decisive element. More fundamental was his underestimation of the scale of the challenge that confronted him in the east and of the recuperative capability of Soviet industrial and military power.

Stalin has sometimes been portrayed as cluelessly trusting in his attitude to Hitler. This is an exaggeration. The relationship between these two rival despots—who never met—is one of the most intriguing in history. Each was convinced that he had the measure of the other. Each misjudged the other. At some level, it is true, the otherwise paranoid Soviet leader actually seems to have trusted Hitler to honour their compact, if only for a time. Although Soviet intelligence was ill-informed about details of the German order of battle, it did obtain evidence from reliable diplomatic sources, reconnaissance reports, and agents, notably the Tokyo-based Soviet master-spy Richard Sorge, that a German attack was impending. In April Churchill, relying on ULTRA intercepts, sent Stalin a personal message drawing attention to German troop concentrations near the Soviet border. Such reports were uniformly categorized as doubtful by General F. I. Golikov, head of the Red Army's Intelligence Division (GRU); but the primary element in Golikov's classification system, like that of most senior Soviet officials, was calculation of what his master wanted to hear.[62] In any case, Stalin brushed aside the accumulation of warning signals, apparently expecting that he could stave off any German attack at least until 1942.

In the meantime he did everything possible throughout 1940 and early 1941 to avoid giving Hitler any pretext for complaint. The Soviet Government formally congratulated the Germans on their victory over France. German Communists who had taken refuge in the Soviet Union and who had survived the purges were handed over to the Nazis. Margarete Buber-Neumann, for example, who worked for the Comintern as a translator, was arrested in 1938, found guilty of counter-revolutionary agitation, sentenced to five years' reformatory labour, and sent to the Karaganda camp in Kazakhstan. In 1940 she was transferred to German custody, together with other anti-Nazis. She spent the next five years in the Ravensbrück concentration camp but survived to tell her tale. In December 1940 Molotov went so far as to present the German ambassador with a proposal for a formal Nazi–Soviet alliance in return for recognition of Soviet territorial claims in Finland, the Balkans, the Caucasus, and north Sakhalin (the Germans never replied).[63] In January 1941 Stalin handed over $7.5 million in gold to the Germans in return for the Suwalki district on the border of Lithuania and East Prussia (it was reoccupied by the German army six months later but, needless to say, the purchase price was not reimbursed). In May Stalin further attempted to curry favour with the Führer by recognizing the Rashid 'Ali regime in Iraq. Until the eve of the German attack, the USSR continued to supply Germany with oil, iron ore, manganese, copper, nickel, phosphate and other raw materials that were used to supply the war machine soon to be turned against the Soviet Union itself.

While seeking to appease Hitler, Stalin, like Chamberlain before him, simultaneously rearmed. The period September 1939 to June 1941 was marked by breakneck expansion of Soviet military strength: seven thousand tanks and seventeen thousand aircraft were added to the arsenal and 3.9 million men were recruited to the Soviet forces. In late March 1941 Stalin acceded to pressure from Marshal G. K. Zhukov, Chief of the General Staff, and permitted the call-up of several hundred thousand reservists. One constraint on Soviet strategic deployment was removed on 13 April, when the Japanese Foreign Minister, Matsuoka Yosuke, visited Moscow and signed a non-aggression pact with Molotov. In an undeclared war in the summer of 1939 Japanese forces in the Far East, operating out of the Japanese puppet state of Manchukuo, had engaged in fierce fighting with the Red Army. The Matsuoka–Molotov agreement gave Stalin some reassurance that he could station the main weight of his armed forces in Europe.

In a semi-secret speech to a military audience on 5 May, Stalin urged the merits of an offensive strategy. The next day he appointed himself Soviet Prime Minister (hitherto he had merely been Secretary-General of the Communist Party). Some troops were moved up to the western border. But when, on 13 June, the Soviet Defence Commissar, Timoshenko, urged further deployments in an offensive posture, Stalin exploded: 'You propose mobilization and moving troops to the western frontier? That means war! Don't you understand that?'[64] Five days later Timoshenko and Zhukov met Stalin again at the Kremlin with maps showing German troop concentrations near the border. They urged that the Red Army be placed in a state of 'full military readiness'. Stalin blew up and launched a minatory tirade against his visitors, culminating in a personal threat: 'If you're going to provoke the Germans on the frontier by moving troops there without our permission, then heads will roll, mark my words!'[65] Whereupon he walked out of the room, slamming the door.

The fact that the Red Army was nevertheless deployed in substantial strength in offensive formations near the frontier in June 1941 has led some writers to speculate that Stalin was planning a pre-emptive strike against Hitler. This was indeed alleged by Germany in her declaration of war, handed to the Soviet ambassador in Berlin a few hours after the German onslaught began. The proposition is far-fetched.[66] In 1940 and early 1941 Russian strategists had analysed the German campaigns in Poland and France as well as their own miserable performance against the Finns in the Winter War but they failed to draw appropriate lessons. Soviet, like French, military doctrine remained stuck in a pre-1939 time-warp. The Red Army's war plans called for concentration of its strongest mechanized forces near the frontier with a view to blunting the initial force of an attack and then moving the battle on to enemy territory. In particular, they failed to take account of the speed with which the Germans would succeed in bringing the main weight of their armies into battle. Soviet forces were, in any case, largely unready for combat in 1941: the officer corps had still not recovered from the purge of the late 1930s; the mass of new recruits to all three services was ill-trained, poorly fed, and lacked adequate transportation, fuel, radio communications equipment, and, in many cases, weapons and ammunition supplies.

In May 1941, in a comic-opera diversion from the serious business of war, the hitherto unremarkable Rudolf Hess, deputy Führer (strictly, number three in the Nazi hierarchy after Hitler and Göring), suddenly flew to Scotland on a self-appointed 'peace mission'. Hitler was reported to be in tears at the news and Goebbels said it was more serious than the desertion of an army corps.[67] The flight led to wild rumours and dark conspiracy theorizing, especially in Moscow. Stalin suspected that British intelligence had somehow lured Hess to England and the episode aroused Soviet fears of a possible secret deal between Britain and Germany. The unexciting truth was that Hess had acted entirely alone, inspired by a mad notion that his pre-war acquaintance with the Duke of Hamilton might somehow enable him to negotiate peace. He was interned for the duration of the war.

In a draft directive prepared eleven days before the attack on Russia, Hitler looked forward confidently to the new order that would follow victory. 'Germany and Italy will be military masters of the European continent with the temporary exception of the Iberian peninsula.' Spain would at last be compelled to cooperate in driving the British out of Gibraltar. British dominance in the Middle East would be crushed by German advances on Iraq from the Caucasus and on Egypt and Palestine from North Africa.[68] This was, to say the least, an optimistic prognosis. On 21 June 1941, the eve of this ambitious enterprise, Hitler devoted energy to the most frivolous of tasks: together with Goebbels, he spent considerable time trying out various alternative forms of fanfare to be broadcast on the radio to hail the forthcoming victory. Meanwhile a deserter from the German army, a secret Communist, crossed the Soviet lines and told Red Army interrogators that a German offensive was scheduled to begin at 4.00 a.m. the next day. The news was reported to Stalin, who ordered the man to be shot for supplying 'disinformation'.[69]

On 22 June 1941 three German army groups, comprising 152 divisions, with 3,350 tanks and over three million German troops, as well as 2,510 aircraft, attacked the Soviet Union. This was the largest invasion force ever assembled in history. The defenders had 177 divisions mobilized, with 2.8 million soldiers. They had twenty thousand tanks, more than the rest of the world put together, but most were obsolete types: fewer than two thousand were modern KV and T-34 models. The air force inventory was similarly huge but out of date: seven to eight thousand aircraft, of which only about 1,500 were recently produced high-performance fighters, notably the MiG-3. There were not enough trained pilots to fly the planes that they had. The total strength of the Red Army was 4.8 million men. But full mobilization would take up to two weeks. In the meantime, the Russians' strongest mechanized forces were positioned close to the border in forward positions that left them, as well as their bases and supplies, highly vulnerable to German envelopment.

The initial attack caught the Russians completely off guard. German bombers destroyed communications centres, naval bases, and airfields. By the end of the first day they had eliminated 1,811 planes (1,489 on the ground) and achieved air supremacy over the battlefield. Total Luftwaffe losses that day were only thirty-five aircraft. Soviet logistics were thrown into utter confusion. German tanks smashed through the half-completed defence lines in the recently annexed western territories and advanced rapidly towards the interior. Stalin, woken at 4.30 a.m. with news of the invasion, was stunned and at first took refuge in the notion that this was a mere 'provocation'. His voice was not heard on the radio until eleven days later when he addressed his Soviet 'brothers and sisters' directly for the first time and called the conflict a 'patriotic war'.[70] Henceforth it would be known in Soviet parlance as 'the Great Patriotic War'.

Within ten days the Germans captured Vilna, Kovno, Minsk, and Lvov. Their advance was so swift that by 14 July Hitler was already looking beyond victory to a reduction in the strength of the German army and navy.[71] Two days later Guderian's Panzers reached Smolensk, where he was shocked to find that the cathedral had been turned into a Museum of

Atheism. By now the Germans had captured nearly three-quarters of a million prisoners. Meanwhile the Luftwaffe had destroyed nearly seven thousand planes and lost only 550 of its own.

As the Germans advanced, the Soviet apparatus of government scrambled ineffectually to cobble together some semblance of organized resistance. On 19 July Stalin took over from Timoshenko as Defence Commissar and chairman of the *Stavka* (general headquarters) and on 8 August declared himself Commander-in-Chief of the armed forces. Over the next four years Stalin, like Hitler, came to believe in his own strategic genius, overriding military advisers and committing the Red Army to expensive military blunders. Like Churchill and Hitler, Stalin was ruthless towards generals who lost battles. But whereas Churchill sent them off out of sight (Ironside into retirement, Gort to Malta, Wavell to India) and Hitler demoted them and stripped them of decorations, Stalin went further. He had the commander of the Western Special Military District, General D. G. Pavlov, put on trial for negligence in the first phase of the invasion: he received the death sentence. Pavlov was not alone. Soldiers at every level who were judged wanting were lined up for execution. Zhukov was spared: he was merely dismissed from his staff position and sent to direct the defence of Leningrad. By this uncharacteristic act of mercy Stalin changed the course of history: to Zhukov, one of the few Soviet generals who dared to contradict Stalin, more than to any other single individual, would redound the credit for the Allied victory in the Second World War.

By 27 July the German High Command reached the premature conclusion that 'the mass of the operationally effective Russian army has been destroyed'.[72] But instead of ordering his forces to drive on to Moscow, as most of his senior commanders advocated, Hitler decided on 21 August that the immediate objectives should be the completion of the conquest of Ukraine, because of its economic resources, and Crimea, 'that Soviet aircraft carrier for attacking the Romanian oilfields'.[73] On 19 September the encircled Ukrainian capital, Kiev, fell: the Germans captured a further 667,000 Russian prisoners.

To the north, Leningrad, besieged on all sides, seemed on the verge of submission by 9 September when the fall of the nearby fortress of Shlisselburg, at the outlet of the River Neva into Lake Ladoga, severed land communications with the rest of the country. Heavy Luftwaffe air raids had already destroyed most of the city's food stocks. Eight days later the Germans captured the suburban Alexandrovka tramcar terminus, just

7.5 miles from the city centre, and intensified their artillery bombardment of the city. At that point the defenders prepared to destroy major buildings rather than allow them to fall into German hands. Hitler, however, decided to surround and strangle the city into surrender rather than storm it. So began the epic 872-day siege by German and Finnish forces. Zhukov led the desperate defence effort that achieved the 'miracle on the Neva' and, at immense human and material cost, staved off the conquest of the city. By the end of September the Germans' assault had run out of steam and, after further unproductive attacks and counter-attacks, the two armies settled down to the greatest test of endurance in modern military history.

Agreeing belatedly to a resumption of the drive towards Moscow, Hitler ordered the Soviet capital to be captured before winter. But the Red Army, reinforced by contingents removed from the Far East, put up stiff resistance. Zhukov was transferred from Leningrad to lead the defence of the capital. When he arrived there he found Stalin talking to the secret police chief, Beria, about putting out peace feelers to Germany.[74] On 19 October Stalin ordered an evacuation of government offices to Kuibyshev on the Volga, five hundred miles to the east. Amid something close to panic, martial law was declared in Moscow. Andrei Sakharov, then a student at Moscow University, watched 'as office after office set fire to their files, clouds of soot swirled through streets clogged with trucks, carts, and people on foot carr[ied] household possessions, baggage, and young children'.[75] Over a million people left the city.

But the Germans' earlier diversion of effort to the south was to preclude any chance of conquering Moscow, let alone of outright victory, before winter weather halted their advance. Already autumn rains were bogging vehicles down in mud on the unpaved roads. As the temperature dropped, German-manufactured anti-freeze proved inadequate to combat Russian winter temperatures and tanks and supply vehicles crunched into immobility. Horses collapsed in the cold and the entire German logistic apparatus seized up. The Wehrmacht, it now became apparent, was not equipped for a long war. So great had been Hitler's (and his high command's) confidence in rapid victory that most of the army in the east had not even been supplied with winter uniforms. By the end of November German tanks were less than twenty miles from the Kremlin. A few days later, amid blizzards, the German offensive ground to a halt.

In less than six months the invaders had conquered an area larger than the whole of western Europe, had captured Kharkov and the Donbas industrial region, and had reached the River Don. The occupied territory held

40 per cent of the USSR's pre-war population, 85 per cent of its aircraft factories, 60 per cent of its armaments production capacity, two-fifths of the railway network and half the grain-producing area. The Germans had captured 3.8 million Soviet prisoners of war and killed or wounded several hundred thousand more. They had destroyed twenty thousand tanks and over eight thousand aircraft.

But they had not conquered the Soviet Union. After a shaky first four months, Soviet mobilization began to replace men and formations faster than they were lost. In spite of its gargantuan casualties, the Red Army's total personnel, at around eight million, was much higher than it had been in June. Meanwhile the Germans' casualties had reached 750,000, a quarter of their entire attacking force, a loss rate so high that they were unable to replenish their depleted units adequately with fresh troops.

On 5 December, aided by the icy conditions, Zhukov launched a counter-offensive. Three days later a new, apologetic note entered Hitler's war directives: 'The severe winter weather which has come surprisingly early in the east, and the consequent difficulties in bringing up supplies, compel us to abandon immediately all major offensive operations and to go over to the defensive.'[76] Guderian's Panzers were forced to pull back. The attack on Moscow was called off and the German army settled down into defensive positions, though these were often unfavourable because of Hitler's refusal to countenance withdrawals. Hitler blamed his generals and dismissed the head of Army Group South, Field Marshal Gerd von Rundstedt, who had committed the grave crime of ordering a retreat. Some of the generals meanwhile began to blame Hitler: 'I would never have believed that a really brilliant military position could be so b. . . . d up in two months,' Guderian wrote on 8 December.[77] On 19 December Hitler himself took over from Brauchitsch as Commander-in-Chief of the German Army. Guderian and other generals were also removed from their commands. Any lingering independence of spirit in the German High Command was henceforth virtually snuffed out. Over the next few weeks, in temperatures that reached −40 °C, the Germans were relentlessly ground down and forced to pull back 175 miles from Moscow. As the cold plumbed numbing depths, Hitler's troops shivered miserably in their bivouacs; frostbite inflicted more casualties than the enemy; large numbers froze to death. For the rest of the war conscription to the eastern front became for German soldiers tantamount to consignment to hell. The collective experience left an enduring mark on the national consciousness and contributed to the brutalization of Hitler's army and its readiness to participate in barbaric atrocities.

Germany had been joined in her assault on the Soviet Union by several junior allies. The Romanian dictator, Antonescu, sent two armies into northern Bukovina and Bessarabia and, with German help, succeeded in conquering these provinces and re-attaching them to Romania. The Romanians then crossed the Dniester into Ukraine and on 16 October, again with German assistance, captured Odessa. Hungarian, Slovak, and Italian forces as well as units of Spanish, French, Belgian, and Croat volunteers were all represented on the eastern front. None of these, however, made a major contribution to the fighting.

Finland, uneasy at her alliance of convenience with Germany, did not participate directly in the initial attack, though she allowed German forces to operate from her soil. But on 25 June, she declared war on the USSR and seized the opportunity to regain territory lost in the Winter War. The Finns did not, however, stop there but advanced into Soviet Karelia. On 6 December Britain declared war on Finland, a 'most painful' decision, Churchill told Mannerheim in a private message.[78] As the campaign in the east continued unexpectedly beyond the winter of 1941, the Germans' fraying manpower resources led them to rely increasingly on troops from their allies. With the exception of the Finns, they were a dubious military asset and most eventually proved to be a heavy liability.

During the winter of 1941/2, as German operations froze to a standstill, Soviet forces dented the front line at various points but failed to secure a breakthrough. In Leningrad they conducted a limited supply operation by lorries across the frozen ice of Lake Ladoga. For their coming summer offensive the Germans concentrated all their efforts on the southern front. In early May 1942 General von Manstein smashed Soviet defensive positions in the Crimea and captured 170,000 prisoners. A few days later a Soviet army group, led by the former Defence Commissar Timoshenko, launched an ambitious offensive to recapture Kharkov. But German military intelligence in the east, headed by Reinhard Gehlen, obtained accurate advance information about the planned attack. Panzer forces encircled Timoshenko's forces: the Russians lost another quarter of a million men and 1,200 tanks. In June the Germans attacked in strength in the south, aiming at a breakthrough towards the Caucasus. They hoped to gain access to Soviet oil-producing regions and cut off Allied supply lines to Russia through Iran. They captured Rostov-on-Don and an army group under

Field-Marshal List bulldozed towards the Northern Caucasus. Stalin, facing another crisis, decided to grant professional military officers greater leeway in decision-making. The war-winning team of Zhukov and A. M. Vasilevsky henceforth proved more than a match for their German opponents. The results were soon felt in the south, where List's momentum decelerated as the Germans found it necessary to give priority to supplying fuel and ammunition to their forces engaged in what developed into one of the decisive battles in the history of the world.

Stalingrad, formerly Tsaritsyn, occupied what, in the eyes of both Hitler and Stalin, was a key strategic position on the Volga. To both men it seemed to represent the last barrier against German conquest of the whole of European Russia as well as the Caucasus. Stalin had led its defence against the 'White' General Denikin during the Russian Civil War; hence the renaming of the city in 1925. In late August 1942 the German Sixth Army, commanded by General von Paulus, pummelled through to the Volga and embarked on a siege of the city. On 6 September the Germans captured part of it but Stalin ordered his forces to stand their ground whatever the cost. Commanded by General V. I. Chuikov, who acquired the sobriquet 'General Stubbornness', they did so. The epic five-month battle marked the turning-point of war on the eastern front. This was the 'Soviet Cannae' (see plate 27). Repeated German onslaughts were met with resistance from makeshift bunkers and dugouts as well as in the streets, squares, factories, power stations, railway stations and sidings, river barges, apartment buildings, basements, and sewers. Both sides wielded every kind of weapon from artillery and dive-bombers to flamethrowers, grenades, bayonets, and clubs. Paulus failed to obliterate the Soviet defenders and, as the Russians moved more forces to the area, found himself in an exposed pocket. On 25 September an exasperated Hitler dismissed the army chief of staff, Halder, and replaced him with Colonel-General Kurt Zeitzler, who immediately recommended that Paulus be allowed to withdraw. But Hitler would not hear of such a thing and the Sixth Army was condemned to its fate. The besieger now found himself besieged. In order to reinforce German troops in the city, parts of the front in the surrounding region were turned over to Romanian forces. Paulus attacked again and again, and in early November came close to conquering the centre of the city but in desperate hand-to-hand fighting the Russians staved off defeat.

Meanwhile, the Red Army brought large reinforcements and supplies into the area. Operation *URANUS*, a vast pincer plan designed to encircle the Germans, was launched on 19 November. Soviet units in the centre of Stalingrad were on the verge of collapse. But the relief forces greatly outnumbered and outgunned the enemy and succeeded in breaking through Romanian-held lines north and south of the city. Paulus's Sixth Army was encircled. On 24 November he was about to order a break-out. But Hitler ordered him to stand fast and gave his personal assurance that 'Fortress Stalingrad' would be supplied from the air. Over the next two months, however, the Luftwaffe failed to deliver more than a fraction of what was required and Paulus's freezing army was reduced to starvation rations. Soldiers slaughtered their horses and gnawed at their bones. Manstein, with a scrambled-together relief force, tried to save the troops trapped in the Stalingrad pocket but failed. The Russians offered Paulus an opportunity to surrender but this was rejected. Finally, in January 1943 General K. K. Rokossovsky's Army Group of the Don enveloped and destroyed the remaining German forces. On 30 January the last radio message from Paulus to the German High Command reported that the German flag was still flying and that German soldiers would never capitulate. Two days later all German resistance ended. Paulus was persuaded by the Russians to denounce his former master and join a 'Free Germany Committee'. At least 110,000 German prisoners, among them twenty-four generals, passed into captivity: only five thousand would ever return home.[79] A million Russians had died in the siege of the city. In this single battle the Red Army had eliminated twenty-two German divisions. Hitler had been the author of the German disaster at Stalingrad. Yet he blamed everyone but himself. His only self-criticism was for having promoted Paulus to the rank of Field-Marshal on 30 January, since no German officer of that rank had ever been captured alive. Paulus, he said, 'should have shot himself' rather than surrender.[80] Stalin, displaying a curiously parallel preoccupation with rank, promoted himself to Marshal of the Soviet Union. Henceforth he was known (like Franco) as 'Generalissimo'.

World War

In 1937 Churchill had said, 'I will not pretend that, if I had to choose between Communism and Nazism, I would choose Communism.'[81] Since 1938, however, he had advocated British association with the USSR against Hitler. During Finland's Winter War, he reverted to belligerent anti-Sovietism. Yet immediately after assuming office as Prime Minister he sent a special envoy, Sir Stafford Cripps, to Moscow to try to improve relations. Upon the German attack on the Soviet Union, Churchill did not hesitate. In a broadcast the same day he declared, 'I will unsay no word that I have said about [Communism], but all this fades away before the spectacle which is now unfolding.'[82] On 12 July 1941 an Anglo-Russian treaty was signed promising mutual assistance in the war and undertaking that no armistice or peace would be negotiated except by mutual agreement.

Stalin received British assistance, as well as the much larger help that was to reach Russia later from the United States, with ill grace. Soviet publicity rarely mentioned it. On the contrary, the major theme of external propaganda over the next two years was the need for the immediate opening of a 'second front' in the west to alleviate the pressure on the Soviet Union. In spite of the alliance, British officials in Russia were often treated more like enemy agents than friendly visitors. When Churchill called on Stalin in Moscow in August 1942 and explained that the opening of a second front would not be feasible that year, he was treated to a diatribe about British cowardice. Stalin refused to disclose his own strategic plans while constantly demanding that the western powers reveal theirs.

The outbreak of the German-Russian war led to a renewal of relations between the USSR and the Polish government-in-exile in London headed by General Władisław Sikorski. In a treaty signed on 30 July 1941, the Soviet Union declared that the Soviet–German treaties of 1939 'as to territorial changes in Poland' had 'lost their validity'.[83] The USSR agreed to the formation of a Polish army on Soviet soil, to be composed of Polish prisoners of war held by the Russians since 1939. Sikorski came under severe criticism from more nationalistic members of his government for accepting less than explicit Soviet recognition of Poland's pre-war frontier. In a broadcast on 31 July he defended the agreement, which, he said, 'does not permit even of the suggestion that the 1939 frontiers of the Polish state could ever be in question'.[84] Here lay the origins of what was to be a slow-working poison in Russo-Polish relations.

The Anglo-Soviet alliance produced other reversals of attitude. Pro-Sovietism in Britain was transformed overnight into a patriotic position and left and right vied in their enthusiasm for all things Russian. The Communist Party of Great Britain declared, 'Britain's honour now depends on whether she starts an invasion in the west.'[85] More surprising was the support that the 'second front' campaign received from the arch-conservative Lord

Beaverbrook, who pronounced in April 1942 that 'Communism under Stalin has won the applause and admiration of all the western nations'.[86] The French Communists were compelled to perform yet another volte-face: '*Ni Berlin, ni Londres*' was torn off walls; instead new posters appeared calling for a united, national, anti-Fascist front in alliance with democratic England and the Soviet Union '*odieusement agressée*'.[87]

As the Germans and Russians grappled in their no-holds-barred struggle on the eastern front, a sudden change in the strategic equation was effected by Japan's attack on American naval vessels at Pearl Harbor, Hawaii, on 7 December 1941. On the same day Japan attacked Hong Kong, Malaya, and the International Settlement at Shanghai. Britain and the United States declared war on Japan the next day. Hitler took the initiative in declaring war on the United States on 11 December. No doubt the Americans would, in due course, have saved him the trouble. They had already moved close to direct involvement in the Battle of the Atlantic by deploying US naval vessels to escort convoys carrying Lend-Lease supplies to Britain. In July 1941 US troops had replaced the Canadian garrison in Iceland (which had declared its full independence from Danish rule following the German occupation of Denmark). Jean Monnet (see plate 20), a French official at that time working for the British Supply Council in North America, wrote to the Cabinet Office in London: 'We assume and believe that the USA will be in the war in 1942.'[88] In August Churchill and Roosevelt, meeting at Placentia Bay, Newfoundland, had issued the 'Atlantic Charter', supporting 'the right of all peoples to choose the form of government under which they will live', declaring that territorial changes should take place only in accordance with 'the freely expressed wishes of the peoples concerned', affirming economic and social rights, and calling for the establishment of 'a permanent system of general security'—in effect a statement of democratic war aims.[89] In November Congress had amended the Neutrality Acts so as to allow armed US merchantmen to enter war zones. Some mystery nevertheless remains why Hitler so eagerly flung down the gauntlet, when a more prudent course might well have been to delay in the hope that the United States might choose to concentrate its efforts on the war in the Pacific. The declaration of war was accompanied by a 'no-separate-peace' agreement with Japan and it may be that Hitler felt that the 'Asian sword' of Tokyo would at least limit the effect on the European theatre of United States involvement.

The Japanese attack had the immediate effect of offering Stalin greater assurance that he would not face a Japanese threat to Soviet territory in east Asia. Both he and the Japanese now shared at least a temporary interest in observing the neutrality to which they were committed by treaty. The American entry into the war offered the Allies the prospect of almost unlimited industrial resources being brought to bear against the enemy. But given the backward condition of American rearmament and military readiness, this reassurance was long-term in nature. Meanwhile the danger remained that both Japan and Germany might quickly seize so much in the way of territory and resources in Russia, the Middle East, and east Asia that they too would be able to contemplate with confidence the outcome of a long-drawn-out struggle.

In this race against time, Japan scored some startling victories. Just two days after Pearl Harbor, Japanese aircraft sank the *Prince of Wales* and the *Repulse*, the pride of Britain's battle fleet in the Far East. The following day the Japanese moved into Burma. Hong Kong capitulated on 26 December. In January 1942 Japan attacked the Dutch East Indies and soon overran those islands with their valuable oilfields. Most disastrous of all to British prestige in the Far East, the whole of Malaya as well as the great naval base at Singapore fell to the Japanese on 15 February 1942 after an unimpressive defence by the British forces there. By April 1942 the Japanese stood on the borders of British India. With Japanese aircraft based in Borneo bombing Darwin, the threat of an onslaught on Australia seemed real. Optimistic Axis planners could envisage a conjunction between German forces moving through the Middle East from Egypt and the Caucasus and Japanese conquerors of India.

Against this expanded threat, Anglo-American cooperation, already close, now became ever more intimate. This was a decisive long-term change in international relations. Not so long before, in the late 1930s, the United States still had contingency plans for war against Britain. Now the USA and UK became each other's closest ally and remained so into the next century. At the Washington Conference of 22 December 1941 to 14 January 1942, Churchill and Roosevelt agreed on the creation of a Combined Chiefs of Staff committee. This presided over integrated planning of munitions, supply of raw materials, communications, intelligence, transportation, and almost every other aspect of the war effort. In spite of occasional friction and frequent disagreements over strategy, the mechanism worked effectively until the end of the war.

The first and most basic decision was to pursue a 'Germany first' strategy. But although British and American planners agreed on that principle, they diverged on its application. The Americans favoured the earliest possible assault on western Europe in order to relieve pressure on the Russians and strike a decisive blow against Germany. The British view was that such an invasion was impractical until overwhelming forces had been recruited, trained, and supplied, and until the complex logistical problems involved in any amphibious attack against a well-defended coastline had been solved. That would take years. The difficulties involved were demonstrated by the embarrassing failure of a British–Canadian cross-Channel raid on Dieppe in August 1942: the attackers lost all their equipment and 73 per cent of their men. The Allies were in reality very far from being fit to mount any serious assault on western Europe.

The British therefore proposed an initial attack against north-west Africa. The Americans were dubious. North Africa was not regarded as a decisive theatre. Churchill was suspected of seeking imperial goals. But in default of any other practical possibility for action against Germany in 1942, the Americans reluctantly agreed.

In North Africa, however, the war was going badly for the Allies. In December 1941 Operation *CRUSADER* pushed the Axis forces back through Cyrenaica. But the effort drained British resources and was soon reversed. In June 1942 Rommel's *Afrika-Korps* captured Tobruk with its 35,000-strong Allied garrison. This German triumph caused worldwide shock. Churchill was distraught, calling it not merely a defeat but a disgrace. The British were driven back into Egypt and officials in Cairo began to burn secret papers and dust contingency plans for withdrawal from Egypt. This proved, however, to be the limit of Rommel's achievement in North Africa. In August General Bernard Montgomery took command of the British Eighth Army—the 'desert rats', as their opponents dubbed them, but they wore the nickname with pride. Spurred on by Churchill, greatly reinforced, and emboldened by ULTRA intelligence that provided him with details of the enemy's deployment and assured him of the superiority of his forces in men, tanks and guns, Montgomery launched his counter-punch at El Alamein in the Western desert on 23 October. After thirteen days he won a decisive victory that determined the outcome of the campaign in North Africa.

In November 1942 the Americans at last entered the fray on land against the Germans, when forces under General Dwight D. Eisenhower initiated

Operation *TORCH* against French north-west Africa. Franco's Spain judiciously remained inactive as Allied forces built up at Gibraltar. Darlan, who was in Algiers at the time of the Allied landings, ordered French forces to lay down their arms without a fight. He and the other French military commanders in Morocco and Algeria, bending with the western wind, quickly switched allegiance to the Allies, so that both countries were occupied without resistance. Darlan paid dearly for his repeated tergiversations: he was assassinated soon afterwards. The Germans, caught between Montgomery's forces advancing from the east (too slowly, according to some retrospective critics) and Eisenhower's in the west, regrouped in Tunisia for a final stand.

TORCH had far-reaching consequences on the French mainland. Some senior French army commanders in unoccupied France thought to seize the opportunity to turn against the Germans. But Pétain resisted suggestions that he move with the government to Algiers. Instead he ordered the French army in North Africa to resist the invaders. The only part of the French Government that decamped to Algiers was the *Deuxième Bureau* (military intelligence service). Instead of providing the Vichy regime with the opportunity to redeem itself in the eyes of the Allies, *TORCH* led the Germans to enter the Unoccupied Zone on 11 November in order to ensure continued French collaboration. Mussolini was rewarded with an enlarged occupation zone in the south-east plus Corsica. The whole of the hexagon was now under Axis occupation.

In November 1942 Axis domination of Europe thus reached its largest territorial extent. Either directly or through his junior allies and minions, Hitler ruled a greater area of the continent than Trajan, Charlemagne, or Napoleon had ever done. Each of these predecessors had used his immense power to inaugurate vast civilizing projects. Hitler used his to enforce an unprecedented descent into organized barbarism.

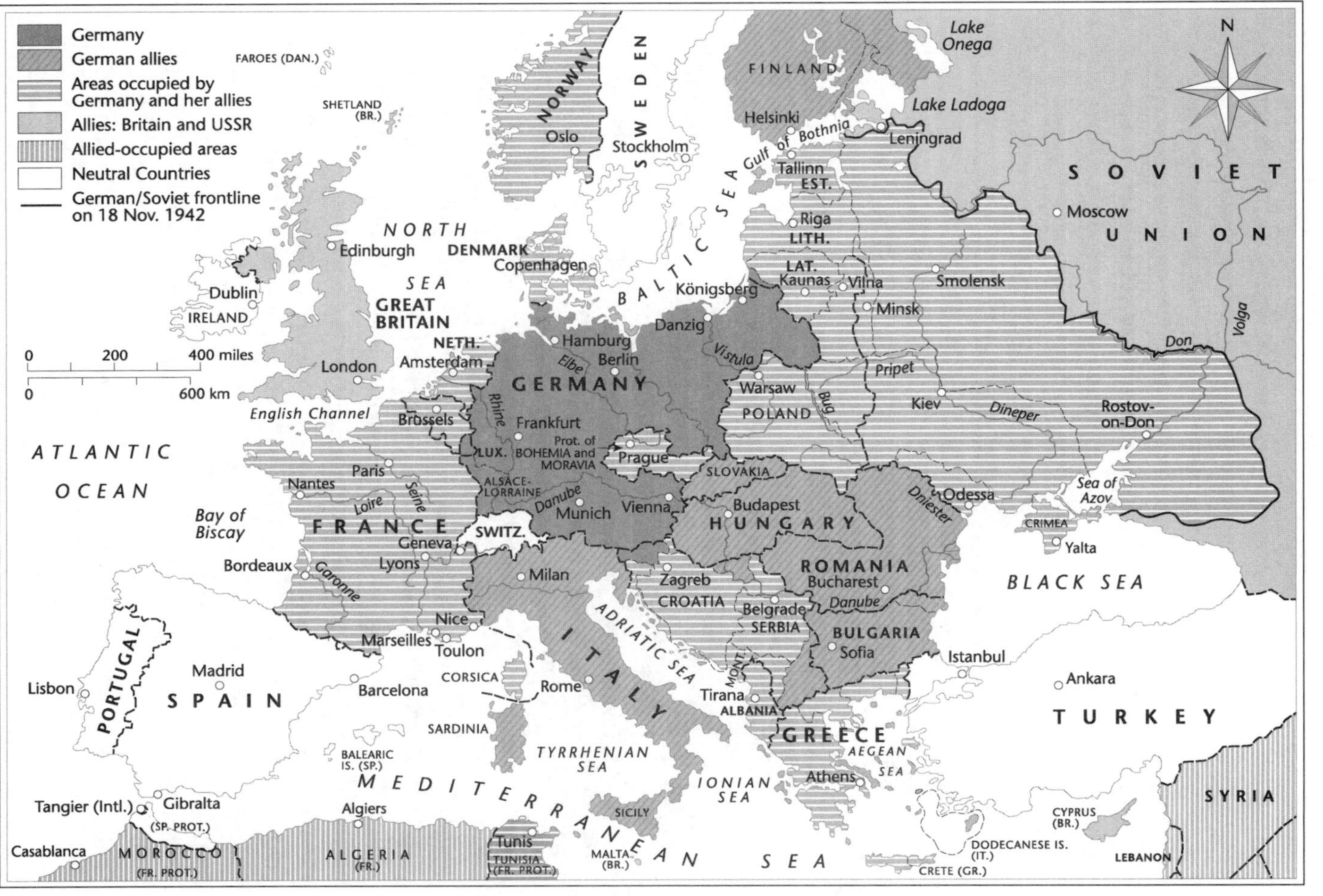

Map 5. Axis-dominated Europe (late November 1942)

9

Life and Death in Wartime

Black milk of daybreak we drink it at sundown
We drink it at noon in the morning we drink it at night
We drink and we drink it

*Paul Celan, Czernowitz, 1944**

War economies

With the failure of the Blitzkrieg strategy, the conflict changed in character. Blitzkrieg had been based on the notion that Germany could achieve decisive victory without full-scale adaptation of her economy to the demands of long-term total war. By the winter of 1941/2 Hitler's concept of warfare had frozen into oblivion in the ice near Moscow. The two coalitions were instead now engaged in a struggle that would be determined by a strategic equation in which command of raw materials, industrial infrastructure, mass production capacity, manpower reserves, advanced technology, transportation capability, and flexibility of social organization ultimately translated into military power. In all these spheres, the Allies were able, eventually, to build a decisive foundation for victory.

In spite of all the fears engendered by Germany's remilitarization in the late 1930s, her economy was ill-adapted to the demands of a long war. All German planning assumptions until late 1941 had been based on the expectation of short, sharp victories. Raw materials, such as coal, oil, iron ore, and rubber were in short supply and depended heavily on imports or substitution. Especially after the German push towards the Soviet oilfields in the Caucasus stalled, the Germans became heavily reliant on Romanian oil

* From 'Death Fugue', translated from the German by Michael Hamburger. *Poems of Paul Celan*, New York, 1995, 63.

from Ploeşti. But production there was inadequate to meet German demand. In addition to lack of fuel in the winter of 1941/2, the German army in the east suffered other shortages—of aircraft, vehicles, and ammunition. German industry was slow in gearing up to make good the deficiencies in weapons and equipment. The 1,660 German fighter planes produced in the second half of 1941 did not replace the 1,823 lost by the Luftwaffe in the same period. Bomber production too fell short of losses. The Wehrmacht was told that food supplies from Germany were unavailable and soldiers would have to forage and live off the land.

Only in late 1941 did Germany's economic strategy change. Movement towards an economic policy based on recognition that Germany faced a long war began under the direction of Fritz Todt, Minister of Armaments and Munitions. The conversion gathered pace under Albert Speer, who succeeded Todt in February 1942, after the latter's death in an accident. Speer secured a relatively free hand from Hitler to centralize and rationalize the German war economy. He expanded the power of the ministry and redirected resources and energies away from civilian consumption towards mass production of war *matériel*. In spite of setbacks on the battlefield and large-scale enemy bombing, output tripled over the next three years, attaining its peak as late as September 1944 (according to one estimate even later, December 1944). In the second half of 1944 Germany produced five times as many tanks as Britain. Germany manufactured 41,000 planes (and her ally Japan another 28,000) in 1944. But even this colossal effort could not compete with the Allies: the US, USSR, and UK together in the same year made 163,000. Overall wartime armaments production by the Allies is estimated to have exceeded that of the Germans by a ratio of 9:2. This figure alone spelt the ultimate doom of the Third Reich. The Germans could compensate to some extent by the superiority of much of their weapons, the generally higher fighting quality of their forces, and their lower loss rate of equipment in the field. But over the long haul the Germans, with their shrinking territorial base, could not match the combined resources of their enemies.

From 1941 onwards, as Germany encountered resource limits at home, she turned to occupied Europe to replenish her raw materials, manufacturing potential, and labour needs. Her aim was to build a self-sufficient *Grosswirtschaftsraum* (Great Economic Area) in Europe under her domination: a core industrial region, based on the expanded Reich, was to be supplied with raw materials and food by a periphery of politico-economic dependencies. Existing manufacturing capacity in occupied territory, mainly in western Europe, was to be exploited but was accorded secondary priority in new investment. Soon after the armistice, French firms began manufacturing warplanes, ships, optical equipment, communications cables, sheet metal, turbines, and motors for their former enemies. The submarine base at Saint-Nazaire, vital for the Germans in the Battle of the Atlantic, and the 'Atlantic Wall', a vast defensive barrier against potential Allied invasion and the largest construction project in wartime France, were constructed by labourers (many of them forced) working for French companies that made handsome profits out of such contracts. By late 1943 40 per cent of French industrial output was for German purposes. Dutch industry, both management and workers, similarly supplied German military needs as a top priority. The head of the Dutch economics ministry, Hans Max Hirschfeld, was, in spite of his German-Jewish origin, exceptionally retained in his post by the German occupation authorities throughout the war. By 1944, under his direction, half of Dutch industrial production, rising to more than 80 per cent in the electrical, shipbuilding, aircraft, and precision engineering sectors, was devoted to meeting orders from Germany.

Nazi exploitation of industry in occupied Europe, however, ran into a roadblock arising from Germany's ever-more-acute domestic labour shortage. The inexorable drain of military mobilization and battlefield casualties on civilian manpower was so severe that the total number of Germans in the German industrial labour force decreased from 10.4 million in July 1939 to 7.5 million five years later. Speer favoured even more vigorous exploitation of industrial capacity and available labour in occupied Europe. But on this he was overriden by the Reich Plenipotentiary-General for Labour, Fritz Sauckel, who preferred transferring labour to Germany to meet the clamant requirements of German industry. Rather than seeking to expand manufacturing capacity elsewhere to the full, therefore, the Germans moved large numbers of foreign workers to factories or labour camps in Germany. By August 1944 7.6 million foreigners, most of them forced labourers, were at work in Germany. Of these 1.9 million were prisoners of war, the rest civilians. One-third of the total were women. Many worked in conditions akin to slavery. And some were actual slaves.

The overall results were probably counter-productive for the German war effort. While German output increased, elsewhere in the Nazi empire it shrank. In France industrial production fell steadily during the occupation: by 1943 it had diminished to 56 per cent of 1939 levels. Foreign workers, even under brutal labour camp regimes, were less productive in the long run than they might have been at home. Moreover, nothing so fuelled hatred of the occupiers as the demand for forced labour. In France, for example, industrial workers were initially invited by the Vichy government to go to work in Germany voluntarily, as a patriotic duty, in return for which French prisoners of war would be repatriated. But few volunteered and even fewer prisoners returned. Under the *Service du Travail Obligatoire* (STO) law of February 1943, large numbers of French workers were compulsorily recruited for labour service in Germany. Over a million were conscripted but the law served also as a recruiting sergeant for the resistance.

In this as in other ways, the Germans failed to draw efficiently on the productive potential of occupied Europe. Until too late, their economic policies in captured territory amounted more commonly to 'smash and grab' than to a coherent long-term strategy. At the most primitive level, Germany's war of annihilation in the east, with its corollary concept of 'useless mouths', offered scope for ruthless economic exploitation. Wherever the invaders went, the standard of living of the civilian population was greatly reduced as resources of all kinds were utilized in the interest of the Reich. In Poland, the occupied Soviet Union, and elsewhere, the local population was reduced to starvation rations while food was sequestered for the German army or for export to Germany. The Germans' very brutality defeated their own long-term interests. The Wehrmacht requisitioned or stole grain, cattle, horses and winter clothing; peasants were displaced from their houses; the order was even issued that 'felt boots be ruthlessly taken off the civilian population'.[1] In many parts of Nazi Europe, the agrarian economy virtually collapsed. In Greece German exactions led in the winter of 1941/2 to a terrible famine in which an estimated 300,000 people perished. Inevitably the bootless, homeless, horseless, starving peasant, who might have been violently anti-Bolshevik on the eve of the occupation, became economically inactive and politically anti-Nazi.

Whereas Germany's economic coordination with her Italian and Japanese allies was almost non-existent, Anglo-American coordination was intimate, systematically organized, and effective. The objectives of pooling resources, manufacturing capacity, and transportation (especially shipping) were generally achieved. Under the pressure of war, these capitalist economies moved with greater alacrity than the National Socialists towards planning, controls, and centralization. The Allies, especially after the German setback in the Battle of the Atlantic, were able to use their command of the oceans to tighten their economic blockade of Nazi Europe and to augment the Soviet war effort. Allied (mainly American) assistance reached the USSR by Arctic convoys and across the Bering Strait, as well as by land through Iran. It mainly took the form of military equipment and vehicles. In 1943 and 1944 such aid is estimated to have contributed as much as 20 per cent of total Soviet net national product. For the war as a whole its value was ten billion dollars. This massive transfer was a one-way flow: taking its name from the original programme of assistance to Britain, it was still called 'Lend-Lease' but it was really a gift. Stalin was never satisfied, frequently complaining to Churchill and Roosevelt about the quantity and quality of deliveries and pointing out with some bitterness that the Soviet Union bore the overwhelming brunt of the fighting.

For the most part, though, the Soviets had to rely on themselves. Soviet survival and eventual victory were built on almost endless geographical depth and almost infinite capacity to absorb human losses. They also recouped their investment in heavy industry in the 1930s, creating a manufacturing powerhouse for tanks, planes, and other weapons of war that made up in sheer quantity for what was often their inferior quality, particularly in precision items, as compared with German *matériel*. They succeeded in moving factories, machinery, and 25 million people wholesale from the western parts of the USSR to regions beyond the Urals that were secure from German land forces or air attack. As early as 29 June 1941, a scorched-earth policy had been decreed, calling for 'removal of all rolling stock, leaving the enemy not a single locomotive, not a truck, not a kilogramme of bread, not a litre of fuel. Collective farmers must drive away their cattle . . . all property of [any value] . . . which cannot be taken away must, without any exceptions, be destroyed.'[2] Soviet national income declined in 1941–2 owing to loss of territory in the west and barely recovered by the end of the war. Nevertheless, between 1940 and 1944 Soviet war production quadrupled. In 1942 24,000 tanks and 21,000 military aircraft were produced (the equivalent figures for Germany were 9,300 tanks and 15,000 aircraft). Total Soviet munitions production in 1942 was double the previous year's in spite of the catastrophic losses of fixed capital in the western occupied regions. Altogether during the war the USSR produced 100,000 tanks, 130,000 aircraft, and 800,000 field guns and mortars.

This emphasis on defence production was at a terrible cost and led to gross imbalances in the Soviet economy. In the first year of the war, output of steel, coal, non-ferrous metals, and ball-bearings all decreased. The civilian economy teetered on the brink of collapse. Agricultural output declined catastrophically as a result of the loss of the 'black earth' regions of Ukraine and southern Russia, the slaughter of herds, de-mechanization, disappearance of draught animals, and absence of able-bodied manpower. Total food production in 1943 was barely half that for 1940. Much of the population hovered on the brink of death from starvation in 1942–3. The centrally planned Soviet system, temporarily thrown into chaos at the outbreak of war, took more than two years to achieve something approaching an optimal balance.

Home fronts

The Soviet Union was the most extreme case but throughout the continent allocation of resources to war production meant that civilian consumption declined and populations were condemned to ever-more-meagre rations. German rationing policy in occupied Europe was organized on a racial scale: Germans got most, Norwegians a little less, French less still, Slavs a lot less, Jews least. For example, the bread and flour ration for Jews in occupied Poland in October 1941 was 580 grams a week; for Poles it was 1,490 grams a week. These were official levels: often the level of actual supply was lower. By comparison, Germans in April 1942 were being allocated 2,000 grams and German heavy-industry workers between 3,400 and 4,400 grams. When, later that year, cuts in food rations were instituted in Germany, there was serious popular discontent and the government was careful not to go further so long as additional limitation could be avoided. Until almost the end of the war, the German civilian population was the most amply fed in Europe. In Britain, butter, sugar, and meat were rationed, but not bread or potatoes. Official policy forced the population on to a healthier diet that included more brown bread, milk, and vegetables. Nutritious but unappetizing items such as whalemeat, snoek, and 'spam' provided much scope for national grumbling. The Ministry of Food encouraged various forms of substitution, such as 'mock cream' (made from milk, margarine, and cornflour), and 'mock goose' (potatoes, cooking apples, and cheese). In Italy coffee was banned from cafés, though many continued to serve it so long as it was available. French caloric intake is said to have suffered the steepest decline in western Europe—to an average of around 1,500 per day, though, of course, there as elsewhere the average masked big differences between town and country. Populations of neutral states were rationed no less than belligerents: in Sweden, notionally self-sufficient in food production, 70 per cent of all foodstuffs were rationed by 1942. The worst privations were felt in the Balkans and the Soviet Union. Red Army soldiers and some manual workers, such as miners, were assigned a nutritionally adequate food ration—but often they did not receive the official allocation. Soviet peasants, most of whose output was seized by the state, were driven to depend on their tiny private allotments. Most of the Soviet urban population subsisted between 1941 and 1944 on the edge of starvation. In besieged Leningrad, where the only supply route in the first winter of the siege was across the frozen Lake Ladoga, a million civilians, a third of the population, perished, mainly from hunger and disease; famished people gnawed at old boots, dead cats, and rats; there were reports of cannibalism.

Rationing applied not only to food but also to clothing, fuel, soap, and in some places tobacco. In Britain controls were introduced on the manufacture of domestic appliances, pots and pans, furniture, toys, jewelry, cosmetics, umbrellas, and even pencils. Across Europe fuel was earmarked almost entirely for military and industrial uses, leaving civilians with little heat and frequent power cuts. In Sweden a government decree in 1942 forbade the use of hot water in private homes without special permission. In most countries private motor cars were allowed only minimal amounts of petroleum and were often converted to alternative fuels or laid up for the duration of the war. Vehicles were propelled by wood or charcoal derivatives. In Paris and other cities shortage of petrol led to the proliferation in city streets of pedal-powered taxis and horse-drawn carts. Bicycle traffic increased (in Sweden three million bicycles were in use in 1942 as against almost no private cars), though in the Netherlands and elsewhere the Germans tried to sequester cycles.

Queuing, particularly for food, became an inevitable and time-consuming activity, especially for women. People survived by recourse to 'black' and 'grey' markets or to what was called in France *Système D* ('D' for *débrouillage*). In Britain and other countries, rackets developed in stolen or 'lost' ration-books and coupons or those allegedly destroyed in air raids. Almost everywhere non-rationed food could be found for sale at multiples of the official price. Eggs and poultry were smuggled from Ireland to Britain. In Italy, where pasta was rationed, it was available on the black market. Sugar too was rationed but peasants in Italian mountain regions, who often had no tradition of using it, happily sold their allocations. Shortages inevitably fed inflation. In Greece the official price of bread rose in the year after June 1941 from 70 to 2,350 drachmas; the black-market price, of course, was much higher. In many places money ceased to have value and people resorted to barter or used gold, cigarettes, or other commodities as currency.

Everywhere people worked harder. Unemployment declined in all the major belligerent states: in Britain and Germany it disappeared and was replaced by acute labour shortage. So too in the USSR, where unemployment had officially never existed since the revolution. Working hours increased—in Britain to an average of fifty per week in 1943. Strikes were banned in most European countries: in Britain they were not eliminated altogether but the number of workdays lost to labour disputes declined below one million, the lowest figure since records began, though stoppages rose again towards the end of the war.

The most significant change in the labour market was the rapid proportional increase in women's employment. The shift was registered most decisively in the USSR, where women's share of industrial employment rose from 38 per cent in 1940 to 57 per cent by 1943. A quarter of all Soviet mineworkers were women in 1942. By the end of the war 80 per cent of the labour force on collective farms was female (the remainder were mainly children and old people). In Britain an additional 2.5 million women went out to work between 1939 and 1943; their share in the labour force rose from 27 to 37 per cent. Generally, however, they continued to be paid at lower rates than men. In Germany ideological preconceptions at first prevented maximization of the potential for women's labour. Wives of servicemen in Germany received much higher allowances than in Britain and so were less attracted to work. After Stalingrad women between seventeen and forty (like men between sixteen and sixty-five) were made liable to labour conscription, though until September 1944, at Hitler's insistence, housemaids were exempt. By 1944 just over half the civilian labour force (excluding foreign workers) was female. But most of these were in non-industrial employment: the number of German women working in industry in mid-1944 was no greater than it had been at the start of the war. Elsewhere, wartime stringencies often led to a dichotomy between official ideology and social reality: in Vichy France, for example, which, like Nazi Germany and Fascist Italy, stressed the role of women in the home and family, economic pressures forced increasing numbers of women into the workplace.

Although the home front was, in general, a much grimmer environment in this than in the previous world war, one dimension of human suffering eased. Medical advances before and during the war greatly alleviated the pain and diminished the mortality rate of the wounded, civilian as well as military. On the battlefield the ratio of killed to wounded rose ('As the precision and lethality of weapons increase, the proportion of killed among the casualties enlarges,' the British official history laid down). At the same time the recovery rate of the wounded also increased ('As the power to control infection and to counteract the effects of haemorrhage enlarges, as surgical techniques improve and as evacuation becomes more speedy and comfortable, the recovery rate rises').[3] The stationing of emergency surgical units nearer the front line as well as more efficient motorized and airborne ambulance services helped many more of the injured to survive. New techniques in orthopaedics saved the limbs of many wounded men. Until the late 1930s blood could be stored only a few hours. The invention in 1939 of the first sterile, vacuum-type blood storage unit increased the maximum storage period from a few hours to twenty-eight days, thus making blood banks practicable. The storage of dried blood plasma became routine during the war, first in the British, later in the German army. Blood transfusions played a major part in saving lives of military and civilian wounded. Immunization greatly reduced the death rate from tetanus. Venereal disease was treated by the use of sulphonamide drugs and, in the later part of the war, by penicillin. Although discovered by Sir Alexander Fleming in 1928, its enormous therapeutic efficacy became understood only as a result of the research at Oxford of Howard Florey and Ernst Boris Chain. They showed that it could be concentrated as a stable dry powder. It began to be manufactured on a large scale in 1942 (in the USA) and was used by the British army, later elsewhere, to treat a wide range of bacterial infections.

As in all previous wars, one of the commonest causes of military death was not hostile action but disease, often the result of poor sanitation and hygiene. Typhus, tuberculosis, diphtheria, dysentery, malaria, and hepatitis claimed millions of victims, especially in southern and eastern Europe. In Greece malaria caused greater damage to the German army than the activities of the resistance. European troops stationed in other continents were particularly vulnerable to disease, as were those who endured squalid conditions in Japanese, Russian, and German POW camps. The German army, we are told, 'exhibited, to a much greater degree than their British counterparts, an anachronistic masculine code that viewed sickness as a sign of weakness and medicine as a form of pampering'.[4] The superior hygiene of the British Eighth Army in Egypt helped it field a much higher proportion of its fighting troops than Rommel's *Afrika Korps*. On the other hand, the Germans operated on more realistic principles than the British in dealing with sexually transmitted diseases. The chief venereologist for British forces in the Middle East insisted in 1942 that 'control of V.D. is a matter of discipline and "morale" much more than of medical measures. Self-discipline comes first.'[5] The Archbishop of Canterbury agreed, condemning the distribution of prophylactics to soldiers on the ground that it would encourage fornication. 'A man can keep fit without a woman,' was the message instilled in a pamphlet handed to convalescent British soldiers in 1943.[6] Montgomery, however, took a different view: he established a hygienically controlled military brothel in Alexandria, arguing that his men 'deserved it'.[7]

The home front, like the battlefront, in this war was not static. Millions of people were persuaded or forced to leave their homes, in some cases several times, often never to return. Ethnic Germans in eastern Europe were dragooned into a process of *Wiedereindeutschung* ('becoming German again'). They and many other Germans were settled in newly conquered territories as a supposed vanguard of the new empire. Polish names of cities and streets were Germanized. The main thoroughfare of every Polish city was renamed Adolf-Hitler-Strasse. An estimated 1.5 million Poles were forcibly moved out of German-annexed territories into occupied areas and at least 160,000 children were torn away from their parents and sent to Germany to be 'Germanized'. After the fall of France 200,000 French citizens were expelled from Alsace by the German authorities. The Soviets, like the Germans, engaged in wholesale movement of populations regarded as hostile or under suspicion. Between 1941 and 1944 Stalin's secret police chief, Lavrenty Beria, supervised the deportation of over a million Chechens, Ingushetians, and other peoples of the northern Caucasus, as well as Volga Germans and Crimean Tatars (among whom the Nazis had recruited volunteer units), from their homelands to Siberia, Kazakhstan, and Uzbekistan. Thousands were shot or died in the course of deportation. Many were sent to forced labour camps from which a high proportion never returned.

Wars of the mind

Propaganda, now subsumed in the 'fourth arm' of 'psychological warfare', played an even more prominent role in this war than in the First World War. The main media of persuasion were radio, film, newspapers, and leaflets. In the course of the war British-based aircraft alone dropped no fewer than six billion leaflets over Nazi Europe. Paper allocation for this enterprise averaged a thousand tons a month. Both sides also introduced new, sometimes ingenious techniques, including the 'talking tank', spoof newspapers (such as *Paris noir*, a German parody of *Paris soir*) and the dissemination of forged enemy currency and *Passierscheine* (documents promising safety to soldiers who surrendered). So long as the Germans held the upper hand in the battlefield, their intimidatory and propaganda onslaught was irrepressible. But when the fortunes of war shifted in the winter of 1942/3, their message lost conviction both at home and abroad. Goebbels, for one, understood this and warned newspaper editors in January 1943 that German propaganda had pursued an erroneous course: 'first year of the war: we have won. Second year of the war: we shall win. Third year of the war: we must win. Fourth year of the war: we cannot be defeated.' Such a progression, he maintained (prophetically) was 'catastrophic'.[8]

Radio became the primary means by which leaders communicated with their peoples. Churchill's radio speeches, in spite of rhetorical flourishes better adapted to Parliament or the platform, stiffened the resolve of the nation. Daladier was an effective radio performer but French broadcast propaganda in the first year of the war was widely criticized. Pétain's paternalistic authority was enhanced by his addresses over the airwaves. André Gide wrote on 16 June 1940 that the Marshal's 'words console us more than all the blowhards of the radio'.[9] Hitler's rasping screech, heard with diminishing frequency in the later part of the war, seemingly ill-adapted to the medium, nevertheless enabled him to maintain his mesmeric hold on German popular feeling.

The BBC's reputation for reliability and accuracy in its news reporting was unmatched during the war years. By December 1943 it was broadcasting forty-three hours a week in German, thirty-nine in French, twenty-nine in Italian, and for shorter periods in at least eighteen other European languages. Its news bulletins were listened to, often in secret and at great risk (the penalties were severe) throughout occupied Europe. Except for a short time in 1942–3, there were no regular BBC broadcasts to the Soviet Union during the war: initially it was reckoned that the Soviet population with their mainly 'wired' sets would not be able to receive them; later the policy was maintained, on Foreign Office insistence, so as not to upset the Soviet government. The BBC probably came closer than any other broadcasting organization during the war to separating news from propaganda—'straightforward news good or bad, told simply but with punch'.[10] Its overseas transmissions were, however, subject to guidance from the Political Warfare Executive, headed by the former intelligence agent Robert Bruce Lockhart. The BBC's German Service scored a hit with a programme of hot jazz and swing music, banned by Goebbels in Germany. But it was for long hampered by a directive not to employ anti-Nazi German émigrés, although this was eventually relaxed.

Radio could not reach everybody. In southern and eastern Europe relatively few private homes boasted a set. In much of Nazi-occupied Europe, particularly Poland and the Netherlands, radio ownership was prohibited and sets were confiscated. The Germans, Italians, and Russians jammed enemy broadcasts. So did the French in 1939–40. The Russians sometimes broke into German home broadcasts with interpolations such as 'Lies! Lies!' The British did not jam: A BBC statement in May 1940 boldly declared, 'The jammer has a bad conscience . . . He is afraid of the influence of the truth. . . . In our country we have no such fears.'[11] The BBC also laid down that 'normal courtesy titles' such as 'Herr Hitler' and 'Marshall Goering' would be generally used in broadcasts.[12] A policy memorandum on *Children's Hour* warned that 'jokes about Nazi leaders' were 'sternly discouraged'.[13]

By contrast with the sophisticated approach of British broadcasters, most German radio propaganda to Britain was woefully ineffective. The Germans' star English-language performer, the American-born former Mosleyite, William Joyce, became something of a laughing stock and acquired the unflattering sobriquet 'Lord Haw-Haw' (a strange misnomer apparently arising from a confusion of identities between him and another Berlin announcer). His French-language equivalent, Paul Ferdonnet, 'the traitor of [Radio] Stuttgart', was easily heard on the Maginot Line and plugged an insidiously anti-British line, designed to sow inter-Allied disaffection.

Domestic programmes in Germany were directly controlled by Goebbels; in Britain the BBC's home service was susceptible to more gentle steering (no political questions were allowed on the immensely popular *Brains Trust* discussion programme). During the Battle of Britain the BBC broadcast British aircraft losses fairly accurately but greatly exaggerated German ones; German radio made hugely disproportionate claims in both spheres. Both the BBC and German home radio stations broadcast widely influential commentaries on the news: in Germany by Hans Fritzsche, in Britain by J. B. Priestley. In the early campaigns of the war, propaganda units attached to the advancing German armies broadcast vivid 'Front Reports' that the BBC began to emulate only in 1944.

After the French armistice in 1940, French radio was divided between the German-directed Radio Paris and Radio Vichy, controlled until 1942 by the French. The BBC French service, animated by brilliant figures like the theatrical director Michel Saint-Denis, helped kindle a resistance spirit in France with programmes such as *Les français parlent aux français*. In addition to de Gaulle, whose broadcasts from London attracted growing attention, other speakers won a large audience in occupied France. Maurice Schumann, who was to serve from 1969 to 1973 as French Minister of Foreign Affairs, broadcast more than twelve hundred five-minute commentaries to occupied France from London between 1940 and 1944.

Radio propaganda afforded a convenient terrain for political theatre, deception, and subterfuge. The battle of the airwaves sometimes led to strange conjunctions. For example, the 'V for victory' campaign, launched by the BBC in 1941, using the morse code sign for the letter (the rhythm of the opening bar of Beethoven's Fifth Symphony) as a station identification signal, was accorded the ultimate accolade: appropriation by the Germans who adopted it themselves, creating a certain confusion in occupied Europe. 'Black' broadcasting, the use of dummy stations that disguised their real location, sponsorship, and objectives, was pioneered by the Germans in 1939 with 'Radio Humanité' and 'La Voix de la Paix', both supposedly based in France. In February 1940 the 'New British Broadcasting Station', based in East Prussia, began beaming would-be demoralizing propaganda to Britain. This was followed by 'Radio Caledonia' which called for a separate peace between Germany and Scotland. After the invasion of the USSR the Germans started a 'National Bolshevik' station that used Communist jargon to appeal to Russian workers and peasants to throw out the traitor Stalin who had 'sold out the Socialist fatherland to the plutocrats'.[14] The talented British mastermind of 'black' broadcasting, Sefton Delmer (his motto: 'never lie by accident, only deliberately'),[15] created the imaginative 'Gustav Siegfried Eins' and 'Soldatensender Calais' stations, although one BBC official complained that the latter was so funny that it might raise rather than depress the morale of its enemy audience. Some bright ideas had to be abandoned: for example, in 1944 it was proposed that an exiled German actor who was an expert Hitler impersonator might be employed on a 'black' station to broadcast a dummy 'Hitler' speech in which the Führer would call on all German soldiers in the west to leave their posts immediately and move to the east to confront the Communists: this was rejected by the Americans who feared that Stalin might take it seriously as evidence of collusion between the western allies and Hitler. Remarkably, the proposal was almost a mirror-image of the suggestion by a Russian propagandist in 1942 that the Soviets should set up a 'black station' that would broadcast bogus messages by 'a group of old German generals' calling for Russo-German cooperation; the objective would be to scare the western allies with the prospect of a separate Soviet–German peace, thus hastening their implementation of a 'second front'.

After news, most people listened to the radio for music. The greatest hit song of the war, one which soared over all frontiers and ideologies into men's hearts, was a haunting, sentimental German ballad composed by Norbert Schultze in Vienna in 1938 to words written during the First World War by a German soldier, Hans Leip. For a time *Lili Marlene* was banned in Germany (Goebbels disapproved) but after Rommel lent it his imprimatur the melody crossed from the *Afrika Korps* to the British Eighth Army and then to the world. Curiously, although the lyric expressed a soldier's yearning for his sweetheart, all the most popular performances were by female artists. It was heard on disc, radio, and stage in every major European language. After the first German recording by Lale Andersen, others were issued by Ann Shelton, Vera Lynn, Marlene Dietrich, and (the most beautiful) by the Hungarian film star Ilona Nagykovácsi. The BBC broadcast an anti-Hitler version; perhaps by way of counter-attack, there was also an indifferent rendering by the choir of the sixth Panzergrenadier division.

Like broadcasting, newspaper and book publishing throughout Europe were subjected to censorship, sometimes in the form of 'guidance', elsewhere in more heavy-handed form. Throughout occupied Europe the Communist and Socialist press was closed or driven underground. In Britain there was little formal censorship, except of military dispositions, but the Communist *Daily Worker* was banned during the early part of the war and the mass-circulation *Daily Mirror* was denounced by Churchill in 1941 for 'rocking the boat' and threatened with closure a year later.[16] Censorship also applied in other spheres. All foreign and much domestic mail was subject to official examination. Telephone calls were intercepted. Weather forecasts were banned in most belligerent countries on the ground that they might aid the enemy.

Except when disrupted by bombing, cinema attendance remained high during the war. Everywhere there was an insatiable hunger for newsreel, which German propaganda used to good effect, at any rate so long as the Germans were winning. American films were banned in Germany after late 1940. German wartime productions, closely supervised by Goebbels, sought to compensate by focusing mainly on escapist lightweight entertainment. But propaganda films also attracted wide audiences, notably the anti-Semitic *Jud Süss* (1940), directed by Veit Harlan. His costume drama *Kolberg* (January 1945), the most expensive film ever made in Nazi Germany, portrayed the resolute defence of a Prussian fortress under French siege in 1807; a cinema was specially rebuilt for it in bombed-out Berlin but renewed massive bombardment meant that few people were able to see it. Hitler and Goebbels pronounced the film 'more useful than a military victory'.[17] They were not the only ones to take comfort from cinematic fantasy: Jan Struther's *Mrs Miniver*, published in 1939 before the outbreak of the war, transformed on the screen into a display of stiff British upper lip during the Blitz, was pronounced by Churchill to be worth six divisions to the war effort.

Book publishing during the war purveyed a similar mixture of propaganda and escapism. Within Germany, although Jewish and left-wing authors were banned, literature was not totally suffocated by ideological strictures. The best-selling books of the war years tended to be non-political: escapist fiction and romantic novels. According to an analysis of the top forty German wartime best-sellers, only ten were 'genuinely Nazi'. The rest included such works as *Gone with the Wind* and Karl May's stories of the wild west, the latter much loved by Hitler.[18] In France most publishers conformed without protest to the Germans' censorship lists. Soviet writers poured forth patriotic reportage, such as the novels of Konstantin Simonov (notably *Days and Nights*, a depiction of the battle for Stalingrad). They also produced anti-German hate propaganda. Ilya Ehrenburg, in his press commentaries, raided the zoological lexicon, calling German soldiers 'brown lice', 'skunks', 'spiders in a bottle', 'lousy dogs', 'beasts of prey', 'reptiles', 'pigs', 'mad wolves', 'scorpions', 'bugs', 'vermin', 'vipers', and 'rats'. 'The rivers', he declared, 'will cast out their foul bodies and the earth will vomit their remains.'[19] Not for nothing was Ehrenburg called a 'literary machine-gun'.[20] As in the First World War, artists and intellectuals happily volunteered to fling verbal mud at the enemy and justify war crimes.

Nor were men of the cloth exempt from patriotic mobilization. The Church of England supported the war against Nazism as a crusade: the Bishop of Exeter called it a war between 'the pagan and the Christian way'. Archbishops Temple of Canterbury and Garbett of York both defended obliteration bombing of Germany. It was left to the Bishop of Chichester, George Bell, to caution that the Church must not become the State's 'spiritual auxiliary'. But in May 1941 his speech to the Upper House of Bishops denouncing reprisal bombing of Germany was shouted down by his episcopal brethren and censored so that not a word of it reached the public.[21] In 1943 he was barred from preaching at a Battle of Britain commemoration service in his own cathedral.

In the USSR the Orthodox Church, under somewhat stricter state control, was given great public prominence during the war. Churches reopened and the Moscow Patriarchate, unoccupied since 1925, was restored in 1943. One motive was to mobilize patriotism; another to help integrate Orthodox populations in the annexed western territories; and a third to present the illusion of Soviet religious freedom to Stalin's western allies. These objectives were imperfectly attained but the war years saw an outpouring of long-suppressed religious sentiment.

Elsewhere too religion enjoyed something of a resurgence during the war as humanity sought solace, inspiration, and hope for a better future. This was true even in neutral Sweden where, in 1941, the Riksdag (parliament) and the Assembly of the state Lutheran Church held a common session in which they affirmed that 'the Swedish way is the Christian way'.[22]

Little space remained anywhere for the individual non-conformist conscience. With the exception of Britain, where conscientious objection to military service was legally less cumbrous and socially somewhat less unacceptable than in earlier wars, most states insisted on their right to harness the minds and bodies of their subjects. In Germany and the Soviet Union no right to refrain from military service was admitted. The handful of objectors in Germany, most of them Jehovah's Witnesses, almost all paid for their refusal with their lives.

Neutrals

Individuals could not abstain from warfare; sovereign states could—and six did. The Irish Free State, Portugal, Spain, Switzerland, Turkey, and Sweden succeeded in remaining aloof from the fighting through all, or most, of the war. Yet while maintaining formal neutrality, these countries found themselves sucked inexorably into the whirlpool. Neutrality was a relative, not an absolute, concept in the conditions of Nazi Europe. Military, economic, and diplomatic pressures from all sides pulled neutrals towards one or other of the combatants. Most of the neutrals were, in effect, neutral in favour of Germany in the period 1940 to 1942, when German power was at its zenith. After that, as the tide turned, even Fascist Spain adjusted her foreign policy to evolving realities and began to curry favour with the Allies.

The neutrals found themselves hemmed in by the economic warfare of both belligerent coalitions. Portugal, Spain, Sweden, and Turkey were important sources of metallic ores vital to the German war effort. After the attack on the Soviet Union, which had sold wolframite (tungsten) to the Nazis, the Germans depended on mines in Portugal and Spain for imports of this mineral. With the highest melting point and lowest vapour pressure of all metals, it was critically important in armaments production: Hitler in 1943 called it *kriegsentscheidend* (decisive for the outcome of the war).[23] The British devoted great diplomatic and naval efforts to restricting the supply of such ores to Germany by the neutrals although it was only in the later part of the war that they were able to persuade producing countries to reduce these exports. The foreign trade of Sweden, in particular, was severely affected by British blockade restrictions and by the occupation of Norway and Denmark. As British supplies of coal and coke were cut off, these were imported from Germany, which had always been Sweden's largest trading partner. Such economic considerations rather than political sympathy lay behind the Swedish decision in 1940 to permit the Germans to move military forces and equipment by rail across the country to German-occupied Norway and later to Germany's ally, Finland.

Istanbul, Stockholm, Berne, and Lisbon became arenas for competitive intelligence jousting by agents of the warring parties. In these neutral capitals discreet contacts could be maintained and 'peace feelers' explored, enemy newspapers could be obtained and analysed, and spies could carry out acts of derring-do. In Lisbon a British double agent code-named 'Tricycle', in fact a Yugoslav citizen, Duško Popov, tricked the German secret service into thinking he was a faithful servant of the Reich, dispatching misleading information to Berlin that proved of great value to the Allies. In Turkey a German agent, 'Cicero' (Elyesa Bazna), obtained employment as the British ambassador's valet and stole high-security papers from his master's safe.

Switzerland differed from the other neutrals in that whereas they were neutral by opportunistic political choice, Switzerland's perpetual armed neutrality had been recognized in international law since the Congress of Vienna in 1815 and was implicitly affirmed in her constitution. But there as elsewhere strategic and economic pressures, ideological sympathies, and personal prejudice also played their parts in determining what form neutrality would take. Among German-speakers (nearly three-quarters of the country's population) some were sympathetic to Nazism, though rarely to the extent of compromising Swiss independence. The feeling was not reciprocated by Hitler who regarded the Swiss as 'the most disgusting and miserable people'.[24] He occasionally contemplated invading Switzerland though he found her useful as a neutral. Surrounded as she eventually was by German or German-occupied territory, Switzerland found it necessary to accede to German requirements. She therefore tolerated German violations of her airspace. She complied with a German demand for a night-time blackout of all buildings (so as not to aid British air raids on German border areas). She continued to feed 40 per cent of the electrical power supply of southern Germany. Her specialized industries exported high-quality technical equipment to the Reich. Her banks notoriously provided a haven until

March 1945 for gold looted by the Germans. And the International Red Cross (international in name, in reality a private Swiss organization), cowed by Nazi power and conforming to Swiss foreign-policy needs, did little to give succour to victims of Nazi war crimes.

The long history of nationalist antagonism against the British weighed against any prospect that the Irish Free State would enter the war at Britain's side or fulfil British requests for naval facilities. Yet seventy thousand Irishmen volunteered to serve in the British forces (not including fifty thousand servicemen, all also volunteers, from Northern Ireland). Ten thousand were killed in British uniforms. In addition, nearly 200,000 workers from the Free State emigrated to work in the British war economy between 1939 and 1945. 'Who are we neutral against?' was the question often asked in the country in the early phases of the war. The pro-Fascist Secretary to the Department of External Affairs, Joseph P. Walshe, alleged in 1940 that the British were 'now using against us all the tricks and wiles which they commonly use against small peoples'.[25] Throughout the war the Irish government denied the British access to the former 'treaty ports' that would have shortened the transatlantic supply routes for convoys sailing to Britain. All the Irish government's anti-British bluster notwithstanding, secret meetings between British and Irish officers were held from the spring of 1941 until 1944 to coordinate against the eventuality of a German invasion of the island. The military planners agreed on a contingency plan whereby British troops would advance from British-held Northern Ireland into the south to meet any German landing. Until the end of the war the Irish nevertheless inflicted irritating symbolic pinpricks on their former rulers. On 2 May 1945, following news of Hitler's death, De Valera, the Taoiseach (Prime Minister) and Minister of External Affairs, took the extraordinary step of paying a 'condolence call' on the German legation in Dublin. 'I could have had a diplomatic illness,' he explained, 'but as you know I scorn that sort of thing.'[26]

Of all the neutrals, the one in closest ideological sympathy with Hitler (and the one that owed him most) was Franco's Spain. After the fall of France, Franco was tempted to seek a cheap spoil from Hitler's war and, with German cooperation, to seize Gibraltar. But he hoped for some further tangible reward from Hitler for such a foray. On 23 October 1940 the two dictators met at Hendaye, on the French-Spanish border. Franco found Hitler reluctant to meet his demands: large-scale economic and military aid plus colonial acquisitions in North Africa at the expense of the French. After some hard bargaining, a protocol was signed in which Franco promised to enter the war at Germany's side at some future, unspecified date; but this vague undertaking was hedged round with so many conditions as to render it worthless from Hitler's point of view. Hitler said he would rather 'have three or four teeth taken out' than endure a conversation like that again.[27] Having switched from formal neutrality to 'non-belligerency' in June 1940, Spain moved to 'moral belligerency' in mid-1941. But this was all diplomatic wordplay. Franco's apologists later claimed that he had cunningly resisted German pressure to take up arms. The truth was that he was initially keen to do so but his price was higher than the Germans thought worth paying. Hitler's military chiefs, Halder and Brauchitsch, considered Spain internally 'rotten' and 'useless' as an ally and the head of the Abwehr (the German intelligence service), Admiral Canaris, called Franco 'not a hero but a little pipsqueak'.[28] Franco did grant refuelling facilities for German submarines and he dispatched the *División Azul* (Blue Division) of nineteen thousand Spanish volunteers to fight for Hitler on the Russian front. As the fortunes of war moved against the Axis, however, Franco shifted towards the Allies, stimulated in that direction by US and British trade policies. The Allies, noting the acute famine in Spain, rationed food and oil imports from the Americas according to the degree of Spanish compliance with demands for limitation of the export of iron ore and other strategic raw materials to Germany.

Hitler's dissatisfaction with Spain was more than matched by Churchill's disillusionment with Turkey. The prospect of Turkish entry into the war on the Allied side became for Churchill an *idée fixe*. He returned to it again and again. In February 1943, he visited Adana to try to persuade Turkey's leaders that the time had come. But President Inönü proved as adamantine in his resistance to Churchill's charm offensive as his predecessor, Atatürk, had been to Churchill's Dardanelles adventure in 1915. Turkish public opinion, mindful of the disasters that had followed from Ottoman involvement in the First World War, was in no mood for fighting, though Turkey did formally declare war on Germany in February 1945.

And then there was another kind of neutrality: that of some international organizations. A strange anomaly of international relations was the continued functioning, throughout the war, of the Bank for International Settlements in Basel. This 'central bank of the central banks' was felt to be so essential to international payment systems, that the warring powers, even as they engaged in economic warfare against one another, cooperated smoothly in the wartime operation of this bank, a kind of higher echelon of capitalism beyond mere earthly concerns—other than money.

Resistance and collaboration

Most Europeans, not enjoying the luxury of neutrality, were compelled by Axis rule to make choices for collaboration or resistance. In retrospect these were fixed principles and polar opposites. But in practice, resistance and collaboration, like neutrality and belligerency, are better viewed as a spectrum of attitudes. The decision for one or the other was rarely clear-cut. More often sheer personal survival dictated a multitude of shabby compromises in daily life.

Occupation regimes varied in form and character in different parts of Europe. Some areas such as Alsace and the former 'Polish corridor' were annexed and incorporated into the Reich. In central Poland a quasi-colony, the 'General Gouvernement', was ruled by a German governor, Hans Frank. Eastern Poland and the occupied Soviet Union were placed under military administration. Yugoslavia and Greece were divided into a patchwork of German, Italian, and Bulgarian occupation zones: some regions were annexed outright; elsewhere puppet governments were staffed by Axis collaborators. Croatia became nominally independent under the rule of Ante Pavelić, leader of the Fascist Ustaša movement, under whose regime large numbers of Serbs were massacred. Serbia was granted an autonomous status under the quisling administration of General Milan Nedić. In western Europe the Germans generally preferred to retain a larger element of indigenous autonomy. Denmark was ruled by her own government, under strict German supervision, until August 1943 when the Germans assumed direct control. In the Netherlands a Reichskommissar, Arthur Seyss-Inquart, exercised authority over the Dutch civil service which was instructed by the Dutch government-in-exile in London to continue to function 'in the interests of the country'.[29]

Vidkun Quisling, who served as head of the Norwegian government for much of the occupation period, became the eponym and in some ways the epitome of the cadre of collaborationist puppet rulers across Nazi Europe. The son of a rural clergyman, he took great pride in his Viking roots. After service as an army captain he had worked as a businessman in Russia in the late 1920s. He enjoyed a stormy tenure as Minister of Defence from 1931 to 1933. Proclaiming himself the heir of Nansen, in whose Russian relief effort he had served in 1921, Quisling conceived of himself as the saviour of the Norwegian nation. As early as 1930 he contacted the Nazis and the ideology of his small political party was close to theirs, especially in its anti-Marxism and anti-Semitism. By 1940 he was operating as a paid German agent in Norway, supplying military information for use in the German invasion. After his short spell in office in 1940, he wormed his way back into favour with Hitler and was reinstated as Prime Minister in January 1942. His regime sought to implement *Gleichschaltung* on the Nazi model, attacking institutions that might afford a focus for opposition: churches, the teaching profession, the press, and trade unions. In spite of the general popular hostility to his government, Quisling did enjoy some limited support. The Nobel literature laureate Knut Hamsun was strongly pro-Nazi. Five thousand Norwegians volunteered to fight with the Germans on the eastern front. But resistance to Quisling's measures was so widespread that by September 1942 the Reichskommissar, Josef Terboven, had deprived him of almost all save titular authority.

The only British territories occupied by the Germans were the internally self-governing crown dependencies of the Channel Islands. Lying off the eastern coast of Normandy, the islands were regarded by the Germans as the first step in the conquest of Britain and their occupation as an interesting test of the reactions of the British population to German rule. Although the United Kingdom was constitutionally responsible for the defence of the islands, few precautions had been taken against attack, except for the registration of homing pigeons. Concluding that the islands were of little strategic value, the British government decided on 15 June 1940 to leave them undefended. The British garrison was withdrawn and the islands were 'demilitarized'. Amidst chaos and panic about 25,000 civilians were evacuated but the remaining 60,000 inhabitants were left to their fate. Churchill found the withdrawal repugnant but was advised that there was no realistic alternative. The Germans arrived on 30 June. On the small island of Sark three days later, they encountered the formidable unarmed presence of the Dame or feudal ruler, Sybil Hathaway. She gave up her seigneurship for the duration of the occupation but bravely remained throughout with her 471 subjects. Claiming that they had liberated the islands from British colonial oppression, the Germans compelled the island administrations, which continued in office, to pass a series of measures, including anti-Jewish laws, though only a handful of Jews remained. Military brothels, stocked with French prostitutes, were set up; some island women gave themselves to German soldiers for love. About two thousand islanders were deported to internment camps in Germany. Large numbers of forced labourers, including French Jews and Russian prisoners, were imported to work on the fortification of the islands and were held in barbarous conditions in four concentration camps. The islanders carried on their lives as best they could; there was next to no resistance and some willing collaboration. A German soldier contrasted the hostility of the French with the friendliness of the population of the Channel Islands where 'we are greeted spontaneously, and eagerly shown the way when we ask'.[30]

'Collaboration', like 'appeasement', acquired its sinister reputation only after the event. The term originated in France. On 30 October 1940 Pétain, shortly after a meeting with Hitler at Montoire, declared: 'I enter today on the path of collaboration.' He gave a hostage to the future when he added: 'This policy is mine.... It is me alone that history will judge.'[31] The initial popularity of Pétain's regime in France owed much to memories of his role as a national healer at the time of the army mutinies in 1917. He proclaimed a 'national revolution' and appointed the former Socialist Pierre Laval as his Vice-Premier. The constitution of the Third Republic was jettisoned in 1940; in spite of many plans and long debates, it was never replaced during the war. Instead France relapsed into a simulacrum of the *ancien régime.* Pétain took on a fatherly, quasi-monarchical aura as head of the '*Etat Français*'. '*Liberté, Egalité, Fraternité*' was replaced on postage stamps by '*Travail, Famille, Patrie*'. The patriarchalism was reflected in the regime's social policies. The sale of alcohol to children was banned. Religious instruction was restored in schools. Divorce was restricted. Under a family law enacted in 1942 (and not repealed until 1965), the husband was recognized as head of the family with the right to make all important decisions. This was a profoundly conservative, even reactionary regime. It leant heavily on the Church for ideological sustenance; Catholicism responded ambivalently, but in large measure favourably. At least initially, the dominant intellectual voice was that of the royalist Charles Maurras rather than those of Fascists such as Robert Brasillach or Pierre Drieu la Rochelle.

Initially Vichy commanded broad national support. Not a single prefect (regional head of government) resigned after the armistice; one, the future resistance leader Jean Moulin, was dismissed. The Vichy regime sought to capitalize on this mood by placing Daladier, Blum, Reynaud, and Mandel under house arrest in September 1940. The Communists denounced the action on the ground that the treatment of these 'traitors' was too lenient: the former ministers '*mènent la vie de château*', while Communists were suffering in prison. Daladier, Blum, and Gamelin were placed on trial at Riom in 1942 on charges of criminal negligence in their management of French defences between 1935 and 1940. But they surprised their accusers by the vigour of their defence and the regime judged it prudent to halt the proceedings. The accused nevertheless remained in custody and Blum was later sent by the Germans to the Theresienstadt concentration camp.

One of the most serious errors of the Nazis was their failure to capitalize on potential support among occupied populations, particularly among the peoples of the Soviet Union. When the German armies arrived in Ukraine, Belorussia, and the Baltic states in 1941 they were often hailed as liberators from the Soviet yoke and greeted with bread and salt as well as flowers. In the First World War the Germans had intelligently sought to inflame separatist feeling among various groups, including Ukrainians, in the Russian Empire. But now Nazi racial theory impelled them to treat their Slavic subject peoples as inferiors, worthy only of enslavement. Hitler despised the Ukrainians, regarding them as 'every bit as idle, disorganized, and nihilistically Asiatic as the Greater Russians'.[32] Some bands of Ukrainian nationalists, led by Stepan Bandera, gave military support to the Germans and participated in anti-Jewish atrocities. In 1943 an SS division of Ukrainian volunteers from Galicia was formed; it was succeeded in 1944 by a 'Ukrainian National Army'. But Hitler considered it worthless: if it consisted of men from former Austrian Galicia, he said, their weapons should be taken away immediately. 'They were lambs, not wolves. They were terrible even in the Austrian army.'[33] Ukrainian nationalist hopes for an independent state under German auspices were dashed.

Ample evidence exists to suggest that large numbers of Russian prisoners might have been persuaded to fight for the Germans. Many did indeed serve, under varying degrees of encouragement and pressure, in units of so-called *Hilfswillige* or '*Hiwis*' (volunteers). A Soviet general, A. A. Vlasov, who was captured by the Germans in 1942, headed a 'Russian Liberation Army', consisting eventually of two divisions. As many as one million Soviet citizens are estimated to have been serving in the Wehrmacht by 1944. In Thessaly the Italian military occupiers recruited Vlach peasants into a 'Roman Legion'. In Bosnia 15, 000 Muslims, augmented by Albanians and Croats, were formed in 1943 into a division of the Waffen SS (militarized arm of the SS). The division was deployed against partisans. But the Nazis distrusted such turncoats and made only half-hearted use of this potential source of support.

Motives for resistance were various. In some cases, deep ideological conviction led people to join the underground: this was often the case with Catholic and (after the invasion of the Soviet Union) Communist resisters. But the decision was frequently half-forced on resisters by factors beyond their control that thrust them outside normal society: for known Communists and Jews facing a choice between arrest or flight, partisan groups might offer a refuge of last resort. In the later stages of the war the forced conscription of millions of civilians from all over Europe to work in German industry led large numbers to seek to escape by joining the resistance. When the order was given in 1944 for 70,000 Norwegians to be conscripted for service in a labour corps with German troops in the east, there was mass flight to the mountains and only a handful could be found. German labour requisition was probably the greatest stimulus to resistance throughout Europe.

Geography was the most significant condition of successful resistance. The mountainous areas of the Balkans, Italy, and the Massif Central in France offered more favourable opportunities for guerrilla warfare than cities or the flat plain of the Netherlands. The fjords of Norway and the inlets of the Adriatic were more hospitable to the undetected arrival of small supply vessels than the Channel coast. Outside aid was critical. Special Operations Executive (SOE), the British agency for subversive warfare, was set up in July 1940 and famously ordered by Churchill to 'set Europe ablaze!' It organized coordination with resistance movements, parachute drops of equipment and agents, sabotage of military, industrial and communications targets, and escape routes for Allied servicemen in Nazi Europe.

Forms of resistance ranged from action by individuals to large military and social movements. At the simplest level resistance might take purely symbolic (though frequently dangerous) forms, such as the Dutch salutation 'Hallo' (short form for the Dutch phrase for 'Hang all traitors!'). In Poland the resistance developed into something close to an underground state; elsewhere, particularly in the Balkans, it constituted little more than loosely organized banditry. In the Netherlands an estimated 1,300 clandestine newspapers and pamphlets were produced during the occupation. The Dutch resistance organ, *Het Parool*, endured the execution by the Nazis of more than a dozen of its staff and the arrest of many of its printers and distributors, but nevertheless managed to appear each month almost continuously (at first under a different name) from July 1940 until the liberation, achieving a peak circulation of 25,000. In France Henri Frenay's *Combat*, founded in late 1940, became the main voice of the non-communist resistance. Resisters throughout Europe killed German soldiers, disrupted German communications, sabotaged industrial plants or military installations, posted placards and distributed leaflets, organized strikes, set up clandestine air-drops, and provided safe houses for fugitives.

Wherever it appeared, resistance was a minority activity. The Netherlands Institute of War Documentation has assessed the number of Dutch resisters at about 76,000. Estimates of the number in France range from 45,000 to 400,000. At the other end of the spectrum, 45,000 Frenchmen volunteered in 1944 to join the paramilitary Milice whose main function was to suppress resistance. In Greece 30,000 *andartes* are estimated to have been active in guerrilla groups by mid-1943. In the USSR no preparations for partisan warfare had been made before the war, since Soviet military doctrine dictated that the war must move from the outset onto enemy territory. As a result partisan activity in the early months of the war was sporadic and ineffective. Later it developed on a large scale: an estimated one million partisans operated behind the lines, mainly in Belorussia and Ukraine.

Hatred of the occupier did not lead to unity among resisters. Almost everywhere conflict developed between conservative (generally Catholic) and left-wing (mainly communist) forces. In Poland the anti-Communist Home Army, loyal to the government-in-exile in London, was the predominant force. In Greece, the resistance was bitterly divided between the Communist ELAS (National People's Liberation Army) and the smaller, British-backed EDES (National Republican Greek League), led by the duplicitous Napoleon Zervas. There and elsewhere resistance often degenerated into bitter internecine fighting, robbery, exactions from civilian populations, and brigandage. The French resistance, at first a meagre projection of de Gaulle's London-based Free French movement, began to pick up momentum after the invasion of the USSR when French Communists suddenly adopted the fight against Hitler as their own cause. In early 1942 de Gaulle tried to combine all branches of resistance under his leadership, dispatching Jean Moulin, as representative of the French National Committee, to contact Georges Bidault, head of the resistance in Unoccupied France. A unified resistance organization, Forces Françaises de l'Intérieur, was formed in February 1943 but rumbling conflict between Gaullists and Communists continued. The resistance also argued incessantly with its British sponsors. In mid-1943 Moulin was betrayed, captured, tortured, and killed on the orders of the SS chief in Lyons, Klaus Barbie. De Gaulle imprinted his dominance only with difficulty over rival contenders for leadership. He also quarrelled bitterly and repeatedly with Churchill and Roosevelt.

The response of the occupiers to resistance was savage and took no account of the laws of war. Both the Wehrmacht and the SS resorted to collective punishment for resistance attacks; they took civilian hostages and announced they would shoot them in large batches unless perpetrators of attacks surrendered. When two Gestapo men were killed at Tælvåg near Bergen in 1942, the Germans destroyed the village and interned the entire population: thirty-one men died later at the Sachsenhausen concentration camp. After Reinhard Heydrich, Himmler's deputy and Acting Reich Protector of Bohemia and Moravia, was assassinated in May 1942, the entire male population of the village of Lidice was slaughtered. One man who was in hospital with a broken leg was permitted to convalesce, then shot. The women were sent to concentration camps, as were the children, save those judged suitably Aryan in appearance, who were distributed to German families for adoption. None returned from the camps. In June 1944, the villagers of Oradour-sur-Glane in France were murdered in reprisal for resistance activity. Such atrocities were multiplied a hundredfold in eastern Europe and the Balkans.

In Greece, the Italians resisted German pressure for violent repression. The Commander of the Italian Eleventh Army, General Carlo Geloso, ordered: 'Firmness and inexhaustible energy against the guilty . . . must not degenerate into a blind brutality which is out of harmony with traditions of Roman justice in the Italian Army, harmful to our prestige, contrary to our very interests.' Geloso declared the taking of hostages a tactic that 'does not enter our laws of war' and 'an odious procedure'.[34] On the other hand, the Italians too set up concentration camps in their occupation zones in the Balkans: women, old people, and children were among those interned. Thousands of Croat, Slovene, Montenegrin, and Greek prisoners died of malnourishment and ill-treatment in these camps.

The borderline between resistance and collaboration was often far from clear-cut. In a sense, successful resistance almost always involved some degree of at least token collaboration. In Yugoslavia the (mainly Serb) Četniks, led by Draža Mihailović, who was appointed Minister of War by the royalist government in London in November 1941, were accused by SOE of collaborationism. The evidence is indisputable that the Četniks collaborated with the Germans in operations against the Communist partisan movement led by Josip Broz (Tito) (see plate 28). It has been argued that Mihailović's ultimate loyalties, unlike those of Nedić and Pavelić, were anti-Axis. His most immediate objective, however, was to forestall a Communist takeover in the country at the end of the war and to that end he was prepared to make deals with the occupying forces. The British, who had initially urged Tito to submit to the leadership of Mihailović, dumped the Četnik leader unceremoniously in December 1943. For Churchill, in opting for Tito, the question was simple: who would kill more Germans? Yet after Tito's death in 1980 it was alleged that he too had conducted negotiations with the Germans in 1943. The allegation was made by Tito's former hagiographer, Vladimir Dedijer. Such contacts had been disclosed as early as 1962 by Tito's wartime lieutenant, later his political prisoner, Milovan Djilas: 'The occasion for the parley [Djilas wrote] was an exchange of prisoners, but its essence lay in getting the Germans to recognize the rights of the Partisans as combatants so that the killing of each other's wounded and prisoners might be halted.' Djilas reports the suspicions that these contacts aroused in the minds of the Yugoslav Partisans' chief patron in Moscow.[35] Tito pleaded with little success for aid from Stalin: he received far more from the British.

In military terms, except, perhaps, in Yugoslavia and France in the later part of the war, the impact of the resistance was minimal. Some isolated attacks caused serious inconvenience to the occupiers: the blowing-up of the Gorgopotamos railway viaduct in Greece in November 1942; the raids by the Norwegian resistance on the heavy-water plant at Rjukan in 1942 and 1943. An effective *resistenza armata* operated in Italy only after the fall of Mussolini. In most of Europe the resistance began to have any significant impact only in 1944. Overall, given Nazi ruthlessness, resistance probably resulted in less damage to occupiers than harm to occupied populations.

Mass murder

The war in the east and in the Balkans differed fundamentally from that in the west in its ferocity, no-holds-barred brutality, and disregard for the laws and conventions of war. Already in the wake of the Polish campaign in 1939–40, the Germans resorted to mass murder of the Polish intelligentsia and professional classes. Tens of thousands who were not killed immediately were sent to concentration camps where they were subjected to forced labour and starvation rations. Such barbarities intensified after the invasion of the Soviet Union. The German High Command's 'commissar order' of 6 June 1941 ordered that all Bolshevik commissars who fell into German hands were 'to be finished off... at once'.[36] 'Commissar' was interpreted broadly to include any Soviet official. Many were killed by the Wehrmacht in accordance with the order; others were handed over to the security organs to be murdered by them. In some newly occupied areas, German cavalrymen turned mental hospital patients out of doors to be hunted and shot down as sport.

German treatment of Soviet prisoners of war was no less savage—in stark contrast to the comparatively civilized treatment of prisoners on the eastern front in the First World War. While the USSR had signed the 1929 Geneva Convention, dealing with treatment of sick and wounded soldiers in the field, it was not a party to the accompanying convention on prisoners of war. Germany, although she had ratified both treaties, consequently felt under no legal constraint while maltreating Soviet POWs and the International Red Cross was unable to gain access to camps in which they were held. At least two million Russian prisoners out of the 5.2 million captured by the Germans between 1941 and 1945 died in captivity. Many were shot in cold blood after capture. Others were worked to death. Large numbers who could no longer work were starved to death. German army doctors were forbidden to treat wounded Russian prisoners. German soldiers, on orders from above, took winter clothing and boots from Russian prisoners who thereupon often froze to death. Sometimes Russian POWs were used to clear minefields. The German army, collaborating closely with the Nazi security apparatus, played the central role in this historically unparalleled war crime.[37] The Russians behaved with only marginally less barbarism: of the 3.2 million German prisoners of war in Russia an estimated 1.2 million died in captivity; of those who survived the war, many were detained in Soviet labour camps until the mid-1950s. After one Soviet battlefield success in 1943, General Konev boasted jovially to a visitor of the treatment accorded to defeated German soldiers at the end of the engagement: 'We let the Cossacks cut up as long as they wished. They even hacked off the hands of those who raised them to surrender!'[38]

In their more extreme forms the activities of the German army in the east merged into the larger framework of terror, mass murder, and genocide. The chief victims were Jews. The origins of the Nazi effort to annihilate an entire nation were deeply embedded in the history of the continent. The Jews of eastern Europe, unlike those in the west, were a nationality, not merely a religious group, recognized as such legally by the Russian and Habsburg empires and by the successor states thereafter. Where their settlement was thickest, in Russia, Poland, and Romania, they generally spoke a common language unique to themselves—Yiddish (in the Balkans Ladino, also known as Judeo-Español performed a similar function). Throughout the region anti-Semitism could draw on a rich substratum of cultural and religious symbolism. In Catholic and Orthodox teaching, drummed into the faithful by parish priests and by the ecclesiastical hierarchies, the Jew was the Christ-killer. In the mind of the peasant majority, the image of the Jew as child-killer and well-poisoner, a residue of medieval superstition, was deeply imprinted.

Between 1789 and 1917 the nation-states of Europe, starting with France and ending with Russia, had all offered (or purported to offer) equal citizenship to Jews. Only Romania refused to do so; but under Allied pressure, she too relented after the First World War. In eastern Europe in the inter-war period, as in the west during the previous century in the aftermath of emancipation, many Jews rushed to participate in all aspects of life of the societies in which they lived. By far the most urbanized element in the population of all these countries, and among the best educated, they were heavily represented in the professions, particularly medicine and law. They also participated disproportionately in the nascent cultural life of the new states, particularly in journalism, literature, and theatre. Even though only a minority of Jews embraced these national cultures, their contributions were impressive—and deeply resented. Jews also played a major part in commerce and industry. In all this they laid themselves open to the charge that they were an obstacle to the genuine 'nationalization' of the economies and cultures of the new and highly self-conscious nation-states.

Jews thus acquired a social, cultural, and political significance quite out of proportion to their numbers. In no country in Europe did Jews compose more than a small minority. Even in Poland, where they were most heavily concentrated, the 3.2 million Jews in the early 1930s constituted no more than 10 per cent of the population. Moreover, there was no region where they formed a majority. Only in a handful of towns and cities did they come close to doing so. They thus conspicuously lacked what almost every other ethnic group in Europe possessed: a territorial base. Only gypsies shared this characteristic but they were nomads on the fringe of organized society, whereas the Jews, for all their separateness, were deeply involved in societies in which they lived.

To all this was added, in the inter-war period, a new and horrifying vision: the Jew as revolutionary. In Ukraine and Hungary, where rural populations had experienced 'Red terror' at the hands of Bolshevik commissars, frequently identified with Jews, this image coalesced with the older ones to produce a monstrous figure of fear and loathing. It required little coaxing by demagogues to draw all these strands together into a doctrine of contempt and persecution. In the unsettled social climate of the 1930s, anti-Semitism flourished in Europe as never before. Hardly any country was wholly free of it. In eastern Europe it evolved into what one historian has called 'the only really potent internationalistic ideology in the area at that time'.[39]

Germany was a relative latecomer to political anti-Semitism. Although small anti-Semitic parties had been active since the 1890s, it was not till the onset of the Depression that anti-Semitism became a major force. Nazi racist legislation was soon copied by right-radical movements in other countries in central and eastern Europe, drawing on native traditions of Jew-hatred. In Poland in the 1930s Jewish students were forced to occupy 'ghetto benches' in lecture halls (from 1937 on the basis of official orders imposed in all universities) and a *numerus clausus*, limiting the numbers of Jews admissible to universities, reduced the Jewish proportion of the student population from 24 per cent in 1924 to 8 per cent by 1939. Hungary, Romania, and Italy all passed anti-Semitic laws that limited the participation of Jews in government and the professions and that struck at the capacity of Jewish businessmen to earn a living. Yet even among the anti-Semites, few went so far as to talk in the 1930s of annihilating this trans-national nation. The Jews' legal, social, and cultural stigmatization, a symptom of the barbarized value systems of Europe after the First World War, nevertheless paved the way to mass murder.

The terror against German Jews sharpened in the autumn of 1938. On 7 November the Third Secretary of the German Embassy in Paris, Ernst vom Rath, was shot by a young Jew whose parents had been among several thousand Polish Jews deported from Germany a few days earlier. (The deportations were in reaction to the passage of a Polish law, anti-Semitic in inspiration, that denationalized Polish citizens who had lived abroad for more than five years.) The Nazis seized on the assassination as the pretext for a savage onslaught against Jews. On the night of 9–10 November synagogues all over Germany were ransacked and burned. Jewish shop windows were broken (hence the name *Reichskristallnacht*, night of broken glass, given to the episode by the German government), and their contents looted. Jews were attacked and murdered. Twenty thousand were seized and sent to concentration camps. Following this state-sponsored nationwide race riot, the German Jewish community as a whole was presented with a vast collective 'fine'. Jewish property was compulsorily 'Aryanized'. Many Jews sought to emigrate, but those who besieged the foreign consulates found few countries willing to grant them refuge. Britain, France, and the United States alone admitted significant numbers. Earlier in the decade British-ruled Palestine had done so too but immigration there was now restricted in deference to the forcefully expressed opposition of the Arab majority population.

An important first step towards the implementation of mass murder of the Jews was the so-called 'euthanasia' programme, which Hitler authorized shortly before the war. A committee assessed requests from parents for the disposal of handicapped children. Thirty 'paediatric clinics' were set up in hospitals throughout the Reich in which such children were starved to death or given lethal injections. Several thousand children were killed under official auspices.[40] About the same time an adult euthanasia project was launched. Epileptics, schizophrenics, and persons suffering from hereditary illnesses were assessed by panels of doctors and assigned for extermination. They were then transported to special centres, undressed, stamped with a number on the shoulder or chest, examined for gold teeth, photographed, led to a gas chamber disguised as a shower room, and killed. Gold teeth were then extracted and the corpses burnt. An employee of such a centre described the conclusion of the process: 'After the corpses had been burnt, the remnants of the bones which had fallen through the grid would be put into a bone mill and ground to powder. This bonemeal was then sent to the grieving relatives as the remains of their dead. We estimated roughly 3 kg. of such meal for each corpse. Since the work was very exhausting, and, as I said, nerve-racking, we got about a quarter litre of schnaps per day.'[41] Standard 'condolence' letters were sent to relatives of the victims informing them that death had been caused by 'influenza in conjunction with an abscess on the lung' or some such cause. Between 1939 and 1941 at least 70,000 people were murdered under this programme. But in August 1941, after the Vatican declared such killing 'against the natural and positive law of God', the Bishop of Münster, Cardinal von Galen, delivered a sermon describing and denouncing the programme. A few weeks later Hitler ordered a halt to the killings. Although the gassings of mental patients stopped, other 'euthanasia' enterprises continued. Victims, who included slave workers and old people from institutions for the poor, were generally killed by drug overdoses or starvation.

Meanwhile, in Poland in 1939 and 1940, special SS units were sent into action with orders to concentrate Jews in ghettos in the major cities. Large numbers were shot at random. Others were sent to labour camps. Synagogues were destroyed. Jews were ordered to wear yellow stars of David on their outer clothes. Overcrowding in the ghettos was extreme, with several persons crammed into every room. Vehicles, furs, and other valuables were confiscated. German soldiers occasionally amused themselves by cutting beards off Jews in the street or yoking them to carts. Hunger, cold, and disease in the ghettos rendered life almost unendurable. In the Łódź ghetto in 1942 the death rate from such causes was 160 per thousand. Faced with such hopeless conditions, many Jews committed suicide. Some German soldiers were outraged by what they witnessed. General Johannes

Blaskowitz protested against the actions of the police in the area of occupied Poland that was under his charge: he was transferred. Other German officers and ordinary soldiers had fewer scruples and, particularly in the later part of the war, themselves participated in the slaughter.

The order for the so-called 'final solution' of the Jewish question was probably issued in the summer or autumn of 1941, shortly after the invasion of the Soviet Union. The role of Hitler in this decision has been much debated. No specific written instruction by Hitler ordering the mass murder has been found. Some 'revisionists' have adduced this negative fact to suggest that Hitler was distant from or even ignorant of the genocide. The weight of evidence, however, points to the Führer's knowledge and approval and it seems likely that he issued an oral instruction in a meeting with Himmler. On 20 January 1942 at a villa in the Berlin suburb of Wannsee, a conference of senior officials, presided over by Heydrich, discussed organizational details of the mass murder plan. The secretary for the occasion, Adolf Eichmann, head of section IV B4 of the RSHA (the state security service), became chief executive officer of the genocide. He had earned his spurs as the impresario of forced expulsions of Jews from Austria after the *Anschluss*. Eichmann was a sinister figure, but in the narrow, inane, humanoid manner of one of Kafka's repellent bureaucrats. Hannah Arendt's phrase, 'the banality of evil', sticks to him like a barnacle.[42]

Germans in almost every sphere of society participated in some way in the mass murder: not only the SS and concentration camp guards but diplomats, local government officials, railway workers, and engineers; and not only Germans but collaborators drawn from all occupied nations. Although the German army was, in general, not centrally involved in the process, military units helped create the conditions necessary for its implementation. On the eve of *BARBAROSSA*, the German Army High Command ordered all units to facilitate the activities of *Einsatzgruppen*. These special SS killing squads fanned out over the newly occupied areas and shot tens of thousands of Jews to death wherever they found them.

Shooting, however, proved slow and inefficient. The administrators of the genocide therefore set about industrializing the process. The first gas killings took place at Chelmno in December 1941. The gas chamber used there was a technically primitive affair: exhaust fumes were channelled into the back of a van. Seven hundred Jews were in the first group to be murdered in this way. Soon gas chambers and crematoria were constructed at killing centres, mainly in Poland. Between 1942 and 1944 Jews were transported in special trains from all over Europe to these death camps: Bełżec, Majdanek, Sobibor, Treblinka, and Auschwitz (Oświęcim) in Upper Silesia, the largest such installation. It had begun as a labour camp and continued to function as an important industrial centre as well as a site of mass murder. Upon arrival there Jews regarded as fit for work were separated from the rest. The rest were removed to the gas chambers in an area of the camp called Birkenau and immediately killed. Their bodies were then burnt in giant crematoria. Some of the arrivals were selected as subjects for so-called medical experiments by German doctors, among them the notorious Josef Mengele. His victims included sets of twins who were subjected to peculiarly ghoulish tortures in the professed cause of medical science. A few survived their terrible mutilations to tell the tale. The commandant of Auschwitz at its foundation and during the period of mass killings was Rudolf Höss. The autobiography he wrote after the war in Allied captivity is one of the most revealing documents of the Nazi era. Notwithstanding his gruesome daily tasks, Höss enjoyed a happy and seemingly normal bourgeois family life, helping his children with their schoolwork, taking walks in the wood, performing household chores for Mrs Höss—those, that is, that were not undertaken by the servants seconded to the household from among the slave labourers of the camp.[43] At least 1.1 million people were killed at Auschwitz: of these, 960,000 were Jews, 73,000 Poles, 21,000 gypsies, and 15,000 Soviet prisoners of war. According to the most reliable assessment, these 'must be regarded as minimum estimates'.[44] A further 150,000 Poles who were imprisoned at Auschwitz died later elsewhere.

We now have thousands of post-war interrogations, testimonies, trial records, interviews, and memoirs that give us windows into the minds of the perpetrators. Such evidence provides some basis for understanding how they could justify their actions to themselves. Division of the work of mass murder into specialized components facilitated the process. Hundreds of thousands of people throughout Europe participated indirectly, often through small acts, each of which, taken by itself, might appear to lack moral importance. As for the killers, they received guidance in a kind of secular sermon by Himmler in October 1943. Speaking to SS leaders at Posen, he declared:

> Whether other peoples live in plenty or starve to death interests me only insofar as we need them as slaves for our culture.... Whether ten thousand Russian women keel over from exhaustion in the construction of an anti-tank ditch interests me only insofar as the ditch for Germany gets finished.

> I want to tell you about a very grave matter in all frankness. We can talk about it quite openly here, but we must never speak of it publicly.... I mean the evacuation of the Jews, the extermination of the Jewish people. It's one of the things one says lightly: 'The Jewish people are being liquidated,' party comrades exclaim: 'naturally, it's in our programme, elimination of the Jews, extermination, okay, we'll do it.' And then they come trudging, eighty million worthy Germans, and each one has his one decent Jew. Sure, the others are swine, but this one is an A-1 Jew. Of all those who talk this way, not one has seen it happen, not one has been through it. Most of you must know what it means to see a hundred corpses lie side by side, or five hundred or a thousand. To have stuck this out and—excepting cases of human weakness—to have remained decent, this is what has made us tough. This is an unwritten, never to be written, glorious page in our history.[45]

Between five and six million Jews from all over occupied Europe were murdered in fulfilment of these sentiments. The most vulnerable were the very old and very young who were not fit for work. No social class was exempt, although those with resources were in some cases able to purchase escape or survival by bribing officials or buying forged documents.

This holocaust (the term came to be applied only much later) could not have been perpetrated without the collaboration of puppet regimes and of parts of the populations of Nazi-occupied Europe. In eastern Europe, where the pre-war Jewish populations had been largest, and where anti-Semitic feeling was deeply ingrained, such collaboration was widespread. Romanian troops massacred several thousand Jews in Odessa after they occupied the city in 1941. Ukrainians and Balts served as concentration camp guards, sometimes participating in atrocities. In Poland, the populations of some towns and villages, as in the notorious case of Jedwabne, turned on their Jewish neighbours and massacred them without requiring much encouragement from the Germans.[46]

Not all Germany's allies joined in the killing with equal enthusiasm. In Bulgaria fifty thousand Jews were saved by Tsar Boris and parliamentary and church leaders who resisted Nazi demands that the Jews be delivered up for deportation to the death camps. Unlike Romania, Bulgaria, with her smaller and better integrated Jewish community, had a much weaker anti-Semitic tradition. On the other hand, in 'new' Bulgaria, the annexed Greek and Yugoslav territories, the authorities entered no such reservation and more than eleven thousand Jews were sent to their deaths.

Senior officials in the Italian Foreign Ministry as well as Italian army officers connived at various devices, in defiance of orders from Mussolini and pressure from the Germans, and protected some fifty thousand Jews in

Italian areas of occupation in France, Greece, and Yugoslavia. As one Italian diplomat put it, 'Apart from any other consideration of a moral character, this is an ignoble traffic in which it is extremely humiliating to have a share, even indirectly.'[47] After Mussolini's fall in 1943, however, Italian Fascists too turned Jews over to the Nazis and collaborated in their murder.

Jewish responses to the Nazi onslaught were for the most part confused, disjointed, and individual, rather than coherent or collectively organized. Many Jews tried to escape. But for the most part their exits were blocked. From Poland, the Soviet-occupied Baltic states and the western portions of the Soviet Union, thousands fled or were deported to the east. Tashkent and other remote Asiatic cities suddenly acquired large refugee communities of European Jews. From central and south-east Europe many boarded river steamers down the Danube and crowded onto old steamers in Romanian and Bulgarian ports in the hope of reaching Palestine. In France Jews crossed from the occupied to the unoccupied zone and then sought to make their way over the Pyrenees. Fascist Spain, where Jews were still legally forbidden to reside under the expulsion edict of 1492, was hardly welcoming. Nevertheless, the Franco regime gave refuge to some and allowed others to transit to Portugal and elsewhere. Nearly twenty thousand German and Polish Jews wandered across the world to the International Settlement of Shanghai, the only place on earth where they did not need to show a passport to enter. But by 1941 the Japanese had closed even that loophole. After the invasion of the USSR, for most Jews caught in the Nazi vice, flight was not an option.

Some Jews collaborated. As in the case of the general populations of occupied countries, the line between collaboration and resistance was fuzzy. In many occupied areas the Germans set up so-called 'Jewish Councils' (*Judenräte*) whose function was to secure the compliance of the Jewish populations with Nazi policies. In the ghettos of the east Jewish police forces helped maintain order. In the Łódź ghetto, between 1940 and 1944, the head of the Jewish Council, Mordechai Chaim Rumkowski, set himself up in bizarre fashion as 'king of the Jews'. Under the slogan 'work and peace', he induced his subjects to seek salvation by making themselves indispensable to the German war production effort. Most of the Jews were deported but Rumkowski succeeded in keeping sixty thousand Jews alive in his city until August 1944, when the Red Army was just 75 miles away. Then he and the remaining inhabitants of the ghetto were sent to Auschwitz. After the war, the philosopher and refugee from Nazi Germany

Hannah Arendt denounced the Jewish Council members in a vitriolic diatribe.[48] More recent historians have issued more charitable verdicts, conscious of the immense pressures and tragic dilemmas imposed by the Nazis.[49] Some council members (most of whom were themselves killed in due course) were undoubtedly cynical opportunists. Others deluded themselves that their cooperation with the occupiers prevented even greater evil. Adam Czerniakow, head of the Warsaw Jewish Council, was more clear-sighted, recording in his diary his desperate anguish at being drawn into collaboration in the destruction process: when it became apparent that he could do nothing to halt the deportations from the Warsaw ghetto, he committed suicide.

Raul Hilberg has argued that the generally feeble Jewish response was conditioned by centuries of submissive behaviour towards authority.[50] But significant Jewish resistance erupted in several parts of Europe. In the most famous instance, the remnant of the population of the Warsaw ghetto held out in underground bunkers against murderous SS attack in April–May 1943. 'Black clouds of smoke are rising over the city from the ghetto which has been burning for three weeks,' wrote a German officer there on 9 May. 'Enormous amounts of property have been destroyed and untold numbers of people killed. The police are still not finished. At night there is incessant shooting. Shocking scenes are being played out there. A new, indelible mark of shame for those who will have to answer for it. Indeed a massive disgrace. We can only be glad that we, as the Wehrmacht, have nothing to do with it.'[51] This was the first civilian rising against the Germans in occupied Europe. Smaller-scale revolts took place in other ghettos and even in death camps. One estimate has it that as many as 40 per cent of all partisans operating on Nazi-occupied Soviet territory in the later part of the war were Jews. In France Jews played a significant role in the resistance: some groups of urban resisters and *maquis* (forest and mountain guerrillas) were distinctively Jewish. Unlike other resistance movements, however, those of the Jews received little outside help. The BBC made a few broadcasts to occupied Europe warning against atrocities. A handful of Palestinian Jewish volunteers were parachuted into Europe by the British with the objective of helping Jews threatened with deportation; but most of the parachutists were captured and killed. Apart from these limited instances, next to no aid was made available. Indeed, official British policy seemed, as in the case of the German resistance, to be actively hostile to the notion of promoting such activity. In the case of the Jews it was felt that military training for guerrilla and subversive warfare might rebound against the British in Palestine after the war. Jewish organizations outside occupied Europe set up 'rescue' committees in the hope of saving some of their brethren. But there was next to nothing that they could do. Various fantastic schemes for bribing the Germans or Romanians into allowing Jews to leave came to nothing. So did the macabre proposal in 1944 whereby Eichmann was said to have offered to barter the lives of Jews for lorries. A few small-scale efforts of this sort nevertheless produced results. The activities in Switzerland of Sally Mayer, a Swiss Jew who represented the American Jewish Joint Distribution Committee, led to the release, in return for promises of money, of 1,210 prisoners from Theresienstadt, who were permitted to go to Switzerland in February 1945.[52]

The response of occupied populations was, in general, more sympathetic in western Europe than in the east. In Amsterdam in February 1941 the population observed a two-day general strike in protest against anti-Jewish measures. But this was an isolated case. The Polish government-in-exile drew public attention to the Jewish predicament by helping to relay and publicize evidence of mass murder. At the same time Polish leaders made it clear that their preferred solution to the 'Jewish problem' in Poland remained mass emigration after the war. By then the annihilation of the overwhelming majority of the three million Polish Jews rendered this academic. The Polish Home Army gave next to no aid to the Warsaw Ghetto rebels in 1943. With only small supplies of arms, the Home Army conserved what little they had for their own later use. The response of the general Polish population was rarely sympathetic. Some Poles hid Jews, particularly children, for long periods or helped them escape. But given the widespread anti-Semitism in the country before 1939, it was hardly to be expected that the majority of Poles would suddenly see Jews as companions in misfortune rather than alien competitors.

The case of France was especially poignant. It was later claimed on behalf of Pétain and Laval that they had at least tried to save French, as distinct from alien, Jews from deportation. Perhaps they won that group some time—and in occupied Europe time was often life itself. But the Vichy regime, deeply imbued with the anti-Semitism traditional on the French clerical right, seemed to rush eagerly to anticipate German anti-Jewish measures rather than resist or delay. Without the application of German pressure, the anti-Semitic *Statut des Juifs* was put into effect in 1940 in the unoccupied zone *before* the Germans began their anti-Jewish activities in the occupied zone.

The first Vichy Commissioner-General for Jewish Affairs, Xavier Vallat, was an anti-Semite but also anti-German. He lost his job after an unseemly confrontation with an SS officer in which he declared: 'I have been an anti-Semite far longer than you . . . What's more, I am old enough to be your father.' French police, not Germans, conducted the *rafles* (round-ups) of Jews in Paris in 1941 and 1942. The Prefecture of Police ordered its agents, in carrying out the arrests to 'see that the gas and electricity meters are cut off, the water cut off, any domestic pets handed over to the *concierge* . . . the keys to be handed over either to the *concierge* or to the nearest neighbour'.[53]

Some exceptions stand out amidst the generally dismal response of the occupied nations. In the Netherlands, although a high percentage of the Jewish community was deported to the death camps, an estimated twenty thousand Dutch families gave shelter to Jews. The Norwegian resistance organized the escape of half of the 1,800 Jews in the country. In Denmark which had next to no tradition of anti-Semitism and where Jews were well knit into national life, the bulk of the community, numbering about eight thousand, was evacuated to Sweden by the Danish resistance in the autumn of 1943 just as the Nazis were about to deport them.

The neutral states at the borders of the Nazi realm gave shelter to some refugees from the terror. Most of them, however, set strict limits on the numbers they were prepared to accept. Turkey allowed Jews to cross her territory heading for Palestine only if they were in possession of valid immigration certificates. A few individuals from neutral countries found themselves in a position to take effective action to save lives. Raoul Wallenberg, a Swede, was sent to Hungary as the personal representative of the King of Sweden. He pressed the rights of diplomatic protection far beyond formal limits and was credited with saving thousands of lives.

The attitude of the Vatican presents a special historical problem. Why did the Pope not speak out more forcefully against the Nazis? In his Christmas broadcast on 24 December 1942, Pius XII did make reference to 'hundreds of thousands who, without any guilt, sometimes for no other reason but on account of nationality or descent, were doomed to death or exposed to a progressive deterioration of their condition'.[54] But that was as far as he would go in public. While he refrained from condemnation of the mass murder of the Jews, he was, on the other hand, quick to denounce Italian resistance fighters in 1944 when they resorted to terrorist tactics. The Pope's reticence must be seen against the background of Nazi threats against the Church, particularly in Poland. But there was also a personal element. As papal nuncio in Warsaw in 1920 the future Pius XII had witnessed the Bolshevik war against the Poles. Later, as nuncio in Berlin he had negotiated the concordat between Germany and the Vatican. The published Vatican documents for the wartime period indicate that both the Pope and his closest advisers regarded communism as more of a danger than Nazism.[55] His defenders have suggested that his primary object was to maintain intact 'the structures of the institutional Church, which he saw in exalted, mystical terms'.[56] Whatever his motives, Pius XII never expressed any remorse for his wartime silence.

Jews were not alone in suffering, although only they were singled out for total annihilation. At least two million non-Jewish Polish civilians are estimated to have been murdered during the war; a large proportion were killed by the Russians but the majority died in Nazi concentration camps or mass executions. Perhaps 220,000 gypsies were killed by the Nazis but estimates have varied widely. At least thirteen thousand German gypsies were deported to Auschwitz where nearly three thousand were gassed in one day, 2 August 1944. Over five thousand Austrian gypsies were murdered at Chelmno. Tens of thousands of gypsies were murdered in Yugoslavia and Hungary. Jehovah's Witnesses and homosexuals were also among the victims. Homosexuality, which had flourished openly in German cities in the Weimar period, was made illegal (between males) after 1935. About fifty thousand men were found guilty of 'offences against nature' over the next decade and at least five thousand were deported to concentration camps. Some, however, escaped punishment by agreeing to undergo 'sexual re-education'.

It defies rational explanation that Nazi Germany should have flouted all moral and provident calculations in committing mass murder on such a scale, applying valuable transportation and other resources to the enterprise even when these were urgently needed for the war effort. Some historians have stressed the ideological imperatives underpinning Nazism; others the impersonal functioning of the bureaucratic machine in pressing forward a policy of extrusion and destruction to its extreme limit. In the last days of the war Himmler attempted to bargain for his own safety by releasing some Jewish prisoners. One man, however, remained fixed in his murderous obsession until the end: in his final 'testament' Hitler gloried in the fulfilment of his 'prophecy' of 1939 that Jewry, the real instigators 'of this murderous struggle', would be called to account.[57]

10

End of Hitler's Europe 1942–1945

'*Der springt noch auf*,' said someone over me.

*Miklós Radnóti, Szentkirályszabadja, Hungary, 1944**

The Grand Alliance

In January 1943 Churchill and Roosevelt met at Casablanca to celebrate their bloodless victory in North Africa and to plan the next stage of the war. The strategic challenge that confronted them remained formidable. Only in retrospect can we see that the victories at Stalingrad and Alamein were decisive turning-points. Germany still dominated the entire European land mass and Japan remained paramount in east Asia and the Pacific. At Casablanca the British and Americans argued over future strategy, in particular over how to respond to Soviet demands for the opening of a second front. The western powers were not yet able to mobilize sufficient strength to mount a major attack on the Germans in western Europe. Until the U-boat threat in the north Atlantic had been eliminated, forces and equipment could not be assembled for an amphibious invasion of western Europe. In the end it was agreed that a cross-Channel offensive would not be practicable until 1944. Churchill pressed for an attack in the meantime on the 'underbelly' of the Axis in the Mediterranean. The Americans suspected him of diverting the war effort out of misguided enthusiasm for 'sideshows'. Finally they consented to a landing on Sicily in 1943.

* From 'Postcards', translated from the Hungarian by Clive Wilmer and George Gömöri. Hugh Haughton, ed., *Second World War* Poems, London, 2004, 227. The German means: 'There's some life in him yet.' A few days after writing these words, the poet was shot by his Hungarian guards.

The conference was marked by two striking public episodes on its last day. One was a handshake, engineered by the British and Americans, between de Gaulle and Darlan's successor as French High Commissioner in North Africa, General Henri Giraud. Their reconciliation was short-lived; de Gaulle soon pushed aside his rival for leadership of the Free French cause. Of greater consequence was the proclamation of the 'unconditional surrender' of Germany, Italy, and Japan as the central Allied war aim. The wisdom of the announcement was later questioned and some saw it merely as an off-the-cuff remark by Roosevelt at the final day's news conference. But both leaders subsequently adhered to it without backsliding (except in the case of Italy). The Second World War, unlike the First World War, was to be a fight to the death.

Behind the Anglo-American wrangles at Casablanca was a changing balance within the alliance. The British were uneasily conscious that they were in the process of being overtaken by the Americans on almost every index of strength, most notably armaments production and military manpower. The Americans never wavered from the 'Germany first' strategy. At the same time they were reluctant to be drawn into efforts to preserve the British Empire in the post-war period. Yet such irritations notwithstanding, Anglo-American economic and military cooperation remained intimate. The two powers also pooled nearly all intelligence information.

Stalin had been invited to Casablanca but, in view of the critical state of the battle in Stalingrad, declined to attend. His relationship with Churchill and Roosevelt remained uneasy. He remained deeply suspicious of his allies and was displeased to learn that there would be no second front in 1943. Difficulties with Arctic convoys carrying supplies to the Soviet Union increased his dissatisfaction. The secrets derived from ULTRA were not transmitted to Russia. Nor was any information about the Anglo-American project for the manufacture of the atomic bomb, though Stalin got wind of that as early as 1942 through his intelligence network.

After Stalingrad there were persistent rumours of a possible compromise peace between Germany and the USSR. Some low-level Russo-German contacts took place in Stockholm in 1943. Stalin's promotion of a League of German Officers, composed of cooperative POWs, including such star turns as Paulus, has led some historians to suggest that he may have been toying with the idea of a negotiated peace, if not with Hitler then with other elements in Germany. More likely all this was merely political warfare by Stalin, designed to disorient the enemy and perhaps also as a salutary warning to his allies. Even as he authorized these 'peace feelers', Stalin took some symbolic measures to reassure the USA and Britain. The dissolution of the Comintern in 1943 (though planned since April 1941) indicated a retreat from the concept of imminent international revolution. Probably with the same intent, the *Internationale* was replaced as the Soviet national anthem by the less memorable strains of *The Unbreakable Union of Freeborn Republics*.

Meanwhile Goebbels for a time plugged the idea that Britain's best interests, to which Churchill was the chief obstacle, lay in making common cause with the Germans against Bolshevism. In January 1944 *Pravda* reported wrongly that Ribbentrop had held talks in Spain with British representatives. As German military fortunes declined, the idea of alliance with the western powers against the Soviets became increasingly attractive to many Germans, though not to Hitler. The doctrine of 'unconditional surrender', however, ruled out any such prospect of a reversal of alliances. In spite of all this shadow-boxing, the Grand Alliance held firm.

On the outer fringes of the warring coalition were the minor European allies, whose territories had been overrun by the Axis. London became the temporary resting-place for a Babel of governments-in-exile, Belgian, Dutch, Norwegian, Czechoslovak, Greek, Polish, Yugoslav, as well as de Gaulle's Free French movement. With the governments came royal families (but not King Leopold of the Belgians), civil servants, propagandists, opposition politicians, and remnants of armed forces. London was suddenly transformed into the most cosmopolitan city of the continent as its polyglot guests published newspapers, opened clubs, and engaged in the petty intrigues and manoeuvres customary among émigré politicians. Eaton Square became a little Belgium, Princes Gate a little Czechoslovakia, Knightsbridge a little Poland. Some of the governments seemed to their hosts like weekend guests who had outstayed their welcome. A few were phantoms without any real political weight. Others brought tangible assets in men, intelligence, gold, ships, or colonies. All dreamed of what for long seemed the very distant prospect of return to their homelands. One set of political refugees was excluded from the party: the Allies did not permit German, Austrian, or Italian political refugees to form governments-in-exile.

By contrast with the Allies' (particularly the western Allies') close coordination, the Axis partnership was, in military terms, as Guderian put it, 'so faulty that it might just as well not have existed at all'.[1] The Germans and Italians did not discuss strategy, did not engage in joint economic planning, often competed for glory or booty in occupied territory, and at almost every level barely trusted each other. Mussolini was guided, in his relations with Hitler, more by churning jealousy than by genuine fellow feeling. The Germans, while preserving outward forms, had little respect for their ally, especially given the less than glorious performance of Italian troops in the Balkans and against the Soviets. In May 1942, Himmler reminded one of his subordinates of the Führer's 'close and cordial friendship' with Mussolini and adjured him: 'Permit no jokes or other criticisms of the Italians.'[2] When Rommel, in the presence of Hitler, was asked in July 1943 which Italian officers could be trusted to collaborate with the Germans, he replied: 'There is no such person.'[3]

Mussolini's twilight

In spite of the success of *TORCH*, it took another six months for the Allies to drive all Axis forces out of North Africa. In Libya, where Rommel conducted a sturdy fighting retreat against greatly superior forces, the westward advance of the British Eighth Army was dispiritingly slow. General Alexander captured Tripoli only in January 1943. The Germans and Italians then concentrated in Tunisia to face their enemies on two fronts. A reinforced German army there under General von Arnim succeeded in blocking the Allied advance from Algeria towards Tunis. In February the Germans inflicted a bloody nose on American forces at the Battle of Kasserine. This was the Americans' first substantial engagement on land in the western theatre. Although Axis forces were soon compelled to withdraw, Kasserine was a shock to the Allies, particularly given their preponderance in men, armaments, and intelligence. But von Arnim could not survive without supplies and in the course of the spring Allied air attacks on Italian shipping across the Mediterranean virtually eliminated his lifeline. Tunis was finally captured in May 1943.

The clearing of North Africa and the opening of the Mediterranean to Allied vessels at last rendered feasible the long-awaited Anglo-American assault on the Axis in 'Fortress Europe'. The Allied project for an invasion of Sicily (Operation *HUSKY*) was facilitated by an ingenious deception—'the man who never was'. A corpse in British uniform, bearing bogus military planning documents, was dropped from a submarine off the Spanish coast. The body washed ashore and the documents, duly relayed to the Germans by the Spanish authorities, persuaded them that the target of attack would be Sardinia or the Balkans. On 10 July 1943 the Allied navies began disembarking 478,000 British and American troops in Sicily from nearly two thousand landing-craft. Montgomery's Eighth Army landed on the east coast, the US Seventh Army, commanded by General George S. Patton, on the south-west. The Allies, who enjoyed overwhelming superiority in the air, met with only light initial opposition from the 230,000-strong Italian defending force, many of whom surrendered en masse. The Americans' favourable reception was eased by contacts between US servicemen of Sicilian origin and their contacts in the Mafia. The Allies also received good ULTRA intelligence, though they failed to make optimal use of it. Inter-allied squabbles and tactical errors enabled the German commander, Field Marshal Kesselring, with only forty thousand men, to hold up the invaders for a month, much longer than they had expected. In early August he succeeded in evacuating over a hundred thousand German and Italian troops as well as most of their equipment across the Strait of Messina to the mainland.

The enthusiastic popular acclaim accorded to American troops in Palermo had, in the meantime, indicated the precariousness of Mussolini's political no less than his military position. Other signs of disaffection were already apparent. In the spring of 1943 mass strikes had broken out in Turin and Milan. Court circles made discreet contacts with Allied agents and even Fascist Party hardliners expressed discontent. Within the Italian High Command sentiment was growing for Italian withdrawal from the war.

On 24–25 July, a raucous nine-hour meeting of the Fascist Grand Council, hitherto a rubber stamp body, terminated with a decisive vote against the Duce. Even his son-in-law, Ciano, voted against him. Mussolini was arrested and imprisoned. King Vittorio Emmanuele III appointed Marshal Badoglio as head of a 'technical' government. Most Italians assumed that this meant the end of the war. In a broadcast proclamation, however, Badoglio declared explicitly 'the war continues!'[4] Hitler was not deceived: 'They say they'll fight but that is treachery.'[5] He was right. Badoglio opened secret talks with the Allies. Churchill advocated seizing the opportunity to effect a rapid military takeover of the Italian mainland: 'Why should we crawl up the leg like a harvest-bug from the ankle upwards? Let us rather strike at the knee.'[6] Eisenhower too argued for a bold stroke. But they allowed themselves to be overruled by more cautious Allied planners. Negotiations with Badoglio's representatives, complicated by the Allies' commitment to 'unconditional surrender', dragged on for several weeks in Lisbon, Tangier, and Sicily. They soon came to the attention of the Germans who had in any case started to prepare dispositions for taking military control of the entire country from their erstwhile allies. While the diplomats dallied, eight Wehrmacht divisions, commanded by Rommel, seized Italy's Alpine passes and airborne forces were flown to Ostia, just outside Rome.

On 3 September, as the first British troops landed on the Italian mainland at Reggio di Calabria, the Italians finally signed an armistice. It was not made public until five days later, shortly before Allied forces landed at Salerno, south of Naples. That operation was a fiasco: the attackers failed to achieve surprise, could not provide adequate air cover, and were held on the beaches. Their naval craft came under withering fire and for a time it seemed that the invasion would have to be abandoned. Eventually heavy reinforcements saved the situation but the Germans' stubborn resistance slowed the Allied break-out from the bridgehead. The Germans captured strong points and airfields, occupied Rome and gained control over most of the country except the far south. Badoglio and the king fled to Brindisi, the Italian army disintegrated, and what might have been a brilliant coup for the Allies turned into an expensive military commitment. Allied plans for airborne landings in Rome had to be abandoned. Instead of speedily clearing the Germans out of Italy, the Allies faced a slow, gruelling northward slog against a resourceful enemy.

On 12 September a unit of glider-borne SS commandos engineered Mussolini's sensational escape from detention. Six days later the Duce broadcast from Munich, denouncing the king and Badoglio, as well as 'certain pusillanimous and shirking generals and certain cowardly Fascist elements'. Invoking 'the republican current and its purest and greatest apostle, Giuseppe Mazzini', he announced the formation of a Republican Fascist Party.[7] With German help, he established new headquarters at Saló on Lake Garda, where he proclaimed the Italian Social Republic. But this was a sorry pretence of an independent state. Most of Italy now suffocated under a harsh German military occupation. Beneath the surface a bitter civil war was waged between the Fascist faithful and the growing partisan movement. Ciano and others who had betrayed the Duce were subjected to a show trial at Verona. Mussolini resisted the implorings of his daughter and ordered the execution of his son-in-law. Together with four other defendants, Ciano was shot in the back in January 1944.

Mussolini's deposition had meanwhile led to a German takeover of Italian-occupied areas of France, Yugoslavia, and Greece. Efficient German brutality now took the place of Italy's relatively lax occupation policy. Italian troops in those areas were disarmed and taken prisoner by the Germans. In Greece many Italian soldiers sold their weapons and equipment to the local population. On Rhodes and other islands Italians fiercely resisted German attempts to disarm them; on the island of Cephalonia at least five thousand were executed by their former allies after their units had been subdued.

Under the command of Kesselring, the Germans doggedly contested every step of the Allied advance northwards. In late 1943 they dug in behind the 'Gustav line', stretching east–west across Italy, north of Naples. On 22 January 1944 the Allies attempted to cut behind this with an amphibious landing at Anzio, further up the Adriatic coast. The operation proved to be another expensive near-fiasco. This time the Allied achieved tactical surprise and, learning from the lesson of Salerno, assembled strong sea and air support. But they failed to exploit their initial advantage and found themselves stuck on the beaches. Kesselring's forces quickly regrouped and inflicted severe damage on the American and British infantry. It took the invaders five months to break out of the beachhead. Churchill, with his fondness for animal metaphors, commented: 'We hoped to land a wildcat that would tear out the bowels of the Boche. Instead we have stranded a vast whale with its tail flopping about in the water.'[8]

Further inland, one of the jewels of European civilization, the abbey of Monte Cassino, mother-house of the Benedictine order, became an object of murderous contention. The monastery, occupying a commanding position on a hilltop in the Abruzzi mountains, was destroyed by Allied bombardment in February 1944. The military consequences of this decision, taken by General Bernard Freyberg of the New Zealand Corps and endorsed by the Allied commander in Italy, Alexander, were entirely counter-productive, since the Germans were allowed to capture the ruins of the monastery. Three major attempts over the next four months to oust them bled American, New Zealand, and Polish forces dry.

The Allied forces finally subdued German resistance at Cassino and Anzio in May. Alexander hoped to envelop the main body of German forces but US General Mark Clark preferred to dash for glory by heading straight to Rome, which Kesselring had declared an 'open city'. The Italian capital fell on 4 June 1944. But the struggle for Italy was by no means over. The

Germans succeeded in withdrawing their forces skilfully and fortified new defensive barriers north of Rome, the Trasimene Line (held until early July), the Arno Line (until 15 July), and the Gothic Line (until late September). They then retreated to the River Uso (Caesar's Rubicon). In the autumn of 1944 they still held the whole of northern Italy beyond the Po valley. Alexander's hopes of punching through to Austria were still far from realization. The 'soft underbelly' had proved to be virtually impregnable. The real military decision would be sought elsewhere.

From Stalingrad to Warsaw

Many armies would have cracked after a defeat on the scale of Stalingrad: the German army did not. The explanation for its continued cohesion until the end of the war may be found partly in a savage disciplinary system under which at least thirty thousand Germans soldiers were executed in the course of the war (as against only forty-eight in the First World War). Most were killed for desertion, cowardice, or other infractions of the military code. But the majority of German soldiers maintained discipline not merely out of fear but also out of faith: Nazi ideology succeeded in infusing the army with the idea that they were engaged in a struggle for the very survival of the German nation. Stalingrad nevertheless severely dented German morale, both military and civilian, and a mood of grim determination replaced the heady optimism of the years of easy victories.

After Stalingrad, the Soviets reconquered the Donets basin and briefly recaptured Kharkov but they failed to exploit the full potential of these gains and were soon driven back by a determined German counter-offensive led by Field Marshal von Manstein. In the north-east the front lines did not move substantially in 1943, though each side suffered hundreds of thousands of casualties in unproductive mutual battering. The Soviets, however, gained one limited but crucial victory in this sector: in Leningrad a land-based supply route became available after January when the Red Army recaptured a corridor along the southern shore of Lake Ladoga. This made possible the construction of a railway to the blockaded city. The line was built in three weeks under German bombardment. It eased though it did not fully relieve the siege.

During the spring and early summer both sides built up their forces in Ukraine until, in July, the greatest armoured battle in the history of the world opened at Kursk. The Germans, commanded by Field Marshals Kluge and Manstein and Lieutenant General Walther Model, launched an offensive, codenamed *Zitadelle* (Citadel). A total of 900,000 German troops with 2,400 tanks, including the new Panther and the heavier Tiger models, and 2,100 aircraft, confronted superior Soviet forces: 1.3 million men, commanded by Rokossovsky, together with N. F. Vatutin, and I. S. Konev, who had at their disposal 3,400 tanks and 2,900 planes. The new German tanks suffered from technical teething problems and proved no match for the less well-armoured but lighter and faster Soviet T-34. A significant contribution to the victory may have been made by a well-placed Soviet intelligence agent in Britain, John Cairncross, who leaked edited versions of ULTRA intercepts showing the German order of battle. (The Soviets themselves had captured a number of German 'Enigma' encoding machines at Stalingrad but did not make much headway in decrypting current German operational signals.) The German forward movement was halted and then went into reverse. The Soviets maintained the initiative and capitalized on victory at Kursk with a wave of powerful attacks that rolled the Germans back to the west. The numerical superiority of the Soviets in men and machines steadily increased. In October they crossed the Dnieper and in early November recaptured Kiev.

By the end of 1943 German casualties in the east numbered over three million, more than the entire strength of the force that had attacked the Soviet Union in June 1941. The almost bottomless manpower superiority of the Soviets now began to weigh heavily against the Germans, whose reinforcements could not keep pace with losses on such a scale. The German army in the east now numbered barely two million. By contrast the Red Army, in spite of its huge losses, comprised six million, nearly all mobilized against the Germans. In January 1944 the Germans suffered a major defeat outside Leningrad where Hitler's refusal to sanction withdrawal once again compounded the disaster that befell his forces. The cost of raising the siege of the birthplace of Bolshevik rule had been immense: quite apart from the civilian deaths, the Red Army suffered a total of 3.4 million casualties in and around Leningrad—more than the entire pre-war population of the city.

The subsequent clearing of German forces from the Leningrad region enabled the Soviets in June to launch a major offensive against the Finns and drive them out of eastern Karelia. In August the aged Mannerheim assumed the Finnish presidency. Under his leadership, Finland signed an armistice on

19 September. This restored the 1940 frontier and ceded the Arctic port of Petsamo to the USSR. Finland was required to reduce her armed forces, to pay $300 million in reparations to the USSR, to place airfields at the disposal of Soviet military aircraft, and to lease the Porkkala peninsula to the Soviet Union for use as a naval base. German troops were ordered out of the country. Most crossed the Norwegian border but some lingered in the north. When they failed to leave, Finland declared war on her former ally. As they withdrew, the Germans burned down villages, destroying nearly half of all the buildings in Lapland as well as cattle herds and machinery. Three-quarters of the inhabitants of the region were evacuated to Sweden or southern Finland. Fierce fighting continued in Lapland for several months before the last Germans were driven out.

The Red Army's advance meanwhile continued inexorably. In March 1944 the Germans retired across the Bug. Manstein, who was held responsible by Hitler for the setbacks in the east, was dismissed. His departure deprived the German army in the east of its most gifted strategist—and one of the few commanders ready to stand up to Hitler. By the end of the month Zhukov's forces were approaching the Carpathians and threatened to break into Hungary.

In response, the Germans occupied Hungary which until this point had managed to preserve some vestige of independence as a junior ally of Germany. Over the previous few months the Prime Minister, Miklós Kállay, had tried through secret channels to negotiate a separate peace with the western powers, hoping thereby to avoid eventual Soviet occupation. Britain and the United States, however, insisted on nothing short of 'unconditional surrender'. Upon the German occupation Kállay took refuge in the Turkish embassy. He was replaced by the pro-German General Döme Sztójay. Horthy retained the regency but real power was now wielded by the Germans. The Hungarian army, now in effect forced conscripts of the Germans, stood guard on the Carpathians as Soviet forces moved closer.

In April the Red Army launched an offensive on the Crimea. Sebastopol fell on 10 May; 130,000 Romanian troops were evacuated; 78,000 were killed or captured. In July Minsk was recaptured and almost the entire German Army Group Centre was destroyed. By now the Red Army was moving into territories Stalin had annexed following the Ribbentrop–Molotov pact. In the north the Germans retreated into Lithuania and north-east Poland. In the south Konev's First Ukrainian Army swept across

Galicia, one of the great battlefields of the previous war. By the end of the month Soviet forces had reached the Vistula and were within sight of Warsaw.

Now came a tragic episode that severely strained the Grand Alliance and left an enduring residue of acrimony: the revolt against the Nazis in Warsaw of the Polish Home Army. This took place against the backcloth of historic Russo-Polish hatreds, exacerbated by bitter Polish memories of the events of 1939. The Poles had fallen out again with the Soviet Union in April 1943 after the discovery at Katyn in Belorussia of mass graves containing the bodies of four thousand Polish officers and NCOs. These formed part of a group of about fifteen thousand Polish prisoners of war in Soviet custody who had disappeared in 1940. The Germans, who disinterred the remains and gleefully revealed them to the world, claimed that the men had been massacred by the Soviet secret police after the Soviet occupation of eastern Poland in 1939. The decision to execute all of them had, in fact, been formally approved in advance by the Soviet Politburo on 5 March 1940, as Soviet documents made available after the fall of the USSR have confirmed.[9] All but 395 of them were shot soon afterwards. Hitler told Goebbels to make a *cause célèbre* out of the affair and German propaganda had a field day. Fierce recriminations followed the German disclosure. The USSR claimed that the corpses were of Polish POWs slaughtered by the Germans. The Poles, against the advice of the British, demanded an inquiry by the International Red Cross. Thereupon the USSR severed relations with the Polish government, complaining that 'to please Hitler's tyranny' it had 'dealt a treacherous blow to the Soviet Union'.[10]

The Warsaw revolt erupted shortly after broadcasts on Moscow Radio on 23 and 30 July 1944 calling on the Poles to rise up against their occupiers. The Poles, like the French, wanted the glory of liberating their own capital. But they felt an even more urgent need than de Gaulle to forestall their would-be liberators. The Home Army regarded the Soviets with almost as much loathing and apprehension as they did the Germans. They were determined to seize power from the Nazis the better to prevent the communization of Poland under the aegis of Stalin's forces. Hitler assigned the task of suppressing the rising to the SS. The Red Army, on the eastern bank of the Vistula, opposite Warsaw, did not budge until after the end of the rebellion. The Poles became convinced that Stalin had deliberately halted the advance, the better to install his Polish Communist protégés later. Marshal Rokossovsky, commander of the Soviet forces on the Vistula, later indignantly denied the charge, claiming that 'at the time we would have gone to any lengths in order to help the insurgents'.[11] Guderian records that the Germans' impression 'was that it was our defence which halted the [Soviet] enemy rather than a Russian desire to sabotage the Warsaw rising'.[12] Liddell Hart supported that interpretation, arguing that the Red Army, in August 1944, had reached, or even overstretched, the limits of their supply lines and would in any case have had to pause, for purely military reasons.[13] Nevertheless, the diplomatic record of exchanges between Stalin and Churchill (and even more so of those between Stalin and Roosevelt) lends some colour to the Polish complaint. Denouncing the revolt as a 'criminal adventure', Stalin vehemently rejected British and American pleas to facilitate the air-drop of military supplies to the Poles in Warsaw. His acquiescence was required because the long distance to Warsaw from Allied airfields in Britain and Italy meant that supply planes would have had to land on Soviet territory to refuel. Churchill was so outraged that he considered sending aid over Russian objections. In the end, too late to affect the issue, Stalin permitted a small number of flights. It took the Germans two months of brutal street fighting to crush the Poles. The cost in Polish lives was appalling: 20,000 Polish fighters and an estimated 225,000 civilians died. After the revolt had been defeated Hitler ordered the entire city to be razed to the ground.

Normandy landings

Throughout 1943 and early 1944 Stalin remained impatient with what he saw as the dilatoriness of the western allies in opening a second front. Allied planning for an invasion of north-west Europe occupied more than two years. At Anglo-American conferences in Washington in May 1943 and in Quebec in August, Churchill and Roosevelt, accompanied by their military staffs, settled details of the plan for an assault from Britain on beaches in Normandy. They finally agreed on a target date of 1 May 1944. At the first meeting of the 'big three', in Teheran in November 1943, Churchill and Roosevelt reaffirmed their commitment to the enterprise though the date was set back to an indeterminate point during May rather than the first day of the month. The western leaders mollified Stalin by acceding, at least in outline, to most of his territorial demands at the expense of Finland and Poland. Stalin promised to mount an offensive against Germany in the east to coincide with the attack in the west. In return for an undertaking by Stalin to enter the war against Japan after the defeat of Germany, he was promised the return to Russia of southern Sakhalin and the Kurile islands.

Reflecting the looming American predominance in the transatlantic relationship, Eisenhower was chosen as commander of the cross-Channel invasion, Operation *OVERLORD*. Under his direction SHAEF (Supreme Headquarters Allied Expeditionary Force) was set up in February 1944 and a large build-up of American and British forces began in Britain. The army was composed of thirty-nine divisions: twenty American, fourteen British, three Canadian, one Free French, and one Polish. In southern England 140,000 vehicles and 3,500 artillery pieces were held ready under camouflage. A fleet of 6,483 vessels of every kind assembled to carry the invasion force to France. Two giant 'Mulberry' artificial harbours were constructed in great secrecy and prepared for towing across the Channel by 132 tugs (one of the structures was later destroyed in bad weather). PLUTO ('pipeline under the ocean') was set in place to pump oil direct from Britain to the invading forces in France.

In spite of the Germans' reverses since Stalingrad, they were still capable of presenting a stout defence in north-west France. Anticipating the possibility of an Anglo-American attack on the west European coastline, Hitler had issued an order in March 1942 for the construction of what became known as the Atlantic Wall, a 1,670-mile line of fortifications stretching (with some gaps) from the Netherlands to the Franco-Spanish border. The Germans had forty-eight infantry and ten armoured divisions stationed in northern France in June 1944. But most were second-grade troops. The best German forces, over two hundred divisions in strength, were engaged in the desperate struggle on the eastern front. The Germans were encumbered with an unwieldy command structure. The Wehrmacht commander in the west, Rundstedt, thought it would be impossible to drive the invaders off the beaches and that the key to success was a large mobile reserve. But he lacked authority over air forces in France and the navy's coastal defences. He was further hamstrung by Hitler's insistence on keeping a number of reserve units under his direct control. Rommel, who exercised semi-independent command over an army group in northern France, insisted that the battle would be won or lost on the beaches. The 'double-cross system', whereby the British secret service, for the greater part of the war, controlled the entire German agent network in Britain, now achieved its greatest success. The Allies made masterful use of deception techniques to persuade the

Germans that the brunt of the assault would be directed against the Pas-de-Calais rather than Normandy. The defenders accordingly disposed the bulk of their forces in the wrong place.

The D-Day landings on 6 June 1944 rank with Xerxes' crossing of the Hellespont in 480 BC as one of the great logistic accomplishments in the history of amphibious warfare. Like the Persian emperor, Eisenhower commanded a vast army drawn from many nations; both employed the latest technology; both were delayed by bad weather. But whereas Xerxes wept on the eve of the attack, Eisenhower preserved a calm demeanour that reassured his subordinates.

First to land, before dawn on 6 June, were 23,400 British and American paratroopers and glider pilots who dropped under cover of darkness to seize bridges and other strategic points on the Cotentin peninsula. Landing craft transported 133,000 men onto five beaches on the Baie de la Seine on the first day. They achieved tactical surprise. The German defensive force was too widely dispersed to prevent the establishment of a beachhead. Rommel continued to believe that the main thrust of the attack would be mounted in the Pas-de-Calais and retained large forces there until too late. The Allies quickly consolidated their air superiority and started pushing inland. When Hitler visited France, eleven days after the landings, he dismayed his generals by insisting that Cherbourg must be held at all costs. 'Instead of trying to pull the troops out of a hopeless trap,' Rundstedt later recalled, 'Hitler wanted to send more men into it. Of course, we paid no attention to the order.'[14] Cherbourg fell on 27 June. Five days later a frustrated Hitler forced Rundstedt to resign a second time and replaced him with Kluge as Commander-in-Chief in the west. Soon afterwards Rommel was seriously wounded in an air raid and Kluge took over his job as well. But a few weeks after that Kluge came under suspicion of disloyalty: summoned by Hitler, he killed himself en route. Rundstedt was recalled to the colours in his place. Yet in spite of the dislocation caused by these successive changes in command, the Germans proved difficult to dislodge.

The break-out from the Normandy beachheads took the Allies longer than they had hoped. Although they had 800,000 men in France by the end of June, they made slow progress. The terrain of the Norman *bocage* (hedgerow country) proved unfavourable to swift offensive movement. Coordination between Allied armour and infantry was poor. Bad weather delayed supply transportation across the Channel. The Germans had sabotaged the port of Cherbourg before they yielded it; only in September did it become fully operational again. Caen, which the Allies had hoped to capture on D-Day, was partly occupied on 7 July after a massive bombing raid had destroyed much of the city; but hostilities did not end there until 17 August. Relations between Eisenhower and Montgomery, his battlefield commander, deteriorated to near breaking-point. The British general was determined to build up his forces patiently, rather than launch a premature offensive that might cost dearly in his men's lives. Eisenhower chafed at the bit, while Montgomery made fictitious claims of progress.

In spite of their determined resistance, the Germans' position by the late summer was near-hopeless. The fighting value of their forces still equalled or surpassed that of their enemies and their new-design tanks at last proved their worth against the Shermans and Churchills of the Allies. But unlike the Allies, they could no longer replace their losses of men and machines. The Allied expansion of forces in France proceeded relentlessly. ULTRA continued to prove its supreme value to the Allies in this campaign. German military intelligence, by contrast, was woefully inadequate and failed to disclose details of enemy dispositions.

In early August the Americans broke through into Brittany. They soon occupied most of the province but this 'right turn' by General Patton failed in its most important objective: capture of the Atlantic ports. The Germans held Brest until 19 September and a well-fortified pocket in and around Saint-Nazaire until the end of the war. Meanwhile a German counter-offensive in Normandy in early August presented the Allies with an opportunity. A gigantic encircling manoeuvre threatened to envelop 200,000 Germans in the 'Falaise pocket'. But the operation was botched, particularly by Canadian and Polish units: twenty thousand Germans and twenty-four tanks managed to fight their way through a gap in the Allied lines and withdraw across the Seine to the east. The Germans' losses, however, were enormous and they were now clearly on the run. The liberation of France accelerated after 15 August when American, British, and French troops, supported by British and American naval vessels, landed on the French Riviera coast. Operation *ANVIL* was one of the most successful Allied amphibious campaigns of the war, partly thanks to ULTRA. The ports of Marseilles and Toulon returned to Allied hands. The Germans were forced to retreat rapidly northwards.

On 24/25 August Free French forces under General Leclerc liberated Paris, where a rising by the resistance had led an exasperated Hitler to call for the destruction of the city—the order was ignored by the German commander. With patriotic hyperbole, de Gaulle acclaimed 'Paris! Paris outraged! Paris broken! Paris martyred! But Paris liberated! Liberated by herself! Liberated by her own people with the help of the armies of France, with the support and help of the whole of France, of France that is fighting, of France alone, of the true France, of eternal France.'[15] It was as if Eisenhower and the Allied armies had not existed. De Gaulle led a victory parade up the Champs-Elysées: as he marched, he noticed Georges Bidault, head of the National Council of Resistance, beside him; looking down from his immense height, he snarled, 'A little to the rear, if you please!'[16] This was de Gaulle's supreme historical moment and he was determined to enjoy it (see plate 29). But his imperious posturing had rendered him odious to the British and Americans. The Chief of the Imperial General Staff, Brooke, called him 'a most unattractive specimen' and rued the day that the British had decided to make use of him.[17] The only realistic alternative at this stage, however, was the French Communist Party. Accordingly de Gaulle was recognized as head of the provisional French government. He now set about restoring France's position as a great power and as an equal member of the grand coalition.

As Allied forces neared the borders of the Reich a new Anglo-American strategic controversy broke out. In September Eisenhower took direct field command of Allied forces in France, which were divided into two army groups, an American one on the right, commanded by Bradley, and an Anglo-Canadian one on the left, commanded by Montgomery. Bradley demanded to be allowed to push directly east to the Rhine. At the same time Montgomery pressed for permission to outflank the Germans' western defences, the 'Siegfried line', by striking north through the Netherlands and then turning south into the Ruhr. He maintained that by this means he could defeat Hitler by the end of the year. With his two chief lieutenants both claiming priority, Eisenhower adopted a weak compromise. He decided to give Montgomery temporary latitude for an advance into Belgium, whereupon the Allies would resume the original plan for advance on a 'broad front'. On 3 September Brussels fell. The German forces in the west had been severely depleted and now mustered a bare one hundred tanks against the Allies' two thousand and 570 warplanes against the Allies' fourteen thousand. Eisenhower's forces seemed on the brink of total victory but the opportunity was squandered. With the resumption of the 'broad front' strategy, the US Third Army, under Patton, pushed towards the Moselle. There he was checked, complaining bitterly that if he had not earlier been denuded of fuel, for the benefit of Montgomery's forces in the north, he could have broken through into the Rhineland.

In the north, Montgomery, after a pause at Antwerp, launched one of the most disastrous Allied ventures of the war. Operation *MARKET-GARDEN*, the attempt to gain a bridgehead across the Rhine at Arnhem, was approved by Eisenhower, who allocated American airborne troops to help. On 17 September British and American paratroops dropped twenty miles behind German lines. Their aim was to seize the bridges across the river which would then be crossed by armoured troops advancing overland in a 'rapid and violent' thrust.[18] But the Germans captured a copy of Montgomery's battle plan. Allied intelligence failed to detect the presence in the area of two German armoured divisions. Bad weather hampered offensive operations. The attack on the bridges had only limited success and the land forces were repulsed by the Germans. The Allies withdrew after losing seventeen thousand dead, missing, or wounded in nine days of heavy fighting. The Arnhem landings were an expensive lesson to the Allies in the dangers of underestimating the enemy even at this late hour. The Germans subjected the Dutch population to brutal reprisals for sabotage attacks by the resistance in support of the Allied offensive. The Dutch provinces north of the Rhine and Waal rivers remained under German occupation until the end of the war. The *hongerwinter* of 1944/5 was one of bitter endurance for civilians there, deprived of food and fuel and driven to eating cats, dogs, and tulip bulbs and burning furniture, doors, and floorboards for heat.

The July plot

As the war turned against Germany, Hitler was seen and heard less and less by his people. Eventually he retreated into almost total isolation in his field headquarters, the Wolfsschanze (Wolf's Lair) at Rastenburg in East Prussia. German public feeling, while depressed by the succession of military disasters from Stalingrad onwards, did not turn decisively against him. Before 1944 only isolated individuals and small groups took action against the regime. On 8 November 1939 Johann Georg Elser, a furniture repairman, acting entirely on his own, had planted a bomb in a beerhall in Munich shortly before Hitler was due to deliver an address to mark the anniversary of his 1923 putsch. Seven people were killed when it exploded—but Hitler had left fifteen minutes earlier. In 1942–3 the 'White

Rose' group of students, also in Munich, had distributed anti-Nazi pamphlets; they, like Elser, paid with their lives.

The success of the Normandy landings and the Soviet advance from the east foretold the doom of the Reich to those Germans whose eyes were not blinded by Goebbels's propaganda machine. Officers of the army High Command, in particular, many of whom had long been sceptical of Hitler's strategic judgement, only to find their warnings of disaster overruled and, at least until Stalingrad, disproved by events, now felt vindicated. Some of them, alarmed by the prospect of a Red Army advance into Germany, contemplated displacing Hitler and suing for peace with the western Allies on the best terms available.

Repeatedly between 1938 and 1944 Germans hostile to Hitler, particularly members of the old Prussian officer class, had approached the British to ask for help in overthrowing Hitler or for some signal that a post-Hitler German government would secure reasonable terms from the Allies. Such approaches were always brushed off. One reason was that the German opposition was regarded as a negligible political quantity that lacked a sufficiently broad base of support to carry credibility. German Social Democrats and others in exile tried to secure Allied support for the creation of a government-in-exile but British propaganda experts warned that such a body would be of little use to the war effort. The Allies, who had not agreed among themselves about the future political disposition of Germany, had no desire to be beholden to any German political group at the end of the war. After the German invasion of the Soviet Union, and particularly after the 'unconditional surrender' declaration at Casablanca, the British and Americans wished to do nothing that might feed Stalin's suspicions that they aimed at a separate peace. For all these reasons, German resistance received no encouragement from the Allies. Later, this was to be a subject for complaint by German anti-Nazis. But the criticism itself exposes the fundamental weakness of the opposition to Hitler. They did not, after all, require permission from the Allies to take action. In large measure, the search for Allied support was an implicit confession that the resisters lacked either the political courage or (since the personal bravery of many of the resisters is not in doubt) the capacity to take decisive action by themselves. With few exceptions, German resistance was uncertain, hesitant, and late in the day.

The most important group of resisters, the *Schwarze Kapelle* (Black Orchestra) clustered around Carl Goerdeler, a former Oberbürgermeister of Leipzig and Reichskommissar for price-fixing in the early years of Nazi rule. Goerdeler was a fervent Christian who considered Hitler a criminal, a madman, and 'the Anti-Christ'. Of the mass murder of the Jews he wrote that it represented 'a dark blot on our history. This can't be wiped out.' Goerdeler hoped that if Hitler were overthrown a new German government might be able to negotiate peace with Britain and the United States on relatively favourable terms. In meeting after meeting with hesitant military officers, he urged the need for a coup against Hitler. 'We must not await the arrival of the correct psychological moment; we must bring it about,' he wrote to one of his interlocutors in May 1943.[19]

The moment finally came on 20 July 1944, when Count Claus Schenk von Stauffenberg, a staff officer, planted a bomb under a table in the conference room at Rastenburg. The assassination attempt was planned to coincide with a seizure of power by military officers in Berlin. The explosion did not, however, kill Hitler or even injure him seriously. The plotters in the capital, disoriented by confusing news from the east, failed to act decisively. At 12.59 a.m. that night Hitler spoke on the radio to prove that he was still alive. Attributing his survival to Providence, he promised that this 'crime without parallel in German history', committed by a 'tiny gang of criminal elements', would be followed by their 'merciless eradication'.[20]

Hitler wreaked a terrible revenge. 'What happened here . . . gives us the possibility to finally get rid of this abscess (inside) our organization,' he told his generals.[21] Thousands of people, most of whom had had nothing to do with the conspiracy, were arrested and thrown into concentration camps or killed. Some of the participants, including Stauffenberg, were shot without trial. Others, such as the Oxford-educated diplomat Adam von Trott zu Solz, were tried before the *Volksgerichtshof* (People's Court), 'a truly revolutionary tribunal to purify the nation', as its presiding judge, Roland Freisler, called it.[22] Some of the defendants made excuses (one even gave the Hitler salute); others behaved with dignity in the face of vulgar tirades of abuse from the bench. Most were hanged. The former Chief of the General Staff, General Beck, whose support for the plot had been hesitant and half-hearted, took his own life. So did Rommel, who had been only marginally connected with the resistance. Hitler, who now trusted almost nobody in the High Command, dismissed Zeitzler and appointed Guderian as Chief of the Army General Staff.

The conspirators, inspired by a mixture of Christian and patriotic motives, as well as by patrician disgust with the guttersnipe Führer, therefore achieved nothing save to contribute to what has been called 'the alibi of a nation'.[23] Many of the leading resisters, including Stauffenberg and Goerdeler (but not Helmuth James von Moltke, at the centre of the Christian 'Kreisau Circle'), were anti-Semites, albeit not advocates of genocide. The July plot was the last fling of the Prussian military elite that had created the Second Reich and, often against their better judgement, sustained the Third. 'Ah, now, really, gentlemen, this is a little late. You made this monster, and as long as things were going well you gave him whatever he wanted,' was the reaction, in his diary, of the Bavarian arch-conservative and violent anti-Nazi, Friedrich Reck-Malleczewen.[24]

With the failure of the bomb plot, the German militarists' nightmare was realized: war to the death on two fronts.

Bombing

The final stages of the war saw the climax of fighting on another front—the war in the air, which increasingly took the form of indiscriminate bombardment of civilian targets. Aerial bombardment on a vast scale was seen by some strategic enthusiasts as a short cut to victory and was undertaken by all the major belligerents. Although the effectiveness of bombing, in military terms, was questionable, the murderous storm that rained down on urban populations brought the horror of war home to urban populations on a scale unknown in any previous conflict.

The Germans started aerial bombing of cities on 14 May 1940 with their attack on Rotterdam which destroyed the city centre and killed at least eight hundred civilians. This led the next day to the first large-scale RAF air raid on the Ruhr. The targets were mainly military or industrial, particularly oil refineries and synthetic oil production plants. At this stage neither the RAF nor the Luftwaffe had any capability for precision bombing and most bombs fell wide of their mark, often killing civilians. Bombing as a military tactic thus merged for both sides into a strategy of 'area bombing' designed to terrorize entire urban populations.

In 1939 British military planners had expected massive civilian casualties from German aerial bombing. As many as 300,000 deaths, it was feared, might be inflicted on Britain in the first fortnight of war. In the event, the toll from enemy bombardment of the United Kingdom during the entire war was 52,000. In Britain in particular, thanks to radar, lives were saved by the development of efficient civil defence procedures. Early warning systems gave notice of impending air attacks. In London public air raid shelters were set up in underground stations. Otherwise people took refuge in tunnels, cellars, and caves or in Anderson shelters (named after the Home Secretary, Sir John Anderson), rudimentary structures placed in back yards. German air raids over Britain slackened after May 1941, as the Luftwaffe switched its attention to the Soviet Union. There, particularly during the first phase of the siege of Leningrad, German bombers inflicted severe damage on civilian populations.

The Allied aerial bombing campaign against Germany, in particular the 'area bombing' of German cities, arose in part from dark memories of the past and frustrated hopes in the present. British commanders in the Second World War were haunted by the ghosts of the millions of casualties in the trenches on the western front in the previous war; bombing seemed to offer an alternative that might be relatively cheap in British casualties. Moreover, even after the entry of the USA to the war in December 1941, lack of trained manpower and equipment precluded any use of land and naval power to invade western Europe until 1943 or, as it turned out, 1944. Attack from the air was thus almost the only significant form of offensive action that Britain and the United States could take against Germany in Europe at this time.

The first major bombing raid on a German city (as distinct from military or industrial targets) was carried out over Mannheim on 16/17 December 1940. Bombers totalling 134 participated: 240 buildings were destroyed and 34 people killed. The German invasion of Russia increased pressure on the British to attack Germany in the west. On 9 July 1941 RAF Bomber Command was ordered to direct its main effort 'towards dislocating the German transportation system and to destroying the morale of the civil population as a whole and the industrial population in particular'.[25] On 30 May 1942 the first 'thousand-bomber' raid against Germany hit Cologne: 2,500 fires were started, 3,330 buildings destroyed, 469 people killed, and over 45,000 bombed out of their homes. At least 135,000 people fled the city temporarily as a result of the raid. But damage to factories was slight and industrial production and general life in the city were soon restored to normal.

The proponents of large-scale bombing, led by Air Chief Marshal Sir Arthur 'Bomber' Harris, head of Bomber Command from 1942 to 1945, argued vigorously that a sustained campaign directed against German cities could by itself knock Germany out of the war. Such an effort would require priority allocation of resources to bomber construction. In August 1942 Bomber Command comprised only 11 per cent of total RAF strength. Thereafter both British and US bomber forces were rapidly expanded. In December the British Chiefs of Staff informed the War Cabinet that 'the bomber offensive is susceptible of great development and holds out most promising prospects' for 'the attrition of Germany'. The Combined Chiefs of Staff approved a directive to the US and British air forces defining the object of the bomber offensive from the UK as 'the progressive destruction and dislocation of the German military, industrial and economic system, and the undermining of the morale of the German people to a point where their capacity for armed resistance is fatally weakened'.[26] A year later Harris assured the Chief of the Air Staff, Sir Charles Portal, that his force would be able 'to produce in Germany by April 1st 1944 a state of devastation in which surrender is inevitable'.[27] As the official history of British strategic bombing, in an unusually sharp personal observation, put it, 'Harris made a habit of seeing only one side of a question and then of exaggerating it. He had a tendency to confuse advice with interference, criticism with sabotage and evidence with propaganda.'[28] Churchill expressed reservations about Harris's prognosis but blew hot and cold on the issue of area bombing. By March 1944 the number of planes at Harris's disposal had doubled and their quality had greatly improved. They were now equipped with navigational apparatus that enabled them to pinpoint targets much more accurately. American bombers based in Britain concentrated on longer-range daytime bombing of industrial targets. But the British persisted in night attacks on German cities.

From the spring of 1943 British raids on industrial towns in the Ruhr caused increasing damage and disruption. In May, a daring British air attack, on the Möhne and Eder dams, using special 'bouncing' bombs, caused severe damage to the water supply network for the entire Ruhr. The 'dam-busters' achieved the most precise bombing attack of the war.

In late July and early August British night-time and American daytime bombing of Hamburg produced the most devastating results so far. Casualties among the attackers were diminished by the use of 'Window', metallic strips dropped from the planes, which confused German radar. On 27/28 July incendiaries sparked a massive firestorm of almost unimaginable intensity in Hamburg. The 'hurricane of fire', as the city's police chief called it, reached temperatures between 600 °C and 1000 °C.[29] Forty thousand people were killed. A million survivors fled. Goebbels called this 'a catastrophe of unimaginable proportions. . . . I believe we must write off the greater part of the city of Hamburg.'[30] Six more such attacks, Speer said, and the Reich would be reduced to impotence. But the resilience of German society and the limitations of bombing as an offensive strategy were shown when production in the city was restored to close to pre-raid levels within a few weeks. Speer himself was surprised and modified his opinion about the effects of area bombing.

In August American B-17 bombers, based in Britain, attacked the ball-bearings factories at Schweinfurt, critical for German industry, and the Messerschmidt aircraft factory at Regensburg. The latter was badly damaged but returned to limited production within a month. The ball-bearings installations escaped serious damage. American losses were heavy: 71 out of 376 B-17s dispatched were lost. Seven further American attacks on Schweinfurt in 1943 and 1944 destroyed the town and reduced production, but some of the machinery was still intact at the end of the war. The RAF too was urged to target Schweinfurt but Harris was intent on his aim of crushing Germany by his chosen strategy of area bombing. Bomber Command did not attack the factory until February 1944, by which time the Germans had dispersed much of their production. Instead, in November 1943, Bomber Command turned its main attention to Berlin which it saturated with raids for four months. Thousands were killed; dangerous wild animals escaped from the zoo and had to be hunted through the streets. But Harris's forecast that the city would be obliterated and the war ended by April 1944 was not fulfilled.

The bombing campaign also involved attacks on Nazi-occupied countries. A raid in March 1942 on the Renault works at Boulogne-Billancourt, near Paris, killed 367 French workers, a larger casualty list than in any attack on Germany up to that point. In December the Philips radio and valve factories in Eindhoven were badly damaged: 148 Dutch civilians were killed. Some of the attacks were tactically valuable: during the Battle of Normandy in June 1944 accurate RAF bombing of communications targets, such as the Saumur railway tunnel, delayed German efforts to move reinforcements into the battle area. Other raids cost large numbers of lives without yielding militarily useful results: the French ports of Lorient and Saint-Nazaire, where the Germans had built U-boat bases, were bombed devastatingly by American and British planes in 1942 and 1943. A thousand-bomber raid on Saint-Nazaire on 28 February 1943 dropped more than two million kg of explosive and incendiary bombs: 479 people were killed. BBC broadcasts encouraged evacuation of the civilian population of the town, whereupon forty-five thousand people fled 'on lorries, or, more often, on carts, wheel-barrows, or even children's perambulators'.[31] Both towns were reduced to ruins. Yet the German bases, protected by concrete shelters, survived almost intact.

During the last year of the war the bombing campaign against Germany reached its climax. In June 1944 total German air strength of 4,925 serviceable machines was near its wartime peak. But the Luftwaffe was overstretched, lacking sufficient fighters, heavily reliant on obsolete models, and unable to offer effective defence against Allied saturation bombing. Whole cities were virtually annihilated and their populations (particularly women, children, and old people, since able-bodied men were generally in the forces) suffered terribly. In September 1944 Darmstadt, not an industrial target, was flattened: almost all those who were not killed were rendered homeless. By the end of the war one-fifth of all the buildings in Berlin had been destroyed or damaged beyond repair. Cologne had been reduced by bombing and flight to under 15 per cent of its pre-war population.

On 13/14 February 1945 came the most destructive raid of the entire European war: the RAF bombed Dresden on two successive nights followed by a third night of attack by American planes. Dresden's population had been swollen by an influx of refugees. The attacks produced a firestorm that destroyed much of the historic heart of the city. The terror, confusion, and savagery of this night were caught by the diarist Victor Klemperer:

> I was standing . . . in the storm wind and the showers of sparks. To right and left buildings were ablaze, the Belvedere and—probably—the Art Academy. Whenever the showers of sparks became too much for me on one side, I dodged to the other. Within a wide radius nothing but fires. . . . A young man, who was holding up his trousers with his hand, came up to me. In broken German: Dutch, imprisoned (hence without braces) at police headquarters. 'Ran for it—the others are burning in the prison.' . . . Eva [Klemperer's wife] . . . wanted to light a cigarette and had had no matches; something was glowing on the ground, she wanted to use it—it was a burning corpse. . . . [The next morning:] We walked slowly . . . along the river bank . . . Above us, building after building was a burnt-out ruin. Down here by the river, where many people were moving along or resting on the ground, masses of the empty, rectangular cases of the stick incendiary bombs stuck out of the churned-up earth . . . At times, small and no more than a bundle of clothes, the dead were scattered across our path. The skull of one had been torn away, the top of the head was a dark red bowl. Once an arm lay there with a pale,

> quite fine hand, like a model made of wax such as one sees in barber's shop windows... Further from the centre some people had been able to save a few things, they pushed handcarts with bedding and the like or sat on boxes and bundles. Crowds streamed unceasingly between these islands, past the corpses and smashed vehicles, up and down the Elbe, a silent, agitated procession.[32]

The bombing led to a breakdown of civil authority in the city. As a happy by-product, Klemperer, a 'non-Aryan' who had been earmarked for deportation the very next day, escaped with his life. At least 35,000 people were killed (in the early post-war period much higher numbers of dead were suggested but this approximate figure has now been established).

From the beginning to the end of the war, RAF Bomber Command flew a total of 387,416 sorties from Britain against Germany and occupied Europe and dropped 955,044 tons of bombs. Altogether Allied aircraft (including the Americans) unloaded a total of 1,350,000 tons of bombs on Germany. In March 1945 alone, 134,000 tons of bombs were dropped on Germany by the British and Americans—more than twice the tonnage inflicted on Britain by the Germans during the entire war. The Germans suffered nearly 400,000 deaths from bombing. Casualties among the attackers were exceptionally high. Nearly nine thousand British aircraft were lost. Of the 125,000 aircrew who served in Bomber Command, nearly 60 per cent became casualties and 56,000 were killed in action, including more than seventeen thousand from the Dominions and other Allied air forces such as the Czechs and the Poles. Given the high value of trained airmen to the Allied war effort, it is by no means clear that the balance of loss of life was to the Allies' advantage.

As for the material effects, these too were questionable. Although Portal claimed in November 1943 that 'social disruption' caused by bombing threatened 'the structure of the entire [German] home front', post-war British and American surveys concluded that bombing impeded German production much less than had been thought.[33] Even repeated, systematic attacks launched against specific targets had only limited results. The Allies did halve German synthetic oil production between March and June 1944. By July 1944 Speer was reporting to Hitler that the attack on oil was having 'the most dire consequences'.[34] But aircraft and tank manufacturing began to decline only in the autumn of 1944—and only in part because of bombing. Moreover, at least until the last months of the war, bombing of German cities does not appear to have dented German civilian morale significantly.

As conventional bombing inflicted unprecedented suffering without delivering the promised strategic decision, both sides invested in a technological race for the 'miracle weapon' that would administer the 'knock-out blow'. In the development of jet propulsion and rockets, German research was ahead of the Allies. Ten thousand V-1 'flying bombs', powered by pulse-jet engines, were launched against England from June 1944 to March 1945. Nicknamed 'doodlebugs', they caused over six thousand deaths. Of greater potential importance were jet fighters. The Germans succeeded in manufacturing over a thousand of the Me262 jet fighters in the last months of the war. But transportation difficulties and shortage of fuel prevented many from getting into the air. The slower British Meteor became operational around the same time but neither plane played a major role in battle before the end of the war.

The Germans also led in the development of liquid-fuelled rockets. Speer, Himmler, and Hitler himself supported the programme whose technical director was Wernher von Braun, a brilliant engineer and SS officer. 'What I want is annihilation—annihilating effect!' Hitler declared.[35] But the rocket too reached the production stage too late—delayed partly by a successful British bombardment of the Peenemünde rocket research station in August 1943. In 1944 the Germans placed the Messerschmidt 163B into operation. This was a fighter/glider with a rocket motor that produced hitherto unprecedented speed, though only for a short period. More successful were the pilotless rocket-bombs aimed at London in the last year of the war. Between September 1944 and March 1945 the Germans launched 1,300 V-2 rockets towards England and Belgium. Over a million people fled London and 2,754 Londoners were killed. Antwerp lost 3,700 dead to V-1 and V-2 attacks: 567 died when a V-2 landed on the Rex Cinema in December 1944, probably the highest death toll from a single explosive device during the war in Europe. Nevertheless, in spite of their human cost, the V-weapons proved not to be the 'miracle weapons' in which Hitler had reposed his final hopes. They could not be targeted accurately and in strategic terms were little more than an irritant to the Allies.

German research on the ultimate 'miracle weapon', the atomic bomb, was much less advanced, though the Allies could not be certain of this at the time. The key stages on the road to nuclear weapons were the discovery of atomic fission by the German chemists Hahn and Strassmann in 1938, the confirmation of the possibility of a chain reaction by French physicists in

1939, and the memorandum in 1940 by Otto Frisch and Rudolf Peierls, two refugee scientists working in Birmingham, that demonstrated the theoretical basis for the atom bomb. The Germans had lost many of their best scientists to emigration; they failed to allocate large-scale government resources to the project; and they lacked supplies of heavy water. At the Quebec conference in August 1943 the British and Americans agreed to pool their nuclear research efforts, code-named 'tube alloys'. British scientists moved to Los Alamos, New Mexico, to work on what became known, though at first only to very restricted circles, as the 'Manhattan Project'. The successful first test explosion, in New Mexico on 16 July 1945, came too late to affect the war in Europe. But the shadow of the mushroom cloud would hang heavy over the continent for ever after.

Endgame

By the autumn of 1944 Germany's defeat appeared imminent. The disparity in production, armaments, and resources between Germany and her enemies was growing ever wider. On 4 September 1944 the British Cabinet, with the Prime Minister and Chiefs of Staff present, agreed that, 'for the purpose of estimating man-power requirements', it could be assumed that war with Germany would not continue beyond 31 December 1944.[36] As Allied forces approached the borders of the Reich itself, Hitler called on his army to summon up 'fanatical determination'. He admitted: 'There can no longer be any large-scale operations on our part. All we can do is hold our positions or die. Officers of all ranks are responsible for kindling this fanaticism in the troops and in the general population, increasing it constantly, and using it as a weapon against the trespassers on German soil.'[37] On 25 September he announced the formation of a new militia to be known as the *Volkssturm*. All males between sixteen and sixty who were not already serving in the armed forces were to be conscripted to it. Later fifteen-year-old boys and women were enlisted in the final struggle.

Eisenhower's armies in the west and Stalin's on the border of East Prussia were held off for the time being but the Red Army's advance in the south produced crucial changes in south-eastern Europe. As Soviet forces approached Romania, the country's diplomats and opposition politicians, headed by Iuliu Maniu, made a series of approaches to Allied representatives in Stockholm. The Romanian army had sustained severe losses on the eastern front and, as in Poland, non-Communist politicians feared that a Soviet occupation would lead to the speedy installation of a Communist government. Although draft armistice terms were negotiated and approved by the US, UK, and USSR, Antonescu refused to give effect to them, remaining faithful to his military alliance with Germany. On 20 August 1944 the Red Army opened a large-scale offensive against Romania, closing in on the city of Iaşi. Three days later King Michael overthrew Antonescu in a *coup d'état* supported by opposition leaders. The new government switched sides in the war and signed an armistice with the USSR. The Romanian army, sixteen divisions strong, turned to fight alongside the Soviets, who poured troops through the country towards its southern and western borders.

The German position in the Balkans now crumbled. Bulgaria, which had never declared war on the Soviet Union, was nonetheless invaded by Soviet forces. On 9 September a Communist-dominated 'Fatherland Front' seized power in Sofia. Bulgaria too joined the war against Germany. The Red Army next attacked German formations in Yugoslavia in alliance with the Bulgarians and Tito's partisan movement. Belgrade fell on 20 October, though hard fighting against the Četniks and German forces continued for several months longer. The German position in Greece had by this time become untenable as Russian troops controlled the northern border and the British navy dominated the Mediterranean. A pro-Allied coalition government under the liberal George Papandreou returned to Greek soil on 18 October, under the protection of a British military expedition (see plate 31). Anxious to extricate themselves from the Greek 'mousetrap', most of the Germans withdrew, though some, obedient to Hitler's orders, remained until November and then tried to battle their way out, harassed on the way by the Greek resistance.

Soviet and Romanian forces meanwhile ousted German and Hungarian troops from Transylvania and moved onto the Hungarian plain. On 11 October Horthy attempted a pro-Allied coup on the Romanian model. He announced a preliminary armistice with the USSR. The Germans, however, retained sufficient influence in Hungary to organize his deposition four days later. Ferenc Szálasi, leader of the Fascist Arrow Cross, was installed as head of a quisling government. Horthy was dispatched to imprisonment in Germany. At the end of October Russian and Romanian troops invested Budapest. By 26 December ninety-nine divisions surrounded the Hungarian capital. But here, as elsewhere, a German garrison, with its back to the wall, put up dogged resistance. Over the next seven weeks the city endured one of the most destructive sieges of the war.

While the Wehrmacht's position in the south-east disintegrated, it still managed to mount one last offensive in the west. Against their better judgement, Rundstedt and Model submitted to Hitler's insistence on an attack. On 16 December the Germans once again surprised the Allies in the Ardennes. Drawing together his last resources in the west, Rundstedt hurled thirty divisions and a thousand aircraft at the Allied line and succeeded in punching a hole through it. This quickly expanded into a 40-mile-wide and 65-mile-deep pocket. The Battle of the Bulge, as it became known, momentarily shook Allied confidence. The Germans reached the banks of the Meuse and seemed about to recapture Alsace and Lorraine. But lacking air superiority, they could not sustain their momentum. They failed to achieve their objective of breaking through to Antwerp and thus dividing the Allied armies in two, as they had done in 1940. Within eight days the offensive ground to a halt. Rundstedt asked for permission to withdraw but as usual Hitler would not yield an inch. By mid-January the 'bulge' had been eliminated, a hundred thousand German captured, and large quantities of equipment destroyed.

This was Hitler's final offensive. He returned from his field headquarters on the western front to preside over the tenacious defence of his capital. In the *Führerbunker* under the Chancellery building, cocooned from the agony of his people, he moved around pins, representing his increasingly imaginary armies, on military maps, berated his generals, consulted horoscopes, and descended into the self-pitying misanthropy that was at the core of his world-view.

The German economy was on the verge of collapse. The loss of the Romanian and Polish oil-producing regions and the destruction by aerial attack in early 1945 of Germany's synthetic oil production works crippled German industrial production and left tanks and planes immobile for lack of fuel. In spite of massive losses, the Luftwaffe still had 4,566 planes available, hardly less than before D-Day. But this was only a small fraction of the number now available to the Allies. As thousands of German pilots were shot down, their replacements were sent into combat with fewer and fewer hours of flight-training behind them. Inevitably they performed badly against much larger formations of enemy planes.

In mid-January the Soviets, who had expanded their forces to five times the size of those facing them, resumed their westward advance. In the north

Rokossovsky entered East Prussia and besieged Königsberg. In the centre Zhukov crossed the Vistula and bulldozed across Poland into Pomerania and Brandenburg, reaching Küstrin, just forty miles from Berlin. In the south Konev entered Silesia and then joined up with Zhukov's forces on the River Oder.

The Soviet advance led to mass flight by Germans in areas threatened with Soviet occupation. The German civilian population in eastern areas of the Reich had been swollen by evacuations from cities under aerial attack, particularly Berlin. From the autumn of 1944 onwards Germans escaped by rail or road, where vehicles were available, more often in carts, on horse-back, or on foot, sometimes with their cattle. In some areas German military commanders ordered a total evacuation of civilians. In other places civilians were forbidden to leave, for fear of panic or clogged communications. As the Russian army surrounded Königsberg, Danzig, and other cities, over two million panic-stricken refugees crowded onto boats to cross the Baltic Sea to western Germany or Denmark. Several thousand died when ships were sunk by Russian attacks. Hundreds of thousands walked in columns across the ice of Frisches Haff, the lagoon between Königsberg and Danzig, separated from the Baltic by a spit of land. The Soviets bombed the columns from the air, killing many; others fell through the ice or froze to death. One of the refugees later recalled the passage through 'this valley of death': 'On the way we witnessed shocking scenes. Demented mothers threw their children into the sea. Others fell on dead horses, cut flesh out of them and fried the pieces over open fires. Women gave birth to children in carts. Everyone thought only of himself; nobody could help the sick and the weak.'[38] Between October 1944 and May 1945 an estimated five million German civilians fled west. Since nearly the whole adult male population had been called up, the refugees were primarily women, children, and old people. Many died en route of exposure or exhaustion. Most imagined they were leaving their homes temporarily: the majority never returned.

From 4 to 11 February, the big three met again: Stalin acted as genial host at the Crimean resort of Yalta. Their deliberations focused mainly on post-war planning. Of immediate significance was their agreement on the division of Germany into zones of occupation: Russian in the east, British in the north-west, American in the south-west; Roosevelt initially opposed a French zone but eventually relented and a small French zone was carved out of the other two western zones. The Yalta discussions also addressed the issue of Poland's borders. Already at the Teheran conference, Churchill had told Stalin in an after-dinner conversation that 'Poland might move westwards after the war, like soldiers at drill taking two steps left close'.[39] At Yalta the 'big three' agreed 'that the eastern frontier of Poland should follow the Curzon line with digressions from it in some regions of five to eight kilometres in favour of Poland'. By way of compensation, they recognized 'that Poland must receive substantial accessions of territory in the north and the west'. Although no final agreement was reached on the issue, these general statements represented a capitulation by the western powers to most of what the USSR demanded. They felt they had little choice and consoled themselves that they had persuaded Stalin to carry out a pledge of 'free and unfettered elections' in Poland.[40]

Hitler's concentration of his strongest remaining forces on the eastern front to meet the Soviet menace facilitated Eisenhower's task. In February the west bank of the Rhine was cleared of German troops. Half a million German soldiers were killed, wounded, or captured. The retreating Wehrmacht forces, under orders to blow up the bridges over the Rhine, hesitated to do so before evacuating all their men and equipment. On 7 March the Americans captured the bridge across the Rhine at Remagen, near Bonn, and over the next ten days moved five divisions across the river. An enraged Hitler dismissed Rundstedt for a third and last time. Model's army group was surrounded in a pocket in the Ruhr by Allied forces. When they surrendered a few weeks later, Model shot himself.

With the loss of the vital industrial regions of the Ruhr and Upper Silesia, Germany's prospects had become hopeless. By now civilian conditions in much of Germany were pitiful; as Allied bombing pulverized German cities, organized society began to break down. Hitler rejected any suggestion that a separate armistice be sought with the western Allies—not that they would have granted it. Last-minute peace-feelers by Himmler and others came to naught. In increasingly heated meetings with his advisers, in which he frequently descended into frenzied ravings, Hitler turned down flat all proposals for tactical retreats. On 18 March the fortress of Kolberg, site of Veit Harlan's epic film which had been released just a few weeks earlier, was abandoned. Goebbels took steps to ensure that the loss would not be reported: 'We can do without that, given the strong psychological impact of the Kolberg film,' he noted in his diary.[41] On 20 March Hitler issued a scorched-earth order, calling for the destruction, before troops withdrew, of everything within the territory of the Reich that might be of value to the enemy. Speer, who had been convinced at least since January that the war was lost, sought to countermand the implementation of Hitler's decree in order to preserve whatever was possible for the post-war period. When he confessed as much to Hitler, the reply was that the German people, having lost the war, did not deserve to survive.

On 15 April 1945 Hitler issued a hysterical 'order of the day' urging resistance unto death. Suddenly elated by the news of Roosevelt's death ('Fate has removed from the earth the greatest war criminal of all time'), he conjured up a vision of 'countless new units' that would ensure that 'the Bolshevik will meet the ancient fate of Asia—he must and shall bleed to death before the capital of the German Reich'.[42] The next day Zhukov's forces began the final assault on Berlin. Within four days they had almost encircled the city and were fighting their way into the suburbs. On 21 April they captured the communications centre of the German High Command at Zossen on the outskirts of the city. The telephones were still ringing and teleprinters were printing out messages from field commanders. German engineers, proud of their equipment, had put up a sign in Russian, asking the captors 'not to damage the installations'. A Russian picked up a phone and, in response to a demand to talk to a German officer, said: 'Ivan here, you can ★★★★!'[43]

Eisenhower ordered his armies to advance towards Leipzig in the designated Russian occupation zone. Stalin had been consulted and had approved but he nevertheless suspected a last-minute deal between the Germans and the western powers. Eisenhower refrained, however, from sending his forces towards Berlin in spite of Churchill's strongly expressed view that the western Allies rather than the Soviets should take Berlin. 'It didn't seem to be good sense', Eisenhower later recalled, 'to try, both of us, to throw our forces toward Berlin and get mixed up.... It would have been a terrible mess.'[44] On 25 April American and Soviet troops met and shook hands near Torgau on the River Elbe.

Zhukov and Konev shared the glory of conquering Berlin, meeting fierce resistance by the heavily outnumbered German defenders. On 30 April Hitler committed suicide in his bunker beneath his burning capital. He took with him his newly wed wife, Eva Braun, and his beloved pet dog Blondi, poisoned by prussic acid administered by Hitler's personal doctor. Later that day two Red Army soldiers raised the Soviet flag over the burnt-out, bomb-battered Reichstag building (the scene was re-enacted for a famous photograph two days later). Half a million people, 60 per cent of them Soviet servicemen, were killed or injured in the battle for Berlin.

Stalin was awakened to take a telephone call from Zhukov who told him the news of Hitler's death. 'So that's the end of the bastard', was Stalin's response.[45]

The Wehrmacht commander in Berlin surrendered on 2 May. Wolfgang Leonhard, who had spent the Hitler years in Moscow, was among a group of German Communists, headed by Walter Ulbricht, who entered Berlin that day under the protection of the Red Army. He recalled: 'The scene was like a picture of hell—flaming ruins and starving people shambling about in tattered clothing; dazed German soldiers who seemed to have lost all idea of what was going on; Red Army soldiers singing exultantly, and often drunk.... Many people had put on white armbands as a sign of surrender, or red ones to welcome the Red Army. A few of them had even taken the double precaution of putting on both a white and a red armband. Similarly, white or red flags waved from the windows. It could be seen that the red ones had been recently converted from swastika flags.'[46] An American officer described the city shortly afterwards as the 'world's biggest heap of rubble'.[47] The underground railway was flooded. Electricity, gas, and water services had stopped working. According to the careful estimate of one historian, at least 110,000 women in Berlin were raped by festive Russian soldiers.[48] A flood of abortions ensued. The Soviet security agencies later reported to Stalin that Zhukov's personal trainload of loot included 3,420 silks, 323 furs, sixty gilt-framed pictures, twenty-nine bronze statues, and a grand piano.[49] The rampage of violence, destruction, and pillage in the fallen capital of the 'thousand-year empire' was reminiscent of the sacks of Rome by Germanic hordes in 410 and 1527. 'The city which had taken the whole world was itself taken.'[50]

Hitler's designated successor, Grand-Admiral Karl Dönitz, a fanatical Nazi, announced his master's death, though not the manner of it, in a broadcast from his headquarters at Flensburg in Schleswig-Holstein: 'Our Führer, Adolf Hitler, has fallen. The German people bow in deepest sorrow and respect.' Dönitz urged his probably very small audience to continue the fight to 'prevent a collapse'.[51] He still hoped to negotiate with the western powers but was informed that only unconditional surrender would be acceptable. On 7 May at Rheims General Alfred Jodl signed the surrender document which specified that fighting would cease the next day—declared VE (Victory in Europe) Day by Churchill. Stalin, ever suspicious, insisted on a second ceremony which took place at the Soviet military headquarters at Karlshorst in east Berlin shortly after midnight on 9 May. Zhukov, accompanied by US, British, and French representatives, accepted the surrender of the last head of the German Armed Forces High Command, Field Marshal Keitel. Afterwards Zhukov held a reception at which he 'danced *à la russe*, as I used to when I was a lad'.[52]

Large numbers of Allied forces continued to engage Japan for the next four months. The USSR, in compliance with the Yalta accord, declared war on Japan on 8 August. The explosion by the United States of atomic bombs over Hiroshima and Nagasaki on 6 and 9 August compelled Japanese surrender on 2 September. The most devastating war in history was at last over. Meanwhile, a new and more insidious struggle for power in Europe had already begun.

II

Europe Partitioned 1945–1949

A shadow stands in a corner, pointing to his heart,
Outside a dog howls to the invisible planet

Czesław Miłosz, Cracow, 1945 *

Liberation

Liberation came at different times and in different ways to the peoples of occupied Europe. Almost everywhere liberation was a paradoxically passive experience since few people in Hitler's Europe were in a position to liberate themselves. Nowhere was this more true than in Himmler's concentration camp universe which continued to function until the end. One of the first camps to be liberated was Auschwitz, which the Red Army reached on 27 January 1945. By then most of the inmates had either been murdered or sent to labour camps further west. Many died or were murdered on the way. Only 7,600 prisoners remained alive in the camp. The majority had been too ill to move and died within a few days of recovering their freedom. A Polish officer reported that they did not 'look like human beings; they are mere shadows'.[1]

In much of eastern Europe liberation by the Soviets was an ambivalent experience, greeted with little joy save by the small number of Communists who had survived underground. When the Red Army's siege of Budapest was finally victorious on 13 February 1945, the liberators went on a rampage of looting and rape. Homes were raided and searched for expensive watches, with which Russian soldiers seemed to have an obsession. The danger of seizure or robbery in the street continued for several months. Artefacts of all kinds were removed to the Soviet Union. Antique silver was

* From 'A Nation', translated from the Polish by the poet. Czesław Miłosz, *The Collected Poems 1931–1987*, New York, 1988, 91.

melted down, Meissen china smashed, stamp collections burned. Libraries and archives were looted. The Swedish legation, where some Jewish-owned paintings had been deposited for safe keeping, was invaded and artworks were removed, never to be returned. A Hungarian Foreign Office official recalled 'that Genghis Khan's hordes had wrought havoc in Hungary during the thirteenth century, and I wondered how we could survive now and save our country from a similar fate'.[2]

Danzig, the ostensible precipitant of the war, was captured by the Russians on 27 March. In the days before the city's surrender, the Russians set up loudspeakers on the walls and broadcast propaganda interspersed with Strauss waltzes. Before departing, the Germans blew up the docks and evacuated a quarter of a million people; a similar number remained. The liberators deported thousands of Germans from the city to labour camps in Siberia.

In Oslo the liberators failed to arrive on time. VE Day came and went without the appearance of any Allied forces or of the returning government-in-exile or the royal family. The Reichskommissar, Terboven, wanted to continue the fight but German army commanders in Norway refused to follow his lead. When small Allied units began to arrive on 9 May, Terboven committed suicide.

In Prague too liberation was delayed. The hitherto relatively inactive Czech resistance launched a rising against the Germans on 5 May. The Czechs were joined by units of Vlasov's 'Russian Liberation Army' who changed sides for the second time, turning on their former German patrons. By the time Konev's forces arrived on 11 May, the German troops had all fled.

The first Allied forces did not reach the Channel Islands until 12 May. Unopposed by the 27,000-strong German garrison, the landing party was accompanied by a British civil servant with a bowler hat, a briefcase, and rolled umbrella. The Dame of Sark resumed her feudal functions and took supreme command of the 275 German troops on her island until their evacuation.

For others liberation took much longer. Homecoming for the three million French workers in Germany was delayed for several weeks as they picked their way back to France through the debris of collapsed transportation systems. For some of their spouses, who had felt liberated by their absence, the reunion was a mixed blessing: many marriages broke up. For many German prisoners of war in the Soviet Union liberation never came at all. Those still alive at the close of hostilities remained as slave labourers.

Survivors were permitted to go home between mid-1946 and 1956. Most returned in a dreadful state of ill health and malnourishment: of 10,000 repatriated in November 1947, only 7 per cent were capable of work.[3]

The human cost of this war dwarfed that of any previous conflict. Russian military dead were so many that estimates varied widely: a Soviet General Staff inquiry in 1990 arrived at a figure of 8,668,400. Deaths in Germany's armed forces numbered between 2.85 and 3.25 million, nearly double her losses in the First World War. For most other European countries the battlefield death toll was lighter than in the previous war. Britain lost about a quarter of a million, France about the same number (including resistance fighters, Frenchmen who died fighting for the Germans, and prisoners who died in captivity), less than a fifth of her number of dead between 1914 and 1918; Italy lost 149,000, compared with 560,000 between 1915 and 1918. Romania, with 510,000 military dead, and Yugoslavia with 300,000, suffered very severely in proportion to their populations.

In addition to the combat deaths were millions of civilian dead, beyond anything known in the First World War. Poland lost an estimated 5.4 million of whom half were Jews murdered by the Nazis. Of German civilians 2.3 million died, including at least a million who died in the panic flight from the east in 1944–5. Estimates of Yugoslav losses range from 597,000 to 1.7 million. Soviet civilian dead amounted to no fewer than 15 million; this number includes inhabitants of annexed areas, Jews and others slaughtered by the Nazis, prisoners who died in Soviet labour camps as well as Germans, Tatars, and other Soviet national groups deported during the war. Most of the Soviet civilian deaths were from starvation. The demographic effects of the war on the USSR were greater than on any other country and were felt for several decades. A large part of an entire generation of young men had been killed or crippled, with serious effects on the Soviet economy and society. The Soviet birth rate declined precipitously during the war and never recovered to its pre-war level.

The economic losses to the entire continent were so devastating that to some observers it seemed improbable that civilized life could resume for decades. In France national income in 1945 had declined to 54 per cent of its 1938 level. In Norway one-fifth of the country's total 1939 capital stock was gone. In Greece a thousand villages had been destroyed and a million people had lost their homes. In Leningrad, Warsaw, Hanover, Frankfurt, and Dresden, whole cities had been blasted to bits and in many districts hardly a building still stood. Cologne had lost more than half its houses and more than a third of its population. No society had suffered greater destruction than the USSR, where one-third of the 1941 capital stock had been destroyed. In terms of economic output, the war was estimated to have cost the USSR 'two Five-Year Plans'.[4]

In most west European countries liberation did not mean restoration. The social and economic shocks of war had been so great as to rule out a simple return to *anciens régimes*. Royalty regained their thrones in Norway, Denmark, and the Netherlands—but these were purely decorative monarchs. Given his flaccid acceptance of Fascist rule for two decades, King Vittorio Emmanuele III of Italy could not hope that his sudden access of courage at the time of Mussolini's deposition in July 1943 would enable him to retain the crown. He withdrew from public life upon the liberation of Rome. Crown Prince Umberto took his place, initially as *Luogotenente* or regent, and upon his father's abdication in May 1946, as king. Umberto promised to comply with the will of the people, as expressed in a referendum on the monarchy. Although a majority of the Christian Democrats joined with left-wing parties in supporting a republic, the popular vote was narrow: 12.7 million favoured a republic, 10.7 million a monarchy. Leopold III of the Belgians too paid the price of his ambiguous conduct during the war. In spite of a 58 per cent majority in his favour in a referendum on the issue of abdication, and notwithstanding the initial support of the government, he was compelled in July 1950 to abdicate in favour of his son.

In France there was widespread consensus that the institutions of the Third Republic had proved inadequate and were at least partly to blame for the disaster of 1940. In a referendum in October 1945, no fewer than 96 per cent of the electorate opposed a return to the constitution of the Third Republic. There was less agreement on what should replace it. De Gaulle pressed strongly for an end to what he saw as the stranglehold of 'the parties' and advocated a strong executive presidency on the American model. But the left feared what they saw as his Bonapartist tendencies and argued in favour of a strong unicameral parliament. De Gaulle, disgusted at having to rely on the support of ministers from several parties including the Communists, resigned in January 1946, hoping to be recalled on a wave of popular support. He remained out of office for the next twelve years. After lengthy wrangles and two further referenda, a constitution, providing for a bicameral parliamentary system, was approved in October. The preamble set out a Declaration of Rights whose first clause guaranteed equal rights to women. Female suffrage was accordingly introduced for the first time in France. The declaration differed from earlier versions dating back to 1789 in its emphasis on social and economic rights, including rights to employment, trade union membership, health care, and free, public, and secular education. A spirit of renewal pervaded political discourse. Yet what the historian Henry Rousso later called the 'Vichy syndrome' pervaded post-war France. The *grand corps de l'état*, the body of senior civil servants, traversed the late Third Republic, the Vichy period, and the early post-war years virtually intact. Most members of the Vichy judiciary remained on the bench. From the outset the Fourth Republic was governed by shaky coalition governments and beset by ministerial crises. Twenty-four prime ministers held office in its twelve years of existence.

The immediate post-war years saw the emergence of two powerful forces in west European politics. On the centre-right, Christian Democratic parties, advocating socially reformist policies within a capitalist framework, came to the fore in Italy, Germany, and (less effectively) France. On the left, the Communists, their democratic credentials relegitimized by the USSR's participation in the Grand Alliance against Hitler, increased their support significantly both among the urban working class and in intellectual circles. In France they became the largest party in the elections of October 1945 and held the support of around a quarter of the electorate throughout the life of the Fourth Republic. In Italy too they posed a strong challenge, alarming both the Vatican and the United States. But in the elections of April 1948 exhortations from the pulpit and clandestine financial assistance from the Americans enabled the Christian Democrats, led by Alcide de Gasperi, to win, with 49 per cent of the vote against 31 per cent for the 'Popular Democratic Front' of Communists and Socialists.

Memorialization

Political life thus resumed, but the memory of war had burned deep into the collective European psyche and could not easily be discarded—or rather memories, for just as selective memory is a basic defensive mechanism for individuals, so it is too for collectivities. Each country, each national group, each political party fashioned its own version of the war and, as time went on, burnished remembrance and amnesia into self-serving myth. For some peoples, such as Serbs and Jews, a narrative of victimhood was a potion that came to serve as justification for resurgent nationalism. For the British, the lone struggle of 1940–1, the heroism of the few in the Battle of Britain and of the many in the Blitz, reinvigorated national self-consciousness. For the French, the petty day-to-day accommodations that most had made with the occupier were overshadowed by the legend of resistance. Only after a generation did the country begin to come to terms with the fact that the Vichy regime had been made in France and supported, at least initially, by the great majority of the French people.

For Germans the chief components of wartime memory were the agonies of the eastern front, the terror of Allied carpet-bombing of German cities, and the flight of civilian population from the path of the Russian army in East Prussia and elsewhere in the east. As Christian Streit has written, 'The process of repression began even during the war. The memory of the assault in 1941 and of the methods of warfare and occupation policy pursued at that period was superimposed in the minds of most soldiers—as in public awareness in general—with the memory of the embittered, bloody defensive battles against [the] Red Army.... The war of aggression and conquest was recast as a defensive war.'[5] From 1947 onwards the Cold War rendered the earlier struggle of the German army against Bolshevism somehow respectable. Military service on the eastern front became a virtual badge of honour with all responsibility for the attendant atrocities against prisoners of war and civilians shunted onto the shoulders of the disbanded police state apparatus. To the extent, indeed, that the Wehrmacht had shielded the German populations in the east from the wrath of the advancing Russians in the final months of the war, this was later hailed by the historian Ernst Nolte and by a large part of the German public as a historic service to the nation. For many Germans the terrible losses from Allied bombing of German cities somehow cancelled out the crimes committed by the Nazis.

In an opinion poll in the American occupation zone of Germany in November 1945, 70 per cent of those questioned denied that Germany bore any responsibility for the war; 50 per cent considered that Nazism had been a good idea but had been poorly implemented. Such attitudes changed only gradually. Few Germans in 1992 could understand how the British could erect a statue in honour of the man who had ordered the destruction of Dresden, 'Bomber' Harris. In West Germany honour was paid to the heroes of the German Resistance, whose role was deliberately magnified in order to provide a historic thread of legitimacy for German democracy. In the process the true ideas and objectives of many of the resisters, especially of the plotters of July 1944, were subtly transformed to fit the needs of the post-war German consensus. As for Germans who had gone abroad and joined Hitler's enemies, they had to contend with suspicion and incomprehension. Willy Brandt, the Social Democrat Federal Chancellor of West Germany from 1969 to 1974 had to overcome such hostility to his wartime anti-Nazi activity on behalf of the Norwegian resistance. Marlene Dietrich, the anti-Nazi film star, had become an American citizen and entertained Allied troops during the war. When she was buried in her home town, Berlin, in 1992, her coffin was greeted with open animosity by many of the wartime generation.

Austrians, who, save for Jews and leftists, had largely welcomed the *Anschluss* and its consequences, generally took shelter behind the claim that they had been Hitler's 'first victim'. Unlike West Germany, where the state took a number of important symbolic actions to register its acceptance of responsibility for the injustices of the Nazi period, Austria contrived until the 1980s to avoid confrontation with the past. The issue suddenly forced itself to the fore of public attention in 1986, when the former UN Secretary-General Kurt Waldheim, a candidate for the presidency of the republic, was exposed as having lied about his wartime activities as a German officer in the Balkans. Although no war crimes were pinned directly on him, Waldheim was shown to have been much more closely involved in the brutal anti-partisan struggle than he had earlier pretended. His concealment of his wartime record brought him condemnation in much of the rest of the world. But in Austria a vehemently nationalist campaign with anti-Semitic overtones led to his victory in the presidential election. Waldheim's ambivalence and amnesia about the war were representative of a large part of his generation of Austrians.

Italy never fully came to terms with her Fascist past in the way that Germany eventually did. Italy's war crimes in Africa, Italian concentration camps in the Balkans, and the assaults on human rights by Fascism between 1922 and 1945 were jettisoned from collective memory and the past was recollected almost as if Italy had been an occupied country throughout the war. There was little confrontation with responsibility by intellectuals or the political class. The neo-Fascist Party, MSI, was at first treated as beyond the pale. But in 1994 Italy became the first European country to admit neo-Fascists to a government coalition. This amnesia of convenience was part and parcel of the broader demoralization and corruption that characterized Italian politics in the post-war period.

For Russians memories of the war were a compound of grief, pride, and selective rewriting of history. The official name of the conflict was 'the Great Patriotic War' and its dates were 1941 to 1945. In official histories (no others were publishable) Britain and France were criticized for their appeasement policies while the USSR's own pact with Hitler was justified and its secret clauses concealed from the Russian people. The role of Russia's allies in securing the final victory was consistently played down. The significance and scale of collaborationism by sections of the population in Nazi-occupied parts of the USSR and by Soviet prisoners of war were too embarrassing to permit serious study. Popular horror at Nazi atrocities was fanned in order to serve Cold War propaganda directed against West Germany; meanwhile any mention of Stalin's wartime deportations of whole peoples was banned, at least until 1956. Stalin was portrayed as a supremely effective war leader. His moments of panic and his catastrophic orders to the army at the outset of the struggle were ignored. For a while in the 1960s, the general depreciation of Stalin affected also the official view of his performance during the war, but in the 1970s his reputation as a war leader was restored. Only in the 1980s did a more balanced and realistic approach to the history of the war begin to emerge, generally from writers of a generation too young to have experienced it. More important, perhaps, than the flip-flops of official historiography were the direct effects of the war on the collective psychology of the Russian people. In Leningrad the sufferings of the population during the long siege cemented a special civic consciousness unique to that city. In the areas of the USSR forcibly annexed as a result of the war, above all in the Baltic states, a widespread and enduring sense of grievance fuelled nationalist feeling.

Retribution

The vast scale of destruction, particularly in the USSR, provoked demands for reparations from Germany. Recalling the morass into which reparations had led the world after the previous war, Britain and the United States resisted Russian proposals. In the end, they agreed that Russia might take more or less what she wished from her own occupation zone of Germany and in addition would receive large quantities of capital equipment from the western zones. Over the next five years a large part of the remaining assets of the Soviet zone of Germany were confiscated by the Russians. Entire factories were dismantled and transported to the Soviet Union. Altogether the Russians are estimated to have extracted goods to the value of $14 billion from Germany and eastern Europe by 1953. Not included in this figure were cultural trophies: the entire contents of German museums, libraries, and archives (including large quantities of such booty earlier looted by the Germans throughout occupied Europe) were removed to the Soviet Union. The western allies received a total of perhaps $1 billion in reparations from their zones of Germany—but in the same period paid much more to Germany by way of subsidies and aid.

Compensation for material damage, however, was only a small part of the retribution that was exacted. In 1943 the Allied Powers had issued a declaration promising that perpetrators of war crimes would be tried and punished after the war. The pledge was redeemed shortly after VE Day with the establishment of the International Military Tribunal at Nuremberg. From the autumn of 1945 a series of trials took place there before panels of Russian, American, French, and British judges. At the first and most important such trial twenty-four 'major war criminals', among them Göring, Ribbentrop, Hess, and Speer, were indicted for crimes against humanity and conspiracy to wage aggressive war—novel concepts in jurisprudence, rendered more doubtful by their retrospective application. The dominant personality at the trial was Göring, who taunted the Allied prosecutors shamelessly. The only defendant who acknowledged any sense of remorse was Speer, though he, like all the others, pleaded not guilty. Three of the defendants were acquitted. Twelve were condemned to death by hanging, among them Göring, who cheated the hangman by swallowing a cyanide tablet in his cell. Others were sentenced to varying terms of imprisonment and held in the Spandau fortress in Berlin in the joint custody of the four occupying powers. After Speer's release in 1966, Hess remained as the sole prisoner in Spandau, still guarded by the complex four-power system. He committed suicide in his cell in 1987 at the age of ninety-three. This first trial was followed by the so-called 'subsequent Nuremberg proceedings' between 1946 and 1949, in the course of which a further 185 Nazi defendants were tried, of whom twenty-four were executed.

The Nuremberg trials were criticized by some as 'victors' justice'. But they preserved at least the outward forms of judicial decorum. In many parts of Europe a rougher justice was administered without legal punctilio. Mussolini, captured with his mistress as he tried to flee to Switzerland, died a dog's death. The two were shot by partisans; their bodies were taken to Milan and displayed in public, hung upside down on meat-hooks in the Piazzale Loreto. Often resistance groups simply murdered collaborators, a term that, like resistance, acquired a disturbingly concertina-like quality according to personal or political convenience. Everywhere women who had consorted with the enemy were ostracized, abused, or worse. In the Channel Isles they were called 'Jerry-bags'; in France their heads were shaved and they were publicly humiliated (see plate 30).

A torrent of revenge swept across the former Nazi empire. In Czechoslovakia, in a wave of 'national cleansing' (*národní očista*), 32,000 alleged collaborators and war criminals were tried before 'People's Courts' and a further 135,000 were vetted by local tribunals for 'offences against national honour'.[6] Among the latter was the film star Adina Mandlová, convicted of having maintained 'social relations' with a German man.[7] In Norway, ninety thousand, one in forty of the population, were investigated on charges of collaboration: eighteen thousand were imprisoned; though only twenty-two, among them Quisling, were executed. In Yugoslavia 'Uncle' Draža Mihailović was tried and executed in 1946; many of his former followers shared his fate. In Bulgaria at least 1,576 people were executed; some of these, however, were opponents of the newly installed Communist government whose offences were purely political. In Romania at least four thousand were arrested and among those sentenced to death was the wartime dictator, Antonescu.

In France during the early stages of *l'épuration* ('purification'), as it was euphemistically called, murders and lynchings settled old scores throughout the country. At least ten thousand people were killed. Another 767 were executed after some form of judicial process. A further forty thousand had been sentenced to prison terms by the end of 1945, though all but four thousand were released by 1949. Some collaborators could not be found and were sentenced in absentia. A knotty question arose in the case of the French army. Should officers who had remained at their posts under Vichy continue to serve alongside those who had fought with de Gaulle? Some could claim that they had been members of the Army Resistance Organization. But five thousand who had no such excuse were cashiered. What of Alsatians who had been conscripted into the German army and even into the SS? Some were arrested but, after a bitter national debate, amnestied.

The trials of Pétain and Laval were miserable episodes. The eighty-nine-year-old Pétain was found guilty of treason and sentenced to death, with the qualification that, in view of his advanced age, the sentence should not be carried out. He died in prison in 1951. De Gaulle, who had served under Pétain at Verdun and recognized both his historical greatness and his tragic ignominy, spared his life but forbade him any posthumous rehabilitation. Laval's end was gruesome: sentenced to death, he tried to kill himself but survived to face a firing squad.

Vlasov was handed over to the Russians. His last-minute reversion to the Allied cause availed him nothing: he was executed in Moscow in 1946. He was not alone. A total of 45,000 Cossacks, most of them former Soviet soldiers who had been captured by the Germans and agreed to fight for them, were also returned to Soviet custody. Altogether 5.5 million Soviet prisoners of war and civilian forced labourers were returned to the USSR, often involuntarily. Many of these repatriates were imprisoned or executed by the Soviet government on charges of collaboration with the enemy. A large number had undoubtedly collaborated and some had committed atrocities. The guilt of others was proved, in Soviet eyes, by the very fact of their having been captured. The fate of the 'prisoners of Yalta', who included camp-following women and children, aroused passionate recriminations for years afterwards.

Even in Britain, which, apart from the Channel Islands, had not had to endure the test of occupation, there were accounts to be settled. John Amery, black sheep son of the wartime Secretary of State for India, Leopold Amery, was hanged for treason on account of his pathetic attempts in Germany to recruit British POWs to a pro-German fighting unit. William Joyce, alias 'Lord Haw-Haw', whose broadcasts from Berlin had appalled, amused, and ultimately bored British wireless listeners, was also found guilty of treason, despite the fact that he was by birth an American, not a British citizen. He had, however, applied for a British passport in 1933, giving false information. As the historian A. J. P. Taylor later noted, the penalty he paid for that application was not the statutory £2 but the hangman's noose. The humorous writer P. G. Wodehouse, no pro-Nazi, also broadcast from Germany. In 1940, busy at his desk in Le Touquet, hardly aware of the speed of the German advance, he had been snatched up and deposited in an internment camp in Germany. Incautiously agreeing to broadcast for an American radio company, he gave a series of talks, gently mocking his captors. After the war precisians held that his actions constituted collaboration with the enemy. The lyricist of a timeless world of ineffable Englishness found it advisable to spend the rest of his life as a resident of the United States.

In Britain, as elsewhere, punishment was unevenly applied. Not a single collaborator on the Channel Islands was convicted. And a country that could hang the son of a Cabinet minister had no compunction about admitting thousands of anti-Communist refugees from Poland, Ukraine, and the Baltic states or about facilitating the onward movement to the United States, Canada, and Australia of tens of thousands more. Theoretically all these were to be 'screened' to ensure that war criminals and Nazi collaborators would not be admitted. In fact, whole units of Ukrainian pro-Nazi militias were whisked through the procedures and quietly settled in Canada.

Moving frontiers, moving peoples

The USSR's preponderant role in the defeat of Hitler and the dominant position of Soviet forces in eastern Europe in 1945 inevitably shaped the territorial settlement at the end of the war. Stalin demanded and obtained a broad band of territory all along the Soviet Union's western frontier. Each of his western neighbours was compelled to disgorge land in order to satisfy Soviet strategic needs.

In July the American, British, and Soviet leaders met at Potsdam (de Gaulle was not invited). By this time President Truman had succeeded Roosevelt; Churchill was replaced in mid-conference by Clement Attlee, following the Labour Party's general election victory; the senior statesman present, Stalin, found little difficulty in imposing his will on his neophyte colleagues. The new frontiers of Poland were finalized. East Prussia was divided between Poland and the USSR. Königsberg, with its surrounding region, was annexed to the Russian Federation. In 1946 the name of this war-blasted city was changed to Kaliningrad (after the recently deceased Soviet head of state, Mikhail Kalinin) and most of its historic German character was erased. Poland's losses in the east represented 45 per cent of her pre-war territory. In return, she received compensation in the west at the expense of Germany. It was agreed that formerly German territory east of the Rivers Oder and the western Neisse, including cities with largely German populations such as Breslau, would be transferred to Poland. The population of East Prussia, Pomerania, and Lower Silesia had been over 90 per cent German before the war but such statistics, which had so exercised the peacemakers after the First World War, were swept aside by *Realpolitik*.

Poland also received the former Free City of Danzig, also overwhelmingly German-inhabited until 1945.

In February 1947 the Allied powers signed peace treaties with Italy, Romania, Hungary, Bulgaria, and Finland. Italy was treated relatively lightly. She had to give up her overseas empire and also ceded territory in the Alps to France and along the Adriatic coast, including the Istrian peninsula and Fiume, to Yugoslavia. But she was allowed to retain the German-speaking South Tyrol. Albania regained her independence. Italy had to pay reparations amounting to a total of $360 million to the USSR, Yugoslavia, Greece, Albania, and Ethiopia. Her armaments were to be limited for the time being. Fascist movements were outlawed. The major piece of unresolved business was the problem of Trieste. The population of the city was predominantly Italian, although there was a large Slovene minority. In the last days of the war Tito's partisans had occupied parts of Trieste, while New Zealand forces secured the surrender of the German garrison and, together with Americans, held other districts. In 1947 the city and surrounding area were constituted a Free State. But east–west rivalries prevented implementation of this section of the peace treaty. After a long diplomatic tussle, an agreement was concluded in 1954 whereby the city reverted to Italy, while most of its hinterland was annexed by Yugoslavia.

Romania, like Italy, had changed sides a little too late to be allowed to escape the consequences of her wartime alliance with the Axis. The Russians held on to Bessarabia and the northern Bukovina. Romania's wartime loss of the southern Dobrudja to Bulgaria was also confirmed (Romania had never properly digested this province, inhabited by an ethnic hotchpotch of Turks, Tatars, Circassians, Vlachs, Gypsies, Bulgarians, Jews, Romanians, and others), though Bulgaria had to give up her wartime acquisitions from Yugoslavia and Greece. On the other hand, Romania was allowed to repossess northern Transylvania with its large Hungarian population. This cost the Soviet Union nothing, although it stored up potential trouble between two of her future allies. Hungary lost all the other territories she had acquired since 1938: she had to yield to Czechoslovakia the portion of Slovakia that she had seized after Munich and a small additional area opposite Bratislava was also ceded, so that Hungary was reduced to an even smaller size than at Trianon. The Finnish peace treaty confirmed the rigorous terms imposed by the USSR in the armistice of 1944. Bulgaria was the only Axis partner in Europe from which Stalin did not demand reparations, presumably because she had never declared war on the Soviet

Union, though that did not stop the Red Army from requisitioning property that had been used by the Germans, including railway rolling stock and locomotives.

Prior to these arrangements, Stalin had persuaded Beneš in 1943 to cede to the USSR Czechoslovakia's easternmost province, Sub-Carpathian Ruthenia. Czechoslovakia had been an ally of the Soviet Union, not an enemy, and Beneš had been fawningly pro-Soviet during the war. The Czechoslovak President, still deeply affected by the events of 1938–9, had concluded that reliance on the western powers was a thin reed; instead, he resolved to place the fate of his country in the hands of his largest neighbour. He offered up Ruthenia as a placatory sacrifice to a savage god.

In western Europe, apart from the return of territories annexed by Germany and Italy during the war, there were no significant border changes. But the whole continent felt the ripple effects of the political changes in the east, notably in the shape of vast population movements.

At Potsdam the British, Americans, and Russians agreed to 'recognize that the transfer to Germany of German populations, or elements thereof, remaining in Poland, Czechoslovakia and Hungary, will have to be undertaken'. But they specified that 'any transfers that take place should be effected in an orderly and humane manner'.[8] The expulsions were, in fact, conducted in a ruthless and often brutal manner. The departure of Germans from all the countries of eastern Europe was one of the most far-reaching consequences of the war. Some of those who left were recent arrivals, who had been settled in German-conquered territories by the Nazis as part of their long-term plan for German domination of eastern Europe. But the majority came of stock whose ancestors had been settled in the eastern lands for generations and who knew no other place as home.

The *Volksdeutsche*, as the Nazis called them, were, for the most part, victims of a calamity of which they were themselves part-authors. Even before the expansion of the Reich, Nazism had evangelized successfully among the Saxons of Transylvania, the Swabians of the Banat (the area between the Mureş and Danube rivers, divided between the wars between Romania and Yugoslavia), and the Sudeten Germans (as they came to be called) of Czechoslovakia. Not all these were Nazis, but a majority became supporters of Hitler. They saw in Nazism a powerful force that might restore their lost status and redress the grievances that they harboured against the states in which they lived. When the German army arrived, to be greeted by local Germans as liberators, the overwhelming majority of the

Volksdeutsche rallied to what they saw as the patriotic cause. Some served in occupation administrations, others as volunteers in the Waffen SS. Seen by the rest of the population as subaltern followers of the Nazis, they stirred up deep hatred and earned condign punishment.

In the north-east part of East Prussia, annexed by the USSR, the food supply had broken down almost completely in 1945 and people were reduced to eating offal. In Königsberg human flesh was offered for sale as fried meatballs.[9] Seven centuries of German civilization in the city thus ended in cannibalism. Many surviving Germans were plundered and conscripted for forced labour on collective farms. The remainder were forbidden to leave until Russian civilians had moved into the region to take their places at work. Between 1947 and 1949 the last hundred thousand Germans were expelled from the region.

In Czechoslovakia, Beneš, in his first speech in liberated Prague, called for the 'liquidation' of the country's Germans and Hungarians.[10] Thousands were killed. Others were victims of looting and abuse. Some committed suicide. Large numbers were forced to depart, leaving behind everything they owned. Many were marched off to the Austrian border at a few hours' notice and left to fend for themselves. Until April 1947 Germans remaining in Czechoslovakia were accorded lower rations than the rest of the population (at the same level as Jews had received during the occupation). They had to wear special armbands and were required to perform compulsory labour. Since most Germans had acquired Reich citizenship, they were regarded as no longer citizens of Czechoslovakia. Their properties, including farms, were confiscated without compensation and handed over to Czechs. These policies enjoyed wide support. Beneš declared that, while 'the transfer must be carried out in a humane, fair, and correct way, and on a moral basis', there would be no turning back: 'our Germans must and will leave.'[11] The later stages of the transfer from Czechoslovakia were conducted in a somewhat less inhumane way. Proven anti-Fascists and partners in mixed marriages were allowed to remain, though in the prevailing atmosphere of hostility many of these too chose to go. By November 1946 an estimated 2.2 million Germans had been expelled.[12] Among them were Czechs who had found it expedient to Germanize their names during the occupation and were now regarded as traitors.[13]

From Hungary about sixty thousand Germans had already fled before the end of the war, some travelling by boat up the Danube. As if to compensate for their own equivocal attitude during the war, the entire Hungarian political class turned vindictively against the resident Germans. Prompted by the Soviet chairman of the Allied Control Commission, Marshal Voroshilov, the government ordered the deportation and expropriation of most Germans. As their trains left, some of the deportees tried to affirm their loyalty by waving Hungarian flags, singing Magyar folk songs, and chalking in (faulty) Hungarian on the sides of the trains slogans such as '*Nem isten veletek, csak viszontlátásra!*' (We don't say goodbye, only au revoir!). Most were sent to Germany but from some villages the entire adult population was deported to labour camps in the Donets basin of the Soviet Union. Altogether at least 300,000 Germans left Hungary. 'Yesterday the "Jews", today the "Swabians", tomorrow the "middle classes", next the cloth-eared... They herd the guilty and the innocent, children and the senile. This is the demise of the morality of European life,' the writer, Sándor Márai, commented in his diary (such heterodox views could barely be expressed publicly).[14]

In former German areas taken over by Poland, Germans experienced two waves of maltreatment, first by the Russian army, then by Poles. German-owned farms and houses were confiscated. Germans were rounded up by Polish militias and put in camps before being driven out of the country. Tens, perhaps hundreds of thousands were killed. In Romania, from the autumn of 1944, tens of thousands of the Swabian Germans of the Banat and more from the ancient Saxon communities of Transylvania, long-settled outposts of German peasant and mercantile life, loaded their wagons and hitched their horses for the long trek to the homeland. The German population of pre-war Romania had been about 780,000. About 10 per cent left between September 1944 and the end of the war. A similar number were deported to labour camps in the Soviet Union where many died. By 1948 the German population had been reduced by more than half. In Yugoslavia virtually all the half million Germans fled, were expelled, or were sent to labour camps by the victorious Tito forces. An estimated 27,000 were sent to camps in the Soviet Union. Violence against the *Volksdeutsche* here was probably more relentless than in any other country.

Official West German accounts, perhaps exaggerated, later placed the number of Germans killed in the expulsions at not less than 610,000. The number of those who were expelled or who departed voluntarily from eastern Europe amounted to 9.5 million by October 1946 and over 11.5 million by 1950. Of these about two-thirds settled in the western occupation zones, the remainder in the Russian zone of Germany. This was the largest population movement between European countries in the twentieth century and one of the largest of all time.

The horde of Germans from the east who suddenly found themselves in a fatherland that many of them had never seen before became for a while a dangerous element in West German politics, easy prey to nationalist demagogues spouting irredentist talk. The *Vertriebenenverbände* (expellee organizations) demanded a right of return, fiercely denounced Communism, and compared their fate as victims with that of Jews under the Nazis. They pressed for non-recognition of the Oder–Neisse line, the new border between Germany and Poland and, under their influence, most non-Communist politicians continued for many years to pay lip-service to the objective of restoring Germany's 1937 borders, albeit by diplomatic means.

As the German presence in eastern Europe was abruptly terminated, other wanderers were also on the move in the early months of the peace. Nearly two million Poles were transferred from formerly Polish-ruled areas of the USSR to take the place of Germans expelled from Pomerania and Silesia. Poland's population was nevertheless reduced to 24 million, almost a third less than the pre-war figure. Half a million Ukrainians, Belorussians, and others were deported from Poland to the Soviet Union. Ukrainians, Estonians, Latvians, Lithuanians, Croats, and others, fearful of reprisals for wartime collaboration, fled west from all over eastern Europe, most of them hoping to get to North America. In the Balkans the post-imperial separating-out of former rulers and ruled took a different form. In 1949 the Bulgarian government suddenly decided to remove large numbers of Turks (who constituted more than 10 per cent of the population) as well as several thousand gypsies, basing their action on the 'exchange of populations' agreement with Turkey that dated back to 1925. By November 1951 158,000 Turks and gypsies had arrived in Turkey, many having been stripped of their possessions, deprived of their ration cards, and forcibly driven across the frontier. Over a hundred thousand Jews, the surviving remnant of east European Jewry, infiltrated to the western powers' occupation zones in Germany and Austria. Most sought permission to enter Palestine but the British mandatory government denied entry to all save a handful. They therefore remained stuck for years in so-called 'displaced persons' camps'.

The result of these movements was a system of almost homogeneous nation-states in east-central Europe. Whereas ethnic Poles had constituted barely two-thirds of the population of inter-war Poland, by 1951 the country, within new frontiers and shorn of its pre-war Jewish, Ukrainian, and German minorities, was 98 per cent Polish. The two most significant exceptions to the pattern, ominous in their long-term implications, were the multi-national Soviet empire and the Yugoslav federation.

The integration of the millions of refugees in their countries of arrival was not easy. European states were, in the main, too preoccupied with the sufferings of their own citizens and with the tasks of reconstruction to have much compassion to spare. The last refugee camps in Europe were not closed until 1958.

Cold War

Europe in late 1945 was a continent crippled, impoverished, and exhausted. All the economies of the belligerents in the final phase of war had been geared to military production at the expense of civilian consumption. Destruction of infrastructure and wearing-out of machinery had greatly reduced productive capacity. Per capita GDP in France had fallen to its 1891 level and in Austria to that of 1886. The relative position of Europe in the world economy had shrunk. The United States now produced more than half of the world's industrial output. Pre-war tariff barriers and wartime blockade had throttled international trade and abolished Europe's central role in it. As European currencies tottered, the dollar reigned supreme. The United States had assumed Britain's pre-1914 position as the world's financial centre. Any revival of the European economies would inevitably depend on infusions of American capital and resumption of trade with the United States. But the end of the Pacific war in September 1945 brought an immediate termination of Lend-Lease. The sudden halt in the flow of resources from the United States exacerbated the problems of economic transition in Europe, though the presence of large numbers of free-spending US servicemen stimulated some local economies and created black and grey markets in 'liberated' US army 'surplus': 'Lucky Strike' cigarettes, chewing gum, and nylon stockings.

At first the United States saw the solution to the problem of post-war reconstruction in the creation of solid international institutions. A basis had been laid at a conference at Bretton Woods, New Hampshire, in July 1944. Forty-four countries were represented, although the chief decisions were the work of the American and British experts, the latter headed by Keynes.

The conference founded the International Monetary Fund (IMF) and the World Bank and agreed on a system of fixed exchange rates based on an equivalence of $35 to one troy ounce of gold. A Bank of England official called the agreement 'the greatest blow to Britain next to the war'.[15] But this dollar gold standard was the bedrock on which the international trading system was resurrected and on which the post-war economies of Europe revived and thrived over the next quarter of a century. In 1946 negotiations began for the liberalization of international trade. These led the following year to what came to be known as the General Agreement on Tariffs and Trade (GATT). The first 'round' of talks among the twenty-three member states produced agreement on tariff reductions affecting a fifth of world trade.

An international political framework, to replace the defunct League of Nations, was likewise constructed. At San Francisco in June 1945 representatives of fifty Allied states, including some, such as Turkey, that had scrambled at almost the last moment to declare war on Germany in order to qualify, gathered to establish the United Nations Organization.

The UN was less Eurocentric than the League of Nations had been. Its most powerful organ, the Security Council, included three European states, Britain, France, and the Soviet Union, among its five permanent members, each possessing a right of veto over any decision. But of the fifty-one UN founder-members (the fifty that attended San Francisco plus Poland which did not formally participate owing to a quarrel between Communists and non-Communists over who should rightly represent her), only fifteen were European. In the General Assembly, in which all members were to have a single, equal vote, Stalin at first insisted on one for each of the constituent republics of the Soviet Union. Eventually he was satisfied with three, one for the USSR, and one each, anomalously, for Belorussia and Ukraine. The defeated European nations were at first excluded altogether from the UN but by 1955 all except Germany and Austria had been admitted, as had most of the neutral states. Switzerland, however, held aloof until 2002 despite the fact that she acted as host, in the old Palais des Nations at Geneva, to the UN's European headquarters. The first two Secretaries-General, the Norwegian Trygve Lie and the Swede Dag Hammarskjöld, were both Europeans (as had been all three of their League of Nations predecessors); all but one of their successors, for the rest of the century, came from other continents. In the post-war world it was no longer possible for Europeans to run the world—or even international organizations.

From the very outset the United Nations belied its name. Ugly disputes between the USA and the Soviet Union soon dispelled any prospect of international harmony. The conflict had its roots in wartime suspicions and post-war fears. At every stage Stalin's paranoia had led him to believe the worst of Britain and America. The Soviets, for example, were represented at Bretton Woods and were offered generous terms for IMF membership, but Stalin, fearful of western predominance, decided against joining. Given the American monopoly of nuclear weapons in the immediate post-war years, his apprehensions were not altogether irrational. Britain and the United States meanwhile worried about Stalin's designs on eastern Europe and then, as Soviet military dominance grew, even on western European countries such as France and Italy where Communist parties were strong. Historians during the Cold War, themselves affected by its politics, argued bitterly about whether Russia or the western powers bore the primary responsibility for the break-up of the wartime coalition. In the wake of the ending of the conflict, these historiographical disputes have an antiquarian tinge. Western concern about the extent of Stalin's ambitions was somewhat exaggerated. He was prepared to probe what he perceived as the weak spots of western influence, such as Turkey and Iran. But in spite of the rhetorical support that he gave to west European Communist parties, he refrained from sponsoring insurrectionist policies outside what he regarded as his east European sphere of influence. His guiding star was the state interest of the Soviet Union rather than the spread of world revolution.

In the immediate post-war years the western powers stumbled uncertainly towards a common policy against the USSR. The British were the first to take active steps to limit what they regarded as the danger of Communist expansion in Europe. As early as October 1944 the British Chiefs of Staff were already discussing the impending 'threat to our security in the shape of an aggressive Russia'.[16] On a visit to Moscow, that month, Churchill concluded what came to be known as the 'percentages agreement' with Stalin. Late one evening in the Kremlin, the British visitor handed his Soviet host what he later called 'a naughty document': a piece of paper containing nothing but the names of countries with percentages alongside, indicating the balance of influence to be allotted after the war to the USSR and Britain. In Greece the proportion was to be 90:10 in favour of Britain, in Romania, on the other hand, it would be 90:10 in favour of the USSR. In Yugoslavia the share was to be 50:50. In Hungary too it would be 50:50 and in Bulgaria 75:25 in favour of the USSR—both later revised to

80:20 in the Soviet favour.[17] Was this merely, as some have maintained, an arrangement for the composition of the temporary military control commissions to be set up in those countries upon their occupation, pending free elections? Or was it a more far-reaching deal for the division of post-war Europe into spheres of influence? Probably a little of both. This was, in any case, an informal understanding rather than a treaty. The United States was in no way bound but the British attached great importance to it.

A test of its efficacy arose almost immediately. In December the Greek Communists, who exhibited an unusual degree of independence from Moscow, seemed on the verge of taking power in Athens through the resistance organization ELAS which they dominated. Churchill showed he meant business by dispatching a large British force to Greece to bolster the anti-Communists. Under British auspices Archbishop Damaskinos of Athens was appointed to head a Council of Regency and a broad coalition government was formed. Churchill was not impressed by Damaskinos—'a pestilent priest, a survival from the Middle Ages'—but was persuaded by advisers to support him.[18] 'Is Greece a British colony?' a Greek Communist newspaper asked in May 1945.[19] The answer, at any rate so far as Stalin was concerned, appeared to be yes, since his formidable military forces in the Balkans did not challenge the British intervention.

The British nevertheless remained apprehensive about Soviet intentions elsewhere. In late May 1945 British military planners considered 'the possibility of taking on Russia should trouble arise'. Field Marshal Brooke commented, 'The idea is, of course, fantastic and the chances of success quite impossible. There is no doubt that from now onwards Russia is all powerful in Europe.'[20] Three influential telegrams from the British chargé d'affaires in Moscow, Frank Roberts, in the spring of 1946, similar in tone to earlier dispatches to Washington from his US counterpart, George Kennan, maintained that the USSR aimed to extend her influence in the Middle East, the Aegean, and the east Mediterranean. The Soviet regime was 'dynamic and still interested in expansion, though not *as yet* beyond the areas where Russian interests existed before 1917'. Russia's long-term ambitions, Roberts argued, were 'dangerous to British vital interests'. While Russia was unlikely to press issues to the point of an outbreak of fighting, it would be advisable for Britain, eschewing both open hostility and appeasement, to align her response with the United States and to show 'strength without ostentation'.[21] The result was a policy of containment of the USSR that combined force-backed diplomacy with covert political warfare.

President Truman, believing that American public opinion would not stand for prolonged foreign military commitments, was inclined to bring American troops home from Europe as soon as possible after the end of the war. But aggressive Soviet diplomacy against Turkey concentrated minds in London and Washington. The Greek Communists once again flexed their muscles and were now reported to be receiving help from the USSR, though Moscow still had grave reservations about the wisdom of a violent insurrection in Greece. An impoverished Britain could no longer afford to undertake a large military enterprise in the Balkans. With more than half a million occupation troops still stationed in Europe, a hundred thousand trying to keep order in Palestine, and pressing requirements elsewhere in the empire, British armed forces were severely overstretched. In early 1947 the British government decided that it could offer no further military or economic support to Greece and Turkey. The Greek government appealed to the United States for assistance. President Truman thereupon enunciated what became known as the 'Truman Doctrine', promising US economic and military support for 'free peoples who are resisting attempted subjugation by armed minorities or by outside pressures.'[22] Stalin, worried about potential international complications, insisted that the Greek Communist uprising, renewed with full force in December, must end. By 1949, with American economic help and military guidance (no US troops were deployed), the Communists' 'Democratic Army' in Greece had been crushed.

In June 1947 the US Secretary of State, George C. Marshall, in an address at Harvard University, announced a far-reaching programme of US government aid for the reconstruction of Europe. Altogether $13 billion were disbursed between 1948 and 1952. Britain was the largest beneficiary, receiving 23 per cent of the total; France came next with 20 per cent, followed by the western zones of Germany, and Italy. Among the recipients were also countries that had been neutral during all or most of the war: Sweden, Turkey, Ireland, and Portugal. After vehement objections from Britain and France, Franco's Spain was excluded, though the Truman administration granted her a $62 million loan in 1950. Under the European Recovery Program (the Marshall Plan's official name) shipments of fuel, fertilizers, vehicles, machinery, and surplus food were delivered to recipient countries and capital was provided for large civil engineering projects such as the rebuilding of the Corinth Canal. Energetically promoted as a supreme act of disinterested generosity, the plan was seen by US policy-makers as a way to revive the European economies and construct a bulwark against Soviet expansionism.

Stalin, on the other hand, saw the plan as a device by the United States to dominate Europe and unload surplus US production. Under orders from Moscow, none of the east European states was permitted to accept the offer of Marshall Plan assistance. West European Communist parties and Communist-controlled labour unions followed instructions from Moscow to oppose and even attempt to sabotage implementation of the plan. Left joined right in complaining of the 'Coca-colonization' of Europe. The French Communist paper, *l'Humanité*, complained of 'the concentration camp of Marshallized Europe'.[23]

American assistance made an important contribution to economic recovery, which was, however, already under way by mid-1948 when aid began to flow in large quantities. There was no magic recipe. German and Belgian post-war recoveries have been attributed in large measure to the elimination of controls and to tight money policies; Norway's, on the other hand, to direct controls and economic planning. Some regions, such as southern Italy, did not share in the new prosperity. Nevertheless, across much of western Europe a post-war boom gathered steam.

The west European powers simultaneously tried to consolidate their political security. In March 1947 Britain and France renewed their alliance in the Treaty of Dunkirk. This was explicitly directed against Germany rather than the Soviet Union: the stated object was 'preventing Germany again from becoming a menace to peace'.[24] But whereas the French remained fixated on their historic antagonism to Germany, the British were much more concerned with the Soviet danger. The British Foreign Secretary, Ernest Bevin, explained to the House of Commons on 22 January 1948 his 'opinion . . . that they [the Russians] thought they could wreck or intimidate Western Europe by political upsets, economic chaos and even revolutionary methods'.[25] In March 1948 the two countries joined the Benelux states in the Treaty of Brussels, an agreement on 'economic, social and cultural collaboration and collective self-defence'. This promised 'military and other aid' in the event of any 'armed attack in Europe' on one of the signatories. In the autumn of that year the alliance was strengthened by the formation of a joint 'land, sea and air command organization'. At the same time the five governments called for the creation of a 'defensive pact for the North Atlantic'.[26]

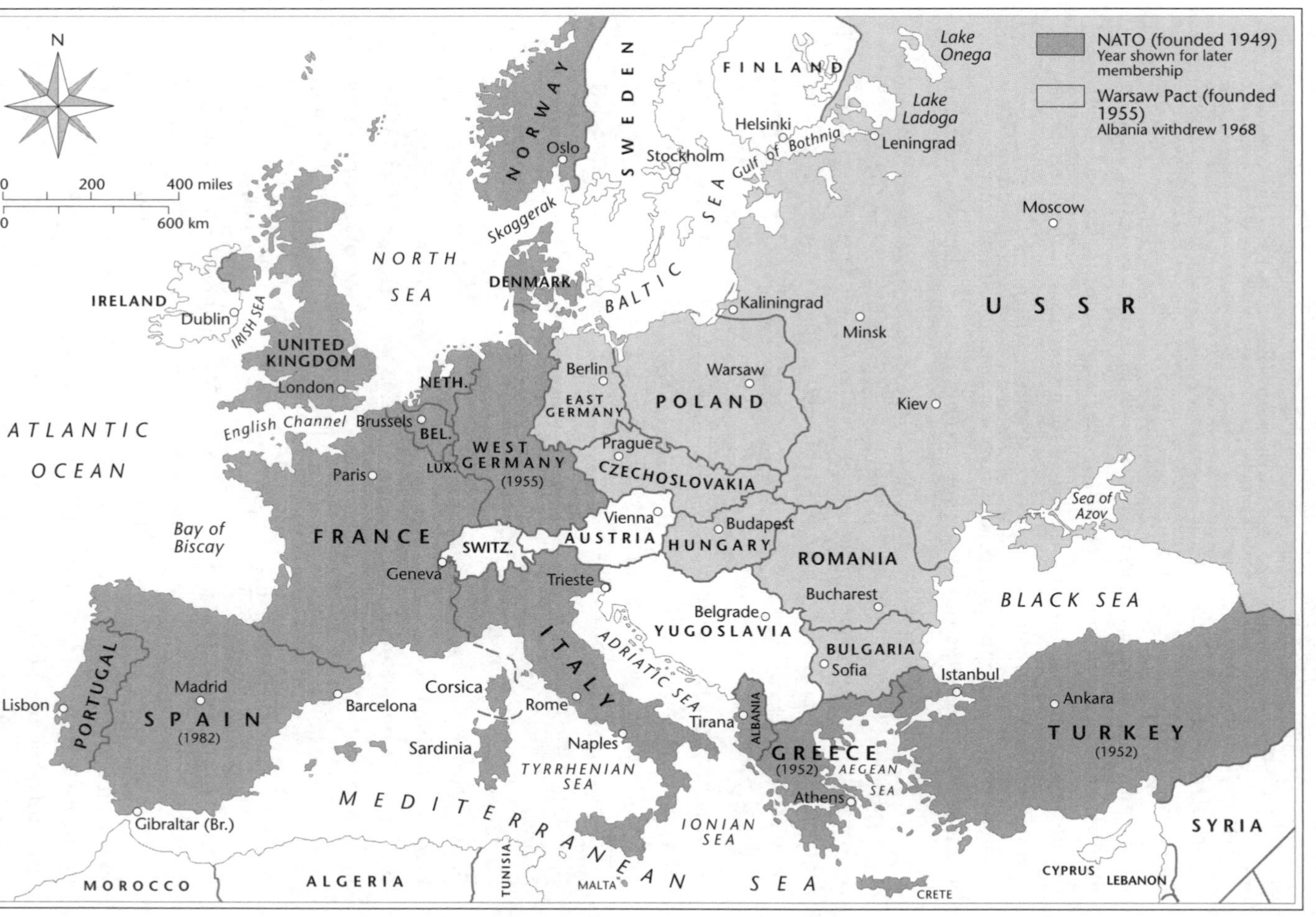

Map 6. Cold War Europe, 1945–1989

The North Atlantic Treaty Organisation came into being in August 1949, a creation of the Treaty of Washington, signed the previous April. The United States and Canada joined the five Brussels Treaty states plus Denmark, Norway, Iceland, Portugal, and a rehabilitated Italy in a mutual security guarantee. Greece and Turkey became members in 1952. The signatories agreed 'that an armed attack against one or more of them in Europe or North America shall be considered an attack against them all'.[27] NATO was not an American imposition on western Europe. Given their fear of Soviet military strength and aggressive intentions, European governments were at least as interested as Washington in maintaining the US security umbrella. The only countries in western Europe not to join were Spain, which was judged inadmissible so long as Franco ruled, Sweden, Switzerland, and Ireland, which jealously guarded their traditional neutrality, Germany and Austria, which had not yet regained independence, and Finland, half in the shadow of the Russians. All these countries maintained capitalist economic systems and all except Spain were multi-party democracies. In peace, as in war, however, neutrality was never absolute. The Finns were bound by treaty and by geographical reality to the USSR. Spain, on the other hand, eventually moved into diplomatic alignment with the United States.

The Soviet alliance system, much more of an unwelcome imposition on its weaker members, grew out of bilateral agreements with the USSR's western neighbours. By 1949 Stalin had concluded twenty-year mutual assistance treaties with Bulgaria, Czechoslovakia, Hungary, Poland, and Romania. Each of these granted the Soviet Union the right to continue its military presence. Unlike NATO, which suffered from lack of uniformity in weapons systems, the eastern bloc allies were all obliged to stock their arsenals mainly with Soviet-built armaments. The division of the continent into two hostile blocs was now the dominant fact of European politics.

Communization in eastern Europe

The partition of Europe into two spheres of influence froze into semi-permanence between 1945 and 1949. The phrase 'iron curtain' (*eiserner Vorhang*, the German term for 'safety curtain' in a theatre) had been used by Goebbels in February 1945 in an article in *Das Reich* which forecast the Bolshevization of a terrorized, Russian-occupied, eastern half of the continent.[28] Others had invoked the image, in both German and English, as far back as the 1920s to denote the barrier between Bolshevik Russia and its western neighbours. But it was Churchill who popularized the phrase and the idea in his famous speech at Fulton, Missouri, in March 1946.

The primary foundation of Communist power nearly everywhere in eastern Europe was the presence of the Soviet army. Stalin himself told one of the Polish Communist leaders: 'When the Soviet Army has gone, they will shoot you like partridges.'[29] Nowhere in the region, with the limited exceptions of Czechoslovakia and Bulgaria, did Communism have a significant pre-war base of popular support. Nor did the conduct of the Soviet army as liberators and occupiers commend Marxist-Leninist ideology to many east Europeans. The presence in the leadership of most Communist parties in eastern Europe of large numbers of returning exiles from the Soviet Union further stamped their doctrine in the eyes of many as an alien imposition. In general Communist parties throughout the region looked to Moscow for guidance and in many cases for direct orders. The techniques used to gain power were often similar; nevertheless, the differing political cultures and specific circumstances of each country produced variations on the basic theme.

Bulgaria became the first state in eastern Europe in which a Communist-dominated government took power after the Second World War (apart from Yugoslavia and Albania where Communist resistance movements maintained control after the end of the war). The Communists in Bulgaria were helped by the fact that this was the one country in the region with a strong tradition of Russophilia. The 'Fatherland Front' government formed after the coup of September 1944 had included members of all the main political groups. But the Soviet-dominated Control Commission that supervised the country until the signature of the peace treaty conducted a purge of non-Communists from the army, police, judiciary, schools, civil service, and trade unions. In February 1945 one hundred right-wing politicians were arrested, put on trial, and shot. The Agrarian and Social Democrat parties were infiltrated and taken over by Communist sympathizers. In elections in November, the 'Fatherland Front', now Communist-dominated, claimed to have won 86 per cent of the votes. Further purges, arrests, and trials of oppositionists followed. After a referendum in September 1946 the boy-king Simeon II, who had reigned since 1943, was ousted and Bulgaria became a Republic. Dimitrov, who had returned home a much-reduced figure since his glory days at the Reichstag Trial and as head of the Comintern, became Prime Minister in November. In mid-1947 the most powerful non-Communist leader, the former Agrarian leader, Nikola

Petkov, was arrested, tried for treason (he was not permitted to present a defence), and executed. Remaining opposition politicians were eliminated soon afterwards and by 1949 all non-Communist parties had been closed down. Bulgaria was declared a 'people's democracy' and a new 'Dimitrov constitution', on the Soviet model, took effect.

In Hungary a Provisional Assembly, meeting in Soviet-liberated territory at Debrecen on 21 December 1944, had elected a multi-party government that ruled the country until elections could be held. Its achievement was the redistribution of about a third of Hungary's arable land to some 600,000 landless peasants, a decisive break with the past and a shattering blow to the landowning gentry class who had hitherto dominated Hungarian politics and society. In the general election of November 1945 the Smallholder Party won 57 per cent of the votes. In 1946 its leader, Zoltán Tildy, became President of the newly declared Republic. The Smallholders called for further land redistribution and 'a genuine democracy, which would be built upon Hungary's democratic traditions and imbued with the spirit of Hungary'.[30] The Communists denounced the Smallholders as heirs of Horthy. In fact, notwithstanding their name, the Smallholders represented not only peasants but also urban bourgeois and other right-wing elements in general. Ferenc Nagy, another Smallholder leader, took office as Prime Minister of a government that, on Soviet insistence, included representatives of other parties, among them Communists. He soon found himself under growing pressure from his partners. A British diplomat summed up his dilemma in March 1946: 'The Prime Minister and Smallholder members of the Government are floundering in a sea of despair. They see Communist push backed up by Moscow and the Red Army. Consequently the Prime Minister, Mr Nagy, has decided to choose what appears to be the lesser of the two evils and to give way to the Communists in order to meet the present crisis.'[31] The wealth and capacity for resistance of the Hungarian bourgeoisie were meanwhile diminished by one of the most savage inflations of history. In August 1946 the currency was stabilized and reformed at a rate of 400,000,000,000,000,000,000,000,000,000 (400 octillion or: 4×10^{29}) pengos to one forint. The Communists claimed this as their achievement. Behind a 'Popular Front' façade, they steadily agglomerated power.

In May 1947 Nagy judged it prudent not to return home from a holiday in Switzerland (the Communists had kidnapped his son and told Nagy he would see him again only if he remained in exile). In parliamentary elections later that year the Communists, with 24 per cent, became the largest party. Non-Communists in the coalition were eliminated or neutered. The Hungarian Communist leader, Mátyás Rákosi, a jovial, pot-bellied Stalinist, a commissar in the short-lived Kun regime in 1919 and political prisoner for sixteen years under Horthy, orchestrated the Communist takeover. He later added a much-repeated phrase to the post-war political lexicon: '"salami tactics", by which we sliced off... the reactionaries'.[32] First various factions of the Smallholders, then the Social Democrats were terrorized into political oblivion. The Roman Catholic Church resisted for a time but the Primate, Cardinal József Mindszenty, was arrested and sentenced to life imprisonment. By 1949 Communist rule was total.

Political change in Romania, as elsewhere, was determined by the overawing presence of the Red Army; in early 1946 at least 600,000 Soviet troops were stationed in the country. The Americans had accepted during the war a tacit understanding that (in the words of Averell Harriman, Roosevelt's emissary to Moscow) 'Romania was an area of predominant Soviet interest in which we should not interfere.'[33] In February 1945 the Russian Deputy Foreign Minister, Andrei Vyshinsky, visited Bucharest and ordered King Michael to appoint Dr Petru Groza, a peasant leader who was on good terms with the Communists, as Prime Minister. Vyshinsky warned the king that failure to comply would imperil the survival of Romania as an independent state. Communists occupied the Defence and Interior Ministries in Groza's Cabinet and used their powers to extend Communist influence. The two largest parties, the Liberals and the National Peasant Party, were excluded from the government. In August the king tried to dismiss Groza but found himself ignored. The results of parliamentary elections held in November 1946 were falsified by the Communists: they claimed 70 per cent support for their 'Bloc of Democratic Parties' whereas the National Peasant Party was said by western observers to have won an outright majority. Opposition leaders protested and boycotted Parliament but in July 1947 the National Peasant leader, Iuliu Maniu, together with others, was arrested. Charged with conspiring with American and British agents, he was sentenced to life imprisonment (he died in gaol in 1953). In December the king was forced to abdicate and a People's Republic was declared. Communists were now in full control of the country.

Resistance to Communism was deepest in Poland. Stalin himself, in a famous phrase, had joked to the Polish Prime Minister, Mikołajczyk, that introducing Communism to Poland would be like 'putting a saddle on a cow'.[34] In the inter-war period the small Polish Communist Party had been little more than an emanation of Soviet foreign policy: it supported Soviet claims to eastern Poland and in 1932 passed a resolution backing German claims to Upper Silesia and Danzig, though it changed its tune after 1934 in response to the new wind from Moscow calling for resistance to Nazism. In 1938, at the height of the purges, Stalin had ordered the party's disbandment and the liquidation of nearly all its leaders. It was resuscitated only in 1942. Communism's dependence on Soviet domination hardly increased its attractiveness to Poles, whose national identity had largely been constructed around the idea of resistance to Russian imperialism. Moreover, in a country where Catholic anti-Semitism remained deeply ingrained, even now that most Jews had been murdered, the disproportionately Jewish composition of the Polish Communist ruling group in the post-war years rendered it even more contemptible in the eyes of much of the population.

In July 1944 the Soviet Union had set up a rival to the Polish government-in-exile in London: the 'Polish Committee of National Liberation' or 'Lublin Committee', including non-Communists but with Communists in key positions. In the autumn of that year, following the failure of the Warsaw rising, the Soviet occupying forces and NKVD (secret police) in eastern Poland arrested thirty thousand members of the Home Army and Ukrainian underground groups. The Secretary of the Communist Party Central Committee, Władisław Gomułka, explained in a speech: 'We must put people who are totally committed to the camp of democratic Poland and who think in the same way as its government in all the key jobs in the civil service, the armed forces and the courts.'[35] Although lacking much of a social base, the Communists succeeded, with Soviet assistance, in taking control of the army, police, and internal security apparatus. The underground networks created by the non-Communist resistance during the war nevertheless remained substantially intact and were turned against the Communists. Eighteen thousand people were killed in the civil war that rumbled on until 1947. The western powers had at first refused to recognize the Lublin Committee as the Provisional Government of Poland but in July 1945 Mikołajczyk and four other members of the London government were persuaded to join an enlarged version of it, pending elections. At Potsdam the western powers agreed to withdraw recognition from the London government and to accord it instead to the enlarged Provisional Government. In January 1947 the long-awaited elections took place against the background of severe repression, censorship, and intimidation, particularly directed against Mikołajczyk's Peasant Party. The result was a victory for the

Communist-controlled 'Democratic bloc'. Mikołajczyk fled the country a few months later. The Communists solidified their rule by continued repression: by January 1948 26,400 political prisoners were being held. Although some institutional centres of social power remained immune from Communist control, notably the Church, political opposition to the regime was, for the time being, snuffed out.

Czechoslovakia in 1945 offered the brightest prospect of a triumph for Communists by democratic means. Building on their strong pre-war base they emerged as the most popular party, securing 38 per cent of the votes in the first post-war elections in May 1946. In the ensuing coalition government they controlled the Ministry of the Interior and, with it, the police and security services. In February 1948 several opposition ministers resigned, hoping to force new elections. Instead they precipitated what amounted to a Communist coup. Supported by some fellow-travelling Social Democrats, the Communist leader, Klement Gottwald, formed a new government that effectively ended parliamentary democracy. Two weeks later the Foreign Minister, Jan Masaryk, who had been retained by the Communists as a decorative face, was found dead, apparently having jumped or fallen from his office window. He was said to have committed suicide, though no note was discovered. Suspicions were widespread that Masaryk was a victim of murder. The truth remains uncertain although a Czech police investigation in 2004 concluded that he was murdered. But even if Masaryk was not pushed, this modern defenestration of Prague signalled the political murder of the second Czechoslovak Republic. The Communist grip on power was formally sealed in May when elections took place on the basis of a single list presented by the Communist-controlled, supposedly all-party 'National Front'. Those who wished to oppose the list were obliged to go behind a screen to register their votes: 11 per cent took the risk of doing so. In September 1948, President Beneš, who had remained in office in the vain hope of preserving some vestige of parliamentary democracy, died. As in the rest of eastern Europe, the one-party state was consolidated by massive repression: within a year the country's gaols held 25,000 political prisoners.

In September 1947 the new dispensation in eastern Europe celebrated a kind of coronation at the founding meeting, held near Wrocław (formerly Breslau) in Poland, of the Communist Information Bureau (Cominform), successor organization to the old Comintern. Cominform was designed to coordinate and confirm the Soviet party's hegemonic control over the international Communist movement. By way of reassurance that the new body would not seek to impose Muscovite imperialism on the international movement, its headquarters were placed in Belgrade, capital of the most reliably Communist state in eastern Europe. Yet within a few months that very country had rebelled against Moscow and earned excommunication from the Cominform. The affair demonstrated vividly the demand of the Soviet party for undeviating conformity from all its fellow members of the Cominform—but also the possibility of successful defiance.

The Tito–Stalin breach was initiated by Stalin, who regarded Tito as too big for his breeches. The Yugoslav partisan leader's independent conduct during the war had aroused the first inklings of suspicion in Stalin's mind. Tito's post-war behaviour in pressing the Trieste issue further than the Soviets thought necessary added to the Soviet leader's irritation. Tito's pursuit of the idea of a Balkan federation that would incorporate Bulgaria and Albania under Yugoslav leadership had at first been supported by the Russians but then became the occasion for the break. The unusual aspect of the case was less Stalin's attack than Tito's readiness to defend himself. Why exactly he did so remains something of a mystery, for in earlier years Tito, a Russian-trained Comintern agent, had been a faithful disciple of Moscow. Other Communist leaders who fell out with Moscow in Stalin's final years behaved like the Russian victims of the purges of the 1930s and duly signed their own death warrants by confessing their ideological sins and indulging in self-mortification. But not Tito. Why? Apart perhaps from the Albanians, the Yugoslavs were the only Communist Party in Europe who could plausibly claim to have installed themselves in power. The Red Army had arrived in Yugoslavia in 1944 but by then partisans already controlled a large part of the country. Soviet troops had withdrawn from Yugoslavia before VE Day. This, more than anything, gave Tito the courage to strike out for independence from the Soviet Union. His defiance of Stalin seemed as stunning a repudiation of established authority as Luther's at Wittenberg. For the first time since 1917 a foreign Communist Party asserted the right to decide its own policy and ideology independently of Moscow.

Even more astounding was the publication of correspondence between the Soviet and Yugoslav parties in which the dispute was laid bare in an unprecedented way. Never before had serious communications between Communist parties, as distinct from fraternal resolutions of solidarity, been published in this way. The exchanges were caustic and direct. The Russians accused Tito of dishonesty, slander, and hypocrisy. They declared that the Yugoslav Party was 'being hoodwinked by the degenerate and opportunist theory of the peaceful absorption of capitalist elements by a Socialist system'. The Yugoslavs responded with the heretical affirmation: 'No matter how much each of us loves the land of socialism, the USSR, he can, in no case, love his own country less.'[36] Stalin was infuriated by Tito's defiance. Nikita Khrushchev later recalled that, at the height of the quarrel, he visited Stalin, who pointed to a letter lately sent to Tito and asked, 'Have you read this?' Without waiting for a reply, he continued, 'I will shake my little finger and there will be no more Tito. He will fall.'[37] The veracity of Khrushchev's account has been questioned.[38] But it certainly reflected Stalin's view.

Tito did not fall. His internal position was secure enough to prevent the Russians from toppling him by deploying agents within Yugoslavia. Their chief such agent until recently had been Tito himself. Without him, and against him, they could achieve little. Plans for Tito's assassination got nowhere. The only alternative was invasion. Frontier incidents were manufactured on the Yugoslav–Bulgarian border. Contingency plans were prepared for an attack on Yugoslavia by the Soviet army, with Hungarian, Romanian, and Albanian support. But the Soviet lines of communication would be very long. The commitment of forces required would be substantial. Moreover, the Russians could not be certain what attitude the west would take to such a move. Even if they did not intervene, they might well supply Tito with arms, as Britain had done during the war. The Russians could be sure that the Yugoslav army, battle-hardened and well-versed in guerrilla warfare on its home soil, would defend the country vigorously. Wisely, Stalin refrained from such an adventure.

Instead he bound his remaining east European clients closer to him by forming the Council for Mutual Economic Assistance (Comecon). Yugoslavia was excluded from membership. The immediate purpose of the organization was to provide an alternative to the Marshall Plan. But one of its first activities was an economic boycott of Yugoslavia. The longer-term aim was to integrate the economies of eastern Europe in a Soviet-dominated trading bloc. This time the error made with the Cominform was not repeated: the headquarters were placed in Moscow.

The German question

The western powers condemned Soviet actions in eastern Europe but gave no serious thought to intervention. The furthest they would go was to offer economic aid to Yugoslavia after its assertion of independence from Moscow. The United States and Britain perforce accepted Stalin's ability, if not his right, to create a cordon sanitaire in eastern Europe. By contrast, east and west engaged in bitter conflict over Germany, which became for the next generation the main arena of the Cold War in Europe. At Potsdam the American, British, and Soviet leaders confirmed their Yalta decisions on Germany and agreed on the 'political and economic principles to govern the treatment of Germany in the initial control period'. Germany was to be disarmed, denazified, and decentralized (the word 'dismemberment', which had been used at Yalta, disappeared from the Potsdam conclusions). The country was to be organized 'as a single economic unit' with common policies for industry, agriculture, trade, currency, and transportation. Primary emphasis would be given 'to the development of agriculture and peaceful domestic industries'. This provision was a relic of the wartime proposal of US Treasury Secretary Henry Morgenthau that Germany should be 'pastoralized' to prevent her re-emergence as an industrial or military power. A five-member Council of Foreign Ministers of China, France, the UK, USA, and USSR was set up, one of whose first tasks would be 'the preparation of a peace settlement for Germany to be accepted by the Government of Germany when a government adequate for the purpose is established'.[39] (In effect, the Chinese, a non-occupying power preoccupied with their ongoing civil war, played little part in this body.)

According to wartime Allied agreements, Berlin, an enclave 110 miles within the Russian zone was to be 'jointly occupied' by Soviet, American, British, and French forces, each of which would be assigned a specified area of the city. The Soviet zone was in the eastern part of the city, the American in the south-west, the British in the west, and the French in the north-west. An Inter-Allied Governing Authority known as the 'Kommandatura', consisting of one military officer from each power, would 'direct jointly the administration of the Greater Berlin area'.[40] Decision-making in this body would be governed by the principle of unanimity. The Kommandatura was set up only in July 1945 after long-drawn-out negotiations between the Soviet and western powers regarding American and British withdrawals from parts of the designated Soviet zone of occupation in Germany and entry by the western forces into their occupation zones in Berlin. The Russians utilized the interval between their conquest of the city at the end of April and the arrival of British and American troops on 4 July to place Communists in key positions in the city administration. Friction soon

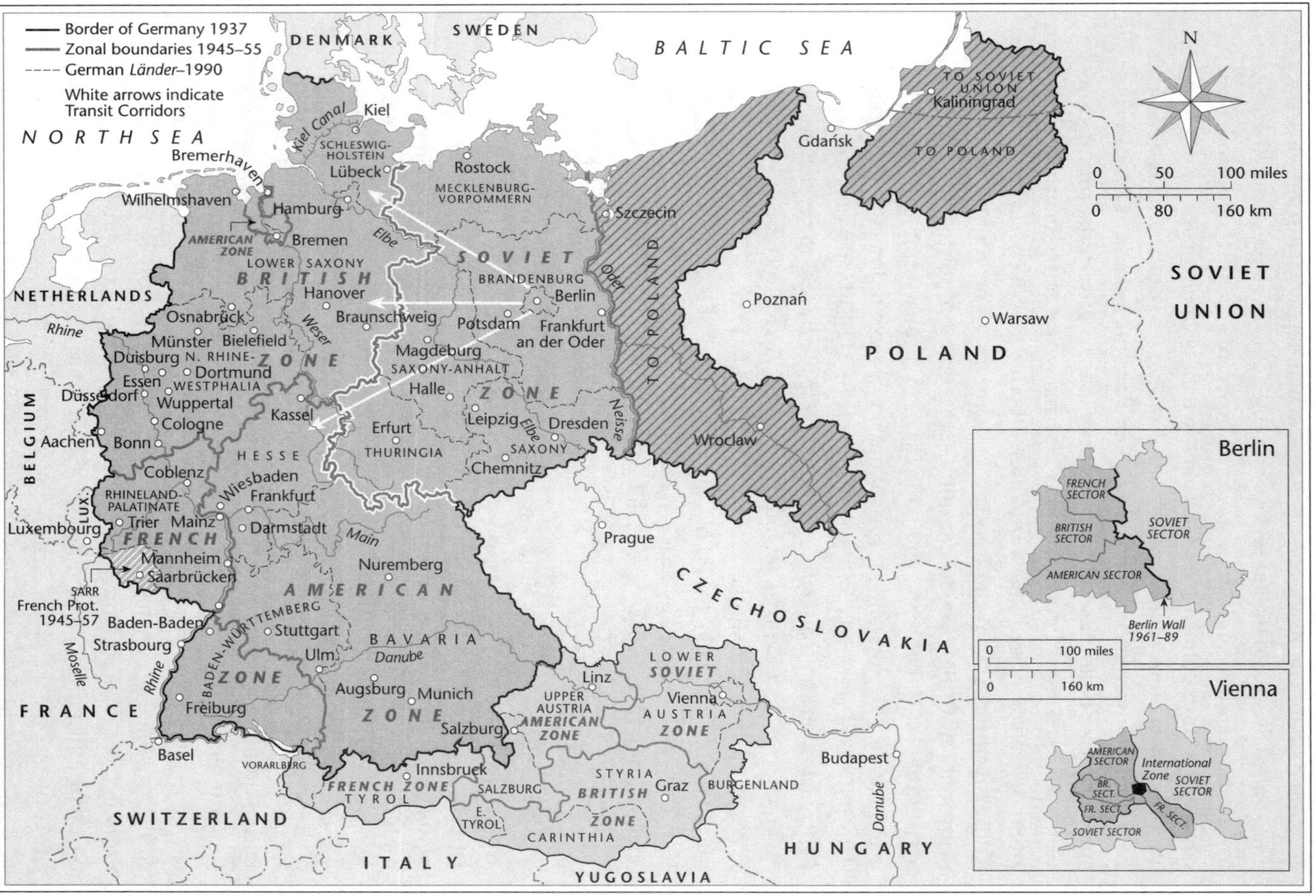

Map 7. Germany and Austria, 1945–1990

developed between Soviet and western representatives on the Kommandatura. In August 1946 all four powers nevertheless agreed to a temporary constitution for the German capital designed 'to restore political freedom and place it in the hands of the people of Berlin'.[41] Elections took place in October 1946. The clear victors were the Social Democrats (SPD) who won 49 per cent of the vote; the Communists, who had formed the Socialist Unity Party of Germany (SED) with a minority of left-wing Social Democrats led by Otto Grotewohl, won only 20 per cent. The new city government, an all-party coalition, took office under the supervision of the Kommandatura. But the Communists, with the help of the Red Army, maintained their grip on levers of power in the Russian sector of the city and by 1947 the SED had 1.8 million members throughout Germany (though mainly in the Soviet zone).

In all four occupation zones a process of denazification was set in train with a view both to rooting out diehard Nazis and to re-educating the German population in the ways of democracy. In the immediate aftermath of liberation, Allied commanders, especially in the American zone, ordered people living in the neighbourhood of concentration camps to be taken on compulsory tours to witness first-hand the crimes that had been committed in their name. Gruesome films of atrocities were exhibited in cinemas to bring home the horrors to the entire German population. The Nazi Party and its offshoots were declared illegal. Nazi laws were abrogated. School textbooks were replaced. In the Soviet zone 520,000 Nazis were dismissed from official posts by the end of 1945. In the western zones every adult was supposed to complete a 131-point questionnaire as a basis for decisions on prosecution, termination of employment, or loss of pension or other rights. Altogether more than six million Germans were eventually investigated. But the undertaking bogged down in bureaucratic difficulties. In spite of denazification, most former party members, including many activists, found it easy to secure a 'Persilschein', the certificate that enabled them to resume normal life. The occupying powers, especially the British, quickly realized that so many Germans had compromised themselves one way or another with the regime since 1933 that there could be no hope of restoring the German economy or rebuilding public administration if all Nazis were excluded from society. 'We have the absolute duty', said one Communist orator at a conference in Leipzig in 1947, 'of enlisting the co-operation of scientists, engineers, technicians, doctors, indeed all those men who are so urgently needed in economic life, above all when they were nominal Pgs

[*Parteigenossen*, members of the Nazi Party].'[42] By 1947 denazification had slowed down and then went into reverse as ex-Nazis regained or retained employment as officials, judges, policemen, or teachers, generally, however, trying to conceal the fact or extent of their complicity with Nazism. After 1951 denazification was halted altogether.

Germany's recovery after the *Stunde Null* ('zero hour') of May 1945 was, at first, halting. During the first two years of the occupation large parts of the country suffered from acute starvation. The British and Americans initially dismantled German heavy industry in their zones, particularly in establishments, such as the Krupp works at Essen, that were identified with armaments production. The Germans were to be forbidden altogether to produce not only armaments but a vast range of goods connected with war-making capability: ships, aircraft, synthetic oil, aluminium, magnesium, ball-bearings, heavy machine tools, heavy tractors, radio transmitting equipment, and others. Further industries were to be severely restricted: steel, machine tools, locomotives, non-ferrous metals, chemicals, dyestuffs, pharmaceuticals, synthetic fibres, and various engineering products. Such massive deindustrialization inevitably created large-scale unemployment, produced a spiral of economic decline, and prevented Germany earning the foreign exchange she required to pay for imported food. Moreover, although the Russians had agreed to treat Germany as 'a single economic unit', they showed no inclination to facilitate a flow of foodstuffs from their zone to the west. The reparations plan postulated a drastic and unrealistic decline in German food consumption. In the British zone fear of food riots led the military administration to import bread from Britain even while it was rationed there. The British thus found themselves paying for food imports to Germany at a time of desperate food (and dollar) shortage in Britain. In May 1946 the Chancellor of the Exchequer told the Cabinet that since VE Day Britain had received less than £2 million in reparations from Germany; meanwhile he estimated expenditure on the British zone, exclusive of occupation costs, would reach £131 million by the end of the year, of which nearly half would go on food. 'Our present policy towards Germany, by which we have become involved in paying her large reparations might rank as the craziest ever—if one did not remember last time,' wrote Keynes.[43] It rapidly became clear to the British and Americans that the only way Germany could pay for food imports was if she were permitted to revive her industrial exports. The Russians, however, who were systematically stripping their zone of every movable asset and also had their eye on goods and equipment in the western zones, were not prepared to cooperate in such a policy. Nor, at first, were the French who had visions of creating a buffer state on the left bank of the Rhine and of incorporating the Saar in a customs union with France.

In January 1947 the American and British zones joined in an economic fusion known as 'Bi-zone'. The Russians refused to participate. The French too were at first unwilling but economic pressures eventually compelled them to come on board, thus forming 'Tri-zone'. Meetings of the Council of Foreign Ministers in May and November failed to produce agreement on terms for a German Peace Treaty. In December the western powers announced their intention of including their occupation zones in the Marshall Plan. In February 1948 they recommended that steps be taken towards the integration and transformation of 'Tri-zone' into a democratic, federal, political structure. The Russians objected vehemently, withdrew from participation in the joint Allied Control Council for Germany, and blocked rail connections from the west to Berlin. The city was, as a result, threatened with economic strangulation. 'Let's make a joint effort,' Stalin said encouragingly to the East German Communist leaders. 'Perhaps we can kick them [the western powers] out.'[44] The head of the military administration in the US zone, General Lucius Clay, expressed his reaction pithily in a teleconference with the Army Department in Washington on 10 April: 'We have lost Czechoslovakia. Norway is threatened. We retreat from Berlin. When Berlin falls, West Germany will be next. If we mean . . . to hold Europe against Communism, we must not budge. We can take humiliation and pressure short of war in Berlin without losing face. . . . This is not heroic pose because there will be nothing heroic in having to take humiliation without retaliation.'[45]

On 20 June a new currency, the Deutsche Mark, was introduced in the western occupation zones of Germany to replace the by now almost worthless Reichsmark. The head of the Soviet military administration, Marshal V. D. Sokolovsky, denounced the currency reform as an attempt to subordinate the German economy to American, British and French monopolies, 'relying for support, in the western zones of occupation, on the big German capitalists and the Junkers who ensured the advent to power of Fascism and prepared and unleashed the second world war'.[46] A separate currency was issued almost immediately in the Soviet zone. The new currencies also circulated in the Soviet and western zones of Berlin, strengthening the tendency to regard them as appendages of the respective occupation zones of the country as a whole. These events, marking, in effect, the economic partition of Germany, paved the way for political separation into east and west German states.

The Russians attempted to exploit the vulnerable military position of the western powers to squeeze them out of Berlin. Asserting that 'the whole mechanism of joint administration is destroyed', they maintained that since Berlin lay within the Soviet zone of occupation of Germany 'the Soviet Military Administration is the only legitimate occupation authority'.[47] On 24 June they imposed a land blockade on west Berlin. The blockade involved the imposition of various technical restrictions, the effect of which was to bar all surface traffic between the western occupation zones of Germany and the western sectors of Berlin. A few days later the Russians withdrew from the Kommandatura, complaining of 'unseemly behaviour' by the American representative. Electricity, which was generated mainly in east Berlin, was cut off to the west. Stockpiles of food and fuel ran low. The position of the western powers in the city seemed untenable since their garrisons there could easily have been overwhelmed by the Russians. US Secretary of State Marshall nevertheless insisted, 'We are in Berlin as a result of agreements between the governments on the areas of occupation in Germany, and we intend to stay.'[48]

Clay proposed testing the blockade by the dispatch of an armed relief force overland to Berlin; but such a measure, which might have led to war, was overruled by Truman. Instead the western powers, which had prepared no contingency plans for the eventuality of a blockade, improvised an airlift of food, fuel, and other supplies to maintain normal life for the 2.4 million civilians in the western zones of the city. The Russians 'buzzed' western aircraft flying through the three air corridors to the city and tried to interfere with flights in other ways but did not take the drastic step of shooting down planes. Stalin, like Truman, hesitated on the verge of a step that might lead to a third world war. The airlift, which began on 26 June, developed into a massive supply operation. Since the main aerodrome at Tempelhof, a Nazi-era showpiece, proved inadequate for the endless stream of Dakotas, a new civil airport was built at Tegel. At the peak of the effort, in the spring of 1949, thirteen thousand tons of supplies a day were being flown into the city. Altogether during the blockade 278,000 flights ferried 2.3 million tons of goods at a cost of more than $200 million.

By then the western powers had proved that they could, if necessary, supply the city indefinitely. If the Russians were to achieve their apparent aim of forcing them out of Berlin, they would have to raise the stakes and resort to military action. Because their position in the city was indefensible, the western powers made it clear that any offensive by the Russians in Berlin would be regarded as a *casus belli* for a larger struggle. This the Russians decided not to risk. In May 1949 they ended the blockade, calling for a meeting of the Council of Foreign Ministers. The crisis turned Berlin into a symbol of western determination to resist the spread of Communism to western Europe. It sealed the American commitment to maintain substantial forces in Europe to achieve that object. And it hastened the division of Germany into two states. When the Council met in Washington, the Russians rejected western conditions for German reunification, which included free elections and a federal government under a four-power High Commission. By this time it was plain that, in spite of general lip-service to the aim of German unity, all four powers were quite comfortable with a permanently divided Germany—the USSR and France emphatically, the US and Britain somewhat less so. The United States saw a revived West Germany as the economic and political pivot of an anti-Communist western Europe. The USSR regarded an East Germany under its exclusive control as preferable to a genuinely independent united Germany.

The western powers decided to merge their zones and create an autonomous political entity, still under occupation but with considerable powers of self-government. On 23 May, a parliamentary council, formed from delegates of the *Länder*, promulgated a constitution or, more properly 'Basic Law' (*Grundgesetz*), for the Federal Republic of Germany. The shape of the new political order grew out of discussions in a constitutional convention as well as out of the practical requirements and experience of the occupation and the *idées fixes* of the occupiers. Over-centralization had supposedly led to dictatorship: hence, federalism was desirable. Prussia was allegedly incorrigibly militaristic: therefore it must be abolished and carved into pieces. The word 'Reich' was eliminated from all official nomenclature. The bicameral parliamentary system would comprise a directly elected lower house (Bundestag) and an upper chamber (Bundesrat) consisting of representatives of the eleven *Länder*. A threshold of 5 per cent of the popular vote was set as the minimum qualification for any party to secure representation in the Bundestag. The Federal Chancellor was given stronger constitutional authority than his predecessors under the Weimar Republic. He had the power to select and dismiss ministers and he held the constitutional power to set general policy guidelines (*Richtlinienkompetenz*).

In a general election in August, the Christian Democrats and their Bavarian Christian Social Union allies won 31 per cent of the vote and 139 seats in the Bundestag to the Social Democrats' 29 per cent and 131 seats. The balance of 52 seats was won by the liberal Free Democrats (FDP) who gained 12 per cent of the vote. The Federal Republic was proclaimed on 20 September. The Communists, with only 6 per cent of the vote, could be dismissed as a negligible factor in West German politics (in 1956 the Federal Constitutional Court, responding to a petition by the government, declared the party illegal). The immigrants from eastern Europe amounted to more than 15 per cent of the West German population. Expellees' organizations remained active for decades. But one of the outstanding achievements of the Federal Republic was the rapid integration of the expellees and refugees and the fading-away of the irredentist impulse as a force in West German politics.

The Christian Democrat leader, Konrad Adenauer, was elected Chancellor by a majority of one vote—his own. Adenauer was still a little-known figure outside his native Rhineland. A former member of the Catholic Centre Party, he had served as mayor of Cologne from 1917 to 1933 and played a not very conspicuous role in Weimar politics. Strongly hostile to the Nazis, he had been arrested in 1934 and again in 1944. On the latter occasion he was earmarked for liquidation but narrowly survived. After the war he was reinstated as mayor but in October 1945 was rudely dismissed by the British military authorities. To this he later attributed his emergence as leader of the Christian Democratic Union (CDU) in the British zone. Given his age, seventy-three in 1949, he was seen by many as a transitional figure. Yet he served as Chancellor for fourteen unbroken years, longer than any of his successors until Helmut Kohl. Adenauer was unsentimental but sensitive to other people, orderly in his habits and private life, conservative in his lifestyle. The Social Democrat leader, Kurt Schumacher, castigated him as 'the Chancellor of the Allies'.[49] But he was no puppet. He favoured a strong defence and foreign policy orientation towards the United States but his goal was to build a moral and political basis for the restoration of German independence. Largely thanks to Adenauer's influence, the small Rhineland city of Bonn, Beethoven's birthplace and former residence of the Archbishop-Electors of Cologne, was chosen in November 1949 as provisional capital of the Federal Republic, pending reunification. The sobriety, modesty, and narrow horizons of this provincial town reflected the limited international ambitions of the new republic.

The Soviet military administration denounced the Federal Republic's leaders as 'yesterday's inspirers of the Hitler regime . . . imbued with open revanchist yearnings'.[50] Somewhat against his initial inclination, Stalin meanwhile gave the green light for the transformation of the Soviet zone into a full-fledged state. In May East Germans were presented with a single list of Communist-approved candidates for the 'German People's Congress': although the election was not secret, 34 per cent voted against the list. On 7 October the German Democratic Republic was proclaimed. Dominated by the Communists, the GDR developed into perhaps the most repressive of the Stalinist police states. Sachsenhausen and other former Nazi concentration camps were adapted for a new generation of political prisoners. More than 120,000 people eventually passed through these camps, of whom 42,889 were reported to have died 'as a result of sickness'.[51] Berlin remained formally under four-power control, although in many aspects of day-to-day life administrative powers in the eastern and western zones were devolved to the East and West German governments respectively.

Welfare state

The pressing needs of reconstruction combined with the ideological imperatives of the Cold War to produce a demand from all sides of the political spectrum in post-war Europe for a new social politics. In eastern Europe nearly all parties agreed in the late 1940s on the urgent need for land-reform measures that would break up the remaining estates of great landowners, including the Church. In western Europe, Christian Democrat parties, such as the Mouvement Républicain Populaire (MRP) in France, tried to break the traditional link between the Church and the established social order, urging a reformist social politics founded on religious faith.

The welfare state that became the European norm in these years therefore commanded widespread consensual acceptance, not only on the left. Government spending everywhere had reached unprecedented levels during the war: in Britain it consumed 74 per cent of national income in 1943, an all-time record. High taxation, rationing, and government controls during the war had inured the possessing classes to a much greater degree of state control of the economy and society. Common sacrifice of soldiers and civilians of all classes had prepared minds for the application of egalitarian policies in the period of reconstruction. The warfare state, it has been argued, shaped the welfare state.[52]

The theory of the welfare state had had a long period of gestation. Its conceptual basis could be found in the writings of British Liberal and Socialist thinkers such as Graham Wallas, Sidney and Beatrice Webb, R. H. Tawney, and G. D. H. Cole. Many of these writers had been connected with the London School of Economics and Political Science, founded at the turn of the century by the Webbs. The LSE became a hothouse of advanced social thought. Although associated primarily with social democracy, the welfare state's progenitors in public policy came from across the political spectrum: Bismarck introduced old-age pensions in the German Empire; agrarian liberals devised a much more far-reaching, universal, non-contributory, state-financed pension law in Denmark in 1891; the Liberal government in Britain between 1905 and 1914 created a system of national compulsory unemployment insurance and enacted other social reforms; conservative governments in Sweden before 1914 levied progressive taxes, socialized mines, and implemented 'people's pensions'. After the First World War Italy, Ireland, and Germany passed compulsory unemployment insurance legislation. The main exponents and executants of such ideas in the inter-war period were Social Democrats in Weimar Germany and Vienna and the Swedish coalition governments headed, after 1932, by Social Democrats. The term *Wohlfahrtsstaat* entered the political vocabulary in Germany that year, as a term of abuse, when the Chancellor, von Papen, attacked the concept as an insupportable burden on the state.[53] In English the first use of the term 'welfare state' appears to have been in 1941 by the Socialist Archbishop of York (later of Canterbury), William Temple.

Sweden's 'middle way' was heavily influenced by the ideas of economists such as Gunnar Myrdal and Ernst Wigforss who, in some respects, were Keynesian *avant la lettre*. Keynes directly inspired Wigforss, who served as Finance Minister (except for a short break in 1936) from 1932 to 1949. The roots of the 'middle way' have been traced to the Swedish culture of 'conflict avoidance' as well as to the 'Christian enlightenment' that inspired Swedish intellectuals of left and right in the nineteenth century, and to a specific Swedish notion of rationality associated with the word *lagom*, which means both 'reasonable' and 'middle-of the road'.[54] The Social Democrats' effort to create a *Folkhemmet* ('people's home') changed the shape of public discourse and policy-making decisively. Unemployment insurance was introduced. Retirement pensions were increased. Public works were launched and subsidies given to industry and agriculture. A large-scale housing programme was initiated. Free health care, prescription drugs, and maternity services were provided. The fundamental characteristic of the Swedish welfare state was universal provision without a means test. In order to pay for all this, short-term deficit budgeting was adopted and taxes on income, inheritance, and wealth were raised and made more progressive. Wigforss pursued a counter-cyclical full-employment policy which succeeded in reducing unemployment from a peak of 186,000 to 18,000 in 1938. In overcoming the depression, the Swedish economy was one of the success stories of the 1930s, although economic historians differ over the extent of the contribution made by stimulatory government policies. The recovery owed much to rapid growth in demand for arms exports to Germany. The distinctiveness of the 'middle way' was as much social as economic. Swedish society was becoming rapidly secularized and adopting a consumerist orientation. The ultimate value of life, some social critics complained, was an ever higher living standard: 'If you have got a place to live in with two rooms and a kitchen, you can always wish for a bathroom, an allotment-garden cottage, or a motor boat. The list can be expanded infinitely.'[55]

The Swedish example was copied by others, for example the Norwegian Labour government elected in 1945. Beyond Scandinavia, the welfare state attained its most comprehensive formulation and implementation in Britain. In 1942 Sir William Beveridge had produced a report on *Social Insurance and Allied Services*.[56] A former Director of the LSE who had worked as a senior civil servant in both world wars, Beveridge was a political Liberal but his report furnished essential elements of the post-war Labour government's programme. Much broader in scope than its title implied, the report proposed a free national health service, a comprehensive system of social insurance, and family allowances. Beveridge propounded fundamental principles that became the bedrock of the future welfare state: universal provision rather than benefits directed only to the needy; full employment policies; central rather than local government responsibility for all welfare. In order to meet the objection that the cost of funding both current and future pensions would be prohibitive, Beveridge accepted Keynes's proposal that pensions should be funded out of current contributions rather than (as in the US Social Security system) out of an accumulated fund. 'The future can well be left to look after itself,' wrote Keynes. 'It will have more resources for doing so than the immediate present.'[57] Beveridge dealt with the problem of potentially spiralling costs also by placing an obligation on the government to keep unemployment low. With its vision of a post-war world relieved of the 'five giants' of 'want, ignorance, squalor, idleness, and disease', the report excited the public imagination, hungry for socially meaningful war aims. In spite of its unpromising title, it became a best-seller and its author an instant celebrity. Churchill was by no means delighted about its recommendations; his initial reaction was to shelve it. But the enthusiastic public reaction prevented that.

Some significant social legislation was passed before the end of the war. In 1944 an Education Act for England and Wales, presented by the Conservative President of the Board of Education (henceforth styled Minister), R. A. Butler, promised to raise the school leaving age to fifteen from 1947. Free secondary education was to be provided by the state in grammar (academic), technical, and 'secondary modern' schools. Although progressive in intent, the act perpetuated class divisions in education: grammar schools (to which admission at the age of eleven was by examination) remained disproportionately middle class, secondary moderns overwhelmingly working class. In June 1945 the long campaign for family allowances, pioneered since the 1920s by the Independent MP Eleanor Rathbone, was crowned with success, though they were paid only for the second and subsequent children. One vital aspect of the scheme inaugurated a shift of power within the family: the allowances were paid to the mother, not the father. This provision was not without its opponents: a government committee concluded that 'it would be destructive of the whole conception of the family to provide a separate income for the wife in this way'. Butler mused: 'If fathers like beer, mothers may also like port and lemon, or gin.'[58] But Rathbone pressed the point and had her way.

The end of the war and the landslide election victory of the Labour Party in July 1945 created conditions for the Beveridge report's implementation. For the first time Labour held an overall majority in Parliament and could govern without dependence on other parties. The new Prime Minister, Attlee, was an undemonstrative, unexciting leader who cut a far from impressive figure in public. 'Was it a wiry toughness or just lack of imagination which kept Attlee cool to the point of obliviousness in a crisis?' mused a left-wing critic.[59] But Attlee turned out to be a crisp decision-maker and he headed a government that wrought the most far-reaching changes in British social policy since before 1914. The aim was a cradle-to-grave system of social security for the entire population. A National Insurance Act in

1946 created a unified system of coverage against sickness, unemployment, old age, and death. The National Assistance Act of 1948 added provision for means-tested 'supplementary benefits' for those whose needs fell outside the general system—a catch-all category that was to grow exponentially in later years.

The National Health Service, founded in 1948, was based on the principles of universal access, comprehensive care, and freedom from charges. Britain was the first capitalist country to introduce such a service. The NHS was funded from tax revenues rather than from insurance contributions (as advocated by Beveridge). It provided free treatment by family doctors ('general practitioners'), specialists, and hospitals as well as free medicines, corrective spectacles, and dental care. The hospitals, hitherto mainly municipal and 'voluntary' institutions, were nationalized and grouped under regional boards. The proposals were, at first, resisted fiercely by the chief doctors' organization, the British Medical Association. But the Minister of Health, Aneurin Bevan, a brilliant, mercurial, left-wing, Welsh Socialist, negotiated with them effectively and secured a compromise settlement whereby a limited private medical sector was permitted to continue alongside the state system. The NHS won broad acceptance and popularity and most of the population endorsed Bevan's claim that its creation represented 'the most civilised achievement of modern Government'.[60] Within a few months 97 per cent of the population and 90 per cent of general practitioners had signed up to the service. But costs rose much faster than expected. By 1949 health spending was three times the 1945 level. Governments soon found themselves compelled to compromise the original, bold vision by setting ceilings on expenditure and initiating charges for ancillary services.

All children in state schools were provided with free milk and with free or subsidized meals, expectant mothers were accorded special rations and they and their infants were also entitled to free orange juice and cod-liver oil, though children abominated the latter and as a result uptake was low except in the middle class. Maternal death in childbirth registered a sharp decline in the 1940s and infant mortality in England and Wales fell from 51 per thousand in 1939 to 27 by 1953. Food prices were kept low by subsidies to agriculture. Expenditure on social services as a whole rose, in real terms, by between 80 and 90 per cent between 1936 and 1950. These costs too became difficult to sustain.

The changes in social policy were enacted within the framework of an economic policy radically different from that pursued by pre-war governments. The key change was the stress on central planning, a legacy of the war that was maintained in peacetime by the Labour government and hardly less by its Conservative successors. This was in line with a general European-wide tendency towards faith in planning that extended across the spectrum from Communists to liberal technocrats of the French Commissariat Général du Plan. National income accounting, almost unknown before the war, became a vital prop of economic planning. A countercyclical full employment policy, based on Keynesian assumptions, became the orthodoxy of the day. The conditions for success were unpromising. Although Britain's had been one of the few European economies to enjoy significant wartime growth, production had been directed overwhelmingly to the war effort. Per capita income had fallen from 90 per cent of that of the United States in 1938 to 51 per cent in 1945. Yet Britain continued to spend much more of her national income on defence than the USA. The country's international trading position had been severely damaged: exports paid for only 30 per cent of imports in 1945. Overseas investments were gone. Once the largest creditor in the world, Britain was now the largest debtor. In 1946 the national debt reached 252 per cent of GDP, the highest point in its history. The country's gold reserves had been exhausted. The pound was over-valued. In 1945 Keynes had negotiated a $3.75 billion loan from the United States. But American public opinion was hostile. As a result, stringent conditions were attached, including a commitment by the British to an early return to sterling convertibility. When that occurred in July 1947, sterling reserves were rapidly depleted and after thirty-seven days the government was obliged to reimpose controls on conversion. The balance of payments in trade returned to the black but the country was buffeted by heavy withdrawals of foreign capital, as a result of which the 'dollar gap' yawned ever wider. By early 1948 the entire US loan had been exhausted. For a time Marshall aid came to the rescue but in 1949 the government was forced to devalue the pound by 30 per cent to $2.80. Within a week twenty other countries, including France, West Germany, Belgium, and Italy, had followed suit with devaluations ranging from 8 to 53 per cent.

Given the weakness of Britain's financial position, welfare was perforce accompanied by austerity. Heavy government social spending and the cost of preserving Britain's role as a world power dictated maintenance of very high levels of taxation and steep progressivity. The harsh winter of 1946/7 brought a severe fuel crisis. Coal, still the main source of home heating, was in short supply. The standard petrol allowance for private motorists was reduced to enough for just 90 miles of driving a month. Rationing of food and clothing continued and in some spheres was even tightened: bread was rationed from 1946 to 1948 ('the most hated measure ever to have been presented to the people of this country', roared the *Daily Mail*)[61] and potatoes were controlled in the winter of 1947/8. A survey in April 1948 reported that 55 per cent of the population complained of an inadequate diet, a higher figure than in 1942/3. Women were particularly affected by rationing: not only did they have to do most of the queuing but items such as nylon stockings and lipstick were considered almost too trivial to waste precious national resources on. And women were supposed to wear 'utility frocks' happily for the public good. A 'bonfire of controls', announced in November 1948 by the President of the Board of Trade, Harold Wilson, eased consumer access to many products but petrol remained rationed until 1950 and many other goods for several years longer.

Although Attlee's government nationalized coal mining, road haulage, civil aviation, electricity generation, gas, iron and steel, the railways, and the Bank of England, it refrained from any attempt to socialize the economy as a whole. In spite of the Labour Party's commitment to 'common ownership of the means of production, distribution and exchange', enshrined since 1918 in the famous 'clause four' of its constitution and printed on all party membership cards, the government stopped short of any attempt to destroy the capitalist system. Even its embrace of planning was half-hearted and less forthright than the *dirigisme* and corporatism characteristic of some other west European economies. For example, public ownership of power generation and public transport did not lead to integrated planning in those spheres. Meanwhile, the Conservatives, although they opposed most of the government's policies in parliament, were themselves moving towards acceptance of the welfare state and of the concept of the 'mixed economy'. What later came to be called 'Butskellism' (a play on the names of R. A. Butler and Hugh Gaitskell, respectively Conservative and Labour middle-of-the-road politicians, both of whom served as Chancellor of the Exchequer) formed the basis of a new consensus.

In most of western Europe in the post-war period the idea of the welfare state became the standard paradigm of social thought and political action. Most Christian Democrats, Liberals, and moderate Socialists came to accept its broad principles even if the form of their application differed. For example, by the 1950s there was general agreement that the state had a duty to ensure health provision for all citizens, whether from direct taxation or from some form of compulsory insurance. (An exception was the Irish Republic where opposition by the Roman Catholic hierarchy to a 'Mother and Child Scheme', designed to provide direct state funding to expectant mothers, led to its abandonment in 1951.) Similarly, there was now little argument about the role of the state in ensuring social payments for the elderly, the disabled, and the unemployed. Public expenditure on health increased sharply: in Britain from 0.6 per cent of GNP in 1937 to 3.3 per cent by 1960, in Austria from 0.2 per cent to 2.1 per cent, and in Sweden from 0.9 per cent to 3.4 per cent. State ownership of utilities, railways, postal and telephone services and other industries came to seem part of the natural order of things and was challenged only by free-market fanatics. As the state grew, the proportion of the labour force who were government employees rose too. The high levels of government spending characteristic of the war years therefore declined only gradually and in most countries did not fall back to pre-war levels but settled at around one third of GDP. On this basis western Europe now entered the period of most dynamic economic growth in its entire recorded history.

12

West European Recovery 1949–1958

VLADIMIR: We have to come back tomorrow.
ESTRAGON: What for?
VLADIMIR: To wait for Godot.
ESTRAGON: Ah! (*Silence.*) He didn't come?
VLADIMIR: No.

*Samuel Beckett, Paris, January 1949**

Towards a common market

The concept of European unity has a long pre-history stretching back to the Roman and Holy Roman empires. In a conversation on St Helena after his deposition, Napoleon declared: 'One of my great ideas was the reunification, the concentration, of those same geographical nations that have been separated and parcelled out by revolution and politics. There are in Europe, dispersed, it is true, more than thirty million Frenchmen, fifteen million Spaniards, fifteen million Italians, and thirty million Germans [note, he omitted the English]; it was my intention to incorporate each of these peoples into one nation. It would have been fine to go forward to posterity with such a train. It would have been a noble thing, earning the blessing of future centuries. I felt myself worthy of this glory!'[1] Nationalist thinkers in the nineteenth century were not necessarily opposed to the idea. Giuseppe Mazzini foresaw a free association of European nations as the natural

* From *Waiting for Godot*, translated from the French by the playwright. Samuel Beckett, *Waiting for Godot* (New York, 1982), 107.

expression and fulfilment of national freedom. In the inter-war period, disgust with the bloody results of nationalist conflict gave rise to a Pan-European movement, headed by the half-Japanese Austro-Hungarian Count Richard Coudenhove-Kalergi. Some, including Churchill, saw him as a visionary, others as a crackpot. Yet in 1930 Ortega y Gasset could write: 'There is now coming for *Europeans* the time when Europe can convert itself into a national idea. And it is much less Utopian to believe this today than it would have been to prophesy in the eleventh century the unity of Spain. The more faithful the national State of the West remains to its genuine inspiration, the more surely will it perfect itself in a gigantic continental State.'[2]

Some transnational institutions in the inter-war period may be seen as precursors of the movement towards European integration. The International Commission of the Danube, for example, established in 1920 (its roots stretched as far back as 1856), took over responsibility for regulating navigation on the river from Admiral Sir Ernest Troubridge, head of the Inter-Allied Commandement de la Navigation du Danube. The river was recognized as an international waterway and, in accordance with an old principle of Roman law, was declared open to the traffic of all nations. The Commission, which had its own flag, was given a legal basis in the Statute of the Danube (1921), signed by all the riparian states as well as Britain, France, Italy, Belgium, and Greece (British shipping, in particular, was an important user of the Danube), and maintained freedom of navigation on the river until shortly before the Second World War. Similar commissions existed for the Rhine (1831) and the Elbe (1922). Another forerunner, involving three of the six founder-members of the European Common Market, was the Benelux Customs Union which took effect on 1 January 1948; its origins dated back to the Belgium–Luxembourg economic union of 1921. More immediately, the Organization for European Economic Cooperation, established in 1948 as a vehicle for implementing the Marshall Plan, accustomed west European countries to the concept of coordinated economic planning.

The real progenitors of European unity, however, were two men. The first was Adolf Hitler, whose vague conception of a German-dominated *Grosswirtschaftsraum* was translated by Albert Speer into imperfectly coordinated economic planning in Nazi-occupied Europe. The second was the Frenchman Jean Monnet, known as 'father of the European Community'. A technocrat with 'the air of a refined peasant',[3] he had served as Deputy Secretary-General of the League of Nations in the early 1920s. In 1940 he had been the chief advocate of the abortive 'union' of France and Britain. During the war he worked as a French, then, after the fall of France, as a British government arms purchasing agent in Washington. He rallied to de Gaulle, with whom, however, his relations were always uneasy. From 1944 until his death in 1979 he played a vital role, mostly behind the scenes, in developing the institutional foundations of what became the European Union. From 1946 to 1952 he presided over French economic reconstruction as head of the Commissariat Général du Plan and in this capacity, with great political skill, impelled French politicians, officials, and businessmen towards the idea of an integrated west European economy.

In 1948 a congress at the Hague, presided over by Churchill, founded a European Movement in order to mobilize public opinion for European political and economic unification. It owed much to the ideas of the Italian anti-Fascist Altiero Spinelli who had founded the Movimento Federalista Europeo in Milan in 1943. The following year agreement was reached by the Brussels Treaty powers (Britain, France, and the Benelux states), as well as Norway, Denmark, Sweden, Ireland, and Italy, on the creation of a Council of Europe with headquarters in Strasbourg. Most west European countries subsequently joined the original signatories. The organization formed a Council of Ministers, a Parliamentary Assembly (not elected but chosen by the parliaments of member states), and in 1959 a European Court of Human Rights. The Council of Europe had no supranational functions but it played a role in protecting human rights and standardizing social and legal practices.

The groundswell of opinion towards supranationalism among the political elites of western Europe meanwhile produced much more far-reaching consequences. On 3 May 1950 Monnet presented a proposal to the French Foreign Minister, Robert Schuman, for a new structure 'which would remove for the Germans the humiliation of endless controls, and for the French the fear of a Germany without controls'.[4] The origins of the scheme were not wholly idealistic or altruistic. The French worried that, following the Berlin airlift, the United States would lose interest in France and focus primarily on German recovery. They hoped to create a framework for limiting the resurgence of German power. And Monnet wanted to ensure French access to German coal and steel resources after the end of the occupation regime. In the United States the Truman administration, as well as much Republican and press opinion, supported the idea of European economic and political integration. Under American pressure, the French had already begun to reverse the policy of dismantlement of German heavy industry decreed at Potsdam. Monnet's proposals were adopted by Schuman and formed the basis of what came to be known as the Schuman Plan.

Born in Luxembourg, Schuman had studied at several German universities, served in a non-combatant unit in the German army in the First World War, and spoke French with a German accent. He called himself a 'cosmopolitan' and asserted his indifference to national difference, 'like many in our border regions, where blood is mixed and national characters confused'.[5] A leader of the MRP and staunch Catholic (after his death admirers were to call for his beatification), he served as Foreign Minister in eight successive French governments between July 1948 and December 1952. Schuman discarded the Germanophobia of de Gaulle and became an apostle of European integration. In October 1948 he met Adenauer at Schloss Bassenheim, near Koblenz, in the French-occupied zone of Germany. Both men were Christian Democrats. Both came from border regions. Both could look back on the destruction of two world wars. They readily found a basis of agreement for Franco-German reconciliation. Adenauer later wrote to Schuman of the meeting that the two of them 'were perhaps called upon by God in a crucial situation for Europe to make a precious contribution towards the achievement of our common goals'.[6] In 1950 they met again and the following year Adenauer visited Paris where he was received with an official and public friendliness that seemed to mark West Germany's return to the circle of West European democracies.

The Schuman Plan called for Franco-German production of coal and steel to be placed under a common 'High Authority', within the framework of 'an organization open to the participation of the other countries of Europe'. The object was explicitly political as well as economic: to ensure that 'any war between France and Germany becomes not merely unthinkable, but materially impossible'.[7] Schuman admitted that the plan was 'a leap into the unknown' ('*un saut dans l'inconnu*') but he considered the risk worth taking.[8]

At a meeting in Bonn on 23 May 1950, Monnet found another kindred spirit. Adenauer told him: 'I have waited twenty-five years for a move like this. In accepting it, my government and my country have no secret hankerings after hegemony. History since 1933 has taught us the folly of such ideas. Germany knows that its fate is bound up with that of Western Europe as a whole.'[9] In France Gaullists and Communists opposed the Schuman Plan but the centre-right-dominated government of Italy found common ground with France and Germany in the concept. The Benelux group joined these three in signing a treaty on 18 April 1951 providing for the formation of a European Coal and Steel Community. It came into force in July 1952 and Monnet was appointed its first President. The creation of the ECSC represented a triumph for those 'functionalists' like Monnet who believed that European unity must be constructed in gradual stages. Founded on the principle of a limited pooling of sovereignty, the ECSC's quadripartite structure of supranational 'High Authority' (composed of officials), Council (politicians), Assembly (non-elected and with advisory powers only), and Court, provided a template for subsequent European institutional developments.

The British stood aloof from the ECSC. Although both the Labour government until 1951 and its Conservative successor paid lip-service to the European idea, Britain saw her economic and political interests as tied more closely to the Commonwealth and the 'special relationship' with the United States—'the central pillar of the whole edifice' as the Foreign Secretary, Harold Macmillan, called it in 1955.[10] Half of Britain's trade was with the Commonwealth, only a quarter with western Europe. In a speech in Zurich in 1946 Churchill had spoken of a 'United States of Europe' but he did not see Britain as part of such a European federation. Under his Indian summer premiership between 1951 and 1955, Britain still conceived of herself as a world rather than a European power. She was indeed still the third economic power in the capitalist world in 1951, producing more than either France or West Germany. The Bank of England considered that British participation in European integration could come only at the expense of financial and fiscal independence. Moreover most British politicians held serious reservations about the idea of political unification of western Europe. Eventually, in early 1955, Britain signed an association agreement with the ECSC but she remained hostile to European federalist ventures.

Britain did, however, participate, albeit after initial opposition, in another, comparatively little-known, cooperative economic enterprise in Europe in the 1950s. The European Payments Union, formed in September 1950 by eighteen non-Communist European countries (Spain was the only important non-member), provided a framework for the mutual acceptance of member countries' still non-convertible currencies in commercial transactions. The agreement furnished an essential basis for the liberalization of trade and paved the way for currency convertibility (and the EPU's own dissolution) at the end of 1958.

Meanwhile the extension of the Cold War had changed the strategic environment. The attack on South Korea in June 1950 by Communist-ruled

North Korea led to a UN Security Council resolution calling on all members to help in the defence of South Korea (the USSR was temporarily boycotting the Council and so did not cast a veto). Belgium, France, Greece, and the Netherlands sent token units; of European states only Britain sent significant forces (two brigades plus some warships). Soviet and American defence spending increased substantially. The Americans now insisted on a greater role by western European powers in their own defence and laid stress on the rearmament of West Germany. Monnet originated a new idea, the European Defence Community (EDC), in which a European army, including German contingents, would take some of the burden of defence from American forces stationed in Europe. The French Prime Minister, René Pleven, embraced the concept in spite of strong hostility to German rearmament in several parts of the political spectrum.

In West Germany too the proposal aroused strong feelings. Adenauer was convinced that Stalin, like Hitler, was bent on an aggressive foreign policy that must not be appeased. He urged support for the EDC as the only way to maintain a strong American commitment to the Federal Republic. Without securing the assent of his Cabinet, he began to discuss German rearmament with the Americans. His Interior Minister, Gustav Heinemann, resigned in protest, declaring: 'God took arms out of our hands twice; we must not take hold of them a third time.'[11] Heinemann was a former member of the anti-Nazi Bekennende Kirche whose founder, Martin Niemöller, also opposed rearmament. The Catholic Church, on the other hand, backed Adenauer's policy. The Social Democrats were divided. Their leader, Kurt Schumacher, was inclined to support rearmament. But other Socialists were opposed. '*Ohne mich!*' (Without me!) was the slogan of the opponents. Adenauer nevertheless moved ahead.

Stalin responded in March 1952 with a formal diplomatic note calling for the reunification and neutralization of Germany. Soviet motives were directed more at hindering the *Westbindung* (integration into the West) of the Federal Republic than at creating a unified Germany. The western powers, probably correctly, interpreted the note as a propaganda ploy rather than a serious proposal. In truth, whatever their protestations, they too had little enthusiasm for German reunification. In May they signed the Bonn agreements with West Germany, granting conditional restoration of German sovereignty. At the same time the six member states of the ECSC signed a European Defence Community Treaty. The agreement also provided for the creation of a European political community. The Bundestag ratified the treaty the following March.

Four other signatories also did so. But in the sixth, France, the issue remained deeply divisive. De Gaulle joined the Communists in root-and-branch opposition to the EDC. The Socialists were split, though many recognized that German rearmament was implicit in the creation of NATO. As the independent newspaper *Le Monde* put it: 'The rearmament of Germany is contained in the Atlantic Pact like the yolk in the egg.'[12] After an impassioned public debate lasting twenty months, the Prime Minister, Pierre Mendès France, finally submitted the issue to a vote in the National Assembly on 30 August 1954. It was defeated, whereupon the opponents broke into a triumphant rendering of the *Marseillaise*. Adenauer was distraught. It was 'crazy' and 'grotesque', he said, 'that I am being forced [by the rejection of the EDC] to create a German national army'. It would be 'a great danger for Germany and for Europe'. 'My God!' he exclaimed, 'What will become of Germany?'[13]

The collapse of the EDC project demonstrated that any further progress towards European integration depended on a fundamental change in Franco-German relations and on at least some rectification of West Germany's anomalous constitutional and diplomatic position. A new round of negotiations in October produced agreements in Paris ending the western powers' occupation of Germany and recognizing the Federal Republic as an independent state entitled to speak for the whole of Germany. The Federal Republic, for its part, undertook never to seek to change its frontiers by force. West Germany was admitted to NATO. American, British, and French forces remained there but as allies rather than occupiers (except in Berlin where they retained formal occupation rights to avoid giving the Russians any pretext for changing the status quo in the city). Following ratification, the agreements entered force on 5 May 1955. After a ten-year hiatus Germany, or at any rate part of it, thus regained sovereignty—a peaceful triumph for Adenauer.

The birth of the Federal Republic marked a radical turn in German history. The old elites were dethroned, conservative ideologies of nation, state, and army were delegitimized. Communist accusations that West Germany was dominated by ex-Nazis were exaggerated. The new Bundeswehr, established in 1955, recruited many former Wehrmacht officers but it nevertheless adopted the concept of a 'citizens in uniform' force that would be strictly under civilian political control. By 1958 it had grown to a strength of one hundred thousand men. But German forces would not engage in offensive action outside Germany's borders for another forty-one years.

To be sure, there were many disturbing elements of continuity. Judges, diplomats, and civil servants who had, with greater or lesser degrees of eagerness, performed their functions under Hitler were, except in the most egregious cases of Nazi enthusiasm, maintained in official employment. The former head of German military intelligence on the eastern front, Reinhard Gehlen, founded a West German intelligence service, at first under American control, that capitalized on existing German networks and expertise to penetrate the Soviet Union and its satellites. Even more controversial was Hans Globke. Although not a Nazi Party member, he had been one of the architects of the Nuremberg Laws. Adenauer rejected all criticism of him and in 1953 appointed him State Secretary, in effect his closest adviser. The two met two or three times a day. 'Talk to Herr Globke' was Adenauer's standard reply to any complicated request. 'Globke was to Adenauer as Père Joseph to Richelieu,' writes Adenauer's biographer (a comparison that might have appealed to the staunchly Catholic Chancellor).[14] Yet notwithstanding such cases, the ruling ideology of the Federal Republic was not racist, militarist, or expansionist but democratic and parliamentary.

The Soviet Union countered the independence of the Federal Republic by forming a collective alliance with its east European client states. The Warsaw Pact created a unified military command and became the basis for Soviet strategic planning over the next three decades. Quite why the USSR chose this particular time to formalize its relationship with its protégés remains unclear. It seems that the step was intended less as a threat to the west than as part of an effort to stabilize the status quo in Europe.[15] Thus while inveighing against supposed West German 'revanchism', the USSR found it expedient to come to terms with Adenauer on some practical issues. In September 1955 he visited Moscow for talks that led to the opening of diplomatic relations between the two countries. The last nine thousand German prisoners of war were released. On 6 October the division of Germany was sealed by Soviet recognition of East Germany as a sovereign state, though the western powers refused to accept its legitimacy. The West German government was alone, however, in clinging to what became known (though the ascription of parentage was mistaken) as the 'Hallstein doctrine', whereby it refused to have diplomatic relations with any country (save the USSR) that recognized the Communist regime in East Germany. While both the eastern and the western blocs continued to call for German reunification, in reality all the powers were satisfied with the status quo. As the junior minister at the Foreign Office, Selwyn Lloyd had written to Churchill in 1953, 'Everyone—Dr Adenauer, the Russians, the Americans, the French and ourselves—feel in our hearts that a divided Germany is safer for the time being. But none of us dare say so openly because of the effect on German opinion.'[16]

Meanwhile, the Saar problem, a thorn in the side of Franco-German relations over the previous decade, moved towards resolution. The creation of the ECSC had calmed French fears of losing the region's valuable coal and steel resources. In 1954 a treaty was signed under which the Saar would be autonomous but in economic union with France. The agreement was subject to approval in a referendum. Twenty years after the referendum of 1935 in which they had opted for Germany, the Saarlanders demonstrated anew their attachment to Germany by decisively rejecting the treaty. A revised Franco-German pact in 1956 led to the Saar's incorporation into the Federal Republic on 1 January 1957.

The settlement of at least this aspect of the German question facilitated a return to the track of west European integration, once again mainly in the economic realm. The Coal and Steel Community, coming on the heels of the Marshall Plan, proved an immediate and outstanding success. By 1953 industrial output in western Europe exceeded the 1938 level by 40 per cent. The removal of internal tariffs on coal and steel within the community led by 1958 to an increase in trade among the members of 151 per cent in steel and 21 per cent in coal over 1950 figures. West Germany enjoyed a spectacular economic recovery that began its return to the status of a major economic power. In the decade 1949 to 1959 she achieved an average annual growth rate of 7.4 per cent: even more remarkably she did so on the basis of virtually full employment, a high rate of growth in productivity, and very low inflation. GDP during the 1950s rose by two-thirds. The *Wirtschaftswunder* ('economic miracle') owed little to state planning or intervention. The Economics Minister from 1949 to 1963, Ludwig Erhard, preferred a laissez-faire approach. He became known as an exponent of the *Soziale Marktwirtschaft* (social market economy), though the originator of this concept was his adviser, Alfred Müller-Armack. The establishment in 1957 of a central bank, with authority over monetary policy, solidified confidence in the mark, which for the next generation became the strongest currency in Europe. West German interest in European integration was, nevertheless, more political than economic. Erhard, indeed, was sceptical about the economic advantage that might be derived from the community.[17] Some suggested that West Germany in this period was an economy in search of a nation. In any case, a broad political consensus favoured closer ties with the BRD's west European partners.

Discussions among the six ECSC members on further steps towards unification led, at a meeting of foreign ministers at Messina in June 1955, to a joint statement that 'the establishment of a united Europe must be achieved through the development of common institutions, the progressive fusion of national economies, the creation of a common market, and the gradual harmonization of their social policies'.[18] Britain was invited to attend the ensuing talks but withdrew after a short time, when it became apparent that the other participants aimed at something much more ambitious than a mere customs union. Britain likewise held aloof from a simultaneous initiative for cooperation in the peaceful use of nuclear energy: Euratom, the European Atomic Energy Community. Unlike most other European institutions, this ambitious project eventually withered on the vine, largely because of insistence by France on guarding national control of her civilian nuclear energy facilities.

Between 1955 and 1957, Monnet, as a private citizen, headed an 'Action Committee' that sought 'to ensure that the Messina declaration . . . should be translated into a genuine step towards a United States of Europe'.[19] The committee's members included Socialists such as Willy Brandt and Guy Mollet as well as Christian Democrats such as Amintore Fanfani and Kurt Georg Kiesinger. As with the EDC, the French attitude was vital to the creation of the European Common Market. In France some businessmen and officials opposed a customs union on the ground that French industry would not be able to compete without tariff protection. Nevertheless, on 25 March 1957 the six member states of the ECSC signed the Treaty of Rome, creating a European Economic Community (EEC). A parliamentary battle over ratification ensued in each country. From self-imposed internal exile in his country home in the small town of Colombey-les-Deux-Eglises in the Haute-Marne, de Gaulle expressed hostility to the project. So did Mendès France. But the Socialists were in favour and the crucial vote in the National Assembly in June 1957 supported adhesion by 342 to 239. Among the other five participants public and official views ranged from unexcited acquiescence in Italy to enthusiasm in the Benelux countries, exemplified in the passionate Europeanism of the Belgian Foreign Minister, Paul Henri Spaak. The Communists everywhere were opposed. But by December all six signatories had ratified the treaty which went into effect on 1 January 1958.

The Treaty of Rome was based on the principle of free movement of goods, labour, services, and capital within a Common Market. Tariff barriers between member states were to be reduced and eventually eliminated.

A common external tariff was to be maintained. On French insistence the treaty provided for a common agricultural policy, designed 'to ensure a fair standard of living for the agricultural community, in particular by increasing the individual earnings of persons engaged in agriculture', thereby protecting France's inefficient but politically influential farming sector. Italy secured advantages for her unevenly developed economy by the creation of a European Social Fund and a European Investment Bank. A powerful Commission, initially with nine members and based in Brussels, headed the Common Market's civil service. It would have the sole right to propose legislation and would work with a Council of Ministers, composed of representatives of each member state. A Court of Justice, sitting in Luxembourg, would decide disputes relating to the treaty. And a European Assembly or Parliament, its 142 members delegated from national parliaments, came into existence in Strasbourg; in the early years, however, it exercised little influence.[20] Over the next half century, as the Common Market widened from the original six to twenty-seven members, it also deepened its institutional foundations, developing into a European Union that was much more than an international organization but still less than a federal polity.

Exit from Asia

The movement towards European unity was accompanied by another historic shift: the beginning of the end of the European overseas empires. The process required drastic mental and strategic adjustments. In the case of four empires, those of Britain, France, the Netherlands, and Italy, the end of colonialism has traditionally been explained primarily in terms of the economic emasculation of the colonial powers by the Second World War. At least one further reason may be suggested—a change in collective consciousness that took shape as a result of the ideological struggles of mid-century. After the war against Hitler's racism, the inherent right of white men to rule the rest of the world was decreasingly defensible to European consciences. All the empires resisted decolonization, though some did so with greater energy than others. Most regretted the loss of their colonies. Yet in the long run all gained by jettisoning what had become, in almost every case, an intolerable burden.

The greatest loss of territory was suffered by Britain, which entered the period as mistress of the greatest empire the world had ever known and was reduced within half a century to a shadow of her former glory. Her most momentous imperial exit came with the termination in 1947 of the 190-year-old Raj in India. Britain's entire imperial strategy had for long been focused on the defence of India and in 1946 the subcontinent was still Britain's largest customer, taking 8 per cent of her exports. But the Indian nationalist movement could no longer be repressed, nor mollified with half-measures. Influenced by the views of the Fabian Colonial Research Bureau, formed in 1940, the British Labour Party sympathized with the aims of the Indian National Congress, led by Mahatma Gandhi and Jawaharlal Nehru. Churchill's long-standing commitment to maintenance of British power in India took the form of denunciation of a policy of 'scuttle'. This was easily overriden by the Labour government's large parliamentary majority. Attlee had more difficulty coping with reservations from Bevin and other Cabinet members about a precipitate end to British rule in the subcontinent. Wavell, who seemed uncooperative and pessimistic about the possibility of peaceful evacuation of British forces, was replaced as Viceroy by the well-connected Louis Mountbatten. He negotiated with Indian leaders an arrangement for partition of the country into a Muslim-dominated Pakistan and a secular India. But independence for the two states on 15 August 1947 was marred by horrific communal violence and by vast refugee movements. India had been by far Britain's most important overseas possession. Yet its loss caused barely a ripple in British society and hardly affected the British economy.

Withdrawal from India was followed in early 1948 by the independence of Burma and Ceylon. In one of their few remaining Asian possessions the British stayed a little longer. In June 1948 a Communist insurgency in Malaya led the colonial authorities to declare a state of emergency. Viewing the revolt in the context of the Cold War, the British resolved not to withdraw until the Communists had been beaten. Foreign-exchange earnings from Malayan rubber may also have had something to do with the decision. National service was extended from twelve to eighteen months. It took fifty thousand British and Australian troops a decade to defeat the rebels at a cost of more than £500 million. In October 1951 the British High Commissioner, Sir Henry Gurney, was assassinated. His successor, General Sir Gerald Templer, served simultaneously as military commander and was granted unprecedented powers. He combined harsh measures, such as collective punishment, with Malayanization of the administration and armed forces. Under his leadership the British gradually gained the upper hand. Malaya was granted independence in 1957 before the insurgency was defeated but British troops remained in the country under the Anglo-Malayan Defence Agreement.

The end of British rule in most of south Asia did not mark a general retreat from empire. In spite of its anti-imperial outlook, the Labour government of 1945–51 regarded the colonies in sub-Saharan Africa as too primitive for early independence. It did, however, promote constitutional reform there, although it bent to the hostility to such schemes of white settlers in Kenya and central Africa. It fell to its Conservative successors to take the next decisive steps in dismantling the empire.

The British model of semi-voluntary decolonization in Asia was generally regarded as a success. By contrast, the rearguard efforts of the Dutch and the French to retain their possessions in the region embroiled them in costly and ultimately disastrous commitments. After the ousting of the Japanese from the Netherlands East Indies in 1945, the Dutch had hoped to reassert their power. But Sukarno, a nationalist who had collaborated with the Japanese, issued a declaration of independence. British troops who landed to take over authority from the Japanese were attacked and suffered severe casualties. Urged by the British to negotiate with the nationalists, the Dutch reached an agreement with Sukarno in November 1946. But this soon broke down and the Dutch launched a determined effort to reassert control by force. They won a pyrrhic military victory. The United States and the United Nations applied pressure that compelled them to yield. In December 1949 more than three centuries of Dutch rule came to an end (save in western New Guinea). The Dutch had hoped to be able to retain control of their significant economic interests after independence but within a decade these had been seized and most Dutch citizens expelled.

The attempt of French forces to reinstall colonial rule in Indo-China was even more calamitous. Between 1941 and 1944 French forces there, loyal to Vichy, had been permitted by the Japanese to maintain a measure of subaltern authority. But after the liberation of France in 1944 the position of the French in the Far East became untenable. In March 1945 the Japanese launched a surprise attack on the sixty-thousand-strong French garrison. At Lang Son the Japanese presented the French commander with a demand for the immediate disarmament of his troops. Upon its rejection, he and the French administrator of the province were decapitated with sabres and the entire force was massacred. What remained of the French army in Indo-China was interned until the end of the war. This humiliation, like that of the British in Singapore in 1942, severely dented the prestige of the colonial power. But whereas the British in Malaya adroitly succeeded in uniting most of the population against the Communists, the French in Vietnam aroused much of the country against themselves.

In September 1945 British and French forces arrived in South Vietnam to take over from the Japanese. North of the thirty-sixth parallel, Chinese forces were authorized to take temporary control but the nationalist Viet Minh, under the political leadership of Ho Chi Minh and the military command of Vo Nguyen Giap, were armed by the Japanese and seized power in Hanoi and Tonkin. The following March General Leclerc landed at Haiphong and once again raised the *tricolore*. But the French were unable to restore their authority. Savage French bombardment of Haiphong in November, in an attempt to flush out the Viet Minh, resulted in six thousand deaths. Over the next eight years the French attempted, at ever-increasing cost, to reclaim their former colony.

The Communist victory in China in 1949 endowed Ho Chi Minh with a vital source of supplies. In 1951 the French commander, Marshal Jean de Lattre de Tassigny, tried to draw the Viet Minh into a decisive confrontation at Hoa Binh. But Giap instead attacked French supply lines and in early 1952 forced de Lattre to withdraw. As the conflict escalated, casualties mounted. So did costs. According to one estimate French expenditure on the war was greater than the country's receipts under the Marshall Plan. By the spring of 1954 the French position was so desperate that the government requested American air support. The Americans consulted the British about joint action. But Churchill rejected this outright, declaring that the war could be won only by use of 'that horrible thing', the atom bomb.[21] In early May the French 'offensive outpost' at Dien Bien Phu, near the Laotian border, succumbed. The French objective, to draw the enemy out of hiding, had succeeded only too well: Giap's forces, who included fearless *hommes-suicides* wearing explosives on their persons, surrounded and overwhelmed the French garrison. The defeat dealt a devastating blow to French morale but the crisis called forth unusually strong leadership in Paris.

Pierre Mendès France, who took office in June 1954 as the sixteenth head of government since 1944, was the most substantial Prime Minister of the Fourth Republic. A Radical of independent views, vigorous intelligence, and masterful personality, he took charge of a demoralized, disillusioned nation. His administration followed the 'trajectory of a comet', as the political scientist André Siegfried put it, though, unlike the celestial body, he streaked across the firmament only once, never to return.[22] During his eight months in power he gave France the most energetic leadership the country had known since the fall of de Gaulle. His campaign against alcoholism and illegal home-distillers (*bouilleurs de cru*) was personalized by the revelation that he drank only milk; protesters raised banners declaring, 'Milk = Misery, Productivity = Ruin.' His weekly broadcast '*causeries de samedi soir*' evoked accusations of 'Bonapartism' but won him popular admiration second only to de Gaulle. The singular achievement of Mendès France's government was the extrication of France from the morass in Indo-China. In his speech to the National Assembly upon taking office, the new Prime Minister astonished his audience and the country at large by declaring that he would reach a settlement in Indo-China within one month, failing which he would present his resignation. He achieved his aim. The Geneva accords, ending French rule in Indo-China and conceding north Vietnam to the Communists, were signed on 20 July and approved by a large majority in the National Assembly.

Suez

The European exit from the Middle East, like that from South-East Asia, was a product of revolutionized power relations after 1945. During the war the USSR, which had hitherto taken little interest in the region, had begun to explore possibilities for extending its influence there. In 1946 Soviet troops entered northern Iran and Moscow began to exert pressure on Turkey, demanding revision of the Montreux Convention of 1936, which had established the international regime for the Straits between the Black Sea and the Mediterranean.[23] Soviet diplomacy was accompanied by threatening naval manoeuvres in the Black Sea. Robust American and British support for Turkey, however, induced the Russians to acquiesce in the status quo in the Straits. Soviet attention in the Middle East henceforth focused more on the Arab countries where it moved towards support for Arab nationalist movements, often at the expense of local Communist parties. The transparent Soviet motive was to undermine the rickety position of Britain and France, formerly the dominant powers in the central Middle East.

As after the First World War, dissension in the Levant soured Anglo-French relations and left a legacy of inter-Allied discord. The French mandatory territories of Syria and Lebanon had been promised independence by Blum's Popular Front government before the war. Upon the fall of

France, however, the French military and civilian authorities declared for Vichy. In 1941 British and Free French forces occupied the territories and, under British pressure, the French again undertook to recognize the sovereignty of the two states. But de Gaulle regarded such British advice as hypocritical. On 17 May 1945 French troops landed at Beirut and attempted to restore French rule there and in Syrian cities. Hundreds were killed in fighting between the French and Syrian irregulars. The British issued an ultimatum demanding French withdrawal and on 3 June the French, isolated diplomatically, complied. British troops remained in occupation until 1946 when the countries' full independence was recognized.

British economic, political, and strategic commitments in the Middle East were much greater than French. The Suez Canal remained a vital passageway for the British merchant fleet, still by far the largest in the world. Even after the decision to leave India, the canal was regarded as a critically important asset in Britain's capability to project force to the Persian Gulf and south Asia in defence of British interests and allies against indigenous and Soviet threats. The British economy, ever more dependent on imported oil, looked to the Middle East for supplies. The Foreign Secretary, Eden, pointed out in a Cabinet memorandum in April 1945 that 'the Middle East is the sole really large source of oil outside America which is available to us'.[24] Hoping to ride the tiger of Arab nationalism, the British in 1944–5 had sponsored the creation of the Arab League. But, like the French, they soon found themselves unable to contain anti-imperial challenges.

The first major test came in Palestine where Britain's thirty-year-old mandate collapsed in ignominy and recriminations. In spite of earlier pro-Zionist party statements, the post-war British Labour government refused to create a Jewish state or to rescind restrictions on Jewish immigration. Caught in crossfire from several sides, the government flailed around without discovering a viable policy. In the western occupation zones of Germany large numbers of Jewish survivors of Nazism clamoured for admission to Palestine. The Zionists organized illegal immigration of Jews to Palestine and extremist Jewish groups engaged in anti-British terrorism there. In the United States, on which Britain was heavily dependent for economic aid, the Zionists mobilized effectively as a political lobby. The Truman administration called for concessions to the Zionists. But the Arab League demanded that Britain concede the Palestinian Arab demand for an independent Arab state in Palestine. The British government feared that the entire British position in the Middle East, including the Suez Canal and the oilfields of Iraq, might be endangered if it acceded to Zionist demands; at the same time, it feared the consequences for relations with the United States if it gave in to the Arabs. The result was a long period of irresolution and drift. In the autumn of 1945 the British and American governments agreed on the appointment of an Anglo-American Committee of Inquiry to look into the problems of Palestine and of the Jewish 'displaced persons' in Europe. The committee reported in April 1946. Its main immediate recommendation, for the admission of 100,000 Jewish refugees to Palestine, was rejected by Attlee, who announced that an essential precondition would be the disarming of all illegal forces in Palestine. The Zionists would not agree to that and the government was consequently again left without a policy.

Meanwhile the British military situation on the ground deteriorated in spite of an increase in British forces to a hundred thousand men. Terrorist incidents such as the massive bomb explosion in July 1946 at the King David Hotel in Jerusalem, which claimed ninety British, Jewish, and Arab lives, led to a partial breakdown of morale in the British army in Palestine. Some British soldiers resorted to counter-terrorism against Jewish targets. At the same time Arab–Jewish violence also increased. Further efforts by the British government to obtain a settlement by agreement failed. In 1947 the government therefore announced that it would return the mandate to the United Nations, as successor of the League, and would withdraw from Palestine. The United Nations sent a committee to Palestine to investigate the position and on the basis of its proposals the UN General Assembly, on 29 November 1947, voted in favour of the partition of Palestine into separate Jewish and Arab states. During the remaining five and a half months of British rule Palestine descended into chaos. By April 1948 a full-scale civil war was in progress between Jewish armed forces and Arab irregulars supported by the armies of surrounding Arab states. As the last British High Commissioner prepared to leave on 14 May, the Zionist leader, David Ben Gurion, declared the State of Israel. With Israel's victory in the ensuing war with her Arab enemies, including the surrounding Arab states, and the departure of the greater part of Israel's Arab population, the way was open for large-scale Jewish immigration. The majority of Jews remaining in displaced persons' camps in Europe opted to move there, as did many Jewish survivors from east-central Europe, particularly Poland, where anti-Semitism remained widespread. Britain's policy in the last stages of the Palestine mandate was guided primarily by a desire not to endanger her broader interests in the Middle East. But the outcome was a legacy of bitterness that overshadowed British relations with the Arab world for the next generation.

In the aftermath of their Palestine fiasco, the British faced growing hostility throughout the Middle East. In 1951 a nationalist government in Iran, headed by Dr Mohammed Mossadeq, nationalized the assets of the British-owned Anglo-Iranian Oil Company, later known as British Petroleum or BP. Refusing to acquiesce in the loss of their largest single overseas investment, the British government organized a worldwide embargo on Iranian oil and referred the issue to the International Court of Justice at The Hague. The court found in favour of Iran but the company and the Iranian government failed to resolve their differences. As Mossadeq began to lean towards the Communist-inspired Tudeh Party, the western powers feared the growth of Soviet influence. In August 1953 a clandestine operation, jointly organized by the CIA and MI6 in collusion with Mohammed Reza Shah Pahlavi, overthrew Mossadeq. A pro-western regime was installed that, in the following year, reached an oil agreement with Britain and in 1955 joined the UK, Iraq, Turkey, and Pakistan in a military alliance, the Baghdad Pact.

Meanwhile, however, as the British shored up the 'northern tier' of the Middle East against Soviet penetration, a threat to their dominance in the region appeared elsewhere. In 1951 a nationalist government in Egypt abrogated the Anglo-Egyptian Treaty of 1936, thus undermining the right of the British to remain in their Suez Canal base. The new Conservative government in London confirmed its predecessor's orders to reinforce the British garrison in the canal zone until it reached a strength of eighty thousand. In January 1952 fighting broke out between British troops and Egyptian police at Ismailia and riots against British, Jewish, and foreign interests erupted in Cairo. In July the discredited royal regime of King Farouk was overthrown in an officers' coup. Gamal Abdul Nasser, who pushed aside rivals by early 1954, was the CIA's favoured candidate for Egyptian leadership and at first showed himself willing to negotiate with the British. He signed a new Anglo-Egyptian agreement in October, calling for all British troops to leave Egypt by June 1956, though the Suez base was 'to be kept in efficient working order' for British use in the event of an attack 'by an outside power' on any Arab League member state.[25] In April 1955 the main British proponent of the new treaty, the Foreign Secretary, Sir Anthony Eden, succeeded the ailing, eighty-year-old Churchill as Prime Minister.

Eden and Nasser, the two main protagonists in the Suez drama, both operated on mistaken assumptions that led them into dangerous courses. Nasser thought he could play off the Russians against the western powers. In September 1955 he revealed an arms purchase agreement with Czechoslovakia (acting as surrogate for the USSR). The deal threatened to upset the precarious arms balance between Israel and Egypt and open the way towards the long-threatened 'second round' between the two countries. On 13 June 1956, in accordance with the treaty, British troops evacuated the Suez base. Among the prominent foreign guests at the three-day celebrations held to mark the event was the new Soviet Foreign Minister, Dmitry Shepilov. Angered by Nasser's apparent slide towards the eastern bloc, the Americans cancelled their offer of financial aid for Nasser's showpiece project, the Aswan High Dam on the Nile. Nasser responded on 26 July by announcing the nationalization of the Suez Canal. It was owned by the Suez Canal Company, a Paris-based concern in which the British government held a 44 per cent share. The company operated the canal as a concessionaire and its position was safeguarded in the 1954 treaty of which Nasser's action was thus a direct breach. Two-thirds of western Europe's oil supplies passed through the canal and Eden saw the Egyptian action as a threat of economic strangulation. He reacted to the nationalization with outrage, denouncing Nasser as a tinpot dictator and insisting that Britain must not again make the mistake of appeasing an aggressor. 'If we lose out in the Middle East,' he said, 'we shall be immediately destroyed.'[26] But the British Prime Minister was out of step with the development of thinking in Whitehall, where an inter-departmental committee concluded that Britain 'has ceased to be a first-class Power in material terms'.[27] Eden nevertheless resolved to overthrow Nasser and, together with the leaders of Israel and France, began planning a military campaign against Egypt. Each of these had reasons for seeking a showdown with Nasser.

The Israeli Prime Minister, Ben Gurion, aimed at a pre-emptive war, designed to knock out the Egyptians before they could absorb eastern-bloc arms supplies and pose a serious challenge to the Jewish state. The French government wanted to cut off the conduit of arms supplies from Egypt to the Algerian rebels against French rule. Socialist leaders, notably the Prime Minister, Mollet, and the Foreign Minister, Christian Pineau, a former deportee to Buchenwald, were sympathetic to Socialist Zionism and agreed to supply Israel with arms, including modern warplanes. Mollet assured the visiting Israeli special envoy, Shimon Peres, that he would 'never be a Bevin' (referring to the former British Foreign Secretary's betrayal of his Zionist friends).[28] Like Eden, the French were affected by the 'Munich syndrome'. Mollet compared Nasser to Hitler and the Egyptian leader's *Philosophy of the Revolution* to *Mein Kampf*.

Britain was anxious not to increase the wrath of pan-Arab nationalists by advertising her alliance of convenience with Israel. Hence the extreme secretiveness of the British contacts with the Israelis. In order to provide a suitable pretext for the Anglo-French occupation of the Canal Zone, it was agreed that Israel would first attack Egypt in Sinai, the French providing a protective air shield for Israeli cities. Britain and France would then issue an ultimatum to both Israel and Egypt demanding that their forces withdraw from the canal. Egypt was expected to reject the ultimatum, whereupon the British and French forces would move into the Canal Zone, supposedly as its protectors. Ben Gurion remained suspicious of British motives and reliability. At a secret meeting with French and British representatives in a former resistance 'safe house' at Sèvres on 24 October, he therefore insisted that the arrangement must be set down in writing as a formal record. A Foreign Office official reluctantly signed the agreement. A furious Eden tried, without success, to persuade the French and Israelis to destroy all copies of the document. British diplomats dispatched to the Quai d'Orsay for this purpose were ushered to a waiting room and left there for several hours. When they eventually decided to leave for dinner, they found that all the officials had gone home and the building was locked up. Subsequently Eden and other British ministers denied in the House of Commons any foreknowledge of the Israeli attack on Egypt.

Militarily the Suez expedition was bungled in an appalling manner. The long period of semi-public preparation of attacking forces at Cyprus and Malta was reminiscent of the prelude to the Gallipoli campaign—not a propitious historical precedent. The Israelis, secure under a French aerial umbrella protecting their cities, attacked Sinai on 29 October. The next day the British and French issued their ultimatum calling on both parties to withdraw from the canal (which Israeli forces had not yet reached). The Egyptians rejected the ultimatum. On 31 October Anglo-French air attacks on Egypt began. Echoing the Chamberlain of September 1939, Eden addressed the nation on the evening of 3 November: 'All my life I've been a man of peace, working for peace, striving for peace, negotiating for peace.'[29] But he insisted that the lesson of the 1930s was that peace must not be sought at any price. The next day the Egyptians sank ships in the canal, blocking passage through it. Early on 5 November British and French paratroops landed near Port Said and Port Fuad.

Hardly had the invasion of Egypt been launched than the British Cabinet began to have cold feet. The Soviet Union made bellicose noises in support of the Egyptians. The French appealed to the United States for an unequivocal assurance that the North Atlantic pact would apply if Britain and

France were attacked by the USSR. Eisenhower, who faced his second presidential election on 6 November, was furious: 'Of course,' he said to an aide, 'there's nobody in a war I'd rather have fighting alongside me than the British . . . But this thing! My God!'[30] Far from offering a guarantee, the Americans demanded unequivocal Anglo-French acceptance of an immediate cease-fire and withdrawal of troops. In London the Chancellor of the Exchequer, Harold Macmillan, earlier a strong proponent of military action, warned the Cabinet that sterling would come under irresistible pressure if the war were not halted forthwith. The British thereupon decided, without consulting their French ally, to stop fighting. Relations between London and Paris and between the British and French military commanders in Egypt dissolved into mutual recriminations. On 6 November, the Israelis, having conquered the Sinai peninsula, agreed to a cease-fire. The next day, the British and French ceased hostilities, having failed to topple Nasser or attain their military objectives. By 22 December they had departed from Egypt, this time for ever, to be replaced by a United Nations peacekeeping force. Eden later claimed that, viewed as 'a short-term emergency operation', Suez had 'succeeded';[31] but the canal remained under Egyptian control.

Suez divided British public opinion like no other foreign question since Munich. The declared purpose of the intervention, separation of Israeli and Egyptian forces, was so transparently bogus that allegations were soon heard that the British and French had 'colluded' in advance with the Israelis, though this was hotly denied by the government. But the charge of 'collusion' stuck and permanently stained Eden's reputation. The Labour Party and most liberal opinion strongly opposed the attack on Egypt as a species of gunboat diplomacy inappropriate to the post-imperial age.

Suez destroyed Eden, who suffered a physical and nervous collapse and resigned in January 1957. His replacement, Macmillan, a more subtle and deft politician, rebuilt confidence in the Conservatives and presided over one of the more successful administrations of the post-war period. Suez was the last major campaign in which conscripts fought in the British army. For the next quarter-century the memory of the disaster was to serve as a salutary warning to British politicians contemplating military action.

The ignominious end of the affair was widely judged to betoken a watershed in the national standing of both Britain and France. Their pretensions to great power status were henceforward increasingly difficult to sustain. Nasser's successful defiance of the former colonial powers exalted his prestige in the Arab world. Arab nationalism over the next few years was on a roll. In 1958 the pro-British Hashemite regime in Iraq was overthrown by a military coup. Yet in spite of considerable soreness in both London and Paris at the lack of support from Washington, the damage to the cohesion of the western alliance was soon repaired.

The French drew somewhat different lessons from the debacle. A post-mortem by the Quai d'Orsay blamed Britain, which had 'for long worked against us in the Arab world' and had shown herself 'hesitant to take action, maladroit in its execution and infirm of purpose at the moment of truth'. The crisis had revealed 'with implacable clarity' France's dependence on the American alliance. Britain and France alone lacked sufficient weight to defy the United States. The long-term solution must lie in a united Europe.[32] French public opinion, except for the Communists and some others on the left, generally supported the expedition and the government remained in power, though the Socialists were seriously divided. *Jusqu'auboutistes* concluded that France must no longer allow herself to be egged on and then abandoned by over-cautious allies, as in Indo-China in 1954 and Egypt in 1956. Instead she must resolutely and unflinchingly pursue her own interests to the furthest limit. The politicization of the French army, which had its origins in the events of the Second World War, and had been exacerbated by the defeats at Dien Bien Phu and Suez, now reached a peak. The result, within two years, was to turn a rebuff into a catastrophe that overwhelmed the Fourth Republic.

The fall of the Fourth Republic

The catalyst was the revolt of the Front de Libération Nationale (FLN), the organization of native Algerian Muslim rebels against French rule in Algeria. The insurrection, which began in November 1954, opened against a background of political concession by the French in North Africa. In a speech at Carthage in August 1954 Mendès France had announced his government's readiness to open negotiations on internal autonomy in Tunisia. Reforms were promised in French Morocco. But Mendès France was determined to maintain French control over Algeria, as was his Minister of the Interior (with authority over Algeria), François Mitterrand. Jacques Soustelle, a Gaullist appointed Governor-General by Mendès France shortly before his fall from power in February 1955, initiated plans for political reforms. But he insisted that 'France is at home here, or rather Algeria and all its inhabitants form an integral part of France, one and indivisible. That is the alpha and omega. Everybody should know, here and elsewhere, that France will as soon quit Algeria as Provence or Britanny.'[33] Soustelle's proposals for granting political rights to the Muslims horrified the French settler community without winning over the Algerian nationalists. The revolt only grew in strength. For the next three and a half years the republic wrestled with the demon until in the end it was consumed by it.

The French stake in Algeria was not just a matter of national pride. Algeria had been under French rule since 1830 and in 1848 it had been proclaimed an integral part of France. By any reckoning, it was France's most important overseas possession. The French population of Algeria, known as *pieds noirs* (supposedly because, unlike the barefoot *indigènes*, they wore black shoes), was larger than in any other overseas possession. In all of Indo-China there were only 67,000 European residents of all nationalities; in Algeria in 1954 there were over a million, constituting 10 per cent of the population. They felt fully at home in Algeria, where 83 per cent of them had been born. Only a minority were of French origin. The rest were mainly immigrants, or their descendants, from Italy, Spain, or Malta. Also included among the 'Europeans' were Algeria's 130,000 Jews, heirs to a community dating back to Roman times, most of whom had enjoyed full French nationality since 1870 (except during the Vichy period). Almost all Christians and Jews in the country identified closely with French culture and feared for their survival under Muslim rule. A far smaller proportion of the *colons* than of the population of metropolitan France was engaged in agriculture: under 10 per cent. Most of these farmed very small tracts. The rest were small shopkeepers, artisans, civil servants, and (more than half the European population) working-class wage-earners. Their standard of living was in general far below that of their equivalents in France, though much higher than that of the Muslims among whom they lived.

In May 1945 fierce communal riots had left over a hundred Europeans and thousands of Muslims dead. Under the Fourth Republic various proposals had been advanced for expanding the Muslim franchise and increasing Muslim political rights but these did not satisfy the nationalists: they demanded independence.

France's determination to maintain authority was not merely a reflection of settler interests. The discovery in 1956 of huge oil deposits at Hassi Messaoud and of gas at Hassi R'Mel offered France the prospect of energy independence. But at the same time Algeria was a heavy burden on the French taxpayer: between 1945 and 1960 its budget depended every year on a subsidy from France, quite apart from the ballooning military costs of repressing the revolt.

The war was a sordid and messy affair. French soldiers were seriously demoralized as a result of the terrorist tactics, first of the FLN, later of militant French settlers. The army was ill-equipped by training, by mentality, or by ideology to fight a campaign against urban guerrillas who planted bombs in marketplaces and then retreated to the rabbit warren of the *casbah*. The number of French troops in the country in 1954 was 54,000. By the end of 1956 450,000, including conscripts and reservists, were engaged in a conflict that the government resolutely refused to term a 'war' (the word did not enter official vocabulary until 1999). The widespread use of torture against prisoners sullied the army's honour. Captured terrorists were frequently shot without trial. 'It was rare,' recalls one French officer, 'that prisoners interrogated at night would still be alive by early morning. Whether they had talked or not, they were generally neutralized.'[34] Contrary to ministerial instructions, the army used napalm against the rebels. But such tactics merely bound the Muslim population more closely to the rebel cause and contributed to the growing demoralization of the army.

The conflict poisoned French politics and society. The Indo-China war, serious though its impact was on French military morale, had been far enough away from the *métropole* to have only limited effects in France herself. Algeria was different. Nearly all the major institutions of French society in the *hexagone*, including the security services, the judicial system, the universities, and the media were affected. Censorship of the press, cinema, and state-controlled broadcasting extended far beyond levels acceptable in most liberal democracies. Journalists who fell foul of the government were thrown in prison.

Meanwhile, other dislocations caused by rapid economic change fuelled a general mood of unrest. This found expression in a movement led by Pierre Poujade, a populist demagogue who appealed to the small-shopkeeper class. Poujadism rode a wave of protest voting that briefly disconcerted the political establishment. In normal times 'Poujadolf' would have been no more than an irritant; now his success seemed to indicate the bankruptcy of the political system.

In the elections of January 1956 the centre-left won a parliamentary majority and the Socialist leader, Guy Mollet, formed a government. Poujadist candidates won 2.6 million votes and 53 seats. During the election campaign Mollet had talked of 'an imbecile war that has reached a deadlock'.[35] But his prescription for resolving the conflict was vague to the point of opacity. When he visited Algiers in February, he was pelted with tomatoes by *pieds noirs*. In

March the French recognized the independence of the neighbouring French protectorates of Morocco and Tunisia, though France was to retain military and naval bases for several years. In the same month Mollet opened secret talks with the FLN but after six months failed to persuade them to accept anything less than total independence. In May 1957 the Mollet government fell, to be succeeded by transient and weak coalitions.

France was now as divided as during the Dreyfus affair, perhaps even as under Vichy. As in those earlier defining episodes, it was no simple matter of left versus right. Not only men of the left, such as Jean-Paul Sartre, but also intellectuals of the centre-right, such as François Mauriac and Raymond Aron, denounced the use of torture and called for an end to the war. The Algerian-born Albert Camus trod a lonely middle way, supporting French rule in Algeria but condemning the abuses by which it was maintained. Soustelle, the darling of the *colons* since his dismissal from Algiers in 1956, was their most eloquent spokesman in France. In the press *Le Monde* was the only daily paper apart from the Communist *L'Humanité* to oppose the war. Old Fascists like Jean-Louis Tixier-Vignancour emerged from the shadows, to join with Poujadistes like Jean-Marie Le Pen in calling for a 'national revolution'.

The death of the Fourth Republic was part euthanasia, part suicide. It was also, in some measure, a *coup d'état*. The failure of Mendès France and the complicity of the Socialists in the wars of Suez and Algeria consigned the republic's traditional defenders to impotence. Parliamentary manoeuvring and revolving-door ministries disgusted a public that, as in 1940, looked for the man on horseback to get rid of what was seen as a corrupt and ineffective party system and save them from a disastrous war. In 1940 that man had been Pétain. Now it was his nemesis: Charles de Gaulle.

The catalyst was a message to the President of the Republic on 9 May 1958 from four army generals stationed in Algeria, Salan, Allard, Jouhaud, and Massu, and an admiral, Auboyneau, in which they declared: 'The army is troubled by a sense of its responsibility towards the men who are fighting... towards the French population at home who feel abandoned... and towards French Muslims who have placed their confidence in France.... The army would unanimously consider the abandonment of this national patrimony an outrage. Its reaction in despair could not be forecast.'[36]

On 13 May, as a new government under Pierre Pflimlin took office in Paris, demonstrations by Europeans in Algiers led to the takeover of government buildings by crowds and to the declaration of a Committee of Public Safety, headed by General Massu. He demanded the creation of a 'government of national salvation' in Paris under the leadership of de Gaulle. His fellow army commanders colluded in what amounted to an insurrection. There was talk of parachutists descending on Paris. Immured at Colombey, the previously silent de Gaulle decided to seize his moment. In a brief, imperious statement issued on 15 May, he deplored the 'degradation' to which the republic had succumbed, recognized that the country 'in its depths, has placed confidence in me to lead it as a whole towards its salvation', and declared himself 'ready to assume the powers of the republic'.[37]

Over the next two weeks a struggle for power pitched de Gaulle, supported by old *fidèles* plus a bandwagon of new political recruits, the army, and the *pieds noirs*, against the Communists and some Socialists and radicals. Soustelle returned to a hero's welcome from the insurgents in Algiers. The army Chief of Staff resigned. De Gaulle moved to Paris and gave a press conference in which he lauded the army's actions in Algiers, again offered to be 'useful to France', and denied that 'at the age of sixty-seven' he could have any intention of 'starting a career as a dictator'.[38] The government monitored de Gaulle's movements without knowing how to contend with him. At a Cabinet meeting on 21 May the Minister of the Interior, Jules Moch, solemnly reported that de Gaulle had stopped his car en route to Paris in order to take a piss and had bantered with the policeman detailed to follow him while he too relieved himself.[39] The Communist-controlled CGT trade union movement declared a general strike. Army chiefs plotted a military takeover. De Gaulle announced he would not countenance such an action. But the looming threat nevertheless caused politicians to gravitate towards him as a saviour. The alternative potential strongman, Mendès France, notwithstanding his sympathy with some aspects of de Gaulle's thinking, declared that he was not disposed to 'gain peace in Africa in exchange for Fascism in metropolitan France'.[40] A decisive majority of the political class swung to de Gaulle as the guarantor of order. The crisis reached its climax with the resignation of the Pflimlin government and the installation of de Gaulle as Prime Minister. In the decisive vote in the National Assembly on 1 June, only 49 out of 95 Socialists joined the Communists, some Radicals around Mendès France and Mitterrand, and a few others in opposing the grant to de Gaulle of full powers to restore order and draft a new constitution.

In his first statement to the National Assembly as Prime Minister designate, de Gaulle set out his programme. He spoke of the 'rapidly accelerating degradation of the State' and of the danger of civil war and asked that his government be invested with full powers for a period of six months. His first task would be to propose constitutional reform to be submitted to the country for approval in a referendum.[41] In early June de Gaulle visited Algeria. In Algiers he gave the settlers the impression that he supported their cause. 'Je vous ai compris,' he declared from a balcony to a cheering crowd of Europeans in Algiers.[42] The phrase was Delphic in its simplicity and ambiguity. In a television address to the French people on 13 June, he was more explicit, announcing his intention of pacifying Algeria 'in such a way that it will, forever, be body and soul with France'.[43] His first Cabinet rewarded those who had brought him to power: it included Mollet, Pinay, and, as Minister of Information, Soustelle. But they were little more than ciphers. Real power was vested in the hands of one man. In the referendum of 28 September the greater part of the right, centre, and moderate left rallied to support of the proposed new institutions. De Gaulle's proposals secured the approval of 79 per cent of voters.

The constitution of the Fifth Republic, which passed into law in October 1958, reflected de Gaulle's long-standing preoccupation with transferring the locus of power from parliament to the presidency. The decorative head of state of the third and fourth republics was now replaced with a strong executive presidency, to be elected by a presidential college composed of about eighty thousand people, mainly members of municipal councils. The Prime Minister's tenure henceforth depended on the continuing confidence of the President, not merely on a majority in parliament. Politics polarized and the centre-left Radical Party, which had held the balance of power for much of the first half of the century, dwindled into an insignificant remnant. De Gaulle's supporters founded a new party, the Union pour la Nouvelle République, which, under various names, dominated French politics for the next generation. On 21 December de Gaulle was overwhelmingly elected first President of the Fifth Republic. His extraordinary quasi-coup was now complete and over the next decade he used the semi-despotic authority granted to him by the French people to recreate France in his own image.

Imbalance of terror

Western fear of the Soviet Union had been suddenly heightened in August 1949 by the detonation in Kazakhstan of the first Soviet atomic bomb. The test was publicized a few weeks later by the Americans. The Soviets at first denied the report, claiming that 'large-scale blasting work' in building hydroelectric stations was responsible for the blast. At the same time they claimed, falsely, that 'the Soviet Union [had] possessed the secret of the atomic weapon [as early as] 1947'.[44] Stalin had, in fact, ordered an intensification of the USSR's nuclear research programme after the American detonations of atomic bombs over Hiroshima and Nagasaki in August 1945. Although Soviet scientists played a significant part in the development of their country's nuclear project, its success owed much to the activity of Soviet spies in Britain and the United States during and after the Second World War. The first to be arrested in Britain, in 1946, was Allan Nunn May, a scientist who had worked on the wartime Anglo-American nuclear enterprise. In 1949 a German émigré physicist, Klaus Fuchs, fell under suspicion and was arrested and imprisoned. Bruno Pontecorvo, an Italian atomic expert also working in Britain, thereupon confessed that he too had spied for the USSR; he was not arrested but shortly afterwards fled to the USSR. All these men acted out of ideological rather than financial motives. Although their cases did not evoke in Britain the extremes of anti-Communist hysteria that were aroused at this period in the United States, they hardened suspicion of Soviet aims and tactics. The role of the spies in the Soviet nuclear effort was one of acceleration rather than discovery. Estimates of the advance gained range between two and ten years. But once the USSR had access to sufficient supplies of uranium, found at the time mainly in the Soviet zone of Germany, it would, even without espionage, have been merely a matter of time before the Soviet Union produced an atomic bomb.

The Soviet success, which took US and British intelligence by surprise, inaugurated a feverish arms race. In November 1952 in the South Pacific the United States detonated its first thermonuclear device, a thousand times more powerful than the bomb dropped on Hiroshima. The first deliverable US hydrogen bomb was exploded on Bikini atoll in March 1954. Meanwhile the Soviets detonated their first hydrogen bomb in Kazakhstan in August 1953. Unlike the Soviet atom bomb, this was largely a homegrown Soviet scientific achievement, one in which Andrei Sakharov, the future Nobel peace prize laureate, played a prominent part.

During the 1950s, and particularly after the end of the Korean War in 1953, Europe remained the main arena of the Cold War. By now it was clear that the United States would keep substantial forces in Germany on a permanent basis, as would the British and French. In 1957, the peak year for US troop strength in Europe between 1950 and the end of the Cold War, 439,000 US servicemen, out of a total US armed forces strength of 2.8

million, were stationed in Europe. Of these 244,000 were in Germany, 72,000 in France (where NATO headquarters were initially situated), 63,000 in Britain, and smaller numbers on the territory of other NATO member states.

In addition the Americans maintained bases around the edges of Europe. Denmark initially resisted continuation of the wartime American military presence at Thule in Greenland for fear of Soviet reaction. The Americans went so far as to offer to buy Greenland outright in 1947. In 1951, however, against the background of the Korean War, the Danes relented and signed a base agreement with the United States. This was public knowledge but the decision in 1957 of the Danish Prime Minister, H. C. Hansen, to permit the deployment of US nuclear weapons in Greenland remained secret. Iceland, whose independence from Denmark had been recognized by the USA in 1944, made her membership of NATO in 1949 conditional on non-stationing of foreign troops (she had no armed forces of her own). But she too agreed in 1951 to allow US troops to return and re-establish a base at Keflavik, though it was so unpopular among Icelanders that for a time servicemen were forbidden to go off-base. The American air base on the Azores also dated back to the Second World War: after the war Portugal permitted it to remain, although there too an agreement regularizing the arrangement was signed only in 1951. The Americans had an easier time in the case of the Wheelus air base in Libya, since most of this former Italian colony was administered by Britain until 1951. After Libyan independence in that year the western-inclined monarchical government readily agreed to the continuation of the US presence.

The American strategic objective in this period of 'containing' the Soviet Union derived from a fear both of Soviet expansionist intentions and of its disproportionate military capabilities in Europe. Under Khrushchev the total armed manpower of the Soviet Union declined from 5.7 million to around three million, of whom half a million were stationed on the territory of its Warsaw Pact allies, the remainder mainly in the western regions of the USSR. The main reasons for the troop reductions were the desire to switch resources to industrial production and a greater reliance on nuclear power. But even after this slimming-down, Soviet conventional military strength in Europe remained superior to that of the west.

Western plans in the Cold War were largely defensive but included more than a grain of opportunistic offensive calculation. A British Chiefs of Staff report in June 1950 declared that 'the enemy's aim' was 'quite clear—it is a

Communist world dominated by Moscow'. The western objective, 'which must be achieved if possible without real hostilities' should involve 'first, a stabilization of the anti-Communist front in the present free world and then, as the Western Powers become militarily less weak, the intensification of "cold" offensive measures aimed at weakening the Russian grip on the satellite states and ultimately achieving their complete independence of Russian control'. In the event of a 'hot war' the western aim must be to prevent the Russians from overrunning western Europe by bringing about 'the destruction of Russian military power and the collapse of the present regime'. The Chiefs did not have any illusions about the capacity of west European armies to resist a Russian advance. 'European civilization could not', they opined, 'survive a Russian occupation of all Western Europe'. Hence the imperative need for German rearmament and for the integration of the future West German army within a coordinated west European defence strategy.[45]

Yet even if Germany were rearmed, and even if the United States maintained its substantial military presence in Europe, NATO conventional forces would not be able to withstand a Russian attack. One indication of western military planners' lack of confidence was the establishment in several west European countries of underground anti-Communist cells, programmed to go into action as paramilitary resistance forces in the event of a Soviet occupation. This 'stay-behind' network was initiated in 1950 and supervised by an Allied Clandestine Committee of NATO. It was set up with the cooperation of the secret services of member countries. Branches were formed throughout western Europe as well as in neutral Austria and Switzerland. By 1952 the enterprise had 6,594 personnel and a budget of $82 million from the CIA. Arms caches, medical supplies, and communications equipment were stockpiled in hundreds of locations. Agents were trained in sabotage and guerrilla warfare techniques. As fear of Soviet occupation receded, the network was gradually put into cold storage but elements of the system remained in existence until the end of the Cold War. Its existence was not revealed until 1989. As in other respects, this was a looking-glass war: the NATO secret army had its bizarre mirror-image in Soviet arms caches and sabotage plans in West Germany, Italy, Austria, and Switzerland.

Both east and west engaged in multifarious forms of covert warfare, propaganda, and information-gathering. American and British intelligence services lent support to remnants of wartime anti-Soviet underground movements in eastern Europe, particularly in the Ukraine. Guerrilla groups there remained active until the early 1950s when they were infiltrated by the Soviet secret police and liquidated. From 1949 onwards the CIA funded propaganda broadcasts to the eastern bloc by Radio Free Europe (later also by Radio Liberty). It provided clandestine support through the Congress for Cultural Freedom to a number of liberal, anti-Communist, intellectual magazines in western Europe, notably *Encounter* in Britain and *Der Monat* in Germany. The eastern bloc, for its part, provided financial aid to Communist and fellow-travelling parties, newspapers, and 'front organizations' in western Europe. In 1955 the CIA supervised the excavation of a 500-yard-long tunnel from west to east Berlin in order to tap telephone lines between Soviet military and intelligence offices in east Berlin. A total of 443,000 conversations were recorded and transcribed. But this Herculean labour was of limited value. Even before the tunnel had been opened, the secret was betrayed to the KGB by a Soviet agent in the British Secret Intelligence Service, George Blake. The KGB did not wish, however, to compromise Blake and so the tunnel remain operative for nearly a year (it remains unclear whether the KGB informed its rival, the Soviet military intelligence organization, GRU).[46]

The Soviets meanwhile scored an impressive victory in intelligence warfare through the work of their Cambridge group of spies. The existence of this ring became public in 1951 when Guy Burgess and Donald Maclean, both Foreign Office officials, fled to Moscow, narrowly avoiding arrest. The identity of the 'third man' who had tipped them off, enabling them to escape, was not revealed for more than a decade. He turned out to be the highest-level 'mole' ever planted by Soviet intelligence: Kim Philby, who had served in the British Secret Intelligence Service, MI6, since 1942. He headed the section devoted to counter-intelligence against Soviet espionage and subversion outside Britain and after 1949 was head of the service's Washington station. Following the defections of his two colleagues, Philby was investigated and obliged to retire from MI6, although there was insufficient evidence for a prosecution. He remained free and worked as a journalist. In 1963, fearing exposure, he too fled to the Soviet Union. A year later a most improbable 'fourth man' made a partial confession to MI6: Sir Anthony Blunt, Surveyor (later Adviser) for the Queen's Pictures and the world's greatest authority on Poussin. He was never punished and retained his position at Buckingham Palace until 1978. His treason was revealed publicly only in 1979. A fifth member of the ring was John Cairncross, a senior civil servant who had worked in the wartime decipherment enterprise at Bletchley. All five men had been converted to Communism while students at Cambridge in the 1930s. They furnished information of inestimable value to the USSR although their effectiveness was limited by Soviet controllers' strong suspicion in the early years that the men were British double agents intent on supplying disinformation.

The western record in intelligence during this stage of the Cold War still remains only partially revealed. The most important achievements, in which the United States and Britain certainly surpassed the eastern bloc, were less in the old-fashioned wiles of 'humint' (human intelligence, i.e. agents in the field) than in technical areas such as communications interception. The United States devoted considerable resources to locating Soviet nuclear establishments and missile sites. Such knowledge was regarded as vital in order to limit the Soviets' defensive and offensive capacity and to maintain a 'second-strike capability' in case of a Soviet nuclear attack. Some American methods of information-gathering were primitive. In 1956 hundreds of polyethylene balloons, equipped with cameras and radio beacons, were launched from Scotland, West Germany, and Turkey. The devices were carried over the Soviet Union by the jet stream and some sent back usable data. Others were shot done by Soviet MIG fighters and displayed in Moscow by an indignant Soviet government. President Eisenhower ordered an end to the scheme and the CIA instead deployed high-flying U-2 spy planes for the same purpose—a decision that was later to have fateful diplomatic consequences.

By the mid-1950s both the US and the USSR had built up large stockpiles of nuclear weapons. The Soviets also set about the construction of defences against nuclear attack on Moscow. From 1957 the Soviet capital was protected by three thousand anti-aircraft missiles and ringed by a large radar network.

The Cold War, like the Second World War, drew neutrals into unacknowledged involvement in many spheres. Sweden, for example, although formally neutral throughout the Cold War, conducted all her defence planning with an eye to the danger of invasion from the Soviet Union. Publicly the country's relations with the United States were cool: no Swedish Prime Minister visited the White House between 1952 and 1987, while there were ten such visits to Moscow between 1956 and 1988. At the same time, however, the country maintained secret contacts with NATO with a view to making Swedish airbases available in the event of war and, if necessary, evacuating the Swedish government to Britain. As General Bengt Nordenskjöld, commander of the Swedish air force, told a British colleague in 1949: 'Let us be practical. What does it matter whether Sweden is or is not in the Atlantic Pact? You know perfectly well that when the balloon goes up the Swedes are bound to fight the Russians.'[47] The United States shared military technology with the Swedes and made advanced weapons available, sometimes even ahead of supplies to NATO allies. Sweden's security policy also included a strong Nordic dimension. Secret military and intelligence cooperation was organized among the Nordic countries. In the 1950s the Swedish air force, mustering over a thousand aircraft, was the largest in western Europe after the RAF and effectively provided air defence not only for Sweden but also for Norway and Denmark, both NATO members. Switzerland too, although adhering publicly to her historic neutrality, engaged in undisclosed military cooperation with NATO. Ireland, which declared itself a republic, wholly independent of Britain, in 1949, accepted Marshall Plan aid and considered joining NATO on condition the British ceded Northern Ireland, but that price was too high for the British.[48]

As the constricted room for manoeuvre by the neutrals demonstrated, the international system was now largely controlled by the two superpowers (that expression entered into general usage in this period). The Russo-American duopoly of nuclear power inaugurated a bipolar strategic environment in which the pretensions of Britain and France to great-power status were barely plausible. Although assured under the NATO treaty of protection by the American nuclear umbrella, the west Europeans remained restive, unsure whether, in a crisis, they could really rely on Washington. Hence the movement by Britain and, a little later, by France towards the creation of independent nuclear forces.

Britain had at first hoped that the wartime nuclear cooperation with the United States would continue in peacetime. But in 1946 the McMahon Act in the United States laid down that American nuclear technology would henceforth be shared with no other power. The British thereupon set about the construction of their first nuclear reactor, at Harwell, Oxfordshire. In January 1947 Attlee resolved on the development of a British nuclear weapon. Only a few senior ministers were consulted and neither Cabinet nor Parliament was even informed. In June 1948 the British permitted the stationing of American air bases in Britain but no agreement was reached on whether British approval would be required before their use for launching a nuclear attack. The British as a result feared that they would be a priority target for the USSR. With her dense population, Britain would be outstandingly vulnerable to nuclear attack. Throughout the Cold War Britain remained alive to the threat of what one senior official called 'the sword of

Damocles of a Russian attack on the Pearl Harbor model'.[49] Possession of independently produced, controlled, and deliverable nuclear bombs was seen both as a direct deterrent against nuclear attack and as a lever for resuscitating wartime nuclear cooperation with the United States. As the USA obstinately continued to guard its nuclear secrets, the British turned to justifying membership of the 'nuclear club' as essential to the maintenance of Britain's position as a world power.

Britain exploded her first atomic bomb off Western Australia in October 1952. The weapon was designed to be delivered by a force of V-bombers: Valiants, and later, Vulcans and Victors, all British-made. But the British nuclear force was far smaller than those of the United States and the USSR and it was unclear how many such bombers could be expected to succeed in evading Soviet defences. It was not until 1956 that the first Valiant squadron capable of delivering nuclear weapons entered service. The logic of the British independent deterrent was less creation of a nuclear balance than redressing of the existing Soviet advantage in conventional armed strength in Europe. The bomb was seen as a deterrent not merely against the use by the USSR of nuclear weapons but also against any offensive action, whether conventional or nuclear. As the British Chiefs of Staff put it in 1954: 'If war came in the next few years, the Allies would have to make immediate use of the full armoury of nuclear weapons with the object of countering Russia's overwhelming superiority of man-power.'[50]

In the same year Churchill's government embarked on production of a hydrogen bomb. This time the decision was made by the Cabinet. The first British thermonuclear weapon was detonated in the Pacific Ocean in May 1957. Like the British A-bomb, the H-bomb was intended to impress the Americans at least as much as the Soviets. US recognition of Britain as a great power, the British ambassador in Washington maintained, depended on Britain's possession of 'megaton as well as kiloton weapons'.[51]

The next stage of the arms race involved a switch in delivery systems from planes to missiles. At the end of the war both the Russians and the Americans had captured and imported teams of German rocket scientists and, with their help, both powers initiated ambitious missile development programmes. Space served as an ersatz field of competition and provided a convenient method for enthusing the general public and gaining support for missile projects. In October 1957 the Soviet Union won the first round in the 'space race' by launching an artificial satellite, 'Sputnik', followed a month later by another containing the first 'space-dog', Laika. These public triumphs belied a more modest military reality: the USSR at this stage had a total arsenal of only four dubiously usable intercontinental ballistic missiles (ICBMs) to deliver nuclear warheads. Nonetheless, the Soviet Union's startling advances in space and its nuclear rocket-rattling shook Washington and led to an intensification of the American missile programme and a commitment to overtake the USSR in manned space flight.

The first American ICBM, the Atlas, became operational in 1958 but it would be some years before ICBMs could be deployed by the United States on a grand scale. In the interim, the Eisenhower administration decided to station nuclear-armed, intermediate-range Thor and Jupiter rockets (IRBMs) in Europe. Only Italy, Turkey, and the UK accepted these dangerous gifts. The British, anxious to restore relations with the Americans after the Suez disaster and concerned about the threat to their own security posed by Soviet missiles, permitted the deployment of sixty Thor missiles in Britain. These would be under dual control and operated jointly by the RAF and the USAF. In July 1958 Britain and the United States concluded an Atomic Energy Defence Agreement providing for a wide-ranging exchange of nuclear secrets and coordination of nuclear targeting. This at last renewed the wartime nuclear partnership and remained in force until after the end of the Cold War.

Believing that they were in the stronger position, because of their superiority in conventional forces in Europe, and anxious to forestall the new American missile deployments, the Soviets lent their support to a proposal by the Polish Foreign Minister, Adam Rapacki, for the creation of a nuclear-free zone in central Europe. The Rapacki plan aroused favourable interest in western public opinion but Adenauer regarded it as a Russian trap that 'would lead to the disintegration of NATO'.[52] The US administration's view was that 'while it might have some surface attraction, it poses totally unacceptable risks'. The plan countered 'agreed NATO strategy . . . which calls for integrated nuclear capability in NATO shield forces'. It would also prevent implementation of a decision to 'extend tactical nuclear weapons . . . to forces of other nations (warheads remaining [in] US custody). Without such weapons Soviet superiority becomes overwhelming in light [of] their much greater conventional forces.' The State Department noted that while the 'dangers of [the] plan [were] self-evident to those with any knowledge of [the] subject', the real problem would seem to lie in combating 'what appears to [the] public on [the] surface as [a] reasonable proposal'.[53]

American fears on this count were prudent, as public anxiety in Europe about the arms race fed anti-American feeling and calls to 'ban the bomb'. In Britain the Campaign for Nuclear Disarmament (CND), supported mainly by the left wing of the Labour Party, demanded unilateral nuclear disarmament. At Easter 1958 ten thousand protesters marched fifty miles from Trafalgar Square in London to the Atomic Weapons Research Establishment at Aldermaston. The event became an annual fixture in the festive calendar of the left but had no effect on government policy. In reality the independent deterrent was based on a cross-party consensus. It fell to Bevan, darling of the Labour left, to disconcert his supporters at a party conference with his warning not to send a British Foreign Secretary 'naked into the conference chamber'.[54]

As competitive nuclear testing between the USSR and the USA reached new heights, the Russians won additional propaganda points in March 1958 by announcing a unilateral moratorium on further tests. A few months later the United States and Britain agreed to match the Soviet commitment for one year and to open talks with the USSR on a permanent test ban treaty.

These developments, however, alarmed the French who feared that they might be permanently locked out of membership of the nuclear club. From as early as 1950 voices in the French military establishment had argued in favour of French nuclear armament, though opinion remained divided on the issue. The Suez affair, in the view of Mollet and other French leaders, demonstrated that if France were to regain great-power status and avoid further humiliations she must have her own deterrent. Nuclear weapons research was stepped up and in April 1958 the Prime Minister, Félix Gaillard, announced that France would conduct a nuclear test.

Both Britain and France saw nuclear weapons not only as a safeguard of their great-power status but as a 'strategic equalizer' that could enable the weak to deter the strong. Both, however, were able to build only small arsenals of nuclear weapons and neither at this stage possessed independent missile delivery systems, though France later developed one. What their nuclear forces achieved, at enormous cost, was not a balance but an imbalance of terror in which, as successive Cold War crises would show, they remained tied to the apron-strings of their American ally.

13

Stalin and his Heirs 1949–1964

the dead are taking stock of the living
the dead will not rehabilitate us

*Tadeusz Różewicz, Poland, 1957**

Stalinism: the last phase

Life in the Soviet Union in the final years of Stalin's rule was grim. Buildings and infrastructure had been shattered or run down during the war. The housing shortage in cities was exacerbated by rapidly rising population. Average living space per person in Soviet homes in 1950 was estimated at less than 5 square metres. Investment was once again steered towards heavy industry at the expense of consumer production. The Soviet countryside was a disaster area where lack of capital, low productivity, and exactions for urban needs combined to produce widespread distress and, in bad harvest years, acute famine. In 1946–7 hundreds of thousands died of hunger in Ukraine. The flight of peasants from rural misery to the towns accelerated in the early 1950s. The role of party officials in social life increased in these years, as did the trend towards consolidation of a class of professional bureaucratic apparatchiki.

Cultural constraints tightened. Political intrusions into science, the arts, literature and scholarship multiplied. The Soviet cultural supremo, Andrei Zhdanov, acting in close consultation with Stalin, delivered a speech attacking the poet Anna Akhmatova as 'half-nun, half-harlot, or rather both nun and harlot, mingling fornication and prayer'.[1] She was expelled from the Writers' Union, prevented from earning a living, and watched by the secret police; her son, Lev Gumilev, was arrested and sent to a prison

* From 'Posthumous Rehabilitation', translated from the Polish by Adam Czerniawski. Tadeusz Różewicz, *They Came to See a Poet*, London, 2004, 72–3.

camp. Zhdanov denounced Prokofiev, Shostakovich, and other composers for alleged 'formalistic distortions' and 'confused neuropathological combinations that turn music into cacophony' that reminded him of a dentist's drill.[2] 'Socialist science' was said to be fundamentally different from and superior to 'capitalist science'. The theory of relativity, already criticized in the 1930s as 'anti-materialist',[3] was now derided as 'reactionary Einsteinism'.[4] Trofim Lysenko advanced the theory, generally derided in the west, of the heritability of acquired characteristics. Russian nationalist pressures distorted scholarship in ethnography, linguistics, and history. The Russians, it appeared, had pioneered almost everything. A certain 'Kryakutnoy of Nerekhta', an eighteenth-century Russian inventor, was hailed as having built the first hot-air balloon long before the Montgolfiers. Radio had originated not with Marconi but rather with A. S. Popov. As for penicillin, it had been discovered not by Fleming but by A. G. Polotebnov as early as 1871. No doubt the Russian-born Samuel Born, inventor of the automated lollipop-making machine, would have been added to the pantheon—had he not emigrated to the United States in his youth.

The Soviet economic model became the paradigm for all the countries of east-central Europe. By 1949 the pattern of Communist rule in the region was set. In spite of local differences, its main characteristics varied little. Opposition parties, save of the extreme right, were not altogether banned; instead, they were condemned to a shadowy life after death, as cowed participants in pseudo-coalitions or forced mergers. Elections were held on a regular basis and, in the absence of genuinely secret ballots, invariably returned near-unanimous support for Communists and their allies. Five-year plans contorted economies to fit Stalin's prescription for growth: 'primitive accumulation', whereby capital was ploughed back into investment in heavy industrial projects. Consumption was squeezed. Industrial and commercial concerns were nationalized. Private businesses were closed. Except in Poland, most private farming gave way to collectivization or state farms. Trade patterns were arranged to suit the convenience of the USSR, which dumped products on its protégés while taking their exports at artificially high rouble exchange rates. The satellites were discouraged from seeking investment from abroad or from trading with the west.

Mini-Stalins imitated the literary style, cultural tastes, and ideological twists and turns of their master. Sycophantic personality cults celebrated their superhuman qualities. A Soviet-style secret police system, with informers in all major institutions, factories, and dwelling-places, kept watch for expressions of dissent or deviations from the party line. Travel to non-Communist countries was restricted to reliable functionaries and even these were generally not permitted to take family members with them. Visits by foreigners to eastern Europe were also restricted in these years to persons regarded as essential, reliable, or impressionable. Non-Communist newspapers were closed or emasculated. Correspondence to and from the west was routinely opened and read by censors, as was much internal mail. Telephones were tapped. In schools and universities the study of Marxism-Leninism became compulsory. Russian replaced German, French, or English as the main foreign language (though many educated people in the satellite countries managed to acquire or retain a good knowledge of western languages). Most independent or church schools and universities were placed under strict ideological control. Instructors who exhibited any ideological non-conformity courted dismissal and imprisonment. The judicial system, the trade unions, and other major institutions were restructured on the Soviet model. With minor exceptions this pattern held true even in Yugoslavia whose rebellion against Moscow was by no means a repudiation of the basic tenets of Stalinism.

Tito's defection from the Soviet bloc provoked a renewed outburst of paranoia in Stalin. If Tito could succeed in asserting the right to independence, what might other east European Communist leaders be preparing? As in the past when dealing with internal opposition, real or imaginary, so now with an external enemy, Stalin's repressive apparatus struck, almost indiscriminately, at friend and foe alike. Most of the victims were like the Old Bolsheviks of the 1930s, Communist faithful who had adjusted to every wobble in the party line over the previous two decades.

The East European show trials of the late Stalinist period followed the model of the pre-war Soviet trials. Hungarian, Czechoslovak, Romanian, and Bulgarian prosecutors grotesquely aped the rebarbative courtroom style of Vyshinsky. As in the cases of Bukharin and his fellow Russian victims of the 1930s, the defendants were accused of a bizarre concoction of mutually contradictory political associations—Titoism, Trotskyism, Fascism, and Zionism—as well as collaboration with foreign intelligence agencies.

In Hungary, in May 1949, the former Interior Minister, László Rajk, a man with an unblemished record of fealty to Communism, was arrested, subjected to a show trial, persuaded to confess to conspiratorial activity with Titoist and western intelligence services, and executed. His last words before his execution were reportedly, 'Long live Communism!'[5]

In Czechoslovakia the hunt for a 'Czechoslovak Rajk' was assisted by two Soviet security experts whose aid was requested in September 1949 by the Communist leaders Klement Gottwald and Rudolf Slánský.[6] The atmosphere of paranoia was fanned by Slánský, General Secretary of the party, who told a meeting of activists in December: 'Nor will our Party escape having the enemy place his people among us and recruit his agents among our members.... Aware of this, we must be all the more vigilant, so that we can unmask the enemies in our own ranks, for they are the most dangerous enemies.'[7] The first batch of victims consisted mainly of members of the Socialist, Catholic, and Social Democratic parties. The next were churchmen who were arraigned in the 'Trial of Vatican Agents' in December 1950. Meanwhile, in March 1950 the Foreign Minister, Vladimír Clementis, a Slovak, was dismissed and accused of bourgeois nationalism and hostility to the USSR (he had disapproved of the Nazi–Soviet Pact in 1939). He resorted to 'self-criticism' but the accusations of ideological deviation soon broadened into charges of espionage and anti-state activity.

In mid-1951 Slánský himself came under suspicion. On orders from Stalin, he was demoted to Deputy Prime Minister. He too submitted to self-criticism but in vain. In November a personal emissary from Stalin, Anastas Mikoyan, arrived suddenly in Prague, carrying a letter to Gottwald in which the Soviet leader demanded Slánský's immediate arrest. Gottwald hesitated but soon gave way. The secret police arrested Slánský and several other prominent figures and charged them with 'anti-Party and anti-State conspiracy'. A public campaign against the 'traitors' was immediately orchestrated. Within a month 2,335 resolutions, letters, and telegrams had reached party headquarters, all approving the arrests and many demanding application of the death penalty. In a letter written three days after his arrest, Slánský denied he was any kind of traitor to the party: 'there must be some terrible mistake.'[8] But after failing in an attempted suicide, Slánský yielded to his interrogators and admitted the charges. He was tried with Clementis and others for high treason, espionage, and sabotage. Of the fourteen accused, eleven were Jews, a fact emphasized by the prosecution. As in all the show trials, the script was finalized in advance of the judicial proceedings, which were broadcast live on Prague radio. The Communist leadership also decided the verdicts in advance: three defendants were sentenced to life imprisonment; Slánský, Clementis, and nine others were sentenced to death and executed in December 1953. Slánský's last words were reported as: 'Thankyou. I am getting what I deserved.'[9] The executed men's ashes were handed over for disposal to a driver and two interrogators. They put them in a potato sack and drove out into the country to scatter them in the fields. But as the roads were icy they spread them instead on the roadway. The driver later joked 'that he had never before carried fourteen people in his little Tatra, three living and eleven in the sack'.[10]

In addition to the well-known leaders, tens of thousands of lesser victims were imprisoned and hundreds judicially murdered during the purges. In Czechoslovakia in May 1950, out of a total prison population of 28,281, more than a third, 9,765, were serving sentences for 'offences against the State'.[11] The use of torture to obtain the required confessions was widespread. Only Poland managed to avoid show trials, although there too party leaders suspected of 'nationalist deviation', notably the party General Secretary, Władisław Gomułka, were removed from power.

Many of the victims were Jews, who had been disproportionately represented in the leadership of the Communist parties of the region, particularly among the exiles who had taken refuge in Moscow until 1945. In Romania, for example, the Foreign Minister, Ana Pauker, reputed to be the daughter of a rabbi, was among those purged on the orders of the party leader, Gheorghe Gheorghiu-Dej. Stalin's personal anti-Semitism, which sharpened in the last years of his life, was no doubt mixed with a canny sense that the endemic popular hatred of Jews in most of eastern Europe would ensure that this particular group of victims would find few defenders. When Israel was established in May 1948, she won immediate Soviet recognition and support for her initially anti-British posture. But the enthusiasm for the Jewish state shown by Soviet Jews at a demonstration of welcome to the first Israeli envoy in Moscow, Golda Meir, evoked official disapproval. The few remaining Jewish cultural institutions in the USSR were closed. Under the direction of Zhdanov, and of his successors after his death in 1948, a propaganda campaign was launched against so-called 'rootless cosmopolitans', a phrase that was understood to indicate Jewish members of the intelligentsia. Between 1948 and 1952 several leading figures of Soviet Yiddish culture who had survived the war were murdered by the secret police or executed after a secret trial.

Stalin's supremacy in his final years was unchallenged. By means of periodic culls, purges, and reprimands of high officials, he ensured that no rival centre of power could form. Over five million political prisoners remained in camps and special settlements in these years. Political debate largely took the form of fawning obeisance to the leader. Mikoyan, the minister in charge of food supplies, criticized by Stalin for 'breeding thieves around our supplies', wrote to apologize: 'Of course, neither I nor others can frame questions quite like you. I shall devote all my energy so that I may learn from you how to work correctly . . . under your fatherly guidance.'[12] Zhdanov was forced to disown his own son, who had made the mistake of crossing swords with Lysenko over genetics; yet after Zhdanov's death Stalin took the young man under his wing and married him off to his daughter Svetlana. The Foreign Minister, Molotov, was obliged in 1948 to acquiesce in Stalin's demand that he divorce his wife, Polina Zhemchuzhina, a former People's Commissar of Fisheries. Of Jewish birth, she was accused of links with 'Jewish nationalists', expelled from the party, and exiled to Siberia. Molotov abstained on the expulsion vote in the Politburo but wrote a cringing letter to Stalin in which he acknowledged his 'heavy sense of remorse for not having prevented Zhemchuzhina, a person very dear to me, from making her mistakes and from forming ties with anti-Soviet Jewish nationalists'.[13]

In the last months of Stalin's life repression reached a new level of grotesque horror with the unveiling of the so-called 'doctors' plot'. On 13 January 1953 Moscow radio announced the discovery of a 'criminal group of killer doctors' intent on murdering Soviet leaders. Several doctors, most of whom were Jews, were arrested on charges of murdering Zhdanov and others. The accused were said to have been 'connected with the bourgeois nationalist organization, the "Joint" [the American Jewish Joint Distribution Committee, a charitable body]'[14] and with US intelligence. After a bomb exploded at the Soviet embassy in Tel Aviv, the USSR broke off relations with Israel and Soviet propaganda denounced Zionism in scurrilous terms. Fearful whispers circulated that Stalin was planning the mass deportation of Soviet Jews to Siberia (though evidence from the Soviet archives so far does not substantiate these rumours).

Stalin's sudden death in March 1953 came for some as a release from terror. Yet he was genuinely and deeply mourned by his subjects, or at any rate by the many who saw in him an embodiment of their resistance to Nazism and their achievements over the past generation. A vast multitude filed in homage past his sarcophagus in the Hall of Columns, once the scene of show trials. In nearby Trubnaya Square the crush of bodies was so great that several people suffocated to death. The dictator's corpse was embalmed and placed next to Lenin's in the mausoleum on Red Square. Thousands of proposals for Stalin's memorialization poured in to the Central Committee, including one for the construction of a 'fountain of tears'.[15] Half a century later, after all the revelations of Stalin's responsibility for the massacre of millions of his fellow countrymen, 29 per cent of Russians still considered that, on balance, he did more good than evil.

The 'thaw'

As no successor had been anointed and none of the potential aspirants was in a position to impose his authority alone, a troika of leaders took initial charge of affairs. Georgy Malenkov, who became First Secretary of the party and Prime Minister, appeared to be primus inter pares. Beria remained for a time head of the security apparatus, and Molotov returned to the Foreign Ministry. All three had been close associates of Stalin and had participated, with Khrushchev and a few others, in decision-making during the dictator's frequent absences from Moscow in the last two years of his life. A number of symbolic acts indicated the new regime's intention to relax the harshest features of the Stalinist terror. In early April the accused doctors were released and rehabilitated. At the same time 1,202,000 people, nearly half the population of the Gulag, were amnestied and set free. Those released included criminals as well as political prisoners: one immediate effect was a crime wave that included a 66 per cent increase in the murder rate.

The thaw (the Zeitgeist of the immediate post-Stalin period took its name from the title of a novel by Ilya Ehrenburg published in 1954) extended also to eastern Europe, where Stalin's death and the gestures of the new Soviet leadership aroused hopes for liberalization. But political relaxation quickly revealed far-reaching discontent with the entire Communist system. In early May 1953 labour trouble surfaced at a tobacco depot in Plovdiv in Bulgaria. A few weeks later strikes, demonstrations, and riots erupted into something close to an insurrection at Plzeň in Czechoslovakia. But it was in East Germany that Communism faced its most formidable popular challenge.

'Germany', wrote Victor Klemperer, a member of the East German Parliament during the 1950s, 'is an earthworm cut in two: both parts squirm, both contaminated by the same Fascism, each in its own way.'[16] The East German leader, Walter Ulbricht, a former carpenter with a goatee beard and an 'unpleasant castrato voice',[17] had been a political commissar in Spain during the Civil War and had spent the war years in the Soviet Union. He presided over a regime that sought to comply with punitive Soviet requisitions while somehow preserving some vestige of indigenous legitimacy. Yet compared with West Germany, the German Democratic Republic was a pygmy: its population was one-third that of the west, its industrial output barely one-fifth. Ulbricht tried to earn credit both at home and in Moscow by social and economic reform on the Stalinist model. In 1950 a five-year plan was adopted. The Junkers were dispossessed and agriculture collectivized. 'Formalism' in art was prohibited and compulsory study of Marxism-Leninism imposed in universities. None of this won the regime much popularity. So long as the frontier remained open, hundreds of thousands of Germans moved to the west. Anxious to staunch this exodus, Ulbricht obtained permission from Moscow in May 1952 to close the border between East and West Germany. But the flight continued through the open sectoral boundary in Berlin. In the course of the year at least 182,000 people left for the west.

In late March 1953 the Soviet authorities rejected an East German request to seal the border in Berlin, warning (presciently, as it turned out) that such a move would have severely negative consequences for the East German regime and the USSR and 'would evoke bitterness and dissatisfaction from Berliners'.[18] In May the East German government announced a draconian economic package that included a 10 per cent increase in work norms as well as tax and price rises. Alarmed at reports of growing unrest in East Germany, the Soviet government decided on 2 June that an 'incorrect political line' had hitherto been adopted there. Instead it 'recommended' to the East German leaders that further collectivization of agriculture should be suspended, small-scale private capital encouraged, development of heavy industry curtailed, 'crude interference' in church affairs ended, and measures taken 'to strengthen legality', including abstention 'from the use of severe punitive measures which are not strictly necessary'.[19] 'If we don't correct now,' Malenkov told a hastily summoned Ulbricht in Moscow, 'a catastrophe will happen'.[20] Similar instructions to change direction were issued to other east European satellite states.

The extreme fragility of the East German regime's social basis was revealed a few days later, when the government admitted that some mistakes had been made, declared its intention to pursue a 'New Course', and announced concessions, including an amnesty for some political prisoners, an easing of travel restrictions, and an end to confiscation of land. There was no mention, however, of rescinding the increased work norms.

Disturbances broke out in east Berlin on 16 and 17 June, spreading to seven hundred towns and villages all over East Germany. Hundreds of thousands of protesters went on strike and stormed prisons, state offices, and party buildings, demanding free and secret elections. The government immediately revoked the increase in work norms, but for the rest it relied on repression. Martial law was declared and Soviet tanks moved into the streets. Demonstrators jeered, 'Soviet swine!' and raised the cry, '*Wir wollen freien Menschen sein und keine Sklaven*' (We want to be free men, not slaves).[21] Thousands were arrested, hundreds injured, and an estimated 125 people killed (see plate 33). The East German Politburo took refuge in the Soviet military headquarters near Berlin and began discussing possible evacuation with their families to Moscow. For a moment Communist power in East Germany seemed paralysed. But Soviet forces eventually restored order.

Unable to comprehend that what had occurred was a spontaneous popular upsurge, the authorities in both Berlin and Moscow explained the episode (to themselves as well as the world) as a 'Fascist putsch attempt' perpetrated in the interests of 'west German monopoly capitalism and Junkers'.[22] The dramatist Bertolt Brecht, who had returned to (East) Germany from exile in America, ironized famously that 'the people had forfeited the confidence of the government'. Perhaps the solution would be, he suggested, for 'the government to dissolve the people and elect another one in its place'?[23] At the same time, however, he issued statements supporting the regime and attacking the hypocrisy of the west. A year later he proudly accepted the Stalin Peace Prize in Moscow, though he kept his Austrian passport, Swiss bank account, and West German publisher.[24]

The rising was a major blow to Communist prestige and the Americans scored a further propaganda success with a large-scale food-aid programme for East Germany. In an effort to restore stability, the Soviet government increased its food supplies to East Germany and terminated reparations as of 1 January 1954. The East German leaders reaffirmed their commitment to the 'New Course' and increased wages, while at the same time doubling the size of the secret police. Ulbricht survived, in spite of serious criticism within the East German Politburo, but it was plain that his regime was upheld only by alien force. Emigration from East to West Germany reached a peak of 408,000 in 1953.

One casualty of the events in east Berlin was Beria, who was charged by his rivals with advocating the abandonment of Communism in East Germany and the establishment of a unified, neutral, non-socialist German state. At a meeting of the Soviet Communist Party Presidium (as the Politburo was called between 1952 and 1964) on 26 June, Khrushchev, who arrived with a gun in his pocket, denounced Beria, who was immediately arrested by Marshal Zhukov. From prison the former secret police chief wrote a pathetic letter to Malenkov, confessing 'inadmissible rudeness' and other sins but insisting that he was 'a faithful soldier of our Motherland' and offering to prove his loyalty, if necessary, 'in a small position' on a collective farm.[25] To no avail. He was tried on a charge of treason and executed the following December, the last Soviet politician to suffer this fate. After his death was announced, subscribers to the *Great Soviet Encyclopaedia* were advised to use 'a small knife or razor' to excise his entry and to replace it with an expanded article on the Bering Sea.[26]

In September Khrushchev was appointed First Party Secretary, the post in which, like Stalin before him and others after, he was able to consolidate supreme power. A professional apparatchik of peasant origins, Khrushchev was an ebullient, impulsive, mercurial, and, according to some analysts, hypomanic personality. As he himself recorded, he had 'no education and not enough culture'.[27] He had served as Moscow party boss (1934–7 and 1949–53), as Ukrainian party chief (1937–41 and 1944–9), and during the war as a political commissar on several fronts, including Stalingrad and Kursk. As First Secretary he managed to sideline and eventually topple Malenkov. By mid-1954 he was the senior (although not yet undisputed) leader.

The reaction against Stalinism reached its climax at a two-day closed session at the end of the twentieth congress of the Communist Party of the Soviet Union on 24–25 February 1956. Khrushchev delivered a speech that reverberated through eastern Europe and the entire world Communist movement. He condemned the Stalinist 'personality cult', declaring it 'impermissible and foreign to the spirit of Marxism-Leninism to elevate one person, to transform him into a superman possessing supernatural characteristics, akin to those of a god'. While careful to emphasize that Lenin had 'denounced every manifestation of the cult of the individual', he drew attention to the statements in Lenin's so-called 'Testament' and other letters written late in Lenin's life, in which he had expressed doubts about Stalin's political capacity.

At the same time Khrushchev paid tribute to what he described as Stalin's 'positive role' in the struggles against Trotskyism and against the Bukharinites. In his memoirs, published much later, Khrushchev recalled that he and his colleagues had decided not to include a specific denunciation of the show trials in order not to embarrass 'representatives of fraternal Communist parties present' at the trials who had gone home and testified to the justice of the sentences. 'So we indefinitely postponed the rehabilitation of Bukharin, Zinoviev, Rykov, and the rest. I can see now that our decision was a mistake. It would have been better to tell everything. Murder will always out. You can't keep things like that secret for long.'[28] Khrushchev nevertheless denounced the process of judicial murder in general terms as well as the concept, whose invention he attributed mistakenly to Stalin, of the 'enemy of the people': 'We must assert that, in regard to those persons who in their time had opposed the party line, there were often no sufficiently serious reasons for their physical annihilation. The formula "enemy of the people" was specifically introduced for the purpose of physically annihilating such individuals.' Khrushchev revealed for the first time the extent of the purges of the political elite. He hinted at Stalin's responsibility for the murder of Kirov. Drawing on his own recollections, he severely criticized Stalin's wartime leadership. He admitted that the 'doctors' plot' had been a total fabrication. And he denounced the 'monstrous crimes' of Beria.

Khrushchev's speech was a repudiation of Stalinism, but in no way of Marxism. Stalin's acts were portrayed as excesses and deviations from the true path laid down by Lenin. At the end, Khrushchev reaffirmed faith in 'the Leninist principles of party leadership, characterized above all by the main principle of collective leadership, by the observance of the norms of party life described in the statutes of our party, and, finally, by the wide practice of criticism and self-criticism'.

Of course, an unkind critic (and there were many) might point out that Khrushchev's utterance, extraordinary though it was, notably lacked any self-criticism. He himself, after all, had ascended to power within the Stalinist system and had been complicit in many of the decisions that he now denounced as crimes. Obliquely Khrushchev confessed that his chief excuse was fear of Stalin: 'Possessing unlimited power, he indulged in great wilfulness and choked a person morally and physically. A situation was created where one could not express one's will.'[29]

Khrushchev's speech was a shocking event, unprecedented in the history of Communism. It shattered the apostolic line of succession by which the rulers of the Soviet Union claimed to be the direct heirs of the founders and subsequent expositors of the Marxist gospel. Old Stalinists such as Molotov were dumbfounded. Although the speech remained formally secret and was not published in the USSR until 1989, its text was read to groups of party activists and was leaked to the western press. The speech did not, however, herald decisive change in the Soviet system. Rearguard resistance within the party hierarchy forced Khrushchev to retreat from any attempt at root-and-branch de-Stalinization (that term was never used in public discourse in the Khrushchev era: instead, official rhetoric referred to 'overcoming the cult of personality'[30]). Molotov, removed from the Foreign Ministry, nevertheless remained a member of the Presidium. Some more political prisoners were released but 782,000 remained in the labour camps.

Polish October, Hungarian November

The most immediate impact of the speech was felt not in the Soviet Union but in the client states of eastern Europe where its contents spread like wildfire. One of the earliest responses came in Czechoslovakia where, in the spring of 1956, writers and students staged anti-Stalinist protests. A firm response by the Czechoslovak government damped down this opposition. The Czechoslovak Communist leader, Antonín Novotný, who ruled from 1953 to 1968, held fast to Stalinist-style controls, and explicitly condemned de-Stalinization, which, he said, stood for nothing more than 'the idea of weakening and giving way to the forces of reaction'.[31] These were the sentiments also of Ulbricht in East Germany, though he prudently dropped all mention of Stalin from his six-hour address to the third congress of the East German Communist Party (SED) in late March. In Poland and Hungary, however, Khrushchev's denunciation of Stalin evoked tumultuous responses that included new interpretations of Communist doctrine and called into question the very survival of the Communist regimes.

Whether out of consternation at Khrushchev's speech or by coincidence, the Polish party chief, Bierut, fell ill at the Moscow congress and died shortly afterwards. Some said he had committed suicide. His successor, backed by Moscow, was Edward Ochab. But he proved incapable of containing unrest. In late June 1956 strikes and demonstrations at Poznań, Poland's fourth-largest city, turned into riots and a virtual revolution that was put down with a heavy hand by armed force. Sixty people were killed. The government denounced the disturbances as a capitalist-sponsored provocation and the Prime Minister, Józef Cyrankiewicz, warned that such indiscipline would not be tolerated: 'Let any madcap provocateur who would dare to raise his hand against the people know that this hand will be severed by the people with the full approval of the working class.'[32]

The riots and the government's fierce response produced a crisis in Polish Communism. A reformist section of the party, known as 'Pulawanie' (they reputedly met at a house on Pulawska Street) favoured installing a new leader, Władisław Gomułka, who had been imprisoned between 1951 and 1954, accused of 'Titoism'. He had the reputation of being opposed to collectivization and to attacks on the Church. The reformists hoped that Gomułka might become a 'national Communist' leader on the Tito pattern but with Soviet approval. A more conservative section known as the 'Natolin group' (after a Warsaw suburb) opposed any concessions in the face of violence. Ochab and others warned that further popular disturbances might precipitate Soviet military intervention.

On 19 October the Central Committee of the Polish Communist Party met, in defiance of a Soviet suggestion of postponement, intending to install Gomułka as First Secretary and to depose the Minister of Defence, Marshal Rokossovsky (of Polish birth but a Soviet citizen, he had hastily been granted Polish citizenship upon his appointment in 1949). The proceedings were interrupted by the unannounced arrival at Warsaw airport of a Soviet delegation, headed by Khrushchev. Meanwhile Soviet troops and Polish forces under the command of Rokossovsky manoeuvred threateningly near Poland's cities. The Polish leaders and Khrushchev shouted at each other for several hours. Khrushchev shook his finger threateningly under Gomułka's nose and bellowed, 'We are ready for active intervention.'[33] Gomułka gave as good as he got, threatening to break off discussion 'if you talk with a revolver on the table'.[34] Soviet military intervention seemed imminent. But the Russians were dubious about the loyalty of the Polish armed forces. Back in Moscow, Khrushchev admitted to his colleagues in the Presidium on 24 October: 'Finding a reason for an armed conflict [with Poland] now would be very easy; but finding a way to put an end to such a conflict later on would be very hard.'[35] In the end, Khrushchev, in effect, gave in. The Poles were permitted to choose their own leadership.

Gomułka was transformed into a national hero. He promised a 'Polish road to socialism' and a general liberalization, though he warned that 'we shall not allow anyone to use the process of democratization to undermine socialism'.[36] Forced collectivization of agriculture was halted. Rokossovsky was sent home. The Catholic primate, Cardinal Stefan Wyszyński, who had been interned in a remote monastery since 1953, was set free. In addition 35,000 other political prisoners were released.

While the Poles exulted in their new-found, if limited, freedoms, events in Hungary took a very different course. As in Poland, the trigger for change was Khrushchev's speech. But sensing the political atmosphere accurately, a British diplomat in Budapest in March 1956 cited the Latin dictum: *quod licet Iovi, non licet bovi* (What is permitted to Jupiter is not permitted to the ox).[37] The 'thaw' in Hungary led to a flood—and then a refreeze.

Imre Nagy, leader of the reformist wing of the Hungarian Communist Party, came of peasant stock. Like Tito's and Gomułka's, his Communist credentials, if judged by his early career, were impeccable. After joining the party at an young age, he had spent two years in Horthy's prisons. From 1930 to 1944 he lived in Moscow, working in an agricultural research institute. In the late 1930s he appears to have served as an informer for the Soviet secret police.[38] On his return to Hungary at the end of the war he became Minister of Agriculture and acquired popularity for his agrarian reforms, which involved large-scale redistribution of land from large landowners (including the Church) to peasants. In 1948 he took a stand against collectivization of agriculture, fell out with Rákosi and suffered a period of eclipse. In the wake of Stalin's death, however, when reformists in the Soviet Union sought local surrogates in each part of the Soviet empire, Nagy seemed a suitable candidate. On orders from the USSR, he became Prime Minister in July 1953 and, like the East Germans, promptly announced a 'New Course'. Unlike Ulbricht, however, he seems to have believed in it. Political prisoners were released and some of the uglier excesses of Stalinism modified. Investment priorities shifted from heavy industry to consumer goods, housing, and agriculture. But Rákosi, who remained First Secretary of the party, retained substantial power. In 1955 the fall of Malenkov, Nagy's patron in the Kremlin, undermined his position and he was once again dismissed from office and expelled from the party.

Khrushchev's anti-Stalin speech in 1956 finally led to the toppling of Rákosi, whose Stalinism now seemed out of date. He was replaced by Ernő Gerő, a new face but an adherent of neo-Stalinist policies. Gerő was hardly more popular than Rákosi and the seeming obduracy of the party heightened popular unrest. Demands for far-reaching change began to be voiced publicly in mid-October as a direct consequence of events in Poland.

The Hungarian revolution was begun by intellectuals. The Writers' Association, especially through its organ, *Irodalmi Újság* (*Literary Gazette*), and a group of young intellectuals around the Petőfi Circle (named after Hungary's national poet and hero of the 1848–9 revolution, which, as all Hungarians recalled, had been suppressed with the help of Russian forces) were prominent in calling for greater cultural freedom. Student demonstrations in support of the Polish reformists soon developed into a movement for reform within Hungary. On 18 October a group of fifty writers presented the party Central Committee with a memorandum denouncing 'the brutal interference of the administration in Hungarian literary life' and demanded 'a stop to anti-democratic practices'.[39] The popular mood was inflamed rather than assuaged by a radio address by Gerő in which he attacked the critics and insisted: 'We, of course, want a socialist democracy and not a bourgeois one.'[40]

On 23 October violence between student demonstrators and secret policemen broke out in Debrecen, followed shortly afterwards by disturbances in Budapest. Crowds yelled 'Rákosi into the Danube!' and 'Out with the Russians!'[41] In a desperate effort to avert a popular explosion, the central committee decided to recall Nagy to office as Prime Minister. That night Soviet tanks entered Budapest in a show of strength. At the same time, without the approval of the Hungarian government, further Soviet forces arrived in Hungary to reinforce those stationed there under the terms of the Warsaw Pact. On 25 October the unpopular Gerő was replaced as First Secretary by János Kádár. But neither Nagy nor Kádár was able to restrain the fury that erupted in the streets as mobs lynched secret policemen and assaulted Soviet tanks, Communist Party offices, and statues of Stalin.

Senior Soviet emissaries, Mikoyan and Mikhail Suslov, as well as the Soviet Ambassador, Yury Andropov, apparently hoping that Nagy and Kádár would be able to reassert control on the basis of a Gomułka-type reformist policy, assured Nagy that the Soviet troops would be withdrawn. At the same time Andropov submitted to Nagy for his signature a formal request, backdated to 24 October, for the intervention of Soviet troops. He refused to sign, whereupon Andropov obtained the signature of Nagy's predecessor, András Hegedűs, and then forwarded the document to Moscow. On 30 October the USSR issued a formal statement promising to respect the independence of fellow members of the socialist bloc. Soviet troops were to be withdrawn from Budapest.

But in the meantime, Nagy, driven forward by the momentum of revolutionary fervour in Hungary, took decisive, and in Soviet eyes heretical, steps. He released political prisoners, abolished the secret police, and opened the way to a multi-party system. He invited non-Communists such as Zoltán Tildy to join his government. He freed the Catholic primate, Cardinal Mindszenty, from imprisonment. And on 1 November, in a move that enraged the Russians, Nagy announced Hungary's withdrawal from the Warsaw Pact and declared that the country would henceforth pursue a policy of neutralism.

All this was too much for Khrushchev who later recalled that 'Budapest was like a nail in my head'.[42] On 31 October the Soviet party Praesidum adopted a resolution instructing Zhukov to 'prepare a plan of action [*plan meropriatii*] in connection with the Hungarian events'.[43] Khrushchev rushed round eastern Europe, shoring up the support of satellite leaders. In a conversation on 2 November on the island of Brioni, where Tito kept a holiday home, Khrushchev asked emotionally: 'What is there left for us to do? If we let things take their course, the West would say we are either stupid or weak, and that's one and the same thing.'[44] For all his neutralism and erstwhile reformism, Tito believed that the very survival of Communist rule in Hungary was in danger. Sharing Khrushchev's fear that the anti-Communist contagion might spread, he added his seal of approval to Soviet military intervention.

On 3 November Hungarian negotiators, led by General Pál Maléter, who had been appointed Minister of Defence by Nagy that day, met Russian military representatives for talks which the Hungarians hoped would lead to a complete Russian military withdrawal from Hungary. The discussions continued into the night. Around midnight, General Serov, the Soviet security chief, burst in and announced he had come to arrest the Hungarians.

The next day Russian tanks re-entered Budapest. Sixteen Soviet divisions and the air force participated in the operation. Resistance against what was seen as a foreign invasion lasted three days. At least 2,500 Hungarian fighters and 669 Soviet soldiers were killed. The result, however, could not be in doubt. Desperate pleas to the west for help were answered with sympathy but no more tangible response. Once again the Soviets accused the western powers of fomenting trouble. In fact, far from being organized from the west, the revolution caught the United States, then in the final stages of a presidential election campaign, by surprise. Britain and France were preoccupied with their intervention in Egypt. NATO would not risk nuclear war for the sake of Hungary. More than two hundred thousand refugees fled, among them the national football star, Ferenc Puskás, who found refuge in Franco's Spain. But in May 1957 the Hungarian government started installing landmines along the border with Austria. It would remain closed to illegal emigrants until 1989.

Desirous of some figleaf of local support, the Russians succeeded in turning Kádár, hitherto a vociferous public supporter of what, as late as 1 November, he had called the 'glorious uprising', into a collaborator in its destruction.[45] In Moscow the next day he had privately warned that the use of Soviet military force would be resisted, and would cause 'the morale of the Communists [in Hungary] to be reduced to zero'.[46] Kádár had endured torture and imprisonment in the last Stalin years. He nevertheless now agreed to accept the role of a quisling.

Why did the USSR, which had withdrawn from the brink of intervening in Poland, of all the satellites the most vital to Soviet security interests, take armed action in Hungary? The public statements of Soviet representatives referred to 'grave mistakes and deviations' of the Hungarian leaders and alleged that 'reactionary Fascist elements' were organizing to seize power, egged on by the west. Dr. Otto Habsburg, mild-mannered son of the last Habsburg Emperor, was said to have conspired with the sons of Horthy and Gömbös to carry out a putsch with help from the United States. While the charge of extreme-right activity was introduced primarily for propaganda effect, there was just enough of a tincture of truth in it to carry conviction in some quarters, for example, among the dwindling band of fellow-travellers in the west.[47] The aged Horthy, in exile in Lisbon, helped no one by issuing an appeal for assistance to the British Prime Minister. Some of the street-fighters were ultra-nationalists. During the revolutionary days anti-Semitic slogans had again appeared on walls in Budapest, prompting many Jews to join the refugees who trudged across the frontier into Austria. Although western foreign ministries studiously avoided encouraging the revolutionaries to expect outside help, the BBC Hungarian service had since the spring been offering satirical suggestions as to what might be done with Stalin statues; during the revolution the CIA-financed Radio Free Europe urged the continuation of armed resistance and hinted that the west might intervene. All this was grist to the Soviet propaganda mill but these were not the main dynamic forces in the events. The revolution was at heart a spontaneous outburst in favour of national independence. The primary reasons for its suppression by the Russians were undoubtedly politico-strategic: fear that their entire empire in eastern Europe would be endangered if Hungary were permitted to secede from the Warsaw Pact.

Khrushchev expected Nagy to recognize political realities and resign. Instead he broadcast a defiant message and, with several supporters, took refuge in the Yugoslav Embassy. Mindszenty fled to the American Embassy where he remained for the next fifteen years. After discussions between the Kádár government and the Yugoslavs, Nagy and his companions were persuaded to leave the embassy on 22 November. They did so with a guarantee of safe conduct from Kádár. The moment they left the embassy, however, Soviet secret policemen arrested them and took them as prisoners to Romania, which announced that it had given them asylum at their own request. In the autumn of 1957 they were returned to Hungary and early the following year legal proceedings were started against Nagy, Maléter, and seven others. Nagy was charged with 'initiating and leading a conspiracy aimed at subverting the people's democratic order of state'.[48] His trial in Budapest was conducted in secret. Unusually for a Communist politician in such circumstances, he obstinately denied his guilt. The court found him guilty and decided that his 'stubborn impenitence, his double-dealing treachery, and his undying hatred, rooted in excessive ambition, precluded the possibility of... giving weight to his forty years in the workers' movement'.[49] Together with Maléter and two others, he was sentenced to death. They were executed on 16 June 1958. The bodies were bound in ropes and sacking and thrown face down in an unmarked grave in lot 301 of the municipal cemetery in Rákoskeresztúr, a site earmarked for the interment of dead animals from the Budapest zoo.

The Soviet intervention in Hungary and Nagy's subsequent execution prompted outrage in the west. Communist parties were gravely embarrassed and lost thousands of members as well as the support of intellectuals such as Jean-Paul Sartre, hitherto a sympathizer, though never a member, and the historian Christopher Hill in England. The editor of the Italian party newspaper resigned in protest when the party leader, Palmiro Togliatti, defended the executions. In the east, the court verdict was hailed as a triumph: 'Fascist murderers are not handled with velvet gloves', declared a commentator on East German radio.[50] The Polish Communist Party initially condemned the Soviet troop deployment in Hungary. Gomułka, who, in different circumstances, might have shared the fate of Nagy, pleaded privately with Khrushchev for Nagy's life. But in public he dutifully denounced the Hungarian leader as 'a revisionist... [who] moved step by step towards capitulation to the counter-revolution'.[51]

From the Hungarian nationalist point of view (that of the great majority of the Hungarian people in 1956), Kádár's conduct during the revolution amounted to brazen treachery. He had acclaimed and been a prominent participant in a revolution that he later helped defeat and that he denounced as a counter-revolution. He promised Nagy immunity from prosecution and later took responsibility for his judicial murder. Yet Kádár succeeded within a few years in earning if not the affection at least the grudging respect of many of those he ruled. This in spite of the ferocity of the vengeance wreaked on his former comrades: 28,000 were arrested and at least six hundred executed between 1956 and 1961. Many more were dismissed from their jobs or suffered other reprisals. Opposition parties were suppressed and the Writers' Union was dissolved. But once the regime had secured itself, Kádár relaxed ideological controls a little, adopting a more tolerant attitude to dissidents, an approach encapsulated in his dictum, 'He who is not against us is with us.'[52] Kádár's 'goulash Communism', in which limited market elements were permitted, produced an upturn in the economy and eventually secured acquiescence from the bulk of the population.

'National Communist' resistance to domination by Moscow did not end with the Soviet intervention in Hungary. In Poland it continued in a milder form judged barely acceptable by the USSR. Further afield it bubbled up in, for the Russians, much less palatable ways. Khrushchev's efforts with Tito to repair the damage caused by what he called 'the cloudy period in our relations' had only limited success: Yugoslavia maintained its irritating neutralism. Romania, from which Soviet troops were withdrawn in 1958, took the opportunity in the early 1960s to move towards an independent diplomatic stance, without, however, withdrawing from membership of the Warsaw Pact or Comecon. In 1963 Romania even made a secret approach to the United States promising neutrality in the event of an east–west war.[53]

Most ominously for the Kremlin, China's Communist leadership, tired of what they saw as Russian domination of the world Communist movement, struck out on their own and from 1960 onwards began public criticism of Soviet 'revisionism'. Khrushchev denounced Mao Tse-tung as a 'scumbag'.[54] Soviet technical experts were withdrawn from China and the two countries hurled offensive jeers and Marxist slogans at each other. But China was too formidable to be called to heel after the manner of Hungary. Mao succeeded not only in asserting his own independence but in encouraging another Communist malcontent to cock an impudent snook at Moscow.

Peking's European proxy was Enver Hoxha, a partisan leader in the Albanian resistance during the Second World War, who had seized power in 1945. Until 1948 he pursued a pro-Yugoslav policy but in the Tito–Stalin conflict he sided with Moscow, remaining loyal until the late 1950s. In the autumn of 1949 Albanian exiles, organized by the British secret service, MI6, landed on the coast with the intention of promoting a rebellion. But the Soviet agent Kim Philby, at that time a senior official in MI6, betrayed the secret. The invaders were quickly rounded up. Further rebel operations until 1952, organized by MI6 and the CIA, met with similar results. An idiosyncratic despot, whose literary tastes embraced Goethe, Jerome K. Jerome, and Rudyard Kipling, Hoxha defied internal conspirators and external enemies. His closest political associate, Koci Xoxe, was accused of Titoism and strangled on Hoxha's orders in 1948. In the late 1950s Hoxha feared that Albania might become a sacrificial victim of the Belgrade–Moscow rapprochement that seemed to be in the making. When Khrushchev visited the country in 1959 he advised Hoxha to concentrate on development of peanuts, tea, and citrus fruit. Hoxha took offence, complaining that the USSR sought to turn Albania into a banana republic. In his memoirs Hoxha recalled that Khrushchev's behaviour 'made my flesh creep'.[55] Khrushchev left in a hurry. When they met again in Moscow in 1960 the quarrel grew worse and, according to Hoxha, Khrushchev 'screamed': 'You are spitting on me. It is impossible to talk to you. Only Macmillan has tried to speak to me like this.'[56] The split became definitive and Hoxha looked elsewhere for support. China offered Albania help and was far enough away not to constitute a threat. Radio Tirana soon began broadcasting Chinese-style denunciations of Soviet revisionism. Hoxha's ability to defy the Soviet Union stemmed in large measure from his immunity from attack. A Soviet land assault was not really practicable because of the mountainous terrain and in any case would have had to move through Yugoslavia, which would certainly have resisted. In 1962 Albania ceased active participation in the Warsaw Pact and in 1968 withdrew from the organization altogether.

The 'New Class' in power

Whether they parroted the Moscow line or pursued a more independent course, all the European Communist states in the late 1950s hardened their internal policies. Although there was no return to the terror of the late Stalin years, political arrests resumed, censorship intensified, efforts towards pluralism were reversed. Nevertheless, in the same period Communism began to evolve from a revolutionary and dynamic system into a 'Thermidorean' phase of corruption, stagnation, and bureaucratization.

The struggle for supremacy between Khrushchev and his opponents reached a climax in June 1957. His enemies succeeded in assembling a majority in the Presidium but Khrushchev countered by calling a meeting of the entire Central Committee where he enjoyed a built-in majority of political dependants. After a marathon six-day session of arguments, accusations, and backbiting, Khrushchev berated the opposition with insults and taunts. Molotov, Malenkov, and others, dubbed the 'anti-party group', were disgraced, although, unlike those who fell out of grace in the Stalin era, they were not executed, tried, or imprisoned. Molotov was packed off to Ulan Bator as ambassador to Outer Mongolia; Malenkov to Kazakhstan as manager of a hydroelectric station. Four months later the Soviet Defence Minister, Zhukov, regarded by Khrushchev as dangerously popular, was accused of 'Napoleonic aspirations' and of plotting a *coup d'état* and was dismissed.[57] In early 1958 the Prime Minister, Nikolai Bulganin, was induced to resign and Khrushchev added that job to his first secretaryship. For the next six years his position as paramount Soviet leader was undisputed.

In 1961 Khrushchev presided over the drafting of a new economic programme that, he claimed, would enable the USSR to surpass the USA in per capita production by 1970. The organization of the agricultural economy was reformed. Continuing a policy of concentration that had begun in 1950, collective farms were organized into larger units: the number dropped from 69,000 in 1958 to 26,000 in 1965. Informal peasant markets developed in which produce from the small permitted private plots was sold. But output remained disappointing and food shortages continued in many parts of the country. Much agricultural production was loss-making: price rises were consequently judged necessary. But when these were enacted in 1962 serious protests broke out in a number of cities. A demonstration in Novocherkassk ended with shooting by the security forces: twenty-six people were killed. After a disastrous harvest in 1963, the USSR was humiliatingly obliged to order grain imports from Canada and the United States.

The anti-Stalin policy reached a peak in the early 1960s. Stalin's embalmed body was removed at night from its place next to Lenin in the

Red Square mausoleum, reburied round the back of the building, and for good measure covered with cement. Statues of the former dictator were demolished, except in his native Georgia. The city of Stalingrad was renamed Volgograd.

Soviet nationalities policy eased somewhat under Khrushchev and allowed a certain latitude to non-political forms of national expression, for example in the Baltic provinces. A Yiddish literary monthly, *Sovyetish Haymland*, was permitted to appear, though, as its name implied, with the object of countering rather than reinforcing any tendency to Jewish national feeling.

Cultural policy loosened a little. Unorthodox novels were published, notably Vladimir Dudintsev's *Not by Bread Alone* (1956), a brave stab at the power of the Soviet bureaucracy, and Alexander Solzhenitsyn's *A Day in the Life of Ivan Denisovich* (1962), a portrayal of prison-camp life. Publication of such works would have been inconceivable before Stalin's death and even now both of these had to be sanctioned personally by Khrushchev, though he criticized Dudintsev's book for its 'tendentiously selected negative facts'.[58] The courageous editor of the literary journal *Novy mir*, Aleksandr Tvardovsky, acted as a patron to many writers at the margin of the permissible. Among those of the younger generation, Yevgeny Yevtushenko seemed to enjoy special high-level protection as he swung in his poetry from fawning subservience to the dictates of cultural commissars to outspoken defiance. Critics dismissed much of his work as lightweight, but his poetry readings attracted audiences of thousands. And some of his work, including 'Babi Yar' (1961), an assault on anti-Semitism, and 'The Heirs of Stalin', published in *Pravda* in 1962, seemed to herald a new period of openness to criticism in Soviet society.

But these were rare exceptions. In general the half-dead hand of the censor and the self-censorship inherent in the activities of the Soviet Writers' Union continued to lie heavy on all Soviet literature. Writers in the USSR, in Ehrenburg's phrase, had to 'live with clenched teeth'.[59] The limits of the 'thaw' were already evident in 1958 when Boris Pasternak, author of the recently published *Dr Zhivago*, was awarded the Nobel Prize for Literature. The novel, perhaps the greatest literary depiction of Russia in revolution, was first issued in the west by the Italian Communist publisher Feltrinelli, after its appearance in Russia had been prohibited. Pasternak regarded it as his testament, a work that would, in the words of Pushkin, 'lay waste with fire the hearts of men', and he was determined to see it published regardless of the consequences.[60] He was expelled from the Writers' Union, forced to decline the award, and denounced as a 'tool of bourgeois propaganda', a 'Judas', 'a frog in a bog', and (evidently the most damaging accusation of all) 'an aesthete and decadent'.[61] In the other arts too the philistine attitudes of the Soviet culture minister, Yekaterina Furtseva, the only woman in the top Soviet leadership, restrained innovation.

Cultural repression, however, carried a price. The Russians were particularly embarrassed by several high-profile cases of flight to the West by performers such as the ballet dancer Rudolf Nureyev in 1961 and the pianist Vladimir Ashkenazy two years later. In the case of Nureyev the Soviet image was not enhanced by accounts of KGB (Soviet secret police) agents trying to grab the recalcitrant star, and haul him onto a plane at Le Bourget airport near Paris. Such episodes strengthened the hand of those in the Soviet hierarchy who regarded intellectual and cultural contact with the west as potentially dangerous sources of infection and defection.

Khrushchev himself alternated between moments of expansive liberalism and a more usual incapacity to transcend the bounds of official cultural doctrine. A typical example was his behaviour at an exhibition of avant-garde art in 1962, when he rounded on the sculptor Ernst Neizvestny. Khrushchev later regretted the incident. So did his victim. After Khrushschev's death his son invited Neizvestny to sculpt a bust to be placed on his tomb, a commission that the sculptor willingly executed.

The most influential critique of Communism as it was practised in these years came damagingly and disturbingly for his fellow Marxists from the pen of one of the leading figures in the Communist world, a former right-hand-man of Tito, Milovan Djilas. A Montenegrin who had played a major role in wartime partisan resistance and had been a liaison between Tito and Stalin, Djilas had fallen out with Tito in 1954 and was expelled from the Communist Party. His book *The New Class*, published in 1957, was all the more powerful an indictment because it analysed the Communist system using many of the tools of Marxist analysis itself. The core of his critique lay in his rejection of the 'illusion' that Communism had created a classless society. On the contrary, he argued, it had given birth to a new class: the *nomenklatura*, the bureaucracy spawned by the centralized state system. This was a property-owning class: 'As defined by Roman law', he wrote, 'property constitutes the use, enjoyment, and disposition of material goods.

The Communist political bureaucracy uses, enjoys, and disposes of nationalized property.' Turning the Marxist concept of 'false consciousness' against his former comrades, he claimed that

> the new class is also the most deluded and least conscious of itself. Every private capitalist or feudal lord was conscious of the fact that he belonged to a special discernible social category. He usually believed that this category was destined to make the human race happy and that without this category chaos and general ruin would ensue. A Communist member of the new class also believes that without his party, society would regress and founder. But he is not conscious of the fact that he belongs to a new ownership class, for he does not consider himself an owner and does not take into account the special privileges he enjoys. He thinks that he belongs to a group with prescribed ideas, aims, attitudes, and roles. That is all he sees. He cannot see that at the same time he belongs to a special social category: the *ownership* class.

Djilas further maintained that the 'totalitarian dictatorship of the Communist Party oligarchy' was not some chance aberration, but inherent to the system—'its body and soul, its essence'. The internal logic of Communism tended both towards concentration of power in a dictator and towards corruption in the bureaucratic elite. He detected a 'cult of force' that led Communist rulers to trample on their own laws. As for the centrally planned economy, its pretensions to efficiency were demonstrably false: the Communist economy was 'perhaps the most wasteful economy in the history of human society'. Far from liberating the working class, Communism had reduced the workers to something not far short of slavery. To this demolition of Communism as a system, Djilas attached some withering comments on Tito. He was rewarded for what Tito called 'the destructive character of his writing about our realities' with a total of nine years' imprisonment but he won an admiring audience in the west and a significant, albeit surreptitious one in the east.[62]

Djilas's critique contained powerful insights. In so far as Communism purported to represent the fulfilment of working-class interests it was by this stage a palpable failure and fraud—as much so as Nazism's claim to advance the interests of the nation. Yet unlike Fascism, which nowhere achieved anything approaching a social revolution, Communism had changed its world. It created a society that, in a crude and ruthless way, represented a form of class revenge, rooting out the old elites of eastern Europe and replacing them with a technocracy that was not all that dissimilar from the emerging white-collar class in the west.

'Peaceful co-existence'?

Stalin's successors introduced a more accommodating tone in relations with the west. From early 1954 their speeches and propaganda began to use the phrase 'peaceful coexistence'. One sign of an easing of tension was agreement over Austria where the Soviets decided on a prudent withdrawal. The Communist movement in Austria was weak: a quasi-putsch in September/October 1950 had failed owing to strong Socialist opposition and Soviet reluctance to offer more than half-hearted support. Soviet-occupied eastern Austria, unlike East Germany, was clearly unviable as an independent state. Even before Stalin's death, therefore, the USSR had indicated readiness to end the occupation, provided Austria never became part of the western defence system. The western allies initially opposed neutralization of Austria for fear that that might set a precedent for Germany. They rejected a Soviet proposal for a four-power guarantee of Austrian neutrality lest that furnish a pretext for future Soviet intervention. But the occupation was costly to all four powers. Moreover, with the creation of the Warsaw Pact, under which the USSR could station troops in Hungary, Soviet leaders no longer saw a military presence in Austria as serving a vital security purpose. Under the Austrian State Treaty of 15 May 1955 the four powers agreed to withdraw their forces and recognize the country as a sovereign state. The treaty prohibited unity with Germany and restoration of the Habsburgs but said nothing about neutrality. Shortly afterwards, however, the Austrian Parliament incorporated into the constitution an amendment declaring that 'Austria of her own free will declares herewith her permanent neutrality... [and] will never in the future accede to any military alliances nor permit the establishment of military bases of foreign states on her territory'.[63] Under the new dispensation, Austria regained respectability, was admitted to the United Nations, and soon became one of the most prosperous countries in Europe.

The Soviet leadership seems to have seen the Austrian treaty as part of a larger pattern whereby the USSR might consolidate its gains in eastern Europe behind a buffer of neutral states. Another element in such a framework was Finland, which, alone among the defeated European states in the Second World War, preserved a real, albeit precarious and limited, independence in the post-war period. Mindful of their troubled historical relationship with Russia, the Finns operated within narrower constraints than the Austrians. Throughout the Cold War they applied a delicate self-censorship to their diplomacy and media. The Finnish Communist Party, unlike the Austrian, was a serious political force. On the other hand, the Finns would almost certainly have offered fierce resistance to any attempt by the Red Army to impose Communist rule. Stalin, no doubt also recalling the Winter War, found it more convenient to bend Finland to his will diplomatically by the Finnish–Soviet Treaty of Friendship (1948). Finland deferred to Moscow and declined to participate in the Marshall Plan. She was the only non-Communist European state not to vote against the Soviets at the United Nations over Hungary, prompting one opposition member of the Diet to complain that the country had dwindled into a kind of 'neutral satellite' of the USSR.[64] The cautious leadership of Urho Kekkonen, Finland's President from 1956 to 1981, led the Russians to grant the country some leeway. They went so far as to hand back the Porkkala naval base in 1956. But some, particularly Franz Josef Strauss, West German Defence Minister from 1956 to 1962, began to warn of the danger of a 'Finlandization' of western Europe.

In July 1955 Khrushchev joined Eisenhower, Eden, and the French Premier, Edgar Faure, at a four-power conference in Geneva, the first meeting of top US and Soviet leaders since Potsdam ten years earlier. This was the first summit conference in which the French participated on an equal basis with the other three major powers. It was also the last. All future summits were to be either narrower (USA and USSR alone) or broader. By now the 'four powers' were being replaced by the 'two superpowers'. Although no specific agreements were reached at Geneva the atmosphere was relatively relaxed. In 1956, however, the events in Hungary as well as the Suez affair abruptly halted the improvement in east–west relations.

Western resolve was tested in two further crises over Berlin in 1958 and 1961. In a formal note to the other three occupying powers, on 27 November 1958, the USSR repudiated the agreements on the four-power occupation of Berlin that had been reached in 1944 and 1945. Arguing that the rearmament of West Germany constituted a violation of the agreement, the USSR declared that its 'very essence' had 'vanished'. The note announced that the Soviet government would enter negotiations with the East German authorities 'at an appropriate moment, with a view to transferring to the German Democratic Republic the functions which the Soviet authorities have exercised temporarily in accordance with these Allied agreements'. It proposed that Berlin should become 'a free city', demilitarized, self-governing, and separate from both Germanies. The document was given the character of an ultimatum by the setting of a deadline of six months within which a settlement of the Berlin question would have to be reached, failing which the Soviet Union would 'effect the planned measures by agreement with the German Democratic Republic'.[65] At a press conference the same day Khrushchev declared that west Berlin was a 'malignant tumour' and that the Soviet Union had decided to embark on 'some surgery'.[66]

The initiative seems to have been Khrushchev's personal idea. The Foreign Minister, Andrei Gromyko, heard about it when he visited Khrushchev's office with his proposals and was told to throw his notes away and listen to the First Secretary dictate. Dictation over, Khrushchev slapped his knee and said, 'Ha! They really will be thrown in the West. They will say: "Khrushchev, that son of a bitch, has now thought up a 'free city'!"'[67] Khrushchev hoped his ultimatum would force the west to negotiate a new arrangement over Berlin that would solidify the Ulbricht regime and stop the continuing flow of departures to the west. Meanwhile the Soviet Union secretly deployed medium-range nuclear-armed missiles near Berlin, the first time such weapons had been stationed outside Soviet borders.

The western powers had continued to maintain garrisons in west Berlin. But these were only a few thousand strong and would be merely a symbolic tripwire in the event of any military action against the city. The exposed and isolated nature of west Berlin as an enclave in East Germany was judged by western experts to render the city indefensible by conventional forces. Any attack on west Berlin therefore ran the risk of escalating quickly into a nuclear exchange. This crisis erupted at a time of heightened international tension over the arms race. Hence the worldwide anxiety.

In the following six months east and west waged a war of words over Berlin. The Governing Mayor of West Berlin, the Social Democrat Willy Brandt, dismissed Khrushchev's offer as less a '*freie Stadt*' than a '*vogelfreie Stadt*' (outlawed city).[68] The western powers rejected the Soviet note out of hand, as did West Germany. But the British Prime Minister, Harold Macmillan, wavered: against the advice of Adenauer and the Americans, he visited Moscow in February 1959 in an effort to reduce tension. He achieved nothing except to annoy Adenauer. In the course of discussions with Macmillan, however, Khrushchev let slip that his deadline was flexible.[69] It emerged that he had no intention of risking a war over Berlin. On 10 June the Soviet Foreign Minister, Andrei Gromyko, announced that the

USSR was 'prepared not to insist on the immediate and complete abolition of the occupation regime in West Berlin'.[70]

In September 1959 Khrushchev visited the USA, the first Soviet leader to do so. He engaged in some awkward confrontations with American citizens (he was outraged when security considerations were cited as a reason for denying him a visit to Disneyland). Talks with Eisenhower produced no tangible results but led to agreement on the convening of another four-power summit. This was eventually set for mid-May 1960 in Paris. But two weeks before that the Russians shot down an American U-2 spy plane flying over the Soviet Union. US and British planes had conducted such missions for several years but most flew at high altitudes, beyond the range of Russian interceptors. Although Russian radar tracked the planes, there was nothing they could do to stop them except issue diplomatic protests. The Americans exulted over the plane's capabilities. 'The U-2 gave us eyes to see inside the Iron Box,' recalled a future Director of the CIA. 'It instantly became a major source of our intelligence about the Soviet Union. It constituted nothing less than a revolution in intelligence.'[71] On this occasion, however, a lucky hit by a Soviet SAM missile damaged the plane. The pilot, Gary Powers, who parachuted to the ground, neglected to use the poison pill with which he had been supplied and was captured alive by the Russians. Khrushchev turned up in Paris for the summit but deliberately brought it crashing to a halt with a ferocious denunciation of the Americans for the U-2 incident, after which he refused to attend any further sessions.

Khrushchev's conduct infuriated the western leaders and accelerated the deterioration in east–west relations. His boorishness alarmed some of his Kremlin colleagues too. Even his friend and ally Mikoyan complained of his 'inexcusable hysterics. . . . He simply spat on everyone. . . . He was guilty of delaying the onset of détente for fifteen years.'[72] But Khrushchev was irrepressible. His petulant behaviour reached something of a climax that autumn when he took off his shoe in the United Nations General Assembly and banged the table in protest against an offending speaker. In June 1961 he met President Kennedy at a summit in Vienna. The abortive CIA-sponsored Bay of Pigs invasion of Cuba a few weeks earlier, an attempt to depose Fidel Castro's revolutionary regime there, soured the atmosphere and the encounter achieved nothing. Soon afterwards the USSR resumed nuclear testing.

Against this background, Berlin yet again became a dangerous flashpoint. The city by this time was already divided by an invisible wall. West Berlin, where large subsidies from the Federal Republic helped restore a prosperous economy, was often called a 'shop window for the west'. Since 1955, while still technically under occupation, it had been a *Land* of the Federal Republic. In east Berlin and East Germany generally, the political immobilism of the regime and its palpable economic failure by comparison with its dynamic capitalist neighbour engendered growing popular discontent and consequent emigration to the west. Although the East Germans had cut off telephone communications as well as tram and bus lines between the Russian and other sectors in 1952, the underground railway remained open, serving the city as a whole. There was therefore no physical impediment to East Germans seeking to move to the west. In December 1957, however, alarmed by the rate of emigration, the East German Volkskammer passed a law making 'flight from the Republic' an offence punishable by up to three years' imprisonment. Rumours that the law might be strictly enforced only increased further the numbers leaving. Dangerous jokes abounded: a notice left on the door of an East German optician after he fled to the west: 'The near-sighted should go to the eye clinic. The far-sighted should follow me.'[73] In July 1961 departures rose to thirty thousand. On 9 August 1,926 refugees registered at reception camps in west Berlin, the highest single-day figure thus far recorded. By that point 3.5 million East Germans had moved west since 1949. The East German government evidently faced the spectre of an ever-diminishing population. The East German foreign intelligence chief, Markus Wolf, expressed the general official despair: 'The state was haemorrhaging its workforce.... I felt that we were swimming through mud.'[74]

Contingency plans for the construction of a wall between east and west Berlin had been prepared as far back as 1952. Khrushchev initially resisted the idea but in the end relented. With Russian approval, the East Germans decided on drastic action in early July. Implementation, however, was delayed owing to a shortage of the necessary materials: 303 tons of barbed wire, 31.9 tons of mesh wire, 1,700 kg of connecting wire, 1,100 kg of clamps, 2,100 concrete pillars, and a large quantity of timber.[75] After a few weeks the technical preparations were complete. Following a meeting on 3–5 August with Khrushchev and other eastern bloc leaders, Ulbricht ordered closure of the border.

On 13 August 1961 East Germany began the construction of barricades between east and west Berlin. At the same time four Soviet divisions secretly took up position near the city. Barbed wire was soon strengthened by concrete blocks. When finished, the wall stretched along the entire sectoral boundary as well as around the frontier (as it had become) between west Berlin and East Germany. It was patrolled by border guards under orders to shoot at would-be escapers. Trains that picked up passengers in east Berlin no longer stopped at stations in the west.

The decision to enforce 'stronger protection and control on the border with West Berlin' was announced and justified in an East German government decree that accused the Bonn government of having 'drawn the conclusion that the piratical policy of the German monopoly capital and its Hitler generals must be tried once more'. West Germany was said to be 'systematically luring citizens of the German Democratic Republic and organizing regular slave traffic'.[76] A Warsaw Pact statement published the same day complained that West Germany, 'through deceit, bribery, and blackmail' had been persuading 'unstable elements' in East Germany to leave for the west where they were trained to be sent back as 'spies and saboteurs'.[77] At the same time, a secret directive by the head of the East German secret police (*Stasi*), Erich Mielke, stated the true motive: 'Measures will be taken against flight from the Republic.'[78]

West Berlin, West Germany, and the western powers reacted with impotent fury. The US and West German intelligence services were caught by surprise. Brandt, whose defiant stance transformed him overnight into a world figure, demanded actions, not words, from the western allies. Britain, France, and the United States protested and reaffirmed their rights under the wartime and post-war agreements but no government was prepared to risk war in central Europe. As Harold Macmillan readily admitted between holes on the Gleneagles golf course, 'Nobody is going to fight about Berlin.'[79] Any thought of western intervention, in any case militarily unfeasible, was moderated by an assurance from the Soviet Commander-in-Chief in Germany, Konev, that western rights in the city would remain inviolate.[80] West Berliners felt betrayed. Western assurances and guarantees, it seemed, were worthless. Brandt later recalled that it was as if 'a curtain had been pulled back to reveal an empty stage'.[81]

The 'anti-Fascist protective barrier' achieved its object in abruptly terminating the unauthorized exodus from East Germany, although at a high diplomatic, public-relations, and human price. Over the next twenty-eight years around nine hundred people died while trying to escape from East Germany, most of them shot by East German border guards. Another 72,000 were imprisoned for planning or trying to cross the border illegally.

Even the wall, however, could not completely dam the pressure for escape. More than 150,000 people were permitted to emigrate legally from East Germany in the decade after the wall was built. What the wall enabled the East German authorities to do was control the flow so as to provide a safety valve for getting rid of dissidents without mass population loss. The wall also had another function. It enabled the regime to conduct a 'slave traffic' of its own: between 1963 and 1989 the GDR released to the west at least 29,766 political prisoners in return for ransom payments amounting in total to more than 3.4 billion marks.

The three crises over Berlin had made clear the limits for both sides of 'brinkmanship', as it had come to be called. Ulbricht saw the wall as a stage in the process of pushing the west out of Berlin. But he was restrained by the Russians. In spite of their threats, they were not willing to risk war by ejecting western forces from the city. For all its inhumanity, the immediate effect of the wall's construction was to crystallize rather than change the status quo. The western powers were prepared to react to any aggression against west Berlin but not to go any further. In this impasse lay the makings of a modus vivendi. In June 1963 President Kennedy visited Berlin and uttered his famous '*Ich bin ein Berliner*' speech in front of the Schöneberg Rathaus. But this was no more than rhetoric. The west's aims remained cautiously defensive; the Russians too now reconciled themselves to the status quo. Western acquiescence in the existence of the wall resulted in a stabilization of the Berlin problem. Meanwhile the primary arena of east–west conflict shifted elsewhere.

The Soviet achievement in April 1961 in putting Yury Gagarin in space had heightened public alarm in the United States about the 'missile gap' and provided a strong base of support both for the American space programme and for increased spending on missile development. US concern was increased by the Soviet resumption of nuclear bomb testing in the atmosphere in the autumn of 1961. In fact, the Americans had a 17:1 advantage in deliverable nuclear warheads. US and British intelligence agencies understood that the 'missile gap' was a useful bogey rather than a reality. They possessed quite accurate data on Soviet missile development thanks, in part, to the U-2 flights and to the services of their most successful double agent of the entire Cold War. Oleg Penkovsky was a Soviet military intelligence officer who worked as a double agent for the British and the Americans. Like the Soviet atom spies and the 'Cambridge five', he appears to have been motivated mainly by ideology, though he did request payment in dollars to be deposited in an American bank. Between 1960 and 1962 he passed copies of thousands of documents on Soviet missiles, nuclear weapons, and agents' names to MI6 and CIA agents. In late 1962 he was discovered and arrested by the Soviet security service and was shot the following year.

The Cuba crisis of October 1962 was another product of Khrushchev's impulsiveness. Fearing humiliation if the Americans succeeded in ousting the revolutionary regime of Fidel Castro, he saw the secret installation of Soviet missiles and nuclear warheads on the island as a deterrent. In spite of warnings from advisers, Khrushchev failed to take account of the likely US reaction. Soviet success in deploying missiles to Cuba would reduce potential warning time of nuclear attack on the United States to close to zero. President Kennedy's declaration of a 'quarantine' around Cuba on 22 October raised the prospect of war if US naval vessels sought to impede Soviet ships delivering missiles to Cuba. The Americans feared that if they took military action in Cuba, the Russians would respond in Berlin. Khrushchev wrote an emotional letter to Kennedy warning that if both sides did not withdraw they would 'clash like blind moles and then reciprocal destruction will begin'.[82] Khrushchev blinked first: the Soviet ships were ordered to turn back before reaching the quarantine line. After six days the Russians agreed to withdraw missiles from Cuba in return for an American pledge not to invade the island. The Americans also undertook informally to remove Jupiter missiles based in Turkey. Kennedy spoke to Macmillan by telephone every day during the crisis but these were little more than courtesy calls; he paid next to no attention to the Prime Minister's views. Although British as well as American nuclear forces were put on high alert, neither Britain nor other European powers could affect the outcome. During the tense days in which nuclear war seemed closer than ever before or since, they were reduced to the role of spectators, facing what came to be called 'annihilation without representation'.

The easing of international tension in the wake of the Cuba crisis provided a more propitious atmosphere for east–west negotiations. In June 1963 the two superpowers signed an agreement initiating a 'hot line' between Washington and Moscow to enable leaders to communicate directly in cases of urgency. The next month a three-power (US, USSR, UK) nuclear test-ban treaty was signed in Moscow, outlawing all nuclear testing in the atmosphere, under water, and in space, though not underground. Ninety other states signed within two years, but not France or

China, which both continued to test nuclear weapons in the atmosphere. The agreement was nevertheless hailed as a first step towards broader east–west negotiations.

Meanwhile, after a decade in power, Khrushchev began to look vulnerable. He had undermined his position by his boastful predictions of economic advance, followed, as they were, by shortfalls in agricultural production. He had alienated his military elite by large cuts in conventional forces. His wavering attitude to de-Stalinization had unsettled conservatives without attracting a solid support base of liberals. His public boorishness, culminating in undignified scenes on an official visit to Egypt in May 1964, exposed the socialist superpower to ridicule. A conspiracy against him crystallized in the spring of 1964. The chief plotters were his Presidium colleagues Leonid Brezhnev, Nikolai Podgorny, Aleksandr Shelepin, and Dmitry Polyansky. According to the later recollections of V. Y. Semichastny, head of the KGB, Brezhnev suggested that Khrushchev should be poisoned, though this seems far-fetched. Khrushchev's son got wind of the plot and warned his father, who seems not to have taken it seriously. Khrushchev was holidaying on the Black Sea when a telephone call from Suslov asked him to return to Moscow for urgent consultations 'on agricultural questions'. Upon arrival, instead of the usual welcoming delegation of Presidium members, he was greeted by Semichastny who said, 'They've all gathered at the Kremlin. They're waiting for you.'[83] In a meeting of the Presidium on 13 and 14 October Khrushchev faced his accusers. One after another they accused him of thoughtlessness and haste, of insulting colleagues and not listening to their opinions, of nepotism and arrogance, and of sponsoring a new personality cult. The most serious criticisms were directed at Khrushchev's agricultural and food-supply policies. Khrushchev made only half-hearted efforts to defend himself. 'I'm upset,' he said, 'but I'm also glad that the party has gotten to the point that it can rein in even its first secretary.'[84] He retired on formal grounds of advanced age and ill health: and spent the rest of his life in obscurity. His overthrow may be termed a palace revolution. But as Khrushchev's remark indicated, its manner marked a kind of coming of age of the Soviet system which for the first time had passed the political scientists' test of peaceful transfer of power between rival politicians.

14

Consensus and Dissent in Western Europe 1958–1973

We can't complain.
We're not out of work.
We don't go hungry.
We eat.

Hans Magnus Enzensberger,
*Frankfurt am Main, 1964**

The fat years

The *trente glorieuses* was the name given in France to the three decades after the war; in economic terms the glory was shared by much of western Europe. The post-war boom, the longest period of sustained prosperity since before the First World War, was achieved under conditions of almost full employment and low inflation. Production was stimulated by increases both in domestic demand and in exports. Higher government expenditures and new patterns of consumer spending boosted output and encouraged investment. Productivity improved as a result of technological innovation, better communications, and reallocation of labour, though the latter was limited by the restrictive practices of powerful trade unions, especially in Britain. Most economies enjoyed growth rates in excess of 4 per cent per annum. EEC members, led by West Germany, headed the pack, with rates of over 5 per cent. Scandinavia was not far behind. Britain, however, lagged at under 3 per cent. Inflation generally remained at a low

* From 'Middle Class Blues', translated from the German by Hans Magnus Enzensberger, Michael Hamburger, Rita Dove, and Fred Viebahn. Hans Magnus Enzensberger, *Selected Poems*, Riverdale-on-Hudson, NY, 1994, 33.

single-digit level that most countries found acceptable, though in this sphere too Britain performed much less well than West Germany. Unemployment remained under 5 per cent of the workforce in all the major economies—2 per cent or lower in West Germany. Many of the less industrialized, peripheral regions of Europe, though not Ireland, also expanded rapidly: Spain and Greece achieved over 6 per cent growth per annum on average between 1950 and 1970.

In much of the region, notably France and Sweden, the state played an important role in steering investment both in nationalized concerns and also, through fiscal and other incentives, in private industry. Public expenditure drifted steadily upward, reaching levels of between 40 and 50 per cent of GNP in most countries by 1973. Switzerland was an exception, at only 27 per cent, but even there the increase, from 21 per cent in 1950, was palpable. The chief cause was rising social transfer expenditures. These at least doubled as a percentage of GNP almost everywhere between 1950 and 1973; in the Netherlands and Norway they more than tripled.[1]

In contrast with the inter-war years, fluctuations in economic activity were relatively moderate, as governments used tax, interest rate, and other mechanisms of demand management to modify cyclical oscillations. Such stability had not been known since before 1914, leading some economists to speculate that in Keynesianism a panacea had been discovered that could produce steady economic growth on a basis of full employment and only moderate inflation. Keynesian prescriptions became the new economic orthodoxy, embraced by bankers, economists, and trade unionists alike. Capitalism was to be steered by macro-economic planning under the supervision of a new breed of professionally trained technocrats, exemplified in France by the '*énarques*', graduates of the Ecole Nationale d'Administration founded in 1945.

Liberalization of international trade, particularly after the GATT-sponsored 'Kennedy round' of tariff reductions in 1964–7, led to swift expansion in west European exports and imports. Overall, exports rose by more than 8 per cent per annum between 1950 and 1970, though here again the British economy, heavily dependent on exports, performed unimpressively. EEC member states' trade patterns reoriented, taking advantage of the abolition of internal tariffs: in 1958–60 a third of France's exports went to other EEC countries; by 1968–70 more than half did so.

Trade growth was aided by relative currency stability. The Bretton Woods system remained the basis of international payments until 1971. International institutions such as the IMF smoothed short-term upheavals in the currency markets. On 1 January 1959 all the non-Communist states of Europe, except Iceland, Spain, and Turkey, returned to convertibility, though most still placed some limitations on capital movements. Sterling, exchange of which had been restricted for almost the whole period since 1939, once again became a 'hard' currency. The move enabled the City of London to resume its position as a major international financial centre. By 1970 Britain's share of foreign assets held by deposit banks was a quarter of the world total. West Germany, Switzerland, the United States, and Japan together held just under a third. Also on 1 January 1959 France introduced the 'nouveau franc', worth 100 old francs. At the same time the French currency was devalued by 15 per cent. De Gaulle saw a strong franc as an essential basis to national greatness and as a counter to 'American imperialism . . . [which] takes all forms but the most insidious of all is that of the dollar'.[2] Under the influence of the economist Jacques Rueff, a liberal opponent of *planification* and Keynesianism, the new franc was backed by mountainous gold reserves. De Gaulle's Finance Ministers, starting with Antoine Pinay, adhered to sound money policies that quickly restored confidence. But the champion currency of western Europe, safeguarded by a powerful, independent, and conservative central bank, was now the Deutsche Mark, which was revalued upwards by 5 per cent in 1961.

While manufacturing and service sectors prospered, agricultural production throughout western Europe declined as a share of total economic output. French agriculture, in particular, remained uncompetitive, although government efforts to consolidate holdings, modernize methods, and increase productivity began to produce results by the late 1960s. The number of independent peasants in France fell from 4 million to 2.5 million and the number of employed agricultural labourers from 1.2 million to 584,000 between 1954 and 1968. The Common Agricultural Policy (CAP) of the EEC was developed ostensibly to secure European food supply but in reality primarily to protect farmers, particularly small producers in France, from the rigours of the international market. The European Commission pressed strongly for the CAP's adoption, seeing it as a vanguard of broader supranational policy-making. The result was chronic over-production, as peasants were paid subsidies to fill economically superfluous wine 'lakes' and accumulate butter 'mountains'. Other producers, including the United States (which subsidized agro-business heavily) and, later, less developed countries, complained bitterly about such market interventionism. European consumers suffered by paying artificially high prices for food. And the EEC's finances were held to ransom by the cost: for many years as much as 90 per cent of the Community budget was spent on this one item.

The British, with their much smaller and more efficient agricultural sector, saw nothing attractive in the EEC's preparations for implementing the CAP. But they nevertheless soon rued their decision to remain outside the Common Market. By the end of the 1950s French GNP was overtaking British for the first time in living memory. Macmillan for a time played to the xenophobes in the gallery, railing against the six and denouncing 'a boastful, powerful "Empire of Charlemagne"—now under French control but later bound to come under German control'. He vaguely threatened to withdraw British troops from Germany but this was an obvious bluff.[3] Britain's first serious response was to initiate the formation of the European Free Trade Association (EFTA), or 'outer seven', with Austria, Denmark, Norway, Portugal, Sweden, and Switzerland (Finland joined as an associate member in 1961). Conceived as a kind of rival to the EEC, it was a loose trading group rather than an economic union. By 1967 all internal tariffs had been eliminated. But there was no common external tariff and no plan for political integration. The British calculated on using EFTA as a bargaining base to negotiate a broad tariff reduction agreement with the EEC. But this hope proved illusory, partly because of American objections to what was seen in Washington as an attempt to lock US exports out of Europe.

In April 1961 the British Cabinet, viewing the success of the EEC as a threat to British trade and to the country's position as the foremost American ally in Europe, decided, after all, to apply for membership. Macmillan carried his party, apart from a right-wing fringe, in support of the venture. In October 1962 the Labour Party decided to oppose membership, at any rate on the terms then apparently on offer. This was the beginning of what became over the next half century a pattern in British politics: when in opposition, the major parties grumbled about European integration; when in government, they acquiesced in it, though often *à contre-coeur*. A team headed by Edward Heath opened negotiations but these bogged down in disputes over British insistence on preferential treatment for imports from Commonwealth countries. In January 1963 the talks came to an abrupt halt when de Gaulle announced at a press conference that France would veto British membership. This snub was seen by many as belated revenge for the wartime humiliations that de Gaulle felt he (and in his person, France) had suffered from Churchill and Roosevelt. De Gaulle expressed his animosity even more pointedly in conversation with his intimates: 'England has become a satellite of the United States. As for the Netherlands, the Scandinavians, and *tutti quanti*, they're satellites of Britain. They're Russian dolls. All that happy breed don't love us and they detest our policies. It's natural, therefore, that we should refuse to go down on our knees before the Anglo-Saxons.'[4] 'This man has gone crazy—absolutely crazy,' a frustrated Macmillan told Kennedy. 'French duplicity has defeated us all,' the British premier wrote despairingly in his diary.[5] For the time being, however, there was nothing the British could do to overcome the French veto.

De Gaulle's haughty nationalism caused renewed trouble in July 1965, when the French walked out of the EEC's main institutions in protest against proposals to limit the national veto in Common Market decision-making. The origin of the crisis lay in an ambitious project by Walter Hallstein, the German who served as first President of the European Commission, to initiate steps towards supra-nationalism. Fusion of the three communities (EEC, ECSC, and Euratom) and their respective commissions into one 'European Community' was approved. But implementation was delayed because of a row with the French. The immediate French objective was to thwart the Commission's proposal to reform the annual budget process, shifting power from the Council to the Commission and the Assembly. Since the budget was primarily devoted to financing the Common Agricultural Policy, due to take full effect on 1 July 1967, de Gaulle regarded the proposal as an assault on vital French interests. For him it was more a matter of national sovereignty than protection of peasants, for whom, at least privately, he had little sympathy. They were 'never satisfied', he said. 'It's always the rich peasants who are the biggest cry-babies.' He called dairy farmers 'a pile of little chaps who live off the piss of their cows and don't know how to make a living any other way'.[6] In a conversation with his Minister of Agriculture, Edgard Pisani, he raged against the Commission and its allies: 'They're all a mafia of supranationalists! . . . They're scum that we've got to get rid of.'[7] The 'empty chair' crisis virtually paralysed the business of the EEC over the next six months. In the end, pressure from the French business community and from French farmers forced a settlement. The so-called 'Luxembourg compromise' of January 1966 permitted each member state to exercise a veto where its vital interests were at stake. Since each member retained the right to define those interests, this was, in effect, a victory for the French. The 'fused' European Community did come into being in 1967 but the national veto stymied EC decision-making for the next two decades.

Wind of change

De Gaulle's first task on regaining power was to resolve the problem of empire, of which the most pressing issue was the future of Algeria. He had vaulted to power with the help of a military rebellion. At that point he appeared to be the only barrier against civil war spilling over into France herself. 'The necessity to put an end to the Algerian war seemed to me the only possible justification for the paternalist monarchy introduced under the cover of the constitution of 1958,' wrote the influential centre-right political commentator Raymond Aron.[8]

In early 1959 General Maurice Challe, the French commander in Algeria, launched a vigorous offensive designed to wipe out the Algerian rebels' underground cells. Hundreds of thousands of Muslim civilians were removed from their homes to primitive 'regroupment camps'. In the evacuated areas, rebels were pursued without mercy. The FLN suffered serious reverses. Challe's campaign succeeded in wiping out the greater part of the rebel forces. Within a year the French came close to a military triumph. Yet the bulk of the Muslim population sympathized ever more strongly with the nationalist cause. The cost of the war, in political, human, and financial terms, was meanwhile proving more than France could bear. By November more than 1.4 million soldiers, at least 200,000 of them Algerian Muslims, had served in the French army in Algeria.

The conflict was also waged on diplomatic, propaganda, and psychological fronts. Whatever the military outcome, it was by now plain that Algerian Muslims would not accept indefinite French rule—and that most European settlers would not accept anything short of that. Public opinion in France grew ever more anguished. Britain and the United States became distinctly hostile to French policy. The French commitment of sixteen divisions in Algeria drained NATO of much-needed troop strength: instead of the fourteen divisions France was supposed to contribute to the alliance, she maintained only 3.67 divisions in Germany.

Gradually de Gaulle's thinking shifted towards the previously unthinkable: Algerian independence. In March 1959 he spoke of 'self-determination'. In a broadcast to the nation on 16 September he went further and spelled out clearly for the first time that he was prepared to offer the Algerians a genuine choice: secession, full integration in France, or 'government of Algerians by Algerians, backed up by French help and in close association with her'. He made no bones about what he expected would be the result of a decision for independence: 'the most appalling poverty, frightful political chaos, widespread slaughter, and, soon after, the warlike dictatorship of the Communists'. Only the timing of the proposed referendum remained in question. With characteristic arrogance de Gaulle said: 'I will decide upon it in due course, at the latest four years after the actual restoration of peace.' He reiterated his earlier promise to the FLN of a 'peace of the brave' in which rebels who ceased the armed struggle would be permitted to take part actively in politics.[9] In spite of all the reservations, this speech marked a decisive turning-point: Algerian independence was no longer ruled out and de Gaulle himself had evidently travelled a long way on the path of intellectual adjustment towards its acceptance.

De Gaulle could not, however, altogether ignore men who had brought him to power and who might, if not handled with care, attempt to depose him. The French army, having tasted the power of king-making, was not disposed to return calmly to its barracks and officers' clubs, the less so when it saw that the main issue on which it had staked its fortunes, preservation of a French Algeria, was about to be betrayed. In January 1960 General Massu was recalled to Paris and dismissed from his post after giving an interview to a German newspaper in which he criticized de Gaulle's Algerian policy. Massu's dismissal was the signal for renewed insurrection in Algiers. On 24 January firing broke out between police and a crowd of European demonstrators. Seventeen gendarmes and nine demonstrators were killed. European civilians, supported by army officers, erected barricades in the streets. The Prime Minister, Michel Debré, visited Algiers and negotiated with the mutinous colonels, who told him flatly that they would disobey orders to shoot at the rebels behind the barricades. They insisted that de Gaulle must withdraw from his commitment to self-determination or make way for General Challe or some other military combination.

But the rebels did not command the full support of the army, nor of the population in metropolitan France. De Gaulle would not yield. On 29 January he delivered his response on television, wearing military uniform 'in order to show that it is General de Gaulle who speaks, as well as the Chief of State'. He refused to withdraw his commitment to self-determination. He dismissed the men behind the barricades as 'agitators' and 'usurpers', who were 'aided by the accommodating uncertainty of various military elements'. He warned that the French army would become 'but an anarchic and absurd conglomeration of military feudalisms if it should happen that certain elements made their loyalty conditional'.[10] This was one of de Gaulle's greatest oratorical performances, stamped with such an air of personal authority that, in effect, he obliterated the rebellion by sheer force of personality.

In a referendum on 8 January 1961 de Gaulle's policy of '*l'autodétermination des populations algériennes*' (still an ambiguous formulation) secured support from 75 per cent of voters. Secret government contacts with the FLN opened a month later. The army commanders, however, would not accept the popular verdict. In April Generals Challe, Salan, Zeller, and Jouhaud attempted to execute a *coup d'état* in Algiers. In another masterly televised address de Gaulle denounced the 'quartet of retired generals' and made it clear he would have no truck with them: 'The future of the usurpers should only be that provided for them by the rigour of the law.' He ended with the dramatic appeal: '*Françaises, Français, aidez-moi*!'[11] Most army units remained loyal to the government. The insurrection collapsed.

The final stages of the war intensified divisions within French society. The government was now engaged in a struggle on two fronts: against the diehard proponents of continued French rule in Algeria and against those of Algerian independence. The most intransigent of the former, headed by Salan, founded the Secret Army Organization (OAS). Its leaders included former resistance fighters and senior politicians such as Soustelle and Bidault. The OAS enjoyed the support of the majority of Europeans in Algeria as well as of many army officers. In desperation, it resorted to terrorist attacks against Muslims, Communists, and senior civil servants. In September 1961 it launched the first of a series of unsuccessful assassination attempts against de Gaulle.

As the war in Algeria dragged on, many of its most unpleasant features were replicated in France. Press censorship in Algeria could not be effectively maintained without being exercised in France too. Television journalists who failed to toe the government line were dismissed. The banning of the Algerian Communist Party was almost meaningless unless measures were taken also against the French Communist Party. When a group of 121 left-wing intellectuals, among them Sartre, called on soldiers in Algeria to desert, the government threatened legal action. The violence also spilled over ever more menacingly into metropolitan France. Following an Algerian nationalist demonstration in Paris in October 1961, eleven thousand demonstrators were arrested: at least a hundred were killed by the Paris police, commanded by Maurice Papon (a former Vichy official who was to be imprisoned in 1999 for his role in wartime deportations of Jews). Many of the bodies were dumped into the Seine.

In late 1961 de Gaulle grasped the nettle and authorized the opening of formal talks with the FLN. By March 1962 these produced an agreement at Evian on a cease-fire that was to be followed, after a brief transition period, by Algerian independence. A referendum on 8 April 1962 secured a remarkable 90 per cent vote in France in favour of the agreement. Algeria became independent on 3 July. For the rest of his life de Gaulle claimed, with some justice, that this was the greatest service he had rendered France in his entire career.

The price was paid by those who had once been his most ardent supporters. At the end of 1961 the French government had expected that perhaps as many as 150,000 Europeans might arrive from Algeria over the next few months. By the end of 1962 710,000 had fled to France. A further 105,000 followed over the next two years. Almost the whole European population of Algeria thus left. About a quarter settled in the southern *départements*, a sixth in Paris, and the rest spread out over the rest of the country. They became, for a while, a disturbing element in French politics, lending support to extreme right-wing politicians. The OAS *plastiqueurs* continued to plant bombs but soon lost public support. Salan was captured in April 1962 and court-martialled. Bidault took refuge in Brazil. Soustelle too fled the country. In spite of French government efforts to exclude them, 93,000 *harkis*, Muslims who had fought for the French, also found sanctuary in France, fleeing massacres in which fifty thousand of their former comrades were slaughtered.

Elsewhere in Africa the French retreat from empire was relatively peaceful. Soon after his return to power, de Gaulle offered all of France's black African colonies a choice between total independence or a form of autonomy combined with membership in a French *Communauté*. All but one accepted this form of association with France. The single exception was Guinée. The French immediately withdrew all personnel, aid, and armed forces from Guinée, which assumed an at first naked, later Communist-bloc-supported, independence. From 1959 onwards the other French colonies in Africa were granted full independence, while retaining close economic, political, and military links with France.

Nearly all the remaining European colonies in the continent, except for those of Portugal, were wound up in the 1960s. The most precipitate and irresponsible act of decolonization was the Belgian withdrawal from the Congo in 1960. This left a country that had been gouged by Europeans for its mineral wealth over the previous seventy-five years without the basic infrastructure of a modern state. In the ensuing chaos, the USSR backed the central government of Patrice Lumumba, while the Belgians and other western powers supported the separatist southern province of Katanga, where Belgian mining interests held sway. The Katangan secessionists were eventually suppressed by a United Nations military operation. Among those who lost their lives in the process were the UN Secretary-General, Dag Hammarskjöld, killed in an air crash en route to Katanga in September 1961.

The greatest imperial power in Africa withdrew the most readily. In 1957 the Gold Coast became the first British colony in sub-Saharan Africa to gain independence, taking the name Ghana. The fiercest resistance to the transfer of authority to black Africans came from the small white settler communities in east and central Africa. They had traditionally looked to the Conservatives, the party of empire, as their patrons. In Kenya for a time the British fought a ruthless campaign to suppress a revolt by nationalists organized in the conspiratorial Mau Mau movement. But revelations of the torture of African prisoners at the Hola detention camp led to protests in the House of Commons, including an eloquent speech that established the parliamentary reputation of the Conservative MP Enoch Powell. After Suez, the Conservatives quickly adjusted to realities and began to prepare for withdrawal from Africa. For a time the white settlers enjoyed an influential spokesman in the Cabinet, the fifth Marquess of Salisbury, but he resigned (on another issue) in 1957. Thereafter the predominant voices in determining policy were no longer sentimental imperialists but rather liberal-minded realists such as Iain Macleod, Colonial Secretary from 1959 to 1961. Altogether, between 1957 and 1964, nineteen colonies, including eleven in Africa, gained independence from Britain.

In February 1960, on a visit to South Africa, Macmillan delivered his 'wind of change' speech in the Parliament in Cape Town, warning the South Africans, and by implication also white colonists elsewhere in Africa, that 'African national consciousness . . . whether we like it or not . . . is a political fact'.[12] The Afrikaner (mainly Dutch-origin) white National Party government in South Africa, insistent on maintaining their policy of *apartheid* (white domination euphemized as 'separate development') withdrew from the Commonwealth the following year and declared the country a republic.

As the Union Jack was lowered in most of Africa, it continued to flutter in one colony, Southern Rhodesia. Uniquely among settler communities in Africa, the whites there had enjoyed internal self-government, on the basis of a whites-only franchise, since 1923, when Churchill, then Colonial Secretary, had failed in an attempt to incorporate the territory into the Union of South Africa. In 1953 the British, in another effort at consolidation, created an autonomous Central African Federation, combining Southern and Northern

Rhodesia with Nyasaland, all under white control. But London resisted settler demands for independence under white rule. The Federation broke up in acrimony in the early 1960s. Britain thereupon gave way to the nationalist tide. Northern Rhodesia and Nyasaland became independent under black rule as Zambia and Malawi in 1964. In Southern Rhodesia, however, the Europeans entrenched themselves behind ever more militant leaders and refused to make any concessions to African nationalism.

In November 1965, fearing that they would be bulldozed by the British into submission to black African nationalism, the Southern Rhodesian whites issued a unilateral declaration of independence. Their government, headed by Ian Smith, failed to secure recognition from a single country but defied their opponents and asserted sovereign authority over the country in spite of British opposition. Commonwealth prime ministers, particularly those of recently independent African states, urged vociferously that Britain should use force to crush the rebellion. The British found themselves in an uncomfortable minority in the councils of their former empire. The Prime Minister, Harold Wilson, professed himself 'deeply committed' to the Rhodesian regime's overthrow and declared he would 'throw the book' at Smith.[13] But the Defence Secretary, Denis Healey, advised that an invasion would require the withdrawal of 'a large number of units from Germany' and would 'carry serious implications, not least in terms of strain on the loyalty of our own troops'.[14] Instead, therefore, the British secured United Nations approval for the imposition of economic sanctions on Rhodesia. The rebels, however, received covert assistance from South Africa and Portuguese Mozambique and proved adept at evading the trade embargo. In an effort to resolve the crisis by diplomacy, Wilson held two meetings with Smith, the first aboard the destroyer HMS *Tiger* off Gibraltar in December 1966, the second on HMS *Fearless* in 1968. But he failed to induce the Rhodesian leader to return to constitutionality. Further efforts in 1971–2 by the Conservative government of Edward Heath were similarly unavailing. Not until 1980 did the whites, under pressure from guerrilla war and diplomatic isolation, finally give way.

The only three colonies in Europe, Gibraltar, Malta, and Cyprus, each posed for the British peculiarly vexing problems. Gibraltar, ceded to Britain by Spain in the Treaty of Utrecht in 1713, remained of strategic importance to Britain. Its population was strongly pro-British, and there could, in any case, be no thought of turning them over to Spain so long as Franco remained in power. A referendum on the Rock in 1967 returned an almost unanimous verdict in favour of continued British rule.

Malta, British since 1814, had proven its value to Britain during the Second World War and again at the time of the Suez expedition. The island had enjoyed a measure of self-government since 1947 but nationalist feeling led in 1964 to the grant of full independence. By treaty Britain retained a base there but the rise of the militantly anti-western Dom Mintoff to power in 1971 led to a long tussle that ended only in 1979 with the closure of the base and the withdrawal of all British forces.

Even more troublesome was Cyprus, which had been acquired for Britain by Disraeli at the Congress of Berlin in 1878 and had been a Crown Colony since 1925. Because it was under British rule, the island, unlike most other areas of intermingled Greek–Turkish population in the region, had been unaffected by the Graeco-Turkish 'exchanges of population' carried out under League of Nations auspices in the 1920s. But relations between the Greek majority and the Turkish minority were poor. From 1955 the British fought a bitter war against a Greek nationalist rebellion. Georgios Grivas, a former Greek army colonel and royalist resistance fighter during the war, headed the guerrilla movement EOKA (National Organization of Cypriot Struggle), which carried out terrorist attacks and called for *enosis*, union of the island with Greece. The Turkish minority responded with proposals for *taksim* (partition). The issue inflamed feeling in both Greece and Turkey and led to anti-Greek riots in Turkey. In early 1956 Eden's government decided to arrest the Greek Cypriot ethnarch, Archbishop Makarios III, and remove him to detention in the Seychelles. After Suez, Macmillan released him, allowed him to go to Greece, though not to return to Cyprus, and agreed to negotiate with him. A settlement was eventually reached in 1959 whereby the Greek Cypriots gave up their demand for *enosis*. Instead a republic was to be founded, in which Greek and Turkish Cypriots would share power. The British would retain sovereign bases on the island. The arrangement was jointly guaranteed by Britain, Greece, and Turkey. Cyprus became independent in 1960 but communal violence soon erupted between Greeks and Turks. Only strong American pressure prevented Turkey from sending forces to protect the Turkish Cypriots. By 1964 communal relations on the island were so acrimonious that a United Nations peacekeeping force had to be sent to the island. For the next decade the UN preserved an uneasy peace but the underlying political conflict remained unresolved.

By 1965, with most of its former responsibilities gone, the Colonial Office felt able to prepare plans for 'a final liquidation of our colonial empire' within the next year.[15] In 1966 the Colonial Office itself disappeared by amalgamation with the Commonwealth Office. Most of Britain's remaining dependencies were indeed being prepared for imminent independence but, having supposedly acquired her empire in a fit of absence of mind, Britain found it remarkably difficult to divest herself of the last bits and pieces. Several small colonies, such as the Pacific island of Pitcairn with eighty-six inhabitants, were judged unfit for sovereignty. Others remained geopolitically important. And two, Hong Kong and the Falkland Islands, bedevilled the efforts of successive governments to arrive at an agreed solution with China and Argentina respectively.

At the same time as Britain tried to close the final chapter in the history of her empire, the Foreign Office concluded that 'British policy today is essentially reconciled to the view that white men cannot expect indefinitely to maintain military bases in non-white territory'.[16] This principle, however, conflicted with strategic requirements in several parts of the world. Between 1963 and 1966, for example, the British found themselves involved in the defence of Malaysia against Indonesian 'confrontation'. Nevertheless, in 1967 the British announced their intention to withdraw the bulk of their forces from 'east of Suez' within the next few years. In November 1967 they left Aden, uniquely in the British imperial experience up to that point handing over power to a Marxist government. Bahrain and Qatar became independent in 1971, though some British officers remained on duty in the Gulf area on supposedly private contracts with local potentates. In 1971 Singapore, the Royal Navy's largest base outside the United Kingdom, was evacuated. Under a five-power agreement with Malaysia, Singapore, Australia, and New Zealand, Britain retained some forces in the region. Otherwise, with minor exceptions, such as the small garrison in Hong Kong and a gurkha battalion in Brunei, British soldiers were, for the first time in modern history, absent from Asia and Africa.

Fraying consensus

Unlike most of its west European neighbours, West Germany enjoyed the luxury in this period of not having to cope with the problem of decolonization. It was itself emerging from foreign rule and confronting profound difficulties of transition and adjustment. Thanks in large measure to Erhard's *Wirtschaftswunder*, the Christian Democrats were victorious in election after election. In 1957, in combination with their Bavarian wing, the Christian Social Union (CSU), they won over 50 per cent of the vote, a record for any German party in a free national election. The Social Democrats, after this, their third successive defeat, entered a period of self-examination. Two years later a party conference at Bad Godesberg produced fundamental changes in doctrine. The Bad Godesberg programme renounced nationalization, except for the coal-mining industry. It moved away from advocacy of Marxism and class conflict and towards the British Labour model of advocacy of a mixed economy and social reform. In 1960 the Social Democrats explicitly renounced neutralism and endorsed West German membership of NATO. The younger generation of pro-western leaders, headed by Willy Brandt and Helmut Schmidt, reoriented the party solidly towards *Westbindung* and, from 1961 onwards, formed a warm relationship with the newly elected Kennedy administration.

The construction of the Berlin Wall weakened Adenauer's political position, especially after he delayed visiting the city for the first ten days of the crisis. In national elections a month later, the CDU suffered a setback, though Adenauer was able to form a new government with support from the Free Democrats. The sealing of the border by East Germany led to calls for new thinking in the Federal Republic. The historian Golo Mann (son of Thomas Mann), for example, urged acceptance of the Oder–Neisse line as Germany's eastern frontier and suggested an end to the taboo on contacts with the East German regime. Adenauer himself conceded privately in October 1961 that 'every thinking person' understood that 'the existing situation' in the east could not be 'rolled back'.[17] Gerhard Schröder, the Christian Democrat West German Foreign Minister from November 1961 until 1966 (not to be confused with the later Social Democrat Chancellor of the same name), advocated a *Politik der Bewegung* (policy of movement), abandonment of the Hallstein doctrine, opening of diplomatic relations with Communist countries other than the GDR, and broadening of trade with the eastern bloc. But diplomatic inertia, opposition within the Christian Democrat Party, pressure from the expellee lobby, and the Cold War environment conspired to ensure that for the time being, apart from minor commercial agreements, little changed in West Germany's *Ostpolitik*.

In October 1962 a divisive scandal erupted after the appearance in the iconoclastic news magazine *Der Speigel* of articles attacking the Defence Minister, Franz-Josef Strauss. The magazine's publisher, Rudolf Augstein, and members of his staff were arrested and charged with treason on the ground that they had published material that might endanger national security. Augstein remained in prison for 103 days. The episode prompted outrage in the press and the political world. Strauss, the rumbustious and outspoken leader of the Bavarian CSU, had joined Adenauer's Cabinet in 1953. His pugnacity endeared him to his Bavarian electorate but set him apart from the reserved style of most CDU politicians. Adenauer had appointed him Defence Minister in 1956 only with great reluctance. Strauss had reduced the planned size of Germany's forces but his vigorous espousal of a greater say for Germany in NATO nuclear defence created alarm. Suspicion grew that he aimed at an independent German nuclear capability. In fact, this was an option that Adenauer privately favoured.[18] In response to criticism, the Chancellor went on the offensive, accusing Augstein of base commercial motives for descending into an 'abyss of treason'.[19] A group of leading writers, among them Günter Grass and Hans Magnus Enzensberger, issued a manifesto of solidarity with Augstein. Even conservative newspapers such as the *Frankfurter Allgemeine Zeitung* and *Die Welt* criticized the government. The Free Democrat ministers in the Cabinet resigned. Skilful political manoeuvring by Adenauer, however, led them to return, though their price was the dismissal of Strauss and the Chancellor's reluctant commitment that he himself would resign not later than October 1963.

When '*der Alte*' finally laid down the reins of office at the age of eighty-seven, he was succeeded by Erhard. Although popular, the new Chancellor lacked Adenauer's immense personal authority. His flexibility and penchant for compromise earned him the nickname 'the Rubber Lion'. His predecessor carped from the back seat and Strauss, still out of office, chafed at the bit. Within the CDU fierce arguments broke out between pro-American 'Atlanticists', headed by Erhard and Schröder, and 'Gaullists', with Adenauer and Strauss in the lead, who favoured alignment with France. Although the ruling coalition comfortably won the 1965 elections, the Social Democrats made further gains. Erhard lacked his predecessor's guile and determination and in October the following year a budget wrangle led to the collapse of his coalition with the FDP.

The result, on 1 December 1966, was a 'grand coalition' of the large parties. Kurt-Georg Kiesinger, an ex-Nazi (he had joined the party in 1933), replaced Erhard as CDU leader and became Chancellor. Brandt became Foreign Minister and Strauss Finance Minister. The three years of coalition government marked the high water mark of consensus politics in West Germany. A mild recession in 1967, the first in the West German economy since the war, led the coalition to pass a Keynesian-inspired Stability and Growth Act that became the bedrock of the country's economic policy. The 'magic triangle' of high employment, price stability, and balance of payments equilibrium was now to be transformed into a 'magic square', with the addition of economic growth as a basic policy-making goal for both the government and the central bank. The government also aimed to secure the cooperation of the trade unions in the implementation of a voluntary policy of wage restraint. But this proved difficult to realize, especially when growth resumed in 1968. In the event, the rate of growth declined in each succeeding decade for the rest of the century.

In Italy superficial political turbulence masked deep structural stability. Revolving-door coalitions, invariably headed by the Christian Democrats, presided over the country's brisk, if uneven, modernization as well as over a corrupt spoils system dubbed *sottogoverno* (subterranean government). An old-fashioned and cumbersome civil service slowed down efforts to reform administration. The judiciary remained highly politicized. Italy nevertheless shared in the general prosperity, enjoying growth in industrial production of over 8 per cent per annum in the 1960s. The gap between the developed north and the backward south, however, remained obstinately wide and between 1950 and 1970 over four million people moved north seeking new employment opportunities.

In Scandinavia, governments dominated by Social Democrats continued to expand the public sector. The Swedish Prime Minister, Tage Erlander, who served continuously from 1946 to 1969, spoke of building 'the strong society'.[20] Large resources were invested in housing programmes, social welfare, and education. Most of the reforms were supported, if not in detail then in fundamental principle, by a broad spectrum of political opinion. Labour relations remained relatively harmonious, governed by the 'spirit of Saltsjöbaden', the system of centralized agreements between employers and trade unions that had prevailed since 1938.

In Britain too consensus prevailed. The mixed economy and the welfare state remained unquestioned axioms of both Labour and Conservative thinking, endorsed by socialists like Tony Crosland and Conservatives like Sir Edward Boyle. The economy boomed and 'Supermac', as he was portrayed by the cartoonist 'Vicky', led his party to a landslide victory in the 1959 general election. But in 1962 'the old actor-manager', as his ministerial colleague Enoch Powell called him,[21] began to lose his hitherto almost magical political touch. The Prime Minister's studied Edwardian languor, owlish flippancy, and shooting holidays on Scottish grouse moors seemed out of tune with the national mood. The government was criticized for its 'stop-go' economic policy and suffered spectacular by-election defeats. On 13 July 1962, 'acting on the principle of protecting the future,' as he later put it, Macmillan executed the most ruthless Cabinet reshuffle of the twentieth century.[22] In his 'night of the long knives', he dismissed a third of his senior ministers, including the Chancellor of the Exchequer, Selwyn Lloyd. 'Greater love hath no man than this', quipped the Liberal MP Jeremy Thorpe, 'that he lay down his friends for his life.'[23]

Macmillan was further weakened in 1963 by a scandal that led to the resignation of the Secretary of State for War, John Profumo, who admitted having lied to the House of Commons over his relationship with a prostitute. As Foreign Secretary at the time of Suez, Selwyn Lloyd had lied to the House over the issue of 'collusion' with Israel. But his lie was for the sake of *raison d'état*; he was later appointed Speaker of the House of Commons. Profumo's lie about his private life terminated his political career in ignominy, though he later rehabilitated himself, earning public respect for years of social work in the east end of London. The sensational aspects of the affair, involving sex, espionage, and high-society high jinks, were gleefully exposed by the media, in particular by a stinging new satirical journal, *Private Eye*, and its television sibling, *That Was The Week That Was*. Macmillan badly mishandled the episode and his remark in Parliament, 'I do not move among young people much myself,' was quoted against him repeatedly and tellingly.[24]

That autumn Macmillan fell ill and, facing a long convalescence, resigned. The news unleashed an unprecedented and undignified scramble for the leadership. The obvious successor, Butler, enjoyed strong support on the liberal wing of the party. But 'Rab' was an uninspiring speaker and lacked the determination to make a forceful bid for power. When the Queen visited the Prime Minister in hospital, he recommended the appointment of the Foreign Secretary, Lord Home, 'a man who represents the old governing class at its best'.[25] This was the last occasion in British history on which an unelected figure was appointed Prime Minister and the last on which the Conservative Party chose its leader without some form of internal election. Home renounced his peerage and secured a seat in the House of Commons as Sir Alec Douglas-Home. He nevertheless seemed an antiquarian choice to lead a party that wished to pose as a modernizing force. As Conservative fortunes ebbed, he delayed calling an election until the last possible moment, in October 1964.

When the nation finally went to the polls, thirteen years of Conservative rule came to an end with the victory of the Labour Party, led by Harold Wilson. A professional economist by training, he had succeeded to the leadership after the sudden death of Hugh Gaitskell in 1963. For most of his career Wilson had been regarded as a man of the left. But eschewing the old ideological disputes, he stressed the moderate, reformist elements in Labour's programme and sought to portray his party as more modern, technological, and attuned to new social ideas than the Conservatives. His triumph was by the narrowest of margins, a majority of just five over all other parties in the House of Commons. The new Cabinet boasted a formidable array of talent, including intellectuals such as Roy Jenkins, Tony Crosland, Richard Crossman, and Denis Healey. Yet Wilson's premiership exposed the limitations of traditional social democracy and proved a sad disappointment to its keenest supporters.

The major problem that confronted the Wilson government throughout its first three years of office and conditioned almost all its policies was economic management. One of its earliest decisions was to rule out devaluation, this even though the trade balance was highly unfavourable and experts considered the pound overvalued. In retrospect the decision was an error but once it had been taken Wilson believed there was no turning back. Defence of the pound became almost a test of manhood for the government. With the exception of the renationalization of most of the steel industry, Labour did not embark on any major initiatives that could be characterized as socialist. George Brown, the most prominent figure on the right of the party, appointed to head the newly created Department of Economic Affairs, was charged with the preparation of a much-vaunted 'economic plan'. Unveiled with much ballyhoo in September 1965, it proved as short-lived as the ministry that produced it. In the hope of damping down inflation, the government created a Prices and Incomes Board. But the 'norms' set by this body soon became base points for negotiation in the minds of trade union collective bargainers. The government, which depended heavily on trade union financial support for the Labour Party, could not bring itself to introduce compulsory wage controls.

In the hope of increasing his wafer-thin parliamentary majority, Wilson called a new election in March 1966. He at last achieved for Labour the convincing majority that had eluded it at every election since its landslide victory in 1945. Secure in power, he did not, however, change his policies, except on one issue. Having switched to a pro-European stance, he launched a renewed membership bid for the EC. But this was once again blocked by de Gaulle, this time before negotiations had even opened.

The Middle East crisis of 1967 administered a death blow to the sterling parity. The closure of the Suez Canal as a result of the June Arab–Israel war hit the British economy hard. Oil imports from the Middle East now had to travel by the much longer Cape route. British merchant shipping, still the largest user of the waterway, was severely affected. The adverse effect on the UK's balance of payments was estimated to be at least £100 million. That was more than sterling could bear. In November, after three years of vain struggle, Wilson had to surrender to the 'gnomes of Zurich' (an updating of the 1931 'bankers' ramp'): the pound was devalued from $2.80 to $2.40. Devaluation gave a much-needed fillip to the British economy but it set in motion ripples of international currency instability. Many of Britain's trading partners, including Ireland, Denmark, Finland, and Spain, devalued at the same time. In August 1969 France devalued by 11.1 per cent and in October Germany revalued by 9.3 per cent. The long-term consequences for the international currency system were to be enormous.

The British decision was seen as a national humiliation and the Chancellor of the Exchequer, James Callaghan, resigned. In a television broadcast, Wilson characteristically fudged, pointing out, in what became a notorious phrase, that the 'pound in your pocket' remained worth just the same after devaluation as before. But what was seen as casuistry fooled nobody and the episode marked a turning-point in the government's fortunes. In 1969, in the hope of restoring some discipline to the labour market, the government issued a White Paper (policy statement) entitled *In Place of Strife*. This outlined proposals for legislation designed to curb unofficial strikes. But the plan aroused heated opposition from the trade unions and the government was embarrassingly obliged to backtrack and accept a 'solemn and binding' undertaking from the unions. 'Sir Solomon Binding' failed, however, to have the desired effect and was soon forgotten. In June 1970 Wilson called an election, which, to general surprise, he lost. But the new Conservative Prime Minister, Edward Heath, like Wilson, soon became embroiled in industrial disputes. Consensus by this time was fraying at the edges—and not only in Britain.

In two areas of western Europe it did not merely fray; it snapped. The first was Northern Ireland, the second was Belgium. Since 1922 Ulster had been the only major part of the United Kingdom to have its own elected provincial government, with broad autonomy in internal affairs. The Irish government in Dublin asserted its theoretical sovereignty over the whole island, but took no steps to realize the claim. The Unionist Party, representing the Protestant majority, ruled Northern Ireland continuously throughout the period. Lord

Craigavon, the province's first Prime Minister, called the provincial assembly at Stormont 'a Protestant Parliament for a Protestant people'.[26] Roman Catholics, who numbered about a third of the total population of 1.5 million, were on average poorer than the Protestants and were subject to discrimination in electoral arrangements, housing, and employment. Many supported nationalist demands for unity with the Irish republic. Rancorous enmity, quasi-tribal in character, separated the two communities.

For a time in the mid-1960s it seemed that the gulf might be bridged. In January 1965 a reformist Northern Irish Prime Minister, Terence O'Neill, invited the Taoiseach, Sean Lemass, to Stormont. The meeting was the first encounter between leaders of northern and southern Ireland. But such contacts offered no clear solutions. Continuing anti-Catholic discrimination in the north led to the growth of a civil rights movement. Its demonstrations were suppressed, with much-publicized brutality, by the Royal Ulster Constabulary, a mainly Protestant police force. O'Neill's programme of moderate reform aroused opposition in his own party and in April 1969 he resigned. Outbreaks of inter-communal violence in Londonderry and Belfast persuaded the British government in August 1969 to dispatch forces from mainland Britain to maintain order. By 1972 British troop strength had reached 22,000.

Initially, the British army was seen as the protector of the Catholics: soldiers in Catholic districts, the Falls Road in Belfast and Bogside in Londonderry, were welcomed with cups of tea by local residents. But Catholic feeling changed following the outbreak of a campaign of terrorism by the Provisional IRA, an offshoot from the Irish Republican Army, a long-established militant group that was now controlled by pro-Moscow Marxists. Bombings by both 'Officials' (supplied with arms by Moscow)[27] and 'Provos' and intimidation of potential witnesses led the Northern Irish government in August 1971 to introduce internment without trial of hundreds of republicans suspected of involvement in terrorism. Many were maltreated while in captivity. This presented the IRA with a civil liberties issue around which it could mobilize widespread support in Northern Ireland, Britain, and among Americans of Irish ancestry. In January 1972 a large demonstration of republicans in Londonderry was fired on by British troops and thirteen died. After this 'Bloody Sunday', opinion polarized further. Intercommunal anomosities were whipped up by the Protestant Unionist demagogue the Reverend Ian Paisley and the Irish nationalist termagant Bernadette Devlin, who had been elected to the House of Commons in 1969 at the age of twenty-one as the youngest ever woman MP.

By March 1972 the conflict between the two communities had reached such a pitch of ferocity that the British government decided to suspend the Northern Irish Parliament and take over direct responsibility for ruling the province. Unionists bitterly resented the end of their half-century of domination. The 'official' IRA suspended its campaign, lest the province descend into sectarian warfare, but the Provisionals intensified their terrorism in the hope that direct rule might be a stage towards British withdrawal. With a view to demonstrating the democratic legitimacy of the union, the government held a referendum in March 1973: almost all Catholics boycotted the poll; 98 per cent of those voting (57 per cent of the total electorate) favoured continuation of the union with Britain.

Recognizing the need somehow to draw the Catholics into the political process, the government persuaded all the major parties, save the Protestant and Nationalist extremists, to agree to a new form of provincial autonomy. Northern Ireland would be governed by a power-sharing Executive responsible to a newly elected Assembly. The Executive would carry out most administrative functions except maintenance of law and order. Hardly had this new body assumed office, however, when its leader, the Unionist Brian Faulkner, was repudiated by his own party. In May 1974 a peaceful general strike of Protestant workers, orchestrated by Paisley, forced the Executive's demise. Direct rule from London, inter-communal hatred, and IRA terrorism remained the lot of the province for the next two decades.

In Belgium endemic tension between Dutch-speaking Flanders and francophone Wallonia threatened the stability of the state. The division had its origins in the line established in the third century between rude Frankish tribes, who conquered the north, and the Gallo-Roman civilization of the south. From the establishment of Belgium in 1830 until after the Second World War, French-speakers dominated the country. But thereafter they found themselves steadily overtaken, demographically, economically, and politically by their Flemish neighbours. By 1970 Dutch speakers outnumbered Walloons by 5.4 million to 3.1 million. French speakers' insecurity was aggravated by the changing economic balance. In 1955 per capita income in Flanders overtook that in the less industrialized Wallonia; by 1974 it was 13.7 per cent higher. The language conflict was temporarily resolved in the late 1960s by agreement on cultural autonomy for Dutch- and French-speaking areas and bilingualism in Brussels, where an estimated 80 per cent or more of the population spoke French as their first language. In 1968, in a sad capitulation to ethno-linguistic pressures, the Catholic

University of Louvain (Leuven) split into Dutch- and French-speaking institutions. After being burned down by the Germans in both world wars, the university library now suffered a third blow at the hands of the Belgians themselves: its book stock was split in two. This piece of cultural barbarism reflected the rifts within all the main political 'families' in the country, each of which broke into two distinct, linguistically based parties in the late 1960s. In 1970 the constitution was revised, beginning movement towards a federal model. But the two communities remained deeply polarized and Belgian national identity became ever more fractured.

Meanwhile consensus politics throughout Europe encountered a head-on challenge, amounting to a wholesale rejection of the post-war generation's social and political value system.

The revolt of the young

The student revolution of the late 1960s broke sharply with the politics of consensus. Although a trans-national phenomenon, the rebels' objectives were often surprisingly localized, even in West Germany and France where the movement developed national political importance. The initial impetus, and the model for much that followed, came from student rebellions in the United States, especially the 'free speech' movement on the university campus at Berkeley, California, that began in 1964. The rallying issues of civil rights and opposition to conscription for the Vietnam War, central to the growth of American student radicalism, were virtually absent in Europe, although hostility to the Vietnam War added an edge of anti-Americanism to the movement there.

The goals of European student rebels were vehemently expressed but often incoherently defined. In spite of the effervescence of colourful *groupuscules* of Trotskyists, Maoists, and anarchists, most participants were mobilized less by ideology than by a vague sense of generational solidarity against an establishment seen as boring, smug, self-interested, authoritarian, patriarchal, bureaucratic, and hypocritical. They saw themselves as liberating, spontaneous, and uncontaminated by commercial or other special interests. The vogue words were 'contestation', 'transformation', and 'imagination'. The image of the Argentinian-born revolutionary Ernesto 'Che' Guevara, who was killed in Bolivia in 1967, became a totem. The movement was strongest in West Germany, Italy, and, most of all, France. In all three countries mass higher education in the post-war period had placed great strain on academic facilities.

Libraries were overcrowded, lecture halls overflowed, professors became remote figures, heard through loudspeakers—or not at all. Sympathizers portrayed the rebellion as a natural and healthy generational revolt; critics denounced it as nihilistic, violent, and intolerant.

Although the rebels saw themselves as leftist, their favourite authors were not the canonical Marxists but writers such as the anti-colonial psychiatrist Frantz Fanon, a propagandist and activist in the Algerian revolutionary struggle, and two elderly gurus: Sartre, who had parted company with the Communists after the Hungarian revolution and whose ideological trajectory was now moving towards Maoism; and the Berlin-born, Frankfurt School neo-Marxist Herbert Marcuse, in exile at Brandeis University in Massachusetts from 1954 to 1965, thereafter in California. Marcuse's visits to Berlin in 1967 and to Paris in May 1968 excited student radicals. But his main influence came through books. His *One Dimensional Man* sold hundreds of thousands of copies in several languages.[28] In *Repressive Tolerance* he provided his admirers with a philosophical sanction for direct action and violence. Commending Robespierre's distinction between the terror of liberty and the terror of despotism, he maintained that 'in terms of historical function, there is a difference between revolutionary and reactionary violence, between violence practised by the oppressed and by the oppressors. In terms of ethics, both forms of violence are inhuman and evil—but since when has history been made in accordance with ethical standards? To start applying them at the point where the oppressed rebel against the oppressors, the have-nots against the haves, is to serve the cause of current violence by weakening the protest against it.'[29]

In West Germany the existence of the grand coalition between 1966 and 1969 left little outlet within the political system for anti-government feeling and strengthened what became known as the *ausserparlamentarische Opposition* (APO, Extra-Parliamentary Opposition). It organized demonstrations, sit-ins, and marches directed against the Shah of Iran and the Vietnam War. Targets closer to home like the conservative Springer newspaper group, which owned 40 per cent of the West German press, and university authorities, portrayed as accomplices in the crimes of the ruling class and as traitors to the Humboldtian ideal of the free university. The students saw themselves as rebels against the *Tätergeneration* ('generation of perpetrators'). Rudi Dutschke, leader of the radical *Sozialistischer Deutscher Studentenbund* (SDS) in West Germany, wanted to expose the 'fascism inside the structure'.[30] The students' enemies accused them of *Traumtanzerei* (dream-dancing).

In November 1967 students occupied the Palazzo Campana, home of the University of Turin's law, education, and humanities faculties. After the occupiers were forcibly evicted in early 1968, they turned to street violence, attacking the office of *La Stampa* newspaper, owned by the Fiat motor company, and engaging in battles with the police. 'Only violence helps where violence reigns!' was the cry.[31] Demonstrations in Milan and Rome in March 1968 led to confrontations between students and police. Ripples of student radicalism spread north to Scandinavia, crossed the Iron Curtain to Poland and Czechoslovakia, and washed over the Channel to England, although the impact was limited in the much more elitist British university system. Demonstrations took place at Warwick and Leicester Universities, a building was occupied in Oxford, and a porter at the London School of Economics died of a heart attack suffered during a student protest there. A small New Left, influential mainly among university intellectuals, especially in the humanities and social sciences, remained active in Britain for some years but never attained any political importance.

Nowhere did the student revolution shake established institutions more alarmingly than in France. By the late 1960s de Gaulle had ruled the country longer than any political leader for a century. His paternalism seemed increasingly at odds with the society that he governed and in some ways despised. His hubris grew with age. It was said of him that he 'identified with France, not with the French, and saw his destiny as dragging the French upward'.[32] He reinforced his legitimacy by occasional referenda and, in 1962, by restoring direct election of the presidency for the first time since 1848. His ministers, including Michel Debré, Prime Minister from January 1959 until 1962, and Debré's successor, Georges Pompidou, were loyalist retainers. Parliament was virtually emasculated. As in Germany and Italy, the young generation felt alienated from a political class that seemed to have sold out to the interests of the 'military-industrial complex'.

In November 1967 social sciences and humanities students in the soulless, factory-like buildings of the new university campus at Nanterre, near Paris, went on strike. They succeeded in persuading the academic authorities to grant many of their demands for participation in administration, for improvement in university facilities, and for abolition of separation of the sexes in student residences. But the movement did not stop there. Agitation continued against an educational system that, as a tract distributed at Nanterre in April 1968 put it, bred graduates like 'stuffed geese'. Daniel Cohn-Bendit, a twenty-three-year-old anarchist of German-Jewish parentage, propounded a theory of 'revolutionary detonation', whereby student rebels would act as the trigger for a broad, working-class uprising. The sociologist Edgar Morin suggested that whereas in 1958 the French had appealed for salvation to a father figure, in 1968 de Gaulle drew on himself 'the old parricidal heritage imprinted on the French political subconscious since the death of Louis XVI'.[33] The students' anti-authoritarian authoritarianism distressed intellectual critics: Raymond Aron deplored the 'delirium' of the student movement and its 'assassination of the liberal university'.[34]

In early May 1968 serious riots broke out in Paris. During the *événements* in the Latin Quarter, police and the CRS (special militia forces) battled demonstrators. Students erected barricades and hurled cobblestones. Intellectuals protested and paraded. University buildings were occupied and draped with red and black flags and portraits of revolutionary heroes. The Odéon theatre provided the stage for round-the-clock psychodrama and impassioned oratory. All the hallowed symbols of revolutionary *journées* reappeared, sometimes transmuted into emblems of radical chic by poster-designers in the Atelier Populaire des Beaux-Arts. Graffiti on the walls proclaimed: '*Il est interdit d'interdire*; *Soyez réalistes, demandez l'impossible*; *Rêve + evolution = révolution*'.

Within a few days the students succeeded in persuading workers in the Renault automobile factories near Paris to stop work. Soon seven million workers all over France were on strike. Trains stopped and passenger aircraft were grounded. Telephone and telegraph services were interrupted. Some workers occupied factories, although these were a minority of employees in the enterprises concerned: only about 250 of ten thousand workers at the Renault factory at Flins were occupiers and a few hundred of the thirty thousand at the plant at Boulogne-Billancourt. The strikers demanded not merely better pay and conditions but *autogestion* (literally 'self-management', conveying to its advocates varying degrees of worker participation) and a fundamental change in the structure of industry. The *élan* of the young rebels had already aroused the antagonism of the leaders of the Communist Party who feared lest their own authority over the trade union movement and their own credentials as revolutionaries might be impaired. In an article in *l'Humanité*, the Communist politician Georges Marchais condemned the 'pseudo-revolutionaries' led by 'the German anarchist Cohn-Bendit', who 'purport to give lessons to the workers' movement'.[35]

The student movement struck momentary terror into the possessing classes. On 11 May Pompidou appeared on television and attempted to pacify spirits. Far from calming the militants, his speech further emboldened those who claimed they now had the authorities on the run. The government brazenly ignored the supposed independence of the state broadcasting system and directly censored television reporting on the disturbances. On 20 May state broadcasting workers at ORTF began a strike in protest against such interference. Radio journalists who took control of their studios in order to broadcast what they regarded as impartial news were forcibly removed by the police.

Often the student rebels seemed to be performing in a theatre of the absurd. But in de Gaulle they faced their country's greatest master of the art of political drama. In the early stages of the crisis he remained silent. From 14 to 18 May he proceeded on a state visit to Romania that he had refused to postpone. François Mauriac, in his *bloc-notes*, published in *Le Figaro Littéraire*, deplored his decision but, recalling the war, noted that his behaviour had at least one merit: '*c'est qu'en cas de péril on pourra toujours le rappeler!*' (In the worst case, we could always summon him back!)[36] On his return the President told his advisers, in an untranslatable phrase that became public, '*La réforme oui! La chienlit, non*'.[37] A few days later he addressed the French people, proposing a referendum on reforms. He seemed distant and out of touch; Alain Peyrefitte, the Minister of Education, confessed that the universal response was one of disappointment. In a Cabinet meeting on 27 May, de Gaulle fumed: 'Enough of these mass meetings! They should no longer be tolerated . . . If the police can't do it, we'll call on the army.' But his ministers remarked privately that he seemed all at sea and overwhelmed by events.[38]

On the same day Pompidou sought to quell the strike movement in collusion with the government's sworn enemy, the Communist Party. At Grenelle (an industrial quarter of Paris) he reached an agreement with business leaders and the trade unions that involved significant concessions to workers' demands. Wages were to be increased by 10 per cent across the board and the minimum wage was raised by 35 per cent. Working hours were to be reduced and unions received new rights in factories. But workers remained on strike, rejecting what was called the government's *escroquerie* (swindle). The revolution now approached its climax. De Gaulle's fate and even that of the Fifth Republic seemed to hang in the balance.

On 29 May, without informing the Prime Minister or any of his other advisers, de Gaulle left Paris and paid a mysterious, secret visit to Baden-Baden. There he met Massu, now commander of the French armed forces in Germany. '*Tout est foutu!*' were his first words to his old comrade. He talked of resigning but Massu stiffened him up and revived his spirits. The President returned to Paris in a more confident mood.[39] His unexplained absence had created panic and consternation in the capital. In its theatricality the episode recalled Ivan the Terrible's sudden disappearance from Moscow in 1564 (the Tsar eventually acceded to pleas to return—on his terms). Rumours of all kinds abounded. De Gaulle wrung political profit from the mood of uncertainty. Back in Paris he delivered another broadcast address (on radio only). This time it was a bravura performance. He declared that, having received the mandate of the nation, he would not resign. He dissolved the National Assembly and called new elections. He warned that France was 'menaced with dictatorship'. And he indicated that he would not hesitate to assume emergency powers if order were not restored.[40] The speech, just four and a half minutes long, was suffused with an air of authority and determination. This broadcast was the decisive turning-point. Hundreds of thousands of people, headed by Malraux and Debré, immediately rallied in a mass demonstration at the Champs-Elysées in support of de Gaulle. The multitude congregated 'like snails after the rain (may the snails forgive me!)', lamented a young student leftist.[41] Like a late-spring squall, the revolution was suddenly over.

Workers drifted back to their jobs. Student occupiers were ejected from university buildings. The parliamentary election, a month later, resulted in a landslide Gaullist victory. Remarkably, and a testimony to the fundamental restraint on all sides in spite of the immense passions aroused, no more than a dozen deaths directly attributable to political violence occurred during the two months of turbulence.

De Gaulle's election victory restored his authority for the moment. To his supporters he appeared yet again as saviour of the republic. He took the opportunity to reward his Prime Minister by sacking him. Pompidou's six-year premiership had been the longest since Guizot's more than a century earlier. In summarily disposing of his loyal lieutenant, de Gaulle seems to have been concerned to reassert the supremacy of the president and at the same time to rid himself of an over-popular crown prince. In Pompidou's place he appointed Maurice Couve de Murville, who had served as Foreign Minister from 1958 to 1968 and then briefly as Finance Minister. A diplomat and technocrat rather than a politician with an independent base, Couve faithfully but colourlessly executed his master's instructions.

In the year that followed de Gaulle talked of reform but he seemed to many to be out of touch with the public, almost a relic of the past. His sense of his own indispensability grated on many. In April 1969 he decided to put his public standing to the test by calling the long-promised referendum. He chose, however, to stake everything on what seemed to many the rather arcane issues of decentralization to the regions and reform in the powers of the Senate. He declared that he would regard the vote as one of confidence in him personally. When he lost it narrowly, he issued a peremptory one-sentence communiqué announcing his resignation and returned, this time for ever, to his home in Colombey.

De Gaulle's sudden eclipse presented his republic with another critical test. Were the political institutions of the Fifth Republic so heavily focused on his personality that, like the Second Empire after the defeat of Napoleon III, they would simply collapse upon his deposition? In the event, the French surprised themselves by the smoothness of the transition. In the ensuing presidential election Pompidou stood as the Gaullist candidate. Alain Poher, President of the Senate, tried to rally the centre. The left presented a sorry spectacle of disunity, offering four candidates who received altogether less than a third of the votes. In the second round, Pompidou won decisively. He was a Gaullist but not an *intransigeant*. He declared that for him Gaullism was 'not a doctrine but an attitude'.[42] De Gaulle was gone but Gaullism, mildly reformulated, survived.

Ludwig Erhard called 1968 'the end of the post-war era'.[43] But the long-term effects were more psychological and intangible than institutional. The New Left melted away almost as suddenly as it had appeared. Its leaders moved in various directions. Dutschke was shot and seriously wounded at a demonstration in April 1968. He moved to England but was deported. He died in Denmark in 1979 as a result of complications attributed to the assassination attempt. Cohn-Bendit was expelled from France, entered conventional politics in Germany, embraced environmentalism, and represented the Green Party on the Frankfurt City Council and later in the European Parliament; by 2005 he was advising the French left to accept that 'we live in a world of market forces'.[44] Other *soixante-huitards*, especially in Italy and Germany, embraced terrorism. And others again threw aside their youthful enthusiasms and joined the conventional rat-race of the consumer society. What remained of their revolution was widespread disdain among the young for traditionalism, a collapse of respect for elders, and a readiness for social and cultural experimentation.

Third force?

European defence policies in the missile age were inexorably dominated by the rivalry between the two superpowers. Most European states except

Britain continued to recruit conscript armies, with the length of compulsory service generally eighteen months in western Europe and two years in the Warsaw Pact. But no conventional wars were waged in Europe between 1945 and the end of the Cold War. European armies' combat experience was therefore restricted to colonial campaigns outside Europe and, in some cases from the early 1970s onwards, to guerrilla wars against terrorists. Only Britain and France clung to some semblance of strategic independence, in each case with only limited success.

In 1960 Britain cancelled her Blue Streak intermediate-range, surface-to-surface missile programme, on the development of which £60 million had already been spent, and instead purchased the American Douglas Skybolt air-launched ballistic missile (ALBM), which could be fired from the UK's existing fleet of V-bombers. As part of the deal, Macmillan agreed to the stationing of a Lockheed Polaris submarine-launched ballistic missile (SLBM) base at Holy Loch on the west coast of Scotland, near Glasgow. The Prime Minister confessed to President Eisenhower his concern about situating such a base 'so near to the third largest and the most overcrowded city in this country. As soon as the announcement was made, Malinovsky [the Soviet Defence Minister] would threaten to aim his rockets at Glasgow.'[45] Such qualms were increased by the continued American reluctance to give a cast-iron guarantee that they would consult the British prior to using nuclear weapons based in the UK. Macmillan nevertheless felt compelled to agree to the Holy Loch base as the price of obtaining Skybolt. He was all the more shocked, therefore, to be informed two years later of the US cancellation of the Skybolt programme. The British were affronted at what they regarded as an American lack of consideration that accorded ill with their conception of the much-vaunted 'special relationship' between the two allies. The survival of the independent British nuclear deterrent seemed threatened. At a conference with Kennedy at Nassau in December 1962, Macmillan agreed that Britain would buy Polaris missiles at a cut-rate price and install her own nuclear warheads.

The Labour Party had meanwhile succumbed to left-wing pressure and adopted a programme demanding unilateral nuclear disarmament. Its leader, Gaitskell, told the 1960 party conference that he would 'fight, fight, and fight again' to reverse the unilateralist policy.[46] His successor, Harold Wilson, criticized the Polaris agreement and the Labour election manifesto in 1964 complained of the independent deterrent that 'it will not be independent and it will not be British and it will not deter'.[47] But Labour in power made virtually no change in nuclear policy. Britain consequently retained a nuclear capacity that was nominally independent but in fact dependent on American-supplied missiles and American strategic direction.

De Gaulle's foreign and defence policy proceeded from profound chagrin at the decline in French power. He belonged to a generation that had twice seen governments flee Paris before an invader, had twice seen the fruit of victory shrivel and turn rotten. He was deeply convinced that at two critical moments in French history, in 1940 and 1958, he had incarnated in his own person the continuity of the French state. Determined not to betray that legacy either in word or in deed, he would not accept the idea of France as a client of the United States within NATO. If Macmillan deluded himself with the notion that Britain could be the Greeks to America's Rome, de Gaulle did so with the idea that France, as leader of Europe, could be an arbiter between the two superpowers. He spoke of a Europe stretching 'from the Atlantic to the Urals'. His tragedy, it was said, was that, though 'born to govern an empire . . . [he] had at his disposal only a state of the second rank'.[48]

De Gaulle viewed the French nuclear programme as an essential building-block of French power. He approved the first test of a French atomic bomb in the Sahara in 1960 and the detonation of the first French thermonuclear weapon over the Pacific Ocean in August 1968. France, unlike Britain, would not rely on American delivery systems. Instead, the French bomb would be delivered by Mirage aircraft and, from the early 1970s, by independently developed underground and submarine missile systems. The nuclear *force de frappe* would free France from humiliating dependence on the American nuclear umbrella and allow her to regain strategic independence. Given the uncertainties of the age, the French nuclear deterrent must be targeted, according to the Commander-in-Chief of the armed forces, General Charles Ailleret, not against a 'privileged enemy', such as the Soviet Union, but '*tous azimuts*' (in all directions).[49] France refused to sign the test-ban treaty in 1963. And she refrained from signing the non-proliferation treaty agreed by the United States, the USSR, and Britain in 1968 (by 2007, 190 countries had signed, including France which did so only in 1992).

Realizing the limits of France's power if she acted alone, de Gaulle sought to turn his country into the leader of an independent-minded bloc of west European nations. Before he came to power he had been against the Treaty of Rome. But after 1958 the economic success of the EEC soon led him to moderate his view. Moreover, he came to see Franco-German friendship as the key to his hope of turning western Europe into a third force in international affairs. In this, although for different reasons, Adenauer became a willing partner. The relationship between the two old men calls to mind the Briand–Stresemann relationship a generation earlier. That had ended in disaster because of circumstances beyond the control of individual statesmen. The new Franco-German symbiosis had a happier outcome. In January 1963 the two countries signed a treaty definitively terminating nearly a century of hostility. It provided for regular meetings between French and German leaders, twice yearly for the President and Chancellor and more frequently for ministers. The Paris–Bonn axis, thus inaugurated, survived changes in leadership in both countries and endured despite differences, for example over British entry to the Common Market. The magnitude of the transformation may be appreciated by recalling that only nine years earlier the project for a combined European army had foundered on the rock of the French National Assembly's fear of German rearmament.

But de Gaulle's hope of turning France into the core of a third force between the two superpowers was doomed to frustration. The West German political establishment, both CDU and SPD, although keen to mend relations with the French, remained wedded to the United States alliance and saw the American military presence on German soil as the best guarantee of security. In early 1966, as the Mirage IV bombers entered service, eliminating French dependence on the NATO nuclear umbrella, de Gaulle abruptly announced that France would withdraw from the integrated military command of NATO, though not from the more intangible political aspects of the alliance. He also evicted NATO headquarters from Paris and all NATO bases from the country. But the French, like the British, soon discovered that full strategic independence in the nuclear age was an unaffordable luxury for medium-sized powers. Within a year secret military contacts with NATO were resumed and after de Gaulle's resignation France once again edged closer to collaboration with, if not full participation in, the alliance.

Britain and France thus gained little from their efforts to maintain independent nuclear capabilities. Both in size and in delivery capabilities, the two countries' nuclear forces remained pygmies by comparison with those of the superpowers. By contrast, a non-nuclear power that deliberately shunned the status of a great power succeeded in the late 1960s in breaking the logjam in east–west relations in central Europe.

Ostpolitik

The creation of the grand coalition in West Germany in 1966 and the appointment of Willy Brandt as Foreign Minister led to a significant modulation in the Federal Republic's policy towards the east. Egon Bahr, Brandt's chief adviser, had made a powerful speech to the Evangelical Academy in Tutzing in July 1963 advocating direct contacts with East Germany with a view to '*Wandel durch Annährung*' (change by rapprochement). He argued that 'contact with the Communist east might lead to its penetration by western ideas, which would then engender gradual change'.[50] Bahr became head of planning in the Foreign Ministry and an architect of the new *Ostpolitik*. In January 1967 Bonn finally discarded the Hallstein doctrine by opening diplomatic relations with Romania. With Kiesinger's approval, secret talks began with the USSR on a treaty renouncing the use of force in changing European borders. In May Kiesinger, while still refusing to recognize the East German regime formally, exchanged letters with his East German counterpart, Willi Stoph, on enhancing intra-German people-to-people contacts.

In the elections of September 1969 the Social Democrats advanced from 202 to 224 seats in the Bundestag. Most of the Socialists' gains were at the expense of the Free Democrats who declined to thirty seats. The CDU/CSU alliance was reduced by only three seats to 242. The Free Democrats, however, who held the balance of power, decided to support the SPD. The result was that the Social Democrats, for the first time since the formation of the Federal Republic, were enabled to form a government in which they were the dominant party. Brandt became Chancellor and Walter Scheel, the Free Democrat leader, became Foreign Minister.

The new Chancellor was the most innovative and, after Adenauer, the most authoritative, political leader produced up to that point by the Federal Republic. Born Herbert Frahm, the illegitimate son of a shop assistant in Lübeck, he took the name Willy Brandt as a political *nom de guerre* at the age of nineteen in 1933. An anti-Nazi émigré to Norway and Sweden between 1933 and 1945, he acquired Norwegian citizenship and worked as a journalist while maintaining contact with the German resistance. He infused German politics with a moral passion and an internationalist outlook that differentiated him from the common ruck of provincial and often narrow-minded West German politicians. As mayor of west Berlin during the wall crisis he displayed leadership qualities and a popular touch that made him a plausible, albeit unsuccessful, candidate for the Chancellorship in 1961 and 1965. A mixture of apparent contradictions, he was a populist and yet something of an *Einzelgänger* (lone wolf); a radical Socialist but not an ideologue; a patriot but not a nationalist; a symbol of resistance to Communism who became the architect of reconciliation between the two Germanies.

Following the 1969 elections Brandt felt empowered to pursue a more vigorous policy of opening to the east. By this time nearly 70 per cent of West Germans considered the now Polish lands east of the Oder–Neisse line as irretrievably lost. Brandt immediately signalled a radical change by dropping the West German claim to be the sole authentic German state; he spoke instead of 'two German states in one nation'.[51] In November 1969 he eased a major Soviet anxiety by disavowing any West German interest in nuclear weapons.

The first fruit of the new phase of Brandt's *Ostpolitik*, now unfettered by coalition considerations (since the Free Democrats enthusiastically supported the policy), was a non-aggression treaty between West Germany and the Soviet Union, negotiated by Bahr and signed in August 1970. This gave the Russians what they most craved: acceptance of the territorial status quo, including explicitly the Oder–Neisse line as the border between Poland and East Germany. In December Brandt visited Warsaw and signed an agreement with the Poles, reaffirming recognition of the Oder–Neisse line. The treaty also provided for the resumption of diplomatic relations and for 'repatriation' of ethnic Germans still living in Poland. During his visit Brandt showed a sense of historical propriety by kneeling in homage at the memorial on the site of the former Warsaw ghetto. The gesture was not particularly welcome to his Polish hosts who had just recently passed through an officially sponsored revival of anti-Semitism. Demagogues at home used the incident to try to weaken Brandt. Expellees' organizations condemned the treaties as a betrayal but by this time their influence was waning. More dangerously, Brandt came under attack from Christian Democrat leaders for alleged over-eagerness to make one-sided concessions. And the US National Security Advisor, Henry Kissinger, while not opposing Brandt's policies outright, expressed private concern to President Nixon lest their very success 'create a momentum that may shake Germany's domestic stability and unhinge its international position'.[52]

As his support dwindled, Brandt faced a choice between withdrawing from an exposed position or trying to accelerate the process in order to demonstrate that he could produce beneficial results. Courageously, he chose the latter alternative. He was aided by the favourable international atmosphere of superpower détente. The replacement of Ulbricht as East German leader by the somewhat more flexible Erich Honecker in May 1971 removed one obstacle to a Berlin settlement. After complex negotiations, a four-power agreement on Berlin was signed on 3 September 1971. The wartime allies now accepted the status quo in the city. Although the wall would remain, other aspects of life in Berlin were humanized and the Russians undertook not to impede access from West Germany to west Berlin. Defending the agreement in a newspaper interview, Brandt declared: 'Of course, the Berlin agreements cannot solve all long-term problems for the city. This will only be possible when we have come substantially closer to a European peace order. "The Wall" is still there but it is less impenetrable.'[53] At the end of the year Brandt returned to Oslo to receive the Nobel Peace Prize.

Subsequent agreements between the two Germanies in December 1971 and May 1972 settled outstanding details regarding Berlin and paved the way for ratification of the 1970 treaties with Russia and Poland. Bundestag elections in November 1972 were fought on the issue of *Ostpolitik*. The outcome was a solid endorsement of Brandt's policy. The Social Democrats advanced to the highest percentage of the vote in their history, 46 per cent, overtaking the CDU/CSU for the first time. The restored SPD/FDP coalition was therefore able to proceed in December 1972 to a *Grundlagenvertrag* ('Basic Treaty') with the East Germans, whereby the two German states, while withholding *de jure* recognition from each other, agreed to exchange diplomatic missions and increase cross-border contacts. The Christian Democrats carped but, weakened by internal conflicts between opponents of the treaty, led by Strauss, and a minority of supporters, notably Richard von Weizsäcker, the party cut a poor figure. The Bundestag ratified the treaty in May 1973, opening the way to somewhat more normalized relations between the two Germanies and, for the first time since the 1930s, to a measure of stability in the heart of Europe.

15

Europe in the 1960s

I'd love to turn you on.

*John Lennon and Paul McCartney, London, 1967**

Children, women, and men

In the 1960s, for the first time since 1914, a cohort came of age in Europe that (except in Greece and Hungary) had never known the horrors of war, revolution, or famine. The children of the post-war 'baby boom' were the best-fed, best-educated, healthiest, least sexually repressed, most self-confident generation in European history. A youth cult reigned supreme. It threw overboard deference to convention, tradition, and respect for elders and betters. Western Europe basked in the sun of unprecedented affluence and ease. Eastern Europe groped towards a less repressive form of Communism. Talk of 'convergence' of the two systems was in the air. Men re-examined some of their ingrained prejudices and began to adopt a more egalitarian view of women and of sexual deviants. Capital and corporal punishment disappeared from much of the continent. Even the most conservative of institutions, like the Catholic Church, embraced *aggiornamento* (modernization). As the European imperial powers retreated from their overseas possessions, their societies discarded or modified colonial and racial attitudes of the past. In architecture, literature, music, the arts, fashion, and design, a spirit of freedom and experimentation swept aside congealed styles, canonical standards, and fossilized mental structures. In the overflowing new universities, new subjects, especially the social sciences, replaced the classical curriculum that had changed little since the previous

* From 'A Day in the Life'. The Beatles, *Sergeant Pepper's Lonely Hearts Club Band* (LP album, released June 1967). The song was banned by the BBC on account of this line.

century. Everything seemed possible. Man walked on the moon. Supermarkets gave out green stamps redeemable, when saved up, for hitherto undreamed-of 'rewards'. Working-class people in northern Europe could afford holidays on the Black Sea or the Mediterranean. Yet in the end, as in all ages, the high optimism of youth dashed against the rocks.

The 1960s marked the start of a secular demographic change. European birth rates declined to, or even below, population replacement level. In Czechoslovakia, Hungary, and Bulgaria the fall began in the late 1950s; in the Soviet Union, Poland, and Romania in the early 1960s. In Britain, the number of live births, which peaked in the early 1960s at over a million a year, the highest since the late 1940s, declined to 700,000 by 1975. By the end of the 1960s net reproduction rates in Bulgaria, Hungary, and Romania had fallen below replacement level. The decline was not evenly spread across societies. Some groups, for instance gypsies and Muslims in the Balkans, still maintained disproportionately high birth rates, giving rise to ethno-nationalist concerns among their neighbours.

A number of reasons for the declining birth rate have been proposed: rising levels of women's education, high participation by women in the workforce, a consumerist culture of self-gratification, constricted housing conditions. None of these is fully persuasive. One further reason was undoubtedly the long-term effect of the war. Apart from neutral countries such as Sweden and Switzerland, the demographic shape of much of the continent had been deeply affected by the bloodletting. The impact of the war on the population of the USSR was still visible in the severe imbalances in age distribution and sex ratio recorded in the 1959 census, the first to be conducted there after the war. The shortage of men led to a sharp decline in the proportion of women who were married and in the fertility rate. These trends were particularly felt in the European regions of the USSR, which had been most directly affected by wartime occupation. Government efforts to reverse the trend, for example by honouring 'Heroic Mothers' and issuing 'Motherhood Medals', had no visible effect.

A few countries displayed somewhat different patterns. In France, a post-war marriage boom led, as elsewhere, to a baby boom in the late 1940s (and the other way round too). But it lasted longer there: 846,000 births, a record, were registered in France in 1946 and the number remained above 800,000 every year until 1973. The population grew to 52.7 million by 1975, a gain of nearly one-third since the end of the war and the fastest rate of population growth in modern French history. Not all these children, however, were planned: according to a survey in French maternity hospitals in 1959–62, a third of pregnancies were unwanted.

West Germany too experienced fast population growth—from 49 to 60 million between 1949 and 1970—though much of this was due to immigration. Both Germanies suffered a fertility decline to well below replacement level from the mid-1960s onwards. East Germany, however, with negative net migration, was the only European state apart from Ireland to suffer absolute population decline in the 1960s: between 1955 and 1961 the population of the GDR fell from 17.8 to 17 million, mainly owing to emigration. The construction of the Berlin Wall put a virtual halt to emigration but not to population loss. The net reproduction rate declined from 1.17 in 1964 to 0.73 by 1975 and never again attained population replacement level (a rate of one equals replacement).

The main reason for the decline in fertility was undoubtedly conscious human choice. Across the continent, couples decided to limit the size of their families. They were aided by the newly invented contraceptive pill. In spite of the rigid opposition of the Roman Catholic Church to all forms of birth control, except the so-called 'rhythm method', the pill gained widespread acceptance as the safest and most convenient form of contraception. In 1967 the National Health Service in Britain began prescribing it to unmarried as well as married women. In Catholic and Communist countries its spread was slower. In France provision of the pill was not legalized until passage of the *loi Neuwirth* in 1967, and even then on a restricted basis: only for married women, only by doctor's prescription, and only upon filling-out of complicated forms. In Italy the Fascist-era prohibition on birth-control information was not repealed until 1971. In Ireland the importation, sale, or advertising of any form of contraceptive remained illegal until 1974. In eastern Europe concern over declining birth rates led governments to restrict availability of the pill. The impact of this first 'lifestyle' drug, should therefore not be exaggerated. In 1972 only 6 per cent of French women were taking it. As late as the 1980s, although the great majority of married couples in Europe were using some form of contraception, not a single country recorded a majority of women of reproductive age as relying on the pill. Other devices such as the diaphragm and IUD were popular before the arrival of the pill and continued to be used thereafter, especially after health scares associated with its use. The fertility reduction in much of western Europe in any case antedated large-scale use of the pill, which should therefore be seen as an accelerator rather than an initiator of demographic decline.

Lower fertility was not, as might be imagined, accompanied by growing childlessness. On the contrary, childlessness decreased in most of western Europe (except Germany) between the first and the third quarters of the twentieth century. The fall in number of births was the result not of abstention from bearing children at all but rather of a combination of postponed and reduced childbirth, another indication that it was a matter of conscious decision-making by women, especially given that improved diet was probably leading to heightened biological capacity to conceive.

Illegitimate births, which had fallen in the first half of the century, began to rise again after 1945. Unlike other births, the great majority of these were unplanned. Women, especially where young and poor, had illegitimate children because they lacked the information, means, and legal framework to exercise choice. Already before the First World War at least a third of all women who married in large cities in Germany were pregnant before their weddings. But whereas then illegitimacy was regarded as a social disgrace, in the 1960s there was greater acceptance of sexual activity before marriage and less pressure to marry in haste in order to legitimize offspring. In Sweden 28 per cent of births were illegitimate by 1965. In France in the period 1960–9 55 per cent of women told pollsters they had engaged in intercourse before marriage. This compared with 33 per cent in the 1940s and 1950s. Opinion polls, it seemed, had replaced confessionals, except that most of those talking to them did not seek absolution for what they no longer regarded as sins.

One form of choice that women could now make legally, at least in some places, was abortion. This was not without a struggle, especially in Catholic countries. Unlike Britain, where abortion was legalized in 1968, it remained illegal in Ireland into the new millennium, in Italy until 1978, in Portugal until 1984, and in Spain until 1985; even thereafter the abortion laws in both Portugal and Spain were very restrictive. In France abortions were illegal in the 1960s, although as many as half a million were performed annually and large numbers of women died as a result of botched operations. In 1971 343 prominent Frenchwomen published a *Manifeste des 343* in the left-wing weekly magazine *Le Nouvel Observateur*, in which they publicly stated that each of them had had an abortion. They included the film star Catherine Deneuve and the writers Marguerite Duras and Françoise Sagan. A mass movement developed in favour of legalization. Success was achieved with the passage in 1975 of the *loi Veil*, followed in 1981 by a measure that provided for abortions to be paid for by social security.

The contrast with much of eastern Europe was striking. In the USSR, where abortion was relegalized in 1955, eight million terminations were officially registered annually in the mid-1960s. The decision to permit abortion again seems to have been connected with the general social relaxation of the post-Stalin period. It was also partly a response to popular pressure in the form of very large numbers of illegal abortions. There were more abortions than live births in the Soviet Union throughout the three decades from 1960. Elsewhere in eastern Europe abortion was by far the most common form of birth control until the collapse of Communism. In Romania in 1965 there were four abortions for every one birth. Alarmed at the consequences for the country's population, the government banned abortion except in a limited number of cases, such as incest. The birth rate doubled the following year, then fell back once more as illegal abortionists resumed their trade.

Thanks in part to the larger proportion of births taking place in hospitals, infant mortality rates continued to fall, in many regions below what had, in the inter-war period, been regarded as the 'biological minimum' of around fifty per thousand. In eastern and southern Europe, where the rates were still highest, they fell sharply: in Yugoslavia from 121 per thousand live births in 1950 to 57 per thousand in 1970; in Italy in the same period from 68 to 29 per thousand. Maternal mortality also fell. For the first time in human history, birth was largely shorn of the terror that it would be accompanied or immediately succeeded by death.

Better health meant that the great majority of those born could expect to survive for a complete lifespan. Average life expectancy increased everywhere, in the Soviet Union from forty-seven in 1938–9 to seventy by 1962–3. (This improvement occurred in spite of the fact that Soviet spending on health, 2.8 per cent of GNP in 1968, was far lower proportionately than that of most other European countries.) As fewer children were born and people lived longer, the balance of old and young in the population changed. Paediatric medicine became mainly a matter of prevention of disease while the costs of geriatric care soared. Cleaner public water supplies, an improved diet, and enhanced public health services eradicated diseases that had been scourges of previous generations. New vaccines became widely available: against measles in 1964, mumps in 1967, and rubella in 1969.

The last major polio epidemic in Europe, at Cork in southern Ireland in 1956-7, struck after the Salk vaccine had been developed in the United

States in 1955 but before it had become generally available in Europe. This was the disease that terrified more than any other, perhaps because it attacked children on a seemingly random basis and because it could paralyse for life. The local authorities and the *Cork Examiner*, anxious to prevent a panic that might affect trade and, by causing mass flight, spread the infection further, insisted there was 'no occasion for undue alarm'.[1] Perhaps fifty thousand people were infected, most without realizing it, although only 499 were diagnosed and twenty died.

The nuclear family of the late industrial age, characterized by high levels of female domesticity, low average age of marriage, high marriage and fertility rates, and low divorce and illegitimacy rates, thus began to fray at the edges in much of Europe. Average age of marriage was one exception to the pattern; it fell in western Europe in the 1960s. But it began to rise after 1970 and thereafter reached unprecedented heights. The disintegration of the family correlated in large measure with religion: majority-Protestant and highly secularized countries led the way, Catholic ones followed, and mainly Orthodox south-east Europe occupied the rear.

Whereas divorce rates had remained static in most west European countries in the 1950s, they shot up in the 1960s. One reason was that legal barriers were lowered. Many countries abandoned the concept of the 'marital offence', replacing it with 'no fault' divorce. In England and Wales the number of divorces per annum, already five times as high as in the pre-war period, rose from 25,000 in 1960 to 45,000 in 1968. In France too, in spite of the strictures of the Catholic Church, the rate rose steadily, though until 1975 divorce was granted only in cases of proven adultery or violence. In Italy divorce was forbidden until 1970: in a few thousand cases each year state tribunals granted legal separations; a few hundred church marriages (99 per cent of the total at the time) were terminated after a long and humiliating process of 'annulment'. A campaign spearheaded by the Radical Party finally led to enactment of a divorce law in 1970. In a rearguard action, the Christian Democrats, spurred on by the Vatican, forced a referendum on the issue in 1973: but only 41 per cent of those voting supported repeal of the law. Divorce was commoner in the northern, Protestant countries of Europe than in southern, Catholic ones. In the Soviet Union, the limitations on divorce of the Stalin years were relaxed after 1965 when there was a return to divorce on demand. The divorce rate shot up over the next two decades, becoming the highest in Europe. Male alcoholism was the chief cause, cited in over half of all cases. Elsewhere in eastern Europe, especially in East Germany, divorce rates also rose and in the region as a whole were much higher than in western Europe.

All these changes in the structure of the European family reflected a transformation in relations between the sexes in the 1960s. The feminist movement, so prominent in the United States, at first mobilized rather weakly in Europe. One reason for its subdued nature in western Europe may have been that the welfare state there typically provided a range of rights and benefits not available in the United States. Simone de Beauvoir's *Le deuxième sexe* (1949), later hailed as a great feminist text, was little noticed upon its first publication. The most influential feminist writers in Europe in the 1960s were mainly non-Europeans like the American Betty Friedan and Germaine Greer, an Australian immigrant to Britain. It was not until the late 1960s that a women's liberation movement, strongly influenced by the example of American feminists, emerged in Europe, especially in West Germany, France, Italy, and Britain. The student revolts of 1968 gave feminism a strong impetus. In West Germany young women radicals revolted against their status as 'brides of the revolution' and asserted autonomous rights and demands.

In eastern Europe feminism was much weaker, no doubt because its contemporary American flavour rendered it suspect, also because autonomous socio-political movements could barely function under Communism, and perhaps also because women in Communist countries had already gained, at least on paper, many rights for which the movement elsewhere fought, including equal pay and easy divorce and abortion. A further reason has been suggested. In the west, feminism was in large measure a reaction to the sexual exploitation to which men subjected women in the 1960s as part of the era's valorization of private pleasure. In the prudish and intrusive societies of Communist Europe, where the principle of individual gratification was not embraced to the same extent, the conditions for this kind of feminist revolt barely existed.

Whereas in the early part of the century the women's movement had been largely political, its aims in the 1960s were different. Female suffrage was no longer a significant issue. Women had gained the vote in France and Italy at the end of the Second World War. In Switzerland they did so at the federal level in 1971 but some cantons continued to refuse women suffrage; the last holdout, the tiny, north-eastern half-canton of Appenzell Innerrhoden, yielded in 1990 only after an order from the Federal Supreme Court. The right to vote was merely the first step on the long road to sexual equality. In France, for example, wives until the 1960s were legally analogous to minors, essentially subordinate to their husbands. Until 1965 a married woman had to obtain her husband's permission before going out to work or opening a bank account. A new family law in 1970 recognized spouses as equal but the husband remained legal manager of family property until 1985. Feminists in the 1960s, therefore, aimed at broader legal and social equality which, especially in western Europe, remained lacking in several spheres.

As at the time of the suffragettes, the new generation of feminists encountered hostility on the left only marginally less than on the right. Demands for equal employment opportunities and equal pay and for safeguards against sexual harassment in the workplace were often resisted by male-dominated labour unions, fearful of the effects on their mainly male members. Although article 119 of the Treaty of Rome required 'application of the principle that men and women should receive equal pay for equal work', application was, in fact, withheld for many years. A European Commission report in 1965 stated that not a single member country of the EEC had implemented the article. Although France, which was constitutionally bound by the same principle, supported immediate enforcement, other countries resisted it. Only in the 1970s, as a result of a decision by the European Court of Justice (*Defrenne* vs. *Sabena*, 1976) and enforcement action by the Commission, was the clause at last translated into social reality.

Women still worked outside the home less than men. In Sweden 45 per cent did so in 1961 but in southern Europe the proportion was much lower. In general, the traditional model of female role segregation remained more prevalent in Catholic than in Protestant societies. As peasants moved to the city, women who had previously worked unpaid on family farms tended to leave the labour force. In Italy non-domestic workers declined from a third to a quarter of the adult female population between 1960 and 1973. Although more jobs opened up to women, they continued to concentrate in certain fields regarded as 'women's work': light industries, the lower ranks of office work, and the 'caring professions', including relatively new and rapidly expanding ones such as social work.

In eastern Europe women were much more fully integrated into the workforce. In East Germany over 70 per cent went out to work in the early 1960s. In Hungary the proportion of women who were 'housewives' fell from 64 per cent in 1952 to just 5 per cent thirty years later. This was partly a result of a number of government initiatives and incentives. Work hours were made flexible and childcare was provided at some workplaces. A childcare allowance that was introduced in 1967 enabled women to take up to three years' maternity leave from work. But while more women worked than in western Europe, the sexual barriers to promotion to senior positions were no less formidable: in Hungary in 1970 women constituted only 7 per cent of 'managers and directors', 8 per cent of 'leaders in public administration', and only 2 per cent of 'technical managers, chief engineers, and works managers'.[2]

Although its achievements, when viewed quantitatively, were limited and patchy, the sexual revolution of the 1960s deserves its name. Particularly among the younger generation a decisive change in consciousness worked its way, fitfully, incompletely, but inexorably, through European societies in the course of the rest of the century. The slow speed was partly a consequence of the enduring effects of poor women's education. But in the post-war period sexual inequalities in education decreased in much of the continent. Segregation of girls from boys in separate schools was abolished in eastern Europe under the Communists and declined in western Europe in the 1960s and 1970s. Expansion of secondary and tertiary education particularly benefited females, traditionally excluded from equal opportunity at these levels. In some countries, for example Poland, they came to constitute the majority of students attending the *lyceum* and universities. As women acquired higher qualifications, it became more difficult to discriminate against them in employment.

Another sphere of sexual relations also underwent a drastic change at this time: homosexuality came 'out of the closet' (the phrase, in its restricted meaning, appears to have been imported to Britain from the United States: its first recorded use was by the American-born poet Sylvia Plath, at that time resident in London, in the *London Review* of 16 January 1963). Except in Finland, lesbianism was not illegal anywhere in western Europe but a lengthy struggle was required before male homosexual relations were decriminalized. In this, there was no clear difference between Catholic and Protestant countries, nor between capitalist and Communist ones, nor between northern and southern Europe. Turkey had never had a law against homosexuality. Luxembourg had decriminalized it in 1792, Spain in 1822, Denmark in 1930, and Portugal in 1945. In the Soviet Union, after its recriminalization under Stalin, homosexuality remained illegal until after the fall of Communism. Poland, which had decriminalized homosexual intercourse from the age of fifteen in 1932, went so far as to legalize homosexual prostitution in 1969. In Belgium homosexuality had never been illegal, save under the German occupation. The same was true in the Netherlands where, by the 1960s, homosexuality found broad public acceptance. Amsterdam became 'not only a magic kingdom for hippies but also a Mecca for homosexuals'. In Britain until the 1950s disclosure of male homosexuality was the stuff of political scandal and social tragedy. But a more tolerant attitude was signalled by the report of the Wolfenden Committee in 1957. The Sexual Offences Act of 1968 permitted homosexual acts in private between consenting adults in England and Wales (but not elsewhere in the UK, not in the armed forces, and not below the age of twenty-one). In both Germanies a law enacted in 1871 that prohibited 'coitus-like acts' between men remained on the statute book after the Second World War; it was abolished in East Germany in 1968 and in West Germany in 1969. In France change came more slowly. One by-product of the radical disturbances in France in 1968 was the foundation of a Front homosexuel d'action révolutionnaire: but it was not until 1982 that homosexual conduct became legal, with the age of consent set, as for heterosexuals, at fifteen.

As in all revolutions, the enemies of sexual emancipation seized on the utterances of militants in order to discredit the movement as a whole. Ridicule was poured on those who maintained that the sex of an individual was determined by social pressures rather than biology and could be redefined by personal decision-making. Feminist Marxists who sought to show that discrimination against women was part of a male-hegemonic, gendered, class system often encountered sneers and ribaldry. Extreme lesbians depicted all heterosexual intercourse as rape and proposed the creation of separatist, all-women organizations and societies. A Frankfurt Women's Committee in 1968 issued a leaflet calling for women to wield an axe against male penises.[3] But the women's liberation movement also participated in constructive social action: from the early 1970s onwards it inspired the foundation of battered women's refuges and rape crisis centres, as well as efforts to counter female sexual exploitation and slavery.

The assault on sexual repression inevitably involved a fierce social conflict, both within the state, hitherto its policeman, and within the institution most directly involved in providing an intellectual basis and justification for it: the Church. The ecclesiastical response, as the cases of divorce and abortion illustrated, was primarily one of defensive reaction. But the sexual revolution nevertheless played a major role in the process of spiritual renovation through which European Christianity, in particular the Roman Catholic Church, confronted the challenges posed by an increasingly secular society.

Faith in the secular society

European Christianity at mid-century was in crisis, as a faith and as a social institution. Some sociologists, such as David Martin, contested the view that modern industrial societies were heading down a one-way street of secularization.[4] However, much of Martin's evidence was drawn from outside Europe. Statistical data regarding beliefs in Europe before the 1960s are too fragmentary to permit confident generalizations about whether Europeans were indeed, as many other contemporary observers argued, becoming less God-fearing. Nevertheless, if behaviour is any guide to underlying systems of values, then taking Europe as a whole, particularly its Protestant and urban areas, the decade marks a watershed in twentieth-century religion. The creeping secularization of the continent, observable since the Enlightenment, now gained an overwhelming momentum.

Admittedly, the trend was not universal. In many rural Catholic areas such as those of Ireland, Brittany, southern Italy, and the Basque country, more than 90 per cent of the population in 1960 still attended mass regularly. Sites of Christian pilgrimage in Europe, such as Lourdes in south-west France, Knock in Ireland, and the shrine of the Black Madonna at Częstochowa in Poland, continued to attract millions of visitors a year. Most shrines were very old, some dating back to pre-Christian times, but some continued to be founded in the twentieth century: for example, Fátima in Portugal, site of an alleged Marian apparition in 1917. Christian imagery and faith still suffused the calendar of festivities in much of the continent: Easter week processions, such as those at Seville and Assisi, passion plays, especially the one staged every ten years at Oberammergau in Bavaria, the parade of the *gigantes* in front of the cathedral of Burgos on Corpus Christi Day, the Ascension Friday 'Blood Ride' by thousands of horsemen at Weingarten in Upper Swabia, and the annual offering of live snakes to the relics of San Doménico Abate at Cocullo in the Abruzzi mountains of central Italy. In Hungarian villages the annual *búcsú*, or village fete, was still held on a fixed date annually; it was the major social event of the year, though, in deference to the Communist authorities, its religious content was somewhat diluted.

Most of these examples, however, relate to unmodernized, rural areas of Europe. The churches themselves evidently felt that they were confronted by a new and formidable set of challenges to their doctrinal and institutional authority. Their responses were both theological and evangelical.

Among the most influential European theologians of the post-war period were the German Lutherans Rudolf Bultmann and Paul Tillich. They sought to demythologize the New Testament, to reduce the emphasis on the historical Jesus, and to ground theology in human experience. Tillich was much affected by the Jewish thinker Martin Buber, whose *I and Thou* (1923), 'a philosophic poem',[5] rather than a work of theology, became a best-seller, especially after its publication in English in 1958.[6] Buber's 'dialogic' spirituality appealed to Christians at least as much as Jews. Bultmann, Tillich, and Buber influenced Anglicans such as John Robinson, Bishop of Woolwich, whose *Honest to God* (1963) sold over a million copies in seventeen languages. The book caused a storm in England with its expression of sympathy with 'those . . . who urge that we should do well to give up using the word "God" for a generation'.[7] 'I cannot understand how a man can appear in print claiming to disbelieve everything that he presupposes when he puts on the surplice. I feel it is a form of prostitution,' was the response of the popular religious writer C. S. Lewis.[8]

Theological anti-supernaturalism helped feed debate over the 'death of God'. The term had been used by Hegel and popularized by Nietzsche in *Thus Spake Zarathustra* (1883–5); it was much discussed in the United States in the 1960s and the concept returned to Europe, where it was taken up by radical theologians and by atheists such as the French historian and influential cultural theorist Michel Foucault.

The theologians had a profound effect on the practices as well as the doctrines of the Protestant churches. The World Council of Churches, formed in Amsterdam in 1948 with Protestant and Orthodox members, called for ecumenism and reconciliation among the churches. In 1960 the Archbishop of Canterbury, Geoffrey Fisher, visited Rome for the first encounter between an Anglican Primate and a Roman Pontiff since 1397. The Lutheran and Calvinist churches also set an example in their expressions of remorse for their past commission of the 'sin against God and man' of anti-Semitism.[9] And even before the rise of the women's liberation movement, Lutherans pioneered a new attitude towards women. This was particularly the case in Scandinavia, where, in spite of near-universal formal membership of the state churches, only a small minority still attended services regularly. In 1958 the Swedish Lutherans became the first church in Europe to permit women to take holy orders.

In the Roman Catholic Church much of the pressure for change came from France. The progressive Catholic theologian Jacques Maritain applied Thomist metaphysics to contemporary problems, arriving at a theocentric humanism. He too had long called for ecumenism, freedom from authoritarianism, and a clear break with the deeply ingrained anti-Semitic doctrines of the Church. The horrors of the occupation and the supportive attitude of the greater part of the Church towards the Pétainist regime led after the war to a certain introspection and self-criticism among Catholics. This found expression in the social-religious philosophy of left-Catholic thinkers like Emmanuel Mounier, founder and editor of the journal *Esprit*. The 'worker-priest' movement that started in Paris in 1944 was one outcome. But the experiment aroused controversy between conservative and reformist wings of the Church and was terminated in 1959. Meanwhile, the Jesuit mystic palaeontologist Pierre Teilhard de Chardin attempted a 'mega-synthesis' of Darwinism with Christianity. However, his suggestion that the earth had been born '*par un coup de hasard*' ('by chance')[10] aroused the disapproval of his superiors. His works were placed under a ban until his death in 1955. Thereafter they achieved a strange posthumous vogue. All this ferment, which was not unique to the Gallican Church, was but the prelude to a momentous period of reform in the Church as a whole.

The election in 1958 of Cardinal Angelo Roncalli as successor to Pope Pius XII initiated a cascade of change. John XXIII presented a striking contrast with his predecessor. He gave the impression of a warm-hearted village priest rather than a cold diplomat, a simple-hearted soul rather than a sophisticated casuist. Whereas Pius had too often seemed concerned primarily with the survival of the Church as an institution, John's call for *aggiornamento* reinvigorated its spiritual mission. The new Pope's five-year reign was marked by the sweeping away of a number of Vatican traditions, by a quickening of the pace of ecumenical outreach to other churches, and above all by his decision, announced in January 1959, to summon the first Council of the Church since 1870.

The Second Vatican Council, which opened in October 1962, instituted the most fundamental innovations in Roman Catholic doctrine and practice since the Counter-Reformation. The 2,498 councillors from all countries wrested, for a while, effective control of the business of the Council from the mainly Italian Curia, in itself a remarkable political shift. Vatican II seemed for a time to mark the beginning of the end of the Church's long association with political conservatism in Europe, with refusal to countenance freedom of thought, and with rejection of the democratic ideas of the French Revolution and of 1848. Although John XXIII died in June 1963, the Council continued its work until December 1965 under his more traditional successor, Paul VI. The Council produced sixteen documents whose cumulative effect on the life and doctrine of the Church was little short of revolutionary.

The most profound changes were theological. The 'Dogmatic Constitution of the Church' reformulated Church doctrine with a stress on historical context and the demands of the 'new era'. Growing out of a more universalist and less hierarchical emphasis in theology was a new schema for the government of the Church, according greater authority to the universal college of bishops.

The Council called on all Roman Catholics to work in an ecumenical spirit towards reconciliation with the other churches. In 1964 the Pope met the Ecumenical Patriarch Athenagoras I in Jerusalem and in 1965 the mutual excommunications between Rome and Constantinople, that had sealed the schism between the eastern and western churches in 1054, were lifted. Over the next few years meetings between the Pope and heads of other churches became common occurrences.

The Council affirmed the right of religious liberty for all. In one of its most controversial declarations, issued in its final session in 1965 only after lengthy debate and some watering-down, it stated that 'even though the Jewish authorities and those who followed their lead pressed for the death of Christ, neither all Jews indiscriminately at that time nor Jews today, can be charged with the crimes committed during his passion'.[11] The declaration deplored anti-Semitism and called for dialogue with Jews and other non-Christians.

A further product of Vatican II, less noticed at the time, was a new translation of the Bible into Latin, the *Nova Vulgata*, a version that introduced radical changes into the traditional interpretation of the text (compare, for example, the old and new renderings of Lam. 4: 20).

The crowning achievement of the Council was the Pastoral Constitution on the Church in the Modern World, *Gaudium et spes* (Joy and Hope), promulgated by the Pope in December 1965. An impressive summation of humanistic Catholic social outlook and its practical consequences, this, the Council's lengthiest document, redefined the mission of the Church and of the 'people of God'. As the President of the Commission charged with its drafting stated, it was less a statement of doctrine than 'the Church directing her gaze upon the modern civilization'.[12] It accepted 'the autonomy of earthly affairs' and insisted that 'the Church, by reason of her role and competence, is not identified in any way with the political community nor bound to any political system'. While hardly budging from strict doctrinal certainty on matters such as the indissolubility of marriage, it manifested a readiness for dialogue and a listening rather than a triumphalist attitude.[13]

The decisions of the Council inaugurated a period of turmoil in the Church. Of all the reforms, none, perhaps, hurt the faithful more than change in the liturgy, particularly the use of the vernacular. The Council's sessions themselves were conducted entirely in Latin, without simultaneous translation, in spite of protests by some participants. Latin had been the language of the western Church since the third century when it superseded Greek. The language of the Tridentine mass, established by Pius IV at the Council of Trent in the sixteenth century, had come to be regarded by many of the devout as virtually a holy tongue. The Vatican Council's 'Constitution on the Sacred Liturgy' was conservative in form, but it gave an opening to reformers of which they took full advantage: 'The use of the Latin language . . . is to be preserved in the Latin rites. But since the use of the vernacular, whether in the Mass, the administration of the sacraments, or in other parts of the liturgy, may frequently be of great advantage to the people, wider use may be made of it.'[14] Within a few years, use of the daily spoken language of the locality, instead of being permissible, became obligatory. The liturgical reforms aroused distress and resistance among many who loved the Tridentine mass. Paul VI said: 'This rite has become a symbol, like the white flag of the monarchists after the French Revolution—a symbol of opposition to the Council.'[15] Hostility to liturgical change was particularly pronounced in France, where some traditionalists followed Archbishop Marcel Lefebvre's defiant stance on this and other issues, culminating in 1988 in his excommunication from the Church.

The Church's continued refusal to permit artificial contraception (reaffirmed by Paul VI in his encyclical *Humanae vitae* in 1968), as well as its ban on divorce and on marriage of priests aroused further controversy. In western Europe lay Catholics increasingly ignored the first and second prohibitions. In the Netherlands, where many Catholics, both clergy and laity, demanded much more far-reaching reforms in Church doctrine, fierce disputes broke out over these issues and liberal priests were inclined to wink at the infractions of their flocks. The later years of the pontificate of Paul VI, marked by a slowing of the reformist impulse, disappointed many who had been inspired by Vatican II. The Swiss-born theologian Hans Küng, who had served as an expert consultant ('*peritus*') for the Council, found himself out on a limb in the late 1960s when he questioned the very basis of papal authority. He was eventually stripped of the right to teach as a Catholic theologian. With bitter overstatement, he later recalled: 'The Vatican authorities, like the political police of the Soviet empire, ... [are] in fact above the law.... It is no exaggeration to say that just as the KGB understands itself as "the sword and the shield of the Party" in order to safeguard its rule, so too, according to a statement which he himself makes, Cardinal Ottaviani [a leading Vatican conservative and Pro-Prefect of the Congregation of the Doctrine of the Faith, successor to the Inquisition] understands himself... as "the old *carabiniere* (policeman) of the church".'[16]

Just how far-fetched this comparison was may be gathered from a brief survey of religious life in eastern Europe in this period. In the Soviet Union the 1960s were characterized by renewed official efforts to stamp out, or at least damp down, religion. All religious bodies continued to be controlled by the state, and large numbers of churches, mosques, and synagogues, as well as monasteries and seminaries were closed. The number of Orthodox priests declined from 11,123 to 6,800 between 1959 and 1965. The onslaught encountered some spirited resistance. The country's three million Protestants, mainly Baptists, secretly egged on by western churches and the CIA, persisted in instructing their children in religion and in holding services. The Greek Catholic Church in the western Ukraine also succeeded in maintaining some degree of independence. Jewish religious practice was discouraged and rendered increasingly difficult under Stalin and Khrushchev and all Jewish institutions were subjected to close control by government agents.

Elsewhere in eastern Europe, religious life proceeded with less external interference. Rural areas, in particular, remained devoted to the Church, to the yearly cycle of Church holidays, and to traditional rites of passage, although observance of fast days declined. In Hungary the more relaxed atmosphere after 1956 permitted local initiatives for religious organization. In the village of Tázlár, south-east of Budapest, for example, a new Catholic church was built by voluntary effort, followed in the 1960s by a Reformed chapel. 'Everyone', we are told by an anthropologist who studied the area in the 1970s, 'but a handful of white-collar communist families, has an affiliation to some denomination and is anxious that his children should grow up with the same affiliation.'[17] At the same time, however, church attendance was slowly declining and participation in voluntary religious instruction in the local school fell from 76 per cent in 1957 to under 50 per cent by the mid-1970s.

Poland offered a striking example of religious persistence. The government after 1956 did not dare to attack the Roman Catholic Church directly. Over 70 per cent of the population in the 1960s regularly attended Sunday Mass, nearly the entire population observed the rite of baptism, and most weddings took place in church. More than ever the Church in Poland furnished a symbolic and institutional basis for national collective identity.

At the other extreme, the most militantly anti-religious country in Communist Europe was Albania, which declared itself 'the first atheist state in the world' in 1967.[18] All places of worship were closed and religious practice was proscribed. The head of the autocephalous Albanian Orthodox Church, Archbishop Damianos of Tirana, was sent to prison, where he died in 1973.

New Europeans

Until around 1960 Europe remained a continent of emigration. During the 1950s the net outflow has been estimated as three million. In the 1960s, however, the balance began to alter: about as many people arrived in the continent as left. The change affected mainly western Europe. Communist countries generally made emigration difficult or impossible, particularly for those deemed useful to the economy. There were a few exceptions: Romania, for example, allowed Germans and Jews to leave in a steady trickle in return for capitation payments by West Germany and Israel. After the arrival of Communism, as before, eastern Europe attracted few immigrants. Western Europe, by contrast, received large numbers, including, for the first time since the barbarian invasions of the fifth century, many originating in other continents.

Not all the intercontinental immigrants, however, were ethnic aliens. The end of empire and the antagonism of newly independent nations to their former rulers led to the extrusion of former colonists and members of ethnic and religious minorities from Asia and Africa. Not only *pieds noirs* from Algeria but Italians from Libya, Greeks from Egypt, and Dutch from Indonesia, people whose ancestors had in many cases been settled in those lands for several generations, were expelled and often at the same time expropriated.

Not all migration was intercontinental. France received more immigrants than any other European country in this period (around four million between 1955 and 1974) but after the Algerian influx in 1962 the majority of new arrivals came from elsewhere in Europe, especially the Iberian peninsula and Italy. The creation of the Common Market, with its provision for free movement of labour, led to increased migration between member states. But there was large-scale movement across other borders too. Switzerland, a non-member of the EEC, took in 1.7 million people, mainly from elsewhere in western Europe: relative to its population it was the largest importer of people during the decade. Spain, Portugal, Italy, and Greece were still net exporters. Proportionately the Republic of Ireland was the champion exporter: four hundred thousand people out of its population of only three million left, mainly for Britain, between 1951 and 1960.

Not all immigrants, even after many years of residence, were allowed to become citizens of their countries of settlement. In 1970 3.3 million unnaturalized aliens were living in France (6.5 per cent of the population) and three million in West Germany (4.9 per cent). Many were non-Europeans. The great majority of non-white immigrants to Europe in the 1960s tended to settle in cities, often clustering together in ethnic quasi-ghettos. Their skin colour rendered them vulnerable to discrimination, both in ex-imperial countries, familiar with the 'colour bar', and in others where they were often exotic objects of suspicion and fear. For the first time in modern European history, ethnic hostility within Europe between Europeans and non-Europeans became a major social phenomenon and political issue.

Racial tensions became particularly visible in Britain, in spite of the fact that, throughout the period from 1950 to 1975, more people emigrated than immigrated. Natural increase was well below the European average and, for most of the period, unemployment was at a level where acute labour shortages were felt in some economic sectors. A majority of immigrants in the 1960s were white. But few people in Britain at the time would have recognized any of those facts. On the contrary, the popular conception was that the country was being inundated by a flood of non-white immigrants. Most of the newcomers came from former dependent territories. Of the 1.1 million arrivals during the decade, one-third came from the 'New

Commonwealth', mainly the east and west Indies and east Africa, that is, were black or brown, while a quarter were from the 'Old Commonwealth', that is, were mainly whites (these figures exclude Irish immigration).

What was called at the time 'coloured' immigration to Britain from the former empire had begun on a significant scale in 1948 with the arrival of five hundred West Indians aboard the *Empire Windrush*. They and those who followed them found jobs in the public sector as bus conductors, postmen, railwaymen, and nurses. As their numbers grew so did opposition to their entry. In 1958 the first serious race riots in Britain broke out in Nottingham and in the Notting Hill area of London: mobs of white youths embarked on 'nigger-hunts'. The government had rejected restriction of Commonwealth immigration in the mid-1950s. In the aftermath of the riots it was reluctant to appear to yield to violence. But by 1962 the volume of arrivals and of hostility to immigrants persuaded it to legislate. The 1962 Commonwealth Immigrants Act for the first time limited the right of Commonwealth citizens to settle in Britain. Fuelled by labour shortages, the inflow nevertheless continued: by 1964 there were estimated to be 800,000 non-white immigrants in the country. In 1968 popular feeling against them was given voice by a former Conservative minister, Enoch Powell, in a powerful speech in which he demanded a halt to new immigration and voluntary repatriation of immigrants already in the country. 'Like the Roman,' he warned, 'I see the river Tiber foaming with much blood.' Powell was disowned by the Conservative Party, which he later abandoned, but his message resonated with the public mood. The government had already enacted a law limiting the right of overseas British passport-holders, principally Asians expelled from Kenya and Uganda, to settle in Britain. Later the same year it passed a race relations act banning discrimination in housing, employment, and services. But racial tensions remained high.

The West German economy, with its rapid growth rate, had an even more insatiable demand than the British for labour in this period. Given full employment, the demand could be met only by immigration. The solution, from 1955 onwards, was the so-called *Gastarbeiter* (guest worker) system, whereby workers from southern Europe, especially Italy and Yugoslavia, came to work in West Germany, supposedly on a temporary basis. The drying-up of the influx from East Germany after the erection of the Berlin Wall in 1961 compelled employers to look further afield. In 1961 a *Gastarbeiter* agreement was signed with Turkey. By 1966 there were 1.3 million guest workers in the Federal Republic. The millionth Turk arrived in 1969: he was presented with a television set. Many of the guest workers returned home after a few years. Others stayed and established homes and families in the country. By 1973 there were nearly four million foreign residents, including 2.6 million guest workers, in West Germany.

Not all migration was international. Everywhere the movement from country to city continued, hastened by high rates of industrial growth. Throughout eastern Europe the heavy industrialization of the 1950s led to a large-scale exodus to towns. In the USSR ten million peasants moved to urban areas during the 1960s. The urban/rural ratio changed from 32 : 68 in 1939 to 54 : 46 by 1967. In Poland, however, where most land remained in the hands of small, inefficient, private farmers, the shift was slower. In western Europe it was particularly marked in Italy where the peasantry shrank from 43 per cent of the working population in 1951 to 18 per cent in 1971. There rural–urban migration also involved continued movement from south to north: in the 1950s 1.75 million people, 10 per cent of the population, left the south. Heavy investment in new industries in the south brought only limited numbers of new jobs. In the 1960s a further 2.3 million people moved north. Poverty drove them away from the countryside; relative prosperity welcomed them to the city.

Consumer society

The 1960s were years of almost full employment nearly everywhere in Europe. Behind the bald statistics, the structure of work was changing. In earlier times, when the majority of people lived and worked on the land, the concepts of unemployment and retirement had hardly existed for the rural masses, who worked, often without limitation of sex or age, in accordance with the rhythms of the seasons and the requirements of their crops and livestock. In the urban environment to which ever-growing numbers of Europeans were translating themselves, most were disciplined into working fixed hours for limited periods of their lives. Strong trade unions operating in tight labour markets were able to restrict weekly working hours, expand annual holiday provisions, and, in some cases, negotiate retirement at the age of sixty or even younger. The extension of secondary education and the start of mass higher education meant that the working life of many in the middle class began only in their early twenties. State pension provision and longer life expectancy enabled the poor to leave work with a modicum of security and look forward to lengthy retirements. The 'full employment' society of the 1960s was one in which most people worked fewer hours of the week, fewer days of the year, and fewer years of their lives than ever before.

This was a society in which, for the first time in European history, nearly everyone could read and write. Pockets of illiteracy in the early 1960s were to be found only in a few rural areas of southern Europe: in Portugal more than a third of the population and in southern Italy (including Sicily and Sardinia), 16 per cent were illiterate in 1961, though the latter figure was a significant improvement from the 25 per cent recorded a decade earlier. Most illiterates were now old people, though some groups on the edge of organized society, especially gypsies, remained disengaged from formal educational systems and therefore disproportionately illiterate.

The 1950s and 1960s brought massive expansion in educational provision throughout the continent. Until after the Second World War most children in Europe attended only elementary schools. Even many of those who entered secondary schools did not finish them but left in their early teens to enter employment or further training. A series of educational reforms, such as those in Britain in 1944, in Sweden in 1962, in France in 1963, and in the Netherlands in 1968, aimed at widening access to education and improving its quality. School leaving ages were raised and much larger numbers of children received at least some secondary education. Most countries continued to follow the traditional system of distinguishing in secondary education between the selective *gymnasium/lyceum/lycée/*grammar school, which followed a strictly academic curriculum designed for an intellectual elite, and vocational or technical schools for larger numbers of pupils who would not go forward to university. In Sweden, however, egalitarian social philosophy produced a trend towards non-selective, 'comprehensive' secondary schools. Primary and secondary education throughout the continent was generally free and state-controlled, although private schools, often religious ones, continued to function in some areas of western Europe, especially in England, where expensive, fee-charging 'public' schools remained the favoured reserve of the rich.

The role of the Church in education receded, though only slowly. In Germany, traditional segregation in public schools between Catholics and Protestants gave way in the 1960s to non-denominational schools. In Britain all state schools began the day with an 'act of worship', generally Christian, and religious instruction remained a compulsory part of the curriculum. Educational debates in France were still dominated by the schism between the Church and secularists. Pressure from the Church led in 1959 to the *loi Debré*, whereby private (mainly religious) schools received a number of concessions, including increased state funding.

Higher education greatly expanded in the 1960s. In France the number of university students rose from 150,000 in 1956 to 605,000 in 1968. In Britain, the Robbins report of 1963, recommending expansion of universities, led to the foundation of a number of new institutions, some of which, such as the University of Warwick, attained high distinction. But the universities still catered mainly for the children of the better-off. The Open University, founded by the Labour government in 1969, was an imaginative attempt to democratize higher education by using television for long-distance instruction. Most universities in western Europe were funded mainly by the state and therefore heavily influenced by government policies. Nevertheless, interference with teaching and research was modest in the liberal democracies. In eastern Europe matters were very different. With the single exception of the Catholic University of Lublin, all institutions of higher education in the Communist bloc were state-controlled, Marxism-Leninism was a compulsory part of the curriculum, and the hand of party orthodoxy lay heavy on lecturers and researchers.

The overall growth in education in the 1950s and 1960s failed to narrow the social gap in educational opportunity. Save in a few countries, such as Sweden and the Netherlands, where the educational gap between classes was already small, the middle classes continued to perform significantly better in educational attainment and to gain access much more readily to colleges and universities. Studies of Poland, Czechoslovakia, and Hungary show that there too inequalities in educational opportunity were little affected by government efforts to improve access to education for the urban and rural working classes.[19] In Hungary, for example, school fees were abolished in 1949 and preferential scholarships were provided for children of peasant and proletarian origins. In the 1950s a quota system operated whereby at least half of secondary-school and university students had to come from such backgrounds. Yet the results of such policies were disappointingly meagre. Egalitarian policies were subverted by the application of *protekció* (influence) or outright bribes. People from privileged backgrounds reconstructed their family histories to conceal their class origins. The percentage of children from non-manual backgrounds attending university barely changed. From the 1960s onwards quotas were relaxed and then abolished. Rather than opening space for children from hitherto deprived classes, the Communist system was manipulated by the old middle class and by the 'new class' of bureaucrats to enable their own children to gain privileged access. In East Germany the process was facilitated by defining all offspring of party functionaries as belonging to the working class. The effects on patterns of social mobility in east-central Europe hardly accorded with the regimes' proclaimed social aims. One study in 1972 found 'hard evidence from Czechoslovakia, and it is a fact of common observation in Hungary and Poland, that it is the pre-revolutionary white-collar classes who provide most of today's rich. The old professional classes have probably done less well. Many children of capitalists have come down in the world—and many have not; peasant families continue poor; children of proletarians, the victorious class, have a random relation to the new positions of wealth.'[20] Was it for such a 'random relation' that the children of the revolution had been compelled to make immense sacrifices?

Even if distribution, in east as in west, remained unequal, economic growth nevertheless translated into rapidly improved living standards for most sections of society in both halves of Europe in this decade. Progressive taxation and welfare state measures, as well as full employment, resulted in a general trend towards greater income equality, which was embraced by many governments as a deliberate objective of policy. In Britain it was possible, in 1962, for a leading social commentator to suggest that, in terms of public perceptions, 'the wealthy were a disappearing class.'[21] So too were the very poor. Beggars, a familiar presence in the great European cities between the wars, vanished almost entirely from the streets.

The welfare state reached its highest point in this period of relative affluence. North European countries, notably Sweden and Norway, offered the most generous and comprehensive social payment provisions. By 1965 Portugal was the only west European country that lacked an unemployment insurance scheme. Most Communist countries also had none, since officially no unemployment existed. All European countries had some form of old-age pension scheme, though the size of benefit and the conditions attached varied greatly.

Many governments regarded it as part of their duty of welfare provision to expand public housing, sometimes also to provide incentives for private construction. Housing shortages throughout Europe had been aggravated by the destruction and privations of the war. But it was not until the 1960s that really large-scale expansion and improvement of the housing stock got under way. In the USSR, where the shortage was most acute, Khrushchev forecast in 1961 that it would disappear within a decade. Under his rule the rate of Soviet housing construction doubled. More housing was built during the five years 1956–60 than in the entire period 1918–46. In the 1960s and 1970s the country built on average 2.2 million units a year, an outstanding achievement. The one-room-per-family, communal apartments in which millions of Soviet city-dwellers had lived since the revolution began to be exchanged for small, modern flats. Average space per person increased by the mid-1970s to 8 square metres (10 in Moscow). But the new apartment blocks were drab, shoddily designed, often jerry-built, and, by any standard, grossly overcrowded. Overall, housing conditions were still 'the poorest of any industrialized nation' and in 1974 30 per cent of urban families still shared apartments and an additional 5 per cent (mainly single people) lived in factory hostels.[22] Urban conditions were not much better in east-central and southern Europe. Public housing in those countries was often poorly planned, densely inhabited, and far from workplaces or public amenities. In western Europe large-scale 'slum clearance' operations were set in motion in many run-down urban areas but too often, as in the Gorbals district of Glasgow, the inhuman tower blocks that replaced the old tenements soon degenerated into a more modernized form of squalor.

By 1960 most homes in Britain, West Germany, and Scandinavia boasted an indoor flush toilet and a bath or shower. But this was still not true elsewhere. In France nearly one in five homes had no running water, two in five had running water only in the kitchen, and only 28 per cent had a shower or a bath. In Belgium under half of all dwellings had an indoor toilet and under a quarter had a bath or shower. In the USSR only one-third of urban households had any indoor plumbing at all. Rural conditions were generally far worse than urban. In Hungary 93.5 per cent of the rural population had no modern conveniences; as for the other 6.5 per cent, we are told, the bathroom, like other prestige items, often remained 'a spotless receptacle', either because it could not be heated in winter or because its possessors clung to old habits.[23] In the course of the 1960s and 1970s, however, rapid improvements in such amenities were registered in much of the continent.

In western Europe, especially Britain, the 1960s brought a new stage in the retailing revolution. Self-service supermarkets arrived and their aggressively competitive pricing, particularly in food and household products,

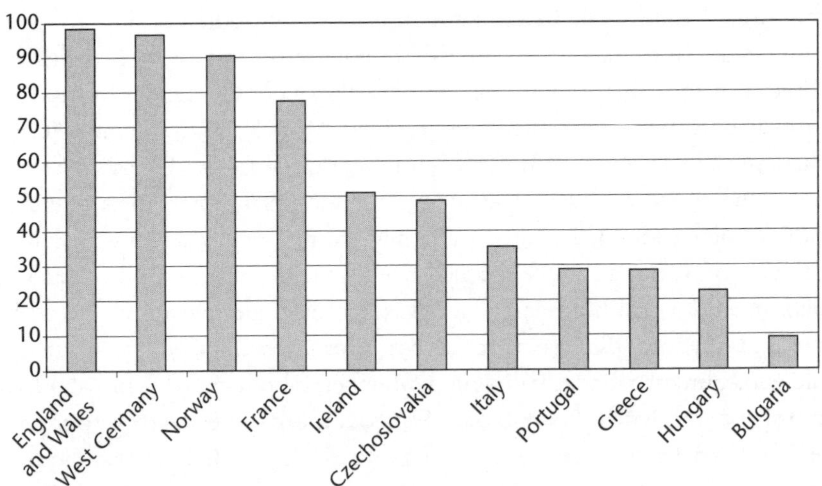

Figure 6. Proportion of dwellings with piped water in selected countries, *c.*1960

Source: UN Economic Commission for Europe, *A Statistical Survey of the Housing Situation in European Countries around 1960* (New York, 1965).

forced many small shops out of business. 'Hire-purchase' (a form of payment over time) became widely used in the sale of durable goods and cars. Credit cards were introduced, although their use at first was not widespread except in Britain. Even in eastern Europe planners began to utilize market research and advertising, consumer goods became more readily available, and women began to be able to indulge tastes for chic fashions and fancy hairstyles.

Cheap ready-made clothing became much more widely available. Distinctions between male and female dress diminished, most strikingly in the leisure attire of young people. Jeans, frowned on for women in the 1950s, became normal casual wear for both sexes. The elastic girdle was displaced by 'control-top' pantyhose. Middle-class men stopped wearing shirts with detachable collars and instead bought 'drip-dry' shirts or, if they were young, informal, American-style, collarless 'T-shirts'. For no very clear reason, most men in cities stopped wearing hats in the 1960s.

Household consumer goods, such as refrigerators, washing-machines, vacuum cleaners, and dishwashers, were becoming standard equipment even in many working-class homes. In France, for example, the proportion of homes with refrigerators rose from 17 per cent in 1957 to nearly 90 per cent by 1974. Automation of the home led to a speed-up in housework.

The average time spent on housework and childcare by a non-employed West German woman declined from 58 hours a week in 1952–4 to 42 hours by 1977. Urban styles and fashions penetrated rural areas: factory-made three-piece suites, convertible sofa-beds, coffee tables, and double beds replaced old-fashioned handmade furniture. In village homes in southern and eastern Europe pictures of saints and 'holy corner' shrines were yielding pride of place to the new household gods: radiograms and televisions.

In western Europe the telephone was gradually becoming standard equipment in most households. In 1969 Sweden had fifty-two telephones for every hundred people, Switzerland had forty-three, and West Germany nineteen; but France still had only fifteen and Portugal seven. In eastern Europe Czechoslovakia led the pack with twelve for every hundred people; the Soviet Union had only four. The installation of a telephone was generally a long-drawn-out affair, often necessitating the deployment of official connections, and invariably involving application, waiting time, allocation of a line, and rental of standardized equipment. Long-distance calls were expensive, overseas ones prohibitively so. Automatic exchanges were spreading but many calls were still connected by operators, usually female. In Communist countries telephone conversations, like almost all forms of communication, were potentially subject to monitoring and were frequently tapped.

Ownership of motor cars was fast extending down the social scale. In the 1950s few working-class families could afford a car. Between 1961 and 1971 ownership doubled in Britain and France and more than quadrupled in Italy. By 1971 most non-Communist countries in Europe had more than twenty cars for every hundred people. But the poorer countries had fewer: Ireland fourteen, Portugal four, and Greece only two. In eastern Europe private car ownership had not spread beyond the ranks of the *nomenklatura*: East Germany had five cars for every hundred inhabitants, Czechoslovakia four, and Romania only one. The Soviet Union had fewer than five private cars for every *thousand* inhabitants. Russian roads remained appalling and inter-urban highways, with a few showcase exceptions such as the 44-hour Moscow–Crimea motorway, were often below the quality of secondary roads in western Europe. In much of the Russian and east European countryside the horse-drawn cart was still the commonest form of wheeled transport. In western Europe fast motorways and comfortable cars made driving something close to a pleasure and the car overtook the train as the favoured form of inter-urban transport. In east and west alike, the increase in vehicles led to an epidemic of deaths on the road. Measured in terms of accidents per vehicle mile travelled, France had the worst rate in western Europe. In West Germany too the casualty rate was grim: over eighteen thousand deaths a year were caused by road accidents and over half a million injured.

As travel by road and air increased, passenger railways and shipping fell into decline in western Europe. Dr Richard Beeching, head of British Railways, became an object of national vilification for seeking to rationalize the system: he closed down half the stations, eliminated service on branch lines amounting to one third of the track, and reduced personnel by 70,000. In eastern Europe railways, which remained cheap, carried most passenger traffic between cities. Most freight in Russia was carried by rail even on short journeys. For want of oil pipelines, a large part of Siberian oil production too was still being transported to European Russia by rail.

Air travel, a rich man's luxury in the 1950s, became the chief mode of long-distance travel in the 1960s. Almost every European country established its state-owned airline. Aircraft manufacturing too was gradually consolidated into 'national champion' companies. The first international commercial jet airliner service in the world was inaugurated in 1951 by the British Overseas Airways Corporation (BOAC), when the British-made de Havilland Comet flew from London to Johannesburg. With five stops, it took 23 hours and 34 minutes. But six crashes, resulting in 99 deaths, ended the commercial career of the plane in 1954. In 1957 air overtook sea in volume of transatlantic passenger traffic. A year later the number of air passengers across the Atlantic exceeded a million for the first time. During the 1960s international air traffic multiplied sixfold. European passenger aircraft manufacturing, however, lagged behind American. The US-made Boeing 707 became the best-selling aircraft of the period and dominated international routes for the next decade. The Soviet Union's first jet airliner, the Tupolev 104, entered service in 1956 but only the Soviet and Czechoslovak airlines bought it and it was grounded in 1960.

Planning for a supersonic airliner began separately in Britain and France in 1956. In 1962 the two governments agreed to join forces and produce the plane together. The project was plagued by rows and budget overshoots. Eventually one billion pounds in development costs had to be written off at the expense of British and French taxpayers. The test flight of the prototype Concorde 001 took place in 1969 but the plane entered commercial service only in 1976. Although initial orders were placed for one hundred aircraft, no more than seven were ever produced. The prohibitive cost of Concorde's operation meant that the only two purchasers were Air France and British Airways. Protests against its loud noise limited the number of airports that would allow it to land. The Soviet supersonic Tupolev 144 entered service in 1977 but faced similar obstacles and was withdrawn a year later. Concorde continued to operate but a crash in 2000 at Charles de Gaulle airport in Paris that killed 113 passengers and crew, grounded it. Although it eventually returned to service, Concorde was finally retired in 2003.

Millions meanwhile travelled on turbo-prop and jet airliners in group charter flights from north-west Europe to 'package holidays' on the Costa Brava and Costa del Sol, the Algarve, and the French and Italian Rivieras. Yugoslavia and Bulgaria too developed major tourist industries. Old-established holiday resorts elsewhere that catered to nearby population centres began to decline. Deauville, Blackpool, Skegness, and Knokke could not compete in sunshine, social *cachet*, or glamour with St Tropez, Ibiza, or Mykonos. Tourism became Greece's most important foreign-currency-earning industry, transforming once placid islands into vulgar pleasure-dromes and polluting the Aegean and Ionian Seas with effluent from aircraft, shipping, and human waste.

The huge expansion of tourism was merely one aspect of the vast increase in leisure industries of all kinds in western Europe, in the 1960s. Fewer babies, shorter work hours, less housework, and higher incomes meant that men and women could afford to spend more time enjoying themselves. One pastime, in particular, outpaced all others and, at any rate in terms of time devoted to it, became the foremost recreational activity of most European adults—if 'activity' is the proper term to use of such a passive form of entertainment as watching television.

By 1960 every major country in Europe had established a television service; the last to do so were Finland and Norway in 1960 and the Republic of Ireland in 1961. The space race adventitiously aided the spread of television through the use of satellites for relaying signals that, because of the curvature of the earth, could not otherwise be transmitted over long distances. In July 1962 the Telstar satellite caused excitement in two continents when it relayed the first television programmes between the United States and Europe. In 1965, the Soviet Union, with its vast land area stretching across eleven time zones, became the first country in the world to employ satellites for domestic programme distribution. By the end of the 1960s the use of satellites for television relays had become almost commonplace. The first colour television service in Europe began in Britain in 1967 (CBS had broadcast in colour in the United States since 1953 but used an inferior system). West Germany and France followed soon after. When Americans walked on the moon in 1969, much of Europe (but no Communist countries except Poland and Romania) watched the event live.

By the end of the decade a television could be found in the great majority of homes in western Europe. In West Germany, for example, ownership grew from only 4 per cent of households in 1956 to 77 per cent by 1970. In eastern Europe television owners were still a minority, although there too the audience grew fast. Czechoslovakia was quickest off the mark and had more televisions per head than France in the 1960s, although with the introduction of colour television the proportion of French viewers leapfrogged over the Czechoslovak.

Television programmes in Communist countries were deadly dull, as even the Soviet Communist Party's Central Committee complained in 1960 and 1964. News bulletins omitted mention of untoward domestic events, such as air crashes or other disasters, and reporting about the west frequently had a crude propaganda edge. But viewers generally ignored political programmes and watched sports, quiz shows, or other light entertainment. Classical music broadcasts were frequent. Popular music, however, presented ideological problems. The director of music on Soviet Central Television warned in 1964 against 'evil influences, banality, decadent moods, naturalism, vulgarity, and erotic lyricism'. He added that dancing shown on television must avoid 'exaggerated twisting of the hips, an unnatural stance with the legs astride, and . . . erotic movements'.[24] Reflecting the prudishness and social conservatism characteristic of all Communist societies in the 1960s, the Czechoslovak President, Antonín Novotný, declared: 'All right, let them dance, but we will not allow these modern dances to degenerate into vulgarisms and thus actually cultivate dark lusts in our people.'[25] East European populations derived much of their knowledge of the west from images in films and on television. In the 1960s such American programmes as *Bonanza* and *Dr Kildare* and the BBC's adaptation of John Galsworthy's *The Forsyte Saga* were imported. But television viewers in some Communist countries were able to form a more realistic view of life on the other side of the Iron Curtain by tuning in to western stations. Finnish television, for example, could be viewed in Estonia. And West German and Austrian television could be received and were widely watched in much of East Germany, although incompatibility of systems hampered reception quality. Dresden was in one of the few areas of East Germany unable to receive West German television; hence its derisive nickname, '*Tal der Ahnungslosen*' ('valley of the clueless').

In western Europe, as in the east, television in these years was mainly state owned but not directly state administered. The most common form of organization was the public corporation, often, as in Britain, financed by licence fees paid by television owners. In West Germany there were independent regional broadcasting organizations and in Belgium separate ones for the Flemish and Walloon populations. Italy, Sweden, and Switzerland had publicly regulated private corporations. In several countries proposals for the introduction of advertising led to political rows. In the Netherlands in 1965 debate over the issue became so acrimonious that it led to the fall of the government. In Britain the BBC maintained a monopoly of television broadcasts on its single channel until the introduction of Independent (commercial) Television (ITV) in 1955. No advertisements were permitted on the BBC and the prevalent tone was one of stuffy respectability. ITV's lighter, more populist approach immediately attracted a huge following. Within two years the BBC commanded only a 28 per cent audience share. Under Sir Hugh Carleton-Greene, Director General from 1960 to 1969, however, the BBC, while continuing to resist commercialization, transformed itself from the staid 'Auntie' of the nation into a more adventurous reflector and propagator of new cultural trends. By the end of the decade almost all other European television systems, except those of Scandinavia and the Vatican, carried advertisements. Strangely, all the Communist countries' services except Albania's did so too, although mainly for state-produced goods.

Whereas the British and West German broadcasting organizations were relatively balanced in their political coverage and only rarely succumbed to governmental pressures, the same was not true of their counterparts in some other west European countries. In Italy until 1975 the state-owned monopoly, RAI, operated mainly in the interest of the ruling Christian Democrat Party. Thereafter a carve-up was agreed between the two main coalition parties: RAI-TV 1 was controlled by the Christian Democrats and RAI-TV 2 by the Socialists. In France there was strong criticism of government control of the political content of broadcasting, particularly during the Algerian war. In an effort to meet this, the government created the Office de Radiodiffusion-Télévision Française (ORTF) in 1964. It was supposed to be an independent public institution, similar to the BBC.

Complaints nevertheless continued and the responses were not always wholly reassuring. In 1965, for example, the Minister of Information, Alain Peyrefitte, explained: 'In ordinary times it is not reasonable that the opposition express itself as often as the Government. The Government has something to say, since it manages the nation's affairs. The opposition can only criticise.'[26]

Cinema attendance declined as television ownership ballooned. In France the number of tickets sold nearly halved between 1960 and 1970. European film-making nevertheless flourished in the 1960s. In Britain a stream of socially realistic films depicted working-class life: Karel Reisz's *Saturday Night and Sunday Morning* (1960), Lindsay Anderson's *This Sporting Life* (1963), and John Schlesinger's *Billy Liar* (1963). In spite of its artistic achievements, the British film industry, unlike those of many other European countries, enjoyed no government subsidy or protection. By the end of the decade the Hollywood invasion had swamped and destroyed most of what was left of British film production. In France, on the other hand, de Gaulle's Culture Minister, André Malraux, instituted the system of *avance sur recettes*, whereby a proportion of all cinema ticket sales was returned to film-makers. The French industry weathered transatlantic competition much better. The 'new wave' directors or 'auteurs' Jean-Luc Godard (*A bout de souffle*, 1959, and *Une femme est une femme*, 1961) and François Truffaut (*Jules et Jim*, 1962) raised cinema to the most influential art form of the decade. In Italy Federico Fellini (*La dolce vita*, 1959, and *8½*, 1963) and Michelangelo Antonioni (*La notte*, 1961, and *Blowup*, 1966) moved beyond realism to explore the limits of representation and expression. In this decade too the German film industry burst in new vitality under the aegis of directors like Rainer Werner Fassbinder and Werner Herzog. But the most enigmatic, also the most influential, director of the late 1950s and 1960s was the Swede Ingmar Bergman. His haunting, allusive, allegorical tales, such as *The Seventh Seal* (1956), dwelt on the problem of 'God's silence' (Bergman was the son of a Lutheran pastor) and penetrated to the heart of painful human relationships with an uncompromising and troubling directness.

Even the ideological straitjacket constricting Soviet film loosened a bit. Joseph Heifitz's charming *The Lady with the Lapdog* (1960), based on the Chekhov story, abstained from any genuflection towards 'socialist realism'. More adventurous was Andrei Tarkovsky's *Andrei Rublev* (1965). Based on the story of a fifteenth-century monkish ikon-painter, it flouted most of the rules of official cinematography and was banned. Released in Paris in 1969 to great acclaim, it later received restricted showings in the USSR. Like many other Soviet creative artists, Tarkovsky felt crushed by such official interference: he emigrated and died in Paris in 1986. In Russia the majority of films shown tended to be domestic productions or imports from other Communist countries. In the satellite states ideological controls were somewhat more relaxed. Directors like the Pole Andrzej Wajda (*Ashes and Diamonds*, 1958), the Czechs Jiří Menzel (*Closely Observed Trains*, 1966) and Miloš Forman (*The Firemen's Ball*, 1967), and the Hungarian Miklós Jancsó (*The Round-up*, 1965) had greater success in stretching the limits of official complaisance.

But European film's most creative decade was also its swansong. It would take another generation and the advent of new technology before it could begin an uncertain revival.

Contrary to some forecasts, the arrival of television did not similarly hurt radio. Almost every country developed its own interminable, family-centred radio soap opera: in Britain *The Archers*, 'an everyday story of countryfolk'; in Hungary the Szabós, 'a collection of hardworking but not perfect people'; in Poland the Matysiaks, 'the longest-running radio soap opera in the world' (actually *The Archers* started earliest, in 1951; all three were still being broadcast in the next millennium). Although peak-time evening audiences fell, sound broadcasting enjoyed something of a renaissance, partly thanks to the invention of the transistor. Whereas televisions were large, immobile objects, occupying pride of place in sitting-rooms, small portable transistor radios, widely available at cheap prices, could be carried around and heard anywhere. They became a favourite of children and teenagers, who tuned in, sometimes under the sheets after 'lights-out', to commercial popular music stations such as Radio Luxemburg, Radio Monte Carlo, or the 'pirate' station aboard a ship in the North Sea, Radio Caroline. The craze for these stations fed the popular music boom of the 1960s and forced broadcasters such as the BBC and ORTF to devote whole channels to popular music.

The USSR in the 1960s still sought to limit the number of 'over the air' radio sets; as late as 1972 half of all radios in the country were 'wired'. Of course, these could not normally receive the American propaganda stations, Radio Liberty and Radio Free Europe, broadcasting to the east from transmitters in central Europe. Such stations, as well as the Voice of America and the BBC, were often jammed by the Russian and other east European governments to prevent reception even by 'over the air' sets.

In east and west alike, television and radio united mass audiences for public events, mass entertainment, and sport. The BBC's broadcast of the coronation of Queen Elizabeth II in 1953 was the most ambitious outside broadcast undertaken by television up to that time. The annual 'Miss World' contest, inspired by the American 'beauty pageants', was broadcast from 1959 by the BBC. It won record international audiences, though it came to be denounced by feminists in the late 1960s as sexist exploitation. Even some eastern bloc states ultimately succumbed to its lure. Mass culture attained an 'ecstatic experience of music and nationalism' in the Eurovision Song Contest, initiated in 1956.[27] By 1965 eighteen countries, including Communist Yugoslavia, competed, watched by over two hundred million people. The breathtaking climax of the 1966 football World Cup final between Germany and England (the winner in extra time), attracted one of the largest audiences in sporting history.

Popular entertainment crossed borders and permeated cultures. European television networks tended to buy expensively produced, fast-paced, American programmes rather than one another's products. Legal dramas such as *Perry Mason* and *The Defenders* and musical performers such as Perry Como and Liberace won audiences throughout Europe that few European entertainers could match. France was the country most resistant to what guardians of all things Gallic saw as an Anglo-Saxon invasion. But official quotas on the importation of American television programmes and films could not suppress demand for them. In Yugoslavia the American television series *Peyton Place* was broadcast for two years before it was withdrawn on the ground that it fostered 'petit bourgeois values'.[28]

Thanks partly to television, a new youth culture, born in Britain, spread throughout the continent. Its most prominent exponents were, in popular music the Beatles and the Rolling Stones, in photography David Bailey, in hairdressing Vidal Sassoon, and in fashion the designers Vivienne Westwood and Mary Quant. The nameless mannequin was transformed into the celebrity super-model: among the first were Jean Shrimpton, popularizer of the mini-skirt, and the 6½ stone (91 lb/40.2 kg) waif 'Twiggy' (Lesley Hornby)—'an x-ray, not a picture', as the cultural critic Marshall McLuhan called her. The use of illegal, hallucinogenic drugs, especially marijuana, confined before the 1960s to fringe groups, became widespread among young people.

Why did Britain lead the way? One reason may have been the abolition of compulsory military service, which still prevailed in almost all other

European countries. The consequent lack of discipline or deference in the youth generation in Britain was new and infectious. Another reason was that English was by now the most commonly understood second language on the continent.

The 'mop' hairstyles of the Beatles and the ultra-short mini-skirts of Carnaby Street were replicated across the continent, even behind the Iron Curtain. In Hungary *galeri* (hooligans), clad in *csöves* (drainpipes), akin to the 'mods and rockers' of 1950s Britain, became a major object of police concern. They were accused of forming gangs, committing petty crimes, and 'entertain[ing] themselves utterly freely, without restraint, according to their own tastes and ideas'.[29] Some identified with western 'hippies'. They enjoyed the music of the guitarist Béla Radics whose band, Sakk-Matt, held a beat mass in memory of Rolling Stones guitarist Brian Jones after his death in 1969. The East German regime, particularly allergic to western cultural influences, denounced the 'twist' as 'NATO music' and condemned western jazz and rock and roll as 'the culture of apes'.[30] Russia too had its hooligans: *stiliagi* raised hackles among the ideologically correct on account of their interest in western fads and fashions and their predilection for chewing-gum.

Vladimir Vysotsky, a much-loved actor, poet, and troubadour, likened to Georges Brassens in France or Bob Dylan in the United States, became the grainy, unofficial voice of his generation. His songs were unpublished in the USSR in his lifetime but, distributed on *magnitizdat* (unofficial recordings), they became wildly popular. One of the notable differences between the USSR and the west was the virtual absence in Russia, even in Moscow and Leningrad, of the evening entertainment culture that flourished in western Europe. Apart from high cultural events such as ballet, theatre and classical music concerts, there were few restaurants, cafés, bars, dance-halls, or night-clubs. Since there was almost nowhere to go, most Russians stayed at home in the evening. Nor, until the late 1960s, were most of them able to watch television: in 1960 there were still only 4.8 million sets in the country. The better educated read; the rest, at any rate the men, drank. No official figures for alcohol consumption were issued, but informed estimates suggested that the USSR was the largest consumer per head of distilled spirits in the world. Thus Russia became one of the best-read and remained one of the most alcoholic societies in Europe.

In the satellite states Poland headed the league table in consumption of spirits, Czechoslovakia in beer, and Hungary in wine. In western Europe alcohol consumption appeared to be in decline. In 1968 the British drank an estimated 21 gallons of beer per head, compared with 28 in 1909. Belgian consumption fell from 49 gallons in 1905 to 30. The French downed 25 gallons of wine per head as against 34 in 1905. These apparent declines, however, masked other changes. Britons now drank more wine, and Frenchmen more beer, so that total alcoholic intake probably remained roughly comparable with the earlier period. The striking difference was not in level of consumption but in social attitudes. The temperance movement had disintegrated. Religious objection to drink, strong in many Protestant areas of Europe in the early part of the century, had greatly diminished. Alcoholism, once regarded as a moral failing and a sign of lack of character, was now widely viewed as a disease.

Consumption of the other socially accepted drug of the time, tobacco, reached a peak in the 1960s. Evidence of the link between cigarette smoking and lung cancer, first discovered by Richard Doll, an Oxford medical research scientist, and published in 1960, led to a short-lived dip in tobacco sales. It was to be another generation before smoking became socially unacceptable in parts of Europe.

In the capital cities of east-central Europe a dim residue of the animated cultural life of the inter-war years endured. Something of a theatrical renaissance occurred in Prague, although the plays of many of Czechoslovakia's foremost playwrights could not be performed there, save for a brief period of liberalization in 1968. The tradition of political satire in cabarets had not vanished altogether from Berlin even under the Ulbricht regime. The dissident Marxist singer Wolf Biermann won a huge following in East Germany with his subversive ballads. His work was banned and denounced as 'toilet-stall poetry'.[31] He became a hit in West Germany too and, upon being allowed to visit Cologne in 1976, found that his East German citizenship had been revoked.

In western Europe the growth of what conservative critics called 'permissiveness' in sexual attitudes and in the arts led to a relaxation of censorship in several spheres. A significant milestone in cultural history was the court case in London in 1960 in which Penguin Books, publishers of D. H. Lawrence's *Lady Chatterley's Lover*, vindicated their right to issue the work in unexpurgated form. On the English stage, the iconoclastic and sometimes absurdist spirit represented by playwrights such as John Osborne, Samuel Beckett, and Joe Orton, by directors such as Peter Brook, and by the critic Kenneth Tynan, led in 1968 to the Lord Chamberlain, the theatrical censor, being almost literally laughed off the stage. Film censorship in Britain, mainly on grounds of sex or violence, was considerably relaxed in the 1960s. In France, on the other hand, it was strictly enforced but primarily political. Films dealing with the Algerian war, including Godard's *Le Petit Soldat* (1960) and Gillo Pontecorvo's *La Bataille d'Alger* (1966), were banned for several years. Not until the 1970s was French film censorship reformed and, save for protection of minors, administered less restrictively. Spanish film censorship was even stricter than French (*Casablanca* and *La dolce vita* were among the films banned). In the course of the 1960s, however, as the Franco regime cautiously opened to the rest of the world, pre-publication scrutiny of books was abolished and newspapers and film-makers were given more breathing space. In Greece right-wing politicians and the Orthodox Church enforced censorship even of some classical writers: a presentation of Aristophanes' *The Birds* in Athens was banned repeatedly in the course of the 1960s on the ground that 'some of its scenes were presented in such a way as to offend the religious sensibilities of the people'.[32]

The Taganka Theatre in Moscow, opened in April 1964 by the director Yury Lyubimov, sought, like its Athens equivalent, to fulfil the age-old function of drama by conveying to its audience uncomfortable and taboo-breaching truths. In 1968 the play *Alive*, based on a short story by Boris Mozhayev and depicting a cunning peasant's struggle against the collective farm system, was banned after the Culture Minister, Yekaterina Furtseva, interrupted a rehearsal by shouting 'Does this theatre have a party cell in it or doesn't it?' Wasn't he ashamed to be participating in such a 'dreadful exhibition', she asked one of the actors.[33] Lyubimov was old enough to have known the work of the great Russian directors of the early twentieth century, Stanislavsky and Meyerhold. He stuck it out until 1984 but was then expelled from the USSR (he survived to return to his homeland and see the play performed at the Taganka in 1989).

The cultural life of western Europe was enormously enriched by the arrival of creative and performing artists in flight from the east. After his 'leap for freedom' in 1961, Nureyev performed at Covent Garden with Margot Fonteyn in one of the most celebrated balletic partnerships of the century. Such defections were more than just a cultural drain. Each one advertised the Soviet Union as a country that nurtured but then stifled artistic sensibility and creativity. The Soviet system's failure, both at home and abroad, to overcome this stultifying cultural conservatism contributed, in the late 1960s, to a renewed moral and political crisis in Communist Europe.

16

Strife in Communist Europe 1964–1985

If you have to scream, please *do it quietly (the walls have*
ears), if you have to make love,
please *turn out the lights*

*Stanisław Barańczak, Poznań, 1980**

Brezhnev's Russia

In the mid-1960s the position of the Soviet Union as one of the two superpowers seemed unassailable. Notwithstanding the furious hostility of Maoist China and the flea-like irritation of Hoxha's Albania, Moscow's pre-eminence in the world Communist movement seemed secure. In the newly independent countries of Africa and Asia, Soviet support for national liberation movements assured it of new allies and placed it on the crest of the historical wave of the moment. Some analysts, taking Soviet statistics at face value, projected that the USSR would overtake the United States as the world's leading economy within a generation. Yet behind the façade, the Soviet system after Khrushchev was a decrepit giant, slow to adjust to economic and social challenges and lacking capacity for revitalization.

Khrushchev was succeeded by a 'collective leadership' headed by Leonid Brezhnev as First Secretary and Alexei Kosygin as Prime Minister. By comparison with their erratic predecessor, both were safe choices, grey men with little political vision beyond maintenance of the status quo. As after the death of

* From 'If you Have to Scream, *Please* Do It Quietly', translated from the Polish by Frank Kujawinski. Czesław Miłosz, ed., *Postwar Polish Poetry*, Berkeley, 1983, 184.

Stalin, 'collective leadership' soon degenerated into dominance by one man. Brezhnev, who secured his position as paramount leader by 1966, offered the country a measure of stability and predictability. Stalin was partially rehabilitated but there was no return to mass terror. The prison camp system continued to be wound down, though not eliminated. Troublesome dissidents were no longer shot; they were diagnosed as mentally ill and placed in lunatic asylums. The practice became so common and notorious that the reputation of the entire Soviet psychiatric profession was compromised and in 1983 Soviet psychiatrists were forced out of the World Psychiatric Association.

Brezhnev's eighteen years in power were characterized by corruption, clientelism, and reinforcement of the privileges of the *nomenklatura*. He promoted family members, surrounded himself with cronies, and awarded himself a chestful of medals. Unlike the rest of Soviet society, members of the elite could obtain or at least aspire to some of the sweets of Soviet life: decent housing, luxury cars, high-quality medical care, access to special canteens (as at the Soviet Academy of Sciences) and to foreign-currency *beryozka* (literally 'silver birch') stores, in which they could buy imported goods unavailable to the general public. Many also acquired a dacha of 'villa' standard, rather than the miserable hutted allotment that was the most that ordinary people could aspire to.

Soviet economic growth declined from around 4 per cent per annum in the late 1960s to about 1 per cent a decade later (the exact figures are still debated). Defence occupied a growing proportion of national income. In spite of the country's much-publicized successes in space, technological innovation was much slower than in capitalist countries. The USSR lagged far behind the United States and Japan in the development and utilization of computers. Industrial equipment became steadily more obsolete and productivity remained low. Protectionist trade policies feather-bedded loss-making enterprises. The 'black' and 'grey' markets, especially in home-brewed alcohol and pilfered state property, increased according to most estimates to at least 10 per cent of GNP. Recognizing that some structural changes were required, the government embarked on half-hearted economic reforms. Some foreign investment was permitted, notably the establishment of a large Fiat motor-car plant on the Volga. Managers of enterprises were accorded a little more room for independent decision-making. Some interest was shown in 'scientific' management techniques. And a certain amount of labour flexibility was promoted. None of this had much effect.

The Soviet oil industry became enormously important to the economy as a whole and, according to some accounts, alone prevented the collapse of the Soviet Union for more than a decade. The country enjoyed an enormous windfall with the rapid increases in the world price of oil and natural gas in the 1970s. Thanks to the discovery of large new oilfields in Siberia, the USSR in 1974 became again the world's largest oil producer, surpassing the United States. At this time the USSR was the only major industrial power wholly self-sufficient in oil. With the development of natural gas exports to western Europe, the country also became the world's largest energy exporter. Between 1973 and 1985 80 per cent of the USSR's entire hard-currency earnings came from energy exports. The east European satellites were supplied with oil from the Volga–Urals through the Comecon pipeline, opened in 1964. But the petroleum industry was ill-equipped, old-fashioned, and wasteful in its production methods. The opportunities offered by the oil bonanza were squandered. Internal energy prices were kept low and little was invested in new exploration and technology. Much of the blame has been laid at the door of the 'perversity of the Soviet incentive system' that, for example, rewarded oil drillers according to metres drilled rather than oil discovered.[1] In spite of the Soviet Union's large reserves, oil production started to decline in the mid-1980s.

Consumer goods became more readily available in the 1960s and 1970s but the quality of Soviet manufacturing was shoddy, choice was limited, and queues remained long. The waiting period for new housing, a state monopoly (three-quarters of urban housing was publicly owned and officials controlled allocation of most of the rest), could often be ten years. Just obtaining a place on the waiting list was a bureaucratic nightmare. A car cost four times the average annual salary of an industrial worker but even if the money were to hand, it was virtually impossible to obtain because of the long waiting list. Once acquired, a car was in any case of use only in or near urban areas: inter-urban roads were poorly engineered and abounded with potholes.

Three areas of vulnerability in the Soviet system became more visible under Brezhnev: agriculture, the nationalities question, and the political awakening of part of the Russian intelligentsia. State-owned agriculture, a flagship sector for the Soviets ever since collectivization, proved to be an expensive embarrassment for the regime. Like the USA and the EEC, the USSR allocated massive sums in subsidies to prop up the agricultural economy. Heavy investment was directed to agricultural modernization and some incentives were introduced. Output increased but overall Soviet agricultural yields were lower than those of any European country except Romania. Permission for peasants to cultivate private plots was expanded. These became important to the peasant economy both as sources of food and as supply points for a burgeoning private market. Although covering only 3 per cent of the cultivated area of the USSR, they produced a third of all livestock products and a tenth of all crops in the late 1970s. One-third of the income of the typical peasant family was derived from the sale of produce from such plots. But the country's overall performance in agricultural production was unimpressive. The USSR's chronic dependence on imported grain contrasted uncomfortably with late Tsarist Russia, which had been a heavy exporter of grain to other parts of Europe. In the late Brezhnev years the country was importing a quarter of all its grain needs and was also a large net importer of meat.

Mainly because of the low Russian birth rate by comparison with those of most other Soviet nationalities, particularly those of Asia, the share of Russians in the USSR's population declined sharply in these years, from about 54 per cent in 1966 to near parity two decades later. About 15 per cent of Russians (around twenty million people) lived outside Russia in the 1960s. Another ten million lived in non-Russian nationality units of the Russian Federation. Russians were the country's most urbanized nationality, apart from the Jews, accounting for two-thirds of the USSR's urban population. Although 'union nationalities' were given a larger share of high positions in the governments of union republics in these years, Russians remained the politically dominant ethnic group. Average incomes in the Russian Federation remained higher than anywhere else in the USSR except for the Baltic republics. Although overtly nationalist opposition to Russian domination was minimal, ethnic resentments simmered near the surface in the Baltic republics, west Ukraine, the Caucasus (where Georgians and Armenians were allowed some room for expression of national distinctiveness), and the Muslim regions of Central Asia. At the same time, national passions were stirring within Russia itself. Brezhnev showed some sensitivity in his handling of national issues but these loomed steadily larger under his rule and one in particular became a serious nuisance to the government.

The Jewish question, in one sense a nationality issue, remained *sui generis*. Although they constituted not much more than 1 per cent of the Soviet population, the two million Jews were, despite persistent discrimination in admission to universities, the best-educated national group in the USSR, and an indispensable part of the technocratic elite. In 1970, 6.9 per cent of all scientific and academic workers in the country were Jews and in the upper reaches of some fields, particularly physics, mathematics, and medicine, the percentage was even higher. Most Jews no longer took much interest in Yiddish culture or Jewish religious practice. The victory of Israel in the 1967 war and the simultaneous breach in relations between the USSR and Israel nevertheless marked the beginning of a resurgence of Jewish national feeling in the Soviet Union that led in the following decade to serious political and diplomatic complications for the Soviet government. In early 1971 a group of Soviet Jews held an unprecedented public demonstration outside the Supreme Soviet building to demand the right of emigration. Partly as an internal safety valve, partly to meet outside, mainly American, pressure that endangered détente, the Soviet government decided in 1971 to permit limited Jewish emigration to Israel. In the course of the 1970s more than a quarter of a million Jews departed, though many 'dropped out' en route and headed to the United States or Canada. The concession failed to solve the old problems while stirring up new ones. The more Jews left, the more applied to leave; other Soviet citizens, seeing that Jews could achieve results by causing a fuss, began to wonder whether they might do the same.

In the cultural sphere, Brezhnev opted for a less elastic policy but with no happier results. In October 1966 the authorities issued a revised law, forbidding dissemination of material hostile to the state. Rather than damping down intellectual dissent, the new law aroused more. Two writers, Andrei Sinyavsky and Yuly Daniel, were tried on charges of illegally publishing anti-Soviet works in the west and were sentenced to long terms in the labour camps. Their cases evoked strong criticism in the west. In 1967 new arrests of intellectuals led to public protests by well-known writers and statements signed by more than four hundred intellectuals. *Chronicle of Current Events*, a dissident journal recording abuses of human rights and protests against them, began appearing in 1968. It circulated as *samizdat* (a term denoting underground publications, generally typed or cyclostyled and secretly distributed) for several years, forming a point of contact for human rights campaigners. Members of the intellectual opposition, like their forebears a century earlier, were only a narrow segment of urban society and by no means represented the country as a whole. But they included some illustrious names and their persistence and ingenuity made it impossible for the government to ignore them.

Two cases exemplified the Brezhnev regime's difficulties in dealing with critics and the varied methods it used to try to damp down dissidence. Each became a cause célèbre. And each gravely damaged the internal and international prestige of the Soviet government.

The first was that of Alexander Solzhenitsyn, who fell out of favour after Khrushchev's fall and was not published in the USSR after 1966. His critique of the entire Soviet system sharpened in his novels *Cancer Ward* and *The First Circle*. Both were first published in 1968 in the west (so-called *tamizdat*, literally 'published over there') and circulated in *samizdat* in Russia. For a while Solzhenitsyn's international fame sheltered him from attack but in late 1969 the Soviet Writers' Union expelled him from membership. He stood accused of allowing his works to be used as part of a 'campaign of slander against our country'.[2] Seventy members of the Union protested as did three hundred other Soviet intellectuals as well as many foreign Communists. A few months later Solzhenitsyn was awarded the Nobel Prize for Literature. As in the case of Pasternak in 1958, the award roused the ire of Soviet officialdom. The Writers' Union condemned the Nobel Committee's decision as 'an unworthy game . . . dictated by speculative political considerations'.[3] Then came *August 1914*, the first part of *The Gulag Archipelago*, a projected multi-volume, semi-fictional history of the Russian Revolution portrayed from an uncompromisingly anti-Communist viewpoint. With its unsparing 'history of our sewage disposal system', it was a shattering onslaught against the very foundations of the Soviet system. Solzhenitsyn recognized that publication would render his continued freedom to work in Russia highly improbable and he had therefore suppressed the book for several years. But after a copy was seized by the KGB he decided to authorize publication in the west in 1973. The following year the Soviet government finally lost patience. He was arbitrarily deprived of his Soviet citizenship and bundled onto a plane to Frankfurt. In exile Solzhenitsyn's bitter enmity to Communism and his distaste for the meretricious commercial culture of the west accentuated his idiosyncratic neo-Slavophile position. But if the Soviets thought, by expelling Solzhenitsyn, to neuter or isolate him, they gravely miscalculated. From his eyrie in Vermont he hurled imprecations against the false gods in the Kremlin—'the quintessence of dynamic and implacable evil'.[4]

The second case was that of Andrei Sakharov, father of Russia's hydrogen bomb. Sakharov's work in nuclear physics had elevated him to the apex of the Soviet scientific establishment at an unusually young age: he was elected to the Soviet Academy of Sciences in 1953, at the age of thirty-two. During the early part of his career his behaviour was generally conformist, although he expressed some undoctrinaire views in the late 1950s. By 1962 he had formed the view that nuclear bomb testing in the atmosphere was 'a crime against humanity' and, after the fall of Khrushchev, he moved towards open dissent.[5] In 1968 he published in *samizdat* a long statement entitled *Reflections on Progress, Peaceful Coexistence, and Intellectual Freedom*. In this he argued for the possibility and desirability of convergence of the capitalist and Soviet systems and called for an open, pluralistic society in the USSR. When the essay was published abroad and extracts were broadcast back to Russia it created a great stir and Sakharov was invited to sign a declaration that the published text was fraudulent. He refused. Two years later he was one of three founders of a Committee for Human Rights and thereafter he led a small group of intellectuals who repeatedly denounced the government's violations of rights. In 1973 he convened a press conference at which he described the Soviet Union as 'one big concentration camp'.[6] His fellow academicians were persuaded to sign statements denouncing him. When he was awarded the Nobel Peace Prize in 1975, the government's reaction, as in the case of Solzhenitsyn, was open fury. He was refused permission to travel to Oslo to accept the prize and called a 'Judas'. The KGB chief, Andropov, at a meeting of the security agency's Collegium, denounced him as public enemy number one.[7] In January 1980 he was arrested and sent to internal exile in Gorky (formerly Nizhny Novgorod), 400 kilometres east of Moscow. Notwithstanding the government's attempts to cut off his contacts with the outside world, he managed to smuggle out political statements. When he went on hunger strike in 1985 he was subjected to forcible feeding. His fate aroused international protests and further discredited the Soviet regime.

Each of these cases showed the inability of the state to achieve a satisfactory modus vivendi with crucial groups in Soviet society—the cultural intelligentsia and the scientific establishment. Solzhenitsyn might be a reactionary fanatic, but he could not be dismissed on that account, not just because he was also Russia's most gifted living prose writer (in the European country that, more than any other, revered imaginative writers as founts of ethical truth) but because his martyrdom was that of Russian literature as a whole under the philistine thumb of the apparatchiks. Sakharov struck some as a prig and a monomaniac but he too could not be shrugged off, and not just because the eyes of the world were fixed on him as Russia's most eminent scientist. His protest spoke for the silent majority of the Russian scientific and technological elite whose access to the good life, Soviet-style, and whose limited contact with the west, far from satisfying them, enabled them to compare their working and living conditions with those of their peers there. The comparison did not redound to Soviet credit and led many to equate modernization with a more open society. For a regime that prided itself on perceiving the historical route to modernity, theirs was a disturbing critique, one that found even more challenging expression elsewhere in the Soviet empire.

Socialism with a human face

In many ways Czechoslovakia was an unlikely place for a reformist movement to appear in 1968. The country had given the Soviets no trouble since their protégés had seized power there in 1948. Unlike Poland, Hungary, and East Germany, Czechoslovakia had not risen in revolt. Unlike Yugoslavia, Albania, and Romania, she had not asserted a claim to national independence from Moscow. Yet Czechoslovakia was the one east European country with strong democratic traditions, a bourgeois culture that had not been totally snuffed out, and a Communist Party that, unlike some of its neighbours', was more than an artificial Soviet imposition. If Soviet domination had anything to fear from the remnants of a dynamic political culture, it was here.

In the early 1960s disputes over economic policy within the Czechoslovak party leadership intensified, as what had once been one of the most prosperous economies in Europe, with a reputation for skilled craftsmanship, high production standards, and modern management, deteriorated into a morass of inefficiency. In 1962 the government openly admitted failure to achieve production targets and abandoned the third five-year plan. Thereafter Novotný made some grudging concessions to recommendations from experts for economic liberalization. But the so-called 'New System of Management' produced inflation, a deficit in the balance of foreign trade, and little improvement in the supply of consumer goods. Economic grievances fuelled ethnic tensions between Czechs and Slovaks that long pre-dated the Communist regime. Slovak party leaders complained that their region was not receiving its fair share of new investment. Slovak particularism focused especially on demands for rehabilitation of Slovak victims of the Stalinist purges. Novotný, skilled in the politics of manoeuvre, calculated that his best hope of survival lay in a cautious alliance with those advocating further liberalization. He believed that he could ride the tiger; in the event it devoured him

Intellectual unrest focused on symbolic issues such as the demand, led by Professor Eduard Goldstücker, for the rehabilitation of Kafka, whose works had been banned and denounced as decadent and bourgeois. A congress of the Writers' Union in 1963 called for intellectual freedom and for sweeping de-Stalinization. Some cultural relaxation followed, particularly in the theatre and cinema where the works of avant-garde young playwrights like Václav Havel and directors such as Miloš Forman indicated a new openness. But this was a loosening of the reins rather than genuine freedom. In 1967 rows over censorship led to a government attempt to impose strict discipline on the Writers' Union, whose members had daringly promoted public discussion of 'positive socialist alternatives'. Ominously, their rebellious mood recalled similar attitudes in the Hungarian Writers' Union on the eve of the revolution there in 1956.

Discord came to a head at a Central Committee plenum in December 1967. Novotný's response to criticism was to threaten to call up the army reserves. But he had alienated the new Soviet leaders by daring to criticize the dismissal of Khrushchev in 1964. Their abstention from support for Novotný spelt his political demise. A further Central Committee meeting in early January led to the decision to oust him and install Alexander Dubček as First Secretary of the Czechoslovak Communist Party, although Novotný retained the honorific post of President.

Judged by his formal record, Dubček, like Nagy before him, was a thoroughly loyal and conformist Communist. He had joined the party at the age of eighteen in 1939. During the war he worked as a blacksmith and in the 1950s received political training in Moscow. But in the early 1960s he pressed for the rehabilitation of victims of the Stalinist purges and became identified with the party's liberal wing. In 1963, riding the first, hesitant wave of de-Stalinization, he became First Secretary of the party in Slovakia. Notwithstanding his liberal stance, at no time before his assumption of power did Dubček betray significant evidence of ideological waywardness. To all appearances a model apparatchik, untainted by suspicion of either corruption or self-aggrandizement, he seemed a respectable choice for high Communist office. The KGB called him 'Our Sasha'.

The events of the next eight months marked a watershed in the history of international Communism, determining whether it could evolve peacefully into a system of government by consent. Most members of the new leadership in Czechoslovakia probably intended a gradual shift towards economic and social reform. But they soon found that such movement, once begun, generated an irresistible momentum that carried them forward further and more quickly than could be imagined at the outset.

The first and most urgent task, economic reform, was addressed in a series of proposals prepared by Ota Šik, the foremost economic expert among the new leaders. He urged less centralized control, a reduction in the role of state monopolies, restriction of state enterprises to sectors such as public utilities, transportation, and forestry, the creation of profit-making industrial and agricultural cooperatives, freedom for small businesses, greater worker participation in industrial management, and the revival of genuinely free trade unions. The reformers also proposed a cautious relaxation of price controls and sought Soviet permission to raise a large western loan. Implementation of these ideas was expected to improve industrial efficiency, rendering Czechoslovakia's products more appealing to western markets. As trade with the west increased, the country's dependence on Comecon would be correspondingly reduced. But open discussion of such far-reaching ideas excited public opinion within the country and rang alarm bells in Moscow.

From March onwards the pace of reform quickened. Censorship virtually disappeared and the newly liberated press published ever more daring articles on previously taboo themes such as alleged Soviet involvement in the deaths of Jan Masaryk and Rudolf Slánský. Radio and television became more open to non-official views. The Social Democratic Party and other opposition groups began to reorganize with semi-official acquiescence. Under pressure from newly vocal public opinion, Novotný was forced out of the presidency. His replacement, General Ludvík Svoboda, was approved by the Soviets but only because they strongly opposed the other candidates, all radical reformists. In the event, Soviet confidence in Svoboda, as in Dubček, turned out to be misplaced. In the gathering crisis, he proved faithful to old-fashioned patriotism rather than to the Soviet conception of socialist internationalism.

In April the Central Committee of the Communist Party approved an Action Programme that proposed greater market freedom, 'economic competition among enterprises of all kinds', 'submitting our economy to the pressure of the world market', and movement towards currency convertibility.[8] While it reaffirmed the 'leading role' of the Communist Party and the alliance with the USSR, the statement promised a further easing of censorship, democratization of party organs, and curbs on abuses of power by the secret police. The programme was a detailed exposition of what came to be called 'socialism with a human face' (the phrase was attributed to Dubček, although whether or when he first used it remains uncertain). Outspoken reformists moved into positions of power: Oldřich Černík became Prime Minister and Josef Smrkovský President of the National Assembly. At the end of May the date of the next party congress, originally scheduled to take place in 1970, was advanced to early September 1968, with the specific purpose of replacing those conservatives who remained in positions of influence and consolidating the reformers' grip on power.

On 27 June four Prague newspapers published a statement drafted by the writer Ludvík Vaculík and signed by a large number of other intellectuals and public figures. Known as '2000 Words', it presented the most forthright enunciation of the credo of the Prague Spring. The document castigated the pre-Dubček regime as one that destroyed basic human relationships. Not only could people not have faith in their government: 'what was still worse was that we could hardly trust each other anymore.' The country's 'spiritual health and character' had been endangered by the system. The reform movement had begun to make necessary changes. But more was needed. 'Truth is not victorious here; truth is what remains when everything else has gone to pot. . . . Somehow we must complete our aim of humanizing this regime. If we don't, the revenge of the old forces would be cruel.' This call for a quickened pace of reform was not overtly anti-Communist. Rather, it called on the Communist Party, at its forthcoming congress, to continue the process of democratization. Alluding to the possibility of Soviet intervention, the writers urged dignified restraint.[9] This was a plea for moderation and discipline rather than a call to arms. But '2000 Words' had an electric effect, especially in Moscow. Brezhnev telephoned Dubček to complain before the Czechoslovak leader had even read it.

The Soviet leaders observed the Czechoslovak reform process, at first with cautious concern, then with increasingly stern disapproval. At successive meetings with Czechoslovak leaders they sought to rein in the reformist tendency. Brezhnev told the Politburo of his fear that events in Czechoslovakia were 'moving in an anti-Communist direction'. The Ukrainian party boss, Pyotr Shelest, warned Brezhnev that the Czechoslovak example was 'causing unsavoury phenomena here in Ukraine as well'.[10] The KGB head, Yury Andropov, recommended consideration of 'extreme measures', including 'military action'.[11] When exhortation failed, the Soviets decided to act. Since there were no Soviet forces permanently stationed in Czechoslovakia, it was decided to stage Warsaw Pact military manoeuvres, obviously intimidatory in purpose, and to prepare contingency plans for an occupation of the country.

In these measures the Soviets were able to rely on support from most of their Warsaw Pact allies. The Prague Spring alarmed the Polish and East German party leaders who worried that demands for reform might spill over into their countries. At a Warsaw Pact conference in March Ulbricht warned that if the Czechoslovak reform process continued 'all of us here will run a very serious risk which may well lead to our downfall'.[12] He and Gomułka therefore urged the Soviet leaders to take a firm line against Dubček. He sought to reassure the Russians, but the ever more militant statements issued in Prague, not only by intellectuals but by members of the reformist Communist leadership themselves, heightened Soviet consternation.

On 16 July the leaders of the Soviet, Bulgarian, Hungarian, East German, and Polish parties dispatched a 'Dear comrades' letter to the Czechoslovak party's central committee. It was reminiscent in tone of the Stalin–Tito correspondence in 1948 and, unusually for communications of such delicacy between Communist states, it was made public. It warned that 'the offensive of reaction, backed by imperialism, against your party and the foundations of the socialist system of the Czechoslovak Socialist Republic threatens in our deepest conviction to push your country from the road of socialism, and thereby threatens the interests of the entire socialist system'. The letter took particular exception to '2000 Words' which it termed 'an outright call for struggle against the Communist Party'. Adopting an almost pleading tone, Czechoslovakia's allies continued: 'Don't you see these dangers, comrades? Is it possible, in such conditions, to remain passive?'[13] The Czechoslovak leaders, however, refused to change course. Amid growing anxiety that an invasion might be imminent, public opinion solidified for the reform leadership: a poll showed 78 per cent support for Dubček.

At the end of the month Brezhnev and Kosygin led a Soviet delegation to meet the Czechoslovak leaders at the small town of Čierná nad Tisou, in Slovakia, near the Soviet border. Brezhnev denounced the abolition of censorship: 'It is madness for you to let your so-called "free writers" dictate your policies for you. They are either hired agents of the imperialists or at least they do what the imperialists want.'[14] Violent arguments broke out, in the course of which Shelest let fly with anti-Semitic insults directed at one of the most vociferous of the Czech reformers, František Kriegel, a Jew. At that point Dubček got up and walked out with the other Czechoslovak negotiators. Later the Soviets apologized and the talks resumed. They ended after four days without written agreement but with what the Soviets understood as Czechoslovak undertakings to rein in their press and return to respectable standards of Communist behaviour. Before departing, Brezhnev fired a Parthian volley at his hosts: 'We rely on your Communist word. We expect that you will act and behave as Communists. If you deceive us once more, we shall consider it a crime and a betrayal and act accordingly.'[15]

Dubček broadcast to the people, insisting that the government would 'stand firm on the positions of our post-January policy', which he defined as offering a 'profoundly democratic' society 'in which our citizens would be able to decide their own fate for themselves and according to their own cognition and conscience'. He claimed that the Soviets had confirmed the 'inalienable right of every party to solve its own problems independently'.[16] But this was a very optimistic interpretation of what had occurred. The published communiqué had, in fact, been conspicuously silent on that point.

Warsaw Pact forces, which had been conducting menacing manoeuvres in Czechoslovakia, were withdrawn and the crisis seemed to have passed. But on 3 August a pro-Soviet member of the Czechoslovak leadership, Vasil Bilák, held a secret rendezvous with Shelest in a public lavatory and handed over a letter, written at Soviet request and signed by several anti-reformist members of the Czechoslovak party praesidium. Addressed to Brezhnev, the document reported that a counter-revolution was under way and requested intervention 'with all the means that you have'.[17]

The letter provided the Soviets with what they regarded as a useful pretext for invasion. The imminence of the Czechoslovak party congress, which seemed likely to accelerate rather than arrest the momentum of reform, finally impelled them to intervene. Sceptics in the Soviet Politburo, such as Kosygin and Suslov, fell into line. Kádár, who had shown some sympathy for the Czechoslovak position over the previous months, held a last meeting with Dubček in which he begged him to conform: 'Do you *really* not know the kind of people you are dealing with?'[18] Dubček, however, would not be moved, and in spite of the many signs seemed curiously oblivious to the danger of Soviet military intervention.

On the night of 20/1 August the invasion began. At least 350,000 Soviet and 70,000 Polish, Hungarian, East German, and Bulgarian troops participated in Operation DANUBE. It came as a shock to Dubček, as did the treatment to which he and his colleagues were subjected by the invaders. They were arrested at gunpoint by Soviet soldiers, who severed all the telephone lines out of Dubček's office. When the prisoners asked to call Moscow, the Soviet ambassador told them the lines were not working. They were flown to a KGB internment camp in the Carpathian mountains. According to one report, they were manacled and the Prime Minister, Černík, had to be carried bodily onto the plane.

The official Soviet explanation for the invasion was published in *Pravda* on 22 August. It claimed that 'party and government leaders' (note: not 'the government') of Czechoslovakia had asked the USSR and other allied states 'to render the fraternal Czechoslovak people urgent assistance'. The intervention was justified on the basis of an alleged 'threat to the socialist system in Czechoslovakia'. The original Soviet plan had called for the creation of a revolutionary 'workers' and peasants' government', headed by Czechoslovak collaborationists, which would issue an appeal for fraternal assistance from the Warsaw Pact. But the Russians could not find a plausible Czechoslovak Kádár to lend some tincture of legitimacy to their intervention. Pro-Soviet elements in the Czechoslovak party leadership were outmaneouvred by reformers who for a short time retained control of television and radio stations. The reformists also succeeded in convening the party congress ahead of schedule. It elected a new central committee and presidium that excluded pro-Soviet elements. The National Assembly met in extraordinary session and passed resolutions opposing the occupation. Unable to implement their original political strategy, the Soviets instead decided to bully the existing leadership into submission.

This proved difficult. President Svoboda broadcast to the nation, declaring the Soviet action illegal and pointing out that it had taken place without the consent of the constitutional authorities. 'We are living through an exceptionally grave moment in the life of our nation,' he said. 'There is no question of our turning back. The programme of the Communist Party and Government expressed the vital interests of the Czechoslovak people. Do not lose faith.'[19] On 23 August he broadcast again, announcing that he would visit Moscow. He asked for support in his efforts 'to find an honourable and dignified way out of the present situation, which is threatening to have tragic consequences for our people and their fatherland'.[20]

Dubček and his fellow captives had meanwhile been flown to Moscow for a dressing-down by their masters. 'I believed in you,' Brezhnev admonished the Czech leader, 'and I stood up for you against the others. . . . Our Sasha is a good comrade, I said. And you disappointed us all so terribly.'[21] Two days later Dubček disappeared from the discussions. Fearing for his safety, his colleagues demanded to be taken to him. Headed by Svoboda, they were led to his room. One of the group later described the scene: 'He was lying in bed, naked to the waist. He lay there limply, and obviously under sedation. He had a small plaster on his forehead covering a tiny wound, and his face wore the absent expression of someone who has been drugged. When I entered the room, he stirred, opened his eyes, and smiled. I was suddenly reminded of traditional paintings of the martyrdom of St Stephen, who smiled under torture.'[22] The arresting simile came rather strangely from a dialectical materialist—but these events strained the limits of Marxist interpretation.

The next day the Czechoslovaks, except Kriegel, consented to a protocol invalidating the decisions of the Czechoslovak party congress, undertaking to maintain the 'leading role' of the party, promising to restore censorship, and agreeing to conclude a new treaty that would regularize the presence of Warsaw Pact forces in Czechoslovakia. The Czechoslovak leaders consoled themselves that they had refused to sign any justification of the invasion and had been able to insert a reference to the occupation as 'temporary'; but these turned out to be paper victories. A telling episode occurred when the enforced guests arrived at the airport to take a plane home. They noticed that one of their number, Kriegel, was missing. He had been the most hostile and contemptuous in his behaviour towards his hosts. The fear was that he was destined for the Gulag. All refused to board the plane until he was produced.

While the Czechoslovak leaders negotiated the terms of their submission with their captors in Moscow, the population of the occupied country reacted with a fury born of impotence. Clandestine radio and television broadcasts and underground newspapers condemned the invasion. Satirical wall-posters appeared and restaurants issued menus offering 'Brezhnev Brain in its own Juice' and 'Braised Wild Kosygin'.[23] But the Czechoslovak army obeyed orders to remain in its barracks and physical resistance to the occupiers was rare. Not more than a hundred Czechoslovaks died.

Why did the USSR decide to intervene? One motive was hidden from view at the time: Soviet desire to retain control of three unfinished nuclear warhead storage sites in Czechoslovakia. Another cause for concern in Moscow was the proposed convertibility of the Czechoslovak crown. This represented a real threat to the Soviets, since, if it were to be achieved, the price of Czechoslovak finished industrial goods within Comecon would rise appreciably, with serious consequences for other member states. But the fundamental reason for the Soviet decision was undoubtedly political. The Russians understood that, whatever the protestations and intentions of the Czechoslovak party leadership, the dynamics of the Prague Spring were moving the country inexorably out of the Soviet orbit. The Soviet leaders were enraged and baffled by the Czechoslovaks' obduracy regarding freedom of the press, a concept alien to Soviet thinking and hitherto unheard-of in any Communist society. Their fears, however, were not misplaced. Whatever the Czechoslovak leaders might say, the Soviets were right in thinking that a free press would almost certainly lead to free elections and in the long run to an end of one-party rule. If such a process were possible in Czechoslovakia, there seemed, as Ulbricht and Gomułka so urgently warned, every likelihood that the infection would spread to the USSR's other east European satellites, perhaps even to the Soviet Union itself. The course of events in eastern Europe two decades later lends considerable retrospective support to such forebodings.

Why did Dubček not call for armed resistance? Although the outcome would have been certain, fighting would, after all, have deepened the shame of the occupation. But Dubček had before him the terrible precedent of thousands of lives wasted in fruitless resistance in Hungary twelve years earlier. Even more than Nagy, he realized that there could be no question of western intervention. Unlike Poland or Hungary, the national tradition in the homeland of *The Good Soldier Švejk* was, in any case, not one of heroic national resistance (unless one were to look back to the Thirty Years War—a disastrous precedent). Defending his decision more than two decades later, Dubček argued that 'presenting a military defence would have meant exposing the Czech and Slovak peoples to a senseless bloodbath'.[24] He therefore chose the path of accommodation, hoping at least to salvage something from the ruins. Any such expectation, however, was delusory. The Moscow Protocol has been called 'a triumph' for the Czech reformers 'that fighting would probably not have won'.[25] But this 'triumph' merely allowed the Russians to pretend that the Czechoslovak leadership had set its seal of approval on their actions.

As the leaders arrived home, protesters gathered in Wenceslas Square and marched on the Parliament building, shouting: 'We want to know the whole truth,' and 'We don't want to die on our knees.' Dubček gave a broadcast during which he several times broke down in sobs. Later Smrkovský delivered a speech in which he outlined the brutal choices that had faced the leaders in Moscow and the reasons that had led them to capitulate. Svoboda too spoke: he stressed that he had returned with

Dubček and the other reformists and that they were 'forthwith resuming the offices to which they have been democratically appointed'. He continued: 'We have, above all, achieved fundamental agreement on the gradual implementation of the complete departure of the [Soviet and other occupying] armies. Pending this, their presence is a reality.'[26] The broadcast speeches of the country's leaders in this period deserve a special place in the history of political oratory. More than any other Communist leadership in eastern Europe before or after, they spoke directly and candidly to their people, seeking to convey their emotional identification with the general popular sense of outrage, while urging restraint and forbearance.

Now followed the period known to its supporters as 'normalization' and to its opponents as 'Absurdistan'. Dubček was humiliatingly compelled to remain in office, though not in power, for a short time in order to lend a patina of legitimacy to the new reality. The Soviets realized that the few men of whose loyalty they could be sure, like Bilák, were generally despised and could not plausibly be groomed for leadership. Dubček was retained as a figurehead until April 1969. Then, after a brief spell as ambassador to Turkey, he was brought home and demoted to menial positions, ending as a clerk in the Slovak Forest Administration. Thousands of leaders of the reformist movement, particularly intellectuals, including Goldstücker and the former Foreign Minister, Jiří Hájek, fled abroad. Others who remained were consigned to lowly jobs cleaning windows or stoking furnaces. Official intellectual life returned to the Marxist straitjacket. Censorship was restored. Television resumed coverage of the celebration of Lenin's birthday and improvements at hydroelectric dams.

In October 1968 Soviet domination over Czechoslovakia was enshrined in a treaty that spelled out with stark specificity the master–servant relationship between the two countries. Soviet forces would remain on Czechoslovak soil 'temporarily . . . for the purpose of ensuring the security of the countries of the socialist commonwealth against the increasing revanchist aspirations of the West German militarist forces'. As if to rub in the humiliation, the treaty required Czechoslovakia to pay the Soviet Union 'the necessary sums in Czechoslovak crowns for expenses connected with the temporary sojourn of Soviet forces on the territory of Czechoslovakia'.[27]

With this imposed accord in his pocket, Brezhnev contrived an ideological justification of the invasion. In a speech to the Polish party congress in November 1968 he formulated in its clearest expression what became known in the west as the 'Brezhnev Doctrine'. He affirmed 'strict respect for the sovereignty of all countries' and reminded his Polish audience that 'the CPSU has always advocated that each socialist country determine the concrete forms of its development along the path of socialism by taking into account the specific nature of their national conditions'. But he continued:

> It is well known that there are common natural laws of socialist countries, deviation from which could lead to deviation from socialism as such. And when external and internal forces hostile to socialism try to turn the development of a given socialist country in the direction of restoration of the capitalist system, when a threat arises to the cause of socialism in the country—a threat to the security of the socialist commonwealth as a whole—this is no longer merely a problem for that country's people, but a common problem, the concern of all socialist countries.[28]

Czechoslovakia was reduced to a Muscovite satrapy for the next eighteen years.

Gustáv Husák, whom the Soviets installed as puppet ruler, administered the country as a loyal *fidus Achates* of Brezhnev. He never succeeded, as Kádár did in Hungary, in earning the grudging admiration of his people. That does not seem to have been his aim. As a young man, Husák had suffered greatly for his beliefs. He had been imprisoned during the war. Arrested again at the time of the Slánský trial in 1951, he had been tortured and secured release only in 1960. During the Dubček period he had been regarded as a 'centrist' but once in power he ruled like an old-style Stalinist. Perhaps he felt that it was an act of kindness that Dubček and his other former colleagues were neither imprisoned nor, like Nagy, murdered, but merely reduced to the status of non-persons.

After the initial wave of resistance had subsided, most of the population relapsed into sullen acquiescence. But in January 1969 a martyr appeared: Jan Palach, a twenty-one-year-old student at the Charles University, burnt himself to death in Wenceslas Square. His self-immolation was interpreted as a protest against the invasion although his suicide note was limited to a demand for an end to censorship. A vast throng gathered at his funeral. Three other young men followed Palach's example. Over the next two decades pilgrimages to his grave on the anniversary of his death became one of the few forms of public protest open to dissidents.

In 1970 a thorough purge of the Czechoslovak Communist Party began. All membership cards were recalled and more than 450,000 members suspected of liberal tendencies, one-third of the entire party, were expelled. They included 64 of the 150 members of the Central Committee. The purge blotted out any lingering hope that at least some of the economic reforms of the Prague Spring might survive its political termination. In contrast to Hungary, Czechoslovakia remained one of the most culturally repressive regimes in the eastern bloc. The works of Kafka were again prohibited in his homeland. Most of the leading writers of the Prague Spring, including figures of international standing such as Milan Kundera, Bohumil Hrabal, Jaroslav Seifert, and Václav Havel, were also banned. Even non-political phenomena that were judged potentially subversive were suppressed. In 1976, for example, members of an underground rock music group, Plastic People of the Universe, were gaoled for 'disturbing the peace'.

The Soviet tanks in Prague in 1968, like those in Budapest in 1956, aroused revulsion and protest in the west. The loyalty to Moscow of the French and Italian Communist parties was severely strained. The French party was still suffering from internal convulsions as a result of the *événements* of the previous May but, under the leadership after 1972 of Georges Marchais, it ultimately resumed submissive obedience to Moscow. The reaction of the Italian Communists was different: for them 1968 marked a decisive break and the point at which their evolution into a left-Socialist parliamentary party acquired irresistible momentum. In eastern Europe too, the poodle-like participation in the invasion by Czechoslovakia's four Warsaw Pact allies aroused shame among thinking people and helped to delegitimize the regimes that had collaborated in these decisions. In general, however, the invasion did not seriously disrupt east–west relations or the movement towards greater stability in central Europe.

By suppressing the Prague Spring, the Kremlin leaders and their east European acolytes thus overcame a short-term challenge—but at the price of the long-term legitimacy and viability of their system. Communism, as it was clamped onto eastern Europe, became, in spite of claims to the contrary, a profoundly conservative force. Repressing the self-critical dynamics that are a prerequisite for development, it decayed over the next two decades into a change-resistant social order that proved unable to compete effectively in the modern world.

Détente

In the course of the 1960s both superpowers deployed growing numbers of intercontinental and medium-range missiles as the main delivery vehicle for nuclear weapons. The USA's much larger missile force was augmented in

1964 by the deployment of nuclear submarines, each capable of launching up to sixteen Polaris missiles. Hopes that the Test Ban and Non-Proliferation Treaties would slow the arms race were soon belied. Both sides entered the horror chamber of arcane mathematical calculations of 'second strike capability', based on the assumption that large parts of their respective populations and industrial capacities would have been destroyed in a first strike by the other side. Perturbed by reports that the USSR was deploying anti-ballistic missiles (ABMs) around Moscow, the United States accelerated development of its own ABM system.

Debate on the implications of these new weapons eventually produced changes in NATO strategy. In 1968 the alliance formally abandoned reliance on 'massive retaliation' and instead adopted the doctrine of 'flexible response' and 'graduated deterrence', involving recourse to relatively small-scale 'tactical' nuclear weapons. Such ideas had been promoted since the early 1960s, particularly by Kennedy's Secretary of Defense, Robert S. McNamara. Under the new approach, full-scale nuclear retaliation would be the last, rather than the first, reaction to a Soviet attack. Conventional incursion would be met initially by conventional defence; escalation would be gradual. NATO deployed a variety of tactical nuclear weapons in West Germany and other west European countries from the 1960s onwards. Although designed to reduce the danger of nuclear catastrophe, the new policy did not allay European anxieties. Some strategists doubted that it would be possible, once any nuclear bombs, even relatively small-scale devices, were used, to prevent rapid escalation to all-out nuclear war. Fears were also expressed that these weapons, if used, might have an inconvenient side-effect: radio-active fallout from them might endanger those firing them as well as those at whom they were directed. Many Europeans remained fearful of their cities being sacrificed in defence of the United States. Unlike strategic intercontinental missiles, therefore, tactical nuclear weapons were subjected to a veto by host states on their use. This was the so-called 'dual key' system (from a procedure at the Bank of England whereby two directors had keys to separate locks to the door of the strong-room). The Soviet Union, for its part, deployed its own tactical nuclear weapons in eastern Europe, though without any 'dual key' arrangement.

In the late 1960s the Soviet Union nearly caught up with the United States in ICBM strength: by 1969 the USSR had 1,028 against the Americans' 1,054. The Americans maintained their advantage in submarine-launched ballistic missiles (SLBMs) with 656 to the Soviets' 196; but in this sphere too the Russians were catching up fast. Overall, the American force nevertheless remained the more formidable, since US missiles were more sophisticated and accurate, particularly after the development of MIRVs ('multiple independently targetable re-entry vehicles'), warheads that divided into several attacking components in space after launching.

The United States, embroiled in war in Vietnam and anxious that it was being overtaken by the USSR in nuclear delivery capability, was, however, keen to avoid conflict elsewhere. The Soviets, in the aftermath of the Czechoslovak events of 1968, had their own reasons for seeking to reduce tension in Europe. When President Nixon took office in January 1969, Moscow found a willing partner in negotiations on arms control and on European issues. The process was facilitated by a secret 'back channel' of discussions between Kissinger and the Soviet ambassador in Washington, Anatoly Dobrynin. In 1971 the superpowers signed agreements on cooperation in space and on improving the Washington–Moscow 'hot line'. Soviet interest in an improvement in relations quickened as a result of the American opening to China in 1971–2 and its portent, ominous for Moscow, of a Sino-American alignment against the USSR. In May 1972, three months after his historic trip to China, Nixon visited Moscow and signed a large number of agreements including two of major importance. The first was a treaty on the limitation of antiballistic missile systems: each side was permitted two such defensive systems, one to protect its capital, the other its launching area for land-based intercontinental ballistic missiles. The second was the so-called SALT agreement, a product of the Strategic Arms Limitation Talks that had begun in 1969. The SALT treaty allowed the USA to deploy 1,710 land- and sea-based missiles; the Soviet Union was permitted 2,347 missiles but as the USSR was still far behind the USA in the development of multiple warheads the treaty left the missile balance roughly even. This was not a disarmament agreement since no weapons were to be withdrawn or destroyed. But it paved the way to further, more ambitious steps towards superpower détente and disengagement.

The chief Soviet diplomatic aim in Europe was to achieve general recognition of the post-war territorial status quo. The treaty with West Germany in 1970 and the Berlin agreements of 1971–2 went a long way towards that goal. At the suggestion of the USSR a Conference on Security and Cooperation in Europe (CSCE) convened at Helsinki in July 1973 in which the USA, Canada, the USSR, and every European state except Albania participated. The conference produced the so-called Helsinki Final Act in August 1975. Although not a 'treaty' in the strict sense, and not even signed by the participants, it was recognized as binding by all of them. While the document fell short of Soviet demands that the western powers formally recognize the post-war frontiers in eastern Europe, thereby legitimizing, for example, the Soviet seizure of the Baltic states during the Second World War, it stated that all participants 'regard as inviolable all one another's frontiers as well as the frontiers of all States in Europe and therefore they will refrain now and in the future from assaulting these frontiers'. It also called for 'confidence-building measures' in the military sphere in central Europe and, at western insistence, contained declarations affirming human rights and the principle of non-interference in the internal affairs of other states.[29] Soviet endorsement of all this did not lead to any significant change in its policies at home or in its east European satellites. Western negotiators hoped that pinning the Soviets down to these commitments might nevertheless yield results in the long term.

The Helsinki agreement palpably reduced tension in Europe. It spawned follow-up meetings at Belgrade (1977–8), Madrid (1980–3), and Vienna (1986–9) as well as a permanent secretariat. But its consequences in eastern Europe were double-edged. Not everybody in the Soviet satellite states was delighted at the sanctification of the post-Yalta division of the continent. A dissident Hungarian writer grumbled that 'the present status quo in Europe represents the petrifaction of an exceptional state of post-war occupation.'[30] The Soviet leadership appeared to think it could pay lip-service internationally to human rights norms, as it had for years done internally, without any consequences. Gradually, however, it was disabused of this notion. In May 1976 dissidents in Moscow, headed by the physicist Yury Orlov, founded a group that became known as the 'Helsinki Watch' committee. It purpose was to monitor Soviet compliance with the agreement and to publicize infringements. To this end it established contact with similar groups that sprouted up elsewhere in the Soviet bloc and in the west. Italian and Spanish 'Euro-Communists' took up the refrain in international Communist gatherings, where it was difficult for the Soviets to shut them up. Predictably, the Soviet authorities took measures to harass and discredit what the KGB chief, in a report to the Central Committee, called 'anti-social elements'.[31] Orlov was arrested in February 1977, tried in secret, and sentenced to seven years in a 'strict regime' labour camp plus another five years of internal exile. But his fate generated a new wave of protests, thus strengthening the dynamic initiated by Helsinki—precisely the outcome the Soviet leadership had wished to avoid. The Carter administration in the United States between 1977 and 1981 placed an unprecedented emphasis on human rights in its diplomacy. But in response to Carter's first letter to him after taking office, Brezhnev brushed off 'interference in our internal affairs, whatever pseudo-humanitarian slogans are used to present it'.[32]

Both the SALT agreement and the Helsinki Final Act were intended by their authors to mark stages on the roads to further treaties. In the case of arms control, Brezhnev signed an agreement with US President Ford at Vladivostok in November 1974 in which the two superpowers set a new limit of 2,400 delivery vehicles each, of which not more than 1,320 might carry multiple warheads. Critics remarked that it was a strange form of arms control that ratified such large increases in the deployment of nuclear weapons. Defenders pointed out that without such an agreement the arms race might spiral even higher. The original SALT agreement had envisaged completion of a follow-up treaty within five years. In the event, further negotiations were complicated by the rapid technological advances in missile weaponry. A SALT II agreement was finally signed by Brezhnev and Carter in June 1979. This froze the overall number of delivery vehicles at 2,400 and provided for reduction to 2,250 by 1981. It also set limits for each category of missile and for multiple warheads. But SALT II was never ratified by the United States Senate.

The main reason was the Soviet invasion of Afghanistan in December 1979. The initiative for this, the first full-scale military offensive by the Soviet Union outside its recognized sphere since 1945, was taken by the Defence Minister, Dmitry Ustinov, but it was opposed by high-level military officers, including the Chief of Staff, General Nikolai Ogarkov. Why did Brezhnev consent to the launching of this ill-fated enterprise? Afghanistan itself was not worth the candle, although the apparently imminent defeat of Soviet protégés in the civil war there would, no doubt, have dealt a blow to the USSR's prestige. Andropov argued in favour of intervention that a mere two battalions of Soviet troops would be 'entirely sufficient' to 'establish Leninist principles in the party and state leadership of Afghanistan'.[33] What the Soviet leadership seems to have assumed is that the creation of a satellite state in Afghanistan would position the USSR to take advantage of opportunities that might arise in the area of the Persian Gulf from the collapse of the Pahlavi dynasty in Iran in February 1979. The decision to intervene proved to be a catastrophic miscalculation. Over the next few years Soviet armed forces were mercilessly harried by Afghan guerrillas, who enjoyed support from the United States and certain Muslim states. Afghanistan turned out to be the 'Soviet Union's Vietnam'. Eventually the Russians sent in not two battalions but hundreds of thousands of troops and all manner of advanced equipment but found that they could not suppress resistance.

The Afghan venture was to have disastrous consequences for the Soviet Union internally. It also destroyed the (in any case luke-warm) support for SALT II in the United States. The Americans dealt a bruising snub to the USSR by boycotting the 1980 Olympic Games in Moscow. More than sixty other countries joined the boycott, although most west European states participated. For a while, western European leaders still hoped to salvage some elements of détente. After a meeting with Brezhnev in May 1980, the French President, Giscard d'Estaing, told his Cabinet that it would be 'dangerous and harmful' to abandon détente. 'Why should the United States have a monopoly on relations with the USSR? That would result in an altogether unacceptable devaluation of the world role of France.'[34]

Superpower antagonism was sharpened by apparent threats to the stability of the nuclear balance of terror. In 1976 the USSR had started to deploy intermediate-range mobile SS-20 missiles, each carrying three independently targetable nuclear warheads. The missiles were deployed not only in the USSR but also in East Germany. With a range of 2,700 miles these missiles could reach anywhere in western Europe or the Middle East. In January 1979, at summit meeting of western leaders at Guadeloupe, Carter, Giscard, and the British Prime Minister, James Callaghan, agreed with the West German Chancellor, Helmut Schmidt on a plan for the deployment of American intermediate-range missiles in western Europe. Schmidt, who was concerned about what he saw as potential dangers to the strategic balance in Europe arising from the SALT agreements, committed West Germany to the stationing of such missiles on her soil, provided at least one other country on the European continent (i.e. not counting Britain) did likewise. A NATO meeting in December 1979 reached a 'two-track' decision: negotiations with the USSR on arms control would continue; in the meantime, NATO would proceed towards deployment by 1983 of 572 intermediate-range Pershing II and cruise missiles in Germany, Britain, Italy, Belgium, and the Netherlands.

The decision fuelled anti-Americanism in NATO countries and stimulated a protest movement. This was mainly leftist in inspiration and support but, like the 'Ban the Bomb' campaign a generation earlier, it won some support across society. In Britain, West Germany, and Greece clerics were among its vocal exponents. A women's protest camp at Greenham Common in Berkshire, near a US Air Force base, was set up in August 1981 and was not wound up until 2000. The movement received some secret financial support from Communist countries.[35] A parallel peace movement in eastern Europe was at first designed as a propaganda ploy. When it began, particularly in East Germany, to develop some characteristics of spontaneity and autonomy from government control, it discomfited Communist governments, to whom, in fact, it should have served as a warning of what was to come. The protest movements did not prevent NATO from starting to deploy intermediate-range missiles in Europe in late 1983, whereupon the Soviets walked out of negotiations on missile limitation.

President Reagan's administration, which took office in the United States in January 1981, embarked on far-reaching rearmament, building up naval strength in particular. Reagan's Strategic Defense Initiative, dubbed 'Star Wars', aroused fierce Soviet complaint that activation of plans for a US missile defence system would constitute a violation of several treaties. The Americans, for their part, complained of Soviet violations of the ABM Treaty, citing the construction of a radar early-warning station at Krasnoyarsk. The Russians denied the charge indignantly, though a few years later the Soviet Foreign Minister, Eduard Shevardnadze, candidly admitted that the violations had occurred. The renewed arms race placed immense pressure on the industrial capacity of the Soviet Union. Estimates of Soviet military expenditure in the early 1980s range from 12.5 per cent of national income to 25 per cent or even higher. Even the lower figure was unsustainable in the long run—and in the long run was not sustained.

As the Cold War thus resumed, the USSR faced yet another challenge to its dominance in eastern Europe, one that began unravelling the entire Soviet system.

Solidarity in Poland

'The last proletarian revolution', as one of its theoreticians later called the *Solidarność* (Solidarity) movement in Poland in 1980–1,[36] broke out against a background of severe economic distress and social upheaval. The roots of the crisis stretched back as far as the 'Polish October' of 1956. The bright prospect of Gomułka's 'Polish road to socialism' had dimmed in the eyes of most Poles, as his regime jettisoned liberalizing policies. But two segments of society remained to some extent insulated from communization. The

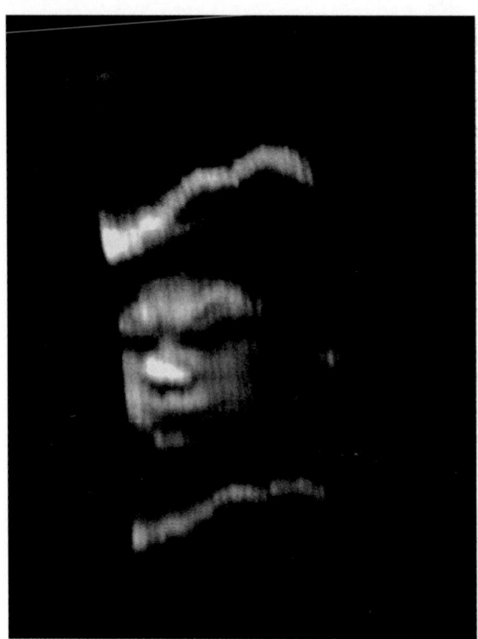

21 (*left*). The face that launched a billion screens: William Taynton (1910–1973), John Logie Baird's office boy, aged fifteen. This is the untouched photo of his image as it appeared on the 'screen' of the first 'Televisor' on 2 October 1925 (Copyright Victoria and Albert Museum, courtesy of Strathclyde University Archives)

22 (*below*). Generalissimo Francisco Franco delivering a speech in his squeaky voice, June 1936 (Imperial War Museum)

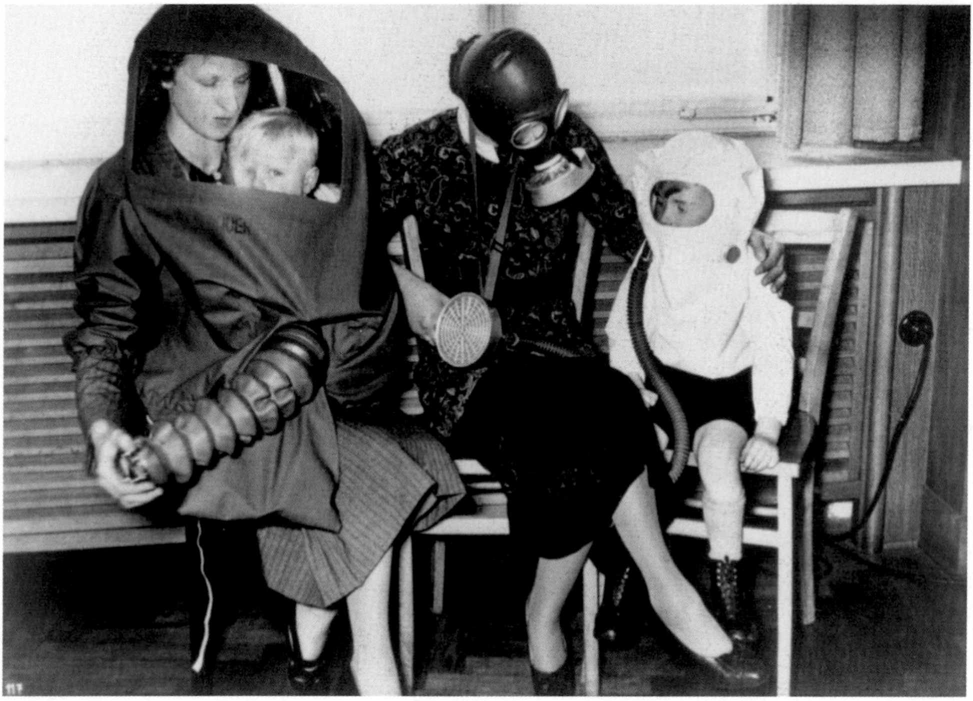

23. A German mother-and-child gas mask on display, January 1939 (Imperial War Museum)

24. Inside the defences on the Maginot Line, the fortification system that stretched along France's frontier with Germany, from Switzerland to Luxembourg. The line was broken by a gap at the Ardennes. In May 1940 the Germans advanced through the gap (Imperial War Museum)

25 (*above*). '*Peace for our time*': Neville Chamberlain (*centre*) arrives at Heston Aerodrome after the Munich Conference, 30 September 1938 (Imperial War Museum)

26 (*left*). '*We have placed ourselves at the side of scoundrels . . . . We shall be robbers of corpses!*' Count Pál Teleki (*left*), Prime Minister of Hungary, welcomed to Rome on 2 April 1940 by the Italian Foreign Minister, Galeazzo Ciano. A year later Teleki committed suicide in despair at the consequences of Hungary's alignment with Germany and Italy (Imperial War Museum)

27. The Battle of Stalingrad, winter 1942–3: German lorry drivers build igloo walls around their vehicles to protect them from sub-zero temperatures (Imperial War Museum)

28. Tito (Josip Broz) (1892–1980), wartime partisan chief, ruler of Yugoslavia, 1945–80 (Imperial War Museum)

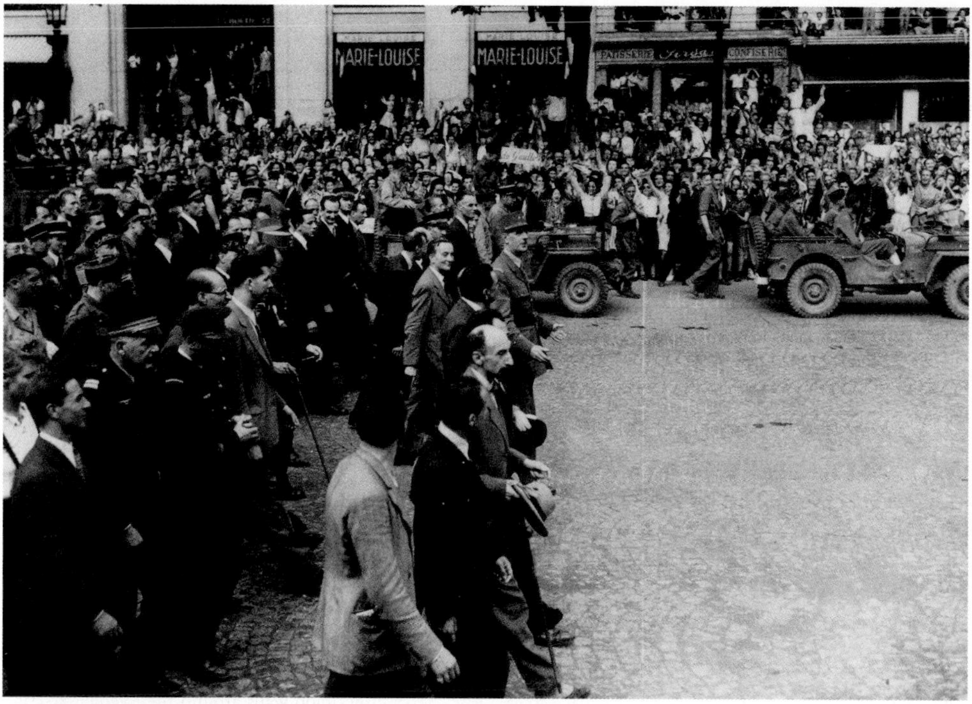

29. General de Gaulle (*centre*) leads victory parade up the Champs-Elysées. Beside him and '*a little to the rear*', Georges Bidault, head of the National Council of Resistance, 28 August 1944 (Imperial War Museum)

30. Alleged 'horizontal collaborators', their heads shaved, swastikas painted on their faces, their clothes partly torn off, carrying their shoes, frog-marched through Paris to an uncertain fate, August 1944 (Imperial War Museum)

31 (*above*). George Papandreou (*centre*), Prime Minister of Greece, accompanied by General Ronald Scobie, Commander of British Land Task Force in Greece, arrives in Athens and ascends Acropolis to rehoist the national flag, 18 October 1944 (Imperial War Museum)

32 (*right*). Liberation of Bergen-Belsen concentration camp, April 1945: women and children, former prisoners, herded together in one of the barrack blocks (Imperial War Museum)

33. Berlin rising, June 1953: a man with a stick attacks a Soviet T34/85 tank (Imperial War Museum)

34. '*Life punishes those who come late.*' Mikhail Gorbachev (*left*), with Erich Honecker saluting at his side, at parade to mark 40th anniversary of foundation of the German Democratic Republic, Berlin, 7 October 1989 (Imperial War Museum)

35. The Berlin Wall comes down. The wall dividing east from west Berlin was opened on 9 November 1989. Within twelve months it had been almost completely razed to the ground (Imperial War Museum)

36. '*We are the Warsaw Ghetto.*' Even though a burnt-out bus and empty freight containers form a barricade, people still run through 'Sniper's Alley' to minimize the risk from Serbian fire during the siege of Sarajevo, 1992 (Imperial War Museum)

first was the independent peasantry: following some decollectivization by Gomułka, 83 per cent of agricultural land was left in private hands. The second was the Church which retained greater institutional freedom and a larger flock than in any other Communist country.

Gomułka succeeded, after a fashion, in transforming the economy. In Poland, as elsewhere, the pre-war dominance of the agrarian sector ended for good as the country entered the industrial age. Industrial production increased 700 per cent between 1950 and 1970. By the 1970s the balance of the population had shifted to an urban majority. As in other Communist countries by then, health services were provided free of charge to the entire population. Rents and transportation costs were low. Cultural production, notably theatre and film, was heavily subsidized and attained impressive levels. But inflation eroded nominal gains in income, housing conditions were grim, and access to consumer goods lagged far behind the west.

By the mid-1960s cracks began to appear in the Communist structure. 'Revisionist' intellectuals such as Adam Schaff and Leszek Kołakowski wrote far-reaching critiques of the Marxist system. Young dissidents like Jacek Kuroń and Adam Michnik went even further and called for revolution. In early 1968 students in Cracow demonstrated in support of the Czech reformers. As Gomułka aged, a struggle for the succession broke out among the party hierarchs. It took the bizarre form in March 1968 of an outburst of officially sponsored 'anti-Zionism', the immediate target being the country's tiny remaining Jewish population. The anti-Semitic drive was a cynical and successful device to drive a wedge between the intelligentsia and workers. The architect of the campaign, the Interior Minister, General Mieczysław Moczar, commanded support from nationalists and Second World War veterans and drew on popular anti-Semitism that was still prevalent in many parts of Polish society. Gomułka, whose wife was Jewish, was vulnerable to this oblique form of attack. Jews in prominent positions in the party, the bureaucracy, and universities were dismissed and many left the country. Gomułka survived for the time being, though Rapacki and others resigned. Kuroń, Michnik, and others were imprisoned and dissent was temporarily subdued.

Two years later, however, the government was confronted by renewed unrest. The spark was the announcement of large price rises for basic foodstuffs and fuel. In December 1970 protest demonstrations and strikes in Gdańsk and other major industrial centres spread throughout the country. The government declared a state of emergency and dispatched security forces to restore order. Fighting in Gdańsk continued for several days, leaving at least forty-five dead. A measure of calm was restored only after it was announced on 20 December that Gomułka had resigned as First Secretary. His successor, the Silesian party boss, Edward Gierek, offered a more technocratic style of leadership. He adopted a mollifying tone towards the protesters, rescinded the price increases, and made conciliatory gestures towards the Church.

In the early 1970s the Polish economy achieved high growth rates but Gierek failed to address some of its basic weaknesses, among them a backward agricultural sector, an unrealistic price structure, and a growing and dangerous dependency on foreign loans. Peasants found it worthwhile to feed subsidized bread to their pigs. Dollars, cigarettes, and vodka circulated as alternatives to the official currency. The system became notorious for *korupcja* and *protekcja*.

By 1976 the government was finding difficulty in meeting short-term obligations. Again it sought to reduce food subsidies, that is, to raise prices. The reaction on the streets was immediate. Taking fright, the government once again withdrew the increases, this time within a matter of hours. Hundreds of protesters were imprisoned. The government's prestige suffered a severe blow. A group of intellectuals, including Michnik and Kuroń, founded a committee to help provide legal defence for those arrested. Over the next four years, the Workers' Defence Committee (*Komitet Obrony Robotników*, KOR), became the engine-room of the political opposition in Poland.

In October 1978 a Pole, Cardinal Karol Wojtyła, Archbishop of Cracow, was elected to the papacy. John Paul II was the first non-Italian Pope for four centuries. In June 1979 he gave a dramatic boost to nationalist sentiment in Poland when he visited his native land. Millions of the faithful gave him an emotional reception. Even the regime felt constrained to welcome him as an honoured guest (Brezhnev failed to persuade Gierek not to receive him). The humiliating obeisance of the country's Communist rulers to their visitor symbolized a larger surrender of spiritual authority. A vital link of ideological control over the population suddenly snapped.

The great crisis of the Polish Communist regime arrived in the summer of 1980. Since 1971 Poland's hard-currency debt to western lenders had ballooned from $1 billion to $21 billion. Eight-five cents of every dollar that Poland earned from exports now went to servicing debt. Yet again the government announced food price increases. Yet again the popular reaction was immediate, widespread, and vehement. But on this occasion, unlike

1970 and 1976, opposition was effectively organized on a nationwide basis. Strikers in a number of factories elected an Inter-factory Strike Committee that was advised on strategy by the KOR intellectuals. From late August the strikers adopted the slogan *Solidarność*, which later became the name of their movement. Instead of staying at home, the strikers occupied their workplaces and remained there for several weeks. Instead of becoming atomized and demoralized, the strikers attained a new collective sense of their own power that, in other circumstances, Communists might have called class consciousness. Solidarity was indeed privately recognized by some of the more open-eyed members of the Soviet leadership as a truly working-class movement.

Lech Wałęsa, a thirty-seven-year-old electrician from the Lenin shipyard at Gdańsk, rose to leadership of Solidarity, borne on a tide of fury against the regime. A pious Catholic, doggedly determined but flexible, unsophisticated but ready to listen to the advice of intellectuals, he disclaimed any interest in politics. 'I am a union man,' he insisted, claiming that Solidarity was interested solely in asserting workers' rights.[37] As strikes spread throughout the country, the government found itself compelled to negotiate. The ensuing talks between the strike leaders and the government afforded a spectacle unprecedented in a Communist country. On 31 August 1980 the two sides signed a historic agreement—historic because, for the first time, a Communist government had been compelled to acknowledge openly that its claim to represent the proletariat was an imposture sustained only by superior force. Free trade unions were to be permitted, the right to strike was recognized, all political prisoners were to be released, censorship was to be eased, and the state radio would broadcast Mass every Sunday, a startling innovation in a Communist country. At the canny insistence of the strike leaders, the end of the negotiations was broadcast live: there would be no secret deals and the government would be seen to be bound by whatever it agreed. Wałęsa declared: 'We have spoken as Poles to Poles. . . . There are no winners and no losers.'[38]

In truth, this was a gigantic triumph for the opposition and a humiliation for the government. If the Polish or Soviet Communist leaders imagined that the August agreement was an end rather than a beginning, they were to be rudely disabused. Five days later Gierek resigned, for health reasons, so it was said. He was replaced by Stanisław Kania, a loyal but colourless apparatchik with close links to the KGB. The Communist Party's authority was reeling and, as the economic crisis worsened, Solidarity made new demands for changes in the economic structure of the country. With the easing of censorship, the formerly underground oppositionist media were now widely disseminated and expressed the feeling of radicalization in the country. Solidarity's leaders were torn between a realistic appreciation that there were limits to Soviet tolerance and an increasing sense of their own social strength. Kuroń coined the phrase 'self-limiting revolution' to indicate that the Solidarity leaders understood that, as he said, 'it was important not to lure the Soviet wolves out of the woods.'[39]

The first sign of opposition strength after the August agreement was the formal establishment of the Solidarity federation of free trade unions, the first non-official labour union in the Communist world. Within a few months it claimed ten million members. Another three million joined its peasant affiliate, 'Rural Solidarity', whose chief demand was protection of private property rights in land.

Solidarity's programme, announced in February 1981, repudiated any intention of seeking to overthrow Communist state power: 'As a labour union, we do not intend to take over the job of the state apparatus of power.' At the same time it called for a policy of economic reform that amounted, in effect, to the demolition of the existing system: 'Central planning should be deprived of its prescriptive and command characteristics, which means that it must not transfer its tasks to enterprises by means of commands and prohibitions.' Nor did the programme shy away from political demands including 'civil liberties . . . such as the right to profess one's own views, freedom of speech and the press, the rights to honest information, to assembly, and to free association'. The movement's basic values were defined as four: 'The nation's best traditions, Christianity's ethical principles, democracy's political mandate, and socialist social thought'. The central role of the Church in national life and in the outlook of most Solidarity members was laid bare in the reference to 'the cross hanging side by side with the white eagle in many union rooms [that] reminds our members of their moral origins and fills them with faith in the justice of our cause'.[40] This religious basis, more than anything, distinguished Solidarity from most other opposition movements in eastern Europe.

The Soviet leadership and its east European allies contemplated the direction of events in Poland with mounting consternation. *Pravda* had denounced the August agreement from the outset as an attempt by 'enemies of Poland' to overturn the status quo in eastern Europe.[41] The East German leader, Erich Honecker, who had replaced Ulbricht in 1971, fearing that the rot might spread to his own subjects, urged 'collective action', by which he meant at least the threat of an invasion of Poland. 'Any delay in acting would mean death—the death of socialist Poland', he wrote to Brezhnev in November 1980.[42] The Czechoslovak and Bulgarian leaders echoed this view. Kádár, alone among the satellite chiefs, advised a more cautious approach. But at an emergency meeting of the Warsaw Pact in December, Brezhnev declared that the 'situation in Poland and the danger emanating from Poland' were 'not simply Polish matters. . . . They affect us all.'[43] Military preparations were at an advanced stage for a Soviet intervention in Poland. In the end, however, Brezhnev held back, perhaps impressed by a warning from Kania that 'if there were an intervention there would be a national uprising' and that 'even if angels entered Poland they would be treated as bloodthirsty vampires'.[44]

The Polish government's attempts to regain the initiative, however, were inept. In January it announced an economic reform package that included proposals for workers' self-management and a gradual move away from centralized planning. In February 1981 Moscow gave the nod to the elevation of the Minister of Defence, General Wojciech Jaruzelski, to the office of Prime Minister. This was the first time in the history of Communist eastern Europe that a military officer had been appointed head of government. Almost from the moment of his appointment, perhaps even earlier, he came under Soviet pressure for military repression of Solidarity. Although impatient with what they called Jaruzelski's 'well-known waffling', Soviet leaders believed that there were 'in fact no other officials who might take over the party and the country'. They decided, therefore, to press Jaruzelski to take a firmer line while 'as a deterrent to counterrevolution, maximally [to] exploit the fears of internal reactionaries and international imperialism that the Soviet Union might send its troops into Poland'.[45] Economic conditions in Poland meanwhile continued to deteriorate, further angering the population. Exports declined, prices increased, and the government reintroduced rationing of basic commodities.

A Solidarity Congress in September called for free trade unions throughout eastern Europe. The appeal was a red rag to a bull. The Soviet party and government sent a message to their Polish counterparts that ominously echoed those of 1948 to Yugoslavia, of 1956 to Hungary, and of 1968 to Czechoslovakia: the Soviets expected that the Polish party and government would 'immediately take decisive and drastic measures to stop the slanderous anti-Soviet propaganda and to put an end to hostile acts directed against the Soviet Union'.[46] In October Brezhnev telephoned Jaruzelski and told him 'without wasting time, to take the decisive measures you intend to use against the counterrevolution'.[47] When, after a month, nothing had happened, Brezhnev berated Jaruzelski for his delaying tactics and demanded immediate action.

On 13 December, the Polish government declared martial law and sent security forces into the streets. Solidarity was banned and several thousand activists, including most of the movement's leaders, were imprisoned. In a radio address Jaruzelski justified these measures, maintaining that the country had been 'on the edge of an abyss'. He insisted that there was no intention of embarking on a military dictatorship. 'We must bind the hands of adventurers before they push the country into civil war,' he declared. To this end, he announced, 'a group of people threatening the safety of the country has been interned. The extremists of Solidarity are included in this group as well as other members of illegal organizations.'[48]

Then and later the Polish leaders justified their action on the ground that the only alternative would have been Soviet military intervention. Jaruzelski, in retirement in post-Communist Poland, recalled meetings with Soviet army chiefs in the autumn of 1981 in which they warned him of their readiness to invade Poland. Evidence of contacts between the Polish and Soviet security arms that became available later suggests that in reality Polish Communist leaders were beseeching the Soviets for military assistance but that the latter were reluctant to comply.[49] The KGB chief, Andropov, told the Soviet Politburo on 10 December, 'We can't risk such a step. We do not intend to introduce troops into Poland. That is the proper position and we must adhere to it until the end. I don't know how things will turn out in Poland, but even if Poland falls under the control of Solidarity that's the way it will be.'[50] It is plain from the minutes of this meeting that Andropov was expressing the general view of the Politburo which was endorsed by the Soviet High Command. Whether the Soviets could really have lived permanently side by side with a Poland in which the Communist government was steadily yielding more and more ground to Solidarity remains questionable. Nevertheless, the Soviet aim at this critical juncture was evidently to overawe the Poles by the threat of intervention rather than by actual use of force.

Solidarity was driven underground rather than crushed. The events of the previous two years had struck much deeper roots in Polish society and institutions than the Prague Spring in Czechoslovakia. Some of Solidarity's leaders evaded the initial wave of arrests and fled abroad or continued to organize from hiding. The union's weekly newspaper continued to appear. Over the next few years Poland survived on two levels: that of government edicts, scorned by the populace, and that of 'civil society', a term that came to be understood as denoting an autonomous, unofficial social sphere in which free thought, speech, and action remained possible. The Polish people fell back even more on the one institution that represented the national will to resist: the Church. In 1983 the Pope revisited his native country and millions (including Jaruzelski) paid homage to him. A few months later Wałęsa was awarded the Nobel Peace Prize. Like many Nobel laureates from Communist countries who had preceded him, he was prevented from accepting in person. In the lecture that was read out on his behalf in Oslo, he quoted from the Pope's words during his visit to Poland and from the Psalms, stressing his unshaken faith in 'real dialogue between the state authorities and the people' as the only way forward.[51]

The Solidarity movement marked the last major appearance, as an independent actor on the European stage, of the organized working class. Its overall impact on the history of the continent had been slighter than was forecast by Marx. Save in the aftermath of the First World War and in the 1930s, proletarian revolution had not been the overwhelming force that both its enemies and its champions expected. Now it turned against those who had usurped and sullied its name. In Gdańsk the heirs of the sailors of Kronstadt and the workers of Barcelona stood their ground and reclaimed the banner of freedom.

Communism grown old

By the beginning of the 1980s Communism in eastern Europe had entered a phase of ossification. Economic growth rates declined, particularly in Poland, which experienced three successive years of big falls in output in 1980–2. The system as a whole creaked at the joints, reflecting the age of its leaders, all but one of whom had been born before the First World War.

In 1980 the oldest, Tito, died, leaving the federal political structure of Yugoslavia under severe strain. Unable to agree on a successor, his colleagues decided on an annual rotation of the country's presidency and of the party leadership among representatives of the component republics of Yugoslavia. The decision diminished the authority of the federal institutions and dangerously reinforced centrifugal tendencies. In 1981 ethnic disturbances broke out between Albanians and Serbs in the Kosovo region. Within a decade the resultant intensification of national rivalries brought about the dissolution of the Yugoslav federation.

The next-oldest of the east European leaders, Enver Hoxha of Albania, ended his political career as he had begun it, with a bloodbath. In 1981 he launched a final purge, demoting his closest colleague and heir apparent, Mehmet Shehu, who committed suicide, and ordering the execution of several others. Hoxha died in 1985, leaving his country, after forty years of Communist rule, as it had been at the outset, the poorest, most isolated, and most primitive in Europe.

The mantle of seniority now fell on the Bulgarian ruler, Zhivkov. He had been appointed First Secretary in 1954 and liked to boast that he had served longer than any other world leader apart from Emperor Hirohito of Japan (he unaccountably ignored Queen Elizabeth II). Bulgaria differed from most of the other Soviet satellites in that Russia, as patron of her independence in the late nineteenth century and her liberator in 1944, could draw on a deep reserve of historic fellow feeling. Anti-Communism here was driven not so much by resentment of Russian imperial domination as by disgust with the corruption of the Zhivkov regime, which for a time seemed to be developing dynastic ambitions. But the death of Zhivkov's Oxford-educated daughter, Ludmilla, in 1981 ended any such pretensions. A 'new economic mechanism', applied to the economy in 1982, failed to raise productivity, improve manufacturing standards, or make consumer goods more readily available.

Communism in Czechoslovakia too was showing signs of dilapidation. Living standards remained high and foreign borrowing low by comparison with other east bloc countries. But high internal consumption and low external debt were sustained at the price of low industrial investment, which eventually reduced Czechoslovak industry to what even the Prime Minister, Lubomír Štrougal, called 'a museum of the industrial revolution'.[52] A dissident movement, Charter 77, founded in 1977, drew encouragement, like KOR in Poland, from the Helsinki Conference's declaration on civil and political rights. The Charter called for 'a constructive dialogue with the political and state power'.[53] Three men were named in the document as 'authorized spokesmen': the religious philosopher Jan Patočka, the playwright Václav Havel, and the former Foreign Minister during the 'Prague Spring', Jiří Hájek. The Charter was signed initially by 243 people. Nearly all were Czechs, a symptom of the regional imbalance in the democratic opposition and an omen of later schism in the federation. Many of the signatories were dismissed from their jobs and subjected to petty harassment. Others were gaoled. The impervious arrogance and philistinism of the regime may be gauged from an episode in 1982. During one of Havel's spells of imprisonment a representative of the Czechoslovak Culture Ministry was questioned by a journalist about cultural conditions in the country and about Havel's work in particular. The official complained that 'the literature Havel writes is against his own nation. . . . His work has nothing in common with Czechoslovak culture.' After similarly disparaging comments about other imprisoned or exiled dissidents such as Milan Kundera (his latest work was 'a disappointment') and Ludvík Vaculík ('not a meaningful personality'), the official declared: 'Our people can live without them. They don't need these adventurers.'[54] At one level this was an assessment that, whatever its value as literary criticism, represented crude political reality. Charter 77 failed to galvanize mass opposition to the regime. The group nevertheless persisted in efforts to open a 'dialogue', albeit a very one-sided one. Like Wałęsa in Poland, Havel and his colleagues waited for their day to dawn.

More than any other Soviet satellite, East Germany remained faithful to Stalinist norms almost to the end. Although the harsh edges of terror were moderated, the Stasi (Ministerium für Staatssicherheit, i.e. secret police and domestic intelligence agency) remained the foremost instrument of power in the land. The number of its full-time employees nearly doubled between 1973 and 1989 and was much larger than that of the Gestapo at its height. Yet at the same time the regime became ever more dependent on its hated rival in the west. According to its propagandists, the productivity of East German industry was overtaking that of Britain; in fact, it never produced more than 10 per cent of the GDP of West Germany. Hundreds of millions of marks were pumped into the east each year by the West German government in the 1970s and 1980s. In 1983 bankruptcy was staved off only with the help of a billion-mark loan from the Federal Republic. The construction of the Berlin Wall had reduced emigration to a trickle, though the West German government quietly bought freedom for some with hard currency: 121,000 emigrated legally, as a result, between 1977 and 1988. Strangely, West German politicians who had once insisted on reunification as a goal now hardly spoke of it, referring instead to the need for 'coexistence'.

Of all the east European countries, Hungary offered the closest to a success story in these years. In 1982 a dissident Hungarian writer could compare Kádár almost affectionately with 'our King Franz Josef, who mercilessly crushed the Hungarian people's struggle for independence in 1849 with Russian help, then went on to rule by the grace of God for sixty-seven years and in the meantime sealed a constitutional compromise with us, opening the way to an era of rapid development'.[55] Under Kádár's 'New Economic Mechanism', inaugurated in January 1968, central control of the economy was reduced, although not eliminated, and some incentives were introduced. Bolder reforms followed in 1978. The pricing structure was liberalized and foreign-exchange controls were relaxed. Kádár's pragmatic policies created an economy poised uneasily somewhere between central planning and the free market. But the country had run up a foreign debt of $10 billion by 1980. The cost of servicing loans was so great that Hungary stood on the verge of default. In the hope of shoring up her international financial position, she joined the IMF and the World Bank in 1982 (at that time Romania and Yugoslavia were the only other Communist member states). The decision was taken without asking or even informing the Soviet Union and represented a significant assertion of sovereign decision-making. Over the next few years Hungary was granted a series of credits and stand-by arrangements. The economy nevertheless continued to deteriorate and the government continued to issue fraudulent economic statistics. By the mid-1980s Kádár was coming to be viewed less as a gifted, if unscrupulous, political operator and more as a dinosaur.

The youngest of the east European leaders, Nicolae Ceauşescu, born in 1919, was the only one who exhibited a kind of political dynamism in these years. In his initial phase in power after 1965 he had flirted with liberal ideas, even permitting some elections with multiple candidates to take place. In 1978 he had launched a campaign for *autoconducerea*, workers' self-management. Under the influence of his powerful wife women were advanced to greater participation in politics and society. Ceauşescu continued to win sterling opinions in the west by repeatedly snubbing the Soviet Union. In 1978 he was accorded the ultimate accolade, a state visit to Queen Elizabeth II at Buckingham Palace.

By the 1980s, however, Ceauşescu's megalomania was driving his country into a deep pit. Observing the plight into which foreign indebtedness had driven his Polish neighbours, he determined at all costs to pay off Romania's loans. Every other economic objective was subordinated to this goal. In particular, consumption was cut back ruthlessly in order to conserve foreign currency. Nationalist hostility to foreign capital had precedents in Romanian history but Ceauşescu carried this to inhuman extremes. The national debt, which had amounted to $11.4 billion in 1982, was reduced within seven years to $1 billion at huge social cost. Romania had once been an important energy exporter but by the 1980s her oil reserves were virtually exhausted and coal production failed to meet the planners' targets. Chronic shortages of fuel led to great hardship, with heat and light cut off for long periods in the cold Romanian winters, during which the maximum permitted indoor temperature was 14 °C (58 °F). In the mining district of the Jiu valley blocks of flats were built without chimneys lest workers steal coal from the mines. Food shortages became endemic in a country that had once produced a large agricultural surplus. In 1982 the government complained that the population was overeating. A Rational Nourishment Commission was created to supervise the nation's diet. Such governmental nannying too had precedents in the pre-Communist era: in the 1930s King Carol had hit on the bright idea of dispatching to remote regions a 'sanitary train' in which grumbling peasants were compulsorily bathed. The benefits to national hygiene were dubious but the underlying intention was no doubt benign. Ceauşescu's programme, however, was driven less by concern for the health of his people than by obsessive determination to pay off debt at whatever cost. His model diet was thin gruel indeed. The bread ration was reduced to 300 grams a day per person. Potatoes and eggs were often unobtainable and coffee disappeared from shops altogether. The country produced large quantities of meat, but most of it was exported to the Soviet Union rather than made available at home.

Economic hardship went hand in hand with repressive social policies. Ceauşescu's ban on almost all abortions failed to raise the birth rate permanently. By the 1980s it had fallen back below replacement level. In the hope of alleviating the demographic deficit, Ceauşescu enforced draconian natalist policies. Childless couples were subjected to punitive taxation. Contraceptives were virtually unavailable. Women were subjected to compulsory monthly gynaecological examinations at their workplaces in order to detect pregnancies, which were then to be carried to term. The consequences included large numbers of illegal abortions, a high maternal death rate arising from botched abortions, and large numbers of unwanted children dumped in overcrowded orphanages.

Discontent with the regime and with Ceauşescu personally increased as complaints of corruption and nepotism became widespread. The personality cult of the leader reached extraordinary heights: sycophants saluted him as the 'genius of the Carpathians'. But enemies dubbed him 'Maoşescu'. Transmissions by state television, limited in 1984 to four hours a day in order to conserve power, chronicled the exploits of Ceauşescu and his wife, who was appointed First Deputy Prime Minister and took charge of education and cultural policy. Dissent was monitored and repressed by the sixteen thousand officers of the *Securitate*, the secret police force. Although there was no return to the mass terror of Stalinism, standard *Securitate* techniques included torture, forced labour, telephone taps, and the compulsory registration of every typewriter in the country.

Ignoring the simmering discontent, the government pressed ahead with two vast projects of social engineering. A new city plan was devised for Bucharest: it involved the wholesale destruction of old quarters, including architecturally important religious buildings, to make way for a broad 'Victory of Socialism Boulevard' and a vast palace, built of white stone. This gargantuan structure rivalled Versailles, in size if not in taste. Ceauşescu also approved a long-mooted scheme for creating large 'agro-industrial centres' in which, by the year 2000, the inhabitants of 7,500 small villages were to be forcibly concentrated.

In November 1982 the biggest beast in the ageing European Communist menagerie, Leonid Brezhnev, finally succumbed to an illness that for some time had rendered him both physically and politically debilitated. His successor, Yury Andropov, was aged sixty-eight—the average age of the Politburo's membership by this time. He was probably the most intelligent and least hidebound leader of the Soviet Union since Lenin. Andropov was said to have a 'Hungarian complex' arising from his experience as Soviet ambassador in Budapest at the time of the 1956 revolution, when he had been perturbed by the lynchings of secret policemen by the revolutionaries. As a realistic and astute head of the secret police apparatus since 1967, he came to understand the need for renewal and institutional change as the price of maintaining Soviet power. Upon assuming office he tried to give renewed impetus to the Soviet economy without, however, countenancing significant political reform. But Andropov survived for only fifteen months in office. He died in February 1984. From his deathbed, he tried but failed to engineer the appointment of a young protégé, Mikhail Gorbachev, as his successor. The Politburo's choice, instead, of the seventy-two-year-old Konstantin Chernenko represented the last throw of the Soviet gerontocracy. Chernenko suffered from lung disease and could barely speak without gasping. He ruled only thirteen months, during which no important policy initiatives were registered. Upon his death in March 1985 the Soviet system could no longer avoid its moment of truth.

17

Stress in Liberal Europe 1973–1989

On and on and on
Keep on rocking baby
'Til the night is gone
On and on and on
'Til the night is gone
On and on and on
Keep on rocking baby
'Til the night is gone

*Benny Andersson and Björn Ulvaeus, Stockholm, February 1980**

End of the post-war era

The economic crisis after 1973 hit the west European economies with the force of a hurricane. The almost unbroken period of rapid economic growth since the late 1940s came to an abrupt halt. Several countries experienced absolute declines in economic activity. Unemployment rose to levels that had not been seen since the 1930s. Fluctuating commodity prices transformed terms of trade. Currency values gyrated wildly. But whereas the Great Depression had been accompanied by deflation, this one involved large-scale inflation. The phenomenon gave rise to the term 'stagflation'. Economists were puzzled and the Keynesian doctrine toppled from its pedestal. Marxist commentators contemplated, with a certain amount of *Schadenfreude*, what they hoped might be the terminal crisis of capitalism. Yet in spite of the battering that it received, west European society exhibited

* From 'On & On & On', lyric of song performed by Abba. Cf. Auden's song 'On and on and on', in W. H. Auden, *Collected Poems*, ed. Edward Mendelson, New York, 1991, 272.

remarkable resilience and, after difficult adjustments, weathered the storm. It took a decade, however, until a sustained economic recovery was under way in most of western Europe.

The immediate precipitant of the crisis was the Arab–Israeli war of October 1973. The Arab oil-producing states, in an expression of solidarity with the cause of the liberation of Palestine, declared an embargo on oil exports to the USA and the Netherlands, both regarded as friendly to Israel. At the same time they induced the Organization of Petroleum Exporting Countries (OPEC) to raise the price of oil drastically from around $3 per barrel in October 1973 to over $13 by January 1974. The American Secretary of State, Henry Kissinger, called the increase 'one of the pivotal events in the history of this century'.[1] Yet although, in the public memory, the recession of the mid-1970s was closely associated with the events of October 1973, its causes ran much deeper and largely antedated the war.

Three interlocking changes in the early 1970s in the structure of the international economic system were largely responsible for the crisis. The first was a worldwide economic boom, in which Europe shared, and which, according to some analysts, represented the final stage of 'catch-up' by European economies after the reconstruction and high-growth phases following the Second World War. The second was the collapse of the dollar-based, gold-backed, fixed-currency system established at Bretton Woods in 1944. The third was the shift in power from oil consumers to oil producers.

The boom of the early 1970s, in part a consequence of massive US government spending associated with the Vietnam War, reached a climax in 1972–3. Very rapid growth rates were achieved by the main European economies, as well as by the United States and Japan: in 1973 the fifteen leading west European economies (not including Switzerland or Norway) grew by 6 per cent. Industrial production grew even faster, by 7.8 per cent. The United States sucked in European exports and developed a gaping balance of payments deficit. Pressure on the dollar and worldwide inflation followed.

The Bretton Woods system had been founded on the supremacy of the dollar and the preponderance of the American economy in world trade. In the early 1970s, however, flight from the dollar reached unprecedented proportions. Between 1969 and 1973 West German foreign-exchange reserves multiplied tenfold. In May 1971 the mark was floated and soon gained heavily against the dollar. In August that year further currency outflows forced the United States, for the first time since the 1930s, to cease

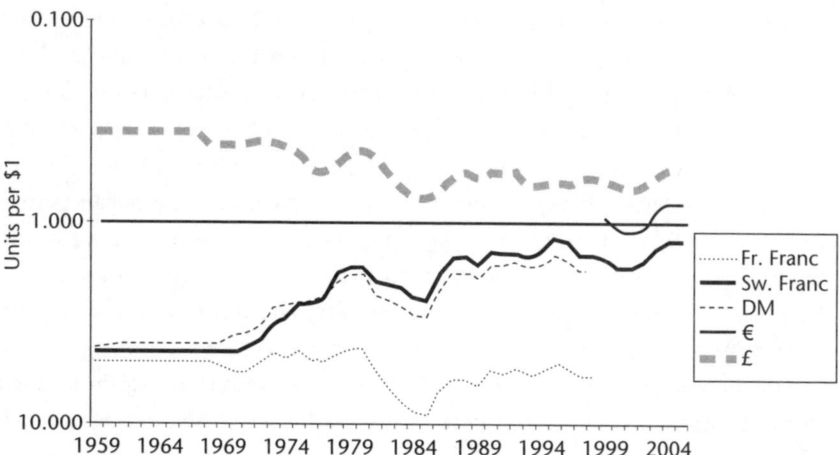

Figure 7. Currency movements relative to US dollar, 1959–2004
Source: IMF.

exchanging the dollar holdings of other countries for a fixed price in gold. With its demonetization, the value of gold, which had been held at $35 per ounce since 1934, moved sharply upwards, rising above $800 by 1980.

While 'closing the gold window', the United States sought to preserve some vestige of the fixed-rate system. In December 1971 a meeting at the Smithsonian Institution in Washington DC of representatives of the 'Group of Ten' leading capitalist countries agreed on new currency values and on flexible 'bands' for currency trading. Under conditions of surging international capital movements and worldwide economic expansion, the Smithsonian agreement soon came under strain. In March–April 1972 the European Community, together with Britain and other countries, set up a 'snake-in-the tunnel' currency system whereby their currencies could fluctuate narrowly within a 'tunnel' of broader movement against the dollar. But within three months speculative pressure on the pound led to its sudden withdrawal from the arrangement. In January 1973 the Swiss franc was floated and the next month the dollar had to be devalued again. In February the Italian lira left the 'snake'. The US Treasury Secretary, John Connally, bluntly warned America's allies: 'The dollar may be our currency but it's your problem.'[2]

Alliances, however intimate, have their limits. On 1 March the Bundesbank (the German Central Bank) had to spend $2.7 billion, the most ever in a single day, to support the dollar. Exchange markets closed for several days.

When they reopened, the era of fixed exchange rates was over. From then onwards the world's major currencies floated freely against the dollar. For a time the Europeans tried to preserve their band of exchange rates with each other but by January 1974 the 'snake' was dead, a casualty of the broader economic crisis that was engulfing the world.

Like the collapse of Bretton Woods, the oil price increase began before the October war. In fact, the two developments were linked, since oil trading was denominated entirely in dollars. As the international value of the dollar declined, oil producers became more and more restive about the price they were receiving for what was, for most of them, their only significant export. OPEC had existed since 1960 but it was not until economic conditions matured in the early 1970s that it was able to capture effective control of the market. The boom led to greatly increased demand for oil in both western Europe and North America. Because of the near-exhaustion of known reserves, oil production in the United States was unable to meet the swiftly rising demand and for the first time in the century the country became a net importer of oil.

In the past, sudden fluctuations in the price of oil had been prevented by collusion among the 'seven sisters', the major companies that exercised vertical control over the entire oil industry (except behind the Iron Curtain), from production through transportation and refining, to marketing. These companies, five American ones plus Anglo-Dutch Shell and British Petroleum, regarded a low and stable price as in their long-term interest. But even before the outbreak of the Middle East war, their capacity to control the market had been deteriorating. In 1969 a military government, headed by Colonel Muammar Gaddafi, seized power in Libya, where large new reserves had recently been discovered. He soon succeeded in taking advantage of the sudden increase in demand created by the economic boom. Libyan oil could command a premium because of its low sulphur content and because the closure of the Suez Canal since 1967 added to the transportation costs to Europe of all the other large Middle East oil producers. Libya now demanded a higher price for her oil. In former times the 'seven sisters' would simply have refused to deal with Gaddafi. But demand for Middle Eastern oil was now irrepressible. In September 1970–1 a small American company, Occidental Petroleum, struck a deal with Libya involving a price rise of nearly a third. This was the beginning of a sea-change in the oil market. The deal broke the control of the oil 'majors' over the oil price. A buyers' ring was soon replaced by a sellers' cartel. The companies and the importing countries found themselves, at least for the time being, obliged to submit.

Western Europe at this time was more dependent than ever before in its history on oil as a source of energy. In 1950 three-quarters of the region's energy needs had been met by coal, most of it domestically produced. By 1973 oil supplied 63 per cent of total energy needs. Use of other fuels, in particular coal, had diminished over the previous two decades, since oil appeared to be cheaper, cleaner, more easily available, and technologically more versatile. Oil was the prime energy source for industry, home heating, and automobiles; it was projected to supply an increasing share of European energy requirements over the next decade; and it was impossible to switch quickly to alternatives. With almost no indigenous sources, the EC was obliged to import 98 per cent of its oil consumption. The rest of western Europe was in a similar position. Most of the oil was supplied by Middle Eastern OPEC members.

As the price of oil rose, west European countries perforce continued to import it, as a result building up large balance of payments deficits. The direct effect of the embargo on oil exports to the Netherlands was small, since the oil 'majors', which still controlled most of the world's oil shipments, were able to contrive various mechanisms for circumventing it. But the price increase and another in 1979, following the revolution in Iran that overthrew the Shah, administered crushing blows to business confidence. The crisis led the EC to adopt a suddenly (some said grotesquely) humble attitude towards OPEC in general, and its Middle Eastern member states in particular. The oil producers agreed to make an effort to 'recycle' their newfound wealth on international capital markets in an orderly way but they would not relent on the oil price. Moreover, they began to take over direct control of oil production, refining, transportation, and marketing from the 'majors', in order to ensure that western oil companies would never again be able to control the oil market.

The impact of the events of 1973 on all aspects of the west European economy was devastating. Stock prices plunged immediately: between October and December 1973 the London Stock Exchange suffered its greatest fall since the war. Growth in the EC declined from 4.8 per cent per annum in the period 1960–73 to 2.4 per cent over the next decade. In 1975, the lowest point of the cycle, most of western Europe experienced a significant decline in industrial output. In the same year inflation reached double digits in almost every country. By 1983 more than 11 per cent of the labour force in the EC were jobless. Everywhere high state unemployment payments and reduced economic growth contributed to further increases in government expenditure in proportion to national income. In several countries state spending rose well above 40 per cent of GDP and in Belgium, the Netherlands, and Sweden above 50 per cent by 1980.

Conventional economic policies seemed inadequate to restore order at either the international or the domestic level. The Keynesian economic consensus, on which most west European governments had based their policies since the war, became discredited. A new economic orthodoxy, based on the monetarist thinking of the 'Chicago school' of economists headed by Milton Friedman, took its place. The guru of the philosophy was the elderly Austrian-born economist Friedrich von Hayek. His wartime philippic *The Road to Serfdom* became the bible of the neoclassical economists, though Keynes himself had written to Hayek, upon its publication in 1944, that he found himself 'morally and philosophically . . . in agreement with virtually the whole of it; and not only in agreement but in a deeply moved agreement'.[3] Detecting a parallel between all forms of socialism and the totalitarianism of the 1930s and 1940s, Hayek denounced planning and called for a return to pure liberalism and a minimalist state, with only limited concessions to market regulation and social welfare. Such prescriptions attracted increasing support on the right of the political spectrum but it was to be several years before governments would dare to think in such terms.

For two countries partial salvation lay on the horizon in the shape of oil and gas in the North Sea. Large deposits had been discovered there a few years earlier. The cost of production was much higher than that of Middle East oil but the increase in the oil price rendered North Sea extraction much more commercially attractive. Norway and Britain shared in the bonanza which by 1980 made both countries self-sufficient in oil and turned Stavanger and Aberdeen into Klondike-style boom towns. Norway became one of the richest countries in the world per head of population. But the exploitation of North Sea oil took some time and was, in any case, cold comfort to countries like Italy that produced no oil or coal at home.

They were obliged to seek other remedies. Everywhere efforts were made to conserve fuel and switch to alternative sources. Total west European consumption of oil fell by a quarter between 1973 and 1982. New construction codes were enforced to make buildings more efficient at preserving heat: by 1987 homes built in western Europe required roughly

40 per cent less energy than those built in 1970–3. In November 1973 West Germany banned driving on motorways on some Sundays. As the price of petrol shot up, the average size of cars on European roads began to go down. Manufacturers started to build more fuel-efficient vehicles. Domestic appliances were made more energy-efficient. There was a flurry of interest in wind and tidal power. But it soon became clear that such expedients could offer only limited succour.

Nuclear power seemed a much more practicable long-term proposition. It was embraced with the greatest vigour by France, where in 1974 the Prime Minister, Pierre Messmer, announced a new programme under which it would provide half of all France's energy needs by the end of the century. As early as 1982 more than half of all electricity in France was generated by nuclear power. Over the next seven years five or six nuclear power stations were commissioned in France each year. Elsewhere, however, the nuclear option encountered political hostility. In Sweden it had been uncontroversial in the 1960s and the construction of eleven reactors was approved almost unanimously by the Riksdag in 1970 and 1971. But after 1973 an anti-nuclear coalition, composed of the Centre Party, Communists, and environmentalists, opposed further reactors. A referendum in 1980 produced a majority in favour of a slow phase-out of nuclear power.

The long-term effects of the crisis on western Europe were immense and included large-scale changes in economic and social structure. The era of full employment ended. Labour unions, unable to prevent the return of mass unemployment, lost membership and political power. Old-established heavy industries, such as steel and shipbuilding, that were highly energy-dependent and that had been regarded as bedrocks of the economy, declined. In some cases they capitulated almost entirely to cheap-labour producers in eastern Europe or south-east Asia.

At the time the crisis evoked frequent comparisons with that of the 1930s. Yet in retrospect it was both less deep and more easily, although more slowly, overcome. Unlike the 1930s, political systems were not overthrown and the out-of-work masses were not mobilized into extremist political movements. The two main reasons were the cushion provided by the welfare state and the robustness of international financial institutions. The unemployed of the 1970s were frustrated and angry. But they were not hungry. Consequently they did not listen to rabble-rousers or march in the streets; they stayed at home and watched television or went out for a drink. The existence of the huge internal market of the EC diminished any tendency to repetition of the protectionist policies of the 1930s. And such bodies as the IMF, that had not existed in the previous depression, helped smooth out the worst financial effects of the crisis. The recession nevertheless left deep social and political wounds and paved the way for a decisive ideological shift away from the social market/welfare state consensus of the previous quarter-century.

The rise of neo-liberalism

The major west European economies each experienced the crisis in a different way and with different political outcomes. Yet some common patterns may be discerned: after initial efforts to spend their way out of the crisis, most governments resorted to deflationary policies that reduced domestic demand and increased unemployment. Strenuous efforts by trade unions to defend working-class incomes, using increasingly militant methods, drove more people out of jobs and eventually out of unions. Neo-liberal ideas gained increasing strength and by the 1980s began to be internalized to some extent even on the centre-left. Various novel means were devised to try to calibrate the effects of the crisis; for example, a 'misery index', comprising the sum of unemployment and inflation rates. Of course, no such measure could be more than crudely impressionistic. Overall, however, the social and political effects on the major economies were felt most acutely in Britain, Italy, and Sweden; somewhat less so in France and West Germany.

In Britain the sudden increase in the oil price emboldened militants in the coal miners' union, who reasoned that market logic dictated a general rise in energy prices. Their demand for a large pay increase was denied and they declared an overtime ban and then a strike, coinciding with a stoppage by electric power engineers. Edward Heath's government, concerned lest concessions to the miners accelerate what was already an inflationary wage spiral, encouraged the management of the nationalized coal industry to stand firm. A national state of emergency was declared on 13 November 1973. The Bank of England raised the bank rate to the unprecedented level of 13 per cent. As coal stocks at power stations dwindled, the government was compelled to declare a 'three-day week', with factories, offices, schools, and public institutions closed on four days out of seven. A government minister earned ridicule by urging citizens to brush their teeth in the dark to conserve fuel. As winter descended there were power cuts in many areas.

Heath decided to gamble on an appeal to the electorate. In the election of February 1974, no party won an overall majority. Heath tried to form a government with the support of the Liberals but was unable to meet their price, electoral reform. Harold Wilson, to his surprise, returned to power as head of a minority administration. A second election in October produced a Labour majority of just three.

The Labour governments of 1974–9, headed first by Wilson, and, after 1976, by James Callaghan, confronted the most intractable economic difficulties faced by Britain since the late 1940s. In 1975 unemployment rose over a million for the first time in a generation. GDP was in decline. Inflation rose to an unprecedented 27 per cent. Public expenditure reached a peacetime high of 46 per cent of GDP in 1975–6 and government borrowing rose to 9 per cent of GDP. The oil price increase led to a yawning balance of payments deficit that renewed pressure on the pound. Interest rates were raised even further but the flight from sterling persisted. In 1976 the Chancellor of the Exchequer, Denis Healey, had to turn to the European and US central banks for a $5.3 billion standby credit and then to the IMF for a further $3.9 billion loan, the largest in the fund's history. This was granted, conditional on a package of government spending cuts and deflationary measures, including a 'social contract' with the trade unions. The government's attempt to fulfil this pledge, however, led to a renewed series of bitter struggles to contain wage demands in the public sector.

These culminated in what came to be known as the 'winter of discontent', a traumatic episode that lodged in the national memory for the next generation. Public sector workers, dissatisfied with wages that failed to keep pace with inflation, struck. Rubbish piled up uncollected. Dead bodies lay unburied. Hospital patients died because of strikes by ambulance workers and hospital support staff. Both trade union membership and the number of working days lost through strikes reached a post-war peak. Public indignation against trade unions mounted and the government lost support. Anti-Labour feeling was fanned by the apparently smug unconcern of Callaghan, at least as portrayed in the largely Conservative press. 'Crisis? What crisis?' was the famous headline in the *Sun* on 11 January 1975 after the premier's return from the summit of western leaders in Guadeloupe (though he never said it). Because of Labour by-election losses, Callaghan came to head a minority administration. He depended for political survival on the support of the Liberals or other small parties. This was no basis for effective government and in the spring of 1979 Callaghan decided to go to the polls. The result was a devastating loss for Labour and the start of eighteen years of Conservative rule.

The new Prime Minister, Margaret Thatcher, had defeated Edward Heath for the Conservative party leadership in 1975. The first woman party leader in Britain and the first woman Prime Minister in Europe, she was intelligent but not an intellectual, forceful but not particularly thoughtful, respected (her own party held her in awe) but not widely loved. Her imperious manner, hard-hitting negotiating style, natural tendency towards polarization rather than consensus, and bold public pronouncements ('The lady's not for turning!'),[4] all represented a breathtaking change from the emollient euphemisms of the previous generation of British political leaders. Energetic, single-minded, and impatient of criticism, she swept aside the old conventions of Cabinet government and reinforced the tendency to concentrate power at 10 Downing Street. Her habit in Cabinet was to give ministers a maximum of one and a half minutes each to express their views at meetings.

Thatcher came from a similar lower-middle-class shopkeeping background to Heath and like him had been educated at Oxford. She had taken elocution lessons as a schoolgirl to make her speech sound more genteel. Yet she was no snob. Heath surrounded himself with Conservatives of the old school who might as well have graced a Macmillan Cabinet. Thatcher preferred self-made men, Jews like David Young, and brash vulgarians like Norman Tebbit who advised the unemployed to do what his father had done in the 1930s and 'get on their bike'.[5] Both Heath and Thatcher were modernizers. Both sought economic efficiency even at the price of hurting cherished institutions. As a minister in Macmillan's government, Heath had angered small shopkeepers by abolishing resale price maintenance for most goods; he thus opened the way for the retail revolution in Britain whereby supermarket chains undercut and destroyed most old-style, independent, specialist purveyors. But Heath and other Conservatives in his mould accepted and even embraced some elements of the welfare state. Thatcher, by contrast, seemed fundamentally opposed to its basic premises. 'Who is society?' she famously asked—then (as she often did) answering her own question: 'There is no such thing! There are individual men and women and there are families.'[6] Entranced by the ideas of Hayek, she surrounded herself with anti-Keynesian, monetarist economic advisers. Taking the principles of individualism and capitalist economic rationality to their logical extremes, she had no compunction about attacking some of the most powerful vested interests in the country, many of them hitherto strong supporters of the Conservative Party. One after another they bowed to her government's new-broom policy of whisking away the cobwebs around privileged corporate institutions—the stock exchange, the legal profession, the universities.

A central feature of the Thatcher government's policy was its effort to diminish the power of trade unions. Apart from the obvious political benefits of undermining the financial and institutional base of the Labour opposition, the policy was also designed to improve labour discipline, reduce strikes, get rid of restrictive practices, and increase elasticity in the labour market. In 1979 and 1981 legislation was enacted to provide for secret ballots before strikes, to prevent secondary picketing (of premises of enterprises not directly involved in disputes), and to render trade unions liable to civil action for damages caused by unlawful strikes, eliminating an immunity that stretched back to before the First World War.

In a year-long test of strength with the coal miners in 1984–5 the government won a victory over this most militant of unions, led by an articulate but politically inept ultra-leftist, Arthur Scargill. The strike was the longest and one of the most violent in British industrial history. More than at any time since the war, Britain came close to an atmosphere of class warfare. There were fierce clashes between police and 'flying pickets' trying to block coal deliveries to power stations. But the National Coal Board, headed by a Thatcher devotee, had laid in large stocks of coal. And gas was gradually displacing coal and oil as an industrial and domestic fuel. The union refused to hold a strike ballot and eventually split. The strikers were brought decisively to heel. The victory enabled the coal industry to close down loss-making pits and concentrate its effort on high-yield, low-cost fields where advanced technology could produce large productivity gains. The number of coal miners in Britain, which had been over a million in 1914, and 700,000 at the time of nationalization in 1947, fell to 41,000 by 1992, and the number of collieries from over 900 to just forty-nine. Coal production, which had been 287 million tons in 1913 and 128 million in 1981, fell to 75 million by 1992.

Previous post-war Conservative governments had generally not sought to reprivatize industries nationalized by Labour. The single important exception was steel. But the Thatcher government embarked on a series of privatizations of major state enterprises that changed the balance of the economy decisively. One after another, state holdings were auctioned off:

British Petroleum, British Aerospace, the national telephone system (it had been the first major enterprise to be nationalized as far back as 1911), British Airways, the gas, electricity, and water supply industries, and Rolls-Royce (which had been nationalized by Heath to save it from bankruptcy). There was also talk of denationalizing the BBC, the railways, and the Post Office and of creating fast-track toll roads of the sort that existed in France and other west European countries. The Conservative objective of creating a 'share-owning democracy' moved somewhat closer to realization. Between 1979 and 1991 the number of individuals owning stocks nearly quadrupled to 11.1 million or 25 per cent of the adult population. On the other hand, large institutional stockholders simultaneously increased their domination of the market: most private holdings were very small, and the proportion of total stocks held by individuals decreased from 28 per cent in 1981 to 21 per cent a decade later.

The British economy in the 1980s benefited greatly from the windfalls of North Sea oil and the proceeds of privatization of nationalized industries. Productivity in manufacturing industry increased. From 1977 to 1987 the country enjoyed a balance of payments surplus. Inflation fell to 3.4 per cent by 1986. The City of London's importance as an international financial centre grew, enhanced by a 'big bang' of deregulation in 1986. By the late 1980s London was transacting more foreign-exchange business than New York. But the price of all this was high. Unemployment reached a post-war peak of 3.3 million (11.5 per cent of the workforce) in 1984 and remained over two million until 1988. The value of sterling fell from $2.40 in 1980 to an all-time low of $1.04 in February 1985.

The Thatcher years altered the socio-economic balance in other ways. Tenants in public housing were encouraged to buy their homes: by 1991 more than two-thirds of the population were homeowners. Income taxes were reduced, particularly at the higher levels, but indirect taxes were increased. The period after 1979 saw a striking reversal of the trend towards greater equality of wealth and income that had characterized British society continuously since the war.

Thatcher's eleven-year reign (that is not too strong a term) was a phenomenon of international as well as British significance. She anchored her foreign policy in the alliance with the United States, forming a close ideological and policy partnership with the Reagan administration. Her government finally completed the decolonization of Rhodesia, which achieved independence under black-majority rule as Zimbabwe in 1981.

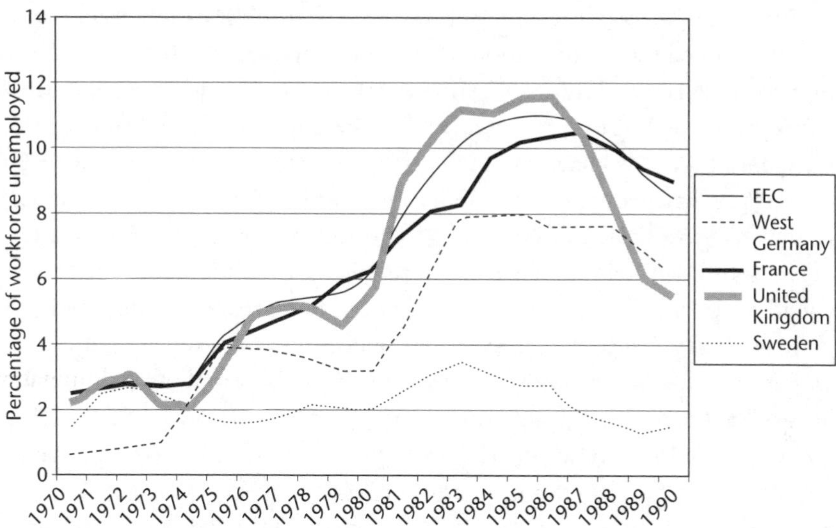

Figure 8. Unemployment, 1970–1990

Source: OECD.

Her implacable resolve (or, as her opponents saw it, her mulish obstinacy) brought victory in a tragi-comic war with Argentina in defence of the British-ruled Falkland Islands in 1982. In its basic pointlessness, the conflict was compared to 'two bald men quarrelling over a comb'.[7] The Argentinean military dictatorship was toppled but Thatcher's left-wing critics, who had spent years in fruitless demonstrations against the junta, clucked disapprovingly. The Archbishop of Canterbury, Dr Robert Runcie, infuriated her with what she held to be his insufficiently triumphalist sermon at the thanksgiving service held in St Paul's Cathedral after the war. Undaunted, she took the salute at a victory parade. In 1984 she signed an agreement with China whereby Britain's rule over her last significant colony, Hong Kong, would end in 1997.

Yet the central Thatcherite objective of diminishing the power of the state was not achieved. Contrary to Thatcherite intentions, the neutering of old elites and institutions magnified the power of central government. Although the number of civil servants fell, public spending in real terms was 16 per cent higher in 1987 than in 1979. In 1988 the government was taking in 37 per cent of GDP in taxes and other imposts, more than in the famously high-tax late 1940s. The proportion of GDP devoted to public expenditure rose from 45 per cent in 1979–80 to 48 per cent in 1982–3, though it dropped back to below 40 per cent in 1989–90.

Thatcher's victories in three successive general elections in 1979, 1983, and 1987 owed much to divisions among her opponents. The Labour Party in the 1980s dissolved into severe internal wrangling as Trotskyite and other 'entryists' battled against the centrist mainstream. Under the leadership of the radical orator Michael Foot, the party swung to the left and campaigned for nuclear disarmament and withdrawal from the European Community. Labour retained some footholds in local government but the antics of its so-called 'loony left' in municipal administrations in London, Liverpool, and elsewhere gave Thatcher a pretext to abolish the Greater London Council in 1986. For the next fourteen years London was the only capital city in western Europe that had no genuine form of self-government. Meanwhile, in 1981 a breakaway group from Labour, under the leadership of Roy Jenkins, founded a new Social Democrat Party that formed an alliance with the Liberals. They won a quarter of the total vote in the 1983 election but the first-past-the-post electoral system awarded them only twenty-three seats. Their immediate achievement, repeated in 1987, was to help ensure the Conservatives' re-election.

Governments in Britain in the 1970s and 1980s continued to wrestle unsuccessfully with the problem of Northern Ireland. Here the breakdown in consensus politics was absolute. Throughout this period terrorism by the Provisional IRA, both in the province, and, from 1973 onwards, in England, aimed at promoting the idea of British withdrawal from Northern Ireland. The organization received financial and propaganda sustenance from Irish-Americans and supplies of arms and explosives from eastern Europe and Libya. In the early 1970s both Conservative and Labour governments held secret discussions with IRA leaders but without result. After the mid-1970s British policy reverted to refusal to have any truck with terrorists. Instead the British sought a solution by negotiation with the main political parties in Northern Ireland and the government of the Irish Republic. Labour and Conservative governments alike repudiated any suggestion of withdrawal from the province except by the consent of a majority of the population in Northern Ireland itself. They maintained this stance in spite of rising sentiment in Britain in favour of washing its hands of the province. The cost was high. Among the more than three thousand lives lost was that of the Northern Ireland Secretary in Thatcher's government, Airey Neave: he was killed by a bomb outside the House of Commons in 1979. By the end of the 1980s British taxpayers were transferring £1.5 billion a year net to Northern Ireland, exclusive of military expenditures.

A breakthrough of sorts was achieved in December 1985 when Margaret Thatcher signed an agreement with the Taoiseach, Dr Garrett FitzGerald. The Irish Republic did not abandon its claim to the north but agreed that 'any change in the status of Northern Ireland would only come about with the consent of the majority of the people of Northern Ireland'. The Republic further recognized formally that the 'present wish' of the majority was for no such change. In return the British agreed to a consultative arrangement between the British and Irish governments whereby the Republic would, for the first time, have a limited say in the affairs of the province. The treaty was denounced by some Protestants as 'treason' and by some Catholics as 'a sell-out'. It improved relations between London and Dublin but not between Catholic west Belfast and the mainly Protestant eastern districts of the city. There and elsewhere in the province the ancient quarrel continued its murderous course.

Thatcher, who narrowly avoided death from an IRA bombing of the Conservative Party conference in Brighton in 1984, was immovable in her refusal to give way to terrorism (Edward Heath, by contrast, had negotiated a deal with Palestinian plane hijackers in 1970). She saw herself, and was seen by many of her followers, as a 'conviction politician' who would set an example for the rest of the world. Her personality and ideas jarred with most of her European counterparts, especially those from the centre-left. Yet during the 1980s, and even more thereafter, they found themselves forced, often against the grain, onto similar courses. All succumbed in some degree to the ascendant social philosophy of the age that came to be known eponymously as 'Thatcherism'.

The west European country that seemed to come closest to systemic collapse in the aftermath of 1973 was Italy. Inflation remained in double digits for a decade. The balance of payments was in deficit every year between 1973 and 1989. Unemployment increased every year but two in the same period, rising to over 10 per cent in 1986. The shadow economy was by all accounts the largest of any EC member, no less than 20 per cent of GDP according to some estimates. In spite of large-scale investment, including help from the EC Regional Fund, the socio-economic gap between north and south had hardly changed since the war: average incomes in the south in 1971 were still, as they had been two decades earlier, barely half those of the rest of the country. Italy in the 1970s was still 'a society which was dominated by distrust' of landlords, of politicians, of the state.[8]

Like Britain, Italy was threatened by terrorism. But in this case the violence was not primarily regional in nature. It took the life of a former Prime Minister and came close to threatening the survival of the Republic. Terror came from the extremes of both left and right. The neo-Fascists of *Ordine Nuovo*, with support from elements within the country's Secret Intelligence Service, adopted a strategy of destabilization that led them to commit a series of bomb attacks: in Milan in 1969 (sixteen dead), on the Rome–Munich express train in 1974 (twelve dead), and at Bologna railway station in 1980 (eighty-five dead). Terrorists of the left grew out of the student movement of the 1960s. They emerged from a political sub-culture whose inhabitants happily deployed the language of violence while disclaiming responsibility when their words were taken seriously. Like the anarchists of the late nineteenth century, the 'Red Brigades' and other such groups saw 'terrorism of the deed' as a spark that might kindle the dormant revolutionary spirit of the masses. Some were grotesque amateurs: the leftist publishing millionaire Giangiacomo Feltrinelli killed himself by mistake while planting a bomb near Milan. Others were more serious: in March 1978 'Red Brigade' terrorists kidnapped the Christian Democrat leader and former Prime Minister Aldo Moro. He was held for fifty-four days, then murdered. The assassination provoked mutual recriminations by right and left and reinforced disillusionment with the effectiveness of the Italian state.

While republican institutions were threatened by violence from without, they were undermined by endemic corruption from within. Much of the political class, from left to right, as well as big business and the Mafia were implicated. The worst offenders were Christian Democrats and Socialists, but the Communists, who liked to pose as more pure in such matters, were also on the take. In 1976, for example, the Italian Communist Party (PCI) received $6.5 million in secret aid from Moscow, this in spite of intense Soviet irritation with the party's incorrigibly independent line.[9]

Italian Communists nevertheless tried hard in this period to render themselves politically respectable. They became the most effective exponents of a new, parliamentary, and non-revolutionary 'Euro-Communism'. In September 1973 the party's leader, Enrico Berlinguer, offered a 'historic compromise', under which the Communists would cooperate with other parties, including the Christian Democrats, to protect republican institutions. As evidence of good faith they even endorsed Italian membership of NATO. The PCI's share of the vote rose in 1976 to 34 per cent, its highest ever. For the next three years the party gave parliamentary support to Christian

Democrat-headed governments. Although it did not furnish ministers it did reap rewards under the country's notorious *lottizzanzione* spoils system. The Communists did not, however, realize their governmental aspirations. There was strong hostility among both Christian Democrats and Communists to cooperation with the traditional enemy. By killing Moro the ultra-leftists eliminated the Christian Democrats' most prominent supporter of reconciliation. The Russian invasion of Afghanistan completed the divorce even before the marriage had been consummated.

In the early 1980s both the Communists and the Christian Democrats lost electoral ground. For the first time in the history of the Republic prime ministers took office who were not Christian Democrats: a Republican, Giovanni Spadolini, in 1981–2 and a Socialist, Bettino Craxi, in 1983–7. Although the Christian Democrats still formed the makeweight of coalition governments, their predominance was slipping. After the suppression of Solidarity in Poland the PCI finally made a clean break with the Soviet Union. But '*lo strappo*' seemed belated and with the sudden death of Berlinguer in 1984 the party lost its most popular leader. As the political system became engulfed in an unending series of scandals, the entire political class was discredited and a sense developed that the country was running on auto-pilot.

Like Britain and Italy, Sweden encountered severe difficulties in coping with inflation, unemployment, and labour conflict after 1973. Her paradigm of a mixed economy and consensual labour relations came under severe strain. The Social Democrat government, headed since 1969 by Olof Palme, governed without a majority after the 1973 election produced a deadlock in parliament. Swedish industrial production declined in seven out of eight years from 1975 onwards. Unemployment nevertheless remained low throughout the period, partly because labour laws made it almost impossible for workers to be dismissed. In 1976 the Social Democrats, who had led governments for most of the previous forty-four years, were defeated in a general election. They had been weakened by their support for nuclear power. Their centre-right successors did not dare to dismantle the welfare state: public spending increased and, as in Britain, the government resorted to heavy borrowing. During the 'ten days that shook Sweden' in 1980, the country suffered its largest strike since 1909. In 1981 the government was forced to devalue the krona and adopt an austerity programme. The Social Democrats, as a result, regained popularity and Palme won re-election in 1982. His new government, however, abandoned some cherished Socialist ideals. Embracing the market economy, it restrained expansion of state spending, especially on welfare, reduced trade union power, and increased wage differentials.

Palme's assassination in February 1986 was a shocking event in a country with traditionally peaceful politics. Neither the murderer's identity nor the motive for the crime were ever conclusively established, though both gave an opening for a number of inventive and disturbing conspiracy theories. Palme's disappearance from the political scene did not, however, change the course of Swedish politics, which continued to head in a neo-liberal direction. His successor, Ingvar Carlsson, introduced regressive fiscal changes modelled on President Reagan's 1986 tax reform in the United States. In the 1930s the Swedish Social Democrats had provided a model for the welfare state that the British Labour Party followed after the war. In the 1980s they blazed the trail for Tony Blair's 'New Labour' a decade later.

France, like her neighbours, had to cope with political terrorism from a variety of angles: radical leftists of the group Action Directe, Palestinians who attacked Jewish targets like the synagogue on rue Copernic in Paris in 1980, and separatists in Corsica. Nevertheless, in spite of, or perhaps because of, her close brush with political instability in 1968, France found a way through the economic travails after 1973 without having to confront serious threats to the institutions of the Republic.

In the process, right and left (though not their extreme elements) shed some of their most deeply rooted ideological nostrums. In 1969 the French Socialists refashioned the SFIO as a new Socialist Party and over the next few years drew various independent leftist elements under their umbrella. Following the signature of a 'Common Programme' in 1972, Socialists and Communists embarked on an uneasy and mutually suspicious partnership. The legislative elections of 1973 produced significant gains for the left, although the Gaullists and their allies comfortably retained their majority. In April 1974, however, Pompidou died, and the ensuing presidential election presented the unusual spectacle of unity on the left and division on the right. François Mitterrand, standing for the Socialists, enjoyed the support of the Communists. The Gaullists, however, were unable to agree on a common candidate. Most supported their official candidate, the former Prime Minister Jacques Chaban-Delmas; others backed Valéry Giscard d'Estaing who headed a loosely defined group of centre-right elements. In the first round Chaban-Delmas was beaten into third place. For the first time in France the major presidential contenders debated directly with one another on television. The encounter between Giscard and Mitterrand on 10 May attracted an audience of 23 million. On the second ballot Giscard won by a hair's breadth: he secured 50.7 per cent of the votes to Mitterrand's 49.3 per cent.

The youngest President of the Fifth Republic (he was forty-eight at the time of his election), Giscard was a characteristic product of the post-war French technocratic elite. A *polytechnicien* and an *énarque*, he had been appointed an Inspecteur des Finances at the age of twenty-eight and Finance Minister at thirty-six, serving in that post from 1962 to 1966 and again from 1969 to 1974. His presidency brought a further transmutation of classic Gaullism, in particular in its stress on domestic problems. He depended for support on Gaullists in the National Assembly and therefore appointed one of their number, Jacques Chirac, as Prime Minister. The partnership was uneasy and Chirac resigned in a huff two years later. The economic predicament that confronted Giscard upon assuming the presidency was dire. He called for redeployment and restructuring of the French economy. But although the government used liberal language, its policies remained *dirigiste*. The state intervened repeatedly to bail out *canards boiteux* (lame ducks) in the steel, textile, and other industries. In 1975 no less than 9 per cent of GDP was spent on state subsidies for business. Gaullist-style fascination with *grands projets* such as Concorde absorbed further massive resources. Chirac's successor as Prime Minister, Raymond Barre, a centrist former professor of economics, gradually moved away from interventionism and towards more market-oriented policies. 'It is up to industry, not the State, to put its own house in order,' he insisted.[10] In 1978 his government, which Maurice Papon had now joined as Budget Minister, introduced an austerity policy designed to promote industrial recovery. Subsidies for public transport were reduced and, in a symbolic move, the state, for the first time for a century, stopped fixing the retail price of bread. But the second oil price 'shock' set the economy reeling again. In May 1981 Giscard ran for re-election, once more challenged by Mitterrand. Chirac, who stood as the Gaullist candidate, came third and then refused to call on his supporters to vote for Giscard on the second round. The division of the right proved a godsend for Mitterrand. Weakened by revelations in the satirical newspaper *Le Canard Enchaîné* of lavish gifts from his hunting companion, the cannibalistic self-styled 'Emperor' Jean-Bédel Bokassa of the Central African Republic-turned-Empire, Giscard narrowly lost.

The first Socialist President of the Fifth Republic, Mitterrand was the son of a vinegar manufacturer from Cognac. Bookish and aloof, barely capable of rapport with ordinary people, Mitterrand was an improbable leader for a left-wing party. In his youth he had flirted with the extreme right but he rallied to de Gaulle during the war. In 1950, at the age of thirty, he had been the youngest minister in France for a century. Upon his election to the presidency, the Socialists held only 117 of the 491 seats in the National Assembly and Mitterrand thus faced the daunting prospect of governing without a supportive majority. He decided to capitalize on his victory by calling immediate legislative elections. The Socialists won and thus found themselves, for the first time in French history, simultaneously holding an absolute majority in parliament and control of a powerful executive presidency. Left-wingers dreamed that the millennium was at hand. But Mitterrand, who had moved away from his earlier opposition to the institutions of the Gaullist republic, proved himself, particularly on defence matters, de Gaulle's most faithful heir. In spite of his earlier criticism of the independent nuclear deterrent, he committed France to developing a new generation of nuclear submarines armed with MIRV-warhead missiles. Led by Mitterrand France became 'perhaps NATO's staunchest European pillar'.[11]

In its initial phase the Socialist-Communist government, under the premiership of Pierre Mauroy, sought to implement far-reaching reforms in French society and economy. Thirteen of the twenty largest industrial enterprises in France were nationalized. The working week was reduced to thirty-nine hours. The government tried to promote an expansionist rush for growth. It failed. Successive devaluations of the franc in October 1981, June 1982, and March 1983 fuelled inflation and necessitated a painful switch to austerity. After less than two years in office the Socialists were obliged to perform an excruciating U-turn. The parallels with the 'pause' of February 1937 and the three devaluations of the Popular Front were miserable. But unlike Blum, Mitterrand stuck to office. In 1984 he replaced Mauroy with the more opportunistic Laurent Fabius. The Socialists abandoned their early, heady ambitions and settled into a modernizing, managerial, reformist mould.

The Communist ministers left government, never again to return. Their party moved into terminal decline. Unlike the Italian Communists, the French party signally failed to reform their thinking, organization, or platform. They did not latch on to newly fashionable left-wing concerns such as feminism and the environment. Intellectuals, disgusted by what they saw as the philistine and unimaginative attitudes of the party leadership, left in droves. By 1986 the party's electoral support had fallen below 7 per cent.

By then public disenchantment with the failure of the Socialists' economic programme was widespread. In the legislative elections of March 1986 the Gaullists trounced the left and Jacques Chirac again became Prime Minister. The resultant enforced 'co-habitation' between a Socialist executive President and an energetic conservative premier seemed a recipe for deadlock. Mitterrand maintained the *domaine réservé* allocated to the President under the constitution: he vetoed legislation with which he disagreed and continued to exercise significant influence on policy-making, particularly in foreign affairs and defence. Given the consensus among the main parties in those spheres, there was little friction between him and Chirac. To the surprise of some, the arrangement worked and indeed served as an impressive test of the solidity of the Fifth Republic.

West Germany, the most powerful economy in western Europe, initially appeared best able to weather the recession. Although unemployment in December 1973 increased to over a million for the first time since the foundation of the Federal Republic, growth resumed at a fairly brisk pace in 1976. Exports remained strong. Thanks partly to the rigorous interest-rate policy of the Bundesbank, inflation never reached the heights attained by Britain and Italy: the peak was 7 per cent in 1973–4.

Brandt's SPD–FDP coalition had come to office with high ambitions for internal reform as well as external initiatives. The Chancellor's attention, however, was focused on inter-German and foreign affairs. His government's main domestic accomplishments were costly extensions to state welfare provision. In May 1974, however, Brandt suddenly resigned following the disclosure that one of his closest advisers, Günter Guillaume, was a Communist spy. Brandt had been warned a year earlier that Guillaume was a security risk but had nevertheless continued to trust him. The loss of Brandt was a blow to the government, though he remained chairman of the SPD and a powerful voice in West German politics.

Brandt's successor as Chancellor, Helmut Schmidt, was a less original statesman but his sober administrative competence suited the country's mood. He played the organ, took snuff, and got on well with statesmen such as Kissinger and Giscard d'Estaing. An efficient administrator rather than an innovator, he called himself 'managing director of the Federal Republic'.[12] Schmidt, however, faced strains within his coalition between the SPD left wing, who clung to utopian Socialist hopes, and his Free

Democrat partners, who insisted on financial rectitude. Major structural reforms were therefore few, though in 1976 the government overcame bitter employers' opposition and enacted a law providing for workers to enjoy parity of representation with shareholders on the supervisory boards of large companies. At FDP insistence, however, employers retained a determining vote. Such 'co-determination' preserved Germany's relatively harmonious industrial relations but at the price of inflexibility in the labour market.

The Germans, like their neighbours, had to face terrorism, both imported and home-grown. At the Munich Olympics in 1972, Palestinian terrorists killed two Israeli athletes and took others hostage. A botched rescue operation by West German security forces left all nine hostages as well as five terrorists dead. Left-wing terrorism too attained menacing proportions. The Red Army Faction, led by Andreas Baader and Ulrike Meinhof, hence often known as the Baader–Meinhof group, like their counterparts elsewhere were products of the student revolution of the late 1960s. They carried out bomb attacks, kidnappings, and assassinations. Their motives remained obscure, beyond a general wish to destabilize capitalist society. In 1977 the group kidnapped the head of the West German employers' association, Hanns-Martin Schleyer, demanding the release of imprisoned terrorists. Shortly afterwards they hijacked a Lufthansa airliner, killing the captain before the plane landed in Mogadishu, Somalia. After a unit of German anti-terrorist commandos stormed the plane and freed the hostages, three of the terrorists' leaders, imprisoned in Germany, including Baader, committed suicide. But Schleyer was found dead in the boot of his car. Although terrorism decreased in the 1980s, remnants of the group remained active and it was not formally disbanded until 1998.

The second oil crisis, in 1979–80, affected West Germany more deeply than the first. In 1980, for the first time since 1950, the trade balance ran into deficit. Growth in the 1980s was anaemic. Unemployment reached two million in 1982 and never returned to the full employment levels of the pre-1973 era. Public spending increased by leaps and bounds. With the shortest work hours and the longest paid holidays of any major industrial power, Germany struggled to keep pace with more productive competitors. Schmidt found himself increasingly isolated, particularly over nuclear energy which, against opposition within his party, he favoured. In 1980 a group of ex-1968 radicals, environmentalists, feminists, anti-nuclear activists, and pacifists came together to form the Green Party. In the course of the next decade it attracted considerable support from the disillusioned left of the SPD. Assailed from all sides, Schmidt, echoing Karl Kraus's famous quip about Germany as a land of '*Richter und Henker*', warned she must not become a land of '*Saturierten und Manipulierten*' (satisfied and manipulated).[13] In 1981 the government was forced into austerity policies that alienated more supporters.

Sensing the way the wind was blowing, the FDP, which favoured even more far-reaching cuts in government expenditure, switched its parliamentary support in 1982 from the Social Democrats to the Christian Democrats. Schmidt consequently lost a vote of confidence in the Bundestag and a new CDU–FDP coalition took office. The CDU Chancellor, Helmut Kohl, was a former lobbyist for the chemical industry who had served as Minister-President of the Rhineland-Palatinate. Compared with his polished, cerebral predecessor, he seemed like a provincial bumpkin. Franz-Josef Strauss, leader of the Bavarian wing of the party, pronounced him totally unfit for the job. But Kohl was a much more sophisticated politician than he appeared. He proved adept at out-manoeuvring internal party rivals, at handling coalition partners, at delegating decisions, and at forging close relations with other world leaders. He won four elections in a row and retained office for sixteen years, longer than any of his predecessors since Bismarck. He achieved what all previous Chancellors of the Federal Republic could only dream of—the reunification of Germany. Yet all turned to dust: his career ended in ignominy and tragedy.

Kohl's first test in office was restoration of the West German economy. Enjoying strong support from big business, Kohl directed a turn towards market-oriented policies. Government expenditures and taxes were cut. State enterprises, such as the Lufthansa airline, were privatized. Recovery in the mid-1980s was aided by a sharp fall in the price of oil. The trade balance returned to robust health and West Germany's exports overtook those of the United States for the first time. Unemployment fell, even if only slowly. The 'German model' seemed to be working again.

Democratization on the southern tier

Portugal, Spain, Greece, and Turkey, although all part of liberal Europe in the sense that they were anti-Communist, were nevertheless embarrassments to the democratic pretensions of the western alliance in the early

1970s. Portugal and Spain had been ruled by authoritarian regimes since the inter-war period; Greece and Turkey both endured military rule. Yet all four countries succeeded, in spite of the economic and social pressures of these years, in re-establishing democratic institutions.

The Salazar regime in Portugal, it has been said, was 'firmly set against the twentieth century'.[14] Authoritarian, anti-parliamentary, and 'corporativist' (the term favoured by Salazar himself), it exhibited many similarities with Fascism, especially in the extensive authority accorded to the secret police. On the other hand, it did not engage in large-scale political violence nor in mass political mobilization. Salazar in fact abolished the country's most Fascist-like movement in 1934, complaining that its members were 'always feverish, excited and discontented... shouting, faced with the impossible: "More! More!"'[15] His rule was not so much Fascist as conservative-traditionalist, resting on a long-term alliance with the Church, army, and landowners.

After 1958, during his last decade in power, Salazar retreated to reclusive supervision of affairs. Portugal shared in the post-war economic boom and during the 1950s and 1960s enjoyed a respectable average growth rate of 5.1 per cent per annum (8.6 per cent in manufacturing). But it nevertheless remained the most backward country in western Europe. Salazar's notion of social welfare was primitive: 'To govern', he said, was 'to protect people from themselves'.[16] During the 1960s more than 10 per cent of the population shunned such protection: fleeing poverty, lengthy military service, and social stagnation, 900,000 people emigrated, mainly to France, West Germany, and Brazil. The dictator survived a military coup in 1961 but in the same year the first sign of weakness appeared from another quarter.

Salazar's regime was closely identified with Portugal's overseas empire. The Portuguese was the oldest of the European empires, stretching back to the fifteenth century. One of its most prized possessions was Goa on the west coast of India, which had been conquered in 1511. In December 1961 India seized the territory by force, a devastating blow to Salazar, who was shown weeping on television. The outbreak in the same year of an anti-Portuguese revolt in Angola, followed by others in Mozambique and Portuguese Guinea, presented the regime with a further challenge that, with fatal results for itself, it chose to confront by brute force.

In 1968 Salazar was incapacitated by a brain clot. The old guard who surrounded him picked as his successor the former Rector of Lisbon University, Marcelo Caetano. In spite of his conservative background, Caetano embarked on cautious economic and political reforms. But 'Fascism with a human face', as it was called,[17] failed, above all because Caetano would not contemplate withdrawal from Africa. The grim, unending struggle there drained the country's dilapidated economy and sapped the vitality of society. By the early 1970s the 150,000-strong conscript army, hopelessly bogged down in an unwinnable war, began to question its purpose. When the regime insisted that the war must continue at all costs, soldiers began to question the legitimacy of the regime itself. The army's demoralization reflected that of much of Portuguese society. Half the population were still without domestic plumbing, sewerage, or electricity. The oil price rise contributed to an inflation rate of over 30 per cent, the highest in western Europe. In these conditions, the government could mobilize little popular support.

In early 1974 General António Spínola, commander of Portuguese forces in Guinea, published a book urging a new policy of acceptance of majority rule in the colonies. Caetano reacted by ordering the country's 120 generals to swear loyalty to the government but Spínola and several others refused. The festering unrest in the army led junior officers to form an insurrectionary Armed Forces Movement (MFA). Most of its members were left-wingers who had been radicalized by the experience of colonial warfare.

The bloodless Portuguese 'revolution of flowers' erupted on 25 April 1974. The MFA, directed by Major Otelo Saraiva de Carvalho, seized power, subdued the secret police, and arrested Caetano. The revolution evoked an overwhelming collective euphoria, akin to that in St Petersburg in February/March 1917.

Over the next two years Portugal endured whirling political turmoil, with six provisional governments, two unsuccessful coups, and three elections. Spínola, who found himself appointed provisional President, tried to steer the revolution on a centrist course. But many of the MFA leaders had, in an unusual inversion, internalized the revolutionary doctrines of their Marxist anti-colonial antagonists in Africa. They embraced the Communist Party, whose leader, Alvaro Cunhal, an unreconstructed Leninist, returned from Moscow to a hero's welcome. The Communists had the most formidable underground organization of any political party in the country. They joined the provisional government and for a time seemed on the verge of establishing a Soviet-style regime. Under the premiership of the far-left General Vasco dos Santos Gonçalves, banks, businesses, the media, and large landed estates were nationalized. Gaols that had recently been emptied of leftist political prisoners filled up with rightists. In September Spínola resigned, warning that 'under the false flag of liberty, there are being prepared new forms of slavery'.[18]

In elections to a Constituent Assembly in April 1975, however, the Socialists, led by Mário Soares, won 38 per cent of the vote and the Communists just 12 per cent. These were the first truly free and inclusive elections in the country's history. Allegedly the Socialists received covert support from the Americans who were worried about Communist influence. Kissinger had earlier told Soares: 'You are a Kerensky. I believe in your sincerity but you are naïve.' Soares responded, 'I don't want to be a Kerensky.' Kissinger said: 'Neither did Kerensky.'[19] But Soares, a reformist Socialist in the west European mould, outmanoeuvred the Communists. In November a coup by the left-wing 'Group of Nine' army officers was suppressed by anti-Communist military units commanded by Colonel António Ramalho Eanes. Gradually, moderate elements in the armed forces overcame the radicals. The 1976 constitution, although paying lip-service to a 'transition to socialism' and granting a privileged role to the army, provided a basis for the development of parliamentary democracy.

Eanes was elected first President under the new constitution and Soares became Prime Minister at the head of a minority government. It faced formidable difficulties. Decolonization produced a chaotic exodus of whites from Angola and Mozambique. The arrival of 600,000 impoverished and clamorous *retornados* placed an immense strain on Portugal's economy and its underdeveloped social services. Unemployment reached 14 per cent, industrial unrest was rife, and continuing economic upheaval obliged the government to turn to the IMF. The condition for its support was a strict deflationary policy. But implementation proved difficult and cost the government votes. In 1978 Soares fell from power, replaced first by technocrats, later by right-wingers. Altogether nine ministries held office between 1976 and 1983. Average real incomes dropped every year until 1984. But eventually the new political system stabilized. The radical economic measures of the early revolutionary years were curtailed and in some cases reversed. In 1982 a constitutional revision led to a reduction in the powers of the President, created a constitutional court, and eliminated the military Council of the Revolution. The 'captains of April' retired into obscurity and the threat of army intervention in politics evaporated. Under centre-right governments between 1985 and 1995, the country enjoyed growing prosperity and restoration to the European mainstream.

Spain's peaceful return to democracy after the death of Franco in November 1975 was one of the political wonders of the age. In the early post-war years Franco had been regarded internationally as something of a pariah on account of his Fascism, but with the onset of the Cold War his anti-Communist credentials stood him in good stead. Although residual hostility on the west European left had blocked Spain's admission to NATO, the Eisenhower administration concluded an executive agreement (in effect, a treaty, but in a form that did not require ratification by the US Senate) with Spain in September 1953 under which American naval and air bases were located in Spain in return for large-scale military and technical aid from the USA. 'Now I have won the Civil War!' Franco allegedly said after the agreement was signed.[20] In the same year Spain signed a concordat with the Vatican. The government adhered to an autarkic economic model and growth in the 1950s remained slow. Between 1951 and 1960 more than half a million people emigrated to other parts of Europe or to Latin America. Franco retained the structure of the Fascist dictatorship: a one-party regime with unlimited power concentrated on the *Caudillo*. The country nevertheless slowly re-entered polite international society, gaining admission to the World Bank, the International Monetary Fund, and, in 1955, the United Nations.

In the 1960s cracks appeared in the Fascist edifice. The ideology of the Falange came to seem more and more anachronistic. New technocratic elements appeared, some associated with Opus Dei, a conservative and elitist Catholic secular order. Millions of tourists, especially from Britain, flocked to the Costa Brava: by 1965 tourism was earning Spain over a billion dollars a year and was the country's largest source of foreign currency. The share of agriculture in the economy declined as industrial production more than doubled during the decade. Between 1961 and 1973 Spain enjoyed a growth rate of 7.2 per cent per annum, the highest of any country in Europe. But labour unrest in the Asturias coal mines and separatist terrorism in the Basque country were clumsily suppressed by the government. More ominously for the internal cohesion of a regime that had aimed to revive 'National Catholicism', the Spanish Church, under the leadership of the progressive Cardinal Vicente Enrique y Tarancón, slowly disengaged from the regime.

In his last years Franco's ability to control events waned. There were some concessions: *aperturistas* (reformists), such as Manuel Fraga Iribarne, were appointed ministers; censorship was relaxed a little; and in 1973 a

Prime Minister, Admiral Luis Carrero Blanco, was appointed for the first time to head a Francoist Cabinet. But the hallmarks of the regime remained corruption, state violence, and scorn for democracy. One response was revolutionary counter-violence, especially from the Basque terrorist movement, Euskadi Ta Askatasuna, founded in 1959. In June 1973 Franco suffered a devastating blow with the assassination of Carrero Blanco, for which ETA admitted responsibility. The new Prime Minister, Carlos Arias Navarro, sought to carve out a path of limited, moderate reform. But his government showed its harsh side by ordering the execution of two anarchists who had been convicted of attacks on the forces of order.

Franco's death at the age of eighty-three in November 1975 was celebrated with dancing in the streets in Bilbao and champagne toasts in Barcelona. His disappearance left a political vacuum. Six years earlier, after a long period of deliberate ambiguity about the succession to his regime, Franco had designated Prince Juan Carlos, grandson of Alfonso XIII, as the future king. The prince's exiled father, Don Juan, who had hoped to become a reconciling 'king of all Spaniards', was regarded as too much of a liberal constitutional monarchist. So long as the Caudillo was alive, Juan Carlos, who, with his father's acquiescence, had been educated in Spain, observed his oath of fidelity to Franco's principles and person. But he maintained close links with liberal Catholics and his private predilections were for a restoration of democracy. Upon Franco's death, he immediately assumed the throne. Without initially making a clear rupture with existing institutions, Juan Carlos used the powers that he had been granted to steer Spain towards the peaceful restoration of parliamentary democracy. Throughout the process he showed great political sensitivity and skill.

The socio-economic structure of Spain had by 1975 changed so greatly that the regime was totally out of touch with society. The Francoist 'bunker' remained strong, however, especially in the army, and Juan Carlos had to proceed cautiously. At first he had no choice but to reappoint Arias as Prime Minister. At the same time a *Comisión Mixta*, composed of Cabinet ministers and members of the *Consejo Nacional*, was charged with recommending democratic reforms. But Arias did not inspire confidence that these would amount to much when he informed the Comisión's first meeting in February 1976 that 'as long as I'm here or still in political life, I'll never be other than a strict perpetuator of Francoism in all its aspects and I will fight against the enemies of Spain who have begun to dare to raise their heads'.[21] Over the next few months a trial of strength developed between the 'bunker' and a resurgent left that was organizing strikes and demonstrations all over the country.

In July 1976 Juan Carlos took the decisive step of appointing Adolfo Suárez, a former Franco loyalist, now a reformer, as Prime Minister. Suárez formed a carefully balanced Cabinet that included a number of reform-minded Catholics and businessmen. He used television skilfully in building public support for his programme of peaceful democratization. He developed a respectful relationship with the Socialist leader, Felipe González, and also put out feelers to the Communists. Under Suárez *reforma pactada* gave way to *ruptura pactada*. Juan Carlos visited Catalonia and, in a significant gesture, delivered a speech in Catalan. Political prisoners were freed and exiles returned. A Law on Political Reform was approved in a referendum in December, paving the way for a multi-party regime.

The peaceful nature of the change checked any tendency towards a drastic settling of accounts over the past. All the main opposition groups committed themselves to a non-retributive transition to democracy. This had the positive effect of preventing renewed bloodshed. On the other hand, it meant that several institutions that were seriously compromised by their role in the Franco years avoided self-examination. For example, judges who had administered the laws of the Fascist regime remained on the bench and in some cases resisted democratization measures, as in the vote of the Supreme Court in 1977 against legalization of the Communist Party. In that case, however, Suárez circumvented the court by issuing a decree law. Unlike its Portuguese counterpart, the Spanish Communist Party, strongly 'Euro-Communist', exhibited a readiness to abide by the rules of the parliamentary game.

In June 1977 the first free elections to the Cortes since 1936 gave Suárez's centre-right party victory. It won 34 per cent of the vote; the Socialists came second with 29 per cent; the Communists won 9 per cent; and the Francoist remnants only 8 per cent. A new democratic constitution was approved by Parliament and ratified in October 1978. The monarch was recognized as 'chief of state, symbol of its unity and continuity'. Except at moments of crisis the monarchy was henceforth limited to a mainly decorative role, on the north-west European model. Politics settled into a multi-party system in which power alternated between two main formations: a free-market-oriented centre-right and a Socialist Party that, in 1979, followed other west European Socialists and explicitly jettisoned its historic Marxist ideology.

Unlike France, where regional separatism was strongest in economically backward regions such as Corsica, in Spain it re-emerged powerfully in the advanced Catalan and Basque countries. The Catalan and Basque languages, suppressed under Franco, once again flourished in the open. Statutes of autonomy for Catalonia and the Basque country (defined as the provinces of Vizcaya, Guipúzcoa, and Alava, but not Navarre, which was also claimed by Basque nationalists) were approved in referenda in 1979. In spite of some rhetorical grandstanding, most Catalans were satisfied with the compromise. So were most Basques. But ultra-nationalists in the Basque country, who commanded the support of a sixth of the electorate, remained uncompromising in their demand for full independence and ETA's terrorist campaign claimed new victims.

Democracy faced one further challenge. In late January 1981 Suárez, who had lost support within his own party, decided to resign. Rumour abounded that his departure was the result of right-wing military pressure. The new Prime Minister, Leopoldo Calvo Sotelo, was to be sworn in on 23 February. As the proceedings were in progress, disgruntled militarists, led by Lieutenant-Colonel Antonio Tejero, attempted a seizure of power, holding government and parliament hostage. The king refused to countenance any concession to the rebels, rallied the Captains-General of the regions by telephone, and appeared on television at 1.15 a.m. that night affirming that he would stand by the constitution. The coup collapsed. Calvo Sotelo was duly installed in office two days later. But his government failed to deal convincingly with a contracting economy or with continuing political violence, especially from Basque terrorists. In October 1982 the Socialists won a landslide election victory. Felipe González took office as head of the first all-Socialist government in Spanish history. It remained in power for the next fourteen years.

After 1975 Spanish society changed with startling rapidity, moving close to the norms and values of western Europe. The Church lost a great deal of its authority. The proportion of self-declared practising Catholics dropped from 91 per cent in 1960 to 34 per cent in 1982. Contraception and abortion were legalized. A divorce law was passed. Pornography became freely available at news kiosks. In 1981, amid emotional scenes of national reconciliation, Picasso's *Guernica* finally completed its long odyssey and was installed in the Prado Museum in Madrid.

Greece, like Spain, was haunted for decades by the memory of its bitter civil war. During the 'stone years' of the 1950s and 1960s the left–right schism in the country remained profound and the palace and army habitually intervened in politics, generally in support of the right. American influence was reinforced by military and economic aid. In the mid-1960s the centre-left government of George Papandreou encountered fierce resistance to its attempts to curb the power of the king and the army. Months of political tension exploded in April 1967 into a military coup, led by Colonel George Papadopoulos. King Constantine II shilly-shallied and compromised himself. He was not a party to the coup but he initially acquiesced in it and lent the new government a veneer of legitimacy. The following December, having realized his mistake, he helped launch a botched counter-coup. After its failure he fled to exile in England. This was the end of the monarchy in Greece. The military regime provoked condemnation from enlightened opinion in western Europe but Greece's NATO allies took only symbolic action against it. The colonels remained in power although they alienated even conservative opinion in Greece by their arrogance, brutality, and sometimes preposterous behaviour. An instance of the latter was Papadopoulos's plan to rebuild the Colossus of Rhodes. Philosophy, another of the regime's leaders maintained, had not merely been invented but exhausted as a subject by the Greeks.

The United States had at first been decidedly cool towards the junta. But the assumption of office by President Nixon in January 1969 brought a gradual warming. Nixon's Vice-President, Spiro Agnew, a Greek-American, helped in this direction, aided by Greek-American members of Congress. American policy was guided in part by the US Navy's need for facilities in the east Mediterranean. Soviet naval activity there was increasing and the military coup in Libya in 1969 led to the closing of US and British bases there. In 1971 Washington opened negotiations with the junta for the establishment of a further US naval base in Greece that would serve as a 'home port' for the US Sixth Fleet. While the talks dragged on, the administration did its utmost to deflect criticism of the regime. The economy was deteriorating as a result of the oil crisis: in 1973 Greece suffered the deepest recession of any European country. Inflation reached over 30 per cent. Domestic opposition grew but a projected coup by naval officers was snuffed out and a student revolt in November was crushed by force, leaving many dead and injured. A few days later Papadopoulos was deposed by fellow army officers. General Dimitrios Ioannides replaced him but neither the nature of the regime nor its policies changed.

Democracy returned to Greece suddenly in 1974, as a result of a dramatic sequence of events on Cyprus. On 15 July a small group of Greek nationalist adventurers, led by Nikos Sampson, a former EOKA terrorist fighter, ousted President Makarios and proclaimed *enosis* with Greece. Sampson enjoyed the support of the Greek government. When Makarios slipped away from Nicosia, Ioannides telephoned Sampson and told him: 'Nikolaki, I want Mouskos' head—you'll get it for me, eh Nikolaki?'[22] Greece and Turkey edged close to full-scale war. The United States was concerned about the prospect of fighting between NATO allies, the first such conflict since the formation of the alliance. Britain, which still held significant forces in sovereign bases on Cyprus, had, with Greece and Turkey, jointly guaranteed Cypriot independence, territorial integrity, and security at the time of independence in 1960. In 1974, however, Britain interpreted her treaty obligations narrowly: she regarded herself as bound only to 'consult' with the other parties. The British Foreign Secretary, James Callaghan, pronounced lofty moral injunctions but otherwise did nothing to enforce the guarantee.

Frustrated by the inaction of Britain and the United Nations, the Turkish government of Bülent Ecevit decided to take military action to safeguard the Turkish minority. But the regime of the colonels, for all its militarism, had not turned the Greek armed forces into a match for the Turks. Between 20 July and 16 August Turkey's thirty-thousand-strong invading force occupied the northern third of Cyprus. Amidst bitter communal bloodshed, an exchange of populations followed, whereby Cyprus was divided into a Greek-populated independent state of Cyprus in the south, and a 'Turkish Federated State' in the north, populated by Turkish Cypriots as well as settlers later brought in from Anatolia. The 112-mile 'Attila line' between the two sectors cut across the island and through the heart of the capital, Nicosia. Meanwhile, after seven days, the legitimate government on the Greek side of the island reaffirmed its authority and removed Sampson, though Makarios remained in exile in London. Turkey came under pressure from the United States, where the Greek lobby in Congress remained strong, but refused to withdraw her forces. Subsequent attempts by the United Nations to resolve the dispute were unavailing. In 1983 North Cyprus declared independence, although no country in the world save Turkey recognized it. The small UN peacekeeping force maintained an uneasy vigil on the island into the new millennium.

The effects of these events on Greece herself were far-reaching. The colonels' regime collapsed in disgrace. The conservative politician Konstantinos Karamanlis returned from exile in Paris and presided over a peaceful transition to democracy. A referendum confirmed the abolition of the monarchy and a new constitution was approved. Greek politics moved away from clientelism towards a more genuinely democratic system, though leadership continued to be dominated by the rival dynasties of Karamanlis on the right and Papandreou on the left.

In 1981 the left-wing PASOK party, led by Andreas Papandreou, son of the former Prime Minister, George Papandreou, won power. A Marxist economist who had spent many years in exile in the United States, Papandreou announced that he would socialize the economy, take over church land, withdraw Greece altogether from NATO, expel US bases from the country, and close down the British and American schools of archaeology in Athens (they were seen as hotbeds of imperialism). It was all hot air. While spouting anti-American rhetoric, the Papandreou government maintained Greek membership of NATO and retained US bases. The USSR, which at first had high hopes of Papandreou, soon became disillusioned. The Orthodox Church, which retained powerful support in the country, successfully resisted nationalization of its lands. The government's efforts at economic reform ran into trouble and were eventually reversed. The archaeological institutes were untouched, though there was some sympathy in Britain for the campaign by Papandreou's Culture Minister, the former film actress Melina Mercouri, for the restitution from the British Museum of the Parthenon marbles, removed to England by Lord Elgin in 1806. Papandreou was re-elected in 1985 and, after a hiatus between 1989 and 1993, won a third term in office. But his government became mired in scandal and he was largely discredited by the time of his death in 1996. Under the next generation of leaders, Kostas Karamanlis and George Papandreou, Greece modernized rapidly and developed into a more open and less nationalistic society.

For the Turks the Cyprus adventure was totally counter-productive. Turkey had already suffered two military coups since the war. After the first, in 1960, the Prime Minister, Adnan Menderes, and two of his ministers were hanged. The second, in 1971, a 'coup by communiqué' by the army high command, led to the resignation of the Prime Minister, Süleyman Demirel. In both cases parliamentary government was restored within a short time. But the army, virtually a state within the state, remained the country's most powerful institution, regarding itself as the guarantor of the legacy of Atatürk. Ecevit, who became leader of the Republican People's Party in 1972, was the first politician with a non-military background to head the movement most closely associated with Atatürk. He steered the party in a social democratic direction and, after victory in the general election of 1973, became Prime Minister as head of a coalition that included the National Salvation Party, an Islamist group at odds with the secularist legacy of Atatürk. The marriage did not prove a success and the invasion of Cyprus brought unexpected woes, including an American arms embargo. The economy collapsed under the weight of the oil crisis and of misconceived economic policies by Ecevit and Demirel who each served as Prime Minister three times between 1974 and 1980. Turkish citizens were used to double-digit inflation but in 1980 they had their first encounter with a triple-digit rate. The Turkish lira collapsed and social unrest grew.

By 1980 the economy was paralysed by unmanageable foreign debt and political life was overshadowed by bloody clashes between neo-Fascist and Marxist groups. Army chiefs once again seized power and declared martial law. They closed all the political parties, temporarily exiled their leaders, and arrested thousands of militants of the far left and far right. The military rulers redesigned Turkey's political system, strengthening the presidency, and tried to confine politics to a contest between approved parties of the centre-right and centre-left. They brought in Turgut Özal, a free-market economist, to administer a stabilization programme that proved highly successful. A new constitution was approved in a referendum in 1982. By then Özal had broken with the military. In 1983 he and his Motherland Party won an easy victory in parliamentary elections. As Prime Minister (1983–9) and President (1989–93), he reaffirmed Turkey's linkages to the west, steering the country towards fuller democracy, trade liberalization, and free markets.

The restoration of democracy in Portugal, Spain, Greece, and Turkey facilitated their closer integration into international institutions. Greece, which had been forced out of the Council of Europe during the military dictatorship, was readmitted in 1974. Portugal was admitted in 1976 and Spain a year later. (Turkey, a founder-member, came close to being forced out in 1981.) In 1986 Spain was admitted to NATO, though, in deference to feeling on the Spanish left, she remained outside the military framework of the alliance and US bases were withdrawn by 1996. But the most significant diplomatic consequence of democratization lay in facilitating the development of closer integration with the European Community.

Expansion of the European Community

By its very existence, the European Community played an important role in moderating economic fluctuations and preserving a measure of social peace and political stability in Europe after 1973. It also provided a new model of supra-nationalist partnership that attracted emulation and new candidates for membership.

The departure of de Gaulle renewed British hopes of entry into the Community. In December 1969 the most important barrier was set aside when Pompidou indicated his removal of the French veto on British admission. Negotiations opened in June 1970. Denmark, Ireland, and Norway, for all three of which Britain was the largest trading partner, joined the talks with the EC at the same time. Sweden considered doing so too but many Swedes endorsed the view expressed earlier by Gunnar Myrdal that the EC had 'a more primitive form of social organization than ours'.[23] In March 1971 Palme announced that his country would not apply for membership. After some hard bargaining with the four applicants, accession treaties were signed in January 1972. Only three of them, however, joined the Community.

In Norway, the government and much of the political class favoured membership but a loose coalition of farming, nationalist, and left-wing elements campaigned effectively against ratification of the treaty. The Labour Party was riven: most of its leaders supported membership but strong opposition developed at the grassroots. City and country were deeply divided: Oslo was in favour but rural areas overwhelmingly against. In a referendum in September 1972 53.5 per cent voted against and 46.5 per cent in favour of membership. Although it was technically only consultative, the referendum decided the issue. The result brought down the Labour government. Its centre-right successors negotiated a free trade agreement with the EC that won unanimous support in the Storting.

Denmark held a referendum a month after Norway. That produced a solid vote in favour of membership. Two Danish possessions, however, chose different paths. The inhabitants of the Faeroe Isles, who had gained a measure of home rule in 1948, feared their fishing industry would suffer from the EC's Common Fisheries Policy. They therefore elected to remain outside the Community. Greenland, which also enjoyed autonomy, joined the EC with Denmark; but in a referendum in 1982 decided, also because of the fisheries policy, to withdraw—the only instance of any territory ever renouncing membership.

In Ireland any constitutional amendment required approval in a referendum. Since membership of the EC was regarded as diminishing Irish sovereignty, a referendum was mandatory. When it was held in May 1972, the two largest parties, Fianna Fáil and Fine Gael both supported entry; the small Labour Party opposed it. Membership was approved by 83 per cent of those voting.

In Britain, in accordance with precedent, the accession treaty was ratified by Parliament, not by popular vote. Edward Heath easily overcame mutterings among some right-wing Conservatives and secured approval for the agreement. The United Kingdom (but not the Channel Islands nor the Isle of Man), Ireland, and Denmark accordingly became members of the EC on 1 January 1973. The British people, however, did not so much endorse entry into the Community as acquiesce in it half-heartedly. Unlike other parts of Europe there were few sections of society outside the political class that were enthusiastic proponents of European integration. After his victory in the election of February 1974, Harold Wilson fulfilled an electoral pledge to 'renegotiate' British membership and to submit the issue of membership to the electorate—the first national referendum in British history. The negotiations were a transparent piece of face-saving for Wilson: little of substance changed in the terms that had been negotiated by the Conservatives. In the referendum campaign, government ministers were granted freedom to campaign for or against the renegotiated terms of membership, though most, including Wilson himself, urged approval. The opponents included left-wingers such as Michael Foot and right-wingers such as Enoch Powell. The far left of the Labour Party were generally suspicious of the EC as a 'capitalist club'; sections of the Conservative Party were hostile to the socialistic tendencies that they detected in 'Brussels bureaucracy'. Only the Liberals were united in support of British entry. The result, in June 1975, was decisive: a 2:1 majority in favour of remaining in the Community.

In the 1980s three more applicants joined: Greece in 1981, Spain and Portugal in 1986. In each case membership was delayed as much by political as economic considerations. In 1961 Greece had been the first country to sign an association agreement with the EC and she looked forward to full membership in due course. But the association was frozen during the rule of the colonels. After 1974, with the restoration of democracy, membership was embraced as a new 'Great Idea' by Karamanlis. On the other hand, PASOK strongly opposed membership. In the 1981 election campaign its leader, Andreas Papandreou, coined the slogan '*EOK-NATO to idio syndikato*' (The EEC and NATO are the same syndicate).[24] He demanded that a referendum be held on EC membership. But the treaty had already been signed and ratified and had entered into force. After he won the election,

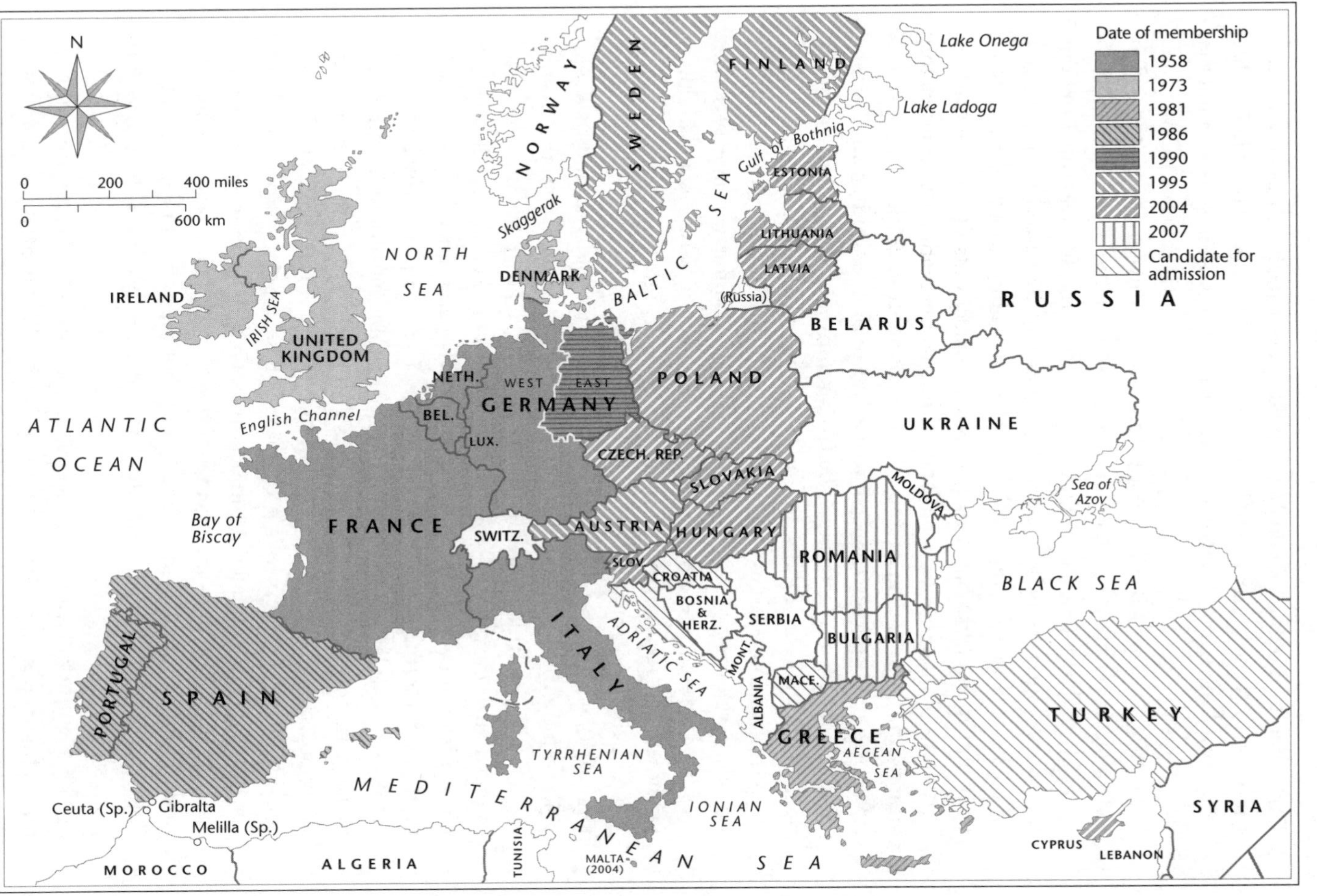

Map 8. Growth of the European Union

Papandreou found he was unable to hold a referendum. Under the constitution of 1975 the prerogative of calling one rested with the presidency; that office was now held by Karamanlis who had no intention of reopening the question.

Portugal had signed a free trade agreement with the EC in 1973. She lodged an application for membership in 1977 for which Soares lobbied tirelessly in all the member countries. Entry into the EC was supported by the entire political spectrum, save the Communists. Spain had first lodged an application in 1962 but while the EC was willing to sign a preferential trade agreement with Spain in 1970, it refused to consider Spanish membership in the absence of democratization. After long and difficult negotiations with the two countries, both were admitted in 1986.

All the new members, in particular the poorer ones, benefited enormously from EC membership. The Community's agricultural and regional policies brought an inflow of funds to impoverished regions. Greece, Portugal, Ireland, and Spain enjoyed some of the highest growth rates in Europe in the late 1980s. Increasing prosperity transformed these societies, creating a strong middle class, reducing the power of old elites, and building public support for the Community.

The benefits of membership for the richer new members, Britain and Denmark, were, in the eyes of their populations, less easily demonstrable. In both countries 'Euro-scepticism' increased. In Denmark it appeared mainly on the left, in Britain on the right. But the Danish Social Democrats softened their hostility to the Community after the mid-1980s whereas the British Conservatives hardened theirs. Margaret Thatcher, in contrast to Edward Heath, was always a reluctant European. She irritated many other European leaders by her stubborn bargaining at summit meetings and by her resistance to proposals for fuller European integration. In particular, she opposed anything that smacked of surrender of British sovereignty. The anti-EC British Conservative press took delight in portraying her wielding her handbag like a blunderbuss in negotiations with her European partners. In 1984 she secured an arrangement whereby the UK was to receive an annual rebate of its allegedly outsize contribution to the European budget. For more than two decades Britain remained the only country to gain such a concession.

The Community in the 1970s and 1980s, far from moving towards any form of federal state, suffered from what some diagnosed as 'Eurosclerosis'. Although the Treaty of Rome and subsequent agreements had created a common trading area, a host of national barriers, anomalies, closed shops, and traditional arrangements had prevented realization of genuinely open markets. No effective action was taken on a call in December 1975 by the Belgian Prime Minister, Leo Tindemans, for the Community to be transformed by 1980 into a political union with common foreign and defence policies. In 1978–9 EC members made a second attempt to coordinate their currencies. The European Monetary System was somewhat more successful than the 'snake' of 1972–4 and lasted until 1993. It was a flexible structure, particularly in the early years: there were twelve realignments in currency values between 1979 and 1990. But the EMS was still a far cry from a common currency.

Some attributed the lack of dynamism in the EC to a 'democratic deficit'. A step towards rectifying this was taken in 1979, when the first direct elections to the European Parliament were held, but the Parliament at this stage exercised very little power and was remote from the concerns of most Europeans.

In 1985 the Commission President, Jacques Delors, secured agreement on the 'Single European Act' which aimed to create genuinely open European markets by sweeping away internal obstacles. The Act also provided for so-called 'qualified majority voting' in the European Council on many, though not all, issues. The original champion of the national veto had been France. Now it was Thatcher's Britain. In 1988 Thatcher delivered a speech at Bruges in which she conjured up the alarming demon of a 'European super-state exercising a new dominance from Brussels'.[25] Yet much of this was posturing for home consumption. The Single European Act, which the British had, in fact, played a large part in formulating, was endorsed by the British Parliament, as by all the other member countries. Its implementation over the next five years represented a major step towards genuine economic union.

18

The Collapse of Communism in Eastern Europe 1985–1991

An uproar rose over the heads
To the heavy, overcast sky.
It had no words.
It couldn't be bugged.
But they all understood.

*Miroslav Holub, Prague, 1989**

Gorbachev's Russia

Mikhail Gorbachev was fifty-four years old when he attained supreme power in the Soviet Union on 11 March 1985. The son of peasants from southern Russia, he was the first Soviet leader born after the revolution and the first to hold a university degree. Both his grandfathers had suffered arrest and persecution under Stalin. Like Nagy and Dubček, he had risen through party ranks in a fairly conventional career pattern for a Communist apparatchik. Although regarded as leaning to the reformist wing of the party, he too had given little indication before attaining the highest office that he would seek to carve out a radically new direction for his country. As a student in the law faculty at Moscow University in the 1950s, Gorbachev developed a close friendship with a fellow student, the Czech Communist Zdeněk Mlynář, who was to play an important role in the reformist movement of 1968. Mlynář later recollected that in his student years

* From 'The Third Language', translated from the Czech by David Young, Dana Hábová and Miroslav Holub, in Peter Forbes, ed., *Scanning the Century: The Penguin Book of the Twentieth Century in Poetry*, London, 2000, 470–2.

Gorbachev, 'like everyone else at that time, was a Stalinist'. But he added: 'In order to be a true reforming Communist you have to be a true Stalinist.'[1] One perceptive figure recognized Gorbachev's potential at an early stage: when he visited Britain in December 1984, Margaret Thatcher had a long private discussion with him, at the end of which, as she later recalled, 'I hoped that I had been talking to the next Soviet leader. . . . This was a man with whom I could do business.'[2]

As a protégé of Andropov, Gorbachev secured speedy promotion to voting membership of the Politburo. His suave manner, charm, and quick wit, as well as his readiness to listen were all unusual characteristics for a Soviet politician. A long-winded speaker in the Kremlin tradition, he was nevertheless capable of arresting formulations and eventually learned to communicate effectively on television. Shortly after his visit to Britain he delivered a speech in Moscow in which he introduced some of the concepts that would become guiding principles of his policy in power, among them *glasnost* ('openness') and *perestroika* ('restructuring'). And he criticized those in the USSR who attempted 'to squeeze new phenomena into a Procrustean bed of moribund conceptions'.[3]

Gorbachev's appointment as Chernenko's successor was not automatic. But efforts to gather support for the conservative, elderly Moscow party chief, Viktor Grishin, had only limited success. Gorbachev enjoyed the backing of V. A. Kryuchkov, head of the KGB, like Gorbachev a former protégé of Andropov. In spite of considerable misgivings on the part of the old guard in the Politburo, Gorbachev secured endorsement as leader, aided by a pervasive feeling that generational change was long overdue. When the news reached Sakharov, still exiled in Gorky, he said, 'It looks as if our country's lucky. We've got an intelligent leader.'[4]

Gorbachev surrounded himself with reformists, including Georgy Shakhnazarov, a domestic affairs adviser described as 'a closet social democrat within the Central Committee apparatus',[5] the Georgian Eduard Shevardnadze, who became Foreign Minister in mid-1985, and the radical Alexander Yakovlev, a political adviser to whom Gorbachev was especially close. But for much of his tenure in office he had to contend with a strong rearguard of conservatives.

His conduct during his six years in high office consequently gave such an appearance of vacillation and prevarication that many of his countrymen damned him as an opportunist without consistency of purpose or principle. Gorbachev himself was almost certainly not aware of where his policies would lead. Often he gave the impression of being carried along by the current of events. Nevertheless, there was from the outset a bold thrust of innovation in his policies. Unlike Khrushchev, who groped clumsily towards a post-Stalin reformulation of what Communism might mean, Gorbachev based his policies on a sophisticated analysis of the dead end to which the Soviet economy and Soviet society had been driven.

Between 1985 and 1989 three dimensions of life were revolutionized in the Soviet Union: first, *glasnost* liberated the arena of public discourse; secondly, *perestroika* created a framework for the transformation of Soviet political institutions; thirdly, *perestroika*'s economic arm began the process whereby market mechanisms replaced the command economy. Gorbachev undoubtedly saw all this as a way of saving the Soviet Union; what neither his supporters nor his critics foresaw was how quickly it would lead to its dissolution.

Glasnost was a concept that originated with Russian liberals in the nineteenth century as a basis of their demands for transparency rather than secrecy in public affairs. It was revived by Solzhenitsyn at the time of his expulsion from the Writers' Union in 1970: '*Glasnost*,' he declared, 'honest and total *glasnost*—this is the first requisite for any society's health, including ours'.[6] Gorbachev's deliberate use of this term was therefore full of symbolic meaning, particularly for the Russian intelligentsia. His public commitment to the idea antedated his appointment to the leadership in 1985. He had elaborated on it in December 1984 when he said that the young member of the new Soviet generation 'won't accept simplistic answers to questions, and keenly senses the falsehoods produced by an inability or fear to reveal the real contradictions of socialist development. . . . To that person we are bound to speak the truth.'[7]

Although *glasnost* formed part of Gorbachev's thinking from the outset, he at first took only cautious steps towards its realization. The continuing limits on Soviet openness were demonstrated in April 1986 when a serious accident occurred at a nuclear power station at Chernobyl, a hundred kilometres from Kiev in northern Ukraine. This was not the first such accident in the Soviet Union: in 1957 an explosion in a tank containing chemical radioactive waste had caused many deaths at a nuclear plant at Kyshtym in the Urals: ten thousand people had to be evacuated from an area of 1,000 square kilometres. At Chernobyl thirty-one people were killed immediately, 116,000 were evacuated from the surrounding area, 220,000 were later permanently relocated, and a 4,300 square kilometre exclusion zone was demarcated. Thyroid cancer rates among children in Ukraine multiplied over the next decade, although most of those affected were able, with medication, to lead relatively normal lives. Authoritative UN reports in 2000 and 2005 concluded that otherwise there 'was no evidence of a major public health impact related to ionizing radiation . . . no increases in overall cancer incidence or mortality that could be associated with radiation exposure. . . . The risk of leukaemia, one of the most sensitive indicators of radiation exposure [was] not found to be elevated even in the accident recovery operation workers or in children . . . [and there was] no scientific proof of an increase in other non-malignant disorders related to ionizing radiation.'[8] A maximum of four thousand people may have died from cancer caused by exposure to radiation. The casualties were fewer than those caused by industrial accidents in the USSR in an average year.

The economic and political fallout from the disaster was nevertheless immense. By 1990 the costs of Chernobyl to the USSR alone were estimated at $90 billion. At the time and for many years afterwards there was worldwide panic, exaggeration of the health consequences, and severe criticism of the Soviet government both for the poor design and careless maintenance that had led to the explosion and for lack of candour in its aftermath. The Soviet media acknowledged what had happened only after the news had been broadcast from the west and become widely known in the USSR. The chief Soviet censor later confessed that this was the first occasion on which the principle that the government alone should decide what the people might know had faltered.[9] Gorbachev himself said nothing about it on television until 14 May. Chernobyl temporarily dented his credibility. The incident produced an outbreak of edgy, anti-government jokes ('What is the best anti-radiation device in the USSR: Tass.' 'What is Gorbachev's official title? "First Isotope" '). Looking back later, Gorbachev saw Chernobyl as 'a turning-point' in Soviet information policy.[10] The accident accelerated movement towards *glasnost*.

Soon afterwards Soviet press and broadcasting began to show a new openness. State television news began to place less emphasis on reports of industrial production successes, and more on hitherto taboo or little-discussed topics. Moscow Radio overseas broadcasts too became less stridently propagandistic in tone. Radio and television stations in the various republics, particularly in the Baltic States, acquired distinctive voices of their own, for the first time in Soviet history, and became channels of expression for nationalist feeling in these areas. Jamming of foreign radio stations stopped in 1987. Non-Communist foreign newspapers and magazines, previously almost unobtainable by ordinary citizens, became available to the general public. Independent newspapers and magazines vied to take advantage of the new permissiveness: *Ogonyok* ('Little Fire', edited by Vitaly Korotych; *Oktyabr*, which published Vasily Grossman's masterpiece *Life and Fate*, written in the 1950s but long banned in the USSR; *Argumenty i fakty*, a weekly that claimed a circulation of ten million in 1988 and 33 million by 1990; and the multilingual *Moscow News*. Even the staid official publications, *Pravda* and *Izvestiya*, shed a little of their dour uninformativeness.

In December 1986 Gorbachev gave an unmistakable signal of movement towards freedom of speech. A telephone was hurriedly installed in Sakharov's apartment in Gorky and Gorbachev called to inform him that he and his wife were being released. 'You can return to Moscow together. . . . Go back to your patriotic work!'[11] What was striking about the episode was not just that Gorbachev had informed Sakharov personally but that he indicated that Sakharov was being freed not as an act of mercy but in order to resume the very activities for which he had originally been exiled.

Freedom of the press was enshrined in a new law that was presented to the Presidium of the Supreme Soviet in 1987. Approved after two years of debate in November 1989, it came into force only in July 1990. In the meantime several previously banned books were published. In 1986 the novels of Vladimir Nabokov began to appear. In February 1987 Boris Pasternak was posthumously rehabilitated by the Soviet Writers' Union and the following year *Dr Zhivago* was published officially in Russia for the first time. Solzhenitsyn, however, whose root-and-branch hostility to Communism continued to frighten Soviet leaders, remained unpublished in his country for the time being. An official spokesman in March 1987 explained that Solzhenitsyn was 'too strong in political opposition to us'.[12] Increased cultural freedom at first bound the majority of the intelligentsia enthusiastically to Gorbachev.

An important aspect of the new freedoms was the fresh light thrown on the darkest features of Soviet history. As in the Khrushchev period, revelations about past misdeeds became weapons in current political struggles. But the new openness went much further than earlier selective disclosures. For the first time since the 1920s genuinely free debate on divisive historical issues became possible. Documentary sources for the most painful aspects of Soviet history were thrown open. In April 1989 Khrushchev's secret speech to the closed session of the twentieth party congress in 1956 was at last published in Russia.

Among the most astonishing official reversals was the posthumous rehabilitation in June 1988 of Nikolai Bukharin, whose execution half a century earlier had been one of the most sensational episodes of Stalin's purges. Earlier in 1988 Bukharin's case had been reviewed by the Soviet Supreme Court and his conviction annulled. The court commented that Bukharin had been a victim of 'gross violations of socialist legality' and that admission of guilt had been 'wrung from the accused through unlawful methods'.[13] Several other prominent victims of the purges were rehabilitated at the same time. Bukharin's rehabilitation was announced on Soviet state television and on the front page of *Pravda*. Bukharin's widow, who had been imprisoned until 1945 and then lived next to a pig farm in Siberia for many years, had campaigned for his vindication since the 1950s and survived to learn the news.

The Soviet Union had always been specially secretive about all aspects of its diplomatic history. The Gorbachev era brought unprecedented disclosures. The secret additional protocols to the Molotov–Ribbentrop pact, whose existence had long been denied by Soviet historians, even though their contents were known in the west from German documents, were published in an abridged form in the Estonian newspaper *Sovetskaya Estoniya* in 1988. In 1989, after an Estonian delegate to the Soviet Parliament had read them out during a parliamentary session, they appeared in *Izvestiya* as part of its parliamentary coverage. Only then were they officially acknowledged to be genuine. Nevertheless, even the liberal-minded Yakovlev, while admitting the authenticity of the protocols, insisted that it was 'far-fetched to seek some kind of interconnection between the present status of the three [Baltic] republics and the non-aggression treaty'.[14] In a similar two-steps-forward, one-step-back manner, the government finally acknowledged Soviet responsibility for the massacre of Poles at Katyn in 1940.

Gorbachev and his advisers saw open public debate as an essential basis for their larger project of political and economic reconstruction. Confronted at his accession to power with what appeared to be a choice between focusing on economic or political reform, Gorbachev, allegedly following advice given some years earlier by Enrico Berlinguer, opted to accord top priority to political change. This did not yet mean multi-party politics. But influenced by European Social Democrat leaders such as Felipe González and Willy Brandt, Gorbachev successively jettisoned core elements of Leninism. By 1987 he was speaking of the need for 'socialist pluralism'. Such talk provoked criticisms that came to a head at the nineteenth party conference in June/July

1988 where democrats and conservatives clashed in an unprecedented and public manner. Boris Yeltsin, who had succeeded Grishin as Moscow party boss in December 1985 but been demoted in 1987 for criticizing Gorbachev, demanded a faster pace of reforms. He was sternly reproved by Yegor Ligachev, a former ally of Gorbachev, now champion of the conservatives: 'You don't rush in politics; it is not like slurping cabbage soup.'[15]

The conference took the momentous decision to create a new legislature. The resulting unwieldy, two-tier system of government was a halfway house to parliamentarism. At the lower level, a Congress of People's Deputies would consist of 2,250 members, of whom two-thirds would be directly elected and the remainder chosen by 'social organizations' such as the trade unions and the Academy of Sciences. The Congress would choose one-third of its own number who would form the new Supreme Soviet.

The elections to the Congress in March 1989 were the first contested elections in the history of the USSR—and the last. Turn-out was an impressive 90 per cent. The Communist Party applied great pressure to secure the return of officially sponsored candidates. Most of the deputies elected were party members. But in Leningrad and Kiev conservatives were roundly defeated by reformers. In Moscow Yeltsin was elected with 83.5 per cent of the vote. 'The apparat wouldn't give me my rehabilitation, but the people did,' he exulted.[16] After a vigorous internal battle in the Soviet Academy of Sciences, Sakharov won a seat as its representative. In the Baltic republics nationalist candidates swept the board. Although the government secured a majority, the results were a severe blow to the party.

The proceedings of the Congress, with Gorbachev in the chair, were, at his insistence, televised live across the country. In a highly charged confrontation, Gorbachev rejected a demand by Sakharov for the immediate elimination of the 'leading role' of the Communist Party. But when the former 'public enemy' died a few weeks later, Gorbachev paid homage at his coffin. And a few weeks after that, in February 1990, Gorbachev himself persuaded the Central Committee to agree to what Sakharov had demanded.

Freedom of speech and open political competition created an environment in which Gorbachev could take some hesitant steps towards economic reforms. The Soviet Union by the mid-1980s had reached an economic impasse. The fall in the price of oil in 1986 deprived the USSR of its largest source of hard currency. The military budget, swollen by the war in Afghanistan and the arms race with the United States, was becoming insupportable. The technology gap with the west yawned ever wider. Alongside the state-controlled command economy, and partly overlapping with it, a second or shadow economy had developed in which *shabashniki* (moonlighters) offered services on the private market ranging from construction to auto parts. Inaction was clearly not an option and some of Gorbachev's advisers urged drastic changes from the start. In a note to Gorbachev on 3 December 1985, Yakovlev had recommended that the market economy be restored, with freedom to own property, a capital market, and an end to the monopoly of the 'order of the sword-bearers', as he described the Communist Party.[17] But Gorbachev sensed that such revolutionary change would encounter opposition that might endanger his entire enterprise.

Instead Gorbachev opted for *uskorenie* (acceleration), a final attempt to make the socialized economy function effectively. Efforts were to be concentrated on increasing efficiency and productivity, updating technology, and improving quality control. Much of this collided with the entrenched interests of managers of state enterprises and with the faith of the dwindling number of true believers. Resistance grew to the 'market socialism' or mixed economy towards which Gorbachev's policies were pointing. Soviet economic performance between 1985 and 1989 was not impressive. Foreign debt rose from $29 billion to $54 billion. The budget deficit reached 10 per cent of GNP. Almost the only area of the economy to accelerate was inflation.

Some of Gorbachev's new policies aroused strong popular resistance. He set great store by an anti-drink campaign which, it was hoped, would not only reduce widespread alcoholism but alleviate chronic absenteeism and generally improve the country's social atmosphere. The results of the campaign were almost entirely counterproductive: higher production and consumption of *samogon* (bootleg liquor, often impure), a shortage of sugar (used in the manufacture of moonshine), a serious loss of state revenues, and increased drug addiction.

Gorbachev's internal policies were necessarily predicated on relaxation of international tension, reduction in military spending, and retraction from foreign commitments. Four weeks after taking office he announced an unconditional moratorium on the deployment of further intermediate-range missiles. The following August he announced a unilateral five-month ban on nuclear weapons testing and promised to make it permanent if the United States would do the same. At two summits with Reagan, at Geneva in November 1985 and at Reykjavik in October 1986, Gorbachev persuaded the Americans that he was serious about much more sweeping disarmament agreements. The Intermediate-Range Nuclear Forces (INF)

Treaty signed by the United States and the Soviet Union in 1987 was the first arms-control agreement to eliminate an entire class of weapons. The USSR undertook to destroy 1,752 short- and medium-range missiles on its own territory and in east-central Europe; for its part the United States would destroy 867 of its missiles in western Europe. The two countries opened each other's missile production facilities to inspection. Shortly afterwards the five west European states that had agreed to the stationing of US missiles on their territories agreed to permit Soviet inspectors to verify US compliance *in situ*.

In December 1988 Gorbachev announced that the four-million-strong Soviet armed forces would be cut by 500,000 men over the next two years. He also announced the withdrawal of 10,000 tanks, 8,500 artillery pieces, and 800 combat aircraft from eastern Europe (including European Russia). Although, even with these reductions, Warsaw Pact conventional land forces would still remain numerically superior to NATO forces in Europe, the unilateral cuts evoked growing dismay in Soviet military circles. The Chief of the General Staff, Marshal Sergei Akhromeyev, who opposed the cuts, resigned in protest. Under Russian influence, the Warsaw Pact adopted a new, defensive military doctrine. Two months later the USSR ended its decade-long military involvement in Afghanistan, a major goal of Gorbachev since his accession to power. The war had been a disaster for the Soviet Union. The official cost was 15,000 military deaths and 37,000 wounded, but unofficial estimates were much higher.

It is doubtful whether Gorbachev had already concluded by 1988–9, as had Yakovlev, that 'Marxism was a utopia and a mistake from the very beginning'.[18] His thinking was nevertheless clearly moving in a direction that had as its ultimate destination not revision but wholesale abandonment of Marxist-Leninist dogma. If the leaders of the Soviet Union could even begin to contemplate such a radical ideological transformation, what hope could there be of maintaining old-style Communism in the Soviet satellite states?

Evolution in Poland and Hungary

The changes in the Soviet Union after 1985 were at first met with a wait-and-see response from all sides in eastern Europe. Communist chiefs in East Germany, Czechoslovakia, Bulgaria, and above all Romania and Albania, were highly dubious about the merits of *perestroika*. But (except for the last two) their entire position was based on the infallibility of Moscow. They were like Roman Catholic bishops watching a Pope embrace Protestantism. Since, as dialectical materialists, the satellite leaders could not conscientiously pray for divine intervention, nothing remained except to wring their hands. The old saw that 'the fish begins to stink at the head', which old-style Communists had been wont to lob at each other in the course of internal disputes in the past, now had an unexpected and peculiar application to their own predicament. As for reformers, their caution arose from bitter memories of Hungary in 1956, Czechoslovakia in 1968, and Poland in 1981. True, Gorbachev's reforms went far beyond anything seen in the first 'thaw' under Khrushchev. But Khrushchev, after all, had backtracked and had then been overthrown. Gorbachev's internal position seemed weaker than Khrushchev's and his political survival based less on a solid political constituency than on consummate skill in holding the balance between contending forces. All sides preferred to husband their resources and wait until the signals from Moscow were unambiguous.

The essential prerequisite for change in the Soviet satellites was an end to the threat of Russian military intervention. None of their regimes could expect to survive for long without that visible buttress. Nevertheless, as early as November 1986, Gorbachev told a meeting of Comecon leaders that each party had the 'right to make sovereign decisions about the problems of development in its country, its responsibility to its own people'.[19] In part, Gorbachev's discarding of the Brezhnev doctrine was a matter of logic. At a time when he himself was adopting much of the language and substance of the Prague Spring, how could he reasonably oppose similar policies in eastern Europe? But logic is not, by itself, a sufficient explanation of the switch in Soviet policy. We may be sure that in case of necessity, explanations supported by appropriate citations from canonical texts would have been forthcoming from the ideological machine that had dealt effectively with the no less perplexing contradictions of Soviet domestic and foreign policy in 1921, 1939, and 1956. The shackles binding eastern Europe to the USSR were loosened not so much by the dialectics of *glasnost* as by the inexorable pressures of *perestroika*. The attainment of Gorbachev's objective of modernizing the Soviet economy depended on an end to the Cold War. The Afghan adventure had wrecked détente under his three predecessors. With the hardline Reagan administration in power in the United States, any military enterprise in eastern Europe would certainly elicit a negative reaction in Washington and defeat Gorbachev's entire strategy. Not all elements in the Soviet leadership, especially in the military and security establishments, concurred in this analysis. Hence his wariness. Nevertheless, in October 1988 Gorbachev told his aides to prepare a speech that would be 'Fulton in reverse' (referring to Churchill's 'iron curtain' speech of 1946).[20] The result was Gorbachev's address to the UN General Assembly on 7 December 1988 in which he declared that 'freedom of choice' was a 'right of peoples' and 'a universal principle and there should be no exceptions'.[21] When it became clear that Gorbachev meant what he said and that the USSR would not, perhaps could not, repeat its actions against Hungary in 1956 and Czechoslovakia in 1968, nor even its intimidation of Poland in 1981, the dam protecting east European Communism burst and inundated its epigones.

The effects of Moscow's policy reversal were felt first in Poland. Jaruzelski, acutely sensitive to atmospheric changes in Moscow, began tacking in a different direction soon after Gorbachev's accession to power. In January 1986 a limited amnesty for political prisoners was announced, followed in September by a broader one. In December Jaruzelski created a Consultative Council in which he tried to persuade opposition groups to participate. Wałęsa expressed a readiness 'for an honest dialogue of all important social forces in Poland'[22] but refused to be drawn into a body that would have purely decorative functions. Gradually, however, the political balance shifted in favour of the opposition. The main reason was the parlous state of the Polish economy. The system was locked into a structure of technological obsolescence and overmanning, protected by unrealistic price structures and an ever-growing mountain of foreign debt. The regime hoped to achieve acceptance on the basis of Kádár-style economic reforms. But these foundered on the rock of public opposition to the harsh consequences that would follow from any opening of the tottering Polish economy to even limited market forces. Like Gierek, Jaruzelski presided over an economy in which, for political reasons, inflationary concessions were repeatedly made to consumers unconstrained by the discipline of a genuine internal market. By 1987 Poland's foreign debt had climbed to over $40 billion. In November that year Jaruzelski sought to mobilize support for economic reform by holding a referendum seeking approval for large price increases. For the first time since the war voting was genuinely free. Predictably the result was a resounding no.

Jaruzelski was now hoist by his own petard. He had openly acknowledged that popular support was necessary for economic reform. He therefore moved towards acceptance of the necessity of compromise with non-Communist political forces. He hoped to satisfy them with some limited power-sharing while preserving the essential levers of power, defence, internal security, and foreign affairs, firmly in Communist hands. But instead of co-opting the revived Solidarity movement into the existing power structure, he found himself presiding over a 'negotiated revolution' in which the opposition took power from the Communists. A wave of strikes in April and May 1988 led the government to propose direct talks with the opposition. After several months of manoeuvring, in which the Church played an important role by its support for the opposition, 'round table' negotiations began in February 1989. These produced agreement in April on the framework for a slow transition to parliamentary democracy over a period of five years. Partly free elections would take place, paving the way for the formation of a coalition government of Communists and non-Communists—a genuine coalition rather than the fraudulent 'united front' arrangements of the past. Censorship was abolished. Solidarity re-emerged into legality.

In earlier times such developments would have aroused fury in Moscow. But Gorbachev's reaction was a confession of helplessness: Poland, he told the Politburo, was 'crawling away from us. . . . And what can we do? Poland has a $56 billion debt. Can we take Poland on our balance sheet in our current economic situation? No. And if we cannot—then we have no influence.'[23] When Jaruzelski turned up in Moscow to report to him, Gorbachev pointedly refrained from any criticism and treated his guest to a disquisition on the importance of democratization, pluralism, and 'real participation of working people in running the economy'.[24]

In the general election of June 1989, the Communists had, under the April agreement, reserved for themselves in the Sejm (lower house of parliament) 173 seats out of 460, plus a further 126 for their hitherto docile allies, the Peasants and Democrats, remnants of the inter-war parties of the same names. Contested elections therefore took place only for the remaining 161 seats in the Sejm and for all one hundred seats in the newly established Senate. The Communists' insistence on assuring themselves (with their allies) a guaranteed majority in advance showed how little confidence they had in facing the electorate. Nevertheless, they marshalled their resources for the election campaign in order to obtain at least a respectable outcome. The result was a damning repudiation of Communism's claim to rule by popular consent. Solidarity candidates won every single seat they contested in the Sejm and ninety-nine out of the hundred Senate seats. The Solidarity leaders themselves were astounded and at first barely realized that power was theirs for the grasping.

The Communists, stunned by their debacle at the polls, floundered. Meanwhile, the shift in the wind affected many of the Peasant and Democrat representatives, on whose uncontested elections the Communists had relied as a guarantee of continuing power. A majority of these members decided to support a Solidarity-led government. Even some Communist deputies defected. After weeks of manoeuvring, the Communists realized they had no choice but to concede defeat. They agreed to a modified coalition, in which they would keep the key ministries of defence and the interior (thus controlling the military and police apparatus), and retain the presidency, while allowing the opposition to nominate a Prime Minister.

On 12 September 1989, the first government in eastern Europe since 1948 that was not dominated by Communists took office in Poland. Headed by Tadeusz Mazowiecki, a Catholic journalist who edited Solidarity's weekly newspaper, it moved fast and courageously to implement economic reforms.

Meanwhile a similar pattern of events in Hungary proceeded, fugue-like, beginning a step or two behind the Poles, but later leaping ahead. By 1987 Kádár, aged seventy-five, had been in power for more than three decades. Kádár's main claim to respect was his relative success in reforming the Hungarian economy. But by the mid-1980s 'goulash Communism' was encountering severe difficulties. Growth, robust in the 1970s, slowed. The Hungarian National Bank, facing a liquidity crisis, escaped insolvency only by obtaining loans from the IMF, which Hungary had joined in 1982. As always with such loans, the IMF attached stringent requirements for implementation of a stabilization programme, involving price reform, monetary control, and budgetary limitation. Inspired partly by Solidarity in Poland and by Gorbachev's reforms in the USSR, democratic ideas made headway in Hungary in the mid-1980s both outside the Communist Party and within it. At a party congress in May 1988 Kádár finally and reluctantly bowed out of office. His replacement as party secretary, Károly Grósz, had earned a reputation as an economic modernizer but he resisted pressure for political reform from the radical reformist wing of the party headed by Imre Pozsgay. The new leadership was immediately faced with a crisis when the IMF refused to allow any more drawings as its policy conditions had not been met. Grósz visited Moscow to ask for economic assistance. Gorbachev gave him a pat on the back for carrying out institutional reforms but could offer no tangible aid. Consequently, by early 1989 Hungary was on the edge of bankruptcy.

As in the Soviet Union, one sign of political evolution was a revision of the official version of history. In February 1989 the Hungarian party Central

Committee officially endorsed the view that the revolution of 1956 had been a popular uprising (good) rather than a counter-revolution (bad). In June, in a symbolic act of great significance, the government permitted the reburial with full state honours of the body of Imre Nagy. A quarter of a million people attended and the ceremony was broadcast live on state television. Several of the speakers, among them veterans of the 1956 revolution, took the opportunity to turn the occasion into a political demonstration. Miklós Vásárhelyi, one of Nagy's co-defendants in the secret trial of 1958, called for 'a peaceful transition to a free and democratic society'.[25] Seven days later Grósz was forced out of the leadership of the Communist Party, giving way to a collective leadership of what was now a deeply divided and demoralized movement.

Following the Polish example, the government opened round-table talks with opposition groups. Twenty-eight 'political associations' (parties) had already appeared in what for the previous generation had been a one-party state. The talks concluded on 18 September. By this time a non-Communist government was already in office in Poland. The Hungarian round table, with this model before it, produced much more far-reaching results than the earlier agreement in Poland. Instead of power-sharing based on a partly free election, the Hungarian Communists accepted the concepts of true multi-party politics and free elections. A blueprint for transition to a west-European-style parliamentary regime was approved. The Communist Party (its official name had hitherto been the Hungarian Socialist Workers' Party) was reborn on 7 October 1989 as the Hungarian Socialist Party. Even before elections took place the National Assembly voted to declare the 'Hungarian Republic' *tout court*, deleting the word 'socialist'. In the elections of March–April 1990 the ex-Communists came fourth, with only 11 per cent of the votes. The largest party, with 25 per cent, was the right-of-centre Democratic Forum, led by József Antall, son of a former Smallholders Party minister. A coalition government, dominated by Democratic Forum and excluding the former Communists, was formed shortly afterwards.

The peaceful transfer of power in Poland and Hungary and the simultaneous movement towards a pluralist system in the Soviet Union obviously imperilled the remaining Communist regimes in eastern Europe, all of which seemed stuck in a time warp, oblivious to the cascading changes that were transforming the political environment in which they operated. Unlike the Poles and Hungarians, Honecker, Husák, Zhivkov, and Ceauşescu were not inclined to adapt in order to survive. One by one each of them now reaped the whirlwind.

The Berlin Wall falls

The fall of the Berlin Wall on 9 November 1989 was the decisive political event of the second half of the twentieth century in Europe. None of the chief participants foresaw it. Few of them even wanted it. Yet once it had happened, all immediately sensed that it was irreversible.

In January 1989, speaking at the 500th birthday commemoration of Thomas Münzer (the radical Protestant had been adopted as a working-class hero by the East German regime), Honecker had declared that the Berlin Wall would still be standing 'in fifty or a hundred years' so long as the conditions that gave rise to it had not been removed.[26] By the end of the year the wall was gone and Honecker, who had spoken of 'shedding no tears'[27] over the departure of dissatisfied citizens from his country, had himself been removed from office. The man who would later seek Gorbachev's protection made no secret before 1989 of his disapproval of Gorbachev's policies. Like Ulbricht, Honecker had a high opinion of his own standing as a Communist theoretician and was one of the few East German leaders who dared to contradict the line emanating from Moscow. Some of Gorbachev's early speeches were censored in East Germany and several newly outspoken Soviet publications were banned from distribution there. At a Central Committee meeting in December 1988 Honecker declared that East Germany would not 'march towards anarchy'.[28] Yet within a few months the footsteps of hundreds of thousands of demonstrators were leading his country inexorably in that direction.

Three interrelated developments led to the opening of the wall: the precarious condition of the East German economy; renewed pressure for emigration and the impossibility, in the changed political geography of eastern Europe, of stopping it; and Soviet abstention, for the first time since 1945, from interference in East German affairs.

On the surface, the East German economy was the least problematic in eastern Europe. As late as the summer of 1989 a well-informed western observer could describe it as having 'not only maintained but actually improved its position as the most successful socialist economy in the world'.[29] In fact, as these words were written, it was on the brink of collapse. In May 1989 the head of the State Planning Commission reported to party leaders that if things continued as they were the country would be insolvent within two years. The report was top secret but found reflection in popular collapse of faith in the system. By June 1989 12 per cent of the entire population of East Germany had lodged applications to emigrate.

The catalyst for revolution was the decision of the Hungarian Government, reported to Gorbachev on 3 March 1989, literally to dismantle the Iron Curtain. It did so in a demonstrative manner, sending troops to tear down barbed wire fences, switch off the power on electrified barriers, and demilitarize fortifications along the 165 miles of border with Austria. The Soviet leader's response to this epochal event was studied nonchalance. The West German government rewarded Hungary for opening the border with one billion marks in loans. The Hungarian decision was made public in May and on 27 June the Hungarian Minister of Foreign Affairs publicly switched off the electronic alarm system and cut the wire fence. Soon alleged 'pieces' of the Iron Curtain were being offered for sale in gift shops in Austria.

East Germans quickly realized that a convenient, if circuitous, route to the west had opened. Nobody could be sure how long the escape hatch would remain open. Thousands of East German 'tourists' arrived in Hungary and the West German embassy grounds in Budapest turned into a giant encampment as the travellers awaited visas to enable them to cross to the west. On 10 September, the Hungarian government opened the border to free exit. Hungarian police at the town of Hegyeshalom found themselves confronted with traffic jams of overladen 'Trabies' (Trabants, the most common small East German cars), spewing exhaust fumes at the approach road to the Austrian frontier. The refugees overwhelmed the capacity to absorb them of Austrian and West German immigration services. Citing an old treaty in which the two Communist regimes promised to prohibit the free emigration of each other's nationals to the west, the East German authorities protested to Budapest. But the Hungarians refused to close the frontier. In the course of September 33,000 people moved west. Thousands more were besieging West German and US embassies throughout central Europe. On 3 October the East German government, which until then had permitted free movement to and from Czechoslovakia, closed that frontier 'temporarily' except to those with valid passports and visas. By agreement between the two German states, special sealed trains carrying several thousand East German refugees from Czechoslovakia and Poland crossed East German territory to West Germany. The East German government hoped that this concession would be a safety valve. But when the trains passed through Dresden, there was a riot at the station as more people tried to get on board. These disturbances merged into a nationwide uprising.

One area of relative institutional independence in East Germany, the Protestant Church, had become a rallying-point for opposition to the regime that encompassed religious, peace, student, and environmental groups. Although participants came from all classes, the core of the movement, unlike that of 1953, was drawn from the intelligentsia. Since the early 1980s weekly 'peace prayer' services had been held each Monday in the Nikolaikirche in Leipzig. By the autumn of 1989 these had developed into regular anti-regime demonstrations that attracted hundreds, later thousands, of people chanting '*Wir wollen raus*' ('We want out') and 'Wir *sind das Volk*' ('*We* are the people'). Gradually the protests spread and grew in size. The authorities considered using force to put down the protests but in the end thought better of it, realizing that bloodshed would eliminate any hope of financial aid from the west.

Until this point the Russians, deeply preoccupied with their own affairs, had pursued not so much a policy as a non-policy towards eastern Europe. The main element was withdrawal of the threat of military intervention. As Fyodor Burlatsky, a reformist-Communist supporter of Gorbachev, put it in April 1988: 'We have given our allies so much bad advice in the past that we now hesitate to give them good advice.'[30] But on a visit to East Berlin on 5 October to celebrate the fortieth anniversary of the establishment of the German Democratic Republic, Gorbachev urged liberalization and warned Honecker that 'life punishes those who come late'[31] (see plate 34). In issuing this admonition, Gorbachev seems to have believed that a liberalized Communist regime would stand a better chance of surviving. Greeted with cheers and cries of 'Gorby! Gorby!' by crowds in East Berlin, the Soviet leader later confessed that 'he had felt very uncomfortable standing at Erich Honecker's side'.[32]

On 17 October Honecker was ousted by restive colleagues. His replacement was Egon Krenz, a late convert to reform. The new leader inspired more derisive humour than confidence. Earlier that year he had flown to China to congratulate Deng Xiao-ping after the Tiananmen Square massacre. Now he was dubbed 'Krenz Xiao-ping'. He did not, however, share Honecker's faith in a 'Chinese solution'. Instead, he announced his readiness for internal political dialogue. The Czechoslovak border was opened again. Altogether, 57,000 people emigrated during October. But the government in Prague, anxious about the effect on its own population of the spectacle of hordes of East Germans passing through Czechoslovakia to the west, objected and told the East Germans they must solve the problem themselves. In the last week of October half a million people took part in demonstrations all over East

Germany, calling for free elections and free emigration. The following week the number of demonstrators more than doubled.

When Krenz met Gorbachev in Moscow on 1 November he told the Soviet leader that East German border guards had been given orders not to shoot at escapers and that liberalized regulations on foreign travel were about to be issued. The minutes of the conversation make it clear, however, that Krenz did not envisage demolishing the wall. On the contrary, he pointed out that 'certain precautionary measures' would have to be taken 'to prevent the masses from attempting to break through the wall'. He appealed to Gorbachev for economic assistance. He reported that the foreign exchange balance of East Germany at the end of year would be: 'Income $5.9 billion; expenditure $18 billion. The deficit thus ran at about $12.1 billion. This meant they had to take on new loans. It was likely', he added, 'that this imbalance would increase further'. An 'astonished Gorbachev asked whether these numbers were exact. He had not imagined the situation to be so precarious'. But Krenz assured him the grim picture was accurate and explained that the only alternative to new loans was an austerity programme involving an immediate lowering of the East German standard of living by 30 per cent. 'This', however, he judged 'not feasible politically.' Gorbachev was unmoved. Rather than offering any aid, he suggested that the East German government would have 'to find a way to tell the population that [they] had lived beyond their means in the last few years'.[33] This reply, similar to the brush-offs administered earlier to Jaruzelski and Grósz, amounted for Krenz to a political sentence of death.

As a last resort, the East Germans dispatched a secret emissary, Alexander Schalk-Golodkowsky, a veteran of shady, clandestine contacts with the west, to Bonn to ask for new loans. His subsequent report to Krenz on his negotiations there shows him adopting simultaneously the stance of beggar and blackmailer. He informed his West German interlocutor, Wolfgang Schäuble, that 'generous regulations' for travel would shortly be announced but explained that 'implementation of these measures [would] create significant . . . costs'. To cover these, East Germany 'would be prepared to take out long-term loans' of up to ten billion marks and in addition would require additional lines of credit from 1991 of 2–3 billion DM. Schäuble replied that any new financial aid would be contingent on political reform in East Germany, specifically including a multi-party system, free elections, and 'making this border [in Berlin] more passable'. No immediate agreement was reached. Under acute pressure from the rising tide of demonstrations, the East German government published new travel regulations on 6 November, permitting its citizens to go abroad for up to thirty days a year, though they would be permitted to take only 15 marks in foreign exchange with them. The news was greeted with sarcasm on the streets: 'Around the world in thirty days—without money!'[34]

Three days later the East German Government, almost without realizing what it was doing, allowed free passage through the Berlin Wall. Günter Schabowski, the Politburo member who announced the decision (if the muddled draft policy directive can be dignified with that label), gave confused answers in an eight-minute-long televised press conference. When asked specifically whether the wall would now be open, his answer was: 'The issue of travel, (um) the ability to cross the wall from our side . . . hasn't been answered yet and exclusively the question in the sense . . . So this, I'll put it this way, fortified state border of the GDR (um) We have always said that there have to be several other factors (um).'[35] Schabowski's stumbling locutions lacked the lapidary eloquence of Cyrus' edict freeing the Hebrews. Yet his declaration, like the Persian monarch's, would 'break in pieces the gates of brass, and cut in sunder the bars of iron'.[36] Somehow he conveyed to his listeners the underlying message: border guards would no longer shoot escapers and nothing, therefore, would prevent East Germans crossing through the wall to the west. They seized the opportunity with a joy akin to that of the Babylonian slaves returning to Jerusalem.

Within hours the first tentative venturings turned into a multitude of delighted east Berliners whose numbers swamped the perfunctory efforts of border guards to stamp their passports. Crowds of young people clambered on top of the wall, dancing, drinking, singing, and wielding mallets with which they chipped away at the concrete slabs (see plate 35). Chunks of the wall quickly became favoured souvenir items. Over the next few days hundreds of thousands of east Berliners visited the west.

All sides were caught by surprise. When Gorbachev was informed, he said that the East Germans 'had taken the proper action'. The 350,000 Soviet troops in East Germany remained firmly ensconced in their barracks. Gorbachev agreed with Shevardnadze that Soviet military intervention 'would have started World War III'.[37] Shevardnadze told the press that the 'correct, clever, and wise decision' to open the wall was 'entirely an affair of the new leadership [of East Germany] and wished them much success'.[38] A divided Berlin was where the Cold War had begun forty-four years earlier; a reunited Berlin was where, overnight, it ended.

Revolutions in eastern Europe

The revolutions of 1989 erupted with such volcanic force, moved across eastern Europe with such velocity, mobilized so many previously disengaged ordinary people, and overthrew authoritarian governments with such ease that people at the time naturally looked back for comparison to the 'springtime of nations', the revolutionary year 1848. The analogy carried within it a transparent anxiety that, as in 1849, the revolutionary successes might be short-lived. The more recent cases of Hungary in 1956 and Czechoslovakia in 1968 were not promising. True, Gorbachev was no Metternich but the Communist Party remained entrenched in the USSR, the security in power of reformists there was questionable, and the Soviet military machine was still encamped in East Germany, Poland, Hungary, and Czechoslovakia. Hence the edge of fear, bordering on paranoia, with which many east Europeans viewed prospects for genuine independence of their states.

Even as reverberations of the collapse of the Berlin Wall echoed through eastern Europe, another ruler was being toppled. Zhivkov ruled with a lighter touch than Honecker but Bulgaria too was plagued by poor economic performance as well as by a spill-over of reformist ideas from the Soviet Union (Bulgarian state television broadcast the first channel of Soviet television on a live feed from Moscow). In the late 1980s, perhaps looking for a scapegoat, the government roused popular antagonism against the Muslim minority, around 10 per cent of the country's 8.9 million population. In 1950 about 154,000 Muslims had emigrated to Turkey under an arrangement agreed upon by the two governments. Those who stayed in Bulgaria were subjected to a policy of involuntary assimilation and religious persecution. In 1984 the government ordered all citizens with Muslim-sounding names to adopt new ones. The practice recalled attempts by Bulgarian governments earlier in the century to force name changes on minorities. Muslim protest demonstrations in May 1989 were violently suppressed by Bulgarian police. The government expelled two thousand alleged ringleaders and challenged the Turkish government to open its borders. Turkey acquiesced but was overwhelmed by a rush of Muslims fleeing Bulgaria. By August more than 300,000 had arrived and the government in Ankara, hard put to cope, restricted admission.

Unlike Poland, Bulgaria did not spawn a significant political opposition movement during most of the Communist period. But in 1988–9 social unrest found expression in an attempt to form an independent trade union, Podkrepa ('Support'), on the model of Solidarity, though at first its members came mainly from the intelligentsia. A number of independent citizens' groups appeared, notably the environmentalist-reformist organization Ecoglasnost. Initially, however, none of these had much political weight. The early stages of the Bulgarian revolution took the form of a palace coup headed by the Foreign Minister, Petar Mladenov. In a letter to the Communist Party Central Committee on 24 October 1989, he complained of Zhivkov's 'rude' behaviour and asserted: 'We have even reached the point where we are estranged from the Soviet Union and we find ourselves entirely on our own, in the same pigs' trough as the rotten dictatorial family regime of Ceauşescu. In a word, with his policies Zhivkov has forced Bulgaria outside the currents of our age.'[39] Gorbachev, who did not like Zhivkov, approved of Mladenov's apparent reformism and seems to have given the 'green light' for a coup.

At a meeting of the Politburo on 9 and 10 November 1989, Zhivkov was forced to resign after thirty-four years in power. He was replaced by Mladenov. The Communist Party embarked on an extensive process of internal reform, later renaming itself the Bulgarian Socialist Party. The Communists hoped to retain power on a reform platform but opposition elements in the Union of Democratic Forces, led by the writer Zheliu Zhelev, gathered strength. With the benign approval of Moscow, the Communists agreed to a round-table conference with the opposition. Both sides agreed to avoid recourse to force, though Mladenov's words, 'Maybe we should call in the tanks', uttered during a demonstration on 14 December, were recorded and later used against him. Substantive talks began in January 1990 and soon led to agreement on democratic reforms, including an end to censorship and free elections for a constituent assembly.

In the next scene the action moved to Prague. For politically conscious Europeans old enough to recall the events there in August 1968, the peaceful revolution in Czechoslovakia in November 1989 had a cathartic quality unmatched even by the drama in Berlin. The return from oblivion of Alexander Dubček, the apotheosis of an unlikely playwright, Václav Havel, as leader of the nation, and the choice of the Magic Lantern Theatre as the Prague headquarters of the democratic movement all gave the peaceful 'velvet revolution', as it came to be known, a character of improvisation and carnival.

The Czechoslovak opposition movement had observed Gorbachev's reforms in the USSR with initial scepticism, then with slowly rising hope.

The Husák regime, for its part, watched Soviet developments with increasing apprehension. But unlike the Polish and Hungarian Communists, who sought to take advantage of the increased room for manoeuvre offered by change in Russia, the Czechoslovak government dug in and tried to batten down the hatches. Some halting economic reforms were introduced in 1987 and the government gingerly adopted phrases from the new political lexicon in Moscow. But cultural controls remained strict. In March members of a banned musical group, the 'Jazz Section', were sentenced to prison terms for conducting 'an unauthorized business venture'.[40] The fundamental reason for the government's anxiety emerged clearly in November when signals from Moscow indicated a possible change in the official Soviet line affirming the rightness of the invasion of Czechoslovakia in 1968. As Jiří Dienstbier, a leader of the democratic opposition, put it: 'If the question is opened, it will open a new situation here. The people who have run this country for nearly twenty years are the men of that intervention. Their only legitimization in power derives from it.'[41]

In December 1987 Husák was replaced as party chief by Miloš Jakeš, a reliable party-liner who had overseen the post-Dubček purge. Husák, however, retained the office of President. Signalling that the change in leadership did not signify any shift in policy, the party newspaper, *Rudé právo*, launched a renewed attack on Dubček, pronouncing it a 'crude lie' to compare the reforms in the Soviet Union with those of the Prague Spring.[42] Dubček himself, in a rare interview given to an Italian Communist paper, 'saluted' Gorbachev's programme 'because I find in it a profound connection with what presented itself to us twenty years ago'.[43]

As in Poland and East Germany, one source of resistance that the government found difficult to deal with was the Church. The Archbishop of Prague, Cardinal František Tomášek, had been critical of Charter 77, but under the influence of Pope John Paul II he became an outspoken advocate of human rights and a thorn in the side of the regime. In January 1988 he signed a petition calling for religious freedom. A mass demonstration in Bratislava supported it and by May half a million people had signed. In June the government bent a little. After negotiations with the Vatican, it permitted the consecration of two new bishops, the first for fifteen years.

Far from satisfying the opposition, however, such gestures sharpened the appetite for political change. In August, twenty years after the Soviet invasion, several thousand protesters marched in Prague in the largest protest demonstration there since 1968. The names of Dubček and Palach were heard again.

Police charged with dogs. Demonstrators shouted: 'We have the truth, you have the dogs!'[44] Further demonstrations followed over the next few months. When President Mitterrand visited Prague in December, he met representatives of Charter 77, including Václav Havel who later told a crowd of demonstrators: 'Our society is beginning to recover from a long slumber.'[45]

Fifty-two years old, the country's most celebrated playwright (though his plays could not be performed publicly in his homeland), Havel was an earnest and cautious intellectual with a moralizing streak. He had the good fortune always to look like an amateur in politics. Until almost the end the Communist leadership made the great mistake of not taking him seriously. In common with most observers, they tended to dismiss the Charter 77 activists as a small group of Bohemian intellectuals, isolated from the masses. But as anti-government demonstrations slowly grew in size, it became clear that the Chartists' long years of lonely witness had endowed them with an unparalleled legitimacy in the eyes of many of their countrymen. After yet another demonstration in January 1989, held in commemoration of the suicide of Palach, Havel was arrested on a charge of 'hooliganism' and held for four months.

On May Day the security forces of a Communist state could be seen performing the strange act of tearing to shreds portraits of Gorbachev that had been raised by demonstrators as a rebuke and taunt to the Czechoslovak leadership. Calls by the opposition for 'dialogue', on the pattern set by the Poles and Hungarians, evoked a warning in *Rudé právo* against 'playing with fire'.[46] The Prime Minister, Ladislav Adamec, told the Soviet newspaper *Izvestiya*: 'It is very difficult to find a common language with such people.'[47] But the opposition had learned how to exploit one of the oldest and best methods of arousing support: the cultivation of a cycle of protest, followed by forcible repression, which itself generated further protest.

In spite of the gathering domestic opposition, the government was probably influenced more by pressure for reform from the Soviet Union. A relaxation in cultural policy began to be felt: banned works by Kafka and Kundera were announced for publication. Jamming of western radio stations stopped. Travel restrictions were eased. But as the momentum of change in surrounding countries accelerated, the snail-pace adjustments of the Prague regime seemed wholly out of step with the times.

Several bizarre episodes in 1989 turned the government into something of a laughing stock. In August the Presidium of the Czechoslovak Parliament issued a grotesque statement protesting against the Polish Parliament's expression of regret for that country's participation in the 1968 invasion: 'a gross interference in the internal affairs of Czechoslovakia', declared the statement referring not to the invasion, but to its repudiation by the Poles.[48] A little later, a tape recording was mysteriously released of a rambling speech by Jakeš to a closed conference of Communist officials. Jakeš could be heard saying that the arrest of Havel was an error, since it had caused an international uproar; it would be better to pick on less well-known figures. The tape was broadcast repeatedly by Radio Free Europe, causing acute embarrassment to Jakeš. Shortly afterwards the government added inconsistency to involuntary candour when it briefly rearrested Havel. Dubček, still unable to speak in public in his own country, appeared on Leningrad television to discuss the events of 1968. For the leaders of a regime that based its entire *raison d'être* on submission to Russia, this was a peculiarly cruel twist.

During October, as crowds of hundreds of thousands in East Germany endangered the regime, the demonstrations in Prague were still on a much smaller scale. After the fall of the Berlin Wall the Soviet party sent a message to Prague warning the Communist leadership there that they would suffer the same fate as Honecker unless they embraced more radical reforms. Fissures began to appear within the party as Adamec tried to carve out a position for himself as leader of a reformist faction. But he was soon swept aside by the rush of events.

On 17 November a series of daily demonstrations in Prague began. They were repressed with heavier than usual police brutality: one man was reported to have been killed and several injured. The report of the killing was denied by the government-run television news and later turned out to have been false. The rumour nevertheless ignited a storm of indignation. Two days later a meeting convened by Havel created a unified organization, Civic Forum, as the main focus of the opposition. In Slovakia a parallel body, known as Public Against Violence, was formed. The next day, 200,000 people joined in the largest anti-government march in Prague since 1968. Demonstrators also marched in Bratislava and Brno. Television news and part of the press reported fully on the demonstrations, suggesting that the government was now loosening (or losing) its hitherto tight control of the media.

This was an indication of a more general loss of self-confidence by the government. Jakeš could not call in external support on the model of 1968. In a Politburo meeting on the night of 21/22 November Jakeš proposed military repression in the style of Poland in 1981. This was seriously considered but there could be no guarantee that the Czechoslovak army would perform such a role in 1989. The only alternative was dialogue. Adamec therefore opened discussions with Havel who, operating from his makeshift headquarters in the Magic Lantern Theatre, emerged as the central figure of the opposition.

As the demonstrations grew day by day, Havel spoke to vast crowds urging persistence, patience, and non-violence. Meanwhile factory workers indicated that they would observe a general strike called by Civic Forum. There could be no doubt now that the opposition extended beyond the ranks of students and intellectuals. The writing was on the wall for Jakeš. On 24 November the news of his resignation and that of the entire Politburo produced an outpouring of emotion that reached a climax when the crowd in Wenceslas Square saw Dubček appear on a balcony by the side of Havel. In a gesture mingling pathos with joy, he stretched out his arms as if to embrace the crowd. People danced and cried.

The Communist leaders' hope that dialogue with the opposition and espousal of a programme of limited reforms might enable the system to survive were soon shown to be misplaced. Although they clung tenaciously to power, their bargaining position was infinitely weaker than that of their Polish and Hungarian comrades just a few months before. In the wake of events elsewhere in eastern Europe, the talks took on the aspect of negotiation of terms of surrender. Critics complained that the Communists' change of heart amounted to too little too late. A more dispassionate reading suggests that the Hungarian-Polish models of more concessions earlier would simply have led more quickly to the Hungarian-Polish conclusion: the end of Communist power. In the last week of November public clocks in Prague were deliberately stopped with the hands showing 5 to midnight to suggest that time was up for the Communist Party. A torrent of public hostility to Communism in any form obliged the party to give way. Even *Rudé právo* complained that the party leadership were 'political mummies'.[49] A two-hour general strike on 27 November was widely observed. Havel declared: 'History has begun to develop very fast in this country. In a country that has had twenty years of timelessness, now we have this fantastic speed.'[50] The next day the party bowed to the inevitable and conceded that it would no longer insist on its 'leading role' in society. On 3 December a new Cabinet was announced in which five out of fifteen members were non-Communists. The opposition rejected it outright. Finally, after renewed mass demonstrations, a new 'government of national understanding', headed by a Communist but with a non-Communist Cabinet majority, was sworn in on 10 December. On the same day, President Husák, who within the space of a month had been transformed from elder statesman to political albatross, resigned. At the end of the month the federal parliament, from which some Communists resigned to make way for co-opted opposition representatives, elected Dubček chairman of the Federal Assembly and Havel President of the country. After the presidential election had been completed, the country's leaders gathered in St Vitus's Cathedral for a Te Deum, the public recitation of which on the last day of the year earns a plenary indulgence.

The last of the revolutions of 1989, and the only one that involved serious violence, broke out in Romania. The first signs of serious disaffection with the regime had appeared two years earlier. Workers at the Red Flag truck and tractor plant in Braşov, enraged by wage cuts, rioted, shouting 'Down with Ceauşescu' and 'We want bread'.[51] Disturbances spread to other cities, and, ominously for the government, assumed a political character, with crowds singing the nationalist anthem 'Romanians Awake'. In the face of earlier workers' protests, for example a strike by miners in the Jiu valley in 1977, Ceauşescu had deftly mixed concession with repression. On this occasion, however, the protests were put down without mercy by security forces. Ceauşescu insisted that he would not veer from the rapid foreign debt repayment policy which, he said, was setting the country on a path towards 'the radiant summits of Communism'.[52] The omnipresence and ruthlessness of the *Securitate* precluded the organization of any opposition movement. In 1988–9 a number of Romanian intellectuals, including the poet Mircea Dinescu and the philosopher Andrei Pleşu, issued public statements praising Gorbachev and calling on the regime to respect human rights and institute reforms. More threateningly for Ceauşescu, in March 1989 six senior members of the Communist Party, including two former general secretaries and a former ambassador to the United Nations, Silviu Brucan, issued an open letter in which they accused Ceauşescu of discrediting the idea of socialism and appealed to him to change course 'before it is too late.'[53] Ceauşescu's response was to accuse them of being enemy agents and to place them under house arrest.

As popular discontent grew, Ceauşescu, like Zhivkov, played the ethnic card. The victims were the Hungarians of Transylvania. As a former ruling nationality, now a minority, they, like the Turks in Bulgaria, could easily be turned into targets of nationalist hostility. In 1988 their plight became a diplomatic issue as large numbers fled from Romania and were granted asylum in Hungary. Opposition groups in Hungary took up the Transylvanian cause and the Hungarian government felt bound to take action. A senior party spokesman assured the Transylvanian Magyars that they had 'the backing of the mother-nation'.[54] An anti-Ceauşescu demonstration in Budapest in July 1988 attracted 50,000 people. A few weeks later Imre Pozsgay, leader of the liberal wing of the Hungarian Politburo, said that the 'incomprehensible and idiotic political program' of Ceauşescu was 'an injury to European civilization, a crime against humanity.'[55] By July 1989 the Hungarian Government was complaining of 'military threats' by Romania.[56] The escalating conflict with Hungary, the growing unrest within Romania, and the example of reform set by Gorbachev all presented Ceauşescu with a crisis to which he seemed unable to respond effectively.

The spark that kindled revolution was an incident in the Transylvanian city of Timişoara on 16 December 1989. Police attempted to arrest a pastor of the Hungarian Reformed Church, László Tőkés, a stubborn dissident and hero among Magyars of the region. A large crowd gathered round his house to protect him. Demonstrations followed that were put down by force on orders from Ceauşescu. Rumour fanned the numbers killed in the ensuing massacre to over four thousand. An official inquiry some months later calculated the real number as ninety-seven; and a recent historical estimate further reduces it to no more than seventy.[57]

Ceauşescu met the crisis with defiance. He summoned a large demonstration in Bucharest on 21 December and addressed the people from a balcony. As usual, claques of party faithful were positioned to deliver applause but catcalls from the crowd disrupted the meeting and disconcerted the leader. State television, which was covering the event live, caught Ceauşescu's expression of baffled rage just before it cut off the transmission. The demonstration turned into a riot, then into an insurrection. Ceauşescu and his wife narrowly escaped from the presidential palace in a helicopter. After frantic wanderings in the Romanian countryside, they were captured and subjected to an improvised trial before a military court in the lecture hall of a provincial barracks building. The trial was held in secret and its conduct was political rather than judicial in nature. The deposed leader refused to acknowledge the legitimacy of the court and expressed confidence that the working class would rally to his support 'until they have eliminated this gang of traitors . . . who with foreign help organized a *coup d'état*.'[58] The proceedings lasted a total of 55 minutes, at the end of which the court pronounced the accused guilty of genocide and other charges. They were sentenced to death, taken out, put up against a wall, and shot. Videotaped extracts from the trial and photographs of the bodies were later distributed round the world.

Ceauşescu's abrupt flight had left a vacuum of power in Bucharest. A National Salvation Front (NSF), composed of various opposition figures and some disaffected former supporters of the regime, took control, at first very shakily. In confused fighting over the next few days, the army protected the new regime against sporadic attacks from members of the *Securitate*. A majority of the 1,104 people killed in the course of the revolution were civilians and a large number appear to have been victims of 'friendly fire'. The main university library in Bucharest was burned to the ground and nearly half a million books were destroyed. (Among the few that were saved were the collected works of Ceauşescu, which were held in a special display room.) With the news of the dictator's execution, however, fighting died down and the new government consolidated its authority.

The NSF was headed by Ion Iliescu, a former Communist youth leader who had fallen out with Ceauşescu in the 1970s. From the outset he faced accusations that he and several of his colleagues were merely the old guard in a new guise. Ever more ingenious conspiracy theories concerning the revolution circulated. The hasty trial and execution of the Ceauşescus were attributed to a desire to prevent embarrassing disclosures of alleged continuity between the old and new orders. More than any of the other revolutions of 1989, the Romanian left a filthy detritus of mutual suspicion and collective guilt. With the fall of the old regime, the Romanians, unlike the Czechs, Poles, and East Germans, seemed to have no alternative ideology to fall back on. Their new rulers seemed hard put to formulate a programme or even to give a sense of direction that could provide a framework for post-Communist politics.

Within three months all the Communist regimes of east-central Europe had melted away (only the Albanian lingered a little longer). The Warsaw Pact was formally disbanded in early 1990. Comecon clung to a faint afterlife until it too was dissolved. As the spectre of Communism faded away, another ghost from the past reappeared to haunt the continent, that of a united Germany. Within a year this moved from a distant and, to many, frightening prospect to a generally welcomed reality.

German reunification

Publicly, western leaders expressed delight at the opening of the Berlin Wall; privately they were unnerved. When the US President, George H. W. Bush, met Gorbachev in Malta on 2 December, he told him that 'some Western allies, while outwardly supportive of reunification, should the German people make this choice, are in reality worried by this possibility. . . . We won't take any rash steps, make any attempts to speed up the resolving of the unification problem.'[59] Henry Kissinger was one of the few observers who understood that the end of the wall would lead almost automatically to German reunification. 'In some form,' he wrote, '[it] has become inevitable, whatever the misgivings of Germany's neighbors and World War II victims.'[60] Kissinger foresaw that free elections in East Germany would be contested by eastern surrogates of the West German political parties and that, shorn of its Communist mission, the German Democratic Republic would lose its *raison d'être*.

In East Germany popular pressure for reunification leapt ahead of the diplomats and the politicians. On 11 December at the Monday demonstration in Leipzig, the placards that had hitherto declared '*Wir* sind das Volk' were amended to 'Wir sind *ein* Volk'. Meanwhile emigration to the west assumed the character of a wholesale exodus: more than 300,000 people left East Germany in the first four months after the opening of the wall. Hans Modrow, the mayor of Dresden, who had a reputation as a reformer, became Prime Minister of East Germany on 14 November at the head of a Cabinet of twenty-seven ministers of whom twelve were non-Communists. On 3 December a tearful Krenz resigned together with his entire Politburo and round-table talks opened between Communists and other parties. But efforts by the former East German secret police, the Stasi, to destroy papers (the organization held 179 kilometres of files on six million persons, half the adult population of the country) led to new demonstrations and the storming of Stasi buildings in order to safeguard the files. In late December Kohl visited Dresden and was greeted by vast crowds calling for unification. The continuing pressure on the streets quickened the pace of political change, forcing the Communists to agree to free elections. Very soon it became clear that these would constitute a referendum on the issue of reunification.

This, however, was not merely an intra-German issue but an international diplomatic question of the first order. Its resolution, and the speed with which it was implemented, owed most to the hitherto underrated Kohl, who in this crisis displayed a historic sense of purpose and leadership. After initially proposing a confederation of the two German states, he quickly came to realize that East Germany was no longer viable as an independent entity. Over the next few months he guided an at first uncertain German people and an even more doubtful Europe towards the objective of a single German state.

The essential precondition was the withdrawal of the Russian veto. That was Gorbachev's contribution. In December 1989 Gorbachev still felt able to assure his Central Committee that Soviet leaders would 'see to it that no harm came to the GDR'.[61] Yet just two months later, when Kohl arrived in Moscow, his briefcase brimming with proposals for German loans to the Soviet Union, Gorbachev assured him that the USSR would not stand in the way of reunification. The main explanation for Gorbachev's switch was the rapidly deteriorating Soviet economic position. The Bush administration helped Kohl by offering Moscow economic and strategic inducements. Both Thatcher and Mitterrand were initially fearful that a reunited Germany would prove too powerful for the balance of Europe. But once the Russians and Americans approved, there was not much they could do about it. Mitterrand was furious: 'What is Gorbachev thinking? . . . How much did Kohl pay him?'[62] The price was, in fact, higher than anyone could have imagined at the time. By 1997 the Federal Republic had paid 133 billion marks to the Soviet Union and its successor states.

Free elections in East Germany on 18 March 1990 produced an overwhelming victory for the 'Alliance for Germany', the eastern extension of the Christian Democrats, who won 48 per cent of the vote. They had entered the election as explicit supporters of reunification. The Social Democrats, who were more mealy-mouthed about unity, won only 22 per cent. As for the reformed Communists, their vote was a humiliating 16 per cent. The Christian Democrats' leader, Lothar de Maizière, succeeded Modrow to become East Germany's last Prime Minister, at the head of a transitional coalition government. He immediately began to negotiate terms of reunification with Bonn. The essential basis was East German acceptance of the constitution of the Federal Republic. What this amounted to was West German annexation of East Germany.

Following the precedent of the early nineteenth-century *Zollverein*, political unity was preceded by economic. On 18 May the two German states signed an agreement to join their currencies and economic systems. This took effect on 1 July when, to their immense enrichment, East Germans discovered that they could exchange most of their own currency for West German marks at a rate of one for one. The market value of the East German mark was only a fraction of the West German. The decision on a parity exchange was Kohl's. Later he was greatly criticized for this. But it had a reassuring psychological effect at the time that was important in reconciling doubters in East Germany.

At the end of May Gorbachev and Bush met for another summit in Washington. Gorbachev was anxious to conclude a new trade agreement with the United States. He also sought $20 billion in western credits to keep the Soviet economy afloat. A deal was being held up by opposition in the US Senate, sympathetic to demands by Lithuania, Latvia, and Estonia for independence from the Soviet Union. Desperately in need of economic aid if *perestroika* were not to founder, Gorbachev made two critical commitments. He secretly undertook to resolve the dispute with the Baltic provinces without resort to force; and he conceded that the Soviet Union would not stand in the way of a united Germany remaining a member of NATO. In return he was granted the trade agreement. In subsequent negotiations the USSR agreed, in return for massive German financial assistance, to withdraw all its forces from Germany by 1994. The western powers sugared the pill for the USSR by promising that no non-German NATO forces would be permanently stationed on former East German territory and that nuclear weapons would not be deployed there.

On 31 August 1990 East and West Germany signed a Unification Treaty providing for the accession of the eastern *Länder* to the Federal Republic. On 12 September, the two Germanies plus the four wartime allies signed what became known as the '2 + 4' agreement. It specified that Germany had no territorial claims whatsoever against other states; that she would renounce the manufacture, possession, and control of nuclear, biological, and chemical weapons; that her armed forces would be limited to a maximum strength of 370,000; and that the rights of the four wartime allies in Berlin would terminate. On 3 October 1990 Germany was finally reunited. But it was not a marriage of equals. East Germany was, as the common saying of the time went, *geschluckt* ('swallowed') by the Federal Republic.

In the course of its forty-one years of existence many had scoffed at the German Democratic Republic's pretensions to exemplify 'real existing socialism'. If only in the manner of its departure, however, it realized perfectly the prophecy of Engels regarding the ultimate fate of the socialist state: 'When at last it becomes the real representative of the whole of society, it renders itself unnecessary.... the state is not "abolished," it withers away.'[63]

The disintegration of the USSR

Between 1989 and 1991, as Germany was reborn, the Soviet Union endured a protracted death agony. While Gorbachev struggled to cope with the worsening economic crisis, nationalist antagonisms, the dark secret of Soviet society rose to the surface. The Communist Party's loss of ideological legitimacy was shown by official resort to violence against demonstrators in Tbilisi, Georgia, in April 1989; by rising ethnic conflicts in Soviet central Asia; by miners' strikes in Siberia, Vorkuta, and the Donbass in July; and by demands in the Baltic republics for independence from the USSR. Over the next two years the political forces that Gorbachev had helped conjure up battled for supremacy and in the end consumed him along with the entire Soviet state.

For most Soviet citizens, *perestroika*'s most immediate gifts were greater hardship, an unfamiliar sense of insecurity, and, most disturbingly, growing food and fuel shortages. The new freedoms, rather than assuaging discontent, provided, for the first time in the country's history, licence for its expression. During 1990 the price of bread rose from 4 to 15 roubles per kilogram and of a litre of milk from 13 to 65 kopeks. Against this background some of the cosmetic changes of the era merely increased the general vexation. The first McDonald's fast-food restaurant to open in Moscow was wildly successful as a commercial operation; but amidst growing hunger it symbolized economic inequality not consumer affluence. Nor did the KGB improve its reputation when it inaugurated a public relations centre in Moscow and announced the election of a 'Miss KGB' who was said to wear a bullet-proof vest, to have the 'sophisticated softness' of a Pierre Cardin model, and to be able 'to deliver a karate kick to the head of an adversary'.[64] As new ikons appeared, old ones fell. In western Ukraine, where nationalist fever was in the ascendant, sixteen cities demolished statues of Lenin.

The efforts of the government to maintain control of events amidst accumulating social tensions became ever more unconvincing. Gorbachev tried to steer a 'centrist' line between conservatives within the Politburo, such as Yegor Ligachev, and radicals who included his closest economic advisers as well as newly assertive mayors and regional bosses. In March 1990 the Congress of People's Deputies elected Gorbachev President of the USSR, though the vote was far from unanimous. He had been ceremonial head of state since October 1988 but this was to be a powerful executive presidency under the newly emerging constitution. Gorbachev found, however, that his authority was stronger on paper than in reality. Hoping to speed movement of power from party to state institutions, he took the revolutionary step of advocating elimination of the constitutional protection of the Communist Party's 'leading role'. This would open the way to a multi-party system. The proposal was approved by the Congress but was greeted with outrage by conservatives. Gorbachev's popularity waned as he tacked to and fro between conservative and reformist courses. Meanwhile, a formidable rival for public affections was emerging. In May Yeltsin was elected Chairman of the Supreme Soviet of the Russian Republic and he used that position to present himself as a popular tribune and to assert that Russia would no longer be subordinate to the central institutions of the USSR. Later in the year Gorbachev was awarded the Nobel Peace Prize. Irony of ironies, whereas in the past Nobel prizes to Soviet dissidents had aroused fierce denunciation by the government, now that the head of the Soviet state was himself a recipient the widespread reaction in the country was one of indifference and even hostility. Lauded overseas, the Soviet leader found himself steadily more isolated at home.

Convinced that the most urgent problem facing the country was the louring economic crisis, Gorbachev had appointed a working group, headed by Stanislav Shatalin and including Grigory Yavlinsky and other liberal economists, to produce a blueprint for reform. Their 'programme for transition to a market economy' became known, from the proposed period set for implementation, as the '500 Days Programme'. No longer bothering even to pay lip-service to socialism, it denounced 'the giant state machine', stressed 'the right to property', affirmed the 'rights of the republics [of the USSR] to economic sovereignty', and called for privatization, decentralization, and liberalization.[65] Gorbachev assured the visiting British Foreign Secretary, Douglas Hurd, that the programme was just 'the beginning of the process. It'll take some time, it'll last until we have a full-blown market economy with all the mechanisms, with an infrastructure, with social security for the people.'[66] But the Soviet leader came under renewed conservative pressure and, after many revisions, the programme was set aside.

The apparent slide away from reform, personified by the conservative, Valentin Pavlov, newly appointed as Prime Minister, led in December 1990 to the resignation of the Foreign Minister, Eduard Shevardnadze. In an arresting speech to the Congress, he prophesied, 'A dictatorship is approaching.'[67] Two days later the head of the KGB, Kryuchkov, indicated where he stood. He denounced 'economic sabotage' and the 'activities of some Western secret services' as well as 'self-seekers' and 'rogues' who were 'using the privatization of property' in order to 'accumulate capital, enough for generations of their relatives.'[68] Following the withdrawal of a planned television documentary on

Shevardnadze's resignation, fears grew that censorship of the news media might be reintroduced. In a 'Dear George' letter to Bush on 25 December, Gorbachev confessed that he was 'particularly upset' by the resignation but he affirmed that 'our new policies . . . will continue'.[69]

Early in the new year conservative elements within the Communist Party and the military apparatus decided to take matters into their own hands with a view to restoring their version of a proper order. Their efforts focused on the Baltic republics where elected nationalist governments were flexing their muscles in opposition to rule from Moscow. The Soviet constitution in theory permitted secession of a union republic. In the past no republic had ever sought to activate such a right. But now the demand was vociferously voiced by the Baltic republics. The problem for Gorbachev was that they were by no means alone. If the Baltics were allowed to go their own way, how could the rest of the Soviet Union be held together? Gorbachev's response appeared flippant. He suggested that he would have no objection to Lithuanian independence, provided that the $33 billion that the USSR had supposedly invested in Lithuania were repaid. This fine debating point cut little ice with the Lithuanians while it infuriated the guardians of Soviet rectitude.

The attack on the Baltics began in Lithuania. On 13 January 1991 Soviet security forces in the Lithuanian capital, Vilnius, made a determined effort to destroy Lithuania's government. Under cover of darkness, tanks and machine guns began moving into the city. Fierce fighting between Soviet troops and Lithuanian civilians broke out around the republic's Parliament and broadcasting station. Loudspeakers repeated a message in Lithuanian and Russian announcing the creation of a 'National Salvation Committee' that was evidently intent on restoring the republic's subordinate relationship to Moscow. Thirteen people were killed and many more wounded. Soviet central authorities exhibited a mixture of bluster and incompetence. The latter was typified by their inability to exercise full control over even their own media. On the evening of 14 January Radio Moscow's short-wave service, instead of broadcasting its usual programme, retransmitted reports in Russian from Radio Riga (capital of Latvia) featuring denunciations of Gorbachev and tape of underground broadcasts from Kaunas (Lithuania). It took some time before the rogue transmissions were interrupted and normal service was restored. Five days later, Soviet television broadcast a statement by an 'All-Latvian Committee of National Salvation' announcing that it had taken over power in Latvia. The next day a small unit of OMON, the Soviet Interior Ministry's special forces unit, seized the Latvian Interior

Ministry building, killing four civilians. Gorbachev's role in these events remains unclear. His immediate response was fumbling and incoherent. Eventually, however, he dissociated himself from the repressions and even affirmed 'the constitutional right of a republic to secede from the union.'[70] Military operations in the Baltic republics were halted and the republics' governments regained their authority.

In the course of 1991 the Soviet economy degenerated towards almost total breakdown. The budget deficit reached 21 per cent of GNP. Banknote printing was almost the only sector to register increased production: more money was created in 1991 than in the entire previous thirty years. Partly as a result of the Gulf War, which halted throughput of Iraqi oil for re-export, petroleum exports declined by more than half in 1991. Miners' strikes helped reduce coal exports for the year by one-third. The loss of hard-currency earnings had a catastrophic impact on the country's ability to pay for desperately needed imports of foodstuffs. Price liberalization led to further huge increases in prices and to widespread hunger. Complaints of hoarding and theft of food were heard everywhere. Economic nationalism exacerbated political unrest, as union republics resorted to protectionism, forbidding food exports to their neighbours. Central direction of the economy was replaced not by free markets but by chaotic, improvisational dirigisme in each of the republics.

In March 1991 Gorbachev attempted to recapture the political initiative and to halt the slide of power away from the centre by holding a referendum on 'the preservation of the USSR as a renewed federation of equal sovereign republics'.[71] The result was overwhelmingly favourable. But the Baltic republics as well as Armenia, Georgia, and Moldavia boycotted the vote. Elsewhere the impact of the positive vote was muddied by the addition to the ballot of other questions. In western Ukraine, for example, there was an 88 per cent vote in favour of Ukrainian independence. In Russia Yeltsin invited views on whether Russia should have its own president: 70 per cent of voters said yes. An election to that position three months later was a political triumph for Yeltsin, whose thunderous attacks on Gorbachev became more and more insulting. Yeltsin was elected President of the Russian Federation with 57 per cent of the vote. Unlike Gorbachev's election as Soviet President the previous year, Yeltsin's was by direct popular vote. This gave him an irreproachable democratic mandate.

Gorbachev succeeded, however, in persuading the heads of nine of the republics, including Yeltsin, to negotiate the terms of a new Union Treaty. Only the Baltic states, Armenia, Georgia, and Moldavia, as before, would not take part. The so-called 'nine plus one' treaty devolved considerable power to the republics while preserving at least the shell of the Soviet Union. The centre would retain authority over foreign affairs and defence but most other matters would be controlled by the republics. The treaty was initialled on 1 August and was due to be signed on 20 August.

Lenin's heirs now made their last bid for survival. At a meeting in a KGB sanatorium on 5 August, the head of the KGB, Kryuchkov, met with the Soviet defence and interior ministers and other anti-Gorbachev elements. They constituted themselves a 'State Committee for the State of Emergency in the USSR'. They ordered the printing of 300,000 arrest forms and the preparation of 250,000 pairs of handcuffs.[72] The impending coup was one of the worst-kept secrets in political history, in this eerily echoing the October Revolution of 1917, which had also been widely forecast. Gorbachev himself had told a West German politician as early as the autumn of 1989 that if he failed, 'his successor in the Soviet Union might be a fierce military dictator'.[73] In June 1991 the American ambassador warned Gorbachev directly that a coup was in the making. On 16 August, Yakovlev resigned from the Communist Party warning that a Stalinist putsch was imminent.

The impending signature of the Union Treaty was the plotters' cue for action. They felt it was imperative to prevent the treaty going into effect, fearing that once that happened the old centralized structure would disintegrate beyond hope of repair. What the conspirators did not realize was that the Soviet Humpty Dumpty had already fallen and broken into pieces and could not be put back together. The authority of the centre no longer held. It was too late to try to reassert it by a show of force.

At 6.00 a.m. on 19 August Moscow Radio announced that Gorbachev's ill health had required his replacement by Vice-President Gennady Yanayev. A State Emergency committee that included Pavlov, Yanayev, Kryuchkov, and the Defence Minister, Marshal Dmitry Yazov, announced that it had taken power. It declared a state of emergency and issued a statement explaining its programme. This document was notable for the complete absence of any mention of socialism, the Communist Party, Lenin, or any of the customary rhetorical flourishes that had adorned Soviet policy statements in the past. In their justification of the putsch, the leaders sought to capture the nationwide mood of frustration: 'Lack of faith, apathy and despair', they wrote, 'have replaced the original enthusiasm and hopes.' They deplored the inter-ethnic conflicts, political confusion, and economic collapse. They also revealed some strange preoccupations:

> Never before in national history has the propaganda of sex and violence assumed such a scale, threatening the health and lives of future generations. Millions of people are demanding measures against the octopus of crime and glaring immorality . . .
>
> Whereas only yesterday a Soviet person finding himself abroad felt himself a worthy citizen of an influential and respected state, now he is often a second-rate foreigner, the attitude to whom is marked by either contempt or sympathy.

Behind such concerns lay the affronted dignity of the apparatchik class, profoundly conservative in its social values (as, for example, in matters of sex) and, of course, the only group in the Soviet Union whose member might 'find himself abroad' with any regularity. The coup represented a last-ditch attempt to salvage the prerogatives of that class. That the objectives of the coup had little to do with socialism was apparent from the declaration 'we shall support private enterprise, granting it necessary opportunities for the development of production and services'. Strikingly absent from the statement was any personal criticism of Gorbachev, who was mentioned only once, in an apparently positive sense, as the initiator of 'the policy of reforms'.[74] The lacuna reinforced the impression that the rebels hoped to persuade Gorbachev to cooperate with the new dispensation.

The KGB surrounded Gorbachev's holiday home in the Crimea and cut him off from control of the 'nuclear briefcase'. Colonel-General Albert Makashov, commander of the Volga–Urals military district, in a cipher message on 20 August, ordered all regimental officers in his area, 'to strengthen patriotic work in military units . . . to arrest emissaries, cosmopolites, traitors to our Motherland and the Soviet Union, interrogate them and give them to Security once their identities have been established'.[75] But few other generals backed the coup. Rumours flew around: of an imminent attack on the Moscow White House, the seat of government of the Russian Federation; of a 'super-secret psychotropic weapon that could be used against the defenders'; of a plan by Gorbachev to return to Moscow to rule under the auspices of the coup leaders.[76] During the coup the Prime Minister, Pavlov, appeared in public palpably drunk. The Foreign Minister, Alexander Bessmertnykh, was reported to be in bed ill—*not* a diplomatic illness, he later explained to sceptical foreign journalists.

A critical confrontation developed at the White House between security forces and a crowd of tens of thousands. Yeltsin declared himself Commander-in-Chief. Some senior officers sat on the fence, waiting to see which side would emerge victorious. But the commander of the military forces surrounding the building, General Alexander Lebed, told his superiors that he would not participate in any assault on the building. KGB officers also resisted the idea of an attack.

Meanwhile Gorbachev remained with his family under house arrest, clandestinely listening to BBC short-wave radio news. His wife, Raisa, suffered a breakdown and Gorbachev himself was shaken by the treachery of some of his closest comrades. He told an aide, 'Yes, this may not end well. But you know, in this case I have faith in Yeltsin. He won't give in to them, he won't compromise.'[77] The confidence in his long-time critic, soon to be his nemesis, was touching and, as it turned out, entirely justified. Yeltsin's victory at the White House brought the swift collapse of the coup.

After the suppression of the revolt, the Russian penchant for conspiracy theorizing ran rampant, with many people persuaded by wild rumours that Gorbachev himself had engineered the coup for some hidden Machiavellian purpose. Several of the putschists including Marshal Sergei Akhromeyev, the former Chief of Staff, committed suicide. Others were arrested, though none was ever convicted.

Gorbachev's return to the capital was anything but triumphant. He seemed bewildered by the pace of events, uncertain whom to trust, and out of touch with the public mood. At a news conference in Moscow he made the cardinal error, in the eyes of many, of reaffirming his faith in the Communist Party and in socialism. A few days later, under pressure from Yeltsin and others, he resigned as General Secretary of the Communist Party. Yeltsin humiliated him before the Russian Parliament, wagging his finger at him intimidatingly and treating him to a political dressing-down. Gorbachev's saviour was now his gaoler. Yeltsin savoured his new-found power and used it to destroy not only Gorbachev but also what remained of the Soviet Union.

The events of August accelerated the break-up of the multi-national Soviet empire. On 24 August Ukraine issued a declaration of independence though this was not recognized by the USSR. Two weeks later, however, the independence of the Baltic states was accepted. By the end of September eight other republics had declared independence. Accordingly Gorbachev began negotiations with the heads of the republics for a new treaty creating a 'union of sovereign states'.

Meanwhile, the economy was lurching towards utter catastrophe. As the value of money collapsed, much of the country reverted to barter exchange. In November Gorbachev wrote two begging letters to the British Prime

Minister, John Major, in his capacity as chairman of the G7 group of major industrialized countries, pleading for 'liquid assets in any form you consider suitable' to enable the USSR 'to hang on for a few months in our finances and food supplies, until market mechanisms kick in more or less effectively'.[78] The G7 countries responded with a multi-billion dollar emergency package of food and medical aid as well as a rescheduling of Soviet foreign debt payments. It was all too late.

On 1 December a referendum in Ukraine produced a 90 per cent vote in support of independence. A week later Yeltsin met the leaders of Ukraine and Belarus (as Belorussia henceforth preferred to be known) and agreed that the USSR was dead and would be replaced by a Commonwealth of Independent States (CIS). Gorbachev was not even consulted. Eleven republics, all the former members of the USSR save the Baltic states and Georgia, signed a declaration establishing the CIS on 22 December.

Three days later Gorbachev resigned and the Soviet Union faded into history. When the end came, it seemed almost an anticlimax. Gorbachev seemed by this stage so out of tune with popular sentiment that he was almost an irrelevancy. His fall was unlamented by most citizens of his country who blamed him for the wretched economic plight in which they found themselves. Yeltsin rubbed salt into the wound by unceremoniously ejecting Gorbachev from his Kremlin office suite. In his farewell broadcast on 25 December, Gorbachev reminded his audience of what they had gained over the previous six years: 'Free elections have become a reality. Free press, freedom of worship, representative legislatures and a multi-party system have all become a reality.'[79] Alas, in the absence of many of the basic necessities of life, few of his fellow citizens, as they now were, set much store by such freedoms.

This inglorious diminuendo not only terminated Europe's last empire. It also spelt *finis* to a movement that, over the previous century, had inspired many of Europe's finest minds with a utopian vision of human justice and brotherhood. It had conquered half of Europe. It had drowned millions, including its own followers, in blood and trampled its ideals in shame. Now, little mourned, it turned to dust.

19

After the Fall 1991–2007

The National Library burned for three days last August and the city was choked with black snow.
Set free from the stack, characters wandered the streets, mingling with passers-by . . .

*Goran Simić, Sarajevo, 1993**

The zigzag road to European unity

The end of the division of Europe did not automatically lead to a united Europe. But it did open the prospect of one. As the structures of the Cold War were dismantled, the old and new nation states of the continent embarked on a zigzag road that, with many false starts, detours, and dead ends, nevertheless brought for most of them an unprecedented degree of strategic, economic, and political integration.

With the end of the Cold War Europe was no longer an arena of superpower conflict. A rapid process of demilitarization of the continent ensued, involving both nuclear and conventional forces. In July 1991, in the last major diplomatic agreement between the United States and the USSR, Bush and Gorbachev signed the 'START' (Strategic Arms Reduction) Treaty. More than seven hundred pages in length, it provided for nuclear weapons arsenals to be limited to 1,600 deployed ICBMs and SLBMs, and six thousand 'accountable warheads' each. Before the treaty could be ratified, however, one of the signatory states had ceased to exist.

The whole nature of the strategic equation henceforth changed. 'The Russian problem', as Lawrence Freedman puts it, 'ceased to be one of

* From 'Lament for Viječnica', translated from the Serbo-Croat by David Harsent. Goran Simić, *The Sorrow of Sarajevo*, Manaccan, Cornwall, 1996, 9. These lines form part of the libretto of the opera *Sarajevo* by Nigel Osborne (1994).

excessive strength and became one of excessive weakness.'[1] Over the next few years the Russians and Americans worked together in what became known as the Cooperative Threat Reduction Program under which the United States offered Russia and other successor states to the USSR assistance in the safe dismantling of nuclear installations. By agreement with Ukraine, Belarus, and Kazakhstan, strategic nuclear sites in those countries were closed down and the weapons and delivery systems removed or destroyed. Movement of short-range nuclear weapons from the ex-Soviet republics to Russia was completed by mid-1992. With the elimination of all ex-Soviet nuclear weapons from elsewhere in eastern Europe, Russia became the only nuclear power in the region.

'START I', as it now came to be called, was ratified by the United States and Russia (as legal successor to the USSR) in 1992. Meanwhile Bush and Yeltsin agreed on a 'START II' treaty that would further reduce the number of deployed nuclear warheads to between 3,000 and 3,500, of which 1,750 might be SLBMs. Signed in the Kremlin with much hoopla on 3 January 1993, the agreement was ratified by the US Senate in 1996 and, after some difficulties with recalcitrant Russian nationalists, by the Duma in 2000. Overtaken by events, it never entered into force, though the two governments nevertheless agreed in 1997 to implement its provisions. In December 2001 the United States formally withdrew from the 1972 ABM treaty. The Russians reacted by withdrawing from the START II treaty. George W. Bush, however, pledged to reduce the American nuclear arsenal of 'operationally deployed strategic nuclear warheads' to 'between 1,700 and 2,200 over the next decade'.[2] The Russians undertook to do the same but insisted that the arrangement be codified in a formal agreement. The two powers did so in a new treaty, replacing START II, that was signed in 2002 and known as SORT (Strategic Offensive Reductions Treaty). Just three pages long, this was extraordinarily simple and straightforward by comparison with earlier strategic arms agreements, exemplifying the more harmonious relationship that had developed between the two countries.

The two west European nuclear powers also reconfigured their forces. Britain in the 1990s replaced the ageing Polaris submarine fleet with Vanguard nuclear submarines armed with American-made Trident II missiles with multiple warheads. France too modernized her nuclear force. But she cut nuclear weapons spending by 45 per cent between 1990 and 1995, and abandoned ground-based missiles and tactical nuclear weapons in the late 1990s. Both British and French nuclear strengths remained puny by comparison with even the slimmed-down US and Russian forces: whereas the latter two powers in 2003 each still possessed over five thousand strategic delivery systems (Russia mainly in the form of land-based ICBMs, the USA mainly SLBMs), France had only 338 (mainly SLBMs) and Britain 185 (entirely SLBMs).

In the same period the Russians and the Americans reduced their conventional forces in Europe. For Russia this was partly a matter of economic necessity. Defence spending dropped from 10 per cent of GNP in the last years of the USSR to 5 per cent of (a much smaller) GNP in the mid-1990s, still higher than any other European country save Turkey, but much lower than in the late Soviet period. Russian military expenditure in 1996 was barely one-sixth of that of the USSR in 1988. Retrenchment affected both manpower and equipment. By 2003 Russia's armed forces had a total strength of 1.1 million (compared with a Soviet strength of 5.3 million in 1985).

Withdrawal of Russian military forces from former Warsaw Pact countries was generally frictionless. In the case of Poland it was completed by October 1992 and in that of East Germany, as had been agreed, by 1994. But in spite of the vast sums paid out by the Germans, supposedly to offset the costs of accommodation and redeployment of Russian troops, returning soldiers faced an acute housing shortage and miserable conditions of service. Budget cuts left the Russian army badly housed, underfed, and ill-equipped. Large numbers of conscripts evaded service and the suicide rate in the ranks mounted.

In one region, the Russians initially resisted pressure for military withdrawal. Immediately upon regaining independence, the Baltic states demanded the departure of all the ex-Soviet troops, numbering over a hundred thousand, stationed on their territories. But some Russian commanders regarded a permanent military presence there as a strategic imperative. Russian nationalists also pressed Yeltsin not to withdraw the troops. For a time Russian negotiators proposed that Russian forces should stay, paid for by their hosts, supposedly in order to help protect their security. The notion that they should subsidize their own continued occupation was fiercely resisted by the governments of the Baltic states, who enjoyed the support of the United States. Russian forces were finally withdrawn from Lithuania in 1993 and from Latvia (except at a leased base) and Estonia the following year. Relations with Russia, however, remained cool.

The United States too reduced its standing forces in Europe, from 315,000 in 1989 to 107,000 by 1995. Their strength was held near that level for the next decade. European states meanwhile scaled down the size of their armies. Turkey continued to maintain the largest armed forces of any European NATO member, numbering 515,000 in 2003. But French armed strength fell from half a million in 1990 to 254,000 by 2004. The Germans' declined below the limit agreed at the time of unification to 284,000 in 2004. In most European countries conscription was dropped altogether in the course of the 1990s. In France and Germany the length of compulsory military service (for males only) was reduced in 1994 from one year to ten months. By 2004 the liability was nine months in Germany with the alternative of ten months of civilian service; but only 10 per cent of the age cohort was actually drafted.

With the Iron Curtain dismantled, the question arose whether NATO still served any useful purpose. The alliance sought a new role in providing a regional security framework for the whole of Europe. A sign of renewed confidence in the alliance was the French announcement, in December 1995, that it would return to full participation in the military command of NATO, three decades after de Gaulle's withdrawal. All three Baltic states as well as most former Warsaw Pact members sought admission to the alliance shortly after the collapse of the USSR. But Russia hotly objected to an advance by NATO to her borders and the applicants' admission to the alliance was delayed. In January 1994, in an effort to allay the anxieties of Russia and other Soviet successor states that an expanded NATO would endanger their security, they were all invited to join a 'Partnership for Peace' with NATO. Fourteen of the former republics of the USSR accepted (Tajikistan was the sole recalcitrant), as did Austria, Bulgaria, Finland, Romania, Sweden, and Switzerland. Also included were Albania (where Communists had been ousted from government by 1992), Slovakia (independent from 1993), and Slovenia and the former Yugoslav Republic of Macedonia (both independent from 1991). The arrangement, however, raised Russian hackles. In May 1997, therefore, it was agreed that admission of new NATO members would be preceded by a new treaty with Russia. The NATO–Russia Founding Act on Mutual Relations, Cooperation and Security reiterated a NATO commitment, first made in December 1996, that the alliance had 'no intention, no plan, and no reason' to station offensive nuclear weapons on the territory of new member states (i.e. former Warsaw Pact members).[3] A few days later NATO and Ukraine initialled a Charter designed to reassure Ukraine too that the enlargement of NATO had no offensive purpose. Following these agreements, as a further gesture of reassurance, Russia was admitted to full membership of the 'Group of Seven', thereafter 'Group of Eight' (G8), most advanced industrial economies, whose leaders met in an annual summit. In July 1997 NATO formally invited the Czech Republic, Hungary, and Poland to begin talks about entry to the alliance. In March 1999 they acceded to the NATO Treaty and formally became members of the organization. By 2004, with the accession of the Baltic states, Bulgaria, Romania, Slovakia, and Slovenia, membership of the alliance had grown from the original twelve to twenty-six.

As the new security regime in Europe took shape, economic and political integration also gathered pace. The European Community after 1989 faced a historic challenge: should its first priority be deepening the relationships among existing members or broadening membership to include east European states? Advocates of the latter approach argued that rapid expansion towards the east would ease the pain of transition to market economies for ex-Communist countries and would help ensure political stability at a critical moment in European history. But these voices were not heeded. The Community chose to adopt the first priority, though not excluding the second in the longer term.

At a Community summit meeting in Maastricht in December 1991, agreement was reached on a Treaty on European Union that would create a single European currency (an official objective of the Community since 1969) and a European central bank, as well as on the formulation of common foreign and defence policies. The agreement also provided for the creation of a 'Cohesion Fund' whereby, for the first time, direct transfers would be made to the four poorest member states (Portugal, Greece, Ireland, and Spain) rather than to regions. The treaty was signed by all twelve members of the Community in February 1992, though Britain and Denmark reserved their positions on the currency issue.

The ratification process, however, opened up a Pandora's box. In June 1992 a Danish referendum on ratification led to a narrowly negative result. Denmark was a small country and it was felt that this setback could somehow be reversed. A second referendum in May 1993 did indeed produce the desired positive outcome. More serious difficulties arose from a decision by President Mitterrand to present the issue to the French people for decision in a referendum there. He was under no constitutional requirement to submit the treaty to a popular vote, but hoped to bolster the sagging popularity of the French Socialist government by demonstrating what was expected to be strong support for his European policy. The referendum campaign, however, threw up a powerful, if incongruous, alliance of extreme rightists, Communists, and other disaffected elements. They argued that monetary union was the first step towards surrender of national sovereignty. Their view drew strength from the insistence of the German central bank on maintaining high interest rates, regarded as necessary to finance the cost of German reunification without inflation. The high German rates forced up rates in other countries with weaker currencies, thus stifling economic growth. Hence the fear that a common European currency would lead to an enforced common economic policy in which the Germans' historic aversion to inflation would limit economic growth throughout the Community. When French voters approved the treaty in September 1992 it was by the narrowest of margins.

Meanwhile, Margaret Thatcher's successor as Prime Minister, John Major, signalled a shift in British policy towards Europe when he told a German audience that he wanted the United Kingdom to be 'at the heart of Europe'.[4] His government ratified the Maastricht Treaty by parliamentary vote rather than referendum, though at the cost of severe internal disturbances in the Conservative Party, in which 'Eurosceptics' were becoming a significant force. Britain's participation in the European Exchange Rate Mechanism (ERM), designed as a forerunner to the common currency, proved short-lived. Strong speculation against the pound in the currency markets led to sterling's enforced exit from the ERM on 'Black Wednesday', 16 September 1992. The episode cost Britain nearly £4 billion and severely discredited the government. The Chancellor of the Exchequer, Norman Lamont, was compelled to resign, and the Conservatives' reputation as the party of sound financial management suffered a shattering blow from which it did not recover for many years.

With the approval of the treaty, the Community took the symbolic step of changing its name to European Union. But Maastricht, intended as a trumpet-blast of European unity, emitted instead an uncertain toot. Bitter recriminations between German ministers and some of their EU partners, particularly the British, lent substance to the foreboding expressed in 1990 by a former European Commissioner: 'Europe has remained a fair-weather concept for the majority of German politicians and for many of their advisers as well.'[5] To the Germans might now be added other nationalities, and to politicians and advisers large parts of the population of Europe.

One reform that it was hoped might assuage the concerns of those who feared the growth of a heavy-handed, unanswerable European bureaucracy was the strengthening of the European Parliament. In the course of the 1990s it slowly acquired more authority at the expense of other institutions. In 1999, for the first time, it forced the resignation of the entire European Commission, after a report showing mismanagement and corruption. But participation in the Parliament's elections remained, almost everywhere, much lower than in national elections, and its multilingual proceedings seldom excited much popular interest.

As a first step towards expansion of the EU, it was decided to open discussions with those non-member states that already had mature capitalist systems and would present few transition problems upon entry. By 1992 Norway, Sweden, Finland, and Switzerland were all moving towards the Union. In May the members of EFTA signed an agreement with the EC to establish a tariff-free European Economic Area. But here too obstacles appeared. In a referendum in December 1992 German–Swiss cantons, apparently fearing that the treaty would compromise the country's historic neutrality, voted against the treaty, overwhelming the pro-treaty votes of the historically more cosmopolitan French-speaking cantons. (Switzerland later signed a series of bilateral treaties with the EU on trade, taxation, and labour migration.) Treaties for the admission to the EU of Austria, Sweden, Norway, and Finland were submitted to national referenda in 1994 with a view to membership in January 1995. In Sweden the left campaigned fiercely against approval, portraying the EU as a neo-liberal enterprise and 'club for the executives of the multinational corporations' that was at odds with the Swedish welfare state and 'the *folklig* community'.[6] The Norwegian electorate again opted to remain outside the Union. The other three countries approved joining. The expansion of the twelve to fifteen gave heart to other would-be members; but applicants such as Poland and Hungary seemed condemned to a frustratingly long wait.

A forward step of a different kind was taken in 1995 when a core group of EU members, comprising Germany, France, and the Benelux states, began implementing the Schengen (a town in Luxembourg) agreement, whereby frontier controls among them would be scrapped and cross-border police and judicial cooperation enhanced. They were later joined by several other EU members (though not Britain) as well as by Norway, Iceland, and, after a referendum in 2005, Switzerland. As a result, for the first time since 1914, it became possible to travel across large parts of Europe without showing a passport.

Meanwhile, preparations moved ahead for the introduction of the common currency. In 1997 the participating countries (all the EU members except Britain, Denmark, and Sweden) agreed on a European Stabilization and Growth Pact. It was clearly modelled on the West German Stabilization and Growth Act of 1967 which had laid the foundation for two decades of successful operation of the Bundesbank. The problem was that the new document was a pact and not an act. An act is made to be obeyed; a pact is liable to be broken. Whereas the act had merely laid down very general long-term objectives for the West German government and central bank, the pact was very specific. It obliged participating governments to set the 'medium-term objective of budgetary positions close to balance or in surplus . . . ' which would 'allow all Member States to deal with normal cyclical fluctuations while keeping the government deficit within the reference value of 3% of GDP'.[7]

The euro was launched 'virtually' (i.e. for electronic transactions) in January 1999 and in the form of circulating notes and coins three years later. But it got off to a rocky start. The 'convergence criteria' that had been agreed were egregiously breached by Germany and France, both of which, under pressure from severe recession and high unemployment, expanded their outlays beyond the agreed limit of 3 per cent of GDP. With a starting value of $1.17, the euro depreciated in 2000 to 83 cents. Then, in late 2004, a yawning US payments deficit led it to shoot up to $1.36. These twists and turns undermined confidence and in 2005 voices were even heard in Germany and Italy calling for national withdrawal from the project.

Eastward expansion of the Union finally took place in May 2004 when ten new states joined: the Baltic states, Poland, Hungary, the Czech Republic, Slovakia, Slovenia (the only former member of the Yugoslav federation), Malta, and Cyprus. Accession had been delayed by lengthy negotiations and by the conditions laid down for new members. Each had to put into effect the so-called *acquis communautaire*, the corpus of EU law, comprising more than eighty thousand pages of legislation.

Further applicants were knocking at the door. Romania and Bulgaria signed accession treaties in 2005, providing for their membership from 2007. Turkey had signed an association agreement with the EEC as early as 1962 and had applied for membership unsuccessfully in 1987. Her revived candidacy a decade later aroused strong feeling from many European politicians, particularly in France and Germany, who felt that Turkey was too Islamic to fit into the Union. Popular suspicion directed at Muslim immigrants in Europe as a result of Islamist terrorist attacks did not help the Turkish cause, even though Turkey herself was a victim of such assaults. In December 2004 the EU Council nevertheless agreed to open negotiations on Turkish membership, although it was expected to take at least a decade before she could have any chance of gaining entry.

By 2007 the EU contained twenty-seven states with 490 million people. It was the largest trading community in the world. But although its members had pooled many parts of their sovereignty, it remained an association of independent states rather than a genuine Union. Its pretensions to a common foreign and security policy were belied in 2003 when Britain, Italy, and Spain joined the USA in an invasion of Iraq, while Germany and France ostentatiously held aloof. In spite of the growing power of the European Parliament, the Union's 'democratic deficit' remained acute. The project was therefore revived of formulating a constitution that would address these problems and provide greater transparency for the workings of the Union. In 2002–3 a convention, presided over by the former French President Giscard d'Estaing, produced a draft constitution. But the European Council soon became bogged down in haggling over its terms. For example, several countries demanded a more explicit reference to Europe's Christian heritage. An amended text, 485 pages in length, was finally approved by a summit of European leaders in June 2004. Its preamble did not mention Christianity, instead referring to 'the cultural, religious and humanist inheritance of Europe'. This text was ratified by several of the signatory states. But referenda in France and the Netherlands in mid-2005 rejected it, throwing the EU into renewed turmoil.

In spite of these ructions, Europe since 1989 had seen a remarkable tumbling-down, not only of the Iron Curtain and the Berlin Wall, but of a myriad other barriers, economic, political, and cultural. The continent was now closer than ever before to unity by consent. One vast region, however, remained largely excluded: the European successor states of the USSR.

Post-Communist Russia and the 'near abroad'

Only eleven of the fifteen former republics of the Soviet Union joined the Commonwealth of Independent States at its inception in 1991. The Baltic states refused to do so; Georgia became a member only in 1993; Turkmenistan joined but withdrew in 2005. One still overshadowed the others in almost every way: the Russian Federation was greater in territory and population than all the states of the 'near abroad' put together. In area she was still the largest country in the world. She was the most populous in Europe: three-quarters of her total population of 149 million lived in European Russia. Diplomatically, she was a wounded giant, hardly qualifying any more as a superpower. Economic catastrophe conditioned everything else in the country in the immediate post-Communist years.

Between 1991 and 1998 Russian national income shrank by about half, one of the steepest peacetime falls ever recorded anywhere—greater, for example, than that suffered by any major economy in the Great Depression. In 1992 economic activity shrank by 19 per cent, inflation reached 1,354 per cent, and real incomes fell 46 per cent. In 1992–4 investment fell by 60 per cent. Foreign debt reached $126 billion in 1994, making Russia the most heavily indebted country in the world. Capital flight was immense: in 1994 alone it was estimated at $50 billion. By contrast foreign investment in Russia in the same year was a mere $1.4 billion. Productivity continued to decline. There was much talk of privatization of industry; critics said the reality was more akin to 'piratization' in the form of asset grabs by managers of state concerns.[8] At the same time, a 'primitivization'[9] of the Russian economy occurred. In particular, manufacturing declined while extractive industry, especially oil, natural gas, and coal, increased their shares of the country's total production and exports.

The dominant force in the management of the Russian economy in the transition from Communism was a young economist, Yegor Gaidar, who became First Deputy Prime Minister in May 1992 and in effect executive head of the government under Yeltsin. Teams of western advisers recommended a 'shock therapy' solution to Russia's economic woes. There was no easy route to a market economy, it was argued, and the best medicine, therefore, would be immediate, total immersion. The result has been termed 'shock without therapy'.[10] Private business was legalized. Commercial banking was introduced. Price liberalization in January 1992 was 'an operation without anaesthesia'[11] that left millions of pensioners and other dependent people defenceless. Faced with rapid inflation and rocketing interest rates, the Russian State Bank alternated between attempts to limit the money supply and surrenders to socio-political pressure to print more money. The consequences of the latter were often crudely visible. When Yeltsin visited Siberia in June 1992, he took with him a planeload of newly produced banknotes to meet the local shortage of cash that was preventing state enterprises there, as elsewhere, paying their employees. The government's economic planners aimed towards rouble convertibility. But there were many barriers en route. One problem was that, after the establishment of the CIS, the rouble continued to serve as the currency of all its members. The Russian Central Bank was therefore reduced to the status of a jobbing printer of banknotes for its former branch offices. No wonder Gaidar himself repeatedly compared his team of economic reformers to 'kamikaze pilots'.[12]

In 1992 Russia was admitted to full membership of the International Monetary Fund and the World Bank. The IMF set stiff conditions for the hard-currency loans that would be required to support a convertible rouble. The major industrial countries pledged billions of dollars in aid to Russia. Germany, which had perhaps the greatest interest of all the donors in ensuring a peaceful transition from Communism, took the lead. In spite of the vast burden already borne by the German economy in integrating the new *Länder*, Kohl's government committed a larger amount to Russia than all other European countries put together. Between 1989 and the end of 1992 Germany transferred nearly $50 billion mainly in the form of credits for machinery and food purchases. But much of the foreign aid was siphoned off and as much as $10 billion was deposited in foreign bank accounts. The Russian Central Bank subsequently admitted that it had systematically lied in its reporting to the IMF and the Fund's president confessed in 1999: 'We contributed to creating an institutional desert in a culture of lies, [and the] taking of advantages inherited from the Communist régime.'[13]

As the power of the police state evaporated, a 'wild west' economy replaced the centralized command structures of old. Criminality and corruption became endemic. *Blat* ('pull', connections), *tolchok* (the black market), *reket* (protection racket), and *vziatka* ('the take', bribery) became key organizing concepts of the new economy. While the bulk of the population struggled with the daily grind of queues and economic survival, a few successful entrepreneurs prospered, many of them at or over the borders of legality. Conspicuous consumption by the new class of would-be capitalists began to replace inconspicuous consumption by the old class of would-be socialists. In many cases the persons involved were identical, since members of the *nomenklatura* were often adept at moving fast to seize business opportunities. Foreign automobiles, hitherto unknown in the USSR, became commonplace: in 1992 the Russian Ministry of Autos estimated that nearly a thousand cars a day were being imported. Meanwhile, swarms of street pedlars, often old women, offered used clothing and other pathetic items for sale. Child malnutrition increased. A massive redistribution of wealth took place in the 1990s not only between classes but between regions, with Moscow in particular gobbling up a disproportionate share of national income and assets. Not surprisingly, popular resentment was soon directed against the newly rich 'oligarchs' and 'kleptocrats'.

A financial crisis in August 1998 culminated in default on state debt and a savage devaluation of the rouble. Russia's credit rating dropped below those of Yemen and Ethiopia. The number of registered banks in the country declined from 2,300 to 1,400. Almost half of Russia's entire industrial output was now 'resource extraction' (oil production, coal mining, timber, etc.). Pensions and wages had fallen in real value by 60 per cent since 1991. But wages were often paid late or not at all. Tax collection was in a state of collapse. The underground economy was said to constitute 40 per cent of GDP.

This, however, proved to be the bottom of the Russian economic roller-coaster. Thanks in particular to the devaluation, revival, when it came, was spectacular. After 1998 Russia enjoyed eight straight years of economic expansion with high rates of growth. Unemployment fell from 13 per cent in 1998 to 7.5 per cent in 2005. After 2000, while the rest of the world's stock markets stagnated, Russian stocks rose to record heights. Russian state bonds, once a joke, were raised to 'investment grade' status in 2003. Inflation fell from triple digits in 1993–5 to below 10 per cent by 2006. Foreign debt declined from 90 per cent of GDP in 1998 to 28 per cent in 2005. In the same year foreign-currency reserves reached $146 billion. The dramatic turnaround in the economy was mainly due to the increase in the price of oil; in 2004 fuels accounted for more than half of all the country's export earnings. But the IMF also ascribed the improvement to 'good macro-economic policies, notably that of taxing and saving oil revenues'.[14]

What emerged was not liberal capitalism but rather what has been called a 'mutant market economy'[15] or 'wild' (*dikii*) capitalism that coexisted with a parasitic state apparatus. Russia still lacked a strong framework of commercial law. Inequality and poverty ballooned. More than 60 per cent of the economy had been privatized but the greater part ended up in the hands of 'robber barons'. As much as a quarter of all economic activity was estimated to be in the 'informal' sector. The liberal economist and politician Grigory Yavlinsky wrote in 2000, 'Graft permeates the country, from street crime to mafia hits to illegal book deals in Kremlin corridors to rigged bids for stakes of privatized companies.'[16] The Russian economy, which some western experts had once forecast would overtake the American, remained only semi-developed both in structure and by many numerical measures. GDP per capita in 2005 was less than half that of Greece.

The social pain of the transition inevitably generated political friction. Bitter rivalry developed between the executive power, headed by Yeltsin, and the Russian legislature where ex-Communists, nationalists, and populists resisted market-oriented economic reform. In the autumn of 1993 these tensions erupted into violence. On 21 September Yeltsin announced the dissolution of Parliament and new elections. In doing this he exceeded his constitutional authority. His opponents, headed by Ruslan Khasbulatov, Chairman of the Parliament, sought to remove him and swore in the Vice-President, Air Force General Alexander Rutskoi, as acting President. He attempted to rally military forces against Yeltsin. Only a handful of officers responded to his call. In Moscow fighting broke out between pro- and anti-Yeltsin factions. Yeltsin ordered a blockade of Parliament while anti-government units tried to capture broadcasting stations and government buildings. Most of the army and security police, however, remained loyal to Yeltsin. In a decisive confrontation on 4 October, Yeltsin ordered tanks and troops to attack the White House. Surrounded in the besieged building, Rutskoi shouted into a radio transmitter: 'I appeal to military pilots, I implore you, I demand: send the planes into the air.'[17] The building was set on fire. One hundred people died. Khasbulatov and Rutskoi were arrested. Yeltsin triumphed.

Ruling by decree, he imposed censorship and for a time banned opposition parties. Notwithstanding these interferences with civil liberties, western governments offered him support, seeing him as the only realistic bulwark against a return to Communism. In parliamentary elections in December 1993 the extreme nationalist Liberal Democrats, led by Vladimir Zhirinovsky, emerged as the largest party. 'Russia's Choice', an equally misnamed party that was closely identified with market-oriented reform, came second. But Yeltsin's position was strengthened by approval of a new constitution that gave the presidency greater powers, including the ability, in certain circumstances, to override and dissolve Parliament. Yeltsin remained committed to free-market capitalism. In 1996, in spite of having suffered two heart attacks, he managed to secure re-election in an extraordinary political comeback. But thereafter his clownish behaviour (he frequently appeared in public drunk) and the continuing slide in Russian economic performance eroded his popularity. During the financial crisis of 1998, he sacked his Prime Minister, Sergei Kiriyenko, but for several weeks was unable to find a replacement who would command a majority in the Duma. Yeltsin's approval rating sank to 2 per cent and for the remainder of his term he lost his grip on power as Russian government spun almost out of control.

During the late 1990s Russia seemed to be heading towards further balkanization. Even shorn of the former republics of the USSR, the country retained large minority populations comprising more than 20 per cent of its inhabitants. They included 130 recognized national groups scattered over thirty-one autonomous republics and regions. These increasingly asserted their freedom from central political as well as economic control. Not only ethnic minorities but Russians in far-flung provinces shook off irksome interference by Moscow. For example, in the far northern autonomous Republic of Komi, home to vast mineral wealth, an ambitious local ruler, Yury Spiridonov, in alliance with 'generals' of local industrial interests, asserted the region's right to collect and keep taxes and to conduct an independent international trade policy. The 1993 constitution did not really resolve the problem. The power of the central government was crippled by continuing economic chaos and by the weakening of the military and internal security apparatus.

The most disastrous case of centre–periphery conflict arose in the Caucasus where Chechen nationalists made a determined bid for total independence. The region was important to Russia for strategic and economic reasons: the capital, Grozny, was Russia's largest oil-refining centre. Yeltsin initially favoured conciliation: 'Intervention by force is impermissible,' he announced on television in August 1994. 'There would be such a commotion, there would be so much blood that nobody would ever forgive us.'[18] Yet spurred on by Russian nationalists, and fearing that concessions to the Chechens would lead to the unravelling of what was still in many ways a multi-ethnic empire, the government decided, after all, to suppress the rebellion by force. In December Russian troops launched a full-scale campaign to regain control over Chechnya. The campaign cruelly exposed the deficiencies of the Russian armed forces. Hundreds of soldiers were killed in a Russian assault on Grozny. Pictures of dogs feeding on their frozen bodies outraged the nation. By mid-1996 five thousand Russian troops and many times more Chechen fighters and civilians were dead or missing.

In June 1996 General Lebed, who had come third in the first round of the presidential election, made a deal with Yeltsin whereby, in return for his support in the second round, he would be appointed National Security Adviser. Immediately upon taking up that office, he went to the Caucasus and by August negotiated an agreement to end the fighting. The Russians undertook to remove their forces from Chechnya. The question of Chechnya's constitutional position was left open for resolution by 2001. The popular general was lauded as a peacemaker. He sought to exploit the acclaim by taking effective control of the government from Yeltsin. For a short time Lebed looked like the man on horseback who might save the country. But it was a Boulanger-like bubble. Yeltsin rewarded him for his trouble by dismissing him. Lebed rode off into the sunrise, securing election in 1998 as governor of the Krasnoyarsk region of eastern Siberia, thus eliminating himself from contention in national politics. He died in a helicopter crash in Siberia in 2002.

The humiliating defeat in Chechnya completed the demoralization of the Russian armed forces. The proud army that had routed the Wehrmacht was now reduced to a starving, ill-equipped rabble. In the late 1990s soldiers were being issued with dog food. Some were reduced to selling their medals and uniforms and to foraging in forests for mushrooms, nuts, and berries. On Armed Forces Day in 1997 the Defence Minister, Igor Rodionov, lamented: 'I am the minister of a disintegrating army and a dying navy.'[19]

On 31 December 1999, Yeltsin surprised the world by announcing his resignation. This was the first time in modern Russian history that a leader had yielded power voluntarily. His hand-picked successor, Vladimir Putin, a former KGB agent, had served as Prime Minister for five months. 'The man from nowhere'[20] was Yeltsin's fifth Prime Minister in less than two years. He had suddenly achieved popularity in September 1999 following mysterious apartment block bombings in Moscow that killed over two hundred people. Although no conclusive evidence regarding their origin was discovered, the attacks were attributed to Chechen terrorists. Putin's reaction was to order the Russian army to move back into Chechnya to destroy the rebel movement. 'We shall not allow the national pride of Russians to be trodden upon,' he told a Kremlin reception at the end of the year. 'We are sure of the power and prosperity of our country.'[21] It was a fateful decision that was disastrous for Russia though, in the short term, highly profitable for Putin. His automatic succession to Yeltsin under the constitution was followed by a presidential election in March 2000. Lebed, perhaps the only man who might have defeated him, decided not to run. Putin, exploiting the mood of nationalist enthusiasm, won an absolute majority of the votes. His nearest rival, Gennady Zyuganov, head of the revived Communist Party, received 29 per cent of the vote. Yavlinsky came a poor third with only 6 per cent, an indication of the limited constituency of liberalism in post- (even more than in pre-) Communist Russia.

Putin's cool, low-key, businesslike, no-nonsense demeanour was very different from his predecessor's bombastic buffoonery. In spite of an early blunder in August 2000, when he failed to react swiftly to the accidental sinking of the *Kursk* nuclear submarine, in which 118 crewmen lost their lives, he maintained a reputation for competence. At the price of serious restriction of civil liberties, including interference with freedom of the press and broadcasting, he succeeded in reversing the erosion of central government authority. His decision to appoint regional governors directly, rather than allowing them to be elected, helped rein in rogue satraps. The power of the oligarchs, or at any rate some of them, was abridged. One, Boris Berezovsky, an early backer of Putin, fled the country. Another, Mikhail Khodorkovsky, head of the Yukos oil company and Russia's richest man, was arrested in October 2003, charged with embezzlement and tax evasion, found guilty, and imprisoned. His company was, in effect, renationalized. Putin established cordial relations with US President George W. Bush, particularly in their common fight against Islamist terrorism. But Putin's mission to bring Chechnya to heel led to a bloodbath. Chechen extremists engineered a series of terrorist incidents including hostage sieges in a Moscow theatre in 2002 and in a school in Beslan (in North Ossetia in the northern Caucasus, not far from Chechnya) in 2004. Botched rescue operations by Russian security forces led in both cases to hundreds of civilian deaths. For the Russian army, Chechnya became a new Afghanistan.

Russia's relations with her immediate neighbours of the 'near abroad' after 1991 were heavily influenced by the legacy of Communism. Sixty million people in the former Soviet Union lived outside their ethnic homelands. Among these were 25 million Russians, formerly imperial top dogs, now reduced to vulnerable minority status. In the Baltic states Russians were deprived of citizenship and treated as aliens in countries in which many of them had been born. Estonia, where 40 per cent of the population was Russian at independence, declared that only those who could show that they or their parents had lived in the country in 1938, that is, before the Russian occupation, might automatically become citizens. Others would have to wait a year before being allowed to take an examination in the Estonian language to qualify for naturalization. The objective was plainly to limit or reduce the Russian element in the population. A few Russians left, but most had nowhere to go.

Nor was this the only problem to sour Russia's relations with the Baltic states. The issue of Russia's access to her exclave of Kaliningrad, bordered by Poland and Lithuania, bedevilled relations with Lithuania. The region contained important military and naval installations, including the headquarters of the Russian Baltic Fleet, now cut off from the rest of Russia. The port was Russia's only ice-free access to the Baltic Sea and therefore of great strategic importance. Its population, thrown adrift by the collapse of the Soviet Union, was plagued by a wave of criminality and smuggling. After the accession of Poland and Lithuania to NATO and the EU, border tensions eased but Kaliningrad remained a historical anomaly and a potential source of friction.

In the former Soviet Republic of Moldavia, now the independent state of Moldova, a separatist movement of Russians and Ukrainians in the Trans-Dniester region led to civil war. Moldova, an area a little larger than Belgium with a population in 1990 of 4.5 million, consisted of Romanian territory seized by Stalin during the Second World War, as well as the Trans-Dniester region, formerly part of Ukraine. That area contained important industrial centres. More than half of its population of about 630,000 were Russians and Ukrainians who had no wish to be ruled by the new Moldovan state or by Romania, with which some Moldovans talked of uniting. The Dniestrian Moldovan Republic asserted independence, with its capital at Tiraspol. The President of Moldova, Mircea Snegur, announced that his country was 'at war' with Russia.[22] Units of the 14th Russian army, stationed in Moldova, intervened to protect Trans-Dniester Russians from attempts by the Moldovan government at Kishinev to assert its authority. In April 1992 Yeltsin sent General Lebed to take command of the Russian forces. He directed artillery fire at the Moldovans and denounced Snegur as a 'Fascist'. By June an estimated 1,500 people were dead as a result of the war. Large numbers of refugees arrived in Russia, fleeing the economic and political turmoil in Moldova. Thanks to the Russian intervention, the secessionist government survived, although no country recognized it. The region became notorious for smuggling, money-laundering, and trafficking in drugs and women. Meanwhile, the economy of Moldova itself went into free fall, with a 31 per cent decline in GDP in the single year of 1994. In 1999 the Russians signed a treaty undertaking to withdraw their troops as well as 50,000 tons of military equipment by 2002. They withdrew some forces but about 1,800 'peacekeepers' were still there in 2005 and international efforts to resolve the dispute remained unavailing. A modest economic revival in Moldova began after 2000 but the country remained one of the poorest, most backward, and most isolated in Europe.

The richest country of the CIS per capita at independence was Belarus. About the size of Kansas, it had a population of over ten million and a strong industrial base. But what a World Bank study called 'suboptimal economic policies that sought to cushion if not avoid the transition to a market economy'[23] produced a spiral of economic decline. Between 1990 and 1996 prices multiplied 50,000 times. Industrial production meanwhile shrank by a quarter. Alexander Lukashenka, elected President in 1994, pursued a policy of 'market socialism' and tied the economy closely to that of Russia. But the economic structure changed much more slowly than in Russia: 87 per cent of economic activity in 1997 was still state-controlled. The country's political culture remained suffused with Communist values. In 1996 70 per cent of those voting in a referendum were said to have approved virtually dictatorial powers for Lukashenka. The Chairman of the Central Electoral Commission, who refused to confirm the result, was dismissed. He later disappeared and was never seen again. Opposition was suppressed and civil freedoms barely existed. Belarus was the one country of the 'near abroad' where reintegration with Russia remained popular. Lukashenka and Yeltsin signed a Treaty of Union in 1997. This served as an earnest of Russia's interest in preserving a sphere of influence to her west and helped maintain the two countries' economic connections. The latter bore fruit after 1998 when Belarus enjoyed some spin-off from Russia's economic recovery. But GDP per capita in 2004 was barely half that of 1991 and, like Moldova, Belarus remained cut off from the European mainstream. Its ranking in the 2005 United Nations Human Development Index was 67, one of the lowest in Europe.[24]

By far the most important country of the 'near abroad' was Ukraine (no longer *the* Ukraine: foreigners were asked to detach the definite article in deference to the republic's sovereign status). Unlike most of the other successor states to the USSR, Ukraine possessed important economic assets and some real prospects. She was rich in natural resources and had a comparatively well-educated and skilled workforce. Before 1991 she had produced 20 per cent of the USSR's industrial and 18 per cent of its agricultural output. Nevertheless, the initial phase of independence saw a big fall in production and an inflation rate even higher than Russia's. In 1991 and 1992 the former breadbasket of the Soviet Union found itself humiliatingly obliged to import grain. Like Belarus, Ukraine languished for a decade in economic depression and political authoritarianism.

For several years after 1991 Ukraine and Russia bickered over territorial issues and the disposition of military assets. A particularly contentious dispute arose over the Crimea, a historic Russian territory that had been presented as a 'gift' to Ukraine by Khrushchev in 1954 to mark the three hundredth anniversary of the union of Ukraine with Russia by the Treaty of Pereaslavl. Two thirds of the Crimean population in 1989 were ethnic Russians, most of whom had moved there since the war. In the early 1990s there was talk among local Russian politicians of secession of the region from Ukraine. Differences over the question appeared within the Russian government: Vice-President Rutskoi courted popularity by plugging a militantly nationalistic line, while the Foreign Minister, Andrei Kozyrev, stressed that borders should be changed only by agreement.[25] The controversy was linked with a row over the future of the 300-vessel Soviet Black Sea fleet, whose home base was at Sebastopol, the main city of the Crimea. The newest of the ships had been built in 1982 and, as a fighting force, the fleet was a pathetic, rusting behemoth. In January 1992 Yeltsin trumpeted: 'The Black Sea Fleet was, is, and will be Russian.'[26] But both he and the Ukrainian leader, Leonid Kravchuk, a Communist apparatchik transformed into a nationalist, sensed that the conflict must be kept within bounds. So did the naval commanders: at the height of the dispute, amidst rows over whether the Russian or the Ukrainian flag should be hoisted on board vessels, Admiral Eduard Baltin resolved the issue temporarily by ordering that the Soviet naval ensign, shorn of the red star, hammer, and sickle, be raised. In August 1992 Yeltsin and Kravchuk signed an accord providing for joint command of the fleet and its bases until 1995, after which it would be divided between the two countries. But Russian nationalists in the Duma objected. The conflict dragged on until 1997 when a new treaty was signed that fixed borders and divided the fleet, with Russia keeping 83 per cent of it. Crimea was recognized as part of Ukraine but the port facilities in and near Sebastopol were leased to Russia for twenty years. At a joint ceremony in Sebastopol, the Tsarist naval ensign, bearing the cross of St Andrew, was raised to celebrate the settlement.

In spite of these disputes, both Kravchuk and his successor, Leonid Kuchma, tied Ukraine's economy closely to Russia. The main reason was geopolitical. Ukrainian politics was characterized by division between the eastern regions, where more than a third of the population was Russian and where half the country's industrial production was located, and the more markedly Ukrainian western and central regions. The population in the east remained pro-Russian and generally hostile to a market economy. In the west there was greater attraction to the European Union and support for the development of a capitalist system. In its voting patterns, the east was much more Communist, the west more nationalist.

These differences came to the fore in a disputed presidential election in 2004. There were widespread allegations of government manipulation in favour of retiring President Kuchma's nominee, Viktor Yanukovich, who was also supported by the Russian government. At first the result was declared in his favour. But a series of peaceful demonstrations in Kiev, staged by supporters of the anti-government candidate, Viktor Yushchenko, were followed by a Supreme Court decision annulling the election. Yushchenko, whose support came mainly from western Ukraine and who also enjoyed strong backing from the United States and the EU, was victorious in the rerun in January 2005.

This 'Orange Revolution' was portrayed by its supporters as another in the sequence of popular anti-Communist ebullitions in eastern Europe since 1989. While prudently seeking to reaffirm ties with Russia, Yushchenko made it clear that his primary aims were to root out corruption, install a market economy, bolster the rule of law, and prepare Ukraine for membership of the European Union. Within a few months, however, he was forced to fire his Prime Minister, Yulia Timoshenko, amid allegations of corruption and favouritism in the disposal of state assets. In 2006, after parliamentary elections in which supporters of the 'Orange Revolution' suffered a reverse, Yanukovich secured Yushchenko's nomination as Prime Minister. Whether Ukraine's destiny lay with its western or eastern neighbours remained an open question.

Mitteleuropa reborn

Ukraine was not alone. Freed from bondage to Russia, almost every country in eastern Europe sought to join 'the west'. But of the countries of the 'near abroad' only the Baltic states definitively succeeded by the end of the century in making the leap. In the Soviet satellites, even before the end of Communism, the cult of a revived 'Mitteleuropa' had been growing among intellectuals. 'Left to our own inclinations, we turn more to the West than the East,' wrote Hungarian George Konrád in 1982.[27] After 1989, this *Drang nach Westen* became irresistible as economists, entrepreneurs, designers, artists, journalists, tourist operators, educators, and engineers all looked to western Europe and North America for models, advice, and investment. 'East-central' Europe became the preferred classification of the region, as most of its peoples spurned the stigma that attached to the east.

Throughout ex-Communist Europe, as in the former Soviet Union, the end of the old order brought a flurry of other label-changes. Sign-painters and cartographers enjoyed a sudden boom in demand. In Prague Red Army Square was renamed Jan Palach Square. In Poland the Lenin shipyard was rebranded as the Gdańsk shipyard. In Budapest the Karl-Marx University, whose origins went back to the Habsburg-period K. K. Joseph Polytechnikum, became the Budapest University of Economic Sciences (in 2004, the name was changed again, this time to Corvinus University, after the fifteenth-century King of Hungary, Matthias Corvinus). By one estimate as many as fifteen thousand place names changed as a result of this process of onomastic de-Communization.

Symbolic demolition went beyond names. In Bulgaria the embalmed body of Dimitrov was removed from its mausoleum in the main square of Sofia and cremated, after protesters demonstrated with placards bearing such slogans as 'Bulgaria is no ancient Egypt', 'We don't need any Pharaohs', and 'It stinks!'[28] The tomb, an imposing edifice, remained standing empty. In 1999 the government decided to blow it up, but the marble building proved impervious to dynamite and still stood upright, though leaning somewhat to the left. Humorists suggested NATO planes should be invited to bomb the site. Eventually seven days' efforts by professional demolitionists succeeded in reducing the building to debris.

So much for the dead. As for the living, the revenge exacted against former Communist rulers was relatively mild, as compared with the White terror of 1918–21 or the Red terror of 1945–53. Of the former leaders only one, Ceauşescu, was executed. Kádár and Husák died opportunely, the one shortly before, the other shortly after the fall of their regimes, so that the question of their being put on trial never arose. Zhivkov was found guilty of corruption and sentenced to seven years, which he was permitted to serve under house arrest. In Czechoslovakia the former Prague Communist

Party chief, Miroslav Štěpán, was imprisoned for his part in the suppression of demonstrators in 1989: he served less than two years.

Honecker, who had sought shelter in the house of a pastor, was hounded from there by a mob shouting 'Pig! Pig!' In January 1990 he was briefly arrested. After being released on ground of ill health, he took refuge in a Russian military hospital. When a warrant for his rearrest was issued, he was spirited off to the Soviet Union, ostensibly for further medical treatment. The German government protested vociferously and demanded his return to stand trial. But Gorbachev resisted handing him over. After the collapse of the USSR Honecker took refuge at the Chilean embassy in Moscow. He was eventually persuaded to fly back to Germany to face charges of ordering East German border guards to shoot dead would-be escapers. The charges were dismissed and he spent his last days miserably in Chile.

The strangest case was that of Jaruzelski who handed over the Polish presidency in December 1990 to his nemesis, Lech Wałęsa. Jaruzelski was not a man who inspired personal affection. But many Poles, even among his opponents, accorded him a grudging respect and some accepted his argument that his actions in 1981 had been dictated by a desire to preserve some limited degree of Polish independence against what had seemed to him at the time imminent danger of Russian military occupation. No legal proceedings were taken against him. In Poland, as in Hungary, it was rumoured that, prior to the fall of the old regime, a 'gentlemen's agreement' had been made between the Communist leaders and their opponents, whereby the former were promised immunity from prosecution.

By 2001, twelve thousand case files on former East German officials had been opened; but only twenty-eight had led to prosecutions. As so often happens in such cases, there was a public sense, to some extent justified, that the smaller fry were being netted while big fish swam free. Former East German border guards were arrested on charges of shooting at escapers. Four senior politicians, including the former East German Prime Minister, Willi Stoph, were also apprehended. But when the former trade union chief, Harry Tisch, was found guilty of misappropriation of funds (he had spent union money on expensive holidays for his family), he received a light prison sentence and was allowed to go free immediately, having already served fourteen months in detention.

The long duration of the Communist governments and the extent to which they had permeated societies prevented any wholesale replacement of established elites. A study of social stratification in the Czech Republic,

Hungary, and Poland in the 1990s found that, apart from the growth of a new group of entrepreneurs and some transfers towards the service sector, 'no substantial changes in the social structure of the population occurred'.[29] Nor, again contrary to popular perceptions, was there a strengthening in the application of meritocratic criteria in appointments to skilled positions. In other words, members of the former *nomenklatura*, far from losing ground, 'underwent a significant improvement in their life-chances during the transition'.[30] There were some exceptions: in East Germany and Czechoslovakia about half the judges either resigned or were dismissed. East German universities were subjected to a wholesale purge of Communist appointees. In Hungary a hundred employees of the state broadcasting system were dismissed in 1994 on ground of their alleged Communist affiliations. But in general in post-Communist Europe, as in Germany, Italy, and France after 1945, most officials, including many directly implicated in the repressions of the previous regime, remained in their posts.

In Czechoslovakia after 1989 a powerful mood of public revulsion against the Communists, and in particular against the secret police system, led to a process called 'lustration'. In ancient Roman ceremonial this had been a purificatory ceremony involving animal sacrifice and processions with the object of warding off evil. In Prague it became a device for blackmail, settling old scores, venting unsubstantiated suspicions, and poisoning the political atmosphere of the reborn democracy. Overriding a veto by President Havel, the federal Parliament passed legislation providing that all senior Communist officials as well as tens of thousands of people listed in secret police files as agents or informers should be deprived of the right to hold public office.

Elsewhere, Communist-era secret police files on millions of individuals were ordered to be sealed for long periods in order to prevent witch hunts. But in Germany it was decided that democratic transparency required that the Stasi archives be opened. Six million files had survived and they proved to contain deeply embarrassing secrets. Husbands were found to have informed on wives and vice versa. Several prominent politicians, among them the Christian Democrat Lothar De Maizière, last Prime Minister of the GDR, and his rival, Ibrahim Böhme, leader of the Social Democrats in the elections of March 1990, were unmasked as informants for the old regime and were compelled to withdraw from public life. Apart from such personal disasters, other disturbing facts emerged. The East German government was revealed to have sponsored and financed terrorist activities in West Germany and to have hired criminals to carry out 'murder contracts'.

The victims, said to number five hundred, included defectors and outspoken critics of the GDR.

The economic consequences of the fall of Communism were, at first, distressing. All the former Communist states experienced negative growth in 1990 and 1991. In Hungary, for example, industrial production shrank by a quarter between 1989 and 1991. Perhaps misled by triumphalist western exponents of the merits of free markets, many east Europeans had expected early, tangible gains from the switch from a command to a demand economy. The reality was profoundly disillusioning. No magic formula could be discovered to ease transition. Much of the basic infrastructure for efficient operation of markets, such as a modern banking system, barely existed. As in Russia, economists recommended 'shock therapy', involving overnight elimination of subsidies and the introduction of real market prices. Only governments confident in their stock of public support dared embark on this road. The Polish government tried it and lost power. The Czechoslovak government tried it and lost Slovakia. Fear of the political cost led other post-Communist regimes, notably the weak Iliescu government in Romania, to opt for a more gradualist approach. But this too was at a price, since the IMF and western investors proved reluctant to steer capital towards economies that had not made a fundamental shift towards market pricing and a legal framework for capitalism. Some governments, unsure or divided within as to whether to pay the political or the economic price, floundered unproductively between the two approaches.

All over east-central Europe there was widespread agreement on the desirability of breaking up big, unproductive state enterprises, but much less on the method by which this should be done. The most likely purchasers were former Communist managers, though the prospect of the *nomenklatura* transmogrifying itself shamelessly into a property-owning bourgeoisie raised protests. A particularly thorny question was whether state-owned housing and agricultural land should be sold to the highest bidder, made available to existing occupants, or restored to previous owners or their descendants (including, in millions of cases, murdered Jews or expelled Germans). No easy solutions to such questions could be found, but so long as property rights were blighted by legal uncertainty, domestic and foreign entrepreneurs were deterred from investing.

Hungary was, at first, the most successful country in the region in attracting foreign capital: $5.5 billion flowed in between 1990 and 1994. Poland's larger but more troubled economy drew only $3.04 billion and the

Czech Republic $2.3 billion. Investors showed little interest in Slovakia, Romania, and Bulgaria in the early 1990s. Gradually, however, a number of west European firms, particularly motor manufacturers, sought to take advantage of low labour costs and corporate tax rates in eastern Europe by investing in new manufacturing plants there. Volkswagen opened a factory at Bratislava in Slovakia, Audi at Györ in Hungary. BMW and Daimler-Chrysler chose to move closer to home by building new plants in eastern Germany.

The largest single investor in ex-Communist Europe was the European Bank for Reconstruction and Development, founded with much fanfare by the European Community in 1991. It got off to a wobbly start, gaining notoriety for the marble splendour of its London headquarters. Its first head, Jacques Attali, a protégé of President Mitterrand, was obliged to resign. Nevertheless, by 1999 it had invested €14.7 billion from its own funds in eastern Europe and helped to mobilize a further €35 billion from other sources. In that period 20 per cent of the EBRD's investments were in Russia and these were mostly lost in the crash of 1998. Embezzlement and corruption elsewhere led to further losses.

Closure of uneconomic state concerns, reductions in military establishments, disruption of existing markets, and lack of investment produced high rates of unemployment all over eastern Europe in the early 1990s. Now that borders were open, emigration became an attractive option for hundreds of thousands of discontented east Europeans, impatient for the creature comforts of the consumer society. Poles moved to Germany and the United States. Greeks from Odessa and Baku left for Greece. Most of the remaining ethnic Germans in Romania and many from Poland moved to Germany.

Throughout eastern Europe the death of Communism led to a sharp increase in economic inequalities. This extended beyond the obvious cases of the suddenly very rich and very poor to the broad wage-earning population. In the Czech Republic, for example, the earnings of miners fell between 1988 and 1998 from 210 per cent of the average wage to 143 per cent and of seamstresses from 78 per cent to 65 per cent; on the other hand, those of judges rose from 152 per cent to 412 per cent and of financial specialists from 107 per cent to 194 per cent. Almost everywhere the balance of economic rewards changed. Teachers, for example, who had been relatively well paid under Communism, became one of the worst rewarded occupational groups.

In Poland the Mazowiecki government's economic programme adhered to strict fiscal rectitude, restrained income growth, set realistic interest rates, began to privatize state enterprises, and liberalized foreign trade. GDP fell by 12 per cent in 1990. By the end of 1990 unemployment had reached nearly a million. Peasant incomes shrank within two years by 40 per cent. Shops stocked up with consumer goods, which, given the collapse of real wages (down 31 per cent in 1990), few people could afford to buy. Inflation declined from 640 per cent in 1989 to 60 per cent in 1991. By 1992 a recovery was under way and between 1994 and 1997 the country enjoyed the highest growth rate in eastern Europe. The social cost was high: rationalization of inefficient industries led to a labour shake-out and unemployment rose from 11 per cent in 1997 to 20 per cent in 2002.

Czechoslovakia's privatization, starting in 1992, took the form of the distribution of shareholding 'vouchers' to the general population. The objective was to spread ownership among a large number of small investors rather than allowing it to become concentrated in the hands of 'oligarchs'. By 1996 70 per cent of the population of the Czech Republic were shareholders, the highest proportion in the world. But most owners quickly sold their shares and in later state asset sales the buyers were mainly financial institutions. The large Škoda automobile works were sold by the Czechoslovak government to Volkswagen for $6.4 billion. Between 1990 and 1997 the proportion of the labour force working for the state sector in the Czech Republic declined from four-fifths to one-fifth of the total.

By 1994 economic growth had resumed in most of east-central Europe. Romania, Bulgaria, and Slovakia lagged behind, partly because populist governments lacked the courage or capacity to take difficult economic decisions. The prospect of entry into the European Union, however, increased confidence in all the affected economies, and boosted foreign investment, trade, and growth. By 2005 east-central Europe was the fastest-growing region of the continent.

Politics in most of the post-Communist states in the 1990s was sadly non-consensual, often fractious, and sometimes violent. Yet all these states experienced peaceful elections leading to orderly transfers of power in the course of the fifteen years after 1989. Poland experienced five changes of government in five elections between 1989 and 2005.

The difficulties of economic transition brought a startling return of ex-Communists to government in several countries. In Poland the Mazowiecki government's compliance with IMF restrictions on public spending and monetary growth led in September 1993 to an electoral comeback by the Democratic Left Alliance, as the former Communists now called themselves. They became the largest party in the Sejm and the dominant element in a new coalition government. But they were a chastened, perhaps even emasculated party, in no way revolutionary, no longer tied to foreign apron-strings, and hardly less committed than their opponents to a mixed economy and an open society. Ex-Communists also returned to government in Lithuania in 1993, and in Hungary and Bulgaria in 1994. In all these cases they refrained from seeking a return to a command economy, generally confining themselves to welfare-state policies of the west European Social Democrat type and supporting entry to the EU.

In no country in eastern Europe did a monarchical restoration take place. Attempts to revive monarchist feeling in Romania, Yugoslavia, and Albania found little support. In Bulgaria, however, ex-king Simeon II, who had reigned as a boy from 1943 to 1946, returned home in 1996. Styling himself Mr Simeon Saxe-Coburg Gotha (Saxcoburggotski), he secured election as Prime Minister in 2001. His ideologically indeterminate 'national movement' pledged to achieve rapid improvements in living standards on the basis of a return to a market economy. He led the country into NATO in 2004 but after losing an election in 2005 was forced to share power in a coalition with the ex-Communists. He did, however, succeed in preparing Bulgaria for EU entry in 2007.

Post-Communist politics were particularly turbulent in Romania. In part this arose from acute economic distress. At the outset the National Salvation Front government took a number of popular steps, such as increasing the availability of electricity and heat, distributing salamis from the *Securitate*'s private stockpiles and so forth. But unlike Poland and Czechoslovakia, Romania did not embrace a free-market economic policy for some time, with the result that assistance from overseas was minimal. In the first post-Communist elections, in May 1990, Iliescu won 85 per cent of the vote in the presidential contest and the NSF won two-thirds of the seats in Parliament. Nevertheless, social unrest continued to simmer and in June 1990 fisticuffs broke out in Bucharest between anti-government demonstrators and miners from the Jiu valley who were transported into the city en masse to beat up government opponents and sack opposition party buildings. The distribution of railway passes to the miners and their organization into a violent intimidatory force recalled ugly practices in the country in the inter-war period. The violence further discouraged foreign investment and retarded economic recovery. In 1996 the NSF suffered electoral defeat but its centrist successors were disunited and unable to overcome a deep recession. Only after 2000 did Romania begin to enjoy sustained growth and move towards a more civil form of politics.

In Czechoslovakia, where democratic traditions and the enlightened leadership of Havel had offered the brightest hope for a smooth political transition, centrifugal pressures soon overwhelmed the federation. Suspicions between Czechs and Slovaks in the anti-Communist movement had long been evident and the coalition that brought about the 'Velvet Revolution' soon disintegrated. Nationalists in the less-developed Slovak region complained that western investment seemed to be directed almost exclusively to the Czech lands. Slovakia was being forced to close down armaments factories and obsolete heavy industries that had been major sources of employment. Separatist feeling bubbled up and calls were heard for the posthumous rehabilitation of the Nazi puppet ruler, Jozef Tiso. When Havel proposed dropping the word 'Socialist' from the Czechoslovak Republic's official name, the suggestion prompted the outbreak of a 'hyphen war': Slovaks demanded redesignation of the country as 'Czecho-Slovakia', as it had been known briefly in 1938–9. The decision to adopt the clumsy 'Czech and Slovak Federative Republic' satisfied few.

In a general election in June 1992, the liberal forces that had led the 'Velvet Revolution' were overwhelmed. No party won an overall majority in either region, but a populist Slovak party led by Vladimír Mečiar became the largest party in Slovakia. In the Czech lands the victors were a right-wing party led by Václav Klaus, who described himself as a 'Thatcherite Conservative'.[31] Neither party had campaigned on a separatist platform but once elected both moved to dissolve the federation. Klaus's insistence on rapid progress towards a market economy was contested by Mečiar. After negotiations failed, they speedily agreed to the creation of two sovereign states. In July the Slovak Parliament voted in favour of Slovak independence. The same day Havel resigned as President of the federation, acknowledging that he had lost the confidence of the Slovak region (he was later elected President of the Czech Republic). Dubček and many of those who had been active in the revolution of 1989 opposed the schism. So did representatives of the Hungarian minority, fearing cultural discrimination in a Slovak state. Economists warned that Czechoslovak scission would weaken Slovakia's fragile economy. All to no avail. By the end of the year the country that had been refounded in joyous spirits just three years earlier split into two sovereign states, the Czech Republic and Slovakia.

The end of Czechoslovakia was a sad repudiation of the vision of Masaryk. Yet at least the 'velvet divorce' was relatively amicable and wholly bloodless, in striking contrast to the savage hatreds that wrenched to pieces the last of the three European Communist federations.

Balkan wars

The disintegration of the Yugoslav federation that had been created by Tito at the end of the Second World War produced the first major war on the European continent since the Greek civil war of the late 1940s. At least 300,000 people died unnatural deaths during nearly a decade of bloodshed.[32] Two million refugees were forced from their homes in what became known as 'ethnic cleansing'. The savage assaults on unarmed civilians, particularly prisoners and women, horrified Europe. Some European powers eventually intervened, albeit reluctantly, with limited effectiveness, and late in the day. The war brutally exposed the limitations of the European diplomatic system and its inability to resolve conflict arising from profound ethno-religious cleavages.

The cumbersome power-sharing arrangement instituted in Yugoslavia after Tito's death in 1980 was compared to a *perpetuum mobile*.[33] It lasted for a decade but then suffered the fate of all such devices. The agent of its collapse, Slobodan Milošević, rose to power in Serbia through the Communist *apparat*. Trained as a lawyer and economist, he worked his way up, securing the directorship of a large Belgrade bank and, in 1986, the chairmanship of the Serbian League of Communists. Like many members of the 'new class', he came from a Communist, partisan background. He was exposed to violence early in life when both his parents committed suicide, although the influence of these episodes on his later conduct cannot be determined. Milošević vaulted to power on the basis of a crude appeal to Serbian nationalism. He mobilized the hopes and fears—or more accurately the ambitions and paranoias—of Serbs both in Serbia and scattered throughout the rest of Yugoslavia, exploiting their self-conception as a victim-nation that had suffered multiple atrocities in the course of history at the hands of Muslims and Croats.

In April 1987 riots broke out in the Serbian province of Kosovo. Serbs there, a minority of about 10 per cent of the population, complained bitterly of persecution by the Albanian majority who had exercised power in the region since it was granted autonomy in 1974. Kosovo held mythical significance for Serbian nationalism, arising from historic memory of the Battle of Kosovo of 1389, in which the Serbs were defeated by the Turks. Immediately after the riots, Milošević visited the area and responded to local Serbs' allegations of ill-treatment with the words: 'No one should dare to beat you.'[34] Overnight the pronouncement turned him into a national hero and in 1989 he secured appointment as President of the Serbian Republic. He immediately stripped Kosovo of its autonomy. Tables were now turned there and the Serb minority ruled the roost. The Albanians protested against their renewed vassalage but for the time being could do little about it.

The fall of Communism elsewhere in eastern Europe led in 1990 to the first multi-party elections in all six republics of the Yugoslav federation. In the northernmost republic, Slovenia, these were followed by a referendum in which an overwhelming majority endorsed independence. The most developed and prosperous member of the former federation, Slovenia historically looked west and north for commercial and cultural links. On 25 June 1991 she declared independence from Yugoslavia. The Yugoslav air force bombed Ljubljana airport and Yugoslav army troops advanced across Croatia towards Slovenia. There were a few scuffles between Yugoslav soldiers and Slovene militiamen at border posts. But unlike all the other Yugoslav republics, Slovenia had an almost homogeneous population (91 per cent Slovene according to the 1991 census). There was no significant Serb minority whose cause might be taken up by Serbia. On 3 July the ruling Socialist (i.e. Communist) Party of Serbia announced: 'Serbia has nothing against Slovenia's secession; it does no harm to our interests and we have no reason not to accept their separation, if it is conducted in a peaceful way.'[35] Bolstered by European Community recognition, the Slovenes succeeded in negotiating a withdrawal by the Yugoslav army. Slovenia thus escaped the horrors that were to engulf much of the rest of Yugoslavia. Alone among the Yugoslav succession states, she succeeded over the next decade and a half in gaining entry into NATO and the European Union. By 2005 Slovenia was ranked 26 on the UN Human Development index, higher than any other ex-Communist state.[36]

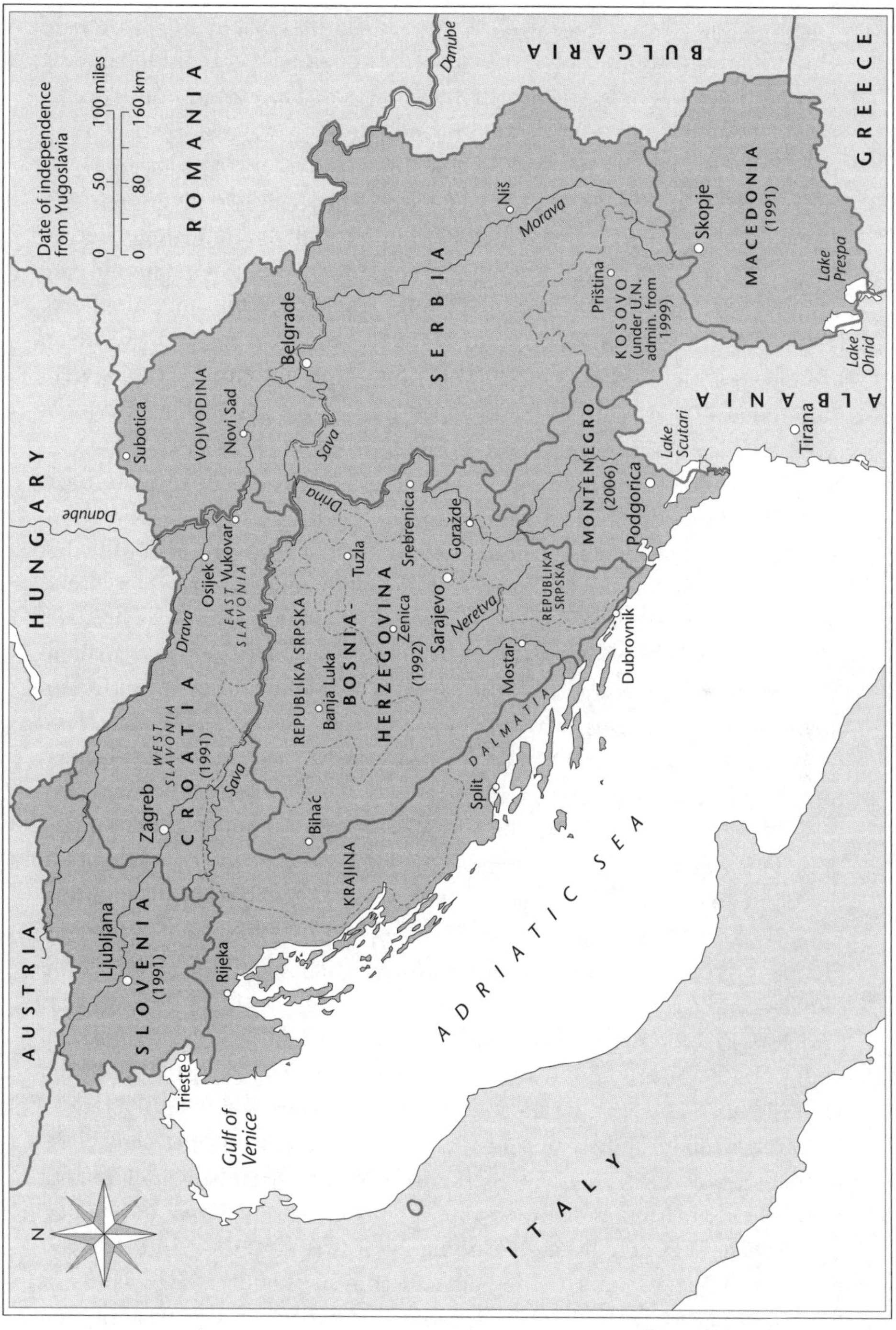

Map 9. Disintegration of Yugoslavia

Meanwhile Croatia took afront at the refusal of Serbia to accept a Croat who had been nominated as President of Yugoslavia under the agreed rotation procedure. Croatia declared her independence on the same day as Slovenia. More than half a million Serbs lived in Croatia (12 per cent of the population) and the Serbian government whipped up allegations of mistreatment by the Croats. The Croatian government in Zagreb fed Serbian fears by striking nationalist attitudes and discriminating against Serbs. Memories of wartime atrocities committed by the Croatian Ustaši against Serbs and by the Serbian Četniks against Croats embittered the conflict. The Croatian President, Franjo Tuđman, a nationalist historian, had fought with his fellow Croat Tito against the Nazis. But he claimed that the numbers of Jews and of Serbs killed during the war had been greatly exaggerated and he restored Ustaša symbols in the newly independent state. Serbia embarked on a military onslaught against Croatia. In August 1991 Serbs in Croatia declared an autonomous republic of Krajina. This was an area in which Serbs were a majority and the Belgrade government gave the rebels covert support. Fighting raged in several parts of Croatia where Serbs and Croats had previously lived side by side. One of the worst massacres of the war was committed at Vukovar in eastern Slavonia (Croatia) in November. After the capture of the town by the Serbs, at least 260 Croatian men, including patients from the town hospital, were slaughtered. The old Croatian port city of Dubrovnik in Dalmatia was besieged for three months and placed under a sixty-eight-day Serbian naval bombardment from October to December. Dozens of civilians were killed and hundreds of buildings destroyed. By 3 January 1992, when a cease-fire, negotiated by the United Nations, took imperfect effect, the Serbs controlled a third of Croatia. A 14,000-strong UN force was dispatched to keep the peace and Germany browbeat its EU partners into recognizing the independence of Slovenia and Croatia.

Before the conflict between Serbs and Croats had been brought to an end, a third war erupted in February 1992 in the republic of Bosnia and Herzegovina. This was the most ethnically mixed republic of Yugoslavia. Of the 4.4 million population of the province in 1991, 44 per cent were Muslims (since 1967 they had been encouraged to regard themselves as a national rather than a religious group), 33 per cent were Serbs, and 17 per cent Croats. War here broke out primarily as a result of the effort of Serbs in the republic to unite with Serbia. Radovan Karadžić, a psychiatrist for the Sarajevo football team, became leader of the Serb minority in

Bosnia. Encouraged by Milošević, he conceived a plan for seizing two-thirds of the territory of the province and styling it the 'Serbian Republic of Bosnia-Herzegovina' with himself as its chief. As for Sarajevo, the Bosnian capital, this would be divided along a 'green line', like Nicosia, into ethnically pure neighbourhoods. Thus the Stari Grad or old Turkish bazaar quarter, inhabited predominantly by Muslims, would become the nucleus of an eastern sector linked to Bosnia, while the newer western portions of the city, in which Serbs constituted about a third of the population, would become an ethnically pure Serb district. The latter would be joined to Serb-dominated regions of Bosnia that would be cleared of Muslims and eventually linked up with Serbia to form a Greater Serbian state. It was widely (and correctly) rumoured that a secret agreement on partition of Bosnia-Herzegovina and of Sarajevo had been reached between Milošević and Tuđman.

The Bosnian Serbs set up their own 'Republika Srpska', which, however, was recognized by no other state. In several parts of Bosnia that were dominated by Serbs, Muslims were forcibly driven out, their homes looted and burned. Hundreds of thousands fled abroad, particularly to Germany. Želiko Raznatović, known as 'Arkan', leader of a Serbian paramilitary group in Bosnia, acquired folk hero status among Serbian nationalists that his involvement in war crimes did little to dent. He was but one of several bandit chieftains, of several nationalities, who turned much of former Yugoslavia into an anarchic hell in these years.

Bosnia's independence was recognized by the United Nations in April 1992. In the same month Serbian fighters began to besiege Sarajevo. The civilian population withstood murderous bombardment by Serbian irregulars encamped on the surrounding hills (see plate 36). At least seven thousand people were killed in the first ten weeks. After a year of siege one in six inhabitants of the city had been killed or injured. All the animals in the municipal zoo died, some after eating their mates. Before the civil war Sarajevo had been one of the architectural jewels of the Balkans. Now many of its historic sites, including mosques, outstanding examples of Ottoman style, churches, and the city's synagogue, were destroyed or damaged.

The outside world sympathized overwhelmingly with the Bosnians who were seen as innocent victims of Serbian aggression. No doubt there were elements of wilful myopia in this black-and-white picture. The fact that Milošević was almost the last remaining Communist ruler in Europe did not enhance his reputation. That atrocities were in many cases two-sided or three-sided, that the Muslims in Bosnia enjoyed support from some very dubious elements in the Muslim world, and that the Serbs' self-image was one of defence in a war for national survival—all this failed to register in the west. Authenticated reports of atrocities against Muslims, particularly in Serb-controlled detention camps, and open espousal by some Serbian leaders of 'ethnic cleansing' aroused revulsion throughout Europe. Apart from Greece and Russia, which felt bound to Serbia by ties of religion and gave some limited support, the Serbs were internationally isolated and retreated into a miasma of collective self-pity and Manichaean hatred of their enemies.

Several attempts were made to halt the war by outside mediation. Lord Carrington, a former British Foreign Secretary and NATO Secretary-General, Cyrus Vance, a former U S Secretary of State, and David Owen, another former British Foreign Secretary, all tried their hands fruitlessly. Time after time, truces were agreed between the combatants, only to break down within hours. An economic blockade and arms embargo of Serbia were declared by the UN Security Council in May 1992. The Serbian economy was severely affected. The dinar became nearly worthless.

But almost unlimited supplies of weaponry seemed to be available to the Serbs from old Yugoslav army stockpiles and on the international black market. Fourteen thousand tons of *matériel*, for example, were purchased from Christian militias in Beirut. Another source of arms was the ordinary Yugoslav household. In 1968 Tito's government had created territorial defence forces, requiring all householders to keep weapons at home to use in the event of invasion. As a result there were said to be more guns than washing machines per household in the country.

By the summer of 1992 there was considerable pressure for military intervention by the United Nations, by the European Community, or by the United States. But none of these seemed willing to undertake the large commitments that would be necessary to achieve results. Few outsiders felt that the war touched on vital national interests, not even Italy which was a neighbour of former Yugoslavia and a recipient of much of the refugee overload from the conflict. Non-intervention, a murderous sham in the Spanish Civil War a generation earlier, became here a murderous reality.

At the end of June the Bosnian President, Alija Izetbegović, sent a despairing personal message to President Mitterrand of France: 'We have no food left, no arms, no hope. We are the Warsaw ghetto. Is the Warsaw ghetto going to be allowed to die once again?' Declaring that 'the urgency grabs one by the throat', Mitterrand made a theatrical personal descent on Sarajevo.[37] His initiative emboldened the UN Security Council to dispatch 1,100 troops to provide protection for the delivery of food and medical relief through Sarajevo airport. From small beginnings, the supply of Sarajevo grew into the largest operation of its kind in history, dwarfing even the Berlin airlift of 1948–9.

As the war dragged on into 1993 it threatened to develop into a broader conflict that might engulf the whole of former Yugoslavia as well as surrounding states. Arab states and Iran expressed growing solidarity with their Bosnian co-religionists. Volunteers from all over the Muslim world began to gather in Bosnia. Greek public opinion became highly excited about Macedonia. There was wild talk in Turkey and Albania of intervention in defence of the Muslim Albanians of Kosovo. The threat of a regional conflagration led to a more determined effort at pacification. During 1993 more than 26,000 United Nations troops were stationed on the territory of the former Yugoslavia; but their presence failed to halt the fighting. Only the threat of NATO bombardment of Serbian gun emplacements near Sarajevo brought an easing of the siege in February 1994.

A critical point in the war came in March 1994 when Croatia switched sides. She signed an agreement with Bosnia-Herzegovina which a year later was turned into a formal alliance. The change in the Croatian stance from collusion with the Serbs to alliance against them proved to be decisive. The USA and several European states gave arms and other help to the Croats and the Bosnians as a result of which the tide began to turn against the Serbs.

The single worst atrocity of the war was committed in July 1995 at the town of Srebrenica in Bosnia. The area was one of several that had been declared 'safe havens' by the United Nations and forty thousand Muslim refugees had found shelter there. They were protected only by a token unit of 429 lightly armed Dutch troops. Bosnian Serb forces under the command of General Ratko Mladić took over the town and slaughtered more than seven thousand unarmed Muslim men. The Dutch soldiers stood by and did not intervene. The episode shamed the UN and the Dutch and caused international outrage. Seven years later, after a strongly critical report by the Netherlands Institute of War Documentation, the Dutch Prime Minister and his Cabinet resigned (this is the only known occasion on which historians have brought down a government). But more than a decade afterwards the chief perpetrator of the massacre, Mladić, and his accomplice, Karadžić, were still free men.

After Srebrenica, however, the Serbs were forced into wholesale retreat. In August the Croats reconquered the Krajina and expelled 170,000 Serbs from there into Serbia. Serbian forces, sensing defeat, resorted to ever more extreme methods. In August they shelled the Sarajevo market place, killing thirty-seven people. Serbian propaganda portrayed this as an atrocity committed by the Bosnians in order to arouse world sympathy. NATO aircraft now bombed Serb encampments around Sarajevo.

As the Serbs were pushed back militarily, they made diplomatic concessions, leading, in November 1995, to a peace agreement concluded under United States auspices at Dayton, Ohio. Bosnia, though nominally remaining a single state, was effectively partitioned between a Muslim–Croat federation, with its capital at Sarajevo, and an autonomous Bosnian Serb republic that held a little under half the territory. A large NATO force was deployed to police the Dayton accords. Refugees were supposed to be able to return to their homes. But ten years later, out of an estimated 2.2 million people displaced by the war in Bosnia, fewer than half had returned.

Elsewhere in the former Yugoslavia, an old and bloody source of countless Balkan intrigues and feuds had in the meantime re-emerged onto the diplomatic scene. In September 1991 a referendum in Macedonia led that republic too to declare independence. Officially its ethnic composition was two-thirds 'Macedonian' and 21 per cent Albanian. In reality the population was a complex ethnic brew of Greeks, Bulgars, Serbs, 'Macedo-Slavs', Albanians, and gypsies. The economic viability of the former Yugoslavia's poorest republic was very questionable. In 1991 its economy contracted by 18 per cent, it had a GNP per capita of just $3,110, an unemployment rate of 20 per cent, and an inflation rate of 118 per cent. In the course of the decade it came to be a major transhipment entrepôt for drugs. Unlike Slovenia and Croatia which secured widespread recognition by early 1992, Macedonia found her path to international acceptance blocked. Greece, whose northernmost province was also called Macedonia, claimed an exclusive historic right to the name. Most members of the EU, while irritated by what seemed to them a senseless dispute, felt obliged to pay attention to their fellow member's susceptibilities. Greek nervousness was manifested in the decision to place on trial leaders of a 'Macedonian Cultural Association' from the Florina district in northern Greece. In 1993 the United Nations admitted Macedonia to membership but, in order to pacify the Greeks, insisted on calling her the 'former Yugoslav republic of Macedonia (FYROM)'. In the same year the newly re-elected PASOK government in Greece, led by

Andreas Papandreou, installed an economic blockade of the frontier with Macedonia. A small contingent of American troops arrived in 1994 to serve as a 'tripwire' in the hope of forestalling intervention by any of the republic's neighbours. Macedonia signed an agreement with Greece in 1995 and with Yugoslavia (now reduced to a rump of just Serbia and Montenegro) in 1996. Greece lifted its blockade but internal relations between the Slavic majority and the large Albanian minority deteriorated. By 2001 civil war had broken out between the government and Albanian rebels who drew arms and support from Kosovo and Albania. After six months of fighting, a cease-fire agreement was signed and a British-led NATO force arrived to supervise its implementation. An uneasy peace was restored but ethnic tensions continued to simmer.

The Dayton agreement did not end the fighting elsewhere in the former Yugoslavia. Encouraged by the Serbian defeat in Bosnia, Albanian nationalists in Kosovo embarked on a guerrilla campaign to oust the Serbs from that region. In the spring of 1999 the Kosovo crisis came to a head. The United States and other powers sponsored negotiations at Rambouillet, near Paris, between the Yugoslav government (i.e. the Serbs) and leaders of the Albanians of Kosovo. The Serbs, however, refused to accept the imposition of an agreement that would return internal autonomy to the Albanian majority in Kosovo. Fighting intensified between the Yugoslav army and an extreme group of Kosovar Albanians, the Kosovo Liberation Army. As earlier in Bosnia, atrocities and mutual accusations of 'ethnic cleansing' abounded.

Driven to act by the blatant violations of human rights and exasperated by the petulant obstinacy of Milošević, NATO decided to launch air strikes, the first offensive campaign undertaken by the alliance in its half-century of history. NATO missiles and warplanes, operating from bases in Italy and Hungary as well as from American ships in the Adriatic, unleashed a massive assault on military and strategic targets in Kosovo and Serbia. German aircraft, operating under NATO command, joined the assault, the first offensive action undertaken by forces of the Federal Republic since its foundation. The declared object was to 'degrade' the Yugoslav army's capacity to assault Albanian civilians in Kosovo. But the most immediate result was an intensification of the Serbian onslaught on Kosovar Albanians. Hundreds of thousands fled across the frontiers to Albania and Macedonia, threatening the precarious stability of both countries. The NATO offensive eventually succeeded, however, in forcing the Serbs to remove their forces from the province. On 9 June 1999 a cease-fire was signed. An international force, 'KFOR', took over as peacekeepers in Kosovo. The United Nations assumed responsibility for administering the province, though it remained nominally part of Serbia. Most of the Albanian refugees returned and it was again the turn of the Serb minority to feel threatened.

Defeat in Kosovo finally punctured Milošević's credibility in the eyes of his people. In October 2000 he was defeated in a presidential election. His refusal to accept the election result led to a popular insurrection in Belgrade in which he was overthrown. In 2001, under pressure from the United States and the EU, the new government handed him over to the International Criminal Tribunal for the Former Yugoslavia, which had been established in 1993 at The Hague. There he faced charges of genocide and crimes against humanity. His trial dragged on for years and he died in custody in 2006 before the proceedings had concluded.

Yugoslavia meanwhile approached the end of the road in 2002 when, by agreement between its last two members, it was reorganized into a loose federation of virtually independent states, Serbia and Montenegro. But the violence that had dogged the region since 1991 did not end even then. Both Serbia and Montenegro were plagued by a wave of political murders, including, in March 2003, the assassination of the Serbian Prime Minister, Zoran Djindjić. What remained of the federation unravelled further in May 2006 when a referendum in Montenegro produced a narrow majority in favour of complete separation from Serbia. The next month Montenegro declared her independence. Nor was the 'Balkanization' of the former Yugoslavia yet complete: Kosovo seemed the most likely next candidate for independence, as the Albanian majority there sought international support for a formal severance of its nominal link with Serbia.

Nevertheless, in spite of continuing tensions, international reconstruction aid began to take effect and as Serbia, Croatia, and Bosnia handed over war crimes suspects to the Hague tribunal, an uneasy calm returned. A small step towards overcoming the decade of horrors was the reconstruction of the picturesque Stari Most (Old Bridge) across the River Neretva at Mostar in Herzegovina. The bridge, built by the Ottomans in 1566, had been deliberately blown up by Croat forces during fighting in 1993. Its reopening in 2004, celebrated with much publicity, symbolized renewed hope for peace in the troubled region.

Western Europe since 1991

Although western Europe was spared the afflictions that beset the ex-Communist states in the 1990s, it suffered many indirect consequences of the troubles in eastern Europe. The burden fell most heavily on reunited Germany which found that the economic and other costs of integrating the eastern *Länder* were far greater than was realized at the outset. The German economy reeled under the impact and had still not recovered by 2005. Germany's increased weight within the EU was such that most of the rest of western Europe was also affected. Economic stagnation bred political disillusionment with national governments and with the European Union. Only Britain, among the major economies of the region, managed to avoid recession between 1991 and 2006. After the tumults of the 1970s and 1980s she also returned to political stability. In Tony Blair she found, after 1997, a new style of leader. But Britain still held aloof from full involvement in the continent and it was the limping German giant that set the pace for Europe.

In June 1990 Kohl incautiously forecast that the new *Länder* would be transformed into 'blooming landscapes'.[38] He thought the process might take three or four years. But the West Germans had accepted much too readily East German claims about the achievements of the Communist regime. Much of the East German infrastructure was far below western standards and had to be replaced from scratch. The supposed industrial assets of East Germany turned out to be obsolete junkheaps: productivity in East German industry was one-third of that in West Germany. In the course of the 1990s the country pumped 4 per cent of GDP a year in subsidies into the east. Privatization of east German industry, far from benefiting state revenues, cost a fortune in restructuring and employee compensation costs, resulting in a net loss of 2 per cent of GDP in 1990–2. As the government deficit ballooned to unprecedented levels, taxes were raised, social benefits were reduced, and interest rates remained high. The German economy entered its deepest recession since the war and unemployment rose by mid-1993 to 3.5 million. The unemployment rate remained around 10 per cent for the rest of the decade.

The economic landscape of eastern Germany, instead of 'blooming', remained bleak. In 1990 GDP of the region dropped 17 per cent, in 1991 a further 30 per cent. The number of people in full-time employment fell from about 10 million in 1989 to half that number by 1991. Distress was eased by a number of cushions: social payments, such as old-age pensions, greatly increased the purchasing power of large parts of the population; many of the unemployed found part-time work under government schemes. Private investment too began to flow eastwards. By the end of the decade some big cities, notably Leipzig, were transformed. Kurt Biedenkopf, a former Secretary-General of the Christian Democrat Party, was one of several enterprising west Germans who moved to Saxony to help regenerate the region. As Minister-President of 'Silicon Saxony', he helped attract big firms such as Siemens and Motorola to its capital, Dresden. The resplendent Frauenkirche cathedral, which had been almost totally destroyed in wartime bombing, was painstakingly rebuilt. Biedenkopf was very popular but other such immigrants were resented as a kind of colonial ruling class. The eastern *Länder* in general stagnated economically. Unemployment remained at least twice as high as in the rest of Germany and young people left to seek their fortunes in the west. The population of the east shrank from 15.4 million at the time of unification to just 14 million in 2001.

The disparity between economic conditions in east and west Germany produced severe social tensions. '*Ossis*' resented what they saw as the domineering and patronizing attitudes of '*Wessis*' and complained that their country had not been reunited but conquered by '*Besserwessis*' (a pun on '*Besserwissers*'—'know-it-alls'). Such feelings were captured in a play by Rolf Hochhuth, performed in 1993 and entitled *Wessis in Weimar: Scenes from an Occupied Land*. Disputes erupted between former property owners who returned to the east to stake claims to homes now occupied by others. The PDS (*Partei des Demokratischen Sozialismus*), successor party to the Communists, nurtured a still significant constituency of East Germans wallowing in what their opponents dubbed *Ostalgie* for the former *Fürsorgediktatur* (welfare dictatorship).

Meanwhile a mass immigration of hundreds of thousands of refugees, profiting from the liberal asylum provisions of the Federal Republic's constitution, provided a convenient target for accumulated frustration. Attacks on gypsies, Turks, Vietnamese, and other easily identifiable foreigners became endemic in east Germany: mobs of young neo-Nazis rampaged through Rostock, Berlin, and other cities, burning down immigrant hostels (in some cases killing those inside), raising a vicious spectre from the past and leading to pressure for the tightening of immigration laws.

Berlin, Germany's restored capital, exemplified the problems and prospects of the reunited country. Almost all trace of the wall soon disappeared as the two sides of the city were brought under one administration. But a sense of separateness proved slow to eradicate, especially in deprived working-class areas of east Berlin, among the former East German *nomenklatura*, and among ex-Communist intellectuals, once lionized, now marginalized. It took several years before 'Ossies' stopped being immediately identifiable in the street by their clothing and demeanour. The city was turned into the largest building-site in Europe by the arrival of much of the federal government in the city and by large-scale projects such as the massive Potsdamerplatz development. In 2005 unified Berlin, with its population of 3.4 million, was the largest city between London and Istanbul. But its demographic make-up was heavily skewed towards the elderly. Foreigners constituted 13 per cent of the population. Although it attracted people, it did not attract much industrial investment. Unemployment, especially in east Berlin, remained high. Local political pressures prevented the amalgamation of showpiece eastern and western institutions such as the city's three opera houses and two major orchestras. In spite of federal help, the capital of Europe's most powerful economy fell into virtual bankruptcy.

In 1999 the Bundestag moved from Bonn into the restored former Reichstag building in the centre of Berlin. The parliamentary move coincided with a change in government. Kohl's defeat in the general election of September 1998 had brought the sixteen-year rule of the 'Unification Chancellor' to an end. Soon afterwards he was implicated in party financing scandals and forced to withdraw in disgrace from political life. Disappointment with his failure to produce the promised 'blooming landscapes' contributed to his fall. But his successor, the Social Democrat Gerhard Schröder, gave his own hostage to fortune when he declared in the course of the election campaign that if he did not reduce unemployment he would not deserve to be re-elected. Schröder formed a coalition with the Greens and his government tentatively dallied with economic radicalism. But the resignation of the leftist Finance Minister, Oskar Lafontaine, after only six months in office, signalled a swift return to economic orthodoxy. There was a modest recovery in 1998–2000 but unemployment stuck at over four million.

In spite of failing his own test, Schröder won re-election by a whisker in 2002. But growth slowed almost to a standstill. Public debt soared to nearly two-thirds of GDP by 2004, compared with less than one-third in 1980. The country's generous welfare provisions became an almost insupportable drag on growth: in 2004 social security contributions by employers and employees were taking an average of 42 per cent of gross salaries, compared with 27 per cent in 1970. Schröder struggled with recalcitrant leftists in his own party to introduce more flexibility into the labour market. By early 2005 there were over five million jobless workers in the Federal Republic, the highest number in its history. In consequence, the Social Democrats steadily lost popularity. By 2005 they had forfeited control of nearly all the *Länder* and therefore of the upper house of the federal parliament, the Bundesrat. Effective government was, as a result, almost impossible and Schröder therefore decided to gamble on an early election. The outcome, in September 2005, was a stalemate in which neither major party secured a workable majority. A new grand coalition of the CDU and SPD took office under the CDU's Angela Merkel, Germany's first woman Chancellor. In spite of a modest upturn in growth, Germany seemed condemned to a further period of political indecision and economic stalemate.

The long German recession dragged down the economies of other members of the EU. In France too adherence by governments of both left and right to strong social protections inhibited growth. Jacques Chirac, elected President in succession to Mitterrand in 1995, made an injudicious decision to dissolve Parliament and call elections in 1997. The Socialists won and until 2002 Chirac was forced to rule in 'cohabitation' with a Socialist government headed by Lionel Jospin. The Socialists' main object was to cut unemployment. With this aim, they reduced the maximum working week to thirty-five hours. The primitive economic notion behind this expedient was that work would be shared around more fairly among the unemployed. After a temporary blip, the unemployment figures rose again and hovered obstinately around 10 per cent for several years. Chirac's re-election in 2002 was an unimpressive vote of no confidence in his main challengers: in the first round, Jospin was humiliatingly driven into third place; in the second, left-wingers, holding their noses, voted for Chirac in order to block the election of Jean-Marie Le Pen, leader of the extreme-right Front National. Chirac's second term, like Mitterrand's, became mired in accusations of corruption: his close associate, Alain Juppé, a former Prime Minister, was forced out of public life in 2004 after being convicted of financial malpractices years earlier. Although the centre-right recaptured power as a result of legislative elections in 2002, France remained mired in recession and political malaise.

If neither Germany nor France could offer convincing models of liberal capitalism to their neighbours to the east, how much less could this be said of Europe's fourth-largest economy. By 1993 Italy had had fifty-two governments in forty-five years. At this point a chain-reaction corruption scandal, nicknamed 'Tangentopoli', disgraced a large part of Italy's ruling class. Between February 1992 and March 1994 over three thousand of Italy's most prominent politicians and businessmen were exposed as bribe-takers or as having had links to the Mafia. The two parties that had dominated government since 1948, the Christian Democrats and the Socialists, were most heavily implicated and found themselves outflanked by revivified neo-Fascist and Communist movements and by new political forces such as the populist Northern League, which called for a decentralized, federal form of government.

In parliamentary elections in March 1994 a right-wing alliance that included neo-Fascists and the Northern League trounced left-wingers grouped round the former Communists. Socialist representation in Parliament was obliterated and the Christian Democrats (renamed Popolari) were reduced to insignificance. 'Ciao, ciao, First Republic!' was the headline in one newspaper. The conventional wisdoms that had governed Italian politics since 1948 had collapsed spectacularly but the electorate seemed to have voted against a discredited past rather than for any clear vision of the future. The leader of the conservative *Forza Italia*, Silvio Berlusconi, Italy's wealthiest man, took office as Prime Minister. He had come to prominence as owner of the TV company Telemilano as well as of residential and commercial property holdings, the publishing house Mondadori, the AC Milan football club, and the right-wing Milan newspaper *Il Giornale*. Although he lost power after seven months he bounced back in 2001 and for the next five years headed Italy's longest-lived post-war administration. But his reputation was deeply soiled by accusations of judicial corruption and he failed to resolve the structural problems afflicting Italy's economy, in particular heavy government indebtedness.

By contrast with stagnation in much of the rest of western Europe, the British economy in these years enjoyed its longest period of sustained economic growth since before the First World War. The period was also marked by a sea-change in British politics. In 1990 Margaret Thatcher's eleven years of power ended abruptly when she was disowned by her own party, which had tired of her domineering style. Her successor, John Major, cut an unassuming figure. If Thatcher was a reincarnated Boadicea, he seemed more like Ethelred the Unready. In an election in April 1992 he nevertheless won a fourth consecutive victory for his party, albeit with a reduced majority. But his government was fatally wounded by the 'Black

Wednesday' episode. Although Major clung to power for five years, his majority in Parliament was eroded and finally eliminated by a series of by-election defeats.

Britain's longest period of one-party rule in modern times came to an end in 1997. After eighteen years, the Conservatives were decisively defeated in a landslide victory for the Labour Party, headed by Tony Blair. He was a new type of British politician. Although educated at an expensive Scottish private school and Oxford, he seemed the most genuinely classless leader the country had ever had. Whereas Thatcher had taken elocution lessons to simulate upper-class tones, Blair modulated his speech towards a socially neutral 'Estuary English'. His 'New Labour' government cast aside many of the traditional axioms of socialism and embraced the market economy with the enthusiasm of the new convert. There were no renationalizations and no adventures in redistributive taxation. The Chancellor of the Exchequer, Gordon Brown, pursued a rigorously prudent policy in the government's first term, concentrating in particular on reducing state debt. Public expenditure fell as a proportion of GDP. The economy prospered, unemployment and inflation both declined to levels unknown since before the post-1973 economic crisis, and Britain's growth exceeded the anaemic levels attained by her large European Union partners.

Blair's government also enjoyed some other successes. After three decades of violence in Northern Ireland that had left three thousand dead and thirty thousand injured, the 'Good Friday Agreement' of 1998 at last offered hope of a political settlement. After endorsement by referenda in both parts of Ireland, a new power-sharing constitutional structure was set in place in the north. Although there were a number of renewed terrorist outrages, further political setbacks, and continued bitter wrangling, a new page seemed to be turning in the history of the troubled province.

Meanwhile in Britain's other Celtic regions, the government carried through measures of devolution that produced a Welsh Assembly with limited autonomous powers, and, in 1999, a more substantial Scottish Parliament, the first since 1707.

Blair maintained his predecessors' intimate relationship with the United States. As in the Gulf War in 1991, Britain was the USA's closest ally in the Kosovo campaign of 1999. The economy continued to boom, though public expenditure crept up again, from 37.7 per cent of GDP in 1999–2000 to 41 per cent in 2003–4. Blair was rewarded with two further election victories in 2001 and 2005, an unprecedented achievement for a Labour Prime

Minister. But his premiership was clouded by the decision in 2003 to join the United States in occupying Iraq. In September 2006 he was forced by rumbling hostility within his own party to undertake that he would step down from office within a year.

Any pretensions of the European Union to a common foreign policy were smashed by the Iraq crisis. Germany and France refused point-blank to follow the United States into the war against Iraq's brutal military dictator, Saddam Hussein. Britain, once again sticking close to the American line, was the only European state to send significant military forces to Iraq, though Poland, Spain, and Italy sent small contingents. The 'Coalition of the Willing' also included token participation by Albania, the Baltic states, Bulgaria, the Czech Republic, Denmark, Hungary, Macedonia, the Netherlands, Romania, Slovakia, and Ukraine as well as some non-European states. It was an impressive list but as the going got tough, several of these countries withdrew from what began to look like a coalition of the unwilling. The war generated strong opposition, especially in Britain, Spain, and Italy. Anti-war feeling increased in 2004 when it emerged that Saddam Hussein had not possessed the weapons of mass destruction that had been advanced as a primary justification for his deposition.

Spanish involvement had momentous consequences at home. In March 2004 an Islamist extremist group planted bombs in Madrid railway stations that killed 190 people, the largest toll in any terrorist attack in Europe since the Second World War. The outrage occurred three days before a general election which the governing conservative Popular Party, led by José María Aznar, was expected to win. But premature government attribution of responsibility to Basque terrorists was widely seen as an electoral gambit. When the true source of the attack turned out to have been elsewhere, a sudden reversal of popular opinion led to electoral victory for the Socialists.

In July 2005 further bomb explosions, on public transport in London, killed more than fifty people. The Islamist terrorism that had suddenly struck America on 11 September 2001 with attacks on Washington and New York now clearly threatened Europe too. Bitter argument broke out over whether the attacks in Europe were a consequence of the Iraq war or had a deeper explanation. But the heightening everywhere of collective suspicions, deepening hostility between natives and Muslim immigrants, and growing curtailment of civil liberties boded ill for the future of liberal societies.

20
Europe in the New Millennium

Good God, he says, looking at his watch.
Is that the time? The century ticks
inside their hearts. They feel the sun's light touch
on their foreheads.

*George Szirtes, Budapest/Wymondham, Norfolk, 29 June 2003**

Then and now

Europe has gone down in the world over the past century. Between 1914 and 2007 its share of world population declined from 27 per cent to 11 per cent. In 1913 the European economy produced more than half of global output; in 2004 around a third. In 1913 Europe's share of world merchandise trade was 59 per cent; in 2004 it was 48 per cent. In 1913 around 90 per cent of foreign capital investment was European (Britain's share alone was 43 per cent); in 2003 the European share of foreign direct investment was 60 per cent (Britain's share was 9 per cent). In 1914 European-owned merchant shipping constituted more than four-fifths of the world's fleet; by 2005 only about half.

In 1914 European imperial powers bestrode the earth, ruling about half the land surface of the globe (in addition, Britannia ruled the waves). The only colonies of Europe remaining by 2005 were such tiny relics as the French island territory of Réunion, in the Indian Ocean, and the British mid-Atlantic island of St Helena. Two of the three British colonies in Europe in 1914, Cyprus and Malta, were now sovereign states and members of the EU, though northern Cyprus was still occupied by Turkey. The third, Gibraltar, remained a British possession and a minor irritant in Anglo-Spanish relations.

* From 'Cities'. George Szirtes, *Reel*, Tarset, Northumberland, 2004, 96.

Similarly, Spain's north African exclaves of Ceuta and Melilla occasionally embroiled her in disputes with Morocco. Most of the post-colonial states retained close commercial and cultural links with their former rulers and small contingents of British and French troops were stationed as peacekeepers or stabilizing forces in some former dependencies, especially in Africa. But the age of anti-imperialism was past and the spirit of decolonization was dead. Colonies were no longer objects of European diplomacy.

In 1914 six of the eight great powers were European: Russia, Germany, France, Britain, Austria-Hungary, and Italy. Only Japan and the United States ranked with these, though the collapsing Ottoman Empire still claimed great-power status. Europe's armed strength dwarfed that of the rest of the world in terms of expenditure, manpower, and naval might (Europe's share of naval capital ships was over 80 per cent). Britain spent more on defence than any other country in the world and had the most formidable navy; Russia had the largest army in the world and Germany the most powerful. In 2006 the United States and China each had larger armed forces than any two European powers. The United States navy alone was more powerful than those of all European states together. Out of seven acknowledged nuclear powers in the world in 2006, only three were European. Of these, the Russians' nuclear force still ranked on paper with that of the United States but its delivery systems were ageing and inferior. In terms of advanced technology, the American armed forces were far ahead of those of all other countries; in Europe only Britain attained a similar qualitative (but much lower quantitative) level. Defence spending by the United States amounted to 4 per cent of GDP in 2000, compared with an average of less than 2 per cent among other NATO members.

In 1914 European universities and laboratories, particularly those of the German-speaking *Kulturraum*, led the world in science and technology. A century later Europe was clearly second to the United States. Of the fifteen Nobel laureates in Physics, Chemistry, and Medicine between 1910 and 1914, all but one were Europeans. Of the forty-three recipients of these prizes between 2000 and 2004, only twelve were Europeans; of the remainder, twenty-four were from the United States.

The balance within Europe also shifted in the course of the period. In 1914 Europe had consisted of twenty-three states (counting Austria-Hungary as one and including the newly independent Albania), plus five micro-states (Liechtenstein, San Marino, Andorra, Monaco, and the Vatican City).

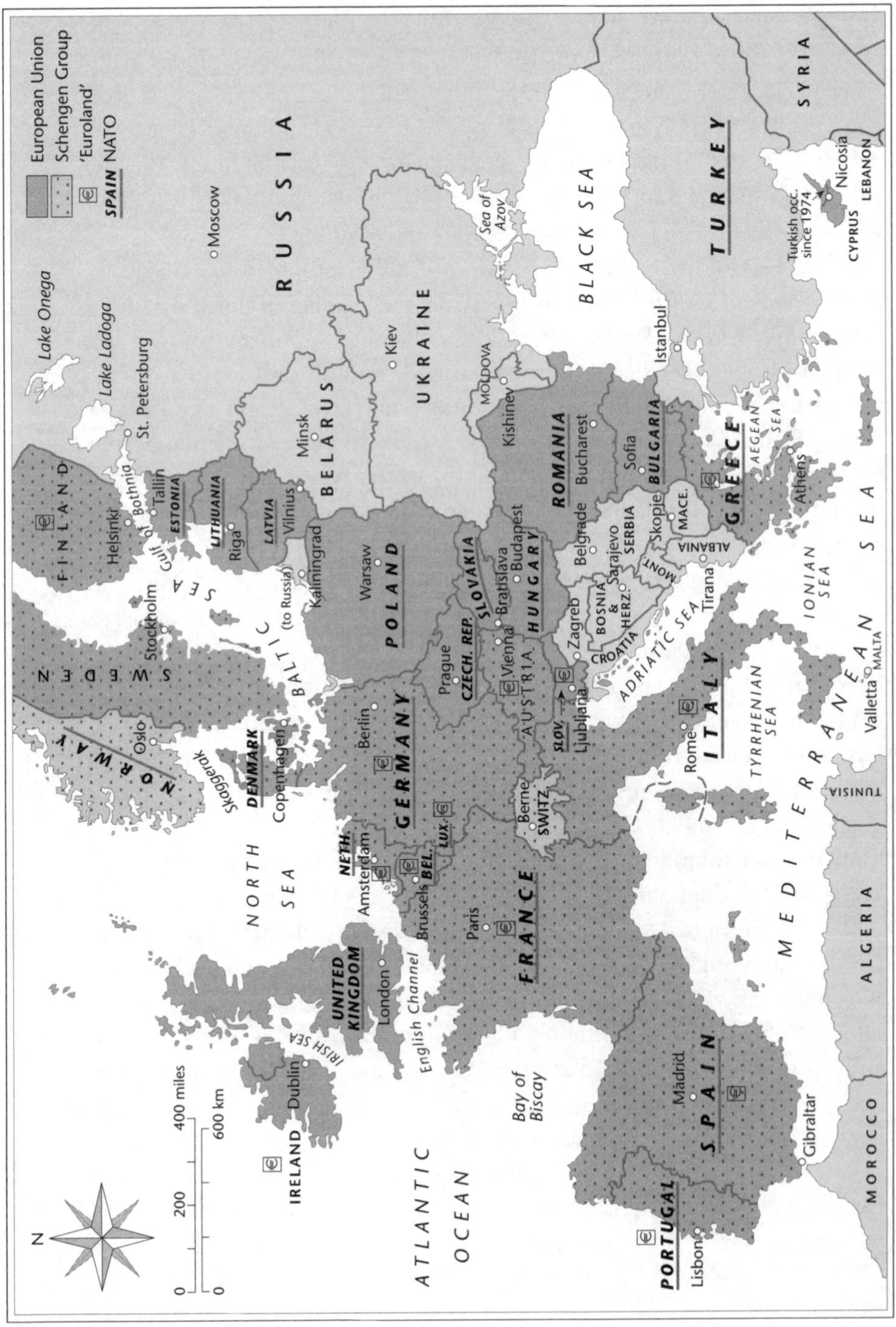

Map 10. Europe in 2007

In 2007 there were forty-one: the twenty-seven members of the EU, four successor states to the USSR (Russia, Ukraine, Belarus, and Moldova), five successors to Yugoslavia (Serbia, Montenegro, Croatia, Bosnia-Herzegovina, and Macedonia), plus Albania, Turkey, Norway, Iceland, and Switzerland (not counting the unrecognized 'Turkish Federated State' in North Cyprus and the Trans-Dniestrian Republic in Moldova). Remarkably, the five micro-states had all survived and, each in its own way, had prospered.

In 1914 the Russian Empire, which covered one-sixth of the land area of the world, had been the most populous state in Europe with 166 million people (140 million in Europe). In 2004 Russia, in much reduced borders, still had the largest population, with 142 million (106 million in Europe), but it was now one of the most rapidly shrinking populations of any European country and the decline particularly affected Russia's European regions. Russia remained the least densely populated European country, bar

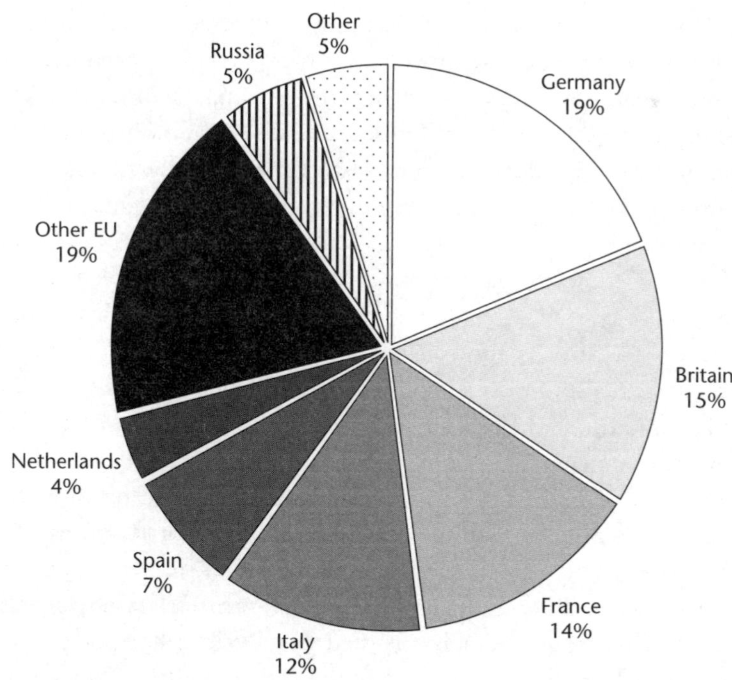

Figure 9. GDP of selected countries as share of total European product, 2005
Source: IMF.

only Iceland. Germany, with 83 million people, compared with 65 million in 1914, was still Europe's second-most populous country, even though she too had lost large parts of her former territory.

In 1913 Russia, although a primitive economy, had the largest GNP of any European country, comprising 20 per cent of the output of the continent. Germany ranked second with 19 per cent, Britain third with 17 per cent, and France fourth with 11 per cent. These four countries alone thus produced two-thirds of the entire output of Europe. In 2004 the four largest European economies were Germany (again 19 per cent of the European total), Britain (15 per cent), France (14 per cent), and Italy (12 per cent). Russia was now the sixth largest, after Spain. The extent of Russia's relative decline may be gauged by the fact that her economy was now about the same size as that of the Netherlands, a country with a population less than one-eighth that of Russia.

In 1914 coal production was regarded as an important index of national political and economic strength. Coal was then the most important source of energy in Europe, leaving aside human and animal draught-power and wood. Britain and Germany together produced 42 per cent of world output of coal. By the early twenty-first century King Coal had been dethroned. Germany's coal production had fallen from 277 million tons in 1913 to 27 million in 2002 (though she still produced large quantities of brown coal or lignite). British production fell no less sharply, from 287 million tons in 1913 (the peak year in the history of the British coal industry) to just 28 million in 2003.

In 1913 the age of oil was just beginning as ships and land vehicles began to use it heavily. Other energy sources, such as gas and hydro-power, supplied only a small fraction of needs. In the early twenty-first century nuclear energy also made a major contribution. France and Lithuania derived four-fifths, and Belgium, Slovakia, and Sweden more than half of their electricity generation from nuclear power. By 2005, however, the great majority of nuclear power stations in Europe were between fifteen and thirty years old; some of these were due to be retired and hardly any new ones were being built. Germany and Sweden, under pressure from environmentalists, were still planning to phase out nuclear power stations altogether. Sweden accordingly invested heavily in other power sources such as hydroelectricity. In 2005 she tested the world's first 'bio-gas' train, powered by decomposing organic material. With the third oil price 'shock' in 2004–5, oil production again became what coal had been in 1914, a crude index of economic might. In 2004, as in 1914, Russia was the world's largest oil producer, briefly overtaking Saudi Arabia before settling back into the number two position. Britain and Norway were the only other large producers in Europe but their reserves were much smaller than Russia's and, after a quarter of a century of oil self-sufficiency, Britain was once again a net importer.

Overall real incomes of Europeans have risen faster over the past century than in any other period in recorded history. Between 1913 and 1990 alone they are estimated to have multiplied in Norway and Sweden ninefold, in Italy sixfold, in Austria, France, and Germany fivefold, and in the UK threefold. Britain's slow relative decline was notable. In 1913 Britain enjoyed the highest per capita income in Europe. By 1990 she was poorer per head than all the countries just named. But reversals can be rapid. Between 1990 and 2005, as most European economies stagnated, Britain enjoyed faster growth than most of her neighbours. As a result, by 2004 British GDP per capita had again overtaken those of France, Germany, and Italy. The richest country in Europe per capita, by far, was now Luxembourg, followed by Norway and Switzerland. The inhabitants of all three countries were, on average, richer than those of the USA. Incomes in the poorer countries of Europe also multiplied several times during the century. Perhaps the most dramatic change in relative economic ranking came in Ireland: in 1913 she had one of the most backward economies of the continent; in 2004, largely thanks to EU membership, her people had become, by some measures, almost as rich as the Swiss. Eastern European economies in the early twenty-first century were in general more buoyant than those of the west and economic growth in most of the region was higher, albeit from a much lower base. But countries such as Moldova and Albania nevertheless remained economically primitive and poverty-stricken, as they had been in 1914.

Economic growth came at the price of environmental degradation, uglification, noise, the fouling of the air, earth, rivers, lakes, and seas—the greatest, most sudden, and most deleterious artificial transformation of the European landscape since the dawn of civilization. Europe was still the most densely populated and most heavily industrialized continent. But by the last quarter of the twentieth century a new environmental consciousness had found a footing in politics and in civil society engendering hope for a new equilibrium between humanity and natural resources.

Economic inequalities within European countries probably decreased substantially in the course of the century, although calculations of the extent run into serious methodological complications. In particular, growth in home-ownership and spikes in property values render comparisons over time and space difficult. At what point should immigrants be included in such comparisons? High progressive taxation, particularly during and after the Second World War, certainly pushed several countries towards greater equality. In those for which estimates have been attempted, for example Denmark and the UK, there was a decline in the share of the top decile of incomes between 1900 and 1970 and redistribution to middle and lower strata. Finland appears to be one of the few countries where income inequality increased in that period. After the 1970s, however, egalitarian pressures decreased. Even in Sweden, once a pioneer of redistributive taxation, direct taxes after the 1980s accounted for only about a quarter of state revenue, compared with more than half in the 1960s. Nevertheless, the Scandinavian countries remained the most egalitarian in distribution of income in western Europe and Switzerland the most inegalitarian. In eastern Europe, characterized by a high degree of inequality in wealth and income in 1914, Communism, at least in its initial phases, undoubtedly brought considerable redistribution from the top downwards. The extent of further redistribution after the 1960s is less clear. After 1989, throughout ex-Communist Europe, there was a swift return to extremes of wealth and poverty.

One of the most remarkable transformations of the century was in the labour market. Unemployment statistics of the modern type were not collected in the years before the First World War. The concept barely existed. No doubt there was considerable hidden un- and underemployment, particularly in the backward agrarian economies of eastern Europe. Economists are nonetheless generally agreed that there was comparatively little unemployment in most European countries in 1913. In the inter-war period large-scale industrial unemployment was endemic throughout the continent. Between the end of the Second World War and 1973 it more or less disappeared. But in the last quarter of the twentieth century it re-emerged as a seemingly ineradicable social phenomenon. In 2004 twenty million people, 9 per cent of the workforce, were jobless in the EU and rates in the non-member countries were generally higher. Britain and Sweden were almost alone among large European economies in having significantly lower unemployment rates but they had large hidden unemployment in the shape of high numbers of people registered for incapacity benefits, double the number of officially unemployed in both countries. Unthinkable as such high unemployment figures were to the economic planners of the early post-war period, what was perhaps even more remarkable was that the return to unemployment levels of the 1920s and 1930s did not produce any social explosion comparable to the turmoil of inter-war Europe. Under enormous strain, the welfare state, for all its defects, maintained a safety net of basic provision that eased discontent and prevented social breakdown.

In 1913 inflation, like unemployment, was virtually unknown, as the gold standard and the world dominance of sterling kept most currency values stable. Massive inflation in the 1920s, particularly in eastern and central Europe, was followed by drastic deflation in the 1930s, then by runaway inflation in the 1940s. A period of relative stability during the Bretton Woods years of dollar dominance between the late 1940s and 1971 was succeeded by renewed inflation in the 1970s. But by the early twenty-first century, inflation had declined to under 3 per cent in most major European economies except Russia and Ukraine, and according to some economists had been 'wrung out of the system'.

The tentacular extension of the state, mainly as a result of the two wars and the costs of social welfare, health, and education, showed no sign of easing in the late twentieth century in spite of the 'neo-liberal' trend. Sweden was the most extreme case: state expenditure there rose from 10 per cent of GDP in 1913 to 64 per cent by 1996. Even in Switzerland, where the government's power to tax was severely constrained by law, public spending rose from 14 per cent of GDP in 1913 to 39 per cent by 1996. The proportion of workers in public employment grew from between 2 and 5 per cent in west European countries in 1913 to between 15 and 30 per cent by the 1990s. From the mid-1990s, however, growth in public expenditure as a proportion of GDP eased in most countries. In 'Euroland' total government outlays peaked at 49 per cent in 1995 and then declined to 45 per cent by 2000. Eastern Europe was not immune to the trend. By 2004 the figures for the five former Communist countries that were now members of the EU were all below 50 per cent of GDP, that is, below the levels of Sweden and France.

Broadly speaking, social attitudes had become gentler. In 1914 the only European countries that managed without a death penalty were Portugal, the Netherlands, and Norway. By 2005 it had been abolished almost everywhere. The only states in which it remained on the statute book (aside from under military jurisdiction or conditions of national emergency) were Russia, where the last execution took place in 1996, and Belarus, where executions continued until at least 2003. Beating in schools and as court-ordered punishment also disappeared.

In the early part of the century even the authoritarian empires, such as Russia, regarded themselves as *Rechtsstaaten*, observing legal norms and recognizing judicial autonomy. The Communist and Fascist regimes of the mid-twentieth century viewed such distinctions with scorn and imprisoned and killed their citizens arbitrarily. But in the later part of the century a greater degree of respect for human rights settled on most of the continent. Crimes against humanity, such as those committed in former Yugoslavia in the 1990s, were regarded as aberrations whereas in the 1930s and 1940s such conduct had come almost to be accepted as a regrettable norm. Before 1914 undemocratic regimes interfered in the lives of the majority of ordinary people far less than the most liberal European governments of the new millennium. This was the paradox of the contemporary liberal state: it intruded in many unprecedented ways into the private sphere; yet liberty of the individual, measured by most reasonable criteria, had enormously increased in Europe by 2005 by comparison with 1914.

Two competing tendencies emerge from the dislocations of the past century: on the one hand a growth of ruthlessness, manifested in wartime atrocities, criminality, and heightened racial hatreds; on the other, a growth of tenderness, exemplified in changed attitudes to the treatment of the mentally ill, the disabled, prisoners, children, and animals.

The second demographic transition

In 2005 Europe's population had reached what experts predicted would be its all-time peak of 740 million. For the first time since the Black Death, the continent's population as a whole was expected to decrease over the next generation. Almost every country in Europe had a below-replacement level of natural increase. Absolute population decline in the period 2000 to 2005 was reported for nearly all the former Communist states as well as Switzerland and Italy. Here too Ireland stood out: the country that had historically lost population continuously since the 1840s was one of the handful in Europe to report an annual rate of increase above 1 per cent. Decline was most marked in the former Soviet Union: Russia's population dropped precipitously between 1991 and 2005, from 149 million to 143 million, one of the sharpest falls in peacetime for any country in European history. France was one of the few countries that departed from the general pattern. There, partly because of the high fertility of immigrant women from Africa, the birth rate remained above replacement level, leading optimistic French demographers to predict that France would overtake Germany in population by 2050.

The main cause of population decline was a fall in fertility below replacement level. The trend was especially marked in eastern Europe where birth rates had been declining since the mid-1980s and fell even further after the collapse of Communism. In east Germany the rate dropped by almost half between 1989 and 1991. In Romania and Ukraine it fell by 30 per cent. Most disastrously, in the early twenty-first century deaths were exceeding births in Russia by nearly a million a year. The dislocations of post-Communism were undoubtedly one cause of the fertility decline but there were others. Russia's population still suffered from a huge sexual imbalance: according to the 2002 census there were 78 million women but only 68 million men. In the case of Romania, another cause was the legalization of abortion, which had been a criminal offence under Ceauşescu.

Remarkably, Catholic countries such as Italy, Spain, and Portugal were among those with the lowest average number of children per mother. Clearly, Church doctrine prohibiting artificial birth-control was being

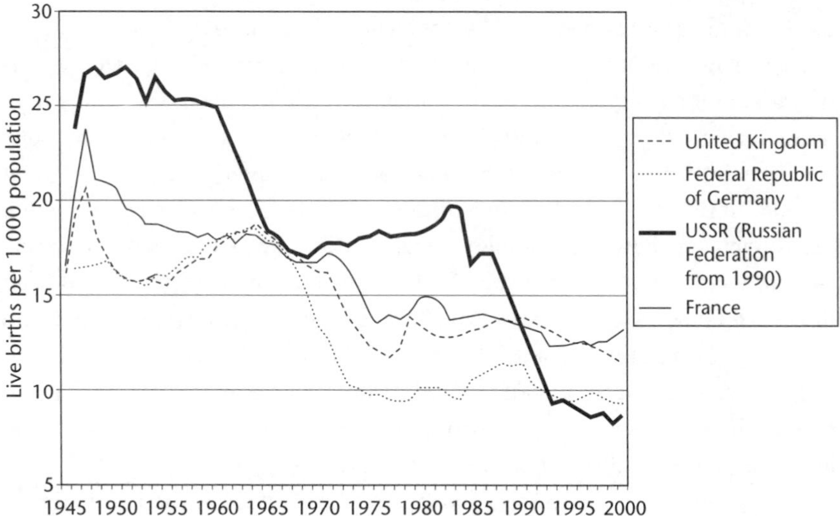

Figure 10. Birth rates in selected countries, 1945–2000

Sources: UN Statistical Office; B. R. Mitchell, *International Historical Statistics, Europe 1750–2000* (New York, 2003).

widely flouted. In Italy, for example, birth control devices were widely available and surveys suggested that most Catholics felt able to reconcile their use with Church teaching. In 1993 deaths exceeded births in Italy for the first time since 1914 and the 'missing child' (*il bambino negato*) became an object of national concern.

Governments worried and, as in the 1930s, pursued natalist policies to try to reverse the trend—but to little effect. Demography proved impervious to social engineering. Millions of individual human decisions combined to yield results that had immense collective consequences.

Population decline accelerated in spite of a further fall in the infant mortality rate. In 1914 it had stood at around one hundred per thousand in most of Europe. By 2003 it had fallen to under ten per thousand in much of the continent. Iceland claimed the lowest rate in the world: just 2.4 per thousand. Improvements in this sphere had been a proud boast of Communist states. Now every European state that had a rate above ten per thousand was ex-Communist.

Women were not only having fewer children; they were having them later. In 2002 the average age at which women bore their first child was twenty-nine in the Netherlands, Spain, and Switzerland and above twenty-five in much of the rest of the continent.

In 1914 life expectancy at birth in Europe was between forty and fifty. By 2005 it had risen to over seventy for males and near eighty for females in most European countries. But there were sharp variations between countries and among regions. Life expectancy for men in Russia was lower than in any other European country: it had declined to only fifty-eight by 1996 (for females it was seventy-two) and edged up only a little over the next decade. In Dzerzhinsk, a heavily polluted city 240 miles east of Moscow, site of a Soviet-era chemicals complex, men in 2003 could expect to die at forty-two and women at forty-seven. Even in Britain, men in the Shettleston district of Glasgow could expect to die by the age of sixty-three. The causes were similar in both places: drink, drugs, pollution, poor diet, smoking, and lack of exercise. Not coincidentally, Glasgow was now the poorest city in Britain. There, as elsewhere, a wide divergence was observed between the life expectancy of rich and poor.

Falling birth and death rates led by the early twenty-first century to a rapid ageing of populations. The percentage of people over sixty rose from around 10 per cent in western Europe in 1900 to near 20 per cent by 2000. In 2003 the United Nations Population Division surveyed the countries with the highest percentage of population older than sixty-five and reported that nineteen of the top twenty were European. Italy had the highest median age of any country in the world: forty-two.

As the age profile of populations increasingly came to resemble an inverted pyramid, the cost of social support for the high proportion of economically inactive elderly people became a major burden. Geriatric medicine had to deal with increased incidences of illnesses specially prevalent among the old, such as hypertension (affecting 59 per cent of a representative sample of people aged over seventy in Berlin in the 1990s), congestive heart failure (65 per cent), varicose veins (73 per cent), urinary incontinence (38 per cent), osteoporosis (34 per cent overall, but much higher among women), poor hearing and sight, as well as psychological conditions such as dementia. The compilers of the Berlin study found that 96 per cent of their sample had at least one, and 30 per cent suffered from at least five medical, neurological, or orthopaedic illnesses. More than a third were unable to go shopping or travel on their own.[1]

Old people were probably lonelier at the end of the century than in 1914. Changes in family structure had stranded many who in earlier times would have received closer social and psychological support from their children. Fewer than before now lived near their children or grandchildren, who were, in any case, far less numerous than in previous generations. Widows on average outlived their husbands for longer than before. In 1914 the old were still revered, especially in rural areas, as repositories of wisdom and useful experience. In the youth-oriented culture of the twenty-first century, they were patronized as 'senior citizens', infantilized by social workers, and often felt that they had been thrown on the dust heap by society.

Although the old lived longer, Europeans worked less. Before the 1970s most workers in Europe did not retire until their mid-sixties. But by the end of the century the average retirement age in the EU had fallen below sixty. In most of western Europe in 2000 the age at which workers could generally start receiving state pensions was sixty-five. In much of eastern Europe it was sixty-two. In Italy workers could retire at fifty-seven and receive full state pensions if they had worked for thirty-five years. In consequence, most actually did so, with the result that the average retirement age in 2003 was fifty-seven. All over Europe state pension schemes and many private ones too faced the prospect of insolvency. By 2002 old-age and other pensions were consuming 15 per cent of Italian GDP, more than anywhere else in Europe. Pensioners made up 28 per cent of the Italian population. Yet proposals there and elsewhere to raise the retirement age and to lower state pension provision produced strong opposition from old people, now a major voting block and political lobby.

With fewer old people working and fewer young ones to take their places, the economically active portion of the population shrank fast. The only recourse for the advanced economies of Europe, if they were to maintain a productive demographic balance, was to increase immigration. A report in 2001 by the Population Reference Bureau stated that if France, Germany, Italy, and the United Kingdom wanted to maintain their populations at current fertility rates, they would have to triple immigration, from 237,000 a year in the mid-1990s to 677,000 a year, with the greatest increase in Italy. Furthermore, 'to maintain the 1995 labor force, immigration would have to increase to 1.1 million a year, and to "save social security," [i.e.] to keep the ratio of 18-to-64 year-olds to those 65 and older at 1995 levels, immigration would have to increase 37-fold, to almost 9 million a year'.[2]

Europe had changed in the course of the century from a continent of emigration to one of immigration. Faced with a spiral of depopulation by natural decrease and with rapidly ageing societies, the advanced economies struggled to cope with the effects of mass immigration.

By the early twenty-first century all the countries of western Europe had large immigrant populations. Even traditional countries of emigration, such as Greece and Ireland, acquired big immigrant populations from the 1990s onwards. The immigrants were of several types. The most numerous were fellow Europeans, either moving within the EU or from the Balkans or eastern Europe to the west. The most visible were dark-skinned Africans and Asians. Of the latter a majority were Muslims. In France, Italy, and Spain the largest numbers came from North Africa, in Britain from the Indian subcontinent. Most of the immigrants were legal but many were illegal and some lived in a grey zone of semi-legality, often in miserable conditions, easy prey for exploiters of all kinds.

The fall of Communism brought new pressure for migration to the west from the impoverished societies of eastern Europe. To their consternation, west European states that had protested for years against the barriers to emigration from the east were now confronted with a flood of immigrants seeking entry to economies that already suffered from high unemployment and overstretched social services. Illegal immigrants from Poland, Ukraine, Romania, and Albania filtered into Germany, Italy, and other countries of the European Union. Throughout Europe governments struggled to cope with the influx and its consequences. The physical and legal barriers that had formerly kept people from leaving were now resurrected on the other side of frontiers to prevent people entering. Most countries enacted restrictive laws and regulations designed to limit immigration to those who would be most useful to the economy and least dependent on social support. In June 1992 Austria set a limit of thirty thousand immigrants per annum and posted two thousand border guards along the frontier with Hungary to stop illegal crossings. Even after the expansion of the EU in 2004, new members' accession terms limited until 2011 the rights of their nationals to settle in most other EU countries; only Britain, Luxembourg, and Ireland permitted free entry from the outset, leading to a huge wave of migration, especially from Poland to Britain. Meanwhile, illegal immigration to western Europe continued, some of it organized by ruthless traffickers transporting their clients or victims from as far away as China.

From the 1990s onwards a growing number of immigrants to western Europe from the Balkans and later many from elsewhere claimed to be 'asylum-seekers', fleeing persecution in their homelands. Countries that were signatories to the European Convention on Human Rights were obliged not to expel asylum-seekers who might face torture or other breaches of human rights in their homelands. This position had been established by case law even though the Convention itself made no direct reference to a right of asylum. By 2005 forty-five countries were signatories to the Convention. The richer EU countries, in particular, found themselves besieged by hundreds of thousands of claimants to asylum, each of whose bona fides had to be examined and, in case of rejection, potentially tested in court. The outcome was a bureaucratic, judicial, and humanitarian nightmare. The general response was to try to prevent such people arriving in the first place. Border patrols by land and sea were increased, particularly in the Mediterranean, in the hope of blocking the influx. Hardly had the old Iron Curtain across the centre of Europe been drawn back than a new one seemed to be descending around its edges.

In western Europe the largest number of immigrants settled in Germany. Between 1991 and 2003 14.2 million Germans and foreigners moved to Germany and 9.6 million moved away. By the end of 2003 7.3 million foreign citizens (including 2.3 million from other EU countries) were living in Germany, constituting 8.9 per cent of the population. Of these, at least 1.7 million were Turkish citizens. The rest were mainly from former Yugoslavia, Poland, Greece, and Italy. One-fifth of the foreign citizens had been born in Germany. More than 60 per cent of the immigrants had lived in Germany for over a decade. They were not evenly spread throughout the country but concentrated in big cities, such as Hamburg and Munich where they formed nearly a quarter of the population. In 1999 German citizenship law, which dated from the imperial period and was governed by the principle of *ius sanguinis* (based on the criterion of descent), was modified. The new law allowed some room for the principle of *ius soli* (based on place of birth) to permit at least children born in Germany to immigrant parents to qualify for German citizenship. Unlike many European countries, however, Germany did not permit dual citizenship. This deterred many of those qualified from applying for citizenship under the new law. Nevertheless, by 2005 an estimated 700,000 of the 2.4 million people of Turkish origin in Germany were German citizens.

Immigrants inspired both love and hatred. Many of the newcomers married natives. Their children, often of mixed ethnic and religious background, constituted a new element in European societies. The result in many spheres was to enrich and broaden hitherto parochial cultures. A new generation of German-Turkish, Dutch-Moroccan, and British-Indian writers gained popularity and critical acclaim.

Hostility to immigrants was more widespread and took many forms: de facto housing segregation, racist rhetoric, and violence. Extreme-right political parties playing on fears of immigration won significant support in France, Switzerland, Austria, Belgium, and the Netherlands. Some sections of the established political spectrum, including the Communists, were not immune to infection by the anti-immigrant mood. Violence involving immigrants took many forms. In Britain in 1981 fierce riots broke out in Brixton (London) and Toxteth (Liverpool), both deprived areas with large immigrant populations. Further riots erupted in Bradford in 1995 and 2001 and in Burnley and Oldham in 2001. These were mainly riots by young immigrants rather than against them. In Germany, on the other hand, a wave of violence after 1989 was directed by young German neo-Nazis, particularly disaffected youths in the east, against Turkish and other immigrants.

Early in the new millennium the European country with the largest number of immigrant residents, by far, was Russia with 13.3 million persons of 'migrant stock', the great majority Russians who had arrived from other parts of the former Soviet Union after 1991. Ukraine had 6.9 million immigrants for similar reasons. Yet the total populations of the two countries declined between 1991 and 2005 in spite of these colossal human accruals. Usually migrants seek better economic conditions. But immigration to Russia peaked between 1991 and 1998 when the economy was severely depressed; after 1998, when the economy improved, immigration slackened. The number of arrivals in 2001 was 186,000, compared with 1.1 million in 1994. One explanation was that the main sources of immigration, the states of the 'near abroad', were themselves affected by the economic upturn in Russia and as a result pressure for emigration from them decreased after 1998. Whatever its cause, the decline of immigration to Russia in the early twenty-first century had potentially catastrophic implications so long as the fertility rate remained below the 2.1 replacement level. In 1999 it was just 1.17.

In both eastern and western Europe, therefore, the new millennium opened with a demographic crisis unprecedented in the modern era. Its resolution would depend on some combination of developments affecting both migration and natural increase. The latter would inevitably reflect the extent and nature of sexual relations. But these too were in an unprecedented flux.

Sex and sexuality

By the 1990s the nuclear family unit was in an advanced state of dissolution in Europe. The decline of marriage was evident almost everywhere save in Greece and Turkey. In France in 1993 and 1994 the number of marriages was the lowest ever recorded in peacetime. Twenty per cent of women aged thirty-five and 15 per cent of those aged forty had never been married at all. The age of first marriage was rising. Only in Ireland, where late marriage was traditional, did the mean age of first marriage decline between 1960 and 1990: from twenty-seven to twenty-six.

In northern Europe, in particular, unmarried cohabitation had become common. The number of children born to unmarried mothers increased sharply: in 2000 they constituted more than half of all children born in Iceland, Sweden, and Estonia. Britain and France were not far behind. More than a third of births in Britain in the 1990s were to unmarried mothers. Illegitimacy, however, no longer carried a taint. In 1987 Belgium stopped distinguishing in law between legitimate and illegitimate births. Germany followed suit in 1997.

Between the 1960s and the 1990s divorce laws continued to be liberalized throughout western Europe. After big increases in divorce in the early part of the period, however, the rate declined somewhat in the 1990s, possibly a consequence of the sharp decline in the marriage rate. The reduction in divorces was most significant in the former Communist countries. The last country to legalize divorce was Ireland. A referendum on the issue took place there in 1986, but after a vigorous campaign by the Church against proposed legislation, the electorate decisively rejected any change. In a second referendum, in 1995, all political parties urged approval against continued Church opposition: the popular vote sanctioned divorce by a very narrow margin. But the divorce rate in Ireland in 2004 remained one of the lowest in Europe. In general, Catholic countries such as Italy and Spain had relatively low rates. The countries of the former Soviet Union, the Czech Republic, and the United Kingdom had the highest in Europe and among the highest in the world.

Whether because of divorce or unmarried parenthood, a growing proportion of children now lived in one-parent families. In Britain by 1994 21 per cent of all families with children included only one parent. The proportion was lower elsewhere, especially in Catholic countries (13 per cent in Spain, 12 per cent in Portugal), but was rising everywhere.

Forms of contraception continued to evolve. In Britain the contraceptive pill, fashionable in the 1960s, was overtaken in the early 1990s by sterilization as the most popular method. In eastern Europe abortion ceased to be the most common means of birth prevention, although it remained much more frequent there than in the west. In Russia, Belarus, Ukraine, Romania, and Bulgaria in 2000 there were more abortions than live births. In Catholic countries, especially Poland and Ireland, the Church continued to fight rearguard actions against the legalization of abortion. The reunification of Germany posed the problem of reconciling the abortion laws of east and west. West Germany's law had hitherto been among the most restrictive in Europe, whereas East Germany, like most Communist countries, permitted abortion virtually on demand until the twelfth week of pregnancy. In June 1992 the Bundestag approved a new law permitting abortion in the first three months of pregnancy. In spite of opposition from most Christian Democrat members, the law passed, thanks to the defection of about twenty CDU members who voted with the opposition. A year later, however, the Supreme Court ruled the law unconstitutional and ordered that women contemplating abortion must be informed that 'the unborn child has its own right to life'. Abortion was declared '*rechtswidrig aber Straffrei*' (unlawful but exempt from punishment).[3] The judgment outraged many, but its practical effect was limited: abortion in the first trimester remained freely available.

In general, by the early twenty-first century most European women possessed—and exercised—the right and means to control their reproduction both negatively and positively. *In vitro* fertilization and artificial insemination enabled many who would otherwise not have had children to do so.

Men now took a much larger share of responsibility for child-rearing and household tasks. But in spite of changing attitudes towards gender roles, the legal and social tendency remained to regard women as the more natural child-rearers. This was reflected in custody decisions by courts upon divorce: in France in the early 1990s, for example, only 20 per cent of divorced fathers sought custody of their children and only 9 per cent were granted it.

Women's employment increased greatly in the last quarter of the century while men's declined. In Germany the proportion of men between fifteen and sixty-five who were employed fell between 1975 and 2004 from 83 per cent to 71 per cent; during the same period women's employment rose from 46 per cent to 59 per cent.[4] But women's employment did not seem to have been at the expense of men's. Rather, men tended to enter the workforce later and leave it sooner than in the previous generation. The percentage of women not in paid employment declined between 1960 and 1990: in Belgium from 73 per cent to 51 per cent, in the Netherlands from 76 per cent to 45 per cent, and in Portugal from 82 per cent to 46 per cent. Early in the new millennium women formed around half the labour force in most of eastern Europe, above 40 per cent in most of northern Europe and above 30 per cent in southern Europe.

The gap between the earnings of men and women was narrowing but remained substantial. In France women earned on average 24 per cent less than men in the early 1990s. In general, women were much more likely to be temporary or part-time employees. In Germany under 5 per cent of management positions in large companies were held by women in 2004.

Old bastions of male-only employment were nevertheless collapsing. In 1960 the first woman priest in the Swedish Lutheran Church was ordained. The Anglican Church was deeply divided over the issue but followed suit from 1994 onwards. By the 1990s women were serving in combat roles in the armed forces of several European countries. In Norway they could serve in any unit. In Britain, Denmark, and the Netherlands they served in some combat roles. In the German and Russian armed forces, however, both of which had placed some women in combat units in the Second World War, women now served only in support positions.

In politics women moved towards equality most rapidly in northern Europe. Following Margaret Thatcher's victory in Britain in 1979, Vigdís Finnbogadóttir became President of Iceland in 1980, Gro Harlem Brundtland of Norway in 1986, Edith Cresson of France in 1991, and Hanna Suchocka of Poland in 1992. In France the newly elected President Mitterrand created a Ministry of the Rights of Women in 1981. But women remained a small minority in the French parliament—only 6 per cent of the National Assembly in 1993. In 2003 women's membership in parliament ranged from 5 per cent in Ukraine (which, however, had a woman Prime Minister, Yulia Timoshenko, for a few months in 2005) to 45 per cent in Sweden. Leftist parties tended more than right-wing ones to include women in senior positions. In West Germany twenty-four of the forty-two Green members of the Bundestag in 1987 were women. Twenty per cent of Italian Communist parliamentarians in the same year were women, compared with only 2.5 per cent of Christian Democrats. Some left-wing parties set quotas for women's participation in contests for elected bodies. The Norwegian Labour Party decided in 1983 that no fewer than 40 and no more than 60 per cent of its candidates must be women. In Iceland in that year a Women's Alliance party secured representation in parliament and, by its existence, greatly increased female representation in other parties. With 221 women out of 732 MEPs in 2005 (30 per cent), the European Parliament had one of the highest proportions of female membership of any legislature in the world.

Attitudes to sexuality more generally were liberalizing. By the 1990s homosexual relations were legal throughout Europe (except perhaps in the Vatican City where they were forbidden although not explicitly mentioned in the legal code). Among the last countries to decriminalize homosexual intercourse were Russia in 1993 and Albania in 1995. In Romania a ban was effectively lifted in 1996 but homosexuals there continued to complain of discrimination; only in 2000, in fulfilment of requirements for membership of the European Union, was homosexuality fully decriminalized.

In 1988 Sweden granted certain legal rights to homosexual couples. The following year Denmark became the first country to grant a right of 'registered partnership' (a little short of legal marriage) to homosexual couples. But the established Lutheran Church was divided over the issue and would not recognize such unions. Nevertheless, in Germany in 2001 a more far-reaching law was passed granting recognition to homosexual unions for most purposes. By 2004 same-sex marriage was legal in the Netherlands and Belgium and some form of civil union was recognized in much of western Europe. Even in Spain, where homosexuality had been illegal until after the death of Franco, a law was introduced in 2004 granting homosexuals the same rights to marry, divorce, and adopt children as heterosexuals, this in spite of strong opposition from the Catholic Church.

More important than changes in law were those in attitudes: in the early twentieth century homosexuality had been regarded by respectable society as a form of deviance. It was something to be hidden and to be ashamed of. As a result many lives and careers were blighted. By the end of the century, homosexuality was chic and it was no longer necessary to keep it secret. Annual 'Gay Pride' processions took place in many major cities. Although the Roman Catholic Church still condemned homosexuality, other churches were moving towards a more relaxed view. By 2001 open homosexuals were serving as mayors of Paris and Berlin. Homosexuality remained, however, a minority taste: British men were sometimes regarded by other Europeans (for example by Edith Cresson in a notorious outburst) as particularly inclined towards their own sex; but a survey in Britain in 1994 indicated that only 3.5 per cent of men had ever had a homosexual relationship and only 1.4 per cent had had one within the previous five years. Figures for lesbianism were similar.

In the early twenty-first century sex was not only liberalized as a matter of private choice. It also appeared much more openly in the public arena. In the former Soviet Union, pornography, which had been strictly banned until the late 1980s, proliferated. Russian cinema started to copy western readiness to depict explicit sexuality. More tolerant attitudes developed to public displays of affection: kissing in public, frowned on in most parts of Europe in 1914, was generally now viewed with equanimity. The *outré* 'Love Parade', a giant festival of 'techno' music and sexual display, held almost every year after 1989 in Berlin, attracted vast crowds of participant-observers.

How Europeans live now

Compared with most of the rest of the world, life in Europe around the turn of the millennium was good. A continent-wide survey of 'lifestyles' in 1992 suggested that Europeans were generally contented with their lot: perhaps not surprisingly, the happiest nations were among the richest: the Danes, the Dutch, and the Finns, 95 per cent of whom said they were satisfied with life; the least happy were reported to be the Hungarians (58 per cent) who, perhaps not coincidentally, continued to suffer one of the highest rates of suicide.

In 2005 fifteen out of the top twenty countries in the UN Human Development Index were European. The top-ranked country was Norway, which, with its $190 billion Petroleum Fund, was also one of the richest countries per capita in the world. But wealth alone was not the whole story. Not a single other major oil producer, apart from the United States and United Kingdom, was in the top thirty. Russia, the world's second-largest oil exporter, ranked only sixty-two, below Libya and other Middle East oil producers.

The health of Europeans in 2005 had improved beyond anything that was imaginable in 1914. Diseases that had been terrible scourges virtually disappeared from Europe: typhoid, smallpox, polio, and above all, pneumonia, once known as the 'captain of the men of death'. Deaths from industrial accidents decreased significantly, thanks to safety regulations pushed through by trade unions and to the decline of dangerous heavy industries, notably coal mining. Among the medical advances of the later part of the century that particularly affected Europeans were transplants of organs such as the heart, lungs, kidney, liver, and pancreas.

Two major causes of death in the twentieth century, cancer and road accidents, began to be contained. Early diagnosis, especially of breast cancer, extended many lives. The decline in smoking in many parts of Europe from the 1960s onwards had a dramatic effect on the incidence of lung cancer. In Britain the male death rate from the disease declined by two-thirds between 1955 and 2005; by then the British rate was among the lowest in the developed world. Declining exposure to such hazards as asbestos and the combustion products of coal as well as the discovery of the carcinogenic effects of certain infectious pathogens offered long-term hope of further reductions in cancer deaths. As for the roads, over a hundred thousand people a year were dying in traffic accidents in Europe around 2000. But when set against the great increase in traffic volume, that represented an improvement from a decade or two earlier, mainly due to increased use of seat belts. In 2000 Norway and the UK were the safest countries in Europe to drive in, Greece and Lithuania the most dangerous.

Throughout the continent health was still heavily conditioned by poverty—of societies and individuals. The relatively poor former Communist countries had the highest rates of death from heart disease in the world. Standards of health care varied greatly even in western Europe. For example, hospitalizations were more than twice as frequent in France as in Spain around the turn of the millennium. The high costs of geriatric care and new medical technology forced even the wealthiest societies to dilute the welfare state principle of free health care for all. In most countries much of the cost of dental treatment, eyeglasses, hearing aids, and prescribed medicines was borne by patients.

By the early twenty-first century, total health spending had risen to between 7 and 10 per cent of GDP in western Europe (over 11 per cent in Germany and Switzerland). The state on average bore, in one form or another, four-fifths of the cost of health care. But consumers were now making a substantial contribution, not in taxes or public insurance payments but by purchase of private provision: in France, Germany, and Italy such private payments amounted to at least a quarter of health expenditure from the early 1990s onwards.

In eastern Europe the end of Communism led to the semi-collapse of health systems, especially in the CIS. Over the next fifteen years spending on health was significantly lower than in western Europe, except in the Czech Republic, Hungary, and Slovenia. In Russia it hovered around 3 per cent of GDP, though, with economic growth in the new century, it rose to 6 per cent by 2004. Private spending on health increased, particularly in Poland and Hungary; even in the supposedly public sector under-the-table payments were often required in order to obtain decent treatment. Smoking was still highly prevalent or even increasing in many east European countries and, as a result, cancer rates continued to rise. Alcoholism, drug addiction, and AIDS were also major health hazards, particularly among men in Russia. Incidence of the 'red death', tuberculosis, which had been reduced to very low levels in western Europe, increased greatly in the former Soviet Union after 1991, especially in overcrowded Russian prisons.

Dental health in Europe improved in the second half of the century. In 1914 a majority of old people on the continent no longer had any of their own teeth. Thanks to fluoridation of water, tooth loss declined steadily; but the Berlin study of the elderly in the 1990s reported that 43 per cent of the sample were completely toothless.[5] Dental disease, like other forms of health, was closely connected to socio-economic condition and ethnic origin. For example, a survey of children of asylum seekers in Geneva in 1994–5 found that children of Bosnian and Kosovar refugees had, on average, two to seven times more decayed or missing teeth than children of refugees from Africa (where dental hygiene was traditionally much better).[6]

Much of the improvement in all forms of health was due to changed eating habits. Thanks mainly to better diet, the average European male at the end of the twentieth century was at least 10 per cent taller than his counterpart two hundred years earlier. In many countries people switched from heavy traditional fare to lighter California-style salads and convenience foods. The Germans ate less sausage, the Irish fewer potatoes. Younger people tended not to eat at fixed mealtimes but to 'graze' whenever they felt like a nibble. The old-fashioned British breakfast of bacon and eggs or kipper gave way to fruit juice, cereal, and yoghourt. Of course, such changes were not universal or evenly distributed. They occurred more slowly in the north of England and in eastern Europe. In Albania, Britain, Germany, and Ireland in 2004 more than a fifth of the population was obese.

Clothing, like eating, became less formal and ritualized. There was a growing tendency towards more casual dress and towards less differentiation between classes in clothing. A century earlier a person's place in society could easily be detected by what he wore. Now it required a keener eye to differentiate among the wearers of mass-produced clothing in crowds at football matches or other public events. Improvements in central heating reduced the prevalence of heavy woollen underclothing, 'long johns' and the like, save in the very coldest parts of the continent. Headgear also changed and often disappeared. The movement of women to towns led many to discard the head-shawls characteristic of their peasant forebears (though many Muslim women wore them for religious reasons).

Housing throughout the continent changed beyond recognition in the course of the century. In 1914 a majority of Europeans, like their ancestors since the dawn of man, huddled for shelter from the elements, hugger-mugger in miserable rural hovels or filthy urban slums. In 2007 most lived in homes with indoor plumbing, central heating, cheap electric light and power, and a reasonable amount of room. The Netherlands had the newest housing stock in Europe: three-quarters of all homes had been built since 1945. By the late twentieth century central heating was a standard fixture in most new construction throughout the continent, though run-down systems in eastern Europe often produced heat sporadically and uncontrollably. With fewer children, Europeans had more free space: even in one of the poorest countries of the continent, Moldova, the average apartment in 1996 had 57 sq. m.: city-dwellers had 18 sq. m. per head and country people 22 sq. m. In Russia density per person decreased from 16 to 20 sq. m. between 1990 and 2002. In western Europe in the late 1990s homes were larger: in France the average was 43 sq. m. per head, in Ireland 33 sq. m., and in Portugal 28 sq. m. The number of inhabitants per room was much lower in the west: 0.5 in Germany and 0.6 in Norway compared with one in Poland and 1.2 in Russia.

Nevertheless, even some of the richest countries in Europe still had large concentrations of sub-standard housing. In Vienna in 1990 58,000 homes, comprising 8 per cent of permanently occupied dwellings, lacked indoor toilets or water supply. In 1991 49 per cent of dwellings in both Italy and Luxembourg were judged 'unfit, lacking amenities, or in serious disrepair'.[7] Conditions for poor people in eastern Europe remained primitive and in many cases grim. Maintenance of public housing under Communism had been minimal with the result that much of the stock was in a dismal condition by 1989. The continuation, under political pressure, of subsidized rent policies in the early post-Communist period rendered modernization and repairs difficult. In Russia in 2002 more than a quarter of homes had no running water and nearly a third had no sewage disposal.

In some rich countries rental housing remained common: in Germany, for example, 62 per cent of occupancies in 1995 were rental (most were private leases but a large part 'social housing'). In the last quarter of the century the heavy promotion of public housing by left-wing governments gave way, especially in Spain, Italy, Ireland, and Britain, to a more market-oriented approach and to the privatization of public housing. By 1994 only 18 per cent of households in the EU lived in public housing. And by the end of the century more than half the population of the EU were owner-occupiers.

In some parts of eastern Europe private ownership of homes was widespread even before the large-scale privatization of public housing that followed the fall of Communism. In Hungary, for example, three-quarters of homes were owner-occupied in the late 1980s. In Czechoslovakia and Poland houses that had been taken into state ownership were in many cases restored to their original owners after 1989.

Decreased availability of public housing led to an increase in homelessness in many countries. Growth in the number of 'street people' was also fed by alcoholism and drug abuse and by the release of large numbers of mental hospital patients under so-called 'care in the community' policies. In Britain a total of over 400,000 homeless people was reported in 1991, a 165 per cent increase since 1979. In France in 1994 there were said to be 627,000, more than 1 per cent of the population. The problem was most acute in the former Soviet Union where, in the 1990s, as in the years after the revolution, hordes of orphans and runaways were wandering the country in search of food and shelter. Moscow city authorities estimated that there were thirty thousand people sleeping rough in 1995 (unofficial estimates ranged as high as 300,000); the number of hostel places for such people in the city at that time was twenty-five. In 2002 there were estimated to be more than four million people in Russia without homes, of whom half had been without fixed abode for more than two years. Mendicancy, which had practically vanished from the streets of most European cities in the 1960s, made a striking return by the 1990s: beggars became a common sight from London to Moscow.

More than three-quarters of the population of Europe in 2004 lived in urban settlements. One-third of the urban population lived in cities of half a million or more people. The largest city in Europe in 2005 was once again Istanbul (as it had been for much of its history, under its old name of Constantinople), with about 11.3 million inhabitants. Moscow was second with 10.4 million and London third with 7.4 million. The proportion of city-dwellers in 2004 ranged from 44 per cent in Albania to 97 per cent in Belgium. In advanced countries, however, where most of the population already lived in cities, the process of urbanization had slowed or even gone into reverse as segments of the middle class moved to suburban or rural areas within easy commuting reach of the workplace, and as those who could afford it among the growing elderly population chose to retire to the countryside.

Eastern and southern Europe were still more heavily rural and agricultural around the turn of the century than the rest of the continent. In Romania more than a third of all workers were farmers. In most of western Europe the percentage had declined to under 5 per cent, in Britain to under 1 per cent. Not only the old heavy industries such as steel and mining but also newer consumer goods manufacturing industries declined as sources of employment, owing to mechanization and globalization. In 1914 large-scale heavy industrial employment had been a characteristic of the most advanced economies. Now countries with the largest industrial employment sectors included both some of the richest, such as Germany and Italy, and some of the poorest, such as Belarus and Macedonia. A striking feature of the new occupational distribution at the start of the twenty-first century was the growth of the community and social services sector. In Britain over 80 per cent of the labour force was engaged in service occupations. This was one part of the economy that women workers dominated nearly everywhere, though males still generally held more senior positions.

The second half of the twentieth century was marked by accelerating change in class structures: the peasantry continued to dwindle; the urban working class shrank; the middle class grew. Within classes, there were major shifts in occupational distribution: from manual to non-manual labour, from less skilled to more skilled, and from low-grade to professional, administrative, and managerial jobs. In France, for example, those working in the professions and in *cadres supérieurs et moyens* grew from 1.7 million in 1954 to 7.4 million in 1990. In the latter year, for the first time in recorded history, there were fewer than a million independent peasant farmers in France; by 2005 there were only 600,000. In Italy the proportion of the working population engaged in agriculture shrank from 28 per cent in 1960 to 7.5 per cent by 1995. In not a single country in Europe did the agricultural proportion increase over that period. In western Europe the traditional working class of manual workers was everywhere a minority by the first decade of the new millennium. Before 1989 these trends transcended the Iron Curtain and they continued unabated in eastern Europe after the fall of Communism. In the Czech Republic, for example, the proportion of farm workers in the labour force declined steadily, from 7 per cent in 1983 to 1.7 per cent in 1997; and of unskilled workers from 31 per cent to 20 per cent.

By the end of the twentieth century, therefore, a great transformation had taken place in the shape of social relations in Europe. The two largest classes of 1914, the peasantry and the urban proletariat, had greatly diminished in importance. The class that was now growing into a majority, the white-collared middle class, was no longer synonymous with the 'bourgeoisie', as that term was used in the nineteenth century. It was a possessing class in the sense that its members often owned their own dwellings and held investments, mainly through pension funds, in stocks and shares. But it was not a property-owning class in the sense that, like the French peasantry in the nineteenth century, it saw its basic interest as lying in the defence of small lots of agricultural land; nor in the sense that, like the British industrial middle class of the nineteenth century, it saw capital and the right to use it with complete freedom as a fundamental condition of survival and therefore as a tenet of faith. Indeed, the emerging middle-class majority of the early twenty-first century was hardly a class in the traditional sense at all. Unlike the traditional proletariat or peasantry, it had little collective sense of social identity. This almost classless class came to dominate a society in which the very concept of class was being drained of much of its meaning.

With the decline of the working class and the enfeeblement of socialism as an ideology, the political and economic power, as well as the membership, of labour unions declined. In Britain, for example, they held their own only in the public sector. By 2004 75 per cent of workers in the EU were non-union. Union membership was above half the workforce in only eight of the twenty-five member states of the EU. In eastern Europe, where membership had been, in effect, compulsory in the Communist period, it declined drastically in the 1990s. Even in Poland, birthplace of free trade unionism in eastern Europe, it stood at only 14 per cent.

How Europeans communicate

Several great transportation projects in the last quarter of the twentieth century exemplified the trend towards European integration. The 1,074-metre Bosporus suspension bridge, completed in 1974, was the first fixed link between Europe and Asia since the pontoon bridge constructed by Mandrocles of Samos for the Persian Emperor Darius in 490 BC. In 1988 a second, slightly longer bridge was opened a little further north. Growth in traffic across the waterway led to the construction of an 8.5-mile underground railway tunnel, scheduled to be completed by 2007. These connections contributed to the huge expansion of the 'Asiatic side' of Istanbul. The Channel Tunnel, between Dover and Calais, planned for nearly two hundred years, opened to rail traffic in 1994. It proved an engineering triumph but a commercial catastrophe. In 1992 the Swiss electorate voted to approve a 57-kilometre-long St Gotthard high-speed railway tunnel under the Alps that would improve communication between the industrial heartlands of Germany and Italy and ease environmental damage caused by road traffic through Switzerland. Upon its completion, scheduled for 2015, this would be the longest railway tunnel in the world. Thus natural obstacles that had troubled invaders since ancient times no longer presented barriers to travellers.

In 1914 railways carried much more freight than road transport. By the early twenty-first century about 80 per cent of freight in western Europe and 55 per cent in the former CIS travelled by road. Increased prosperity in eastern Europe in the early twenty-first century led to great increases in car ownership, though the number of passenger vehicles was still lower than in the west. Russia, for example, had 148 cars per thousand people in 2002 compared with 462 in Spain and over 500 in Italy, Germany, and Switzerland. Albania, Moldova, and Turkey still had under 70 per thousand. After 1989 the great motorway systems of the west were extended also to eastern Europe with the result that it became possible to drive from one end of the continent to the other in comparative ease in two or three days.

New telecommunications technology also brought radical changes in social behaviour. The computer revolution, both in the workplace and the home, affected almost every aspect of daily life. The private letter faded out of general use as people increasingly resorted to electronic mail. The portable cellular phone rapidly displaced the fixed landline home telephone. In most European countries in 2005 there were more than 500 mobile phone subscribers per thousand of population. In Italy, Sweden, and Luxembourg there were more mobile phones than people. Russia was among the laggards with only 120 per thousand; even backward Albania had 358 per thousand.

By 2005 260 million people in Europe had access to the internet, amounting to a 36 per cent penetration rate. Increasingly they were connected by high-speed broadband. The rate of connection was highest in the richer countries of the European Union such as Sweden (74 per cent), much lower in new members such as Poland (28 per cent) and very low in the poorer countries of eastern Europe such as Russia (16 per cent) and Ukraine (6 per cent). As internet usage ballooned, television audiences shrank and fragmented. The spread of cable, digital, and satellite television and the multiplication of local and specialist stations reduced the great monolithic audiences enjoyed a generation earlier by state-run broadcasting monopolies. In 2004 85 million European subscribers were spending more than €20 billion per annum on 'pay-per-view'(PPV) television.

Information diffusion changed radically. Newspaper circulations declined and newspapers changed in character, printing in colour, producing more magazine and 'lifestyle' sections, and disseminating round-the-clock internet editions. The tendency to press concentration accelerated as western publishing concerns bought east European papers.

The most fundamental form of human communication, language, was deeply affected by the trends towards political and economic integration in the continent. The massive language-translating apparatus of the European Union's bureaucracy was a tribute to the very national prides that the EU was designed to surmount. The Union employed a veritable legion of translators, at a cost of €220 million a year, to render intelligible more than a million pages per annum of official documents, this quite apart from the battalions of simultaneous interpreters deployed at meetings. But by the early twenty-first century English was edging out French and German as the main official language of EU business. The European Central Bank conducted all of its business in English, which was also becoming the main working language of the Commission. Only the European Court of Justice worked exclusively in French.

In 1914 German had been the number one language of science, French of diplomacy, Latin of prayer, and English (perhaps) of business. In the new millennium English was Europeans' common second language, the Latin of the new Europe.

In 1956 a leading French intellectual could still claim that 'if English is becoming more and more the language of business, French remains the language of culture'.[8] But such pretensions grew ever more unrealistic. The French government's Minister for Francophonie laboured to maintain the status of French as a world language. The *loi Toubon* of 1994 forbade use of foreign words without translation in fields such as advertising. French committees of linguistic purity tried to lay down that such terms as *toile d'araignée mondiale* and *page d'accueil* should prevail over 'worldwide web' and 'home page' but with limited effect: a sample search of the internet in 2001, limited to French-language sites, produced more than ten times as many returns for 'worldwide web' as for its officially endorsed francophone equivalent. Linguistic nationalism dictated that in France, almost alone in the continent, English should not be the sole language of communication used by air traffic controllers: it took a fatal accident through consequent misunderstanding by a monoglot British pilot in 2001 to force reconsideration of this policy.

Signs of creeping English linguistic imperialism could be seen in advertising all over the continent. Many academic journals published in France and Germany now routinely carried English synopses. Most significantly, medical and scientific journals began to appear in English only. English also insinuated itself into the general press. In 2005 a random day's *Jurnalul*

Național (Bucharest) contained references to 'videoclip', 'teleshopping', and 'download-eze'. The cultural section of the same day's *Expressen* (Stockholm) sported headlines with such 'Swenglish' words as 'insidertips', 'output', 'crazy' and 'Queerneval'.[9] Anglicisms invaded every other language. In Greece, for example, chic stores in the upper-class Kolonaki district of Athens took to displaying signs in English without Greek translation. The foremost private universities in Turkey operated entirely in English. By the end of the decade English was also paramount on the internet. French capitalism proved unable to resist 'le venture capital', 'le hot money', and 'le takeover'. In 2005 an estimated 97 per cent of German university students knew English. Out of 2,888 translated works of fiction published in Germany in 2003, 1,072 were from English. The next largest group, translations from French, numbered just 227. On the other hand, only twenty-eight German novels were translated into English in that year. A similarly uneven 'literary balance of trade', reflecting the dominance of Anglo-American culture, could be found in most other European countries. In eastern Europe, where Russian had been imposed as a second language for half a century, and where German and French were widely known before the war, English became the foreign language of first choice in schools. English-language private schools for the children of the nouveaux riches sprouted in Russia and in central Europe.

The break-up of the USSR brought attempts to revive languages such as Ukrainian and Belarusian that had been smothered in the Soviet period. But even the Ukrainian Cabinet in the early 1990s conducted its meetings in Russian.[10] Belarusian was made the official language in Belarus in 1990 but only 10 per cent of the population used it in everyday intercourse and President Lukashenka was at one with a majority of his countrymen in deriding the language and expressing preference for Russian.[11] In 1995 Russian was restored as a joint official language and thereafter Belarusian once again declined. In rural areas a hybrid dialect of the two languages known as *trasyanka* (literally a mixture of hay and straw) was used but was denounced by language purists and became an object of fierce political controversy in the 1990s. In spite of much nationalist posturing, Russian remained the lingua franca of the CIS.

The small languages of Europe continue to decline: for example, Ladino (or Judaeo-Español, spoken until the early twentieth century among the Sephardic Jews of the Balkans and Turkey), Lappish (of which various dialects were spoken by a few thousand people in Norway, Sweden, and

Finland) and Livonian (a language akin to Finnish, once spoken in parts of Latvia). Yiddish, the first language of millions of east European Jews in 1914, had been wiped out by Hitler and Stalin and was now spoken in Europe only by a remnant of ultra-orthodox Jews in Antwerp and a few other cities. In many cases governments and/or private enthusiasts made special efforts to help preserve such languages but with limited success. In Ireland, where compulsory Gaelicization measures were enacted in the 1930s, the number of native speakers of Irish (Gaelic) in the *Gaeltacht* halved between 1922 and 1939. By 1990 only 180,000 people, 5 per cent of the population, in the Irish Republic spoke Irish as compared with 582,000, 12 per cent of the population of the whole island, at the 1911 census. Scottish Gaelic and Breton waned in spite of earnest efforts to sustain them by governments and the European Union. British government efforts to preserve Welsh slowed its decline but did not reverse it: 16 per cent of the population of Wales spoke the national language at the 2001 census, compared with 37 per cent in 1931.

On the other hand, Lusatian, the language of the Sorbs or Wends, a Slavic ethnic enclave in East Germany, survived precariously. Romanche, recognized since 1938 as one of the four national languages of Switzerland (actually a generic name for two Celtic-Roman dialects used mainly in Grisons and Engadine), was still spoken as a native tongue by forty thousand people, a number little changed since the early part of the century. Regional autonomy in Spain after 1979 gave an impetus to the revival of Catalan, spoken by more than 60 per cent of the population in the *Principat*. Only about 20 per cent of the population of Euskadi, however, spoke Basque.

In Norway language remained a matter of political and social controversy, with sharp distinctions among the various dialects: *Riksmål* ('national language'), traditional standard Norwegian, was paradoxically the least 'Norwegian' form, since it was heavily influenced by Danish; *Bokmål* ('book language'), which developed out of it, was generally held to be less conservative; *Nynorsk* ('new Norwegian') was supposedly, in spite of its name, the more authentic, 'old' Norwegian dialect. *Riksmål* and *Bokmål* were more common in newspapers and belles-lettres, though some important literary figures wrote in *Nynorsk*. *Bokmål* and *Nynorsk* (known before 1929 as *Landsmål*) had both been officially recognized since 1885 and continued to be used in the liturgy of the state church, education, and, later, in broadcasting. *Bokmål* was more prevalent in Oslo and in northern and eastern Norway; *Nynorsk* in rural areas.

In many countries in the late twentieth century, official efforts to dam or guide the flow of living language were engulfed by popular resistance. France and Germany tried to enforce language simplification measures. Germany, for example, officially abolished most uses of the letter ß, though with only limited success. In Greece, the PASOK government encountered initial resistance to its efforts to promote the demotic language at the expense of the artificial, formal, literary *katharevousa*. Conservatives objected to the abolition of breathing marks and to the reduction of study of ancient texts in schools. Some of these works were restored to the curriculum in the 1990s but by then the victory of the demotic was clear.

Education in the new millennium

In 1914 fewer than one in ten children in Europe attended secondary schools; by 2000 over nine out of ten did so and the majority stayed on until eighteen. In general, northern Europe was better educated than southern and boasted the highest secondary school completion rates. Public expenditure on education greatly increased in the later part of the twentieth century. It more than doubled as a proportion of GNP between 1950 and 1992 in the fifteen (in 1992) countries of the European Union. In Sweden it rose during that period from 3.5 per cent to 8.3 per cent, the highest in Europe.

In the former Soviet Union education spending rose from 1.7 per cent of GDP in 1950 to 7.6 per cent in 1975. In 1991 Yeltsin had promised that it would be raised to 10 per cent; instead, in the following year it fell back to just 3.4 per cent. In real terms educational expenditure in Russia shrank by no less than 73 per cent between 1990 and 1994. The school leaving age was lowered and the proportion of children aged fifteen to nineteen attending school declined. Yet the CIS countries continued to employ much larger proportions of their labour forces in their education systems than other European countries, nearly 10 per cent in the case of Russia in the early 1990s, almost twice as many as in other advanced economies. The inevitable consequence was that the real value of teachers' salaries collapsed, in Ukraine, for example, to just 10 dollars a month in 1994. Many teachers in the CIS were obliged to moonlight in other jobs, to give private lessons, to charge for good grades or school certificates, or to flee the profession.

Most pupils in Europe in the late twentieth century attended free public schools. In Germany the private sector remained quite small: about 5 per cent of pupils were enrolled in private, mainly upper-level secondary schools. Elsewhere demand for private education was growing. In Italy around 7 per cent of children attended private schools. About 8 per cent of children in Britain attended independent fee-charging schools that were mainly nurseries for the business and professional classes. In spite of its traditional hostility to what it termed 'educational apartheid', the Labour government of Tony Blair, like all its predecessors, did nothing to interfere with the privileges, including tax concessions, of the private sector.[12] So-called 'faith schools', particularly Church of England primary, Catholic primary and secondary, as well as a few Jewish and Muslim schools, received state subventions. In the Netherlands and Belgium more than two-thirds of children attended private denominational schools at public expense. In eastern Europe hundreds of new private schools opened after the fall of Communism. Most catered mainly to the children of the nouveaux riches. Many were confessionally based. In Hungary by 1999 8 per cent of secondary schools and one-fifth of *gymnasiums* (the most prestigious type of academic secondary school) were private religious institutions that enjoyed some tax-payer support. Nevertheless, in many of these cases, any religious motive of parents in sending children to such schools was secondary to other social and educational objectives.

More than any other country, France adhered to the principle of *laïcité* (secularism), particularly in public ceremonial and education. Yet about a fifth of pupils attended non-state, mainly Catholic schools. More 'zapped' between private and public education; including the zappers, more than a third of French children received a religious education. An issue that aroused huge controversy from 1989 onwards was the question whether Muslim girls might wear a religious headscarf (*foulard/hijab*) in state schools. In 2004 the headscarf, together with other religious symbols such as Jewish skullcaps, Sikh turbans, and large crosses, were banned from all state schools. The *affaire du foulard* provoked violent controversy and fuelled racist xenophobia as well as Islamist extremism.

In other parts of Europe religious symbolism was permitted or even mandated in state schools. In staunchly Catholic Bavaria, for example, where, as in the rest of Germany, schools were still organized mainly on a confessional basis, crosses were traditionally hung on the wall in classrooms. In 1995 the Federal Constitutional Court ruled against the practice on the ground that 'taken together with universal compulsory schooling, crosses in schoolrooms mean that pupils are, during teaching, under State auspices and with no possibility of escape, confronted with this symbol and compelled to learn "under the cross"'.[13] The judgment did not, however, lead to the disappearance of most crucifixes in classrooms, since it was interpreted to mean that they could remain unless there were an objection.

In 1914 only a tiny proportion of the population, mainly upper-and middle-class males, attended universities. By 2005 a larger proportion of the population was gaining a higher education than ever before: in advanced countries over a third of the age cohort did so. In Sweden, Finland, and Norway more than four-fifths were receiving some form of tertiary education in 2004. But students were still disproportionately drawn from the middle class. In Germany 49 per cent of children of civil servants attended university in 1988; only 8 per cent of children of blue-collar workers did so. Things were no different in eastern Europe. In the Czech Republic in the 1990s, for example, children of parents with tertiary education were eight times as likely to go to university themselves as those of parents with less than higher secondary education; nor was this a result of the fall of Communism; it merely represented a further strengthening of a trend visible there since the 1960s.

Inequalities between the sexes in higher education were diminishing. In Britain the heavily male composition of Oxford and Cambridge had changed in the course of the 1970s, as nearly all of the two ancient universities' colleges, most hitherto single-sex, decided to admit both men and women. But although women were now a majority of the student population almost everywhere (Turkey and Switzerland were the only significant exceptions), differentiations between the sexes in registration for certain subjects and institutions were still highly visible. For example, the student bodies in the French *grandes écoles*, such as the *Ecole normale supérieure* and the *Ecole polytechnique*, remained overwhelmingly male.

In higher as in secondary education there was a trend towards private financing of teaching, research, and institutional structures. In Scandinavia, public attachment to the principle of free higher education remained strong. But in much of the rest of western Europe many students were required to pay at least a share of the cost of their education. In eastern Europe too some students were obliged to pay fees. By 2001 at least a third of university students in Russia were estimated to be paying full fees.

The leisure age

Europeans—and not only the unemployed—worked less in the new millennium than at any previous time in their history. In 2004 French workers in employment worked 10 per cent and Germans 6 per cent fewer hours in the year than they had done in 1990. Europeans also worked much less than people in other advanced countries. Dutch workers, for example, averaged 25 per cent fewer hours than Americans. Productivity in the European Union in 2003 remained lower than that of the United States, although the gap had narrowed since 1970. Far more than ever before, work was a part-time activity. 'Leisure services', in their various forms, now constituted major industries, employing millions.

In the early twenty-first century, as a hundred years earlier, drinking was probably the second-most popular leisure activity. The EU was the heaviest drinking region of the world. The Portuguese, Swiss, Italians, and French consumed the most wine. Czechs and Germans were top of the beer-drinking league, an achievement the more remarkable in that they were also very heavy consumers of spirits. In Scandinavia strict controls on the sale of alcohol remained in force. In Sweden the only retail outlets for alcohol above 3.5 per cent proof were *Systembolaget*, a government-licensed chain of stores. In England and Wales, on the other hand, where violence by drunken young louts developed into a serious threat to public safety on weekend evenings in many cities, the government relaxed the hitherto strict licensing laws in 2005 so as to permit round-the-clock opening hours in pubs. In Russia, where forty thousand people a year were said to be dying from consumption of impure alcohol, President Putin called in 2005 for the resumption by the state of its monopoly on the sale of liquor.

Tobacco after the 1990s became what alcohol had been in some parts of Europe before 1914—a highly popular but increasingly disreputable drug. Although cigarette smoking declined from its peak in the 1960s as evidence accumulated of its adverse effects on health, around 40 per cent of adult Europeans still smoked in the early twenty-first century. In Russia, Spain, and much of the Balkans, average annual consumption was more than six cigarettes per head per day in 2004. By 2005 Ireland, Norway, Sweden, and Scotland had enacted total bans on smoking in enclosed public places. Heavy taxation was also deployed as a deterrent: a packet of cigarettes in Britain in 2004 cost more than twice as much as in Germany and nearly ten times as much as in Poland. The European Union forbade nearly all tobacco advertising and required outsize health warnings on all cigarette packets. But such efforts were not much more effective than those of teetotal campaigners a century earlier.

Sport, albeit often only as a spectator activity, boomed in the late twentieth century and became big business. Shares in football clubs were quoted on stock exchanges. A generation earlier, professional football players had been paid little more than any other worker; now stars received salaries in the millions. The top tennis players competing at Wimbledon in the 1960s were all amateurs; by the end of the century they too were millionaire professionals. In 2005 leading athletes such as the Russian-born tennis star Maria Sharapova, the German racing driver Michael Schumacher, the English footballer David Beckham, and the golfer Annika Sörenstam were among the highest-paid professionals in the world.

Some sports engendered a nasty tendency to violence, especially in Britain and Italy. As in ancient Rome and Byzantium, fans of rival teams would engage in fighting. Sometimes the combat took on a political, racial, or sectarian character. In 1985 at the Heysel stadium in Brussels English football supporters went on a rampage during a match between Liverpool and Juventus: a wall collapsed and thirty-nine spectators died.

Foreign tourism, once regarded as a luxury, was now almost a birthright. France was the most popular destination in Europe in 2004 with 75 million visitors. For some regions in Europe, such as the Mediterranean coast and scenic mountain areas of Switzerland and Austria, tourism became the foremost industry.

Hunting, shooting, and fishing were still popular, although increasingly under attack from many sides. In Italy environmentalists sought to limit the hunting of wild birds. This was a very widespread activity: 1.5 million Italians held shooting licences in 1990. Hunters there also used traps to catch wildfowl, doves, orioles, hoopoes, and even small birds such as nightingales and robins. In some regions of the country trees were virtually denuded of birds as a result. The griffon vulture, once common in the peninsula, could now be found only in Sardinia. Environmentalists forced a referendum on the issue in June 1990 and produced a majority in favour of a limiting law; but the number of ballots cast was below the minimum necessary to render the result binding. The slaughter did not abate. In Britain fox-hunting on horseback with hounds remained popular, particularly among the rural upper classes and aspirants to such status, in spite of a sometimes violent campaign against the sport. Opposition from animal rights campaigners was tinged with class antagonism. After several years of bitter debate a bill for abolition was approved in 2004; but not before an unprecedented incursion by protesters on to the floor of the House of Commons.

Old forms of mass entertainment were being transformed by new technology. The cinema faced a new threat in the form of large high-definition television sets that showed films bought or borrowed and viewed at home. The giant film palaces of the mid-twentieth century had now mostly been divided up into small 'multiplex' auditoriums. Videotape recorders, common items of household equipment in the 1970s, were retired around 2000 in favour of DVD players. By 2004 more than half the homes in western Europe were equipped with them. Meanwhile compact discs had replaced vinyl long-playing records and cassette tapes as the most popular format for recorded music. Vinyl discs disappeared from the market in western Europe and sales of pre-recorded cassette tapes also declined. By 1991 27 per cent of homes in Britain were equipped with compact disc players. But by 2007 the pre-recorded CD too was on the way out as popular music increasingly was being marketed over the internet and downloaded direct by consumers onto computers and mobile electronic listening devices.

A better-educated population resorted to more highbrow recreations. In West Germany 62.4 million visits were paid to museums in 1986 as against only 7.9 million in 1958. In spite of repeated forecasts of the demise of the book, the number of titles published rose rapidly, in France, for example, from 38,000 in 1998 to 52,000 in 2004.

Yet the coarseness of much public discourse and the vulgarization of many forms of aesthetic expression, literary, theatrical, musical, and artistic, suggested that green shoots of barbarism were sprouting within this most sophisticated civilization. Did the most literate, best-educated, most leisured generation in European history have a value system that could cope with the challenges that beset it from all sides?

Values in a post-Christian era

Europeans of the new millennium were the first post-Christian generation in history. Religious attitudes and behaviour were characterized by continuing, albeit uneven, secularization. The least religious countries were

Protestant north European ones such as Estonia, Great Britain, and Sweden; the most religious were Poland and Romania.

State churches were maintained in Belgium (Roman Catholic), England (Anglican), Scotland (Presbyterian), Greece (Orthodox), and Norway, Denmark, and Iceland (Lutheran). Finland continued to have three established sects: the Russian Orthodox Church, and the separate Finnish and Swedish Evangelical Lutheran churches. Romania re-established her Orthodox Church as a state Church after the fall of Communism. But elsewhere, as societies became more multi-confessional and pluralist, monopolist state religions receded, giving way to the conception of churches as voluntary associations, even if with a privileged relationship to the state, for example in taxation. The Swedish Lutheran Church was disestablished in 2000, with the compulsory Church tax replaced by a voluntary levy to be used to support all religious denominations. In Italy the 1929 Concordat with the Vatican was revised in 1984: Catholicism was no longer to be the state religion but it retained various privileges. The new law also enabled other sects and religions, such as the Waldensians (Protestants of pre-Reformation origin, numbering about 45,000, mainly in Piedmont) and Italy's small but ancient Jewish community, to be granted an *intesa* (accord) that would give them state recognition and equivalent rights.

Religious rites of passage, such as baptism, church marriage, and burial, fell out of fashion. Cremation was taking over from religious interment as the predominant means of disposal of the dead in many parts of Europe. It was pioneered in Britain, where the percentage of cremations rose from 4 per cent in 1939 to over 70 per cent by the 1990s. Elsewhere the practice spread rapidly, particularly in Scandinavia. Although sanctioned by the Roman Catholic Church in 1964, cremation remained less popular in Catholic countries. In 1999, for example, the rate was only 4 per cent in Italy as against 68 per cent in Sweden.

Britain, with the possible exception of Sweden, was the most secular country in Europe. One study in 2003 reported a 'terminal decline of virtually all the large, organised conventional Christian Churches in Britain' as well as 'the permanent decline of the common and pervasive Christian culture to which most Britons had adhered . . . for centuries'.[14] In once-Calvinist Scotland, where the General Assembly of the Church of Scotland had once thundered forth pronouncements whose echoes reverberated across the world, the Catholic Church was now the more vital spiritual force, though it too was in decline. All told, only 12 per cent of the population of Britain considered themselves church members. Even fewer attended church more than very occasionally and these were disproportionately old people. Sunday school enrolment, around 77 per cent in the early twentieth century, was estimated at 5 to 8 per cent in the 1990s. The number of clergy fell in the course of the century by half in England and by two-thirds in Scotland. What the British had a generation earlier scorned as the 'continental Sunday' had now become a venerated British institution even in Scotland: shops, cinemas, pubs, and restaurants stayed open till all hours, often in defiance of antique Sunday observance statutes that were still on the books. Many churches were sold off and turned into restaurants, bingo halls, or discount warehouses. The only exception to the general trend was Northern Ireland: there, perhaps because sectarianism remained the main marker of collective identity, secularization was much less pronounced than in the rest of the United Kingdom.

Catholicism was in a downward spiral almost everywhere. In Italy in the late 1980s only one-third of the population was still attending church, as against around two-thirds in the 1950s. In Spain, once the most militantly Catholic country in Europe, church attendance declined substantially in the post-Franco era. At Maynooth seminary in Ireland, where there had been six hundred students in the 1960s, there were sixty in 2005. In Ireland, as in other countries, the Church lost legitimacy as a result of a series of scandals, particularly those involving paedophile priests. In France church attendance, christenings, church weddings, and belief in God all declined sharply between the 1960s and the 1990s. By 2005 there were only 22,000 priests in the country, compared with 45,000 in 1960. The number of nuns had shrunk by nearly half to 52,000. Over 60 per cent of priests were over sixty and only 5 per cent under forty. The number of ordinations per year, formerly about a thousand, had dwindled to a hundred. In order to minister to its dwindling flock, the Gallican Church was obliged to import new priests from francophone Africa. The 'crisis of vocation' affected most of western Europe, as the number of recruits to the priesthood declined everywhere.

John Paul II's papacy from 1978 to 2005 was the second longest of modern times (after Pius IX, 1846–78). He created 232 cardinals, the great majority in his own deeply conservative mould. He undertook 104 pastoral visits outside Italy, including eight to his native Poland. In 2001 he became the first Pope to visit Greece since the Schism of 1054. There he asked forgiveness for acts of omission or commission against 'Orthodox brothers and sisters', specifically apologizing for the sack of Constantinople during the Fourth Crusade in 1204.[15] His was an energetic, intellectually coherent, and politically successful pontificate. But measured by the criteria of religious sociology it was an abysmal failure; the numbers of the faithful steadily declined.

The one area where Christianity could record some gains was in eastern Europe after the end of the Cold War. Notwithstanding three-quarters of a century of Communism, only 5 per cent of the population of Russia in 2000 defined themselves as atheists. Half the population claimed to belong to a religious denomination and nearly two-thirds pronounced themselves in some sense 'religious persons'. On the other hand, only 9 per cent attended religious services more than once a month. Overall, church attendance in the Baltic states, Russia, Belarus, and Ukraine was twice as high as in western Europe; and whereas it was decreasing in the west, it was increasing in the former Soviet states.

In many areas religion was closely associated with nationalism. In Lithuania Roman Catholicism and in Latvia and Estonia Lutheranism reasserted themselves as national faiths. In south-west Ukraine (eastern Galicia), where the Greek-rite Catholic Church had been suppressed under Soviet rule, conflict broke out between Orthodox and Catholics: each accused the other of stealing church property and souls. Elsewhere in Ukraine further divisions, replete with accusations of sexual misconduct and even murder, appeared within the Orthodox fold between those who remained faithful to the Moscow Patriarchate and followers of the Ukrainian Orthodox Church, which declared itself independent of Moscow under the Patriarchate of Kiev. This sect was not to be confused with the smaller Autocephalous Ukrainian Orthodox Church, founded in 1921, suppressed in 1930, and revived in 1991, which also insisted on its distinct character. The two latter churches were identified with nationalist feeling in west-central Ukraine, whereas the Moscow-leaning Orthodox found support mainly in the east of the country with its large Russian population.

The religious revival in eastern Europe, however, was not universal and there seemed little prospect of the churches recovering the position in society that they had held before the advent of Communism. There was no question of returning the churches' large landholdings nor of restoring their once dominant role in education, though some church schools were reopened and Catholic universities revived.

In Poland, where the Catholic Church had been at the heart of the struggle against Communism, it found difficulty after 1989 in coming to terms with a more open, pluralist society. It secured the reintroduction of religious instruction in public schools but, after a long struggle, it failed to outlaw abortion. Its opposition to sex education in schools, its failure to dissociate itself in the popular mind from the militantly right-wing Radio Marya, and the equivocal attitude of the primate, Cardinal Glemp, towards anti-Semitism all contributed to the Church's loss of authority, especially in more sophisticated, educated social strata.

Whereas the Protestant churches of Europe, with only a few exceptions, focused their efforts on evolving in harmony with a rapidly changing society, the response of the Roman Catholic Church was, in general, different. Under John Paul II a kind of Counter-Reformation set in. On such issues as homosexuality, birth control, abortion, female priesthood, and euthanasia, the Church resisted demands for change. Echoing the denunciations of almost everything modern in the 'Syllabi of Errors' issued by his predecessors Pius IX (in *Quanta Cura*, 1864) and Pius X (in the decree *Lamentabili sane exitu*, 1907), John Paul II warned, in his encyclical *Evangelium vitae* (1995):

> A new cultural climate is developing and taking hold, which gives crimes against life a new and—if possible—even more sinister character, giving rise to further grave concern: broad sectors of public opinion justify certain crimes against life in the name of the rights of individual freedom, and on this basis they claim not only exemption from punishment but even authorization by the State, so that these things can be done with total freedom and indeed with the free assistance of health-care systems.... We are confronted by an even larger reality, which can be described as a veritable structure of sin. This reality is characterized by the emergence of a culture which denies solidarity and in many cases takes the form of a veritable 'culture of death'.[16]

John Paul's successor, the German Cardinal Joseph Ratzinger, who took the name Benedict XVI upon his election in 2005, had previously served as Prefect of the Congregation for the Doctrine of the Faith, successor to the Inquisition. His homily to his fellow cardinals on the eve of his election signalled his uncompromising hostility to modernist trends: 'Today, having a clear faith based on the Creed of the Church is often labelled as fundamentalism. Whereas relativism, that is, letting oneself be "tossed here and there, carried about by every wind of doctrine," seems the only attitude that can cope with modern times. We are building a dictatorship of relativism that does not recognize anything as definitive and whose ultimate goal consists solely of one's own ego and desires.'[17]

Many non-Catholic observers would have agreed with his diagnosis. There was a discernible and measurable rise in individualism in much of Europe as well as a widespread rejection of Christian dogma. An ambitious comparative, trans-national European Values Study conducted since the 1980s across much of the continent showed a clear trend towards privatization around the turn of the millennium, visible, in particular, in relation to the family and sexual relations.

Some sociologists of religion argued that traditional forms of religious expression were giving way to 'believing without belonging'.[18] Certainly some residual religious beliefs remained. In 1990 the numbers renouncing any belief in God or a spirit ranged from only 1 per cent of the population in Ireland to no higher than 20 per cent in Denmark. But other evidence pointed in the opposite direction: belonging without believing. In every European country examined by the European Values Study, except the Netherlands, the proportion of the population belonging to a religious denomination was greater than that of people who defined themselves as 'a religious person'.[19] In Sweden, where the great majority of the population belonged to a church, 44 per cent were in no other way religious

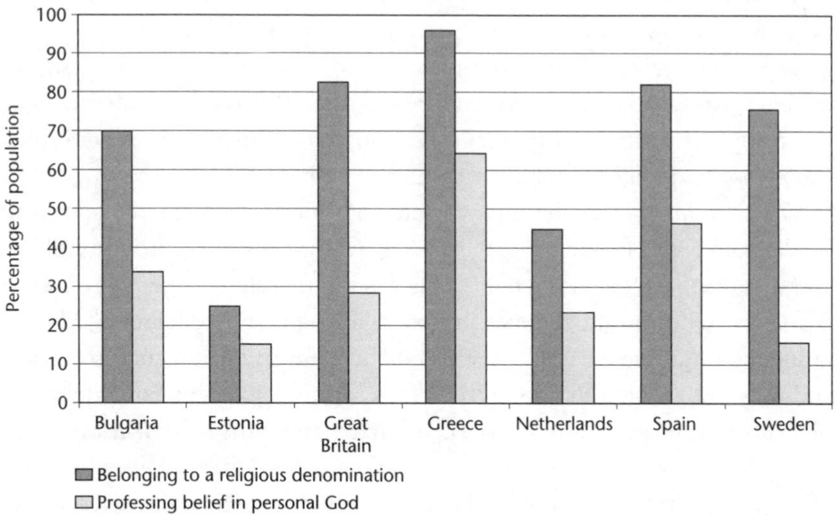

Figure 11. Religious belief and adherence in selected countries, *c.*1999

Source: EVS Foundation, *European Values Survey*, 1999.

and only a small minority said they believed in the existence of a personal God. In Britain social surveys recorded reduced numbers believing in God, the Devil, heaven, hell, and life after death. Between 1990 and 2005 the secularizing trend became even more marked. Religion was no longer the 'sacred canopy' of European society.[20]

Other observers rejected the concept of secularization, arguing instead that people were replacing institutionalized religion with a more personal faith or with a 'diffused spirituality'.[21] This might be seen as part of the larger process of individualization and privatization in contemporary society. Certainly mass credulity still knew few bounds if one were to judge by the popularity of 'New Age' philosophies or commercialized cults such as Scientology, the Unification Church of the Korean Reverend Sun Myung Moon (the 'Moonies'), or 'Transcendental Meditation'. In many European bookshops early in the new millennium 'New Age' works outnumbered those dealing with normative religion. Vague spirituality fed the market for 'alternative medicines', 'psychic healers', astrology, and organic vegetables. It also added to a widespread public distrust of science. At the end of the twentieth century no fewer than 125 million Europeans each year were estimated to undertake some form of pilgrimage: even if some of these journeys were little more than a form of tourism, their number nevertheless betokened a real spiritual hunger.

What was clear, however, was that in the new millennium religion was no longer necessarily a reliable repository of moral beliefs. For example, in regard to the central Christian injunction to 'love thy neighbour', survey evidence showed that in West Germany and the Netherlands in 1990, practising Christians (both Catholic and Protestant) were significantly more prone to xenophobia than committed atheists.

What could replace religion as a source of values? Marxism, the dominant intellectual force in much of western as well as eastern Europe until the 1960s, was in retreat everywhere. This was not merely a consequence of the fall of the Communist regimes in eastern Europe. The decline of Marxist influence on intellectual life, in Poland and Hungary as much as in France and Italy, ante-dated the political collapse. Indeed, one fundamental cause of that collapse itself was undoubtedly Marxism's loss of dynamism as an intellectual current after the 1960s. A variety of doctrines, mainly re-treads of old ideas, rushed into the intellectual vacuum: neo-liberalism, feminism, deconstructionism. None, however, provided the scaffolding for an alternative social morality that could satisfy a majority in society.

Civilization and barbarism walked hand in hand in Europe in the course of the past century. They were not polar opposites but, as Walter Benjamin maintained, locked together in a dialectical relationship.[22] 'The more civilization advances, the more it is compelled to cover the evils it necessarily creates,' another perceptive social observer had written in 1884.[23] The contemporary history of the continent is, in essence, an uncovering of those evils. Some were indeed necessary, in the sense that they were dictated by the predicaments in which Europeans found themselves. Others were the result of conscious human choices. As early as 1919 Anna Akhmatova pronounced the twentieth century 'worse than any other'.[24] It is impossible, contemplating the record, to disagree. Who can read of the killing fields of Flanders, the Somme, Caporetto, Stalingrad, and Leningrad, of the bombardments of Guernica, Rotterdam, Coventry, Hamburg, and Dresden, of the slaughter of innocents in Lidice and Oradour, of the grotesquely misnamed 'civil' wars in Russia, Finland, Ireland, Spain, Greece, and Yugoslavia, of the slave-labour camps of the Gulag, of the charnel-houses of Auschwitz, Treblinka, Sobibor, Majdanek, Bełżec, Mauthausen, and Jasenovac, and of the victims of political terrorism in Bologna, Istanbul, Madrid, and London, without acknowledging the barbarism deeply implanted in the heart of our civilization? Evil stalked the earth in this era, moving men's minds, ruling their actions, and begetting the lies, greed, deceit, and cruelty that are the stuff of the history of Europe in our time.

Notes

PREFACE

1. Walter Benjamin, 'Über den Begriff der Geschichte', in *Gesammelte Schriften*, ed. Rolf Tiedmann and Hermann Schweppenhäuser, vol. i, part 2, Frankfurt, 1978, 696.
2. Erich Eyck, *Geschichte der Weimarer Republik*, Erlenbach-Zürich, 1956, ii. 10.
3. Cicero, *Orator*, 120.
4. John Lukacs, *The End of the 20th Century: And the End of the Modern Age*, New York, 1993, 1.

1. EUROPE AT 1914

1. H. G. Wells, *Anticipations of the Reaction of Mechanical and Scientific Progress upon Human Life and Thought* (London, 1902). The book was translated into French, Polish, Spanish, Russian, Dutch, and German.
2. Steven Lukes, *Emile Durkheim: His Life and Work: A Historical and Critical Study*, Harmondsworth, 1975, 544.
3. Richard Ellmann and Charles Feidelson, eds., *The Modern Tradition: Backgrounds of Modern Literature*, New York, 1965, 433.
4. Reinhard Bendix, *Max Weber: An Intellectual Portrait*, London, 1966, 464.
5. H. G. Wells, *Experiment in Autobiography*, London, 1969 (first published 1934), ii. 652.
6. See Paul Bairoch, 'Europe's Gross National Product, 1800–1975', *JEEH* 5: 2 (1976), 273–340.
7. Stefan Zweig, *The World of Yesterday: An Autobiography*, London, 1943, 16.
8. Ralf Dahrendorf, *Society and Democracy in Germany*, New York, 1979, 39.
9. Michael Howard, *The Continental Commitment: The Dilemma of British Defence Policy in the Era of the Two World Wars*, Harmondsworth, 1972, 11.
10. See Modris Eksteins, *Rites of Spring: The Great War and the Birth of the Modern Age*, Boston, 1989, ch. 1.

11. Reginald Bray, quoted in George K. Behlmer, *Child Abuse and Moral Reform in England 1870–1908*, Stanford, 1982, 209.
12. There are no settled criteria for distinguishing between urban and rural areas. Different definitions have been used at different periods in different places. Comparative data must therefore be used with caution. See e.g. Dov Friedlander, 'The Spread of Urbanization in England and Wales, 1851–1951', *Population Studies*, 24: 3 (1970), 423–43; David Moon, 'Estimating the Peasant Population of Late Imperial Russia from the 1897 Census: A Research Note', *EAS* 48: 1 (1996), 141–53; Northern Ireland Statistics and Research Agency, *Statistical Classification and Delineation of Settlements—February 2005*, Belfast, 2005 (http://www.nisra.gov.uk/archive/urbanreport.pdf).
13. Eugen Weber, *Peasants into Frenchmen: The Modernization of Rural France, 1870–1914*, Stanford, 1976, 148.
14. Gaston Schmit, *Un village solognot: Vannes*, Paris, 1961, 99.
15. Pino Arlacchi, *Mafia, Peasants and Great Estates: Society in Traditional Calabria*, Cambridge, 1983, 60–1.
16. Anatol Lieven, *The Aristocracy in Europe, 1815–1914*, London, 1992, 63.
17. *Visions and Beliefs in the West of Ireland*, 'Collected and Arranged by Lady Gregory with Two Essays and Notes by W. B. Yeats', New York, 1970 (first pub. London, 1920), 327–8.
18. Tekla Dömötör, *Hungarian Folk Beliefs*, Bloomington, 1981, 163.
19. David Daiches, *Glasgow*, London, 1982, 213.
20. Theodore Zeldin, *France, 1848–1918: Ambition and Love*, Oxford, 1979, 111.
21. John Lukacs, *Budapest 1900: A Historical Portrait of a City and Its Culture*, New York, 1988, 148.
22. James Joll, *The Origins of the First World War*, 2nd edn., London, 1992, 228.
23. Joachim Remak, 'The Healthy Invalid: How Doomed the Habsburg Empire?' *JMH* 41: 2 (1969), 127–43.

2. EUROPE AT WAR 1914–1917

1. Joachim Remak, '1914—The Third Balkan War: Origins Reconsidered', *JMH* 43: 3 (1971), 353–66.
2. Sir F. Cartwright to Sir A. Nicolson, 31 Jan. 1913, in G. P. Gooch and Harold Temperley, eds., *British Documents on the Origins of the War, 1898–1914*, vol. ix, part II, London, 1934, 467.
3. Vladimir Dedijer, *The Road to Sarajevo*, London, 1966, 337.
4. Ibid. 145.
5. Ibid. 445.
6. Friedrich Graf von Szapáry to Leopold Graf von Berchtold, 24 July 1914, in I. Geiss, ed., *July 1914: The Outbreak of the First World War: Selected Documents*, New York, 1974, 176–8.

7. Text of Serbian reply with accompanying commentary by Austro-Hungarian government in Luigi Albertini, *The Origins of the War of 1914*, Oxford, 1952, ii. 364–71.
8. Hew Strachan, *The First World War*, vol. i, *To Arms*, Oxford, 2001, 72.
9. Albertini, *Origins*, ii. 138–9.
10. Ibid. i. 486.
11. James Joll, *The Origins of the First World War*, 2nd edn., London, 1992, 215.
12. Paul von Hindenburg, *Aus meinem Leben*, Leipzig, 1920, 72.
13. Gunther E. Rothenberg, *The Army of Francis Joseph*, West Lafayette, Indi., 1976, 177.
14. Friedrich von Bernhardi, *Germany and the Next War*, London, 1914, 68, 83, 85.
15. T. von Bethmann Hollweg, *Reflections on the World War*, London, 1920, 27.
16. Ibid.
17. 'Impressions dans la tourmente: le journal d'Etienne Clémentel dans l'été 1914', *Guerres mondiales et conflits contemporains*, 39: 156 (1989), 89–103 (diary entry dated 6 Aug. 1914).
18. Gerald D. Feldman, *Army, Industry and Labor in Germany, 1914–1918*, Princeton, 1966, 27.
19. Erich von Ludendorff, *Meine Kriegserinnerungen, 1914–1918*, Berlin, 1919, 29.
20. J. F. C. Fuller, *The Conduct of War 1789–1961*, London, 1972, 156.
21. *Mémoires du Maréchal Joffre*, vol. i, Paris, 1932, 143.
22. See Strachan, *First World War*, i. 190–8.
23. Announcement reproduced in J. Paulov-Boncour, *Entre deux guerres: Souvenirs sur la IIIe République: les luttes républicaines 1877–1918*, Paris, 1945, facing p. 213.
24. For a contrary view, see Strachan, *First World War*, i. 252–61.
25. Alistair Horne, *The Price of Glory: Verdun, 1916*, London, 1964, 44.
26. Horne, *Price of Glory*, 227.
27. Allain Bernède, *Verdun 1916: le point de vue français*, Le Mans, 2002, 342. Other sources give higher estimates, but these are the most plausible as is shown by Paul Jankowski in his forthcoming study of the battle.
28. Gordon A. Craig, *Germany, 1866–1945*, London, 1978, 373.
29. Ludendorff, *Kriegserinnerungen*, 5.
30. B. H. Liddell Hart, *History of the First World War*, London, 1972, 254.
31. Norman Stone, *The Eastern Front, 1914–1917*, New York, 1975, 122.
32. Ibid. 125.
33. Ludendorff, *Kriegserinnerungen*, 173.
34. Stone, *Eastern Front*, 240–54.
35. Strachan, *First World War*, i. 680.
36. Arthur J. Marder, *From the Dardanelles to Oran: Studies of the Royal Navy in War and Peace, 1915–1940*, London, 1974, 1.
37. David French, 'The Origins of the Dardanelles Campaign Reconsidered', *History*, 68: 223 (1983), 216.
38. Robert Rhodes James, *Gallipoli*, New York, 1965, 38.

39. Ibid. 186.
40. Erich von Falkenhayn, *Die Oberste Heeresleitung 1914–1916 in ihren Entschliessungen*, Berlin, 1920, 154.
41. B. H. Liddell Hart, *Strategy*, 2nd rev. edn., New York, 1991, 186.
42. Holger H. Herwig, *The First World War: Germany and Austria-Hungary, 1914–1918*, London, 1997, 32.
43. Cyril Falls, *Caporetto 1917*, London, 1966, 53.
44. Falkenhayn, *Oberste Heeresleitung*, 181.
45. Ludendorff, *Kriegserinnerungen*, 245.
46. Joffre memorandum dated 10 Nov. 1914, quoted in Patrick Facon, 'Aperçus sur la doctrine d'emploi de l'aéronautique militaire française (1914–1918)', *Revue historique des armées*, 3 (1988), 80–90.
47. Jean-Jacques Becker, *The Great War and the French People*, Leamington Spa, 1985, 36.
48. Karl Clausberg, *Zeppelin: Die Geschichte eines unwahrscheinlichen Erfolges*, Munich, 1979, 139.
49. Georg Christoph Lichtenberg, *Schriften und Briefe*, vol. ii, *Sudelbücher II, Materialhefte, Tagebücher*, Munich, 1971, 569.
50. Joll, *Origins*, 166.
51. David Lloyd George, *War Memoirs*, London, 1934, i. 101.
52. Feldman, *Army, Industry and Labor*, 173.
53. Lloyd George, *War Memoirs*, i. 101.
54. Feldman, *Army, Industry and Labor*, 150.
55. Estimate by Max Rubner quoted in Avner Offer, *The First World War: An Agrarian Interpretation*, Oxford, 1991, 33.
56. Ibid. 53.
57. Roderick Phillips, *Untying the Knot: A Short History of Divorce*, Cambridge, 1991, 188.
58. Becker, *Great War*, 48–9.
59. Ibid. 162–3.
60. Eksteins, *Rites of Spring*, 93.
61. Strachan, *First World War*, i. 1123.
62. Becker, *Great War*, chs. 14 and 15.
63. Guy Pedroncini, *Les Mutineries de 1917*, Paris, 1967, 136–7.
64. Lloyd George, *War Memoirs*, ii. 1247.
65. Ibid. 1247, 1248, 1277, 1320.
66. Jean Martet, *Le Silence de M. Clemenceau*, Paris, 1929, 222.
67. Jean Jules Henri Mordacq, *Le Ministère Clemenceau: journal d'un témoin*, Paris, 1930, i. 13–15.

3. REVOLUTIONARY EUROPE 1917–1921

1. Ronald Kowalski, *The Russian Revolution, 1917–1921*, London, 1997, 25–7.

2. W. E. Mosse, 'Interlude: The Russian Provisional Government 1917', *SS* 15: 4 (1964), 412.
3. George Katkov, *Russia 1917: The February Revolution*, London, 1969, 476.
4. Orlando Figes, *A People's Tragedy: The Russian Revolution, 1891–1924*, London, 1997, 351.
5. Ibid. 415.
6. Robert V. Daniels, ed., *A Documentary History of Communism*, vol. i, Hanover, NH, 1984, 55–7.
7. Kowalski, *The Russian Revolution*, 55.
8. Michael T. Florinsky, *The End of the Russian Empire*, New York, 1961, 229.
9. N. N. Sukhanov, *The Russian Revolution 1917: A Personal Record*, ed. and trans. Joel Carmichael, Princeton, 1983, 362, 374.
10. Figes, *People's Tragedy*, 423.
11. Remark attributed to General M. V. Alekseev: Richard Pipes, *The Russian Revolution*, New York, 1990, 441.
12. 'To the Workers, Peasants, and Soldiers!', Oct. 1917, in *Collected Works of V. I. Lenin*, vol. xxi, New York, 1932, 59–60.
13. Daniels, *Documentary History* i. 72–3.
14. Leon Trotsky, *History of the Russian Revolution*, vol. iii, *The Triumph of the Soviets*, London, 1967, 289.
15. Alexander Rabinowitch, *The Bolsheviks Come to Power: The Revolution of 1917 in Petrograd*, New York, 1978, 303–4.
16. Daniels, *Documentary History*, i. 91–2.
17. David Shub, *Lenin: A Biography*, rev. edn., Harmondsworth, 1966, 328.
18. Daniels, *Documentary History*, ii. 19–21.
19. John W. Wheeler-Bennett, *Brest-Litovsk: The Forgotten Peace: March 1918*, London, 1938, 213.
20. Ibid. 268.
21. B. H. Liddell Hart, *The First World War*, Oxford, 1984, 399.
22. Jean Jules Henri Mordacq, *Le Ministère Clemenceau: Journal d'un témoin*, 4 vols., Paris, 1930–1, ii. 62.
23. Raymond Recouly, *Le Mémorial de Foch: mes entretiens avec le Maréchal*, Paris, 1929, 162.
24. Paul von Hindenburg, *Aus meinem Leben*, Leipzig, 1920, 364.
25. Arthur J. May, *The Passing of the Habsburg Monarchy, 1914–18*, vol. i, Philadelphia, 1966, 434.
26. Arthur Rosenberg, *The Birth of the German Republic, 1871–1918*, London, 1931, 245.
27. Text of armistice in H. W. V. Temperley, ed., *A History of the Peace Conference of Paris*, London, 1920–4, i. 459–76.
28. Klaus Epstein, *Matthias Erzberger and the Dilemma of German Democracy*, Princeton, 1959, 281.

29. Stanley Weintraub, *A Stillness Heard Round the World: The End of the Great War: November 1918*, Oxford, 1987, 157.
30. B. H. Liddell Hart, *Foch: Man of Orleans*, Harmondsworth, 1937, ii. 427.
31. Hindenburg, *Aus meinem Leben*, 403.
32. Paul-Marie de la Gorce, *The French Army: A Military–Political History*, New York, 1963, 144.
33. Liddell Hart, *First World War*, 463.
34. Rosenberg, *Birth of the German Republic*, 252
35. Allan Mitchell, *Revolution in Bavaria, 1918–1919: The Eisner Regime and the Soviet Republic*, Princeton, 1965, 311.
36. Maureen Healy, *Vienna and the Fall of the Habsburg Empire: Total War and Everyday Life in World War I*, Cambridge, 2004, 77.
37. L. B. Namier, 'The Downfall of the Habsburg Monarchy', in Temperley, *History of the Peace Conference*, iv. 90.
38. Zara Steiner, *The Lights That Failed: European International History, 1919–1933*, Oxford, 2005, 51.
39. D. Perman, *The Shaping of the Czechoslovak State: Diplomatic History of the Boundaries of Czechoslovakia, 1914–1920*, Leiden, 1962, 43.
40. Dragolioub Jovanović, 'The Serbian Exodus', in David Mitrany, *The Effect of the War in Southeastern Europe*, New Haven, 1936, 247.
41. Arvo Tuominen, *The Bells of the Kremlin: An Experience in Communism*, Hanover, NH, 1983, 27.
42. Harry Hill Bandholtz, *An Undiplomatic Diary*, New York, 1933, 15. See also E. L. Woodward and Rohan Butler, eds., *DBFP*, ser. 1, vol. i, 394–6, 468–70, 498–500, 505–6, 629–32.
43. Daniels, *Documentary History*, i. 81–2.
44. Ibid. 84–5.
45. John Channon, 'The Peasantry in the Revolutions of 1917', in E. R. Frankel, J. Frankel, and B. Knei-Paz, eds., *Revolution in Russia: Reassessments of 1917*, Cambridge, 1992, 120.
46. Robert Service, *Lenin: A Biography*, London, 2002, 365.
47. Decree 'on the press' of 9 Nov. 1917, Daniels, *Documentary History*, i. 82–3.
48. Albert Resis, 'Lenin on Freedom of the Press', *RR* 36: 3 (1977), 274–96.
49. Wheeler-Bennett, *Brest-Litovsk*, 254.
50. David Carlton, *Churchill and the Soviet Union*, Manchester, 2000, 15.
51. Evan Mawdsley, *The Russian Civil War*, Edinburgh, 2000, 61.
52. Extract from Trotsky, *Terror and Communism* (1920), in Daniels, *Documentary History*, i. 121–3.
53. Daniels, *Documentary History*, ii. 44–7.
54. George Bernard Noble, *Policies and Opinions at Paris, 1919*, New York, 1935, 358.

55. Abbreviated text of treaty in J. A. S. Grenville and Bernard Wasserstein, eds., *The Major International Treaties of the Twentieth Century*, 2 vols., London, 2001, i. 100–12.
56. In his speech 'Politik als Beruf' (Politics as a Vocation), delivered on 28 Jan. 1919, quoted in Wolfgang Mommsen, 'Max Weber and the Treaty of Versailles', in Manfred F. Boemeke, Gerald D. Feldman, and Elisabeth Glaser, *The Treaty of Versailles: A Reassessment after 75 Years*, Cambridge, 1998, 546.
57. Harold Nicolson, *Peacemaking, 1919*, New York, 1965, 370.
58. Noble, *Policies and Opinions*, 34–5.
59. Robert Skidelsky, *John Maynard Keynes*, vol. i, *Hope Betrayed, 1883–1920*, London, 1983, 378.
60. J. M. Keynes, *The Economic Consequences of the Peace*, New York, 1920, 83, 168, 268, 277. The first edition appeared in London in 1919.
61. Skidelsky, *Keynes*, i. 383.
62. Ibid. 384,

4. RECOVERY OF THE BOURGEOISIE 1921–1929

1. *The Times*, 6 May 1925, quoted in Charles P. Kindleberger, *A Financial History of Western Europe*, London, 1984, 338.
2. Report by V. A. Antonov-Ovseyenko, 20 July 1921, in Jan M. Meijer, ed., *The Trotsky Papers, 1917–1922*, vol. ii, The Hague, 1971, 494–5.
3. Orlando Figes, *A People's Tragedy: The Russian Revolution, 1891–1924*, London, 1997, 777.
4. Text of manifesto in Robert V. Daniels, A *Documentary History of Communism*, vol. i, Hanover, NH, 1984, 137–8.
5. Paul Avrich, *Kronstadt 1917*, New York, 1970, 3.
6. Lenin, 'The Tax in Kind', in Daniels, *Documentary History*, i. 143–4.
7. Meier, *Trotsky Papers, 1917–1922*, ii. 790–5.
8. A. V. Lunacharsky, *Revolutionary Silhouettes*, London, 1967, 65.
9. Ibid. 62.
10. Leonard Schapiro, *The Communist Party of the Soviet Union*, rev. edn., New York, 1971, 299.
11. Speech by Stalin, 23 Oct. 1927, in J. V. Stalin, *Collected Works*, vol. x, Moscow, 1954, 177–81.
12. Politburo resolution, 8 July 1929, text in Lars T. Lih, Oleg V. Naumov, and Oleg V. Khlebniuk, eds., *Stalin's Letters to Molotov, 1925–1936*, New Haven, 1995, 150.
13. Robert Service, *Stalin: A Biography*, London, 2004, 38–9.
14. Leon Trotsky, *Stalin*, vol. i, London, 1969, 16.
15. Charles Kessler, ed. and trans., *Berlin in Lights: the Diaries of Count Harry Kessler, 1918–1937*, New York, 1999, 167.

16. E. H. Carr, *A History of Soviet Russia: The Bolshevik Revolution, 1917–1923*, London, 1953, iii. 369–70.
17. F. L. Carsten, *The Reichswehr and Politics, 1918–1933*, Berkeley, 1973, 140.
18. Hans W. Gatzke, 'Russo-German Military Collaboration During the Weimar Republic', in Gatzke, ed., *European Diplomacy Between the Two Wars, 1919–1939*, Chicago, 1972, 47.
19. Raymond J. Sontag, *A Broken World, 1919–1939*, New York, 1972, 120.
20. G. C. Paikert, *The Danube Swabians: German Populations in Hungary, Romania and Yugoslavia and Hitler's Impact on their Patterns*, The Hague, 1967, 102.
21. Jonathan Wright, *Gustav Stresemann: Weimar's Greatest Statesman*, Oxford, 2002, 2.
22. Piotr S. Wandycz, *France and Her Eastern Allies, 1919–1925: French–Czechoslovak–Polish Relations from the Paris Peace Conference to Locarno*, Minneapolis, 1962, 367.
23. A. J. P. Taylor, *English History, 1914–1945*, London, 1990, 128–9.
24. Kessler, *Harry Kessler Diaries*, 75.
25. Norman Davies, *God's Playground: A History of Poland*, vol. ii, Oxford, 1981, 402.
26. G. Ionescu-Siseşti and N. Cornătzianu, *La Réforme agraire en Roumanie et ses conséquences*, Bucharest, 1937, 37.
27. David Mitrany, *The Land and the Peasant in Rumania: The War and Agrarian Reform, 1917–21*, London, 1930, 181.
28. Dennis Mack Smith, *Mussolini*, London, 1983, 282.
29. Ibid. 147.
30. Ibid. 131.
31. Charles F. Delzell, *Mediterranean Fascism, 1919–1945*, New York, 1971, 22–5.
32. Ibid. 27–37.
33. Adrian Lyttelton, *The Seizure of Power: Fascism in Italy, 1919–1929*, 2nd edn., Princeton, 1987, 95.
34. Mack Smith, *Mussolini*, 94.
35. Delzell, *Mediterranean Fascism*, 57–61.
36. Alfonso Manaresi, *Storia Contemporanea per i Licei classici, scientifici e gli Istituti magistrali*, Milan, 1939, 360.
37. Lyttelton, *Seizure of Power*, 419.

5. DEPRESSION AND TERROR 1929–1936

1. Remark attributed to Lord Passfield (Sidney Webb) by A. J. P. Taylor, *English History, 1914–1945*, London, 1965, 297.
2. Barry Eichengreen, *Gold Fetters: The Gold Standard and the Great Depression, 1919–1939*, New York, 1995, 21.
3. David S. Landes, *The Unbound Prometheus: Technological Change and Industrial Development in Western Europe from 1750 to the Present*, Cambridge, 1969, 387.

4. Zara Steiner, *The Lights that Failed: European International History, 1919–1933*, Oxford, 2005, 687.
5. Jonathan Steinberg, *Why Switzerland?*, Cambridge, 1976, 144.
6. David S. Landes, *Revolution in Time: Clocks and the Making of the Modern World*, Cambridge, Mass., 1983, 335.
7. *League of Nations Economic Committee: The Agricultural Crisis*, vol. i, Geneva, 1931, 2.
8. George Kagan, 'Agrarian Regime of Pre-War Poland', *Journal of Central European Affairs*, 3: 3 (1943), 252.
9. Martin Hill, *The Economic and Financial Organization of the League of Nations: A Survey of Twenty-Five Years' Experience*, Washington, 1946, 55.
10. Ian Kershaw, *Hitler 1889–1936: Hubris*, London, 1998, 287.
11. See Henry Ashby Turner, Jr., *German Big Business and the Rise of Hitler*, New York, 1985.
12. Larry Eugene Jones, *German Liberalism and the Dissolution of the Weimar Party System 1918–1933*, Chapel Hill, NC, 1988, 395.
13. William L. Patch Jr., *Heinrich Brüning and the Dissolution of the Weimar Republic*, Cambridge, 1998, 269.
14. Harold James, *The German Slump: Politics and Economics, 1924–1936*, Oxford, 1986, 35.
15. Erich Eyck, *A History of the Weimar Republic*, vol. ii, New York, 1963, 427.
16. Kershaw, *Hitler: Hubris*, 421.
17. Martin Broszat, *The Hitler State: The Foundation and Development of the Internal Structure of the Third Reich*, London, 1981, 338.
18. Karl Dietrich Bracher, *The German Dictatorship: The Origins, Structure and Consequences of National Socialism*, Harmondsworth, 1973, 336.
19. Ibid. 337.
20. Ibid. 342.
21. Alan Beyerchen, 'Anti-Intellectualism and the Cultural Decapitation of Germany under the Nazis', in Jarrell C. Jackman and Carla M. Borden, eds., *The Muses Flee Hitler: Cultural Transfer and Adaptation, 1930–1945*, Washington, 1983, 38.
22. Franz Neumann, *Behemoth: The Structure and Practice of National Socialism, 1933–1944*, New York, 1963, 398.
23. From a lecture by SS Brigadeführer and President of the Reich Chamber of Writers, Hanns Johst, *c.*1935, quoted in Uriel Tal, *Structures of German 'Political Theology' in the Nazi Era*, Tel Aviv, 1979, 22.
24. Ian Kershaw, *The 'Hitler Myth': Image and Reality in the Third Reich*, Oxford, 1987, 109.
25. Ludwig Volk, *Das Reichskonkordat vom 20. Juli 1933*, Mainz, 1972, 65.
26. A. O. Ritschl, 'Nazi Economic Imperialism and the Exploitation of the Small: Evidence from Germany's Secret Foreign Exchange Balances, 1938–40', *EcHR* 54: 2 (2001), 324–45.

27. See James, *German Slump*, 379.
28. Hans Mommsen, *From Weimar to Auschwitz*, Princeton, 1991, 170–4.
29. *League of Nations: Journal of the Monetary and Economic Conference, London, 1933*, 5 (15 June 1933), 27.
30. Alec Nove, *An Economic History of the USSR*, Harmondsworth, 1972, 144.
31. Text of speech, 19 Nov. 1928, in Stalin, *Collected Works*, vol. xi, Moscow, 1954, 255–302.
32. Text of speech, end Jan./start Feb. 1929, ibid., 332–40.
33. Lynne Viola, *Peasant Rebels under Stalin: Collectivization and the Culture of Peasant Violence*, New York, 1996, 75.
34. S. G. Wheatcroft and R. W. Davies, 'The Crooked Mirror of Soviet Economic Statistics', in R. W. Davies, Mark Harrison, and S. G. Wheatcroft, eds., *The Economic Transformation of the Soviet Union, 1913–1945*, Cambridge, 1994, 29.
35. J. D. Barber and R. W. Davies, 'Employment and Industrial Labour', in Davies et al., *Economic Transformation*, 104.
36. Lewis H. Siegelbaum, *Stakhanovism and the Politics of Productivity in the USSR, 1935–1941*, Cambridge, 1988, 234.
37. Maurice Dobb, *Soviet Economic Development since 1917*, London, 1966, 470.
38. Siegelbaum, *Stakhanovism*, 302.
39. Jerrold L. Schecter and Vyacheslav V. Luchkov, *Khrushchev Remembers: The Glasnost Tapes*, Boston, 1990, 24.
40. Nadezhda Mandelstam, *Hope Against Hope*, Harmondsworth, 1975, 38.
41. Osip Mandelshtam, *Selected Poems*, trans. David McDuff, New York, 1975, 131.
42. *Report of Court Proceedings: The Case of the Trotskyite–Zinovievite Terrorist Centre, 19–24 August 1936*, Moscow, 1936, 164.
43. Stalin to Kaganovich, 23 Aug. 1936, in R. W. Davies et al., eds., *The Stalin–Kaganovich Correspondence, 1931–36*, New Haven, 2003, 337.
44. *Report of Court Proceedings in the Case of the Anti-Soviet Trotskyite Centre, Moscow, January 23–30, 1937*, Moscow, 1937.
45. See Wolfgang Leonhard, *Child of the Revolution*, Chicago, 1958, 38.
46. Bukharin letter dated 20 Feb. 1937, translated text in *NYT*, 15 June 1992.
47. Leonard Schapiro, 'Bukharin's Way', in *Russian Studies*, London, 1986, 301.
48. Bukharin letter dated 13 March 1938, translated text in *NYT*, 15 June 1992.
49. E. H. Carr, 'The Legend of Bukharin', *TLS*, 20 Sept. 1974.
50. George Katkov, *The Trial of Bukharin*, London, 1969, 126.
51. David Caute, *Communism and the French Intellectuals, 1914–1960*, New York, 1964, 129.
52. David Caute, *The Fellow-Travellers: Intellectual Friends of Communism*, rev. edn., New Haven, 1988, 138–9.
53. Arthur Koestler, *The Invisible Writing*, London, 1954, ch. 37.
54. See Walter Laqueur, *Stalin: The Glasnost Revelations*, New York, 1990, 321–32; also *NYT*, 6 and 8 Feb. 1988.

55. Dmitri Volkogonov, *Stalin: Triumph and Tragedy*, London, 1991, 294.
56. Oleg V. Khlevniuk, *The History of the Gulag: From Collectivization to the Great Terror*, New Haven, 2004, 287–329; Robert Conquest, *The Harvest of Sorrow: Soviet Collectivization and the Terror-Famine*, New York, 1986, 295; Robert Conquest, *The Great Terror: A Reassessment*, New York, 1990, 465–6; Adam B. Ulam, *Stalin: The Man and his Era*, New York, 1973, 345; *NYT*, 21 March 1988.
57. Alexander Solzhenitsyn, 'Misconceptions about Russia are a Threat to America', *FA* 58: 3 (Spring 1980).
58. *NYT*, 4 Feb. 1989.
59. S. G. Wheatcroft and R. W. Davies, 'Population', in Davies et al., *Economic Transformation*, 57–80. The debate continues: see e.g. the articles by Wheatcroft and Conquest in *EAS* 51: 2 (1999), 315–45 and 51: 8 (1999), 1479–83.
60. Boris Nicolaevsky, ed., *The Crimes of the Stalin Era: Special Report to the 20th Congress of the Communist Party of the Soviet Union*, New York, 1962, 34.
61. Article reprinted in *Was Stalin Really Necessary? Some Problems of Soviet Political Economy*, London, 1964, 17–39.
62. See Moshe Lewin, 'The Immediate Background of Soviet Collectivization', in Lewin, *The Making of the Soviet System: Essays in the Social History of Interwar Russia*, London, 1985, 91–120.
63. Roy A. Medvedev, *Let History Judge: The Origins and Consequences of Stalinism*, London, 1976, 416–18.
64. Suetonius, *Life of Caligula*, xxii.
65. See e.g. [Joseph Stalin], *Stalin on Lenin*, Moscow, 1939.
66. Ilya Ehrenburg, *Memoirs, 1929–1941*, New York, 1966, 426.
67. Edward Gibbon, *The History of the Decline and Fall of the Roman Empire*, London, 1776, vol. i, ch. 3.

6. EUROPE IN THE 1930S

1. Jörg Vögele, 'Urbanization, Infant Mortality and Public Health in Imperial Germany', in Carlo A. Corsini and Pier Paolo Viazzo, eds., *The Decline of Infant and Child Mortality: The European Experience, 1750–1990*, The Hague, 1997, 109–27.
2. The figure for 1940–1 is an estimate for the USSR as a whole. The rate for Moscow in that year was 100. See Frank Lorimer, *The Population of the Soviet Union: History and Prospects*, Geneva, 1946, 122.
3. These figures omit some areas of the Soviet Union.
4. Jacques Dupâquier, *Histoire de la population française*, vol. iv, *De 1914 à nos jours*, Paris, 1988, 187.
5. Paul Ginsborg, 'The Politics of the Family in Twentieth-Century Europe', *CoEH* 9: 3 (2000), 426.

6. Victoria de Grazia, *How Fascism Ruled Women: Italy, 1922–1945*, Berkeley, 1992, 69.
7. Ginsborg, 'Politics of the Family', 428.
8. J. Noakes and G. Pridham, eds., *Nazism: A History in Documents and Eyewitness Accounts 1919–1945*, 4 vols., Exeter, 1983–98, i. 457–8.
9. *Hitler's Secret Conversations, 1941–1944*, New York, 1961, 103.
10. Louise A. Boyd, *Polish Countrysides: Photographs and Narrative*, New York, 1937.
11. Ginsborg, 'Politics of the Family', 435.
12. Alix Holt, ed. and trans., *Selected Writings of Alexandra Kollontai*, New York, 1980, 229.
13. Basile Kerblay, 'Socialist Families', in André Burguière et al., *A History of the Family*, vol. ii, London, 1996, 445.
14. *Pravda* editorials of 28 May and 9 June 1936, in Robert V. Daniels, *A Documentary History of Communism*, vol. i, Hanover, NH, 1984, 247.
15. Martine Segalen, 'The Industrial Revolution: From Proletariat to Bourgeoisie', in Burguière et al., *History of the Family*, ii. 399.
16. Ginsborg, 'Politics of the Family', 429.
17. Gerhart Luetkens, 'Romania Today', *IA* 17: 5 (1938), 682–95.
18. *Economist*, 13 May 1939.
19. Andrea Graziosi, *A New, Peculiar State: Explorations in Soviet History, 1917–1937*, Westport, Conn., 2000, 240.
20. Robert Friedel, *Zipper: An Exploration in Novelty*, New York, 1994, 159.
21. Ibid. 162.
22. Robert W. Desmond, *Crisis and Conflict: World News Reporting Between Two Wars, 1920–1940*, Iowa City, 1980, 405.
23. Derek Jones, 'Art', in Jones, ed., *Censorship: A World Encyclopedia*, vol. i, London 2001, 102–12.
24. Alan Riding, 'An Artist Who Stayed in Hitler's Germany', *NYT*, 18 Feb. 2003.
25. Albrecht Mendelssohn Bartholdy, *The War and German Society: The Testament of a Liberal*, New Haven, 1937, 290.
26. Ernest K. Bramsted, *Goebbels and National Socialist Propaganda, 1925–1945*, London, 1965, 63.
27. Michel Dorigné, *Jazz, Culture et Société*, Paris, 1967, 79.
28. Jim Godbolt, *A History of Jazz in Britain, 1919–1950*, London, 1984, 29.
29. S. Frederick Starr, *Red and Hot: The Fate of Jazz in the Soviet Union, 1917–1980*, New York, 1983, 89–90.
30. Ibid. 127.
31. Barbara Keys, 'Soviet Sport and Transnational Mass Culture in the 1930s', *JCH* 38: 3 (2003), 413–34.
32. Christopher Thompson, 'The Tour in the Inter-War Years: Political Ideology, Athletic Excess and Industrial Modernity', *International Journal of the History of Sport*, 20: 2 (2003), 79–102.

33. José Ortega y Gasset, *The Revolt of the Masses*, London, 1961, 14.
34. Sigmund Freud, *Civilization and its Discontents*, London, 1930, chs. 3, 4, 5, 8.

7. SPIRAL INTO WAR 1936–1939

1. Speech on 'the fundamental principles of the revolution', 30 June 1930: http://www.cphrc.org.uk/sources/so-md/fund-1.htm.
2. Lecture by the Guardist intellectual Nae Ionescu, quoted in Mihail Sebastian, *Journal 1935–1944: The Fascist Years*, Chicago, 2000, 9 (diary entry dated 30 March 1935).
3. James K. Pollock, 'The Saar Plebiscite', *American Political Science Review*, 29: 2 (1935), 275–82.
4. Lord (Robert) Vansittart, *The Mist Procession: The Autobiography of Lord Vansittart*, London, 1958, 520.
5. Treaty of Mutual Assistance between the Soviet Union and France, 2 May 1935, in J. A. S. Grenville and Bernard Wasserstein, eds., *The Major International Treaties of the Twentieth Century*, 2 vols., London, 2001, i. 194–5.
6. Keith Neilson, 'The Defence Requirements Sub-Committee, British Strategic Foreign Policy, Neville Chamberlain and the Path to Appeasement', *EHR* 118: 477 (2003), 651–84.
7. Hansard, HC (series 5), vol. 270, col. 632 (10 Nov. 1932).
8. Hansard, HC (series 5), vol. 292, col. 2339 (30 July 1934).
9. McGregor Knox, *Mussolini Unleashed, 1939–1941: Politics and Strategy in Fascist Italy's Last War*, Cambridge, 1982, 14.
10. Zachary Shore, *What Hitler Knew: The Battle for Information in Nazi Foreign Policy*, New York, 2003, ch. 3.
11. Hoesch (London) to German Foreign Ministry, 9 March 1936, *DGFP*, ser. C, vol. v, 57.
12. Speech to Reichstag, 7 March 1936, in Norman H. Baynes, ed., *The Speeches of Adolf Hitler, April 1922–August 1939*, London, 1942, 1300.
13. L. B. Namier, *Europe in Decay: A Study in Disintegration, 1936–1940*, London, 1950, 10.
14. *Die Tagebücher von Joseph Goebbels: Sämtliche Fragmente*, ed. Elke Fröhlich, vol. ii, Munich, 1987, 581.
15. Ian Kershaw, *Hitler, 1889–1936: Hubris*, London, 1998, 591.
16. Jean Lacouture, *Léon Blum*, Paris, 1977, 205.
17. Dimitrov cable to Thorez, 12 May 1936, quoted in Alexander Dallin and F. I. Firsov, eds., *Dimitrov and Stalin, 1934–1943: Letters from the Soviet Archives*, New Haven, 2000, 34–5.
18. Kenneth Mourse, '"Une Eventualité Absolument Exclue": French Reluctance to Devalue, 1933–1936', *FHS* 15: 3 (1988), 479–505.
19. Lacouture, *Blum*, 407.
20. Ibid.

21. Joel Colton, *Léon Blum: Humanist in Politics*, rev. edn., Durham, NC, 1987, 192.
22. Ibid. 195.
23. Ismael Saz, 'Foreign Policy under the Dictatorship of Primo de Rivera', in Sebastian Balfour and Paul Preston, eds., *Spain and the Great Powers in the Twentieth Century*, London, 1999, 53.
24. Paul Preston, *Franco: A Biography*, London, 1995, 618.
25. Ibid. 144.
26. William J. Callahan, *The Catholic Church in Spain, 1875–1998*, Washington, 2000, 349.
27. Ian Gibson, *Federico García Lorca: A Life*, London, 1989, 464, 468.
28. *DGFP*, ser. D, vol. iii, 892–4.
29. *DGFP*, ser. D, vol. iii, 932–3.
30. Paul Preston, 'Italy and Spain, 1936–1943', in Balfour and Preston, *Spain and the Great Powers*, 166.
31. Preston, *Franco*, 215.
32. Colton, *Blum*, 234–5.
33. Text of speech in George R. Esenwein, *The Spanish Civil War: A Modern Tragedy*, New York, 2005, 29.
34. R. N. Carew Hunt, 'Willi Muenzenberg', in David Footman, ed., *St Antony's Papers 9: International Communism*, Carbondale, Ill., 1960, 72–87; but see also Sean McMeekin, *The Red Millionaire: A Political Biography of Willi Münzenberg, Moscow's Secret Propaganda Tsar in the West*, New Haven, 2003, which minimizes Münzenberg's direct role in activity related to Spain.
35. Knox, *Mussolini Unleashed*, 6.
36. Antony Blunt, *Picasso's 'Guernica'*, New York, 1969, 9.
37. Herschel B. Chipp, *Picasso's Guernica: History, Transformations, Meanings*, Berkeley, 1988, 171.
38. Speech by Lord Cranborne, 11 Dec. 1937, League of Nations *Official Journal*, 18: 1 (Jan. 1937), 11–13.
39. Preston, *Franco*, 322–3.
40. Barbara Jelavich, *Modern Austria: Empire and Republic, 1815–1986*, Cambridge, 1987, 195.
41. Kurt von Schuschnigg, *The Brutal Takeover*, London, 1971, 106.
42. *The Economist*, 7 Nov. 1936.
43. Charles A. Gulick, *Austria from Habsburg to Hitler*, vol. ii, Berkeley, 1948, 1765.
44. Joachim Fest, *The Face of the Third Reich*, Harmondsworth, 1972, 271.
45. Schuschnigg, *Takeover*, 3.
46. Erwin A. Schmidl, *März 38: Der deutsche Einmarsch in Österreich*, Vienna, 1988, 106.
47. Remark attributed to Helmut Andics in Norbert Leser, 'Austria Between the Wars', *AHYB* 17/18 (1981–2), 134.
48. Arnold J. Toynbee, *Survey of International Affairs, 1938*, vol. i, London, 1941, 246.

49. Unsigned minute, probably by Weizsäcker, 19 Aug. 1938, *DGFP*, ser. D, vol. ii, 593.
50. German General Staff to Hitler, 24 Aug. 1938, *DGFP*, ser. D, vol. ii, 618–19.
51. Hugh Seton-Watson, 'Conflict in Bohemia', *TLS*, 19 Aug. 1977.
52. Katriel Ben-Arie, 'Czechoslovakia at the Time of "Munich" ': The Military Situation', *JCH* 25: 4 (1990), 434.
53. Zara Steiner, 'The Soviet Commissariat of Foreign Affairs and the Czechoslovakian Crisis in 1938: New Material from the Soviet Archives', *HJ* 4: 3 (1999), 751–79.
54. N. H. Gibbs, *Grand Strategy*, vol. i, *Rearmament Policy*, London, 1976, 645.
55. Runciman's report, dated 21 Sept. 1938 (reflecting his recommendations to the government upon his return to London on 16 September), in Paul Vyšný, *The Runciman Mission to Czechoslovakia, 1938: Prelude to Munich*, Basingstoke, 2003, 344–9.
56. R. G. D. Laffan, *Survey of International Affairs 1938*, vol. ii, *The Crisis over Czechoslovakia, January to September 1938*, London, 1951, 390.
57. Ibid. 416–17.
58. Keith Feiling, *The Life of Neville Chamberlain*, London, 1946, 376.
59. Elisabeth du Réau, *Edouard Daladier, 1884–1970*, Paris, 1993, 277.
60. Feiling, *Chamberlain*, 381.
61. Contemporary newsreel clip incorporated in Philip Whitehead and Cate Haste's film, *Munich: The Peace of Paper* (Brook Productions/Thames Television, 1988).
62. Note du Deuxième Bureau de l'État-Major de l'Armée, 25 Sept. 1938, *DDF*, série 2, *1932–1939*, vol. xi, Paris, 1977, 536.
63. *NZZ*, 19 April 2002.
64. Edouard Daladier, *Journal de captivité, 1940–1945*, Paris, 1991, 15; Réau, *Daladier*, 285.
65. Laffan, *Survey 1938*, ii. 451.
66. *Punch*, 12 Oct. 1938.
67. Harold Nicolson, *Diaries and Letters 1939–1945*, ed. Nigel Nicolson, London, 1967, 35 (diary entry dated 20 Sept. 1939).
68. David J. Dallin, *Soviet Russia's Foreign Policy 1939–1942*, New Haven, 1942, 6–7.
69. Peter Jackson, 'Intelligence and the End of Appeasement', in Robert Boyce, ed., *French Foreign and Defence Policy, 1918–1940: The Decline and Fall of a Great Power*, London, 1998, 251.
70. Anne M. Ciencala, *Poland and the Western Powers, 1938–1939: A Study in the Interdependence of Eastern and Western Europe*, London, 1968, 224.
71. Gibbs, *Grand Strategy*, i. 811.
72. Jackson, 'Intelligence', 243.
73. J. Noakes and G. Pridham, eds., *Nazism, 1919–1945: A History in Documents and Eyewitness Accounts*, 4 vols., Exeter, 1983–98, ii. 737.

74. G. Bruce Strang, 'Once More into the Breach: Britain's Guarantee to Poland, March 1939', *JCH* 31: 4 (1996), 723.
75. A. J. Prazmowska, 'Poland's Foreign Policy: September 1938–September 1939', *HJ* 29: 4 (1986), 863.
76. Geoffrey Roberts, *The Soviet Union and the Origins of the Second World War: Russo-German Relations and the Road to War, 1933–1941*, Basingstoke, 1995, 92.
77. Speech to 18th Congress of Communist Party of the Soviet Union, 10 March 1939, in Jane Degras, ed., *Soviet Documents on Foreign Policy*, vol. iii, London, 1953, 322.
78. Hans von Herwarth, *Zwischen Hitler und Stalin: Erlebte Zeitgeschichte 1931 bis 1945*, Frankfurt, 1982, 186.
79. Boris Meissner, 'The Baltic Question in World Politics', in V. Stanley Vardys and Romuald J. Misiunas, eds., *The Baltic States in Peace and War, 1917–1945*, University Park, Pa., 1978, 142.
80. Grenville and Wasserstein, eds., *Major International Treaties*, i. 229–30.
81. Donald Cameron Watt, *How War Came: The Immediate Origins of the Second World War, 1938–1939*, New York, 1989, 462.
82. Jerrold L. Schecter and Vyacheslav V. Luchkov, *Khrushchev Remembers: The Glasnost Tapes*, Boston, 1990, 46.
83. Ian Kershaw, *Hitler, 1936–1945: Nemesis*, London, 2001, 208–9.
84. Henderson to Sir A. Cadogan, 25 Aug. 1939, *DBFP*, ser. 3, vol. vii, 257.
85. Gerhard Weinberg, *A World at Arms: A Global History of World War II*, Cambridge, 1994, 46.
86. Memorandum handed to British ambassador in Berlin by Ribbentrop at 11.20 a.m., 3 Sept. 1939, *DBFP*, ser. 3, vol. vii, 539.
87. Text of Chamberlain speech: http://www.yale.edu/lawweb/avalon/wwii/gb3.htm.

8. HITLER TRIUMPHANT 1939–1942

1. Jean-Jacques Rousseau, *Considérations sur le gouvernement de Pologne* (written 1771, first published Geneva, 1782, ch. 3).
2. B. H. Liddell Hart, *History of the Second World War*, London, 1970, 27.
3. G. D. Sheffield, 'Carton de Wiart and Spears' in John Keegan, ed., *Churchill's Generals*, London, 1991, 328.
4. Paul W. Doerr, '"Frigid but Unprovocative": British Policy Towards the USSR from the Nazi-Soviet Pact to the Winter War, 1939', *JCH* 36: 3 (2001), 423–39.
5. Alan Bullock, *Hitler: A Study in Tyranny*, rev. edn., Harmondsworth, 1962, 556.
6. David J. Dallin, *Soviet Russia's Foreign Policy, 1939–1942*, New Haven, 1942, 70–1.
7. Ivo Banac, *The Diary of Georgi Dimitrov, 1933–1949*, New Haven, 2003, 115.
8. Adam Ulam, *Stalin: The Man and his Era*, New York, 1973, 519.

9. Translated transcript in Keith Sword, ed., *The Soviet Takeover of the Polish Eastern Provinces, 1939–41*, Basingstoke, 1991, 295–300.
10. Francis King and George Matthews, eds., *About Turn: The British Communist Party and the Second World War: The Verbatim Record of the Central Committee Meetings of 25 September and 2–3 October 1939*, London, 1990, 27 and 69–70.
11. David Caute, *Communism and the French Intellectuals, 1914–1960*, New York, 1964, ch. 4.
12. Jean-Louis Crémieux-Brilhac, *Les Français de l'an 40*, Paris, 1990, i. 179.
13. Väinö Tanner, *The Winter War: Finland against Russia, 1939–1940*, Stanford, 1957, 27.
14. Ibid. 30.
15. Alexander Elkin, 'Finland', in Arnold Toynbee and Veronica M. Toynbee, eds., *Survey of International Affairs, 1939–1946: The Initial Triumph of the Axis*, London, 1958, 76.
16. W. M. Carlgren, *Swedish Foreign Policy During the Second World War*, New York, 1977, 23–5.
17. Ibid. 33.
18. Alan Bullock, *Hitler, and Stalin: Parallel Lives*, New York, 1991, 662.
19. Hansard, HC (series 5), vol. 360, col. 1150 (7 May 1940).
20. Ibid. col. 1283 (8 May 1940).
21. Field Marshal Lord Alanbrooke, *War Diaries, 1939–1945*, ed. Alex Danchev and Daniel Todman, London, 2002, 534 (entry for 23 March 1944).
22. Ibid. 590 (entry for 10 Sept. 1944).
23. Ian Kershaw, *Hitler, 1936–1945: Nemesis*, London, 2001, 293.
24. Heinz Guderian, *Panzer Leader*, London, 2000, 105–6.
25. Liddell Hart, *Second World War*, 66.
26. Carl von Clausewitz, *Vom Kriege*, 18th edn., Bonn, 1973, 377 and 388; see also Baron [Antoine Henri] de Jomini, *The Art of War*, Philadelphia, 1862 (repr. Westport, Conn., 1973), 176 and 322.
27. See Ernest R. May, *Strange Victory: Hitler's Conquest of France*, London, 2000, 347–61.
28. Martin Gilbert, *Winston S. Churchill*, vol. vi, London, 1983, 339–40.
29. Ibid. 346–7.
30. Ibid. 350.
31. Ibid. 377.
32. Martin Middlebrook and Chris Everitt, *The Bomber Command Diaries: An Operational Reference Book, 1939–1945*, London, 1990, 43–55.
33. Thomas J. Knight, 'Belgium Leaves the War 1940', *JMH* 41: 1 (1969), 46–67.
34. Paul-Marie de la Gorce, *The French Army: A Military–Political History*, New York, 1963, 301.
35. Charles de Gaulle, *Mémoires de guerre*, vol. i, *L'Appel*, Paris, 1954, 49.

36. P. M. H. Bell, 'The Breakdown of the Alliance in 1940', in N. Waites, ed., *Troubled Neighbours: Franco-British Relations in the Twentieth Century*, London, 1971, 220–7.
37. Alanbrooke, *War Diaries*, 80.
38. Gilbert, *Churchill*, vi. 358.
39. Ibid. 368.
40. Ibid. 607.
41. Marc Ferro, *Pétain*, Paris, 1987, 85.
42. De Gaulle, *Mémoires de guerre*, i. 267–8.
43. Robert Paxton, *Vichy France: Old Guard, New Order, 1940–1944*, New York, 1972, 22.
44. Text in Charles F. Delzell, *Mediterranean Fascism, 1919–1945*, New York, 1971, 213–15.
45. Bullock, *Hitler*, 592.
46. Hugh Trevor-Roper, ed., *Hitler's War Directives, 1939–1945*, London, 1966, 74–9.
47. Bullock, *Hitler*, 594–5.
48. Trevor-Roper, *Hitler's War Directives*, 79–80.
49. Klaus Maier et al., *Germany and the Second World War* vol. ii, Oxford, 2000, 402.
50. J. R. M. Butler, *Lord Lothian (Philip Kerr), 1882–1940*, London, 1960, 307.
51. Robert Skidelsky, *John Maynard Keynes*, vol. iii, *Fighting for Britain, 1937–1946*, London, 2000, 99.
52. Galeazzo Ciano, *Diario 1939–43*, vol. i, Milan, 1963, 353.
53. Guderian, *Panzer Leader*, 141.
54. Kershaw, *Hitler: Nemesis*, 362.
55. Gyula Juhász, *Hungarian Foreign Policy, 1919–1945*, Budapest, 1979, 185.
56. Mark Mazower, *Inside Hitler's Greece: The Experience of Occupation, 1941–44*, New Haven, 2001, 16.
57. Jürgen Förster, 'Hitler's Decision in Favour of War against the Soviet Union', in Horst Boog et al., *Germany and the Second World War*, vol. iv, Oxford, 1996, 26.
58. Trevor-Roper, *Hitler's War Directives*, 93–8.
59. Kershaw, *Hitler: Nemesis*, 356.
60. Ibid. 345.
61. Guderian, *Panzer Leader*, 141.
62. David M. Glantz, *Stumbling Colossus: the Red Army on the Eve of World War*, Lawrence, Kan., 1998, 233–51. Bullock, *Hitler and Stalin*, 719; Gabriel Gorodetsky, 'Filip Ivanovich Golikov', in Harold Shukman, ed., *Stalin's Generals*, London, 1993, 77–87; and Konstantin Bakhtov, 'Uneasy Days in France', *International Affairs* (Moscow), 13: 1 (1992), 98–105.
63. Steven Merritt Miner, 'His Master's Voice: Vyacheslav Mikhailovich Molotov as Stalin's Foreign Commissar', in Gordon A. Craig and Francis L. Loewenheim, eds., *The Diplomats, 1939–1979*, Princeton, 1994, 79.

64. Cynthia Roberts, 'Planning for War: The Red Army and the Catastrophe of 1941', *EAS* 47: 8 (1995), 1293–326.
65. Gabriel Gorodetsky, *Grand Delusion: Stalin and the German Invasion of Russia*, New Haven, 1999, 299.
66. Ibid., *passim*.
67. Rudolf Semmler, *Goebbels—the Man Next to Hitler*, London, 1947, 33; Kershaw, *Hitler: Nemesis*, 375–6.
68. Trevor-Roper, *Hitler's War Directives*, 130–4.
69. John Erickson, *The Road to Stalingrad: Stalin's War with Germany*, vol. i, London, 1983, 105–6.
70. Ibid. 141.
71. Trevor-Roper, *Hitler's War Directives*, 135–9.
72. Erickson, *Road to Stalingrad*, 174.
73. Guderian, *Panzer Leader*, 200.
74. Viktor Anfilov, 'Gregory Konstantinovich Zhukov', in Shukman, *Stalin's Generals*, 343–60.
75. Andrei Sakharov, *Memoirs*, London, 1990, 43.
76. Trevor-Roper, *Hitler's War Directives*, 166–70.
77. Guderian, *Panzer Commander*, 261.
78. *The Memoirs of Marshal Mannerheim*, London, 1953, 436.
79. Rüdiger Overmans, 'Das andere Gesicht des Krieges: Leben und Sterben der 6. Armee', in Jürgen Förster, ed., *Stalingrad: Ereignis—Wirkung—Symbol*, Munich, 1993, 419–55.
80. Bullock, *Hitler and Stalin*, 788.
81. David Carlton, *Churchill and the Soviet Union*, Manchester, 2000, 57.
82. Ibid. 83.
83. Antony Polonsky, ed., *The Great Powers and the Polish Question, 1941–1945*, London, 1976, 82–3.
84. Ibid. 19.
85. Dallin, *Soviet Russia's Foreign Policy*, 408.
86. A. J. P. Taylor, *Beaverbrook*, Harmondsworth, 1974, 677.
87. A. Rossi [Tasca], *La Guerre des papillons: quatre ans de politique communiste, 1940–1944*, Paris, 1954, pp. v–xxvi.
88. Sir Richard Clarke, *Anglo-American Economic Collaboration in War and Peace, 1942–1949*, Oxford, 1982, 92.
89. Text in Grenville and Wasserstein, *Major International Treaties*, i. 234.

9. LIFE AND DEATH IN WARTIME

1. Omer Bartov, *Hitler's Army: Soldiers, Nazis, and War in the Third Reich*, New York, 1991, 78.
2. John Erickson, *The Road to Stalingrad: Stalin's War with Germany*, vol. i, London, 1983, 138.

3. Sir Arthur Salusbury MacNalty and W. Franklin Mellor, eds., *Medical Services in War: The Principal Medical Lessons of the Second World War*, London, 1968, 136–7.
4. Mark Harrison, *Medicine and Victory: British Military Medicine in the Second World War*, Oxford, 2004, 5.
5. Ibid. 98.
6. Ibid. 148.
7. Ibid. 104.
8. Jeremy Noakes, 'Germany', in Noakes, ed., *The Civilian in War: The Home Front in Europe, Japan and the USA in World War II*, Exeter, 1992, 52.
9. Jean-Louis Crémieux-Brillac, *Les Français de l'an 40*, Paris, 1990, i. 604.
10. BBC 'weekly note', 31 March–6 April 1942, in Asa Briggs, *The History of Broadcasting in the United Kingdom*, vol. iii, *The War of Words*, London, 1970, 420.
11. Ibid. 67.
12. Ibid. 103.
13. Ibid. 115.
14. Rudolf Semmler, *Goebbels—the Man next to Hitler*, London, 1947, 48.
15. Briggs, *War of Words*, 433.
16. Hugh Cudlipp, *Publish and Be Damned: The Astonishing Story of the* Daily Mirror, London, 1953, 156ff.
17. Ian Kershaw, *Hitler, 1936–1945: Nemesis*, London, 2001, 713.
18. Tobias Schneider, 'Bestseller im Dritten Reich', *VfZ* 52: 1 (2004), 77–97.
19. Ilya Ehrenburg, *Russia at War*, London, 1943, 22, 53, 60, 160, 231–2, 258, 272, 275–7.
20. Joshua Rubenstein, *Tangled Loyalties: The Life and Times of Ilya Ehrenburg*, London, 1996, 194.
21. Andrew Chandler, 'The Church of England and the Obliteration Bombing of Germany in the Second World War', *EHR* 108: 429 (1993), 920–46.
22. *Sweden: A Wartime Survey*, Press Bureau of the Royal Ministry for Foreign Affairs, Stockholm, 1942, 20.
23. Christian Leitz, *Nazi Germany and Neutral Europe during the Second World War*, Manchester, 2000, 131.
24. Ibid. 14.
25. Aengus Nolan, 'Irish Diplomats at Home and Abroad', in Dermot Keogh and Mervyn O'Driscoll, eds., *Ireland in World War Two: Diplomacy and Survival*, Cork, 2004, 134.
26. Joseph T. Carroll, *Ireland in the War Years*, Newton Abbot, 1975, 160.
27. Alan Bullock, *Hitler: A Study in Tyranny*, rev. edn., Harmondsworth, 1962, 605.
28. Paul Preston, *Franco, a Biography*, London, 1993, 394–5.
29. Gerhard Hirschfeld, *Nazi Rule and Dutch Collaboration: The Netherlands under German Occupation, 1940–1945*, Oxford, 1988, 155.
30. Charles Cruikshank, *The German Occupation of the Channel Islands*, London, 1975, 153.

31. Text of speech in Margaret Carlyle, ed., *Documents on International Affairs, 1939–1946*, London, 1954, 126–7.
32. Kershaw, *Hitler: Nemesis*, 401.
33. Helmut Eiber and David M. Glantz, eds., *Hitler and His Generals: Military Conferences, 1942–1945*, London, 2002, 713.
34. Mark Mazower, *Inside Hitler's Greece: The Experience of Occupation, 1941–44*, New Haven, 1993, 146–7.
35. Milovan Djilas, *Conversations with Stalin*, New York, 1962, 9–10.
36. Jürgen Förster, 'Operation Barbarossa as a War of Conquest and Annihilation', in Horst Boog et al., *Germany and the Second World War*, vol. iv, Oxford, 1996, 507–13 and 1225–35.
37. See Christian Streit, *Keine Kamaraden: Die Wehrmacht und die sowjetischen Kriegsgefangenen, 1941–1945*, Stuttgart, 1978. But cf. Boog et al., *Germany and the Second World War*, vol. iv, 852 n. 71, and 1172–9.
38. Djilas, *Conversations with Stalin*, 54.
39. Joseph Rothschild, *East Central Europe Between the Two Wars*, Seattle, 1977, 10.
40. J. Noakes and G. Pridham, eds., *Nazism: A History in Documents and Eyewitness Accounts*, vol. ii, New York, 1988, 1001–9.
41. Ibid. 1026.
42. Hannah Arendt, *Eichmann in Jerusalem: A Report on the Banality of Evil*, London, 1963.
43. Steven Paskuly, ed., *Death Dealer, The Memoirs of the SS Kommandant at Auschwitz by Rudolph Hoess*, Buffalo, 1992.
44. Franciszek Piper, 'Estimating the Number of Deportees to and Victims of the Auschwitz-Birkenau Camp', *Yad Vashem Studies*, 21 (1991), 49–103.
45. *Trial of the Major War Criminals before the International Military Tribunal*, vol. xxix. Nuremberg, 1948, 110–73 (doc. 1919-PS).
46. Jan T. Gross, *Neighbors: The Destruction of the Jewish Community in Jedwabne, Poland*, Princeton, 2001.
47. Jonathan Steinberg, *All or Nothing: The Axis and the Holocaust, 1941–1943*, London, 1990, 59–60.
48. Arendt, *Eichmann in Jerusalem*.
49. Isaiah Trunk, *Judenrat: The Jewish Councils in Eastern Europe Under Nazi Control*, New York, 1972.
50. Raul Hilberg, *The Destruction of the European Jews*, 1st edn., Chicago, 1961; rev., 3-vol. edn., New York, 1985.
51. Thomas Vogel, ed., *Wilm Hosenfeld 'Ich versuche jeden zu retten': Das Leben eines deutschen Offiziers in Briefen und Tagebüchern*, Munich, 2004, 714.
52. Yehuda Bauer, '"Onkel Sally"—Die Verhandlungen des Sally Mayer zur Rettung der Juden 1944/5', *VfZ* 25: 2 (1977), 188–219.
53. Orders issued by police chief Emile Hennequin, 12 July 1942: text in Michael R. Marrus and Robert O. Paxton, *Vichy et les Juifs*, Paris, 1981, 412–13.
54. Günter Lewy, *The Catholic Church and Nazi Germany*, London, 1964, 299.

55. *Actes et Documents du Saint Siège*, 11 vols., Città del Vaticano, 1965–81.
56. George Bull, 'The Vatican, the Nazis and the Pursuit of Justice', *IA* 47: 2 (April 1971), 353–8.
57. Kershaw, *Hitler: Nemesis*, 822.

10. END OF HITLER'S EUROPE 1942–1945

1. Heinz Guderian, *Panzer Leader*, London, 2000, 142.
2. Jonathan Steinberg, *All or Nothing: The Axis and the Holocaust, 1941–1943*, London, 1990.
3. Michael Howard, *Grand Strategy* vol. iv, *August 1942–September 1943*, London, 1972, 470.
4. Charles F. Delzell, *Mediterranean Fascism, 1919–1945*, New York, 1971, 223.
5. Howard, *Grand Strategy*, iv. 472.
6. Ibid. 502.
7. Delzell, *Mediterranean Fascism*, 235–7.
8. Field Marshal Lord Alanbrooke, *War Diaries, 1939–1945*, ed. Alex Danchev and Daniel Todman, London, 2002, 527 (entry for 29 Feb. 1944).
9. George Sanford, 'The Katyn Massacre and Polish-Soviet Relations, 1941–43', *JCH* 41: 1 (2006), 95–111.
10. Molotov to Polish Ambassador in Moscow, 25 April 1943, in Antony Polonsky, ed., *The Great Powers and the Polish Question, 1941–1945*, London, 1976, 126–7.
11. Richard Woff, 'Konstantin Konstaninovich Rokossovsky', in Harold Shukman, ed., *Stalin's Generals*, London, 1993, 177–96.
12. Guderian, *Panzer Leader*, 359.
13. B. H. Liddell Hart, *History of the Second World War*, London, 1970, 583–4.
14. Charles Messenger, *The Last Prussian: A Biography of Field Marshal Gerd von Rundstedt, 1875–1953*, London, 1991, 193.
15. Charles de Gaulle, *Mémoires de guerre*, vol. ii, *l'unité 1942–1944* (Paris, 1956), 709.
16. Jean Lacouture, *De Gaulle*, vol. i, *Le Rebelle, 1890–1944*, Paris, 1984, 837.
17. Alanbrooke, *War Diaries*, 212 (entry for 16 Dec. 1941).
18. Montgomery's directive quoted in L. F. Ellis, *Victory in the West*, vol. ii, London, 1968, 29.
19. Ludwig Kaiser, 'The Goerdeler Movement', in Donald S. Detwiler, ed., *World War II German Military Studies*, vol. xxiv, section C: German Opposition to Hitler, New York, 1979, MS # B-285, 61.
20. Ian Kershaw, *Hitler, 1936–1945: Nemesis*, London, 2001 684.
21. Helmut Eiber and David M. Glantz, eds., *Hitler and His Generals: Military Conferences, 1942–1945*, London, 2002, 465.
22. H. W. Koch, *In the Name of the Volk: Political Justice in Hitler's Germany*, London, 1997, 6.

23. Ibid, 210.
24. Friedrich Reck-Malleczewen, *Diary of a Man in Despair*, London, 2000, 216.
25. Sir Charles Webster and Noble Frankland, *The Strategic Air Offensive against Germany, 1939–1945*, London, 1961, iv. 135–7.
26. Howard, *Grand Strategy*,iv. 605, 607, 623.
27. Martin Middlebrook, *The Berlin Raids: RAF Bomber Command Winter 1943–44*, London, 1990, 3.
28. Webster and Frankland, *Strategic Air Offensive*, iii. 80.
29. Ibid. iv. 312.
30. *Die Tagebücher von Joseph Goebbels*, ed. Elke Fröhlich, part II, vol. ix, Munich, 1993, 190 (entry for 29 July 1943).
31. Marthe Barbance, *Saint-Nazaire: Le Port, La Ville, Le Travail*, Moulins, 1948, 623.
32. Victor Klemperer, *To the Bitter End: The Diaries of Victor Klemperer, 1942–1945*, London, 1999, 391–3.
33. Webster and Frankland, *Strategic Air Offensive*, ii. 256.
34. Ibid. iv. 326.
35. Michael J. Neufeld, *The Rocket and the Reich: Peenemünde and the Coming of the Ballistic Missile Era*, New York, 1995, 192.
36. Alec Cairncross, *Planning in Wartime: Aircraft Production in Britain, Germany and the USA*, Basingstoke, 1991, 35.
37. Order dated 16 September 1944, H. Trevor-Roper, *Hitler's War Directives*, 281.
38. Theodor Schieder et al., eds., *Die Vertreibung der Deutschen Bevölkerung aus den Gebieten östlich der Oder-Neisse*, Bonn, 1954–60, vol. i/1. 82.
39. Robin Edmonds, *The Big Three: Churchill, Roosevelt and Stalin in Peace and War*, London, 1992, 352.
40. 'Report of the Crimea Conference', 11 Feb. 1945, *FRUS: The Conferences at Malta and Yalta 1945*, Washington, 1955, 968–75.
41. *Tagebücher von Joseph Goebbels*, ed. Elke Fröhlich, part II, vol. xv, Munich, 1995, 542 (entry for 19 March 1945).
42. Trevor-Roper, *Hitler's War Directives*, 300–1.
43. John Erickson, *The Road to Berlin*, Boulder, Col., 1983, 581.
44. Donald E. Shepardson, 'The Fall of Berlin and the Rise of a Myth', *JMilH* 62: 1 (1998), 135–53.
45. Erickson, *Road to Berlin*, 608–9.
46. Wolfgang Leonhard, *Child of Revolution*, Chicago, 1958, 298.
47. Edgar McInnis, Richard Hiscocks, and Robert Spencer, *The Shaping of Postwar Germany*, New York, 1960, 103.
48. Barbara Johr, 'Die Ereignisse in Zahlen', in Helke Sander and Barbara Johr, eds., *Befreier und Befreite: Krieg, Vergewaltigungen, Kinder*, Munich, 1992, 46–73.
49. Robert Service, *Stalin: A Biography*, London, 2004, 528.
50. Jerome, Letter CXXVII (To Principia).

51. Margaret Carlyle, ed., *Documents on International Affairs, 1939–1946*, London, 1954, ii. 17–18.
52. Viktor Anfilov, 'Gregory Konstantinovich Zhukov', in Shukman, *Stalin's Generals*, 357.

11. EUROPE PARTITIONED 1945–1949

1. Martin Gilbert, *Auschwitz and the Allies*, London, 1981, 338.
2. Stephen D. Kertesz, *Between Russia and the West: Hungary and the Illusions of Peacemaking, 1945–1947*, Notre Dame, Ind., 1984, 22.
3. Frank Biess, *Homecomings: Returning POWs and the Legacies of Defeat in Postwar Germany*, Princeton, 2006, 71.
4. Susan J. Linz, 'World War II and Soviet Economic Growth, 1940–1953', in Linz, ed., *The Impact of World War II on the Soviet Union*, Totowa, NJ, 1985, 25.
5. Christian Streit, *Keine Kameraden: Die Wehrmacht and die sowjetischen Kriegsgefangenen, 1941–1945*, Stuttgart, 1978, 10.
6. Benjamin Frommer, *National Cleansing: Retribution against Nazi Collaborators in Postwar Czechoslovakia*, Cambridge, 2005, 2.
7. Ibid. 205.
8. 'Report on the Tripartite Conference of Berlin', 2 Aug. 1945, *FRUS: The Conference of Berlin 1945*, 2 vols., Washington, 1960, ii. 1499–514.
9. Theodor Schieder et al., eds., *Die Vertreibung der Deutschen Bevölkerung aus den Gebieten östlich der Oder-Neisse*, Bonn, 1954–60, vol. i/1, 90E; vol. i/2, 121.
10. Frommer, *National Cleansing*, 42.
11. Radomír Luža, *The Transfer of the Sudeten Germans: A Study of Czech-German Relations, 1933–1962*, New York, 1964, 275.
12. Ibid. 287.
13. For a local instance, see Jeremy King, *Budweisers into Czechs and Germans: A Local History of Bohemian Politics, 1848–1948*, Princeton, 2002, 184 and 190–200.
14. Sándor Márai, 'Journals', *HQ* 46: 171 (2003), 18.
15. Robert Skidelsky, *John Maynard Keynes*, 3 vols., London, 1983–2000, iii. 358.
16. Lord Alanbrooke, *War Diaries 1939–1945*, ed. Alex Dancher and Daniel Todman, London, 2002, 598 (entry for 2 Oct. 1944).
17. Hugh Thomas, *Armed Truce: The Beginnings of the Cold War, 1945–46*, New York, 1987, 93 and 555.
18. Alistair Horne, *Macmillan, 1894–1956*, London, 1988, 233.
19. Thomas, *Armed Truce*, 388.
20. Alanbrooke, *War Diaries*, 693 (entry for 24 May 1945).
21. Thomas, *Armed Truce*, 530–1.
22. Truman message to Congress, 12 March 1947, in Margaret Carlyle, ed., *Documents on International Affairs, 1947–1948*, London, 1952, 2–7.

23. Marc Lazar, 'The Cold War Culture of the French and Italian Communist Parties', in Giles Scott-Smith and Hans Krabbendam, eds., *The Cultural Cold War in Western Europe, 1945–1960*, London, 2003, 217.
24. Carlyle, *Documents, 1947–1948*, 194–7.
25. Ibid. 201–21.
26. Communiqué issued after meeting of Brussels Treaty Consultative Council, 26 Oct. 1948, ibid. 232–4.
27. J.A.S Grenville and Bernard Wasserstein, eds., *Major International Treaties of the Twentieth Century: A History and Guide with Texts*, 2 vols., London, 2001, i. 359.
28. *Das Reich*, 25 Feb. 1945. Goebbels also used the phrase repeatedly in his diary: *Die Tagebücher von Joseph Goebbels*, ed. Elke Fröhlich part II, vol. xv, (Munich, 1995, 498, 535, and 540 (entries for 14, 18, and 19 March 1945).
29. Norman Davies, *God's Playground: A History of Poland*, rev. edn., 2 vols., Oxford, 2005, ii. 558.
30. Jörg Hoensch, *A History of Modern Hungary, 1867–1986*, London, 1988, 167.
31. W. M. Carse (Budapest) to Foreign Office, 12 March 1946, British National Archives, Kew, CAB 121/441.
32. *Társadalmi Szemle*, 7: 2–3 (Feb.–March 1952), 134. Although the phrase is generally identified with Rákosi, it would appear from the context (a speech to a party audience on 29 Feb. 1952) that he did not claim to have coined it.
33. Thomas, *Armed Truce*, 282.
34. Ibid. 254.
35. Antony Polonsky and Bolesław Drukier, *The Beginnings of Communist Rule in Poland*, London, 1980, 77.
36. Texts of letters dated 27 March and 13 April 1948 in Gale Stokes, ed., *From Stalinism to Pluralism: A Documentary History of Eastern Europe since 1945*, New York, 1991, 58–65.
37. Boris Nicolaevsky, ed., *Crimes of the Stalin Era: Special Report to the 20th Congress of the Communist Party of the Soviet Union*, New York, 1962, 48.
38. Adam Ulam, *The Communists: The Story of Power and Lost Illusions, 1948–1991*, New York, 1992, 125.
39. 'Report on the Tripartite Conference of Berlin', 2 Aug. 1945, *FRUS: Conference of Berlin 1945*, vol. ii, 1499–1514.
40. Agreement of 14 Nov. 1944, as amended 1 May 1945, in Wolfgang Heidelmeyer and Gunter Hindrichs, eds., *Documents on Berlin 1943–1963*, Munich, 1963, 6–8.
41. Kommandatura statement, 13 Aug. 1946, in Heidelmeyer and Hindrichs, *Documents on Berlin*, 28.
42. Gareth Pritchard, *The Making of the GDR, 1945–1953: From Anti-Fascism to Stalinism*, Manchester, 2000, 195.
43. Alec Cairncross, *The Price of War: British Policy on German Reparations, 1941–1949*, Oxford, 1986, 100.
44. John Lewis Gaddis, *We Now Know: Rethinking Cold War History*, Oxford, 1997, 47.
45. Text in Heidelmeyer and Hindrichs, *Documents on Berlin*, 57.

46. Proclamation dated 19 June 1948 in Carlyle, *Documents, 1947–1948*, 576–9.
47. Text of article in *Tägliche Rundschau*, official newspaper of Soviet military administration, 24 June 1948, in Heidelmeyer and Hindrichs, *Documents on Berlin*, 66–7.
48. Statement on 30 June 1948, ibid. 67.
49. Michael Ermarth, ed., *America and the Shaping of German Society, 1945–1955*, Providence, RI, 1993, 13.
50. Statement by General V. I. Chuikov, 8 Oct. 1949, in Beate Ruhm von Oppen, ed., *Documents on Germany under Occupation, 1945–1954*, London, 1955, 422–3.
51. Norman M. Naimark, *The Russians in Germany: A History of the Soviet Zone of Occupation, 1945–1949*, Cambridge, Mass., 1995, 376–7.
52. See e.g. Jytte Klausen, *War and Welfare: Europe and the United States, 1945 to the Present*, New York, 1998; and James E. Cronin, *The Politics of State Expansion: War, State and Society in Twentieth-Century Britain*, London, 1991.
53. Peter Flora and Arnold J. Heidenheimer, eds., *The Development of Welfare States in Europe and America*, New Brunswick, NJ, 1981, 19.
54. Göran Rosenberg, 'The Crisis of Consensus in Post-War Sweden', in Nina Witoszek and Lars Trägårdh, eds., *Culture and Crisis: The Case of Germany and Sweden*, New York, 2002, 170–201.
55. Arvid Runestam, *Äktenskapets etik*, Stockholm, 1935, 108, quoted in Johan Söderberg, 'Controversial Consumption in Sweden, 1914–1945', *Scandinavian Economic History Review*, 48: 3 (2000), 16.
56. William Beveridge, *Social Insurance and Allied Services* (The Beveridge Report), Cmd. 6404, London, 1942.
57. Keynes to Beveridge, 17 March 1942, quoted in José Harris, *William Beveridge: A Biography*, Oxford, 1977, 408.
58. Susan Pedersen, *Family, Dependence, and the Origins of the Welfare State: Britain and France, 1914–1945*, Cambridge, 1993, 348–9.
59. Michael Foot, *Aneurin Bevan: A Biography*, vol. ii, London, 1973, 27.
60. Charles Webster, *The National Health Service: A Political History*, 2nd edn., Oxford, 2002, 1.
61. *Daily Mail*, 3 July 1946, quoted in Ina Zweniger-Bargielowska, *Austerity in Britain: Rationing, Controls, and Consumption, 1939–1955*, Oxford, 2000, 216.

12. WEST EUROPEAN RECOVERY 1949–1958

1. Comte de Las Cases, *Mémorial de Sainte-Hélène, ou Journal où se trouve consigné, jour par jour, ce qu'a dit et fait Napoléon durant dix-huit mois*, vol. vii, Paris 1824, 265–6.
2. José Ortega y Gasset, *Revolt of the Masses*, London, 1961, 136.
3. Valéry Giscard d'Estaing, quoted in François Duchêne, *Jean Monnet: The First Statesman of Interdependence*, New York, 1994, 27.
4. Julius Friend, *The Linchpin: French–German Relations, 1950–1990*, New York, 1991, 17.

5. Raymond Poidevin, *Robert Schuman*, Paris, 1988, 1.
6. Hans August Lücker and Jean Seitlinger, *Robert Schuman und die Einigung Europas*, Luxembourg, 2000, 73.
7. Poidevin, *Schuman*, 78.
8. Lücker and Seitlinger, *Schuman*, 90.
9. W. W. Rostow, 'Jean Monnet: The Innovator as Diplomat', in Gordon Craig and Francis L. Loewenheim, eds., *The Diplomats, 1939–1979*, Princeton, 1994, 260.
10. Simon Burgess and Geoffrey Edwards, 'The Six Plus One: British Policy-Making and the Question of European Economic Integration, 1955', *IA* 64: 3 (1988), 396.
11. Hans-Peter Schwarz, *Adenauer: Der Aufstieg, 1876–1952*, Stuttgart, 1986, 773.
12. Ronald J. Granieri, *The Ambivalent Alliance: Konrad Adenauer, the CDU/CSU, and the West, 1949–1966*, New York, 2003, 38.
13. Schwarz, *Adenauer: Der Aufstieg*, 152.
14. Ibid. 660–1.
15. Vojtech Mastny, 'The New History of Cold War Alliances', *JCWS* 4: 2 (2002), 55–84.
16. Selwyn Lloyd to Churchill, 22 June 1953, in Christian F. Ostermann, ed., *Uprising in East Germany, 1953*, Budapest, 2001, 252–4.
17. Friend, *Linchpin*, 26–8.
18. Text of Messina Declaration at http://www.eu-history.leidenuniv.nl/index.php3?m=10&c=52.
19. Duchêne, *Jean Monnet*, 288.
20. Text of Treaty of Rome, 25 March 1957, in J.A.S. Grenville and Bernard Wasserstein, *The Major International Treaties of the Twentieth Century: A History and Guide with Texts*, 2 vols., London, 2001, ii. 530–44.
21. George C. Herring and Richard H. Immerman, 'Eisenhower, Dulles, and Dienbienphu: "The Day We Didn't Go to War" Revisited', *Journal of American History*, 71: 2 (1984), 343–63.
22. André Siegfried, *De la IIIe à la IVe République*, Paris, 1956, 168.
23. See text of the Convention in Grenville and Wasserstein, *Major International Treaties*, i. 128–31.
24. 'Defence of the Middle East', War Cabinet memorandum by Eden, 13 April 1945, in *BDEE*, series B, vol. iv, part 1, London, 1998, 6–9.
25. Text in *BDEE*, ser. B, vol. iv, part 3, London, 1998, 320–4.
26. *BDEE*, ser. A, vol. iii, part 1, London, 1994, p. xxxiv.
27. Memorandum dated 17 July 1956, quoted ibid., p. xxviii.
28. Georgette Elgey, *Histoire de la IVe Répuliqe*, vol. iv, Paris, 1997, 73.
29. Keith Kyle, *Suez: Britain's End of Empire in the Middle East*, 2nd edn., London, 2003, 425.
30. Peter G. Boyle, *The Eden–Eisenhower Correspondence, 1955–1957*, Chapel Hill, NC, 2005, 201.
31. *The Memoirs of the Rt. Hon. Sir Anthony Eden: Full Circle*, London, 1960, 577.

32. French Foreign Ministry memorandum, 10 Nov. 1956, *DDF*, série 7, *Depuis 1954*, vol. iii, Paris, 1990, 271–7.
33. Elgey, *Histoire de la IVe Républiqe*, vol. iv, 531.
34. Paul Aussaresses, *Services spéciaux: Algérie, 1955–1957*, Paris, 2001, 153.
35. Paul-Marie de la Gorce, *The French Army: A Military-Political History*, New York, 1963, 422.
36. Jean Lacouture, *De Gaulle*, vol. ii, *Le politique, 1944–1959*, Paris, 1985, 461.
37. Charles de Gaulle, *Discours et messages*, vol. iii, Paris, 1970, 3.
38. Transcript of press conference, 19 May 1958, ibid. 4–10.
39. Lacouture, *De Gaulle*, vol. ii, 473.
40. Jean-Louis Rizzo, *Mendès France ou la rénovation en politique*, Paris, 1993, 199.
41. Statement by de Gaulle, 1 June 1958, official text issued by French Embassy, Washington.
42. Speech on 4 June 1958, De Gaulle, *Discours et messages*, vol. iii, 15.
43. Text of address, 13 June 1958, issued by French Embassy, Washington.
44. David Holloway, *Stalin and the Bomb: The Soviet Union and Atomic Energy, 1939–1956*, New Haven, 1994, 265–6.
45. Report by the Chiefs of Staff, 7 June 1950, in *DBPO*, ser. II, vol. iv, London, 1991, 411–31.
46. Christopher Andrew and Vasili Mitrokhin, *The Sword and the Shield: The Mitrokhin Archive and the Secret History of the KGB*, New York, 1999, 399.
47. Juhana Aunesluoma, *Britain, Sweden and the Cold War, 1945–54*, Basingstoke, 2003, 81.
48. Paula L. Wyle, *Ireland and the Cold War: Diplomacy and Recognition, 1949–1963*, Dublin, 2006, 43 and 60.
49. General Sir Ian Jacob, Military Assistant Secretary to the War Cabinet, 1939–1946, quoted in Stephen Twigge and Len Scott, *Planning Armageddon: Britain, the United States and the Command of Western Nuclear Forces, 1945–1964*, Amsterdam, 2000, 251.
50. Chiefs of Staff memorandum for Cabinet Defence Committee, 23 Dec. 1954, *BDEE*, ser. A, vol. iii, part 1, 52–7.
51. John Baylis, 'Exchanging Nuclear Secrets: Laying the Foundations of the Anglo-American Nuclear Relationship', *Diplomatic History*, 25: 1 (2001), 33–61.
52. Hans-Peter Schwarz, *Adenauer: Der Staatsmann, 1952–1967*, Stuttgart, 1991, 383.
53. State Dept. to US Mission to NATO, 21 Jan. 1958, *FRUS 1958–60*, vol. x, part 1, 1–4.
54. Michael Foot, *Aneurin Bevan: A Biography*, vol. ii, London, 1973, 574.

13. STALIN AND HIS HEIRS 1949–1964

1. Anna Akhmatova, *The Word That Causes Death's Defeat: Poems of Memory*, ed. Nancy K. Anderson, New Haven, 2004, 108.

2. David Caute, *The Dancer Defects: The Struggle for Cultural Supremacy During the Cold War*, Oxford, 2003, 381.
3. Andrei Sakharov, *Memoirs*, London, 1990, 46.
4. Boris Kagarlitsky, *The Thinking Reed: Intellectuals and the Soviet State 1917 to the Present*, London, 1988, 130.
5. Christopher Andrew and Oleg Gordievsky, *KGB: The Inside Story of its Foreign Operations from Lenin to Khrushchev*, London, 1990, 341.
6. Jiří Pelikán, *The Czechoslovak Political Trials, 1950–1954: The Suppressed Report of the Dubček Government's Commission of Inquiry, 1968*, Stanford, 1971, 76.
7. Ibid. 78.
8. Slánský to Chairman of Central Committee of Czechoslovak Communist Party, 26 Nov. 1951, in Karel Bartosek, *Les Aveux des archives: Prague—Paris—Prague, 1948–1968*, Paris, 1996, 375.
9. Igor Lukes, 'The Rudolf Slánský Affair: New Evidence', *SR* 58: 1 (1999), 160–87.
10. Czech newspaper account quoted in Patrick Brogan, *The Captive Nations: Eastern Europe 1945–1990*, New York, 1990, 90.
11. Pelikán, *Czechoslovak Political Trials*, 56.
12. Yoram Gorlizki and Oleg Khlevniuk, *Cold Peace: Stalin and the Soviet Ruling Circle, 1945–1953*, Oxford, 2004, 25.
13. Ibid. 76.
14. Benjamin Pinkus, *The Soviet Government and the Jews, 1948–1967: A Documented Study*, Cambridge, 1984, 219–20.
15. Elena Zubkova, *Russia After the War: Hopes, Illusions, and Disappointments, 1945–1957*, Armonk, NY, 1998, 153.
16. Victor Klemperer, *The Diaries of Victor Klemperer, 1945–1959: The Lesser Evil*, London, 2004, 525 (entry dated 31 Dec. 1958).
17. Ibid. (entry dated 10 Aug. 1957).
18. 'Draft Instructions for General Vasilii Chuikov and Vladimir Semyonov regarding GDR Control of Borders', 18 March 1953, in Christian F. Ostermann, ed., *Uprising in East Germany 1953*, Budapest, 2001, 50.
19. Order by USSR Council of Ministers, 2 June 1953, in Ostermann, *Uprising*, 133–6.
20. Notes by Otto Grotewohl on meetings of East German and Soviet leaders, 2–4 June 1953, ibid. 137–8.
21. Gareth Dale, *Popular Protest in East Germany, 1945*–1989, Abingdon, 2005, 20.
22. Martin Krämer, *Der Volksaufstand vom 17. Juni 1953 und sein politisches Echo in der Bundesrepublik Deutschland*, Bochum, 1996, 7; and Ostermann, *Uprising, passim.*
23. Bertolt Brecht, 'Die Lösung', *Gesammelte Werke 10: Gedichte 3*, Frankfurt am Main, 1967, 1009–10.
24. Mark W. Clark, 'Hero or Villain? Bertolt Brecht and the Crisis Surrounding June 1953', *JCH* 41: 3 (2006), 451–75.
25. Beria to Malenkov, 1 July 1953, in Ostermann, *Uprising*, 155–7.

26. Christopher Andrew and Vasili Mitrokhin, *The Sword and the Shield: The Mitrokhin Archive and the Secret History of the KGB*, New York, 1999, 2.
27. William Taubman, *Khrushchev: The Man and his Era*, New York, 2003, 43.
28. Strobe Talbott, ed., *Khrushchev Remembers*, Boston, 1970, 353.
29. Boris Nicolaevsky ed., *Crimes of the Stalin Era: Special Report to the 20th Congress of the Communist Party of the Soviet Union*, New York, 1962, *passim*.
30. Polly Jones, ed., *The Dilemmas of De-Stalinization: Negotiating Cultural and Social Change in the Khrushchev Era*, Abingdon, 2006, 2.
31. Galia Golan, *The Czechoslovak Reform Movement: Communism in Crisis, 1962–1968*, Cambridge, 1971, 4.
32. Adam B. Ulam, *The Communists: The Story of Power and Lost Illusions, 1948–1991*, New York, 1992, 143.
33. Johanna Granville, 'Reactions to the Events of 1956: New Findings from the Budapest and Warsaw Archives', *JCH* 38: 2 (April 2003), 266.
34. Gomułka's report to meeting of Polish United Workers' Party Politburo, 19–21 Oct. 1956, *CWIHPB* 5 (1995), 39–40.
35. Record of meeting of Soviet party Presidium, 24 Oct. 1956, *CWIHPB* 5 (1995), 53–6.
36. Konrad Syrop, *Spring in October: The Polish Revolution of 1956*, London, 1957, 108.
37. L. A. C. Fry (Budapest) to H. A. F. Hohler (Foreign Office), 21 March 1956, in Eva Haraszti-Taylor, *The Hungarian Revolution of 1956: A Collection of Documents from the British Foreign Office*, Nottingham, 1995, 22–5.
38. See report by KGB chief, V. A. Kryuchkov, 16 June 1989, and accompanying documents, *CWIHPB*, 5 (1995), 36–7.
39. Congress for Cultural Freedom, *The Truth about the Nagy Affair*, London, 1959, 129–30.
40. Ulam, *Communists*, 159.
41. György Litván, ed., *The Hungarian Revolution of 1956: Reform, Revolt and Repression, 1953–1963*, London, 1996, 55.
42. Taubman, *Khrushchev: The Man and his Era*, 296.
43. János M. Rainer, '1956—The Other Side of the Story: Five Documents from the Yeltsin File', *HQ* 34 (129): 100–13 (translation slightly amended).
44. Notes by Yugoslav Ambassador to Moscow on Brioni talks, 2/3 Nov. 1956, in Csaba Békés, Malcolm Byrne, and János M. Rainer, *The 1956 Hungarian Revolution: A History in Documents*, Budapest, 2002, 348–54.
45. Congress for Cultural Freedom, *Nagy Affair*, 9.
46. Mark Kramer, 'The Soviet Union and the 1956 Crises in Hungary and Poland: Reassessments and New Findings', *JCH* 33: 2 (April 1998), 163–214.
47. David Caute, *The Fellow-Travellers: Intellectual Friends of Communism*, rev. edn. New Haven, 1988, 340–2.
48. Alajos Dornbach, *The Secret Trial of Imre Nagy*, Westport, Conn., 1994, 52.
49. Court judgment, ibid. 114.

50. Broadcast on 19 June 1958, Congress for Cultural Freedom, *Nagy Affair*, 172.
51. Speech at Gdańsk, 30 June 1958, ibid. 174.
52. Kádár speech to National Council of People's Patriotic Front, 9 Dec. 1961, quoted in Ferenc A. Vali, 'The Regime and the Nation', in Tamás Aczél, ed., *Ten Years After: The Hungarian Revolution in the Perspective of History*, New York, 1966, 138. Kádár here reversed a statement attributed to Rákosi, in turn echoing Luke 11: 23.
53. Raymond L. Garthoff, 'When and Why Romania Distanced itself from the Warsaw Pact', *CWIHPB* 5 (1995), 111.
54. Taubman, *Khrushchev: The Man and his Era*, 471.
55. Jon Halliday, ed., *The Artful Albanian: The Memoirs of Enver Hoxha*, London, 1986, 220.
56. Ibid. 237.
57. Brian D. Taylor, *Politics and the Russian Army: Civil–Military Relations, 1689–2000*, Cambridge, 2003, 186.
58. Kagarlitsky, *Thinking Reed*, 159.
59. Joshua Rubenstein, *Tangled Loyalties: The Life and Times of Ilya Ehrenburg*, London, 1996, 4.
60. See Isaiah Berlin, *Personal Impressions*, London, 1980, 185–6.
61. Olga Ivinskaya, *A Captive of Time: My Years with Pasternak*, London, 1978, 246, 272, 278, 290.
62. Tito to Aneurin Bevan, 22 Feb. 1954, in Michael Foot, *Aneurin Bevan: A Biography*, London, 1973, ii. 422–3.
63. Barbara Jelavich, *Modern Austria: Empire and Republic, 1800–1980*, Cambridge, 1987, 267.
64. Tuure Junnila quoted in M. Cresswell (Helsinki) to Selwyn Lloyd (British Foreign Secretary), 5 Dec. 1956, http://www.fco.gov.uk/Files/kfile/britain-finland3956_37.pdf.
65. Text in H. Hanak, ed., *Soviet Foreign Policy since the Death of Stalin*, London, 1972, 106–11.
66. Taubman, *Khrushchev: The Man and his Era*, 397.
67. Account by A. M. Aleksandrov-Agentov quoted in Hope M. Harrison, *Driving the Soviets up the Wall: Soviet-East German Relations, 1953–1961*, Princeton, 2003, 109.
68. Willy Brandt, *Erinnerungen*, Berlin, 1994, 34.
69. John P. S. Gearson, *Harold Macmillan and the Berlin Wall Crisis, 1958–62: The Limits of Interests and Force*, Basingstoke, 1998, 71.
70. Wolfgang Heidelmeyer and Gunther Hindrichs, eds., *Documents on Berlin, 1943–1963*, Munich, 1963, 257.
71. George Tenet, 'The U-2 Program: The DCI's Perspective', paper read at CIA Center for the Study of Intelligence public symposium at the National Defense University, Fort McNair, Washington, DC 17 September 1998, http://www.odci.gov/csi/studies/winter98_99/art01.html.

72. Taubman, *Khrushchev: The Man and his Era*, 468.
73. John Rodden, *Repainting the Little Red Schoolhouse: A History of Eastern German Education, 1945–1995*, Oxford, 2002, 109.
74. Markus Wolf, *Memoirs of a Spymaster*, London, 1998, 103.
75. Harrison, *Driving the Soviets*, 188.
76. Decree dated 12 Aug. 1961, in Heidelmeyer and Hindrichs, *Documents on Berlin*, 271–2.
77. Text of statement dated 13 Aug. 1961, in Hanak, *Soviet Foreign Policy*, 112–3.
78. Harrison, *Driving the Soviets*, 205.
79. Harold Evans, *Downing Street Diary: The Macmillan Years, 1957–1963*, London, 1981, 159.
80. Oleg Rzheshevsky, 'Ivan Stepanovich Konev', in Harold Shukman, ed., *Stalin's Generals*, London, 1993, 91–107.
81. Detlef Junker et al., eds., *Die USA und Deutschland im Zeitalter des Kalten Krieges 1945–1990: Ein Handbuch*, 2 vols., Stuttgart, 2001, i. 267.
82. Taubman, *Khrushchev: The Man and his Era*, 569.
83. William Taubman, ed., *Khrushchev on Khrushchev*, Boston, 1990, 133–4.
84. Taubman, *Khrushchev: The Man and his Era*, 15.

14. CONSENSUS AND DISSENT IN WESTERN EUROPE 1958–1973

1. Jürgen Kohl, 'Trends and Problems in Postwar Public Expenditure Development in Western Europe and North America', in Peter Flora and Arnold J. Heidenheimer, eds., *Development of Welfare States in Europe and America*, New Brunswick, NJ, 1981, 307–44.
2. Alain Peyrefitte, *C'était de Gaulle*, vol. ii, Paris, 1997, 74 (entry dated 27 Feb. 1963).
3. Jeffrey Glen Giauque, *Grand Designs and Visions of Unity: The Atlantic Powers and the Reorganization of Western Europe, 1955–1963*, Chapel Hill, NC, 2002, 40.
4. Alain Peyrefitte, *C'était de Gaulle*, vol. i, Paris, 1994, 299 (entry dated 30 May 1962).
5. Alistair Horne, *Macmillan, 1957–1986*, London, 1989, 446–7.
6. Peyrefitte, *C'était de Gaulle*, ii. 356–8 (entries dated March–April 1963).
7. Ibid. 291 (entry dated 1 July 1965).
8. Raymond Aron, *Mémoires*, Paris, 1983, 385.
9. Charles de Gaulle, *Discours et messages*, vols. iii–v, Paris, 1970. iii. 117–23.
10. Ibid. 162–6.
11. Ibid. 308.
12. Horne, *Macmillan, 1957–1986*, 195.
13. Harold Wilson to Kenneth Kaunda, 13 Dec. 1965, *BDEE*, ser. A, vol. v, part 2, 213–5.
14. Healey to Wilson, 20 Jan. 1966, BDEE, ser. A, vol. v, part 2, 231–2.

15. Draft Colonial Office memorandum, August 1965, *BDEE*, ser. A, vol. v, part 3, 32–5.
16. Foreign Office memorandum, 6 July 1965, *BDEE*, ser. A. vol. v, part 3, 18–30.
17. Hans-Peter Schwarz, *Adenauer: Der Staatsmann, 1952–1967*, Stuttgart, 1991, 687.
18. Marc Trachtenberg, *Constructed Peace: The Making of the European Settlement, 1945–1963*, Princeton, 1999, 233–8.
19. Schwarz, *Adenauer: Staatsmann*, 787–8.
20. Stig Hadenius, *Swedish Politics in the 20th Century*, Stockholm, 1997, 101.
21. Horne, *Macmillan, 1957–1986*, 153.
22. Harold Macmillan, *At the End of the Day, 1961–1963*, London, 1973, 93.
23. Keith Laybourne, *Fifty Key Figures in Twentieth Century British Politics*, London, 2002, 177 (cf. John 15: 13).
24. Horne, *Macmillan 1957–1986*, 481.
25. Simon Ball, *The Guardsmen: Harold Macmillan, Three Friends, and the World They Made*, London, 2004, 369.
26. Conor Cruise O'Brien, *States of Ireland*, St Albans, 1974, 17.
27. Christopher Andrew and Vasili Mitrokhin, *The Sword and the Shield: The Mitrokhin Archire and the Secret History of the KGB*, New York, 1999, 384–5.
28. First published in English in 1964, in German and Italian in 1967, and in French in May 1968.
29. Herbert Marcuse, 'Repressive Tolerance', in Robert Paul Wolff, Barrington Moore, Jr., and Herbert Marcuse eds., *A Critique of Pure Tolerance*, Boston, 1969, 117.
30. Claus Leggewie, 'A Laboratory of Postindustrial Society: Reassessing the 1960s in Germany', in Carole Fink, Philipp Gassert, and Detlef Junker, *eds., 1968: The World Transformed*, Cambridge, 1998, 286.
31. Stuart J. Wilwig, 'The Revolt against the Establishment: Students versus the Press in West Germany and Italy', in Fink et al., *1968*, 340.
32. Stanley Hoffman, 'The Foreign Policy of Charles de Gaulle', in Gordon Craig and Francis L. Loewenheim, eds., *The Diplomats, 1939–1979*, Princeton, 1994, 240.
33. Edgar Morin, Claude Lefort, and Jean-Marc Coudray, *Mai 1968: la Brèche: Premières réflexions sur les événements*, Paris, 1968, 78.
34. Raymond Aron, *La Révolution introuvable*, Paris, 1968, 13–14.
35. Text of article in *L'Humanité*, 3 May 1968, reprinted in Adrien Dansette, *Mai 1968*, Paris, 1971, 383–5.
36. François Mauriac, *Le dernier bloc-notes, 1968–1970*, Paris, 1971, 60 (entry for 11 May 1968).
37. Peyrefitte, *C'était de Gaulle*, iii. 527 (entries dated 19 May 1968).
38. Ibid. 546–9 (entries dated 27 May 1968).
39. Ibid. 550–777 (entries for 28 May–14 June 1968); Jacques Massu, *Avec de Gaulle: Du Tchad 1941 à Baden 1968*, Monaco, 1998, 159–94; Jean Lacouture, *De Gaulle*, vol. iii, *Le Souverain 1959–1970*, Paris, 1986, 702–10.
40. Charles de Gaulle, *Discours et messages*, vol. iv, Paris, 1970, 292–3.

41. Dansette, *Mai 1968*, 431.
42. Georges Pompidou, *Entretiens et discours, 1968–1974*, Paris, 1975, 16.
43. Leggewie, 'Laboratory', 279.
44. *Independent*, 23 May 2005.
45. Horne, *Macmillan, 1957–86*, 277.
46. Patrick Gordon Walker, 'Hugh Gaitskell', in Hugo Young, ed., *Political Lives*, Oxford, 2001, 351.
47. Stephen Twigge and Len Scott, *Planning Armageddon: Britain, the United States and the Command of Western Nuclear Forces, 1945–1964*, Amsterdam, 2000, 137.
48. Michel Winock, *La République se meurt: Chronique, 1956–1958*, Paris, 1978, 137.
49. [Charles] Ailleret, 'Défense "dirigée" ou défense "tous azimuts"', *Revue de défense nationale*, 23 (Dec. 1967), 1923–32.
50. Gottfried Niedhart, 'Ostpolitik: The Role of the Federal Republic of Germany in the Process of Détente', in Fink, et al., *1968*, 175.
51. Josef Joffe, 'The Foreign Policy of the Federal Republic of Germany', in Roy C. Macridis, ed., *Foreign Policy in World Politics*, 6th edn., Englewood Cliffs, NJ, 1985, 101.
52. Kissinger to Nixon, Feb. 1970, in Jussi M. Hanhimäki and Odd Arne Westad, eds., *The Cold War: A History in Documents and Eyewitness Accounts*, Oxford, 2004, 338.
53. Interview with Brandt in *Die Zeit*, quoted in speech by Aase Lionæs at Nobel Peace Prize award ceremony, Oslo, 10 Dec. 1971, http://nobelprize.org/peace/laureates/1971/press.html.

15. EUROPE IN THE 1960S

1. Patrick Cockburn, *The Broken Boy*, London, 2005, 52.
2. Rózsa Kulczár, 'The Socioeconomic Conditions of Women in Hungary', in Sharon L. Wolchik and Alfred G. Meyer, eds., *Women, State, and Party in Eastern Europe*, Durham, NC, 1985, 199.
3. Geoff Eley, *Forging Democracy: The History of the Left in Europe, 1850–2000*, New York, 2002, 367.
4. David Martin, *A General Theory of Secularization*, Oxford, 1978.
5. Paul Mendes-Flohr, 'Buber's Rhetoric', in Paul Mendes-Flohr, ed., *Martin Buber: A Contemporary Perspective*, Jerusalem, 2002, 23.
6. Martin Buber, *I and Thou*, trans. Ronald Gregor Smith, Edinburgh, 1958.
7. John Robinson, *Honest to God*, London, 2001, p. xiii.
8. C. S. Lewis, *God in the Dock: Essays on Theology and Ethics*, Grand Rapids, Mich., 1994, 260.
9. Statement by World Council of Churches, 1948, quoted in Geoffrey Wigoder, *Jewish–Christian Relations since the Second World War*, Manchester, 1988, 165.
10. Pierre Teilhard de Chardin, *Le Phénomène humain*, Paris, 1955, 66.

11. Austin Flannery, OP, ed., *Vatican Council II: The Conciliar and Post Conciliar Documents*, rev. edn., Northport, NY, 1992, 741.
12. Cardinal Claudio Hummes, 'Theological and Ecclesiological Foundations of *Gaudium et spes*', paper delivered at conference on 'The Call to Justice: The Legacy of *Gaudium et spes* forty years later', Vatican City, 16 March 2005.
13. Text of *Gaudium et spes* at http://www.vatican.va/archive/histcouncils/ii_vatican_council/documents/vat-ii_cons_19651207_gaudium-t-spes_en.html.
14. Flannery, ed., *Vatican II*, 13.
15. Peter Hebblethwaite, *In the Vatican*, Oxford, 1987, 124.
16. Hans Küng, *My Struggle for Freedom: Memoirs*, Grand Rapids, Mich., 2003, 374.
17. C. M. Hann, *Tázlár: A Village in Hungary*, Cambridge, 1980, 116.
18. Jon Halliday, *The Artful Albanian: The Memoirs of Enver Hoxha*, London, 1986, 14.
19. Yossi Shavit and Hans-Peter Blossfeld, eds., *Persistent Inequality: Changing Educational Attainment in Thirteen Countries*, Boulder, Col., 1993.
20. P. J. D. Wiles and Stefan Markowski, 'Income Distribution under Communism and Capitalism. Some Facts about Poland, the UK, the USA and the USSR. Part I', *SS* 22: 3 (1971), 353.
21. Richard M. Titmuss, *Income Distribution and Social Change: a study in criticism*, London, 1962, 15.
22. Henry W. Morton, 'Who Gets What, When, and How? Housing in the Soviet Union', *SS* 32: 2 (1980), 236.
23. Tibor Valuch, 'From Long House to Square: Changing Village Living Conditions in Sixties Hungary', in János M. Rainer and György Péteri, eds., *Muddling Through in the Long 1960s: Ideas and Everyday Life in High Politics and the Lower Classes of Communist Hungary* (Trondheim Studies on East European Cultures and Societies, No. 16), Trondheim, 2005, 153.
24. Burton Paulu, *Radio and Television Broadcasting in Eastern Europe*, Minneapolis, 1974, 162.
25. Galia Golan, *The Czechoslovak Reform Movement: Communism in Crisis, 1962–1968*, Cambridge, 1971, 29.
26. Burton Paulu, *Radio and Television Broadcasting on the European Continent*, Minneapolis, 1967, 153.
27. Philip V. Bohlman, *The Music of European Nationalism: Cultural Identity and Modern History*, Santa Barbara, 2004, 3.
28. Paulu, *Broadcasting in Eastern Europe*, 491.
29. Sándor Horváth, 'Hooligans, spivs and gangs. Youth subcultures in the 1960s', in Rainer and Péteri, eds., *Muddling Through*, 210.
30. John Rodden, *Repainting the Little Red Schoolhouse: A History of Eastern German Education, 1945–1995*, Oxford, 2002, 125, 127.
31. David Caute, *The Dancer Defects: The Struggle for Cultural Supremacy during the Cold War*, Oxford, 2003, 304.
32. Gonda A. H. Van Steen, *Venom in Verse: Aristophanes in Modern Greece*, Princeton, 2000, 125.

33. Anatoly Smeliansky, *The Russian Theatre after Stalin*, Cambridge, 1999, 43.

16. STRIFE IN COMMUNIST EUROPE 1964–1985

1. Bülent Gökay, 'History of Oil Development in the Caspian Basin', in Michael P. Croissont and Bülent Aras, eds., *Oil and Geopolitics in the Caspian Sea Region*, Westport, Conn., 1999, 15.
2. David Burg and George Feifer, *Solzhenitsyn*, New York, 1973, 288.
3. Ibid. 321.
4. 'Mr Solzhenitsyn and his Critics', *FA* 59: 1 (1980), 200.
5. Andrei Sakharov, *Memoirs*, London, 1990, 225.
6. David Caute, *The Dancer Defects: The Struggle for Supremacy during the Cold War*, Oxford, 2003, 434.
7. Christopher Andrew and Vasili Mitrokhin, *The Sword and the Shield: The Mitrokhin Archive and the Secret History of the KGB*, New York, 1999 325.
8. Galia Golan, *Reform Rule in Czechoslovakia: The Dubček Era, 1968–1969*, Cambridge, 1973, ch. 2.
9. Gail Stokes, ed., *From Stalinism to Pluralism: A Documentary History of Eastern Europe since 1945*, New York, 1991, 126–30.
10. Mark Kramer, 'The Czechoslovak Crisis and the Brezhnev Doctrine', in Carole Fink, Philipp Gassert, and Detlef Junker, eds., *1968: The World Transformed*, Cambridge, 1998, 144.
11. Kramer, 'Czechoslovak Crisis', 125.
12. Jiri Valenta, *Soviet Intervention in Czechoslovakia, 1968: Anatomy of a Decision*, rev. edn., Baltimore, 1991, 24.
13. *The Times*, 19 July 1968; and H. Hanak, ed., *Soviet Foreign Policy since the Death of Stalin*, London, 1972, 261–8.
14. Karen Dawisha, *The Kremlin and the Prague Spring*, Berkeley, 1984, 256.
15. Ibid. 263.
16. *The Times*, 3 Aug. 1968.
17. Kieran Williams, *The Prague Spring and its Aftermath: Czechoslovak Politics 1968–1970*, Cambridge, 1997, 123.
18. Dawisha, *Kremlin and the Prague Spring*, 289.
19. *The Times*, 22 Aug. 1968.
20. *The Times*, 24 Aug. 1968.
21. Zdeněk Mlynář, *Night Frost*, London, 1980, 239.
22. Ibid. 211.
23. Kai Hermann, 'The Fall of Prague', *Encounter*, 31: 5 (Nov. 1968), 85–93.
24. Foreword by Dubček to Valenta, *Soviet Intervention in Czechoslovakia*, p. x.
25. William V. Wallace, *Czechoslovakia*, London, 1977, 341.
26. *The Times*, 28 Aug. 1968.

27. J. A. S. Grenville and Bernard Wasserstein, *The Major International Treaties of the Twentieth Century: A History and Guide with Texts*, 2 vols., London, 2001, ii. 399–402.
28. Stokes, *Stalinism to Pluralism*, 132–4.
29. Grenville and Wasserstein, *Major International Treaties*, ii. 828–35.
30. George Konrád, *Antipolitics*, San Diego, 1984, 2.
31. Report dated 15 November 1976, Jussi M. Hanhimäki and Odd Arne Westad, eds, *The Cold War: A History in Documents and Eyewitness Accounts*, Oxford, 2004, 531–2.
32. Daniel C. Thomas, *The Helsinki Effect: International Norms, Human Rights, and the Demise of Communism*, Princeton, 2001, 138.
33. Personal memorandum from Andropov to Brezhnev, early Dec. 1979, Hanhimäki and Westad, *Cold War*, 546–7.
34. Georges-Henri Soutou, 'L'Anneau et les deux triangles: les rapports franco-allemands dans la politique européenne et mondiale de 1974 à 1981', in Serge Bernstein and Jean-François Sirinelli, eds., *Les Années Giscard: Valéry Giscard d'Estaing et l'Europe, 1974–1981*, Paris, 2006, 73.
35. Markus Wolf, *Memoirs of a Spymaster*, London, 1998, 242–6.
36. Bronysław Geremek at symposium to mark the 25th anniversary of Solidarity, Warsaw, 29 Aug. 2005.
37. Richard J. Hunter and Leo V. Ryan, *From Autarchy to Market: Polish Economics and Politics, 1945–1995*, Westport, Conn., 1998, 49.
38. Ibid. 52.
39. Gideon Baker, *Civil Society and Democratic Theory: International Perspectives*, London, 2002, 17. (The term 'self-limiting revolution' has also been ascribed to Jadwiga Staniszkis.)
40. Text in Robert V. Daniels, ed., *A Documentary History of Communism*, 2 vols., Hanover, NH, 1984, ii. 420–5.
41. *Pravda*, 1 Sept. 1980, quoted in Matthew J. Ouimet, *The Rise and Fall of the Brezhnev Doctrine in Soviet Foreign Policy*, Chapel Hill, NC, 2003, 138.
42. Honecker to Brezhnev, 28 Nov. 1980, *CWIHPB* 5 (1995), 124.
43. *NYT*, 12 Jan. 1993.
44. Vojtech Mastny, 'The Soviet Non-Invasion of Poland in 1980–1981 and the End of the Cold War', *EAS* 51: 2 (1999), 189–211.
45. Report to Soviet Politburo by K. Chernenko, Y. Andropov, D. Ustinov et al., 16 April 1981, *CWIHPB* 5 (1995), 130–1.
46. Adam B. Ulam, *The Communists: The Story of Power and Lost Illusions, 1948–1991*, New York, 1992, 375.
47. Transcript of telephone conversation, 19 Oct. 1981, *CWIHPB* 5 (1995), 132.
48. Text in Daniels, *Documentary History*, ii. 425–7.
49. See extract from notebook of Lt.-Gen. V. I. Anoshkin regarding conversation on 11 Dec. 1981 between Soviet Marshal Victor Kulikov and Polish General Florian Siwicki, Hanhimäki and Westad, eds., *Cold War*, 571–3.

50. Minutes of CPSU CC Politburo, 10 Dec. 1981, in Malcolm Byrne, 'New Evidence on the Polish Crisis 1980–1981', *CWIHPB* 11 (1998), document 21, 165.
51. Text of Nobel lecture, 11 Dec. 1983: http://nobelprize.org/peace/laureates/1983/walesa-lecture.html.
52. *NYT*, 26 Nov. 1987.
53. *Voices of Czechoslovak Socialists*, London, 1977, 126–32.
54. *NYT*, 18 Jan. 1982.
55. Konrád, *Antipolitics*, 163.

17. STRESS IN LIBERAL EUROPE 1973–1989

1. *Economist*, 11 Aug. 1990.
2. Peter B. Kenen, ed., *Managing the World Economy: Fifty Years After Bretton Woods*, Washington, 1994, 36.
3. Skidelsky, *Keynes*, vol. iii, 284–5.
4. Speech at Conservative Party Conference, Brighton, 10 Oct. 1980: http://www.margaretthatcher.org/speeches/displaydocument.asp?docid=104431.
5. Shirley Robin Letwin, *Anatomy of Thatcherism*, New Brunswick, NJ, 1993, 314.
6. Interview for *Woman's Own*, 31 Oct. 1987: http://www.margaretthatcher.org/speeches/displaydocument.asp?docid=106689.
7. Sir Michael Howard (quoting an unnamed Latin American) in a review in *EHR* 121: 490 (2006), 261.
8. Paul Ginsborg, *A History of Contemporary Italy: Society and Politics, 1943–1988*, London, 1990, 34.
9. Christopher Andrew and Vasili Mitrokhin, *The Sword and the Shield: The Mitrokhin Archive and the Secret History of the KGB*, New York, 1999, 298, 306; Christopher Andrew and Oleg Gordievsky, *Comrade Kryuchkov's Instructions: Top Secret Files on KGB Foreign Operations, 1975–1985*, Stanford, 1991, 170.
10. Vincent Wright, *Conflict and Consensus in France*, London, 1979, 92 (translation amended).
11. Sten Rynning, *Changing Military Doctrine: Presidents and Military Power in Fifth Republic France, 1958–2000*, Westport, Conn., 2002, 126.
12. Heidrun Abromeit, 'The Chancellor and Organised Interests', in Stephen Padgett, ed., *Adenauer to Kohl: Development of the German Chancellorship*, London, 1994, 170.
13. Speech at Mainz on 10 May 1981.
14. Kenneth Maxwell, *The Making of Portuguese Democracy*, Cambridge, 1995, 17.
15. Robert O. Paxton, *The Anatomy of Fascism*, London, 2005, 150.
16. Maxwell, *Making of Portuguese Democracy*, 18.
17. Ibid. 42.
18. Ibid. 66.

19. Tad Szulc, 'Lisbon and Washington: Behind the Portuguese Revolution', *Foreign Policy*, 21 (1975–6), 3.
20. Francisco J. Romero Salvadó, *Twentieth-Century Spain: Politics and Society in Spain, 1898–1998*, Basingstoke, 1999, 146.
21. Paul Preston, *The Triumph of Democracy in Spain*, London, 1986, 80.
22. C. M. Woodhouse, *The Rise and Fall of the Greek Colonels*, New York, 1995, 155.
23. Lars Trägårdh, 'Crisis and the Politics of National Community: Germany and Sweden, 1933/1994', in Nina Witoszek and Lars Trägårdh, eds., *Culture and Crisis: The Case of Germany and Sweden*, New York, 2002, 93.
24. Richard Clogg, *Parties and Elections in Greece: The Search for Legitimacy*, London, 1987, 138.
25. Eric J. Evans, *Thatcher and Thatcherism*, London, 1997, 86.

18. THE COLLAPSE OF COMMUNISM IN EASTERN EUROPE 1985–1991

1. Donald Morrison, ed., *Mikhail S. Gorbachev: An Intimate Biography*, New York, 1988, 59–60.
2. Margaret Thatcher, *The Downing Street Years*, London, 1993, 463.
3. Archie Brown, *The Gorbachev Factor*, Oxford, 1996, 32 and 78–80.
4. Ibid. 37.
5. Ibid. 101.
6. David Burg and George Feifer, *Solzhenitsyn*, New York, 1973, 288–90.
7. Brian McNair, *Glasnost, Perestroika and the Soviet Media*, London, 1991, 53.
8. United Nations Scientific Committee on the Sources and Effects of Ionizing Radiation, *Report to the General Assembly, with Scientific Annexes*, United Nations, 2000, vol. ii, annex J, 516; see also Report of the UN Chernobyl Forum Expert Group 'Environment', *Environmental Consequences of the Chernobyl Accident and their Remediation: Twenty Years of Experience* (Aug. 2005) and International Atomic Energy Agency, *Chernobyl's Legacy: Health, Environmental and Socio-Economic Impacts* (Vienna, Sept. 2005).
9. Steven Richmond and Vladimir Solodin, '"The Eye of the State": An Interview with Soviet Chief Censor Vladimir Solodin', *RR* 56: 4 (1997), 585.
10. Brown, *Gorbachev Factor*, 163.
11. Andrei Sakharov, *Memoirs*, London, 1990, 615.
12. *NYT*, 6 March 1987.
13. *NYT*, 6 Feb. 1988.
14. *NYT*, 19 Aug. 1989.
15. Adam B. Ulam, *The Communists: The Story of Power and Lost Illusions, 1948–1991*, New York, 1992, 432.
16. *Washington Post*, 28 March 1989.
17. Jean-Marie Chauvier, 'Retour, vingt ans après, sur la perestroïka gorbatchévienne', *Le Monde Diplomatique*, June 2005.

18. Alexander Yakovlev, *The Fate of Marxism in Russia*, New Haven, 1993, p. xvii.
19. Hans-Hermann Hertle, 'The Fall of the Wall: The Unintended Self-Dissolution of East Germany's Ruling Regime', *CWIHPB* 12/13 (2001), 132.
20. Vladislav M. Zubok, 'New Evidence on the End of the Cold War', *CWIHPB* 12/13 (2001), 9.
21. Brown, *Gorbachev Factor*, 225.
22. Wałęsa to Council of State, 2 Oct. 1986, *CWIHPB* 12/13 (2001), 94.
23. Zubok, 'New Evidence', 11.
24. Report by Jaruzelski to Polish Politburo, dated 9 May 1989, on visit to Moscow on 28 April 1989, *CWIHPB* 12/13 (2001), 112.
25. Rudolf L. Tőkes, *Hungary's Negotiated Revolution: Economic Reform, Social Change and Political Succession, 1957–1990*, Cambridge, 1996, 330.
26. Egon Krenz, *Herbst* '89, Berlin, 1999, 19.
27. The phrase appeared in a statement by the East German news agency on 1 October 1989 and was generally attributed to Honecker: Krenz, *Herbst* '89, 74, and Elizabeth Pond, *Beyond the Wall: Germany's Road to Unification*, Washington, 1993, 100 and 300.
28. Daniel Hamilton, 'Dateline East Germany: The Wall Behind the Wall', *Foreign Policy*, 76 (Autumn 1989), 186.
29. Ibid. 179.
30. Zubok, 'New Evidence', 10.
31. Brown, *Gorbachev Factor*, 249.
32. Hans-Hermann Hertle, *Der Fall der Mauer: Die unbeabsichtigte Selbstauflösung des SED-Staates*, Opladen, 1996, 462–82.
33. Ibid.
34. Hertle, *Der Fall der Mauer*, 135.
35. Transcript of press conference, 6.53–7.01 p.m., 9 Nov. 1989, *CWIHPB*, 157–8. The ellipsis marks in the text indicate hesitations by the speaker, not omissions from the record.
36. Isa. 45: 2.
37. Hertle, *Der Fall der Mauer*, 138.
38. Ibid.
39. Mladenov to Central Committee, 24 Oct. 1989, *CWIHPB* 12/13 (2001), 169–70.
40. Sabrina P. Ramet, *Social Currents in Eastern Europe: The Sources and Consequences of the Great Transformation*, Durham, NC, 1995, 129.
41. *NYT*, 10 Nov. 1987.
42. *Independent*, 5 Jan. 1988.
43. *NYT*, 10 Jan. 1988.
44. *MGW*, 28 Aug. 1988.
45. *NYT*, 11 Dec. 1988.
46. *Le Monde*, 1 July 1989.
47. *NYT*, 6 Sept. 1989.
48. *NYT*, 19 Aug. 1990.

49. *NYT*, 28 Nov. 1989.
50. *NYT*, 29 Nov. 1989.
51. *Le Monde*, 24 Nov. 1987.
52. *FT*, 15 Dec. 1987.
53. *Les Temps Modernes*, 552 (Jan. 1990), 42–5.
54. *Le Monde*, 27 April 1988.
55. *Time*, 5 Sept. 1988.
56. *NYT*, 11 July 1989.
57. Peter Siani-Davies, *The Romanian Revolution of December 1989*, Ithaca, NY, 68, 281.
58. Ibid. 139–40.
59. Anatoly S. Chernyaev, *My Six Years with Gorbachev*, University Park, Pa., 2000, 239–40.
60. *Newsweek*, 4 Dec. 1989.
61. Timothy Garton Ash, *In Europe's Name: Germany and the Divided Continent*, New York, 1993, 349.
62. *Der Spiegel*, special international edn., 4 (2005) 'The Germans: Sixty Years after the War', 75.
63. Friedrich Engels, *Anti-Dühring* (1878), part III, ch. 2.
64. David Satter, *Age of Delirium: The Decline and Fall of the Soviet Union*, New Haven, 2001, 213.
65. These quotations are from the revised version of the programme drawn up in August 1990: G. Yavlinsky et al., *500 Days (Transition to the Market)*, New York, 1991.
66. Chernyaev, *My Six Years*, 287.
67. *NYT*, 21 Dec. 1990.
68. *NYT*, 23 Dec. 1990.
69. Chernyaev, *My Six Years*, 312–13.
70. Brown, *Gorbachev Factor*, 282.
71. John Keep, *Last of the Empires: A History of the Soviet Union, 1945–1991*, Oxford, 1996, 435.
72. Christopher Andrew and Vasili Mitrokhin, *The Sword and The Shield: The Mitrokhin Archive and the Secret History of the KGB*, New York, 1999, 393.
73. *NYT*, 12 Nov. 1989.
74. *NYT*, 20 Aug. 1991.
75. Quoted in Yuri L. Bessmertny, 'August 1991 as Seen by a Moscow Historian', *AHR* 97: 3 (1992), 803–16.
76. Electronic mail message distributed on 22 Aug. 1991 by Vladimir Butenko, Moscow State University.
77. Chernyaev, *My Six Years*, 376.
78. Ibid. 386.
79. BBC News, 25 Dec. 1991.

19. AFTER THE FALL 1991–2007

1. Lawrence Freedman, *The Evolution of Nuclear Strategy*, 3rd edn., Basingstoke, 2003, 415.
2. Statement by President Bush at joint press conference with President Putin, 13 November 2001, http://www.state.gov/t/ac/trt/18016.htm 6.
3. Treaty dated 27 May 1997, J.A.S Grenville and Bernard Wasserstein, *The Major International Treaties of the Twentieth Century: A History and Guide with Texts*, 2 vols., London, 2001, ii. 946–52.
4. David Childs, *Britain Since 1945: A Political History*, London, 2001, 275,
5. Ralf Dahrendorf, *Reflections on the Revolution in Europe*, London, 1990, 127.
6. Lars Trägårdh, 'Crisis and the politics of National Community: Germany and Sweden 1933/1994', in Nina Witoszek and Lars Trägårdh, eds., *Culture and Crisis: The Case of Germany and Sweden*, New York, 2002, 94–5.
7. Resolution of European Council on the Stability and Growth Pact, Amsterdam, 17 June 1997 (97/C 236/01).
8. Marshall I. Goldman, *The Piratization of Russia: Russian Reform Goes Awry*, London, 2003.
9. Stefan Hedlund and Niclas Sundström, 'The Russian Economy after Systemic Change', *EAS* 48: 6 (1996), 900.
10. Andrew Jack, *Inside Putin's Russia*, London, 2005, 34
11. Natalya Rimashevskaya, quoted ibid.
12. Hedlund and Sundström, 'Russian Economy', 905.
13. BBC News, 31 Aug. 1999.
14. Concluding Statement of IMF Mission to Russia, 6 June 2005, http://www.imf.org/external/np/ms/2005/060605.htm.
15. Michael Ellman, 'The Russian Economy under El'tsin', *EAS* 52: 8 (2000), 1419.
16. Serguey Braguinsky and Grigory Yavlinsky, *Incentives and Institutions: The Transition to a Market Economy in Russia*, Princeton, 2000, 5.
17. Brian D. Taylor, *Politics and the Russian Army: Civil–Military Relations, 1689–2000*, Cambridge, 2003, 294.
18. Anatol Lieven, *Chechnya: Tombstone of Russian Power*, New Haven, 1999, 88.
19. Taylor, *Politics and the Russian Army*, 310.
20. Jack, *Inside Putin's Russia*, 42.
21. BBC News, 1 Jan. 2000.
22. *MGW*, 28 June 1992.
23. *Belarus: Prices, Markets and Enterprise Reform*, World Bank, 1997, 1.
24. *Human Development Report 2005*, United Nations, 2005, 219.
25. Kozyrev interview in *Le Monde*, 6/7 June 1992.
26. Taylor, *Politics and the Russian Army*, 274.
27. George Konrád, *Antipolitics*, San Diego, 1984, 155.
28. *NYT*, 20 July 1990.
29. Jiří Večerník and Petr Matějů, eds., *Ten Years of Rebuilding Capitalism: Czech Society after 1989*, Prague, 1999, 179.

30. Ibid. 180.
31. Abby Innes, *Czechoslovakia: The Short Goodbye*, New Haven, 2001, 86.
32. One sober estimate for the period 1991–5 alone is 300,000: Richard H. Ullman, ed., *The World and Yugoslavia's Wars*, Council on Foreign Relations, New York, 1998, introduction: Columbia International Affairs Online, http://www.ciaonet.org/book/ulr01/ulr01a.html.
33. Ivo Banac, 'Historiography of the Countries of Eastern Europe: Yugoslavia', *AHR* 97: 4 (Oct. 1992), 1092.
34. Robert Thomas, *Serbia under Milošević: Politics in the 1990s*, London, 1999, 44.
35. Sabrina Ramet, *Nationalism and Federalism in Yugoslavia, 1962–1991*, 2nd edn., Bloomington, Ind., 1992, 256.
36. *Human Development Report 2005*, 219.
37. *Le Monde*, 30 June 1992.
38. K. Stuart Parkes, *Understanding Contemporary Germany*, London, 1997, 74. Kohl used the phrase on a number of occasions, notably in a debate in the Bundestag on 21 June 1990.

20. EUROPE IN THE NEW MILLENNIUM

1. Paul B. Baltes and Karl Ulrich Mayer, eds., *The Berlin Ageing Study: Ageing from 70 to 100*, Cambridge, 1999, 138–9, 389, 486.
2. Philip Martin, *Europe: A New Immigration Area?*, Population Reference Bureau, May 2001.
3. Atina Grossmann, *Reforming Sex: The German Movement for Birth Control and Abortion Reform, 1920–1950*, New York, 1995, 214–15.
4. The 1975 figure is for West Germany only.
5. Baltes and Mayer, eds., *Berlin Ageing Study*, 137.
6. Sophie Durieux-Paillard and Francesca Murati-Rossi, 'SMILE: A Tooth Decay Prevention Project among Children of Asylum Seekers in Geneva', in Pierre Chauvin, ed., *Prevention and Health Promotion for the Excluded and the Destitute in Europe*, Amsterdam, 2002, 150–3.
7. Paul Balchin, ed., *Housing Policy in Europe*, London, 1996, 9.
8. Jacques Vernant, quoted in Georgette Elgey, *Histoire de la IVe République*, rev. edn., 4 vols., Paris, 1993, iv. 57.
9. *Jurnalul National* and *Expressen*, 9 Feb. 2005.
10. Information from Alec Nove.
11. Steven M. Eke and Taras Kuzio, 'Sultanism in Eastern Europe: The Socio-Political Roots of Authoritarian Populism in Belarus', *EAS* 52: 3 (2000), 523–47.
12. Neville Harris, 'Regulation, Choice, and Basic Values in Education in England and Wales: A Legal Perspective', in Patrick J. Wolf and Stephen Macedo, eds., *Educating Citizens: International Perspectives on Civic Values and School Choice*, Washington, 2004, 101.

13. German Constitutional Court decision of 16 May 1995 (1 BvR 1087/91), BVerfGE 93,1 (Classroom Crucifix Case).
14. Hugh McLeod and Werner Ustorf, *The Decline of Christendom in Western Europe, 1750–2000*, Cambridge, 2003, 29.
15. Papal address to Holy Synod, Athens, 4 May 2001, http://www.catholic-forum.com/saints/pope0264qp.htm.
16. *Evangelium Vitae*, Introduction and chapter 1, http://www.osjspm.org/cst/ev.htm.
17. Homily pronounced at Mass 'Pro Eligendo Romano Pontifice', Vatican Basilica, 18 April 2005, http://www.vatican.va/gpII/documents/homily-pro-eligendo-pontifice_20050418_en.html.
18. Grace Davie, *Religion in Britain since 1945: Believing without Belonging*, Oxford, 1994.
19. Wil Arts and Loek Halman, eds., *European Values at the Turn of the Millennium*, Leiden, 2004, 283–385.
20. The concept of the 'sacred canopy' was adumbrated by Peter Berger in *The Sacred Canopy*, New York, 1967.
21. McLeod and Ustorf, *Decline of Christendom*, 63.
22. See above, p. vi. For a discussion of Benjamin's thinking on this point, see Michael Lowy, *Fire Alarm: Reading Walter Benjamin's 'On the Concept of History'*, London, 2005, 46–57.
23. Friedrich Engels, *Origins of the Family, Private Property, and the State* (1884), chapter IX: 'Barbarism and Civilization.'
24. From 'Plantain' (Petrograd, 1919) in *Anna Akhmatova: Selected Poems*, trans. D. M. Thomas, London, 1988, 49.

Bibliography

WEBSITES

Avalon Project: Twentieth Century Documents, http://www.yale.edu/lawweb/avalon/20th.htm
BBC History, http://www.bbc.co.uk/history/
Berlin Wall Online, http://www.dailysoft.com/berlinwall/
British Foreign and Commonwealth Office, http://www.fco.gov.uk/
British official documents (The Stationery Office), http://www.official-documents.co.uk/
Central and East European Library, http://www.ceeol.com/
Central European History Virtual Archive, http://www2.tltc.ttu.edu/kelly/Archive/
CIA World Factbook, http://www.cia.gov/cia/publications/factbook/index. html
Cold War International History Project, http://www.wilsoncenter.org/index.cfm?fuseaction =topics.home&topic_id=1409
Columbia International Affairs Online, http://www.ciaonet.org/
The Economist, http://www.economist.com/
Eurodocs: West European Historical Documents, http://eudocs.lib.byu.edu/index.php/Main_Page
European Union gateway, http://europa.eu.int/index_en.htm
EU History website (University of Leiden), http://www.eu-history.leidenuniv.nl/
European University Institute Virtual Library European History Project, http://vlib.iue.it/history/index.html
Eurostat (European Commission Statistical Office), http://europa.eu.int/comm/eurostat/
European Values Study, http://www.europeanvalues.nl/
First World War Document Archive, http://www.lib.byu.edu/estu/wwi/

French Foreign Ministry, http://www.diplomatie.gouv.fr/en/
German Foreign Ministry, http://www.auswaertiges-amt.de/
German History in Documents and Images, http://germanhistorydocs.ghi-dc.org/index.cfm
German Propaganda Archive (Nazi and East German), http://www.calvin. edu/academic/cas/gpa/index.htm
Glasgow Digital Library, http://gdl.cdlr.strath.ac.uk/index.html
Great Buildings Collection (history of architecture), http://www.GreatBuildings.com/gbc.html
Guardian Century (*Manchester Guardian* articles 1899–1999), http://www.guardiancentury.co.uk/
Gutenberg-e (online historical monographs), http://www.gutenberg-e.org/index.html
History of the Soviet Union, http://www.uea.ac.uk/his/webcours/russia/welcome/
History Online, http://historyonline.chadwyck.co.uk/info/home.htm
Imperial War Museum (online exhibitions), http://www.iwm.org.uk/online/index.htm
Infonet-Austria, http://infonet.onb.ac.at/cgi-db/infonet.pl
International Labour Organization, http://www.ilo.org/
International Monetary Fund, http://www.imf.org/
Le Monde Diplomatique, http://mondediplo.com/
National Security Archive: The George Washington University, http://www.gwu.edu/~nsarchiv/
NATO, http://www.nato.int/
Neue Zürcher Zeitung, http://www.nzz.ch/index.html
Norwegian Ministry of Foreign Affairs, http://odin.dep.no/odin/
Nuremberg War Crimes Trials (Avalon project), http://www.yale.edu/lawweb/avalon/imt/imt.htm
Parallel History Project on NATO and the Warsaw Pact, http://www.isn. ethz.ch/php/index.htm
Radio Free Europe/Radio Liberty, http://www.rferl.org/
Russian Archives Online, http://www.russianarchives.com/rao/archives/index.html
Sea and Cities: (Environmental History of NE Europe), http://www.valt.helsinki.fi/projects/enviro/
Der Spiegel Online, http://www.spiegel.de/
U.K. National Archives (Public Record Office), http://www.nationalarchives.gov.uk/
United Nations Economic Commission for Europe, http://www.unece. org/
V2 rocket website, http://www.v2rocket.com/

Zeitgeschichte Information System (University of Innsbruck Institute of Contemporary History), http://zis.uibk.ac.at/

BOOKS AND ARTICLES

The volume of historical writing on Europe over the past century is greater than that on all previous periods put together. Priority here is given to works that have had a major historiographical impact, to more recent writing, and to works available in English.

General

Statistics: B. R. Mitchell, *International Historical Statistics, Europe, 1750–2000* (New York, 2003).

Demography: Maria Sophia Quine, *Population Politics in Twentieth Century Europe: Fascist Dictatorships and Liberal Democracies* (London, 1996); John R. Gillis, Louise A. Tilly, and David Levine, *The European Experience of Declining Fertility, 1850–1970: The Quiet Revolution* (Cambridge, Mass., 1992); Carlo A. Corsini and Pier Paolo Viazzo, eds., *The Decline of Infant and Child Mortality: The European Experience, 1750–1990* (The Hague, 1997).

Economic history: Derek Aldcroft, *The European Economy, 1914–2000* (4th edn., London, 2001); Gerold Ambrosius and William H. Hubbard, *A Social and Economic History of Twentieth-Century Europe* (Cambridge, Mass., 1989); Vito Tanzi and Ludger Schuknecht, *Public Spending in the 20th Century: A Global Perspective* (Cambridge, 2000); Youssef Cassis, ed., *Finance and Financiers in European History, 1880–1960* (Cambridge, 1992); Paul Bairoch, 'Europe's Gross National Product, 1800–1975', *Journal of European Economic History*, 5: 2 (1976), 273–340.

Women, family, sexuality: Edward Shorter, *The Making of the Modern Family* (New York, 1975); Angus McLaren, *Twentieth-Century Sexuality* (Oxford, 1999); Gisela Bock and Pat Thane, eds., *Maternity and Gender Politics: Women and the Rise of European Welfare States, 1880s–1950s* (London, 1991); Susan Pedersen, *Family, Dependence, and the Origins of the Welfare State: Britain and France, 1914–1945* (Cambridge, 1993); Roderick Phillips, *Untying the Knot: A Short History of Divorce* (Cambridge, 1991); Paul Ginsborg, 'The Politics of the Family in Twentieth-Century Europe', *CoEH* 9: 3 (2000) 411–44.

Diplomacy: *Akten zur Deutschen Auswärtigen Politik, 1918–1945; Documents on British Foreign Policy, 1919–1939; Documents on British Policy Overseas; Documents Diplomatiques Français; I Documenti Diplomatici Italiani; Diplomatische Dokumente der Schweiz*; J. A. S. Grenville and Bernard Wasserstein, eds., *The Major International Treaties of the Twentieth Century: A History and Guide with Texts* (2 vols., London, 2001); *Survey of International Affairs* (Royal Institute of International Affairs, London, 1920–62) and companion series, *Documents on International Affairs*; Gordon Craig and Felix Gilbert, eds., *The Diplomats, 1919–1939* (Princeton, 1953); Gordon Craig and Francis L. Loewenheim, eds., *The Diplomats, 1939–1979* (Princeton, 1994).

Cultural history: Donald Sassoon, *The Culture of the Europeans* (London, 2006); Peter Watson, *A Terrible Beauty: A History of the People and Ideas that Shaped the Modern World* (London, 2000); Hermann W. von der Dunk, *Kulturgeschichte des 20. Jahrhunderts* (2 vols., Munich, 2004); Modris Eksteins, *Rites of Spring: The Great War and the Birth of the Modern Age* (Boston, 1989); Philip V. Bohlman, *The Music of European Nationalism: Cultural Identity and Modern History* (Santa Barbara, 2004); H. Stuart Hughes, *Consciousness and Society: The Reorientation of European Social Thought, 1890–1930* (New York, 1977).

Architecture: John R. Gold, *The Experience of Modernism: Modern Architects and the Future City* (London, 1997); Charles Jencks, *Modern Movements in Architecture* (London, 1973); Henry-Russell Hitchcock and Philip Johnson, *The International Style* (New York, 1966).

Left and right: Geoff Eley, *Forging Democracy: The History of the Left in Europe, 1850–2000* (New York, 2002); Donald Sassoon, *One Hundred Years of Socialism: The West European Left in the Twentieth Century* (London, 1996); Hans Rogger and Eugen Weber, *The European Right* (Berkeley, 1965).

National histories: Miranda Vickers, *The Albanians* (London, 1999); Barbara Jelavich, *Modern Austria: Empire and Republic, 1815–1986* (Cambridge, 1987); Peter Clarke, *Hope and Glory: Britain, 1900–2000* (London, 2004); R. J. Crampton, *A Short History of Modern Bulgaria* (Cambridge, 1987); D. G. Kirby, *Finland in the Twentieth Century* (London, 1979); Maurice Larkin, *France since the Popular Front: Government and People, 1936–1996* (Oxford, 1997); René Rémond and Jean-François Sirinelli, *Notre siècle: de 1918 à 1991* (Paris, 1991); Gordon A. Craig, *Germany, 1866–1945* (Oxford, 1978); Lothar Kettenacker, *Germany since 1945* (Oxford, 1997); Jörg K. Hoensch, *A History of Modern Hungary* (London, 1984); Roy Foster, *Modern Ireland, 1600–1972* (New York, 1988); Martin Clark, *Modern Italy, 1871–1995* (London, 1996); Norman Davies, *God's Playground: A History of Poland* (rev. edn., 2 vols., Oxford, 2005); Keith Hitchins, *Rumania, 1866–1947* (Oxford, 1994); T. M. Devine, *The Scottish Nation: A History, 1700–2000* (London, 2000); Raymond Carr, *Spain, 1808–1975* (Oxford, 1982); Stig Hadenius, *Swedish Politics in the 20th Century* (4th edn., Stockholm, 1997); Jonathan Steinberg, *Why Switzerland?* (Cambridge, 1976); Andrew Wilson, *Ukrainians: The Unexpected Nation* (New Haven, 2002); Geoffrey Hosking, *The First Socialist Society: A History of the Soviet Union from Within* (rev. edn., Cambridge, Mass., 1990); Kenneth O. Morgan, *Rebirth of a Nation: Wales, 1880–1990* (New York, 1981).

Rural life: Eugen Weber, *Peasants into Frenchmen: The Modernization of Rural France, 1870–1914* (Stanford, 1976); Gaston Schmit, *Un village solognot: Vannes* (Paris, 1961); Richard J. Evans and W. R. Lee, eds., *The German Peasantry: Conflict and Community in Rural Society from the Eighteenth to the Twentieth Centuries* (New York, 1986); A. J. B. Wace and M. S. Thompson, *The Nomads of the Balkans: An Account of Life and Customs among the Vlachs of Northern Pindus* (London, 1914); Pino Arlacchi, *Mafia, Peasants and Great Estates: Society in Traditional Calabria* (Cambridge, 1983); Ben Eklof, *Russian Peasant Schools: Officialdom, Village Culture, and Popular Pedagogy, 1861–1914* (Berkeley, 1986); Anatol Lieven, *The Aristocracy in Europe,*

1815–1914 (London, 1992); A. M. Anfimov, 'On the History of the Russian Peasantry at the Beginning of the Twentieth Century', *RR* 51: 3 (1992), 396–407.

Urban society: Robert Eric Dickinson, *The West European City* (2nd edn., London, 1961); John Lukacs, *Budapest 1900: A Historical Portrait of a City and its Culture* (New York, 1988); Mark Mazower, *Salonica: City of Ghosts* (London, 2004); Norman Davies and Roger Moorhouse, *Microcosm: Portrait of a Central European City* (London, 2003); Timothy J. Colton, *Moscow: Governing the Socialist Metropolis* (Cambridge, Mass., 1995); Anthony Read and David Fisher, *Berlin: The Biography of a City* (London, 1994); Jerry White, *London in the Twentieth Century: A City and its People* (New York, 2001); Irene Maver, *Glasgow* (Edinburgh, 2000); Colin Jones, *Paris: Biography of a City* (London, 2004); Marthe Barbance, *Saint-Nazaire: Le Port, La Ville, Le Travail* (Moulins, 1948); Josef Mooser, *Arbeiterleben in Deutschland, 1900–1970* (Frankfurt, 1984); Bernard Marrey, *Les Grands Magasins des origines à 1939* (Paris, 1979); W. Hamish Fraser, *The Coming of the Mass Market, 1850–1914* (Hamden, Conn., 1981); Michael B. Miller, *Le Bon Marché: Bourgeois Culture and the Department Store, 1869–1920* (Princeton, 1987).

Nationality problems in south-east Europe: Oscar Jászi, *The Dissolution of the Habsburg Monarchy* (Chicago, 1929); Barbara Jelavich, *History of the Balkans*, vol. ii, *The Twentieth Century* (Cambridge, 1983); John F. Cadzow, Andrew Ludyani, and Louis J. Elteto, eds., *Transylvania: The Roots of Ethnic Conflict* (Kent, Oh., 1983); Michael A. Nagelbach, *Heil! and Farewell: A Life in Romania 1913–1946* (Chicago, 1986); Robert J. Donia, *Islam under the Double Eagle: The Muslims of Bosnia and Hercegovina, 1878–1914* (New York, 1981); Ivo Banac, *The National Question in Yugoslavia: Origins, History, Politics* (Ithaca, NY, 1984).

The First World War

War origins: Thomas E. Griess, ed., *Atlas for the Great War* (Garden City Park, NY, 2003); James Joll, *The Origins of the First World War* (2nd edn., London, 1992); R. J. W. Evans and H. J. O. Pogge von Strandmann, eds., *The Coming of the First World War* (Oxford, 1988); Luigi Albertini, *The Origins of the War of 1914* (Oxford, 1952); Fritz Fischer, *Germany's Aims in the First World War* (New York, 1967); idem, *War of Illusions: German Policies from 1911 to 1914* (New York, 1975); idem, *World Power or Decline: The Controversy over Germany's Aims in the First World War* (London, 1975); I. Geiss, *July 1914: The Outbreak of the First World War: Selected Documents* (London, 1967); Zara S. Steiner and Keith Neilson, *Britain and the Origins of the First World War* (2nd edn., Basingstoke, 2003); Samuel R. Williamson Jr., *Austria-Hungary and the Origins of the First World War* (Basingstoke, 1991); D. C. B. Lieven, *Russia and the Origins of the First World War* (London, 1983); Michael Howard, *The Continental Commitment: The Dilemma of British Defence Policy in the Era of the Two World Wars* (Harmondsworth, 1972); Paul M. Kennedy, ed., *The War Plans of the Great Powers, 1880–1914* (London, 1979); Gunther E. Rothenberg, *The Army of Francis Joseph* (West Lafayette, Ind., 1976).

Military history: Hew Strachan, *The First World War* (3 projected vols.; vol. i, *To Arms*, Oxford, 2001); B.H. Liddell Hart, *History of the First World War* (London, 1972); Keith Robbins, *The First World War* (Oxford, 1984); Holger H. Herwig, *The First World War: Germany and Austria-Hungary, 1914–1918* (London, 1997); István Déak, *Beyond Nationalism: A Social and Political History of the Habsburg Officer Corps, 1848–1918* (New York, 1990); Paul-Marie de la Gorce, *The French Army: A Military-Political History* (New York, 1963); Martin Kitchen, *The German Officer Corps, 1890–1914* (Oxford, 1968). Norman Stone, *The Eastern Front, 1914–1917* (New York, 1975); Robert Rhodes James, *Gallipoli* (New York, 1965); Allain Bernède, *Verdun 1916: le point de vue français* (Le Mans, 2002); Alistair Horne, *The Price of Glory: Verdun 1916* (London, 1993); Cyril Falls, *Caporetto, 1917* (London, 1966); Brian Bond, ed., *The First World War and British Military History* (Oxford, 1991); John Terraine, *The Western Front, 1914–1918* (Philadelphia, 1965); Guy Pedroncini, *Les Mutineries de 1917* (Paris, 1967); John Horne and Alan Kramer, *German Atrocities, 1914: A History of Denial* (New Haven, 2001); Richard Hough, *The Great War at Sea, 1914–1918* (Oxford, 1983); John H. Morrow Jr, *German Air Power in World War I* (Lincoln, Nebr., 1982); Karl Clausberg, *Zeppelin: Die Geschichte eines unwahrscheinlichen Erfolges* (Munich, 1979).

Memoirs and diaries: Erich von Falkenhayn, *Die Oberste Heeresleitung 1914–1916 in ihren wichtigen Entschliessungen* (Berlin, 1920); Paul von Hindenburg, *Aus meinem Leben* (Leipzig, 1920); Erich von Ludendorff, *Meine Kriegserinnerungen, 1914–1918* (Berlin, 1919); Theobald von Bethmann Hollweg, *Reflections on the World War* (London, 1920); Hartmut Pogge von Strandmann, ed., *Walther Rathenau, Industrialist, Banker, Intellectual and Politician: Notes and Diaries, 1907–1922* (Oxford, 1985); *Mémoires du Maréchal Joffre* (2 vols., Paris, 1932); Philippe Pétain, *La Bataille de Verdun* (Paris, 1929); Jean Jules Henri Mordacq, *Le Ministère Clemenceau: Journal d'un témoin* (4 vols., Paris, 1930–1); Raymond Recouly, *Le Mémorial de Foch: Mes Entretiens avec le Maréchal* (Paris, 1929); David Lloyd George, *War Memoirs* (6 vols., London, 1933–6); Gary Sheffield and John Bourne, *Douglas Haig: War Diaries and Letters, 1914–1918* (London, 2005).

Economic and social history of the war: James T. Shotwell, ed., *Economic and Social History of the World War* (Carnegie Endowment for International Peace, general series; national series for Austria-Hungary, Belgium, Britain, France, Germany, Italy, the Netherlands, Rumania, Russia, Scandinavia, and Turkey; and translated and abridged series, New Haven, 1921–38); Gerd Hardach, *The First World War, 1914–1918* (Berkeley, 1977); Jean-Jacques Becker, *The Great War and the French People* (Leamington Spa, 1985); Jürgen Kocka, *Facing Total War: German Society, 1914–1918* (Leamington Spa, 1984); J. M. Winter, *The Great War and the British People* (Basingstoke, 2003); Arthur Marwick, *The Deluge: British Society and the First World War* (London, 1965); Richard Wall and Jay Winter, *The Upheaval of War: Family, Work and Welfare in Europe, 1914–1918* (Cambridge, 1988); Jay Winter and Jean-Louis Robert, eds., *Capital Cities at War: Paris, London, Berlin, 1914–1919* (Cambridge, 1997); Maureen Healy, *Vienna and the Fall of the Habsburg Empire: Total War and Everyday Life in World War I* (Cambridge, 2004); Magnus Hirschfeld,

The Sexual History of the World War (New York, 1937); John N. Horne, *Labour at War: France and Britain, 1914–1918* (Oxford, 1991); Avner Offer, *The First World War: An Agrarian Interpretation* (Oxford, 1989); Niall Ferguson, *The Pity of War* (London, 1998); Stanley Weintraub, *A Stillness Heard Round the World: The End of the Great War: November 1918* (Oxford, 1987).

Wartime politics and diplomacy: Z. A. B. Zeman, *A Diplomatic History of the First World War* (London, 1971); David Stevenson, *The First World War and International Politics* (Oxford, 1988); Cameron Hazlehurst, *Politicians at War, July 1914 to May 1915* (London, 1971); John Turner, *British Politics and the Great War: Coalition and Conflict 1915–1918* (New Haven, 1992); John Rae, *Conscience and Politics: The British Government and the Conscientious Objector to Military Service, 1916–1919* (London, 1970); Gerald D. Feldman, *Army, Industry and Labor in Germany, 1914–1918* (Princeton, 1966); Winston Churchill, *The World Crisis* (6 vols., New York, 1923–31).

Occupied Belgium and France: Adolf Solansky, *German Administration in Belgium* (New York, 1928); Henri Pirenne, *La Belgique et la guerre mondiale* (Paris, 1928); Richard Cobb, *French and Germans, Germans and French: A Personal Interpretation of France under Two Occupations, 1914–1918/1940–1944* (Hanover, NH, 1983).

Russian Revolution: Orlando Figes, *A People's Tragedy: The Russian Revolution, 1891–1924* (London, 1997); Richard Pipes, *The Russian Revolution* (New York, 1990); E. H. Carr, *A History of Soviet Russia* (London, 1950–78); Dominic Lieven, *Nicholas II: Emperor of all the Russias* (London, 1993); Leon Trotsky, *The History of the Russian Revolution* (3 vols., London, 1932–3); Leonard Schapiro, *The Russian Revolutions of 1917: The Origins of Modern Communism* (New York, 1984); Ronald Kowalski, *The Russian Revolution, 1917–1921* (London, 1997); Alexander Rabinowitch, *The Bolsheviks Come to Power: The Revolution of 1917 in Petrograd* (New York, 1978); O. Radkey, *The Election to the Russian Constituent Assembly of 1917* (Cambridge, Mass., 1950); E. R. Frankel, J. Frankel, and B. Knei-Paz, eds., *Revolution in Russia: Reassessments of 1917* (Cambridge, 1992); J. W. Wheeler-Bennett, *Brest-Litovsk: The Forgotten Peace: March 1918* (London, 1938); Robert V. Daniels, *A Documentary History of Communism* (2 vols., Hanover, NH, 1984).

Revolutionary leaders: Richard Abraham, *Alexander Kerensky: The First Love of the Revolution* (New York, 1987); Robert Service, *Lenin: A Biography* (London, 2002); Isaac Deutscher, *Trotsky* (3 vols., London, 1954–63); Israel Getzler, *Martov: A Political Biography of a Russian Social Democrat* (Cambridge, 1967); Israel Getzler, *Nikolai Sukhanov: Chronicler of the Russian Revolution* (Basingstoke, 2002).

Inter-war Europe

Revolution and counter-revolution in central Europe: Arthur Rosenberg, *The Birth of the German Republic, 1871–1918* (London, 1931); J. P. Nettl, *Rosa Luxemburg* (2 vols., London, 1966); Allan Mitchell, *Revolution in Bavaria, 1918–1919* (Princeton, 1965); F. L. Carsten, *Revolution in Central Europe, 1918–1919* (Berkeley, 1972); Bruno Thoss, *Der Ludendorff-Kreis, 1919–1923: München als Zentrum der mitteleuropäischen Gegenrevolution zwischen Revolution und Hitler-Putsch* (Munich, 1978); Johannes

Erger, *Der Kapp-Lüttwitz Putsch* (Düsseldorf, 1967); E. Könnemann and G. Schulze, eds., *Der Kapp-Lüttwitz-Ludendorff-Putsch: Dokumente* (Munich, 2002); Rudolf L. Tőkés, *Béla Kun and the Hungarian Soviet Republic: The Origins and Role of the Communist Party of Hungary in the Revolutions of 1918–1919* (New York, 1967); David Mitrany, *The Effect of the War in Southeastern Europe* (New Haven, 1936).

The Paris Peace Conference: H. W. V. Temperley, ed., *A History of the Peace Conference* (6 vols., London, 1920–4); Margaret Macmillan, *Peacemakers: The Paris Conference of 1919 and its Attempt to End War* (London, 2001); J. M. Keynes, *The Economic Consequences of the Peace* (London, 1919); Manfred F. Boemeke, Gerald Feldman, and Elisabeth Glaser, *The Treaty of Versailles: A Reassessment after 75 Years* (Cambridge, 1998); André Tardieu, *The Truth about the Treaty* (Indianapolis, 1921); Georges Clemenceau, *Grandeurs et misères d'une victoire* (Paris, 1930); Harold Nicolson, *Peacemaking, 1919* (New York, 1939); Sally Marks, *Innocent Abroad: Belgium at the Paris Peace Conference of 1919* (Chapel Hill, NC, 1981).

Inter-war Europe: Raymond J. Sontag, *A Broken World, 1919–1939* (New York, 1972); Jay Winter, *Sites of Memory, Sites of Mourning* (Cambridge, 1995); Charles Meier, *Recasting Bourgeois Europe: Stabilization in France, Germany, and Italy in the Decade after World War I* (Princeton, 1975); Deborah Cohen, *The War Come Home: Disabled Veterans in Britain and Germany, 1914–1939* (Berkeley, 2001); James Joll, *Three Intellectuals in Politics* (London, 1960); Piers Brendon, *The Dark Valley* (New York, 2000).

France: Eugen Weber, *The Hollow Years: France in the 1930s* (New York, 1996); Stanislas Jeannesson, *Poincaré, la France et la Ruhr, 1922–1924 Histoire d'une occupation* (Strasbourg, 1998); Philippe Bernard and Henri Dubief, *The Decline of the Third Republic, 1914–1938* (Cambridge, 1985); Paul F. Jankowski, *Stavisky: A Confidence Man in the Republic of Virtue* (Ithaca, NY, 2002); Eugen Weber, *Action Française: Royalism and Reaction in Twentieth Century France* (Stanford, 1962); Julian Jackson, *The Popular Front in France: Defending Democracy, 1934–38* (Cambridge, 1988); Danielle Tartakowsky, *Les Manifestations de rue en France, 1918–1968* (Paris, 1997); Joel Colton, *Léon Blum: Humanist in Politics* (rev. edn., Durham, NC, 1987); Jean Lacouture, *Léon Blum* (Paris, 1977); Ilan Greilsammer, *Blum* (Paris, 1996); Jules Moch, *Rencontres avec Léon Blum* (Paris, 1970); Elisabeth du Réau, *Édouard Daladier, 1884–1970* (Paris, 1993).

Britain: Charles Loch Mowat, *Britain Between the Wars, 1918–1940* (London, 1955); A. J. P. Taylor, *English History, 1914–1945* (London, 1965); Robert Graves and Alan Hodge, *The Long Weekend: A Social History of Great Britain 1918–1939* (New York, 1963); Randolph S. Churchill and Martin Gilbert, *Winston S. Churchill* (8 vols., London, 1966–88 and documentary Companion vols.); Charles Townshend, *The British Campaign in Ireland, 1919–1921* (London, 1975); David Marquand, *Ramsay MacDonald* (London, 1977); Diane B. Kunz, *The Battle for Britain's Gold Standard in 1931* (London, 1987); Keith Middlemas and John Barnes, *Baldwin: A Biography* (London, 1969); A. J. P. Taylor, *Beaverbrook* (London, 1972); Bernard

Wasserstein, *Herbert Samuel: A Political Life* (Oxford, 1992); Robert Skidelsky, *Politicians and the Slump: The Labour Government of 1929–1931* (Harmondsworth, 1970); Harold Nicolson, *Diaries and Letters* (3 vols., London, 1966–8).

Soviet Union under Lenin: Evan Mawdsley, *The Russian Civil War* (Edinburgh, 2000); Orlando Figes, *Peasant Russia, Civil War: The Volga Countryside in Revolution, 1917–1921* (Oxford, 1989); Benjamin M. Weissman, *Herbert Hoover and Famine Relief to Soviet Russia: 1921–1923* (Stanford, 1974); Israel Getzler, *Kronstadt, 1917–1921: The Fate of a Soviet Democracy* (Cambridge, 1983); Roger Pethybridge, *One Step Backwards, Two Steps Forwards: Soviet Society and Politics in the New Economic Policy* (Oxford, 1990); Sheila Fitzpatrick, Alexander Rabinowitch, and Richard Stites, eds., *Russia in the Era of NEP: Explorations in Soviet Society and Culture* (Bloomington, Ind., 1991); Andrea Graziosi, *A New, Peculiar State: Explorations in Soviet History, 1917–1937* (Westport, Conn., 2000).

Weimar Germany: Hans Mommsen, *The Rise and Fall of Weimar Democracy* (Chapel Hill, NC, 1996); Detlev J. K. Peukert, *The Weimar Republic* (London, 1991); Gerald D. Feldman, *The Great Disorder: Politics, Economics and Society in the German Inflation, 1914–1924* (New York, 1997); Stephen A. Schuker, *American 'Reparations' to Germany, 1919–33* (Princeton, 1988); Larry Eugene Jones, *German Liberalism and the Dissolution of the Weimar Party System, 1918–1933* (Chapel Hill, NC, 1988); F. L. Carsten, *The Reichswehr and Politics, 1918–1933* (Berkeley, 1973); Klaus Epstein, *Matthias Erzberger and the Dilemma of German Democracy* (Princeton, 1959); Hans W. Gatzke, *Stresemann and the Rearmament of Germany* (Baltimore, 1954); Manfred Zeidler, *Reichswehr und Rote Armee: Wege und Stationen einer ungewöhnlichen Zusammenarbeit* (Munich, 1993); William L. Patch Jr., *Heinrich Brüning and the Dissolution of the Weimar Republic* (Cambridge, 1998); Heinrich Brüning, *Memoiren, 1918–1934* (Stuttgart, 1970); *Berlin Lights: The Diaries of Count Harry Kessler* (New York, 1999); Jonathan Wright, *Gustav Stresemann: Weimar's Greatest Statesman* (Oxford, 2002); John P. Birkelund, *Gustav Stresemann: Patriot and Staatsmann: ein Biographie* (Hamburg, 2003).

Eastern Europe: Joseph Rothschild, *East Central Europe between the Two World Wars* (Seattle, 1977); David Mitrany, *The Land and the Peasant in Rumania: The War and Agrarian Reform, 1917–21* (London, 1930); Jozo Tomasevich, *Peasants, Politics, and Economic Change in Yugoslavia* (Stanford, 1955); Joseph Rothschild, *Piłsudski's Coup d'Etat* (New York, 1966); Andrew Mango, *Atatürk* (London, 1999); Antony Polonsky, *The Little Dictators: The History of Eastern Europe since 1918* (London, 1975); idem, *Politics in Independent Poland, 1921–1939: The Crisis of Constitutional Government* (Oxford, 1972); Ezra Mendelsohn, *The Jews of East Central Europe between the Wars* (Bloomington, Ind., 1983); V. Stanley Vardis and Romuald J. Misunas, *The Baltic States in Peace and War, 1917–1945* (University Park, Pa., 1978).

Fascist Italy: Adrian Lyttelton, *The Seizure of Power: Fascism in Italy, 1919–1929* (2nd edn., Princeton, 1987); Denis Mack Smith, *Mussolini* (London, 1981); Herman Finer, *Mussolini's Italy* (London, 1935); Frank Snowden, *The Fascist*

Movement in Tuscany, 1919–1922 (Cambridge, 1989); Alice Kelikian, *Town and Country under Fascism: The Transformation of Brescia, 1915–1926* (Oxford, 1986); A. James Gregor, *Italian Fascism and Developmental Dictatorship* (Princeton, 1979); Carl Ipsen, *Dictating Demography: The Problem of Population in Fascist Italy* (Cambridge, 1996); Victoria de Grazia, *How Fascism Ruled Women: Italy, 1922–1945* (Berkeley, 1992).

Great Depression: Barry Eichengreen, *Golden Fetters: The Gold Standard and the Great Depression, 1919–1939* (New York, 1995); Patricia Clavin, *The Great Depression in Europe, 1929–1939* (London, 2000); Charles H. Feinstein, Peter Temin, and Gianni Toniolo, *The European Economy Between the Wars* (Oxford, 1997); Robert Skidelsky, *John Maynard Keynes* (3 vols., London, 1983–2000); Charles P. Kindleberger, *The World in Depression, 1929–1939* (rev. edn., Berkeley, 1986); Harold James, *The German Slump: Politics and Economics, 1924–1936* (Oxford, 1986); William C. McNeil, *American Money and the Weimar Republic: Economics and Politics on the Eve of the Great Depression* (New York, 1986); Richard J. Evans and Dick Geary, eds., *The German Unemployed* (New York, 1987); Sidney Pollard, ed., *The Gold Standard and Employment Policies Between the Wars* (London, 1970); W. R. Garside, *British Unemployment, 1919–1939: A Study in Public Policy* (Cambridge, 1990); Alfred Sauvy, *Histoire Economique de la France entre les Deux Guerres* (3 vols., Paris, 1965–72).

Nazi Germany: Ian Kershaw, *Hitler* (2 vols., London, 1998 and 2000); J. P. Stern, *Hitler: The Führer and the People* (London, 1975); Norman H. Baynes, ed., *The Speeches of Adolf Hitler, April 1922–August 1939* (London, 1942); Ian Kershaw, *The Nazi Dictatorship: Problems and Perspectives of Interpretation* (London, 1985); J. Noakes and G. Pridham, eds., *Nazism, 1919–1945: A History in Documents and Eyewitness Accounts* (4 vols., Exeter, 1983–98); Elke Fröhlich, ed., *Die Tagebücher von Joseph Goebbels* (28 vols., Munich, 1987–98); Karl Dietrich Bracher, *The German Dictatorship: The Origins, Structure and Effects of National Socialism* (London, 1971); Martin Broszat, *The Hitler State: The Foundation and Development of the Internal Structure of the Third Reich* (London, 1981); Helmut Krausnick and Martin Broszat, *Anatomy of the SS State* (London, 1968); Hans Mommsen, *From Weimar to Auschwitz* (Princeton, 1991); Joachim Fest, *The Face of the Third Reich* (Harmondsworth, 1972); Ian Kershaw, *The 'Hitler Myth': Image and Reality in the Third Reich* (Oxford, 1987); idem, *Popular Opinion and Political Dissent in the Third Reich: Bavaria, 1933–1945* (Oxford, 1983); Robert Gellately, *The Gestapo and German Society: Enforcing Racial Policy, 1933–1945* (Oxford, 1990); idem, *Backing Hitler: Consent and Coercion in Nazi Germany* (Oxford, 2001); Henry Ashby Turner Jr., *German Big Business and the Rise of Hitler* (New York, 1985); Gerhard Rempel, *Hitler's Children: The Hitler Youth and the SS* (Chapel Hill, NC, 1989); Jill Stephenson, *The Nazi Organisation of Women* (London, 1981); Günter Lewy, *The Catholic Church and Nazi Germany* (London, 1964); Ludwig Volk, *Das Reichskonkordat vom 20 Juli 1933* (Mainz, 1972); Richard Gutteridge, *Open Thy Mouth for the Dumb: The German Evangelical Church and the Jews,*

1879–1950 (Oxford, 1976); Neil Gregor, *Daimler-Benz in the Third Reich* (London, 1998); Lothar Gall et al., *The Deutsche Bank, 1870–1995* (London, 1995).

Soviet Union under Stalin: Robert Service, *Stalin: A Biography* (London, 2004); Chris Ward, *Stalin's Russia* (2nd edn., London, 1993); Robert V. Daniels, *The Stalin Era: Foundations of the Totalitarian Era* (3rd edn., Lexington, Mass., 1990); Alec Nove, ed., *The Stalin Phenomenon* (London, 1993); J. Arch Getty and Roberta T. Manning, eds., *Stalinist Terror: New Perspectives* (Cambridge, 1993); Alec Nove, *An Economic History of the USSR* (London, 1992); idem, *Was Stalin Really Necessary? Some Problems of Soviet Political Economy* (London, 1964); R. W. Davies, *The Industrialisation of Soviet Russia*, vol. i, *The Socialist Offensive: The Collectivisation of Soviet Agriculture, 1929–1930* (London, 1980), vol. ii, *The Soviet Collective Farm, 1929–1930* (London, 1980); R. W. Davies, Mark Harrison, and S. G. Wheatcroft, eds., *The Economic Transformation of the Soviet Union, 1913–1945* (Cambridge, 1994); Moshe Lewin, *The Making of the Soviet System: Essays in the Social History of Interwar Russia* (London, 1985); Robert Conquest, *The Harvest of Sorrow: Soviet Collectivization and the Terror-Famine* (New York, 1986); Robert Conquest, *The Great Terror: A Reassessment* (New York, 1990); Oleg V. Khlevniuk, *The History of the Gulag: From Collectivization to the Great Terror* (New Haven, 2004); Lynne Viola, *Peasant Rebels under Stalin: Collectivization and the Culture of Peasant Resistance* (New York, 1996); Leonard Schapiro, *The Communist Party of the Soviet Union* (rev. edn., New York, 1971); Vitaly Shentalinsky, *The KGB's Literary Archive* (London, 1995); Stephen F. Cohen, *Bukharin and the Bolshevik Revolution: A Political Biography, 1888–1938* (New York, 1973); Catriona Kelly, *Comrade Pavlik: The Rise and Fall of a Soviet Boy Hero* (London, 2005); George Katkov, *The Trial of Bukharin* (London, 1969); Lars T. Lih, Oleg V. Naumov, and Oleg V. Khlevniuk, *Stalin's Letters to Molotov, 1925–1936* (New Haven, 1995); Lewis Siegelbaum and Andrei Sokolov, *Stalinism as a Way of Life: A Narrative in Documents* (New Haven, 2000); R. W. Davies et al., eds., *The Stalin–Kaganovich Correspondence, 1931–36* (New Haven, 2003); Dmitri Volkogonov, *Stalin: Triumph and Tragedy* (London, 1991); Alec Nove, ed., *The Stalin Phenomenon* (London, 1993); Sheila Fitzpatrick, *Everyday Stalinism: Ordinary Life in Extraordinary Times: Soviet Russia in the 1930s* (New York, 1999); idem, *Stalin's Peasants: Resistance and Survival in the Russian Village after Collectivization* (New York, 1994); Nadezhda Mandelstam, *Hope Against Hope* (New York, 1970).

Great Dictators compared: Alan Bullock, *Hitler and Stalin: Parallel Lives* (New York, 1991); Ian Kershaw and Moshe Lewin, eds., *Stalinism and Nazism: Dictatorships in Comparison* (Cambridge, 1997); Zevedei Barbu, *Democracy and Dictatorship: Their Psychology and Patterns of Life* (London, 1956).

Society and culture between the wars: Helmut Gruber, *Red Vienna: Experiment in Working-Class Culture, 1919–1934* (New York, 1991); H. Stuart Hughes, *The Obstructed Path: French Social Thought in the Years of Desperation, 1930–1960* (New Brunswick, NJ, 2002); Michael B. Miller, *Shanghai on the Métro: Spies, Intrigue, and the French between the Wars* (Berkeley, 1994); George Mosse, *Nazi Culture: Intellectual, Cultural and Social Life in the Third Reich* (New York, 1966); Pamela

Potter, *Most German of the Arts: Musicology and Society from the Weimar Republic to the End of Hitler's Reich* (New Haven, 1998); Jim Godbolt, *A History of Jazz in Britain, 1919–1950* (London, 1984); Michael Kater, *Different Drummers: Jazz in the Culture of Nazi Germany* (New York, 1992); S. Frederick Starr, *Red and Hot: The Fate of Jazz in the Soviet Union, 1917–1980* (New York, 1983); Kate Lacey, *Feminine Frequencies: Gender, German Radio, and the Public Sphere, 1923–1945* (Ann Arbor, 1996); Hugh Cudlipp, *Publish and Be Damned: The Astonishing Story of the* Daily Mirror (London, 1953); Sigmund Freud, *Civilization and its Discontents* (London, 1930); Eli Zaretsky, *Secrets of the Soul: A Social and Cultural History of Psychoanalysis* (New York, 2004); Ian Gibson, *Federico García Lorca: A Life* (London, 1989); Clemens Zimmermann, 'From Propaganda to Modernization: Media Policy and Media Audiences under National Socialism', *German History*, 24: 3 (2006), 431–54; Gary Cross, 'Vacations for All: The Leisure Question in the Era of the Popular Front', *JCH* 24: 4 (1989), 599–621; Johan Söderberg, 'Controversial Consumption in Sweden, 1914–1945', *Scandinavian Economic History Review*, 48: 3 (2000), 5–21.

Fascist movements: Robert Paxton, *The Anatomy of Fascism* (New York, 2004); Eugen Weber, *Varieties of Fascism* (Princeton, 1964); Charles F. Delzell, *Mediterranean Fascism, 1919–1945* (New York, 1971); Philip Morgan, *Fascism in Europe, 1919–1945* (London, 2003); Robert Skidelsky, *Oswald Mosley* (New York, 1975); Sir Oswald Mosley, *My Life* (London, 1968); Richard Griffiths, *Patriotism Perverted* (London, 1998); Andres Kasekamp, 'Radical Right-Wing Movements in the North-East Baltic', *JCH* 34: 4 (1999) 587–600; symposium on 'International Fascism 1920–1945', *JCH* 1: 1 (1966); Mihail Sebastian, *Journal, 1935–1944: The Fascist Years* (London, 2000); Zvi Yavetz, 'An Eyewitness Note: Reflections on the Rumanian Iron Guard', *JCH* 26: 3/4 (1991), 597–610.

Inter-war diplomacy: Zara Steiner, *The Lights That Failed: European International History, 1919–1933* (Oxford, 2005); E. H. Carr, *The Twenty Years Crisis, 1919–1939: An Introduction to the Study of International Relations* (London, 1939); Hans W. Gatzke, ed., *European Diplomacy Between the Two Wars, 1919–1939* (Chicago, 1972); Piotr S. Wandycz, *France and Her Eastern Allies, 1919–1925: French–Czechoslovak–Polish Relations from the Paris Peace Conference to Locarno* (Minneapolis, 1962); Gerhard Weinberg, *Hitler's Foreign Policy: The Road to World War II, 1933–1939* (New York, 2005); Martin Thomas, *Britain, France and Appeasement: Anglo-French Relations in the Popular Front Era* (Washington, 1996); Zachary Shore, *What Hitler Knew: The Battle for Information in Nazi Foreign Policy* (New York, 2003); Robert Boyce, ed., *French Foreign and Defence Policy, 1918–1940: The Decline and Fall of a Great Power* (London, 1998); Edward W. Bennett, *German Rearmament and the West, 1932–1933* (Princeton, 1979); Brian Bond, *British Military Policy between the Two World Wars* (Oxford, 1980); G. C. Peden, *British Rearmament and the Treasury, 1932–1939* (Edinburgh, 1979); James Thomas Emmerson, *The Rhineland Crisis* (London, 1977); Silvio Pons, *Stalin and the Inevitable War, 1936–1941* (London, 2002); Hans von Herwarth, *Zwischen Hitler und Stalin: Erlebte Zeitgeschichte 1931 bis 1945* (Frankfurt am Main, 1982); Wacław Jędrzejewicz, ed., *Diplomat in Berlin: Papers and Memoirs of*

Józef Lipski, 1933–1939 (New York, 1968); Lord (Robert) Vansittart, *The Mist Procession: The Autobiography of Lord Vansittart* (London, 1958); Leonidas E. Hill, ed., *Die Weizsäcker-Papiere, 1933–1950* (Berlin, 1950); Gyula Juhász, *Hungarian Foreign Policy, 1919–1945* (Budapest, 1979); Eva Ingeborg Fleischhauer, 'Rathenau in Rapallo: Eine notwendige Korrektur des Forschungsstandes', *VfZ* 54: 3 (2006), 365–415; C. J. Hill, 'Great Britain and the Saar Plebiscite of 13 January 1935', *JCH* 9: 2 (1974), 121–42; Stephen A. Schuker, 'France and the Remilitarization of the Rhineland, 1936', *FHS* 14: 3 (1986), 299–338; Barton Whaley, 'Covert Rearmament in Germany, 1919–1939: Deception and Misperception', *Journal of Strategic Studies*, 5: 1 (1982), 3–39; Martin Thomas, 'French Economic Affairs and Rearmament: The First Crucial Months, June–September 1936', *JCH* 27: 4 (1992), 659–70.

Spanish Civil War: Hugh Thomas, *The Spanish Civil War* (rev. edn., New York, 1977); George R. Esenwein, *The Spanish Civil War: A Modern Tragedy* (New York, 2005); Paul Preston, *Franco: A Biography* (London, 1993); Gerald Brenan, *The Spanish Labyrinth* (Cambridge, 1943); Paul Preston, *The Coming of the Spanish Civil War: Reform, Reaction and Revolution in the Second Republic* (London, 1978); Paul Preston, ed., *Revolution in Spain, 1931–1939* (London, 1984); Sebastian Balfour and Paul Preston, eds., *Spain and the Great Powers* (London, 1999); Herbert Rutledge Southworth, *Guernica! Guernica! A Study of Journalism, Diplomacy, Propaganda and History* (Berkeley, 1977); Paul Preston and Ann L. Mackenzie, eds., *The Republic Besieged: Civil War in Spain, 1936–1939* (Edinburgh, 1996); Stanley Payne, *The Franco Regime, 1936–1975* (Madison, 1987); Julio de la Cueva, 'Religious Persecution, Anticlerical Tradition and Revolution: On Atrocities against the Clergy during the Spanish Civil War', *JCH* 33: 3 (1998), 355–69; Brian R. Sullivan, 'Fascist Italy's Military Involvement in the Spanish Civil War', *JMilH* 59: 4 (1995), 697–727; R. Geoffrey Jensen, 'José Millan-Astray and the Nationalist "Crusade" in Spain', *JCH* 27: 3 (1992), 425–47; Julius Ruiz, 'A Spanish Genocide? Reflections on the Francoist Repression after the Spanish Civil War', *CoEH* 14: 2 (2005), 171–91.

***Austria and the* Anschluss:** Charles A. Gulick, *Austria from Habsburg to Hitler* (2 vols., Berkeley, 1948); Charlie Jeffery, *Social Democracy in the Austrian Provinces, 1918–1934: Beyond Red Vienna* (London, 1995); Kurt von Schuschnigg, *The Brutal Takeover* (London, 1971); A. Schmidl, *März 38: Der deutsche Einmarsch in Österreich* (Vienna, 1988); Norbert Leser, 'Austria Between the Wars: An Essay', *AHYB* 17/18 (1981–2), 127–42.

Czechoslovakia and Munich: Victor S. Mamatey and Radomír Luža, *A History of the Czechoslovak Republic, 1918–1948* (Princeton, 1973); Zbyněk Zeman, *The Masaryks: The Making of Czechoslovakia* (London, 1976); idem with Antonín Klimek, *The Life of Edvard Beneš 1884–1948: Czechoslovakia in Peace and War* (Oxford, 1997); Igor Lukes, *Czechoslovakia Between Stalin and Hitler: The Diplomacy of Edvard Beneš in the 1930s* (New York, 1996); Telford Taylor, *Munich: The Price of Peace* (New York, 1979); Paul Vyšny, *The Runciman Mission to Czechoslovakia, 1938: Prelude to Munich* (Basingstoke, 2003); Katriel Ben-Arie,

'Czechoslovakia at the Time of "Munich": The Military Situation', *JCH* 25: 4 (1990), 431–46.

The Second World War

Outbreak of the Second World War: Donald Cameron Watt, *How War Came: The Immediate Origins of the Second World War, 1938–1939* (New York, 1989); P. M. H. Bell, *The Origins of the Second World War in Europe* (London, 1986); Geoffrey Roberts, *The Soviet Union and the Origins of the Second World War: Russo-German Relations and the Road to War, 1933–1941* (Basingstoke, 1995); Wolfgang Leonhard, *Der Schock des Hitler-Stalin-Paktes* (Munich, 1989); Anna M. Ciencala, *Poland and the Western Powers, 1938–1939* (London, 1968); Simon Newman, *March 1939: The British Guarantee to Poland: A Study in the Continuity of British Foreign Policy* (Oxford, 1976); A. J. P. Taylor, *The Origins of the Second World War* (London, 1961); G. Bruce Strang, 'Once More into the Breach: Britain's Guarantee to Poland, March 1939', *JCH* 31: 4 (1996), 721–52; A. J. Prazmowska, 'Poland's Foreign Policy: September 1938–September 1939', *HJ* 29: 4 (1986), 853–73.

The Second World War in general: Gordon Wright, *The Ordeal of Total War* (New York, 1968); Peter Calvocoressi, Guy Wint, and John Pritchard, *Total War: The Causes and Courses of the Second World War* (rev. edn., 2 vols., New York, 1989); B. H. Liddell Hart, *History of the Second World War* (London, 1970); Gerhard Weinberg, *A World at Arms: A Global History of World War II* (Cambridge, 1994); John Keegan, ed., *The Times Atlas of the Second World War* (New York, 1989); I. C. B. Dear, *The Oxford Companion to the Second World War* (Oxford, 1995).

Britain at war: Winston S. Churchill, *The Second World War* (6 vols., London, 1948–54); N. H. Gibbs, *Grand Strategy*, vol. i, *Rearmament Policy* (London, 1976); Michael Howard, *Grand Strategy*, vol. iv, *August 1942–September 1943* (London, 1972); Michael Howard, *British Intelligence in the Second World War*: vol. v, *Strategic Deception* (London, 1990); W. N. Medlicott, *The Economic Blockade* (2 vols., London, 1952–9); Richard M. Titmuss, *Problems of Social Policy* (London, 1950); Mark Harrison, *Medicine and Victory: British Military Medicine in the Second World War* (Oxford, 2004); Sir Richard Clarke, *Anglo-American Economic Collaboration in War and Peace, 1942–1949* (Oxford, 1982); Lord Alanbrooke, *War Diaries, 1939–1945*, ed. Alex Danchev and Daniel Todman (London, 2002); Nigel Hamilton, *Monty* (3 vols., London, 1981–6); Alec Cairncross, *Planning in Wartime: Aircraft Production in Britain, Germany and the USA* (Basingstoke, 1991); Andrew Hodges, *Alan Turing: The Enigma* (London, 1983); Angus Calder, *The People's War: Britain, 1939–1945* (London, 1969); F. W. Winterbotham, *The Ultra Secret* (New York, 1974); John Masterman, *The Double-Cross System in the War of 1939 to 1945* (New Haven, 1972); R. V. Jones, *The Wizard War: British Scientific Intelligence, 1939–1945* (New York, 1978); Ina Zweiniger-Bargielowska, *Austerity in Britain: Rationing, Controls, and Consumption, 1939–1955* (Oxford, 2000); Paul Addison, *The Road to 1945: British Politics and the Second World War* (London, 1975); John

Keegan, ed., *Churchill's Generals* (London, 1991); Maureen Waller, *London 1945: Life in the Debris of War* (London, 2004).

Germany at war: *Germany and the Second World War* (Oxford, 1990– , translation of *Das Deutsche Reich und der Zweite Weltkrieg*, Stuttgart, 1979– , series produced by Militärgeschichtliches Forschungsamt, Potsdam); Helmut Eiber and David M. Glantz, eds., *Hitler and His Generals: Military Conferences, 1942–1945* (London, 2002); Hugh Trevor-Roper, ed., *Hitler's War Directives, 1939–1945* (London, 1966); Albert Speer, *Inside the Third Reich* (London, 1970); *The Diaries of Victor Klemperer, 1933–1945* (2 vols., London, 1998–9); Friedrich Reck-Malleczewen, *Diary of a Man in Despair* (New York, 1979); Albrecht Hartmann and Heidi Hartmann, *Kriegsdienstverweigerung im Dritten Reich* (Frankfurt, 1986); Charles Messenger, *The Last Prussian: A Biography of Field Marshal Gerd von Rundstedt, 1875–1953* (London, 1991); Heinz Guderian, *Panzer Leader* (London, 2000); Georg Lilienthal, *Der 'Lebensborn e. V.': Ein Instrument nationalsozialistischer Rassenpolitik* (Mainz, 1985); Omer Bartov, *Hitler's Army: Soldiers, Nazis, and War in the Third Reich* (Oxford, 1991); Alfred Price, *The Luftwaffe Data Book* (London, 1997); Michael J. Neufeld, *The Rocket and the Reich: Peenemünde and the Coming of the Ballistic Missile Era* (New York, 1995); Donald E. Shepardson, 'The Fall of Berlin and the Rise of a Myth', *JMilH* 62: 1 (1998), 135–53.

Polish Campaign, Winter War: Stanisław Maczek, *Avec mes Blindés* (Paris, 1967); Jan T. Gross *Revolution from Abroad: the Soviet Conquest of Poland's Western Ukraine and Western Belorussia* (rev. edn., Princeton, 2002); Keith Sword, ed., *The Soviet Takeover of the Polish Eastern Provinces, 1939–41* (Basingstoke, 1991); Carl Van Dyke, *The Soviet Invasion of Finland, 1939–40* (London, 1997); E. N. Kulkov, O. A. Rzheshevsky et al., eds., *Stalin and the Soviet-Finnish War, 1939–1940* (London, 2002); Väinö Tanner, *The Winter War: Finland against Russia, 1939–1940* (Stanford, 1950); J. E. O. Screen, *Mannerheim: The Finnish Years* (London, 2000).

Fall of France: Joel Blatt, ed., *The French Defeat of 1940: Reassessments* (Providence, RI, 1998); Julian Jackson, *The Fall of France: The Nazi Invasion of 1940* (Oxford, 2003); Charles de Gaulle, *Mémoires de guerre* (3 vols., Paris, 1954–9); Ernest R. May, *Strange Victory: Hitler's Conquest of France* (London, 2000); Marc Bloch, *L'Etrange Défaite* (Paris, 1946); Jean-Louis Crémieux-Brilhac, *Les Français de l'an 40* (2 vols., Paris, 1990); A. Rossi [pseud. = Angelo Tasca], *Les Communistes français pendant le drôle de guerre* (Paris, 1951); Talbot Charles Imlay, 'A Reassessment of Anglo-French Strategy during the Phony War', *EHR* 119: 481 (2004), 333–72.

Italy's war: MacGregor Knox, *Mussolini Unleashed, 1939–1941: Politics and Strategy in Fascist Italy's Last War* (Cambridge, 1982); Martin L. van Creveld, *Hitler's Strategy, 1940–1941: The Balkan Clue* (Cambridge, 1973); Galeazzo Ciano, *Diario di Ciano, 1939–43* (2 vols., Milan, 1963); F. W. Deakin, *The Brutal Friendship: Mussolini, Hitler, and the Fall of Fascism* (London, 1962).

German-Soviet War: John Erickson, *Stalin's War with Germany: The Road to Stalingrad* (London, 1975); idem, *The Road to Berlin* (London, 1983); Robert Cecil, *Hitler's Decision to Invade Russia 1941* (London, 1975); David M. Glantz, *Stumbling*

Colossus: The Red Army on the Eve of World War ((Lawrence, Kan., 1998); Gabriel Gorodetsky, *Grand Delusion: Stalin and the German Invasion of Russia* (New Haven, 1999); Harold Shukman, ed., *Stalin's Generals* (London, 1993); Omer Bartov, *The Eastern Front, 1941–1945* (New York, 1986); Jürgen Förster, ed., *Stalingrad: Ereignis—Wirkung—Symbol* (Munich, 1993); David M. Glantz, *The Siege of Leningrad, 1941–1944* (London, 2001); Evan Mawdsley, 'Crossing the Rubicon: Soviet Offensive War Plans in 1940–1941', *IHR* 25: 4 (2003), 818–65; Cynthia Roberts, 'Planning for War: The Red Army and the Catastrophe of 1941', *EAS* 47: 8 (1995), 1293–1326; Teddy J. Uldricks, 'The Icebreaker Controversy: Did Stalin Plan to Attack Hitler?', *SR* 58: 3 (1999).

War economies: Alan Milward, *War, Economy and Society, 1939–1945* (Berkeley, 1979); idem, *The German Economy at War* (London, 1965); idem, *The New Order and the French Economy* (Oxford, 1970); idem, *The Fascist Economy in Norway* (Oxford, 1972); R. J. Overy, *War and Economy in the Third Reich* (Oxford, 1995); Mark Harrison, *Accounting for War: Soviet Production, Employment, and the Defence Burden, 1940–1945* (Cambridge, 1996); John Barber and Mark Harrison, *The Soviet Home Front, 1941–1945: A Social and Economic History of the USSR in World War II* (London, 1991); Susan J. Linz, ed., *The Impact of World War II on the Soviet Union* (Totowa, NJ, 1985); Ulrich Herbert, *Hitler's Foreign Workers: Enforced Foreign Labor in Germany under the Third Reich* (Cambridge, 1985).

Occupied Europe: Ruth Bettina Birn, *Die Höheren SS- und Polizeiführer: Himmlers Vertreter im Reich und in den besetzten Gebieten* (Düsseldorf, 1986); Mark Mazower, *Inside Hitler's Greece: The Experience of Occupation, 1941–44* (New Haven, 1993); Robert Gildea, *Marianne in Chains: In Search of the German Occupation of France, 1940–1945* (London, 2002); Philippe Burrin, *France under the Germans: Collaboration and Compromise* (New York, 1993); Marie-Louise Roth-Zimmermann, *Denk' ich an Schelklingen: Erinnerungen einer Elsässerin an die Zeit im SS-Umsiedlungslager, 1942–1945* (St Ingbert, 2001); Louis de Jong, *The Netherlands and Nazi Germany* (Cambridge, Mass., 1988, a brief English distillation of idem, ed., *Het Koninkrijk der Nederlanden in de Tweede Wereldoorlog*, 14 vols., 's-Gravenhage/Leiden, 1969–91); Charles Cruikshank, *The German Occupation of the Channel Islands* (London, 1975); Christian Streit, *Keine Kameraden: Die Wehrmacht und die sowjetischen Kriegsgefangenen* (2nd edn., Bonn, 1991); Robert O. Paxton, *Vichy France: Old Guard and New Order, 1940–1944* (New York, 1972); Marc Ferro, *Pétain* (Paris, 1987); Edouard Daladier, *Journal de captivité (1940–1945)* (Paris, 1991); A. Rossi [pseud. = Angelo Tasca], *La Guerre des papillons: quatre ans de politique communiste, 1940–1944* (Paris, 1954).

Resistance: M. R. D. Foot, *Resistance: An Analysis of European Resistance to Nazism, 1940–1945* (London, 1976); Stephen Hawes and Ralph White, eds., *Resistance in Europe, 1939–1945* (London, 1976); Henri Michel, *The Shadow War: Resistance in Europe, 1939–1945* (London, 1972); Rab Bennett, *Under the Shadow of the Swastika: The Moral Dilemmas of Resistance and Collaboration in Hitler's Europe*

(Basingstoke, 1999); Klaus Schmider, *Partisanenkrieg in Jugoslawien, 1941–1944* (Hamburg, 2002).

Collaboration: Catherine Andreyev, *Vlasov and the Russian Liberation Movement: Soviet Reality and Emigré Theories* (Cambridge, 1987); Paul Jankowski, *From Communism to Collaboration: Simon Sabiani and Politics in Marseille, 1919–1944* (New Haven, 1989); Gerhard Hirschfeld, *Nazi Rule and Dutch Collaboration: The Netherlands under German Occupation, 1940–1945* (Oxford, 1988); Ruth Bettina Birn, 'Collaboration with Nazi Germany in Eastern Europe: the Case of the Estonian Security Police', *CoEH* 10: 2 (2001), 181–98.

Propaganda: Michael Balfour, *Propaganda in War, 1939–1945: Organisations, Policies and Publics in Britain and Germany* (London, 1979); Ernest K. Bramsted, *Goebbels and National Socialist Propaganda 1925–1945* (London, 1965); Z. A. B. Zeman, *Nazi Propaganda* (London, 1973); Daniel Lerner, *Psychological Warfare against Nazi Germany: The Sykewar Campaign D-Day to VE-Day* (2nd edn., Cambridge, Mass., 1971); Ortwin Buchbender and Reinhard Hauschild, *Geheimsender gegen Frankreich: Die Täuschungsoperation* 'Radio *Humanité' 1940* (Herford, 1984); Carl Brinitzer, *Hier spricht London* (Hamburg, 1969); Tobias Schneider, 'Bestseller im Dritten Reich', *VfZ* 52: 1 (2004), 77–97; Brett C. Bowles. 'La Tragédie de Mers-el-Kébir and the Politics of Filmed News in France, 1940–1944', *JMH* 76: 2 (2004), 347–88.

Wartime diplomacy: Herbert Feis, *Churchill, Roosevelt, Stalin: The War they Waged and the Peace they Sought* (Princeton, 1957); Robin Edmonds, *The Big Three: Churchill, Roosevelt and Stalin in Peace and War* (London, 1992); Sir Llewellyn Woodward, *British Foreign Policy in the Second World War* (5 vols., London, 1970–6); David Dilks, ed., *The Diaries of Sir Alexander Cadogan OM, 1938–1945* (London, 1971); Gerhard L. Weinberg, *World in the Balance* (Hanover, NH, 1981); David Carlton, *Churchill and the Soviet Union* (Manchester, 2000); Mario D. Fenyo, *Hitler, Horthy, and Hungary: German–Hungarian Relations 1941–1944* (New Haven, 1972); Antony Polonsky, ed., *The Great Powers and the Polish Question, 1941–45: A Documentary Study in Cold War Origins* (London, 1976); Milovan Djilas, *Conversations with Stalin* (New York, 1962); Paul W. Doerr, ' "Frigid but Unprovocative": British Policy Towards the USSR from the Nazi-Soviet Pact to the Winter War, 1939', *JCH* 36: 3 (2001), 423–39; George Sanford, 'The Katyn Massacre and Polish-Soviet Relations, 1941–43', *JCH* 41: 1 (2006), 95–111.

Neutrals: *Actes et documents du Saint Siège relatifs à la seconde guerre mondiale*, 11 vols. (Città del Vaticano, 1965–81); Christian Leitz, *Nazi Germany and Neutral Europe during the Second World War* (Manchester, 2000); Joseph T. Carroll, *Ireland in the War Years* (Newton Abbot, 1975); Dermot Keogh and Mervyn O'Driscoll, eds., *Ireland in World War Two: Diplomacy and Survival* (Cork, 2004); Robert Fisk, *In Time of War: Ireland, Ulster, and the Price of Neutrality, 1939–45* (Philadelphia, 1983); W. M. Carlgren, *Swedish Foreign Policy During the Second World War* (New York, 1977); *Sweden: A Wartime Survey* (Stockholm, Press Bureau of the Royal Ministry for Foreign Affairs,1942); Independent Commission of Experts, *Final Report: Switzerland, National Socialism and the Second World War* (Zürich, 2002).

Genocide: Raul Hilberg, *The Destruction of the European Jews* (2nd edn., 3 vols., New York, 1985); Christopher R. Browning, *The Origins of the Final Solution: The Evolution of Nazi Jewish Policy, September 1939–March 1942* (Lincoln, Nebr., 2004); idem, *Ordinary Men: Reserve Police Battalion 101 and the Final Solution in Poland* (New York, 1992); idem, *The Path to Genocide* (Cambridge, 1992); Ulrich Herbert, *National Socialist Extermination Policies: Contemporary German Perspectives and Controversies* (New York, 2000); Hannah Arendt, *Eichmann in Jerusalem: A Report on the Banality of Evil* (London, 1963); Isaiah Trunk, *Judenrat: The Jewish Councils in Eastern Europe Under Nazi Control* (New York, 1972); Lucjan Dobroszycki, ed., *The Chronicle of the Łódź Ghetto, 1941–1944* (New Haven, 1984); Herman Kruk, *The Last Days of the Jerusalem of Lithuania: Chronicles from the Vilna Ghetto and the Camps, 1939–1944*, ed. Benjamin Harshav (New Haven, 2002); Jonathan Steinberg, *All or Nothing: The Axis and the Holocaust, 1941–1943* (London, 1990); Steven Paskuly, ed., *Death Dealer, The Memoirs of the SS Kommandant at Auschwitz by Rudolph Hoess* (Buffalo, 1992); Martin Gilbert, *Auschwitz and the Allies* (London, 1981); Michaël R. Marrus and Robert O. Paxton, *Vichy et les Juifs* (Paris, 1981); Frederick B. Chary, *The Bulgarian Jews and the Final Solution, 1940–1944* (Pittsburgh, 1972); Omer Bartov, *The Eastern Front, 1941–5: German Troops and the Barbarisation of Warfare* (New York, 1986); Thomas Vogel, ed., *Wilm Hosenfeld: 'Ich versuche jeden zu retten': Das Leben eines deutschen Offiziers in Briefen und Tagebüchern* (Munich, 2004); Jan T. Gross, *Neighbours: The Destruction of the Jewish Community in Jedwabne, Poland* (Princeton, 2001); Franciszek Piper, 'Estimating the Number of Deportees to and Victims of the Auschwitz-Birkenau Camp', *Yad Vashem Studies*, vol. xxi (1991), 49–103; Nathan Rotenstreich, 'The Holocaust as a Unique Historical Event', *Patterns of Prejudice*, 22: 1 (1988), 14–20; James Walston 'History and Memory of the Italian Concentration Camps', *HJ* 40: 1 (1997), 169–83.

German resistance: Peter Hoffman, *The History of the German Resistance, 1933–1945* (London, 1977); Heinrich Hermelink hrsg., *Kirche im Kampf: Dokumente des Widerstands und des Aufbaus in der evangelischen Kirche Deutschlands von 1933 bis 1945* (Tübingen, 1950); Ulrich von Hassell, *Die Hassell-Tagebücher, 1938–1944* (Berlin, 1988); H. W. Koch, *In the Name of the Volk: Political Justice in Hitler's Germany* (London, 1997); Hans Mommsen, *Alternative zu Hitler: Studien zur Geschichte des deutschen Widerstandes* (Munich, 2000).

Bombing of Germany: Sir Charles Webster and Noble Frankland, *The Strategic Air Offensive against Germany, 1939–1945* (4 vols., London, 1961); Martin Middlebrook and Chris Everitt, *The Bomber Command Diaries: An Operational Reference Book, 1939–1945* (London, 1990); Martin Middlebrook, *The Schweinfurt–Regensburg Mission: American Raids on 17 August 1943* (London, 1985); idem, *The Berlin Raids: RAF Bomber Command, Winter 1943–44* (London, 1990); Jörg Friedrich, *Der Brand: Deutschland im Bombenkrieg, 1940–1945* (Berlin, 2002); Götz

Bergander, *Dresden im Luftkrieg* (Würzburg, 1998); Helmut Schnatz, *Tiefflieger über Dresden? Legenden und Wirklichkeit* (Cologne, 2000).

Europe since 1945

Memories of war: Monika Flacke, ed., *Mythen der Nationen: 1945—Arena der Erinnerungen* (Berlin, 2004); Susan Rubin Suleiman, *Crises of Memory and the Second World War* (Cambridge, Mass., 2006); Henry Rousso, *The Vichy Syndrome: History and Memory in France since 1944* (Cambridge, Mass., 1991); Frank Biess, *Homecomings: Returning POWs and the Legacies of Defeat in Postwar Germany* (Princeton, 2006); Wolfram Wette, *The Wehrmacht: History, Myth, Reality* (Cambridge, Mass., 2006); Charles S. Maier, *The Unmasterable Past: History, Holocaust, and German National Identity* (Cambridge, Mass., 1988); Richard J. Evans, *In Hitler's Shadow: West German Historians and the Attempt to Escape from the Nazi Past* (New York, 1989); Norbert Frei, *1945 und Wir: Das Dritte Reich im Bewusstsein der Deutschen* (Munich, 2005); Konrad H. Jarausch and Michael Geyer, *Shattered Past: Reconstructing German Histories* (Princeton, 2003).

War crimes trials: *Trial of the major war criminals before the International Military Tribunal, Nuremberg, 14 November 1945–1 October 1946* (42 vols., Nuremberg, 1947–1949, known, from colour of binding, as 'blue series'); Telford Taylor, *Anatomy of the Nuremberg Trials: A Personal Memoir* (London, 1993); Istvan Déak, Jan T. Gross, and Tony Judt, eds., *The Politics of Retribution in Europe: World War II and its Aftermath* (Princeton, 2000); Benjamin Frommer, *National Cleansing: Retribution against Nazi Collaborators in Postwar Czechoslovakia* (Cambridge, 2005).

Flight and expulsion of Germans from eastern Europe: Theodor Schieder et al., eds., *Die Vertreibung der Deutschen Bevölkerung aus den Gebieten östlich der Oder-Neisse* (5 vols., Bonn, 1954–60); Radomír Luža, *The Transfer of the Sudeten Germans: A Study of Czech–German Relations 1933–1962* (New York, 1964); G. C. Paikert, *The Danube Swabians: German Populations in Hungary, Rumania and Yugoslavia and Hitler's Impact on their Patterns* (The Hague, 1967); Wolfgang Benz, ed., *Die Vertreibung der Deutschen aus dem Osten: Ursachen, Ereignisse, Folgen* (Frankfurt am Main, 1995); Philipp Ther, *Deutsche und polnische Vertriebene: Gesellschaft und Vertriebenenpolitik in der SBZ/DDR und in Polen, 1945–1956* (Göttingen, 1998); Michael A. Nagelbach, *Heil! and Farewell: A Life in Romania, 1913–1946* (Chicago, 1986); Marion Countess Dönhoff, *Before the Storm: Memories of my Youth in Old Prussia* (New York, 1990); Johannes Kaps, *Die Tragödie Schlesiens 1945/6 in Dokumenten* (Munich, 1952–3).

Communization of eastern Europe: Thomas Hammond, ed., *The Anatomy of Communist Takeovers* (New Haven, 1975); Antony Polonsky and Bolesław Drukier, eds., *The Beginnings of Communist Rule in Poland* (London, 1980); Stephen D. Kertesz, *Diplomacy in a Whirlpool: Hungary and the Illusions of Peacemaking, 1945–1947* (Notre Dame, Indiana, 1984); Sándor Márai, *Memoir of Hungary, 1944–1948* (Budapest 1996); Sergiu Verona, *Military Occupation and Diplomacy: Soviet Troops in Romania, 1944–1958* (Durham, NC, 1992); Wolfgang

Leonhard, *Child of the Revolution* (Chicago, 1958); Teresa Toranska, *'Them': Stalin's Polish Puppets* (New York, 1987); Karel Bartosek, *Les Aveux des archives: Prague—Paris—Prague, 1948–1968* (Paris, 1996); Robert Levy, *Ana Pauker: The Rise and Fall of a Jewish Communist* (Berkeley, 2001).

Cold War: Hugh Thomas, *Armed Truce: The Beginnings of the Cold War, 1945–46* (New York, 1987); S. J. Ball, *The Cold War: An International History, 1947–1991* (London, 1998); Jussi M. Hanhimäki and Odd Arne Westad, eds., *The Cold War; A History in Documents and Eyewitness Accounts* (Oxford, 2004); John Lewis Gaddis, *We Now Know: Rethinking Cold War History* (Oxford, 1997); David Holloway, *Stalin and the Bomb: The Soviet Union and Atomic Energy, 1939–1956* (New Haven, 1994); Marc Trachtenberg, *A Constructed Peace: The Making of the European Settlement, 1945–1963* (Princeton, 1999); Lorna Arnold, *Britain and the H-Bomb* (Basingstoke, 2001); Stephen Twigge and Len Scott, *Planning Armageddon: Britain, the United States and the Command of Western Nuclear Forces, 1945–1964* (Amsterdam, 2000); Lawrence Freedman, *The Evolution of Nuclear Strategy* (3rd edn., Basingstoke, 2003); Giles Scott-Smith and Hans Krabbendam, eds., *The Cultural Cold War in Western Europe, 1945–1960* (London, 2003); David Caute, *The Fellow-Travellers: Intellectual Friends of Communism* (rev. edn., New Haven, 1988); idem, *The Dancer Defects: The Struggle for Cultural Supremacy During the Cold War* (Oxford, 2003); Christopher Andrew and Oleg Gordievsky, *KGB: The Inside Story of its Foreign Operations from Lenin to Gorbachev* (London, 1990); Christopher Andrew and Vasili Mitrokhin, *The Sword and the Shield: The Mitrokhin Archive and the Secret History of the KGB* (New York, 1999); Yuri Modin, *My Five Cambridge Friends* (New York, 1994); Juhana Aunesluoma, *Britain, Sweden and the Cold War, 1945–54* (Basingstoke, 2003); Markus Wolf, *Memoirs of a Spymaster* (London, 1998); Christopher Andrew and Oleg Gordievsky, *Comrade Kryuchkov's Instructions: Top Secret Files on KGB Foreign Operations, 1975–1985* (Stanford, 1991); Vojtech Mastny, 'The New History of Cold War Alliances', *JCWS* 4: 2 (2002), 55–84; John Baylis, 'Exchanging Nuclear Secrets: Laying the Foundations of the Anglo-American Nuclear Relationship', *Diplomatic History*, 25: 1 (2001), 33–61; Valur Ingimundarson, 'Between Solidarity and Neutrality: the Nordic Countries and the Cold War, 1945–1991', *CWIHPB* 11 (1998), 269–74.

Germany, 1945–55: Helke Sander and Barbara Johr, eds., *Befreier und Befreite: Krieg, Vergewaltigungen, Kinder* (Munich, 1992); Alec Cairncross, *The Price of War: British Policy on German Reparations, 1941–1949* (Oxford, 1986); idem, *A Country to Play With: Level of Industry Negotiations in Berlin, 1945–46* (Gerrards Cross, Bucks., 1987); James F. Tent, *Mission on the Rhine: Reeducation and Denazification in American-Occupied Germany* (Chicago, 1982); Beate Ruhm von Oppen, ed., *Documents on Germany under Occupation, 1945–1954* (London, 1955); Edgar McInnis, Richard Hiscocks, and Robert Spencer, *The Shaping of Postwar Germany* (New York, 1960); Norman M. Naimark, *The Russians in Germany: A History of the Soviet Zone of Occupation, 1945–1949* (Cambridge, Mass., 1995); Michael Ermarth, ed., *America and the Shaping of German Society, 1945–1955* (Providence, RI, 1993); Wilfried Loth, *Stalin's Unwanted Child: The Soviet Union, the German Question and the Founding of the GDR* (Basingstoke, 1998).

Marshall Plan: Charles S. Maier and Günter Bischof, eds., *The Marshall Plan and Germany: West German Development within the Framework of the European Recovery Program* (New York, 1991); Michael J. Hogan, *The Marshall Plan: America, Britain, and the Reconstruction of Western Europe, 1947–1952* (Cambridge, 1987); Alan S. Milward, *The Reconstruction of Western Europe, 1945–51* (Berkeley, 1984).

Welfare state: W. J. Mommsen and Wolfgang Mock, eds., *The Emergence of the Welfare State in Britain and Germany, 1850–1950* (London, 1981); José Harris, *William Beveridge: A Biography* (Oxford, 1977); Peter Flora and Arnold J. Heidenheimer, eds., *The Development of Welfare States in Europe and America* (New Brunswick, NJ, 1981); Jytte Klausen, *War and Welfare: Europe and the United States, 1945 to the Present* (New York, 1998); Richard M. Titmuss, *Income Distribution and Social Change: A Study in Criticism* (London, 1962); Charles Webster, *The National Health Service: A Political History* (2nd edn., Oxford, 2002); James E. Cronin, *The Politics of State Expansion: War, State and Society in Twentieth-Century Britain* (London, 1991); Alexander Davidson, *Two Models of Welfare: The Origins and Development of the Welfare State in Sweden and New Zealand, 1888–1988* (Uppsala, 1989).

European Common Market to European Union: Jean Monnet, *Mémoires* (Paris, 1976); François Duchêne, *Jean Monnet: The First Statesman of Interdependence* (New York, 1994); Raymond Poidevin, *Robert Schuman* (Paris, 1988); Hans August Lücker and Jean Seitlinger, *Robert Schuman und die Einigung Europas* (Luxembourg, 2000); Alan S. Milward, *The European Rescue of the Nation-State* (2nd edn., London, 2000); Lee Miles, ed., *The European Union and the Nordic Countries* (London, 1996); Jeffrey Glen Giauque, *Grand Designs and Visions of Unity: The Atlantic Powers and the Reorganization of Western Europe, 1955–1963* (Chapel Hill, NC, 2002); Anthony Eden (Earl of Avon), *The Eden Memoirs* (3 vols., London, 1960–65); Peter G. Boyle, ed., *The Eden–Eisenhower Correspondence, 1955–1957* (Chapel Hill, NC, 2005); William I. Hitchcock, 'France, the Western Alliance, and the Origins of the Schuman Plan, 1948–50', *Diplomatic History*, 21: 4 (1997), 603–30; Simon Burgess and Geoffrey Edwards, 'The Six Plus One: British Policy-Making and the Question of European Economic Integration, 1955', *IA* 64: 3 (1988), 393–413; N. Piers Ludlow, 'The Making of the CAP: Towards a Historical Analysis of the EU's First Major Policy', *CoEH* 14: 3 (2005) 347–71; Peter Lange, 'Maastricht and the Social Protocol: Why Did They Do It?', *PS* 21: 1 (1993) 5–36.

Ends of empire: J.D. Hargreaves, *Decolonization in Africa* (London, 1988); John Darwin, *Britain and Decolonisation: The Retreat from Empire in the Post-War World* (New York, 1988); Judith M. Brown and William Roger Louis, eds., *The Oxford History of the British Empire*, vol. iv: *The Twentieth Century* (Oxford, 1999); *Constitutional Relations between Britain and India: The Transfer of Power, 1942–47* (London, 1970–83); *Constitutional Relations between Britain and Burma: The Struggle* *for Independence, 1944–1948* (2 vols., 1983–4); *British Documents on the End of Empire* (London, 1994–); Keith Kyle, *Suez: Britain's End of Empire in the Middle East* (rev. edn., London, 2003); William Roger Louis and Roger Owen, eds., *Suez 1956: The Crisis and its Consequences* (Oxford, 1989); Jules Roy, *La Bataille de Dien Bien Phu* (Paris, 1963); Robert Guillain, *Diên-Biên-Phu: La Fin des Illusions* (Paris, 2004); Alistair Horne, *A Savage War of Peace: Algeria, 1954–1962* (New York, 1978); Martin S. Alexander and J. F. V. Keiger, eds., *France and the Algerian War, 1954–62: Strategy, Operations and Diplomacy* (London, 2002); Paul Aussaresses, *Services spéciaux: Algérie 1955–1957* (Paris, 2001).

Britain 1945–73: Kenneth Morgan, *The People's Peace: British History, 1945–1989* (London, 1990); idem, *Labour in Power 1945–1951* (Oxford, 1984); Peter Hennessy, *The Prime Minister: The Office and its Holders since 1945* (New York, 2001); Michael Foot, *Aneurin Bevan*, 2 vols. (London, 1962–73); Ben Pimlott, *Hugh Dalton* (London, 1985); Peter Clarke, *The Cripps Version: The Life of Sir Stafford Cripps, 1889–1952* (London, 2002); Arthur Marwick, *British Society since 1945* (4th edn., London, 2003); Noel Annan, *Our Age: The Generation that Made Post-War Britain* (London, 1990); Alec Cairncross, *The British Economy since 1945: Economic Policy and Performance, 1945–1990* (Oxford, 1992); Alistair Horne, *Macmillan* (2 vols., London, 1988–9); Simon Ball, *The Guardsmen: Harold Macmillan, Three Friends, and the World They Made* (London, 2004); Richard Lamb, *The Macmillan Years, 1957–1963: The Emerging Truth* (London, 1995); Jacqueline Tratt, *The Macmillan Government and Europe: A Study in the Process of Policy Development* (London, 1996); Harold Evans, *Downing Street Diary: The Macmillan Years, 1957–1963* (London, 1981); Joe Haines, *The Politics of Power* (London, 1977); Richard Crossman, *The Diaries of a Cabinet Minister* (3 vols., London, 1975–7).

West Germany 1955–89: Henry Ashby Turner, Jr., *Germany from Partition to Reunification* (New Haven, 1992); Detlef Junker, Philipp Gassert, Wilfried Mausbach, and David B. Morris, eds., *The United States and Germany in the Era of the Cold War: A Handbook* (Cambridge, 2004); Ralf Dahrendorf, *Society and Democracy in Germany* (first pub. 1965; New York, 1979); Julius Friend, *The Linchpin: French–German Relations, 1950–1990* (New York, 1991); Hans-Peter Schwarz, *Konrad Adenauer: A German Politician and Statesman in a Period of War, Revolution, and Reconstruction* (2 vols., Providence, RI, 1995–1997); Angela E. Stent, *From Embargo to Ostpolitik* (Cambridge, 2003); Ronald J. Granieri, *The Ambivalent Alliance: Konrad Adenuer, the CDU/CSU, and the West, 1949–1966* (Providence, RI, 2003); Pertti Ahonen, *After the Expulsion: West Germany and Eastern Europe, 1945–1990* (Oxford, 2003); Willy Brandt, *Erinnerungen* (Berlin, 1994); Franz Schneider, ed., *Der Weg der Bundesrepublik: Von 1945 bis zur Gegenwart* (Munich, 1985); Stephen Padgett, ed., *Adenauer to Kohl: Development of the German Chancellorship* (London, 1994); Thomas A. Koelble, *The Left Unravelled: Social Democracy and the New Left Challenge in Britain and West Germany* (Durham, NC, 1991).

East Germany, 1953: Martin Krämer, *Der Volksaufstand vom 17. Juni 1953 und sein politisches Echo in der Bundesrepublik Deutschland* (Bochum, 1996); Volker Koop, *Der*

17. Juni 1953: Legende und Wirklichkeit (Berlin, 2003); Hubertus Knabe, *17. Juni 1953: Ein deutscher Aufstand* (Munich, 2003); Christian F. Ostermann, ed., *Uprising in East Germany 1953* (Budapest, 2001); Manfred Hagen, *DDR—Juni '53: Die erste Volkserhebung im Stalinismus* (Stuttgart, 1992); Victor Klemperer, *The Diaries of Victor Klemperer, 1945–1959* (London, 2004); Gareth Pritchard, *The Making of the GDR, 1945–1953: From Antifascism to Stalinism* (Manchester, 2000).

Berlin crises: Wolfgang Heidelmeyer and Guenther Hindrichs, eds., *Dokumente zur Berlin-Frage, 1944–1966* (Munich 1967); I. D. Hendry and M. C. Wood, *The Legal Status of Berlin* (Cambridge, 1987); Rolf Steinger, *Der Mauerbau: Die Westmächte und Adenauer in der Berlinkrise, 1958–1963* (Munich, 2001); Helge Heidemeyer, *Flucht und Zuwanderung aus der SBZ/DDR 1945/1949–1961: Die Flüchtlingspolitik der Bundesrepublik Deutschland bis zum Bau der Berliner Mauer* (Düsseldorf, 1994); Hope M. Harrison, *Driving the Soviets up the Wall: Soviet–East German Relations, 1953–1961* (Princeton, 2003); John P. S. Gearson, *Harold Macmillan and the Berlin Wall Crisis, 1958–1962: The Limits of Interests and Force* (Basingstoke, 1998).

Fourth and Fifth Republic France: Robert Gildea, *France since 1945* (Oxford, 1996); Georgette Elgey, *Histoire de la IVe République* (4 vols., rev. edn., Paris, 1993–); André Siegfried, *De la IIIe à la IVe République* (Paris, 1956); Jean-Louis Rizzo, *Mendès France ou la rénovation en politique* (Paris, 1993); David Caute, *Communism and the French Intellectuals, 1914–1960* (New York, 1964); Michel Winock, *La République se meurt: Chronique, 1956–1958* (Paris, 1978); Charles de Gaulle, *Discours et messages*, vols. iii–v (Paris, 1970); Jean Lacouture, *De Gaulle* (3 vols., Paris, 1984–6); Alain Peyrefitte, *C'était de Gaulle* (3 vols., Paris, 1994–2000); Odile Rudelle, *Mai 58: De Gaulle et la République* (Paris, 1988); Jean-Pierre Guichard, *De Gaulle face aux crises, 1940–1968* (Paris, 2000); Jean-Pierre Le Goff, *Mai 68: l'héritage impossible* (Paris, 1998); Alain Delale and Gilles Ragache, *La France de 68* (Paris, 1978); Vasco Gasquet, *Les 500 affiches de mai 1968* ([Paris], 1978); Alain Schnapp and Pierre Vidal-Naquet, eds., *Journal de la Commune étudiante: Textes et documents, novembre 1967—juin 1968* (Paris, 1969); Raymond Aron, *La Révolution introuvable: Réflexions sur les événements de mai* (Paris, 1968); Edgar Morin, Claude Lefort, and Jean-Marc Coudray, *Mai 1968: la Brèche: Premières réflexions sur les événements* (Paris, 1968); Louis Gruel, *Rébellion de 68: Une relecture sociologique* (Paris, 2004); Jacques Massu, *Avec De Gaulle: Du Tchad 1941 à Baden 1968* (Monaco, 1998); Georges Pompidou, *Entretiens et discours, 1968–1974* (Paris, 1975); Adrien Dansette, *Mai 1968* (Paris, 1971); Sten Rynning, *Changing Military Doctrine: Presidents and Military Power in Fifth Republic France, 1958–2000* (Westport, Conn., 2002); William Andrews and Stanley Hoffman, eds., *The Impact of the Fifth Republic on France* (Albany, NY,1981); Philip Thody, *The Fifth French Republic* (London, 1998); Vincent Wright, *Conflict and Consensus in France* (London, 1979); Serge Bernstein and Jean-François Sirinelli, eds., *Les Années Giscard: Valéry Giscard d'Estaing et l'Europe, 1974–1981* (Paris, 2006).

Southern Europe: Paul Ginsborg, *A History of Contemporary Italy: Society and Politics, 1943–1988* (London, 1990); idem, *Italy and its Discontents: Family, Civil*

Society, State, 1980–2001 (London, 2003); Richard Webster, *The Cross and the Fasces: Christian Democracy and Fascism in Italy* (Stanford, 1960); James Pettifer, *The Greeks: The Land and People since the War* (rev. edn., London, 2000); John O. Iatrides, *Greece in the 1940s: A Nation in Crisis* (Hanover, NH, 1981); Richard Clogg, *Parties and Elections in Greece: The Search for Legitimacy* (London, 1987); C. M. Woodhouse, *The Rise and Fall of the Greek Colonels* (New York, 1985); Feroz Ahmad, *The Making of Modern Turkey* (London, 1993); Andrew Borowiec, *Cyprus: A Troubled Island* (Westport, Conn., 2000); José M. Magone, *The Politics of Southern Europe: Integration Into the European Union* (Westport, Conn., 2003); Kenneth Maxwell, *The Making of Portuguese Democracy* (Cambridge, 1995); Paul Christopher Manuel, *The Challenges of Democratic Consolidation: Political, Economic, and Military Issues, 1976–1991* (Westport, Conn., 1996); Paul Preston, *The Triumph of Democracy in Spain* (London, 1986); Audrey Brassloff, *Religion and Politics in Spain: The Spanish Church in Transition, 1962–96* (Basingstoke, 1998); Walther L. Bernecker, 'Monarchy and Democracy: The Political Role of King Juan Carlos in the Spanish Transición', *JCH* 33: 1 (1998), 65–84.

USSR 1945–85: John Keep, *Last of the Empires: A History of the Soviet Union, 1945–1991* (Oxford, 1995); Ronald Grigor Suny, *The Soviet Experiment: Russia, the USSR, and the Successor States* (New York, 1997); Yoram Gorlizki and Oleg Khlevniuk, *Cold Peace: Stalin and the Soviet Ruling Circle, 1945–1953* (Oxford, 2004); Elena Zubkova, *Russia After the War: Hopes, Illusions, and Disappointments, 1945–1957* (Armonk, NY, 1998); William Taubman, *Khrushchev: The Man and his Era* (New York, 2003); Strobe Talbott, ed., *Khrushchev Remembers* (Boston, 1970); Polly Jones, ed., *The Dilemmas of De-Stalinization: Negotiating Cultural and Social Change in the Khrushchev Era* (Abingdon, 2006); Anatoly Smeliansky, *The Russian Theatre after Stalin* (Cambridge, 1999); Andrei Sakharov, *Memoirs* (London, 1990); Henry W. Morton, 'Who Gets What, When and How? Housing in the Soviet Union', *SS* 32: 2 (1980), 235–59; Susan E. Reid, 'Cold War in the Kitchen: Gender and the De-Stalinization of Consumer Taste in the Soviet Union under Khrushchev', *SR* 61: 2 (2002), 211–52.

Communist eastern Europe: Joseph Rothschild, *Return to Diversity: A Political History of East Central Europe since World War II* (New York, 1989); Gale Stokes, ed., *From Stalinism to Pluralism: A Documentary History of Eastern Europe since 1945* (New York, 1991); Adam B. Ulam, *The Communists: The Story of Power and Lost Illusions, 1948–1991* (New York, 1992); Milovan Djilas, *The New Class: An Analysis of the Communist System* (New York, 1957); Matthew J. Ouimet, *The Rise and Fall of the Brezhnev Doctrine in Soviet Foreign Policy* (Chapel Hill, NC, 2003); Sharon L. Wolchik and Alfred G. Meyer, eds., *Women, State, and Party in Eastern Europe* (Durham, NC, 1985); John Rodden, *Repainting the Little Red Schoolhouse: A History of Eastern German Education, 1945–1995* (Oxford, 2002); Jirí Pelikán, *The Czechoslovak Political Trials, 1950–1954: The Suppressed Report of the Dubček Government's Commission of Inquiry, 1968* (Stanford, 1971); Dennis Deletant, *Ceauşescu and the Securitate: Coercion and Dissent in Romania, 1965–1989* (London,

1995); Nissan Oren, *Revolution Administered: Agrarianism and Communism in Bulgaria* (Baltimore, 1973); Robert R. King, *A History of the Romanian Communist Party* (Stanford, 1980); Jon Halliday, ed., *The Artful Albanian: The Memoirs of Enver Hoxha* (London, 1986); James Mark, 'Discrimination, Opportunity and Middle-Class Success in Early Communist Hungary', *HJ* 48: 2 (2005), 499–521.

Austria: William B. Bader, *Austria Between East and West, 1945–1955* (Stanford, 1966); Günter Bischof and Anton Pelinka, eds., *Austria in the Nineteen Fifties* (New Brunswick, NJ, 1995); Gerald Stourzh, 'Towards the Settlement of 1955: The Austrian State Treaty Negotiations and the Origins of Austrian Neutrality', *AHYB* 17/18 (1981–2), 174–87.

Hungarian Revolution: György Litván, ed., *The Hungarian Revolution of 1956: Reform, Revolt and Repression* (London, 1996); Tamás Aczél, *Ten Years After: The Hungarian Revolution in the Perspective of History* (New York, 1966); Csaba Békés, Malcolm Byrne and János M. Rainer, eds., *The 1956 Hungarian Revolution: A History in Documents* (Budapest, 2002); Alajos Dornbach, *The Secret Trial of Imre Nagy* (Westport, Conn., 1994); George Paloczi-Horvath, *The Undefeated* (London, 1959); Mark Kramer, 'The Soviet Union and the 1956 Crises in Hungary and Poland: Reassessments and New Findings,' *JCH* 33: 2 (1998), 163–214; Johanna Granville, 'Reactions to the Events of 1956: New Findings from the Budapest and Warsaw Archives', *JCH* 38: 2 (2003), 261–90.

Post-war economic history: Nick Crafts and Gianni Toniolo, eds., *Economic Growth in Europe Since 1945* (Cambridge, 1996); E. Owen Smith, *The German Economy* (London, 1994); Robert A. Mundell, 'The Monetary Consequences of Jacques Rueff', *Journal of Business*, 46: 3 (1973), 384–395.

Post-war social change: Colin Crouch, *Social Change in Western Europe* (Oxford, 1999); Carole Fink, Philipp Gassert, and Detlef Junker, eds., *1968: The World Transformed* (Cambridge, 1998); H. Stuart Hughes, *Sophisticated Rebels: The Political Culture of European Dissent* (2nd edn. Cambridge Mass., 1990); Ingemar Wizelius, ed., *Sweden in the Sixties* (Stockholm, 1967); Nina Witoszek and Lars Trägårdh, eds., *Culture and Crisis: The Case of Germany and Sweden* (New York, 2002); János Rainer and György Péteri, eds., *Muddling Through in the Long 1960s: Ideas and Everyday Life in High Politics and the Lower Classes of Communist Hungary* (Trondheim, 2005); C. M. Hann, *Tázlár: A Village in Hungary* (Cambridge, 1980); Jane Jenson, 'Struggling for Identity: The Women's Movement and the State in Western Europe', *West European Politics*, 8: 4 (1985), 5–18.

Migration: Michael R. Marrus, *The Unwanted: European Refugees in the Twentieth Century* (New York, 1985); Andrew P. Geddes, *The Politics of Migration and Immigration in Europe* (London, 2003); D. W. Dean, 'Conservative Governments and the Restriction of Commonwealth Immigration in the 1950s: The Problems of Constraint', *HJ* 35: 1 (1992) 171–94; Abraham Ashkenazi, 'The Turkish Minority in Germany and Berlin', *Immigrants and Minorities*, 9: 3 (1990), 303–16.

Broadcasting: Asa Briggs, *History of Broadcasting in the United Kingdom* (5 vols., London and Oxford 1961–95); Burton Paulu, *Radio and Television Broadcasting on the European Continent* (Minneapolis, 1967); idem, *Radio and Television Broadcasting in Eastern Europe* (Minneapolis, 1974); Ruth Thomas, *Broadcasting and Democracy in France* (Philadelphia, 1976).

Prague Spring and after: Galia Golan, *The Czechoslovak Reform Movement: Communism in Crisis, 1962–1968* (Cambridge, 1971); idem, *Reform Rule in Czechoslovakia: The Dubček Era, 1968–1969* (Cambridge, 1973); Jiri Valenta, *Soviet Intervention in Czechoslovakia, 1968: Anatomy of a Decision* (2nd rev. edn., Baltimore, 1991); Kieran Williams, *The Prague Spring and its Aftermath: Czechoslovak Politics 1968–1970* (Cambridge, 1997); Zdeněk Mlynář, *Night Frost* (London, 1980); *Hope Dies Last: The Autobiography of Alexander Dubček* (New York, 1993); Karen Dawisha, *The Kremlin and the Prague Spring* (Berkeley, 1984); William Shawcross, *Dubček* (2nd edn., New York, 1990); Ludvík Vaculík, *A Cup of Coffee with my Interrogators* (London, 1987); Václav Havel, *Living in Truth* (London, 1987).

Communist Poland: Alexander J. Groth, *People's Poland: Government and Politics* (San Francisco, 1972); C. M. Hann, *A Village without Solidarity: Polish Peasants in Years of Crisis* (New Haven, 1985); Richard J. Hunter and Leo V. Ryan, *From Autarchy to Market: Polish Economics and Politics, 1945–1995* (Westport, Conn., 1998); Douglas J. MacEachin, *U.S. Intelligence and the Confrontation in Poland, 1980–1981* (University Park, Pa., 2002); Vojtech Mastny, 'The Soviet Non-Invasion of Poland in 1980–1981 and the End of the Cold War', *EAS* 51: 2 (1999), 189–211.

Britain since 1973: Kathleen Burk and Alec Cairncross, *'Goodbye, Great Britain': The 1976 IMF Crisis* (New Haven, 1992); Denis Healey, *The Time of My Life* (London, 1989); Hugo Young, *One of Us: A Biography of Margaret Thatcher* (London, 1989); Hugo Young, ed., *Political Lives* (Oxford, 2001); Simon Jenkins, *Accountable to None: The Tory Nationalization of Britain* (London, 1996); Shirley Robin Letwin, *Anatomy of Thatcherism* (New Brunswick, NJ, 1993); Eric J. Evans, *Thatcher and Thatcherism* (London, 1997); Margaret Thatcher, *The Downing Street Years* (London, 1993); Geoffrey Wheatcroft, *The Strange Death of Tory England* (London, 2005); Anthony Sampson, *Who Runs This Place? The Anatomy of Britain in the 21st Century* (London, 2004); Paul Dixon, *Northern Ireland: The Politics of War and Peace* (Basingstoke, 2001).

Decline and fall of the Soviet Union: Steven Kotkin, *Armageddon Averted: The Soviet Collapse, 1970–2000* (Oxford, 2001); Archie Brown, *The Gorbachev Factor* (Oxford, 1996); Anatoly Chernyaev, *My Six Years with Gorbachev* (University Park, Pa., 2000); Alexander Yakovlev, *The Fate of Marxism in Russia* (New Haven, 1993); Jerry F. Hough, *Democratization and Revolution in the U.S.S.R, 1985–91* (Washington, 1997); Brian McNair, *Glasnost, Perestroika and the Soviet Media* (London, 1991); David Satter, *Age of Delirium: The Decline and Fall of the Soviet Union* (New Haven, 1996); Coit D. Blacker, *Hostage to Revolution: Gorbachev and Soviet Security Policy, 1985–1991* (New York, 1993); Dale R. Herspring, *The*

Soviet High Command, 1967–1989: Personalities and Politics (Princeton, 1990); Mark R. Beissinger, *Nationalist Mobilization and the Collapse of the Soviet State* (Cambridge, 2002); G. Yavlinsky et al., *500 Days (Transition to the Market)* (New York, 1991); Susan Senior Nello, 'The Food Situation in the ex-Soviet Republics', *SS* 44: 5 (1992), 857–880; Jeffrey Surovell, 'Gorbachev's Last Year: Leftist or Rightist?', *EAS* 46: 3 (1994), 465–487.

Fall of Communism in eastern Europe: Timothy Garton Ash, *The Magic Lantern: The Revolutions of '89 Witnessed in Warsaw, Budapest, Berlin and Prague* (Cambridge, 1990); idem, *The Uses of Adversity: Essays on the Fate of Central Europe* (New York, 1990); Sabrina P. Ramet, *Social Currents in Eastern Europe: The Sources and Consequences of the Great Transformation* (Durham, NC, 1995); Ralf Dahrendorf, *Reflections on the Revolution in Europe* (London, 1990); Daniel C. Thomas, *The Helsinki Effect: International Norms, Human Rights, and the Demise of Communism* (Princeton, 2001); Marek Jan Chodakiewicz, John Radziłowski, and Dariusz Tołczyk eds., *Poland's Transformation: A Work in Progress* (Charlottesville, Va., 2003); George Konrád, *Antipolitics* (San Diego, 1984); Rudolf L. Tőkés, *Hungary's Negotiated Revolution: Economic Reform, Social Change and Political Succession, 1957–1990* (Cambridge, 1996); Vesselin Dimitrov, *Bulgaria: The Uneven Transition* (London, 2002); Peter Siani-Davies, *The Romanian Revolution of December 1989* (Ithaca, NY, 2005); Nestor Ratosh, *Romania: The Entangled Revolution* (New York, 1991); Mark Almond, *The Rise and Fall of Nicolae and Elena Ceauşescu* (London, 1992); *Les Temps Modernes* (special issue), no. 552 (Jan. 1990); Paweł Machcewicz, 'Poland 1986–1989: From "Cooptation" to "Negotiated Revolution" ', *CWIHPB* 12/13 (2001), 93–129.

German reunification: Timothy Garton Ash, *In Europe's Name: Germany and the Divided Continent* (London, 1993); Hans-Hermann Hertle, *Der Fall der Mauer: Die unbeabsichtigte Selbstauflösing des SED-Staates* (Opladen, 1996); Gareth Dale, *Popular Protest in East Germany, 1945–1989* (Abingdon, 2005); Elizabeth Pond, *Beyond the Wall: Germany's Road to Unification* (Washington, 1993); K. Stuart Parkes, *Understanding Contemporary Germany* (London, 1997); 'Germany in Transition', *Daedalus: Proceedings of the American Academy of Arts and Sciences* 123: 1 (1994); Egon Krenz, *Herbst '89* (Berlin, 1999); Gary Bruce, ' "In Our District, the State is Secure": The East German Secret Police Response to the Events of 1989 in Perleberg District', *CoEH* 14: 2 (2005) 219–44; Albert O. Hirschmann, 'Exit, Voice, and the Fate of the German Democratic Republic: An Essay in Conceptual History', *World Politics*, 45: 2 (1993), 173–202; Stephen Brockmann, 'The Reunification Debate', *New German Critique*, 52 (Winter, 1991), 3–30.

Former Soviet Union: Marshall I. Goldman, *The Piratization of Russia: Russian Reform Goes Awry* (London, 2003); Serguey Braguinsky and Grigory Yavlinsky, *Incentives and Institutions: The Transition to a Market Economy in Russia* (Princeton, 2000); Cameron Ross, ed., *Russian Politics Under Putin* (Manchester, 2004); Andrew Jack, *Inside Putin's Russia* (rev. edn., London, 2005); Daniel R. Kempton and Terry D. Clark, eds., *Unity or Separation: Center-Periphery Relations in the Former Soviet*

Union (Westport, Conn., 2002); Anatol Lieven, *Chechnya: Tombstone of Russian Power* (New Haven, 1999); Andrew Wilson, *Ukraine's Orange Revolution* (New Haven, 2005); Stefan Hedlund and Niclas Sundstrom, 'The Russian Economy after Systemic Change', *EAS* 48: 6 (1996), 887–914; Michael Ellman, 'The Russian Economy under El'tsin', *EAS* 52: 8 (2000), 1417–32.

East-central Europe after 1989: Judy Batt, *East Central Europe from Reform to Transition* (London, 1991); Vladimir Tismaneanu, 'The Revival of Politics in Romania', *Proceedings of the Academy of Political Science*, 38:1 (1991), 85–99; Jiří Večerník and Petr Matějů, eds., *Ten Years of Rebuilding Capitalism: Czech Society after 1989* (Prague, 1999); Abby Innes, *Czechoslovakia: The Short Goodbye* (New Haven, 2001); Helga A. Welsh, 'Dealing with the Communist Past: Central and East European Experiences after 1990', *EAS* 48: 3 (1996), 413–28; Mark S. Ellis, 'Purging the Past: The Current State of Lustration Laws in the Former Communist Bloc', *Law and Contemporary Problems*, 59: 4 (1996), 181–196; Erhard Blankenburg, 'The Purge of Lawyers after the Breakdown of the East German Communist Regime', *Law & Social Inquiry*, 20: 1 (1995), 223–43; Mark Kramer, 'Polish Workers and the Post-Communist Transition, 1989–93', *EAS* 47: 4 (1995), 669–712; Maria Todorova, 'The Mausoleum of Georgi Dimitrov as *lieu de mémoire*', *JMH* 78: 2 (2006), 377–411; David L. Bartlett, 'Democracy, Institutional Change, and Stabilisation Policy in Hungary', *EAS* 48: 1 (1996), 47–83; Wayne C. Thompson, 'Germany and the East', *EAS* 53: 6 (2001), 921–52.

Yugoslavia and its successors: Richard H. Ullman, ed., *The World and Yugoslavia's Wars* (New York, 1998); Misha Glenny, *The Fall of Yugoslavia: The Third Balkan War* (London, 1992); Martin van den Heuvel, ed., *The Disintegration of Yugoslavia* (Amsterdam, 1992); Sabrina Ramet, *Nationalism and Federalism in Yugoslavia 1962–1991* (2nd edn., Bloomington, Ind., 1992); Robert Thomas, *Serbia under Milošević* (London, 1999); Jan Willem Honig and Norbert Both, *Srebrenica: Record of a War Crime* (London, 1996); Noel Malcolm, *Kosovo: A Short History* (London, 1998); Mike Bowker, 'The Wars in Yugoslavia: Russia and the International Community', *EAS* 50: 7 (1998), 1245–61.

Recent Educational issues: Yossi Shavit and Hans-Peter Blossfeld, eds., *Persistent Inequality: Changing Educational Attainment in Thirteen Countries* (Boulder, Col., 1993); Elizabeth Sherman Swing, Jürgen Schriewer, and François Orivel, eds., *Problems and Prospects in European Education* (Westport, Conn., 2000); Patrick J. Wolf and Stephen Macedo, eds., *Educating Citizens: International Perspectives on Civic Values and School Choice* (Washington, 2004); Wolfgang Mitter, 'A Decade of Transformation: Educational Policies in Central and Eastern Europe', *International Review of Education*, 49: 1–2 (2003), 75–96.

Recent social issues: Pierre Chauvin, ed., *Prevention and Health Promotion for the Excluded and the Destitute in Europe* (Amsterdam, 2002); Malcolm Cook and Grace Davie, eds., *Modern France: Society in Transition* (London, 1999); Wolfgang Glatzer et al., eds., *Recent Social Trends in West Germany, 1960–1990* (Frankfurt, 1992); Paul Balchin, ed., *Housing Policy in Europe* (London, 1996); UN Economic Commission for Europe, *Country Profiles on the Housing Sector: Russian Federation* (United Nations, 2004); Arne Kubitza, *Pensions in Europe 2002: Expenditure and Beneficiaries* (Luxembourg, 2004); Office of National Statistics: *Census 2001: Report on the Welsh Language* (London, 2004); Paul B. Baltes and Karl Ulrich Mayer, eds., *The Berlin Aging Study: Aging from 70 to 100* (Cambridge, 1999); Stephen White, *Russia Goes Dry: Alcohol, State and Society* (Cambridge, 1996); Julian Peto, 'Cancer Epidemiology in the Last Century and the Next Decade', *Nature*, 411 (17 May 2001), 390–5.

Religion and secularization: Loek Halman and Ole Riis, eds., *Religion in a Secular Society: The European's Religion at the End of the 20th Century* (Tilburg, 1999); Wil Arts and Loek Halman, eds., *European Values at the Turn of the Millennium* (Leiden, 2004); Mary Lee Nolan and Sidney Nolan, *Christian Pilgrimage in Modern Western Europe* (Chapel Hill, NC, 1989); Austin Flannery OP, ed., *Vatican Council II: The Conciliar and Post-Conciliar Documents* (Boston, 1987); Hugh McLeod and Werner Ustorf, *The Decline of Christendom in Western Europe, 1750–2000* (Cambridge, 2003); Tom Inglis, Zdzisław Mach and Rafał Mazanek, eds., *Religion and Politics: East–West Contrasts from Contemporary Europe* (Dublin, 2000); Peter Hebblethwaite, *In the Vatican* (Oxford, 1987); Steve Bruce, *Religion in Modern Britain* (Oxford, 1995); Grace Davie, *Religion in Britain since 1945: Believing without Belonging* (Oxford, 1994); Hans Küng, *My Struggle for Freedom: Memoirs* (Grand Rapids, Mich., 2003); Bernard Wasserstein, *Vanishing Diaspora: The Jews in Europe since 1945* (London, 1996).

Index

marriage 223, 559, 765
Marseilles 383
Marshall, George C. (1880–1959) 424, 440
Marshall Plan 424–5, 452
Martin, David (b. 1929) 564
Marx, Karl (1818–83) 30, 188
Marxism 29, 146, 792
Masaryk, Jan (1886–1948) 273, 276, 432, 599
Masaryk, Tomáš Garrigue (1850–1937) 103, 155, 272, 732
Massilia 302
Massu, Jacques (1908–2002) 475, 526, 545
Masuria 119
Masurian Lakes, Battle of (1914) 57
Matignon agreements (1936) 254
Matsuoka Yosuke (1880–1946) 315
Matteotti, Giacomo (1885–1924) 162
Mau Mau 529
Mauriac, François (1885–1970) 475, 545
Mauroy, Pierre (b. 1928) 646
Maurras, Charles (1868–1952) 252, 253, 351
Mauthausen 271
Max, Prince of Baden (1867–1929) 95
Maxton, James (1885–1946) 277
May, Ernst (1886–1970) 215
May, Sir George (1871–1946) 168
May, Karl (1842–1912) 344
Mayenne 18
Mayer, Sally (1882–1950) 366
Maynooth seminary 788
Mazowiecki, Tadeusz (b. 1927) 678, 730
Mazzini, Giuseppe (1805–72) 374, 451
Mečiar, Vladimír (b. 1942) 732
medicine 19, 337–8; *see also* health
Medvedev, Roy (b. 1925) 200, 202
Medvedkin, Aleksandr (1900–89) 233
MeFo bills 186
Meinhof, Ulrike (1934–76) 648
Meir, Golda (Goldie Meyerson, 1898–1978) 491
Melilla 751
Memel 119, 155, 280
Mendelsohn, Erich (1887–1953) 215, 216
Menderes, Adnan (1899–1961) 659
Mendès France, Pierre (1907–82) 302, 457, 460, 464–5, 472, 475, 476
Mengele, Josef (1911–79) 362
Menton 311
Menzel, Jiří (b. 1938) 585
  Closely Observed Trains (1966) 585
Mercedes-Benz 218, 238
Mercouri, Melina (1920–94) 659
Merkel, Angela (b. 1954) 746
Mers-el-Kébir 304
Messina
  declaration (1955) 460
  Strait of 373
Messmer, Pierre (b. 1916) 633
Metaxas, Ioannis (1871–1941) 232, 243, 311
Meteor (plane) 394
Metz 96
Meuse, River 297, 298, 397
Meyerhold, Vsevolod (1874–1940) 233, 589
Michael, King (b. 1921) 305, 396, 430
Michaelis, Georg (1857–1936) 77
Michnik, Adam (b. 1946) 615, 616
Mielke, Erich (1907–2000) 516
Miës van der Rohe, Ludwig (1886–1969) 216
migration 16–17, 762–5
Mihailoviç, Draža (1893–1946) 355, 412
Mikhail Aleksandrovich, Grand Duke (1878–1918) 83
Mikołajczyk, Stanisław (1901–66) 430–2
Mikoyan, Anastas (1895–1978) 285, 490, 491–2, 501, 514
Milan 160, 269, 373, 412, 453, 543, 642, 747
Milestone, Lewis (1895–1980) 233
Milhaud, Darius (1892–1974) 237
Milošević, Slobodan (1941–2006) 733–4, 737, 742
Miłosz, Czesław (1911–2004) 403
Milyukov, Pavel Nikolayevich (1859–1943) 48, 82–3, 84, 85
Mindszenty, József (1892–1975) 430, 502, 504
minorities treaties 155
Minsk 317, 378
Mintoff, Dom (b. 1916) 531
Mirbach-Harff, Count Wilhelm von (1871–1918) 109
missiles 394, 485, 513, 514, 517, 548–9, 608–10, 612, 613–14, 646, 673–4, 705–7
'Miss World' contest 586
Mistinguett (Jeanne Bourgois, 1875–1956) 236
Mit brennender Sorge (1937) 185
Mitterrand, François (1916–96) 252, 476, 644–5
  as President 646–7, 688, 709, 738–9, 768
Mladenov, Petar (1936–2000) 686
Mladić, Ratko (b. 1943) 739
Mlynář, Zdeněk (1930–97) 666–7
Moch, Jules (1893–1985) 476
Moczar, Mieczysław (1913–86) 615
Model, Walther (1891–1945) 377, 397, 399
Modrow, Hans (b. 1928) 694, 695
Mogadishu 648
Mohammed Reza Shah Pahlevi (1919–80) 468, 542, 631
Möhne dam 390
Moholy-Nagy, László (1895–1946) 230
Mola Vidal, Emilio (1887–1937) 258–9
Moldavian Soviet Socialist Republic 305, 700
Moldova 721–2, 755, 773
Mollet, Guy (1905–75) 460, 469, 474, 477, 486
Molotov, Vyacheslav (1890–1986) 284–5, 289, 314, 315, 492, 493, 497–8, 507
Moltke, Helmuth von (1848–1916) 39, 44, 47, 49, 50, 52, 59, 62
Moltke, Helmuth James von (1907–45) 388
Mommsen, Hans (b. 1930) 189
Monat, Der 481
Mondadori 747
Monde, Le 457, 475
Monnet, Jean (1888–1979) 325, 452–6, 460
Mons, Battle of (1914) 49–50
Monte Cassino, Battle of (1944) 375